World Encyclopedia of Police Forces and Correctional Systems

SECOND EDITION

Advisory Board

World Encyclopedia of Police Forces and Correctional Systems

SECOND EDITION

VOLUME II
COUNTRIES: M–Z
APPENDIXES
INDEX

George Thomas Kurian

EDITOR

GALE
CENGAGE Learning

Detroit • New York • San Francisco • New Haven, Conn • Waterville, Maine • London

World Encyclopedia of Police Forces and Correctional Systems, Second Edition

George Thomas Kurian, Editor

Project Editors
Kristin Hart, Anjanelle Klisz, Dan Marowski

Contributing Editor
Rachel J. Kain

Editorial Technical Support
Mark Springer

Rights Acquisition and Management
Lisa Kincade, Ron Montgomery

Imaging
Randy Bassett, Lezlie Light, Christine O'Bryan

Product Design
Tracey Rowens, Jennifer Wahi

Composition
Evi Seoud, Mary Beth Trimper

Manufacturing
Wendy Blurton, Dorothy Maki

LIBRARY OF CONGRESS CATALOGING-IN-PUBLICATION DATA

World encyclopedia of police forces and correctional systems / George Thomas Kurian, editor in chief. — 2nd ed.
    p. cm.
    Rev. ed. of: World encyclopedia of police forces and penal systems / George Thomas Kurian. c1989.
    Includes bibliographical references and index.
    ISBN 0-7876-7736-1 (set hardcover : alk. paper) — ISBN 0-7876-7737-X (vol 1 : alk. paper) — ISBN 0-7876-7738-8 (vol 2 : alk. paper)
    1. Police—Encyclopedias. 2. Corrections—Encyclopedias. 3. Criminal law—Encyclopedias. I. Kurian, George Thomas. II. Kurian, George Thomas. World encyclopedia of police forces and penal systems.

    HV7901.W63 2007
    363.203—dc22
                                              2006011381

This title is also available as an e-book.
ISBN 1-4144-0514-6
Contact your Gale sales representative for ordering information.

Macedonia

—■—

Official country name: Republic of Macedonia
Capital: Skopje
Geographic description: Landlocked country in southeastern Balkans
Population: 2,045,262 (est. 2005)

■ ■ ■

LAW ENFORCEMENT

History. The Republic of Macedonia—known officially by the United Nations, the European Union, and North Atlantic Treaty Organization as the Former Yugoslav Republic of Macedonia—is the smallest and newest Balkan country. It is located in southeastern Europe bordered by Albania to the west, Bulgaria to the east, Serbia to the north, and Greece to the south. Because the Republic of Macedonia also includes the Greek region of Macedonia, tensions between Greece and Macedonia continue, as well as some confusion as to where the border lies. Macedonia is a multiethnic nation. Ethnic Macedonians make up 66.5 percent of the population while Albanians, Turks, Roma, Serbs, Muslims, and Vlachs make up 22.9 percent, 4 percent, 2.3 percent, 2 percent, 0.07 percent, and 0.004 percent, respectively. The remainder is made up of foreign nationals and small minorities, including Croatians, Bosnians, and Bulgarians.

Before Macedonia gained independence from the former Yugoslavia in 1991 and became a democracy, the official name of its police force was *Milicija na Republickiot Sekretarijat za Vnatresni Raboti na Socijalisticka Republika Makedonija* (Police of the Socialist

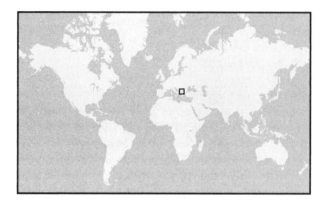

Republic of Macedonia). Following independence, *Milicija* was changed to *Policija*. The official name eventually became *Policija na Republika Makedonija* (Police of the Republic of Macedonia), commonly known as the Macedonian National Police (MNP).

Since independence, Macedonia has been in an ongoing reform process to develop a democratic, ethnically equitable police force and establish Western-style professionalism and ethics. To this end, in 2000 the country embarked on a law enforcement development program through their National Police Academy under guidance from the International Criminal Investigative Training Assistance Program (ICITAP), a program initiated by the U.S. Department of Justice in 1986. As well as providing a democratic policing curriculum and instructor development training, this program provides initiatives for internal review protocols within the MNP under a newly established Professional Standards Unit (PSU). Working in collaboration with the ICITAP and the

Ministry of Interior, in 2002 the PSU began conducting surveys to determine the feasibility of introducing policing at local community and municipality levels throughout the entire country. It also initiated workshops to develop recommendations and determine how community policing would be defined and integrated. By 2004 municipal-level policing was being implemented and becoming accepted in an increasing number of communities, and two community action teams had been established to partner with police in resolving neighborhood issues.

The MNP code of conduct reads: "I will enforce the law in a humane and adequate manner, without any fear, corruption, or bad intent, and I will never use any unnecessary force or violence" ("Balkan Conflicts" 1998). However, police reform is still necessary, and the greatest challenges to that end include:

- Overcoming the inertia of a Communist-era policing model

- Addressing the issue of police accountability

- Establishing the necessary and consistent political will

- Sustainability

Structure and Organization. Macedonia's Parliament, or Sobranje, a single legislative body creates the laws and develops policy. The legal system is based on a civil law system and judicial review of legislative acts. The Supreme Court is the highest court in the country. A hierarchy of trial and appeals courts exists to handle legal cases. Judges for each of these courts are appointed for life by a seven-member judicial council, which in turn is appointed by Parliament. The constitutional court decides constitutional questions and may annul laws that are inconsistent with the constitution.

The Ministry of Interior heads the MNP, including uniformed police, criminal police, border police (shared with the Ministry of Defense), and the state intelligence service, which deals only with external matters. Its director is appointed by and reports directly to the president of Macedonia, with a horizontal link to the government, and is responsible for state security. The Directorate for Security and Counterespionage, which reports to the Ministry of Interior, deals with internal security, organized crime, and counterintelligence. Its director reports jointly to the minister for internal affairs and the prime minister and is appointed by the government on the recommendation of the minister of internal affairs.

Salaries. The average salary of a uniformed police officer is between 9,000 and 11,000 denars per month (US$180–$200) while inspectors earn between 11,000 and 16,000 denars (US$200–$320).

Retirement Age. Officers have the right to retire at a very young age although the normal retirement age is 64 for men and is currently 60.5 for women. (Women's retirement age is being raised from 59.5 to 62 over a period of eight years).

Police-Community Relations. In cooperation with the Organization for Security and Cooperation in Europe (OSCE) Police Development Unit, the Macedonian police have implemented methods to break down barriers and build trust between the police force and civilian communities by forming citizen advisory groups (CAGs), regular informal meetings between local representatives of an area or village and their local police. In these CAGs, matters of mutual interest and concern, whether police issues or not, are discussed.

Deployment of International Community Police Trainers (CPTs) has also been implemented in which the CPTs work with local police, mayors, and municipal leaders to introduce community policing principles and confidence-building measures. The CPTs assist with community policing training, seminars, and workshops; developing relationships between communities, municipal structures, and local police; as well as identifying police stations needing renovation or supplies.

Local Police. There are ten regional offices of the Ministry of Interior, each with a structure identical to that of the ministry as a whole. There are sections for the uniformed police, the police investigators (also called criminal police), and the ministry's civilian work (passport issuance, etc.) According to the Law on Internal Affairs, all section chiefs are appointed by the ministry in Skopje, and by law, local police chiefs are required to provide the local city councils with reports on their work twice a year. Other than these formal reports, there appears to be little to no relationship between the local police and the local government.

Education and Training. Police cadets must have completed at least the fourth degree of secondary school, be between the ages of eighteen and twenty-five, and be citizens of Macedonia. They must be mentally and physically fit, have strong moral character, and demonstrate a commitment to protecting the human rights of all people. They must also have regulated their military service and have no criminal record.

Police are educated and trained at the Police Academy and police-operated high schools. At the high schools, schooling is four years; both male and female students are accepted. The subjects taught at the high school level are:

- Law

- Police administration and management

Police escort Zoran Vraniskovski, a Serbian priest charged with inciting racial and religious hatred, into the district court in Veles, Macedonia, September 20, 2005. *Supporters of the priest believe he was unjustly arrested over endorsing a 2002 proposal that would have put the Macedonian Orthodox Church under control of the Serbian Orthodox Church, a controversy many saw as threatening Macedonian nationhood. Vraniskovski was already serving a two-year sentence and was back in court for alleged misuse of $240,000 in church funds associated with the Macedonian Orthodox Church.* AP IMAGES.

- Criminalistics and criminology

- Other police-related subjects

- General subjects

Graduates are obligated to work for the police force for a minimum of eight years. The high school diplomas earned at these police high schools are recognized as high school diplomas outside the police force.

New police officers receive on-the-job training prior to working independently. In order for candidates to enroll in the bachelor-level police education, they must have been or become employees of the police force first. The proportion of candidates who join the police force for the first time after completing their education at the following levels are:

- High school degree: 60%

- Associate degree: 10%

- Higher professional education degree: 0%

- Bachelor's degree: 30%

- Master's or doctoral degree: 0%

For specialized training, 80 percent of police officers train at a training center only, and 20 percent are trained on the job. Police officers typically receive approximately seventy hours of specialized training per year.

With help, guidance, and training from ICITAP and similar organizations, education and training for Macedonian police is improving. At the Police Academy, cadets receive a more well-rounded education: in addition to other subjects, instruction in policing in democracy, constitutional framework, human rights, use of force, police ethics and code of conduct, policing in a multiethnic society, first aid, domestic violence awareness, gender issues, community policing, patrol procedures, arrest and detention, effective communication, use of firearms, and traffic accident management are part of the curriculum. In a pilot program, the success of which allowed it to be taken nationwide, six components were added to the curriculum specifically addressing policing at the local level:

- A self-paced community policing curriculum for certifying police officers
- Courses in community leadership
- A bicycle community action team
- A community advisory group
- Local presence of the PSU
- A Citizens' Police Academy (CPA)

The first CPA was successful, with ninety officers graduating in 2004. Also in 2004, the MNP recommended that the first community policing station be established in an ethnically diverse community.

To provide training to the judiciary, the European Commission (EC) established a Public Judicial Institute.

Uniforms and Weapons. The traditional standard MNP uniform of camouflage has, for the most part, been replaced with light-blue collared shirts and navy-blue pants, ties, and jackets. Operations in areas such as mountainous regions require the camouflage uniform, however. Police are equipped with body armor and assault rifles, as well as pistols and truncheons.

Transportation, Technology, and Communications. Between 1998 and 2005, the European Commission provided the following amenities to the Ministry of Interior and the MNP:

- 29 vehicles to police and customs
- 115 vehicles to the border police services
- Computers to judicial institutions and the necessary user training
- Technical assistance to the Interior Ministry and judiciary
- Integrated communications network for all border crossing points
- Border search and detection equipment
- Passport reading and computer equipment (to the Ministry of Interior)

The United States also donated vehicles and office equipment to the MNP unit that combats trafficking in humans.

Three helicopters are operated by the MNPs Aircraft Unit (*Avijaciska Edinica na Makedonskata Policija*), two of which they have had since Macedonia was part of former Yugoslavia. The third was purchased in 2000, with the US$5 million the Taiwan government donated. The helicopters are used primarily by the Ministry of Internal Affairs for such tasks as VIP transport, border

monitoring, transport of various cargo and special police units, search and rescue missions, medevac, and traffic surveillance. All helicopters are based at Idrizovo near Skopje, the latter city being the main police base.

Police Statistics.

- Total Police Personnel: 11,000 (6,000 uniformed and 5,000 civilian officers)
- Civilian Reservists: 11,000
- Police Officers per 100,000 Population: 550

HUMAN RIGHTS

Procedural violations by police are common, with the most serious abuse being excessive force when arresting a suspect and physical mistreatment of detainees. Arrests are sometimes made without a warrant and suspects beaten until they confess. All too often, suspects are detained past the twenty-four hours mandated by law, are kept uninformed about the reason for their arrest, and denied immediate access to a lawyer. Also, people are often summoned to police for questioning in an illegal practice called "informative talks." Courts and police often collaborate to backdate arrest warrants, courts often ignore complaints of police abuse, and police are seldom held responsible for breaking the law. As a result, many incidents of police abuse go unreported for fear of retribution from police or the courts. The legal affairs bureau has failed to enforce appropriate punishment, even for repeat offenders. While the Macedonian Constitution prohibits torture and other cruel treatment, there have been isolated reports of such incidents.

According to Global Beat (1998), the Center for War, Peace, and the News Media at New York University:

> One factor behind police abuse is Macedonia's Law on Internal Affairs, enacted after independence in 1991, which strongly centralized the police force. In contrast to the communist period in Yugoslavia, when local police chiefs were appointed by local governments, today they are appointed directly by the Ministry of the Interior in the capital, Skopje. The police, therefore, are still not accountable to the local population, which encourages a culture of abuse and impunity. Macedonian police also do not receive adequate human rights training. ("Balkan Conflicts")

One of Macedonia's reform programs for its police force is the instruction on practical human rights issues for all uniformed officers. The course has been structured in as practical a manner as possible, with various activities and officer/cadet participation, to educate them in identifying when policing violations of human rights norms most frequently appear, which include: the use of force, arrest and detention, and arbitrary interference with privacy.

CRIME

Crime is pervasive in Macedonia, the most pervasive being drug and human trafficking. As Macedonia is just a young nation, its police force has not been as well-trained and regulated as those of more developed countries. However, with new reforms implemented since 2002, the police force and communities are becoming better equipped and educated to deal with crime. Macedonia is the poorest Balkan country, and when police officers are only making the equivalent of US$300 per month, they can often be motivated to criminal behavior.

Organized Crime. Drug smuggling and trafficking, drug-related crimes, money laundering, and trafficking in human beings are the most prominent organized crime problems in Macedonia. While Macedonia is neither a major producer of nor a major destination for illicit drugs, it has nevertheless become vulnerable to drug trafficking and drug abuse in general. Police reforms have begun to deal with the pervasive crime.

Crime Statistics. Offenses reported to the police per 100,000 population (2000): 975.8. Of which:

- Homicide: 2.31
- Robberies: 14.57
- Thefts: 662.48
- Major Assault: 10.14
- Rape: 1.3
- Automobile Theft: 14.92

CORRECTIONAL SYSTEM

The Macedonian corrections system is centralized under the Directorate of Prison Administration within the Ministry of Justice. Each penal and correctional institution, however, is an independent state body.

Prison Conditions. The U.S. Department of State reported in 2001 that prison conditions were generally up to international standards and met basic needs for food, hygiene, and access to medical care. The two deaths reported in custody were contributed to natural causes. Men, women, and juveniles are held separately although crowded facilities sometimes means older juveniles are held with adults. Also, pretrial detainees are held separately from convicted criminals.

Prison Statistics.

- Total Prison Population: 2,256
- Prison Population per 100,000: 113
- Pretrial Detainees: 10.1%
- Female Prisoners: 2.3%
- Juvenile Prisoners: 1.4%
- Number of Prisons: 8
- Official Capacity of the Prison System: 2,225
- Occupancy Level: 101.4%

BIBLIOGRAPHY

"Balkan Conflicts. Police Violence in Macedonia. Human Rights Watch" 1988. *Global Beat* (April). Available online at http://www.nyu.edu/globalbeat/kosovo/HRW0498.html (accessed December 29, 2005).

"Former Yugoslavia Republic of Macedonia: The Protection of Kosovo Albanian Refugees." 1999. Amnesty International. Available online at http://web.amnesty.org/library/Index/ENGEUR650031999?open&of=ENG-MKD (accessed December 29, 2005).

"Macedonia Civil Police." 2001. World Air Forces. Aeroflight. Available online at http://www.aeroflight.co.uk/waf/fyrm/mac-police.htm (accessed December 29, 2005).

Perry, Duncan. 1997. "The Republic of Macedonia: Finding Its Way." In *Politics, Power and the Struggle for Democracy in South-East Europe*, edited by Karen Dawisha and Bruce Parrott. Cambridge, UK: Cambridge University Press.

Roudometof, Victor, ed. 2000. *The Macedonian Question: Culture, Historiography, Politics*. New York: Columbia University Press.

"Size and Structure of the Macedonian Police" and "Laws Regulating the Police." 1998. Human Rights Watch. Available online at http://www.hrw.org/reports98/macedonia/maced2a.htm (accessed December 29, 2005).

Wendy C. Garfinkle-Brown
Nathan R. Moran
Robert D. Hanser

Madagascar

Official country name: Republic of Madagascar
Capital: Antananarivo
Geographic description: Island in the southern Indian Ocean off the southeastern coast of Africa, east of Mozambique; the fourth-largest island in the world
Population: 18,040,341 (est. 2005)

■■■

LAW ENFORCEMENT

History. Early police traditions go back to British and French rule over the island. The French, who prevailed, ruled Madagascar from 1896 to 1960 and established the National Gendarmerie as the principal law enforcement agency. Assisting the gendarmes was the Civil Police, which maintained law and order in towns and urban areas. Madagascar regained independence in 1960.

Structure and Organization. There are six law enforcement agencies:

- National Gendarmerie
- National Police
- Mobile Police Group (*Groupe Mobile de Police*)
- Civil Police
- Civil Service
- Antigang Brigade

All but the National Gendarmerie (which operates under the Ministry of Defense) are outside the command of the National Army (the *Forces Armées Populaires* [FAP], or the People's Armed Forces).

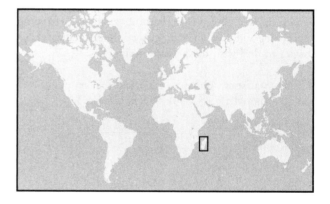

The National Police establishment comes under the jurisdiction of the Ministry of Public Security, which is part of the cabinet. Under the Ministry, there are various departments:

- Directorate of Finance and Administration
- Directorate of Police Intervention Forces
- Directorate General of the National Police
- Directorate of Anti-Corruption
- Directorate of Judicial Police
- Directorate of Public Security
- Directorate of Financial and Economic Crimes
- Directorate of Immigration and Emigration
- Central *Commissariat* of Antananarivo Police

The National Police is the principal law enforcement agency, providing police services throughout all municipalities. It is equipped with automatic weapons, armored cars and aircraft, and its units are connected to the central command by a modern system of radio communications. Although part of the defense establishment, the National Gendarmerie's command structure is entirely separate from that of the army. The Gendarmerie is responsible for policing in rural areas. The Maritime Police is also part of the Gendarmerie.

The Civil Police maintains law and order in towns and urban areas. The head of each prefecture has at least one small contingent under his control. They are less well trained and equipped than the National Gendarmerie. The Civil Service is a paramilitary force. It is a reserve element of the defense forces, and its commanders are military officers in uniform although its operations are nonmilitary. It participates in rural economic and social development programs.

Education and Training. There are two training institutions for the various elements of internal security forces. The first is the National Superior Police School in Antananarivo for officers, and the other is the National School for Police Inspectors and Agents for noncommissioned personnel.

Police Statistics.

- Total Police Personnel: 5,880
- Population per Police Officer: 3,110

HUMAN RIGHTS

The security forces have a poor record of respecting human rights. During the conflict between presidential contenders Didier Ratsiraka and Marc Ravalomanana, law enforcement personnel loyal to both sides committed human rights abuses, including abduction of opponents as well as illegal arrest of suspects and their detention without judicial warrant. Human rights groups have cited numerous instances of violence, theft, and vandalism. Forms of torture, including beating detainees with rifle butts and burning them with lighted cigarettes, have been reported.

CRIME

Crime Statistics. Offenses reported to the police per 100,000 population: 112. Of which:

- Murder: 0.6
- Assault: 12
- Burglary: 0.7
- Automobile Theft: 0.1

CORRECTIONAL SYSTEM

Prisons are under the control of the director of Penitentiary and Surveillance Administration under the Ministry of Justice. Each province has a central prison for prisoners serving sentences for less than five years. There are also twenty-five lesser prisons for persons awaiting trial and those sentenced to less than two years. Courts at the subprefecture level have jails where prisoners serve sentences of less than six months. The largest prison is the Central Prison at Antananarivo, which has a women's section. Hardened criminals and those serving sentences of more than five years are sent to one of the prisons on one of the small coastal islands, such as Nosy Lava or Nosy Be.

Prison Conditions. Prison conditions are harsh, reflecting the nation's general poverty and political violence. Prisoners do not receive adequate food rations, and families are expected to supplement them. Prisoners without relatives go for days without food. Prison cells average less than 1 square yard of space per inmate. Lack of adequate medical care causes a high incidence of malnutrition and a host of infections, many of which are fatal. Prisoners are used as forced labor. Women are sometimes abused and raped, as they were not kept separate from men. Pretrial detainees and juveniles also are kept in the same quarters as hardened criminals.

Prison Statistics.

- Total Prison Population: 19,000
- Prison Population per 100,000: 106
- Pretrial Detainees: 65.4%
- Female Prisoners: 3.4%
- Juvenile Prisoners: 1.4%
- Number of Prisons: 97
- Official Capacity of the Prison system: 13,000
- Occupancy Level: 146.2%

George Thomas Kurian

Malawi

■

Official country name: Republic of Malawi
Capital: Lilongwe
Geographic description: Landlocked country in southern Africa, east of Zambia
Population: 12,158,924 (est. 2005)

■ ■ ■

LAW ENFORCEMENT

History. The Malawi Police Force traces its origins to 1921, when it was set up by the British. It was reorganized in 1946 prior to independence.

Structure and Organization. Under the constitution, the Malawi Police Force is placed under the control of the Police Service Commission. The national police headquarters is at Lilongwe, and there are regional headquarters at each of the three regional capitals. There are four territorial divisions: Central, Southern, Northern, and Eastern, each under a commissioner. There are also stations in each of the country's twenty-four districts and thirty-seven substations, and police posts are scattered throughout the country. All constables, as regular police personnel are called, are under the national headquarters. There are no separate municipal or local forces. Along with its routine operational and patrol units, the force has a Criminal Investigation Division and a Special Branch for the collection and analysis of intelligence data. The Immigration Service is also part of the police. The Police Service Commission, composed of an ombudsman, civil servants, and legal officials, oversees the police and confirms promotions and appointments and conducts disciplinary hearings.

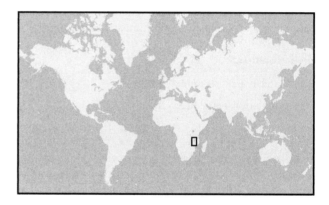

Major ethnic groups, such as the Chewa, Lomwe, and Nyanja, are strongly represented in police ranks. The Ngoni, who make up only 1.2 percent of the population, are disproportionately represented because of their martial traditions. Residents of northern and west central Malawi are also heavily represented in the lower ranks while southerners were predominant in the higher ranks. Women were admitted to the police force in 1971 and now are fully represented.

Special Police.

Police Mobile Force. The Police Mobile Force is a quick reaction force to quell riots and uprisings. Its members are equipped with rifles, light machine guns, and riot gear and move in trucks and lighter vehicles, such as motorcycles. Mobile Force units are stationed at the national headquarters at Lilongwe and at each of the four regional headquarters and are connected by a radio network. Police patrols cover all major towns night and day. Tours lasting as long as a week include visits to most rural settlements. Lake Malawi is patrolled by Malawi Police Force boat and air wings.

Education and Training. After an initial four-year enlistment, members of the force can sign up for continuing service until they qualify for a lump-sum retirement payment at age forty-five, or they may extend their service further to qualify for retirement benefits. Recruits are trained at Kanjedza, near Blantyre, where the basic police course lasts six months. Selected police officers are given special training at Zomba national headquarters. There is an additional police training school at Limbe.

Police Statistics.

- Total Police Personnel: 6,700
- Population per Police Officer: 1,814

HUMAN RIGHTS

Police use of excessive force or negligence results in a number of deaths of detainees. Beating and abuse of detainees is part of police culture. Arbitrary arrest and detention are common procedures. Wires rather than handcuffs are used to restrain prisoners.

CRIME

Crime Statistics. Offenses reported to the police per 100,000 population: 850. Of which:

- Murder: 3.1
- Assault: 82.2
- Burglary: 13.1

CORRECTIONAL SYSTEM

Prisons are administered by the chief commissioner of the Malawi Prisons Service in Zomba under the Ministry of Home Affairs and Internal Security.

Prison Conditions. Malawi's prisons are substandard and fall far short of international requirements in terms of overcrowding, sanitation, nutrition, and health facilities. Many prisoners succumb to HIV/AIDS without proper care. Women are kept separately, but juveniles and pretrial detainees are housed together with convicted criminals. The constitution provides for an Inspectorate of Prisons, but its recommendations are generally never heeded nor implemented.

Prison Statistics. The central prison is at Zomba, and other large prisons are at Lilongwe, Kanjedza and Mzuzu. The government also runs a prison farm for first offenders and a small school for juvenile offenders.

- Total Prison Population: 8,566
- Prison Population per 100,000: 70
- Pretrial Detainees: 23.5%
- Female Prisoners: 1.2%
- Juvenile Prisoners: 9.2%
- Number of Prisons: 23
- Official Capacity of the Prison System: 5,500
- Occupancy Level: 155.7%

George Thomas Kurian

Malaysia

Official country name: Malaysia
Capital: Kuala Lumpur
Geographic description: Three geographically separate territories separated by the South China Sea: Malay Peninsular, bordered on the north by Thailand; and the two states of Sabah and Sarawak on the north coast of the island of Indonesia
Population: 23,953,136 (est. 2005)

■ ■ ■

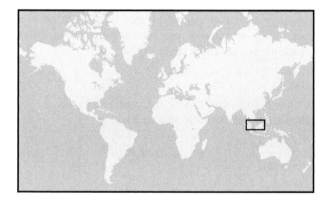

LAW ENFORCEMENT

History. The Malaysian police force predates colonial rule. Even during the fifteenth century, there was a royal official known as *temenggong* whose duties included arresting criminals, building prisons, and executing convicted miscreants. A police force under the *temenggong* patrolled the city streets at night. In the rural areas, the village headman carried out police duties. When the Portuguese conquered Malacca in 1511, they retained this system. Neither the Dutch nor the British, who followed the Portuguese as rulers, made any significant changes. However, the British began to use Indians, especially Sikhs, as police.

The modern Malaysian police force dates from 1806 when the British formed a police force in Penang. In 1824, a similar force was established in Malacca. The Perak Armed Forces was established in 1867, followed by similar organizations in Negeri Sembilan, Selangor, and Pahang. These forces operated independently until 1896 when they were amalgamated into the Federated Malay States Police. These units were trained by noncommissioned officers of the British Army. The unified police force was engaged in constant patrols against the armed retainers of local territorial chiefs and in putting down insurrections and rebellions in various states. By 1920, all states in the peninsula had police forces. Increased immigration by Chinese and Indians in the early twentieth century brought new problems in urban law and order. Police had to cope with urban criminal gangs, with banditry and terrorism in outlying areas, and with the problem of suppressing Chinese secret societies responsible for new forms of organized crime. As a result, the police began to develop sophisticated facilities for criminal investigation, detection, and apprehension. A fingerprint registry was established in 1904.

When the Japanese occupied Malaya in 1942, they used the Malayan police to support their operations. When the Japanese left in 1945, organization and operations of the police were disrupted, and much of the police force was no longer trusted by the people.

On their return, the British found that they needed to extensively retrain the force. In 1946 the Federated Malay States Police and independent forces of the other states were integrated into the Malay Union Police, renamed the Federation of Malaya Police in 1948.

During the prolonged emergency from 1948 to 1960 when public order was threatened by Communist insurgents, police forces in the Malay Peninsular increased sevenfold—to 75,341 (31,164 regular police and 44,177 special constables). They were given greater authority under centralized state control, and increased attention was given to recruitment, training, and equipment. The police were required not only to fight the Communist terrorists as a paramilitary adjunct to regular armed forces but also to develop a role in gathering intelligence.

Law enforcement in Sarawak before the arrival of the first white raja in 1841 was rudimentary and was limited to tax collection. People in outlying areas were not subject to any significant central control. Under the white rajas, a police force initially took the form of troops led by the raja himself. Subsequently, a separate group was formed to perform more conventional duties in the towns. In 1932 these two elements were combined to form the Sarawak Constabulary. When the last of the white rajas ceded the Sarawak to the British in 1946, the British made a major effort to improve the quality and efficiency of these forces by putting increasing emphasis on regular police work rather than paramilitary training and procedures. The Sarawak Constabulary was reorganized as regular police with responsibility for civil police duties. Two units were created: the Field Force to patrol the jungle and rural areas and the Special Force to deal with investigation and control of subversion. In Sabah, the British created an organization similar to that in Sarawak after Sabah was ceded by the British North Borneo Company in 1946. On the amalgamation of Sabah, Sarawak, and the Federation of Malaya into Malaysia in 1963, the three separate police organizations were merged into a single national police force called the Royal Malaysian Police (RMP) under federal authority and control.

Structure and Organization.

Federal Level. At the federal level, the Ministry of Home Affairs is responsible for police activities in accordance with the Police Act of 1963. The RMP is commanded by the inspector general of police, whose powers and responsibilities are delineated in the Police Act of 1967, who reports to the minister of home affairs, and who is assisted by a deputy director general. The Inspector General's headquarters has four departments:

- Internal Security/Public Order (IS/PO)
- Management
- Crime Investigation
- Special Branch

Each department is headed by a director with the rank of commissioner of police and who is immediately subordinated by field commanding officers who implement policy. Other police units perform support or conventional police tasks, such as directing traffic, and maintaining communications. The RMP also has a women's contingent that deals with crimes relating to women or children and maintains various kinds of volunteer units, the largest of which is the People's Volunteer Reserve that supplements the regular force, particularly in times of national emergency.

The major operating units of RMP are the:

- Police Field Force (PFF)
- Federal Reserve Units (FRU)
- Criminal Investigation Department (CID)
- Special Branch
- Marine Police

Police Field Force: The PFF is controlled by the IS/ PO, which has primary responsibility for all public order situations involving suppression of riots and disturbances. The PFF was formed to undertake punitive operations against Communist guerrillas and armed uprisings by other criminal elements operating from bases in the jungle. To facilitate the process, the inspector general is cochairman with the chief of the armed forces staff in the Operational Planning Committee at the national level. PFF functions include patrolling the frontiers and other sparsely populated areas. The unit is organized into brigades, battalions, and companies that can be deployed on long-term, deep-jungle operations either independently or, especially in internal security matters, in conjunction with the armed forces. The PFF is also utilized in support of the General Duties Police in crime prevention measures, disasters, and public order situations. Its seventeen battalions are organized into north, central, southeast, and east brigades. Units are supplied with scout cars equipped with machine guns and radios. The force has a platoon of women police trained in jungle warfare. The unit is headed by a senior assistant commissioner of police as deputy director of administration and logistics.

Federal Reserve Units: The FRUs, also responsible to the IS/PO, are run by a finance and logistics director and deputy director of operations. These are self-contained, specifically designed, and highly mobile units of specially trained police for the suppression of riots, dispersal of unlawful assemblies, protection of important national and foreign dignitaries, and crowd control. They also assist in rescue work during local or national disasters and may be deployed on special tasks in aid of the CID, the Special Branch, or District Police.

Criminal Investigation Department: The CID was created in 1970. Its director is responsible for the prevention and detection of crime and the apprehension and prosecution of criminals. He has two deputy directors. The deputy director of administration and prevention deals with matters pertaining to administration, criminal records, fingerprints, and railways. The deputy director of planning and operations deals with the analysis of crime at both national and international levels, the latter through links with Interpol; technical and forensic investigations into the more complicated criminal events, secret societies, and antinarcotic measures. It also maintains a dog unit and oversees the detective establishment.

Special Branch: The Special Branch is the equivalent of a secret service and is responsible for the collation and dissemination of security intelligence conveyed regularly to the prime minister and the cabinet. This intelligence service operates at district, field, and headquarters level.

Marine Police: The Marine Police patrol territorial and coastal waters to prevent, detect, and investigate breaches of the law, including piracy; protect fishing and other marine craft; assist in maritime search and rescue efforts; and police areas accessible only by water. The Marine Police are particularly active off Sarawak in supporting anti-insurgency operations, delivering materials to ground forces, patrolling, and maintaining blockades. Their vessels consist mainly of patrol and speed boats.

State and District Levels. The Police Commissioners of Sabah and Sarawak and the chief police officers in each state in the Malay Peninsular are responsible for the day-to-day command and administration of police forces. The country is divided into thirteen contingents/components headed by the commissioners of police in Sabah and Sarawak in the Borneo states and chief police officers of the states of Kedah/Perlis, Penang, Kuala Lumpur Federal Territory, Selangor, Negeri Sembilan, Melaka, Johor, Kelantan, Terengganu, and Pahang. Each of these commanders has a headquarters staffed somewhat comparably to the office of the inspector general, with some local modifications based on geography and population. There are three categories of commanding officers in terms of rank:

- Commissioners in Sabah and Sarawak and the chief police officers in Kuala Lumpur, Perak, and Kedah/Perlis have the rank of deputy commissioner of police.

- Chief police officers of Penang, Pahang, Kelantan, Johor, and Negeri Sembilan have the rank of senior assistant commissioner of police

An officer removes a suspicious package from the Australian Embassy in Kuala Lumpur, Malaysia, October 5, 2005. Security in the area was raised after other suspicious packages were found at U.S., British, French, and Russian embassies in Malaysia. The following day, six other foreign ministries received similar packages. All were determined to be fake threats. **AP IMAGES.**

- Chief police officers of Melaka and Terengganu have the rank of assistant commissioner of police

The next level of command is that of the officer in charge of a police district, who is responsible to the commissioner/chief police officer for the command and control of his district. The police district is not always on an equal level with an administrative district. There are seventy-four police districts in the Kuala Lumpur Federal Territory. The lowest rank is that of an assistant superintendent of police in small or rural districts. However, the rank may go up to that of an assistant commissioner of police for the more important urban industrialized districts, such as Ipoh or Petaling Jaya. The lowest level of command is that of an officer in charge of a police station. Each police district is divided into a number of station areas under a junior police officer. There are more than five hundred police stations crisscrossing the country. Each station area is divided into a number of beat and patrol areas.

Education and Training. The composition of the police force reflects the general ethnic makeup of the nation. Most police in the Malay Peninsular are Malay Muslims; in Sabah and Sarawak, most of the lower ranks come from the native ethnic groups. Indians and Chinese are present in all branches, but more visibly in the CID and Special Branch. The force is well trained, and pay and morale are high.

Although local conditions vary, there are three methods of joining the police force. Candidates with at least six years of primary school are recruited as constables, those holding the Malaysia Certificate of Education are recruited as probationary inspectors, and university graduates are recruited as probationary assistant superintendents.

The police training school in Kuala Lumpur offers basic training for constable recruits and refresher courses for junior officers. Higher-level courses are given at the Police College in Kuala Kubu Baharu. There are separate schools for CID and Special Branch personnel, and paramilitary training for the PFF is given at Ulu Kinta in Perak. Unit training is also given where needed. A number of police officers from other countries in Southeast Asia attend the Royal Malaysia Police College, and members of the RMP attend courses in Australia, the United Kingdom, and the United States.

Uniforms and Weapons. Police officers normally wear a full khaki uniform with a bush jacket. Depending on the duties or branches in which they serve, members of the force wear colors as follows:

• Police Field Force: jungle green

• Federal Reserve Unit: dark blue

• Marine Police: white

• Traffic Police: dark-blue trousers or white shorts

• Women Police: light blue-gray

Transportation, Technology, and Communications. The RMP has fleets of mobile patrol vehicles equipped with radio communications deployed in all districts, major towns, and urban areas for round-the-clock, inter-mittent, or special patrols. In addition, highway patrols are deployed.

Police Statistics.

• Total Police Personnel: 29,248

• Population per Police Officer: 818

HUMAN RIGHTS

Human rights are generally respected. However, the police commit a number of extrajudicial killings and on occasion, torture, beat, or otherwise abuse detainees. Detained suspects are denied legal counsel prior to being formally charged. Police use the Internal Security Act to arrest and detain many persons, including members of the opposition party, without charge or trial.

CRIME

Crime Statistics. Offenses reported to the police per 100,000 population: 604. Of which:

• Murder: 3.1

• Assault: 25.9

• Burglary: 155.6

• Automobile Theft: 20.8

CORRECTIONAL SYSTEM

The penal code devised by the British for the Straits Settlements is still in force, with some modifications and amendments. Some elements of Islamic justice have been incorporated, such as whipping. The death penalty may be imposed for a number of crimes, including drug trafficking.

Penitentiaries and jails are run by the Prisons Service under the Ministry of Home Affairs. There are separate prison departments for each of the three constituent states of Malaysia, but they all report to the director general of the Prisons Service. There are 17 corrections facilities in the Malay Peninsular, 7 in Sabah, and 6 in Sarawak. Penal institutions range from conventional, walled compounds to open farms and detention camps.

In the Malay Peninsular, first offenders and well-behaved prisoners are sent to the Central Training Prison at Taiping. Regional training prisons at Penang, Alor Setar, Kuala Lumpur, and Johor Baharu house recidivists. Young male offenders are sent to reform schools in Teluk Mas, Ayer Keroh, and Melaka; girls are sent to a school in Batu Gajah. The Pulau Jerejak Rehabilitation Center and the detention camps at Taiping and Muar hold detainees awaiting trail. A special prison at Seremban receives all classes of prisoners. Local prisons for offenders charged with lesser crimes are maintained at Sungei Petani for young males; Kuantan for adult males; and Kuala Lumpur, Georgetown, Alor Setar, and Pengkalan for females. There is a modern prison complex in Kajang, Selangor, which includes the Prisons Department headquarters and a prison officer's training facility.

Sarawak has a central prison and a women's prison at Kuching, regional prisons at Simanggang, Sibu, Miri, and Limbang and detention camps for men and women at Kuching. Sabah has a central prison, a women's prison, and a detention camp at Kota Kinbalu, regional prisons at Sandakan and Tawau, a minimum security prison at Keningau, and a reform school.

Prison Conditions. In 1953 Malaysia adopted the United Nations' (UN) Standard Minimum Rules for the Treatment of Prisoners and the UN Body of Principles for the Protection of All Persons under Any Form of Imprisonment or Detention but has consistently ignored them. In 2001 the UN Human Rights Commission called for Malaysian prison authorities to provide standard medical treatment and food for prisoners, as well as light, ventilation, and bedding. Torture and inhuman or degrading treatment have been reported. Overcrowding is a major problem. Conditions are particularly harsh in prison camps for illegal immigrants where deaths have been reported as a result of abuse. Juveniles are kept separately but they mingle with adults during communal activities. Children as young as ten are kept in prison for offenses such as petty theft or school fights.

Prison Statistics.

- Total Prison Population: 42,282
- Prison Population Rate per 100,000: 177
- Pretrial Detainees: 39.1%
- Female Prisoners: 8.4%
- Juvenile Prisoners: 3.3%
- Number of Prisons: 45
- Official Capacity of the Prison System: 33,200
- Occupancy Level: 127.4%

George Thomas Kurian

Maldives

Official country name: Republic of Maldives
Capital: Male
Geographic description: An archipelago of coral islands grouped into atolls in the Indian Ocean, south-southwest of India
Population: 349,106 (est. 2005)

■ ■ ■

LAW ENFORCEMENT

Structure and Organization. The national police is the National Security Service, which combines the roles of a militia, *gendarmerie*, and army. It is administered by the Ministry of Public Safety.

Police Statistics.

- Total Police Personnel: 500
- Population per Police Officer: 698

CRIME

Crime Statistics. Offenses reported to the police per 100,000 population: 2,353. Of which:

- Murder: 1.9
- Assault: 3.3
- Burglary: 36.1

CORRECTIONAL SYSTEM

Prisons on the archipelago are administered by the Ministry of Justice. The three major prisons are at

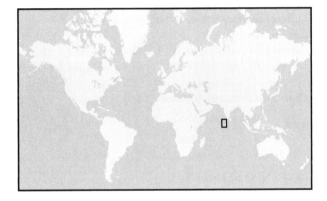

Gaamaadhoo and Dhoonidhoo on North Male Atoll and Maafushi on the South Male Atoll.

Prison Conditions. Prisons are built to conform to international standards but generally do not meet those standards, with some prisoners housed in crowded and unsanitary facilities. Spouses are allowed privacy during visits. Women are segregated from men and juveniles from adults. Guards are trained to respect international conventions. There have been reports of mistreatment—including beatings—of people in police custody, particularly in Maafushi Prison.

Prison Statistics.

- Total Prison Population: 1,098
- Prison Population Rate per 100,000: 310
- Female Prisoners: 26.6%
- Number of Prisons: 9

George Thomas Kurian

Mali

■

Official country name: Republic of Mali
Capital: Bamako
Geographic description: Landlocked west African country southwest of Algeria, occupying a region known as Sahel
Population: 12,291,529 (est. 2005)

■■■

LAW ENFORCEMENT

Structure and Organization. The Malian police are organized along French lines into three units:

- *Gendarmerie*
- National Guard
- Civil Police

The *Gendarmerie* and the National Guard are under the Ministry of Defense. The Civil Police are under the Ministry of Internal Security. The police and the gendarmes share responsibility for internal security; the police are responsible for urban areas and the gendarmes for rural areas.

Police Statistics.

- Total Police Personnel: 7,266
- Population per Police Officer: 1,681

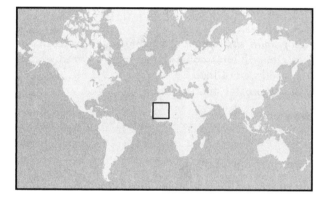

CRIME

Crime Statistics. Offenses reported to the police per 100,000 population: 10. Of which:

- Murder: 0.7
- Assault: 1.5
- Burglary: 0.8
- Automobile Theft: 0.3

CORRECTIONAL SYSTEM

Prison Conditions. Prison conditions are substandard. Most prisons, including the newest one at Bamako, are overcrowded, and medical facilities and food supplies are limited. Outside the Bamako prison, men, women, adults and children are housed in the same facility. The government permits visits to prisons by human rights monitors.

Prison Statistics.

- Total Prison Population: 4,040
- Prison Population Rate per 100,000: 33
- Pretrial Detainees: 67.2%
- Female Prisoners: 2%
- Juvenile Prisoners: 1.2%
- Number of Prisons: 58

George Thomas Kurian

Malta

———■———

Official country name: Republic of Malta
Capital: Valletta
Geographic description: Island in the central Mediterranean, south of Sicily
Population: 398,534 (est. 2005)

■■■

LAW ENFORCEMENT

History. The Malta Police Force was formed in 1814 when, at the conclusion of the Napoleonic Wars, Malta was annexed by the United Kingdom. The force underwent considerable reorganization following independence in 1964.

Structure and Organization. The police force is commanded by a commissioner based in Floriana and assisted by three assistant commissioners, one of whom is responsible for administration, one for operations, and the third for criminal investigations. The assistant commissioner for administration is in charge of liaison and coordination with other government departments and agencies, public relations, legislation, prosecutions, personnel, customs, and stores and equipment. The assistant commissioner for operations is in charge of public meetings, traffic operations, transport, fire fighting, mobile squad patrols, and telecommunications. The assistant commissioner for criminal investigations is in charge of state intelligence, security, crime investigations, immigration, Interpol, weapons office, crime statistics, criminal records, police dogs, police training, research, and planning. Under the assistant commissioners, certain branches, such as the Traffic Branch

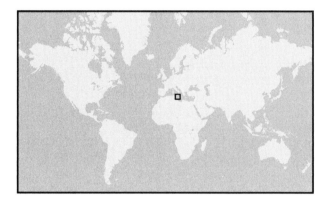

and the Security Branch, are commanded by senior superintendents. The Traffic Branch includes the Traffic Section, the Fire Brigade, Transport Section, Mounted Section, Traffic Citations Office, and the Licensing Bureau. The Security Branch is composed of the detective and uniformed sections of the Criminal Investigation Department.

The force is deployed over 77 police stations, which include 57 on Malta, the main island, 19 on the island of Gozo, and 1 on the island of Comino. The stations are grouped into divisions and districts. There are 5 police districts, each one under a senior superintendent. Divisions are under a senior police officer.

The principal grades in police service are, in descending order:

- Commissioner

- Assistant Commissioner

- Superintendent

- Senior Inspector

- Inspector

- Probationary Inspector

- Sergeant Major First Class

- Quartermaster

- Sergeant

- Sergeant Major Second Class

- Sergeant First Class

- Sergeant Second Class

- Sergeant Third Class

- Constable First Class

- Constable Second Class

- Constable Third Class

Education and Training. Education for all ranks is provided at the Police Training School at Valletta. Assistance in police training is received from the United Kingdom and the European Union.

Uniforms and Weapons. The winter uniform consists of a dark-blue tunic and slacks, a dark-blue peaked cap, black boots, a light-blue shirt, and black tie. The summer uniform consists of khaki slacks and tunic, the winter cap with a khaki cover, khaki shirt, and black tie. During hot summer days, the police may wear half-sleeved shirts. The force is generally unarmed, and patrolmen carry only wooden billy clubs.

Police Statistics.

- Total Police Personnel: 1,678

- Population per Police Officer: 238

HUMAN RIGHTS

The government generally respects human rights, and the law and the judiciary provide effective means of dealing with individual instances of abuse.

CRIME

Crime Statistics. Offenses reported to the police per 100,000 population: 1,841. Of which:

- Murder: 3

- Assault: 35.2

- Burglary: 1,079.2

- Automobile Theft: 243.9

CORRECTIONAL SYSTEM

The prison system is administered by the director of the Department of Correctional Services.

Prison Conditions. Prison conditions meet international standards. The prison is visited regularly by independent human rights observers.

Prison Statistics.

- Total Prison Population: 283

- Prison Population Rate per 100,000: 71

- Pretrial Detainees: 29.7%

- Female Prisoners: 3.9%

- Juvenile Prisoners: 1.1%

- Foreign Prisoners: 35%

- Number of Prisons: 1

- Official Capacity of the Prison System: 300

- Occupancy Level: 94.3%

George Thomas Kurian

Marshall Islands

Official country name: Republic of the Marshall Islands
Capital: Majuro
Geographic description: Group of atolls and reefs in the North Pacific Ocean between Australia and Hawaii
Population: 59,071 (est. 2005)

■ ■ ■

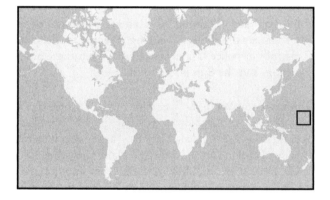

LAW ENFORCEMENT

History. For forty years, the Marshall Islands was a U.S. dependency. The law enforcement was therefore the responsibility of the United States until independence in 1986. The National Police is patterned after U.S. local police departments and follows U.S. regulations and traditions. On independence, the police force was transferred to the republic.

Structure and Organization. The National Police is under the Ministry of Internal Affairs and is headed by a director. There are police stations on each atoll headed by a superintendent. There are few police vehicles, and most policemen conduct their duties on bicycles or on foot.

Police Statistics.

• Police Officers per 100,000 Population: 268.52

HUMAN RIGHTS

Capital punishment is not permitted for any crime in the Marshall Islands. Although victim impact is considered by the criminal justice system, no legislation currently exists to ensure victim participation during criminal proceedings.

CRIME

The Marshall Islands participates in the sixteen-member Pacific Islands Forum in compliance with United Nations rules that require counterterrorism awareness. The myriad of small, impoverished islands in the South Pacific are thought to be hotbeds for networks of organized terrorist cells. Such operations flourish in venues such as the Marshall Islands due to the lack of uniform legislation and human, financial, and technical law enforcement resources.

CORRECTIONAL SYSTEM

There are detention centers on the main islands and a main prison on the Kwajalein atoll.

Prison Conditions. Prison conditions are spare but meet international standards. Male adults and juveniles are housed separately, but female adults and juveniles are housed together. In 1990 prisons were at 154 percent of capacity; however, under international pressure, that rate was reduced to 96 percent by 1994.

Prison Statistics.

- Total Prison Population: 43
- Prison Population Rate per 100,000: 73
- Pretrial Detainees: 34.8%
- Female Prisoners: 4.7%
- Juvenile Prisoners: 2.3%
- Number of Prisons: 1
- Official Capacity of the Prison System: 32
- Occupancy Level: 128.1%

Charles Johnson

Mauritania

Official country name: Islamic Republic of Mauritania
Capital: Nouakchott
Geographic description: Large country on the west coast of northern Africa on the Atlantic Ocean, and bordered by Western Sahara and Algeria to the north, Mali to the east, and Senegal to the south
Population: 3,086,859 (est. 2005)

■ ■ ■

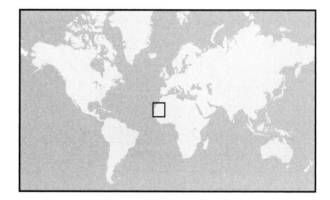

LAW ENFORCEMENT

History. The French colonial administration, which began in 1914, introduced a *Gendarmerie* system in the 1920s, but it was mostly confined to the coastal and southern regions and towns. The country gained independence in 1960.

Structure and Organization. There are three law enforcement agencies:

- *Gendarmerie*
- National Guard
- National Police

The *Gendarmerie* is a specialized paramilitary group under the Ministry of Defense responsible for civil order in and outside of metropolitan areas. The National Guard performs police functions in areas in which the National Police are not present. It and the National Police are under the Ministry of the Interior. Originally organized in two companies, one for the east and one for the west, the *Gendarmerie* was reorganized in 1963 after independence into two companies in the capital and

brigades in each *departement.* Police headquarters is attached to the army headquarters in Nouakchott. One of the two companies in Nouakchott is the Presidential Guard, officially called the Escort and Security Squadron.

The National Police is a nationwide force that exercises ultimate command through the governors of the twelve regions. It is a highly centralized system under a unified command structure. The civil force is organized hierarchically in three ranks in ascending order: policeman, inspector and commissioner. Each prefect and town mayor has a certain amount of discretion and authority in deploying the police under his command.

Education and Training. Training for all ranks is provided at the Police Academy in Nouakchott.

Police Statistics.

- Total Police Personnel: 3,440
- Population per Police Officer: 897

HUMAN RIGHTS

Mauritania is an authoritarian state in which the security services are used by the government to intimidate and suppress dissent. Arbitrary arrests and abuse of prisoners are used by the three law enforcement agencies, and the government rarely, if ever, brings offending personnel to justice. Minority groups, such as the Fulani, Soninke, and Wolof, are singled out as targets of police brutality.

CRIME

Crime Statistics. Offenses reported to the police per 100,000 population: 95.4. Of which:

- Murder: 0.8
- Assault: 27.0
- Burglary: 7.3
- Automobile Theft: 2.5

CORRECTIONAL SYSTEM

Prisons are administered by the director of Penitentiary Administration under the Ministry of Justice.

Prison Conditions. Serious overcrowding in prisons outside Nouakchott, along with lack of proper sanitation facilities, contributes to diseases and a high prison death rate. Medical supplies are inadequate and in short supply. Rich or influential prisoners bring their own food and medicines. Despite regulations against beatings and torture, prisoners are subject to abuse and degrading treatment. Female prisoners are treated much better than men. They have separate facilities, and a private foundation provides a program of education for female prisoners and another program of training for female guards. Another foundation provides substantial aid for juvenile offenders.

Prison Statistics.

- Total Prison Population: 1,185
- Prison Population Rate per 100,000: 38
- Pretrial Detainees: 12.5%
- Number of Prisons: 18
- Official Capacity of the Prison System: 800
- Occupancy Level: 169.3%

George Thomas Kurian

Mauritius

Official country name: Republic of Mauritius
Capital: Port Louis
Geographic description: Island off southern Africa in the Indian Ocean south of Madagascar. Includes the islands of Mauritius, Rodrigues, Agalega Islands, and the Cargados Carajos Shoals (Saint Brandon)
Population: 1,230,602 (est. 2005)

■■■

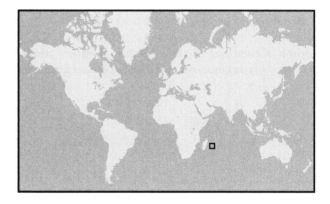

LAW ENFORCEMENT

History. The modern incarnation of the Mauritius Police Force (MPF) has its origins in the colonial experience. Initially settled by French sugar planters dependent on African slave labor, the island was coveted by British imperialists during the Napoleonic Wars as a strategic outpost in the Indian Ocean. On November 29, 1810, the French garrison in Port Louis surrendered to a British amphibious force thus relinquishing effective control, and Mauritius became part of the British colonial empire. Although the Franco-Mauritian planters were permitted to retain their estates, when the British government abolished the slave trade in 1835, it became necessary to find an alternative source of labor. Subsequently, the planter class turned to a system of indentured servitude recruiting extensively from the Indian subcontinent. Within a few decades, the demographic composition of the island shifted to reflect the substantial number of Indian migrants, mostly Hindus and, to a lesser extent Muslims, who responded to the island's labor needs.

A national police force was created in 1859 with a separate unit for Port Louis and modified by the Police

Ordinance of 1893 as the MPF under an inspector general and from 1934 a police commissioner. The role of the MPF during the colonial era, in keeping with the objectives of British imperial policy, was to support the British administrative structure, maintain public order, and preserve what was essentially a feudal social structure. Organized like other colonial forces, the higher echelons of the command structure consisted entirely of British officers responsible for directing resources and maintaining discipline. Indigenous patrol officers executed routine law enforcement, but no native Mauritian could aspire to any rank higher than sergeant. Wary of giving the Indo-Mauritian majority any authority, the police service drew its officers primarily from the Creole sector of the population. Consequently, on the eve of independence, despite the multiethnic character of the nation, the MPF represented a Creole occupational enclave. When the British withdrew in 1968 giving Mauritius its independence, communal tensions erupted in several months of sectarian violence that, in the face of police ineffectiveness, required the intervention of British paramilitary forces. The violence motivated by the fear of exclusion from an Indo-Mauritian-dominated government produced a substantial outward migration of minority communities, including many long-serving Creole officers. As Indo-Mauritians rushed to fill the vacancies, the cumulative effect was to create a police service that reflected a more accurate representation of the nation's diverse ethnic composition. In an island society where communal sensitivities assume great importance, the multiethnic character of the police force facilitated the legitimacy of the MPF, but it also made it subject to political manipulation, as evidenced by frequent administrative changes.

At independence, with the exception of the capital, Port Louis, Mauritius was a nation of tranquil coastal and scattered interior towns, and the establishment of the MPF reflected this social reality. Excluding the Special Mobile Force (SMF), the entire police establishment totaled 1,758 officers. Since most citizens relied on bicycles or horse-drawn transportation, only sixty-four officers were assigned to the Traffic Branch. The two police districts that encompassed the Port Louis metropolitan area were patrolled by a mere 316 officers. Furthermore, only eleven individuals occupied ranks higher than superintendent, suggesting a relatively simple command structure (*Annual Report of the Mauritius Police Force* 1968). By 1980, in the aftermath of the turmoil that had accompanied the immediate postindependence period, the police establishment had more than doubled, totaling 3,805 members. Most of this growth was among the lower ranks. Of the total, almost 3,000 were constables, nearly 450 were sergeants, and 68 were part of a newly created women's police service (*Annual Report of the Mauritius Police Force* 1980). A decade later, the MPF establishment had increased to 6,117 supervised by the commissioner of police assisted by 4 deputy commissioners, 12 assistant commissioners, and 36 superintendents. By this time, a parallel women's service with its own administrative structure headed by an assistant superintendent was beginning to emerge (*Annual Report of the Mauritius Police Force* 1990).

Structure and Organization. Mauritius is an extensively policed society, and the modern MPF invites controversy by having to navigate between its legal mandate to enforce the rule of law and its political role as the most visible agency of state authority. Overall supervisory responsibility for the MPF is exercised by the commissioner of police, who acts under the authority of the prime minister. The commissioner is assisted by 5 deputy commissioners who supervise each division. Next in rank are the 13 posted assistant commissioners in charge of several specialized units (e.g., Port Police, CID). The divisional command structure also includes 37 posted superintendents and 61 posted assistant superintendents in charge of operations, prosecutions, and public relations.

The 16 posted deputy assistant superintendents form the link between the gazetted ranks and the Inspectorate. Police stations are supervised by either chief inspectors (97 posted) or inspectors (274 posted), depending on size and magnitude of responsibility. Sergeants and constables are the lowest ranks in the hierarchy of officers and form the direct-service component of the MPF.

Day-to-day patrol operations are organized into six territorial divisions, consolidating what had been ten police districts:

- Northern
- Eastern
- Southern
- Central
- Western
- South/North, consolidating the two districts that served Port Louis, which covers the entire capital area

Within these divisions are eighty police stations and posts that provide a police presence in every major population center and many smaller communities.

Principal Agencies and Divisions. The MPF consists of 8 branches and 9 units. The branches are:

- Anti-Drug and Smuggling Unit (ADS)
- Central Investigation Division
- Helicopter Squadron
- National Coast Guard
- Passport and Immigration Unit
- Rodrigues Police
- Special Mobile Force
- Special Supporting Unit
- Traffic Branch

The units are:

- Antipiracy Unit
- Complaint Investigation Bureau
- Crime Prevention Unit
- Emergency Response Service
- Police Family Protection Unit
- Police Band
- *Police de tourisme*
- Police Medical Unit
- Port Police

Salaries. The salary schedule for the various police ranks is established by the Pay Research Bureau and ranges from Rs 11,800 (US$389) per month for a constable to Rs 60,000 (US$2,123) per month for the commissioner of police. In addition, a variety of allowances are available for eligible officers: those serving with the ADS are awarded a "risk allowance" of Rs 840 (US$30) per month, and investigators assigned to the CID are granted a "detective allowance" and a "clothing allowance" totaling Rs 660 (US$23) per month.

Retirement Age. In accordance with legislative enactment, all civil servants, including police officers, must accept mandatory retirement at age sixty.

Police-Community Relations. Despite a mission statement that requires officers to enforce the law fairly and impartially and to uphold fundamental human rights, the MPF's emphasis on discipline and order does not merge comfortably with community-oriented policing. To its credit, the MPF has tacitly acknowledged its uneasy relations with the public by instituting an Emergency Response Service (ERS) Bike Patrol in April 2001 to facilitate "contact policing" (*Annual Report* 2001, p. 19). Its central aim, however, is merely to supplement mechanized and foot patrols by assisting in traffic regulation and crime prevention. The department also maintains a Complaints Investigation Bureau (CIB) that responds to citizen complaints about police misconduct. Although this unit is under the administrative control of the commissioner's office, the CIB is required to report all complaints it receives to a judicial board of inquiry within forty-eight hours.

Special Police.

Special Supporting Unit. The Special Supporting Unit (SSU), or Anti-Riot Squad, is charged with assisting the regular police in controlling civil disturbances whenever circumstances expand beyond the control of the latter. It also secures sensitive venues, conducts missing person searches, tracks wanted criminals, and provides escort for dangerous prisoners. Originally constituted in 1937 as a "Police Reserve" by British police administrators in response to a series of labor strikes, the detachment assumed its modern form just prior to independence. Consisting of five operational units and a posted strength of 383 officers, the SSU is based at the line barracks (police headquarters) in Port Louis.

Anti-Drug and Smuggling Unit. Since 1986 the ADS has focused on the growing problem of possession and trafficking in illegal substances. Apart from marijuana, which is easily cultivated amid the cane fields and on remote areas of the island, and opium, a fixture in Mauritius since the colonial period, Mauritius is the only African country with a heroin problem (MacDonald 1996). There is not only a visible addict population, but Mauritius is also easily accessible to Indian suppliers. Employing aerial surveillance and often operating jointly with the SMF (the parliamentary force), the ADS has been modestly successful in eradicating indigenous marijuana plants. Intercepting the importation of heroin, however, has been a more elusive goal. Heroin arrests primarily have been confined to house searches and street arrests.

Traffic Branch. With three major roads all converging in Port Louis, the role of the Traffic Branch in relieving congestion is critical. In a small island nation where there are more than a quarter of a million licensed vehicles, the police are actively involved in directing the flow of traffic, attending to road accidents, and citing motorists for traffic violations. Apart from uniformed officers who move traffic along in Port Louis and the interior cities to the east, a mobile patrol on motorcycles is deployed along the major arteries in each of the six police divisions to monitor traffic during peak hours and enforce ordinances pertaining to parking, speed limits, and driving while intoxicated.

Education and Training. All regular police recruits are obligated to enroll in a six-month training period offered on a revolving basis that includes instruction in routine drills, riot demonstrations, courses in self-defense and first aid, and lectures on general duties and specific areas of law enforcement (e.g., crime-scene investigations, legal implications of the 1970 Geneva Convention). Female recruits undergo separate but similar training augmented by instruction in grooming and public relations. Development courses for newly promoted sergeants and inspectors are designed to enhance the station-level administrative command structure. For officers assigned to the ERS Bike Patrol and those designated for assignment as police prosecutors, special training programs cover the duties unique to those positions. SSU personnel receive special training in crowd control techniques, escort duties, driver education, and mountain climbing exercises. SMF recruits must undergo a rigorous twenty-two-week basic military training period at SMF headquarters in Vacoas.

Uniforms and Weapons. The conventional MPF uniform is a light-blue, short-sleeve shirt with dark-blue trousers (skirts for female officers) and matching cap with gold trim. The insignia appears on the cap brim and both shoulders. The officer's rank can be determined by the chevrons that appear on the epaulets. SSU officers are attired similarly except for a distinctive blue beret and combat boots. An olive-green khaki uniform identifies members of the SMF.

In accordance with their British legacy, regular officers do not carry firearms or any other weapon except for a baton in the course of their normal duties.

Transportation, Technology, and Communications. Most vehicles in the MPF fleet are cars (482) and motorcycles (327), the former equitably distributed throughout the various stations and the latter deployed along the major arteries. The 298 jeeps and 168 vans are mostly employed by the SMF and SSU. The MPF also has seventy-six trucks and an assortment of earth-moving equipment (e.g., mobile cranes, excavators, backhoes) at its disposal, which is useful for rescue operations and clearing debris from the roads when cyclones strike the island. The Helicopter Squadron maintains and operates four helicopters. Based at Sir Seewoosagur Ramgoolam (SSR) International Airport, the two aircraft that form the Maritime Air Squadron are used to conduct search and rescue missions, coastal sorties, and logistical support to the Mauritian territorial islands of Agalega and Rodrigues. The National Coast Guard maintains a fleet of vessels consisting of an Indian naval ship acquired in 1974, 5 Mandovi marine-class boats, 2 Zhuk-class patrol boats, 2 smaller patrol boats, and a Canadian designed, diesel powered, 42-ton ship constructed by a Chilean shipyard and purchased in 1996 (Murthy 1996).

By all measures, the communications and technology capacity of the MPF is rudimentary. The Communications Branch (PCB) consists of a telephone exchange, and a wireless section that oversees the installation and maintenance of mobile, static, and portable telecommunications, facsimile machines, generators, and public address equipment. A Forensic Science Laboratory (FSC) conducts chemical and biological examinations mostly related to crime-scene investigations, drug identification, and testing for blood alcohol levels. There is no capability for conducting DNA analyses. The MPF has come late to computerized law enforcement: In 1999 the department initiated an automated database of fingerprints taken from suspects and crime scenes. The following year, the Automated Finger Print Identification System became the centerpiece of a newly established Information and Technology (IT) Unit, the expanded capacity of which included the coordination and implementation of computer-assisted technology. As of 2001, the link between the main system and the six divisional headquarters became fully operational. The IT Unit would eventually integrate administrative, stores, and payroll records as well as automotive licensing into a single computerized system.

Surveillance and Intelligence Gathering. Internal security is the jurisdiction of the National Security Service (NSS). The NSS was established in May 2001 after its predecessor, the former National Intelligence Unit, was dissolved by legislative enactment. The NSS is supervised by a director-general who reports directly to the commissioner. In the absence of any obvious external

threat to the nation's security, the surveillance of potential domestic challenges to state authority seems to be its principal mandate.

Police Statistics. The approved establishment of the MPF is 8,276, 97% of which is consigned to patrol, traffic, and other direct services to the public.

- Total Police Personnel: 8,697
- Police Personnel per 100,000 Inhabitants: 720
- Women's Police Service: 488

HUMAN RIGHTS

Mauritius is a long-standing parliamentary democracy with all the institutions usually associated with democracies: an elected legislature and executive, an independent judiciary, a free press, and constitutionally guaranteed rights. With a few exceptions, the police generally respect the human rights of the citizenry. The CIB received 186 complaints in 2003 alleging police brutality, most often during attempts to obtain confessions. The most controversial of such cases in the recent past occurred in February 1999 when Kaya, a popular Creole singer, died in police custody, touching off a week of rioting and looting. However, the law prohibits inhumane treatment, and normally, the authorities comply. Moreover, in most instances when someone is taken into custody, the police allow prompt access to family and legal counsel. With regard to freedom of assembly, the commissioner of police must issue a permit for any public demonstration. In 2003, with one exception (later overturned on judicial appeal), no request was denied, and the right of free association has usually been respected in practice ("Mauritius" 2004).

CRIME

Criminal Identification and Forensics. Detecting crime and gathering evidence is the responsibility of the Central Criminal Investigation Division (CCID). It handles all cases of fraud, bribery, homicide, and sexual assault. The CCID has at its disposal a number of support units trained to conduct forensic analysis and maintain records. The Fraud Squad investigates major property crimes, and the Major Crimes Investigation Team inquires into all cases of homicide. The Technical Support Unit and the Scientific Support Service based at Rose Hill conduct crime-scene investigations to secure fingerprints and take photographs, which are stored at the Crime Records Office in police headquarters. There is also a Handwriting Section, which maintains samples for identification in cases of forgery, swindling, and document alterations. Cases involving trace evidence, ballistic tests, drug analysis, arson investigations, and examination of postmortem specimens are the responsibility of the Chemistry and Biology Sections of the Forensic Science Laboratory. Victims of sexual assault are normally examined by police medical officers.

Crime Statistics. Offenses reported to the police per 100,000 population: 3,030.25. Of which:

- Homicide: 2.19
- Rape: 2.28
- Robbery: 98.3
- Burglary: 133.54
- Assault: 909.7

CORRECTIONAL SYSTEM

The prison system is under the authority of the commissioner of prisons; the largest prison is at Beau-Bassin.

Prison Conditions. Although prison facilities are overcrowded, conditions and sanitation generally meet international standards, with sufficient provision of food, water, and medical care available. Women are held separately from men, juveniles from adults, and pretrial detainees from convicted prisoners. Prisoners with HIV/ AIDS are held separately from the general prison population. International organizations are permitted to visit prison facilities.

Prison Statistics.

- Total Prison Population: 2,464
- Prison Population Rate per 100,000: 205
- Pretrial Detainees: 34.3%

- Female Prisoners: 5.6%
- Juvenile Prisoners: 0.4%
- Number of Prisons: 9
- Official Capacity of the Prison System: 1,741
- Occupancy Level: 141.5%

BIBLIOGRAPHY

Annual Report of the Mauritius Police Force. 1968, 1980, 1990, 2001. Mauritius Police Force.

Bowman, Larry W. 1991. *Mauritius: Democracy and Development in the Indian Ocean.* Boulder, Co: Westview.

Dinan, Monique. 1985. Une ile eclatee: Analyse de l'emigration mauricienne 1960–1982. Port Louis, Mauritius: Best Graphics.

MacDonald, Dave. 1996. "Drugs in Southern Africa: An Overview." *Drugs: Education, Prevention and Policy.*

"Mauritius (Country Reports on Human Rights Practices— 2003)." 2004. U.S. Department of State, Bureau of Democracy, Human Rights and Labor.

Murthy, L. C. 1996. "National Coast Guard." *Police Magazine.* Mauritius Police Force.

"Review of Pay and Grading Structures and Conditions of Service in the Public Sector and the Private Secondary Schools." 2003. (Vol. II, Part 1, Civil Service, Police 13.1.) Pay Research Bureau, Office of Prime Minister.

Roth, Frederick P. 2005. "The Prospect of Democratic Policing in Underdeveloped Countries: The Mauritian Model." In *Comparative Criminal Justice: Traditional and Nontraditional Systems of Law and Control,* 2nd ed., edited by Richter H. Moore and Charles B. Fields. Long Grove: Waveland Press.

Simmons, Adele Smith. 1982. *Modern Mauritius: The Politics of Decolonialization.* Bloomington: Indiana University Press.

Frederick P. Roth

Mexico

Official country name: United Mexican States
Capital: Mexico City
Geographic description: Third-largest country in Latin America, south of the United States, in Middle America bordering on both the Pacific Ocean and the Gulf of Mexico
Population: 106,202,903 (est. 2005)

■■■

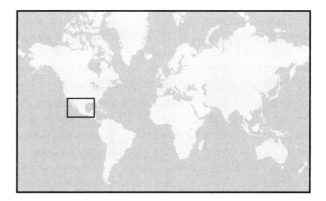

LAW ENFORCEMENT

History. A rudimentary police system existed in Mexico in the nineteenth century. Originally, the police were under the control of the Public Ministry. Its agents were called *fiscals* because one of their principal functions was the collection of fiscal levies imposed by attorneys of the Crown. Later, they were charged with suppressing crime and initiating procedures in criminal cases. They were assigned to police stations where they worked with local police and the judicial police.

Structure and Organization. There is no one particular dominant police force in Mexico. The structure of police organizations is complex, and organization changes frequently. Police forces exist at the federal, state, and municipal levels through many overlapping layers of authority. Each state has its own police department and a judicial police. Larger cities have a judicial police.

Principal Agencies and Divisions.

Federal Police: There are three federal-level forces: The Federal Preventive Police (*Policía Federal Preventiva*, PFP), established in 1999, is responsible for public security and

crime prevention and combat across the country. The Secretariat of Public Security of the Federal District (*Secretaría de Seguridad Pública del Distrito Federal*, SSP), which does not operate on a national level, oversees a combined force of more than ninety thousand in the Federal District and is responsible for public safety and order in central Mexico City, which experiences the highest crime rate and level of insecurity in the country. The Federal Agency of Investigation (*Agencia Federal de Investigaciones*, AFI), established in 2001, is charged with investigating federal crimes. This agency replaced the corrupt Federal Judicial Police (*Policía Judicial Federal*, PJF), and efforts to develop and maintain an uncorrupt agency continue.

The PFP is the primary force and was established after the Mexican Senate ordered the creation of a national police force combining the Federal Highway Police, the Federal Fiscal Police, and the Federal Immigration Police. The PFP is attached to the *Secretaría de Seguridad Pública* and is divided into several divisions:

- Preventive
- Riot
- Auxiliary
- Traffic
- Investigation (formerly called the Secret Service

Slightly less than half of the preventive police work in the Sectoral Police Division, which is distributed geographically into six main regions, with usually three precincts in each and a number of sectors within each precinct. The rest of the preventive police are organized into five main divisions. The Metropolitan Division consists of the Public Transit Police, Tourist Police, Grenadiers, Feminine Police, and the Emergency Rescue Squad. Another division is the Special Squadron, which comprises helicopters, motorcycles, the task force that deals with terrorist threats, and the Alpha Group, which fights drug trafficking. The Federal Highway Police patrol the federally designated highways and investigate auto accidents. Other government agencies and ministries are empowered to maintain their own police forces; these include the Ministry of Public Health, the National Railway of Mexico, the Ministry of Hydraulic Reserves, and Mexican Petroleum. The Federal District has its own police force under the secretary of public security.

The main components of the federal police are the central office for classification of offenses, licensing and traffic control office, prevention of juvenile delinquency division, radio patrol service, special investigations service, and special services. Federal police has its own rescue elements: the Urban Services and Land and Air Rescue Squadron, equipped with motor vehicles, boats and aircraft. The police force is organized on military lines and has a paramilitary role. It consists of thirty-three battalions, of which thirty-one are numbered. The 2nd is the preventive police; the 4th, 5th, 6th, 9th, 12th, 14th, and 22nd are auxiliary; the 31st is the auxiliary private police. A reserve force, the 18th, is administrative, and the 28th is the women's police. The unnumbered battalions are the Grenadiers and the transport battalion. The Grenadiers are a riot control force, which includes a motorized brigade and an internal security squad.

State and Municipal Police: Mexico's thirty-one states maintain both preventive and judicial police forces, which enforce state law (*fuero comun*). The state police enforce state laws within their jurisdiction and assist the federal police in enforcing federal laws. Large cities have special units, such as the Park Police and the Foreign Language Police. The number of state-level preventive police is approximately ninety thousand and judicial police approximately 26,185. The judicial police is the law enforcement agency charged with investigation and prosecution related to local crimes.

Of Mexico's 2,395 registered municipalities, approximately 340 have no police force. Police forces are concentrated in larger municipalities, with approximately 69 percent of preventive police located in the eighty-seven largest cities. This means that the approximately 25 million residents in areas of fewer than 2,500 people lack official police forces and rely on community volunteers to police their towns. Municipal police lack technical equipment, carry outmoded firearms, must supply their own bulletproof vests and often other necessary equipment. Salaries are poor.

Police at Work. In large urban areas there are many precincts, called police delegations; a typical delegation has between 200 and 250 preventive police attached to it. The delegation is under the command of a *comandante*, usually an officer with the rank of a captain. (All police ranks correspond to military ranks.) Lesser officers, usually lieutenants, are in charge of each eight-hour shift and are assisted by first sergeants, second sergeants, and corporals. Most of the men operate out of the command headquarters called a *comandancia*, but part of the company is stationed at fixed points throughout the police delegation, usually at small two-person kiosks accessible to the public. Assisting the preventive police are auxiliary police who patrol the streets on the night-shift only. Agents of the Public Ministry assigned to the delegation have their offices at the *comandancias*. Many of the *comandancias* also have a first-aid facility on the premises with a doctor or medical technician in attendance. Many of the *comandancias* have two kinds of cells: large communal cells, usually without bunks, holding numerous persons sentenced for misdemeanors (with separate cells for men and women) and small cells with bunks to confine persons under arrest for felonies during preliminary investigation. Mexico City has twenty such *comandancias*.

Special Police. Currency and banking offenses are investigated by the Special Investigation Department of the Bank of Mexico. The Bank and Industrial Police is a separate organization that protects banking institutions and includes two specialized units, the Mounted Police and the Patrol Squadron. Numerous small, private police forces are employed by banks, department stores, hotels, and similar institutions or assigned to them by the commercial police branch of the police force. The police assigned to department stores have the right to arrest debtors and keep them locked up in the stores until the debt is paid.

Education and Training. Recruitment is a major problem for the Mexican police, and police units in all jurisdictions are understaffed. Education and training are provided at all levels. The General Directorate of Police and Traffic operates a police academy where intensive courses of from

Police in Mexico City conduct patrols on rollerblades in front of the seventeenth-century Metropolitan Cathedral located in the city's main square, January 14, 2005. The officers are members of a division that patrol the city of over 8.5 million people by also using bicycles and horses. **AP IMAGES.**

four to six months are given to selected new recruits and advanced training is provided to officers and police. The Federal Highway Police runs a small training school for its personnel. The Technical Institute of the Public Ministry gives graduate courses in criminology. A few states have academies for state police. The best are those in Nuevo Leon, Jalisco, and Mexico City. Courses at state academies usually last for four months. In smaller localities, police are appointed on the basis of political patronage.

Police Statistics.

- Total Strength of the Police force: 350,000
- Population per Police Officer: 295

HUMAN RIGHTS

Corruption is widespread in police ranks and combined in many cases with immorality and incompetence. Bribes are commonplace and even demanded for the performance of some tasks. There is also a close relationship in some parts of the country between the police and organized crime, especially with drug dealers. Corruption

is not limited to the lower ranks but extends to the top echelons. Extrajudicial killings and excessive use of force cause concerns to human rights watchers. There are credible reports of disappearances. The police often torture persons to obtain information, prosecutors use such evidence in courts, and the courts admit as evidence confessions extracted under torture. Human rights abuses are particularly severe in the state of Chiapas, where there is an ongoing insurrection against the government.

The government's efforts to improve the human rights situation have led to the creation of an Undersecretariat for Human Rights and Democracy and to the ratification of international conventions and numerous protocols and agreements on human rights issues.

CRIME

Crime Statistics. Offenses reported to the police per 100,000: 108. Of which:

- Murder: 7.3
- Assault: 30.2

CORRECTIONAL SYSTEM

The Federal Criminal Code dates from 1931, with later amendments. It modernized previous laws singled out juvenile delinquency for special attention and made new provisions for controlling traffic in narcotics and dealing with corruption, pandering, and espionage. Crimes are broadly categorized as those against persons, property, state, public morals, and public health. Capital punishment was prohibited by the Federal Code of 1931, but the constitution permits it for parricide, abduction, and highway robbery. The highest punishment is thirty years in prison. The most distinctive feature of the Mexican criminal justice system is the writ of *amparo*, which has no exact English equivalent but is roughly similar to a writ of habeas corpus. An *amparo* may be sought by any citizen for the redress of an infringement of his or her civil rights or against the act of any official, tribunal, police officer, legislator, or bureaucrat. The penal system includes 6 federal penitentiaries, 10 federal district prisons, 365 state prisons, and 70 municipal and regional jails.

Prisons are under the jurisdiction of the Secretaría de Seguridad Pública and are divided into federal, state, and municipal facilities. The constitution requires that penal systems focus on rehabilitation and social readjustment of the prisoner through education and training. The largest of the federal prisons are the Penitentiary for the Sentenced, the Lucumberri Penitentiary, and the Women's Jail. The Federal District also contains 4 centers of seclusion, 3 small jails, and 13 jails in the various *comandancias*. There are 2 federal penal colonies where the most dangerous criminals and those serving long sentences are placed. The most infamous of these is in the Maria Islands, about 70 miles offshore in the Pacific Ocean. Here, married prisoners are permitted to have their families with them and are provided with thatched houses. Unmarried prisoners live in dormitories. All can move freely around the main island but must attend roll call twice daily. Prisoners work to develop the island's resources and work in lime quarries, salt fields, lumber mills, sisal plantations, and workshops, or engage in agricultural pursuits and cattle raising.

All states have state penitentiaries. Some are old and overcrowded while others are modern and fairly large. Among the best are those in Sonora, Durango, Michoacán, Jalisco, and Mexico City. Many have large staffs, including psychologists, psychiatrists, and other doctors. Every prisoner either works in the shops or on the prison farm or goes to school. There are more than 2,500 municipal prisons, including holding cells. Some are fairly large and have separate sections for women and children, but others are primitive and lack toilet and water facilities. In some villages, the prisoners work on public projects, such as street cleaning and gardening.

Prison Conditions. Life in Mexican prisons and jails generally is less grim than in many other countries. Little friction exists between prisoners and guards, and the guards themselves perform small services for the prisoners in return for tips and bribes. Prisoners with skills are permitted to make items and sell them while others engage in such services as barbering and shoe repairing. Prisoners who can afford it furnish their own quarters and have their own personal servants. Some prisons permit commercial workshops to operate on their premises.

Prisoners usually are on their own during the day to work, relax, or engage in sports or games, as most penal institutions do not have full-time organized recreational activities. There are intramural leagues for baseball and soccer with daily games. Idle inmates frequently fight among themselves. Families and other relatives usually are permitted to visit twice a week, Sundays being one of the days set aside for such visits. In women's prisons and in women's sections of state prisons, mothers are permitted to have their small children with them at all times.

Male prisoners have the right to conjugal visits. Wives usually are permitted to spend up to two hours every week alone with their husbands. Some prisons permit wives to spend the entire night with their husbands, and in others, girlfriends and prostitutes are allowed to visit single inmates. No conjugal visits, however, are permitted for women inmates; only fathers or brothers may be alone with them. Prisoners nearing the end of their sentences are permitted to spend weekends with their families.

Health and sanitary conditions are poor. Many prisoners suffer from HIV/AIDS and tuberculosis, which are the leading causes of death in prisons. HIV-positive prisoners are subject to discrimination and mistreatment. Drug and alcohol addictions are rampant. As many as 80 percent of prisoners are reported to use some form of drug, with heroin being the drug of choice, followed by cocaine. Corruption and poor prison conditions often lead to riots and escapes. Convicted criminals and pretrial detainees are often housed together because of overcrowding, which is a serious problem: in Baja California and Sonora, prisons are more than 181% overpopulated. Juveniles aged eleven to eighteen are held outside the prison system.

Prison Statistics.

- Total Prison Population: 201,931
- Prison Population Rate per 100,000: 191
- Pretrial Detainees: 41.9%

- Female Prisoners: 5%

- Number of Prisons: 457

- Official Capacity of the Prison System: 151,692

- Occupancy Level: 125.6%

George Thomas Kurian

Micronesia, Federated States of

Official country name: Federated States of Micronesia
Capital: Palikir
Geographic description: Island group in the North Pacific Ocean, north of New Guinea and between Hawaii and Indonesia
Population: 108,105 (est. 2005)

■■■

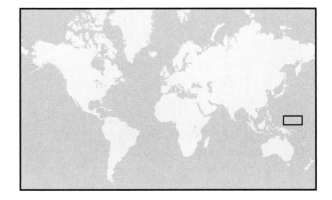

LAW ENFORCEMENT

History. The Federated States of Micronesia (FSM) was a dependency of the United States as a United Nations (UN) Trust Territory until 1986, and its police system was created under U.S. auspices and is modeled on the local municipal forces in the United States. On independence, these forces were transferred to the republic.

Structure and Organization. Each of the four states—Chuuk (*Truk*), Kosrae (*Kosaie*), Pohnpei (*Ponape*), and Yap—has a department of public safety that includes corrections agencies as well. Under the Compact of Free Association, the United States assists local public safety departments in operational matters.

HUMAN RIGHTS

Capital punishment is not permitted for any crime. Although victim impact is considered by the criminal justice system, no legislation exists to ensure victim participation during criminal proceedings.

CRIME

The age of criminal responsibility varies; it is eighteen in Chuuk and Kosrae; however, in Kosrae, a sixteen year old may be tried if at the time the crime is committed he or she is considered physically and mentally mature.

Terrorism. Micronesia officials participate in the sixteen-member Pacific Islands Forum in compliance with UN rules that require counterterrorism awareness. The myriad of small, impoverished islands in the South Pacific are thought to be hotbeds for networks of organized terrorist cells. Such operations flourish in venues such as Micronesia due to the lack of uniform legislation and human, financial, and technical law enforcement resources.

Crime Statistics.

- Number of Reported Criminal Offenses: 6,622
- Felony: 1,602

- Misdemeanor: 2,188

- Minor Traffic: 1,799

- Juvenile: 489

- Serious Drug Offense: drugs are generally not a problem; alcohol is a serious problem, believed to be involved in most crimes

CORRECTIONAL SYSTEM

There are detention centers on most islands and prisons in each of the four states. Prisons are maintained by the Department of Public Safety.

Prison Conditions. Prison conditions generally meet international standards. Inmates are sometimes placed on a work crew but are not provided with organized education or therapy programs. Frequent visits are permitted, and the general atmosphere is informal.

Prison Statistics.

- Total Prison Population: 39

- Prison Population Rate per 100,000: 22

- Number of Prisons: 4

Charles Johnson

Moldova

---■---

Official country name: Republic of Moldova

Capital: Chişinău

Geographic description: Located in Eastern Europe, bordered by Romania to the south and west and Ukraine to the north and east

Population: 4,455,412 (est. 2005)

■ ■ ■

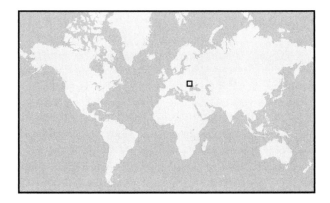

LAW ENFORCEMENT

History. From 1918 to 1940, the police of Chişinău (formerly Kishinev) fell under the direction of the police prefect. In the other cities and districts, the police were under the leadership of city and district prefects. Passage of the Law on the Organization of the General Police on July 21, 1929, brought radical changes in the activities of the police. The law provided for the creation of administrative and criminal police as well as an information service, which was part of the Main Department of Police under the Ministry of Internal Affairs. From 1940, with the creation of the Moldavian Soviet Socialist Republic, a new system of social institutions was developed, the function of which was public order maintenance. In August 1940, by order of the People's Commissariat of Internal Affairs of the USSR, the People's Commissariat of Internal Affairs (NKVD) of the Moldavian Soviet Socialist Republic was formed.

The organizational structure of the NKVD had two levels: the central apparatus; and departments, units, and services. The basic components of the system of internal affairs were the Directorate for the Peasant-Workers Militia, Department of Penitentiary Institutions, Fire Service Department, Archives Department, State Security Service, and Border Security. The August 1940 order also created six district departments of internal security. In this period, the agencies for state security and public order maintenance were all under the NKVD. In 1941 the state security agency was removed from the NKVD and formed into the People's Commissariat for State Security (NKGB). In March 1946 the NKVD was renamed the Ministry of Internal Affairs (MVD). One of the main events in the evolution of the internal affairs agencies was the establishment in 1956 of the principle of double subordination of police—to local government and to national headquarters of the MVD. In the 1960s the internal affairs system underwent several reorganizations. In 1966 the MVD became the Ministry for the Protection of Social Order. In 1968 it was changed back to its old name, Ministry of Internal Affairs. Among the basic components of the MVD were the Administrative Service, Criminal Investigation, Department for the Fight against Theft of Socialist Property and Speculation, Passport and Visa Registration Department, State Auto Inspectorate, Fire Service, and Department of Correctional-Labor Institutions.

After the declaration of sovereignty by the Republic of Moldova on June 23, 1990, a new legal status and structure were established, along with restructured responsibilities of the law enforcement agencies, and the process of forming a national system of internal affairs agencies began. On September 13, 1990, the government of the Republic of Moldova passed Decision No. 321, "On the Reorganization of the Internal Affairs Agencies of the Moldavian Soviet Socialist Republic," which provided for the creation of a central police department as well as regional police departments. The new agencies of internal affairs (police) began to replace the militia. The Law on the Police was passed by the legislature on December 18, 1990.

The process of structural reform continues. The police of the Republic of Moldova boast of a law enforcement agency that serves the public and strictly observes the laws to defend life, health, rights, and freedoms of its citizens from criminal and other illegal encroachments.

Structure and Organization. The Ministry of Internal Affairs is responsible for the police; the head of the Moldovan Police is the inspector general of police, who is also deputy minister of internal affairs. The Information and Security Service (ISS) controls other security agencies. The Department of Border Guards, Tax Police, and Customs constitute separate agencies. The Parliament has constitutional authority to investigate the activities of the Ministry of Internal Affairs and the ISS and to ensure that they comply with the law. Within the context of an authoritarian executive branch, the legislature has relatively little power.

The ISS can investigate crimes but cannot arrest individuals. Civilian authorities maintain control of the security forces. Some members of the security forces are known to have committed human rights abuses. The Tax Police (part of the national tax inspectorate of the Ministry of Finance since 1998) has preventative and investigative powers in cases of tax-related crimes and breaches of fiscal and customs legislation. It is authorized to conduct certain investigations, check the existence and authenticity of certain documents, inspect registers and accounting documents, and seize goods of unproven origin, the income on which taxes have not been paid, and goods that are illegal to manufacture and sell. When such offenses are disclosed, the Tax Police must inform the relevant criminal investigation units.

There is some coordination among various agencies to provide for the guarding of the state borders. These

agencies include the Ministry of Internal Affairs, Border Guard Troops, the Ministry of Defense, Carabinieri, Customs, and other agencies. However, due to some of the more challenging issues facing law enforcement, such as low salaries, lack of equipment, weak legal mechanisms, and widespread corruption, one must consider that the border is not adequately guarded. Due to the fact that the basic work in protecting the border is carried out by the Border Guard Troops, it is frequently regarded as the most important of the agencies. The Border Guard Troops has in its ranks 5,500 military persons who serve in the headquarters unit, frontier groups, frontier commandants' offices, frontier stations, and state border-crossing checkpoints. In the western sector of the state border, there are about thirty frontier posts and frontier commandant's offices and five international state border crossing checkpoints. In the northern and southern sectors, there are about twenty frontier posts and frontier commandant's offices and twelve international state border-crossing checkpoints. Establishment in the northern and southern sectors was begun later and will be enhanced over time. To the east, the state border in the Transdniestr region is the site of ongoing conflict and requires no less than twenty frontier posts and international state border-crossing checkpoints.

A special battalion, the Fulger, was created by MVD Order No. 677-4 on December 5, 1991, for the purpose of strengthening law enforcement's fight against crime and maintenance of public order. Fulger reports directly to the minister of internal affairs under the Ministry of Interior. The group is part of the system of units of special designation *(spetsialnogo naznacheniya)* made up of three rapid-response forces units, one counterterrorism unit, one technical services unit, and others. The primary function of these groups is to prevent terrorist acts and criminal attacks, detain armed criminals, carry out operational or detective work, prevent civil unrest, and the evacuation and rescue of individuals in emergency situations. These groups frequently work in conjunction with law enforcement officers to prevent street crime, burglaries of apartments and in automobiles, and other such activity.

The Carabinieri Troops were formed on the basis of the law "On the Carabinieri Troops of the Republic of Moldova MVD," which passed on December 12, 1991. The Carabinieri are essentially the analogue of the internal troops of other former Soviet republics. Their basic function is to support the police in maintaining public order; defending basic rights and freedoms of the citizenry; protecting personal property and state holdings; guarding embassies, consulates, and other diplomatic missions of foreign governments; providing guard services for particularly sensitive government installations; and other similar functions.

Police at Work. The police of Moldova, as is the case with police in most of the former Soviet states, work in conditions that do not allow for effective law enforcement. Police salaries are low, reflecting the overall economic situation in the country. In 2003 the average monthly salary was approximately $57 (818 lei). The average monthly salary was approximately $66 (941 lei) in the private sector and approximately $46 (657 lei) in the public sector. Frequently, the government is unable to meet employee payrolls; salaries can fall months in arrears. The severe shortages of gasoline or budgetary resources to purchase gasoline are present in Moldova and throughout the former Soviet Union. There is frequently little gas to fuel police cars in order to patrol or to pursue criminals. Police have been known to ride the bus to answer a police call.

Comparatively speaking, law enforcement agencies at the border regions were much better equipped during the Soviet era and have fallen behind the times. Currently, although the borders are considered by Moldovan officials to be satisfactorily equipped, this equipment by and large dates to the 1980s. The lack of modern surveillance equipment requires increasing the number of personnel to compensate for the absence of modern technical equipment. It is believed that the technical upgrading of border facilities is well beyond the financial capabilities of the Moldovan government.

As of January 2001, the Ministry of Internal Affairs was understaffed by nearly 12 percent. Throughout the 1990s, police officials left the service in search of more lucrative opportunities. In 2000, 1,774 employees left the service; this represented an increase of more than three hundred from the previous year. Since 1998 the number of officials leaving the service has exceeded the number of recruits. Also problematic is the crime rate among police and officials alike. In 2000, 5,459 disciplinary sanctions were instituted against Ministry of Internal Affairs officials. Of these, 3,326 were lodged against police employees, 1,897 against Carabinieri troops, and 236 against staff of educational establishments. Four hundred thirty-one officials were dismissed. Nineteen cases of illegal usage of firearms were registered and, overall, criminal proceedings were instituted against 291 police employees and 113 Carabinieri. During the first four months of 2003, sixty-five criminal cases were instituted against police officers for bribery, robbery, and abuse of office.

Education and Training. Historically, there has been little discrimination in the selection of recruits, resulting in the admission of candidates of low caliber. The Ministry of Internal Affairs has expressed deep concern regarding the inadequacy of incoming candidates. Reasons for difficulty in recruiting, at least in part, lie with the low salary, low prestige of police work, unsatisfactory living conditions provided to police, and a failing educational system. The level of professional

training of new recruits through the educational institutions is considered to be low. According to the Ministry of Internal Affairs, the theoretical training of the graduates of the Moldovan Police Academy was once at a level of about 53 percent of what it should be while those graduating from the National Police College were at the 25 percent level. However, in 2001 the International Criminal Investigative Training Assistance Program (ICITAP), established by the U.S. Department of Justice in 1986, began assisting with modernizing technical support and training instructors at the Moldovan Police Academy and the National Police College. The ICITAP also established an internship to facilitate communication between Moldovan officials and law enforcement trainers around the world. In 2002, to help improve police training, the ICITAP assisted in remodeling and providing modern technical equipment to the conference center at the National Police College. This center is accessible to all U.S. agencies.

Police Statistics.

- Total Police Personnel: 13,431
- Total Female Personnel: 500
- Police Staff per 100,000 Population: 300

Also, Moldova has a paramilitary force attached to the Ministry of Internal Affairs that could number about 2,500, along with a riot police force of about 1,000.

CRIME

Crime in Moldova, and everywhere in former Soviet republic, rose dramatically following the demise of the Soviet Union. Economic and drug-related crimes, the most visible and predictable results of the deteriorating economic situations in the newly independent countries, have simply overwhelmed the human and financial resources devoted to them. Often, however, the problem is more extensive than what is acknowledged, as many crimes are not registered. For example, in mid-1995, the Moldovan government stated that overall crime had risen by 29% over the previous year. However, the number of motor vehicles "being searched for" was thirteen times the number of vehicles listed as "stolen."

Organized and economic crime grew in dramatic fashion throughout the 1990s. Moldovan authorities estimated that the income of criminal organizations amounted to more than half the total income in the national economy. This income of criminal organizations comes mainly from trafficking in drugs, arms and oil products, prostitution, theft of assets belonging either to the state or to private individuals, smuggling tobacco or alcohol, bank and financial fraud, and tax evasion. Officials estimate that the value of smuggled goods coming into the country that crosses at the Transdniestr region is at least $900 million.

There are about 2,500 recorded juvenile offenders per year in Moldova. Most of these young people are aged sixteen or seventeen (about 60%), and over 90 percent are boys. While these figures almost certainly mask nonreporting or nonrecording practices, they indicate a relatively low level of juvenile offending countrywide. The majority of juvenile offenders are sentenced for theft (over 60%). Violent offenses are a relative rarity.

Narcotics. Drug-related crimes were reported to have increased between 2001 and 2002 by approximately 35 percent. Initially, Moldova was a drug trafficking route for narcotics moving westward to Europe from central Asia and for raw products moving in the opposite direction. However, the finished product now appears to be marketed through the country from both directions. Moldova also grows its own raw product; it is an agricultural country, with a climate conducive to growing marijuana and opium poppies. Estimated annual production of marijuana is several thousand pounds, and between January and November of 2002 alone, authorized personnel destroyed more than seven thousand pounds of cannabis and eight thousand pounds of poppies. Synthetic drugs are increasingly being imported, especially from Romanian traffickers, who are establishing manufacturing enclaves in Moldova for amphetamines and ecstasy in particular. Organized crime in neighboring countries heavily facilitates Moldovan drug trafficking, as it does trafficking in women.

In July 2001 the Service to Fight against Illegal Traffic in Drugs became a division of the department in the Ministry of Internal Affairs that deals with organized crime and corruption. Moldovan law enforcement authorities continue to pursue the fight against drugs. To that end, drug enforcement capabilities were restructured in 2002, with revisions also being made to the criminal code in relation to drug offenses. The Drug Enforcement Unit is dedicated exclusively to antidrug functions, and although its number of personnel decreased following restructure, the quantity of drugs seized remained similar to that of the previous year, and criminal proceedings increased considerably. Changes to the criminal code also permit arrest and prosecution of individuals not directly involved in trafficking but who facilitate those who are. Maximum penalties for drug trafficking were increased to twenty-five years in prison. With the establishment of the Center for Combating Economic Crimes and Corruption, Drug Enforcement Unit personnel increased to 117—twenty-one are employed in headquarters and support services, and the remaining are located throughout the country.

In 2003 Moldovan counternarcotics efforts underwent significant leadership changes, with the Drug Enforcement Unit of the Ministry of Internal Affairs changing directors three times in a six-month period. The number of law enforcement personnel within the Drug Enforcement Unit remained constant, with ninety-five officers in the field and twenty serving in headquarters or support functions.

Trafficking in Persons. Trafficking in people is prohibited by law, and sentences for such crimes range from seven to twenty-five years in prison, with the most severe being for trafficking groups and pregnant women, as well as for repeat offenders and abuse of power, kidnapping, use of violence, or trickery in capturing people to be trafficked. Trafficking in children brings sentences anywhere from ten years to life. Regardless, Moldova is a major source of women and children trafficked primarily for prostitution to the Balkans, other European countries, and the Middle East. Some sources report that as many as fifty thousand Moldovan women are trafficked annually to Europe alone for prostitution purposes. Moldovan men are transported to Russia and surrounding countries for use in forced labor and begging. Evidence has arisen that men are also trafficked to Japan. Contributing to the widespread nature of this crime is insufficient resources for border control, as is the high degree of corruption found among migration officials and border guards whose low salaries and often intermittent pay make them particularly vulnerable to bribery in this lucrative market.

The government has stepped up efforts to prevent trafficking of women and provide victim assistance, but these efforts have been slow and primarily focused on legislation an prosecution. Only in 2003 was one full-time staff member employed by the National Committee on Antitrafficking. Local regional committees have been established, and the National Committee requires local governmental and ministerial officials to give updates on their antitrafficking efforts. Also, a special unit has been established within the Ministry of Internal Affairs. This ministry and the Ministry of Labor provide training to investigators dedicated specifically to antitrafficking programs, and Moldova's government has begun cooperating with Interpol and certain countries in preventive efforts. From January to September 2003, 290 trafficking investigations were opened, with 137 directly related to former or present laws. There were nine cases of trafficking of minors, along with other cases of children being taken illegally out of the country, illegal hiring of people to work outside the country, and illegal acquisition of persons for prostitution purposes.

Crime Statistics. Crime statistics should always be handled with great care. In the case of Moldova and other former Soviet states, they are relatively meaningless. Locked in an ideological battle with the West, Soviet reality urged the creation of fictitious figures across virtually all sectors of the economy and society in order to portray a positive image to the outside world. The depiction of crime was one of the most important sectors for manipulation as the USSR attempted to demonstrate the superiority of Communism and its promise of the disappearance of crime. According to police officials, the practice of producing fraudulent statistics (*pipiska*) continues long after the demise of the Soviet Union. Latent crime has always been assumed to be rather high.

Offenses reported to the police per 100,000 population: 893.67. Of which:

- Intentional Homicides: 8.13
- Assaults: 28.4
- Rapes: 4.67
- Robberies: 59.29
- Thefts: 416.16

CORRECTIONAL SYSTEM

Prisons fall under the direction of the Ministry of Justice.

Prison Conditions. The Department of Penitentiary Institutions provides separate facilities for adults and minors. There are 17 adult prisons (8 correctional colonies, 3 settlement centers, and 6 prisons) plus 1 prison hospital. For juveniles, there are 5 Isolation Units, which hold juveniles on pretrial detention. There is also 1 prison for juveniles.

Although human rights organizations and the Red Cross are permitted to visit prisons, conditions are harsh, particularly in Transnistria, where many people are arbitrarily arrested, imprisoned, and tortured. Malnutrition and disease, especially tuberculosis, are serious issues. Prisons generally are overcrowded and lack fresh air, recreational, and rehabilitation facilities, and it is usually left up to local and nongovernmental organizations to supply prisoners with clothes, medicine, and other items.

Prison Statistics.

- Total Prison Population: 10,729
- Prison Population Rate 100,000: 238
- Pretrial Detainees: 24.4%
- Female Prisoners: 2.8%
- Juveniles: 0.4%
- Foreign Prisoners: 1%
- Number of Establishments: 20
- Official Capacity of the Prison System: 12,105
- Occupancy Level: 88.6%

BIBLIOGRAPHY

Carasciuc, L., E. Obreja, V. Gasca, N. Izdebschi, C. Lazari, and M. Mazur. 2002. "National Integrity System Indicators: Republic of Moldova." Transparency International. Available online at http://www.transparency.md/Docs/IntegrityInd_en.pdf (accessed January 5, 2006).

"Country Report on Human Rights Practices, 2003." U.S. Department of State. Available online at http://www.state.gov/g/drl/rls/hrrpt/2003/27854.htm (accessed January 5, 2006).

"International Narcotics Control Strategy Report, 2003." U.S. Department of State. Available online at http://www.state.gov/p/inl/rls/nrcrpt/2003/vol2/html/29915.htm (accessed January 5, 2006).

"Moldova: Anti-Trafficking Policies." Crime and Violence. 2004. Gender Issues. Available online at http://www.unece.org/stats/gender/web/genpols/keyinds/crime/moldova.htm (accessed January 5, 2006).

"Moldova Expands Human Trafficking Efforts with More Local Cops." 2003. Deutsche Presse-Agentur (September 2003). Available online at http://www.iabolish.com/news/press-coverage/2003/dpa09-15-03.htm (accessed January 5, 2006).

Moldova Ministry of Internal Affairs. Available online at http://www.mai.md/fulger_ru/ (accessed January 5, 2006).

"Moldova 2001, Prison Conditions." British Helsinki Human Rights Group. Available online at http://www.bhhrg.org/Print.asp?ReportID=161&CountryID=16 (accessed January 5, 2006).

Obreja, Efim, and Lilia Carasciuc. "Corruption in Moldova: Facts, Analysis, Proposals." 2002. Transparency International—Moldova. Available online at http://moldova.org/download/eng/293/ (accessed January 5, 2006).

"Seventh United Nations Survey of Crime Trends and Operations of Criminal Justice Systems." United Nations, Office on Drugs and Crime, Center for International Crime Prevention. Available online at http://www.nplc.lt/stat/int/7sv.pdf (accessed January 5, 2006).

"SPAI General Assessment Report for Moldova," Final Report. Adopted on April 30, 2002, Stability Pact Anti-Corruption Initiative (SPAI). Transparency International. Available online at http://www.transparency.md/Docs/SPAI_GA_Moldova.pdf (accessed January 5, 2006).

"Trafficking in Persons Report, 2003." U.S. Department of State. Available online at http://www.state.gov/g/tip/rls/tiprpt/2004/33192.htm (accessed January 5, 2006).

Joseph D. Serio

Monaco

Official country name: Principality of Monaco
Capital: Monaco
Geographic description: Small area in western Europe bordering the Mediterranean Sea on the southern coast of France
Population: 32,409 (est. 2005)

■ ■ ■

LAW ENFORCEMENT

History. In 1867 the prince of Monaco created the office of the *commissaire* of police who was answerable to the mayor for general policing and to the governor general for criminal matters. Eight years later, the office of director of police was created, aided by three *commissairies*. The director was directly under the governor general. In 1902 the force became the *Direction de la Sûreté Publique*, and in 1929 it was placed under a minister of state in the Office of the Counselor for the Interior.

Structure and Organization. The *Sûreté Publique* consists of three branches: Urban Police, Judicial Police, and Administrative Branch. In addition to the regular police, the *Carabiniers du Prince* perform security functions.

The Urban Police, or the uniformed branch, is headed by a principal commandant under whom there are four grades of officers: peace officers, chief brigadiers, brigadiers, and agents. Agents are organized in four sections, one of which is Reserve and Emergency. It also includes a motorcycle squad under a chief brigadier. The *commissaire* is assisted by a division inspector and several inspectors.

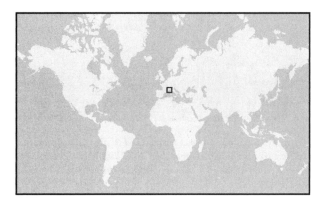

The Judicial Police, or the Criminal Investigation Branch, is headed by a *commissaire* assisted by a division inspector and several inspectors. It also handles criminal records and Interpol activities.

The Administrative Branch is headed by a *commissaire* under whom are a division inspector and several other inspectors. This branch is responsible for such things as licensing and registration.

Other principal branches under the control of the director include the Maritime Police (equipped with a fast launch) under a commandant, the Women Police, Communications Section, and the Prison Service. The latter is under a brigadier chief.

Uniforms and Weapons. The uniforms of the Monaco Police are very colorful and elaborate. The director and the *commissairies* wear uniforms only for special events or ceremonies. This consists of a black peaked cap round which are rows of silver acanthus leaves—two rows for

Officers in Monaco stand beside Ted Maher, an American nurse, as he stands trial for the arson death of his former billionaire employer, November 28, 2002. *Maher claimed he accidentally started a small fire in a wastebasket that soon grew out of control in Edmond Safra's luxury penthouse in 1999. Both Safra and another nurse died after inhaling toxic fumes caused by the blaze.* AP IMAGES.

the director and the divisional *commissairies* and one for the other *commissairies*. A straight cut, open-neck tunic in black bears rows of leaves on the cuff in the same manner as the cap. Black trousers and tie and a white shirt complete the uniform. The director may also wear a silk-covered belt. Commandants wear a black peaked cap bearing four rows of silver braid to indicate their rank. In winter, a black, open-neck tunic is worn with a white shirt and a black tie. Stiff epaulettes on the tunic carry four rows of silver braid. The trousers are dark blue with a wide black stripe.

Peace officers wear the same uniform as commandants but with fewer rows of braid on the cap and epaulettes. In summer, they wear sky-blue, long-sleeved, open-neck shirts with air-force-blue trousers striped with red up the side seams. The shirt has stiff air-force-blue epaulettes and a shoulder patch on the left arm. A white cover is worn on the cap in summer. Uniforms for the brigadiers and agents is similar to that of the peace officers, with the royal cipher in place of the badges of rank on the epaulettes.

Riot Squad personnel wear a special uniform consisting of a padded waistcoat worn under a dark-blue blouse made of fire-resistant material, matching trousers gathered at the ankles, and a black plastic helmet. The Maritime Police wear navy-blue trousers and a double-breasted naval-type tunic. A distinctive anchor badge is worn on cap, epaulettes, and overcoat. In summer, navy-blue trousers are worn with a navy-blue, open-neck, long-sleeved shirt, with the usual shoulder patch. Light-blue overalls are worn on board together with yellow rubber boots. The Women Police wear belted tunics, dark blue in winter and light blue in summer, with matching skirts and Robin-Hood-style caps.

All uniformed personnel carry a Smith and Wesson .38 revolver in a black (white on ceremonial occasions) holster on the right side. Submachine guns are used during road checks.

Education and Training. Basic training is provided at the Police Training School in Monaco under the charge of the *Commissaire* for Administration. Senior officials are sent to France for advanced training.

Police Statistics.

- Total Strength of Police Force: 500
- Population per Police Officer: 64

HUMAN RIGHTS

The government generally respects the human rights of its citizens, and the law and the judiciary provide effective means of dealing with individual instances of abuse.

CRIME

Crime Statistics. Offenses reported to the police per 100,000 population: 3,430. Of which:

- Burglary: 106.7
- Automobile Theft: 70

CORRECTIONAL SYSTEM

The prison system is administered by the *Maison d'Arrêt* under the *Direction des Service Judiciaires.*

Prison Conditions. Prison conditions generally meet international standards. Prisoners with long sentences are transferred to a French prison to serve out their time.

Prison Statistics.

- Total Prison Population: 13
- Prison Population Rate per 100,000: 39
- Total Number of Establishments: 1

George Thomas Kurian

Mongolia

Official country name: Mongolia
Capital: Ulan Bator
Geographic description: Landlocked country in central Asia, bordered by Russia to the north and China to the south
Population: 2,791,272 (est. 2005)

■■■

LAW ENFORCEMENT

History. Modern Mongolian law enforcement history begins with the Communist revolution in 1921 when a Soviet-style police apparatus was set up as much to bolster Communism as to keep law and order. Internal security forces were primarily engaged in surveillance and intelligence gathering and suppression of opposition.

Structure and Organization. The Public Security Force operates under the Ministry of Justice and Home Affairs. The police system comprises the militia and auxiliary law enforcement groups. The ministry is also responsible for a wide range of functions, including passports, fire fighting, traffic control, prisons, border control, and criminal investigation.

The militia has a department in each province and an office in each district. It also conducts criminal investigation under the supervision of procurators. Militia organs, together with local councils administer labor sentences of convicted criminals. The Central Militia Office has a Motor Vehicle Inspection Bureau, and militiamen direct motor traffic and are stationed along railroads. The militia also includes security police and frontier guards.

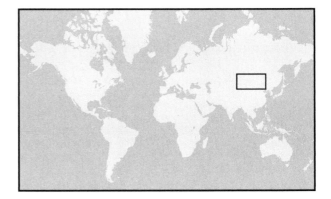

In a number of towns, auxiliary police brigades help the militia in crime detection and prevention. The most important of these bodies, which includes deputy sheriffs and special policemen, are the Crime Fighting and Crime Prevention Councils, which operate without paid staff. They also conduct anticrime education and propaganda programs.

The Ulan Bator Railway Administration has mounted police patrolling the tracks for roaming livestock.

Education and Training. Education for all ranks is provided at the Central Police Academy in Ulan Baton. Senior officials are sometimes assigned to Russia for further training.

Police Statistics.

- Total Police Personnel: 20,475

- Population per Police Officer: 136

HUMAN RIGHTS

After the opening up of Mongolia to democratic influences in the early 1990s, there was significant improvement in the human rights situation. Budgetary constraints have forced the government to cut down on security personnel. The security forces are now under civilian control. However, old police traditions of beating prisoners and detainees to obtain forced confessions continue. Arbitrary arrests and detention are used indiscriminately as means of intimidation. Police corruption also is a burden on the people. In September 2002 a new criminal code was established, giving citizens procedural safeguards against abuse of authority. The government also established a National Commission of Human Rights to monitor complaints from the public and to investigate and discipline errant police officials.

CRIME

Crime Statistics. Offenses reported to the police per 100,000 population: 1,010. Of which:

- Murder: 30
- Assault: 74.7
- Burglary: 486
- Automobile Theft: 2.1

CORRECTIONAL SYSTEM

Prisons are administered by the Department of Court Decision under the Ministry of Justice. There are 28 prisons for sentenced prisoners (15 central and 13 provincial) and 21 for pretrial prisoners (1 in Ulan Bator and 20 in the provinces). The total prison population is 6,400 sentenced prisoners only. The incarceration rate is 246 per 100,000 population. Of the total number of inmates, 4% are females and 2% are juveniles.

Prison Conditions. Tuberculosis is a major problem in Mongolian prisons. The government has constructed a tuberculosis hospital for prisoners, and deaths from the disease have declined significantly. Conditions in detention centers are worse than in prisons. Under the revised criminal code, the prison administration took over the responsibility for detention centers from the police. All female prisoners are held separately in one central prison at Ulan Bator. In 2001 a separate facility for juvenile offenders opened in Ulan Bator with ninety-four children. Outside the capital, juveniles between fourteen and eighteen are kept in the same centers as adults. In 2001 human rights training was initiated for prison and police guards.

Prison Statistics.

- Total Prison Population: 6,400
- Prison Population rate per 100,000: 230
- Pretrial Detainees: 17.4%
- Female Prisoners: 4%
- Juveniles: 2%
- Foreign Prisoners: 0.1%
- Number of Establishments: 28

George Thomas Kurian

Morocco

———•———

Official country name: Kingdom of Morocco
Capital: Rabat
Geographic description: Northwestern tip of northern Africa, west of Spain across the Strait of Gibraltar, bordered by the North Atlantic Ocean to the west, Algeria to the east and southeast, and Western Sahara to the south
Population: 32,725,847 (est. 2005)

■ ■ ■

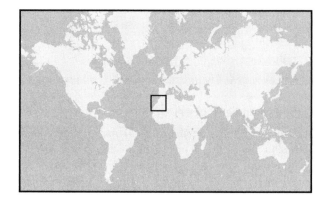

LAW ENFORCEMENT

History. Under French rule, which began in 1907, internal security was maintained by French troops augmented by Moroccan recruits who were organized into four elements: *tirailleurs, goums, makhzanis,* and partisans. The *tirailleurs* were regular soldiers. *Goums* performed a number of duties, including training and buildings schools and hospitals. *Makhzanis* were assigned to rural areas. Partisans were local forces in remote areas recruited for special missions. In 1956, after achieving full independence, Morocco adopted the French system with two branches: the *Sûreté Nationale* and the parliamentary *Gendarmerie*. Eventually, several different forces were established, most parliamentary in nature, with overlapping responsibilities

Structure and Organization. Primary responsibility for the maintenance of law and order and for conducting internal security operations is exercised jointly by the country's three separate police organizations: the *Sûreté Nationale,* the Royal *Gendarmerie,* and the Auxiliary Forces. All three are modeled on their French counterparts and are regarded as paramilitary organizations.

The main law enforcement agency, the *Sûreté Nationale,* is the national police directly responsible to the king. The Royal *Gendarmerie* technically is part of the Royal Moroccan Army (*Forces Armées Royales,* FAR) and is directly responsible to the king. The Auxiliary Forces, as a quasi–national guard, is also within the jurisdiction of the Interior Ministry. The commanders of these forces are directly appointed by the king who approves all major policy decisions. The overlapping of operational functions among the three is maintained deliberately to preclude any possible threat to the throne from any one element.

Sûreté Nationale. The *Sûreté,* with headquarters in Rabat, is under the command and control of a director general. It exercises primary police authority in the principal urban centers and in certain towns. It shares the patrolling of highways with the *Gendarmerie* and responsibility for frontier security with the FAR, and Auxiliary Forces. As the national agency for countersubversion, it conducts overt

Moroccan authorities escort an African immigrant from Mali to a plane in Oujda, Morocco, October 12, 2005. *Mali immigrants who have attempted to reach Europe by crossing through Morocco are often apprehended by authorities and sent back to their home country.* **AP IMAGES.**

and clandestine operations nationwide. To fulfill this responsibility, it maintains careful surveillance of foreigners and assists customs and immigration officials in certain aspects of their work.

The *Sûreté* was established by a royal *dahir* (decree) in 1956. Its structure, procedure, and operational concepts are more French than Moroccan. Except for two reorganizations, the *Sûreté* has existed without any major modification of its structure and responsibilities. During the period after the disastrous Casablanca riots in 1965, the *Sûreté* was removed from the Ministry of the Interior and made autonomous, answerable only to the king.

For administrative purposes, the *Sûreté* has six sub-directorates: Administration, Public Safety, National Security, Documentation and Regulatory Control, Judicial Police, and Inspectorate and Training. It employs four basic police units: the Urban Corps, the Mobile Intervention Companies, the Judiciary Police, and the International Security Police. The country is divided into ten regions (confusingly, each is called a *sûreté*), each under the command of a commissioner.

The uniformed Urban Corps, the largest of the *Sûreté* branches, provides most of the police services in the cities and major towns in foot, bicycle, motorcycle, or automobile patrols. They work in pairs in foot beats and on automobile patrols. They man traffic-control stations and provide crowd control. In some cases, the Mobile Intervention Companies augment the Urban Corps, and the Urban Corps augments the Judicial Police.

The Mobile Intervention Companies (*Compagnies Mobiles pour l'Intervention*, CMI) is a uniformed and motorized police unit. Its major mission includes crowd control, policing public functions, and providing emergency services in times of civil disasters or natural catastrophes. With the *Gendarmerie*, it patrols the major highways. Motorcycle CMI companies serve as guard of honor for dignitaries. The CMI is deployed in Rabat, Casablanca, Fez, Marrakech, Meknes, Oujda, and Tetouan.

Criminal investigation is the responsibility of the Judicial Police. All nonuniformed employees of the *Sûreté* are certified to act as Judicial Police officials. Its operations cover the entire range of criminal offenses, including arrest. It acts in criminal cases under the technical direction of the prosecutor and his deputies. In such cases, it functions as an arm of the court system.

The least-publicized unit of the *Sûreté* is the Subdirectorate for Internal Security, which is the police intelligence service. It is under the direct supervision of the director general, and most of its operations are clandestine. It does not make arrests but passes on its information to the Judicial Police for follow-up, arrest, and prosecution. The Countersubversion Section of this subdirectorate is organized to deal with antimonarchists, radical Islamic groups (such as al Qaeda), Communists, labor unions, and political parties. The Counterespionage Section is concerned with activities of foreign embassies and sensitive industrial and commercial enterprises. All other matters of internal security are assigned to the General Activities Section. These three sections are supported by the Technical Section, which provides communications and technological capabilities. This section utilizes boats, aircraft, and helicopters.

The *Sûreté* plays an important role in immigration and emigration control through the Subdirectorate for General Documentation and Regulatory Control, in particular its Immigration division, which issues bulletins concerning arrivals and departures of certain categories of aliens; maintains lists of persons denied entry; monitors movements of foreign vessels and aircraft in Moroccan air and sea space; expels undesirable aliens; scrutinizes requests for visas and work permits; and keeps records of foreigners who die in Morocco, children born of foreign parents, and marriages between Moroccans and foreigners. The Customs Service is a separate department under the Ministry of the Interior, but the *Sûreté* works in close cooperation with it.

Royal Gendarmerie. The *Gendarmerie* is the main police unit in rural areas. Its commander and many, if not most, of its upper- and middle-level officers are drawn from the army. The rest of its personnel are volunteers who have elected to serve five-year tours of duty. Technically, the *Gendarmerie* is under the operational control of the army, but in practice is personally supervised by the king. In addition to its general mission of enforcing public order, the *Gendarmerie* provides assistance and support to a number of other government agencies. It serves as the army's Military Police, the Truant Police for the Ministry of Education, as tax collectors for the Ministry of Finance in rural areas, and as the statistical arm of the Ministry of Transportation collecting statistics on highway traffic.

With national headquarters in Rabat, the *Gendarmerie* is organized into companies that are deployed throughout the country. The companies are, in turn, divided into sections and brigades, the latter being its basic operational

units. Motorcycle brigades share responsibility for highway traffic control with CMI. Jeep-mounted brigades patrol sections of rural territory, and dismounted brigades operate police posts in small villages. The centrally located Mobile Group is maintained for rapid-response deployment to assist in riot control and other special emergencies.

After coup attempts by elements of the army and air force in 1971 and 1972, the *Gendarmerie* was built by the king as a counterpoise to the military. The Mobile Group was expanded by two companies, and the regular force was expanded by five territorial brigades, an additional brigade to assist the Judicial Police, one parachute squadron, air and maritime units, and four new armories. The *Gendarmerie* also acquired four depots for stockpiling arms, ammunition and other equipment, and air and maritime units for patrolling air- and waterways.

Auxiliary Force. The Auxiliary Force consists of provincial and municipal guards—collectively referred to as the Administrative Makhzani and a contingent known as the Mobile Makhzani. In other countries, this force would be termed the National Guard. They operate under civil administrative authorities at local levels and an inspector general of the Ministry of the Interior at the national level.

Military in character, the nonuniformed Administrative Makhzani personnel are recruited from the local areas to which they are assigned. Many of its members are army or *Gendarmerie* retirees who have some military experience but little, if any, instruction in law enforcement. When assigned to a province, they are under the command of a governor. Their responsibilities include guarding buildings and bridges, patrolling *souks* or markets, acting as messengers and minor clerks for local authorities, serving as arbitrators in the frequent water and grazing disputes, and assisting uniformed police forces whenever needed. It has a limited number of motor vehicles, such as jeeps, light trucks, motorcycles, and bicycles, but some units still use camels for patrolling desert areas.

The larger Mobile Makhzani is a well-equipped, modern paramilitary force. Its companies, each about 150 officers and men, are motorized and are specifically trained to control riots and put down demonstrations. These company-size units are deployed throughout the country, at least one in each province and others near major population centers. Its two principal missions are patrolling the key border areas and rapid intervention in situations beyond the capabilities of the other branches of the police. The companies are controlled operationally by the provincial and prefectural governors, but when employed as intervention forces, they are under the operational control of the *Sûreté* regional chief in urban areas or the *Gendarmerie* commander in rural areas. Both in armament and transport, these mobile companies are greatly superior to the Administrative Makhzani.

Police-Community Relations. Except for the plain-clothes investigations police, others enjoy a relative degree of public confidence. Tourists in Morocco speak well of the efficiency and courtesy of the policemen they encounter.

Education and Training. Entrance to the *Sûreté* is through competitive examinations. Recruits must be fluent in both Arabic and French, be of good moral character, be free from police record, be between the ages of 21 and 35, and have at least primary school education.

Until about 1970 the uniformed police were mostly illiterate and untrained because of poor pay, poor service conditions, long working hours, and limited opportunities for advancement. Following the military-led coups of 1971 and 1972, the king initiated a number of reforms to bring the police to a level comparable to that of the FAR in pay, fringe benefits, and quality of personnel. In addition to a salary commensurate with that paid to other civil servants, the police received subsidized housing, a family allowance, a hazardous-duty allowance, and overtime. In addition, the *Sûreté* maintains medical centers throughout the country for police personnel and their families, and employees receive private hospital insurance plans, pension plans, and medical disability coverage.

Initially, police personnel were trained either on the job or in French, German, British, or U.S. police academies. With French assistance, training facilities were established at two sites in Morocco: Sidi Othmane, near Casablanca, and Sale, on the outskirts of Rabat. The former is a general training school and the latter a specialized training school. In 1965 the National Police Academy was established near Meknes. Personnel assigned to field units received instruction from French specialists in criminal investigative procedures, traffic control, licensing inspections, visa control, laboratory techniques, use and care of firearms, and first aid. Officer training is conducted at the Royal Military Academy near Meknes and the Royal *Gendarmerie* School for Professional Training at Kenitra near Marrakech. The *Gendarmerie* has a network of regional instruction centers.

Uniforms and Weapons. Routinely, the Urban Corps are armed with automatic pistols and rubber billy clubs. In times of riot, the corps is provided with steel and plastic helmets, service pistols, submachine guns, rifles, and tear-gas grenades. The *Gendarmerie* forces are armed with rifles, submachine guns, automatic rifles, tear-gas grenades, and water-pump trucks. To the extent that it is armed, the Administrative Makhzani is equipped with side arms, rifles of World War II vintage, and rubber billy clubs.

Police Statistics.

- Total Police Personnel: 36,482
- Population per Police Officer: 1,007

HUMAN RIGHTS

Members of the security forces commit serious human rights violations. In several incidents through 2000 and 2001, the police beat and violently dispersed demonstrators. Several persons died in police custody. Suspects are held incommunicado and family members are not informed. The government admits past torture and police abuses, which are reported to still occur in order to extract confessions or force prisoners to sign statements. In late 2004 the government drafted a proposal to include severe physical and mental abuse in laws against torture in accordance with the International Convention against Torture.

CRIME

Crime Statistics. Offenses reported to the police per 100,000 population: 366. Of which:

- Murder: 1.4
- Assault: 6.7

CORRECTIONAL SYSTEM

The Moroccan Penal Code, with its three books and 600 articles, reflects the legal traditions of France as well as the Sharia. Offenses are divided into four categories: crimes, *delits*, *delits de police*, and contraventions, which correspond to felonies, misdemeanors, less serious misdemeanors, and minor violations. Sections of the code are expressly designed to protect Islam and the monarchy through harsh punishments. Rounding out the statutory basis of the criminal justice system is the 1959 Code of Criminal Procedure, consisting of seven books with 772 articles.

At independence, the responsibility for the prisons was transferred from the police to the Ministry of Justice. The ministry's Department of Penitentiary Administration operates thirty-four prisons and correctional institutions, including central prisons at Rabat, Meknes, Fez, Settat, Oujda, Marrakech, Kenitra, Casablanca, and Tagounite. Ain Borja and Centrale prisons in Kenitra are maximum-security institutions; the remainder is medium-security institutions. There is one juvenile correctional institution at Kenitra.

Amnesty International identifies seven large detention centers: two in the vicinity of Casablanca, one in Mulay Cherif, another in old workshops that serve domestic flights at Anfa Airport, one at Dar el-Mokri near Rabat, one south of Kenitra on the road to Rabat, and one near Oujda in the far northeast near the Algerian border. French sources cite the existence of similar detention centers at police villages in Agdal, on the Romani Road near the capital, and in Marrakech. Further, they report prison camps at Assa near the Draa River in the southwest and at phosphate quarries in the central part of the country.

Prison Conditions. Prison conditions remain harsh, often as a result of chronic overcrowding, malnutrition, and lack of hygiene. In 2000, fourteen prisoners died in Oakacha Prison in Casablanca due to unhygienic and inhumane conditions. Most prisons lack adequate medical care and personnel. The media also report widespread corruption, drug use, and violence. Young first-time offenders are housed together with hardened criminals. However, there are vaccination programs for some prisoners, the budget for medical care increased 61 percent from 1998 through the end of 2000, and deceased inmates now undergo

autopsies to determine cause of death. Also, alternatives to imprisonment for some crimes are being considered.

Prison Statistics.

- Total Prison Population: 54,200
- Prison Rate per 100,000: 166
- Pretrial Detainees: 40.7%
- Female Prisoners: 3.3%
- Juvenile Prisoners: 0.5%
- Number of Prisons: 53
- Official Capacity of the Prison System: 35,000
- Occupancy Level: 155.1%

George Thomas Kurian

Mozambique

Official country name: Republic of Mozambique
Capital: Maputo
Geographic description: On the east coast of Africa bordering the Indian Ocean, with South Africa to the south; Zimbabwe to the west; and Zambia, Malawi, and Tanzania to the north
Population: 19,406,703 (est. 2005)

■■■

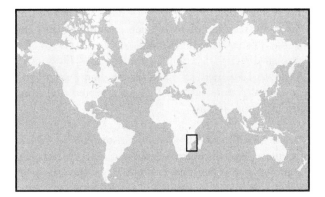

LAW ENFORCEMENT

History. Immediately after the departure of the colonial Portuguese government, lawlessness prevailed in the country for many years. Troops of the ruling organization, Front for the Liberation of Mozambique, organized under Marxism, acted as police, arresting their opponents. Police sweeps were common in the cities, aimed at non-Marxists and social deviants. The Public Security Force, the nation's first national police force, was formed in February 1975. Eight months later, it was transformed into the National Service of Popular Security. At the same time, the Mozambique Police Corps was set as a parallel law enforcement agency. It included the Criminal Investigation Police and the Fiscal Guards, which comprised customs, immigration and port police.

Structure and Organization. Internal security forces are under the Ministry of the Interior. They include three agencies: The Criminal Investigation Police, the Mozambican National Police, and the Rapid Intervention Police. Criminal Investigation is a specialized, plainclothes unit in charge of criminal investigation and apprehension of suspects. Mozambican National Police is the principal law enforcement agency and is under the administrative control of a director based in Maputo. Under him are deputy commissioners in charge of administration, traffic, personnel, operations, and communications. Territorially, there are provincial directors of police who report to the provincial governors. Most towns and cities have police stations under the command of an inspector.

Education and Training. Until the establishment of a Training School in Maputo in the 1980s, most policemen were untrained and owed their jobs to political and party connections. The Training School provides two-year preparatory courses for recruits.

HUMAN RIGHTS

The human rights situation in Mozambique has shown much improvement, but numerous abuses persist, especially excessive use of force, torture, and unlawful killings. These abuses are even more pervasive because of widespread police corruption. Many deaths are reported because of police abuse. Arbitrary arrest and lengthy pretrial detention are common. In 2001, one hundred detainees died in their cells due to asphyxiation. The League of Human Rights reports that police are involved in sexual abuse of women. There are checkpoints in many highways where police detain travelers and demand bribes before allowing them to proceed.

CRIME

Crime Statistics. Offenses reported to the police per 100,000 population: 166. Of which:

- Murder: 4.2
- Assault: 9.2
- Burglary: 45.9

CORRECTIONAL SYSTEM

Prisons are controlled by two ministries: The Ministry of Home Affairs is in charge of maximum security prisons, and the Ministry of Justice is in charge of all others. Maximum security prisons are administered by the head of the prison department and other prisons by the national director of prisons in the National Directorate of Prisons. As well as penitentiaries and central and provisional prisons, there are 42 open centers and some district branch prisons.

Prison Conditions. In general, prison conditions are extremely harsh, overcrowded, and life threatening. Commonly, prisoners are fed once a day, usually with only beans and flour. Families are permitted to bring food, but there have been reports of guards extracting bribes to deliver the food.

Prison Statistics. The principal prisons and their actual population in 2002 were as follows (with official capacity in parenthesis):

- Beira Central Prison: 705 (400)
- Tete Prison: 540 (150)
- Manica Prison: 608 (200)
- Imhambane Provincial Prison: 199 (99)
- Nampula Prison: 724 (100)
- Cabo Delgado Prison: 338 (100)
- Gaza Prison: 222 (100)
- Niassa Prison: 356 (100)
- Zambezia Prison: 446 (150)
- Maputo Central Prison: 2,450 (800)
- Maputo Machava Maximum Security Prison: 600

The National Directorate of Prisons also had an agricultural colony in Mabalane and industrial penitentiaries in Nampula and Maputo.

- Total Prison Population: 8,812
- Prison Rate per 100,000: 45
- Pretrial Detainees: 72.9%
- Female Prisoners: 6.3%
- Number of Prisons: 27 (penitentiaries and central and provisional prisons)
- Official Capacity of the Prison System: 6,119
- Occupancy Level: 144%

George Thomas Kurian

Namibia

Official country name: Republic of Namibia
Capital: Windhoek
Geographic description: Southwest Africa on the South Atlantic Ocean, with Angola to the north, Botswana to the east, and South Africa to the south
Population: 2,030,692 (est. 2005)

■■■

LAW ENFORCEMENT

History. The Namibian Police Force was first organized by the German colonial government and was based in Windhoek. There was little or no law enforcement outside the capital except for mobile patrols. On independence in 1990, the force was transferred to the new government, with few changes in structure and operational controls.

Structure and Organization. The inspector general of police reports directly to the Ministry for Home Affairs, which also controls the paramilitary Special Field Force. Each of the thirteen administrative divisions has a regional headquarters. There are field posts in all major towns. There are 104 police stations, 27 substations, 21 satellite stations, and 19 border posts. Intelligence and criminal investigations are handled by the National Central Intelligence Service (NCIS).

Education and Training. Recruits undergo basic training at the Pius Josef Kaundu Training Center. Senior officials received specialized training at the Patrick Iyambo Police College.

Uniforms and Weapons. Police are armed. They also use *sjamboks*, or heavy leather whips.

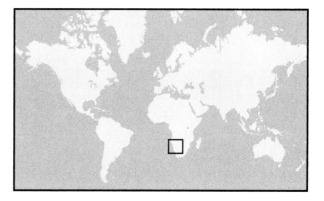

HUMAN RIGHTS

Despite training courses in human rights, policemen continue to commit severe human rights abuses.

CRIME

Crime Statistics. Offenses reported to the police per 100,000 population: 2,006. Of which:

- Murder: 26.3
- Assault: 533.6
- Burglary: 692
- Automobile Theft: 65.8

CORRECTIONAL SYSTEM

The nation's prisons are administered by the Namibia Prisons Service under the Ministry of Prisons and Correctional Services through the Commissioner of Prisons.

Prison Conditions. Although prison conditions are substandard, they are free from the unfavorable excesses found in many other African countries. The main problems are overcrowding and poor maintenance. Victims of abuse are able to pursue legal remedies. Women are separated from men and juveniles from adults, but pretrial detainees are housed together with convicted felons.

Prison Statistics.

- Total Prison Population: 4,814
- Prison Population Rate per 100,000: 240
- Pretrial Detainees: 5.2%
- Female Prisoners: 1.8%
- Juvenile Prisoners: 5.5%
- Number of Prisons: 13
- Official Capacity of the Prison System: 3,822
- Occupancy Level: 126%

George Thomas Kurian

Nauru

Official country name: Republic of Nauru
Capital: Yaren District
Geographic description: Island in the South Pacific Ocean south of the Marshall Islands
Population: 13,048 (est. 2005)

■ ■ ■

LAW ENFORCEMENT

Structure and Organization. One member of the local government council is designated as responsible for maintenance of public order and is designated director of police. He supervises a force of 114 constables.

Police Statistics.

- Total Police Personnel: 114
- Population per Police Officer: 114

CRIME

Crime Statistics. Offenses reported to the police per 100,000 population: 1,650. Of which:

- Murder: 25
- Assault: 400
- Burglary: 100

CORRECTIONAL SYSTEM

The island has only one prison, which is minimum security and administered by a council member

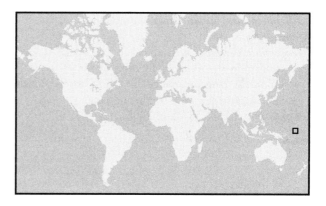

in charge of justice who is responsible to the Nauru Police Department. Most inmates are incarcerated for very short periods, generally for drunkenness or domestic violence.

Prison Conditions. Although basic, the prison meets international standards. Women are segregated from men, juveniles from adults, and pretrial detainees from convicted felons.

Prison Statistics.

- Total Prison Population: 3
- Prison Population Rate per 100,000: 23
- Number of Prisons: 1

George Thomas Kurian

Nepal

Official country name: Kingdom of Nepal
Capital: Kathmandu
Geographic description: Landlocked rectangular-shaped country in the southern foothills of the Himalayan mountain range, bordered by China to the north and India to the west, south, and east
Population: 27,676,547 (est. 2005)

■ ■ ■

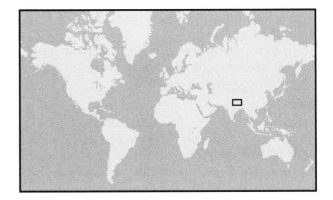

LAW ENFORCEMENT

History. Until the middle of the nineteenth century, police and judicial functions were in the hands of the local princes or rajas who were virtual autocrats. Outside the capital, the local governors appointed headmen and village councils to maintain order, but the scope of police activity varied with local customs. Generally, justice was capricious and punishments harsh. Torture by fire and water or mutilation were not abolished until 1851. Court sentences and police powers were influenced by the caste and social standing of the offenders. Brahmans and women were exempted from capital punishment.

Because of the relative isolation of most communities, law and order were maintained by small detachments of the civil police force supplemented by a few locally recruited policemen. In the mountain areas, there was no effort to enforce central government authority, and local communities maintained their traditional autonomy.

The Ranas, who controlled the government at the turn of the twentieth century, made the first effort to establish a modern police system. Prime minister Dev Shamsher Rana, who ruled from 1901 to 1929, modernized the police forces in the capital. Villages, however, still policed themselves. The militia exercised some police functions, although their main mission was to protect the people from bands of bandits, known as *dacoits*, common in the Tarai border areas.

In 1950–1951, the Ranas were overthrown. The Nepali Congress, which then rose to power, had a paramilitary arm of some five thousand men known as the Raksha Dal. This group was invested with police powers. The new government created four more distinct police organizations: the Civil Police, of 2,000 men; the Randal or Kathmandu Police, of 500 men; the militia, of 15,000; and military detachments attached to police posts of 1,000 men, all under the Ministry of Home Affairs.

Within two years, the police department was shaken by a series of political events. In 1952 the Raksha Dal supported Kunwar Indrajit Singh in his uprising. In

Authorities stand guard outside the Royal Commission for Corruption Control offices in Kathmandu, Nepal, while former Nepali Prime Minister Sher Bahadur Deuba faces interrogators inside, April 27, 2005. Deuba was apprehended at his house that morning after he failed to show up before a commission for charges of suspected corruption associated with a road-building contract. **AP IMAGES.**

1953 a police-inspired plot to overthrow the government was uncovered. More than eighty police officials were arrested, and the inspector general of police was forced to resign. In rural areas, the police were totally ineffective against better-organized party activists.

In 1952 the government requested Indian assistance to overhaul the law enforcement system. A police training school was established, and some Nepali policemen were sent to the Indian police training school at Moradabad near New Delhi. In 1954 the five law enforcement groups were consolidated into a single group under central government control. The militia was disbanded and reconstituted as a "road army" to help build roads. Military detachments doing police duties were returned to their military duties. The Civil Police, Raksha Dal, and Randal were merged into one. The pay and allowances of the personnel were increased. In 1955 King Mahendra promulgated the Nepal Police Act, which marked the beginning of the modern police system in the country.

Structure and Organization. In accordance with the Nepal Police Act, the country is divided for police purposes into five zones or ranges: Far Western, Midwestern, Western, Eastern, and Central, with headquarters at Biratnagar (Eastern Tarai), Kathmandu (Kathmandu Valley), and Nepalganj (Far Western Tarai) respectively. Each zonal headquarters, under a deputy inspector general of police, is responsible for several subsections composed of four or five police districts operating under a superintendent of police. Each station normally is headed by a head constable. He is in charge of several constables who perform the basic police functions. Each constable customarily is responsible for three or four villages. The overall system includes 21 police inspectors, guards for the 32 *bada hakim* (governors), 43 tax collection offices, and personnel for 291 outposts. There are 15 zonal offices, 75 district offices, 340 police stations, and 937 police posts. The Central Police headquarters, under an inspector general of police, is under the Ministry of Home Affairs. The headquarters comprises the Criminal Investigation Division, Intelligence, Counterespionage, Traffic and Radio sections, the Traffic Police Company, the Central Training Center and a band.

Education and Training. All officers in the Nepali Police Force are graduates of the Police Academy at Bhimphedi, southwest of Kathmandu. Bhimphedi also provides refresher courses for midcareer officers.

Police Statistics.

- Total Police Personnel: 45,481
- Population per Police Officer: 608

HUMAN RIGHTS

The continuing Maoist insurgency in Nepal sets the background for human rights abuses committed by police and military forces. Torture is used routinely to extract confessions. The disappearance of persons in custody is a serious problem. There are several instances of deaths while in police custody. A National Human Rights Commission was appointed in 2000 to investigate allegations of police brutality. However, police officers involved in cases of brutality are rarely punished. Police are unwilling to discipline fellow officers, and member of the general population are afraid to bring cases against the police for fear of reprisals.

CRIME

Crime Statistics. Offenses reported to the police per 100,000 population: 9. Of which:

- Murder: 2.8
- Assault: 1.1
- Burglary: 0.8

CORRECTIONAL SYSTEM

The corrections system consists of a central prison at Kathmandu and at least one jail in the district capitals, all administered by the Ministry of Home Affairs.

Prison Conditions. Because of lack of facilities, juveniles are incarcerated with adults. Sick persons are generally transferred to hospitals. Women normally are incarcerated separately from men but under similar conditions. Prisons offer medical treatment, recreational facilities, and visiting privileges for relatives. Prison workshops are supervised by the Cottage Industries Department.

Prison Statistics.

- Total Prison Population: 7,132
- Prison Population Rate per 100,000: 26
- Pretrial Detainees: 59.8%
- Female Prisoners: 8.3%
- Number of Prisons: 73
- Official Capacity of the Prison System: 5,000
- Occupancy Level: 142.6%

George Thomas Kurian

Netherlands

Official country name: Kingdom of the Netherlands
Capital: Amsterdam
Geographic description: In western Europe, bordering the North Sea between Germany and Belgium
Population: 16,407,490 (est. 2005)

■■■

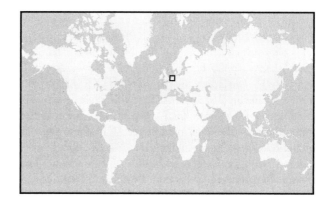

LAW ENFORCEMENT

History. Two foreign occupations of the Netherlands have been influential, both positively and negatively, in the development of the Dutch police forces. The first was the French occupation from 1795 to 1813, from which the Netherlands emerged as a unified state and during which time the modern police system began. The second was the German occupation from 1940 to 1945, which led to drastic reforms in the system.

Before the French occupation of the United Netherlands, police affairs were a matter of local administration and the courts. After the occupation, during which the police were a part of the French State Police, the regional police forces were revived, but their functions, although locally performed, were not completely municipal, and the lines of organization were not clearly drawn. This arrangement resulted from the French-inspired judicial organization in which the prosecuting office is attached to the courts under the authority of the Ministry of Justice. As a result, criminal investigations and prosecutions fall under the authority of the public prosecutor.

Another new force, a statewide military force, originated with the police authority. At first called the Force *Marechaussee*, it was later called *Wapen der Koninklijke Marechaussee* in Belgium, with which the Netherlands was united. It came into being in 1814 to replace the French *Gendarmerie*, which had returned to France.

At first these forces worked only in the south, but later they were spread thinly over the Netherlands and were charged with civil police services. As far as organization and management were concerned, the Force *Marechaussee* fell under the Ministry for War while the police fell under the Ministry of Justice. In 1851 the system was completely overhauled through the Municipal Act, which created a civil police force under the authority of the Ministry of Justice. Called *Het Korps Rijksveldwacht*, it began to function on January 1, 1858, and by World War II consisted of 1,260 men.

Several attempts to unify the forces failed. In fact, until the German invasion of 1940, three kinds of police existed side by side. The first was the city police, based on the Municipal Act of 1851 and regulated by municipal bylaws and which functioned in nearly all communities—in the towns in the form of forces and in the country villages in the form of one or more police officials (*gemeenteveldwachters*). There were also two state police forces of restricted personnel strength—the military *Marechaussee* and the Civil *Rijkveldwacht*. Also in the cities a third type of police: the *Korps Politiegroupen* formed in 1918 to replace the *Koninklijke Marechaussee* in military duty. This was an army unit of no more than seven hundred men who assisted the police, especially in cases of large disturbances. This multiplicity of police forces with overlapping jurisdictions and competing authorities and regulations gave rise to what was known as the Police Question.

During the German occupation, the Germans tried to bring all police forces into a unified organization. However, before it could be accomplished, the war was over, and the unification attempt met considerable resistance from the nationalist police authorities. The organizational chaos the Germans left behind after liberation forced a serious effort to solve the Police Question. The response was the Police Act of 1957, the first legal regulation of police in the history of the Netherlands. The act established two police forces: regional forces (*gemeentepolitie*), appointed by the Crown in urban communities with 25,000 or more inhabitants, and one statewide police force, the State Police (*Het Korps Rijkspolitie*), in other areas, under the authority of the Ministry of Justice. While these two civil police branches were melded together in 1993, each body is discrete with separate organization and function. The *Koninklijke Marechaussee*, on the other hand, continued to function as a military police unit of the army, but it lost all its prewar civil police duties although it may still be called upon to assist the police on special occasions.

Structure and Organization. In police administration, a distinction is made between management and authority. Daily management falls to the mayor, who appoints, suspends, or dismisses all police officials with the exception of the chief commissioners and commissioners, who are appointed by the crown. But the authority to determine official policy, strength, formation, general legal status, recruitment, education, and budget falls under the Ministry of the Interior and Kingdom Relations. The annual police budget is prepared by this ministry. Operational management is based on studies of the police force's effectiveness, quality, and performance. Public opinion on police work is charted periodically by means of *Politiemonitor*, an extensive poll.

The authority and management of the state police fall under the authority of the Ministry of Justice, but the commanding officers are appointed by the Crown. Despite the duality of management and authority, the police operate as a unified body. The police forces are responsible to the mayor for maintenance of law and order and to the public prosecutor for detection of crime and execution of sentences. The Police Act corrected many organizational shortcomings of prewar days but it did not solve the dichotomy in the chain of command. As a result, many attempts have been made since then to reform and modernize the system.

The Dutch police are organized into twenty-six forces, twenty-five of them regional and the twenty-sixth the National Police Services Agency (*Korps Landelijke Politiediensten*, KLPD). The regional forces are divided into districts and units, and districts are generally divided into base units. In terms of jurisdiction, police function under a dual authority:

- The Ministry of Justice, responsible for law enforcement
- The Ministry of the Interior and Kingdom Relations, responsible for local police

Municipal mayors are responsible for maintenance of public order in the municipality in which the force is stationed. The queen's chief constable is the commander of the municipal police in operational matters. Overall control for internal security is the responsibility of the Ministry of Interior and Kingdom Relations, as is the National Police Services Agency, which is commanded by the director general of public order and safety. In matters relating to criminal law and investigation and enforcement of judicial decrees, the competent authority is the public prosecutor. Public prosecutors report to the Board of Procurators' General, which in turn reports to the minister of justice. Thus, the police force combines two functions—maintenance of public order, and investigation of criminal offenses—but have two chains of command. The twenty-five regional forces have a great degree of operational freedom in matters such as finance, personnel, materials and buildings, information, and automation. The mayor of the largest municipality in a region is the commander of a regional police force and is the link between the Ministry of the Interior and Kingdom Relations and the regional police chief, who is the de facto field commander. Police headquarters is usually located in the largest municipality in the region. Major policy decisions are taken by the regional board, which consists of all the mayors of the region and the chief public prosecutor.

Because of the bifurcation of police responsibilities between the two ministries, the jurisdiction of each ministry is clearly spelled out in administrative regulations. The minister of the interior and kingdom relations is the principal person for maintaining public order and security and is indirectly responsible for the twenty-five regional police forces and directly responsible for the National Police Services Agency. He is also responsible for training and education of police personnel and police budgets. The minister of justice is responsible for the enforcement of criminal law and the criminal justice system, including the procurators general.

Police at Work. Working hours are figured on a four-week period of 168 hours divided into a weekly schedule of forty-two hours or a daily schedule of eight and a half hours.

All members of the police force receive various allowances of 8–15 percent in addition to regular salary for irregular service. There is a special pay for shift service, clothing, children, and vacations. Agents are automatically promoted after five years to head agent. Salary scales follow those for general civil servants. All officials get a vacation allowance of 7 percent of annual salary. The official retirement age is 65, but executives may retire at 60. The maximum pension is 70 percent of salary after 40 years of service. Vacation time is linked to salary and varies from 22 to 30 days a year. Police personnel receive between 16 and 23 days of vacation a year. In addition, they receive an extra day of vacation for each 5 years of service after the age of 30. All members of the force have medical coverage under which they may choose their own physician and receive 80–100 percent reimbursement for medical expenses.

Members of the regional police forces are unionized. The major unions are the Dutch Trade Union, the Christian Trade Union, and the Catholic Trade Union. Members of the National Police Services Agency have their own federation. Those of higher rank may join the Organization of Chief Police Officials.

Regional Police.

Regional police forces are characterized by the absence of compulsory central regulations. They are autonomous within their own jurisdictions, which means in principle they exclusively perform police duties in their communities. This rule has a few exceptions during emergencies, when state police services may intervene, as declared in the Police Act.

In larger cities there is considerable specialization and organizational differentiation, but in a middle-size force, a regional police force is divided into three main parts:

- The Uniformed Division (*de Algemene Dienst*), consisting of the patrol squad, the traffic squad, and the Bureau of Licenses and Special Bylaws

- The Detective Division (*de Justitiele Dienst*), consisting of the General Detective Bureau, the Juvenile and Vice Squad, and the Technical Investigation and Identification Bureau

- The Administrative Division (*de administratieve Dienst*)

Most regional police forces have a technical squad that concentrates on technical matters, such as footprints, and fingerprints.

Regional units vary greatly in size. In Amsterdam-Amstelland with over 850,000 residents, the police strength is 5,000, or one police officer for every 169 residents. In Gooi-en-Vechtstreek, with 245,000 residents, there are 550 police officers, or 1 police officer for every 445 residents. Of the 141 smaller units, only 12 have a strength of more than 300, and no less than 97 have less than a strength of 100. Only 5 of the largest cities have more than 500 officers.

A base police unit has one or more police stations. The primary tasks of each station are to:

- Patrol the area by car, motorcycle, bicycle, or foot

- Provide emergency assistance

- Record reports of crime

- Keep in touch with community and neighborhood groups

- Mediate disputes

- Investigate crimes

- Manage traffic flows and investigate traffic accidents

- Enforce environmental regulations

- Enforce local ordinances

Other areas of concern to police are quality-of-life crimes and crimes against public morals, such as child pornography and child prostitution. Even though most laws relating to adult pornography and adult prostitution have been taken off the statute books, those against child pornography and child prostitution are strictly enforced. Several regions have environmental bureaus performing comprehensive environmental policing. Environmental offenses are classified into three categories. The more serious offenses require the intervention of environmental protection officers.

As already noted, management of the regional police is actually a partnership between the state and the community. This means that the state is in charge of making the regulations, determining force strength, and paying costs. In the capacity as chairman of the city council, the mayor of each city has a strong role in management of personnel and materiel, and appoints, promotes and dismisses all police officers with the exception of the chief commissioners, who are appointed by the Crown in consultation with the mayor. The city council functions as a watchdog. Daily management and administration is in the hands of the chief of police, who is always a professional and career official. In communities of 40,000 or more inhabitants (there are 67 such communities) the chief of police has the rank of a commissioner. In communities of 125,000 or more inhabitants, the rank is chief commissioner.

The regional police have two other groups of officials. The first group consists of unpaid officials (*onbezoldigd ambtenaren*), who are public functionaries without formal police status, and social detectives, who are officials in charge of preventing the misuse of public security measures. The second group is the reserve police, first organized in 1948, one function of which is to assist the regular police in countersubversive activities and during war or national emergencies. This group, who are uniformed and armed, perform under the authority of the regular police and are generally volunteers who are appointed by the mayor.

Regional police have the following ranks:

- Commanding officers: head official first, second, and third class; official first, second, and third class; and supernumerary

- Others: adjutant, brigadier (sergeant), head agent, agent, and aspirant

Commanding officers also have functional titles. A chief commissioner can be appointed in the rank of head official first or second class; commissioner in the rank of head official, second, or third class; or official first class. A chief inspector can be appointed in the rank of first or second class. An inspector can be appointed in the rank of official second or third class. An assistant inspector can be appointed in the rank of supernumerary.

Special Police.

Riot Police: In emergency situations, the regular police is augmented by the riot police. There are 45 riot squads in the kingdom, each consisting of approximately 50 members. Nine of these squads have jurisdiction over maritime and river vessels. Large city forces have 4 riot squads each while rural ones have only 1 each. Members of the riot squads have special gear and weapons. A primary function of the riot squads is to control football (soccer) hooliganism, which is a bane of European sports. At the national level, there is a central office for control of football hooliganism located in Utrecht. There is also a computerized Football Data Collection System that maintains surveillance on known hooligans and the clubs they attend.

Detective Division: Within each police force is the detective unit charged with criminal investigation. There are base units at each police station and also regional units. The detective force is supported by allied units, which are often centrally organized. These consist of departments involved in collecting information such as identification and intelligence services. Identification services collect and process hard information and produce computer records. The criminal intelligence unit focuses on soft information, including interrogations and interviews that are privacy sensitive. Some forces also have surveillance teams and arrest squads.

Arrest Squads and Police Infiltration Teams: There are eight arrest squads active in several regions. An arrest squad is responsible for apprehending suspects who are armed and dangerous. Members of these squads receive specialized training and have special equipment. They also guard and protect the transport of witnesses, suspects, and prisoners, and guard and protect valuable objects. Another supraregional group, the Police Infiltration Team, infiltrates terrorist or antisocial groups and gangs. Each region has its own observation team, which provides support for investigations.

Special Assistance Units: A Special Assistance Unit is one that is deployed in case of hostage taking and terrorist acts. It consists of police officers, including marine and army personnel.

National Police Services Agency. The National Police Services Agency comprises the state police force and special officials with police status. The former is the largest police force in the country. The operational head of the force is the inspector general, who holds a rank equivalent to that of a general in the army and is headquartered is in Voorburg, near the Hague. All 217 commanding officers are appointed by the Crown and others below that rank by the Minister of Justice. The National Police Services Agency performs law enforcement duties in all the 676 communities where there are no regional police forces. By far the largest part of the force is made up of the *landdienst*, divided into seventeen districts. These are divided into groups, which, in turn, are divided into posts. The strength of these posts may vary from nine to fifty-three people. Ranks for commanding officers are: inspector general; and directing officials first, second or third class. Below them are adjutants, sergeants, head agents first class; agents, and aspirants.

Principal Agencies and Divisions.

National Criminal Intelligence Service: At the core of the National Police Services Agency is the National Criminal Intelligence Service (NRI), which operates under a chief commissioner and eight commissioners and which is in charge of antiorganized crime activities, fingerprinting, and forensic laboratories. It is the principal contact office for Interpol, Europol, and the *Schengen* Information System. Besides an internal General

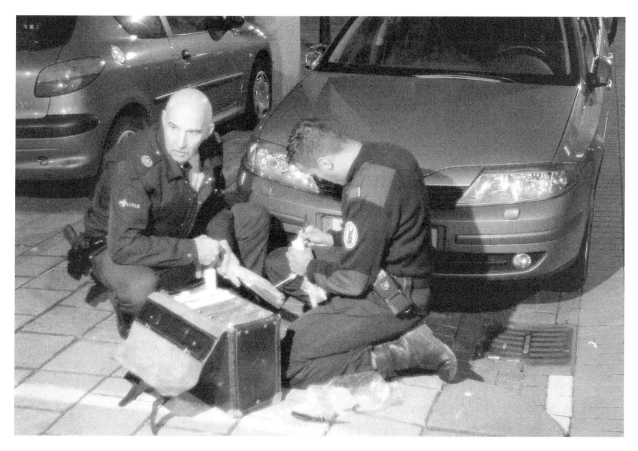

Police in Rotterdam, Netherlands search for evidence near a car that was torched during the night, November 13, 2005.
Authorities said several youths burned four cars during the night and damaged numerous others in a working-class neighborhood of the city. Police were investigating if there was any connection to French riots that occurred nearby in recent weeks. **AP IMAGES.**

Administration Department, the NRI has two external departments. The first is the Information Department, which issues publications such as the *Criminal Investigation Information Bulletin,* and runs a television program similar to the show *Most Wanted* in the United States. The Information Department handles the Central Record Bureau, which stores fingerprints and other police registrations. Another of its subsections is the Circulation Section.

Because combating serious and organized crime requires great expertise, and because most regional police forces are too small to build up pools of expertise in specialized fields, five core teams represent groups of regional police forces. These teams function under the aegis of one of the participating regions. A core team is a relatively small unit of fifty to ninety persons who serve for five years. Core teams focus on one or more of the following special areas:

• Organized crime

• Synthetic drugs, which comprises police and customs

• Military constabulary and fiscal intelligence, which functions in the southeast Netherlands

• Illegal immigration, which functions in the north and east

A sixth core team, the National Investigation Team, also a branch of the National Police Services Agency, concentrates on international and national organized crime and corporate fraud. In addition to the core teams are interregional fraud teams assigned to combat fraud affecting banks and insurers and deal with crimes involving data transport, bank and credit card fraud, bankruptcy fraud, and insurance fraud. Police in these teams work closely with financial professionals, such as accountants and tax auditors.

Criminal Investigation Department: The Criminal Investigation Department consists of nine branches, including an International Branch that works in tandem with Interpol; the Special Branch for preventing terrorist attacks; the Criminal Intelligence Branch; the National Investigation Team, which focuses on fraud; the Detective Team; Transport and Logistics, which targets crimes in the transportation system; and the Digital Crime Investigation Team, which keeps watch on Internet-related crimes.

Specialist Investigation Applications Department: This department, with highly specialized experts in its Research and Development unit, supports the National Police Services Agency in observation, intervention, and infiltration, and provides a witness protection program.

The National Police Services Agency also has separate bureaus that handle specialized law enforcement tasks. Among them are:

- Water Police (*Rijkspolitie to Water*),with a large fleet of patrol vessels and speed boats headquartered in Driebergen, near Utrecht. The Water Police monitors shipping, fishing, and aquatic sports. In cooperation with the Coast Guard, it supervises Dutch territorial waters in the North Sea. The water routes are divided into four districts: Amsterdam, Leeuwarden, Nijmegen, and Dordrecht, which are subdivided into groups and posts. Rotterdam-Rijnmond however, has its own river police at the Rotterdam Harbor.

- General Traffic Service (*De Algemene Verkeersdienst*) (AVD), headquartered in Driebergen, is in charge of police duties on the main highways. Its core tasks include traffic surveillance, speed control, and enforcement of drunk-driving laws.

- Aviation Service (*Die Dienst Luchtvaart*) is headquartered at Schiphol Airport and the national airport at Amsterdam, with subdivisions at the airports of Rotterdam, Beeck, and Eelde. It also serves as the base of *Afdeling Vliegdienst* and collaborates with the Civil Aviation Tribunal. The service runs and maintains all National Police Services Agency's aircraft and helicopters. Aircraft are equipped with special photographic infrared cameras and videos as well as fire extinguishers. Directed from Driebergen, the aircraft direct police action from the air at sporting events and during natural disasters.

Other statewide law enforcement services include:

- State Detective Bureau (*De Rijksrecherche*), which is under the jurisdiction of a commissioner and which investigates complaints against police officers and administrative and judicial authorities

- Safety of the Royal Family (*De Veiligheidsdienst Koninklijk Huis*), which is stationed near the royal police at Soestdijk and which also protects members of the diplomatic corps, mayors, queen's commissioners, members of the judiciary, and public prosecutors

- Judicial Laboratories (*De Gerechtelijke Laboratoria*), which is divided into the Judicial Science Laboratory and the Judicial Health Laboratory.

- Police Communication Service (*De Politieverbindingsdienst*), which is in charge of telecommunications for the National Police Services Agency

- Service Force of the State Police (*De Intendance der Rijkspolitie*), which is headquartered in Apeldoorn and serves the National Police Services Agency as well as the regional police forces in procuring uniforms, armament and repairs, and firearms

- Police Technical Service of the State Police (*De Politietechische Dienst der Rijkspolitie*), which is in charge of procurement and maintenance of motor vehicles and other transportation vehicles, is headquartered in Delft, near the Hague, and has six workshops around the country

Other Law Enforcement Agencies. Apart from the national and regional police forces, there are other law enforcement agencies:

- Military Police of the *Marechaussee*, which performs police duties for the army and security tasks in airports, assists in combating cross-border crimes, enforces immigration laws, escorts the transport of money to state institutions and guards the residence of the prime minister

- Economical Control Service, under the Ministry of Economics, oversees the enforcement of economic regulations.

- General Inspection Service of the Ministry of Agriculture and Fishing, which is in charge of the enforcement of regulations relating to agriculture and fishing. The Inspection Service of the same ministry inspects goods and fish and meat to ensure that they comply with state regulations.

- Revenue-Taxes Service, which enforces tax laws and the collection of taxes and dues. It has two units: The first is concerned with internal revenue and the latter with customs and excise duties. They are governed by the General Law for the State Taxes and the General Law for Customs and Excise.

- Railway Police, called the Railway Detective Division, falls into a special category. Founded in 1919 to prevent transportation theft, although not a state agency, it has grown years to perform a host of duties in a variety of areas on trains as well as on platforms. The commander is a commissioner of state police and all executive officers are unpaid officials of the state police. It is headquartered in Utrecht.

- Immigration Police, established under the Immigration Act, has responsibilities in the field of admission, supervision, detention, and deportation of aliens and the granting, extension, and cancellation of residence permits. They keep a watchful eye on the activities of aliens and their integration into mainstream society.

- Voluntary Police, of which there are approximately 2,500, serve in various capacities in the police forces. Another 4,000 city watchers assist the regular police in neighborhood watches by reporting suspicious events and characters through radiotelephone.

Education and Training. To be appointed as an aspirant in the regional police or the National Police Services Agency, the following requirements are necessary: Dutch origin; blameless character; age between seventeen and twenty-eight years, and successful completion of physical and psychological tests. There are also standards of educational attainment that call for a diploma of the four-year MAVE (school that follows the basic school system but has a more general formal education). After the applicant has met these requirements, he or she may be appointed with a probation time of a maximum of three years. During probation, the aspirant should demonstrate theoretical and practical ability.

For appointment as a commanding officer (inspector of a regional police third class or official of the state police second class), the same regulations apply with two differences: the required age is between twenty and twenty-eight, and attainment of a higher educational level is required, such as completion of high school or junior college. Also, the applicant must have successfully completed the final examination for the inspector of regional police or commanding officer of the state police. This means four years of training at the Police Academy or a university degree.

Promotion is automatic in most cases after a certain numbers of years of service. An aspirant will be promoted after one year to agent and an agent after five years to head agent (agent first class). For the rank of brigadier (sergeant), there is a special requirement of the "B" diploma, which is based mostly on theoretical knowledge. For promotion in the commanding officer ranks, there is no requirement save a minimum service time.

Although regional police personnel, with the exception of the chief commissioners, are appointed by the mayor, Recruitment is being centralized in the State Selection Center for the regional police in Hilversum. Only about 10 percent of applicants are accepted. There are some disturbing geographical factors in recruitment: About half the applications come from the north, east, and south of Holland although the vacancies are more in the western part of the country, in the *Randstad.*

Training and education of police personnel were historically neglected until the 1960s. Before World War II, only the *Marechaussee* and the *Rijksveldwacht* had their own internal training facilities. Police education was mostly in the hands of private groups and police unions who provided courses of study and held examinations. The situation changed radically in 1965, when the training of all police personnel was made the responsibility of the minister of justice. However, most programs offered only legal training because it was generally accepted that all police work was done within a legal context. The Ministry of Justice established the Institute for Training Commanding Police Officers (the name of which was changed in 1967 to the Dutch Police Academy). It continued the work of the Model Police Vocational School in Hilversum, founded in 1919 by the General Dutch Police Union. The school has a one-year course for the police diploma and a two-year course for inspector candidates.

Because of its tradition of centralized management, the state police was the first to start its own training institutes, not only for primary training but also for specialized personnel, such as traffic police. Training for regional police came later. Large cities had their own training centers while smaller ones initiated joint ones. It was not until 1959 that regional training institutions were available for the whole country. After the Police Act of 1957, which made the Ministries of Justice and the Interior less dependent on one another, developments have been much faster. On the initiative of the Department of the Interior in 1959, the Study Center for the Continuous Education of Commanding Officers for both state and regional police personnel was started. Later, a statewide traffic school, a school for staff officials of the regional police, a detective school, and two centers for the training of mobile units, were founded.

Technical selection of police officers takes place at the National Police Selection and Training Institute (LSOP). LSOP trains some 30,000 police officers each year through its five semiautonomous institutes:

- Institute for the Basic Police Function

- Dutch Police Academy

- Police Institute for Public Order and Danger Management

- Police Institute for Traffic and Environment

- Institute for Crime Control and Investigations

In addition, there are two nationwide institutes under LSOP control:

- Institute for Police Recruitment and Selection
- Central Police Examination Bureau

Although police education was privatized in 1992, LSOP retains overall control.

The following training and education institutes serve the police forces in the Netherlands:

For commanding officers of state and regional police:

- The Dutch Police Academy in Apeldoorn, which offers four-year courses. The first year is on an intern basis. The next thirty months are devoted to practical and vocational work. During the last term, the student is expected to prepare a paper and a final report. About 25 percent of admissions are externs who have excelled in lower police ranks and have requested school training.
- Study Center for Commanding Officers in Warnsveld, which offers a series of courses of one to three weeks in length aimed at midcareer professionals. The center also offers a management course for top functionaries and organizes study conferences.

For other personnel:

- Two primary schools for regional police, one in Rotterdam and the other in the Hague, and four regional schools with intern training that lasts for one year.
- One primary training school for the State Police, with a one-year internal training in Apeldoorn and two annexes in Horn and Harlingen.

Continuous training and education:

- Training for the mobile unit of the state police is offered in Neerijnen and for the regional police in Woensdrecht. The basic mobile unit training lasts five weeks. In addition, there is a four-week staff officers' course and a six-week program for firearms instructors.
- Staff training for the rank of sergeant, for which students must have ten years of service and have a "B" diploma. The training takes place in Apeldoorn for the state police and in Zutphen for the regional police. The course lasts eight weeks.

More specialized training courses are also offered:

- Traffic training program for the state police takes place in Bilthoven and in Noordwijkerhout for the regional police. The basic course lasts three weeks; a supplementary driving training course lasts one week.

- Detective training is given in Zutphen. Various courses are offered, including an eight-week basic course, a 6-week primary detective course for commanding officers and members of the prosecutor's office, and a 12-week technical course. There are also courses for squads dealing with juveniles, drugs, fraud, and swindling.
- Sleuth Hounds School of the state police in The Hague for dog handlers and dogs. The training of the dog lasts one year and that of the handlers six months. The school trains dogs for drug sniffing for police and customs work.

Patrol dogs of the state and regional police are trained by local dog brigades.

Training and education are also offered on the job through tutoring and training for the "B" diploma. Young police officers are tutored for thirteen weeks by older colleagues, followed by a six-week introductory course. The "B" diploma is required for promotion to staff ranks, such as sergeant.

As a result of a number of factors, including a low birthrate, a thirty-five-hour workweek in the general population, aging, and increased demands on police resources, there is a growing shortage of personnel in the police force. To meet this shortage and to maintain optimum staffing levels, the Ministry of the Interior and Kingdom Relations launched an initiative called Police Staffing Project. Its purpose is to develop a positive public image of the profession and to discourage the outflow of personnel.

Police training is the focus of new reforms initiated in 2002. Their main features are: uniform job profiles, well-defined professional standards, linkage to higher education, and a dual training system that promotes on-the-job training. The two goals of the reforms are career development and diversity. Career development seeks to ensure that the right people are invited to enter the police service at the appropriate level and that such people are given further opportunities for development. Diversity seeks to ensure that the police force reflects the increasing ethnic diversity of the Dutch population and that immigrants are properly represented at every level.

Uniforms and Weapons. The uniform of state police consists of a blue-black tunic, blue trousers, and a blue-black peaked cap with a band. Municipal police wear a gray-blue tunic, blue trousers, and a dark-blue cape with Prussian blue piping. The Royal Constabulary wear a blue-black tunic, royal-blue trousers, and peaked caps.

Standard-issue arms are a 7.65 service pistol, ammunition (Walther P5 and Action3 bullet) a short baton, and pepper spray. Police always carry steel handcuffs and truncheons. The use of force is strictly regulated under legislation. Riot-squad police are armed with additional equipment, such as shields, helmets, and bulletproof vests. Arrest squads are equipped with electronic batons and semiautomatic Heckler and Koch machine guns. The use of automatic firearms requires prior permission of the minister of justice. In certain situations, police are permitted to use tear-gas grenades.

Police Statistics.

- Total Police Personnel: 31,650
- Population per Police Officer: 202

HUMAN RIGHTS

Human rights observance by the Dutch police is monitored by the Police Inspectorate, an independent organization that reports directly to the Ministries of Justice and Interior and Kingdom Relations. The inspectorate also assesses the way in which the police force provides quality management and investigates all incidents involving the police that result in abridgment or abuse of human rights.

CRIME

Crime Statistics. Offenses reported to the police per 100,000 population: 8,211.54. Of which:

- Murder: 10.9
- Assault: 277.54
- Rape: 10.36
- Burglary: 3,100.4
- Automobile Theft: 241.01

CORRECTIONAL SYSTEM

The two laws governing prisons are the Prisons Act of 1951 and the Prisons Regulation of 1953. As a result of these acts, prisons and prisoners were redefined and reclassified, new prisons were built, and the education of prison officials enhanced. Ultimate responsibility for all penal institutions is vested in the Ministry of Justice, under which prisons are administered by the National Agency of Correctional Institutions. The director of public prosecutions directs the implementation of prison sentences. The Prison Allocation Center, headed by a psychologist, advises the prison authorities on the placement of prisoners.

Each prison is administered through a governor, who supported by a staff that includes chaplains, counselors, doctors, social workers, psychologists, and guards. Supervisory boards oversee all aspects of the treatment of prisoners but have no administrative authority. Prisoners may freely address the board either in writing or in person.

There are two types of penal institutions: houses of detention and prisons. Houses of detention are mainly for those remanded to custody awaiting trial and those serving prison sentences of less than two weeks. The law requires that there be at least one house of detention per court district, but some districts have more than one. Two-thirds of the average population in these houses of detention are those remanded to custody.

Considerable attention is given in prison legislation to the welfare of prisoners. The Criminal Code stipulates that anyone sentenced to serve time in prison should be committed to the institution best suited to his or her disposition and background. Section 26 of the Prisons Act states that the prison sentence should be conducive to preparing the prisoner for return to society. To reduce the dangers of isolation and alienation from society, prisoners are brought into frequent contact with the outside world. Prisoners' committees, as well as prison newspapers, serve as open forums for prisoners. Inmates are allowed to keep their own clothes and personal effects, write letters unsupervised, and visit the outside world for short periods under special circumstances.

Women serve sentences in the Women's Prison at Amsterdam, and the houses of detention in Maastricht and Groningen have separate sections for women inmates. Prisoners who have not been remanded to custody because their offense is not particularly serious and who have received short terms of imprisonment serve their sentences in a semiopen prison at Bankenbosch in Veenhuizen, Ter Peel in Sevenum, Oosterland in Hoorn, De Raam in Grave, or Westlinge in Heerhugowaard. Separate quarters are assigned to prisoners serving short-term (less than six months) sentences and those serving long-term (over six months) sentences. Short-term sentences are served in Boschpoort Prison in Breda or in the semiopen Nederheide Penitentiary Training Institute in Doetinchem. Sentences of less than two weeks may be served in installments. Transfer is possible between one institution and another. At Nederheide, prisoners are expected to participate in a social education program. Longer sentences are served in Esserheem and Norgerhaven prisons in Veenhuizen, Noordschans in Winschoten, Schutterswei in Alkmaar, and in the prison in the Hague. Noordschans Prison accommodates prisoners who are unable to adjust to a communal environment. In smaller prisons, inmates are permitted outside employment with normal wages. Psychologically challenged offenders are committed to mental hospitals for a period not exceeding one year. This sanction is known as a hospital order. A number of provisions incorporated into the Criminal Code of 1925 deal specifically with this group of offenders, who are designated as "psychopaths."

Prisoners between eighteen and twenty-three years who have not been remanded to custody are placed in Nieuw Vosseveld Prison in Vught or De Corridor Penal Training Camp in the village of Zeeland in North Brabant. Longer-term prisoners are accommodated in the prison at Zutphen. These prisoners can be transferred to the open prison at Rozenhof.

The granting of a remission of sentence in respect to a penalty imposed by a court is the prerogative of the crown. Remission may consist of reduction of a sentence or commutation of a sentence to another type. Conditional remission bears some semblance to suspended sentence and release on license.

An organization called the Society for the Moral Improvement of Prisoners was set up as early as 1823 to aid offenders both while in prison and after discharge. The introduction of the release on license in 1886, of probation in 1915, and of conditional remission of sentence in 1976 gave this and similar organizations a role in the criminal justice system by entrusting them with supervision of the fulfillment of special conditions imposed by the court (probation) and by the administration (release on license and remissions). Rehabilitation, probation, and aftercare remain largely in the hands of religious and voluntary social service organizations officially recognized by the Ministry of Justice. There is also an "early intervention" program, introduced in nearly all police districts in 1974, which has been responsible for providing early assistance to suspects in police custody.

Prison Statistics.

- Total Prison Population: 20,747
- Prison Population Rate per 100,000: 127
- Pretrial Detainees: 30.7%
- Female Prisoners: 8.8%
- Juvenile Prisoners: 1%
- Number of Prisons: 102
- Official Capacity of the Prison System: 20,522
- Occupancy Level: 97.5%

George Thomas Kurian

New Zealand

Official country name: New Zealand
Capital: Wellington
Geographic description: Islands in the South Pacific Ocean southeast of Australia, principally the North Island and the South Island separated by Cook Strait.
Population: 4,035,461 (est. 2005)

■■■

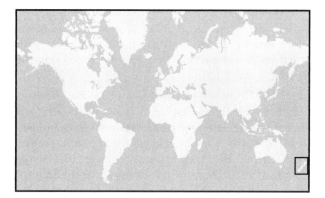

LAW ENFORCEMENT

History. The modern New Zealand police force has its roots in British colonial New Zealand. Governor William Hobson appointed the first police officers in New Zealand in 1840, and legislation mandating a full police force was passed in 1846. The act called for police who would be "fit and able men who would serve as an armed force for preserving the peace, preventing robberies and other felonies, and apprehending offenders against the peace." The structure of the police force was paramilitary and closely resembled that of its British counterpart. It was referred to as the Armed Constabulary Force.

In 1852 further legislation was passed that addressed police governance, and as a result, pseudo police stations were established in the provinces of Auckland, New Plymouth, Wellington, Nelson, Canterbury, and Otago. By 1867 legislation was passed that transitioned the Armed Constabulary Force into the first national police service. Despite its name, officers in this service were unarmed. However, the police force played a significant role in peace keeping during the land wars, and many police died while attempting to maintain civil order. The land wars were fought over a twenty-year period, from 1843 to 1872, and the main protagonists were Maori (New Zealand natives) and allies fighting against varying combinations of the British Army, New Zealand Armed Constabulary, and colonial settlers. The conflict was over provisions in the Treaty of Waitangi (signed in 1840) that addressed land claims and sovereignty. Ironically, many of the early Armed Constabulary Force members were Maori. The police also had a large role to play in peace keeping during the gold rushes in Otago and Canterbury during the 1860s. This job proved especially difficult due to the desperate nature of the gold rush movement and the influx of immigrants with criminal backgrounds, who were attracted to the movement.

The first noncommissioned police officer in New Zealand was Sergeant John Nash, who registered in 1886 after arriving in New Zealand as an officer in the British Army. Nash was initially a constable in Nelson and was later promoted to sergeant. The first police commissioner, General Sir George Whitmore, was appointed in 1886 and served only one year. Whitmore was succeeded by Major Walter Gudgeon, who served until 1903. Both men had played fairly large roles in the land wars.

The first police commissioner to rise through the ranks of the police was John Cullen. Cullen was appointed in 1912 and served until 1916. During his tenure, the first New Zealand Police Association was formed to address police salary levels and working conditions. With only one exception, all commissioners since Cullen have risen through the ranks from that of constable. Even today, it is pointed out to police recruits during training that the potential for promotion all the way up the ladder to the rank of Commissioner is available to all sworn officers.

From very early in the history of the New Zealand police, women have played a significant role. From 1891 to 1913, there were a number of police matrons on staff whose responsibilities centered on the care of female prisoners. The first policewomen were formally admitted to the New Zealand police in 1941. Initially, women were assigned to a separate women's division and were tasked with duties of a community service nature. In 1973 women in the New Zealand police were given equal status and pay and were fully integrated into the service.

In 1958 legislation was passed to remove the word *force* from the name of the New Zealand Police. This was done to better reflect the consensual style of community policing that the New Zealand police still practices today. The current New Zealand police mission is "to serve the community by reducing the incidence and effects of crime, detecting and apprehending offenders, maintaining law and order, and enhancing public safety" (New Zealand Police 2003). Along with this mission came an adoption of New Zealand police values, which are:

- To maintain the highest level of integrity and professionalism

- To respect individual rights and freedoms

- To consult with, and be responsive to, the needs, welfare and aspirations of all police staff

- To be culturally sensitive

- To integrate Treaty of Waitangi principles and Maori values into policing (New Zealand Police 2003).

Structure and Organization. During the fiscal year 2005, the New Zealand Police had approximately nine thousand staff members, which included 2,300 support staff. Police worked from four hundred community-based police stations around the country. Although there is just one jurisdiction in New Zealand, the New Zealand Police is decentralized and organized into twelve districts, each of which has a main station and is overseen by a district commander.

The chief officer is the commissioner of police, who answers to the minister of police (a politically appointed official). A Board of Commissioners comprised of the commissioner and two deputies make most of the high-level decisions. A team of advisers support the board and is made up of finance managers, public affairs personnel, cultural affairs personnel, human resources advisors, and a Maori representative. A separate commissioner's support group, overseen by an assistant commissioner, acts as an oversight authority for the commissioner.

During 2003 women made up 15 percent of sworn officers. Eleven percent of sworn officers were Maori, and 4 percent were Pacific Islanders. Of all personnel in senior management positions, 5.6 percent are women, 10.2 percent are Maori, and 4 percent are Pacific Islanders (New Zealand Police 2003).

The highest ranking officer is the commissioner who is appointed by the governor general, but the candidate is drawn from the lower rank of deputy commissioner or assistant commissioner. Under the rank of assistant commissioner is superintendent, which is preceded by that of inspector. Under the rank of inspector comes senior sergeant, and below senior sergeant is sergeant, with the lowest rank being constable. Approximately 75 percent of the police are constables, 15 percent hold the rank of sergeant, 5 percent senior sergeant, and 5 percent hold ranks above senior sergeant (New Zealand Police Web site). Promotion to the next rank is contingent upon successfully completing qualification examinations and availability of openings.

Principal Agencies and Divisions. The New Zealand Police have three main operational branches:

- General Duties

- Criminal Investigation

- Traffic Safety

There are also a number of other staff groups that provide special assistance, such as:

- Armed Offenders Squad

- Dive Squad

- Dog Units

- Forensic Services

Forensic Services are located in the cities of Auckland, Hamilton, Wellington, and Christchurch. The National Fingerprint Database is maintained in Wellington, as is the document examination team.

The single jurisdiction of the country translates to a wide police mandate. In addition to traditional policing activities, New Zealand Police enforce laws on roads and seas, and in the air. On the water, the police are assisted by the Royal New Zealand Coast Guard, which is a volunteer organization. The Coast Guard is primarily responsible for search and rescue operations, and boating education. The Coast Guard responds to some five thousand calls each year.

Salaries. During 2004 police cadets, or police trainees, earned a salary of NZ$28,824 (approximately US$19,600). Upon graduation, the salary increased to NZ$41,189 (approximately US$28,000). For five years after graduation, officers receive an increase of NZ$2,000 (approximately US$1,359) per annum, and NZ$1,000 (approximately US$680) thereafter, in addition to any promotion increase. During the fiscal year 2002–2003, 173 members of the New Zealand police earned more than NZ$100,000 (approximately US$68,000). The top earnings bracket was between NZ$350,000 and NZ$360,000 (approximately US$238,000 and US$245,000).

Retirement Age. There is no set retirement age for New Zealand Police, as legislation views age limits as age discrimination. Instead, many officers retire upon reaching their fifty-sixth birthday, the age at which they are eligible for government superannuation.

Police-Community Relations. Establishing close ties with the community is the key to ensuring that community policing is effective. The phrase "local solutions, by local people, to local problems" is one that is frequently used and typifies the relationship between the police and the community ("Briefing" 2002). The image that most New Zealand citizens have of the New Zealand police officer is the bobby, or constable, walking through the town center. The bobby is friendly, approachable, and symbolic of safety.

Illustrations of how the New Zealand Police and the community work together were cited in the 2002 police report to the incoming minister of police. Some of these were:

- Partnerships between local government and police to improve public perceptions of safety through improving street lighting and closed circuit televisions

- Joint local government and police ventures to address physical decay and deterioration in communities, such as graffiti problem areas, park clean up operations, and removal of abandoned vehicles

- Coordination of crime prevention programs, the largest of which in New Zealand is the neighborhood watch

- Joint partnerships with service-providing agencies, such as Women's Refuge, victim support services and mental health services ("Briefing")

Historically, one of the most challenging community partnerships police have had to face is with New Zealand Maori, particularly given that Maori are overrepresented in both offender and victim populations. Police have implemented a number of initiatives to improve relations, such as the establishment of a network of police Iwi liaison officers, who are assigned to specific Maori communities and are charged with improving relationships between Maori and police, and helping in the flow of information at the community level. Another initiative was to train incoming police in Maori culture and procedure, and also to recruit more Maori officers. Police are also working with the Ministry of Pacific Island Affairs to establish similar initiatives with Pacific Island people, large numbers of whom reside in major New Zealand cities, such as Auckland.

Complaints made against police are investigated by an independent unit called the Police Complaints Authority, which was established by the governor general. This authority also handles investigations where serious bodily harm or death results from police action. From 2000 to 2002, the number of police complaints decreased by 20 percent. There is a police code of conduct in place that outlines performance and conduct criteria and is tied to remuneration and promotion.

Local Police. The most visible police presence in New Zealand communities are the 3,500 beat and patrol staff, who are likely to be constables. Their mandates vary widely under the community policing doctrine; officers may be involved in activities from crime prevention to dealing with a lost child. Beat and patrol staff are also called upon to help manage large sporting events, demonstrations, and other situations that require crowd control.

In addition to beat and patrol staff are the Criminal Investigation Branch (CIB) detectives stationed around the country. CIB detectives are beat and patrol staffs that have completed extensive training in investigation and law. The CIB is used to investigate serious crime and organized crime and to monitor habitual offenders.

At the local level, police are charged with maintaining safety in communities. The New Zealand Police public relations office describes the different elements of this charge as:

- Providing tools to communities to allow them to attend to matters of community safety

- Creating community partnerships

- Reducing fear of crime by reducing actual crime

- Providing rehabilitative and support services for offenders

- Keeping the peace and maintaining order

- Assisting in trouble-free traffic flow

- Reducing the risk of personal and property victimization

Local police in New Zealand have formed a number of alliances with community agencies and services. One example is Youth Offending Teams, found throughout the country. These teams have representation from the police, the Child, Youth, and Family Agency, the Ministry of Education, and the Ministry of Health. The goal of this collaboration is to improve coordination among agencies that deal with youth offenders, those at risk of youth offending, and those youth who come into contact with government agencies for a variety of other reasons, such as child neglect. From the perspective of the police, services for youth aim to prevent youth from offending and recidivating, hold youth offenders accountable for criminal activities, and prevent youth from becoming victims of crime. Examples of services offered by the police to youth are:

- School education services and school road safety education (including the DARE program)

- Youth Aid

- Youth prosecution and alternatives to prosecutions

- Support for family group conferences

- Youth development programs

Special Police.

Riot Police. The New Zealand Police do not have a designated special riot police division, and policing riots was not given much consideration until the Springboks, South Africa's national rugby team, toured New Zealand in 1981. Their tour was met with numerous, large, and at times violent, antiapartheid protests that police were not prepared for. Largely in response to this event, many police are now trained in riot control. Like the Armed Offenders Squad (AOS), riot police hold other appointments but serve in police riot units if the demand should arise.

Traffic Police. Prior to 1991 traffic police were a separate entity from the regular police and operated under the Ministry of Transport. As a result of legislation passed in 1991, the New Zealand Police and the Ministry of Transport merged, with the merger becoming effective in July 1992. At that time, some 1,100 traffic police joined the New Zealand Police. The new organization of traffic police was in response to high numbers of fatalities and other injuries sustained in crashes on New Zealand roads. In 2000 a special highway patrol unit was established

due to a high proportion of road fatalities. This unit was also charged with increasing police visibility on the roads and decreasing road trauma. By December 2001 some 225 special officers worked in this unit. They are aided by such tools as infrared cameras, radar guns, breath-analyzing flashlights, and speed cameras. Traffic police are distinguishable from other police by special markings on their vehicles.

The 2002 police brief to the incoming minister of police cites deaths on the roads and nonfatal road accidents as an ongoing national concern. Approximately 14.4 road deaths per 100,000 people occur each year, which is significantly higher than rates in Australia (9.5), the United Kingdom (6.9), Sweden (6.1), and a number of other European countries. The New Zealand Police have implemented a strategic plan that addresses policing on the roads through 2006 and is designed to integrate general policing and traffic policing duties and further reduce road trauma and related crime. Traffic police have identified speed black spots, conducted targeted mandatory driver checks, introduced more stringent criteria for driver's licenses, introduced mandatory breath testing, and have aired hard-hitting advertising campaigns on the effects of speeding and driving under the influence of alcohol.

Crashes on New Zealand roads because of drinking and driving have received national attention since the early 1990s, and some initiatives described above, such as mandatory breath testing, have helped alleviate this problem. In 2002 statistics indicated a 6.6 percent decrease in drinking and driving offenses, which is most likely due to the efforts of the highway units (New Zealand Police 2003).

Education and Training. Upon acceptance to the New Zealand police, recruits reside at the Royal New Zealand Police College, located outside of Wellington, for nineteen weeks. Once the recruit has successfully completed the training program, he or she is given probationary constable status, which is held for two years. Training for special police, such as dog handling or AOS, is given to police after the probationary period has been successfully completed, and training varies greatly by division.

The New Zealand police recruits nationally and typically has six intakes each year of between sixty and eighty recruits. The cohorts are referred to as wings. Applicants must be New Zealand citizens or permanent residents, hold valid driver's licenses, have no criminal convictions, and able to converse adequately in English. Potential recruits must undergo a number of other academic and physical tests, such as a literacy, numeric skills, and keyboard skills examinations. At their own expense, potential recruits must obtain first aid credentials, a defensive driving certificate, and a swimming competency certificate. After the initial screening process, there is a

A topless woman is arrested by police following a protest while Britain's Prince Charles arrived in Civic Square, Wellington, New Zealand, March 8, 2005. The prince was there on a five-day tour of the country. AP IMAGES.

three-month evaluation process during which potential recruits undergo physical assessment, medical examination, psychological assessment, interviews, academic tests and assessment, background check, and Surroundings, Conditions, Organization, People, and Effects (SCOPE) testing. Physical assessment comprises a Physical Appraisal Test (PAT) and a Physical Competency Test (PCT). The PAT test assesses body-mass index (the standard set for potential recruits is between 20 and 28), running ability (men must be able to run 2.4 kilometers [1.5 miles] no slower than 10 minutes and 15 seconds, and women must complete the distance in less than 11 minutes and 15 seconds), vertical jump ability (48 centimeters [18 inches] for men and 40 centimeters [16 inches] for women), number of continuous press-ups, and grip strength (the combined total of both hands should be at least 120kg for men, and 80kg for women). The PCT consists of twelve areas of physical competency that officers may encounter on the job, such as running, balance, crawling in confined spaces, and climbing through a window. SCOPE testing is designed to ascertain how a potential recruit will respond to situations and environments that a

police officer may encounter. The test includes an internship at a police station, where the applicant spends forty hours working with officers on a variety of police duties, and applicants are given and tested on a wide variety of police literature.

Uniforms and Weapons. Prior to the tenure of John Cullen as commissioner of police in 1912, the police uniform was very similar to the paramilitary French *gendarmerie*. Cullen had a large hand in changing the police uniform to the navy-blue nonmilitary style tunic with pockets and high collar and blue bobby helmet. The uniform is the same style today.

The New Zealand police have long abided by the philosophy of maximizing safety and minimizing force. To this end, officers are armed with short, side-handle, ASP batons and oleoresin capsicum (pepper) spray. Sworn officers do not carry firearms. However, firearms are available at each police station, with both Remington Model 7 rifles and Glock 17 pistols the standard police firearms. In situations that involve the use of firearms, weapons, or the threat of either, the AOS is called in.

The AOS was established in 1964 and divisions are located in all police districts and other major centers. The AOS is comprised of volunteer police officers who complete rigorous and ongoing training in firearms. Members of the AOS have access to Remington Model 7 rifles, Glock 17 pistols, and a variety of other firearms. The only other units that are armed are the antiterrorist units.

Transportation, Technology, and Communications. New Zealand Police have had a service agreement with Holden (General Motors) since the 1960s. Various models of Holden Commodores are driven by different police units. For example, VT Commodores are used for general duties and highway patrol. Commodore utility vehicles, both VT and VR models, are used for various special activities, including dog transportation, and a more recent model, VX Commodore S, has also been added to the highway patrol fleet. Eleven maritime vessels are operated between the New Zealand Police's two maritime units, one based in Auckland and the other in Wellington. The main vessel in Auckland is a 14.5-meter launch and a similar size launch is kept in Wellington. Mounted police were a part of the New Zealand Police for many years, but budgetary restrictions have precluded their use. However, some districts receive commercial sponsorships for mounted police so that parks, rivers, beaches, and other reserves, can be patrolled on horseback. This is more common in the summer months.

Communications are managed, coordinated, and overseen by one communications center located outside of Wellington. The New Zealand Police has three emergency "111" call centers: one being located in each of the northern, central, and southern regions. They have and ten emergency operating rooms located in various police districts. When individuals call 111, their call is answered by sworn and unsworn personnel at one of the three emergency call centers. Calls are then diverted to dispatchers when deemed appropriate. Ninety percent of 111 calls are answered within ten seconds. If a call is not answered after seventy seconds, it is transferred to one of the other two centers. The national communications network has a 99.99 percent reliability rating. The New Zealand police operate an Ericsson MD110 CA telephony-radio switching platform that is used in all three 111 communication centers and all ten district emergency operating rooms. The three emergency operating rooms receive a total of 1,140,000 calls each year (New Zealand Police Web site). The police also have a land mobile radio network, 3,500 Centrex telephones, which are networked on a virtual private network, and 3,500 IP phones, all of which are regularly updated with newer technology.

Surveillance and Intelligence Gathering. Typically, surveillance and intelligence gathering is conducted by the CIB, with help from officers in other branches when needed. Police surveillance encountered its first legal and public challenges during a period of political surveillance between 1919 and 1935, and as a result, there are a number of legal limitations on surveillance that do not differ greatly from limitations on local police jurisdictions in the United States.

Police Officers Killed in the Line of Duty. There have been twenty-eight police officers killed in the line of duty. The first was Constable Neil McLeod, who was shot by a psychologically disturbed man in 1890. Four officers, Constable Edward Mark Best, Sergeant William Cooper, Constable Frederick William Jordan, and Constable Percy Campbell Tulloch, were all shot and killed by Eric Stanley Graham in 1941. Graham was a farmer during the depression who was convinced the government was persecuting him, and he reacted violently to a police visit to his home. Graham himself was eventually fatally shot by police. Two other police officers, Detective Inspector Wallace Chalmers and Detective Sergeant Neville Wilson Power were both fatally shot while responding to a domestic dispute in Wellington in 1963. A memorial for officers killed in the line of duty is located on the campus of the Royal New Zealand Police College in Porirua. There is also an annual memorial service held at the college.

Police Statistics.

- Total Police Personnel: 7,500
- Population per Police Officer: 538

HUMAN RIGHTS

New Zealand is a democracy, with an independent judiciary. The commissioner of police is accountable to the minister of police. The Commission on Human Rights reports that in 2000, there were no political or extrajudicial killings or disappearances in the country. Such events have not occurred in New Zealand since the settlement wars.

With regard to torture and cruel, inhuman, and degrading treatment, New Zealand has had a small number of reports of police abuse. Between 1998 and 1999, there were eleven cases of police misconduct that involved death. All of these incidents were fully investigated and resolved. An alleged gang rape of a woman by a group of police officers in 1986 eventually came to light. Mistreatment of prisoners by prison officials and staff have also been reported in small numbers, with the most well-known case involving two prisoners who claimed they were stripped and beaten in 1993. This incident was investigated and resulted in a government-issued apology. There are no political prisoners in New Zealand, nor are prisoners exiled from the country for any reason. Citizens of New Zealand are entitled to a fair and expeditious trial.

Other human rights issues that affect the police are the criminalization of spousal rape, the decriminalization of adult prostitution (although the organizing and recruitment of women for prostitution is illegal), and safeguarding children's rights.

CRIME

Criminal Identification and Forensics. Criminal identification is handled largely by CIB in conjunction with beat and patrol staff. In larger districts, the CIB is a stand-alone unit, but in most districts, it is part of the regular police. CIB detectives are trained in forensics. Although some forensic services are available within the police, there is no dedicated group of forensic experts. Most technical forensic services are contracted to Environmental Science and Research (ESR), a Crown research institute owned by the government but which is controlled by an independent board of directors. ESR has forensic experts and technicians available to the police twenty-four hours a day, seven days per week, and these personnel help police with crime-scene investigations, drugs and alcohol investigations, physical evidence, DNA, toxicology, and fire forensics. ESR also provides police training in forensics.

In 1995 the New Zealand Police and ESR joined forces to create a national DNA database, which samples from convicted offenders and volunteers and also from unsolved cases. Individuals who submit, or who are required to submit DNA, are also asked to provide some details about four generations of their ancestry. Using this database, some 34 percent of previously unsolved cases have been solved. In 2003 the Criminal Investigations (Bodily Samples) Amendment Act was passed and implemented. This act updated DNA legislation, extended the range of offenses for which a DNA sample could be obtained, and eliminated the need for police to get a court order for collecting DNA samples from convicted offenders. The act also introduced compulsory testing of offenders incarcerated prior to the implementation of DNA testing so that the database could be enlarged and allows for buccal (mouth) DNA samples as well as blood samples. The act also allows police to request a sample from a juvenile suspected of serious offending provided parental consent is obtained.

Another initiative in which the ESR played a large role in the dismantling of clandestine amphetamine ("P") laboratories. With the recent increase in popularity of amphetamine drugs, there are shortages of chemists specializing in these drugs worldwide. ESR has specially trained chemists in clandestine drug laboratories and currently has eight of these chemists on staff.

Each of the major police centers, Auckland, Wellington, Hamilton, and Christchurch, have fingerprinting facilities that assist CIB and other police personnel in identification of crime-scene fingerprints. The national fingerprint database is housed and maintained in Wellington. Other forensic services available within the police are document examination (Wellington only), armory, which handles ballistics in addition to maintenance and repair of police weaponry, and an electronic crime laboratory. Another forensics resource available inside the police organization is crime-scene photographers, who are specially trained police that work out of all police districts.

Organized Crime. The New Zealand Police recognize drug manufacturing, cultivation, and trafficking; fraud, money laundering; and a number of property offenses as organized crime. Since 1999 efforts have focused on infiltrating groups that manufacture and distribute amphetamine stimulants, particularly clandestine "P" laboratories. Special police laboratory response teams with ESR staff members were established in major centers to assist in this task, and in 2002, 142 methamphetamine laboratories were taken out of commission.

To combat other types of organized crime, the New Zealand Police has instituted connections with police agencies in other countries, for example, with local police and Interpol in Southeast Asia, in order to exchange information about drug trafficking. Other liaison officers have been appointed in Australia, the United States, and the United Kingdom to assist in preventing and detecting financial crimes, terrorist activity, and human trafficking. The New Zealand Police organization is an active supporter of the United Nations Convention against Transnational Organized Crime, and participates in the Financial Action Task Force on Money Laundering. Both are international bodies comprising representatives from numerous police and government agencies around the world.

There are two special police units that deal with financial crime. The first is the Financial Intelligence Unit, which is based in Wellington and monitors large domestic and international cash transactions and aids investigation of money laundering. The second is the Proceeds of Crime Unit, based in three major national centers, which was established by the 1992 act of the same name to oversee seizure of assets and money used or acquired during the commission of illegal activity.

The other formal organization under which investigation of organized crime may be conducted is the Serious Fraud Office, which falls under the jurisdiction of the minister of justice. A serious fraud is one that involves more than NZ$500,000 (US$340,000), is perpetrated in a complex manner, and is of public interest and concern.

Crime Statistics. Crime statistics are collected by police for each fiscal year. Statistics for both recorded and resolved crimes are kept, and are divided into seven categories. In 2005 crime statistics were: Offenses reported to the police per 100,000 population: 9,680.8. Of which:

- Violent offenses: 112.4
- Sexual: 7.8
- Drugs and Antisocial: 125.3
- Property Abuse: 46.5
- Administrative: 29.3

CORRECTIONAL SYSTEM

The New Zealand Department of Corrections is overseen by a politically appointed minister of corrections.

Prison Conditions. The philosophy of the New Zealand correctional system is that of rehabilitation and recidivism prevention. When inmates arrive at a prison, an assessment is made of their offense, history, circumstances surrounding the offense, health, safety, education, other special needs, and willingness to change is made. This assessment helps determine the inmate's sentencing plan, which incorporates the services and programs the offender needs to become successful upon reentry to society. All prisons provide medical, dental, psychological, and counseling services. Chaplains are available at all prisons, as are church services and Bible study groups.

In 1968 New Zealand opened its first and only maximum security facility for male inmates in Auckland, and a similar facility for women was opened in Christchurch in 1974. Unique to these maximum security prisons is the Behavior Management Regime (BMR), designed for inmates who are considered to be a safety risk to staff and other inmates. These inmates are housed in one unit of the prison. The regime is a stepped program of four phases that begins with a fourteen-day assessment period. Inmates have little or no contact with fellow inmates during this period. Continuation to the proceeding phase is dependent on performance and behavior, which is assessed daily. As an inmate progresses through the phases, his or her privileges increase.

Prison Statistics.

- Total Prison Population: 7,444
- Prison Population Rate per 100,000: 181
- Pretrial Detainees: 16%
- Female Prisoners: 6.1%
- Juvenile Prisoners: 1.3%
- Number of Prisons: 20
- Official Capacity of the Prison System: 6,936
- Occupancy Level: 102.2%

BIBLIOGRAPHY

"Briefing to the Incoming Minister." 2002. New Zealand Police. Wellington: Government Printing Office.

Dunstall, Graeme. 1999. "A Policeman's Paradise? Policing a Stable Society, 1918–1945." Palmerston North, New Zealand: Dunmore Press.

"Facts and Statistics." New Zealand Department of Corrections. Available online at http://www.corrections.govt.nz/public/aboutus/Factsandstatistics (accessed January 3, 2004).

Hill, Richard S. 1995. "The Iron Hand in the Velvet Glove: The Modernization of Policing in New Zealand, 1886–1917." Palmerston North, New Zealand: Dunmore Press.

New Zealand Crime Statistics 2002/2003. A Summary of Recorded and Resolved Offenses. Office of the Police Commissioner, Wellington, New Zealand.

New Zealand Police. Available online at http://www.police.govt.nz/ (accessed January 22, 2006).

"Report of the New Zealand Police for the Year Ended 30 June 2003." 2003. New Zealand Police. Presented to the House of Representatives. Wellington: Government Printing Office.

Monica L. P. Robbers

Nicaragua

Official country name: Republic of Nicaragua
Capital: Managua
Geographic description: Central American country bordered by the North Pacific Ocean to the west, the Atlantic Ocean to the East, Honduras to the north, and Costa Rica to the south
Population: 5,465,100 (est. 2005)

■■■

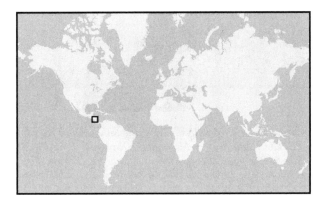

LAW ENFORCEMENT

History. Nicaragua inherited a rudimentary police system from the Spanish colonial regime, but it was active only in the major towns. After independence, the police force was highly political and took partisan sides in the numerous struggles for power. After the civil war of the 1980s, they are required to be nonpolitical. Police personnel may not vote in elections, and they come under military law.

Structure and Organization. The exercise of police functions is the responsibility of the Ministry of the Interior, but police personnel are required to be under the authority and control of the National Guard by constitutional law. As a result, police enjoy all the benefits and pensions of national guard personnel.

The political administrator of the police department, the *jefe politico*, is appointed by the president and has overall responsibility for law enforcement throughout his department. He is part of the Ministry of the Interior and is locally in command of the armed forces, including the police. His police chief, who is a police judge, is the immediate commander of the police forces. Each department has at least one police judge, and two departments, Chinandega and Río San Juan, have two. In addition to the normal complement of police forces, there are special police agents, somewhat above the grade level of regular police, on detached duty throughout the department of Zelaya and in the territory of Cabo Gracias a Dios.

The police force is divided into three categories:

- Urban
- Rural
- Judicial

The police hierarchy consists of, in descending order, colonel, lieutenant colonel, major, captain, lieutenant, sublieutenant, sergeant, corporal, and patrolman.

The urban police is concerned with common offenses, such as vagrancy, drunkenness, prohibited games, counterfeiting, carrying arms without a license,

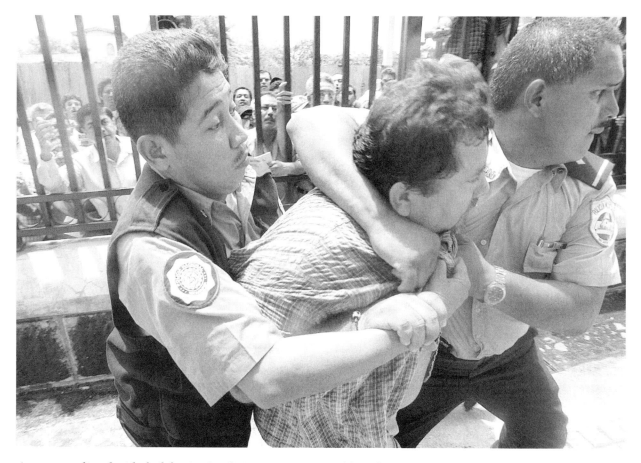

A protestor aligned with the left-wing Sandinista Front is arrested by police near the Telecommunications and Post Office (TELCOR) building in Managua, Nicaragua, June 15, 2005. The protest erupted after President Enrique Bolanos ordered authorities to block new government officials from taking office. Bolanos was upset that Congress had designated these new officials to replace the ones he had named to hold positions in public organizations such as mail and phone companies. **AP IMAGES.**

prostitution, violation of laws concerning quality of life, and maintenance of peace and good order. Peddlers and *curanderos*, or native healers, pose a recurring problem. The rural police enforce hunting and fishing laws and gun licensing and monitor the telegraph system and railroads. The judicial police run jails, provide guard services for the courts, and assist in the investigation of crimes and the apprehension of criminals. There is a security force for the treasury, also under the National Guard.

The secretary of the interior also has jurisdiction over fire departments and the prison system. At the higher jurisdictions, there is a public prosecutor who represents the people in criminal cases, and at municipal and lower levels, a *sindico* performs the same functions.

Education and Training. The police school at Managua is part of the Ministry of Defense. It trains officers through a special curriculum that bears the imprint of U.S. influences.

Uniforms and Weapons. Police uniforms are blue-gray in color, with trousers bloused into boots. Police wear plastic helmets with a triangular-shaped badge with a design of five volcanoes and the cap of liberty. They normally carry pistols and billy clubs. Pay is relatively good by military standards. Room, board, and clothing are free, as are medical care and other benefits.

Police Statistics.

- Total Strength of the Police Force: 62,222
- Population per Police Officer: 88

HUMAN RIGHTS

Even though the human rights situation in Nicaragua has improved since the civil war, members of the security forces still commit extrajudicial killings and beat, abuse, and torture detainees. There is provision for punishment of police who commit abuses, but they generally receive a mild reprimand or suspension.

CRIME

Crime Statistics. Offenses reported to the police per 100,000 population: 7,808. Of which:

- Murder: 25.6
- Assault: 203.8
- Burglary: 110.7

CORRECTIONAL SYSTEM

The Penal Code was drafted in 1968, revising and modifying earlier codes promulgated in 1837, 1871, 1879, and 1898. Prisons are often makeshift in character. Guards are supplied by the judicial police. The principal penitentiary is at Managua, but there are seven other facilities. There is also a national rehabilitation center called Centro Penal de Rehabilitación Social.

Prison Conditions. Overcrowding, once a major problem, has been alleviated as a result of the work of several human rights organizations that managed to free detainees who have spent six months or more in jails without a trial. Prison guards receive human rights training and generally treat prisoners well. However, medical care ranges from inadequate to nonexistent. About one-third of all prisoners have no beds, and some prisoners sleep on concrete floors. The daily expenditure per prisoner for food is only US$0.50. Many prisoners receive additional food from visiting family and friends. Authorities occasionally release prisoners when they can no longer feed them. Conditions in prisons and holding cells remain harsh. Suspects are left in their cells during their trials in an effort to save fuel in transferring them to distant courtrooms. At the Bluefield jail, there are only two showers and four toilets for 102 prisoners. Only Managua has a separate prison for women; outside the capital, women were housed in separate wings of prison facilities. There are no separate facilities for children under fifteen. Sometimes, these children are locked up in totally dark and overcrowded cells and beaten by police wardens.

Prison Statistics.

- Total Prison Population: 5,610
- Prison Population Rate per 100,000: 103
- Pretrial Detainees: 14.4%
- Female Prisoners: 6.5%
- Juvenile Prisoners: 0.6%
- Number of Prisons: 8
- Official Capacity of the Prison System: 5,446
- Occupancy Level: 102%

George Thomas Kurian

Niger

Official country name: Republic of Niger
Capital: Niamey
Geographic description: Landlocked country in western Africa, north of Nigeria and south of Algeria and Libya
Population: 11,665,937 (est. 2005)

■■■

LAW ENFORCEMENT

Structure and Organization. The three principal law enforcement agencies are the Republican Guard, the paramilitary *Gendarmerie*, and the National Security Police (*Sûreté Nationale*), all organized along French lines. The *Sûreté* is headed by a director and organized in brigades. The 1,800-man *Gendarmerie* is a paramilitary force headquartered in Niamey, with four regional *groupements* based at Niamey, Agades, Maradi, and Zinder. The *Gendarmerie* patrols rural areas. The Republican Guard is a ceremonial presidential guard.

Police Statistics.

- Total Police Personnel: 4,842
- Population per Police Officer: 2,350

CRIME

Crime Statistics. Offenses reported to the police per 100,000 population: 99. Of which:

- Murder: 0.9
- Assault: 16.6

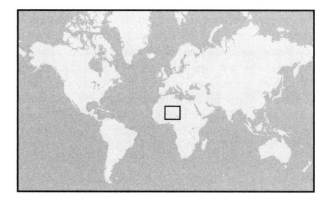

- Burglary: 1
- Automobile Theft: 0.7

CORRECTIONAL SYSTEM

The prison system is administered by the director of the Penitentiary Administration under the Ministry of Justice.

Prison Conditions. Conditions in all prisons are substandard. Prisons are underfunded and understaffed. After 29 prisoners died in 1999 as a result of abuse, the government promised to reform the system but has not done so. Family visits are allowed, and prisoners receive supplemental food from relatives. Prisoners are segregated by gender. Minors and adults are houses separately, but pretrial detainees are housed with convicted felons.

Prison Statistics.

- Total Prison Population: 6,000
- Prison Population Rate per 100,000: 52
- Number of Prisons: 35

- Official Capacity of the Prison System: 8,722
- Occupancy Level: 68.8%

George Thomas Kurian

Nigeria

Official country name: Federal Republic of Nigeria
Capital: Abuja
Geographic description: Located in West Africa on the Gulf of Guinea
Population: 128,771,988 (est. 2005)

■■■

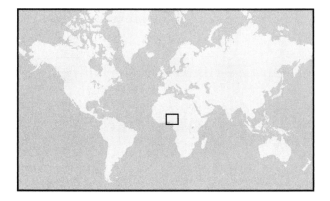

LAW ENFORCEMENT

History. The national police developed from early constabularies raised to protect British personnel and their administrative and commercial interests after they assumed responsibility for the port of Lagos in 1861. The imposition of British rule in the country triggered protests and demonstrations that threatened law and order in the new colony. To combat the unrest, the Lagos Police Force was formed, and it was the first modern police force in Nigerian history. As the British expanded their operations to the interior, the size and reach of the force grew proportionately, and additional constabularies were formed to protect the new administrative and trade centers. In the north the Northern Nigerian Constabulary (the Armed Hausa Police) was formed in 1900 when the British assumed responsibility for the protectorate of Northern Nigeria. The Southern Nigeria Police were created in 1906, six years after the proclamation of the colony and protectorate of Southern Nigeria. The Southern Police Unit absorbed the former Lagos Police Force and Niger Coast Constabulary (the Oil Rivers Irregulars, "Court Messengers"), which had operated in the eastern provinces. In 1930 the Northern Constabulary and the Southern Police Force were merged to form the Nigeria Police Force, which then became the federal law enforcement authority.

Before the consolidation of the Nigeria Police in 1930, the colonial government had left the development and organization of police establishments to the three political administrations in the country: the Lagos Colony and the Protectorates of Southern Nigeria and Northern Nigeria. The main reason for the decentralized approach to law enforcement was the need at that time to allow each segment of the federation to organize a defense compatible with local conditions and political climate. As a result, the pattern and extent of development in the three areas differed. Following the amalgamation of all the units of the country into what is now known as Nigeria in 1914, the various departments of the amalgamated protectorates were systematically merged, one after the other. The police were an exception.

Though quite willing to surrender control of the other departments, the lieutenant governors of the protectorates were worried about relinquishing control over maintenance of law and order to the new federal administration in Lagos. They saw no reason for such a surrender of power, since there was nothing really technical in police operations that lay beyond their competence. For these regional government heads, control of the regional police establishments afforded enormous leverage, especially in view of the poor communications between Lagos and the rest of the country. The amalgamation was eventually effected in 1930 because the federal government saw the need for a "unified controlling authority over matters of police routine and discipline." The powers that were hitherto exercised by lieutenant governors in the provinces and districts were now vested in the inspector general of police, headquartered in Lagos. It was a shift to unitary management that has lasted to this day.

Local forces with any degree of police authority and organized in typical police fashion did not come into existence until 1943, when the northern and western regions of the country established local government police forces quite distinct from the Nigeria Police. In creating these forces these two regions capitalized on section 105(7) of the Nigerian constitution, which made provision for the maintenance of such a force by local authorities, provided men of the force were employed and deployed only within the area of jurisdiction of the local authority that created it. These local or provincial forces played a major role in helping police remote areas of the country, where the Nigeria Police had little or no presence.

In 1958, after the Federal Republic was inaugurated, the control of the Nigeria Police was placed in the hands of the Federal Government. Appointment of the inspector general of the Nigeria Police and the regional commissioners of police was strictly safeguarded by various constitutional provisions, and the training and equipment of all police forces were coordinated by a federal police organization.

Sections 98 to 103 of the Nigerian constitution accordingly provided that:

- The Nigeria Police shall be under the command of the inspector general of the Nigeria Police, and any contingents of the Nigeria Police Force stationed in a region shall, subject to the authority of the inspector general of the Nigeria Police, be under the command of the commissioner of police of that region. The prime minister may give to the Inspector General of the Nigeria Police such directions with respect to the maintaining and securing of public safety and public order as he may consider necessary, and the inspector general shall comply with those directions or cause them to be complied with.

- The commissioner of police of a region shall comply with the directions of the premier of a region with respect to the maintaining and securing of public safety and public order within the region or cause them to be complied with, provided that before carrying out any such directions, the commissioner may request that the matter should be referred to the prime minister for his directions.

Despite these constitutional provisions, the northern and western regional governments refused to amalgamate their forces with the Nigeria Police. Amalgamation, however, was accomplished after the Nigerian Army stepped into the political arena and ousted the recalcitrant politicians. The military government set up a study group to examine all police-related issues and it recommended the gradual integration of all local forces into the Federal Nigeria Police. In 1968 this amalgamation was achieved when the first group of federal police officers reported for training at the Police College in Lagos in 1968. By March 1969 the process had been completed for all forces in the Western State, and within a few years it was complete for all Nigeria.

Structure and Organization. Headquarters of the Nigeria Police is in Lagos and is under the command of the inspector general of police, who is assisted by a deputy inspector general. Its staff operations are supervised by assistant inspectors general.

The duties of the commissioner of police at force headquarters are split into five departments, tagged alphabetically from A to E, each under the command of an assistant inspector general. The functions of these departments are as follows:

- Department A is responsible for general administration, including all matters concerning personnel, assignments, transfers, promotions, leaves, and disciplinary action.

- Department B is the communications branch that supervises operation of the nationwide police radio network that links all state police commands with force headquarters. It is also responsible for operations and transportation, traffic control, and the central motor vehicles registry. This branch also monitors government vehicle licensing policy as it affects the police force.

- Department C is responsible for general financial matters and buildings, work, and capital development. It formerly included pay and quartermaster services, but these functions are now performed by the accounts/internal audit wing of the administration.

- Department D is responsible for criminal records and investigation. Of the various specialized developments assigned to the national headquarters, the largest is the Criminal Investigation Department (CID), which is responsible for the application of scientific methods to the prevention and detection of crime.

- Department E is the Special Branch, responsible for internal security and countersubversive activities. It gathers intelligence and infiltrates extreme groups engaged in terrorism.

Except for special functions that come directly under the national headquarters, control of the force in the field is vested in and exercised through state police commands. The nineteen headquarters of these commands, each under the authority of a police commissioner, are in the various state capitals. Directly below the state commanders or commissioners are the provincial police officers and then the district police officers, down to the station officers. The police stations are usually commanded by a sergeant or inspector of police.

The size and organizational complexity of the state police commands vary depending on the population density of the state and the extent of police authority needed. Police posts and stations are found in the larger urban centers, mainly along rail lines and major highways.

The largest of the state commands is that in Lagos State. Its headquarters in Lagos's Lion Building coordinates the activities of a police laboratory, a CID training school, the division in charge of the registration of aliens, and several specialized operational groups. These include a mobile unit and a police dog unit, both at Obalende; a motor traffic division at Ijora; the Nigeria Ports Authority Police at Lagos and Apapa; the Nigerian Railway Police at Ikeja and Shomolu; and a division of policewomen. Since they are better trained and equipped and have strong CID capabilities, the state commands of the Nigeria Police Force are the first responders in difficult or specialized cases.

Criminal investigations are initially the responsibility of the police station in the area in which the offense is committed. If the initial investigation indicates a serious crime, or that the case will be prolonged, the state CID may be called on for assistance. The latter may also call on the force CID in Lagos if inquiries are required in other states of the country or overseas. Generally speaking, however, the force CID is employed to investigate complicated cases of fraud or murder. It also serves as the central agency for the collection, compilation, classification, and recording of information concerning crimes and criminals and the dissemination of such information as required.

Officers with Nigeria's bomb removal unit search the area surrounding a federal court after concerns that explosives were planted nearby, Lagos, Nigeria, September 13, 2005. Authorities received a bomb threat and evacuated the high court building to search the area. The scare interrupted the country's largest fraud trial, a case where three men were accused of stealing $242 million from a Brazilian bank. **AP IMAGES.**

Criminal Investigations Department. The force CID investigates cases that are either reported directly by members of the public or referred to the department by other police formations from all parts of the country, government departments, the Central Bank of Nigeria, and commercial banks and firms.

The force CID has several operations sections:

- The Crime Section is charged with investigating serious cases, such as murder, robbery, boundary disputes, and complex fraud cases.

- The Missing Persons Section is part of the Crime Section and deals with efforts to find missing or kidnapped persons.

- The Fraud Section deals with cases of fraud, forgery, and allied offenses throughout the country, but especially in Lagos where the Central Bank, commercial banks, and large corporations are the target for criminal elements. Nigeria is notorious as the home of many swindlers who bilk millions out of unsuspecting foreigners who are promised large sums of money in return for loans or bank account numbers.

- The X Squad Section handles various crimes stemming from malfeasance or corrupt practices and abuse of authority by public officials including police officers.

- The Post and Telecommunication Fraud Section is attached to the Posts and Telecommunication Department for investigation of postal crime by postal employees or by civilians.

- The National Central Bureau, Interpol consists of three units: Interpol, narcotics, and antiquities.

- The Interpol Unit deals with investigation of crimes and apprehension of criminals originating in foreign countries. It conducts inquiries on behalf of foreign police organizations into the activities of Nigerian nationals and corporations that are in violation of law.

- Narcotics Unit handles cases involving the possession, smoking, trafficking, and cultivation of marijuana. Most of these cases are dealt with by state police commands. Those cases with international connections are handled by the narcotics section of the Interpol Unit. The usual modus operandi of narcotics dealers is to send it by mail as parcels in newspaper wrappings, books used as containers, wooden carvings, wearing apparel such as clothes and shoes, and empty boxes of detergents. Once caught, the addresses to which they are directed are passed on to the foreign narcotics bureaus.

- The Antiquities Unit deals with the interdiction of smuggled archeological artifacts.

- Section A22, the Police Public Complaint Bureau, serves people who cannot contact the police in person because of fear of being victimized.

- The Ballistic/Counterfeit Investigation Section deals with the classification and identification of forensic ballistics. It also handles cases of counterfeiting and disputed documents and serves as the Firearms Registry and Drawing Office.

- The Counterfeit Investigation Unit serves as the medium between the Central Bank and the police and keeps records of all cases of forgeries and counterfeits.

- The Disputed Documents Unit examines public and private documents for authenticity and classifies them by categories.

- The Drawing Office prepares and prints graphic materials, such as certificates, designs and paints armorial bearings, repairs, mounts, and frames photographs, and handles related technical matters.

- The Firearms Registry registers private guns and firearms and keeps track of them.

- A related Printing Section prints forms and other documents for police use.

- The force CID (*Kaduna*) provides specialized services and training facilities to the northern states in fingerprinting, photography, criminal records, and detection and prosecution of crimes. It compiles criminal statistics for the northern (Muslim) states and files fingerprints of those with a criminal background.

- The Legal Section generally gives legal advice and prosecutes criminal cases that come before the courts. The section also prepares cases to be sent to the deputy public prosecutor.

- The Photographic Training Section produces documentary films to be shown to students and photographs police activities for publication.

- The Statistics and Crime Records of the Force CID is solely responsible for collecting and editing criminal statistics for all states as well as the Railway Police.

Section Units. The Nigeria Police has seven specialized branches. The first is the Mounted Branch formed in 1961 at Kaduna. Earlier, between 1880 and 1890 the Royal Higher Company Constabulary had a Mounted Section known as Carroll's Horses that patrolled installations on the banks of the Niger River. The present-day Mounted Branch also patrols borders and assists Customs and Excise Department personnel in antismuggling operations.

The Police Dog Section was established in Lagos in 1963 and today covers the entire country. Police dogs patrol oil installations, serve as guard dogs, and are used at crime scenes and airports. The Dog Training School in Lagos also trains dogs for prison service and police officers as dog handlers.

The Nigeria Railway Police is the principal law enforcement arm concerned with reducing crimes, such as pickpocketing on trains and in stations. They also put down strikes by rail personnel.

The Port Authority Police combat theft in Nigerian ports, which is in itself a massive problem.

The force Signals Section operates 201 radio stations as well as 17 telex circuits at Abakaliki, Yola, Ijebu-Ode,

Onitsha, Aba, and other centers. A majority of the patrol cars are now equipped with radios.

Department A is the Public Relations Branch, which has a branch in each state command headquarters. It is manned mostly by professional journalists.

The Central Motor Registry is the principal motor vehicle licensing authority. It also keeps records of all driving licenses and registered vehicles in the country.

Force Auxiliaries. The Special Constabulary is a an auxiliary force engaged in combating crime. There are two categories of supernumerary constables. The first consists of personnel serving at force and area command headquarters. The second consists of personnel on official payroll, who are hired out to commercial or public utility firms to protect life and property in which the state has a vested interest.

The Traffic Warden Service, started in 1975 in Lagos, has now expanded to all state capitals. The wardens help to unsnarl the perennial congestion on Nigeria's urban traffic.

A police band with fife, drum, and bugle was introduced in 1897. The present-day Central Band was formed in 1920 and consists of fifes, drums, and pipes. Made up of the Military Band, the Pipe Band, and the Force School of Music and Piping, it is a ceremonial arm of the force headquarters at Ikeja, with branches in six state capitals. It performs in public and private functions and concerts. There are state police bands at Enugu, Kaduna, Maidugiri, Ibadan, Benin, and Jos. Band personnel are trained at the School of Music and Piping.

The Police Medical Service, established in 1975, has 12 functioning clinics, of which 5 are in Lagos, 1 is at the Staff College in Jos, 3 at the police colleges at Kaduna, Enugu, and Maidugiri, and 3 at Owerri, Umuahia, and Aba in Imo State.

Women police were introduced as late as 1955. They are required to be unmarried and meet the same entry standards as their male counterparts except for a lower height. They are generally restricted to nonfield operations, such as radio dispatch, motor traffic control, juvenile offenders, missing persons, and cases involving women.

Ranks. There are seventeen ranks in the Nigeria Police. Of these, the first ten constitute the senior ranks and the remaining seven the lower ranks:

- Inspector General
- Deputy Inspector General
- Assistant Inspector General
- Commissioner of Police
- Deputy Commissioner
- Assistant Commissioner
- Chief Superintendent
- Superintendent
- Deputy Superintendent
- Assistant Superintendent
- Chief Inspector
- Inspector
- Sergeant Major
- Sergeant
- Corporal
- Constable
- Recruit

Education and Training. Recruitment focuses on youth and ethnic diversity. Recruits also have to meet minimum educational standards and qualifications, set in some states at a year short of full high school certificate. Because educational attainments are lower in the north, fewer Muslim applicants are able to cross this barrier. Recruitment takes place regularly at all divisional police headquarters and at the police colleges at Ikeja, Kaduna, Enugu, and Maidugiri. Those who qualify are required to pass a physical and meet tests of character, mental alertness, and financial solvency before they are accepted for training.

All recruits attend a basic six-month course at one of the police colleges. During this training period the young constable is taught basic law and police duties, drill, musketry, and first aid. He or she also undergoes rigorous physical training and participates in a wide variety of sports, such a soccer, field hockey, athletics, boxing, and gymnastics. At the same time, he or she is attached to a particular police command for practical experience in the field.

Uniforms and Weapons. Police officers wear dark-blue uniforms and gray shirts with silver buttons for ceremonial occasions and khaki work uniforms of British design with dark-blue peaked caps. The cap badge depicts an elephant, two crossed batons, and "The Nigeria Police" in scroll, the whole surmounted by an eagle.

Normally, the police officers are unarmed except for a billy club or baton. Many have been trained in the use of light infantry weapons, however, and are armed in emergency situations. They are also trained to use tear gas and firearms in dealing with large demonstrations.

Antiriot drills and parades are held weekly in police situations. For this purpose, police are formed into units of fifty, under the command of an officer. These units contain baton sections, a tear-gas section, a rifle section, stretcher bearers, and buglers. These units are fully mobile, provided with radio communications, and can travel over rough terrain. Great emphasis is placed on using only the minimum amount of force to avoid inflaming the public. One section of seven men in each unit is armed with rifles, but these weapons are rarely used.

Transportation, Technology, and Communications. The size of the country and the scarcity of usable roads enhance the role of radio communications in police work. The force headquarters in Lagos has direct links with all state headquarters. More than thirty-eight stations maintain subsidiary links within the twelve states. In addition, an expanding VHF teleprinter system links Lagos headquarters with state headquarters and the latter with the more important provinces. Many towns also have VHF stations connecting their control rooms to patrol cars engaged in traffic control and crime prevention.

The force also maintains a large fleet of motor vehicles and a number of motor launches. Many villages and towns in the Niger Delta are accessible only by water.

Foot Patrols. The standard patrol is on foot rather than in motor vehicles. Foot patrols are also effective in maintaining good community relations, getting firsthand information on local conditions, and maintaining a police presence in high-risk areas. For certain types of street crimes, foot patrols are the most effective antidote.

The introduction of foot patrols is determined by a number of criteria: the size of the locality, the type of inhabitants, the density of population, the presence of banks and shops, the existence of deserted premises, crime patterns, and the incidence of crime according to the time of day or the day of the week. Over time foot patrols acquire intimate knowledge of local conditions and personalities.

Composition of foot patrols varies, depending on the availability of manpower, the characteristics of the district to be patrolled, and the prior history of criminal victimization. Generally, a patrol consists of at least two police officers, who supported at night by motorized patrols with which they have constant radio contact. The patrolmen stay on their beat for eight hours a day.

Patrol officers reach their beat by foot, bicycles, or motorcycles or are taken there from an assembly point by a police vehicle. The officers are constantly in contact with police headquarters, the nearest police station, or police cars by means of two-way radios. They usually carry a small stick but sometimes are armed at night and during sensitive assignments or accompanied by dogs.

Because the Nigeria Police emphasize foot patrols vis-à-vis motorized patrols, which are concentrated in urban areas, vast areas of the country left virtually unpatrolled and unpoliced. It also makes police officers overworked and frustrated.

Motorized or Car Patrols. Car patrols are of four kinds: roundabout patrols, antirobbery patrols, highway patrol, and police accident patrol.

The roundabout patrol was introduced by the Lagos State Police. It involves assigning police officers to all important roundabouts (called traffic circles in the United States) in urban areas on beat duty. Such men are usually equipped with walkie-talkies, with which they call their operational base for reinforcement or to report a suspicious activity, while, in turn, instructions are communicated to them through the same medium. The system has made it possible for police officers on duty at the roundabout to keep an eye on all movements in the area. It has been particularly effective in locating missing or wanted persons.

Each police station has a mobile antirobbery patrol team. These teams have been particularly effective in stopping armed robbers in their tracks, intercepting and foiling robbery in progress, and apprehending criminals fleeing the scene of the crime.

Highway patrol teams are equipped with radios, ambulance recovery vehicles, and motorcycles, besides highly sophisticated communications equipment. Their duties include clearing roads, booking offending or reckless drivers, recovering stolen vehicles, aiding accident victims and taking them to the hospital, and preventing highway armed robberies.

Introduced in 1975, the reorganized highway patrol has been effective in enforcing traffic laws that had become a dead letter when handled by conventional police patrol units. At least 80 percent of the entire federal highway network is effectively under patrol in eight-hour shifts. Their job is made harder by the absence of uniform traffic regulations and the lack of speed limits.

The police accident patrol is concerned with hit-and-run accidents and the provision of medical aid to victims of road accidents.

Police Statistics.

- Total Police Personnel: 114,035

- Population per Police Officer: 1,129

In 1925 the first cadet inspectors were recruited directly, but the program was abandoned in 1935. Introduced in 1953, direct recruitment to the subinspectorate cadre was designed to attract those with high school certificates. The sole direct recruitment to the upper officer echelon is for the assistant superintendent cadre, the lowest senior officer rank in the Nigeria Police. Entrants are university graduates.

Both inspector and assistant superintendent ranks are also open to officers of lower rank, who may be promoted to those and other positions depending on their performance in prescribed refresher courses or fieldwork and the reports of their superiors.

There are five major police colleges, each serving a specific region. The largest and oldest is at Ikeja, which opened in 1948. It handles basic police training for recruits from the southern states. All police cadet inspectors and senior officers recruited from the civil service or elsewhere are also trained there.

The Kaduna Police College, established in 1949, is the second-largest and second-oldest in the country. It serves the northern states. The Enugu Police College serves primarily Anambra, Bendel, Cross River, Imo, and Rivers states, but also handles overflow recruits from Lagos, Oyo, Ogun, and Ondo states. The Maidugiri Police College that opened in 1973 serves Bauchi, Borno, Gongola, Benue, and Plateau states. The Police Staff College at Jos that opened in 1976 provides police command training for senior police officers.

The courses of instruction in these colleges include police ordinances and regulations, criminal laws, laws of evidence, motor vehicle ordinances, police station duties, such as fingerprinting, taking statements, and preparation of reports and sketches at the scene of a crime or accident. Interpretation of town ordinances and proper methods of keeping books and records are also taught. Practical work includes preparation of mock cases for court presentation. An intensive physical training program includes food drill, arms drill, parades, unarmed combat tactics, and riot control techniques. At every level the instruction tends to be advanced, detailed, and technical. Senior members and selected noncommissioned officers and constables are sent for advanced training in the United Kingdom or the United States in specialized areas, such as fingerprinting, dog handling, handwriting analysis, photography, and forensic science.

HUMAN RIGHTS

The government's human rights record has improved under the civilian administration that came to power at the turn of the twenty-first century. Nevertheless, serious problems remain. In response to increased incidences of armed robbery, the police have instituted a campaign called Fire for Fire, which is responsible for many human rights abuses, including use of excessive force and extrajudicial killings. Torture and beatings of suspects, detainees, and prisoners are common, and police officials are not held accountable for deaths of prisoners as a result of such torture and beatings. Prolonged pretrial detention remains a serous problem. In the north the Sharia-imposed punishments are condemned as barbaric throughout the world, but the government is incapable of enforcing a more humane law in areas where Muslims are in the majority.

CORRECTIONAL SYSTEM

Nigerian criminal law is entirely statutory and is based largely on two separate criminal codes: the Nigerian Criminal Code and the Northern Criminal Code. The former has universal application in the six southern states while the latter applies to the six largely Muslim states in the north. Customary tribal laws have fallen into disuse except where they have been incorporated into either of the criminal codes or are supported by separate legislation. Crimes are punishable only by the state and not by tribal authorities.

The Nigerian Criminal Code is generally based on the unqualified principles of English criminal law. It classifies offenses as felonies, misdemeanors, or simple offenses, each distinguished by a scale of punishment. Besides the criminal code, certain other ordinances apply to the enforcement of criminal law.

The Northern Criminal Code is based on the Sudan Code, which in turn is derived from the Penal Code of India and, ultimately, from the Sharia, or Koranic jurisprudence. It deviates considerably from Anglo-Saxon legal concepts. Provocation, for example, mitigates the punishment for homicide. It prescribes harsh punishments for such crimes as adultery, drinking alcoholic beverages, and insults to the modesty of women, unlike the Nigerian Criminal Code, which does not classify such offenses as crimes. By contrast, the Northern Criminal Code does not contain references to crimes, such as treason, sedition, or counterfeiting, which therefore appear as addenda to the code or as statutory legislation enacted separately.

Punishments are harsh under both codes, although the principle of rehabilitation is acknowledged in theory. Death sentences are carried out in public by shooting. Corporal punishment by light rod, cane, or whip is also administered in public. The Northern Criminal Code, reflecting its Koranic origin, is extremely draconian and barbaric and prescribes amputation and flogging for even minor offenses.

The Nigerian corrections system was established during the British colonial era. Originally, all federal prisons were operated by the police, but in 1908 a separate prisons department was established in southern Nigeria. In 1938 several northern prisons were redesignated federal institutions and placed under the Prisons Department. At independence the federal system was transferred to the central government, while the local prisons continued to operate under provincial and local authorities.

In 1968 the federal military government federalized all prisons and vested their administration in a commissioner of internal affairs and police. At the headquarters the system is headed by a director of prisons, and at each district headquarters by an assistant director of prisons.

The federal prisons are classified as convict, provincial, and divisional. Convict prisons are maximum security institutions that receive all classes of prisoners, while provincial and divisional prisons receive only those whose sentences do not exceed two years. In 1974 the prisons were classified on a functional basis into remand and reception centers, industrial production prisons, industrial training institutions, and prison farms.

The vast majority of the prisoners are male. Consequently, there are no prisons designated as solely for women. Some prisons have segregated sections for women, where they are employed in domestic crafts. Convicted juveniles between fourteen and eighteen years are incarcerated in the juvenile section of the Port Harcourt Prison. There are two reformatories for offenders under the age of twenty-one: the Approved School at Enugu in East-Central State and the Reformatory at Kukuri in North-Central State. In federal prisons male and female prisoners are segregated, and first offenders are segregated from hardened criminals. Prison labor is divided into three main categories: industrial, domestic, and unskilled labor.

Prison Conditions. Most prisons were built under the colonial administration about seventy to eighty years ago and lack basic facilities, such as potable water and indoor plumbing. Diseases are rampant in the in the cramped, poorly ventilated cells and there are chronic shortages of medicines. Many inmates have to provide their own food and are allowed outside their cells for recreation or exercise only rarely. Petty corruption among prison officials makes it difficult even for relatives to bring food into prisons. Beds and mattresses are not provided, and most inmates sleep on concrete floors without a blanket. Prison officials, police, and security personnel deny inmates food or medicine as a means of punishment or to extract money. A number of prisoners die each year as a result of malnutrition and lack of medical care and are buried promptly in the prison compounds without notifying the nearest kin.

Prison conditions are worse in rural areas than in urban ones. Women and juveniles are not separated from adult males in rural areas, which leads to considerable abuse. About 70 to 80 percent of the prison population are detainees awaiting trial. Some have to wait for up to twelve years, sometimes more than the maximum length of their possible sentences. Serious delays are caused by multiple adjournments or missing case files. In 2001 the National Human Rights Commission drafted a new bill that would grant prisoners basic rights under United Nations protocols.

Prison Statistics.

- Total Prison Population: 39,153
- Prison Population Rate per 100,000: 31
- Pretrial Detainees: 64.3%
- Female Prisoners: 1.9%
- Number of Prisons: 147
- Official Capacity of the Prison System: 42,681
- Occupancy Level: 101.5%

George Thomas Kurian

Norway

Official country name: Kingdom of Norway

Capital: Oslo

Geographic description: Northernmost country on the Scandinavian Peninsula, bordering the North Sea

Population: 4,593,041 (est. 2005)

■■■

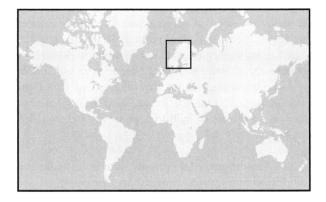

LAW ENFORCEMENT

History. The earliest traces of a legal system in Norway existed over 1,000 years ago. This institution was known as the Allting and was a public gathering of yeomen, who convened to settle disputes and make laws for the local district. During the late thirteenth century regional laws were ultimately consolidated into one coherent codification scheme. This was later followed by a second major codification of Norwegian law that took place in 1687, during a period when Norway was ruled by Denmark. On dissolution of the union with Denmark because of the close of the Napoleonic Wars, Norway adopted a constitution on May 17, 1814. This constitution established Norway as a parliamentary democracy and a constitutional monarchy.

The first comprehensive penal code was enacted in 1842. This was replaced by the General Civil Penal Code of May 22, 1902. Since this time, the penal code remains, though it has been greatly modified through amendments over time. Rules on criminal procedure were first codified in 1887. This statute was replaced by the Act on Rules of Judicial Procedure in Penal Cases, which became official on January 1, 1986. The Penal Code and Criminal Procedure Act continue to be the two main laws governing the civil administration of criminal justice in Norway today.

Structure and Organization. There are five police regions, among which are fifty-four police districts. The districts are led by police commissioners (Politimestre), who have as their immediate subordinates, deputy police commissioners (Politiinspektorer), assistant commissioners (Politiadjutanter), and superintendents (Politifullmektiger). Police commissioners and deputy police commissioners are appointed by the king in council. The other two classes of officials are appointed by the Ministry of Justice and Police.

The police force is administered directly by the Ministry of Justice and Police. It is also subordinate to the Public Prosecution Authority when investigating or prosecuting criminal cases. The police commissioners and their immediate subordinates are ultimately headed by the director general; the director general, in turn, is appointed by, and directly accountable to, the king, independent of the Ministry of Justice.

In rural areas police duties are carried out by sheriffs (Lensmenn), each of whom has general administrative authority in relation to a defined district. There are 370 such districts. As a police officer, a sheriff is accountable to the local police commissioner. There are several special units to the police force, all of which are administered centrally. These include the National Bureau of Crime Investigation (Kriminalpolitisentralen—also known as Kripos), the Police Security Service (Politiets Overvkingstjeneste), the Police Computing Service (Politiets Datatjeneste), the Police Equipment Service (Politiets Materielltjeneste), and the Mobile Police (Utrykningspolitiet). There is also a small specialist antiterror squad based in Oslo.

Furthermore, police are considered separate from the military branch of the government, making it a truly civilian-based form of social control. Similar to other countries, the police can, and sometimes do, seek the assistance of the military. Such assistance may be obtained during times of natural disaster or state emergency. Also, in times when human and physical resources are not adequate for a given task, the police have been known to call on the military for assistance when dealing with a given problem. In these instances military personnel involved in such operations fall under the command of the civilian police and are likewise accountable for their behavior under the same codes that govern civilian police actions.

Principal Agencies and Divisions. There are five police regions, among which are fifty-four police districts. The districts are led by police commissioners, who have as their immediate subordinates, deputy police commissioners, assistant commissioners, and superintendents. In rural areas police duties are carried out by sheriffs (Lensmenn), each of whom has general administrative authority in relation to a defined district. There are 370 such districts. It should be noted that in Norway a sheriff is accountable to the local police commissioner of that district. Lastly, the national police have primary responsibility for internal security, but in times of crisis, such as internal disorder or natural catastrophe, the police may call on the military forces for assistance. In such circumstances the military forces are always under police authority. The civilian authorities maintain effective control of the security forces.

Police at Work. The functions and tasks of the police are many and varied, ranging from the usual maintenance of law and order, the investigation and prevention of crime, to more specialized administrative tasks, such as immigration control and control of lotteries and gambling. Various local and district departments indicate that police at work in Norway engage in the following activities in roughly the following proportions.

With direct police-related work, it is estimated that roughly 40 to 50 percent of their time is devoted to public service, investigation of crimes, crime prevention activities, traffic duty, immigration control, rescue services and licensing tasks related to business operations and social events, and other routine police work.

Public Service. Traffic duty naturally consists of speed surveillance and traffic regulation among the general populace. The police also enforce safety belt controls. The police do have primary responsibility for enforcing laws that pertain to driving while under the influence of alcohol. In addition, Norwegian police initiate, lead and coordinate all operations regarding accidents and hostile situations.

Investigative work consists of investigations of all criminal offenses such as those of violence, those for profit, and drug-related and property crimes. Of course, officers do investigate fire-related scenes and accidents as well. The police are also involved in crime prevention efforts. This includes education components within their school systems as well as direct actions against target groups, special environments, and different specific types of crime.

Roughly 20 to 30 percent of their work has to do with the exercise of civil duties. Particularly time consuming is the role of enforcement officers during force auction sales, the return of stolen property, cases of indebtedness, the announcement of summons and sentences, and so forth. Other duties may include dealing with the estates of deceased persons and the registering of those estates. The remaining 20 percent of their work typically involves administrative functions on a day-to-day basis.

Police-Community Relations. To maintain effective police-community relations in Norway, several mechanisms have been designed to restrain power, to avoid misconduct, and to keep police personnel in line and accountable. One of these mechanisms is to ensure thorough and independent investigation of complaints filed against police personnel. Special Investigatory Bodies, organizationally independent of the police and subordinate to the director general of public prosecution (Riksadvokaten), investigates complaints against the police in Norway. Each of these bodies has three members: a chairman with qualifications equal to a Supreme Court judge, a lawyer with a minimum of two years practicing criminal law, and finally a member with significant experience in police investigation. One substitute is assigned to each of the members of these bodies. The primary mandate of the Special Investigatory Bodies is to investigate all complaints alleging that police have breached criminal law in carrying out their duties. Furthermore, they also investigate all cases in which police actions have resulted in a person's death and/or serious bodily injury, irrespective whether or not a complaint was made. General complaints not in breach of criminal law are handled internally while special committees attached to each police district handle allegations of police acting in breach of discipline. Finally, after concluding their investigation, the Special Investigatory Bodies make recommendations about further action to the state attorney who then makes a final decision about the case.

The annual number of complaints filed has increased steadily since the Special Investigatory Bodies were established in 1988. While only 401 complaints were filed in 1988, the corresponding number for 1999 was 656. During this same period the rate of substantiation was relatively stable, around 7 to 8 percent. The relatively low rate of substantiated complaints has made for a constant source of criticism toward the Special Investigatory Bodies. This, coupled with the fact that most members either are or have been employed in the police force, has fueled the assumption that the Special Investigatory Bodies are biased in favor of the police. However, empirical evidence in Norway and elsewhere shows that the rate of substantiation remains low even if more "civilians" are involved in the process.

Special Police. There are several special units to the police force, all of which are administered centrally. These include the National Bureau of Crime Investigation, the Police Security Service, the Police Computing Service, the Police Equipment Service, and the Mobile Police. There is also a small specialist antiterror squad based in Oslo.

Uniforms and Weapons. The most common type of weapon with which police arm themselves is a wooden baton. Furthermore, "there are two main types of guns available for use by ordinary police officers: U.S. carabineers (30 caliber) and Smith and Wesson revolvers (model 10), and machine guns are available to specially selected police units, such as the anti-terror squad" (Bygrave 1997, p. 13). There are light bulletproof vests for approximately half of the operative police force. They are distributed unequally between the various police districts depending on need. Almost all police officers on patrol in Oslo have bulletproof vests. There are also approximately 2,000 heavy bulletproof vests and helmets distributed between the police districts.

Transportation, Technology, and Communications. As of August 1993 there were approximately 1,620 police automobiles. About 1,000 of these were state owned; the rest were rented. In addition, there were eighty-six motorcycles, all of which were state owned (Bygrave 1997).

Computer technology is used by the police force for a variety of purposes, including reporting crimes, gathering and processing crime statistics, budgeting,

accreditation of officials, and fingerprinting (the Automated Fingerprint Identification System has been in use with the National Bureau of Crime Investigation since the beginning of 1985). All police and sheriff stations have online links to a central computer network maintained by the Police Computing Service. There were plans to mount a fleet of police cars with minicomputer terminals in 2005. Mobile telephones, radio equipment, and radar guns are also widely used.

Surveillance and Intelligence Gathering. There are two comprehensive registration and surveillance systems in operation in Norway. The first is called the Schengen Information System (SIS). It is a data-based registration and surveillance system whose purpose is to maintain public order and security, including state security, and to apply the provisions of this convention relating to the movement of persons, in the territories of the contracting parties, using information transmitted by the system. This stated purpose is broad and comprehensive, comprising both "public order" and "state security." No further definitions of these terms are given, which means that just about everything may be included, from acts of qualified terrorism through various forms of social unrest to political demonstrations deemed to be a threat to public order and/or state security by the governments concerned.

Generally speaking, the information that may be stored in the system may be viewed in terms of three major levels or tiers. First, article 94.3 of the convention specifies the items that may be included in respect to persons: name and forename, and any aliases possibly registered separately; any particular objective and permanent physical features (an example would be skin color); first letter of second forename; date and place of birth; sex; nationality; whether the persons concerned are armed; whether the persons concerned are violent; reason for the report; and action to be taken. In other words, the basic information combines objective (sex) and evaluative (estimated violence) items.

SIS, however, is only one of the systems for information exchange in Schengen. The other system, closely related to and intertwined with SIS, is the Supplément d'Information Requis à l'Entrée Nationale (Supplementary Information Request at the National Entries; SIRENE). "SIRENE is intended to facilitate bilateral and multilateral exchange, mainly of supplementary information about persons and objects registered in the SIS, between the national police authorities in different Schengen countries" (Mathieson 2000, p. 171). In essence, "SIRENE is a complex, network-like structure for bilateral and multilateral police and security cooperation between those countries utilizing the Schengen Information System, including central national offices and a sophisticated computerized information system, enabling the exchange of 'supplementary' data on persons and items before the entry of a report in the SIS, or following a positive search in the SIS" (p. 171). Through the SIRENE system, police authorities in one country that have arrested a person who is registered in the SIS by another country may require supplementary information, not stored in the SIS, from the latter country. The SIRENE system has developed alongside SIS and is far less known and not even mentioned in the Schengen Convention.

Police Statistics. In 2000 there were 11,134 total police personnel, which equates to a rate of one per every 248 citizens in Norway (Centre for International Crime Prevention 2002). There were 3,087 female police in Norway in 1994. These numbers include those officers who serve on the sheriff's force as well. As of 2005 there were two female police commissioners.

HUMAN RIGHTS

A delegation of the European Committee for the Prevention of Torture and Inhuman or Degrading Treatment or Punishment (CPT) visited Norway in September 1999 as a routine spot-check visit on human rights issues. The report noted that the delegation visited a number of police stations, prisons, psychiatric facilities, and establishments for young people, as well as a detention center for aliens. No allegations of torture or other forms of ill treatment of persons held in police establishments were received. However, some allegations were heard of the use of excessive force by police officers at the time of apprehension. Specifically, the report noted that in 1998 and 1999 the director general of public prosecutions issued several new guidelines on a variety of matters, including the transfer of persons remanded in custody from police stations to prisons, the treatment of prisoners on remand, and a detainee's access to a lawyer. The CPT noted that a significant reduction had been achieved in the average length of time that persons remanded in custody spent on police premises and that in most cases the transfer now takes place within twenty-four hours.

With regard to prisons, the CPT focused on two issues of concern: the treatment of remand prisoners subject to restrictions imposed by a court and the quality of prison health care services. The CPT noted the harmful effects of restrictions on prisoners, who were reported to have complained of anxiety, restlessness, sleeping problems, depression, and even suicidal thoughts. The CPT recommended that serious efforts continue to be made by prison staff to offer additional activities and appropriate human contact to prisoners held on remand under restrictions. Health-care services within the Norwegian criminal justice system were found to be adequate. However, the CPT expressed concern at the situation found in Oslo Prison, where an ongoing conflict within the staff could compromise the quality of health care. No allegations were heard of deliberate physical ill treatment of patients by staff at the psychiatric facilities visited. Staff-patient relations appeared to be relatively relaxed and the care staff was evidently dedicated to their work.

The only other major human rights concern that appears worthy of mention in Norway involves the minority group known as the Sami. Aside from a tiny Finnish population in the northeast, the Sami constituted the only significant minority group until the influx of immigrants during the 1970s. In recent years the government has taken steps to protect Sami cultural rights by providing Sami language instruction at schools in their areas, radio and television programs broadcast or subtitled in Sami, and subsidies for newspapers and books oriented toward the Sami. In an unique political statement King Harald V publicly apologized to the Sami people for repression under Norwegian rule. In 1996 this was followed by the appointment of a state of secretary in the Ministry of Local Government and Regional Affairs to deal specifically with Sami issues.

CRIME

Organized Crime. The media reflect that the following are areas of concern with organized crime within Norway: the involvement of eastern Europeans in organized crime, the infusion of the Russian Mafia in organized crime within Norway, and the eastern European Mafia have become aware of the market and profit potentials in Norway. Thus, Norway is becoming an increasingly attractive target.

While it has been determined that organized crime by eastern Europeans is not an epidemic problem, some have been involved in serious forms of organized crime in Norway. Specifically, "the drug import business has been found to be particularly well organised. Heroin is smuggled to a large extent to Norway from Afghanistan, Pakistan and certain neighbouring countries via the Balkans and through Europe." There is also a new itinerary farther north, which passes through former Soviet states and Russia. Amphetamine is smuggled into Norway from Poland and the Baltic states—particularly Estonia (Kittelsbye and Naess 2001).

Likewise, illegal immigration has become extensive and seems to be well organized. The police have documented a close connection between illegal passing of human beings in a country and trafficking in human beings. Trade in women is a form of crime that has been growing during the last few years. The Oslo Police District has analyzed the phenomenon in Oslo and concludes that the number of women working in the indoor prostitution business is growing. Previously, the criminal aspect of this trade was mainly related to prostitution. However, a hardening of the business has taken place and the infrastructure around the women is linked to criminal organizations, which invest the proceeds from this "industry" into other types of illegal activity.

In fact, human trafficking has been identified in Norway as a form of organized crime that has become particularly problematic. While the primary purpose of this trade is sexual exploitation, it also serves as a source of illicit labor. In Norway trafficking represents an aggravated form of sexualized violence that is incompatible with the principle of gender equality. Women and children afflicted by poverty are particularly vulnerable to traffickers, who are motivated by profit and in many cases involved in organized crime. Human trafficking comprises a serious form of organized crime and constitutes a grave violation of human rights.

In 2003 Norway launched its first Plan of Action to Combat Trafficking in Women and Children. This action plan contains measures to protect and assist the victims, prevent human trafficking, and prosecute the organizers. In 2002 the Norwegian government introduced ethical guidelines for civil servants to prohibit the purchase and acceptance of sexual services. The basis for the resolution is the increasing problem posed by international prostitution and the trafficking of women and children for sexual purposes. The guidelines send a clear signal as to the ethical and moral standards Norwegian senior officials and civil servants are expected to observe. The introduction of these guidelines emphasizes the government's role as a good example. In this way the authorities and the government as employers seek to assume the responsibility in principle for preventing people from being degraded as victims of human trafficking for sexual purposes.

Crime Statistics. Roughly 207,000 offenses were reported to the Norwegian police during the first half of 2003. This was a decrease of 11 percent from the first half of 2002. For the second year in a row there was a decline in narcotics offenses. The number of offenses reported to the police varies from year to year, but such a decrease from one year to another as happened in 2002 and 2003 is rare. Crimes declined by 12 percent, and misdemeanors by 8 percent. The change from 2001 was 3 percent and 4 percent, respectively. The preliminary figures are normally 1 to 2 percent lower than the final figures, hence it looks like 2002 had the high figures. It is uncertain to what extent the high figures in 2002 and the following decline in 2003 are, whether they represent changes in the registration system or to other reasons.

There were 106,000 reported offenses for profit during the first half of 2003. This was 10 percent less than the previous year, but the numbers were 2 percent higher than in 2001. Theft was the largest type of offense in this category and constituted about 40 percent of all reported offenses and almost 60 percent of all crimes. Simple larceny decreased by 6 percent from the previous year, and aggravated larceny dropped by 9 percent. The figures for simple larceny have not been as low since 1997, but the numbers for aggravated larceny are—in spite of the decrease from the previous year—still higher than in both 2000 and 2001 (Statistics Norway 2003a).

Similar to other decreases, for the second year in a row, there was a decline in narcotics offenses. There were 19,000 cases in the first half of 2003. This was a decrease of 24 percent compared to the first half of the previous year. The decrease was particularly because of use and possession of drugs, which dropped by 31 and 20 percent, respectively, compared to the first half of 2002. Crimes of narcotics dropped by 25 percent, and serious crimes of narcotics by 13 percent (Statistics Norway 2003a). The overall figures have not been this low since 1997. The exception is serious crimes of narcotics, which are still higher than in 2001. However, the number of reported narcotic offenses might be directly affected by changes in the police registers and may also be highly sensitive to the priorities of the police. Hence, it is difficult to tell if the decline is because of an actual decrease in crimes of narcotics or because of other reasons.

By contrast, there has been a rise in sexual crimes. There were 1,800 reported sexual crimes in the first half of 2003. This is an 8 percent increase compared to 2002. Sexual crimes are the only group of offenses that rose in the first half of 2003. However, sexual crimes are often reported a long time after the crime was committed and hence the numbers reflect to a lesser extent the number of sexual crimes committed the year they were reported (Statistics Norway 2003a). In a particular year, the numbers are also attributed to the inclination to report such offenses. As an example, about 50 percent of the sexual crimes reported in 2003 were committed before 2003.

Readjustment of the Police Registration System. Between October 2002 and March 2003 the police registration system underwent a technical readjustment in relation to the police reform in the same year. As expected, this caused an overall decrease in numbers. In the past, if an offense was reported in one police district and then the case was transferred to another police district, the case was registered again in the new district. This kind of double-entry registration was eliminated through the readjustment of the registration system. As such, double-entry registrations have since been substantially reduced given the new routines for registration. This has had the greatest effect on offenses that are most likely to be transferred to another police district. This is particularly so for narcotic offenses. However, it is not likely that this phenomenon alone can explain the reduction in numbers from 2002 to 2003.

CORRECTIONAL SYSTEM

According to the 2001 United Nations Survey on Crime Trends and Operations of Criminal Justice, there were forty-six adult prison institutions in Norway. The prisons had a total 2,818 beds available to house offenders. Of these prisons, five were central prisons and forty-one were regional prisons. One of the central prisons was for females only. Most other prisons contained prisoners of both sexes. Larger prisons had special sections just for women. As of 2002 there were no prisons solely used for juveniles. There were 1,807 places for prisoners in closed prison institutions and 2,011 places in open institutions. In open institutions there are no special security measures taken to prevent prisoners from escaping, unlike those taken in closed institutions.

Prison Conditions. As a general rule, prisoners are released on parole before the period for which they have been sentenced has expired. Normally, they are released once they have served at least two-thirds of their sentence, which must be at least two months, including time spent in custody. In special circumstances a prisoner can be released on parole after half the sentence has expired, but this rarely occurs.

There are compulsory work schemes for prisoners. However, those serving short prison sentences may avoid having to participate in these schemes if it is difficult to find appropriate work activities for them. Prisoners are paid for their work.

Prisoners can participate in programs run by the Ministry of Education. Furthermore, prisoners have visitation rights, postal correspondence rights, the right to lodge written complaints, and the right to be allowed outdoors for at least an hour each day.

Most prisons have a priest who holds regular church services for prisoners and helps organize social events. At the larger prisons, there are also social workers and sports and recreation advisers whom prisoners can consult. Prisoners are normally allowed to have televisions, radios, and magazines in their cells. In special circumstances they are also allowed to leave prison for short periods, such as to visit a sick relative.

There are no special treatment programs for prisoners beyond ordinary medical services, although it is possible to transfer prisoners to other institutions for special treatment if necessary. It is also possible for a prisoner addicted to drugs to enter into a special contract with the prison authorities. In this contract the prison authorities can offer and provide more privileges on the condition that the prisoner promises not to use drugs and agrees to undergo regular urine tests to ensure the promise is being kept.

Prison Statistics. In 2001, 2,800 inmates were held in Norwegian prisons. This was an increase of about 200 from the previous year. There were 12,000 imprisonments in the course of the year, which was 8 percent more than in 2000. The average number of people in Norwegian prisons also went up by 8 percent. The prison population at the start of the year increased by 11 percent to 2,975. The number of prisons was 46, the official capacity of the prison system was 3,136, and the occupancy level was 94.9 percent. The prison population rate per 100,000 was 65. Pretrial detainees made up 20.6 percent of the prison population, female prisoners 5.2 percent, and juvenile prisoners 0.3 percent. These trends are in part the result of an increase in the capacity of the prison system: There were 109 extra available prison spaces in 2001, and the available spaces were used to a greater extent in 2001 than in the previous year. Still, the number of people waiting to serve a sentence did not decrease in 2001, because of an increase in the number of unconditional prison sentences (Statistics Norway 2003b).

The number of imprisonments to custody, and the number of people held in custody on an average day did not change significantly from 2000 to 2001. There were about 3,800 incarcerations in the course of the year, and 600 people were held in custody on an average day. Hence, the increase in the prison population was only the result of more people serving prison sentences.

The average daily number of prisoners was 2,548, of which 124, or approximately 5 percent, were women. A total of 4 percent of those admitted to prison were foreign citizens residing in Norway. Out of this 4 percent, over half had originally come from Europe (mainly from northern Europe), 9 percent from North America, 14 percent from Africa, and 28 percent from Asia. A total of 5 percent of those admitted to prison were of unknown citizenship (Central Bureau of Statistics 1993). The percentage breakdown by type of offender in Norwegian prisons is:

- Drug Crimes: 9%

- Violent Crimes (includes sexual offenses, various forms of bodily violence, and murder): 12%

- Property Crimes (includes theft): 15%

- Other Crimes (includes fraud, drunk driving, and traffic offenses): 40%

- Unknown: 24%

MOST SIGNIFICANT ISSUE FACING THE COUNTRY

As in other European countries, immigration to Norway has posed many political and social challenges. The building of Norway as a nation and the development of the welfare state in the twentieth century placed great emphasis on cultural equality as the national cornerstone. As the 1980s progressed, it became clear that Norway now had a permanent minority of people with a non-European background. They looked different to ethnic Norwegians and in many important areas they were quite different from a cultural viewpoint. Thus, discrimination issues have been noted to be fairly widespread. It is well known that immigrants have more problems than others do in procuring jobs and homes. Furthermore, more blatant forms of discrimination have been found to occur. For instance, a number of discotheques and nightclubs refuse to admit persons who look as though they come from a non-European country. The discrimination in Norway against immigrants who do not appear European has led many immigrants to change their names so as to sound more European in descent. It has also been asserted that the police treat people differently on the basis of their appearance (Eriksen 2003). Those who do not look like Norwegians risk being stopped on the street and asked for proof of identity. Discrimination is a major obstacle that precludes the successful integration of minorities into Norwegian culture. Lastly, it is clear that during the last few years conceptions of Norway and what it means to be Norwegian have been challenged. This is because of the increasingly multiethnic society developing in a country that has been almost completely homogenous. Being Norwegian no longer implies being culturally the same: The integration of immigrants requires equality on paper as in reality.

BIBLIOGRAPHY

Andenaes, Johs. 1987. *Norsk straffeprosess* [Norwegian Criminal Procedure], vol. 1. 2nd ed. Oslo: Universitetsforlaget.

Andenaes, Johs. 1993. *Norsk straffeprosess*, vol. 2. 3rd ed. Oslo: Universitetsforlaget.

Andenaes, Johs, and Anders Bratholm. 1991. *Spesiell strafferett* [Special Criminal Law], 2nd ed. Oslo: Universitetsforlaget.

Bindal Sheriff Office. 1998. "Bindal Sheriff Office on the WWW." Bindal Sheriff Office. Available online at http://home.c2i.net/lmogstad/e/ (accessed December 23, 2005).

Brenna, Wenke. 1998. "The Sami of Norway." Norwegian Ministry of Foreign Affairs. Available online at http://odin.dep.no/odin/engelsk/norway/history/032005-990463/index-dok000-b-n-a.html (accessed December 23, 2005).

Bureau of Democracy, Human Rights, and Labor. 2001. "Country Reports on Human Rights Practices: Norway." U.S. Department of State. Available online at http://www.state.gov/g/drl/rls/hrrpt/2000/eur/878.htm (accessed December 23, 2005).

Bygrave, Lee. 1997. "Norway." In *World Factbook of Criminal Justice Systems*. Oslo: Norwegian Research Centre for Computers and Law. Available online at http://www.ojp.usdoj.gov/bjs/pub/ascii/wfbcjnor.txt (accessed December 23, 2005).

Central Bureau of Statistics. 1992. *Kriminalitet og rettsvesen* [Criminality and the Legal System], 2nd ed. Oslo: Central Bureau of Statistics.

Central Bureau of Statistics. 1993. *Kriminalstatistikk 1991* [Criminal Statistics 1991]. Norges offisielle statistikk C 73. Oslo: Central Bureau of Statistics.

Centre for International Crime Prevention. 2002. "United Nations Criminal Justice System Compilation: Norway." Vienna: UN Office on Drugs and Crime.

Eriksen, Thomas Hylland. 2003. "Norway: A Multi-ethnic Country." Norwegian Ministry of Foreign Affairs. Available online at http://odin.dep.no/odin/engelsk/norway/social/032091-990909/index-dok000-b-n-a.html (accessed December 23, 2005).

Kittelsbye, Ellen. S., and Elisabeth Naess. 2001. *Crime Committed by People from Eastern Europe: The Police Perspective*. Oslo: Nordiska Samarbetsrådet för Kriminologi.

Law Faculty, University of Oslo. 1992. *Norges Lover 1685–1991* [Laws of Norway 1685–1991]. Oslo: Ad Notam.

Mathieson, T. 2000. "On the Globalisation of Control: Toward an Integrated Surveillance System in Europe." In *Criminal Policy Transition*, edited by Penny Green and Andrew Rutherford. Portland, OR: Hart.

Ministry of Justice and Police. 1980. *Administration of Justice in Norway*, 2nd ed. Edited by the Royal Ministry of Justice in cooperation with the Royal Ministry of Foreign Affairs. Oslo: Universitetsforlaget.

Norwegian Ministry of Children and Family Affairs. 2003. "Trafficking in Women and Children." Norway: The Official Site in the UK. Available online at http://www.norway.org.uk/policy/gender/trafficking.htm (accessed December 23, 2005).

Police Division, Ministry of Justice and Police. 1991. *Politiets yearrbok 1991* [The Police Yearbook 1991]. Oslo: Police Division, Ministry of Justice and Police.

Public Prosecution Authorities and Police in Norway. 1992. Information Office, Oslo Police Department.

Statistics Norway. 2003a. *Offenses Reported to the Police: First Half of 2003—Preliminary Figures Decrease in Reported Offenses*. Oslo: Statistics Norway.

Statistics Norway. 2003b. *Record High Number of Inmates*. Oslo: Statistics Norway.

Thomassen, Gunnar. 1999. *Investigating Complaints against Police in Norway: An Empirical Evaluation*. Oslo: PHS-forskning.

United Nations Human Rights System. 2000. "For the Record 2000: Western Europe and Other." Human Rights Internet. Available online at http://www.hri.ca/fortherecord2000/eng2000pdf/vol6e_weurope.pdf (accessed December 23, 2005).

Robert D. Hanser
Nathan R. Moran

Oman

Official country name: Sultanate of Oman
Capital: Muscat
Geographic description: Located at the southeastern corner of the Arabian Peninsula, bordering the Gulf of Oman and the Persian Gulf
Population: 3,001,583 (including 577,293 nonnationals) (est. 2005)

■ ■ ■

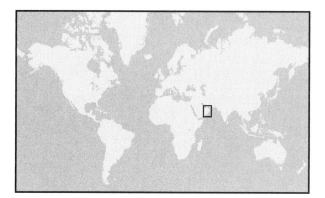

LAW ENFORCEMENT

History. The Royal Omani Police is the descendant of the tribal police composed of *askars* (traditional guards), as well as the more organized Omani Gendarmerie and the Muscat Police Force, the latter formed in 1931. It was created by the British and was staffed by British expatriates who modeled it on British lines.

Structure and Organization. The internal and external security apparatus fell under the authority of the Royal Office, which coordinated all security and intelligence policies. The Royal Oman Police, whose head had cabinet status, performed regular police duties, provided security at airports, served as the country's immigration agency, and maintained a small coast guard.

The commander of the Royal Omani Police is the inspector general of police and customs, who reports to the minister of the interior. Specialized headquarters functions include traffic and criminal investigation. The operational divisions include the Marine Division, the Fire Service, and the Police Air Wing.

Territorially, the Royal Omani Police is divided into field units that correspond to the three governorates and the five regions. The divisional headquarters are at Al-Sharqiyah, Al Wusta, Al Betinah, Al Dahirah, Al Dakiiyah, Muscat, Dhofar, and Mussandam. Regional and governorate police commands are headed by deputy inspector generals who have jurisdiction over a number of rural and urban police stations.

Education and Training. Training for all ranks is provided at the Sultan Qaboos Academy for Police Sciences at Muscat and the Police Academy at Nizwa.

Uniforms and Weapons. Working dress for all ranks consists of khaki shirts and trousers with a black belt and black shoulder epaulettes bearing rank badges. A British-style blue peaked cap with a checkered cap band is also worn. On occasions, an open-necked khaki tunic is worn instead of the shirt. The ceremonial uniform is a white tunic and blue trousers with a broad stripe on the seams.

Police Statistics.

- Total Police Personnel: 5,865
- Population per Police Officer: 512

HUMAN RIGHTS

Oman has a basic charter with the force of law that provides for many human rights. However, in practice the security forces do not observe its injunctions, especially regarding arrest and detention, and due process is denied to those tried in state security courts. The courts are not independent as judges serve at the behest of the sultan, who also has the right to override any judicial decision.

CRIME

Crime Statistics. Offenses reported to the police per 100,000 population: 331. Of which:

- Murder: 1.5
- Assault: 1.8
- Automobile Theft: 14.9

CORRECTIONAL SYSTEM

Prisons are administered by the director of prisons under the Ministry of the Interior.

Prison Conditions. Prison conditions, while spartan, appear to meet international standards. Men are separated from women, juveniles from adults, and pretrial detainees from hardened criminals. However, the government does not permit independent monitoring of prison conditions.

Prison Statistics. There are three prisons in the sultanate with a total population of 2,020. The incarceration rate is 81 per 100,000 people. Of the total prison population, 5 percent are female, 3.3 percent are juveniles, and 20.3 percent are foreigners.

George Thomas Kurian

Pakistan

■

Official country name: Islamic Republic of Pakistan
Capital: Islamabad
Geographic description: Northwestern part of the Indian subcontinent including a part of Kashmir that is still in dispute with India
Population: 162,419,946 (est. 2005)

■■■

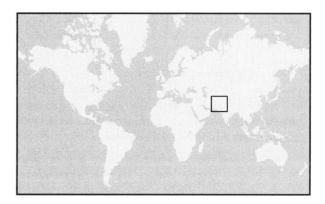

LAW ENFORCEMENT

History. The first modern police force in Pakistan was set up by the British administration in 1843 and formed along the lines of the Royal Irish Constabulary. This force was so successful that it formed the model for succeeding forces created in other parts of the British Raj. The Police Act of 1861 made this police organization the norm to be followed in all provinces under direct British rule. The principal feature of the act was that policing was a civil function exercised by the provincial governments through an inspector general of police. The force was organized hierarchically on the lines of the army. Following independence, the Pakistani police were separated from the Indian counterpart and given jurisdiction over West Pakistan and East Pakistan. In 1971 East Pakistan became independent as Bangladesh, and West Pakistan became what is now known as Pakistan.

Structure and Organization. Under the constitution the maintenance of law and order is a provincial function; consequently, most of the police forces are organized under the auspices of the provincial governments. However, certain national agencies function under the federal Ministry of the Interior, including the Federal Investigative Agency and the Frontier Constabulary. In 1973 a new national-level body, the Federal Security Force, was formed to perform guard duties as a police reserve.

Police forces at the national and provincial levels are highly similar, being uniformly governed by many national regulations carried over almost intact from pre-independence British India. In general, the police are oppressive and corrupt and much disliked by the common Pakistani. Several high-level commissions have studied the police system and recommended many changes. The system as a whole, however, is entrenched and has proven resistant to change. The system is also subject to partisan political manipulation, sectarian and regional rivalries, and an overburdened bureaucracy.

The provincial forces are not integrated vertically, but they function under some common rubrics, making them almost identical in operation and administration. Many administrative matters, such as minimum pay, allowances, and uniforms, are prescribed at the national level. Although the overall organization is of British origin, much of the methods and equipment as well as training reflect U.S. models as a result of U.S. aid programs.

The core of the federal police establishment is the Police Service of Pakistan (PSP), formed at independence with Muslim members of the Indian Police Service as its nucleus. The PSP is not an operational entity and does not function as such. It is a career service from which officers are individually assigned to operational police units. All senior officers both in the national agencies and in the provincial police are members of the PSP.

Two of the principal national-level agencies, both under the Police Division of the Ministry of the Interior, are the Federal Investigation Agency (FIA) and the Federal Security Force. The FIA was formed in 1941 as the Anticorruption Agency. It has investigative powers and may initiate investigations of its own or respond to requests from other governmental departments on matters such as embezzlement, bribery, black marketing, or misappropriation of funds. Its director has the rank of inspector general of police.

The Federal Security Force is a paramilitary police reserve for control of public disturbances and for important guard duties. It is believed to consist of up to nineteen battalions stationed at garrisons in the capital and in key locations throughout the country.

At the national level the best-known paramilitary police is the long-established Frontier Constabulary, commanded and staffed by members of the PSP. Its headquarters are at Peshawar, and it is run under a deputy inspector general of police, who reports to the minister of the interior. Constabulary units are stationed in the North-West Frontier Province, the population of which is heavily Pushtun with sympathies for the radical Islamic elements of Afghanistan. Among their duties is to watch for infiltrators from Afghan tribal areas, al Qaeda terrorists, heroin smugglers, and Taliban fighters on the run. The Frontier Constabulary works in tandem with the army auxiliaries known as the Frontier Corps.

At least three other organizations at the national level are involved in law and order, although they are not directly part of the police structure. The Directorate of Civil Defense under the Ministry of the Interior plans and directs civil relief in disasters and other emergencies. The notorious Central Intelligence Service (CIS) reports directly to the president. The CIS is known as the father of the Taliban and its main funding source. The FIA investigates economic crime, combats corruption in the federal and state governments, and investigates immigration and white-collar crimes.

Because the primary responsibility for the maintenance of law and order rests with the provincial governments, most police personnel are employed by the provinces. The provincial police forces include the regular police, other specialized security forces of the special armed reserve, the railway, highway, and river police, and the village police. The combined strength of these forces is estimated at more than 125,000. The largest segment is in the Punjab, followed by those of Sind, the North-West Frontier Province, and Baluchistan.

Police officers are categorized as gazetted or subordinate, roughly analogous to commissioned and noncommissioned officers, respectively, in the armed services. The subordinate grades are further divided into upper and lower categories. The top five grades, in descending order, are those of inspector general, additional inspector general, deputy inspector general, superintendent, and assistant superintendent. These grades are customarily filled by PSP officers. In the provincial police services the top grade is that of deputy superintendent, which is equivalent to that of assistant superintendent, the lowest grade in the PSP. Below these gazetted ranks are the upper subordinate positions, in descending order, of inspector, subinspector, and assistant subinspector. Below them are the bulk of rank-and-file policemen in the lower subordinate grades, including the head constable and the constable.

Each province is divided for purpose of police administration into a number of divisions. The four provinces have a total of thirteen divisions. Corresponding to each division and coterminous with the divisional commissioner's jurisdiction is the territorial police area called a range. Each range, in turn, is divided into districts; these are further broken down into a varying number of subdistricts, which have a number of police stations called station houses (*thanas*). Some districts do not have subdistricts, and there the station houses report directly to the district headquarters.

In each province the head of the police establishment is the inspector general of police, who reports to the secretary of the home department of the provincial government. The inspector general, who may be aided by an additional secretary general, supervises several deputy inspectors general at the provincial headquarters, each in charge of certain departmental functions, such as criminal investigation, identification, communications, railway security, terrorism, and administrative affairs. Outside the headquarters, the inspector general exercises general supervision over the police ranges in his province, each under a deputy inspector general.

Within the ranges the districts are the fulcrums of police operations. The district chief is the superintendent, assisted by one or more assistant superintendents and a number of inspectors and other ranks. The subdistrict is supervised by an assistant or deputy superintendent; the station house is commanded by one of the upper subordinate grades and manned by ten to twenty head constables and constables. In the larger cities the police are organized on a municipal basis but remain part of the provincial police and answer to the inspector general of the province.

At all levels the senior police officer is linked to a dual chain of command, that of the police organization and that of the designated civil government. This sometimes causes confusion and discord in the chain of command, but the principle of ultimate civilian control was established in the Police Act of 1861 and continued under both civilian and military governments since independence. Thus, at the provincial level the inspector general reports to the home department; at the division, or police range level, the deputy inspector general answers to the divisional commissioner; and at the district level the police superintendent is subordinate to the deputy commissioner, who, as district officer and magistrate, is in charge of tax collection, law and order, and administration of justice. Although the deputy commissioner has no authority to interfere directly in the internal organization and discipline of the police, an important part of his duties is to inspect the police stations of his district at regular intervals. In case the deputy commissioner and the police chief disagree on issues relating to police functions, the former's decision overrides that of the latter. However, the deputy commissioner is dependent on police cooperation in keeping things under control. In case of serious differences, however, both may refer the disputed matter to higher authorities for reconciliation: the deputy commissioner to his commissioner and the superintendent to his deputy inspector general.

The provincial police also include a number of specialized categories. The transportation system is secured by the railway, highway, and river police. The provincial special forces are anticorruption establishments that perform, at a lower level, functions similar to those of the FIA. In each province the inspector general also has the Special Armed Police to deal with such critical functions as protection of public installations in times of civil commotion, armed escort for important public officials, peacekeeping during festivals and sports events, relief and rescue work during natural calamities, and the operation of armored cars carrying strategic or other valuable public properties.

Assisting the regular police in rural areas are semiofficial part-time village constables called *chowkidars* or *dafadars*, who report violations to the nearest police station or apprehend offenders on police orders. The village constables are recruited and controlled locally and given some remuneration, clothing for night duty, and, in some cases, small arms. The number of such constables varies with the size of the village and the incidence of crime.

Police at Work. The Pakistani police are one of the most ubiquitous and pervasive institutions in the country, but they are spread thin, overworked, poorly paid, poorly equipped and trained, and subject to the whims of volatile administrations. The police are also notoriously corrupt, inept, and brutal. Attempts are made periodically to reform the system, with few results.

The last major effort was the Police Commission set up in 1969 with a broad and sweeping mandate. However, the report of the commission, issued in 1971, was overshadowed by the secession of East Pakistan, and the proposals were shelved. Further efforts were made under Prime Minister Zulfikar Ali Bhutto, but with his fall the reforms were abandoned. In August 2000 the Musharraf government introduced a comprehensive package of police reforms. One key change was the transfer of oversight of the district superintendent of police from district commissioners to the elected district mayors. Public safety commissions have also been set up consisting of elected and nonelected members to oversee police ethics.

Police professionalism is low. New officers receive only short training, and many hires outside the PSP are the result of political patronage.

Education and Training. PSP officers are selected through annual, competitive, national examinations conducted by the Federal Public Service Commission. A ranked list of eligible candidates, based on examination grades, is drawn up annually by the commission, and from this list new officer appointments are made according to vacancies and quotas by the Establishment Division. This division also controls training, assignment, promotion, and administrative policy. Typically, only twenty to thirty appointments are made annually. The total strength of the PSP is about 2,500.

The successful PSP entrant—or probationer, as he is called—spends the first half of his two-year apprenticeship at the Pakistan Police Academy at Sihala, near Rawalpindi. During his first year he receives instruction on criminal law, police procedures, forensic medicine, and language, among other subjects. The second year is divided between service with a military unit and service at a district police headquarters. On completion of the second year the probationer is given the rank of assistant superintendent of police and assigned either to a national-level agency or, more likely, to one of the provincial police forces, where he will have charge of several police stations. Although he is then likely to remain in the same province for an extended period, the PSP officer, unlike the non-PSP provincial officers and men, is always subject to transfer to any post in the country.

Provincial police officers are recruited and appointed at the provincial level. Constables are recruited at the district level. Each province has a police training center where the constables receive training for a minimum of six months. In the lower subordinate grades the pay, morale, and educational levels are low and advancement is slow. Women are eligible for police service, but their numbers are small, and they are not actively recruited.

Uniforms and Weapons. Both national and provincial police forces have their own distinct uniforms, the most common being a gray shirt worn with khaki trousers, or a khaki drill tunic and trousers. A blue cap or beret completes the outfit. The force is armed with rifles, stun guns, and revolvers.

Police Statistics.

- Total Police Personnel: 202,722
- Population per Police Officer: 801

HUMAN RIGHTS

Pakistan is a police state. Police commit many extrajudicial killings and abuse and rape citizens. While some officers charged with these abuses are transferred or suspended for their actions, no officer has even been convicted and few have been arrested. According to a human rights watchdog agency, more than a hundred people die from police torture every year. Police also fabricate evidence or stage escape attempts to justify shooting and killing of suspects. In many instances police kill suspected criminals to prevent them from implicating the police in crimes. Police routinely use excessive force to break up demonstrations and strikes.

Police corruption is widespread. They routinely extort money from prisoners and suspects and their families. Police also accept money for registering cases on false charges and torture innocent citizens. People pay the police to humiliate their opponents and to avenge their personal grievances. Police corruption is the most serious at the station house level, where arrest-for-ransom operations flourish.

CRIME

Crime Statistics. Offenses reported to the police per 100,000 population: 318. Of which:

- Murder: 7.1
- Assault: 2.2

- Burglary: 10.4
- Automobile Theft: 9

CORRECTIONAL SYSTEM

Law enforcement and crime and punishment are governed by a number of statutes, some of them inherited from the British Raj. These include the Penal Code of Pakistan, first promulgated in 1860 as the Indian Penal Code, the Police Act of 1861, the Evidence Act of 1872, the Code of Criminal Procedure of 1898, the Criminal Law (Amendment) Act of 1908, and the Official Secrets Act of 1911, as amended. Enacted after independence are the Security of Pakistan Act of 1952 and a host of other laws directed against corruption, terrorism, espionage, and smuggling. In any case, the regular and emergency powers of the constitution, especially articles 232 to 235, give the president and the central government more than ample authority to exercise firm control over all segments of society.

The Penal Code of Pakistan lists all major classes of crime, including what are called offenses against the state. Punishment is divided into five classes: death, banishment from seven to twenty years or more, imprisonment, forfeiture of property, and fine. With the introduction of Sharia, draconian punishments have become mandatory, such as amputation of hands for theft and flogging for adultery. The so-called Hudood Ordinances are designed to enforce the Sharia on Muslims and non-Muslims alike.

Tribal areas are outside the penal code. These areas are administered by centrally appointed political agents and police by the Frontier Corps and the Frontier Constabulary aided by local tribal guards (*khassadars*).

The Frontier Crimes Regulation of 1901 and the tribal customary law, adjudicated by the *jirga*, or council of *Maliks* (tribal elders), are in force in tribal areas supplemented by governmental regulations.

The custody and rehabilitation of prisoners is a provincial function governed by the 1860 penal code, the Prisons Act of 1894, and the Prisoners Act of 1900. The highest official in the prison administration in each province is the inspector general of prisons; at the division or police range level the senior official is the director of prisons and at the district or municipal level the jail superintendent. Below the district jail level are the village police lockups. The central government subsidizes the operations of the provincial prisons and the Central Jail Training Institute at Lahore. There is only a single juvenile jail at Landhi, near Karachi.

Prison Conditions. Even by third world standards Pakistani prisons are grim and harsh, marked by overcrowding, absence of sanitation, and poor living conditions.

Overcrowding is so severe that there are 86,000 prisoners in jails meant to hold around 38,000. In Rawalpindi 4,277 inmates are housed in a facility meant for 2,000; the 16 jails of Sind with a total capacity of 7,759 actually house 14,000; Karachi's prison with a capacity of 991 houses 4,087; the Lahore district jail built to house 1,045 prisoners contains 3,200; and Punjab jails meant for 17,271 hold more than 50,000. Only 2 toilets are available for every 100 inmates.

There are three classes of prisons: A, B, and C. The last category holds common prisoners and those in pretrial detention. Such cells often have dirt floors and no furnishings. Prisoners in these cells suffer the most abuse, including beating and forced kneeling for long periods of time. The daily food budget in the lowest classes of prisons is about $.02 per day. Inadequate food, often consisting of a few pieces of bread, leads to chronic malnutrition for those unable to supplement their diet with help from family or friends. There is no medical care for those who are physically or mentally ill. Foreign prisoners, mostly citizens of African countries, often remain in prison long after their sentences are completed because they have no money to pay for their deportation to their home countries. Conditions in A and B cells are markedly better. Prisoners in these cells are permitted to have servants, special food, and satellite television. A cells are for prominent individuals and B cells are for those politically well connected or those with university education.

Shackling of prisoners is routine. Many prisoners are fettered by the guards in an attempt to solicit bribes. The shackles are tight, heavy, and painful and have led to gangrene and amputation in some cases. Common torture methods include beating, burning with cigarettes, whipping the soles of the feet, sexual assault, prolonged isolation, electric shock, denial of food or sleep, hanging upside down, and forced spreading of the legs with bar fetters.

Female detainees are held separately from men. There is only one jail in every province for convicted prisoners under twenty-one years of age and children are routinely incarcerated along with the general prison population. The Human Rights Watch reports that children are frequently beaten and tortured while in detention, either to extract confession or extort payments from their families. Sexual abuse of child detainees is also a problem.

Prison Statistics.

- Total Prison Population: 86,000
- Prison Population Rate per 100,000: 55
- Pretrial Detainees: 66.1%
- Female Prisoners: 1.7%
- Juvenile Prisoners: 4.5%
- Number of Prisons: 89
- Official Capacity of the Prison System: 38,839
- Occupancy Level: 222.5%

George Thomas Kurian

Palau

Official country name: Republic of Palau
Capital: Koror; a new capital is being built at Melekeok on Babelthuap
Geographic description: Group of islands in the North Pacific Ocean, southeast of the Philippines
Population: 20,303 (est. 2005)

■ ■ ■

LAW ENFORCEMENT

Structure and Organization. The police force is under a chief of police who is responsible to the ministry of justice. The small force of a little under 100 is mostly unarmed. There are police posts on all outlying islands, which are linked to the capital by telecommunications and satellites. The force also has a Marine Law Enforcement Division that patrols the borders.

CORRECTIONAL SYSTEM

The country has only one prison at Koror. It has separate quarters for men and women, juveniles and adults, and pretrial detainees and convicted felons.

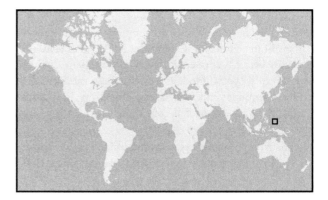

Prison Conditions. Prison conditions meet international standards.

Prison Statistics. The prison can hold up to 100 prisoners. The total prison population is 110 and the prison population rate per 100,000 is 550.

George Thomas Kurian

Panama

———————— ■ ————————

Official country name: Republic of Panama
Capital: Panama City
Geographic description: Located on the Isthmus of Panama connecting the North and South American continents
Population: 3,039,150 (est. 2005)

■ ■ ■

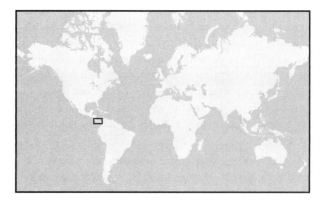

LAW ENFORCEMENT

History. The small Panamanian Army that came into being when the country gained its independence from Colombia, through U.S. maneuvers, lasted only one year before it was demobilized. To replace the disbanded army, the Corps of National Police was formed in December 1904, and for the next forty-nine years it functioned as the country's only armed force. The government decree establishing the national police authorized a strength of 700, and the tiny provincial police that had been operating since independence was incorporated into the new organization. The corps was deployed territorially in the then-existing seven provinces, and by 1908 its strength had grown to 1,000. By the 1940s some organizational stability had been achieved, but it was not until the presidency of José Antonio Remón Cantera in the early 1950s that the corps was institutionalized and renamed the National Guard, a name it bore until the U.S. invasion in 1989. After the invasion, the National Guard was abolished and in its stead was the Panamanian National Police. Additional law enforcement agencies include the Institutional Protection Service, the National Maritime Service, and the National Air Service.

Structure and Organization. The Panamanian National Police (PNP) inherits much of its structure from its predecessor, the National Guard. It is constitutionally a part of the Ministry of Government and Justice. The force is headed by a commandant, and all command lines emanate directly from him and flow to the subordinate units. The commandant is assisted by a deputy commandant and a general staff. The general staff has five sections: personnel, intelligence, operations, logistics, and civil action. The assistant chiefs of staff in charge of these sections have the status of lieutenant colonels.

The PNP is deployed territorially in ten numbered zones: two (the first and the tenth) in Panama City and the other eight in each of the other provinces. By regulation the headquarters of a zone is in the capital city of the province. A zone is commanded by an officer with the rank of lieutenant colonel or major.

A public order unit, a successor to the Public Order Company, assists in maintaining order on special occasions, such as sports events, parades, and festivals, coordinates relief during natural disasters, and puts down disturbances. The Cavalry Squadron is the most colorful unit of the PNP and its functions are purely ceremonial, although it is called on occasionally for crowd control. The Presidential Guard is a specially trained group charged with guarding the president and the presidential palace. On parade, or when mustered to greet foreign dignitaries, the Presidential Guard presents an impressive appearance in khaki uniforms, shiny helmets, boots with white laces, and white belts and rifle slings. Another unit is the Traffic Police, commanded by a lieutenant colonel. Their responsibilities include issuing, renewing, revoking drivers' licenses, registering vehicles, investigating accidents and infractions of vehicle laws, inspecting vehicles, and developing traffic safety programs. The remaining unit of the PNP is the security detachment at the national prison in Panama City.

The Panamanian equivalent of the U.S. Federal Bureau of Investigation (FBI) is the National Department of Investigations (Departmento Nacional de Investigaciones, DENI), established in 1960 as the successor to the National Secret Police, which was founded in 1941. Unlike the latter, which functioned under the Ministry of Government and Justice, DENI is under the attorney general in the Public Ministry. It also maintains an identity and records bureau and a national fingerprint file. DENI headquarters are in Panama City, with branches in Colón and David. Only the Supreme Court may remove the director of DENI from office.

The PNP has three officer categories: company grade (second lieutenant through captain), field grade (major through colonel), and general officer. Noncommissioned officer ranks are corporal, second sergeant, and first sergeant.

The Institutional Protection Service is charged with the protection of public buildings and property. It is supervised by the Ministry of the Presidency. The Judicial Technical Police is a semiautonomous body under the attorney general. Its members are appointed by the Supreme Court, and they perform criminal investigations in support of public prosecutors.

Education and Training. Recruitment to the PNP is based on voluntary enlistment. Most noncommissioned officers come from rural areas while most officers come from the urban middle class. The PNP employs some women, especially as DENI investigators and as traffic police.

Training is provided by the President Belisario Porras Police Training Academy in Panama City and the Police Training Center (Centro de Capacitación Policial). The United States has trained a number of police officers under FBI initiatives.

Uniforms and Weapons. PNP uniforms are either green fatigues or khaki-colored short-sleeved shirts and trousers. Officers wear short-sleeved khaki shirts with dark-green trousers or various (white or dark-green) dress uniforms. Headgear varies from helmets or helmet liners to various colored berets; stiff-sided visored fatigue caps; or visored felt garrison caps similar to those worn by U.S. Army officers. Field-grade and general officers wear gold braid on their visored caps. Combat boots are the most common footgear, but officers wear low-quarter shoes. Officer rank insignia consist of gold bars or stars on an elongated gold oak leaf for the commander. The three noncommissioned officer ranks are designated by chevrons. Distinctive unit shoulder patches are worn by all ranks on the right shoulder of their uniforms. On the left shoulder all ranks wear the familiar blue, white, and red shield showing crossed rifles bisected by an upright saber.

Police Statistics.

- Total Police Personnel: 16,194
- Population per Police Officer: 188

HUMAN RIGHTS

The government generally respects the human rights of its citizens, but there are sporadic incidents of extrajudicial killings by the police and abuse of detainees. Corruption among police officers remains a problem. The PNP has the Office of Professional Responsibility with administrative authority to investigate police misconduct and corruption. On average it receives ten complaints a week from the public, of which some 30 to 40 percent result in punitive action.

CRIME

Crime Statistics. Offenses reported to the police per 100,000 population: 419. Of which:

- Murder: 2
- Assault: 11.8
- Burglary: 25.1
- Automobile Theft: 77.7

CORRECTIONAL SYSTEM

The criminal code defines felonies and misdemeanors as crimes. The code also establishes upper and lower limits for each crime. Capital and corporal punishments are prohibited. The most severe punishment is twenty years' imprisonment.

Penal institutions are governed by article 27 of the constitution, which lays down the principle of the rehabilitation of prisoners. The Department of Corrections was established in 1940 to administer the prisons for the Ministry of Government and Justice. The worst offenders are sent to the Coiba Penal Colony on Coiba Island, founded in 1919. It also houses a minority of offenders awaiting trial. In the main camp there are facilities for rehabilitation training and a small school. Work without remuneration is required of all prisoners, leading to the charge of slave labor. The Model Jail in Panama City was built in 1920 but since then has acquired a reputation that belies its name.

The main prisons in Panama City include the maximum security La Joya, Tinajitas, the Women's Rehabilitation Center, and a juvenile detention facility. Two additional facilities, La Joyita and El Renacer, hold inmates accused of lesser crimes. There are prisons of significant size in David and Santiago. A new prison was opened in 2001 in Colón known as Nueva Esperanza. There is at least one jail in each provincial capital. Most women offenders are sent to the Women's Rehabilitation Center in Panama City, which is run by a Roman Catholic order of nuns. It has acquired a reputation for being one of the best organized, cleanest, and most humane institutions in Central America.

Prison Conditions. Prison conditions remain harsh, despite attempts by the Prison Department to train guards. Most prisons are dilapidated and overcrowded. There is also a lack of separation of inmates according to the type or severity of the crime committed. Medical care is inadequate; tuberculosis, AIDS, and other communicable diseases are common among the prison population. Recurring violence in the prisons has led to the death of 28 inmates and 142 serious injuries since 1996. Conditions in La Joyita led to a hunger strike by inmates protesting against the inhumane conditions, including overcrowding and the lack of sanitation, sleeping facilities, and recreation. Because prison security rests almost entirely with the PNP, tensions arise between PNP officers and their civilian directors. In addition, PNP officers are untrained for prison duty and generally find the assignment distasteful, which contributes to tensions and abuses within the system.

Prison Statistics.

- Total Prison Population: 10,630
- Prison Population Rate per 100,000: 354
- Pretrial Detainees: 55%
- Female Prisoners: 6.9%
- Juvenile Prisoners: 6.7%
- Number of Prisons: 73
- Official Capacity of the Prison System: 7,348
- Occupancy Level: 144.7%

George Thomas Kurian

Papua New Guinea

—■—

Official country name: Independent State of Papua New Guinea

Capital: Port Moresby

Geographic description: Group of islands in southeastern Asia, including the eastern half of the island of New Guinea, between the Coral Sea and the South Pacific Ocean

Population: 5,545,268 (est. 2005)

■ ■ ■

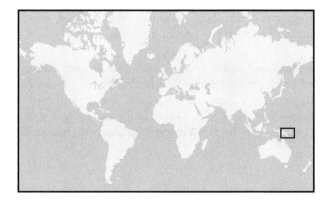

LAW ENFORCEMENT

History. The first administrator of British New Guinea (now Papua), who was appointed in 1888, selected a tribal leader from each village and made him a village constable. These village constables continued to be appointed for the next seventy-five years. As a regular force, an armed constabulary was created in 1890 consisting of twelve constables from the Solomon Islands and two Fijian noncommissioned officers under a British commandant. This small nucleus was later expanded by the appointment of a number of Papuans whose main function was to act as escort to the lieutenant and the resident magistrates. In 1939 the prefix *Royal* was granted to the force, making it the Royal Papuan Constabulary. Meanwhile, in German New Guinea, a small police force consisting of Malays was formed on the British model. Control of these constables was vested in the district officers, or in the case of larger districts, a police master. Their main function was to conduct punitive expeditions against the natives. These two forces were joined together in 1952.

Structure and Organization. The Papua New Guinea Police Constabulary is under the operational control of a commissioner of police who reports to the minister of state for police. The constabulary headquarters is in Port Moresby. The command post comprises four major, functionally organized staff sections: Police, Training, Special, and Criminal Investigation. The first coordinates and directs the daily activities of police stations throughout the country. The second operates the Central Police Training Center at Bomana, near Port Moresby. The third is concerned with internal security and directs the activities of plainclothes police officers. The last maintains the Office of Criminal Records and the Fingerprint Bureau and operates ballistics, photographic, and scientific laboratories.

Besides security duties, the Papua New Guinea Constabulary is associated with a number of other related missions: fire fighting, controlling traffic, licensing of motor vehicles, and regulating the sale and use of liquor, explosives, and firearms. The constabulary also includes a thirty-five-piece band that performs during parades and ceremonial functions.

The constabulary is divided into three operational elements. The Regular Constabulary is the bulk of the force consisting of full-time professional members, who are graded and ranked in quasi-military fashion as follows: commissioners, superintendents, inspectors, noncommissioned officers, and constables. The Regular Constabulary is usually unarmed, but rifles are issued in times of emergency. The Field Constabulary patrols rural and remote interior areas where no Regular Constabulary stations have been established. The Field Constabulary is armed with rifles and operates under the general supervision of the local administrative officers of the Department of District Administration. The size of the Field Constabulary is gradually diminishing as central authority over rural areas expands, new permanent police stations are set up, and field personnel are absorbed into the Regular Constabulary.

The Reserve Constabulary is a permanent corps of part-time volunteers appointed by the commissioner in areas where constabulary strength is not fully needed or where additional strength may be required periodically. Members of the Reserve Constabulary have the same authority, organization, and responsibilities as the Regular Constabulary.

Below headquarters level, the constabulary operates through four territorial commands, each headed by a senior police officer. The first division includes Papua and nearby islands, the second, third, and fourth are in New Guinea and consist of separate commands for highland, coastal, and island areas. Each territorial division is, in turn, divided into districts and subdistricts. Many interior areas, however, have not been brought under full governmental control, and police presence there is sporadic and minimal. In such places police functions are discharged by the field staff of the Department of Local Government.

Education and Training. All officers and personnel are recruited by voluntary enlistment. There are no educational requirements, only good character and health.

Personnel for the ranks are inducted as probationary constables at the Police Training Depot of the Central Police Training Center at Bomana. They undergo six months of training in police procedure, after which they are assigned to regular police stations for two years of training on the job. If at the end of this period they are deemed acceptable, they become full-fledged constables.

Officer training cadets are sent to the Police Training College at Bomana for a course of training that lasts four years. Successful cadets are then assigned to police stations for three years of additional on-the-job training. Graduates are commissioned as subinspectors.

Uniforms and Weapons. The duty uniforms worn by both officers and men are essentially the same except for the headgear. The uniforms consist of a light-blue shirt, dark-blue shorts, a black belt, and black shoes. Officers wear visored caps; other ranks wear berets. Officers and sergeants also have a dress uniform consisting of a light-blue shirt, dark-blue slacks, a Sam Browne belt, a dark-blue tie, and a dark-blue cap.

Police Statistics.

- Total Police Personnel: 7,012
- Population per Police Officer: 791

HUMAN RIGHTS

The government generally respects human rights. However, the police use excessive force, such as beatings, when arresting or interrogating suspects and engage in excessively punitive and violent raids. All police shootings are investigated by the police department's internal affairs office and reviewed by a coroner's court.

CRIME

Crime Statistics. Offenses reported to the police per 100,000 population: 766. Of which:

- Murder: 8.6
- Assault: 66.7
- Burglary: 63
- Automobile Theft: 22

CORRECTIONAL SYSTEM

The corrections system is separate from the police although it operates directly under the administrator in the executive branch of government. Operational control is vested in the Correctional Institutions Branch of the Department of Law, whose director, the controller of corrective institutions, has his office at the main facility of the system at Bomana. All jails are called correctional institutions, regardless of size.

The main facility at Bomana is a detention center for prisoners serving sentences of more than one year. It is a modern and progressive institution that provides literacy and training programs and work shops, and includes penal farms. Penal institutions in district headquarters house prisoners sentenced to less than one year. Short-term prisoners and those awaiting trial are placed in jails attached to each patrol post in urban areas.

Prison Conditions. The prison system suffers from serious underfunding, the deterioration of infrastructure, and the paucity of basic services. Many prisons have been closed because of life-threatening conditions. In 2001 there were a number of prison escapes and at one point there were 200 escaped prisoners at large.

Prison Statistics.

- Total Prison Population: 3,302
- Prison Population Rate per 100,000: 66
- Pretrial Detainees: 35.2%
- Female Prisoners: 4.2%
- Juvenile Prisoners: 5.9%
- Number of Prisons: 17
- Official Capacity of the Prison System: 4,040
- Occupancy Level: 87.4%

George Thomas Kurian

Paraguay

Official country name: Republic of Paraguay
Capital: Asunción
Geographic description: Landlocked country in south-central South America
Population: 6,347,884 (est. 2005)

■■■

LAW ENFORCEMENT

History. In Spanish colonial times formal law enforcement was limited to Asunción and to a few major cities. This situation continued well into the twentieth century, when the first national force was constituted under the Police Law of 1951.

Structure and Organization. The Paraguayan National Police has two branches under separate commands. The older branch, the Policia de la Capital, is the force that maintains law and order in the capital. It is divided into borough precincts; departments—Public Order, Investigations, and Training and Operations; and 4 directorates—Surveillance and Offenses, Identification, Alien Registration, and Political.

A special unit of the capital police is the Security Guard, which is called on during emergencies and ceremonial occasions. It consists of 2 rifle companies, 1 support company, and 1 headquarters company. Another special unit is the Police of the Presidency, which is the plainclothes secret service detail of the president. The Fire Department is also manned by police personnel.

Units of the Interior Police are under the control of the delegate (*delegado*) of the department to which they are assigned. Operational control of these units

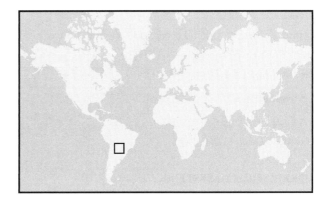

rests with the chief of police (*jefe de policia*). The departments are divided into districts headed by an city judge (*alcalde*), under whose jurisdiction are police conscripts drawn from the district as well as neighboring districts.

The internal security organ is the Director General of Investigations, which handles undercover activities, surveillance, and counterterrorism. The Highways Police operates under the Ministry of Public Works.

Education and Training. There are four training establishments, all at Asunción:

- Police College for basic training

- Higher Police College for specialized training

- Noncommissioned Officer School for noncommissioned officers

- Police Training Battalion for in-service training

Uniforms and Weapons. Khaki uniforms and berets are worn by all ranks in the summer, and navy-blue uniforms and caps are worn in the winter. Different ranks are denoted by different colored facings on the uniforms.

Police Statistics.

- Total Police Personnel: 18,625
- Population per Police Officer: 341

HUMAN RIGHTS

The government generally respects the human rights of its citizens, but there are serious problems in some areas. There are killings by security forces and incidents or torture and abduction. Arbitrary and arrest, which were common during the Stroessner regime, continue. The 2000 Penal and Criminal Procedures Code provides the legal basis for the protection of fundamental human rights.

CRIME

Crime Statistics. Offenses reported to the police per 100,000 population: 418. Of which:

- Murder: 11.5
- Assault: 54.2
- Burglary: 21.4
- Automobile Theft: 30.5

CORRECTIONAL SYSTEM

The criminal justice system is governed by the penal code of 2000. The death penalty was abolished in 1967 and the highest punishment is life imprisonment with hard labor.

Prisons are under the control of the General Directorate of Penal Institutions, which, in turn, is under the Ministry of Justice and Labor. The principal facility is the National Penitentiary at Asunción. Others include the Tacumbu Penitentiary for adult males at Villa Hayes, 20 miles north of Asunción, the Women's Correctional Institute under the supervision of the Sisters of the Good Shepherd, and the Correctional Penitentiary for Minors at Emboscada, 25 miles northeast of Asunción.

In addition, each department has a prison or jail in its capital.

Prison Conditions. Prison conditions are substandard as a result of overcrowding, lack of proper sanitation, and abuse by guards. The worst prison is Tacumbu, the largest prison in the country; designed to hold 800, it has a population of 2,100, two-thirds of whom are awaiting trial. Other regional prisons hold about three times more inmates than their capacity. In the Coronel Oviedo prison more than 500 inmates are crowded into a facility built for 100.

Security is a major problem in all the prisons. The drug use by prisoners is rampant. Drugs, weapons, and knives are frequently smuggled into prisons and lead to hostage takings and killings by prisoners. Escapes and escape attempts are frequent. At Buen Pastor, a women's prison, there are reports of rapes of prisoners by their guards, even though the law prohibits male guards in such facilities. The Congressional Human Rights Commission criticizes the prisons for the poor nutritional value of prison diets. Prisoners are generally served only one meal a day, and it contains no meat or vegetables. Panchito López, a former youth detention center, was burned down in 2001 after complaints of abuse of inmates. In response to criticism, the administration has built new juvenile facilities at Itagua and Fernando de la Mora. The government has also decreed that convicted prisoners should be segregated from those awaiting trial.

Prison Statistics.

- Total Prison Population: 4,088
- Prison Population Rate: 75
- Pretrial Detainees: 92.7%
- Female Prisoners: 5.1%
- Juvenile Prisoners: 10%
- Number of Prisons: 12
- Official Capacity of the Prison System: 2,707
- Occupancy Level: 151%

George Thomas Kurian

Peru

Official country name: Republic of Peru
Capital: Lima
Geographic description: Middle of western South America, bordering the South Pacific Ocean
Population: 27,925,628 (est. 2005)

■ ■ ■

LAW ENFORCEMENT

History. The Peruvian National Police (Policía Nacional del Perú) were created December 6, 1998, by national law 24949 as a result of the union of Peru's previous police forces, the Civil Guard, Investigation Police (Policía de Investigaciones), and the Republican and Health Guard (Guardia Republica y Sanidad) with the purpose of creating a single, more dynamic and professional organization.

As a result of the 1993 Political Constitution of the Peruvian State (Constitucion Politica del Estado Peruano) and article 166 contained within its text, the mission of the Peruvian National Police was set forth years before its final creation. The mission is as follows:

- Guarantee, maintain, and reestablish internal order
- Give protection and help to people and the community
- Guarantee observance of the law and security
- Prevent, investigate, and combat delinquency
- Guard and control the borders

Structure and Organization.

Principal Agencies and Divisions. As outlined in the Organic Law of the National Police on December 22,

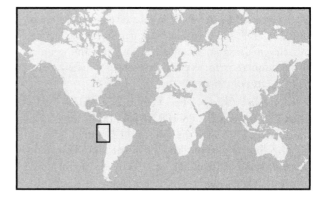

1999, in article 166 of the Peruvian Constitution, the National Police form part of the structure of the Ministry of the Interior. The National Police have the following organizational structure:

- Directorate (Organo de Dirección)
- Assessment Branch (Organo de Asesoramiento)
- Control Branch (Organo de Control)
- Consultative Branches (Organos Consultivos)
- Support Branches (Organos de Apoyo)
- Branches of Instruction and Indoctrination (Organos de Instrucción y Doctrina)
- Branch of Execution (Organos de Ejecución)

  Specialized Branches include:

- Antidrug Branch (Dirección Antidrogas)
- Counterterrorism Branch (Dirección Contra el Terrorismo)

- National Defense and Border Control Branch (Dirección de Defensa Nacional y Control de Fronteras)

- Criminal Investigation Branch (Dirección de Investigación Criminal)

- Highway Police Branch (Dirección de Policía de Carreteras)

- Judicial Police Branch (Dirección de Policía Judicial)

- Prosecutorial Police (Dirección de Policía Fiscal)

- Ministry of the Public Police (Dirección de Policía de Ministerio Publico)

- State Security Police (Dirección de Seguridad de Estado)

- Highway Safety Police (Dirección de Seguridad Vial)

- Tourist and Ecological Police (Dirección de Policía de Turismo y Ecologia)

Territorial Directorates: With the passage of ministerial resolution 0982-2003-IN/Policía Nacional del Perú on June 12, 2003, the Peruvian National Police was divided into eleven directorates spread throughout the country. The headquarters for each directorate is situated near a major metropolitan area.

Aviation Police: The Peruvian Aviation Police (Dirección de Aviacion Policíal, DIRAVPOL) were legally instituted in 1984 with the mission of planning, organizing, directing, and controlling the instruction, flight training, and maintenance of aircraft in Peru. Before this unit's formation, experts and professionals from Latin American airline companies were consulted on the formation of a unit that was capable of aerial operations in a number of different environments.

The history of the aviation police is as interesting as are the exploits that have made this unit famous. On July 31, 1983, during an antidrug operation, three planes intended for use by drug traffickers were confiscated. These planes were taken to Mazamari, where they became the first planes used by DIRAVPOL. This unit also uses helicopters in its operations.

Transit Police: The Directorate of Transit Safety (Dirección de Seguridad Vial) has the mission of regulating transit in Lima and Callao. Among the actions that transit police are charged with are foot patrols, car patrol, and air patrol (through the Aviation Police). One of the chief responsibilities that traffic police must regularly address is the smooth flow of traffic during peak hours in places considered critical such as downtown Lima.

The mission of transit safety is fulfilled by three units within the directorate: the Unit of Transit Control, the Unit of Motorized Transit Control, and the Phoenix Squadron. The Unit of Transit Control either works on foot or in squad cars in four zones in the city of Lima (Central Lima, South Lima, East Lima, and North Lima). The Unit of Motorized Transit Control and the Phoenix Squadron were created to address and combat the inherent problems and complications with traffic in metropolitan and surrounding areas.

Directorate of Special Operations: Based in Lima, the Special Operations Directorate of the Peruvian National Police handles situations that threaten the lives of Peruvians to maintain internal order. Situations that require the training and expertise of this directorate include cases of kidnapping, hostage rescue, and acts of terrorism.

The Special Operations Directorate was originally created in 1987 and integrated former members of special operations teams that had been dissolved. Thus, the new directorate adapted quickly with experience that would prove effective against domestic terrorist groups. The directorate was reorganized in 1993 with a new command structure, internal control, and a new support structure.

Counterterrorism Directorate: The Counterterrorism Directorate (Dirección Contra el Terrorismo) was formed in 1983 to stem the tide of revolutionary terrorism that was taking the country by storm. In 1991 the directorate was reformed as the National Counterterrorism Directorate (Dirección Nacional Contral el Terrorismo; DINCOTE). With this reformation, the directorate became accountable to the General Directorate of the Peruvian National Police.

DINCOTE has been successful against domestic terrorist groups. Among the many successful operations of the directorate was the June 1992 capture of Victor Polay Campos, the leader of the Tupac Amaru Revolutionary Movement. Perhaps the most widely cited success of the directorate was the capture of the Sendero Luminoso (Shining Path) leader Abimael Guzmán in September 1992.

Police-Community Relations. The Peruvian National Police has introduced reforms designed to increase the amount of citizen involvement in maintaining order. One program introduced by the National Directorate of Citizen Participation (Dirección Nacion de Participacion Ciudadana) is known as Vigilant Neighbor (Vecino Vigilante). In essence, the program is a type of neighborhood crime watch where citizen groups cooperate with the police in information sharing.

Another way the citizenry is involved is through juvenile patrols (Patrullas Juveniles). This program is aimed at adolescents at risk of committing crime. Juvenile patrols consist of groups of youths, many of them gang members, who participate in programs designed to give the youths alternatives to crime and delinquency, including art classes, recreational sports, and cultural activities. Successful participants are able to leave the program with a better education and new job skills.

HUMAN RIGHTS

Following President Alberto Fujimori's resignation and Vladimiro Montesino's (former spy chief) arrest because of corruption scandals, the Peruvian government began new investigations into past human rights cases and established the Truth and Reconciliation Commission. In August 2003 the commission released its final report on twenty years of internal conflict and human rights abuses from 1980 to 2000. From the initial burning of ballot boxes by the Sendero Luminoso in Chusqui, Ayacucho, on May 17, 1980, to the eventual flight of former president Fujimori to Japan in November 2000, Peru has witnessed many forms of political violence and human rights violations committed by government forces and insurgent groups.

The Peruvian Human Rights Ombudsman's Office estimates that in since the mid-1980s there have been 30,000 victims of political violence. No less than 4,000 individuals "disappeared," thousands of individuals were arbitrarily detained, 400,000 were displaced, and the victims of torture were too many to be accurately counted. Information gathered from more than 160,000 people in 530 locations around Peru shows that many victims were people from ethnic groups and social sectors historically marginalized and discriminated against. Three successive administrations led by Presidents Fernando Belaúnde Terry, Alan García Pérez, and Fujimori used various strategies and methods to address the situation. During all three regimes state security forces and rebels committed grave human rights abuses.

CRIME

There appears to be a consensus that crime prevention strategies in Latin America that stress deterrence are ineffective and incompetence and corruption on the part of the government, including the police, makes the problem of crime much worse in the region. Four characteristics of Latin American crime have been offered by scholars to explain why Latin American crime is different from other regions. First is the endemic pattern of poverty and inequality. A second characteristic is the cultural pattern of male chauvinism. Third is the presence of corrupt law enforcement that ebbs and flows in intensity depending on the country being examined. The last characteristic is the drug trade, which has become an omnipresent problem in Latin America.

Changes in crime levels in Peru, as well as in other Latin American nations, have been linked to economic, political, and social changes within the society. However, crime statistics in Peru do not provide an adequate description of actual crime levels, considering that some areas do not report their crime statistics as well as the unwillingness of many Peruvians to report crimes to the police. Thus, a dark figure is present. That said, official crime data show dramatic increases in crime throughout the 1980s. Official police figures indicate an increase in crime of approximately 18 percent between 1980 and 1986.

The recorded homicide level for Peru from 1995 to 1997 was approximately 12 incidents per 100,000 citizens. In comparison to other countries such as Colombia or South Africa, this rate appears to be high but not as violent as other countries. The available data does suggest that violent crime in Peru has increased markedly since the mid-1990s. It is approaching the serious levels of the early 1990s.

The occurrence of Peruvian crime can be categorized into three groups. Organized transnational/national crime, which is mostly related to drugs and arms trafficking, money laundering, and so on. It is carried out by well-organized groups, sometimes involving government officials. Street crimes include assaults, attacks, robberies, small-scale drug peddling, racketeering, and so on. They are usually carried out by single or isolated individuals. Juvenile delinquency includes assaults, attacks, robberies, and street violence. It is carried out by juvenile gangs.

Threats to the Criminal Justice System in Peru. In the 1980s Peru was racked by deadly insurgent rebels who formed a terrorist group known as the Sendero Luminoso. The violence peaked in 1983 and 1984 in Ayacucho, one of Peru's poorest provinces. More than 25,000 people were killed during the warring years in Peru. Besides the Sendero Luminoso, which continues to operate on a small scale, Peruvian police must face the threat posed by drug traffickers and organized crime groups.

During Fujimori's presidency (1990–2000) terrorism perpetrated by Sendero Luminoso was greatly reduced. Additionally, a decades-old border war with Ecuador was effectively ended with the signing of a treaty. However, Peru is faced with extreme poverty and high unemployment rates. Since the end of Fujimori's term and the presidency of Alejandro Celestino Toledo Manrique, the country is trying to reinstall democracy and forget the memories of the previous twenty years. One of the problems Peru faces in its mission to erase the images of violence and authoritarianism is a high level of criminal activity and violence from groups spanning the spectrum of organization, arms proliferation, and connections to criminal organizations outside the country.

Drugs. The production of cocaine paste has served as a source of income for impoverished Peruvian families,

Two men are arrested by Peruvian police after spray painting an ancient Incan stone wall in Cuzco, Peru, January 19, 2005. *After appearing in court, bail for the two was set at $30,000 for defacing the wall with graffiti.* AP IMAGES.

especially in the Huallaga Valley, for decades. During the 1980s and 1990s Peru was the major Andean supplier of coca leaf for the production of cocaine. However, the use of the coca leaf is as much embedded in Peruvian culture (coca was used before the country was being colonized by the Europeans), as it is in the economic survival of families, drug traffickers, and rebel groups.

Organized crime groups began to capitalize on coca cultivation in the 1970s and business was good for these groups as well as for rebel groups in the 1980s. Efforts by the government in the 1980s to eradicate coca cultivation proved to be of limited success. A change of strategy in the 1990s concentrated on reducing support by the farmers for Sendero Luminoso rebels by depenalizing coca cultivation. This gave the government more time to concentration on the violent insurgency that had already cost thousands of lives. By the late 1990s Peru was no longer the world's largest supplier of coca leaves; most of the market moved to Colombia, where drug cartels and rebel groups such as the Revolutionary Armed Forces of Colombia and the United Self-Defense Forces of Colombia make millions of dollars each year.

Despite the drop in coca cultivation, drug trafficking continues to be a problem in Peru. This is due, at least in part, to a sustained demand from cocaine in developed countries in North American and Europe. As opposed to large drug cartels that operate in other countries, organized crime groups linked to the drug trade in Peru largely consist of small groups known as *firmas* (firms). The situation has a further destabilizing effect when noting that Peruvian drug trafficking firms, once subordinate and dependent on Colombian organized crime groups, have now become largely independent through the development of new trafficking routes and new ways to process coca paste into cocaine.

The cultivation of coca continues to be legal in Peru, though other uses for the crop remain illegal. In 1999 coca eradication efforts were at an all-time high: 13,800 hectares were destroyed. However, in 2002 slightly more than half of the 1999 level was destroyed (7,100 hectares). To further combat the drug problem, the Peruvian government developed a long-term plan known as the Drug Use Prevention Commission in 1996. Led by President Toledo, the committee was reformulated in 2001. It has developed a 2002–2007 plan to combat the drug problem. The new strategy includes eradication efforts, drug abuse reduction, and alternate development programs to give farmers other economic options.

Statistics on the Drug Problem. According to the Drug Enforcement Administration (DEA), the cultivation of coca has dropped 70 percent since 1995. In 2001 only 34,100 hectares were reportedly used in the country for coca cultivation. This may explain why the number of eradicated hectares has dropped. A smaller area devoted to growing coca will make such areas harder to find. Thus, in the Peruvian case lower figures on eradication may be a good sign. The DEA further estimates that Peru's potential cocaine production has also dropped. The drop in potential production is estimated at 68 percent, mirroring the drop in usable land for cultivation. According to 2000 figures, the estimated cultivation potential for Peru was placed at 145 metric tons. This was in stark contrast to estimates of 460 metric tons for 1995.

CORRECTIONAL SYSTEM

Peru's prisons are administered by 3,075 employees, with a guard staff made up of about 4,000. Article 234 of the constitution of 1979 emphasizes the reeducation and rehabilitative functions of the penal system rather than simply punishment, with the goal of reintegration of the prisoner back into society.

Of a 1990 prison population estimated at 40,000, about half were in the twenty-five jails in Lima. In the early 1990s the government under Fujimori began a program of building new prisons and rehabilitating old ones but financial limitations left the project incomplete. In a survey of the prisons carried out in 1987 to assess their general physical state, only 14 were determined to be in good condition, 59 were average, and 36 were poor; 2 Lima prisons were not surveyed.

Among the most important prisons, all in Lima, are Lurigancho Prison, built in 1968; Canto Grande Prison, built in the 1980s; Miguel Castro Prison; and two women's prisons, Santa Mónica Prison in Chorrillos District, built in the 1950s, and Santa Bárbara Prison.

The National Penitentiary Institute has the mission of directing and controlling Peru's system of national prisons. The goal is the ensure that Peruvian prisons offer the reeducation, rehabilitation, and reinsertion of prisoners into society and the establishment and maintenance of the country's penal infrastructure.

Prison Conditions. In the second half of the 1980s Sendero Luminoso insurgency exacerbated the country's already deplorable prison conditions. One of the Sendero Luminoso's early successes was a March 1982 raid on the Ayacucho Prison, freeing many of the prisoners, including several Sendero Luminoso militants. Even though officials had been warned of a possible attack, prison officials chose to disregard the warning.

Deplorable prison conditions have contributed to rising levels of violence in prisons. Riots have become commonplace in many installations and sometimes result in a cycle of violence perpetrated both by prisoners and correctional personnel. In 1986, for example, the Peruvian military killed 244 Sendero Luminoso inmates while putting down riots at three Lima penitentiaries. In a similar incident in 1992 over thirty inmates were killed during a riot at Canto Grande Prison.

Another problem related to the country's rebel insurgency is the segregation of Sendero Luminoso members from other prisoners. The Sendero Luminoso turned this policy into an advantage by creating minicamps, where the group's ideology continued to flourish. In some instances the inmates were able to virtually control their own lives within the prison through informal contracts with prison guards. There is little doubt that this segregation policy made the coordination of prison riots much easier.

Prison Statistics.

- Total Prison Population: 32,129
- Prison Population Rate per 100,000: 114
- Pretrial Detainees: 69.8%
- Female Prisoners: 7.2%
- Juvenile Prisoners: 0.1%
- Number or Prisons: 81
- Official Capacity of the Prison System: 20,497
- Occupancy Level: 148.3%

BIBLIOGRAPHY

Aguirre, Carlos. 1998. "Crime, Race, and Morals: The Development of Criminology in Peru, 1890–1930." *Crime, History, and Societies* 2 (2), pp. 73–90.

Hojman, David E. 2004. "Inequality, Unemployment, and Crime in Latin American Cities." *Crime Law and Social Change* 41 (1), p. 33.

Instituto Nacional Penitenciario. 2005. Available online at http://www.inpe.gob.pe/proyectoestadistica (accessed December 27, 2005).

"Nuevo Esquema." 1991. *Caretas* (Lima), no. 1169 (July 22), p. 20.

Policía Nacional del Perú. 2005a. "DIRAVPOL: Dirección de Aviación Policíal." Available online at http://www.pnp.gob.pe/direcciones/diravpol/ (accessed December 27, 2005).

Policía Nacional del Perú. 2005b. "Direcciones Territoriales de Policía." Available online at http://www.pnp.gob.pe/regiones.asp (accessed December 27, 2005).

Policía Nacional del Perú. N.d. "Cartilla de Seguridad Ciudadana: 'Vecino Vigilante.'" Pamphlet circulated by the Dirección Nacional de Participación Ciudadana, Policía Nacional del Perú.

Policía Nacional del Perú. N.d. "'Patrullas Juveniles': Para jóvenes y adolescentes en riesgo 2001–2002." Pamphlet circulated by the Dirección Nacional de Participación Ciudadana, Policía Nacional del Perú.

Portal del Estado Peruano. 2005. "Gobierno." Available online at http://www.peru.gob.pe/gobierno/gobierno.asp (accessed December 27, 2005).

Salas, Luis, and José Maria Rico. 1993. "Administration of Justice in Latin America: A Primer on the Criminal Justice System." Center for the Administration of Justice, Florida International University.

Truth and Reconciliation Commission. 2003. "Final Report." Truth and Reconciliation Commission (August 28). Available online at http://www.cverdad.org.pe/ingles/pagina01.php (accessed December 27, 2005).

United Nations Office on Drugs and Crime. 2003. "Country Profile: Peru, 2003." Available online at http://www.unodc.org/pdf/peru/peru_country_profile_2003.pdf (accessed December 27, 2005).

Adam Dulin

Philippines

Official country name: Republic of the Philippines
Capital: Manila
Geographic description: Archipelago in Southeast Asia between the Philippine Sea and the South China Sea
Population: 87,857,473 (est. 2005)

■ ■ ■

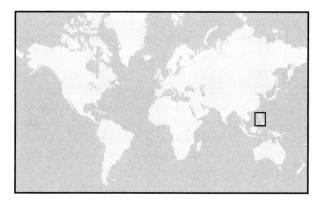

LAW ENFORCEMENT

History. The Spanish colonization in the 1500s ushered in the concept of a formal national police force. The Guardia Civiles (Civil Guards) had the primary obligation of policing the occupied territories (Campos 1991). The U.S. occupation of the Philippines in 1901 introduced a national police concept called the Philippine Constabulary (PC). The PC had nationwide jurisdiction similar to its predecessor, the Guardia Civiles. It was established by the U.S. colonial government to preserve peace and order. The PC also provided the nucleus of the first regular division of the commonwealth's army in 1936. It remained an element within the army (after 1946 as the Military Police Command) until 1950, when it was reestablished as a separate force. It was formally renamed the Philippine Constabulary in 1959.

After its renaming, the PC officially constituted a national police force and essentially operated as a gendarmerie, holding primary authority for law enforcement and domestic security. It was responsible for dealing with large-scale crime, conducting wide area operations, and enforcing the peace and national laws, especially in remote areas where other forces were nonexistent or ineffective.

The constabulary also played a prominent role in combating the Muslim and Communist insurgencies.

Constabulary forces throughout the country were supported and controlled through a system of regional commands, with one command in each of the country's twelve political regions. Under the operational control of the area commands, the regional commands controlled the provincial PC. These 73 provincial headquarters, in turn, supervised 234 constabulary companies, which were the constabulary's line units. Regional Special Action Companies provided backup to the line companies and acted as counterinsurgency strike forces. The constabulary also had a variety of specialized units with nationwide responsibilities that operated independently of the regional command system. These included the Criminal Investigative Service, Highway Patrol Group, Security Group, Crime Lab, and Support Command. The Philippine Constabulary Training Command was responsible for instructing enlisted constables and their officers, whose training paralleled that of the army. In 1983 the constabulary created an elite national reaction force, the Philippine Constabulary Special Action Force, with the capability to combat terrorism, hijacking, and insurgency. These additions contributed to the overall growth of members of the constabulary during the 1980s, from approximately 33,500 in 1980, to an estimated 45,000 members in 1990.

Until the mid-1970s, when a major restructuring of the nation's police system was undertaken, the PC alone was responsible for law enforcement on a national level. Independent city and municipal police forces took charge of maintaining peace and order on a local level, calling on the constabulary for aid when the need arose. The Police Commission, established in 1966 to improve the professionalism and training of local police, had loose supervisory authority over the police. It was widely accepted, however, that this system had several serious defects. Most noteworthy were jurisdictional limitations, lack of uniformity and coordination, disputes between police forces, and partisan political involvement in police employment, appointments, assignments, and promotions. Local political bosses routinely used police as private armies, protecting their personal interests and intimidating political opponents.

To correct such deficiencies, the 1973 constitution provided for the integration of public safety forces. Several presidential decrees were subsequently issued, integrating the police, fire, and jail services in the nation's more than 1,500 cities and municipalities. On August 8, 1975, Presidential Decree 765 officially established the joint command structure of the PC and Integrated National Police (INP). The constabulary, which had a well-developed nationwide command and staff structure, was given the task of organizing the integration. The chief of the PC served jointly as the director general of the INP. As constabulary commander, he reported through the military chain of command, and as head of the INP, he reported directly to the minister (later secretary) of national defense. The National Police Commission was transferred to the Ministry (later Department) of National Defense, retaining its oversight responsibilities but turning over authority for training and other matters to the PC and INP.

The INP was assigned responsibility for public safety, protection of lives and property, enforcement of laws, and maintenance of peace and order throughout the nation. In practice, the PC retained responsibility for dealing with serious crimes or cases involving jurisdictions separated from one another, and the INP took charge of less serious crimes and local traffic, crime prevention, and public safety.

The INP's organization paralleled that of the constabulary. The thirteen PC regional command headquar-

ters were the nuclei for the INP's regional commands. Likewise, the constabulary's seventy-three provincial commanders, in their capacity as provincial police superintendents, had operational control of INP forces in their respective provinces. Provinces were further subdivided into 147 police districts, stations, and substations. The constabulary was responsible for patrolling remote rural areas. In metro Manila's four cities and thirteen municipalities, the INP's Metropolitan Police Force shared the headquarters of the constabulary's Capital Command. The commanding general of the Capital Command was also the director of the INP's Metropolitan Police Force and directed the operations of the capital's four police and fire districts.

As of 1985, the INP numbered some 60,000 people, a marked increase over the 1980 figure of 51,000. Approximately 10 percent of this staff were fire and prison officials, and the remainder were police. The Philippine National Police Academy provided training for INP officer cadets. Established under the INP's Training Command in 1978, the academy offered a bachelor of science degree in public safety following a two-year course of study. Admission to the school was highly competitive.

The INP was the subject of some criticism and the repeated object of reform. Police were accused of involvement in illegal activities, violent acts, and abuse. Charges of corruption were frequent. To correct the INP's image problem, the government sponsored programs to identify and punish police offenders and training designed to raise their standard of appearance, conduct, and performance.

On January 1, 1991, the PC and the INP were combined to form the Philippine National Police (PNP). The PNP was created in 1991 under Republic Act No. 6975. Dramatic changes were planned for the police in 1991. The newly formed PNP was to be a strictly civilian organization pursuant to the constitutional provision that the state shall establish and maintain one police force, which shall be national in scope and civilian in character. The PNP was also removed from the armed forces and placed under a new civilian department known as the Department of the Interior and Local Government (Gutang 1993). Likewise, the PNP took immediate responsibility for most duties of the former INP and the responsibility for the counterinsurgency efforts against Muslim secessionists and Communists.

Structure and Organization.

Principal Agencies and Divisions. The National Police Commission is the agency mandated by the constitution and the major police reform laws such as Republic Act Nos. 6975 and 8551 to administer and control the PNP. Under the Philippine National Police Reform and Reorganization Act of 1998 (R.A. No. 8551), the commission regained the powers to investigate police anomalies and irregularities and to administer police entrance examinations and is granted summary dismissal powers over erring police officers.

In 1966 Congress enacted Republic Act 4864, otherwise known as the Police Act of 1966, to provide the foundation for the much needed police reforms in the country. It created the Police Commission to achieve and attain a higher degree of efficiency in the organization, administration, and operation of local police agencies and to place the local police service on a professional level.

Since 1966 the commission had undergone several changes in its organizational structure. It was reorganized in 1972 as the National Police Commission. Originally under the Office of the President, it was transferred to the Ministry of National Defense in 1975 by virtue of Presidential Decree 765, known as the Police Integration Law. This decree also established the INP with the PC as the nucleus. Ten years later in 1985 it was returned to the Office of the President pursuant to Executive Order No. 1040. In 1989 Executive Order No. 379 placed the INP directly under the command, supervision, and control of the president.

The same executive order vested the National Police Commission with the powers of administrative control and supervision over the INP. With the passage of Republic Act No. 6975 on December 13, 1990, the PNP was established under a reorganized Department of the Interior and Local Government (DILG). A new National Police Commission was created within the DILG for the purpose of effectively discharging the functions prescribed in the constitution and provided in the act.

On February 25, 1998, Congress passed into law Republic Act No. 8551, otherwise known as the Philippine National Police Reform and Reorganization Act of 1998. This act strengthened and expanded the commission's authority over the PNP to include administration of police entrance examinations, conduct of precharge investigations against police anomalies and irregularities, and summary dismissals of erring police members.

The command group consists of officers who control and supervise the entire police organization. The chief of the PNP heads the entire organization. There are three other offices that directly assist the PNP chief in this capacity.

The chief of the PNP commands, supervises, and controls all elements of the police. He or she issues detailed instructions regarding personnel, funds, records, property, correspondence, intelligence, operations, training, and such other matters as may be necessary to effectively carry out the functions of the organization. He or she prescribes, subject to the approval of National Police

Commission, the table of organization and equipment, functions, duties, and powers of various staff, services, installations, and other units of the PNP. The chief of the PNP or the subordinate official he or she authorizes has the power to issue subpoena and subpoena duces tecum in connection with the investigation of cases.

The deputy chief for administration assists the chief of the PNP in the exercise of responsibilities relative to the PNP personnel, human resource (training) and doctrine development, logistics, comptrollership, technical research, and material development activities. He or she likewise assists the chief of the PNP in directing, controlling, and supervising the national administrative support units such as Logistics Support Service, Computer Service, Finance Service, Health Service, Communications and Electronics Service, Chaplain Service, Legal Service, Engineering Service, and Headquarters Support Service. As second in command, he or she exercises duties that may be delegated to him or her or as directed by the chief of the PNP.

The deputy chief for operations assists the chief of the PNP in the exercise of responsibilities relative to PNP operations, intelligence, planning police-community relations, and investigation activities. He or she likewise assists the chief of the PNP in directing, controlling, and supervising the national operational support units such as Maritime Group, Aviation Security Group, Narcotics Group, Special Action Group, Criminal Investigation and Detection Group, Civil Security Group, Intelligence Group, Traffic Management Group, Police Security and Protection Office, Police Community Relations Group, and Crime Laboratory Group. As third in command, he exercises duties that may be delegated to him or her or directed by the chief of the PNP.

The chief of directorial staff primarily coordinates the activities of the PNP Directorial Staff, disseminating instructions of the chief of the PNP, and supervising many command activities. The office has the primary function of ensuring the strict implementation of existing plans and policies, as well as projects and activities pertaining to personnel, training, intelligence, research, community relations, investigation, and other major thrusts of the PNP. He or she coordinates the conduct of command and staff conferences, held both inside and outside the PNP national headquarters and the visits of foreign dignitaries and national leaders, as well as the timely submission of requirements and reports to higher offices on issues, incidents, and matters concerning peace and security including the results of PNP efforts against all forms of criminality throughout the country.

At the PNP headquarters, the director general has ten directorial staff:

• Directorate for Personnel and Records Management

- Directorate for Intelligence
- Directorate for Operations
- Directorate for Human Resource and Doctrine Development
- Directorate for Logistics
- Directorate for Research and Development
- Directorate for Comptrollership
- Directorate for Plans
- Directorate for Police-Community Relations
- Directorate for Investigation and Detective Management
- Administrative and operational support units under the director general

The following are the descriptions of the specific functions of the various directorial offices in the PNP headquarters.

Directorate for Personnel and Records Management: Manpower buildup, proper placement, and instilling discipline among its personnel are the primordial concerns of this directorate.

Directorate for Intelligence: This office primarily gathers, coordinates, and analyzes police intelligence information. It is also responsible for disseminating intelligence information to different units in the PNP and the national government.

Directorate for Operations: The Directorate for Operations is the tactician of the PNP. As the tactician, it plans, directs, controls, coordinates, and supervises PNP operations so that police forces are used to their optimal advantage.

Directorate for Human Resource and Doctrine Development: The directorate's main concern is human resource and doctrine development. It supervises the conduct of in-service training programs, individual training programs, and specialized courses to provide all members of the PNP with specialized skills and technical knowledge necessary to effectively carry out their law enforcement duties.

Directorate for Logistics: This directorate oversees the expenditure of the logistical budget for maintenance and other operating expenses.

Directorate for Research and Development: This directorate determines and develops specifications and standards for all PNP equipment in accordance with acceptable local and international standards. It conducts testing and evaluation of clothing, material, vehicles, and equipment procured or programmed to be procured by this directorate.

Directorate for Comptrollership: This directorate handles the disbursements of funds of the organization. It conducts various management audit and inspections of the different PNP units.

Directorate for Plans: This directorate develops plans and programs to the attain mission and vision of the PNP.

Directorate for Police-Community Relations: This directorate develops and implements plans and programs that promote community and citizen's participation in the maintenance of peace and order and public safety. Its tasks include information and networking activities that help foster a better public understanding of the PNP and its efforts.

Directorate for Investigation and Detective Management: This directorate is mandated to instill investigative skills among the police uniformed personnel (police commissioned and noncommissioned officers) down to the municipal police stations.

Administrative Support Units: The PNP Health Service looks after the health needs of the members of the PNP to promote sound health and well-being for its personnel.

The Communications and Electronics Service is responsible for establishing an effective police communications network. For operational accomplishments, this service provides communications support and assistance to the various PNP activities.

The Engineering Service provides for the overall planning, implementation, supervision, and evaluation of the PNP engineering program relative to administrative, construction and repair projects, land utilization, housing projects, and other activities.

The Logistics Support Service is responsible for the procurement, distribution, and management of all the logistical requirements of the PNP including firearms and ammunition.

The Legal Service provides quality, efficient, and effective legal services to the PNP and assistance to its members' legal dependents.

The Computer Service is responsible for the design, implementation, and maintenance of a database system for the PNP. It is also develops information systems for the different PNP units.

The Headquarters Support Service provides administrative and service support to the national headquarters, PNP, and Camp Crame. This service also keeps Camp Crame worker-friendly through regular garbage collection, clean-and-green activities, demolition of all unregistered structures and establishments, and repair of facilities.

Wilfredo García, the Philippine police chief superintendent, looks over seized firearms collected as part of an initiative to crack down on crime in suburban Manila, August 27, 2005. *García and his forces upped their efforts to address the recent activities of criminal gangs, who were using assault weapons in more frequent daytime robberies and kidnappings.* AP IMAGES.

The Finance Service is responsible for the custody of PNP funds. It implements policies and fiscal directives to address the problem of the PNP personnel concerning finance matters.

The Chaplain Service is a national support unit mandated to provide spiritual and other counseling services for the moral growth of the PNP personnel and their dependents.

Operational Support Units: The Aviation Security Group, in coordination with airport authorities, secures all the country's airports against offensive and terrorist acts that threaten civil aviation, exercises operational control and supervision over all agencies involved in airport security operation, and enforces all laws and regulations relative to air travel protection and safety.

The Traffic Management Group enforces traffic laws and regulations. It promotes safety along the highways, enhances traffic safety consciousness, and renders various forms of assistance to motorists.

The Narcotics Group enforces all laws relative to the protection of the citizenry against dangerous and other prohibited drugs and substances.

The Criminal Investigation and Detection Group undertakes the monitoring, investigating, and prosecuting all crimes involving economic sabotage and other crimes of such magnitude and extent as to indicate their commission by highly placed or professional criminal syndicates and organization. It likewise investigates all major cases involving violations of the revised penal code and operates against organized crime groups, unless the president assigns the case exclusively to the National Bureau of Investigation.

The Maritime Group performs all police functions over Philippine territorial waters and rivers. This group implements Operation Plan Shore Watch, which sets forth the operational guidelines on the heightened security measures and seaborne security patrols. Operation Plan Shore Watch is being implemented by all regional maritime offices within their respective areas of responsibility to prevent possible attacks by various groups and criminal elements targeting innocent civilians and public facilities like ports, piers, ferry terminals, beach resorts, and other vital installations in the Philippine coastal areas.

The Intelligence Group serves as the intelligence and counterintelligence operating unit of the PNP.

The Special Action Force functions as a mobile strike force or reaction unit to augment regional, provincial, municipal, and city police forces for civil disturbance control, counterinsurgency, hostage-taking rescue operations, and other special operations.

The Civil Security Group provides administrative services and general supervision over the organization, business operation, and activities of all organized detectives, watchmen, security guard agencies, and company guard forces.

The Police Security and Protection Office provides security for government officials, visiting dignitaries, and private individuals authorized to be given police protection.

The Police Community Relations Group implements plans and programs that will promote community and citizens' participation in the maintenance of peace and order and public safety.

The Crime Laboratory Group provides scientific and technical investigative aid and support to the PNP and other government investigative agencies. It also provides crime laboratory examination, evaluation, and identification of physical evidences involved in crimes with primary emphasis on their medical, chemical, biological, and physical nature.

Local Police. The local police forces are those that are found in the regions, provinces, cities, municipalities and metropolitan areas. It must be noted that there is continuity of command from the highest officer to the lowest official. Thus, police offices in the local areas receive orders from the national headquarters.

Police Regional Offices. At the different regions, the fifteen regional offices maintain organizational structures that are similar to the national structure. However, the organizational structures in the regions are streamlined. The fifteen regional offices and their locations are as follows:

- Regional Office 1: Camp Gen Oscar Florendo, Parian San Fernando, La Union

- Regional Office 2: Camp Adduru, Tuguegarao, Cagayan

- Regional Office 3: Camp Olivas, San Fernando, Pampanga

- Regional Office 4: Camp Vicente Lim Canlubang, Laguna

- Regional Office 5: Camp Simeon A Ola, Legazpi City

- Regional Office 6: Camp Martin Delgado, Iloilo City

- Regional Office 7: Camp Sergio Osmena Sr., Cebu City

- Regional Office 8: Camp Ruperto K Kangleon, Palo, Leyte

- Regional Office 9: Camp Justice R. T. Lim Boulevard, Zamboanga City

- Regional Office 10: Camp Alagar, Cagayan de Oro City

- Regional Office 11: Camp Catitipan, Davao City

- Regional Office 12: Camp Amado Dumlao Sr., Sultan Kudarat

- Regional Office 13: Camp Rafael Rodriguez, Libertad, Butuan City; ARMM—Camp Salipada Pendatun, Parang, Maguindanao

- Procar Office: Camp Bado Dangwa, La Trinidad, Benguet

- National Capital Region: Camp General Tomas Karingal, Sikatuna Village, Quezon City

The National Capital Region, which covers metro Manila, is divided into five districts, and each one is headed by a district director. The five districts are Western Police District, Manila; Eastern Police District; Northern Police District; Central Police District, Quezon City; and Southern Police District.

Provincial Police. Each region is composed of several provinces. The police provincial director coordinates and administers all police activities in each town and city within the province.

City and Municipal Police. These police offices maintain peace and order in the local area. These cities or municipalities are headed by a chief of police. Local police forces are not substantially controlled by the local executives. Their usual participation is the selection of the chief of police from among three or four nominees that come from the regional or provincial police offices. Nevertheless, local officials also play a role in law enforcement. By presidential decree, the justice system in the *barangays* empowers village leaders to handle petty and less serious crimes. The intent of the decree was to reinforce the authority of local officials and to reduce the workload on already overtaxed Philippine law enforcement agencies.

Hierarchy and Rank. There are sixteen ranks with three major classifications. The first are star-rank officers, who occupy the top commands in the hierarchy. Star-rank personnel are appointed by the president. The next group includes the commissioned officers. These commissioned officers occupy the ranks of inspector to chief superintendent. These officers are appointed to the rank by the PNP and the National Police Commission after satisfying the established criteria. The third group consists of noncommissioned officers. The lowest rank for this group is Police Officer 1 and the top rank is the Senior Police Officer 4. The following are the rank classifications in the PNP arranged from highest to lowest:

- Director General
- Deputy Director General
- Director
- Chief Superintendent
- Senior Superintendent
- Superintendent
- Chief Inspector
- Senior Inspector
- Inspector
- Senior Police Officer 4
- Senior Police Officer 3
- Senior Police Officer 2
- Senior Police Officer 1
- Police Officer 3
- Police Officer 2
- Police Officer 1

Salaries. PNP members receive salaries from the national government, although local government units are authorized to provide extra incentives and allowances. Salaries of police officers are standardized across the country commensurate to their ranks. As of July 2002, the starting salary for a noncommissioned officer was 12,005 pesos (US$214) per month. The starting salary of the lowest ranking commissioned officer (i.e., inspector) was 22,113 pesos (US$402) a month. The uniformed members also receive allowances such as the cost of living allowance, clothing allowance, hazard pay, and longevity pay.

Retirement Age. PNP members remain in the service until the age of fifty-six, which is the mandatory retirement for all police officers. Police officers who have incurred permanent physical disability in the line of duty are also considered retired regardless of their age. Officers who incur partial physical disability are not considered retired but are separated from the service with corresponding severance pay.

Awards and Decorations. The PNP recognizes significant contribution from its members by giving awards, decorations, and citations:

- *Medalya ng Kagitingan* (Medal of Valor)—This is awarded to any member of the PNP for action of the recipient involving conspicuous gallantry and intrepidity at the risk of life and limb above and beyond the call of duty. To justify this award, a member of the PNP must perform in action a deed of personal bravery and self-sacrifice above and beyond the call of duty so conspicuous as to distinguish him- or herself clearly above his or her comrades in the performance of more than ordinary hazardous service.

- *Medalya ng Kabayanihan* (Distinguished Conduct Medal)—This is awarded to any member of the PNP for acts of conspicuous courage and gallantry in the face of an armed enemy or acts of heroism so notable and involving a risk of life so extraordinary as to set him or her apart from his or her comrades.

- *Medalya ng Katapatan sa Paglilingkod* (Distinguished Service Medal)—This medal is awarded to PNP members. The accomplishment of the duty should have been complete before submission of recommendation or, if the person being recommended has been transferred before completion, the accomplishment must have been determined to be exceptional or significant.

- *Medalya ng Katapangan* (Bravery Medal)—This medal is awarded to PNP members.

- *Medalya ng Katangi-tanging Gawa* (Outstanding Achievement Medal)—This medal is awarded to PNP members and civilian personnel of the Republic of the Philippines and of friendly foreign nations.

- *Medalya ng Kadakilaan* (Heroism Medal)—This is awarded to members of the PNP for heroism not involving actual conflict with an armed enemy.

Police-Community Relations. The PNP aims to engage the community so that the community can regularly assist the PNP in its mission of maintaining peace and order. The police at the station level actively participate in the formal community-based organization even at the *barangay* levels. Government organizations, non-governmental organizations, civic organizations, and even business groups actively support the PNP in every undertaking that directly affects the community. This necessitates the institutionalization of the philosophy of the Community-Oriented Policing System (COPS) at all levels of the PNP, where every police officer is expected to become a COPS practitioner. The objective of COPS is to change the perceptions of the public toward the PNP. Specifically, it aims to develop a police officer as someone to be respected, rather than feared; someone who is a friend, a protector, and a community leader.

To reach this stage, the PNP formulated the Medium-Term Development Plan (MTDP). Initially, education efforts are made at the regional and provincial levels to emphasize the importance of community partnership. On the first year of the MTDP, People's Day activities were geared toward imparting skills and knowledge on crime prevention and control.

Aside from these plans, the PNP has developed some strategic programs for developing better community relations. The PNP established the Council of Community Elders, whose members serve as partners of the police on problem solving. As of 2003, there were 1,451 councils with 11,210 members. The PNP has a livelihood and skills development program for the youth called the Out-of-School Youth Servicing toward Economic Recovery. The PNP also targets students by having a school-based protection program that aims to promote peace and order in the schools. The program calls for the creation of councils in schools. This council includes the local police, school authorities, officers of the parent-teachers association, local businesses, and other nongovernmental and civic organizations. The aim of the program is to reduce violence on campuses, particularly gang- and fraternity-related violence.

The PNP has also taken advantage of the cellular phone technology to make it more accessible to the public. The PNP TXT 2920 provides better access to police assistance twenty-four hours a day, seven days a week.

Special Police.

Special Action Force. The Special Action Force (SAF) is assigned to the national headquarters and to regional and provincial barracks for immediate deployment to areas that need special tactics and weapons. The SAF is also deployed in special combat operations, especially in counterinsurgency efforts.

Riot Police. Each local police unit is allowed to maintain civil disturbance units that are primarily involved in crowd control during rallies and demonstrations. These units are support by either provincial or regional reaction groups (in most cases these are SAF

units). These reaction groups are called in to supplement local police forces not only for riots but also for other police emergencies.

Traffic Police. The Traffic Management Group has the primary function of policing and maintaining safety on the highways. City police offices usually create traffic units within their departments. Municipal police departments usually do not have special traffic units but every noncommissioned patrol officer is expected to render traffic services such as taking accident reports, directing traffic, and helping motorists.

Education and Training.

Under Republic Act No. 8551, a baccalaureate degree is a mandatory minimum requirement for entry into the police service. For rank promotion, police officers are required to meet several education and training requirements. The highest educational requirement for promotion to any rank of position is a master's degree. On top of these academic requirements, there are several specific trainings and civil service eligibilities that one must posses to move up the ranks.

Recruitment and Conditions of Service. The applicant must be at least twenty years of age but not more than thirty years old. There is also a height requirement (men: 5 feet, 4 inches; women: 5 feet, 2 inches). However, a civilian applicant may be exempted from the requirement for age, height, or education if he or she has already availed of the corresponding age, height, educational requirement waiver from the National Police Commission, before the filing his or her application for examination. Also, members of the cultural minorities/indigenous communities are automatically exempted from the height requirement on submission of a certification on his or her membership issued by the National Commission on Indigenous Peoples or the Office of Muslim Affairs, whichever is applicable.

Every year about 15,000 men and women go through the rigor of applying for cadetship. These recruits are tested on physical agility, intelligence, and character. Among these applicants about 350 are chosen and on average, about 200 of them graduate to become officers. For the rank and file, about 25,000 apply for police service. On average, about 5,000 are able to serve as police personnel.

Section 27 of the Republic Act No. 6795 provides that the ideal manning level should be 1 police officer for every 500 population and that this ratio should not be less than 1:1,000. The same law also specifies the rank and position for key officials. The purposes of these provisions are for the PNP to have efficient administration, supervision, and control of the members of the organization. Approved through the National Police

Commission Resolution No. 92-23, the Police Manual provides for the rank distribution in the PNP.

As of 2005 the recruitment of PNP officers was primarily established under section 33 of the Republic Act No. 6975, which reads:

> Sec. 33. Lateral Entry of Officers into the PNP— In general, all original appointments of commissioned officers in the PNP shall commence with the rank of inspector, to include all those with highly technical qualifications applying for the PNP technical services such as dentists, optometrists, nurses, engineers, and graduates of forensic sciences. Doctors of medicine, members of the Bar, and chaplains shall be appointed to the rank of senior inspector in their particular technical service. Graduates of the Philippine National Police Academy (PNPA) shall be automatically appointed to the initial rank of inspector. Licensed criminologists may be appointed to the rank of inspector to fill up any vacancy after promotions from the ranks are completed.

Therefore, under the law officers are apparently divided into those who perform line functions and those who perform technical functions. Those who perform line functions enter through the officer's corps either laterally or from the ranks. Graduates of the PNPA and licensed criminologists enter the service laterally and they perform line functions. Promotable senior police officer 4s enter the officer's corps through the ranks. Promotion from the ranks considers only a pool from the promotable senior police officer 4s. Therefore, PNP personnel who are from the ranks have to start with the initial rank of police officer 1.

The technical officers such as doctors, nurses, dentists, engineers, and lawyers are not automatically appointed and they only occupy the technical positions and not the line positions. It must be noted that, except for the graduates of PNPA who have automatic entry into the officer's corps, all the appointees to the officer's corps must undergo some officer orientation course such as Officer's Orientation Course or Officer's Candidate Course.

Uniforms and Weapons. The PNP uniforms may be classified into three types: gala uniforms, general office attire, and combat uniforms. Gala uniforms are worn during formal occasions and functions. This is usually a dark-blue bush coat. At other times, police officers use formal coats with the rank insignia and other regalia. This attire is usually dark blue and its upper garment is a long-sleeved coat. These are mostly worn by top-ranking officers.

General office attires are those that the police wear as part of their daily uniform. Men wear dark-blue pants with a light-blue stripe on its side. Women wear a skirt of the same color. The upper garment is sky-blue with thin white stripes. On some occasions, the chief of police may wear civilian clothes. The prescribed civilian attire may be a coat and tie or a barong tagalog.

Combat uniforms are those that are worn by special forces or those assigned in combat zones. This type of uniform is also worn by special reaction forces such as SWAT teams and the SAF. This type of uniform is usually a light chocolate-brown fatigue, while others use a black fatigue uniform.

The standard weapon of the members of the PNP is a 9-mm caliber automatic pistol. However, special operations units are usually provided M16s as their primary weapon. Some of these special operations officers are provided with grenade launchers. For riot police officers, they are usually equipped with batons and tear gas launchers. Aside from the provision of these traditional lethal weapons, all police officers are required to undergo Arnis training (an indigenous martial arts technique using a long baton).

Badges, Logo, and Heraldry. Officers are issued a badge that contains the logo of the PNP and the commission number of the police officer. The following is an explanation of the PNP logo and the meanings of the symbols:

- Lapu-Lapu (figure of a man with a sword)— The great Filipino hero of Mactan, the prototype of the best and most noble in Filipino manhood who is the symbol and embodiment of all the genuine attributes of leadership, courage, nationalism, and self-reliance and of a people-based and people-powered community defense. The benevolent and heroic warrior who derived added strength from a cohesive, determined, and loyal people is today a fitting symbol and prototype as well of people power to preserve values, customs, traditions, way of life, and the rule of law through a solid community-based police system. Lapu-Lapu also personifies civilian constitutional authority.

- Laurel—A green laurel with leaves symbolizes the fourteen regional commands. It is also a symbol of the honor, dignity, and privilege of being a member of a noble organization where the call to public service is par excellence a commitment to public trust.

- Service-Honor-Justice—Added distinct ideals for the officers of the PNP to ensure efficiency, integrity, cohesiveness, camaraderie, and equanimity, all of which enhance community acceptance and support to attain its mission of peacekeeping and law enforcement.

- Shield—The symbol of the PC, the first national police by virtue of Organic Act No. 175, enacted by the Philippine Commission on July 18, 1901. For nearly ninety years of service, the PC has performed with honor, professionalism, and courage. The PC has carved out a large part of the glorious pages of Philippine history, as attested by its proudly and deservedly garnering eighty-six of the ninety-two Medals of Valor, the highest honor that a grateful Filipino nation can bestow on its gallant sons and daughters in the service of the republic. Most appropriately therefore, the PC became the nucleus of the INP in 1975 to nurture the then embryonic concept of the nationalization of the country's local police forces.

- Three Stars—These stars represent the three major islands in the Philippines—Luzon, Visayas, and Mindanao—and the 1,700 islands and the territorial integrity wherein the PNP must enforce the law and maintain peace and order with professionalism, zeal, and dedication in keeping with the highest ideals and traditions of service to its country and people.

- Sun—This symbolizes the flowering, maturing, and ultimate realization of the glorious evolution of the PC/INP into a national police organization—"national in scope and civilian in character"—as enshrined in the 1986 constitution. The traditional light rays represent the eight first provinces that rose in arms against Spain in the Philippine Revolution of 1896, whose ideals of courage and patriotism the members of the National Police must possess.

Transportation, Technology, and Communications. The PNP uses vehicles such as cars and motorcycles. It has a few helicopters, but these are not used for patrol purposes. It also has motorboats, but rural areas have *bancas* (small paddled boats) that are used to patrol rivers and seashores. The PNP has relatively scarce vehicles and equipment. For example, as of June 2002, the PNP had a total of 2,951 motorcycles in its inventory, which represent less than 30 percent of the required number of motorcycles based on the table of equipment prescribed by the National Police Commission ("162 New Motorbikes to Boost Police Mobility" 2002).

The PNP intends to concentrate on developing its operational capability by focusing its expenditures on ground mobility and fire power. Therefore, it intends to equip its police officers with the necessary firearms as well as the needed resources for faster response.

In a country where cellular phones are almost twice as many as landline phones, the PNP's Central Operations Center installed five additional phone lines. The activation of these phone lines increased the access of the community to the police. The PNP also has a Web site to provide the community with updated information about the police. It also launched an emergency telephone system called REACT 166. This emergency dialing system is similar to the United States' 911 emergency. In addition, the PNP has taken advantage of the cellular text messaging service by establishing Club 2920, where citizens can report emergencies and other police information through text messages dialing the numbers 2920. Even with these modern communications technologies, the PNP maintains the use of two-way radios as a means of communication, especially among its provincial offices and remote areas of operation.

Surveillance and Intelligence Gathering. Local police departments are encouraged to develop their surveillance and intelligence gathering capabilities. However, the local forces are mostly confined to gathering human intelligence (i.e., detecting suspicious characters and activities in their areas of operation). High-level surveillance and intelligence gathering (i.e., those that involve sophisticated equipment and training such as wire taps and infiltration using Deep Penetration Agents) are conducted by the operational support units, primarily the Intelligence Unit. Independently, all the operational support units undertake surveillance and intelligence gathering operations. As of 2001 there were approximately over 13,000 community-based information networks with over 30,000 informants being used for intelligence gathering. Most intelligence operational activities are undertaken to address problems involving organized crime and insurgencies.

The Intelligence Unit also conducts counterintelligence operations to address misconduct and disloyalty among the members of the PNP. It should make its service relevant to all, especially those who are less in power, material goods, and influence. The emphasis is on people-driven efforts because the people know best on what their needs and priorities are. Republic Act No. 8551 created the Internal Affairs Service, which aims to proactively investigate officers who are suspected of abusing their authority and engaging in illegal acts.

Police Officers Killed in the Line of Duty. Southern Philippines and communist terrorist-related incidents have contributed to several deaths of officers in line of duty. The data from the Directorate for Operations and the Directorate for Personnel and Records Management through its Personnel Accounting Information System indicate that there were a total of thirty-eight police personnel killed in action in 2002 and thirty-six in 2003.

CRIME

Criminal Identification and Forensics. The PNP is supported by the National Bureau of Investigation. As an agency of the Department of Justice, the National Bureau of Investigation is authorized to investigate, on its own initiative and in the public interest, crimes and other offenses against the laws of the Philippines; to help whenever officially requested investigate or detect crimes or other offenses; and to act as a national clearing house of criminal records and other information. In addition, the bureau maintains a scientific crime laboratory and provides technical assistance on request to the police.

Executive Order No. 386 as amended by Executive Order No. 145 dated August 27, 1999, provided for the establishment of the National Crime Information System (NCIS) Project. The NCIS aims to develop and institutionalize an information system that systematizes the collection, storage, processing, interpretation, and dissemination of reliable and comprehensive criminal justice statistics and provides decision-support mechanisms in the treatment of offenders, thus contributing toward the enhanced criminal justice performance. This project involves the nine agencies under the criminal justice system: the PNP, National Prosecution Service, the Court, the Bureau of Corrections, the Bureau of Jail Management and Penology, the National Bureau of Investigation, the Parole and Probation Administration, the Board of Pardons and Parole, and the National Police Commission.

With this information system, each of the agencies maintains a database of case information using its own application system. The system, which allows information sharing among the agencies under the criminal justice system, reduces the amount of manual data entry and establishes a standard for data correctness and reliability that would facilitate faster and efficient exchange of crime and offender information among the participating agencies.

Organized Crime. The following describes the success of the PNP in its campaigns against certain organized crimes such as kidnapping, carjacking, smuggling, illegal drugs, illegal gambling, robbing banks, and terrorism and anti-insurgency.

Kidnapping and Serious Illegal Detention. Statistics show that kidnapping incidents have significantly declined (1996 to 2001). The decrease in kidnapping incidents is attributed to the relentless effort and campaign of the PNP to apprehend the perpetrators of these incidents.

The campaign against kidnap-for-ransom gangs has been put on high gear with the activation of the National Anti-Kidnap-for-Ransom Task Force (NAKTF). With the Police Anti-Crime and Emergency Response provid-

ing main operational support, the antikidnap-for-ransom campaign led to the arrest of a significant number of wanted kidnap-for-ransom personalities in the last quarter of 2003, including the four most wanted on the NAKTF list. In addition, 122 suspects were arrested and 31 killed in antikidnap-for-ransom operations. The solution efficiency in 2003 reached 79 percent with sixty-five out of eighty-two cases solved.

The PNP attributes many of the kidnappings and serious illegal detention cases to the worsening Philippine economic conditions. The Southern Philippines Secessionist Group and the Abu Sayaff Group have also turned to kidnap-for-ransom activities primarily to generate resources and to serve as a tool for political leverage.

Carjacking Incidents. The campaign against carjacking has gained headway and has resulted in the number of people being arrested for carjacking. The rate of carjackings peaked in 1997, with it being 7.4 percent higher than in 1996. On the one hand, 2000 posed the lowest number of stolen vehicles with a total of 1,336, approximately 19 percent lower than 1999. The campaign against highway robbery on commodities or hijacking was strengthened in 2003 by a cooperative agreement that bound law enforcers and private-sector organizations to a common action agenda to solve the recurring problem. The Memo-randum of Agreement signed by five government agencies and four private-sector organizations set the stage for more comprehensive police action on the ground, with the full support of the companies and organizations that have been affected by the operations of these hijacking syndicates. By 2003 the PNP was successful in bringing down the average number of cars stolen per day by 23 percent (from 8.1 per day in 2002 to 6.2 per day in 2003).

Smuggling. The PNP's strict implementation of maritime and aviation laws has resulted in a decrease in the number of reported cases of smuggling and an increase in the number of persons arrested and cases filed in court. The PNP, the Bureau of Customs, and other law enforcement agencies have established collaborative efforts in solving the problem of smuggling. Since in 2001 there has been a tremendous drop of cases reported.

Illegal Drugs. The continuing proliferation of illegal drugs in many parts of the country remains to be a major law enforcement concern. The number of reported cases involving dangerous drugs and the number of persons arrested showed a notable increase in 2003. The PNP created the Anti-Illegal Drugs Special Operations Task Force in June 2003. In its six months of operations, this task force seized more than 13.0 billion pesos' (US$237 million) worth of shabu and ephedrine. Sixteen clandestine laboratories and warehouses were dismantled, eleven of which were laboratories with complete manufacturing facilities, and five storage warehouses that contained significant volumes of chemical precursors and laboratory equipment. Since 2003 a total of 23,382 persons have been arrested by the task force and 16,620 cases have been filed in court.

Illegal Gambling. One of the major campaigns of the PNP is to contain illegal gambling all over the country. All regional police offices have been ordered to step up their drive against *jueteng* (a numbers game) and all other forms of illegal gambling. In 2000 the PNP intensified its antigambling operations. For that same year, the anti-illegal gambling campaign led to an increase in the number of persons arrested for the crime and the number of cases filed in court. As a result, the data show a decreasing rate of cases reported since 2001. It is projected that the statistics for illegal gambling will show positive results in the coming years with the drive against illegal gambling operators and financiers. The revitalized campaign against illegal gambling, which is intended to make the Philippines a "no *jueteng*" country, has been marked by not only a sustained effort but also a groundswell of support from the local leaders and religious authorities. Following the December 15, 2002, directive from the chief of the PNP to the regional directors, the compliance has reached a 91.5 percent level, with eighty-six of the ninety-four provincial/city/districts having been certified "no *jueteng*" as of December 29, 2003.

Bank Robbery. The resurgence of bank robbery incidents in the third quarter of 2003 led to the creation of the Philippine National Police Anti-Bank Robbery Special Operations Task Force. This task force is focused on consolidating information and mounting operations against identified bank robbing groups. One of the highlights of this task force was the arrest of more than ten suspects following a series of bank robberies in Palar Village, Taguig, and metro Manila.

Terrorism and Anti-Insurgency. The Philippine contribution to the global war against terrorism has been in the form of arrests of key personalities in the international network of terrorist organizations, including Mukhlis Yunos and Taufek Refke, as well as the prevention and deterrence of possible violent attacks.

The PNP provides support to the armed forces of the Philippines in the anti-insurgency campaign. However, the successive attacks on police stations in far-flung areas since 2002 have heightened police readiness and responsiveness against communist terrorists. Implementing the twin strategy of static and active defense, the PNP has repulsed several New People's Army attacks against police stations in Quinapondan, Eastern Samar; Naga City, Camarines Sur; San Lorenzo Ruiz, Camarines Norte; and Zaragoza, Nueva Ecija. The proactive stance has not only shown police capability in defending its citizenry but

has also highlighted the bravery of its police officers on the ground.

Crime Statistics. In 2003 there was a 2.4 percent decrease in crime volume, from 85,776 in 2002 to 83,704 in 2003. Crime-solution efficiency also improved by 2.1 percent compared to 2002 figures. Responding to the clamor for decisive action against snatchers and thieves that were victimizing the citizenry on the streets, the police reported that the force stopped the trend. As of the latest records, there has been a 42.5 percent decrease in street crimes on a national level since the campaign against street crimes began. Most notable is the 56.2 percent decrease in the national capital region (1,008 incidents in March 2003 versus 441 incidents in October 2003). The three-pronged thrust of checkpoints, walking the beat, and deployment of mobile forces/stations has been identified as the key to this downtrend.

According to the latest PNP crime report, the total crime volume went down in the first quarter of 2003 by 4 percent compared to the same quarter of 2002. The following are the specific crime reports on major classifications:

- 6 percent decrease in index crimes (17,939 in 2003 compared to 19,031 in 2002)

- 2 percent decrease in nonindex crimes (16,793 in 2003 compared to 17,122 in 2002)

There were major decreases in homicide (15%) and physical injury (8%). The number of crimes solved increased by 2.3 percent. Crimes against persons decreased by 2 percent, particularly homicide (down 9.8%). Crime-solution efficiency has improved by 3 percent, with an increase of 5.5. percent for solution efficiency on index crimes. The crime volume was the lowest in 1997 and it started to climb in 1999. At the start of the twenty-first century, the crime volume began to dip again.

HUMAN RIGHTS

Police have often been suspects in a number of arbitrary and unlawful killings, disappearances, illegal detention, and abuse. The Commission on Human Rights investigated twenty-two complaints of killings for the first six months of 2003, the same number as in the first six months of 2002. The Commission on Human Rights included killings by antigovernment insurgents in its investigations. The Task Force Detainees of the Philippines (TFDP), a nongovernmental organization, documented six summary executions of civilians by government forces and insurgents through June 2003. In combating criminal organizations, security forces sometimes resorted to summary execution of suspects, or "salvaging." Police and military spokesmen explained these killings as the unavoidable result of a shootout with suspects or escapees. Statements by various local government officials have condoned extrajudicial killings as an acceptable means to fight crime. The Commission on Human Rights suspected PNP members in a majority of the human rights violations involving deaths that it investigated through June 2003.

The police are also being blamed for disappearances of people and the illegal detention of suspects. Families of Victims of Involuntary Disappearances, a domestic nongovernmental organization, reported twenty-one disappearances in 2003. The Commission on Human Rights investigated seventy-two cases of illegal arrest and detention through June—an increase of 24 percent from the number recorded during the same period in 2002. The TFDP documented thirty-six cases of politically motivated arrests by the government through July 2003. The TFDP and the Philippine Human Rights Information Center, another nongovernmental organization, both estimated the total number of political prisoners in the country at approximately 200 (Bureau of Democracy, Human Rights, and Labor 2004). The 2003 Amnesty International report documents at least a dozen of cases where suspects were illegally arrested, detained, or abused during investigation.

CORRECTIONAL SYSTEM

The Bureau of Jail Management and Penology (BJMP), also referred to as the Jail Bureau, was created pursuant to Section 60, Republic Act No. 6975, which took effect on January 2, 1991. Apparently, this is an upgraded version of its forerunner, the Office of Jail Management and Penology, which was created in 1976.

In the late 1980s institutions for the confinement of convicts and the detention of those awaiting trial included a variety of national prisons and penal farms as well as many small local jails and lockups (Sanchez 1984). In general, the national prisons housed more serious offenders, and those serving short-term sentences were held in local facilities. The prison system at the national level was supervised by the Bureau of Prisons of the Department of Justice. The bureau was responsible for the safekeeping of prisoners and their rehabilitation through general and moral education and technical training in industry and agriculture. The bureau also oversaw the operation of prison agro industries and the production of food commodities.

In 1991 the newly formed BJMP took over administration of local jails. The BJMP is organized similar to the PNP. The command, control, and supervision of the jail personnel are located at the central headquarters in Manila. The head of the BJMP is headed by a director. There are also regional offices in the jail hierarchy.

The prisons are managed on a national level by the Bureau of Corrections. The bureau is attached to the Department of Justice and is headed by a director. The government maintains seven correctional institutions and penal farms. These prisons are each headed by a warden. The nation's largest prison is the National Penitentiary at Muntinlupa, metro Manila. The penitentiary serves as the central facility for those sentenced to life imprisonment or long-term incarceration. It is divided into two camps to separate those serving maximum and minimum penalties. The Correctional Institution for Women is also located in metropolitan Manila. There are also facilities that are combinations of a prison and penal farms. These are located in far-flung areas such as those Zamboanga City, Palawan, Mindoro Occidental, and several others in the Visayas and Mindanao provinces.

Some prison inmates may be eligible for parole and probation. Before serving their sentence, felons, who are not charged with subversion or insurgency or who have not been on probation before, can apply for probation. Probationers are required to meet with their parole officers monthly, to avoid any further offense, and to comply with all other court-imposed conditions. After serving an established minimum sentence, certain prisoners can apply to their parole board for release. The board can also recommend pardon to the president for prisoners it believes have reformed and who present no menace to society. The Parole and Probation Administration is responsible for the administration of prison release programs. This office is also attached to the Department of Justice.

Prison Conditions. Prison conditions in the Philippines are generally poor and prison life is harsh. Among the noted complaint is the overcrowding of prisons. Because of overcrowding, prisoners suffer from physical as well as mental diseases. In 2003 the Human Rights Commission noted that prisoners developed boils, diarrhea, and other respiratory problems because of poor ventilation in prisons. The commission also noted that facilities lacked an adequate supply of medicine and laboratory equipment. Thus, the commission concluded that the facilities were not fit for human confinement.

Aside from the structural problems, the prisons also suffer form logistical problems. The institutions can barely afford to feed their inmates with a measly daily allowance of 30 pesos (US$0.50). Prisoners have to rely on donations from family, friends, and charitable institutions to eat decently. Another problem is the system of mayors, where cells are basically controlled and administered by inmates themselves. This practice promotes gangsters in prison. Finally, inmates complain of violation of their basic human rights such as legal consultation and conjugal rooms and of suffering sexual abuse and harassment. Because of these problems, a European human rights commissioner asked the Philippine government to improve its prison system. As a response, the Philippine government immediately released funds to build new jail facilities.

Prison Statistics. In 2002 the national and provincial prisons held 97,968 inmates (National Statistics Coordination Board 2003). The seven national prisons held 27,582 inmates, including 1,055 females. The prison population rate per 100,000 was 86. Pretrial detainees made up 58.2 percent of the total prison population, while females made up 5.5 percent and juveniles 3.0 percent. The official capacity of the prison system was 45,000 and the occupancy level was 156.4 percent. The New Bilibid Prison in Muntinlupa City, metro Manila, held the most number of inmates (16,134) and was above its capacity limit by 85 percent. The National Correctional Institute for Women also in Manila held approximately 950 prisoners and was also over its capacity limit by 90 percent. The rest of the prisoners were confined in five other institutions and were mostly located in the Visayas and Mindanao areas. Most prisoners were in the maximum security category, where 12,233 (49%) out of 25,002 were in maximum security. According to the 2003 National Statistics Coordination Board survey, the top-three crimes committed by inmates were homicide (26%), murder (23%), and rape (12%). As of 2003 there were about a thousand inmates on death row and twenty-seven of them were women (National Statistics Coordination Board 2003).

There were 3,325 inmates released from prison in 2002 with the following breakdown: released on parole, 2,519; expiration of sentence, 627; pardon, 6; others, 173. It should be noted that there are no alternative community corrections programs because of lack of financial and personnel resources.

BIBLIOGRAPHY

Amnesty International. 2003. "Philippines: Torture Persists: Appearance and Reality within the Criminal Justice System." Amnesty International USA (January 23). Available online at http://www.amnestyusa.org/countries/philippines/document.

do?id=9246AD015D235A2E80256C980016690D (accessed December 19, 2005).

Bureau of Democracy, Human Rights, and Labor. 2004. "Country Reports on Human Rights Practices, 2004: Philippines." U.S. Department of State. Available online at http://www.state.gov/g/drl/rls/hrrpt/2004/41657.htm (accessed December 19, 2005).

Campos, C. 1991. "Law Enforcement Policy and Strategy in the Republic of the Philippines." *Police Studies* 14 (2), pp. 76–104.

Central Intelligence Agency. 2005. "World Factbook: Philippines." Available online at http://cia.gov/cia/publications/factbook/geos/rp.html (accessed December 19, 2005).

Commission on Human Rights. 2004. "The Situation of Philippine Penitentiaries: An Update on the Study on the Conditions of Jails and Correctional Institutions in the Country." Human Rights Monitor. Available online at http://www.hrnow.org/monitor/h000218_sitpeni.htm (accessed December 19, 2005).

"Effective July 2002, PNP Salary Standardization." 2002. *Police Digest* (February).

"Funds for New Jail Facilities Approved." 2003. *Malaya News* (September 4).

Gutang, R. 1993. *Pulisya*. Manila, Philippines: National Bookstore.

National Statistics Coordination Board. 2003. "Factsheets: Correctional Institution for Women, Most Overcrowded National Prison." Available online at http://www.nscb.gov.ph/factsheet/pdf03/fs3_04.asp (accessed December 19, 2005).

"162 New Motorbikes to Boost Police Mobility." 2002. *Police Digest* (August).

Philippine National Police. 2000. "Annual Report." Philippine National Police.

Philippine National Police. 2001. "Annual Report." Philippine National Police.

Philippine National Police. 2003. "Annual Accomplishment Report." Philippine National Police.

"Philippines Asked to Improve Human Rights Conditions." 2003. *Agence France Press* (November 19).

Sanchez, E. L. 1984. "Corrections in the Philippines." Resource Materials Series, no. 26, Tokyo, Japan. United Nations Asia and Far East Institute for the Prevention of Crime and the Treatment of Offenders.

Melchior C. de Guzman

Poland

Official country name: Republic of Poland
Capital: Warsaw
Geographic description: Located in eastern Europe, east of Germany and west of Russia
Population: 38,635,144 (est. 2005)

■ ■ ■

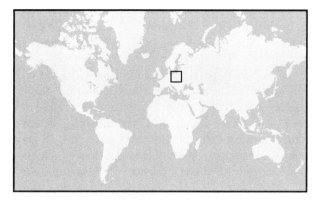

LAW ENFORCEMENT

History. Poland has over a thousand years of tradition. In the early Middle Ages the present-day administrative and judicial police functions were performed by royal officials, such as palatial comes, governors, and castellans. During the Noble Republic police functions belonged among others, such as major-domos, *voivodes*, and *starosts*. During the Four-Year Seym (from 1791) questions of security and public order were dealt by the Police Commission of Both Nations (Poland and Lithuania).

After the republic's fall (1795–1918) police tasks in the Polish territory were taken over by the Russian, Austrian, and Prussian invaders, respectively. Before Poland regained its sovereignty following World War I, various social and civic organizations interested in public order protection were established in the Polish territory. Guards and militias formed by these organizations differed from each other.

Construction of the police organization based on the Law of July 24, 1919, on the State Police was one of the most important goals of reviving the state. The process was realized for a few years. Its course was not easy and different in various parts of the country. The leading authority was the chief commandant of the State Police,

and the country was divided into police districts. On September 1, 1939, the police service in Poland had approximately 35,000 police officers.

After Poland lost its sovereignty to Germany during World War II, the Polish police (*policja granatowa*) became a subsidiary to the German police force that was established in the occupied territory (Generalne Gubernatorstwo). The Polish police were not trusted by their occupants. Several of its officers cooperated with the Polish resistance movement. Meanwhile, the Polish police officers who were captured by the Soviets faced a different destiny. About 6,000 of them were put in Ostaszków camp. Another 9,000 soldiers, government officials, and intellectuals were sent to internment camps in Kozielsk and Starobielsk. These prisoners of war were murdered by Soviet authorities in the spring of 1940.

In 1944 the Civic Militia (Milicja Obywatelska) was organized. The decree on the Civic Militia of October 7, 1944, stated that it was a public law enforcement formation of the Public Security Department. Besides having ordinary police functions, the militia was given an executive role by the communist authorities. In 1954 the Ministry of Public Security was replaced by the Public Security Committee, and the Civic Militia was moved to the newly established Ministry of Internal Affairs. In 1956 the Civic Militia was moved back to the Public Security Committee because a newly established Security Service (Służba Bezpieczeństwa) was placed in the Department of Internal Affairs. In December 1981 the Civic Militia, alongside the army and other public services of the state, was used to enforce and maintain a state of emergency. In other cases the Civic Militia was used to restrain unrests and social dissatisfaction. In 1983 *voivode*-ship and regional headquarters of the Civic Militia were renamed to voivode-ship and regional offices of internal affairs.

Following the political upheaval in Poland and subsequently in Central and Eastern Europe in 1989, the Civic Militia and Security Service were dissolved one year later. In their stead the police and the Office of State Protection (at present the Internal Security Agency and the Intelligence Agency) were established. The basic legal act is the Law on the Police of April 6, 1990 (with further amendments). The present philosophy of the police is not to act by way of repression but in close cooperation with society and according to a rule of political disengagement. The Polish police cooperate with the police forces from other countries within the Interpol and Europol systems. Police officers have been or actually are in missions abroad (peacekeeping or democracy building operations) organized under the auspices of international organizations (e.g., United Nations, Organization for Security and Cooperation in Europe, European Union, and Western European Union) in the following countries: former Yugoslavia, Iraq, Croatia, Bosnia and Herzegovina, Tajikistan, Albania, and Kosovo. The Polish police also have liaison officers in a few countries (e.g., the Netherlands, Russia, Ukraine, and Baltic states). Police officers are members of International Police Association and International Association of Chiefs of Police.

Structure and Organization. According to the Law on the Police of April 6, 1990, the police are a uniformed and armed formation serving society and intended for protection of people's security and for maintaining security and public order. The name *Police* belongs to this formation exclusively. Besides the police, there are several other types of law enforcement agencies, such as Border Guards, Internal Security Agency, Intelligence Agency, Customs Inspection, Railway Guards, Prison Service, Government Protection Bureau, State Fishing Guards, State Game-Keepers Guards, State Fire Guards, municipal and communal guards, and various special armed protective formations. Police tasks in the military are performed by the Military Police.

The basic duties of the police are:

- To protect the life and health of the people and their property

- To provide security and public order in public places, in public transportation and communication, on the highways and streets, and on the waterways designated for common use

- To prevent crimes and criminal activity by cooperating with state agencies, self-governmental bodies, and public organizations

- To detect crimes and misdemeanors and pursue the offenders

- To provide supervision via municipal guards and special armed forces

- To cooperate with the police services of other nations and international organizations

- To gather, process, and transmit criminal information

- To maintain the National Information System

Principal Agencies and Divisions. The Polish police are composed of the following kinds of services: criminal (33% of police officers), preventive (58%), and supporting the police activity in organizational, logistic, and technical fields (9% of police officers). Their separate organizational entities are:

- Court Police

- Higher School of Police, police training centers and police schools

- Prevention units and antiterrorist subunits

- Research and development units

Other kinds of the police service can be established by the chief commander of the police with approval of the minister of internal affairs and administration. The chief commander, who is subordinated to the minister of internal affairs and administration, is responsible for the protection of the people and the maintenance of public safety and civil order. The chief commander is appointed and dismissed by the prime minister at the request of the minister of internal affairs and administration. The chief commander has three deputies who are appointed and dismissed by the internal affairs minister. The chief commander's office is the National Police General Headquarters, which is composed of bureaus managed by directors. The most important is the Central Bureau of Investigation (about 2,000 officials). There is also the Chief Commander's Cabinet, the Protection of Classified

Information and Inspection Bureau, the Internal Affairs Bureau, the Internal Audit Unit, the Police Strategy Bureau, the Crime Intelligence Directorate, the Central Forensic Laboratory, the International Police Cooperation Bureau, the Logistics Bureau, the Financial Bureau, the Communication and Automation Bureau, the General Staff Bureau, the Crime Combat Tactics Bureau, the Police Academy, and the National Center of Criminal Information.

The following organs are responsible for the protection of the people and the maintenance of public safety and civil order: *voivode*-ship commandants (Szczecin, Gdańsk, Bydgoszcz, Poznań, Olsztyn, Białystok, Gorzów Wielkopolski, Łódź, Lublin, Kraków, Wrocław, Opole, Katowice, Rzeszów, Kielce, and Radom) and metropolitan commandant (Warsaw), commandants of specialized police stations (railway, water, airport, and metro—15), county commandants (270), municipal commandants (65), and police station commandants (618). Their supporting offices are respectively: *voivode*-ship headquarters of the police, Warsaw Metropolitan Headquarters of the Police, specialized police stations, county headquarters of the police, municipal headquarters of the police, and police stations. The *voivode*-ship (metropolitan) commandant of the police is appointed and dismissed by the minister of internal affairs and administration at the request of the chief commander of the police in agreement with the *voivode*. The county (municipal) commandant is appointed and dismissed by the *voivode*-ship commandant in agreement with the *starost* of a district. The police station's commandant is appointed and dismissed by the county (municipal) commandant after consulting a chief officer(s) group of villages (mayor or president of a city).

Salaries. The police service ensures a relative stability of employment; however, it does not guarantee particularly high salaries. Salary depends on several factors, the most important being classification, which comprises eighteen professional groups (categories). As such, the basic salary is 1,355 Polish złotys. To determine the actual salary, one can multiply this by the respective coefficient. For the lowest group (1) it is 0.65, for the highest group (18) it is 4.41.

The basic salary is supplemented by allowances. An allowance for a term of service becomes available after two years' service. One percent is applied for each year of service, up to 20 percent. Between twenty and thirty years of service the allowance increases by 0.5 percent per year, coming up to maximum amount of 25 percent. The following are sample allowances (in złotys) for the respective police rank: private (320), sergeant (440), staff ensign (595), commissioner (635), supercommissioner (640), inspector (790), and inspector general (990). The following are more specific examples of allowances

(in złotys): private with two years of service (1,400 złotys), a sergeant with five years of service (1,900 złotys), a subcommissioner with fifteen years of service in a position of specialist (2,684 złotys), a commissioner with eighteen years of service in a position of an expert (3,310 złotys), a supercommissioner with twenty years of service in a position of the police station's commandant (3,490 złotys), a subinspector with twenty years of service in a position of commandant of district police (4,870 złotys), a subinspector with twenty years of service in a position of head of division in National Police General Headquarters (5,200 złotys), an inspector with twenty-one years of service in a position of deputy commandant of regional police (6,230 złotys), an inspector with twenty-two years of service in a position of director of bureau in National Police General Headquarters (7,060 złotys), a superinspector with twenty-two years of service in a position of commandant of regional police (7,210 złotys), and an inspector general with twenty-five years of service in a position of chief commander of the National Police (12,490 złotys).

Functional allowances are granted in three categories according to the position held: in the amount of 60 percent of basic salary (e.g., police spokesman), 70 percent (e.g., head of division) and 80 percent (e.g., chief of the police station). An official (service) allowance is granted in an amount up to 50 percent of the basic salary. A uniform allowance is paid once a year; its amount depends on rank (and to a small degree on sex). The following are sample uniform allowances (in złotys) for the respective police rank: inspector general and superinspector (2,930 złotys), commissioned officers (2,056 złotys), and noncommissioned and other police officers (2,020 złotys).

Retirement Age. Equal retirement rules refer to officials of the police, Internal Security Agency, Intelligence Agency, Border Guards, Government Protection Bureau, State Fire Guards, and Prison Service. Retirement assessment is based on the police officer's last occupied post. Retiring pensions come under valorization. Minimal retirement rights require a minimum of fifteen years of service; then, the retiring pension amounts to 40 percent of its assessment basis. For each year of service above the minimum of fifteen years, a retiring pension is raised by 2.6 percent. The retiring pension is also raised for various types of service performed in conditions particularly dangerous to life and health. Finally, a total amount of retiring pension cannot exceed 75 percent of its assessment basis. In the case of a full term of service (thirty years) a retired police officer obtains a retiring pension equal to his or her previous salary (in other words 100%) for twelve months. The age of a police officer is of no importance to gaining retirement rights.

Hierarchy and Ranks. The Ministry of Internal Affairs and Administration supervises the police, Border Guards, and State Fire Guard. The minister is the superior of the chief commanders of all these services. One of deputies of the minister is to supervise police work. The chief commander of the police is superior to all police officers. The *voivode*-ship commandant and county (municipal) commandant are superiors to police officers in the area of their activity. Besides their own tasks (investigation, prevention, and detection of crimes) the police also execute court, prosecutor, state administration, and territorial self-government orders. Police officers are subject to particular service discipline. However, if performance of an order issued by a prosecutor, state administration, or territorial self-government will lead to committing a crime, the police officer can refuse the execution of the order. This police officer should, neglecting official channels, report immediately to the chief commander of the police in such a situation. In connection with the performance of official duties, a police officer enjoys protection provided for public officials by the penal code. The following lists the four police corps and the respective police ranks within:

- Corps of Commissioned Officers of the Police (inspector general, superinspector, inspector, junior inspector, subinspector, supercommissioner, commissioner, and subcommissioner)

- Corps of Ensigns of the Police (staff ensign, senior ensign, ensign, and junior ensign)

- Corps of Noncommissioned Officers of the Police (staff sergeant, senior sergeant, and sergeant)

- Corps of Privates of the Police (senior private and private)

Promotion within the privates, noncommissioned officers, and ensigns corps is determined by superiors. A police officer can be promoted to the first commissioned rank (subcommissioner) if he or she has completed the Higher School of Police or, if he or she possesses a university education, has finished a training for graduates from higher schools and has passed an exam for commissioned officers. The president, acting by a proposal made by the minister of internal affairs and administration, promotes police officers to the first commissioned rank and to ranks of superinspector and inspector general. The chief commander of the police can be promoted to other ranks of commissioned officers.

Appointment to the next higher rank should be adequate to an official position taken and depends on an official opinion about the respective police officer. However, promotion to a respective rank cannot be earlier (besides in particular cases of advancement) than after a certain number years of service have been met for each rank: private (1 year), senior private (1 year), sergeant (2 years), senior sergeant (2 years), staff sergeant (2 years), junior ensign (3 years), ensign (3 years), senior ensign (2 years), staff ensign (4 years), subcommissioner (3 years), commissioner (4 years), supercommissioner (4 years), subinspector (3 years), junior inspector (4 years), and inspector (4 years). Police officers dismissed from the service are allowed to use their possessed rank by adding "retired." Deprivation of police rank follows a deprivation of Polish citizenship, conviction with legal validity by a court to an additional penalty of civic rights deprivation, or a penalty of deprivation of liberty for an offense committed with a low motive. In cases provided for by law, the lowering of a police rank is possible (e.g., as a result of a punishment within a disciplinary proceedings).

Police-Community Relations. The need to define in a new manner relations between the police and the local communities developed in Poland in the early 1990s. The term *community policing* is difficult to translate into Polish. In Polish practice it means simultaneously a philosophy; a strategy of police activity; and a partnership of cooperation between the police, individuals, and public and private institutions. Local communities have witnessed the following results: an increase in feeling safe and having a better quality of life, having more influence on police activity, and holding the police responsible for protecting society. The police have experienced more efficient crime prevention, are more successful at combating crime, and have a higher level of acceptance and prestige. However, it depends on mental (awareness of a service role) and organizational changes within the police themselves. At present, decentralization of the police tasks and competencies is being realized.

A fundamental institution is the community police officer. A basis for his or her activity is immediate contact with the local community, flexibility, nonbureaucratic manner of activity, and expedition and efficiency of intervention. The following are a few of the programs that are conducted: "My Community Police Officer" and "Safe Town/City," and within the latter: police educational programs (e.g., "Safe Way to School"), "Neighbor's Anticrime Program," "Be Helpful to the Addicted," and "Be Alert and Cautious." An essential element is building an image of the police within public relations. All police units have public relations people who are responsible for working with the media. Social confidence in the police is still on a high level. Social feeling of security within the neighborhood is an increasing process.

Special Police.

Riot Police. In Poland these units are called prevention troops. They were established in twenty-two of the largest cities by the chief commanders of the police. The troops number 6,000 police officers and are divided into companies and platoons. The troops are held in reserve by the chief commander of the police and are used anywhere in the country to control massive entertainment events and ceremonies, to pursue extremely dangerous criminals, to control protests and gatherings, and to maintain public order during states of emergency, such as during dangerous public disturbances, disasters, calamities and epidemics, and acts of terrorism. The troops stay and perform their tasks in the respective territory of the police *voivode*-ship headquarters. When the troops are not engaged in organized action, they do a patrol service for local police units.

Traffic Police. The most important tasks of the traffic police are to ensure security, order, and fluency of traffic on public roads, to prevent offenses and misdemeanors on the roads, and to apprehend perpetrators. The traffic police use photo radars set up in unseen places to record misdemeanors. These radars record the car, its registration number, its speed, the face of the driver, the date and time, and the location. Misdemeanors are recorded without stopping drivers. Road incidents are also documented by video radar installed in unmarked patrol cars. Every police unit has at least one department (section) of traffic police. Sometimes there is one department common for traffic and preventive police.

Education and Training. After 1990 the system of professional training was modified as regards substantial and methodological matters. The experiences of other countries (Great Britain, United States, France, and Germany) were used to introduce new curricular elements like human rights and freedoms and social communication. An important challenge was the necessity to train a new staff. It resulted in approximately 46 percent of police officers leaving the service between 1990 and 1996.

The professional training of police officers is now conducted on three levels: basic, specialist, and commissioned officer. Successful completion of training for each respective level is required for future career advancement in the police service. New recruits must go through basic professional training, regardless of their level of education. The focus of this level is general preparation for preventive service in the police. Specialist professional training gives a background for performance in one of three basic police functions: preventive, criminal, and logistics. The commissioned officer level is intended for police officers with several years in the service who passed both basic and specialist training. It covers police officers of the previously mentioned kinds of service. The intent of this training is to obtain an officer's rank and to further possibilities, such as seeking the post of command

Members of Greenpeace are detained by police in Warsaw, Poland, February 11, 2005. *Activists were protesting against the importing of genetically modified organisms (GMO) into the country. The protest took place outside the offices of Poland Prime Minister Marek Belka.* AP IMAGES.

in the police. Training focuses on interactive methods (simulating activity) and has a convertible nature because it is combined with professional practice in the police stations.

Until the past few years basic training was conducted by thirteen training centers. Activity at most of them was suspended due to a decline of recruitment to the police. As such, basic training duties were taken over by the police schools, which also handle specialist training (the police schools in Piła and Katowice—criminal service; the police school in Słupsk—preventive service; and the Police Training Center in Legionowo and the Higher School of the Police in Szczytno—all services). Future commissioned officers are trained in the Higher School of the Police in Szczytno, where improvement courses for managerial staff of the police are conducted as well. Future commissioned officers obtain a complete education in such police disciplines as traffic police, prevention, tactics in fighting against various forms of criminality, criminalistics, criminology, and victimology, various law disciplines (e.g., administrative and constitutional law, substantive criminal law, law of criminal proceedings, police, civil, and finance and international law), police professional ethics, human rights and freedoms, philosophy, sociology, psychology, economy and finance, and foreign languages (Russian, French, German, and English). The police officers having a higher education can pass a shortened training for commissioned officers. Within the Police Training Center in Legionowo exists the International Center for Special Police Training, which organizes international courses and conferences, primarily for central and east European countries.

Recruitment and Conditions of Service. Access to the police service is freely open for all men and women who have Polish citizenship, do not have a criminal record, enjoy full public rights, have at least a secondary education, have physical and mental powers (ability) to serve in armed units (formations) amenable to particular internal discipline, and are willing to subject themselves to it. Physical and mental powers are ascertained by medical commissions. Before entering on service duties a police officer takes the following oath:

> "I, the citizen of the Republic of Poland, conscious taking on myself duties of police officer, pledge: to serve the People faithfully, to protect legal order set up by the Republic of Poland's Constitution, to guard security of the state and its citizens, even with a risk of my own life. Performing tasks charged to me, I pledge to respect law strictly, keep loyalty with constitutional organs of the Republic of Poland, comply with an official discipline and fulfill orders of my superiors. I pledge to keep state and official secrets, as well as honor, dignity and good name of the service and to abide rules of professional ethics."

The official relationship of a police officer originates in virtue of an appointment. Appointment for standing follows three years of preparatory service. A competence to appoint a police officer to an official post, to shift, and to release from the post is exercised by the chief commander of the police, the *voivode*-ship (metropolitan) commandants, the county (municipal) commandants, and the commandants of the police schools. Appointment depends on the police officer's level of education, professional qualifications, and duration of the police service. A periodic opinion is given about a police officer. If he or she does not agree with the passed opinion, he or she can submit an appeal to a higher superior in a due term. A police officer can be shifted to perform the service duties or seconded for temporary service in another place, offi-

cially or at his or her own request. The decision on shifting or secondment is taken by the chief commander of the police (the whole state territory) or by the commandants of different levels (*voivode*-ship, city, and county). Term secondment is up six months; in exceptional cases it can be extended to twelve months by the chief commander of the police. A police officer can be seconded, with his or her approval, by the chief commander of the police to perform the service duties outside the police in the country or abroad. A police officer can be charged with performance of official duties at another post in the same place for a term up to twelve months. A police officer has to be shifted to the minor (lower) post in case of sentencing for appointment for the lower post punishment in disciplinary proceedings. He or she may be shifted to the minor post in the following situations:

- Decision issued by a medical commission on permanent inability to perform official duties at a taken post, if there is no possibility to appoint him or her to an equivalent post

- Uselessness as regards the occupied post, which is ascertained in an official opinion in terms of preparatory service

- Being discharged from official duties after receiving two succeeding official opinions issued with at least six months' break between them

- Liquidation of the occupied official post or for other reasons justifiable by organizational needs, if there is no possibility to appoint him or her to another equal post

- At a request of a police officer

A police officer who does not agree with being shifted to a lower post can be released from the service. A police officer has to be suspended from service activities if criminal proceedings against him or her in case of intentional offense prosecuted by the public prosecutor were instituted (usually up to three months). A police officer can be sent (ex officio or at his or her request) to a medical commission in the internal affairs department to determine a state of health and physical and mental ability to the service and to ascertain a causal nexus between respective illness and the service. He or she has to be released from the service in the following cases:

- Decision taken by a medical commission on permanent inability to the service

- Uselessness in the service settled by an official opinion in terms of preparatory service

- Disciplinary sentencing to dismissal from the service

- Valid in law sentencing for intentional offense prosecuted by the public prosecutor

- Renouncement of Polish citizenship or acquisition of a foreign state's citizenship

However, a police officer can be released from the service in the following situations:

- Being discharged from official duties after receiving two succeeding official opinions issued with at least six months' break between them

- Valid in law sentencing for an offense other than an intentional one prosecuted by the public prosecutor

- Appointment to another country's service and taking a function resulting from elections in the local government or in associations

- Becoming qualified for a retirement pension in virtue of obtaining thirty years in the service

- Liquidation of the police organizational unit or its reorganization connected with reduction of staff, if shifting of a police officer to another police unit or to a lower official post is not possible

- Expiration of twelve months from cessation of the service because of illness

In certain situations a reappointment in the service is possible (e.g., when decision on release from the service will be abrogated or recognized as null and void). A policewoman cannot be released from the service when she is pregnant and during a maternity leave (except in situations strictly provided for by the law). A police officer released from the service obtains the service certificate and at his or her own request an opinion on the service. He or she can require correction of the service certificate and appeal in due term to a higher superior as regards the service opinion.

Uniforms and Weapons. According to the law being in force in Poland, the police are a uniformed formation. The law determines the kinds of and wearing manner of a uniform, insignia of rank and identity badges, rules of wearing of uniforms, medals, and badges, as well as uniform standards. The uniforms, insignia of rank, and identification badges are proprietary and are worn exclusively by police officers in the line of duty. There are four types of uniforms: service, official, gala, and training. Service, official, and gala uniforms differ from each other by the kind of material and some accessories (e.g., a gala cord is a supplement to official and gala uniforms). Basic uniform elements are: gray-blue jacket or tunic with shoulder straps on which are insignia of rank, navy-blue trousers (inspector general and superinspector have dark-blue stripes), black leather shoes, gray-blue cap with dark-blue rim (it has a crowned eagle in silver with the inscription *Policja* [Police] on the cap) or navy-blue beret

with an eagle (antiterrorist units), and blue or white shirt (with navy-blue tie). The accessories are leather belt and gloves. In the colder months a short overcoat or overcoat with a navy-blue scarf are worn. In summer time a blue or white short-sleeved shirt (white one with a tie) is worn; there are insignia of rank on the shoulder straps. Uniforms for women differ slightly from the men's (e.g., women wear navy-blue skirts).

The Polish police use handguns, revolvers, smooth-bore rifles, machine guns, rifles, and carbines. P-64 handguns (120,000 pieces) and P-83s (8,600 pieces) are mostly personal firearms for police officers. Since the early 1990s the police have been using modern repeating handguns—Glock 17, Glock 18, and Glock 26 (7,200 pieces) with Parabellum ammunition 9mm gauge, as well as revolvers (mainly Astra, Taurus, and Smith and Wesson; 1,150 pieces). In the early 1990s smooth-bore 12mm gauge rifles (2,500 pieces) were added. They are used by antiterrorist troops, Central Bureau of Investigation units, and preventive and traffic police services. At present, obsolete machine guns—43 and 63 types—have been replaced by Glauberyt machine guns (9mm gauge). Over 11,300 pieces of these weapons have been purchased. Furthermore, police officers of the Central Bureau of Investigation and antiterrorist units use Uzi and MP5A3 machine guns (500 pieces). Since 2000 a weapons modernization program for the police and the Border Guards has been in progress. Among others, P99 Walther automatic handguns have been introduced.

Transportation, Technology, and Communications. The police use patrol and operational cars, field cars, ambulances, trucks, buses, and motorcycles. Some services use special cars, armored transporters, helicopters, and motorboats. They also use bulletproof helmets and jackets, gas masks, shields (including bulletproof ones), all kinds of batons, chemical throwers, water throwers, bullet-resistant coveralls, surveillance mobile robots, as well as police radars and breath tests. For coercive measures they use handcuffs, stingers, horses, and police dogs. In criminalistics there are investigation kits, chromatographic apparatus and spectral ones, portable metal, drug, and gas detectors, and equipment for taking fingerprints and transferring them into the Automated Fingerprint Identification System (AFIS) system.

Technology is obviously the most modern component supporting the police. The teleinformatic infrastructure corresponds to international standards (including European Union ones) and is fully prepared to cooperate and exchange information with other international systems (e.g., Schengen Information System, Europol, and Interpol). Since January 1, 2003, the National Center of Criminal Information has been functioning. Its tasks are gathering and transmitting criminal information. The system enables coordinated exchanges of information about criminality, crimes, and offenders. Applied solutions ensure the highest technological level of security. The system is useful to the police, the public prosecutor's office, Border Guards, Customs, taxation control and taxation offices, the Government Protection Bureau, the Military Police, the general inspector of financial information and financial information authorities, and the public administration authorities competent in matters of citizenship, foreigners, and repatriation.

The basic police informatic system is the National Police Information System, which is based on the most modern technological solutions and on the Oracle database. It can cooperate and exchange information with other systems (domestic and international). Its data provides information about wanted/missing persons, stolen vehicles, documents, objects, and weapons, criminal incidents, and acts of investigation. The system contains data concerning 12 million offenses, 7.8 million persons, and over 2.5 million stolen vehicles, documents, and objects. Access to the National Police Information System and nonpolice databases is secured by 5,000 stationary workstations in the police units and 400 mobile ones in patrol cars. The National System of Criminal Intelligence and Analysis has been working since 2004. It makes it possible to ascertain connections between events, persons, and objects. As of 2005 AFIS and the infrastructure for electronic fingerprinting (live scanners) compatible with Eurodac (regional police and border guards units) were being developed. The police intranet is also used for communication.

Surveillance and Intelligence Gathering. In cases of the most serious and intentional offenses and when other measures appear to be ineffective, a district court may decide on an operational control. A written application for this is submitted by the chief commander of the police (with prior written acceptance of the general public prosecutor) or by the *voivode*-ship police commandant (with prior written acceptance of the district public prosecutor). An operational control concerns the correspondence, delivery, and information transmitted by a telecommunications network. It lasts up to three months. A district court may prolong it in justifiable cases. In these situations it can also be decided on covert purchase or selling items of criminal origin, or objects that manufacturing, possessing, and trading in are forbidden, as well as an acceptance or giving a material profit. The decision belongs to the chief commander of the police (or *voivode*-ship commandant) after a written acceptance is made by a district public prosecutor. This activity lasts up to three months; it can be prolonged in justifiable situations. In these situations the police are allowed to use information concerning contracts of insurance and such data as bank secrets. After receiving an application from the chief commander of the police or *voivode*-ship commandant, the district court will make a decision. The police can also use secret informants.

Duties and Rights of a Police Officer. A police officer is obliged to keep his or her duties embodied in the affirmation formula. He or she has an obligation to refuse exercising of a superior's order or order issued by other bodies if its execution would be connected with the commitment of a crime. A police officer should wear the service uniform and equipment. The chief commander of the police determines situations in which a police officer in the line of duty has no obligation to wear a uniform. A police officer should produce an identity card that provides his or her name and identification and the organ that issued the card. A police officer must not enter into paid work beyond the service without approval of his or her superior. A police officer is obliged to make a report on his or her financial position (situation). He or she is not allowed to be a member of any political party. Such memberships are ended when entering the service. A police officer should inform his or her superior about his or her membership in domestic associations functioning beyond the service. An affiliation to foreign or international organizations or associations requires approval of the chief commander of the police or a superior duly authorized by him or her. A police officer should report to his or her immediate superior on his or her planned abroad travel if it is longer than three days. Police officers can associate themselves in the police trade union. However, there is only one trade union in the police community and police officers have no right to strike.

A police officer obtains a compensation if he or she suffers a detriment to his or her health or sustains damage to property in connection with the line of duty. In case of the death of a police officer in connection with the service, an indemnity is acquired by members of his or her family. Family members left by deceased police officers are entitled to police dependents' pension.

A newly appointed police officer is provided with a uniform free of charge. Later on, he or she is given a currency equivalence to complete his or her uniform. A police officer has a right to annual paid rest leave (26 working days). Police officers who perform their duties in extremely difficult conditions and who have attained a respective age or length of the service are entitled to paid extra holidays (up to 13 working days annually). There is also a possibility of being granted paid sick leave, special leave, and leave without pay for important reasons.

A police officer who does his or her duties satisfactorily, has initiative, and improves his or her professional qualifications may be:

- Awarded a citation

- Awarded a citation by an order

- Given remuneration or material reward

- Given short-term leave

- Awarded a departmental mark of distinction

- Recommended for a national medal

- Given an early promotion to a higher police rank

- Appointed to a higher official position

Police Officers Killed in the Line of Duty. Every year, more than 10 police officers are killed and about 450 are injured in the line of duty. Between the establishment of the police in 1990 and mid-2003, 92 police officers have been killed in the line of duty (2 of them in missions abroad—Iraq and Bosnia and Herzegovina). The names of the dead police officers are enrolled on the Commemorating Plate (at the Police General Headquarters and other police units). In 1997 the chief commander of the police established the Aid Foundation for Widows and Orphans of Dead Police Officers, which renders material assistance to the surviving dependents. In Warsaw there is the obelisk "Republic of Poland—for the Dead Police Officers" commemorating officials who have been murdered or killed in defense of the country since 1919. Memory about them is a stable and important element of tradition of this public service. Every year during the Police Festivity ceremonies take place there.

HUMAN RIGHTS

Before 1990 the attitude toward human rights was informal, both in the state and within the police. Nowadays, the observance of human rights and freedoms is considered to be one of the most essential components of state and progressive policing. Relations between human rights and the police are characterized by the protection of human rights as one of the fundamental police tasks, by the observance of human rights in the line of duty, and by the consideration of a police officer as a specific subject of human rights. Since 1999 the police have been involved in successive and unprecedented worldwide programs of the Council of Europe that are devoted to human rights. The Chief Commander's Plenipotentiary for Human Rights is responsible for the executive coordination of these programs in Poland. In celebration of the fiftieth anniversary of signing the European Convention on the Protection of Human Rights and Fundamental Freedoms, the international conference

"The Police Officer as a Subject of Human Rights" was organized at the end of 2000. In mid-1999 the World Organization against Torture and Center for Human Rights of Jagiellonian University carried out a pilot study on human rights awareness of young police officers in urban centers—Warsaw and Kraków (Mac Veigh 1999). Polish police have also been involved in preparation of the Council of Europe's guide on European Convention's values and human rights standards (Joint Informal Working Group on Police and Human Rights 2000). The Polish Charter on Rights of Victims was issued in 1999. The police are supported by the nongovernmental organizations Helsinki Committee, Helsinki Foundation for Human Rights (School of Human Rights), Center for Rights of Women, and La Strada.

CRIME

An increase in crime and unfavorable changes in its structure were the negative and indirect results following the political transformation in Poland after 1989. The transformation led to a disorganization of social life, unemployment, and a sudden deterioration of status of some social groups. The number of recorded offenses increased by over 60 percent between 1990 and 1989. Unfavorable tendencies in the crime structure included an increase in the threats of offenses against people and to a minor degree against their property; an increase in aggression, violence, and brutalization of criminals; more frequent use of firearms and explosives against individuals and law enforcement officials; the appearance of criminal terrorism and revenge crime; the development of organized crime, its professionalization and internationalization, and an increase in the number of criminal groups and organizations; an increase in the number of foreign perpetrators (e.g., so-called Russian-speaking criminals); an increase in demoralization of juveniles and their participation in the commitment of crime; an increase in economic and financial crime connected with the transformation process (e.g., corruption); the appearance of electronic (computer) crime; and offenses related to mass events (e.g., football matches and concerts).

Criminal Identification and Forensics. The National Police Information System has been functioning since January 1, 2003. It is a basic system of criminal information in the country. It consists of several mutually related modules:

- Incidents that are offenses mostly as well as traps. These are details about the category of crime, date and place of its commitment, and full particulars of crime (among other losses and secured traces).

- Information about perpetrators or suspects, wanted/ missing persons, unidentified persons, and unidentified dead bodies. These data include photos (right profile, frontal, and silhouette), signalment, peculiarities (e.g., scars and tattoos), pseudonyms, fingerprints, addresses, criminal and social contacts, and committed crimes.

- Things (including documents) having a number, thereby enabling unmistakable identification. These are things caused by a crime, used to commit a crime, or having or would have other connections with a crime or its perpetrator, which possessing or trafficking in are illicit.

There are also the National Collection of Cartridge Cases and Bullets from Scene of Crime, the Collection of Arms and Ammunition Samples, the Central Register of Lost Arms, the Central Register of Anonymous Documents, the Central Register of DNA Codes, and the Bank of Smells. Contemporary Polish forensics is a complex discipline. It uses methods and achievements of other domains from psychology and linguistics to chemistry and physics. One of the bureaus within the National Police General Headquarters is the Central Forensic Laboratory; there are also forensic laboratories in *voivode-*ship police headquarters. The secret services, Military Police, Border Guards, and Polish Forensic Association have their own forensic units.

Organized Crime. Organized crime is a relatively new phenomenon in Poland. Its existence was officially confirmed in the early 1990s. Polish criminal law does not use the term *organized crime* in principle. In police practice it is understood as a hierarchical criminal organization established as profit-seeking to commit continual and various crimes and planning to secure its objectives by corruption, extortion, and use of violence. Organized crime includes illegal traffic in narcotic drugs and psychotropic substances, counterfeit currency and securities, frauds causing damage to governmental programs and international funds, crimes against tariffs, tax, and foreign currency exchange regulations by participation in criminal affairs, money laundering, illegal traffic in arms and radioactive materials, environmental crime, crimes against good morals, illegal gambling, racket, and corruption.

The dynamic development of organized crime is linked to the transformation of a political system, an expansion of private property, the development of a banking system and stock exchange, and an increase in goods circulation and in market of services, both in the country and in international relations. There is a threat not only to the private sector and freedom of trade but also to the security of the country. Particularly, connections between criminals and political circles are dangerous. Since 1994 a special police service has been combating organized crime (at present, the Central Bureau of Investigation with its

regional branches in the whole country). Similar organizational units exist within the public prosecutor's office. Combat against organized crime is also conducted by secret services, customs and finance services, Border Guards, military information services, and Military Police. During the last few years new legal solutions have been used (crown witness, incognito witness, controlled purchase, and covertly supervised delivery). Poland cooperates internationally (Interpol, Europol, and Schengen) and is a party to many international agreements.

CORRECTIONAL SYSTEM

The corrections system is overseen by the Ministry of Justice. The prison services are public and the uniformed services are managed by a general director. Besides the Central Board of Prison Service there are fifteen regional inspectorates (Białystok, Bydgoszcz, Gdańsk, Katowice, Koszalin, Kraków, Lublin, Łódź, Olsztyn, Opole, Poznań, Rzeszów, Szczecin, Warszawa, and Wrocław).

The Central Training Center of Prison Service in Kalisz has three components:

- Officer's Division (10 months)—fields of study: penitentiary, security, evidentiary, employment and human resources, working conditions, logistics, financial affairs, and health services (number of graduates in 2003: 283)

- Officer Cadet Division (extension)—fields of study: penitentiary, security, administration, financial affairs, logistics, evidentiary, health services, communication, and employment

- Noncommissioned Officer's Division (5 months)—fields of study: security, evidentiary, logistics, financial affairs, employment, health services, administration, communication, and transportation; there are also 13 Training Centers of Prison Service (in 2003 about 8,000 people completed their courses)

Concerning the penitentiary infrastructure, 96 out of a total 156 prisons and remand prisons were constructed before World War I. Only 36 units were built after World War II. In 1938 Poland had a total of 344 correctional facilities and remand prisons. Concerning the age of these facilities, 8 were built between the thirteenth and eighteenth centuries, 86 date from nineteenth century and the beginning of the twentieth century, 15 were built between 1918 and 1939, and 6 were based on converted World War II prison-of-war camps. At present, there are 70 remand prisons and 86 prisons. Of the latter, 32 are external units and 2 are for mothers with small children.

Concerning prison manufacturing facilities, on December 31, 2003, there were 15 state-run prison manufacturing facilities and 27 auxiliary farmstead penitentiary institutions and remand prisons. Prison manufacturing facilities employ about 3,200 people, including 1,150 prisoners. In 2003 these subjects achieved the highest level of income from sale of products and services—580,000,000 złotys.

The prisons are overpopulated and in bad financial condition. Since 2001 the prison population has increased by over 50 percent, while the total number of the prison officers has increased by only 1.3 percent. There is no place for over 13,000 convicted people (Prison Management in Poland 2004).

Prison Conditions. Reform of the Polish correctional system in the early 1990s was recognized by western European countries as a model solution for central and eastern Europe. The quality of penitentiary activity considerably increased in spite of the relatively small expenditure of money. The prison service officers' treatment of the prisoners was changed because they recognized that the prisoners have some rights. A set of correctional measures was widened. It resulted in the improvement of prisons and an increase in the most important factors determining the efficiency of penitentiary institutions. During the last few years the number of imprisoned people has been increased and at the same time the costs for the correctional system have been reduced. Reproached failures concern penitentiary activity, immediate tutoring, employment policy, and health protection. The United Nations Committee on Human Rights has reservations regarding the practical implementation of minimal imprisonment rules. Among the prisoners there are more and more hardened criminals, members of organized crime groups, and extremely demoralized prisoners. Feelings of safety both among prisoners and the prison service officers has declined.

BIBLIOGRAPHY

Joint Informal Working Group on Police and Human Rights. 2000. "Policing in a Democratic Society: Is Your Police Service a Human Rights Champion?" European Platform for Policing and Human Rights. Available online at http://www.epphr.dk/download/hreng.pdf (accessed December 22, 2005).

Mac Veigh, Johanna. 1999. *Human Rights and Policing in Poland: Trying to Answer Some Important Questions.* Brussels, Belgium: OMCT-Europe.

Prison Management in Poland. 2004. *Guide Book.* Central Board of Prison Service.

Jacek Wegrzyn

Portugal

Official country name: Portuguese Republic
Capital: Lisbon
Geographic description: The most westerly of continental Europe, occupying the greater portion of the western littoral of the Iberian Peninsula
Population: 10,566,212 (est. 2005)

■■■

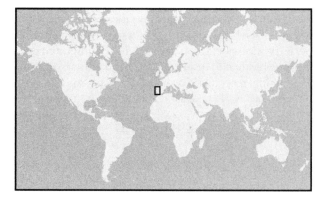

LAW ENFORCEMENT

History. The Portuguese government is a parliamentary democracy with an elected president, a prime minister, and a Legislative Assembly that are all freely elected by an anonymous ballot process. The internal security of the state is mainly the responsibility of the Ministry of Justice and Internal Administration. All security forces are subordinate to the government, and there is a defined distinction between the civilian police force and the military. This is an important point because before the 1970s this was not the case. In fact, the government was much more totalitarian in nature, with civilian criminal law being enforced by military personnel.

This totalitarian form of government ended in April 1974 during the revolutionary overthrow of the Caetano regime, which resulted in the establishment of a democratic government. Problems of fear and mistrust between the citizens and the police were a major issue during this time and this resulted in many revisions of the policing structure and the criminal code in Portugal. The constitution drafted in 1976 specifically addressed the responsibility of the police to defend the new democratic process and sought to ensure that they acted within

the legal parameters stipulated in written codes. This then clearly established limits to their own discretion and authority. The police were to observe the rights, freedoms, and safeguards of all citizens regardless of political patronage.

The constitution of 1976 drastically altered the role of the police to protect the civil rights of the population. This new constitution provided guidelines and obligations for criminal investigation and the treatment of suspects. The constitution also made it clear that citizens would not be held without trial or imprisoned without a defined sentence. This was important because before this it was common for people to be imprisoned for a variety of political crimes with charges that were unclear and with detentions of undetermined periods. Further telling of the changes being made was the fact that habeas corpus was reinstated in Portugal as another safeguard against unfair detentions. The habeas corpus addition applied to both criminal and military courts helping to ensure fairness in the detention of citizens. To add further weight to this provision, it was declared that a judge must answer any habeas corpus request within eight days. This demonstrated how the new government fully intended to expand the rights of citizens within the criminal justice system.

Another central component to the historical change of criminal justice in general and policing in particular was the clear disapproval of torture and other means of forced interrogation of the accused. Principles concerning the legalities of searches, seizures, and interrogations were all included into the constitution. Though these were all positive developments, there was still a period of unrest in the nation during the transition to a democratic form of policing.

During the months that followed the revolution, a sharp rise in crime was experienced that was especially problematic for the nation. This was because of the governmental state of flux that existed and because the police themselves were not always certain about their role within society. The disappearance of social and moral constraints as a result of tradition, regardless of the fact that they emanated from an authoritarian era, led to a state of near chaos in the country. It was not until the civilian police force was completely reorganized and retrained to operate in Portugal's new political environment that the nation saw stability. Furthermore, during this transition period it was necessary for the armed forces to maintain internal order. This initially seemed to breed more of the same mistrust between the policing personnel and the civilian population. However, control of the policing function was returned to civilian control in the form of the Ministry of Administration in 1976. This marked the official beginning of improved policing and police-community relations throughout the nation.

One final piece of history in Portuguese policing is likewise important but has as much to do with Europe in general. In 1985 France, Germany, and the Benelux countries signed an agreement in the Luxembourg border town of Schengen to remove controls at the "internal" borders between participating member-states and to introduce "flanking measures" to tighten up security at their common "external" frontier. That meant establishing common policies on asylum, immigration and visas, police cooperation, and the exchange of information between national immigration authorities. This is often referred to as the Schengen Agreement. This development has also produced the Schengen Information System, which is a database tool used to assist European Union members in internal policing of immigration patterns. In 1995 Portugal joined the Schengen Agreement and since then has been an active member in matching EU policing standards.

Structure and Organization.

Principal Agencies and Divisions. There are two primary divisions within the policing system of Portugal. The Public Security Police (Policía de Segurança Pública, PSP) and the National Republican Guard (Guarda Nacional Repúblicana, GNR). One other prominent division of the Portuguese policing system is the Polícia Judiciária, which is a police force that is highly specialized in technical, scientific, and even academic arenas. The Polícia Judiciária is theoretically autonomous from both the tactical and the investigative point of view. Beyond the Polícia Judiciária, all other types of police are divided by special types of duty.

The GNR was originally formed in 1913 and was a heavily armed quasi-military force that was technically called a constabulary. This constable force was structured in a military fashion up to the battalion level. It was actually meant to be a counterbalance against the military and was first employed to contain revolts from pro-monarchy resisters who were still in the military. Initially, the function of the GNR was to maintain a policing function in the rural areas of Portugal, but over time the GNR began to assist municipal police in riot control during various demonstrations, particularly those dealing with labor unrest. The GNR has typically been stationed in various major cities and district capitals of the various regions of Portugal. Some are also stationed in smaller areas of the more rural areas of Portugal.

By contrast, the PSP is a paramilitary police force that answers to the Ministry of Internal Administration. The basic mission of this police force was to protect property and public security in urban areas. Before 1953 the urban police had been under the control of the various provincial governors. During the colonial wars security police assault units were dispatched to Africa, where they assisted in combat operations against guerilla forces. However, the PSP has been reorganized and retrained since 1975, with its military equipment being given to the Portuguese Army. PSP detachments operate from the divisional headquarters in Lisbon and from the eighteen districts of Portugal. The eighteen districts and two autonomous regions are Aveiro, Azores, Beja, Braga, Bragança, Castelo Branco, Coimbra, Évora, Faro, Guarda, Leiria, Lisboa, Madeira, Portalegre, Porto, Santarém, Setúbal, Viana do Castelo, Vila Real, and Viseu. These districts are further divided into northern, southern, and central regions. Separate headquarters are in Madeira and the Azores.

The Polícia Judiciária is a more specialized branch of the police but is common enough to be considered a separate division of policing. This branch of police acts in conjunction with the court system in investigating crimes, especially those that involve subversion (politically driven) and terrorism. This police force is considered more

A group of Portuguese police officers protest against their poor working conditions and press for better wages and benefits, Lisbon, Portugal, June 22, 2005. AP IMAGES.

elite and prestigious in Portugal. It is a hierarchically organized body of police that reports to the minister of law enforcement. This police force is provided with excellent resources as its special relationship with the judiciary, coupled with the nature of its tasks, creates a demand for state-of-the-art equipment because of necessity.

Salaries. The Federal Research Division (1993) has documented the salaries of police in Portugal. in 1993 a typical patrol officer only earned the equivalent of approximately US$390 a month.

Police-Community Relations. Police-community relations have improved since the 1970s with the overthrow of the Caetano government. However, the use of torture is reportedly used among many of the police and detention personnel in Portugal. Though this is being removed from Portugal's policing tactics, isolated incidents are still reported to occur. This has caused some distrust among the citizens and those who visit the country. Portugal is actively trying to improve the police-community relationship.

Intertwined within the notion of police-community relations is the use of the community policing concept that is common throughout much of the European Union and has thus been adopted within the Portuguese policing system of service delivery. However, improved training is not the only initiative that has emerged in Portugal; the creation of specific programs has been implemented on a nationwide basis. According to the Consultive Counsel for the Formation of Security Services and Forces of Portugal (2003), Portugal has incorporated four specialized programs within each police jurisdiction:

1. Launched in 1996, the Safe Schools Program targets all the school systems in Portugal. This program is designed to protect school children and to sensitize them to the police in an effort to build future police-citizen community relations. Officers work in pairs with police vehicles set aside specifically for this duty. The officers are given specific training for this program. There are about 1,000 officers who are assigned to this program with roughly 450 police vehicles in place at school systems throughout Portugal. Officers are equipped with cell phones and first-aid kits to assist the community. Roughly 6,000 schools are included in this program.

2. The Aid 65, Safety for Senior Citizens provides for the reinforcement of policing in areas frequented by seniors. The police partner with institutions that provide services to senior citizens. Furthermore, teams of police have been created that specialize in security concerns of the elderly. This program is designed to protect citizens who may be in need for reasons beyond security and to improve relations with a generation that may have memories of the older era of policing in Portugal.

3. The Safe Commerce Program is designed to ensure the protection of local shop owners and business vendors. It is designed to improve police reactions to businesses that operate at the neighborhood level and are thus part of the common civilian population's routine economic and cultural development. The program ensures that there is a direct line of communication between shop owners and the police. The police likewise advise shop owners on security matters and invite the citizens of the surrounding area to various evening community training sessions.

4. The Crime Victim Support Program provides reception, guidance, and attendance to crime victims. This program includes partnerships with social service agencies and has officers specially trained for crime-victim trauma support. Also, in police stations throughout most of Portugal, separate physical facilities are provided for crime victims that are designed to provide a receptive environment that is not sterile and mechanistic in appearance.

Special Police. In 1990 the Fiscal Guard (Guarda Fiscal; also known as Treasury Police) was a border control force of 8,500 charged with customs inspections and the collection of import duties. In addition, they investigate smuggling, tax evasion, and illegal financial transactions, particularly those involving import or export businesses and currency exchange. Most of its uniformed and plainclothes police are stationed at frontier crossing points, ports, and terminals of entry. The monitoring of entries and departures by foreigners also produces a flow of information needed by internal security agencies. The Maritime Police have functions similar to a coast guard service.

Recruitment and Conditions of Service. All potential police applicants are required to have Portuguese citizenship and to pass a special criminal inquiry that goes beyond the general requirements. Different specialty divisions may have different types of additional qualifications. For instance, police jobs in public telecommunications,

computer science, and human resources may all require demonstration of skills specific to that line of work.

Requirements for admission to training consist of at least a secondary education. The age of these applicants must be between twenty-one and thirty years. The period of training for most of the policing positions is approximately one year. This is followed by a probationary period in which the applicants demonstrate competency in their given assignments. For the technical jobs dealing with computers or communication technology, applicants have to demonstrate technical expertise and they must be certified with a professional qualification. Some positions require the completion of a degree (the Licenciatura degree, which is the equivalent to a bachelor's degree). This is especially true with the Polícia Judiciária.

Uniforms and Weapons. The uniforms of the Portuguese police vary with the type of police unit. In municipal areas police wear blue uniforms; these police are typically the PSP and will not often be found outside the jurisdiction of their town. In the countryside and beyond municipal districts the police wear green uniforms that are typically quasi military in appearance; these police are the GNP.

Police Statistics. According to the Consultative Council for the Formation of the Security Services and Forces of Portugal (2003), there are approximately 26,000 GNR police and 22,000 PSP police. Furthermore, the GNR have approximately 600 different police stations that are responsible for about 90 percent of Portugal. By contrast, the PSP have approximately 200 different police stations that are responsible for the urban areas of Portugal; this computes to roughly 10 percent of Portugal, but over 40 percent of the Portuguese population (Consultative Council for the Formation of the Security Services and Forces of Portugal 2003). Riot police have typically consisted of the GNR. Traffic police are a special brigade that is stationed throughout various regions of Portugal. In addition, there are another roughly 1,500 specialized officers and investigators. The types of vehicles and equipment used include commando armored cars and at least twelve Alouette II helicopters of German manufacture.

HUMAN RIGHTS

As mentioned earlier, the Portuguese police have had community relations problems because of their previous methods of torture and interrogation. However, this is being eradicated from the policing elements of Portugal. In fact, in 2001 the Committee against Torture inspected the Portuguese criminal justice system and simply suggested that the country should maintain its vigorous measures of moving the police culture in Portugal to one that respects human rights. This clearly shows how the Portuguese government is making acceptable progress to protect the human rights of those who come into contact with its criminal justice system. However, in demonstrating that there is still work yet to be done, the committee did specifically note that criminal investigation and prosecution of public officers should be continued whenever appropriate when it was revealed that acts of torture, or cruel and inhuman or degrading treatment had been committed by them. It also expressed concern at continuing reports of a number of deaths and ill treatment arising out of contact by members of the public with the police and the interprisoner violence in prisons.

According to Amnesty International, citizens enjoy a broad range of civil and other human rights. Civil rights are outlined in the constitution with specific reference to the Universal Declaration of Human Rights. An ombudsman, chosen by the legislature, is Portugal's chief civil and human rights officer. Any citizen may apply to the ombudsman for relief. The ombudsman receives roughly 3,000 complaints annually, with many of these cases of alleging misadministration by the bureaucracy or delays in the judicial process. The principal human rights problem concerns credible reports of beatings of detainees or prisoners by police or prison personnel. It should be noted that these infractions against human rights are becoming less and less common as the police continue to professionalize. The government, criticized for being slow to investigate such reports, has dismissed or forcibly retired some officials found guilty of such abuse.

When considering arrest, detention, and/or exile, it is up to the investigative judge to determine whether an arrested person should be detained, released on bail, or released outright. Persons may not be held more than forty-eight hours without appearing before an investigating judge. Investigative detention is limited to a maximum of six months for each suspected crime. If a formal charge has not been filed within that period, the detainee must be released. In cases of serious crimes (such as murder, assault, or armed robbery), or more than one suspect, investigative detention may be for up to two years and may be extended by a judge to three years in unusual circumstances. A suspect in preventive detention must be brought to trial within eighteen months of being formally charged. If the suspect is not in detention, there is no specified period for going to trial. A detainee has access to lawyers and the nation of Portugal will assume the cost if necessary.

With respect to women, Amnesty International (2003) reports that women's groups have drawn increasing attention to the largely hidden problem of domestic and other violence against women. The law does provide for criminal penalties in cases of violence between spouses. However, Portuguese society maintains traditional social mores based on patriarchy and this discourages many battered women from recourse to the judicial system. In addition, there are criticisms about the services themselves since it seems that Portugal lacks enough facilities to provide relief to battered women. Traditional attitudes of male dominance persist but are changing gradually.

Lastly, concerning the issue of racial and ethnic minorities, Amnesty International finds some points of interest. First, the principal minority groups are immigrants, legal and illegal, from Portugal's former African colonies. African immigrants sometimes do organize and protest perceived institutional racism in Portugal. The government does deny that significant racist offenses have occurred, and for the most part it would appear that these denials are valid in Portugal. However, within the broader Portuguese society, as opposed to the criminal justice system, this is not necessarily as true. The Portuguese media reports of racially motivated incidents that were perpetrated by small, unorganized skinhead groups. Overall, it was reported that the police pursue such incidents as promptly as they pursue other crimes.

CRIME

Crime in Portugal is mostly concentrated in Lisbon, the capital, and Oporto. Regardless, several Portuguese cities have been encouraged, through the European Forum for Urban Safety, to develop municipal prevention plans; by 1990 the highest rise in criminal behavior was in the area of drug-related offenses. Court cases for drug use rose by 54 percent and those for selling drugs by 33 percent. Drug agencies claim that there are 50,000 heroin addicts in the Lisbon region and 50 percent of young people between the ages of sixteen and twenty-one who are arrested are drug users.

Organized Crime. Though not necessarily the most widespread crime problem in Portugal, developments exposing corruption in Portugal while organizing for Euro 2004 nonetheless drew international attention. Police arrested sixteen people, including the Euro 2004 league president for questioning over alleged match-fixing during the games. This was part of a yearlong anticorruption operation that uncovered several crimes of document falsification, sports corruption, and influence peddling.

Beyond the drug problem in Portugal, there is one other major source of organized crime activity that has proven to be particularly troublesome: human trafficking. International trafficking rings take Portuguese women abroad, often to neighboring Spain, and bring foreign women to Portugal. The Portuguese women involved tend to be from poorer areas and are often, but not always, drug users. The vast majority of foreign women come from Brazil, but some come from Africa as well. Many of the

Brazilian women are further transported to neighboring England, Spain, and France to work in the sex industry. Thus, just as with the drug trade, Portugal serves as a major gateway and shipping point for human sex workers. Russian Mafia organizations have emerged in Portugal and are now providing a supply of eastern European women for the sex trade in Portugal. One such network reportedly sells Moldovan and Ukrainian women for the equivalent of around US$4,000 each. The authorities broke up one such ring in 1999 that was headed by a nuclear scientist from the former Soviet Union.

Crime Statistics. Decolonization in Africa has brought over 800,000 unemployed refugees to Portugal, some of whom became involved in crime. Regardless of the reality of this claim, the Portuguese media and mainstream conservatives often portray this as a stark reality. The media frequently point toward young adults and discharged soldiers, unemployed and unable to emigrate, turning to crime. While statistics on the commission of crime between 1984 and 1988 showed a reduction in most categories, crime statistics from 1996 to 2000 showed that Portugal had a 13 percent rise in overall crime (Barclay and Tavares 2002). This is important because among the European Union (EU) nations crime rose an average of only 1 percent. Gordan Barclay and Cynthia Tavares (2002) report that Portugal's rise in overall reported crimes is the third-highest in the EU following Belgium (17 percent) and Austria (15 percent).

Drug offenses increased from 1,154 to 1,782 during the 1980s and continued to soar, resulting in Portugal's ultimate decriminalization of most drug-related offenses (Bureau of Democracy, Human Rights, and Labor 2001). Portugal was an important transshipment point for narcotics because of its geographic position near the North African coast and on the air routes between South America and western Europe. The Portuguese media and government make the claim that indigenous drug use and production are not considered to be major problems, but this is contradictory to the reality in the prison system and in the treatment programs throughout the nation.

With violent crime the situation is much different. Though not unknown in Portugal, violent crimes are somewhat less a concern. Murders are generally crimes of passion and are only infrequently associated with robbery. Premeditated homicide is punishable by a prison sentence of sixteen to twenty years, although mitigating circumstances often lead to reduced terms. In 1988, out of a total of 513 homicide arrests 205 were for negligent homicide; 331 of the arrested received prison terms (Barclay and Tavares).

Comparing homicide rates in various capital cities of the EU, Lisbon had only 85 homicides between 1998

and 2000, putting the homicide rate at only 1.55 per 100,000 citizens. This was well below the EU average of 2.48 per 100,000, making the capital of Portugal less dangerous than many capital cities of the EU member nations. Throughout the nation of Portugal, a total of 116 homicides were reported in 1996 and 127 were reported in 2000. This was an increase of 9 percent over the four-year period. However, when restricting this examination of homicides to between 1998 and 2000, the number of homicides went down by 3 percent (1998 had 150 homicides, followed by 1999, which had 131 homicides, and then 2000, which had 127 homicides). Thus, the number of homicides was higher than in 1996, but the trend toward the increase in numbers seems to have been countered (Barclay and Tavares 2002).

By contrast, of this small rise in EU crime, an average of 14 percent included a rise in violent crime. Portugal had a 28 percent rise in violent crime, which means that while indicators of homicide were lower than average, the amount of violent crimes aside from homicide has increased and is double the average increase throughout the European Union. In 1996 a total of 15,494 violent crimes (assault and sexual assault) were reported in Portugal. This rose in 1997 to 16,733 and then dipped to 15,463 in 1998. This dip in violent crime is ironic because this is the same year that the number of homicides was highest during this same four-year period. Though speculation, it is proposed this is probably the result of the overwhelming drug trade that had plagued Portugal during this time, resulting in an inflated number of homicides that were specifically linked to drug warfare, while throughout the rest of the nation generalized criminal assaults were declining. In 1999 reported cases of violent crime rose to 18,492, followed by yet another corresponding rise to 19,780 in 2000 (Barclay and Tavares).

Domestic burglaries declined between 1996 and 2000, with 22,798 being reported in 1996 and only 21,153 being reported in 2000. This is roughly a 7 percent decrease, but it is not clear if this is a literal decrease or just a failure to report this kind of crime among Portuguese citizens. On the contrary, between 1996 and 2000 there was a 32 percent rise in motor vehicle theft (Barclay and Tavares).

Barclay and Tavares note that the International Crime Victim's Survey of 2000 found that only 15 percent of all Portuguese report crime victimization, putting Portugal on par with nations such as Japan that are considered relatively safe countries in which to live. Among the reporting EU countries, this was the lowest victimization rate and only Northern Ireland reported the same percent of victimization. Thus, Portugal is tied for the lowest percentage of reported crime victimization throughout the EU (Barclay and Tavares).

Larceny was by far the most common form of crime. In 1988 over 41,000 thefts of all kinds were recorded. More specifically, there were 12,800 thefts under aggravated circumstances, 4,000 armed or violent thefts, 7,400 cases of breaking and entering, and 5,300 automobile thefts. In 1988 nearly 4,000 cases of fraud and more than 17,000 cases involving bad checks were reported, although few of the latter resulted in court trials (Barclay and Tavares).

CORRECTIONAL SYSTEM

The Portuguese prison system operates under the Ministry of Justice. The type of prison regime to which an offender is sentenced is determined by the district punishment court on conviction. Youthful offenders are often given opportunities to learn trades. The mastery of a trade while in prison and good behavior are considered in reducing time spent in prison. Individuals convicted three times of the same crime are considered a danger to society and are not usually eligible for parole. Unlike other prisoners, who might be allowed to do farm work, they might be kept to a strict prison regime. All prisoners are allowed to earn money for their work while in prison, and work is considered a necessary part of the rehabilitation process.

Prison Conditions. Amnesty International reports that although investment in prisons has increased and buildings have been renovated in the past few years, the prison system of Portugal is still held to be inadequate. Besides being overcrowded, many of the facilities do not have adequate physical accommodations for long-term human dwelling. Poor hygiene and medical services have also been cited. Some facilities are thought to have problems with infectious diseases as well (International Centre for Prison Studies 2004). In 2004 an inspection was conducted by the ombudsman for justice who recognized that the prison authorities have made an effective effort to improve the living conditions during the past few years. However, these improvements did not offset the rampant contagious diseases and the widespread drug dependency among inmates in the prison population. In fact, the drug dependency issue has become a primary concern among prison officials, particularly when considering that drugs are a major social issue in Portugal. It is hoped that the decriminalization of drugs in Portugal will result in less inmates with drug dependency issues in the prison system. This would most likely reduce the amount of infectious disease within the prison system since the HIV/AIDS issue is so intertwined with the drug dependency issue of inmates in the Portuguese prison system.

The U.S. Department of State reports that health problems such as hepatitis and drug dependency remain a concern and prisoners suffer from a high AIDS infection rate. In 1999 the health-services director of the Bureau of Prisons reported that seven out of every ten convicts entering the prison system were infected with AIDS, hepatitis B, or hepatitis C. An estimated 20 percent of the total prison population is infected with AIDS. Tuberculosis is also on the rise. Prison health services, although still not adequately staffed, have benefited from increased spending on health services, the use of local health-care providers to help prison inmates, and the construction of new health-care facilities in many prisons.

Prison Statistics. As of 2004 there were 59 prisons and 3 military prisons in Portugal. Of the civilian prisons, there were 20 central prisons, 35 regional prisons, and 4 special institutions (International Centre for Prison Studies). The total prison capacity of the Portuguese prison system was 11,603. The Portuguese prison system is overcrowded with more inmates than are designed for these facilities. Because of this, many criminal punishments are handled through fines or probation. There are over 14,000 inmates, of which 6,964 were adult males, 475 were adult females, and 922 were youths under the age of 21 (International Center for Prison Studies). There were 186 military prisoners. The prison population had remained fairly stable between 1984 and 1988. By far, the largest institutions were the central prisons, which had a total capacity of 4,870. The regional prison capacity was 1,758; the special prison, 706; and the military prisons, 299 (Federal Research Division 1993).

The incarceration rate of Portugal is 134 persons per 100,000 as based on an estimated prison population of 13,223 in September 2003. Within the prison population of Portugal, 29.2 percent are held as pretrial detainees or are on remand. About 8.1 percent of the inmate population is female, and another 2.1 percent are juvenile offenders. Further still, roughly 12 percent of the Portuguese prison population consists of foreign offenders (International Centre for Prison Studies).

Seven reformatories held 457 male youths, and 211 female juveniles were detained at three institutions. The remainder were assigned to observation and social action centers at Lisbon, Porto, and Coimbra (International Center for Prison Studies). The average time served in prisons by adult males was about six months. The incarceration ratio in 1990 was 83 per 100,000 population, comparable to the ratios in neighboring Spain and France but only one-fifth that of the United States (Federal Research Division).

MOST SIGNIFICANT ISSUE FACING THE COUNTRY

Perhaps the most significant issue facing this country is the illegal transportation of drugs. According to the European Monitoring Center for Drugs and Drug Addiction (2003), the number of hard-drug addicts in Portugal has escalated since the 1990s, and Portugal has Europe's highest HIV infection rate. Portugal, with a population of 10 million, has between 50,000 and 200,000 drug addicts. By contrast, the Netherlands, with 16 million inhabitants and a liberal drug policy, has an estimated 25,000 addicts (European Monitoring Center for Drugs and Drug Addiction; Tremlett 2001; Bureau for International Narcotics and Law Enforcement Affairs 1997).

Portugal is not a producer of cocaine or heroin, but it is an important transit point for cocaine from South America to the rest of Europe. The country's long coastline and infrequently patrolled waters around the Azorean islands, and a shortage of law enforcement resources encourage traffickers to use Portugal as a transshipment point (European Monitoring Center for Drugs and Drug Addiction; Tremlett; Bureau for International Narcotics and Law Enforcement Affairs 1997). Portuguese law enforcement entities attribute the drop in the quantity of drugs seized in the first half of 1996 to their heightened vigilance; they believe this may have deterred some traffickers or caused them to change their smuggling methods. Portugal was a party to the 1988 United Nations Convention.

Portugal's significance in the international drug trade stems from its location as an entry point to the rest of Europe for heroin and cocaine. Open borders with other western European countries facilitate the trafficking of heroin through the Netherlands and Spain and cocaine trafficking from Brazil. Although the size of the local drug user population is unknown, anecdotal information suggests it has increased in recent years. One indicator of this trend is the increased incidence of AIDS among intravenous drug users, which has grown fivefold over the last five years (Drug Reform Coordination Network 2001; European Monitoring Center for Drugs and Drug Addiction; Tremlett; Bureau for International Narcotics and Law Enforcement Affairs 1997).

Portuguese counternarcotics authorities demonstrated greater efforts at coordination. The government of Portugal organized a national coordination meeting of all relevant law enforcement agencies and departments; several regional meetings followed. The National Institute of Advanced Criminal Science has provided narcotics-related courses for officials from Angola, Mozambique, Cape Verde, and Guinea-Bissau. The PSP has also given counternarcotic courses to various African officials as well. Portugal and Spain signed a joint communication that provides for the establishment of police stations along the border of both of these nations. Each of these stations will have both Portuguese and Spanish personnel working within them.

Because the drug problem is overwhelming Portugal, the government has decriminalized the use of drugs. It was reported that police had stopped arresting suspects and that the courts were dismissing cases rather than enforcing legislatively mandated sentences for up to three years. The drug liberalization is even more progressive and permissive than most other European countries. However, Portugal now observes drug abuse to be a disease rather than a criminal issue.

The Portuguese government has adopted a National Drug Policy Council that coordinates Portugal's demand-reduction and treatment programs. Demand reduction in Portugal has consisted mostly of a few government-funded treatment centers and a few educational programs. Many new private centers have opened in recent years, but their effectiveness has not been subject to any form of scrutiny.

BIBLIOGRAPHY

Amnesty International. 2003. "Portugal 2003 Report." Available online at http://web.amnesty.org/report2003/prt-summary-eng (accessed December 22, 2005).

Anderson, James M. 2000. *The History of Portugal*. Westport, CT: Greenwood.

Barclay, Gordan, and Cynthia Tavares. 2002. "International Comparisons of Criminal Justice Statistics in 2001." *Research Development Statistics* 12/3 (July 12). Available online at http://www.homeoffice.gov.uk/rds/pdfs2/hosb502.pdf (accessed December 22, 2005).

Bureau of Democracy, Human Rights, and Labor. 2001. "Country Reports on Human Rights Practices, 2000: Portugal." U.S. Department of State. Available online at http://www.state.gov/g/drl/rls/hrrpt/2000/eur/880.htm (accessed December 22, 2005).

Bureau for International Narcotics and Law Enforcement Affairs. 1996. "International Narcotics Control. Strategy Report: Portugal." U.S. Department of State. Available online at http://www.hri.org/docs/USSD-INCSR/95/Europe/Portugal.html (accessed December 22, 2005).

Bureau for International Narcotics and Law Enforcement Affairs. 1997. "International Narcotics Control Strategy Report: Portugal." U.S. Department of State. Available online at http://www.hri.org/docs/USSD-INCSR/96/Europe/Portugal.html (accessed December 22, 2005).

Consultive Council for the Formation of the Security Services and Forces of Portugal. 2003. *Community Policing: A New Security Culture*. Lisbon, Portugal: Consultive Council for the Formation of the Security Services and Forces of Portugal.

Drug Reform Coordination Network. 2001. "Drug Possession No Longer a Crime in Portugal." *Drug War Chronicle* (July 6). Available online at http://www.stopthedrugwar.org/

chronicle/193/portugalpossession.shtml (accessed December 22, 2005).

Escola Superior de Policia. 2005. "Instituto Superior de Ciencias Policiais e Seguranca Interna." Escola Superior de Policia. Available online at http://www.esp.pt (accessed December 22, 2005).

European Monitoring Center for Drugs and Drug Addiction. 2003. "Annual Report 2003: The State of the Drugs Problem in the European Union and Norway." Available online at http://ar2003.emcdda.eu.int/en/home-en.html (accessed December 22, 2005).

Federal Research Division. 1993. *Portugal: The Police System.* Edited by E. Solsten. Washington, DC: Library of Congress. Available online at http://www.exploitz.com/Portugal-The-Police-System-cg.php (accessed December 22, 2005).

Hall, B., and A. Bhatt. 1999. *Policing Europe: EU Justice and Home Affairs Cooperation.* London: Centre for European Reform.

International Centre for Prison Studies. 2005. "Prison Brief for Portugal." King's College, London. Available online at http://www.kcl.ac.uk/depsta/rel/icps/worldbrief/europe_records.php?code=160 (accessed December 22, 2005).

Machado, Diamantino P. 1991. *The Structure of Portuguese Society: The Failure of Fascism.* New York: Praeger.

Maxwell, Kenneth. 1995. *The Making of Portuguese Democracy.* New York: Cambridge University Press.

Polícia Judiciária. 2001. "Manutenção e Actualização: Polícia Judiciária." Available online at http://www.policiajudiciaria.pt/ (accessed December 22, 2005).

Saraiva, José Hermano. 1997. *Portugal: A Companion History.* Edited by Ian Robertson and L. C. Taylor. Manchester, UK: Carcanet in association with Calouste Gulbenkian Foundation, Instituto Camo˜es, and Instituto da Biblioteca Nacional e do Livro.

Tremlett, Giles. 2001. "Lisbon Takes Drug Use off the Charge Sheet." *SocietyGardian.co.uk* (July 20). Available online at http://society.guardian.co.uk/drugsandalcohol/story/0,8150,525037,00.html (accessed December 22, 2005).

United Nations Human Rights System. 2001. "For the Record 2001: Western Europe and Other." Human Rights Internet. Available online at http://www.hri.ca/fortherecord2001/v016/portugal.htm (accessed December 22, 2005).

U.S. Department of State. 1995. "Portugal Human Rights Practices, 1995." Embassy of the United States of America, Stockholm, Sweden. Available online at http://www.usemb.se/human/human95/portugal.htm (accessed December 22, 2005).

Wilkinson, Isambard. 2004. "Portugal Police Arrest 16." *Telegraph.co.uk.* Available online at http://www.telegraph.co.uk/sport/main.jhtml?xml=/sport/2004/04/21/sfnur021.xml (accessed December 22, 2005).

Kaine Jones
Mekisha Smith
Robert D. Hanser
Nathan R. Moran

Puerto Rico

Official country name: Commonwealth of Puerto Rico
Capital: San Juan
Geographic description: Island in the Caribbean Sea east of Hispaniola, on the Mona Passage that leads to the Panama Canal
Population: 3,916,632 (est. 2005)

■ ■ ■

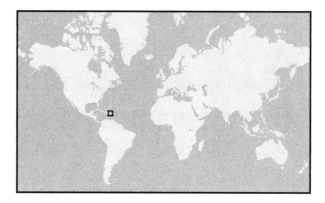

LAW ENFORCEMENT

History. From 1837 to 1898 Puerto Rico was under Spanish military rule. In 1868 the Civil Guard was established by Spain with authority over all Puerto Ricans. After the Spanish-American War Puerto Rico was ceded to the United States under the Treaty of Paris in 1898. In 1900 the island was granted a civil government in which all real power was exercised by the United States and the governor and the executive council were appointed by the U.S. president. In 1901 the Insular Police of Puerto Rico were authorized, but existing municipal forces were retained. In 1946 the island was granted full autonomy with the right to elect its own governor and legislature. The Insular Police continued to exist, but they were all stationed in towns. In the rural areas there were no patrols since the abolition of the Civil Guard. Rural barrios lacked any resident law enforcement personnel.

It was only in 1956 that a true police department was established. It consisted of two separate branches: The Insular Police Commission, which dealt with recruitment and enlistment, only drafted rules and regulations and heard complaints against police for professional miscon-duct or violation of law. The second branch was the Office of the Chief of Police, which handled all operational matters.

Structure and Organization. The office of chief of police consists of four functional branches: Administration, Inspection, Technical Services, and Field Operations. Each branch is headed by a chief of bureau.

The island is divided into five areas: Metropolitan, North, South, East, and West. Each area contains the following cities:

- Metropolitan: Bayamón, Carolina, and San Juan

- East: Caguas and Humacao

- North: Arecibo and Vega Baja

- South: Coamo, Guayama, and Pone

- West: Aguadilla and Mayagüez

Officers in Puerto Rico stand guard at a blockade outside a farmhouse where FBI agents earlier faced a showdown with Puerto Rican nationalist leader Filiberto Ojeda Rios, Hormigueros, San Juan, Puerto Rico, September 23, 2005. Ojeda Rios, who was wanted by the FBI for his involvement in a 1983 armed robbery, died after gunfire erupted when authorities attempted to arrest him. AP IMAGES.

Each area office has five divisions: Administrative, Investigations, Intelligence, Traffic, and Juvenile Delinquency. The areas are divided into zones, which, in turn, are divided into districts. The Metropolitan Area is also responsible for the Capitol Police Force, Airport Police, and Mounted Police. A Detective Bureau operates as part of the Insular Police. A Public Relations Division at the headquarters serves the entire police force.

The chief of the Insular Police is the commanding officer who also heads the three-member Insular Police Commission. The commission establishes regulations and rules of conduct, directs recruitment and enlistment, appoints and removes all police personnel, sets salaries and compensations, and authorizes the annual budget.

The Federal Bureau of Investigation (FBI), U.S. Customs Service, and U.S. Marshals Service maintain bureaus in San Juan.

Police at Work. The normal working day is eight hours a day with a maximum of forty hours a week. Members of the force receive an annual vacation leave of two and one-half days for each year of service and an annual sick leave of one and one-half days for each month of service.

Privates may be promoted to corporal by taking a competitive examination and corporals may be promoted to sergeant on recommendation of the chief of police. Noncommissioned officers are promoted to second lieutenant on the basis of competitive examination. All grades above second lieutenant are filled at the discretion of the governor.

Education and Training. To join the Insular Police Force, candidates must be high school graduates, between the ages of nineteen and thirty-five, 5 feet and 7 inches tall, fluent in Spanish, and have a good character. They must successfully pass physical, written, oral, and psychological tests. The initial appointment is for two years. Officers are commissioned by the governor.

After acceptance, a probationary member must complete a six-month residential study course in the

Police Academy, where he or she is given intensive training in criminal law, departmental rules, first aid, use of firearms, conduct of investigations, report writing, and court procedures. Additional courses cover photography, ballistics, public relations, juvenile delinquency, and racial problems. Outstanding students then proceed to study police science at the University of Puerto Rico and attend the FBI Academy at Quantico in Virginia.

Uniforms and Weapons. Police officers wear navy-blue shirts, trousers, and peaked caps. They carry a .38 revolver and a police baton. All patrols are in regular police cars. There are a few helicopters. Horses are used in the Condado beach area.

HUMAN RIGHTS

In 1972 a Prosecution and Appeals Commission was established to deal with human rights abuses by the police. The commission has five commissioners appointed by the governor. The commission's administrative affairs are handled by a director.

CORRECTIONAL SYSTEM

The Prison Service is headed by a director who oversees the two main prisons and forty-eight smaller penitentiaries. The central prison is located in San Juan. There is women's prison, also in San Juan, and a juvenile detention facility.

Prison Conditions. Prison conditions generally conform to international and U.S. standards.

Prison Statistics.

- Total Prison Population: 15,046
- Prison Population Rate per 100,000: 386
- Pretrial Detainees: 38%

George Thomas Kurian

Qatar

Official country name: State of Qatar
Capital: Doha
Geographic description: Peninsula bordering the Persian Gulf and Saudi Arabia
Population: 863,051 (est. 2005)

■ ■ ■

LAW ENFORCEMENT

History. The Qatar Police was established in 1948 under British auspices as a municipal police force for the town of Doha. At independence in 1971, the force was Arabized, but the British-inspired style and structure were retained.

Structure and Organization. Qatar has efficient security and police services. The civilian security force, controlled by the Ministry of the Interior, has two branches: the Police and the General Administration of Public Security. The Muhabith, a state security investigative unit, reports directly to the Office of the Emir, performs internal security investigations, collects intelligence, and is responsible for sedition and espionage cases. The Mukhabarat, a civilian intelligence service, also reports directly to the emir.

The police force is commanded by a commandant who is a senior military officer. For operational purposes, the emirate is divided into four departments: Airport, Doha, North, and Umm Said. Internal security functions are performed by the Emergency Police Force, which is stationed at Rayman Palace. Specialized sections include the Fire Brigade, the Coast Guard, the Seaport and Marine Section, the Mounted Section, and the Police

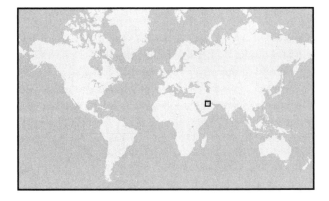

Air Wing. The Riot Division serves as a backup force to deal with demonstrations and civil emergencies.

The principal ranks in the police service are:

- Brigadier
- Colonel
- Lieutenant Colonel
- Major
- Captain
- Lieutenant
- Second Lieutenant
- Warrant Officer
- Staff Sergeant
- Sergeant
- Corporal
- *Shurti* (Policeman)

Education and Training. Training is provided for all ranks at the Police Academy in Doha.

Uniforms and Weapons. Officers wear navy-blue trousers and long-sleeved shirts, while other ranks wear navy-blue trousers and short-sleeved blue shirts. Woolen jackets are worn in winter. All ranks use submachine guns, rifles, pistols, and revolvers.

Police Statistics.

- Total Strength of the Police Force: 11,833
- Population per Police Officer: 73
- Percentage of Women: 4.57 percent

HUMAN RIGHTS

The government generally respects human rights; however, these rights are not guaranteed, but exist at the sufferance of the ruler. Foreigners, who make up over one-half of the population, have no rights and are frequently the target of abuse. The police also harass non-Muslims and those who offend the royal family.

CRIME

Crime Statistics. Offenses reported to the police per 100,000 population: 1,079. Of which:

- Murder: 2.1
- Assault: 7.1
- Burglary: 34.1
- Automobile Theft: 11.5

CORRECTIONAL SYSTEM

Prisons are administered by the director of the administration of the Penal and Reformatory Institutions under the Ministry of the Interior.

Prison Conditions. Prison conditions generally meet international standards. Women are held separately from men, juveniles from adults, and pretrial detainees from hardened criminals.

Prison Statistics. There is only one penal institution in the country, with an inmate population of 570, of whom 35.5 percent are pretrial detainees, 11.8 percent are female, and 55.6 percent are foreigners. There are no known juveniles in the system. The incarceration rate is 95 per 100,000 persons.

George Thomas Kurian

Romania

Official country name: Romania
Capital: Bucharest
Geographic description: Located in southeastern Europe, bordering the Black Sea, between Bulgaria and Ukraine
Population: 22,329,977 (est. 2005)

■■■

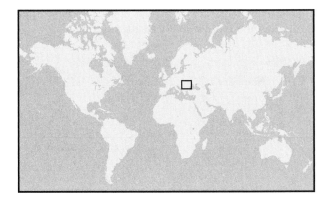

LAW ENFORCEMENT

History. Ethnic Romanians are descendants of the Dacians, one of the Romanized Thracian tribes that inhabited the Balkan Peninsula during the first millennium B.C.E. The region was part of the Roman Empire until 275 C.E., at which point it was occupied by the Goths. Between the sixth and twelfth centuries Romania was overrun by the Huns, Bulgars, and Slavs. In the fifteenth century most of the territory (specifically the provinces of Moldavia and Walachia) was annexed by the Turkish Ottomans, and as the Ottoman Empire entered its long period of decline during the early nineteenth century, Romania came under the Russian sphere of influence. Walachia and Moldavia formally united as Romania in 1861 under the rule of Prince Alexander Cuza. Romania subsequently backed the Russians in their war against the Turks in 1877. After the end of the war the following year, Romania was finally recognized by the major European powers as an independent state ruled by King Carol I; formerly known as Prince Charles of Hohenzollern, who had overthrown Alexander Cuza in 1866.

Romania was at war again in 1913, this time against Bulgaria in the yearlong Second Balkan War, and in 1916 joined the Allied cause in World War I. The postwar reorganization of Europe saw Romania gain several territories from the Hapsburg Empire. During the 1930s, along with European countries, Romania experienced the rapid growth of an indigenous fascist movement, the Iron Guard. However, King Carol II, who suspended the constitution and established an absolute monarchy, prevented any constitutional government from taking power, and in 1940 the Germans occupied Romania and forced Carol to abdicate. The country was placed in the hands of General Ion Antonescu, who promptly joined the Nazis in their war against the Soviet Union. In 1944, with Soviet forces about to occupy the country, the Antonescu regime was overthrown and replaced by a coalition government of Communists, liberals, and social democrats under the titular leadership of Carol II's son, King Michael.

The Communists gradually established their political supremacy within the government, and in 1947 the monarchy was deposed and the government declared the Romanian People's Republic. Nicolae Ceauşescu became the first secretary of the Romanian Communist Party in 1965 and held power in the country until the revolution during Christmas 1989. Despite being a member of the Warsaw Pact and the Council for Mutual Economic Assistance trading bloc, Romania was inclined to pursue independent policies, particularly with regard to military and foreign policy matters. Ceauşescu refused to allow other Warsaw Pact military forces to maintain bases in the country, and in 1968 he vigorously denounced the Soviet-led invasion of Czechoslovakia.

In 1985 Ceauşescu rejected the reformist policies of glasnost and perestroika, which were introduced by Mikhail Gorbachev, the new Soviet leader. Consequently, Romania lost its unique advantage as the maverick of the Soviet bloc. Also, domestic and international opposition increased as the true nature of the government's domestic policies became apparent. This included forced assimilation of minorities, tight rationing of basic items, and severe cultural and political repression. In mid-December 1989 protests in the city of Timişoara triggered a nationwide revolt. A large part of the army defected from the government to join the revolutionaries, and for several days the country was in a state of open civil war as the pro-Ceauşescu Securitate (secret police) mounted a desperate bid to prevent the collapse of the government.

The president and his wife were captured, quickly tried, and executed. The new government, under the provisional leadership of Ion Iliescu (the former secretary of the Communist Central Committee), was faced with a number of acute problems: the pacification of the country, the disbanding of the Securitate, the restoration of the economy, and the need to prepare Romania for peaceful multiparty elections. Iliescu has since become the dominant figure in Romanian politics, serving three terms as president. The next three years were a period of serious instability—occasionally breaking out into violence—as Romania made a painful transition from communist dictatorship to pluralist democracy.

The ruling National Salvation Front eventually split into two factions led by Petre Roman, who was the prime minister for eighteen months in 1990 and 1991, and President Iliescu, who formed his own breakaway party, the Democratic National Salvation Front (later renamed the Social Democratic Party of Romania). Over the next decade it was the Social Democrats who prevailed while the Roman faction dwindled away. However, at the November 1996 elections the Social Democrats lost control of both the presidency and the national assembly to a five-party alliance called the Democratic Convention of Romania.

In April 1998, however, Prime Minister Viktor Ciorbea resigned from office. Two transitional governments, lasting twenty-nine months respectively, held office until the next round of elections scheduled for November 2000. The Social Democrats returned to office and Iliescu took over once again as president.

Although the constant changes of government have confirmed that Romania is now a fully fledged and cohesive democratic state, they have made it difficult to pursue and execute major policy initiatives and this has undoubtedly held back the country's development since 1990. Economic progress has been irregular while Romania has not advanced as far as its east European counterparts toward its twin principal goals: membership in the North Atlantic Treaty Organization (NATO) and in the European Union. In 2002 Romania was formally invited to join NATO to the delight of Adrian Năstase, the government of premier. Membership of the European Union will take somewhat longer, however, and Romania will not be among the next wave of new entrants until after 2007.

Structure and Organization. Although the principal agencies and divisions of Romania are significant, the Romanian police are the governmental institution that citizens are most likely to have direct contact with on a regular, if not daily, basis. To civilians, the police represent "government in action" and thus may influence their overall opinions on and perspectives of the larger government, and its philosophy and applicability to their daily lives. Therefore, the police and their actions are of central concern in the transition to a democratic form of government. The actions of the police may either strengthen or weaken the public support necessary to sustain a viable democracy.

The national police force is the Gendarmerie created in 1850. The Gendarmerie has the following structure: the National Command of the Gendarmerie and the Territorial Command of the Gendarmerie with nine regional divisions at Timişoara, Cluj, Craiova, Constanţa, Braşov, Targu, Mureş, Bacău, and Ploieşti. These divisions are further subdivided into Judet (administrative district) commands, mobile intervention units, specialized subdivisions (such as alpine), the Mobile Intervention Brigade, training centers, and logistic and maintenance units.

Police at Work. The legal framework establishing the activities of law enforcement is primarily made up of Law No. 40/1990, which relates to the organization and functioning of the Ministry of Interior, and by Law No. 26/1994, which specifies the organization and functioning of the Romanian police. These two laws have to be completed with the Statute of the Policeman, the Deontological Code, and the Internal Regulations.

Hierarchy and Ranks. According to Ion Anghel Manastire (1989), the organizational structure of the Romanian police contains the following:

- General Inspectorate
- General Direction of Bucharest Municipal Police
- Police inspectorates (41 counties)
- Police inspectorates for railway, air and naval transports (3)
- Institutes for the training of the officers (3)

The central unit of the Romanian police is the General Inspectorate of Police, which commands, coordinates, and supervises the activity of the other police units. The minister of interior is in charge of the directorates, services, and offices of this organizational structure.

Police-Community Relations. Community policing training and technical assistance is provided for Romania's law enforcement officials and communities. Community policing is used as a form of crime prevention. The concept is based on the idea of a community-oriented, professional, and transparent police force, operating in close contact and mutual understanding with local communities. The aim is that the police see themselves and are perceived by society as a force at its service, not as an agency merely imposing law and order. The police must have the trust of the population. The basis of community policing is built on adequate legislation and support of the political leadership and senior police officials. Moreover, human rights education must be part of regular police training, and mechanisms of civilian control of police work have to be established. Community policing is also a custom-oriented approach to building partnerships to make communities safe and constitutes problem solving at the level closest to the problem. This form of policing involves channeling all the police resources to the neighborhood level to help solve problems and build self-reliant neighborhoods. Police enforcement strategies are based on priorities set through the community's identification of the problems.

The Research and Crime Prevention Institute has set forth some important areas of the Romanian Crime Prevention Partnership Program:

- Prevention of domestic violence
- Police-community partnership
- Prevention of drug and alcohol abuse
- Prevention of juvenile delinquency
- Prevention of property crimes
- Elimination of citizen tension and mistrust within the communities

- Police-community relationship and rights of citizens

Local Police. Local police authorities play an important role in the implementation of government strategies and policies at all local levels. The Romanian Police Department is a specialized state institution that exercises its functions within the Romanian territory. These functions are carried out in accordance with the regulations set in the Romanian Penal Procedure Code and in the Law No. 32/1968, which states the legal framework that is required for the fulfillment of police tasks and activities.

The Romanian police have approximately 52,000 policemen, of which 10,900 are officers, 37,000 are non-commissioned officers and military technicians, and 4,000 are civilians. More than 50 percent of these officers have acquired more than ten years of professional experience, with 17 holding doctorates and another 9,600 holding college degrees. However, because of the size and structure of Romania, the police force is able to have only 1 police officer for every 429 inhabitants.

Special Police. Founded in 1995, the Special Task Force of the Romanian police is assigned the most intricate operations. According to the head of the Special Task Force, some of the most basic operations include:

- Preventing and counteracting terrorist actions, seizing dangerous or armed criminals, and recovering kidnapped victims
- Granting protection to other government officials and police commanders
- Rescuing the victims of natural disasters and other catastrophes
- Defusing explosives
- Seizing radioactive materials

The bomb squad is another special police force of Romania with the basic activity including recognizing, defusing, and destroying explosive devices, which take the form of suspect parcels or vehicles, and any other cases in which explosives are used. Specialists from different regions are used to carry out specific tasks, such as bomb squad officers, chemists, electronics, physicists, and mechanics.

Another independent service of the Romanian Police Force is for control of firearms, explosives, and toxic substances. This department registers stolen and lost firearms and identifies crimes against the government in which explosives, radioactive, and nuclear substances are used. This special police service also supervises the administration that keeps the registration of authorized services dealing in operations with explosives and toxic substances.

Students from the Romania Police Academy participate in a military parade to commemorate the eightieth anniversary of the country's reunification with Transylvania in Bucharest, Romania, December 1, 1998. *The parade took place in front of the palace built by Nicolae Ceauşescu, a former Communist dictator in the country. Opinions about holding the celebration were split among political groups, some of who believed it was too costly in the face of tough economic conditions within the country.* **AP IMAGES.**

Riot Police. The purpose of the riot police is for protection and order maintenance throughout Romania. This force exercises its structures through the different departments such as the specialized forces of the security and order police, along with the road traffic police, which is always present throughout the streets. Security forces in rural areas also carry out specific duties. Romanian riot police officers, who are charged with maintaining peace, are equipped with protective gear, as well as batons, cuffs, and, depending on the circumstances, cars, horses, and dogs. The main objective of the riot police is to prevent disruptive and rebellious acts and impede on any other serious order disturbances. Another priority of the riot police is to undertake and reestablish public order in the streets by means of special intervention units of troops and police.

Traffic Police. The Traffic Police Department coordinates all police actions at the central level. Territorial units and offices direct the regional activities, while rural areas use public order forces to control and monitor road traffic. The most frequent causes of traffic accidents in Romania are speed limit offenses, incorrect driving, trespassing, and jaywalking.

Education and Training. According to the Management and Human Resources Department, it is necessary to train and educate the workforce of the Romanian police "to enable them to fulfill their new tasks, to preserve the public peace and order, and to protect the private and public wealth, and the rights and liberties granted by the Constitution." It becomes a priority to educate and train the police force for them to respond to the developing trends of crime. The Police Academy provides a four-year academic study for the police officers and graduates of the law school. Vasile Lascar, the noncommissioned officers' school, also provides an eighteen-month training period for all the specific activities of the Romanian police. Besides the training provided at the training facilities, a specialized professional training of the police officers takes place each year at each specific police unit.

Surveillance and Intelligence Gathering. As stated by the Informatics Department of the Romanian Police Department, the Romanian police are "presently equipped with mini and macro computers that have provided the necessary technical support for the information system consisting of a three-tier computer network: local, regional, and central levels." The system is designed to provide the department with efficient information on economic and financial crime as well as stolen cars. Public records, traffic police services, and criminal records have also become readily available; as a result, administration and supervisors may now counteract criminal offenses. The Romanian police also use their technology in the field of simulated behavior data processing, such as polygraph techniques and physical-chemical analysis.

HUMAN RIGHTS

The Romanian constitution, under Title 2 of the fundamental rights, freedoms, and duties (articles 22–49), grants all Romanian citizens the right to life, physical and mental integrity, personal freedom, defense, personal and family privacy, information, education, protection of health, vote, be elected, association, labor and social protection of labor, strike, protection of private property, inheritance right, petition, restriction on the exercise of certain rights or freedoms, as well as the freedom of movement, conscience, expression, and assembly.

CRIME

According to the Judicial Police Department Brigade General in Romania, some significant factors that contribute to a high rate of criminal acts are:

- Insufficient education and the lack of a minor's protection system
- Sections of uneducated citizens
- Excessive consumption of alcohol
- Citizen conflicts
- Lack of authority at home and in schools
- Victims of criminal offenses are not given adequate assistance

Criminal Identification and Forensics. The Forensic Institute of Romania classifies, administers, and directs activities related to the use of technical and scientific processes to investigate and help prevent criminal offenses. Highly trained and experienced police officers and specialists, along with trained experts in chemistry, biology, and judicial anthropology, staff the institute and are well known for their expertise and proficiency.

The disciplined and capable police experts are skilled and trained to approach and effectively resolve an extended amount of investigations and inspections such as: dactyloscopy, graphoscopy, ballistics, trace analysis, and microquantitative determinations. These proficient services are used in the investigations of drugs, narcotic, toxicology, explosives, fire traces, different kinds of ink and paper, inorganic analysis, different kinds of paint, glass, soil, and metal, and processing latent fingerprints.

Organized Crime. A specialized organization in counteracting organized crime has been established in Romania to deal with the new forms of crime because of the social and economical changes generated by the transition within the state. Every year, quantities of narcotics and psychotropic substances are seized, while the authorities combat several criminal groups involved in illegal migration, national and foreign currency counterfeiting, smuggling of stolen cars, and the trafficking of humans.

CORRECTIONAL SYSTEM

The General Department of Penitentiaries is a subordinate unit of the Ministry of Justice. In Romania the government, acting through the Ministry of Justice, decides on the prison policy, and by doing so, lays down the guiding principles for the institutional and organizational measures. The basic principles concerning the execution of penalties are provided by Law No. 23/1969, fundamentally amended in 1973, 1990, and 1992. This law contains provisions regarding the rights and obligations of the inmates, their work and wages, the grounds and procedures for their disciplinary responsibilities, conditional release, the surveillance of the convicts, access rights within the penitentiaries, the execution of the punishment at one's workplace, the execution of fines, the execution of the complementary penalties, and the execution of the pretrial detention.

Prison Conditions. Since a number of old prisons are still in use, the Romanian prison system allows more than one prisoner to be housed per cell. At present, overcrowding poses a major problem. During mid-2001 the average percentage of overcrowding was approximately 44 percent beyond the originally planned capacity (National Institute for Research and Development in Informatics 2005).

Prison Statistics.

- Total Prison Population: 38,805
- Prison Population Rate per 100,000: 179

- Pretrial Detainees: 15.7%

- Female Prisoners: 4.4%

- Juvenile Prisoners: 2.1%

- Number of Prisons: 45

- Official Capacity of the Prison System: 37,635

- Occupancy Level: 103.1%

MOST SIGNIFICANT ISSUE FACING THE COUNTRY

In 2001 and 2002 important steps were taken to criminalize illegal activities that posed a serious threat to public security. In Romania "human trafficking, together with all its social and economic implications, constitutes a phenomenon that has reached worrying dimensions." To suppress it, a special law has been adopted to prevent and combat human trafficking. The law includes provisions regarding the prevention of trafficking, the penal measures, victims' protection and assistance, enforced judicial procedures, as well as the promotion of international cooperation.

BIBLIOGRAPHY

Gheorghiu, Irina, and Stefan Gheorghiu. 1998. "Destinations." Available online at http://students.missouri.edu/~romsa/destinations/index.html (accessed December 26, 2005).

International Helsinki Federation for Human Rights. 2002. "Community Policing and Minorities in the Balkans" (October 31). Available online at http://www.reliefweb.int/rw/rwb.nsf/db900SID/OCHA-64CCLN?OpenDocument (accessed December 26, 2005).

Manastire, Ion Anghel. 1989. "Romanian Police." *Tipoart 2001* (July).

National Institute for Research and Development in Informatics. 2005. "Welcome to Romania." Available online at http://www.ici.ro/romania (accessed December 26, 2005).

Project on Ethnic Relations. 1994–1998. "Building Romanian Democracy: The Police and Ethnic Minorities." Available online at http://www.per-usa.org/Police.html (accessed December 26, 2005).

Regional Environmental Center for Central and Eastern Europe. 2002. "Country Report Romania: Networking." Regional Environmental Center for Central and Eastern Europe and Tisza-Szamos Public Benefit Company. Available online at http://www.rec.hu/frame2/RO_network.html (accessed December 26, 2005).

Romania.org. 2002. "About Romania—The Romanian Constitution: Fundamental Rights, Freedoms, and Duties." Available online at http://www.romania.org/romania/constitution2.html (accessed December 26, 2005).

World Travel Guide. 2005. "Romania: History and Government." Columbus Travel Publishing. Available online at http://www.columbusguides.co.uk/data/rom/rom580.asp (accessed December 26, 2005).

Lindsey Bowden
Nathan R. Moran
Robert D. Hanser

Russia

Official country name: Russian Federation
Capital: Moscow
Geographic description: Largest country on the planet, stretching from the Baltic Sea to the North Pacific Ocean and covering northern Europe as well as central and northern Asia; located in the northern latitudes, much of Russia is closer to the North Pole than to the equator
Population: 143,420,309 (est. 2005)

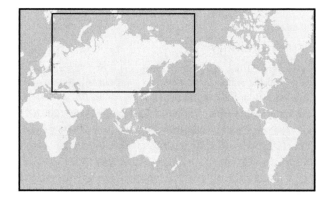

■■■

LAW ENFORCEMENT

History. The Ministry of Internal Affairs (Ministerstvo Vnutrennikh Del, MVD) of Russia was created in 1802 by a decree of Czar Alexander I as an integral part of the country administration system. Since that time, the MVD has been one of the key elements of Russia's internal security apparatus to maintain public order and national security.

Repeated devastating defeats of the Russian Army in World War I combined with a weak economy and uninspired leadership led to widespread rioting in the major cities of the Russian Empire and to the overthrow in 1917 of the 300-year-old Romanov dynasty. The Communists, under Vladimir Lenin, seized power soon after and formed the Union of Soviet Socialist Republics in 1922.

The Bolshevik regime created a police system that proved to be far more effective than the czarist version. It swept away the czarist police, so despised by Russians of all political persuasions, along with other czarist institutions, and replaced it with a political police of considerably greater dimensions, both in the scope of its authority and in the severity of its methods. However lofty their initial goals were, the Bolsheviks forcibly imposed their rule on the people. They constituted a dictatorship of a minority that had to establish a powerful political police apparatus to preserve its domination.

The first Soviet political police, created in December 1917, was the All-Russian Extraordinary Commission for Combating Counterrevolution and Sabotage (Vserossiiskaia Chrezvychainaia Komissiia po Bor'be s Kontrrevoliutsiei i Sabotazhem, VChK; also known as the Vecheka or the Cheka). The Cheka was mostly an ad hoc organization, whose powers gradually grew in response to various emergencies and threats to Soviet rule. No formal legislation establishing the Cheka was ever enacted. It was to serve as an organ of preliminary investigation, but the crimes it was to uncover were not defined and the procedures for handling cases were not set forth.

This situation was the result of the extralegal character of the Cheka, which was conceived not as a permanent state institution, but as a temporary agency to wage war against "class enemies." Given its militant role and extralegal status, it is not surprising that the Cheka, which was headed by Feliks Dzerzhinsky, acquired powers of summary justice as the threat of counterrevolution and foreign intervention grew. After an attempt was made on Vladimir Lenin's life in August 1918, the Cheka unleashed its violence on a wide scale—the so-called Red Terror—that continued until 1920 and resulted in thousands of deaths.

The civil war (1918–1921), the demobilization of the Red Army, and the introduction of the New Economic Policy (NEP) in 1921 brought about a changed atmosphere that seemed incompatible with a terrorist political police agency. Lenin himself spoke of the need for a reform of the political police, and in early 1922 the Cheka was abolished and its functions transferred to the State Political Directorate (Gosudarstvennoe Politicheskoe Upravlenie, GPU). When the Soviet Union was formed in December 1922, the GPU was raised to the level of a federal agency, designated the Unified State Political Directorate (Ob'edinennoe Gosudarstvennoe Politicheskoe Upravlenie, OGPU), and attached to the Council of People's Commissars.

On paper, it appeared that the powers of the political police had been reduced significantly. Indeed, police operations, during the NEP period, were considerably less violent, and the staff and budget of the political police were reduced. Initially, the OGPU was subject to definite procedural requirements regarding arrests and was not given the powers of summary justice that its predecessor had. But the legal constraints on the OGPU were gradually removed, and its authority grew throughout the 1920s. The OGPU was drawn into the intraparty struggles that ensued between Joseph Stalin and his opponents and was also enlisted in the drive to collectivize the peasantry by force, beginning in late 1929, resulting in the death of upward of 5 million people.

In July 1934 the OGPU was transformed into the Main Directorate for State Security (Glavnoe Upravlenie Gosudarstvennoi Bezopasnosti) and integrated into the People's Commissariat of Internal Affairs (Narodnyi Komissariat Vnutrennykh Del, NKVD), which had been given federal status earlier that year. The functions of the security police and those of the internal affairs apparatus, which controlled the regular police and the militia, were thus united in one agency.

The NKVD was a powerful organization. Besides controlling the security police and the regular police, it was in charge of border and internal troops, fire brigades, convoy troops, and, after 1934, the entire penal system, including regular prisons and forced labor camps known as the Gulag.

From 1934 to 1940 the NKVD took charge of many economic enterprises that employed forced labor such as gold mining, major construction projects, and other industrial activity. In addition, the Special Board, which was attached to the NKVD, operated outside the legal codes and was empowered to impose on persons deemed "socially dangerous" sentences of exile, deportation, or confinement in labor camps. The Special Board soon became one of the chief instruments of Stalin's purges.

Stalin's domination over the party was not absolute at this time, however. Dissatisfaction with his policies continued to be voiced by some party members, and elements existed within the leadership that might have opposed any attempt to use police terror against the party. Among Stalin's potential challengers was Sergei Kirov, the chief of the Leningrad party apparatus. Conveniently for Stalin (and perhaps ordered by Stalin), Kirov was assassinated by a disgruntled former party member in December 1934. This provided Stalin with the pretext for launching an assault against the party. Although Stalin proceeded cautiously, a turning point had been reached and the terror machinery was in place. From 1936 to 1938, the NKVD arrested and executed millions of party members, government officials, and ordinary citizens. The military also came under assault. Much of the officer corps was wiped out in 1937–1938, leaving the country ill prepared for World War II. The era in which the NKVD, with Stalin's approval, terrorized Soviet citizens became known in the West as the Great Terror.

The war years brought further opportunities for the political police, under the control of Lavrenty Beria, to expand its authority. The NKVD assumed a number of additional economic functions that made use of the expanding labor camp population. The NKVD also broadened its presence in the Red Army, where it conducted extensive surveillance of the troops. Toward the end of the war, the political police moved into areas formerly under German occupation to arrest those suspected of sympathy for the Nazis. They also suppressed nationalist movements in the Estonian, Latvian, Lithuanian, and Ukrainian republics.

Beria himself steadily gained power and authority during this period. In early 1946, when he was made a full member of the Politburo and a deputy chairman of the Council of Ministers (the new name for the Council of People's Commissars), he relinquished his NKVD post, but he apparently retained some control over the police through his protégés in that organization. In March 1953, following Stalin's death, Beria became chief of the MVD, which combined the regular police and the security police into one organization. Some three months later, he made an unsuccessful bid for power and was arrested by his Kremlin colleagues.

The "Beria affair" and the shakeup in the Kremlin that followed his arrest had far-reaching consequences for the role of the police in Soviet society. The party leadership not only arrested and later executed Beria and several of his allies in the MVD but it also took measures to place the political police under its firm control. From that point onward, violence was no longer to be used as a means of settling conflicts within the leadership and widespread terror was not to be employed against the population at large.

When the MVD was established in the postwar years, the security police was separated from the regular police. The MVD was originally established as a national ministry with headquarters in Moscow. In 1960 the Nikita Khrushchev leadership, as part of its general downgrading of the police, abolished the central MVD, whose functions were assumed by republic ministries of internal affairs. Then, in 1962 the MVD was redesignated as the Ministry for the Preservation of Public Order (Ministerstvo Okhrany Obshchestvennogo Poriadka, MOOP). This name change implied a break with the all-powerful MVD created by Beria as well as a narrower range of functions. The changes were accompanied by increasing criticism of the regular police in the Soviet press for its shortcomings in combating crime.

Following Khrushchev's ouster in 1964, Leonid Brezhnev did much to raise the status of the regular police. In 1966, after placing one of his protégés, Nikolai A. Shchelokov, in the post of chief, Brezhnev reinstated the MOOP as a union-republic ministry. Two years later, the MOOP was renamed the MVD, an apparent symbol of its increased authority. Efforts were made to raise the effectiveness of the MVD by recruiting better-qualified personnel and upgrading equipment and training. Brezhnev's death, however, left the MVD vulnerable to his opponents. Just a month after Brezhnev died in 1982, Shchelokov was ousted as its chief. Shchelokov was later tried on corruption charges. A similar fate befell Brezhnev's son-in-law, Yuri Churbanov, who was removed from the post of first deputy chief in 1984 and later arrested on criminal charges. After bringing several officials from the party apparatus into the MVD, Brezhnev's successor, Yuri Andropov, sought to make it an effective organization for rooting out widespread corruption; Mikhail Gorbachev continued these efforts in the mid-1980s.

The MVD had a wide array of duties. It was responsible for uncovering and investigating certain categories of crime, apprehending criminals, supervising the internal passport system, maintaining public order, combating public intoxication, supervising parolees, managing prisons and labor camps, providing fire protection, and controlling traffic. Until early 1988 the MVD was also in charge of special psychiatric hospitals, but a law passed in January 1988 transferred all psychiatric hospitals to the authority of the Ministry of Health.

As a union-republic ministry, under the Council of Ministers, the MVD had its headquarters in Moscow and branches in the republic and regional government apparatus, as well as in territories and cities. The internal affairs apparatus across the country was subject to dual subordination; local internal affairs offices reported both to the executive committees of their respective local soviets and to their superior offices in the MVD hierarchy.

The MVD headquarters in Moscow was divided into several directorates and offices. The Directorate for Combating the Embezzlement of Socialist Property and Speculation was established in the late 1960s to control such white-collar crime as embezzlement and falsification of economic plan records. The Criminal Investigation Directorate assisted the Procuracy in the investigation of criminal cases. There was a separate department for investigating and prosecuting minor cases, such as traffic violations, and the Maintenance of Public Order Directorate, which was responsible for ensuring order in public places and for preventing outbreaks of public unrest.

The members of the *militsiia* (uniformed police), as part of the regular police force, were distinguished by their gray uniforms with red piping. The duties of the *militsiia* included patrolling public places to ensure order and arresting law violators, including vagrants and drunks. Resisting arrest or preventing a police officer from executing his duties was a serious crime in the Soviet Union, punishable by one to five years in prison. Killing a police officer was punishable by death.

The Office of Visas and Registration was charged with registering Soviet citizens and foreigners residing in each precinct of a city and with issuing internal passports to Soviet citizens. Soviet citizens wishing to emigrate from the Soviet Union and foreigners wishing to travel within the Soviet Union had to obtain visas from this office. The Office of Recruitment and Training supervised the recruitment of new members of the militsiia, who were recommended by work collectives and public organizations. The local party and Komsomol bodies screened candidates thoroughly to ensure their political reliability. Individuals serving in the militsiia were exempt from the regular military draft.

The chief vehicle for party control over the MVD was the State and Legal Department of the Secretariat, which had a special section for supervising the MVD. This section presumably participated in the selection of MVD personnel and evaluated the MVD's work in terms of how well it carried out party directives.

Another means through which the party exercised control over the MVD was the Political Directorate of the MVD. This directorate, a network of political organs existing throughout the MVD, was established in 1983 and operated in a way similar to that of the Main Political Directorate of the Soviet Army and Navy. The Political Directorate was reportedly created because local party officials were not exercising sufficient control over the activities of internal affairs officials, but were colluding with them in committing economic crimes.

In the late 1980s the Soviet Union continued to place great emphasis on ensuring security and internal order. Because it was governed by a monopolistic party whose leaders were not democratically elected, the Soviet system had no legitimacy based on popular support and, therefore, protected itself from internal and external threats by means of a strong security system. The system included the regular police, judicial organs, prosecutorial agencies, and the security police, as well as an external security and foreign intelligence apparatus. Even in the era of perestroika and glasnost ushered in by Gorbachev, the organs of internal security had a key role to play, despite the party leadership's apparent tolerance of criticism of the political system.

The Minister of Internal Affairs was usually a member of the Central Committee, but up to the end of the Soviet era, had never enjoyed membership in the Politburo. Thus, the regular police executed party policy, but had little voice in policy formulation at the national level. At the local level, however, the police chief may have had more impact on decision making in the law enforcement realm because he was generally included on both the local soviet executive committee and the local party committee.

Internal Troops. A component of the armed forces, the Internal Troops (Vnutrennye Voiska, VV), were subordinate to the MVD. Numbering approximately 260,000 men in 1989, they were one of the largest formations of special troops in the Soviet Union. The Internal Troops were first established in 1919 under the NKVD. Later, they were subordinated to the state security police, and then, in 1934, they were incorporated into the expanded NKVD. They were back under the authority of the security police in the early 1950s, but when the MVD was established, control of the Internal Troops shifted to the MVD.

Like the regular army, the Internal Troops, for the most part, were composed of conscripts, who were obliged to serve for a minimum of two years. The Internal Troops accepted candidates for commission both from the ranks of the armed forces and from civilian society. The MVD had four schools for training members of the officer corps, as well as a separate school for political officers.

The Internal Troops supported MVD missions by supplementing the militsiia in ensuring crowd control in large cities and, in emergencies, by helping to fight fires.

These troops also guarded large-scale industrial enterprises, railroad stations, certain large stockpiles of food and material, and certain communication centers that were strategically significant. One of their most important functions was preventing internal disorder that might threaten the regime's political stability. They took a direct role in suppressing anti-Soviet demonstrations in the non-Russian republics and strikes by Soviet workers. In this capacity, the Internal Troops probably worked with the MVD Security Troops.

There was little evidence to support the theory that the Internal Troops would serve as a counterweight to the regular armed forces during a political crisis. Most Internal Troops units were composed of infantry alone and were not equipped with artillery and tanks; in 1989, there was only one operational division of the Internal Troops in Moscow. According to some Western analysts, the Internal Troops were to perform rear security functions in the event of war, just as they did in World War II.

The September 1992 law "On the Internal Troops of the Ministry of Internal Affairs" defined their responsibilities as:

- Assisting Internal Affairs organs in maintaining public order and public safety and in providing the necessary lawful procedures during a state of emergency

- Protecting important state facilities, communications installations, and special cargo as well as assisting in accidents involving nuclear material

- Guarding forced-labor institutions and escorting convicts and prisoners

In November 1993 the VV had nearly 234,000 men, and following the breakup of the Soviet Union the Internal Troops, in theory, became state agencies intended to provide domestic security in peacetime that did not possess the organizational structure for conducting ground combat actions against a foreign enemy. Functions carried out by Russia's Internal Troops include disaster relief and security, counterdrug and counterterrorism efforts, and peacekeeping operations. However, they have been particularly active in the wars against Chechnya, which began in late 1994.

Internal Troop organizational elements include:

- Operational units (divisions and brigades) and troop units (regiments, separate battalions) comprising the MVD federal mobile reserve

- Special motorized troop units that support public order in most of Russia's large cities

- Large units and troop units for guarding important state facilities, including nuclear arms and nuclear energy complexes and special cargo

- Large units and troop units for guarding forced-labor institutions (this responsibility, involving some 100,000 men, has been transferred to the criminal punishment system)

Structure and Organization. As of 2005 the MVD headed the system of the agencies of internal affairs (police forces) and internal troops (gendarmerie). The internal affairs system comprises district divisions (MVD main offices in federal districts), republic ministries of internal affairs, main offices, and offices of internal affairs of other regions of Russia. Each city, depending on its size and population, has regional offices of internal affairs, each serving to enforce the law and public security within its jurisdiction in vertical subordination. The ministry also comprises offices (departments and divisions) of internal affairs for rail, air, and water transport, offices (departments) for especially important and restricted facilities, preliminary investigation agencies, district offices for material, technical, and military support, educational, research and development institutions and other divisions, enterprises, institutions, and organizations.

The System of Internal Troops comprises internal troops commands, formations, military units, military training institutions and institutions for internal troops, and internal troops administrative branches.

MVD activities are governed by the constitution of the Russian Federation, federal laws, presidential decrees, Russian government decrees and regulations, generally recognized principles and norms of International law, and international agreements of the Russian Federation.

The MVD is the central agency in the management of law enforcement and crime control in the Russian Federation. It is comprised of the Criminal Militia Service, the Public Security Service, the Federal Migration Service, and the Logistics Service headed up by deputy ministers.

The Criminal Militia Service consists of Chief Directorate for Criminal Investigation, the Chief Directorate for Combating Financial Crimes, the Chief Directorate for Combating Organized Crime, and the Directorate for Operational Investigation Information and Coordination Office of Criminal Militia Service.

The Public Security Service consists of the Chief Directorate for Public Order Maintenance, the Chief Directorate of State Road Safety Inspection, the Chief Directorate of Internal Affairs for Restricted Facilities, the Chief Directorate of Interdepartmental Security Guard Service, and the Coordination Office of Public Security Service.

The Federal Migration Service consists of the Chief Directorate of Internal Affairs for transport and Special Transportation, the Directorate for Passport and Visa Registration, the Migration Control Office, the Foreign Labor Migration Department, the Legal Office, the Office for Crisis Situations, the Office for Resource Provision, and the Finance and Economy Office.

The Logistical Service consists of the Office for Material and Technical Support, the Finance and Economy Department, the Medical Office, the Office for Communication and Automation, the Office for Capital Construction, the Coordination Office of Logistical Service, and the General Service Office.

The independent divisions are the Office of General Affairs, the Main Office for Internal Security, the Control and Auditing Office, the Internal Troops General Headquarters, the MVD Committee of Inquiry, the Forensic Expertise Center, the Chief Directorate for Organization and Inspection, the Chief Directorate for Special Technical Actions, the Chief Directorate for Investigations, the National Central Bureau of Interpol, the Mobilization Training Office, the Main Center for Information, the Chief Directorate for Staffing and Personnel, the Main Legal Office, the Office for International Cooperation, and the Office for Information and Regional Contacts.

The minister of internal affairs heads the MVD. The minister is a member of the Russian government and the chairman of the board of the MVD. He is appointed and dismissed by the president of the Russian Federation as proposed by the prime minister. The minister of internal affairs bears personal responsibility for the fulfillment of the tasks to be performed by the ministry, subordinate agencies of internal affairs (police forces), and internal troops (type of gendarmerie). The tasks of the minister include:

- Organizing the work of the ministry

- Guiding the police and internal troops activities

- Defining the MVD officials jurisdiction

- Approving staffing and central administration and subordinate structures

- Issuing orders and other normative acts, including those binding on authorities, organizations, and citizens

- Submitting draft orders for consideration by the president and the government

- Appointing and dismissing MVD officials

- Conferring primary specialized titles on middle- and top-ranking officers, primary officer titles, and specialized and military ranks up to general rank inclusive

- Recommending MVD officers for decorations

Officers detain a protestor outside the Belarus Embassy in Moscow, May 4, 2005. *Several protestors gathered outside the embassy in efforts to advocate the release of Belarusian and Ukrainian activists who were arrested in Minsk, Belarus, for taking part in an antigovernment rally.* AP IMAGES.

The minister delegates some of the responsibilities for MVD administration to his deputies and defines their jurisdiction and specific area of responsibility.

Researchers on the Russian police system, most notably Mark Galeotti, have outlined the intentions of the MVD to reform its structure. As of 2003 the ministry was drafting a new Law on the Police that would completely reshape the structure of Russian law enforcement.

Recruitment and Training. To enter the police force, recruits must be Russian citizens between the ages of eighteen and thirty-five with at least secondary-level education. Recruitment is a federal responsibility. The Ministry of the Interior operates twenty-two institutions of higher education and eleven specialized vocational schools for police officers and there are branches of these institutions in every major city. The institutions of higher learning offer five to six years of study and the vocational

schools two to three years of study. Each year about 100,000 cadets attend these institutions.

Police Statistics.

- Total Strength of the Police Force: 700,000

- Population per Police Officer: 205

CRIME

Narcotics. Russia is a transit country for heroin and opium, most of which comes from Afghanistan and is destined for Europe. Given the porous nature of the Russian border with Central Asia and the limited technical and financial support for law enforcement, Russia is ill equipped to check the flow of Afghan heroin into the country.

Heroin from Southwest Asia flows through Central Asia, particularly Tajikistan and Kazakhstan, over the southern border into Russia, for domestic distribution and consumption and for transshipment to Europe and, to a much lesser extent, the United States. The Caspian Sea port city of Astrakhan and the Black Sea port of Novorossiysk are major transit points for Turkish and Afghan heroin into Russia. Vast amounts of daily sea traffic, consisting of passengers, cars on ferries, and bulk goods in trucks are used to conceal heroin moving into Russia. Both routes mentioned earlier are also used in reverse to smuggle multiton quantities of the precursor chemical acetic anhydride to the clandestine laboratories that produce Afghan and Turkish refined heroin. The lack of border controls with China and Mongolia facilitates smuggling, including drug trafficking, through that region.

In the east the Russians continue to import the precursor ephedrine from China for Russian domestic production of methamphetamine in kitchen labs in quantities for personal use. Cocaine traffickers also route Colombian cocaine for transshipment to Europe and elsewhere through Russian seaports and airports.

Russia is also a consumer of heroin because of high availability and low prices. Production of amphetamines and synthetics for domestic consumption is minor, but on the rise. Designer "club" drugs are increasingly popular with Russia's youth. Typically, ecstasy is produced in the Netherlands and Poland. However, in 2003 there were several reports by both the Russian MVD and the Federal Security Service (Federalnaya Sluzhba Bezopasnosti Rossiyskoy Federatsii, FSB) that ecstasy labs now exist in Russia. Although ecstasy tablets produced in Russia are believed to be of low quality, low prices for domestic pills attract Russian youth. Cocaine trafficking is not widespread in Russia, as the prices remain high. Although there have been many reports of cocaine being transported to the Russian port of St. Petersburg, no significant seizures of cocaine occurred in Russia in 2003.

Heroin trafficking and abuse continues to be a major problem facing Russian law enforcement agencies and public health agencies. Since the events in Afghanistan in 2001, opium cultivation and heroin production in Afghanistan has risen dramatically. Given Russia's large and porous borders with Central Asia, Afghan opium/heroin transiting Russia to Europe has become a major problem for Russia. This rise in heroin trafficking is reflected in the increase of drug-related crimes and the number of HIV/AIDS cases.

Drug abuse within Russia is a matter of concern for national health officials. In the beginning of 2003 there were 340,000 registered drug addicts in Russia. This figure only reflects those addicts who are known to health officials. The number of drug users in Russia is estimated to be between 3 million and 4 million people. Most drug users are under thirty and approximately 30 percent are heroin addicts. According to the Ministry of Health, as of October 2003, there were 251,000 officially registered HIV/AIDS cases in Russia, but the actual number is estimated to be between 700,000 and 1.5 million. As of 2005, 70 to 80 percent of all transmissions were through intravenous drug use.

Domestic distribution of drugs is handled by traditional Russian criminal organizations that have long conducted other criminal operations in various regions of Russia. Trafficking into the country is often handled by members of various ethnic groups who tend to specialize in certain categories of drugs in specific areas. Afghans, Tajiks, and other Central Asians mainly import heroin across the southern border with Kazakhstan into European Russia and western Siberia.

In November 2003 the Russian government passed legislation reducing the sentence for possession of drugs for personal use from a maximum of three years in jail to a fine. Additionally, Russia passed legislation increasing the maximum jail terms for drug dealers from fifteen to twenty years.

President Vladimir Putin has stated that controlling corruption is a priority for his administration. However, implementing this policy presents a constant challenge. Inadequate budgets, low salaries, and lack of technical resources and support for law enforcement hamper performance, lower morale, and encourage corruption. In October 2003 five GKPN agents were arrested on charges of extortion. The agents were allegedly taking bribes not to launch a criminal case against a drug trafficker. The agents were former MVD officers.

In October 2003 reports of corruption among newly assigned GKPN officers in Russia's Far East indicated that corrupt officers could earn up to 7,000 rubles (US$230) a month for protecting one drug sales point. A former police officer was sentenced to seven and a half years in prison for drug trafficking. There were no reported cases of high-level narcotics related corruption.

Trafficking in Persons. The law prohibits trafficking in persons; however, trafficking in women and children is a problem. There are no reliable estimates of its scope, but trafficking is believed to be widespread.

In December 2003 the Russian government enacted amendments to the criminal code criminalizing human trafficking and the use of forced labor and expanding criminal liability for recruitment into prostitution, organization of a prostitution business, and the distribution of child pornography. According to these articles, if certain aggravating factors are established, trafficking and use of slave labor are each punishable by a maximum of fifteen years in prison, recruitment into prostitution is punishable by a maximum of eight years, organization of a prostitution business is punishable by a maximum of ten years, and the manufacture and distribution of child pornography is punishable by a maximum of eight years.

Besides the passed amendments, other articles of the criminal code may also be used to prosecute traffickers. These include article 322, which provides for up to five years' imprisonment for unlawful violations of borders by a "group of persons in prior arrangement or by an organized group either using violence or the threat of violence"; article 133, which prohibits compulsion of a person into sexual activity by blackmail, threat, damage, or dependence; article 126, which prohibits the kidnapping of persons; article 132, which prohibits forced actions of a sexual nature; article 135, which prohibits perverse actions with children under fourteen; and article 134, which prohibits sexual intercourse with a person under fourteen. Articles 159, 165, and 182 all prohibit various kinds of fraudulent activity and could potentially be used to prosecute traffickers engaged in fraudulent recruitment efforts. Prostitution itself is not a crime anywhere in the country, but an administrative offense carrying a fine of 1,200 rubles (US$40). Recruitment for prostitution, domestically or abroad, is not a crime, but an administrative offense with a maximum penalty of incarceration for fourteen days.

The most common bases for trafficking prosecutions have been antifraud statutes and the statute prohibiting trafficking in minors. Traditionally, laws relating to the organization and maintenance of prostitution businesses have not been well enforced and it is believed that the MVD itself controls prostitution throughout the country. However, newspaper reports indicate that the Moscow police have begun cracking down on brothels.

Russia is a country of origin and transit for victims of trafficking. There are no reliable statistics; however, nongovernmental organizations, academic researchers, and law enforcement agencies in destination countries indicate that Russia is a country of origin for a significant number of victims of trafficking. Children are also trafficked, but more rarely. The virtual trafficking of pornographic images of children over the Internet is also a growing problem, with Russia becoming a major producer and distributor of child pornography in the last few years. This has led to confirmed cases both of sex trafficking of children as well as child sex tourism to the country. There were also extensive reports of human trafficking within Chechnya. Specifically, government and law enforcement sources reported that Chechen rebels frequently captured Russian soldiers during combat and then enslaved them, traded them among themselves, and ultimately sold them back to their families.

According to the International Organization for Migration (IOM), Russian women have been trafficked to almost fifty countries, including every western European country, the United States, Canada, former Soviet republics, such as Georgia, Middle Eastern countries, such as Turkey and Israel, and Asian countries, including Japan and Thailand. There are also reports of Russian women being trafficked to Australia and New Zealand. Victims often agree to be transported to one location, only to be diverted to, and forcibly held in, another. Sometimes they are "sold" en route, particularly when transiting the Balkans.

Reports indicate that internal trafficking is also becoming an increasing problem, with women and children being recruited and transported from rural areas to urban centers and from one region to another. The migration of young women from the provinces to the major cities to work in sex industries such as stripping and prostitution is sometimes facilitated by traffickers. The young women, who go annually into Moscow, sometimes end up in prostitution, and, once there, find themselves trapped. Smaller numbers of men are also reported to be trafficked internally for manual labor.

There are also reports that children are kidnapped or purchased from parents, relatives, or orphanages for sexual abuse, child pornography, and the harvesting of body parts. When police investigate such cases, they sometimes find that these children are adopted legally by families abroad; however, there are confirmed cases of children trafficked for sexual exploitation. National law enforcement authorities believe that there is a brisk business in body parts, but international law enforcement and other organizations have found no evidence to support this claim.

Reliable statistical estimates with regard to all these forms of trafficking are extremely difficult to develop. Few women who have been trafficked and returned to Russia report their experiences to the police and continue to be fearful of retaliation by the traffickers. Statistics are also complicated by the fact that some trafficked women are of Russian ethnic origin, but citizens of other former Soviet countries, such as Ukraine. Women from such countries as Tajikistan migrate illegally to Russia to seek work, and some are victimized by traffickers. Some migrants become victims of forced labor once they arrive at the destination.

According to an IOM report, women aged fifteen to twenty-five, particularly those interested in working overseas, are the most likely to be trafficked. Some surveys indicate that the profile of female trafficking victims in the country is similar to that of the female population at large. Women who are educated and have job skills also are trafficked. Traffickers offer enough economic hope to persuade even well-educated, mature women to become risk takers and entrust traffickers with their money, documents, and persons. Almost all returned trafficked women report that they traveled to better their lives through work or marriage abroad. Some knowingly agreed to work in sex industries. However, all victims insisted that they never suspected the severity of the conditions, the slavery, or the abuse they would be subjected to. None suspected that she would be deprived of her wages.

According to reports, some employers force workers from countries of the former Soviet Union—such as Uzbekistan—to work without pay. Employers or the individuals who bring the workers into the country withhold the workers' passports or other documentation and threaten them with exposure to law enforcement agencies or immigration authorities if they demand payment. At times, the recruiter demands part or all the worker's wages to avoid deportation.

The rise in trafficking appears to be related to the socioeconomic dislocation that occurred following the collapse of the Soviet Union. Formerly, rigid controls on the movement of persons within and across borders discouraged migration of any kind, and the extensive involvement of the state in social services provided minimal levels of support for women and children. State support is gone, and there is no replacement. Most single parent families are headed by women, who are now more dependent on earned income for family support and less likely to find employment than during the Soviet welfare state. Unemployment is approximately 9 percent, but ranged from 15 to 40 percent in the most hard-pressed regions. According to the Ministry of Labor, 70 percent of the registered unemployed are women. Law enforcement officials report that at least half of trafficked women were unemployed. Nongovernmental organizations report that many women are desperate to find a better level of support. Children are also at a greater risk of trafficking.

According to surveys of law enforcement officials and nongovernmental organizations, unlicensed front companies and agents of legitimate companies with ties to criminal organizations appear to be the main channels for human trafficking. Many place advertisements in newspapers or public places for overseas employment, some employ women to pose as returned workers to recruit victims, some place Internet or other advertisements for mail-order brides, and some victims are recruited by partners or friends. During the tourist season, many fly-by-night firms are created especially to provide particular channels for the smuggling of women. There are also purely criminal firms that find work abroad for prostitutes and intentionally sell young women into slavery.

Information from foreign prosecutions, academic researchers, and law enforcement sources suggest that trafficking is primarily carried out by small criminal groups with the assistance of front companies and more established organized crime groups. Typically, the traffickers use a front company—frequently an employment agency, travel agency, or modeling company—to recruit victims with promises of high-paying work overseas. Once they reach the destination country, the traffickers typically confiscate the victims' travel documents, lock the victims in a remote location, and force them to work in the sex industry.

Traffickers often use their ties to organized crime to threaten the victims with harm to their families should they try to leave. They also rely on ties to organized crime in the destination countries to prevent the victims from leaving and to find employment for the victims in the local sex industry. Trafficking organizations typically pay Russian organized crime a percentage of their profits in return for "protection" and for assistance in identifying victims, procuring false documents, and corrupting law enforcement. They also sometimes pay "protection" money to local organized crime groups in destination countries.

Reports state that individual government officials take bribes from individuals and organized trafficking rings to assist in issuing documents and facilitating visa fraud. Law enforcement sources agree that often some form of document fraud is committed in the process of obtaining external passports and visas, but they are uncertain to what extent this involves official corruption rather than individual or organized criminal forgery and fraud. There are reports of prosecutions of officials involved in such corruption. The penalty for violating border laws with fraudulent documents is up to three years. The penalty for taking bribes is three to seven years. Those who are charged with more than one crime receive heavier sentences.

Journalists, politicians, and academic experts state that trafficking is facilitated and, in many cases, controlled by corrupt elements within the MVD and other law enforcement bodies. Substantial evidence, including information derived from victims, nongovernmental organizations, foreign law enforcement, and criminal prosecutions in Russia, suggest that corrupt elements within the MVD protect trafficking organizations and, in many cases, directly operate trafficking and prostitution businesses themselves.

Nongovernmental organizations claim that consular officials abroad refuse to help trafficked women. The Foreign Ministry confirmed that it has no policy on assistance to victims of trafficking and is working to create appropriate guidance. Victims rarely file complaints against the agencies that recruit them once they return to the country, reporting that fear of reprisals often exceed their hope of police assistance. Law enforcement authorities acknowledge that they rarely open a case following such complaints because, often, no domestic law is broken and law enforcement authorities are evaluated according to the number of cases they close.

There are no government initiatives to bring trafficking victims back to the country. Unless deported by the host country, women have to pay their own way home or turn to international nongovernmental organizations for assistance. Women report that without their documentation, which is often withheld by traffickers, they receive no assistance from Russian consulates abroad. The Russian government does not provide direct assistance to trafficking victims.

CORRECTIONAL SYSTEM

In the 1980s the Soviet Union had few conventional prisons. About 99 percent of convicted criminals served their sentences in labor camps. These were supervised by the Main Directorate for Corrective Labor Camps (Glavnoye Upravleniye Ispravitel'no-Trudovykh Lagerey), which was administered by the MVD. The camps had four regimes of severity. In the strict-regime camps, inmates worked at the most difficult jobs, usually outdoors, and received meager rations. Jobs were progressively less demanding and rations better in the three classifications of camps with more favorable regimes.

The system of corrective labor was viewed by Soviet authorities as successful because of the low rate of recidivism. However, in the opinion of former inmates and Western observers, prisons and labor camps were notorious for their harsh conditions, arbitrary and sadistic treatment of prisoners, and flagrant abuses of human rights. In 1989 new legislation, emphasizing rehabilitation rather than punishment, was drafted to "humanize" the penitentiary system. Nevertheless, few changes occurred in the conditions of most prisons and labor camps before the end of the Soviet period in 1991.

In the post-Soviet period all prisons and labor camps except for fourteen detention prisons fell under the jurisdiction of the MVD. The MVD was previously responsible for 743 correctional labor institutions, 168 pretrial detention facilities, and 13 prisons before their transfer to the Ministry of Justice in 2000. In addition, the MVD maintained 60 educational labor colonies for juveniles. In 1994 the MVD received only 87 percent of its funds allocated by the federal budget. As a result, it is estimated that prisons were able to provide only 60 to 70 percent of the daily food rations they envisioned providing and only 15 to 20 percent of needed medications and medical care. Prisoners and detainees had to rely on family members to provide them with extra food and routine medicines.

In the early and mid-1990s the growth of crime led to a rapid rise in the number of prisoners. Because of over-crowding and the failure to build new prison facilities, conditions in prisons deteriorated steadily after 1991, and some incidents of Soviet-style arbitrary punishment continued to be reported. In 1994 a Moscow prison designed to hold 8,500 inmates was housing well over 17,000 shortly after its completion. Many prisons are unfit for habitation because of insufficient sanitation systems. In 1995 *Nezavisimaya Gazeta* reported that the capacity of isolation wards in Moscow and St. Petersburg prisons had been exceeded by two to two and a half times.

Observers claim that some prisons stopped providing food to prisoners for months at a time, relying instead on rations sent from outside. The lack of funding also led to a crisis in medical care for prisoners. In 1995 President Yeltsin's Human Rights Commission condemned the prison system for continuing to allow violations of prisoners' rights. It cited lack of expert supervision as the main reason that such practices, which often included beatings, were not reported and punished.

In 1995 conditions in the penal system had deteriorated to the point that the Duma began calling for a transfer of prison administration from the MVD to the Ministry of Justice. According to Western experts, however, the MVD's Chief Directorate for Enforcement of Punishment was prevented from improving the situation by funding limitations, personnel problems, and lack of legislative support, rather than by internal shortcomings.

By the mid-1990s Russian penal legislation resembled that enacted in Western countries, although the conditions of detention did not. Post-Soviet legislation has abolished arbitrary or inhumane practices such as bans on visitors and mail, head shaving, and physical abuse. Also, prison officials are now required to protect prisoners who have received threats, and, officially, freedom of religious practice is guaranteed. Prisoners are rewarded for good behavior by being temporarily released outside the prison; in 1993 the MVD reported a 97 percent rate of return after such releases. However, the penalty for violent escape has increased to eight additional years of detention.

Prison Conditions. Prison conditions remain extremely harsh and frequently life threatening. The Ministry of Justice administers the penitentiary system centrally from Moscow. The Ministries of Justice, Health, Defense, and Education all maintain penal facilities. There are five basic forms of custody in the criminal justice system: police temporary detention centers, pretrial detention facilities known as special isolation facilities (sledstvennyi izolyator, SIZOs), correctional labor colonies (ITKs), prisons designated for those who violate ITK rules, and educational labor colonies (VTKs) for juveniles. Responsibility for operating the country's penal facilities falls under the Ministry of Justice's Main Directorate for Execution of Sentences (GUIN). As of August 2003 there were approximately 877,000 people in the custody of the criminal justice system. Men are held separately from women, as are juveniles from adults. The FSB continues to run the Lefortovo pretrial detention center in Moscow, in keeping with a 1998 presidential decree.

The Russian government does not release statistics on the number of detainees and prisoners who have been killed or died in custody, or on the number of law enforcement and prison personnel disciplined. The Moscow Center for Prison Reform estimates that in earlier years, 10,000 to 11,000 prisoners died annually in penitentiary facilities, 2,500 of them in SIZOs. During 2003 these numbers were believed to be somewhat lower. Most die as a result of poor sanitary conditions or lack of medical care (the leading cause of death was heart disease). The press often reports on individuals who are mistreated, injured, or killed in various SIZOs; some of the reported cases indicate habitual abuse by the same officers.

Abuse of prisoners by other prisoners continues to be a problem. Violence among inmates, including beatings and rape, is common. There are elaborate inmate-enforced caste systems in which informers, homosexuals, rapists, prison rape victims, child molesters, and others are considered to be "untouchable" and are treated harshly, with little or no protection provided by the prison authorities.

Penal institutions remain overcrowded; however, there have been some improvements. Mass amnesties offer immediate relief. The authorities are also taking longer-term and more systemic measures to reduce the size of the prison population. These include the use of alternative sentencing in some regions and revisions of both the criminal code and the criminal procedure code that eliminate incarceration as a penalty for many less serious offenses. Many penal facilities remain in urgent need of renovation and upgrading. By law, authorities must provide inmates with adequate space, food, and medical attention; with the dramatic decrease in prison populations, they are believed to be increasingly meeting these standards.

Inmates in the prison system often suffer from inadequate medical care. In 2001 President Putin described the problem of disease in the prison system as a potential "Chernobyl." According to the GUIN, as of July 1, 2003, there were approximately 77,000 tuberculosis-infected persons and 37,000 HIV-infected persons in SIZOs and correction colonies. Public health measures, funded by international aid and by the doubling of government resources for the prison system's medical budget, have effected a limited reversal of the spread of tuberculosis, but have not contained the spread of HIV. Russian detention facilities have tuberculosis infection rates far higher than in the population at large.

ITKs hold the bulk of the nation's convicts. There are 753 ITKs. Guards reportedly discipline prisoners severely to break down resistance. At times, guards humiliate, beat, and starve prisoners. According to the Moscow Center for Prison Reform, conditions in the ITKs are better than those in the SIZOs, because the ITKs have fresh air. In the timber correctional colonies, where hardened criminals serve their time, beatings, torture, and rape by guards reportedly are common. The country's "prisons"—distinct from the ITKs—are penitentiary institutions for those who repeatedly violate the rules in effect in the ITKs.

Conditions in police station detention centers vary considerably, but generally are harsh; however, average periods of stay in such facilities are decreasing, and overcrowding has been greatly alleviated. Implementation in July 2002 of the new criminal procedure code and the overall reduction in the use of pretrial detention for petty criminals reduced both the numbers of persons being held and the length of time they may be held in pretrial detention. Since 2000 the pretrial population has declined by approximately 46 percent, virtually eliminating the problem of overcrowding in those institutions.

Despite these improvements, conditions in SIZOs, where suspects are confined while awaiting the completion of a criminal investigation, trial, sentencing, or appeal, remain extremely harsh and pose a serious threat to health and life. Health, nutrition, and sanitation standards remain low because of a lack of funding. Head lice and various skin diseases are prevalent. Prisoners and detainees typically rely on families to provide them with extra food. Poor ventilation is thought to contribute to cardiac problems and lowered resistance to disease.

Because of substandard pretrial detention conditions, defendants at times claim that they have confessed simply to be moved to comparatively less harsh prison conditions. Defendants' retractions of confessions made under these conditions generally are ignored, as are those who attempt to retract confessions they claim they were coerced to make.

VTKs are facilities for prisoners from 14 to 20 years of age. Male and female prisoners are held separately. As of 2003 there were 526 mothers with children under 3 years old in Russian prisons. In August 2003 the GUIN reported that there were 62 educational colonies, 3 of which were for girls. Conditions in the VTKs are significantly better than in the ITKs, but juveniles in the VTKs and juveniles in SIZO cells reportedly also suffer from beatings, torture, and rape. The Moscow Center for Prison Reform reports that such facilities have a poor psychological atmosphere and lack educational and vocational training opportunities. Many of the juveniles are from orphanages, have no outside support, and are unaware of their rights. There are also 2 prisons for children in Moscow. Boys are held with adults in small, crowded, and smoky cells. Schooling in the prisons for children is sporadic at best, with students of different ages studying together when a teacher can be found.

As in the Soviet period, corrective-labor institutions have made a significant contribution to the national economy. In the early 1990s industrial output in the camps reached an estimated $100 million, and forest-based camps added about US$27 million, chiefly from the production of commercial lumber, railroad ties, and summer cabins. Because the camps supply their products to conventional state enterprises, however, they have suffered from the decline in that phase of Russia's economy; an estimated 200,000 convicts were without work in the camps in early 1994. In 1995 the chief of the Directorate for Supervision of the Legality of Prison Punishment reported that the population of labor camps exceeded the capacity of those facilities by an average of 50 percent.

Prison Statistics.

- Total Prison Population: 846,967

- Prison Population Rate per 100,000: 584 (based on an estimated national population of 145 million in 2003)

- Pretrial Detainees: 16.9%

- Female Prisoners: 5.8%

- Juveniles Prisoners: 2.5%

- Foreign Prisoners: 1.7%

- Number of Establishments: 1,013

- Occupancy Level: 90.2%

- Official Capacity of Prison System: 954,323

Recent prison population trend (year, prison population total, prison population rate per 100,000 of national population):

1992	722,636	(487)
1995	920,685	(622)
1998	1,009,863	(688)
2001	923,765	(638)

BIBLIOGRAPHY

Bureau for International Narcotics and Law Enforcement Affairs. 2004. "International Narcotics Control Strategy Report, 2003." U.S. Department of State. Available online at http://www.state.gov/p/inl/rls/nrcrpt/2003/ (accessed December 20, 2005).

Bureau of Democracy, Human Rights, and Labor. 2003. "Country Reports on Human Rights Practices, 2003: Russia." U.S. Department of State. Available online at http://www.state.gov/g/drl/rls/hrrpt/2003/27861.htm (accessed December 20, 2005).

"Drug-Resistant TB Being Spread from Russian Prisons." 2003. *New York Times* (March 23). Available online at http://newsmax.com/articles/?a=2000/3/23/133748 (accessed December 20, 2005).

Galeotti, Mark. 2003. "Russian Police Reform: Centralisation, Paramilitarisation, and Modernisation." *Crime and Justice International* 19 (70) (February). Available online at http://158.135.23.21/cjcweb/college/cji/index.cfm?ID=762 (accessed December 20, 2005).

GlobalSecurity.org. 2005. "Russia." Available online at http://www.globalsecurity.org/intell/world/russia/mvd.htm (accessed December 20, 2005).

Ministry of the Interior of Russia. Available online at http://eng.mvdrf.ru/ (accessed December 20, 2005).

Moscow Center for Prison Reform. Available online at http://www.prison.org/english/mcpr.htm (accessed December 20, 2005).

"Russian Prison Population Shrank by 100,000 in 2002—Minister." 2004. *Interfax News Agency* (February 18). Available online at http://www.cdi.org/russia/johnson/7066-10.cfm (accessed December 20, 2005).

"Russian Prisons Contain 526 Mothers with Children under Three." 2003. *Pravda RU* (January 15). Available online at http://english.pravda.ru/society/2003/01/15/42030.html (accessed December 20, 2005).

RussiansAbroad.com. 2005. "Russian History." Available online at http://www.russiansabroad.com/russian_history_384.html (accessed December 20, 2005).

Joseph D. Serio

WORLD ENCYCLOPEDIA OF POLICE FORCES AND CORRECTIONAL SYSTEMS, 2ND ED.

789

Rwanda

Official country name: Republic of Rwanda
Capital: Kigali
Geographic description: Landlocked country in central Africa that includes the source of the Nile
Population: 8,440,820 (est. 2005)

■■■

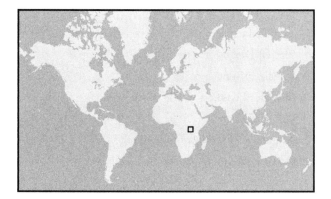

LAW ENFORCEMENT

History. Under Belgian rule law and order was the responsibility of the Force Publique. It consisted of about 800 men, both Congolese and Belgian, under the charge of a director. In 1960 the first Rwandans were recruited to the force.

Structure and Organization. The National Police are commanded by a commissioner general under the authority of the minister of police. Most of the force is assigned to the twelve prefectural administrations. Although responsible to the police headquarters in matters of discipline, promotion, training, and general policy, the prefectural detachments receive their operating instructions from the prefect and his assistants.

Each commune has its own police force commanded by a brigadier appointed by the mayor. The Communal Police are responsible for implementing communal laws, regulations, and ordinances, safeguarding public property, overseeing public markets, and executing court judgments. The maximum size of the Communal Police is fixed at 1 per every 1,000 inhabitants. Under conditions of widespread public disorder, the mayor can appeal to the prefect for additional units of the National Police. The Central Information Service is in charge of criminal investigation and represents Interpol in Rwanda.

Education and Training. The National Police School is located in Ruhengeri. Many of the candidates are those turned down by the National Guard School. Applicants have to take a written examination and receive at least 50 percent scores for acceptance. The six-month course for enlisted personnel includes court procedures, traffic regulations, weapons, self-defense, first aid, and police administration. A similar course is taught in the course for officers.

Uniforms and Weapons. Uniforms are of gray twill. Headwear includes a Belgian cap, a dress cap with a wide brim, and a helmet, often painted white for guard and ceremonial duties. Police weapons are mostly of foreign origin.

Police Statistics.

- Total Police Personnel: 1,590
- Population per Police Officer: 5,309

HUMAN RIGHTS

Security forces took advantage of the unsettled conditions in the country to commit human rights abuses on a large scale. The suspects in the 1994 genocide, reported to be over 100,000, are the primary victims of human rights abuses. The judiciary takes orders from the quasi-military Tutsi government. The worst human rights abuses were committed in the Democratic Republic of the Congo, where Tutsi soldiers destroyed and burned entire villages and tortured, raped, and killed the inhabitants.

CRIME

Crime Statistics. Offenses reported to the police per 100,000 population: NA. Of which:

- Murder: 45.1
- Assault: 114.3
- Automobile Theft: 0.3

CORRECTIONAL SYSTEM

Prisons are administered by the director of prisons, who heads the Rwanda Prisons Service under the Ministry of the Interior.

Prison Conditions. Because of the large number of prisoners, Rwanda does not have the physical infrastructure to house them in conformity with international standards. Private residences are sometimes used as prisons, where prisoners are treated as slaves, beaten, and killed. Sanitation is nonexistent and the government provides only 50 percent of the food and medical treatment that the prisoners require. There are a number of deaths in the prisons each year that are unreported. Minors between the ages of fourteen and eighteen are incarcerated with adults as are pretrial detainees.

Prison Statistics. There are eighteen central prisons in the country (besides communal holding centers) with a prison population of 112,000. Of this, 103,134 are prisoners being detained on suspicion of participation in the 1994 genocide. The incarceration rate is 109 per 100,000 inhabitants. The overcrowding rate is 202.4 percent. Of the total prison population, 2.4 percent are pretrial detainees, 2.6 percent are females, 4.5 percent are juveniles, and 0.3 percent are foreigners.

George Thomas Kurian

Saint Kitts and Nevis

Official country name: Federation of Saint Kitts and Nevis

Capital: Basseterre

Geographic description: Islands in the Caribbean Sea; shaped like a baseball ball and bat, the islands are separated by the Narrows Channel

Population: 38,958 (est. 2005)

■■■

LAW ENFORCEMENT

History. Saint Kitts (alternatively Saint Christopher) and Nevis were first settled in 1623 by the British and became an associated state with full internal autonomy in 1967. In 1983 Saint Kitts and Nevis became completely independent. In 1998 a vote in Nevis to separate from Saint Kitts fell short of the needed two-thirds majority.

Saint Kitts and Nevis is a constitutional monarchy with a Westminster-style Parliament. The judicial system of Saint Kitts and Nevis is based on a British practice and procedure and its jurisprudence is based in English common law.

Structure and Organization. Little information is available regarding police or corrections in Saint Kitts and Nevis. Police in Saint Kitts and Nevis are all members of the Royal Saint Kitts and Nevis Police Force, which does include a Special Service Unit. The police force is headed by a commissioner. Each of the three geographic divisions (Nevis and the two districts on Saint Kitts) is commanded by a superintendent. The Police Service Commission is responsible for recruitment, promotion, and discipline.

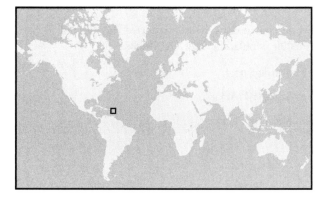

Special Police. The Royal Saint Kitts and Nevis Police Force does include a Special Services Unit, but nothing is known about its function or makeup.

Recruitment and Training. Recruits undergo six months of initial training at the Police Training School. Promotions are based on qualifying examinations and interviews with the Promotions Board.

Police Statistics. The Royal Saint Kitts and Nevis Police Force includes approximately 400 members, with approximately 50 Special Service officers. The population per police officer is 97. Women make up 28 percent of the force.

HUMAN RIGHTS

The constitution of Saint Kitts and Nevis provides for a number of civil rights such as freedom of speech and assembly and protection against inhumane punishment. The police and the government respect these rights as a rule.

There have been minor problems with intimidation of witnesses in high-profile drug-related cases, and government restrictions on opposition to state-controlled media. The government of Saint Kitts and Nevis is exploring the possibility of a program to protect witnesses, jurors, and judges throughout the Caribbean community.

CRIME

Saint Kitts and Nevis are relatively free from crime. Like other Caribbean countries, Saint Kitts and Nevis do experience problems with drug trafficking from South America to the United Kingdom and the United States. There are some reports of burglary, robbery, and sexual assault on the islands.

CORRECTIONAL SYSTEMS

The prison in Saint Kitts was built in 1840 and was intended to house only 60 people. In recent years the prison population has averaged around 100, with women held separately from the men. There is no separate facility for juveniles.

There is one small prison on Nevis, designed to hold 20 people. It suffers from similar problems like the prison in Saint Kitts.

Prison Conditions. Prison conditions in Saint Kitts and Nevis are poor. Prisoners suffer from severe overcrowding, lack of food, and proper security. These conditions have, in the past, contributed to riots, the last occurring in 1994.

Prison Statistics.

- Total Prison Population: 195
- Prison Population Rate per 100,000: 415
- Pretrial Detainees: 21.5%
- Female Prisoners: 0.9%
- Juvenile Prisoners: 14.7%
- Official Capacity of the Prison System: 105
- Occupancy Rate: 128.6%

Jennifer Albright

Saint Lucia

Official country name: Saint Lucia
Capital: Castries
Geographic description: Island in the east Caribbean Sea, part of the Windward Islands group
Population: 166,312 (est 2005)

■■■

LAW ENFORCEMENT

History. The Royal Saint Lucia Police was established in 1834. It was then headed by an inspector of police, who was assisted by three sergeants and twenty-four corporals and constables. The inspector also served as a magistrate and prosecutor.

As the police force grew in numbers, the chief of police was designated as the senior superintendent by the end of World War II. He also served as the chief immigration officer, the head of the prison service, and fire chief. The fire service remained part of the force until 1975. In 1960 the force was renamed the Royal Saint Lucia Police in honor of the visit of Queen Elizabeth II to the island. At the same time, the head of the force was redesignated commissioner.

Structure and Organization. The Royal Saint Lucia Police is headed by a commissioner assisted by four assistant commissioners who are assigned specific divisions: Community Policing and Training, Crime and Police Prosecutions, Operations, and Administration. The support services are the responsibility of an administrative officer. The commissioner also oversees the Coast Guard, Immigration, and the Police Band. The Administrative Division

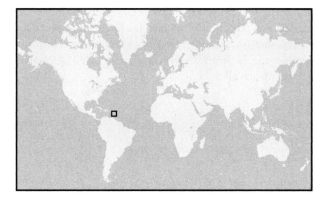

includes the Special Branch, Telecommunications, Criminal Investigation Department, Traffic and Licensing, Passports and Immigration, Transport and Stores, and the Police Band.

For territorial purposes the island is divided into Northern and Southern Divisions, each headed by a superintendent. The Northern Division comprises eight police stations and the Southern Division five.

There is also a Community Relations Branch, which is charge of fostering good relations with the community at large.

There are three auxiliary forces: the Port Authority Constabulary, the Special reserve Police, and the Rural Constabulary.

In 2002 the administration prepared a five-year plan with the help of British experts that included community-based policing, crime prevention, increased professionalism, complaint investigation, and internal review. The Royal Canadian Mounted Police lent an officer to serve as deputy commissioner to strengthen personnel procedures.

Education and Training. To enter the police force, entrants must have a high school diploma or equivalent, good physical and mental health, and be between eighteen and thirty years old. They are also required to pass an oral and written examination.

Successful candidates attend a five-month initial training course at the Police Training School, where the courses include practical police subjects. Graduates are considered probationers for two years when they are deployed in various units.

Sergeants and inspectors receive special supervisory management training and gazetted officers receive senior management and leadership training.

Uniforms and Weapons. Depending on the occasion, gazetted officers wear full dress, service dress, or a working dress. The full dress consists of a white tunic, blue service overalls with silver braid, Wellington boots, sword with steel scabbard, belts and slings, silver sword knot, cap, and blue sash. Service dress consists of a khaki tunic, blue lanyard, khaki trousers, white shirt and collar, and a black Sam Browne belt. The working dress consists of a khaki bush tunic, khaki trousers and a blue lanyard or white shirt, black pants, and a black tie.

Nongazetted personnel and constables wear a full dress consisting of black trousers with white stripe, black boots, a waist belt, and a cap, and a working dress consisting of a white short-sleeved shirt, black trousers with white stripe, a cap, and black boots.

Generally, all ranks are unarmed.

Police Statistics.

- Total Police Personnel: 730

- Population per Police Officer: 228

HUMAN RIGHTS

The government generally respects all human rights. Occasional charges of abuse by the police are investigated promptly.

CRIME

Crime Statistics. Offenses reported to the police per 100,000 population: 4,386. Of which:

- Murder: 17

- Assault: 1,193

- Burglary: 778

CORRECTIONAL SYSTEM

Prison Conditions. Prison conditions are poor because of overcrowding and lack of amenities. Since the controls are lax and prison guards are corrupt, weapons and drugs are smuggled into the Castries Prison. Rival drug gangs often fight within the prison walls. Sanitation is a particular problem with only open-pit latrines.

The focus of the correction program is on containment rather than on training or rehabilitation. There are only a few craft programs. Hardened criminals are housed with detainees, but young offenders and women are kept separate from adult males.

Prison Statistics.

- Total Prison Population: 460

- Prison Population Rate per 100,000: 287

- Pretrial Detainees: 28.4%

- Female Prisoners: 1.7%

- Juvenile Prisoners: 6.5%

- Number of Prisons: 1

- Official Capacity of the Prison System: 500

- Occupancy Level: 92%

George Thomas Kurian

Saint Vincent and the Grenadines

Official country name: Saint Vincent and the Grenadines
Capital: Kingstown
Geographic description: Caribbean islands in the Caribbean Sea
Population: 117,534 (est. 2005)

■■■

LAW ENFORCEMENT

Structure and Organization. Headquartered in Kingstown and headed by a commissioner, the Saint Vincent and Grenadines Police Force is a small force numbering 686. The force has a number of operational divisions, such as the Criminal Investigation Department and the Fire Brigade, and special sections on immigration, traffic, and transport. The force consists of twenty-two units deployed in five geographical divisions (Central, Western, South central, Eastern, and Grenadines). Police officers operate unarmed. In times of emergency a paramilitary unit is activated. Also under the police is a small coast guard, which participates in narcotics interdiction, smuggling prevention, fisheries protection, and search-and-rescue missions.

The government has established an Oversight Committee to monitor police activity and to hear complaints about police misconduct. It also conducts police seminars on human rights and domestic violence.

Education and Training. Basic police training is provided locally by the Police Training Academy. Senior officials go abroad for refresher courses.

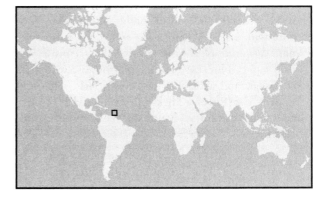

Police Statistics.

- Total Police Personnel: 452
- Population per Police Officer: 260

CRIME

Crime Statistics. Offenses reported to the police per 100,000 population: 3,977. Of which:

- Murder: 10.3
- Assault: 986.9

CORRECTIONAL SYSTEM

Saint Vincent and the Grenadines has three prisons administered by the superintendent of prisons, who heads the Prison Service under the Ministry of National Security. The main prison is a four-building compound in Kingstown. The second prison is a new one built in

2003 at Bellisle on the west coast. It is a US$13 million facility designed to hold 400 inmates with separate areas for juveniles and first-time offenders. The third facility is at Fort Charlottes.

Prison Conditions. Prison conditions are substandard. Two of the prison buildings are old and pose serious health and safety problems. A 2001 Report on Prison Conditions concludes that the main Kingstown prison is a "university for crime" because of endemic violence, understaffing, underpaid guards, uncontrolled drugs and weapons, an increase in HIV/AIDS, and prevalence of unhygienic conditions, such as missing toilets. The report states that inmates have to get protection from gangs and obtain for gang leaders alcohol, drugs, and weapons. If they fail to do this, they are beaten severely. In addition, the report finds that inmates are routinely stabbed for running afoul of gang leaders. Since the report was issued, the government has hired new guards,

has initiated a rehabilitation program, and has established a program with courses in carpentry, tailoring, baking, and mechanical engineering. Inmates are allowed to speak freely to their lawyers but must be within hearing distance of a prison guard when they do so. Female inmates are housed separately. A family court handles criminal cases for children up to age sixteen. Beyond that age they may be housed with convicted felons.

Prison Statistics. The official capacity of the Kingstown and Bellisle prisons is 280, and the total prison population is 302, yielding an occupancy level of 107.9 percent. The incarceration rate is 270 per 100,000 population. Of the total prison population, 16.9 percent are pretrial detainees, 2.6 percent are female, 16.9 percent are juveniles, and 1.3 percent are foreigners.

George Thomas Kurian

Samoa

Official country name: Independent State of Samoa
Capital: Apia
Geographic description: Group of islands in the South Pacific Ocean between Hawaii and New Zealand
Population: 177,287 (est. 2005)

■■■

LAW ENFORCEMENT

History. The Samoan Police Force was originally the Western Samoan Police until 1997. It was formed by the German colonial administration around 1900. In 1914, following the outbreak of World War I, New Zealand took over the islands and renamed the police force Military Controlled Police. In 1921 the Samoan Constabulary was established based on the police system of New Zealand. This force existed until independence in 1962, when it became the Western Samoan Police.

Structure and Organization. The police and penal systems are organized as the Department of Police and Prisons under a commissioner of police, who reports to the prime minister. There are no operating or territorial divisions. The headquarters also includes a public relations office, a Special Branch in charge of internal security, a Firearms Registry, and five departments dealing with crime, technical matters, administration, training, and mobile operations, respectively. The bulk of the force is deployed at Apia. Other units of the police are stationed at the islands of Upolu and Savaii. There are three stations on Upolu and three on Savaii. All the six stations

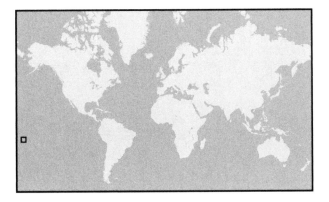

are also responsible for policing outlying islands in the vicinity.

Uniforms and Weapons. The daily working uniform is a light-gray short-sleeved shirt, worn with a light-gray lava-lava, or wraparound skirt. A white helmet is also worn. For ceremonial occasions a white shirt is worn with a lava-lava. Officers wear the same uniform with a dark-blue peaked cap. Traffic officers wear long trousers instead of the lava-lava. All policemen are unarmed.

HUMAN RIGHTS

Samoa is a parliamentary democracy and generally respects the human rights of its citizens. There are no credible reports of abuses or violations.

CORRECTIONAL SYSTEM

The prison service is headed by a police sergeant who controls a force of three corporals and sixteen wardens and administers two penal institutions: a conventional prison at Tafa'igata near Apia and a prison farm at Vaia'ata on Savaii Island. Both are minimum security prisons were inmates receive vocational training.

Prison Conditions. Prison conditions meet international standards, although they are fairly basic with respect to food and sanitation.

Prison Statistics.

- Total Prison Population: 281

- Prison Population Rate per 100,000: 158

- Pretrial Detainees: 6.8%

- Female Prisoners: 6%

- Number of Prisons: 2

- Official Capacity of the Prison System: 260

- Occupancy Level: 108.1%

George Thomas Kurian

San Marino

Official country name: Republic of San Marino
Capital: San Marino
Geographic description: Landlocked enclave within central Italy
Population: 28,880 (est. 2005)

■■■

LAW ENFORCEMENT

History. The first urban police was formed in 1947 with the appointment of area policemen who were seconded to the corps of the Gendarmerie. They were called the Urban Guards under an inspector of police. In 1963 the Corps of Urban Police was formed, first with Italian nationals and later with San Marino citizens.

Structure and Organization. There are two law enforcement organizations. The Corps of Urban Police manned by San Marino citizens and the Corps of the Gendarmerie, who are part of the Italian Carabinieri. The Guardie de Rocca, a national guard, is responsible for the security of Parliament, the public palace, and the Captains Reagent.

The main tasks of the Gendarmerie are criminal investigation and maintenance of public order. In accordance with a seventeenth-century law, all gendarmes, judges, and inspectors must be foreigners. This law was designed to prevent any favoritism being shown to fellow citizens by a gendarme. The Corps of Urban Police is charged with traffic while other sections oversee law enforcement in health, tourism, and commercial sectors. The force is headed by a commandant, who is assisted by four officers.

Education and Training. The Corps of Urban Policemen are trained in Italian police schools.

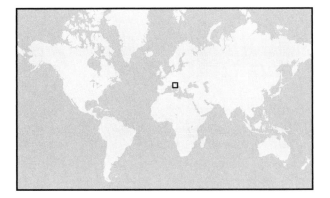

Uniforms and Weapons. The corps has two types of uniforms, one for the winter and one for the summer. The winter uniform is blue, complete with a helmet, a white shirt, gloves, white armlets, black socks, a tie, and shoes. The summer uniform is aquamarine. The force is not normally armed.

HUMAN RIGHTS

The government generally respects human rights in accordance with European conventions.

CORRECTIONAL SYSTEMS

San Marino maintains one small prison, which is unpopulated. All prisoners sentenced to more than six months are transferred to Italian prisons.

Prison Conditions. Prison conditions meet international standards. Male adult prisoners are separated from women and children.

George Thomas Kurian

São Tomé and Príncipe

Official country name: Democratic Republic of São Tomé and Príncipe
Capital: São Tomé
Geographic description: Islands in the Gulf of Guinea straddling the equator, west of Gabon in West Africa; the smallest country in Africa
Population: 187,410 (est. 2005)

■■■

LAW ENFORCEMENT

Structure and Organization. The regular police is the Public Order Police with a strength of over 300. The Public Order Police works mainly in the towns. Rural areas are policed by the National Guard. Many policemen are part-time farmers or fishermen.

Police Statistics.

- Total Police Personnel: 355
- Population per Police Officer: 528

CRIME

Crime Statistics. Offenses reported to the police per 100,000 population: 558. Of which:

- Murder: 4

CORRECTIONAL SYSTEM

There is only one prison in São Tomé and Príncipe. It is administered by the director of the prisons service under the Ministry of Justice.

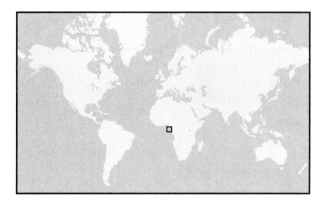

Prison Conditions. Prison conditions are substandard but not life threatening. Food is inadequate. Women and men are housed separately.

Prison Statistics. The official capacity of the prison is 300, but the actual prison population is only 130. The occupancy level is only 43.3 percent. The incarceration rate is 58.5 percent per 100,000 population. Of the total prison population, 58.5 percent are pretrial detainees, 2.3 percent are female, 6.9 percent are juveniles, and 0.8 percent are foreigners.

George Thomas Kurian

Saudi Arabia

Official country name: Kingdom of Saudi Arabia
Capital: Riyadh
Geographic description: Saudi Arabia occupies about 80 percent of the Arabian Peninsula in the Middle East
Population: 26,417,599 (including 5,576,076 non-nationals) (est. 2005)

■■■

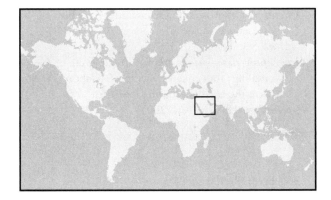

LAW ENFORCEMENT

History. The organization of a modern law enforcement system was one of the more notable achievements of Abd al Aziz, the founder of the Saudi dynasty. Previously, the country had known only rudimentary law enforcement, and even that at only a local level. However, even though the police system has evolved, it has remained partly entrenched in the tribal social order under which the sheikhs remain the primary guarantors of public order within their bailiwicks. Only when local efforts fail is the National Guard brought in. National law enforcement agencies complement but do not intrude on tribal authority.

Structure and Organization. Law enforcement is the portfolio of the Ministry of the Interior under which are four organs: the National Guard, the Public Security Police, the Frontier Force, and the Coast Guard. The core agency is the Public Security Police, the equivalent of a national police force. It is organized at two levels: provincial police directorates and local police directorates. Its units are scattered all over the country and in every province. The provincial governors exercise direct control over the police within their administrative divisions. In addition, the governors and the sheikhs have their personal battalion of guards, who may be deployed on public duties on occasion.

The National Guard is a highly mobile paramilitary force that often works in conjunction with other law enforcement agencies. It is recruited primarily from the noble Bedouin tribes. Its principal allegiance is to the royal family.

The Ministry of the Interior is responsible for most of the other public security agencies, including the Frontier Force and the Coast Guard. Units of all these forces are deployed during the Haj season to control the pilgrims who flock to Mecca from various parts of the world.

Another police agency is the autonomous Religious Police (Mutawwa'in), which is organized under the authority of the Koran. They serve on the quasi-judicial public morality committees charged with ensuring strict compliance with the puritanical concepts of Wahhabism.

Saudi police forces stand guard along a street in Riyadh's industrial area after a shootout with extremists occurred, April 6, 2005. *During the shootout, one of the Saudi Arabia's most wanted Islamic militants was killed. The incident marked a wave of violent confrontations with radical extremists that happened over four days in the kingdom.* AP IMAGES.

Local committees in every town report to two central royal offices: one covering the western provinces and the other covering the Nejd and the eastern provinces. They are notorious for their unrelenting and rigorous enforcement of such Islamic requirements as the five daily prayers, Ramadan fasting, modesty in female attire, and proscriptions against the use of alcohol.

There is a ceremonial force known as the White Army, so-called because of its white uniforms. They are mobile and lightly armed.

Education and Training. In 1960 the government established the Police College at Mecca to train police officers. A secondary school certificate is required for entrance. A separate college, the Internal Security Forces College at Riyadh, also provides training for officers belonging to all services. Both institutions provide training in advanced equipment, including helicopters and radar. Instructors in police colleges are usually Arabs from Egypt.

Uniforms and Weapons. Police uniforms are similar to those of the Royal Saudi Army except for their red beret.

Police Statistics.

- Total Police Personnel: 83,464

- Population per Police Officer: 316

HUMAN RIGHTS

As an autocratic regime, Saudi Arabia's human rights record is among the worst in the world. People are arrested and detained arbitrarily and held incommunicado for long periods. In most cases security forces commit torture with impunity and are not held accountable. Because the minister of the interior is a senior member of the royal family, police do not have to face consequences for their actions. The dreaded Religious Police are the most flagrant offenders against human rights. They detain, intimidate, and abuse both citizens and foreigners for minor infractions of Islamic laws. The government views its interpretation of Sharia as its sole guide and disagrees with internationally accepted definitions of human rights.

CRIME

Crime Statistics. Offenses reported to the police per 100,000 population: 149. Of which:

- Murder: 0.5

- Assault: 0.2

- Automobile Theft: 45.4

CORRECTIONAL SYSTEM

The Saudi penal system is based on the Sharia, which encompasses two categories of crime: those that are carefully defined in the Koran and have prescribed penalties, and those that are only implicit in the Koran and for which penalties may be set at the discretion of the judge (*qadi*). In addition, a third category of crimes has been established since the end of World War II. It consists of governmental decrees and regulations prohibiting certain types of activities. The first two categories are tried in Sharia courts and the third in administrative courts.

For many crimes, penalties under the Sharia are extremely severe and barbaric. Even though they are carried out only infrequently as a last resort, they are still on the books as evidenced by periodic stoning and beheading in public.

Sharia carefully defines six types of major crimes: homicide, personal injury, fornication, adultery, theft, and highway robbery and specifies a penalty (*hudd*) for each. Homicide is not considered a crime against society or state, but only against the victim and his or her family. The victim's family has the right to retaliation, reparations, or blood money. The right of habeas corpus is not recognized. In serious cases, bail is not normally granted and the accused is detained until trial.

Trial by jury is unknown and the single judge who hears the case has great latitude. In Islamic law the testimony of one man is equal to that of two women. The judge does not pass sentence. All papers are sent to the district or provincial governor who, with the advice of Koranic legal scholars (ulema), pronounces the sentence. Imprisonment is virtually mandatory for even relatively minor violations.

Fornication and adultery are considered serious crimes punishable by flogging. However, the law requires rigorous proof, usually four reliable witnesses to the act.

It is extremely unlikely that anyone would commit adultery or fornication in front of four hostile witnesses. Theft is punished by cutting off the right hand of the thief, but theft from relatives is not considered a crime. Highway robbery is punished more severely, by having alternate hands and feet cut off. In robbery involving murder, the prisoner is crucified. Those who commit against public morality, such as drinking, gambling, and not fasting during Ramadan are flogged or fined.

Prisons are under the Ministry of the Interior and are administered by a director.

Prison Conditions. Most Saudi prisons are reported to be filthy, crowded, and unsanitary. Some modern jails have been built in the Eastern province through the efforts of Aramco, the oil company. They are built of cement blocks and have running water, bedding, and toilet facilities. Some of the modern prisons have air-conditioned cells. Prisoners have no rights during incarceration. Saudi Arabia does not permit international human rights organizations to inspect their prisons.

Prison Statistics.

- Total Prison Population: 28,612

- Prison Population Rate per 100,000: 132

- Pretrial Detainees: 58.7%

- Female Prisoners: 5.7%

- Number of Prisons: 30

George Thomas Kurian

Senegal

Official country name: Republic of Senegal
Capital: Dakar
Geographic description: Located in West Africa bordering on the North Atlantic Ocean, between Guinea-Bissau and Mauritania
Population: 11,126,832 (est. 2005)

■■■

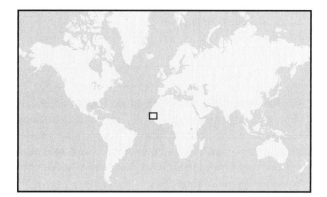

LAW ENFORCEMENT

History. The National Gendarmerie was created in 1843 soon after the French conquest. It was modeled after the French metropolitan force in terms of its mission, organization, and nomenclature. In 1928 a Mobile Gendarmerie was added, along with a mounted squadron. In 1949 it was reorganized on a territorial basis. When Senegal became independent in 1960, the Gendarmerie was retained in its entirety. However, in 1968 it was reorganized as part of the armed forces. The Sûreté Nationale was formed in 1878 to police urban areas.

Structure and Organization. The Senegalese Police follows the French pattern of a dual system consisting of a National Gendarmerie and a Sûreté Nationale (National Police). The former is a paramilitary force controlled by the president through the minister of state for armed forces. The commander of the force is concurrently the chief of the general staff of the armed forces. Units known as legions are maintained in each of the ten administrative regions. Legions are divided into smaller units called brigades—some consisting of only a few men—stationed at key positions throughout the country.

They constitute the rural police force but have other duties and responsibilities. They have well-trained and well-equipped rapid-response companies available for antiriot operations. They also guard the presidential palace, government buildings, airports, harbors, and key border points.

The Mobile Gendarmerie consists of five squadrons, all based at Dakar. The Territorial Gendarmerie consists of seven companies, each with its own reserve squad. The most picturesque unit is the Mounted Squadron, which inherits the colorful traditions of the Mamelukes and the Spahis.

Sûreté Nationale. The Sûreté Nationale is a centrally directed force under the minister of interior at Dakar. It is primarily an urban force The Sûreté Nationale is composed of seven central directorates, of which the largest is the Public Safety Directorate. This directorate comprises two main divisions: Mobile Support Group and Regional Public Safety Services. The former consists of a number of self-supporting mobile companies of riot police. There are two special commissariats: one for the Dakar Airport and the other for ports. Each of the ten administrative divisions has a police headquarters responsible for the town police stations in the region. Each town has at least one *commissariat* (police station); larger towns have *commissariats d'arrondissement* (precinct stations). In the smaller towns there is no Sûreté Nationale presence, and policing is entrusted to the Gendarmerie. The former Republican Guard was absorbed into the Sûreté Nationale in 1970 and now forms one of its units.

There are five separate ranks in the Sûreté Nationale:

- Commissioner
- Police Officer
- Peace Officer
- Police Inspector
- Guardian

Education and Training. The principal training academy is the Police Training College at Dakar, where police personnel from all of Francophone West Africa are trained.

Uniforms and Weapons. The regular uniform of the Gendarmerie is a military-type khaki drill tunic or bush shirt with matching trousers. For ceremonial occasions there is an exotic uniform of wide, baggy trousers tucked into the tops of calf-length boots, a tunic, and an unusual tall cloth cap shaped like a large paper bag. The Mounted Squadron has a flowing cloak or burnoose.

The regular uniform of the Sûreté Nationale is of lightweight khaki and consists of a tunic and/or shirt worn with matching trousers and cap. Dark-blue epaulettes on the shoulders bear the badge of the force and the badges of rank. For general duties, the lower ranks wear a Sam Browne belt, and for certain duties, such as crowd control, a black beret replaces the usual peaked cap. All personnel are normally unarmed.

Police Statistics.

- Total Police Personnel: 13,568
- Population per Police Officer: 820

HUMAN RIGHTS

Guerrilla activity in the Casamance region is responsible for many extrajudicial killings by the security forces. Several disappearances are also reported. Police routinely torture and beat suspects during questioning. Although police abuses are widely reported, the government does not try or punish the police or Gendarmerie for such abuses.

CRIME

Crime Statistics. Offenses reported to the police per 100,000 population: 123. Of which:

- Murder: 0.5
- Assault: 8.8
- Burglary: 2.1
- Automobile Theft: 8.2

CORRECTIONAL SYSTEM

The penal code and the code of penal procedure were promulgated in 1966 and incorporated into the elements of the penal code of metropolitan France. Police powers and procedures are based on regulations derived from the colonial period.

There are thirty-eight prisons and penitentiaries in the country, of which the largest is in Dakar. Women are held separately from men and juveniles from adults, but pretrial detainees are held with convicted prisoners because of limited space.

Prison Conditions. Prison conditions are poor because of overcrowding and lack of medical care.

Prison Statistics.

- Total Prison Population: 5,360
- Prison Population Rate per 100,000: 54
- Pretrial Detainees: 33.1%
- Female Prisoners: 3.7%
- Juvenile Prisoners: 3.2%
- Number of Prisons: 38
- Official Capacity of the Prison System: 2,972
- Occupancy Level: 167.9%

George Thomas Kurian

Serbia and Montenegro

Official country name: Serbia and Montenegro
Capital: Belgrade
Geographic description: Located in southwestern Europe on the eastern side of the Balkan Peninsula
Population: 10,829,175 (est. 2005)

■ ■ ■

LAW ENFORCEMENT

History. Serbia came into existence around 700. In 1918 Serbia became a province within the Kingdom of Yugoslavia, and after World War II it became a part of the Social Federal Republic of Yugoslavia. With the collapse of the Eastern bloc, Serbia regained its sovereignty. As of 2005 it is composed of two autonomous provinces: Kosovo and Vojvodina. In 1990 Slobodan Milošević was elected president of the new republic. Serbia's national status was recognized in 1992 by the United Nations. At this time Serbia formed a loose confederation with Montenegro called the Federal Republic of Yugoslavia. Conflicts in Bosnia led to the imposition of international trade sanctions in 1992. Many of these sanctions were lifted in 1995 when the Dayton Peace Agreement was signed, but that was not the end of Serbia's political and economic turmoil. In 1998, because of the increasing internal warfare in Kosovo, a small land area on the Serbian-Albanian border, even more restrictive sanctions were put into place.

The political and historic dynamics in Serbia and Montenegro, Serbia's partner in the Federal Republic of Yugoslavia, contributed to the violence in this troubled region. Serbia's leader, Milošević, finding his political

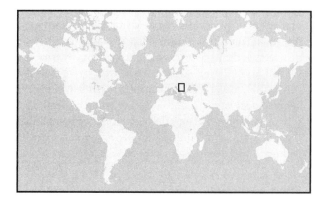

position weakening because of the international sanctions, struggled to maintain political control and enhance his popularity. He gained popular support by appealing to the newly emerging sense of Serbian nationalism and pride. To further strengthen and preserve his political position, Milošević brought hard-line ultranationalists, the Radical Party, into the government coalition and publicly rejected talks with the Albanians over Kosovo. This move alarmed some, as the Radical Party was rumored to have engaged in ethnic cleansing in Bosnia and some members were thought to be responsible for attacks on Serbian minority groups. By 1999 the violence in Kosovo had continued to escalate and further international sanctions were imposed.

In 2000 free elections were held and Milošević lost his political position. The newly elected officials began to take the first steps needed to form a more democratic national government. The new prime minister called for elections, and his actions, as well as other pro-democratic political steps taken over the next two years, helped establish political, legal, and human rights in Serbia. On February 5, 2003, both Serbia and Montenegro formally began to lead their countries away from the chaos and bloodshed that had typified the region in the 1990s when they proclaimed the Constitutional Charter of the State Union of Serbia and Montenegro. This movement away from chaos was strengthened on December 26, 2003, when the Parliament of Serbia and Montenegro ratified the European Convention on the Protection of Human Rights and Fundamental Freedoms.

The philosophical high point in Serbia's newly proposed constitution occurred when the Democratic Opposition of Serbia (DOS) agreed to define Serbia as a "state of its citizens," not as a state of the Serbian nation. The DOS also agreed that the Serbian president would be elected by Parliament and that Serbia, although strongly linked to Montenegro, would maintain its own full rights and powers. In 2002 Serbia developed an active strategy for reforming the judiciary to ensure and protect citizen rights and develop a judicial code of ethics. After the assassination of the Serbian prime minister in March 2003, the army was placed under civilian control and active steps were taken to disassemble the Milošević security apparatus (International Crisis Group 2003). Citizen rights were strengthened in June 2003, when the Parliament of Serbia-Montenegro adopted legislation establishing a separate federal court system. A few weeks later, the Serbian Parliament repealed the police and special prosecutor provisions enacted when Milošević had declared a state of emergency.

Structure and Organization. Serbia is composed of a unicameral assembly, the president, and deputy ministers who oversee various ministries. As of 2003 the president was elected by the Parliament. The legislature of Serbia is a unicameral assembly of 250 deputies are elected in direct general elections for four-year terms. The deputies in the National Assembly elect the government of the Republic of Serbia. The judiciary is independent. The Ministry of the Interior is concerned with public safety and human rights and serves as the law enforcement branch of the Serbian government at the local and national levels.

Principal Agencies and Divisions. The duties and authority of the Ministry of Internal Affairs are noted in article 7 of the Law on Ministries. Some of the duties that the ministry is empowered to carry out include maintaining the security of Serbia; detecting and preventing activities intended to subvert or destroy the constitutional order; protecting lives and property; preventing and identifying criminal activities; apprehending perpetrators and delivering them to the judicial authorities; maintaining public peace and order; protecting the right of assembly; securing persons and buildings as specified;

providing traffic safety; overseeing border crossings and movements in the Green Line; tracking the activities of foreign nationals; monitoring the acquisition, creation, and possession of weapons, ammunition, and explosive substances; providing fire protection services; providing personal identification number and identity cards; examining travel documents; conducting staff training; and other tasks as specified in the law.

According to the Ministry of the Interior, major political and organizational changes in the ministry began in 2001. These changes led to the promulgation of more democratic laws, successful attempts to combat organized crime and corruption, improvements in property and personal security for its citizens, and promotion of human rights, strengthened antiterrorism activities, and improved relationships with the public and with police throughout the world.

These early steps were expanded in 2002 when the ministry changed its organizational structure. Government actions promoted further reform by enacting new legislation, creating guidelines for professional police education, and planning for modernizing equipment. Personnel changes that began in 2001 were continued and communication between the public, local, community groups and Parliament was established. Also, the ministry opened communication with foreign police agencies and various international organizations. The Serbian police are represented at all major regional, European, and world meetings and have strove to become a part of the international policing community. When Major General Milorad Simić, the head of police department, was appointed to the presidency of the Association of Police Chiefs for Southeastern Europe, Serbia's efforts appear to have met with success.

Most law enforcement activities in Serbia are handled by departments and units within the Public Security Sector. This sector is comprised of fourteen units and includes ten separate departments. The departments are:

- Criminal Investigation Department
- Police Department
- Traffic Police Department
- Border Police Department for Foreigners (which includes 37 border police stations)
- Fire Protection Department
- Analytical Department
- Information Technology Department
- General Affairs Department
- Communication Department
- Catering and Accommodation Department

Serbian officers stand in a line to prevent protestors from taking a donkey to a government building in downtown Belgrade, August 19, 2005. *The protestors consisted of dozens of peasants and farmers who were demonstrating against agricultural policies they viewed as having negative effects on their efforts to make a living.* **AP IMAGES.**

The Secretariats of Internal Affairs are composed of 233 police stations, 52 traffic police stations, 6 railway safety stations, and 2 border police stations.

Policing efforts in 2002 resulted in the ministry reaching one of its major goals. The threats to the safety of persons and property had been escalating in previous years, but these trends were halted in 2002 when the number of crimes dropped 21.7 percent (Ministry of Internal Affairs 2003).

Salaries. In 2002 budget appropriations for the Ministry of Internal Affairs totaled almost 21 billion dinars (US$251 million). Salaries accounted for 58 percent of the appropriations, and in 2002 employees received a 10 percent salary increase. However, even with the increase, salaries still remained less than that of employees in other civil service sectors (Ministry of Internal Affairs).

The average net monthly salary for Serbian police officers in October 2002 was 14,200 dinars (US$170). Although the officers' average monthly salaries exceed the minimum salary of 5,396 dinars established in early 2004, it still remained below that of other civilian sectors, which averaged 20,000 dinars a month in 2003 (Ministry of Internal Affairs; Republic of Serbia 2004a).

Hierarchy and Ranks. In 2003 the Ministry of Internal Affairs had 51,218 potential positions and 69.4 percent were filled. Of these, 3,999 had full executive power and authority. Field units of the ministry had 31,358 employees, or 70 percent of the total positions defined by the job classification, 20,870 positions were for uniform police officers, 2,480 officers executed specific duties, 3,045 were for firefighters, and 5,009 filled other positions in the ministry (Ministry of Internal Affairs).

Police-Community Relations. In 2002 almost 2,200 complaints were filed against police officers, of that amount, 9.1 percent of the complaints were judged to have merit. As a result, disciplinary proceedings were instituted against forty-four officers for serious violations of duty. According to the ministry, every complaint that is made is examined and processed.

To improve relations, community policing has been reintroduced, as have patrol sectors, beat patrol officers, and school police officers. The training in and use of modern police methods also help build confidence in the police among citizens and give police a sense professionalism and the importance of their job.

Local Police. Local policing efforts undertaken include "School without Drugs" activities. The police also focus more on prevention measures and introducing a police presence in the schools to help ensure student safety.

Special Police. In an attempt to deal with organized crime in Serbia regional intelligence centers were established. These five centers focus on collecting information on organized crime and the activities of organized criminal gangs in Serbia. This data collection is helped by the development of an information technology system aimed at monitoring the state of organized crime and analyzing the gathered information.

Serbia is a signer of the London Declaration (November 25, 2002), which is aimed at combating organized crime in southeastern Europe. The Ministry of Internal Affairs and the Serbian state have agreed to fight organized crime and its links to terrorism and trafficking in humans. To meet this obligation, funds have been allocated for the special equipment and the training of special tactical units, such as the Special Antiterrorist Unit, whose task is hijack prevention, the Special Operations Unit, which is designed to respond to the most violent and serious terrorism, and the Gendarmerie, which strives to prevent and suppress both internal and international terrorism activities.

Traffic Police. Despite increasing traffic, aging vehicles, and unsatisfactory road conditions, there was a 15.6 percent decrease in traffic accidents in 2002 when compared to 2001. Traffic injuries also declined by almost a quarter. Unfortunately, 847 persons died in traffic accidents in 2002, but this number still represents a 33.6 percent decline from the previous year. In fact, the number of traffic fatalities in 2002 was at its lowest level in fifteen years (Ministry of Internal Affairs).

These dramatic decreases in injury and mortality appear to have been affected slightly by stricter traffic penalties for violations, but the major positive factor appears to be better organization and improved policing techniques. Traffic officers were more aggressive in seeking out serious traffic violations, a 5.7 percent increase from 2001. In Serbia, 22 centralized and 726 localized activities were designed to detect serious offenses. The activities are titled "Road-Worthy Vehicle—Safe Driving." These activities were combined with increased police surveillance. Also, free automobile inspections by vehicle inspection associations were offered so as to decrease the number of unsafe vehicles on the road (Ministry of Internal Affairs).

Education and Training. In 2002 a four-month training program (May through August) was held for 752 female police officers. Starting in September and October, two six-month courses were conducted for 647 male officers. The training used a new curriculum including foreign-language study, courses on United Nations resolutions and conventions related to freedoms, rights, and duties of people, as well as provisions of war and humanitarian law and Police Code of Conduct. In September 2002, 124 students graduated from the first Gendarmerie course (Ministry of Internal Affairs).

A course titled "Introduction to Contemporary Standards of Policing" was held February to December 2003. Over 2,710 police officers attended and completed the course. Attendance was high, with 99.9 percent of police officers from all levels that were expected to attend doing so. During the course particular attention was paid to the lawful use of force by police officers in the line of duty (Ministry of Internal Affairs).

The education and training of police officers is carried out at the Secondary Police School, the Police College, and the Police Academy. Between 2002 and the beginning of 2003, 441 students enrolled in the Secondary Police School, 550 enrolled in the Police College, and 125 students enrolled in the Police Academy. The schools face problems because of a lack of space, up-to-date equipment, and technical resources (Ministry of Internal Affairs).

Recruitment and Conditions of Service. The ministry hired 2,450 new officers in 2002. Most of the officers were hired to serve as uniform police; 152 were hired to serve as criminal investigation officers, 223 as firemen, 47 as information technology officers, and 21 as border police officers. Women are also being sought out and hired by the ministry. Women account for 19.1 percent of all employees (Ministry of Internal Affairs).

There are approximately 2.5 police officers per 1,000 inhabitants, which is an insufficient number given the complexity of the issues facing Serbia. This ratio is also well below European averages in countries of approximately the same size and population.

In 2001, 1,397 ministry employees retired and 499 left for other reasons. In 2002, 622 persons retired because of age or because they were medically unable to perform their duties, another 318 persons left the ministry by mutual consent or because of a disciplinary court decision. In Belgrade about one-third of the police officer positions are unfilled despite active recruitment campaigns (Ministry of Internal Affairs).

Uniforms and Weapons. In 2002 over 9 billion dinars were allocated to the ministry's budget to pay for its operational expenses. Monies were used to purchase new uniforms for the uniform police and equipment, including specialized equipment for the Gendarmerie and Traffic Police (Ministry of Internal Affairs).

Transportation, Technology, and Communications. Although it is difficult to clearly identify exactly what weapons are being used by the Serbian police, reports regarding the use of force do help to paint a partial picture of the weapons commonly in use. In 2002, 65 cases reported the use of a baton, 41 cases reported the use of a firearm, and in the remaining 249 cases other means of coercion excluding physical force were reported (Ministry of Internal Affairs).

The Ministry of Interior purchased Tetra, a state-of-the-art digital radio communication system, making the Serbian police one of the best equipped services in Europe. A major part of the 2003 efforts were directed at equipping the Organized Crime Directorate and the Gendarmerie with Tetra.

The ministry also uses an IBM mainframe computer, server, and workstations in most of the secretariats. New programs are being developed and installed to further expand the information technology system and computer-telecommunications network. The ministry's analytical services are engaged in analyzing security-related incidents and events in the republic. Statistical reporting has been improved through the use of information technology and graphic tools. The ministry maintains and uses criminal investigation records regularly and in one year conducted over 1,040,000 background checks.

Police Statistics.

Serbia:

- Total Strength of Police Force: 27,000

- Population per Police Officer: 275

Montenegro:

- Total Strength of Police Force: 4,227

- Population per Police Officer: 150

CRIME

Organized Crime. The ministry has actively fought against organized crime and the violence it perpetrates in Serbia. The Directorate for Suppression of Organized Crime has been successful in its efforts to deal with organized crime. Shortly after it was established in 2002, the directorate identified and targeted 234 gang members. By 2003 the directorate had arrested 104 of them on charges stemming from 286 major criminal offenses. Significant results have also been achieved by the police as they strive to suppress other forms of economic corruption. For example, in 2003 thirty-seven people were arrested, of whom twenty-six were employees of the Republic Pension Insurance Fund who had accepted bribes so others could falsely acquire disability pensions.

Other organized crimes challenging Serbian police is tax evasion and money laundering. Many of these activities are carried out under the guise of business trans-

actions through phantom firms. In 2002 a total of 619 fictitious or phantom firms were identified. These firms engaged in money laundering through the Centro Banka, a legally registered commercial bank located in Belgrade. A bank officer issued falsified certificates of founding share capital for phantom firms with a value exceeding 1.5 million dinars. These fictitious firms and their transactions enabled the participants to evade tax payments of about 300 million dinars (Ministry of Internal Affairs).

Cigarette smuggling also poses a problem in Serbia. In 2002 approximately 127,624 cartons of illegally imported cigarettes were seized, while the smuggling of a million cartons of cigarettes was prevented. Forged excise stamps were also seized representing 500 million dinars. These activities have preserved the marketing of cigarettes from the legal sources and enabled the collection of excise taxes (Ministry of Internal Affairs).

Another area relating to organized crime has been the collection of evidence on the organization, operation, command structure, and crimes committed by the so-called Kosovo Liberation Army during the armed conflict in Kosovo and Metohija. A total of 9 reports and more than 10,000 pages of evidence relating to crimes committed by 138 members of the Kosovo Liberation Army were turned over to the Federal Ministry of Justice. This material allowed the Hague Tribunal to indict most of these individuals (Ministry of Internal Affairs).

CORRECTIONAL SYSTEM

The Ministry of Justice oversees the prison system in Serbia. Beginning in 2001 the prison system started evaluating and reforming its structure. The Organization for Security and Cooperation in Europe (OSCE) carried out an assessment in early 2001 with the Office for Democratic Institutions and Human Rights and the Council of Europe. A major finding of the study was the need for prison staff training. As a result, the OSCE began a program designed to train in successive stages the prison guards and governors. By 2003 approximately 200 prison guards from Belgrade Central Prison, Padinska Skela Prison, and Belgrade Prison Hospital took part in educational training that included seminars on communication skills, ethics, professional conduct, human rights, and drug awareness in prisons (OCSE 2003a).

Another goal of this reform is to introduce into the prison system a self-sustainable prison training structure. The OSCE hopes to achieve this goal through a program of training for local trainers. On May 12, 2003, OSCE trainers presented twelve police trainers with diplomas of completion (OCSE 2003b).

Table 1. Prisons Statistics, Kosovo, Montenegro, and Serbia

	Kosovo	Montenegro	Serbia
Total Prison Population	1,199	734	7,487
Prison Population Rate per 100,000	63	108	92
Pre-trial Detainees	71.8%	38.1%	27.5%
Female Prisoners	2.0%	2.5%	1.7%
Juvenile Prisoners	5.0%	1.4%	3.4%
Number of Prisons	6	3	28
Official Capacity of the Prison System	937	670	10,184
Occupancy Level	49.1%	109.6%	73.5%

To help foster a new openness with the media, the OSCE has been active in facilitating the development of relationships between the prison system, the media, and nongovernmental organizations. The OSCE has been working with the ministry to help establish an internal but independent mechanism of control that will oversee the prison system.

Prison Conditions. Prison conditions generally meet international standards; however, conditions vary greatly from one facility to another. The Helsinki Committee on Human Rights notes that some prisons are clean and secure while others, notably Belgrade Reformatory for psychiatric prisoners, are filthy and inhumane. Guards receive poor training. Basic educational and training programs are in place in most prisons, but they are limited by lack of resources. Men were separated from juveniles, women from men, and pretrial detainees from convicted felons.

Prison Statistics. Prison statistics are listed in Table 1.

MOST SIGNIFICANT ISSUE FACING THE COUNTRY

Serbia faces the threat of renewed United Nations economic sanctions because of its refusal to turn four generals and police officers over to the Hague Tribunal. The threat of economic sanctions is compounded by an unemployment rate in 2004 of close to 30 percent. The new prime minister hopes to ease the economic crisis by cutting taxes and public spending, easing regulations so the creation of small firms is encouraged, increasing the move toward privatization, and working toward bringing multibillion-dollar foreign debt under control.

Potential decreases in public spending may pose a problem for the Ministry of the Interior, which lacks highly qualified and specialized staff members, sufficient

technical equipment, and office space and in general has poor working conditions. The number of new officers being recruited has been low for years and recruitment has been the most difficult among traffic and general police officers. Recruitment difficulties are spreading to other areas of the ministry. In 2003 there was a scarcity of information technology and communication staff. This problem was aggravated when a number of highly skilled workers either quit, were fired, or retired from their positions. The ministry found it was almost impossible to hire trained staff to replace them and as a result one-third of the analytical and communication job positions at the ministry are now vacant. Finally, the country still remains politically unstable.

BIBLIOGRAPHY

Council of the European Union. 1998a. Common Position (EC) 98/326/CFSP (1) (May 7).

Council of the European Union. 1998b. "Concerning Additional Restrictive Measures against the Federal Republic of Yugoslavia." Council decision of May 10 implementing common position of May 10, 1999/318/CFSP. Official Journal L 123, 13/05/1999.

Council of the European Union. 1998c. "Concerning the Prohibition of New Investment in Serbia." Common Position (EC) 98/374/CFSP of June 8, 1998, defined by the council on the basis of article J.2. of the Treaty on European Union. Official Journal L 165, 10/06/1998.

Council of the European Union. 1998d. "Concerning the Reduction of Certain Economic Relations with the Federal Republic of Yugoslavia." Council Regulation (EC) 926/98, April 27. Official Journal L 130, 01/05/1998.

International Crisis Group. 2003. "Serbian Reform Stalls Again." *Europe Report*, no. 145 (July 17). Available online at http://www.crisisgroup.org/home/index.cfm?id=1719&l=1 (accessed December 26, 2005).

Judicial Reform Council. 2004. "Platform for the Strategy for Judicial Reform in Serbia." Ministry of Justice. Available online at http://www.judicialreform.sr.gov.yu/ (accessed December 26, 2005).

Mihajlović, Dušan. 2003. "Visa Regime Liberalization and Human Trafficking." Speech presented at the European Union Conference of the Ministers of Interior in Belgrade on March 3–4. Available online at http://www.mup.sr.gov.yu/domino/mup.nsf/obracanje (accessed December 26, 2005).

Ministry of Internal Affairs. 2003. "The Ministry of Internal Affairs of the Republic of Serbia 2002 Activity Report." Available online at http://www.mup.sr.gov.yu/domino/mup.nsf/index1-e.html (accessed December 26, 2005).

Office of Communication. 2003. "Extended Police Detention Abolished." Republic of Serbia press release, July 1.

Office of Communication. 2004. "Assembly." Republic of Serbia. Available online at http://www.serbia.sr.gov.yu/cms/view.php?id=1193 (accessed December 26, 2005).

Organization for Security and Cooperation in Europe. 2003a. "Report on Judicial Reform in Serbia." Rule of Law/Human Rights Department, Organization for Security and Cooperation in Europe. Available online at http://www.osce.org/documents/fry/2003/03/13_en.pdf (accessed December 26, 2005).

Organization for Security and Cooperation in Europe. 2003b. "Serbian Prison Guard Trainers to Receive Diplomas from OSCE." Media Advisory, Organization for Security and Cooperation in Europe. Available online at http://www.osce.org/item/7492.html (accessed December 26, 2005).

Republic of Serbia. 2003. "Police to Introduce Tetra System." Republic of Serbia press release, December 24.

Republic of Serbia. 2004a. "Average Monthly Salary in December 2003 Goes over 20,000 Dinars." Republic of Serbia press release, January 23.

Republic of Serbia. 2004b. "Minimum Net Wages up 15 Percent." Republic of Serbia press release, February 3.

Republic of Serbia. 2005. "Organization of the Ministry of Internal Affairs." Available online at http://www.mup.sr.gov.yu/domino/mup.nsf/index1-e.html (accessed December 26, 2005).

Stojanovic, Dušan. 2004. "Official: Serbian War Crimes Not Priority." *PhillyBurbs.com* (February 22). Available online at http://www.phillyburbs.com/pb-dyn/articlePrint.cfm?id=250512 (accessed December 26, 2005).

Roe Roberts
Nathan R. Moran
Robert D. Hanser

Seychelles

Official country name: Republic of Seychelles
Capital: Victoria
Geographic description: Group of islands in the Indian Ocean, northeast of Madagascar
Population: 81,188 (est. 2005)

■ ■ ■

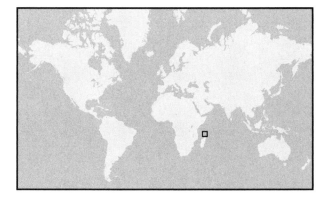

LAW ENFORCEMENT

History. Seychelles was first policed in 1775, when as a dependency of Île de France (Mauritius) fifteen soldiers were sent to Seychelles to perform security duties. This system continued until 1802, when a small police force was established under the command of Citizen Savy, who took orders from Revolutionary officials in France. Seychelles was ceded to Britain in 1814 and between 1822 and 1840 various combinations of policemen and soldiers formed the security forces of the country.

The police station at Victoria, the capital of Mahé, the main island, was destroyed with all the local records in a landslide in 1862, leaving a gap in the history of the force. By 1879 the strength of the force had increased to forty-five and outstations had been established at Victoria, Port Glaud, Anse Aux Pins, and Takamaka.

In 1903 the Mahé Group and Corallines became the separate Colony of Seychelles, by which time the force had grown to seventy-nine, with twelve outstations in operation.

A Special Force unit of forty-five men, paramilitary in character, was established in 1964 to assist the regular police in dealing with civil unrest and disturbance. During 1967 and 1968 radio communication facilities were obtained by police, and women police officers were also appointed. A criminal record office based on fingerprint identification was set up during this same period.

In 1971 when the Seychelles Airport was inaugurated, the Airport Police Section was established, followed by the Police Dog Unit in 1973. The Police Training School was opened in 1974 on the island of Praslin. In 1976 the Marine Section was founded to provide coastal and interisland policing for the inner islands.

When the Colony of Seychelles became independent on June 28, 1976, the police force was transferred with few changes to the new state. More than ten expatriates continued to serve as heads of departments and advisers.

However, the force was significantly affected by the coup d'état of June 5, 1977, which brought France-Albert René to power. The police armories were raided by the rebels to gain the weapons with which they overwhelmed the loyal troops. One police officer was killed in the operation.

Structure and Organization. The Seychelles Police Force is governed by the Police Force Act. They are under the control of the commissioner of police from the headquarters in Victoria. For operational and administrative purposes, the country is divided into four divisions: the Central District, including Victoria, the capital; the North Division; the South Division; and the Praslin/La Digue Division.

Each of these divisions is under the command of a senior police officer. There is a total of seventeen police stations in all the divisions. The Police Training School and the Police Mobile Unit are each under the command of an assistant superintendent who is directly responsible to the deputy commissioner. The force departments are staffed by police officers or civil staff and, in some cases, a combination of both. The organizational structure at the headquarters is as follows:

- Administrative and Support Services (including Prosecution, Marine, Dogs, Training, traffic, and Interpol)
- Criminal Investigation Department (CID)
- Special Force (Police Mobile Unit)
- General Duties
- Special Branch

  Other departments include:

- Traffic
- Marine
- Finance
- Radio and Telephone Communication
- Port Police
- Airport Police
- Transport Branch
- Rescue Unit
- Police Band
- Excise Section
- Canine Section
- Women Branch

Practically all local crime is investigated by uniformed and CID officers in the districts, while headquarters CID investigates certain serious transdistrict crimes, compiles fingerprints and criminal records, and undertakes photography and other specialized duties. It also supplies intelligence information regarding criminal activities to other police stations.

The Police Mobile Unit, under the command of a superintendent, is responsible for the preservation of public order and its restoration in the event of civil unrest or uprising. This unit also has the responsibility for providing personnel for parades.

The Special Branch, which is under the direct control of the commissioner of police, is responsible for the maintenance and operation of security and intelligence services and the prevention and detection of subversive activities. The Seychelles Police Special Constabulary is a permanent volunteer force under the Police Force Act.

Education and Training. The Police Training School at Praslin is under a commandant (who holds the rank of an assistant superintendent) and is responsible for recruit and refresher course training (15 weeks' duration), supervisory officers' courses (2 weeks), the promotion course (2 weeks), and basic courses taught in Creole (2 weeks). Field training is conducted weekly on a district basis. Prepromotion classes are held to prepare candidates for future promotion examinations. Instructors are generally sergeants or inspectors.

Uniforms and Weapons. Regular police inspectors and above wear a white open-necked shirt with royal-blue shorts or trousers. Junior ranks wear a blue shirt with royal-blue shorts. Personnel in the Special Force (Police Mobile Unit) war khaki shirts and shorts. Headgear consists of a dark-blue cap with a white checkered band. Members of the force are usually unarmed but the Police Mobile Unit is heavily armed with rifles and other weaponry.

Police Statistics.

- Total Police Personnel: 695
- Population per Police Officer: 117

HUMAN RIGHTS

The government generally respects the human rights of its citizens, although President René holds unchecked power. Security forces sometimes arbitrarily arrest citizens but detain them for only twenty-four hours under the constitution's charge or release provision.

CRIME

Crime Statistics. Offenses reported to the police per 100,000 population: 5,361. Of which:

- Murder: 3.7
- Assault: 43.4
- Burglary: 378
- Automobile Theft: 40.9

CORRECTIONAL SYSTEM

There are two penitentiaries on the island, of which the Long Island Prison is the main one.

Prison Conditions. There are no reports of abuse of prisoners. Family members are allowed monthly visits and prisoners have access to reading materials, although not to writing materials. Men are held separately from women and juveniles from adults.

Prison Statistics.

• Total Prison Population: 149

• Prison Population Rate per 100,000: 186

• Pretrial detainees: 1.3%

• Female prisoners: 1.3%

• Number of Prisons: 2

George Thomas Kurian

Sierra Leone

Official country name: Republic of Sierra Leone
Capital: Freetown
Geographic description: Located in western Africa on the North Atlantic between Liberia and Guinea
Population: 6,017,643 (est. 2005)

■■■

LAW ENFORCEMENT

History. The beginnings of what is known as the Sierra Leone Police Force date back to 1829, when twenty-six constables, half of whom kept order during day and half by night, were appointed in Freetown, then a British colony. By 1836 the nucleus of a proper police force had taken shape with 1 inspector, 3 subinspectors, and 60 constables. Each was issued one pair of shoes a year, but no uniforms. Senior officers had no prior police experience but were retired noncommissioned army officers or civilians.

When the British annexed Koya and Sherbro Island in 1861, the police role was expanded to cover the new territories. Some military structure and training were introduced into the force. The commander became the inspector general; the force was installed in barracks, armed with carbines, and given uniforms of white tunics and slacks with broad leather belts. By this time the force numbered 200 men.

In 1891 the Frontier Police was formed the guard the borders. In 1894 the civil force was designated the Sierra Leone Police Force in a government gazette. The first police band was formed in 1900, when the total strength was raised to 600. In September 1909 the first commissioner of police was selected. The commissioner formed a riot squad to deal with civil disturbances and started the

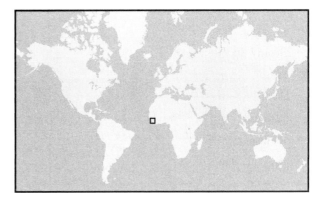

Police Training School at Port Loko. It was later transferred to the naval base at Hastings, where it remains.

In 1948 the force was again enlarged, this time to 1,000, and the first African was promoted to the rank of assistant superintendent. The riot squad was disbanded and every policeman began to receive training in riot control. In 1954 the force was extended to the main towns of the protectorate, replacing the disbanded Court Messenger Force. The first policewoman was recruited in 1947. In 1963 the first native Sierra Leonean was appointed commissioner of police and the last expatriate officer left the force in 1968. Meanwhile, the country began to experience civil unrest on a large scale. In 1968 all senior police officers were arrested by the junior ranks. For the next thirty-five years the police were swept into the turmoil and violence that culminated in a civil war in the 1990s.

Structure and Organization. The Sierra Leone Police Force is commanded by a commissioner, who is a minister of state without portfolio. It is organized into five geographical divisions, including one that guards the diamond industry. Each regional division is subdivided into a number of formations, such as the Criminal Investigations Department, the Special Branch, and the Traffic Division. The Special Branch is concerned with counterinsurgency and counterterrorism activities. The Traffic Division is also concerned with issuing firearms and ammunition licenses. There are separate men's and women's police bands and a Dog Division.

Constables are issued shoes and uniforms and are housed in barracks. Those not housed in barracks are given special housing allowances. All police officers from constable up are entitled to a pension.

The Sierra Leone Police Force has fifteen grades:

- Commissioner of Police
- Deputy Commissioner
- Senior Assistant Commissioner
- Assistant Commissioner
- Chief Superintendent
- Superintendent
- Deputy Superintendent
- Assistant Superintendent
- Chief Inspector
- Inspector
- Subinspector
- Sergeant Major
- Sergeant
- Corporal
- Constable

In addition, there are a number of special police groups, including the Internal Security Unit (ISU). It guards important government installations and constitutes the Presidential Guard. The former ISU-2 was a militia that has since been disbanded.

The Court Messenger Force is a quasi-police force employed by the district commissioners to carry warrants and subpoenas. When the Sierra Leone Police Force was extended to the Protectorate in 1954, the Court Messenger Force was disbanded, but each local authority was permitted to retain its local unit. In 1953 a permanent police force was established to counter illegal diamond smuggling.

Education and Training. Direct entry into the force is limited to those with secondary education. Others are sent to the Police Training School at Hastings for a six-month training course, at the end of which they are appointed constables.

Uniforms and Weapons. The formal uniform is a blue tunic worn with a white shirt and tie or a blue bush shirt worn with matching trousers and a blue cap. Members of the force are normally unarmed.

HUMAN RIGHTS

With the end of the civil war the systematic and serious human rights abuses have ended. The civil liberties suspended during the conflict have been reinstated. However, there are reports of extortion by the police.

CORRECTIONAL SYSTEM

Criminal law in Sierra Leone is contained not in a comprehensive code; instead, it consists of a series of local ordinances. Many English statutes are incorporated into the ordinances.

The most prevalent form of crime is diamond smuggling. Sexual offenses are relatively infrequent. Growing problems for the police are armed robbery, which is usually committed by gangs. There is also concern over the increasing use of drugs by the young, especially the smoking of *djamba*, a form of cannabis. Another kind of crime is ritual murder of children by secret societies, such as the Kieh.

Sierra Leone has twelve prisons, which are administered by the Ministry of Social Welfare. Pademba Road Prison is a maximum-security facility. The major ones are at Bo, Makeni, Kabala, and Kailahun. The Masanki Prison accommodates 500 prisoners. The Mafanta Prison has an agricultural colony. The Freetown Central Prison is the only one with a woman's wing. For juvenile prisoners there are five remand homes—at Wellington, Bo, Kenema, Makeni, and Sefadu.

Prison Conditions. Prison conditions have improved significantly since the end of the civil war. Although the prison in Kenema suffered overcrowding, conditions in Pademba Road maximum-security prison and at Bo and Moyamba are considered acceptable. Male and female prisoners are housed separately, although adults and juveniles as well as convicted prisoners and pretrial detainees are housed together. Conditions in holding cells in police stations are extremely poor.

Prison Statistics.

- Total Prison Population: 1,400
- Prison Population Rate per 100,000: 27
- Number of Prisons: 12
- Official Capacity of the Prison System: 700
- Occupancy Level: 200%

George Thomas Kurian

Singapore

Official country name: Republic of Singapore
Capital: Singapore
Geographic description: Island in Southeast Asia at the end of the Malay Peninsula, separated from Indonesia by the Strait of Singapore
Population: 4,425,720 (est. 2005)

■■■

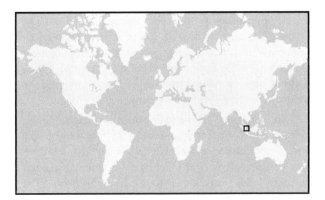

LAW ENFORCEMENT

History. The Singapore Police Force was established in 1827 when Sir Thomas Stamford Raffles, the founding father of Singapore, hired one sergeant and twelve constables to keep the peace. Thirty years later, the Police Act was passed, establishing a regular police force. In 1863 the first police uniforms were introduced. Another twenty-one years passed before the Criminal Investigation Department was set up, but the Criminal Records Office was not founded until 1901. Between then and the end of World War II there were only few developments. In 1916 marine patrols were launched to control piracy. In 1923 the Police Force Training Depot was begun, as the predecessor of the present-day Police Academy. In 1929, as more cars began to appear in the streets, the first Mobile Squad of the Traffic Police began work. Following the end of the Japanese occupation in 1946, the force was reorganized under R. E. Boulger. The Radio Division began operation in 1948. The next year women were first hired by the force and a female police unit was organized. In 1950, as the political landscape began to change, riot squads were formed to deal with street violence and demonstrations. In 1955 the Police Dog Unit became an integral part of the force. In 1959 the Police Force Training Depot became the Police Academy. In 1969, four years after independence, the drab khaki uniforms were discarded in favor of more lively blue ones. In 1972, following the report of the Lee Soon Ann Commission Report, police pay was raised and training facilities were upgraded. Recruitment was streamlined by placing it under the aegis of the National Service. In 1981 the force was reorganized into four commands.

Structure and Organization. The Singapore Police Force is headed by a commissioner of police assisted by four deputy commissioners, each in charge of one of four commands: Administration, Planning, Operations, and Civil Defense. Two departments are directly under the commissioner: the Public Relations Department and the Staff Inspectorate. Each of these departments is headed by a deputy assistant commissioner. The Public Relations Department is the focal point of media relations. It plans major campaigns directed at the public as well as its own personnel. It produces a number of in-house publications and audiovisual education programs, and it organizes exhibitions and community functions to present a better image of the police to the public. The Staff Inspectorate constitutes the eyes and ears of the force. It constantly monitors and assesses the performance of the force and provides feedback to the commission regarding possible changes and reforms.

The deputy commissioner for administration is assisted by three directors in charge of the Manpower and Administration, Logistics, and Training departments. The Manpower and Administration Department oversees all matters pertaining to the force personnel, finances, records, discipline, and welfare. Its welfare program has expanded considerably and now includes recreational facilities, social events, and provision of discounted consumer products and services. The Logistics Department administers workshops in the Marine, Transportation, Communications, and Armaments divisions and handles the Stores and Supplies Division. In addition, it evaluates new equipment and weapons and manages buildings. The Training Department runs the Police Academy and develops course materials through its Training Development Division. Moreover, it supervises the National Police Cadet Corps, a school-level organization designed to familiarize children with police activities.

The Planning Command implements changes in operations and prepares it to become a more efficient force. The deputy commissioner for planning is assisted by three directors in charge of the Operational Planning, Strategic Planning, and Systems and Research departments. The director of the Operational Planning Department supervises two divisions: the Security Planning Division and the Contingency Planning Division. The Security Planning Division formulates policy and doctrine relating to public order and security. It is also responsible for airport security and all entrances and exits out of the country. The Contingency Planning Division prepares for emergencies such as major natural disasters and crises, such as acts of terrorism and hijackings. The Strategic Planning Department is composed of two divisions: the Development Projects Division and the Conceptual Planning Division. The Development Projects Division initiates large development projects and handles the formulation of all building plans and the presentation of cost-benefit studies until the funds are approved. The Conceptual Planning Division is concerned primarily with five-year rolling plans and annual work plans. This involves data collection and analysis, coordination of planning activities among the various units, and work plan seminars. It also reviews from time to time force strategies to see whether they need to be readjusted. The director of the Systems and Research Department supervises three divisions: Organization and Method,

Doctrine, and Computer Systems. The Organization and Method Division reviews and revises work procedures and the organizational structure of various units. It undertakes the research required for demarcation of patrol sectors and adjustment of patrol shifts. It also undertakes feasibility studies on recommended new systems and procedures. The Doctrine Division reviews, amends, and issues force policies, doctrines, police general orders, force directives, and headquarters circulars. It also collects proposed amendments to legislation and prepares answers to parliamentary questions. The Computer Systems Division is responsible for the maintenance and development of computer networks. It translates the requirements of the police into the language of systems analysis and design.

The Operations Command is the front line of the force. This is where the bulk of the force is deployed in constant contact with the public. It has five departments: Areas, Detachment, Criminal Investigation, Traffic, and Crime Prevention. The commander for Areas Department, assisted by a deputy commander, is responsible for eight land divisions, the Radio Division, and the Airport Police. Each land division is headed by a superintendent who oversees crime prevention, patrol, investigation, enforcement, and other functions. The Radio Division is the mobile response force and its primary function is to attend to emergency calls. Headed by a deputy superintendent, it is composed of a large patrol force and a radio communications center; during major crises the latter serves as a combined police-military operations room. The Airport Police work with the Security Planning Division to enforce airport security.

The Detachment Department serves as an umbrella for a number of security units, mainly the Police Task Force, the Marine Police Division, the Security Branch, the Gurkha Contingent, and the Police Dog Unit. The Police Task Force consists of three units that serve many functions. In normal times they are deployed to provide security and control crowds at large public events, such as festivals and sports events. In times of unrest and public disorder, however, they serve as antiriot squads. The Marine Police Division is a large one, and its duties include patrolling territorial waters. It enforces rules and regulations governing the operation of all maritime vessels and looks out for illegal aliens and contraband goods arriving by sea. The Security Branch guards all VIPs. The Gurkha Contingent, composed of ethnic Gurkhas recruited from Nepal, acts as a backup force for any unit that needs such support. The Police Dog Unit trains dogs for guard and security work. The dogs are also used at airports to detect heroin and other drugs brought to the country.

The Criminal Investigation Department (CID) has four divisions, each headed by a superintendent. The four divisions are the Administrative and Specialist Division,

Police forces work to control a small protest in Singapore's financial district, August 11, 2005. *Several protesters gathered to call for more financial transparency in public institutions. The event followed a scandal from the month before, where the CEO of the National Kidney Foundation, Singapore's largest government-backed charity, was removed for suspected misuse of funds.* AP IMAGES.

the Commercial Crime Division, the Criminal Intelligence Unit, and the Secret Society or Organized Crime Division. The Administrative and Specialist Division investigates murders, kidnappings, and organized crime involving gambling vice and gambling syndicates. The Commercial Crime Division handles sophisticated white-collar crime. The division takes over from the Land Division cases that involve large sums of money or those considered too complicated. The Criminal Intelligence Unit collects information on crime and provides essential information to field investigators. The Secret Society Division watches for criminal activities by secret societies (*tongs*), a problem unique to Chinese populations.

The Traffic Police consists of the Operation Division and the Administrative Division. The Operation Division oversees traffic control and management, including patrol and enforcement. It investigates traffic accidents and processes violation reports. It also has a research branch that undertakes data collection, production of management information, and dissemination of road safety information. The Administrative Division oversees testing and licensing of drivers and administers the points demerit system and the training of traffic police personnel.

The Crime Prevention Department has a twofold task. It persuades and educates the general public and the business community to partner in the work of law enforcement and crime prevention through adopting safety measures. It performs this function through mass media campaigns as well as through direct liaison with community groups and business organizations. It has three divisions: the Operations Division, which directs and supervises crime prevention programs, the Liaison and Exhibitions Division, which reaches the community groups through neighborhood gatherings and mobile exhibitions, and the Collation and Research Division, which keeps track of criminal activities and trends.

The last of the four commands is the Civil Defense Command, which consists of two components: the Civil Defense Corps and the Construction Brigade. The Civil Defense Corps is composed of police reservists and it is the first responder in cases of aid and rescue operations in emergencies, such as a terrorist attack.

Education and Training. Recruits are required to have the equivalent of a tenth-grade education, be physically fit, and be between the ages of seventeen and a half and twenty-seven. Basic training lasts for thirty-two weeks and covers procedures, laws, weapons drill, hand combat, first aid, swimming, and civics. Class work is given at the Police Academy and is followed by on-the-job training. Since 1975 national servicemen began serving full time with the police to make up for shortfalls in recruitment.

Uniforms and Weapons. The uniform is a gray shirt, khaki shorts, and a beret or peaked cap.

Police Statistics.

- Total Police Personnel: 18,278
- Population per Police Officer: 242

CRIME

Crime Statistics. Offenses reported to the police per 100,000 population: 783. Of which:

- Murder: 1
- Assault: 2.4
- Burglary: 40.1
- Automobile Theft: 55.2

CORRECTIONAL SYSTEM

Singapore has one of the most severe penal codes in the world. It sanctions caning for a number of offenses including theft, and prescribes the death penalty for trafficking in firearms and kidnapping.

The Prisons Department of the Ministry of Home Affairs is under the immediate control of the director of prisons. He is assisted by a deputy and five superintendents. Women are kept at the Female Prison, a minimum-security facility. The Queenstown Remand Prison, a short-term maximum-security facility, receives and classifies newly convicted adult male offenders, and it also holds people awaiting trial or sentencing. Changi Prison, a maximum-security facility, houses prisoners sentenced to more than three years and those detained indefinitely. There are two medium-security facilities for first- and second-time offenders and those considered to be rehabilitatable: Moon Crescent in Changi and Khasa Crescent Center.

There is a prerelease camp, a minimum-security prison for long-term prisoners serving the last six months of their sentence. Young people under age sixteen are not sent to prisons, but to approved homes for girls and boys. The Reformative Training Center houses young offenders between ages sixteen and twenty-one.

Prison Conditions. Prison conditions, while spartan, meet international standards. However, inmates are chained to their beds at night. Human rights monitors are not allowed to visit prisons.

Prison Statistics.

- Total Prison Population: 16,835
- Prison Population Rate per 100,000: 392
- Pretrial Detainees: 8.9%
- Female Prisoners: 11%
- Juvenile Prisoners: 7.3%
- Number of Prisons: 15
- Official Capacity of the Prison System: 12,650
- Occupancy Level: 144%

George Thomas Kurian

Slovakia

---■---

Official country name: Slovak Republic
Capital: Bratislava
Geographic description: Landlocked country in east central Europe
Population: 5,431,363 (est. 2005)

■ ■ ■

LAW ENFORCEMENT

History. The Slovak Republic came into existence on January 1, 1993. Michal Kováč was elected by the Parliament in February to serve as the president. Vladimír Mečiar was elected and served three times as Slovakia's prime minister. Mečiar began moving toward increasingly authoritarian behavior and was pointed out as the reason Slovakia was eliminated from consideration for both the European Union (EU) and the North Atlantic Treaty Organization (NATO) in earlier years. Slovakia was without a president for more than a year after Kováč finished his term. Finally, the constitution was changed to allow for direct vote, and Rudolf Schuster was elected in May 1999.

Mečiar, the Populist prime minister, was unseated in the 1998 elections by the reformist government of Mikuláš Dzurinda. Mečiar has been blamed for Slovakia's low investment from foreign capital. In April 2000 Mečiar was arrested and charged with paying illegal bonuses to his cabinet ministers while in office. A three-week standoff with police preceded the arrest, ending only when police commandos blew open the door on Mečiar's house and seized him. He was also questioned about his alleged involvement in the 1995 kidnapping of Kováč's son.

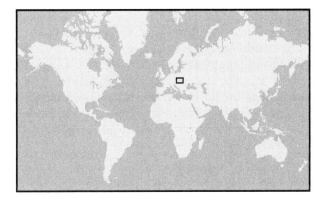

Dzurinda has improved Slovakia's reputation in the West. In 2004 the country became a member of both the EU and NATO. As of 2005 Dzurinda was becoming unpopular within the country because of tough economic policies.

Structure and Organization.

Principal Agencies and Divisions. There are two major law enforcement agencies within Slovakia as well as one major intelligence agency. The State Police, under the jurisdiction of the Ministry of Interior, is the primary law enforcement agency. Besides domestic law enforcement, they also have the responsibility for border security. The State Police are broken into four main categories: Traffic Police, Border and Customs Police, Criminal and Financial Police, and Public Order Police. The second major law enforcement agency is the municipality police that reside within the cities and towns. The Slovak Information Service is an independent organization that reports directly to the prime minister and is responsible for all civilian security and intelligence activities.

Salaries. The average salary for a Slovak police officer is 19,000 Slovak crowns (US$404) per month, which is almost 70 percent above the national average for wages. This average does not apply to the municipal officers and lower traffic officers.

Retirement Age. Legislation has been passed with the goal of retaining workers to produce a more efficient and productive Slovakian economy. Beginning in January 2004 legislation raised Slovakia's retirement age by nine months each year; eventually, the retirement age will be sixty-two years for both men and women. As of 2005 the retirement age for men was sixty years and between fifty-four and fifty-seven years for women, depending on how many children they have raised.

Police at Work. The Police Corps of the Slovak Republic is an armed safety corps responsible for maintaining internal order and safety. The Slovak National Council and government control the police force, which is subordinate to the minister of interior. The activities and responsibilities of the Police Corps are controlled by the constitution and other binding regulations. The corps is totally independent of the military and lacks any connections at either the management or organizational level, though in times of great need, the government may order that the military soldiers join with the Police Corps to secure the state frontier or to guarantee internal public order.

The Police Corps consists of criminal police, public order police, traffic police, object protection police, foreign service police, frontier police, and special task police. The protection of special persons and finances are designated to the special task police. There are separate district, regional, and Slovak investigation offices. The head of the Police Corps is the Police Corps president.

Police Corps law allows for the use of force by police. The type of force to be used is largely dependent on the police officer's interpretation of the situation. Officers exercise a great deal of discretion when it comes to the use of force. Types of force that can be used include basic elements such as truncheons, defense bars, tear gas, electric paralyzing devices, and guns.

The police can apprehend a person in accordance with Police Corps law, which states that a person who threatens life, health, or property or who was caught in the act may be placed in custody for a maximum of twenty-four hours. Investigators can apprehend a suspect who has been caught committing a crime without an indictment or approval from the prosecutor. When the case needs immediate action, the suspect can be apprehended and placed into custody, where justified, without indictment. To conduct this type of apprehension, prosecutor approval is necessary. The suspect can be held for a maximum of twenty-four hours, after which the case must be submitted for trial or the suspect is set free. No cautioning in this stage of apprehension is allowed. The purpose in apprehending a suspect is to assess whether sufficient conditions are met for placing the person in prison.

Most complaints about police behavior concern the activities of the basic corps and involve searches, unproductive investigations, improper public identification of suspects, and activities of traffic police. Complaints are handled by the following authorized persons: commander, district commander, inspection officer of a district commandership, inspection officer of the Inspection Department of the Ministry of Interior, and the formation director of the Minister of Interior.

Police-Community Relations. The police-community relations in Slovakia are best described as tense. The ethnic minorities in the country strongly distrust law enforcement. The police are viewed as corrupt by most and cooperation between communities and the Police Corps has been minimal in the past. African, Roma, Hungarian, and other minorities feel that the police ignore crimes committed against ethnic groups and pay little attention to investigation. Furthermore, skinheads repeatedly attack all ethnic minorities with little interference from law enforcement.

To solve police-community relations problems, Slovakian law enforcement has encouraged foreign agencies to assist with training and education. American law enforcement experts have been traveling to Slovakia to present a modern form of policing. They hope to present the benefits of listening to the community rather than assuming that all the problems are known. Slovakian police tend to jump directly into a situation to gain order and control while it is the goal of the foreign law enforcement aide to present a calmer approach of community cooperation.

Local Police. The local police forces for individual cities and towns are the municipal police. They are usually simple beat cops who walk the streets in pairs to deal with minor street quarrels and provide assistance to those in need. Municipal police have responsibilities similar to those of Public Order Police as seen at the state level, but they also oversee parking in towns. Municipal police do not have authority to issue fines for exceeding the speed limit, although they have authority to punish many other traffic offenses. Municipal police range from the average street cop to the mounted officer.

Special Police. Special police units include organizations like the Border and Customs Police that fall under the

Slovakian security forces on horseback patrol the Bratislava Castle shortly before a summit between U.S. President George W. Bush and Russian President Vladimir Putin is scheduled to take place there, February 23, 2005. Because of the summit, Slovakian authorities increased safeguards at key border crossings and expanded patrols at airports and train stations, along with locking down security in the capital city. **AP IMAGES.**

state policing system. Units such as these are responsible for monitoring border crossings and administering the rules governing foreign residents of Slovakia. There are also special task police that have specific jobs such as guarding private persons and finances.

Riot Police. Riot police are known as intervention units in Slovakia. Intervention units are called in to deal with unruly mobs and situations that are possibly unstable. The Slovakian intervention units have a bad reputation for the use of excessive force. Within the sporting community of Europe, Slovakian intervention units are regarded in a negative light because of the use of excessive force against English soccer fans.

Traffic Police. The Traffic Police are a subdivision of the State Police. Their job consists of monitoring the traffic laws applicable in towns and on highways. Traffic Police make use of cars equipped with radar and transmitters to enforce traffic violations. Some Traffic Police

can also be found on horseback within town and city limits.

Education and Training. To become a member of the Police Corps of the Slovak Republic, a person must be a citizen, be at least eighteen years of age and have passed what is called the school-leaving examination available at a secondary school or have graduated from a university or technical college. The applicant must also be physically and mentally healthy, have finished military duty (if applicable), and have a clean criminal record. A probationary period of up to twelve months is established at the time of appointment. Further education and training of officers is performed in special secondary schools of the Police Corps, the Police Academy of the Slovak Republic, and the Institute for Further Education of Police and Training. Further education also comes from the cooperation with foreign law enforcement agencies dealing with ethnic tolerance and police-community relation issues. American law enforcement experts are among the foreign law enforcement helping Slovakian police gain insight about modern policing.

Uniforms and Weapons. The officers of the Police Corps of the Slovak Republic wear several types of uniforms including official, field dress, and special uniforms for the special units officers. Uniforms vary with regard to the individual police unit as well as with the time of year. Men and women officers both have a variety of uniforms when it comes to seasonal changes and to the changing styles in clothing. Accompanying the officer's dress is the standard armament for a Slovakian officer. The basic armament for an officer includes a belt, handcuffs, truncheon, and extra clips.

Weapons for Slovakian police vary with the needs of the unit. Officers have access to weapons ranging from truncheons, defense bars, protection shields, tear gas, bulletproof vests, and handguns. Three main handguns are issued as standard weapons to most officers: Arrow PS97, Model 82, and EZ75.

Transportation, Technology, and Communications. Several types of vehicles and equipment are used for modern policing. The Civil Police are reported to have a total of seven policing helicopters that are based at the Bratislava-Ivanka Airport. The helicopters include one Mil-Mi-8p and six Mil-Mi2. The Police Corps is equipped with cars, with a ratio of one car to every five police officers.

The Slovakian technology is behind the times but can be seen in most aspects of policing. The command levels of the Police Corps are equipped with computer databases, which contain personal documents and criminal information. The main computer databases are about the highest point of technology pertaining to law enforcement. Police cars are equipped with radar and transmitters as needed, such as with Traffic Police on highways and in major cities. The communications technology is lacking; this can be seen in the case of the infamous police walkie-talkies, which function only at extremely short ranges.

Surveillance and Intelligence Gathering. There are eleven entities within Slovakia that deal with intelligence services, including Borders and Alien Police, Civil Defense, Civil Police, Defense Ministry Intelligence-Security Service, Internal Security, Ministry of Interior, National Anti-Drugs Unit, Office of Civil Protection, Office of Nuclear Surveillance, Reserve Force (Home Guards), and Slovak Information Service. The Slovak Information Service is the main agency responsible for intelligence gathering and reports directly to the prime minister. Technology and communications are outdated within the country, thus causing an obstacle for intelligence gathering and surveillance.

Police Statistics. Most police statistical information for Slovakia is considered restricted.

- Total Strength of the Police Force: 20,208
- Population per Police Officer: 269

HUMAN RIGHTS

The Slovakian government is generally respectful of human rights and aware of their implications in the world. Slovakia has created antidiscrimination legislation and provisions within the penal code. The government's cabinet has approved action plans to prevent all forms of discrimination and intolerance. The government has also created the position of special government commissioner for Roma issues in the Office of Deputy Prime Minister for Human Rights and Minorities. Despite these additions, the government still has not fulfilled the United Nations recommendation to create a national committee for human rights. Although improvements have continued since the early 1990s, there remain obstacles to be overcome.

There are many reports about police indifference, alleged beatings, and abuse of the Roma. Ethnic minorities, in particular the Roma, face discrimination within the Slovakian society. Skinheads frequently attack the Roma, and police sometimes fail to provide adequate protection against these attacks. This represents one of the greatest problems facing Slovakian society. In 1999 a police officer allegedly shot a twenty-one-year-old Roma during an interrogation. Later the next year, the officer was dismissed for violating the law when he interrogated a Roma, during which time he had a gun accessible.

CRIME

Organized Crime. Organized crime is a prevalent concern in Slovakia and the east European countries. The Slovak Intelligence Service reports that most organized crime within Slovakian borders is because of international Mafias, especially Russian, Albanian, and Italian. Slovakia is considered a transport corridor for weapons smuggling because of the lack of adequate legislation in the area. According to the Slovak Intelligence Service director, Russian and Ukrainian Mafia are using their links to the Slovak underworld to smuggle small arms to countries that have military conflict. Slovakia has also become an important part of the "Balcan Route" for drug smuggling.

Slovak police officials speculate that extortion, protection, and silent partnerships are the main rackets of the mobsters within Slovakia's borders. Another problem with organized crime is the growing sex trade as young Slovak women are hired as dancers or bar girls abroad, and then find themselves forced into prostitution. The Slovak police have seen organized crime elements, from within the country and abroad, increase in complexity of crimes and the amount of resources at the groups' disposal. This rising growth in organized crime is because of the emergence of globalization. Slovakia is located between Europe and the Asian continent, so it serves as a natural funneling point for illegal activity across the world.

CORRECTIONAL SYSTEM

The correctional system contains three individual levels of prisons for adult males, the highest level being maximum security. Within maximum security, adult convicts are housed with the goals of education and rehabilitation. Separate prisons are found for juveniles and women.

After those convicted have served half of their prison sentence, or two-thirds in the case of serious crimes, they have the right to be set free on a conditional basis, which can last from one to seven years. Courts are the final say on the decision of rulings and corrections. Convicts must be able to demonstrate their readiness for release by their prison behavior, or the court must accept the guarantee of completion of rehabilitation of the convict.

Prison Conditions. The prison conditions within Slovakia have been vastly improved with the progression of time. In 1987 when Slovakia and the Czech Republic were still joined as Czechoslovakia, prison conditions were poor. Prisoners complained of frequent beatings from authoritative figures and less-than-standard living conditions. Prisoners also told of beatings and ill treatment by fellow prisoners that were possibly encouraged by the guards. Food complaints and disease were widespread and dietary deficiencies led to ailments. Disease ran rampant through the prison and spread quickly to others. Prison conditions in Slovakia were often in Amnesty International reports during the 1970s and 1980s, which concluded that prison conditions in Czechoslovakia fell below "internationally accepted standards." Today, prison conditions and the quality of life for prisoners have improved.

Prisoners are obligated to work while serving time in prison. If an inmate fails to work, the convict is required to pay the cost of his imprisonment and is forced to stay in a special room during the working hours. Those who cannot work and the elder individuals are exempt from the service of labor. Prisoners who exhibit good behavior, good working results, or exemplary action can be rewarded. The convict can be rewarded such things as a temporary release from prison for up to fifteen days, praise, special visit permission, special packet permission, pocket money

increase, or financial and material reward. Prisoners today have certain rights that cannot be alienated while in prison. Inmates have a right to receive and send letters, to receive packets, and to be allowed visitation by relatives. They have the right to use cultural and educational resources, such as the prison library, and to explore sport and hobby opportunities, legal education, and medical education. There are also legal regulations allowing them to further their education.

Prison Statistics.

- Total Prison Population: 8,891
- Prison Population Rate per 100,000: 165
- Pretrial Detainees: 33.1%
- Female Prisoners: 2.5%
- Juvenile Prisoners: 0.7%
- Number of Prisons: 18
- Official Capacity of the Prison System: 9,500
- Occupancy Level: 93.6%

MOST SIGNIFICANT ISSUES FACING THE COUNTRY

The most significant issue facing Slovakia with regard to its criminal justice system is the lack of trust from the community and society toward police. The Police Corps is viewed as a corrupt organization that can be bought with bribes. The ethnic groups within the country do not believe the police will help with racial violence and feel the police ignore the problems plaguing the country.

With regard to the country itself, organized crime is becoming more effective, and with the effects of globalization, it is growing everywhere. Slovakia is a key midpoint for shipment between the Asian continent and the remainder of Europe. The Slovak legislation has loopholes inherent in the system that allows organized crime to flourish and grow within the borders. Drugs pass through the country regularly, and the internally organized crime is beginning to develop a larger production of drugs.

BIBLIOGRAPHY

Bureau of Democracy, Human Rights, and Labor. 2001. "Country Reports on Human Rights Practices: Slovak Republic, 2000." U.S. Department of State. Available online at http://www.state.gov/g/drl/rls/hrrpt/2000/eur/868.htm (accessed January 4, 2006).

Goldman, Minton F. 2004. *Global Studies: Russia, the Eurasian Republics, and Central/Eastern Europe*, 10th ed. Guilford, CT: McGraw-Hill/Dushkin.

Hencovska, Maria. 1992. "World Factbook of Criminal Justice Systems: Slovak Republic." Bureau of Justice Statistics, U.S.

Department of Justice. Available online at http://www.ojp.usdoj.
gov/bjs/pub/ascii/wfbcjslo.txt (accessed January 4, 2006).

Ministry of the Interior. 2003. "Survey on Selected Types of
Crime in 1988–2002 in the Slovak Republic." Available
online at http://www.minv.sk/en/_private/krimisurvey.htm
(accessed January 4, 2006).

Ministry of the Interior. 2005a. "Organisational Chart."
Available online at http://www.minv.sk/en/images/org.htm
(accessed January 4, 2006).

Ministry of the Interior. 2005b. "Uniforms of the Officers of the
Police Force of the Slovak Republic." Slovak Republic.

Available online at http://www.minv.sk/rovnosaty/ (accessed
January 4, 2006).

Pisarova, Martina. 2001. "A Quick Guide to How the Slovak
Police Work." *Slovak Spectator* 7 (19) (May 14–20).

Togneri, Chris. 2001. "Police Begin Sensitivity Training." *Slovak
Spectator* 27 (22) (June 4–10).

Ryan Lacina
Nathan R. Moran
Robert D. Hanser

Slovenia

Official country name: Republic of Slovenia
Capital: Ljubljana
Geographic description: Located in central Europe, bordering the eastern Alps with a small coastline on the Adriatic Sea
Population: 2,011,070 (est. 2005)

■ ■ ■

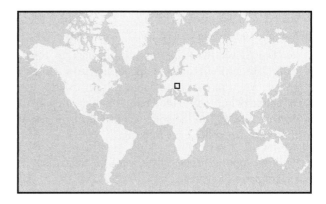

LAW ENFORCEMENT

History. Slovenia came under the rule of Habsburg princes in the late thirteenth century. It would remain a part of the Habsburg Empire until the end of World War I, when it became part of the newly created Kingdom of Serbs, Croats, and Slovenes. In 1929 the Kingdom of Serbs, Croats, and Slovenes was renamed Yugoslavia. Nazi, Italian, and Hungarian forces occupied Slovenia during World War II. After the war Slovenia was one of the republics in Communist Yugoslavia led by Josip Broz Tito. Following the death of Tito in 1980, Slovenia sought more autonomy within communist Yugoslavia. In 1991 Slovenia declared its independence from Yugoslavia and adopted its own constitution.

Structure and Organization. The Slovenian police force is a part of the Ministry of the Interior. It consists of the General Police Directorate (GPD), which operates at the national level. It has eleven regional police directorates and ninety-nine local police stations. The headquarters of the GPD are in Ljubljana. The director general of the police is in charge of the police force and heads the GPD.

The regional directorates are led by directors and the local police stations by commanders.

Principal Agencies and Divisions. The GPD adopts guidelines, determines strategies, and monitors the enforcement of police duties. The police directorates carry out the work of the police force at the regional level. The local police stations perform duties relating to general and transport safety and border security. The commanders of police stations report to the regional directors.

The GPD includes the following components: the Office of the Director General of the Police, the Uniformed Police Directorate, the Criminal Police Directorate, the Operation and Communication Center, the Special Unit, the Police Academy, the Occupational Health and Safety Service, and the Information and Telecommunications Service. Within the Office of the Director General of the Police are found the Supervision Division, the Division for Complaints, Internal Affairs and Assistance to Policemen, the System Analysis Division, the International Cooperation Division, and the Office of Public Relations. Within the Uniformed Police Directorate are found the Public Order Sector, the Road Traffic Sector, the State Border and Aliens Sector, the Sector for the Organization and Development of the Uniformed Police, the Defense Planning and Police Specialties Sector, the Flight Police Unit, the Police Orchestra, and the Aliens Center. Within the Criminal Police Directorate are found the General Crime Sector, the Economic Crime Sector, the Organized Crime Sector, the Special Tasks Sector, the Computer Crime and Crime Analysis Sector, the International Cooperation Sector, the Forensic Research Center, and the Mobile Crime Units. Within the Police Academy are the Police High School and the Police College and the Training and Education Center.

The police directorates at the regional level have the following components: the Office of the Director of the Police Directorate, the Uniformed Police Office, the Criminal Police Office, the Operation and Communication Center, and the Logistic Division. The eleven regional police directorates are Celje, Koper, Kranj, Krško, Ljubljana, Maribor, Murska Sobota, Nova Gorica, Novo Mesto, Postojna, and Slovenj Gradec.

The Slovenian police force is required to operate within laws established by the political system consistent with the constitution of the country. The basic law governing the police force is the Police Act of the Republic of Slovenia. Article 3 of the police act lists the basic responsibilities of the police force as being:

- Protection of people's lives, personal safety, and property

- Prevention, disclosure, and investigation of criminal offenses and misdemeanors, the disclosure and arrest of perpetrators of criminal offenses and misdemeanors, and the implementation of searches for wanted persons and their handover to the proper authorities

- Maintenance of public order

- Supervision and direction of traffic on public roads and unclassified roads currently in use for traffic

- Protection of state borders and the implementation of border control

- Implementation of duties set forth in the Aliens Act

- Protection of certain individuals, agencies, buildings, and districts

- Protection of certain places of employment and classified state information unless otherwise prescribed by law

- Implementation of the tasks set forth in this act, other acts, and executive regulations

Salaries. The Slovenian national currency is the tolar. In 2001 the police force budget totaled 44,831,923,000 tolars, of which 35,115,804,000 tolars (78%) went into salaries. In 2002 the police force budget totaled 50,255,592,000 tolars, of which 39,170,738,000 tolars (77%) went into salaries (Ministry of the Interior 2003a). For every year of service in the police force beyond the first five years, a police officer is entitled to a bonus of 0.5 percent of his or her basic salary. Specific salary schedules by position and rank are not openly published.

Retirement Age. A male police employee of at least forty-five years of age with a minimum of thirty years of qualifying service, or a female police employee of at least forty years of age with a minimum of twenty-five years of qualifying service, including at least fifteen years of service with the status of an authorized officer, according to the Internal Affairs Act, or with the status of a police officer, has the right to retire six months after submitting a request to retire. The retirement pension is estimated to be 65 percent of the basic salary. Every year worked beyond the pension minimum of thirty years for males or twenty-five years for females increases the basic pension by 2 percent to a maximum of 85 percent of the basic salary.

Hierarchy and Ranks. The GPD operates at the national level. The police directorates carry out the work of the police force at the regional level and are subordinate to the GPD. The local police stations report to the police directorates.

The specific ranks, from highest to lowest, in the Slovenian police force are:

- Director General of the Police
- Deputy Director General of the Police
- Chief Police Superintendent
- Senior Police Superintendent
- Police Superintendent First Class
- Police Superintendent
- Chief Police Inspector
- Senior Police Inspector
- Police Inspector First Class
- Police Inspector
- Junior Police Inspector
- Senior Police Officer
- Police Officer First Class
- Police Officer
- Junior Police Officer

- Auxiliary Police Officer

- Cadet of the Police High School

Police at Work. The basic rights and responsibilities of the Slovenian police force at work are outlined in article 33 of the Police Act of the Republic of Slovenia. Article 33 states that "while on duty, police officers may warn, give orders, determine a person's identity and initiate identification procedures, make a security check on a person, issue summons, perform a safety check, deny entry to a certain territory, perform an anti-terrorist search of premises, buildings, instruments and territories, arrest and bring in a person, detain a person, order strict police surveillance, confiscate items, enter a private residence and private premises, make use of transportation and communication means, apply undercover police coercive and any other measures authorized by law."

Police-Community Relations. The Slovenian police force commonly informs the people of important information related to their security. Particular effort is devoted to informing the public of preventive measures to fight crime and the rights of citizens in police procedures. An attempt is made to inform the people of police work through news articles and profiles in the media, open houses, and public meetings. In 2001 the police organized 375 press conferences and issued 3,790 reports, notices, and public information announcements (Ministry of the Interior 2002).

The orchestra of the Slovenian police force regularly performs concerts and is well respected in the country. Teams composed of police force employees routinely participate in national and international sporting competitions.

Local Police. The local unit of law enforcement in Slovenia is the police station. There are standard police stations and stations for the traffic police, border police, airport police, railway police, maritime police, mounted police, and police dog handlers. The total number of police stations is 99. All police stations are considered to have equal status, but their size is not equal. There are at least 20 police officers in a police station. Some have more than 200 officers. The categories of classification used are 1A for stations with 81 or more police officers, category 1 for stations with 51 officers or more, category 2 for stations of 31 officers or more, and category 3 for up to 30 officers. Category 3 typically applies to border, railway, mounted, airport, and police dog handler stations. Police details typically number from 10 to 20 police officers (Kolenc 2003).

Special Police. The special police in Slovenia consist of the Special Unit, mounted police, air police, and police dog handlers. The Special Unit handles criminal activity involving extortion and kidnapping, illegal sale of weapons, explosives, prohibited drugs, vehicle theft, and capturing escaped prisoners. It also examines terrain and buildings to detect traces of criminal activities, assists in the search for missing persons and items, and returns foreign citizens who enter Slovenia illegally. In 2002 the Special Unit was used in thirty-nine operational actions and nine urgent interventions (Ministry of the Interior 2003a).

The air police uses helicopters to monitor road traffic and the state border and to search for criminal offenders. Police dogs are used to detect prohibited drugs and explosives. Mounted police are mainly involved in observation and protection of the public and monitoring state borders.

Riot Police. There is not a specifically designated riot police unit in Slovenia. Mounted police, air police, and Special Unit members perform crowd-control functions. Special Unit members often cooperate with the uniformed police in monitoring high-risk soccer matches and any protest marches. In 2002 mounted police officers were used on one occasion as a means of crowd restraint (Ministry of the Interior 2003a).

Traffic Police. Each regional police directorate has at least one traffic police station. Additionally, local police stations are involved in traffic safety. Traffic police regulate the traffic on public roads and enforce measures against the violators of traffic rules, examine accident sites, and protect special transports and events.

Traffic police use laser speedometers, the video surveillance system ProVida 2000, and a helicopter equipped with the I LEO system to monitor traffic speeds. They use a stationary electronic alcohol tester or etilometer to test for alcohol use. In Slovenia the permitted amount of alcohol in the blood is five grams per kilogram.

In 2002 the police force registered 571,089 traffic violations for which fines were enacted and 102,812 violations for which misdemeanor procedures were justified. There were 39,601 traffic accidents and 269 fatalities. Speeding was the leading cause for traffic accidents, followed by driving under the influence of alcohol (Ministry of the Interior 2003a).

Education and Training. The GPD regulates the planning and implementation of education and training for the police force. It is required that all applicants for the general and criminal police must have at least finished high school. Additionally, they must undergo a six-month training course before they can start to work as a police officer. Those interested in a police career as early as age fifteen may attend the School for Cadets (Police High School) for four years after primary school and the

In an attempt to catch drivers speeding, Slovenian officers stand in a wooden bus shelter and aim a laser radar device at traffic going to Kocevje, a small city 40 miles south of Ljubljana, Slovenia, March 1, 2005. The operations were part of new efforts by Slovenia authorities to introduce traffic laws with higher penalties for violators. **AP IMAGES.**

Higher School for Internal Affairs (Police College) for two years. The principles of the Code of Police Ethics form part of the curriculum at the police schools.

Once employed, the Higher Police Officer Educational Program and Officer Advanced Training Program offer additional educational and training opportunities. Training courses are offered in the areas of general police tasks, criminal investigation, traffic control, border affairs and foreign persons, computer proficiency, police dog handling, social skills, and special police unit training in conjunction with foreign police experts, including the U.S. Federal Bureau of Investigation.

Recruitment and Conditions of Service. A police officer is required to have a minimum of a secondary professional diploma and the appropriate psychological and physical ability to perform police work. A candidate cannot be a convicted criminal and cannot be involved in proceedings for a criminal offense. The candidate must have completed any mandatory service in the military of Slovenia, not be older than thirty years of age, and be both a citizen and permanent resident of the Republic of Slovenia. Women are not required to serve in the military before being employed as police officers.

A candidate who has accepted employment as a police officer must pass an examination before beginning work. After passing the examination, the candidate must take the following oath: "I solemnly swear to carry out my police duties in a conscious, responsible, and humane manner, in accordance with the law and with respect to human rights and basic liberties." A new police recruit signs a statement that he or she accepts the contents of the Code of Police Ethics on joining the force.

A police officer must take a professional, psychological, and physical competency test at least every three years. He or she may retake the test a maximum of two consecutive times. If the test is not passed, the officer is terminated.

Uniforms and Weapons. The Slovenian police force has winter, summer, work, and solemn police uniforms, each with its own special type of cloth and headgear. Component parts of each uniform include rank insignia and police symbols. The basic color of the uniform is blue. Police officers also wear special uniforms, such as camouflage, skiing, pilot, motorcycle, and naval.

The uniformed police may perform some of their tasks in civilian clothes when directed by their supervisors.

Detectives usually wear civilian clothes and they identify themselves with police identification cards. The appearance of the Special Unit is different from that of regular police and the public rarely sees the unit members with their faces uncovered. They usually perform their tasks in work uniforms, which are dark gray and have a panther patch on the right shoulder. The head gear of their solemn uniforms is also different from that worn by the regular police.

The weapons issued and used by the Slovenian police force include pistols, revolvers, automatic pistols, semiautomatic and automatic rifles, heavy machine guns and machine guns, sniper rifles, shotguns, hand grenades, grenade and gas launchers, and pyrotechnical devices. The most basic weapon issued to uniformed police officers is the rubber truncheon.

Standard-issue pistols are the Beretta M92, for the uniformed police, and the Beretta M8000, for detectives. The Berettas have replaced the Crevna Zastava Ml 70, which was used during the 1970s and 1980s. Specific long-barreled weapons include Heckler-Koch machine guns, M70 automatic guns, and M59/66 semiautomatic guns.

Transportation, Technology, and Communications. In carrying out its responsibilities, the Slovenian police force uses bicycles, motorcycles, white-blue patrol vehicles, unmarked vehicles, smaller and larger intervention vehicles, special vehicles for the investigation of sites of traffic accidents, vehicles for the survey of crime scenes, vehicles designed to transport police dogs, all-terrain vehicles, special trailers for the transport of horses and vessels, and armored transporters equipped with water guns. At the end of 2002 the total number of vehicles in use by the Slovenian police force was 2,050, including 812 personal unmarked vehicles, 539 personal police vehicles, 235 all-terrain vehicles, 184 motorcycles, 124 intervention vehicles, and 74 combined vehicles (Kolenc 2003).

Besides vehicles, the Slovenian police force operates a small fleet of helicopters. The police operate five helicopters, two AB-206 Jet Rangers, an AB-212, an AB-412, and an EC-135. They are used for VIP transport, transport of various cargo and the Special Unit, border monitoring, search and rescue missions, medical evacuation, and traffic surveillance (Kolenc 2003).

To monitor and protect the territorial waters of the country, the Slovenian police force uses patrol rescue boats P111 and P66 and the rubber boat P88. Boat P111 is equipped with two radars, a satellite navigator, an electronic map, depth indicators, a printer, and two magnetic compasses (Kolenc 2003).

Similar to the 911 system used in the United States, the Slovenian police force operates a 113 system. In 2001 the police received 801,020 calls from citizens on the 113

number. On the basis of these calls, 166,422 police patrols were referred to the scene of an event. In 2002 the police received 557,137 calls from citizens on the 113 number, a decrease of 30.5 percent from the previous year. While the total number of calls declined, the number of police patrols based on intervention calls increased to 180,391 (Ministry of the Interior 2003a).

The average reaction time of police patrols was sixteen minutes and twenty seconds for emergency interventions, and twenty-two minutes and forty-seven seconds for all events (Ministry of the Interior 2002).

The Slovenian police force has access to Interpol's new I-24/7 Global Communications System. Using the Internet, I-24/7 makes encrypted data and communications tools from around the world instantly available to the Slovenian police.

Surveillance and Intelligence Gathering. The Slovenian police force regularly monitors signaling and security devices in buildings, homes, and facilities. In 2001 police patrols carried out 1,948 responses to the triggering of such signaling and security devices. In more than 90 percent of the cases it was established that the signaling or security devices were triggered either accidentally or for unknown reasons (Ministry of the Interior 2002).

Equipment for the surveillance of the state border include telescope mirrors, endoscopes, carbon dioxide detectors, and ultrasound indicators. Ultraviolet light and magnifiers are used to detect forged travel and other documents and for checking the security features of documents.

Police Officers Killed in the Line of Duty. It is quite rare for a police officer to be killed in the line of duty in Slovenia. For instance, no police officers were reported killed in the line of duty in either the 2001 or 2002 annual report of the Slovenian police.

Police Statistics. As of December 2002 there were 8,931 employees of the Slovenian police force (7,132 men and 1,799 women). The number of uniformed police officers was 5,855 (5,457 men and 398 women). The number of plainclothes police officers was 1,537 (1,317 men and 220 women). The average age of police employees was thirty-three years old (Ministry of the Interior 2003a).

HUMAN RIGHTS

The Constitutional Court of the Republic of Slovenia is the highest authority of judicial power for the protection of the constitution, legality, human rights, and fundamental freedoms. The court exercises the power of judicial review over statutes and executive decrees. It has jurisdiction with respect to constitutional complaints in relation to violations of human rights and fundamental freedoms.

The Code of Police Ethics contains the basic principles that regulate the interaction of the Slovenian police force with the public. The code takes into account and embodies rules included in the General Declaration of the United Nations on Human Rights, the International Treaty on Civil and Political Rights, the Declaration on Protection of All People from Torture and Other Forms of Cruel, Inhuman, or Humiliating Treatment or Punishment, the Declaration on Police, and the constitution, laws, and other regulations of the Republic of Slovenia.

The government of Slovenia routinely permits prison visits by independent human rights observers and the media. The death penalty was abolished in 1989. In 2002 four criminal offenses of incitement of religious, national, or racial hatred were reported by the Slovenian police force (Ministry of the Interior 2003a).

CRIME

Overall, crime rates in Slovenia are below the European average. The country's geographic position, stable economy, and developed financial system are typically offered as reasons why the crime rate is low.

Criminal Identification and Forensics. The Forensic Research Center of the Slovenian police force is equipped with chromatographs, spectrophotometers, electrophoresis, automatic analyzers of genes, and color photography labs with computer systems for fingerprint identification. The center maintains DNA profiles of criminal suspects, fingerprint records, and computer-designed photographs of unknown persons. It routinely performs laboratory investigations related to physics, chemistry, biology, and dactylography.

In 2002 criminal technicians participated in 5,002 inspections of crime scenes. They identified 340 criminal suspects on the basis of fingerprints and offered 934 expert opinions (Ministry of the Interior 2003a). The most frequent requests of the Forensic Research Center were tests for DNA, of samples of illicit drugs, and of traces left behind by criminal suspects.

The Slovenian police force routinely uses polygraph tests to eliminate innocent people from further investigation. Polygraph tests are not admissible in Slovenian courts.

Organized Crime. The Slovenian police force reports organized crime activity in the areas of money laundering and counterfeiting, illicit drugs, illegal weapons, organized car theft, illegal migration and smuggling, prostitution and enslavement, blackmail, kidnapping, bribery, and tax fraud and evasion.

In 2002 the Slovenian police force reported that organized crime was involved in 253 cases of illicit drug trading, 196 cases of illegal migration, 19 cases of illegal weapons trading, 13 cases of blackmail, and 4 cases of illegal explosions (Ministry of the Interior 2003a).

Crime Statistics. There are three categories of punishable acts in Slovenia: criminal offenses, economic offenses, and petty offenses. Statistics for criminal and economic offenses are readily available. In 2002, 77,128 criminal offenses were committed, a 3.2 percent increase from the previous year. Specifically, there were 78 murders, 86 rapes, 410 criminal offenses of serious bodily injury, 449 robberies, 548 illegal national border crossings, 1,534 criminal offenses of illegal drug abuse, and 16,341 burglaries (Ministry of the Interior 2003a).

Also in 2002 the Slovenian police dealt with 8,527 criminal offenses in the area of economic crime, a rise of 18.2 percent from the previous year. Specifically, there were 5 cases of money laundering, 520 cases of embezzlement, 2,079 instances of business fraud, and 2,516 cases of bad checks and unauthorized use of bank cards (Ministry of the Interior 2003a).

CORRECTIONAL SYSTEM

Prison Conditions. Prison conditions in Slovenia generally meet international standards. Male and female prisoners are held separately, juvenile offenders are held separately from adults, and convicted criminals are held separately from pretrial detainees.

Prison Statistics. Slovenia has a prison population of 1,129, which is an incarceration rate of 30 per 100,000. There are fourteen prisons, of which thirteen are for men and one for women. Nine of the prisons are maximum security and five are minimum security. Pretrial detainees make up 27.1 percent of the total prison population, female prisoners 4.1 percent, and juvenile prisoners 1.3 percent. The official capacity of the prison system is 1,103 and occupancy level is 102.4 percent.

MOST SIGNIFICANT ISSUE FACING THE COUNTRY

Slovenia became a member of both the North Atlantic Treaty Organization (NATO) and the European Union (EU) in 2004. Conformance on the part of Slovenia to the policies of both NATO and the EU, particularly the Schengen standards of the EU, are the most significant issues facing the country in the near term. Continued Slovenian participation, including by the police force, in peacekeeping missions in Kosovo, Macedonia, East Timor, and Albania is also of pressing concern.

BIBLIOGRAPHY

Kolenc, Tadeja. 2003. *The Slovene Police.* Translated by Miha Granda. Ljubljana, Slovenia: Pleško.

Ministry of the Interior. 2002. "Annual Report on the Work of the Police, 2001." Republic of Slovenia. Available online at http://www.policija.si/en/statistics/report01/report2001.html (accessed January 3, 2006).

Ministry of the Interior. 2003a. "Annual Report on the Work of the Police, 2002." Republic of Slovenia. Available online at http://www.policija.si/en/statistics/reports.html (accessed January 3, 2006).

Ministry of the Interior. 2003b. "The Police Act of the Republic of Slovenia." Republic of Slovenia. Available online at http://www.policija.si/en/general/acts/police-act.html (accessed January 3, 2006).

Selih, Alenka, and Darko Maver. 1993. "World Fact Book of Criminal Justice Systems: Slovenia." Bureau of Justice Statistics, U.S. Department of Justice. Available online at http://www.ojp.usdoj.gov/bjs/pub/ascii/wfbcjslv.txt (accessed January 3, 2006).

United Nations Office on Drugs and Crime. 2001. "Seventh United Nations Survey of Crime Trends and Operations of Criminal Justice Systems (1998–2000)." Available online at http://www.unodc.org/unodc/crime_cicp_survey_seventh.html (accessed January 3, 2006).

Nathan R. Moran

Solomon Islands

Official country name: Solomon Islands
Capital: Honiara
Geographic description: Group of islands in the South
    Pacific Ocean, east of Papua New Guinea
Population: 538,032 (est. 2005)

■■■

LAW ENFORCEMENT

History. The Royal Solomon Islands Police was the
creation of the British. At independence the force was
indigenized.

Structure and Organization. The Solomon Islands Police
Force (SIPF) is a relatively small establishment containing about 700 officers and men. Its mission includes,
besides conventional law enforcement, immigration control, firefighting, and the administration of prisons. The
force is also called on frequently to participate in ceremonial functions and maintains a small band for that
purpose. Since Solomon Islands does not have a military
establishment, the police are also called on frequently to
handle national security functions.

Administratively, the force comprises six grades of
officers and men: chief of police, officers, inspectors,
noncommissioned officers, constables, and prison wardens. Operationally, the SIPF is divided into four police
districts, which correspond to similar divisions in the
political administration. Each district is commanded by
a police inspector and is assigned operating forces in
accordance with geographical and population needs.
The Western District covers Choiseul Island and the

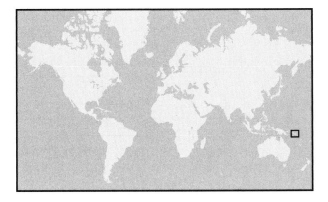

Shortland and New Georgia Island groups from its
headquarters on Gizo Island in the New Georgia
group. The Central District includes Santa Isabel,
Guadalcanal, Bellona, Rennell, and the Russell and
Florida island clusters. Its headquarters is contiguous
to that of the overall force at Honiara. The Malaita
District embraces Malaita Island, Sikaiana, and the
Ontong Java atoll. Its headquarters is at Auki on
Malaita. The Eastern District directs police activities
on San Cristóbal and Santa Cruz from its headquarters
at Kirakira on San Cristobal.

Since the takeover of Honiara in June 2000 by militants from the island of Malaita, the police force has
become factionalized and ineffective. One faction, the
paramilitary Police Field Force, is directed by militant
Malaitans rather than the police commissioner. As many
as 2,000 former untrained militants have been taken into
the police force as "special constables" who are not answerable to the official command structure.

Education and Training. Training for all ranks is carried out at the Police Training School at Honiara. Facilities at this institution are quite limited. Two courses in basic police activities are presented each year, as well as one designed to prepare constables and inspectors for promotion. It also conducts an annual course in criminal investigation. There is no training for direct entry into officer ranks. Advanced training is lacking, but officers and men of the lower ranks requiring specialized training in fingerprinting and administration are regularly sent to the appropriate schools abroad. Among the foreign schools most frequently attended are Bramshill Police College and Herndon Police Training School in England, the headquarters school of the Royal Papua New Guinea Constabulary, and the Nases Police School near Suva in Fiji.

Uniforms and Weapons. Members of the SIPF are issued two uniforms, one for duty wear and the other for ceremonial dress occasions. The working uniform consists of a khaki shirt and shorts, a blue beret, and black sandals; the dress uniform has a white tunic, a blue *sulu* (short sarong), and black sandals. Both types are worn with a black belt superimposed on a red sash.

Police Statistics.

- Total Police Personnel: 780
- Population per Police Officer: 690

HUMAN RIGHTS

The armed conflict between Malaitan and Guadalcanalese militants and the takeover of the government by Malaitans has resulted in a serious deterioration of the human rights situation. The police force, which is dominated by Malaitans, commits many human rights abuses, including killings, abductions, torture, rape, forced displacement, looting, and the burning of homes. The government has not ordered an independent judicial investigation of these abuses.

CORRECTIONAL SYSTEM

All prisons except one were closed following the ethnic conflict between the Guadalcanalese and the Malaitans. Almost all the inmates were either released or were allowed to escape. Some of the escapees joined the militant factions.

Before the conflict, the chief of police was also the superintendent of prisons and ran the country's four major prisons and directed the activities of their wardens and keepers. The Rove Prison at Honiara, serving the Central District, was the largest and best equipped. It housed prisoners condemned to long prison sentences. Similar but smaller prisons, called district prisons, were established at the headquarters of the other police divisions. Official policy was rehabilitation rather than retribution. All prisons provided vocational training and adult education classes.

Prison Statistics.

- Total Prison Population: 275
- Prison Population Rate per 100,000: 56
- Pretrial Detainees: 25.5%
- Female Prisoners: 1.5%

George Thomas Kurian

Somalia

Official country name: Somalia
Capital: Mogadishu
Geographic description: Easternmost country on the Horn of Africa, bordering on the Indian Ocean
Population: 8,591,629 (est. 2005)

■■■

LAW ENFORCEMENT

History. The Somali Police Force ceased to exist by 1991. The Somali Police Force grew out of the police forces employed by British and Italians in British Somaliland and Italian Somalia, respectively. The earliest Somali law enforcement agency was an armed constabulary of about fifteen men established in 1884 to police the northern coast. In 1910 the British formed the Somaliland Coastal Police, and in 1912 they formed the British Somaliland Camel Constabulary to police the interior. The Camel Constabulary took part in the operations against Sayyid Mohamed ibn Abdullah Hassan but were ambushed in 1913, losing their leader and most of their 150-man force. They were later reformed and continued to operate until 1920.

In 1926 the British formed the first properly constituted modern police force in the colony. Called the Somaliland Police Force, it was led by British officers, but included Somalis in the lower ranks. They were aided by uniformed and armed rural constabulary (*illalo*) who brought offenders to court, guarded prisoners, patrolled local townships, and accompanied nomadic townsmen over grazing areas.

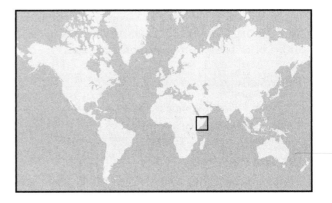

Meanwhile, in Italian-held Somalia military forces were used to maintain public order until 1914, when they developed a small coastal police and a rural constabulary (*gogle*) for that purpose. By 1930 this force comprised some 300 men.

When the fascists took over Italy, Italian administrators reconstituted the former Somali Police Corps into a more efficient force called Corpo Zaptie. The ranks of the older police corps were purged, and Somali, Eritrean, and Arab troops were recruited to bring the strength of the Corpo Zaptie to about 800. Italian Carabinieri officers trained and supervised the new corps, and new barracks were built to house them. When the Corpo Zaptie proved ineffectual against the nomadic population of Benadir, Obbya, and Mijerteyn, other *askaris* (policemen) were recruited from local clans to disarm the unruly tribes. During the Ethiopian War the Corpo Zaptie expanded to about 6,000 men.

In 1941, after an initial defeat and expulsion from the Horn of Africa, the British returned to crush the Italians and recover the area. The British then established a British Military Administration over both protectorates. The Corpo Zaptie was disbanded and replaced by a hastily recruited Somalia Gendarmerie, under British officers. By 1943 this force had expanded to more than 3,000 men, led by 120 British officers. In 1948 the Somalia Gendarmerie was renamed the Somali Police Force. However, the British let the former Italian colony's rural police survive without major changes, since it resembled their own.

At about the same time a school was opened for training Somali officers and noncommissioned men. By 1949 a few of its graduates had reached the rank of chief inspector, the highest noncommissioned rank.

When in 1950 the southern area became the Trust Territory of Somaliland under Italian administration, Italian Carabinieri officers and Somali personnel from the Somali Police Force formed the Police Force of Somalia (Corpo de Polizia della Somali), commanded by Italian officers. In 1958, two years before independence, the force was completely Somalized and redesignated the Police Force of Somalia (Forze de Policia della Somalia). Similar progress was not made in British Somaliland. Somalis did not receive positions of command until just before independence, and British officers were not withdrawn until 1960. At that time the northern and southern forces were integrated.

Of the 3,700 men and officers in the police force at independence, 1,000 belonged to the Mobile Group (Darawishta Poliska). This force was used to keep peace in the interior, where frequent disputes over water and grazing rights often led to fighting between rival clans or lineages. The most serious crisis of this nature happened in 1965, when the police had to declare an emergency and used the infantry to restore order.

A police air wing with Cessna light aircraft and one Douglas DC-3 was formed in 1961 to provide assistance to field police units and to the Darawishta Poliska through airlift of supplies and reconnaissance. A small unit of policewomen was formed, also in 1961, for interrogating female prisoners and for supervising abandoned girls, prostitutes, and female juvenile delinquents.

By the time of the 1969 military coup (marking the beginning of Somalia's disintegration), the Somali Police Force had grown to 6,000 in strength. Aid from Germany, Italy, and the United States had helped to bring the force up to high professional standards.

Structure and Organization. Somalia is what is known as a failed state, in which there are no effective national institutions or any public order. The country has reverted to its traditional state of anarchy in which each tribe or lineage follows legal conventions and norms handed down through generations. According to these conventions, disputes or acts of violence, including homicide, are wrongs affecting not only the parties involved but also the entire group or lineage to which the offenders and victims belong. The offending party and his group would pay *dia*, or blood compensation, often in the form of livestock, to the injured party and his group. After independence, there was some attempt to develop a modern system of criminal and civil laws, but these attempts were aborted by the civil war. In the absence of a civil society, the *dia*-paying legal system is the basis of criminal justice.

Between 1960 and 1991 the Somali Police Force was an active national institution. Public order was the legal responsibility of the minister of the interior (normally a general of the army), regional governors, and district commissioners. The police were part of the armed forces, but the police commandant was under the ministry of justice. The force was divided into various departments, known as divisions, with branches in all jurisdictions. Each region had a regional commandant and each district a commissioned officer. Outside Mogadishu the chain of command ran through group commands, divisional commands (corresponding to the regions), subdivisional commands (corresponding to the districts), station commands, and police posts.

The Mobile Police comprised the Darawishta Poliska and the Riot Unit (Birmadka Poliska). The former operated in remote areas and the frontier, and the latter was a crack emergency unit and an honor guard for ceremonial functions.

Technical and specialized units included the Tributary Division, the Criminal Investigation Division (CID), the Communications Unit, and the Training Unit. The CID handled investigations, fingerprinting, criminal records, immigration, and passports in rural and urban areas. Service units included the Transport Department, Central Stores, and Health Service. The Police Custodial Force consisted of prison guards.

In 1972 the government organized a paramilitary force known as Victory Corps with powers of arrest. In urban and rural areas they constituted a vigilance corps, scrutinizing particularly contacts between Somalis and foreigners. Dressed in green, they were highly visible and much feared. There was also a Treasury Guard based on the Italian force of the same name and with similar duties and a political police known as the National Security Service.

Police ranks were divided into five groups: senior officers, junior officers, inspectors, noncommissioned officers, and *askaris*. Inspectors were equivalent to warrant officers in the army. Pay and allowances were the same as for members of the Somali armed forces.

Education and Training. Recruits to the police force were required to be between seventeen and twenty-five years of age, without any criminal record, and be physically fit. After enlistment, they received a six-month training at the Police Academy at Mogadishu or Mandera. Once this training was complete, recruits took an examination; those who passed served two years in the force. At the end of two years they were offered a contract. Officers underwent a stiff training course for nine months. The Darawishta Poliska received a special training in a six-month tactical course.

Police Statistics.

- Total Police Personnel: 14,357
- Population per Police Officer: 598

HUMAN RIGHTS

Because of the lack of central authority, human rights abuses are common. Kidnapping, murder, and torture are routine occurrences with the complicity of local warlords. Internecine clan warfare has led to a cycle of violence and retribution.

CRIME

Crime Statistics. Offenses reported to the police per 100,000 population: 144. Of which:

- Murder: 1.5
- Assault: 8
- Burglary: 31.2

CORRECTIONAL SYSTEM

The Somalia Penal Code, which was in force from 1964 to 1991, was the first attempt to modernize the legal system and establish the constitutional supremacy of law over all citizens. It replaced customary law with a written code in which penal responsibility was declared to be personal and not collective. Criminal offenses were defined as those committed willfully so as to cause harm to another person, to property, or to the state. The accused was assumed to be innocent until proven guilty beyond all reasonable doubt. The burden of proof rested with the accuser or prosecutor. The penal code classified offenses as with crime or contraventions, the latter being legal violations without criminal intent. It prescribed a maximum and minimum punishment but left the actual sentence to the discretion of the judge. The penal code recognized the social and rehabilitative nature of punishment and its role in restoring the offender to a useful place in society. Matters relating to arrest and trial were governed by the Criminal Procedure Act that also came into effect in 1964. It recognized the right of habeas corpus and required an arrested person to be brought before a judge within twenty-four hours.

Somalia inherited a primitive penal system from the colonial administrations. There were forty-nine correctional institutions in the country, of which the Mogadishu Central Prison was the largest. There was a youth reformatory at Afgoi, on the outskirts of the capital. Other major prisons were at Hararyale, Bossasso, Puntland, Shirkhole, and Hargeisa.

Prison Conditions. Prison conditions are life-threatening and harsh, marked by overcrowding, poor sanitary conditions, a lack of access to adequate health care, and absence of educational and vocational facilities. Tuberculosis is widespread. Abuse by guards is reportedly common. The costs of detention are borne not by the state but by the inmates and their clans. Inmates receive their daily rations from their family members or relief agencies. Ethnic minorities make up a large portion of the prison population.

George Thomas Kurian

South Africa

Official country name: Republic of South Africa
Capital: Pretoria (executive); Bloemfontein (judicial); Cape Town (legislative)
Geographic description: Southernmost country in Africa, occupying land south of the southern borders of Namibia, Botswana, Zimbabwe, and Mozambique
Population: 44,344,136 (est. 2005)

■ ■ ■

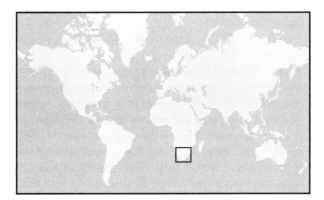

LAW ENFORCEMENT

History. South Africa had an extensive police system even in the nineteenth century. The Boer republics had paramilitary mounted police forces, such as the Transvaal Police and the Orange River Colony Police, and the Cape Colony had the Cape Constabulary, which was modeled on London's Metropolitan Police Force. It was aided by the Water Police, which patrolled the waterfront against smugglers. In rural districts law and order were maintained by constables known as *landdrosts*, who could call on the assistance of local volunteers when needed. In Natal the Mounted Police undertook law enforcement in the neighboring British colony and provided effective support during the Zulu War of 1879.

After the Anglo-Boer War ended in 1902 in British victory, the new British administration reorganized the Mounted Police in Transvaal and Orange Free State. The police forces of the four provinces were consolidated soon after the Act of Union of 1910 and from this amalgamation two law enforcement agencies emerged. The Mounted Riflemen were detailed to rural areas and to border patrol and the South African Police (SAP) to urban areas. When the Mounted Riflemen were conscripted during World War I, the SAP assumed law enforcement duties throughout the nation, although this jurisdiction became statutory only in 1936, when the SAP absorbed the Mounted Riflemen. From 1939 to 1990 the SAP also policed Namibia.

Structure and Organization. The SAP is a centrally organized law enforcement agency operating under the Ministry of Police. All SAP operations are controlled from a central headquarters in Pretoria by a commissioner of police. For police purposes, the country is divided into eighteen divisions, each under a divisional commissioner. Each division comprises a number of police districts, each under a divisional commandant. Within these districts there are over a thousand police stations, each under a station commander.

Operationally, the SAP is organized into three branches: Uniformed, Detective, and Security. The bulk of the force is employed in the Uniformed Branch, where police recruits are initially assigned as recruits. As part of the Uniformed Branch, the Quartermaster Division is responsible for supplies and maintenance of police equipment. The Uniformed Branch also makes extensive use of police dogs trained at Kwaggaspoort Dog Training School in Pretoria. Most of the animals are German shepherds trained for tracking and detecting drugs and sniffing out landmines. They are also given parachute training so they can be dropped from the air into areas inaccessible to motorized police. The Radio Patrol Service, popularly known as the Flying Squad, works in tandem with the SAP Air Wing.

The Detective Branch is a centralized service that includes the Criminal Investigation Division and the Special Branch. The latter is concerned with intelligence-gathering, surveillance, and investigation of subversive activities. The Criminal Bureau serves as a clearinghouse for fingerprints and as an archives for criminal records. The Narcotics Squad investigates drug trafficking. The SAP has a forensic science laboratory that is considered among the best in the continent.

The Security Branch is responsible for border patrol and internal security operations. It is composed of mobile units trained in riot control and counterinsurgency tactics ready for deployment anywhere in the country at short notice. All units are self-sufficient in weaponry communications, transportation equipment, and logistical support. In operational situations they are provided with camouflaged dress, gas masks, body armor, and helmets and are armed with assault rifles, automatic weapons, shotguns, and tear-gas canister launchers. Units are transported in armored personnel carriers and specially designed riot trucks. Besides an array of lethal ordinance, units also rely on rubber bullets, electric prods, Plexiglas shields, and sneezing machines. Riot control is undertaken by platoon-sized units accompanied by dog units.

The other main branches and units are:

- Narcotics Bureau, established in 1974
- Commercial Branch, which deals with company fraud
- Diamond and Gold Branch
- Sock Theft Branch, to curb cattle rustling
- Special Guard Unit, a secret service that provides security to the president and other state officials
- Horse Unit
- Spiritual and Social Services Unit
- Police Band
- Dog School
- Police Museum

A South African policeman stands guard while a woman and child walk near a protest being held by Madala Farm residents in Cape Town, South Africa, July 7, 2005. Protesters demanded housing and basic services for their makeshift settlements from the African National Congress local government. During the protest, confrontations erupted and police fired rubber bullets at crowds who threw stones, burned tires, and created roadblocks. AP IMAGES.

The Police Reserve, established in 1961, is composed of civilian volunteers who perform ordinary police duties when members of the regular force are diverted to other duties. It consists of four separate personnel categories:

- Group A: Reservists who serve full time during emergencies. They receive training and are issued firearms.
- Group B: Home guards who perform part-time police duties in their own neighborhoods.
- Group C: Typically employees of local authorities and key industries who may be called on to protect their employers' property during emergencies.
- Group D: Civilians who serve as a restraining force during the initial stages of an emergency until regular police arrive.

Provincial Police. Commanded by a provincial commissioner, each provincial office is located within its respective capital. The provincial commissioner oversees anywhere between three to eight police areas, each headed by an area commissioner, who is in command of a number of police stations, each headed by a station commander. The station commander is in charge of local patrols. There are over 1,100 SAP police stations nationwide.

Municipal Police. The municipal police are considered separate from the SAP and exist primarily to supplement federal law enforcement. Major urban areas like Johannesburg, Cape Town, and Durban have long had local police forces operating primarily in black neighborhoods.

Education and Training. All senior officers are promoted from the ranks and there is no direct entry into the commissioned ranks.

The SAP places great emphasis on training. The broad scope of technical and academic instruction, coupled with drill and combat training, has led to a high level of professional competence. The four training institutions are: the South African Police Training College in Pretoria, Hammanskraal north of Pretoria, Bishop Lavis Police Depot near Cape Town, and Wentworth, near Durban. Recruits in all four institutions undergo identical training for six months.

Recruit training includes both practical and theoretical instruction in physical conditioning, self-defense, first aid, use of firearms, crowd and riot control, close-order drill, and infantry tactics. Physical training includes karate, jujitsu, boxing and wrestling. Instruction is also given in various police laws and lectures are given on social problems, such as race relations, drug abuse, and alcoholism. After completing basic training, recruits are promoted to the rank of constable and assigned for two months of duty with a metropolitan police station before receiving a permanent station assignment.

Besides training recruits, SAP schools also provide instruction for police specialists, advanced courses in criminology and law enforcement techniques for senior personnel, and refresher courses in the use of firearms and riot-control procedures. Security Branch forces receive intensive training in counterinsurgency tactics. Other courses include crime laboratory work, the use of electronic devices, computer technology, radio operation and repair, motor vehicle operation and maintenance, horsemanship, and veterinary science. A course leading to a degree in law enforcement is offered at the University of South Africa.

Women have been admitted to the SAP since 1972, but female applicants must either be widowed or single.

Uniforms and Weapons. Police uniforms consist of a blue-gray belted jacket worn with lighter gray trousers and a peaked cap. Constables and noncommissioned officers add a black Sam Browne belt. In summer police wear blue-gray bush jackets and shorts. All constables on patrol duty have batons and handguns. All ranks are issued a 9mm Parabellum pistol.

Police Statistics.

- Total Police Personnel: 102,354
- Population per Police Personnel: 433

HUMAN RIGHTS

The SAP was a notorious offender against human rights during the apartheid, and conditions have improved only marginally. Security forces still use excessive force and deaths in policy custody are too many to be condoned. Many members of the force beat, rape, torture, and abuse detainees and suspects. Incidents of police harassment of foreigners have become more frequent in keeping with the general rise in xenophobia in the general population. Police corruption is a problem of national proportions.

The Independent Complaints Directorate (ICD) investigates police abuses, including killings and rapes. In 2002 there were 217 deaths in police custody and 311 deaths as a result of the use of excessive force. It also investigated 23 incidents of torture and 16 rapes committed by police officers. In the same year the ICD received 1,002 allegations of criminal offenses by the SAP. Of these, 35.2 percent dealt with serious assaults, 12.6 percent with attempted murder, and 10.5 percent with corruption and extortion. The ICD also received 2,913 cases of police misconduct. The government made efforts to address these abuses with an official antitorture policy and training programs in human rights. Despite these programs, the reports of abuses have actually increased. For example, cases of reported corruption increased from 30 in 2002 to 106 in 2003.

CRIME

Crime Statistics. Offenses reported to the police per 100,000 population: 7,141. Of which:

- Murder: 121.9
- Assault: 595.6
- Burglary: 896.6
- Automobile Theft: 262.7

CORRECTIONAL SYSTEM

The South African legal system has its roots in Roman-Dutch and English law, reflecting two great Western legal traditions. Although the former was the first to reach the country, later assimilation of English law after the British rose to power in Cape Colony in 1806 resulted in substantial modifications, both in principle and in practice. Court procedures, the jury system, and rules of evidence are all patterned on the English rather than the Roman-Dutch model. The primary source of law is legislation rather than judicial precedent. Acts of parliament, provincial ordinances, municipal bylaws, and administrative regulations govern all legal relationships.

The first Prisons Department was created in 1911 under the Act to Consolidate and Amend the Laws Relating to Convict Prisons, Gaols, Reformatories, Industrial Schools, and for Other Purposes. It remained a separate department until 1980, when the Department of Prisons was merged with the Department of Justice.

The national penal system is administered by the commissioner of the Department of Correctional Services. The department is organized into regional commands, each responsible for the operation of prisons within the command area. Ultimate authority for policymaking rests with the minister in charge, who usually holds the portfolio for justice or police in the cabinet. The senior officer within the department is the commissioner of prisons, who heads the Prison Service. Prisons are staffed by civil servants and their management is subject to review by the Public Service Commission. Operational and maintenance costs of all institutions in the system are met from the state budget. The costs include the building of new prisons or extensions to current ones.

Pay rates for prison personnel, although lower than those for the police, are good and include medical benefits, housing, and pension on retirement at age sixty. Despite such benefits, there is a high turnover of 15 to 20 percent annually, resulting from the resignation of trained prison warders, who frequently accept security jobs with private industrial concerns. Prison Service personnel are trained at Kroonstad, Pollsmoor, Durban, and Baviuanspoort, near Pretoria. The course of instruction emphasizes discipline, suitable methods of punishment, conduct toward prisoners, physical conditioning, self-defense techniques, first aid, firefighting, and close-order drill. All candidates are instructed on the Prisons Act and attend lectures on practical psychology, sociology, criminology, management, legal procedures, and agriculture.

Prison Service personnel work long hours and often have irregular schedules. Warders are armed with billy clubs, but those assigned to maximum-security prisons are authorized to carry firearms. The prisons also employ trained dogs, which are highly effective in tracking down escapees.

Local prisons are usually classified as medium security, however, there are maximum-security facilities as well. Remanded prisoners make up at least 40 percent of the prison population. Reformatories for juvenile offenders are not part of the penal system, but are administered by a separate department. There are also a number of minimum-security prison farms, where prisoners are required to do farming. South Africa has one of the largest prison populations per capita in Africa. Blacks form the vast proportion of the inmates, making up nearly 94 percent of the prison population even though they form only 78.4 percent of the general population.

Although prisons built in the colonial period are still in use, most have extensively modernized since World War II. The trend in new prison construction begun in the 1960s, however, favored the gradual replacement of outdated prison facilities with consolidated complexes, each of which contains a reception center, a maximum-security section, and a prison farm. This concept permitted advancement from closed- to open-prison conditions without the need for transfers and readjustment to new surroundings as prisoners progressed toward completion of their confinement. Typical of modern prisons built on this model were the complexes at Pretoria, Pietermaritzburg, and Paarl in Western Cape Province. Despite the modernization of most prisons, sharp discrepancies exist in physical conditions. In many prisons, standards of hygiene, lighting, sanitary facilities, floor space, and ventilation are substandard.

The oldest prison in the system is located off Cape Town on Ribben Island in Table Way, where Nelson Mandela was once incarcerated. The island originally served as a haven for seamen buffeted by the violent cape storms, but a penal colony was established there in the eighteenth century. It is an impenetrable maximum-security prison, where prisoners are cut off from any contact with the outside world.

Prisoners are classified according to their offenses, past records, and length of sentences, taking also into account their psychological condition and prospect of rehabilitation. About 10 percent are designated Class A and serve in prison farms under minimum security. About 80 percent are placed in medium-security institutions as Class B prisoners. The remainder, assigned to Classes C and D, are assigned to maximum-security units.

Every prisoner serving a sentence of two years or longer is transferred to an observation center after admission. A team of professional social workers, psychologists, educators, and chaplains investigate the prisoners' background, psychological and physical state, rehabilitative potential, and personality makeup as well as aptitudes. The prisoners are then classified into one of several categories. These categories determine where they are sent, the type of work they are required to do, and other aspects of their treatment.

The Prisons Service employs its own team of social workers, chaplains, and psychologists who help the prisoners even after their release. They help them to maintain their family ties, find suitable work, and make suitable psychological adjustments to the new environment. Prison officials may also help them to hone their natural skills or acquire new ones.

Solitary confinement is usually imposed on prisoners guilty of disciplinary violations, with a reduced diet for a period not exceeding six days. For more serious violations, the period may be extended up to one month. Corporal punishment is authorized for only the most incorrigible offenders. Officially, whipping is permitted only after a medical officer certifies that the prisoner is fit to undergo such a punishment.

The release of all long-term prisoners is in the hands of the Central Release Board. There are two types of release: unconditional release and conditional release (also called parole or probation). Depending on the prisoner's conduct, he may be eligible for remission of a part of his sentence.

Prison Conditions. The Prisons Act of 1959 prohibits criticisms of the prison administration and imposes a blackout on information on prison conditions. Prisons do not meet international standards and sometimes do not even meet internal legal standards. The most serious problem is overcrowding, with over 75 inmates living in cells designed for 40. Prisoners are often required to sleep in shifts because of lack of space. In 2002 there were 1,087 deaths, 90 percent of which were HIV/AIDS related.

Prison employees and fellow prisoners abuse and assault prisoners physically and sexually. Rape is the single most common cause for the spread of HIV/AIDS among prisoners. Food is of poor quality and insufficient nutritionally.

The government appointed the Jail Commission in 2002 to investigate allegations of corruption and sexual abuse in prisons. The commission's report mentioned widespread irregularities, including prisoners being allowed to go AWOL, nepotism, drug trafficking, food theft, medical aid fraud, extortion, abuse of parole pro-

cedures, abuse of disciplinary inquiries and appeals procedures, and rape. In 2003, 270 reports of corruption in prisons were received by the Department of Correctional Services.

The Lindela Repatriation Center is the largest detention center for undocumented immigrants. Police regularly conduct sweeps of squatter camps and send illegal immigrants to Lindela. There are reports that these immigrants are routinely assaulted if they do not pay bribes. Immigrant children at Lindela are not provided with separate sleeping facilities.

C-MAX prisons hold the country's most dangerous prisoners. Human rights advocates raise serious concerns regarding the restrictive and solitary conditions of the inmates in these prisons.

Male and female prisoners are housed separately. Nevertheless, women inmates are often raped by male prisoners and guards. Juveniles are normally housed separately, but on occasion are housed with adults. There are credible reports that youths from the juvenile wards are sold by the guards to adult prisoners for sexual exploitation. A Child Justice Section exists within the Sexual Offenses and Community Affairs to meet the special needs of children in the corrections system.

South Africa is a signatory of the United Nations Standard Minimum Rules for the Treatment of Prisoners.

Prison Statistics. There are 241 penal institutions in the country, with a total prison population of 176,893. The prison population rate is 400 per 100,000 population. Of the total prison population, 29.6 percent are pretrial detainees, 2.4 percent are women, 11.4 percent are juveniles, and 2 percent are foreigners. The official capacity of the system is 109,106, yielding an occupancy level of 162.1 percent over capacity.

George Thomas Kurian

Spain

Official country name: Kingdom of Spain
Capital: Madrid
Geographic description: Located on the Iberian Peninsula in southwestern Europe, excluding Portugal, but including the Balearic Islands and the Canary Islands
Population: 40,341,462 (est. 2005)

■■■

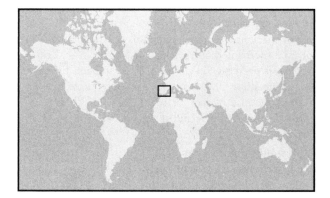

LAW ENFORCEMENT

History. The Spanish penal system was developed during the Middle Ages from local adaptations of its original Germanic heritage. In the eighteenth century it was subjected to the influence of the rationalist thinkers, who asked for the adoption of systematic rules, which resulted during the era of the French Revolution, in requests for the adoption of penal and criminal procedural codes.

The famous book *Dei delitti e delle pene* by Cesare Beccaria first appeared in 1764 and was translated into Spanish some ten years later. Although some conservative authors opposed the book at the time, it led to an enthusiastic movement culminating in the proposal to adopt a penal code.

In 1812 the Spanish patriots who, during the Napoleonic invasion (1808–1813) had taken shelter in Cadiz in the south of Spain, adopted Spain's first political constitution. This liberal constitution included a proposal for the creation of a penal code, but the reestablishment of the absolutist King Ferdinand VII on the Spanish throne (1814) prevented the adoption of the code. A liberal upheaval in 1820 led to the adoption of the first Spanish penal code in 1822. The code was in force for only one year, after which the monarch resumed absolute rule.

In 1848 in a more moderate political situation, a new penal code was adopted, and since then a penal code has always existed and been applied, with some interruptions during times of military rule. Paradigm shifts, inflationary trends, as well as the return to democracy in 1975 have contributed to changes in penal policy over the years. A new penal code was enacted on November 25, 1995, which was still in effect as of 2005. The 1995 code distinguishes between three different types of offenses: major, medium gravity, and minor infractions.

The Spanish Police. The Spanish policing system is characterized as a centralized multiple uncoordinated system. The Spanish model is considered centralized because all police forces operate under the authority of the national government (Ministry of the Interior). The director of state security, who is part of the Ministry of the Interior, is tasked with overseeing the police in Spain.

Spanish police forces trace their history back to the twelfth century, but the first modern version was formed in 1829 with the Carabineros and in 1844 with the Guardia Civil. Under Francisco Franco a tripartite system of police was formalized: the Civil Guard in rural areas; the Armed and Traffic Police (renamed the National Police in 1979), which fulfilled normal police functions in communities with a population of more than 20,000; and the Higher Police Corps of plainclothes police with responsibility for investigating crimes and political offenses. Separate municipal police forces under the control of local mayors were concerned mainly with traffic control and enforcement of local ordinances.

During the Franco era the police had been regarded as a reactionary element, associated in the public mind with internal surveillance and political repression. The Civil Guard and the Armed and Traffic Police were legally part of the armed forces, and their senior officers were drawn from the army. The 1978 constitution effects the separation of the police from the military, and it emphasizes that one of the functions of the police is to safeguard personal liberties. Article 104 of the 1978 constitution states that "the Security Corps and Forces, responsible to the Government, shall have as their mission the protection of the free exercise of rights and liberties and the guaranteeing of the safety of citizens." Although considerably delayed, a subsequent statute, the Organic Law on the Security Corps and Forces, was enacted in March 1986 to incorporate the mandate of the constitution to redefine the functions and operating principles of the police forces. With its passage the final legal steps had been taken to make the police system conform to the requirements of the democratic regime, although most observers concluded that it would be years before the reforms were fully in effect.

The new organic law provided a common ethical code for police practices, affirmed trade union rights, recast the role of the judicial police serving under the courts and the public prosecutors, combined the uniformed and the non-uniformed police into the single National Police Corps, and redefined the missions and the chains of command of the various police elements. The Civil Guard remained a separate paramilitary force, although in operational matters it was under the direction of the Ministry of Interior rather than the Ministry of Defense. In time of war or emergency it would revert to the authority of the minister of defense. In 1986 a new post of Director of State Security was created in the Ministry of Interior to coordinate the activities of the National Police Corps and the Civil Guard. The National Police Corps functioned under the directives of the director general of the National Police Corps, but civil governors of the provinces exercised local supervision where police forces served.

Structure and Organization. There are three separate police organizations: The Guardia Civil wearing green uniforms are responsible for national security, crowd control, and customs. A major focus of Guardia Civil activity is the investigation of crimes against women and children. A group within Guardia Civil is dedicated to crimes involving domestic abuse, sexual assault, trafficking in human brings, sexual exploitation, and child pornography. Another unit of Guardia Civil investigates international criminal activities and organized crime. Its Brigade of Technology Investigations investigates cybercrime and crimes involving new technologies. Its Traffic Police patrol the main highways. The Guardia Civil has 70,000 members, which makes it the largest of the three branches of police The National Police officers wear a black uniform and white shirts. They are heavily armed, as their duties include guarding public buildings, the royal family, and other dignitaries. They deal with most crime investigations. The Municipal Police wear white and blue uniforms and are in charge of local traffic control and parking violations. They report to the mayor and town hall. The Municipal Police are armed only with pistols.

Under the Statute of Autonomy of 1979, the Basque Country and Catalonia were granted authority to form their own regional police forces. Subsequently, this right was extended to ten of the seventeen autonomous regions, but only Basque Country, Catalonia, and Navarre have their own regional forces.

Spanish Courts and Criminal Procedure. Spanish courts consist of the Supreme Court, the National Court, the Superior Justice Courts of the seventeen autonomous regions, fifty provincial courts, single judge courts, and justice of the peace courts. These courts are further subdivided into other courts such as main penal cases courts, appellate civil courts, and examining penal judge courts. The highest court in criminal matters is the Criminal Chamber of the Supreme Court. Decisions of this court create penal doctrine that lower courts are obliged to follow. Because of the presence of the Supreme Court, Spain is characterized as having a concentrated system of judicial review. Specifically, Spain has a single, authoritative legal body that creates precedent for other courts to follow.

In Spain criminal proceedings are initiated when a denunciation is made to a police officer or to an investigating judge. Proceedings can also be initiated if a formal complaint is made, accusing specific persons of committing criminal activity. In all cases a lawyer admitted to the bar, who signs the writ of complaint, must accompany a complainant.

Unlike the United States, judges in Spain are responsible for investigating crimes, although any member of

Spanish forces escort a suspected Islamic terrorist in the city of Santa Coloma de Gramenet, near Barcelona, Spain, June 15, 2005. Several raids in surrounding cities resulted in the arrest of 16 terror suspects. Eleven men arrested were believed to have ties to al Qaeda groups in Iraq responsible for recruiting people for ongoing suicide attacks. AP IMAGES.

Spain's different police forces can assist. For this reason, all of Spain police officers, regardless of agency, are considered members of the judicial police. When an investigating judge determines that a person has committed a crime, the arraignment process begins. During this time, suspects have the right to remain silent and to retain a practicing lawyer as counsel.

Once an investigation is completed, the accused appears before the court. During this phase, the prosecutor receives the results of the investigation. In this pretrial phase the prosecutor is in charge of preparing the writ of accusation. The writ consists of the prosecutor's description of the facts of the case, how the offense occurred, an explanation of the facts of the case fit into the legal description of the offense committed, and any mitigating circumstances. At the end of the writ the prosecutor states the evidence that will be presented during the trial. After presentation of the writ of accusation the court decides on the competence of the prosecutor's case and sets a date for trial. At this time, the court may decide not to proceed, for example, if a crime is not committed voluntarily, or at least through imprudence. In Spain the principle of strict liability is not recognized.

During the trial phase of criminal proceedings, questioning follows a specific order. The accused is questioned

first by the prosecutor; then, if any victims are to testify, the defense lawyer proceeds with questioning. Finally, the defendant is questioned by his or her counsel. Cross-examination is possible during trial, but it is not frequently used.

After questioning and presentation of all evidence, the parties submit oral statements. The accusing parties give oral statements first, followed by the defendant's counsel. Oral statements consist of each side's view of the case. Afterward, the court has three days to hand down a sentence.

The pretrial and trial phase of criminal proceedings in Spain are similar in many ways to the criminal proceedings in the United States. Both systems have a pretrial process that is inquisitorial in nature. Also, the trial phase in adversarial. There are important exceptions such as the judge's role in the investigative process as well as the lack of emphasis placed on cross-examination in Spanish courts. Another key difference between the United States and Spain is the role of the jury during trial.

After a long absence, the jury trial was reintroduced to Spain in 1995. The Spanish legislature granted the right to a trial by jury for cases falling under the jurisdiction of provincial courts, on the basis of the magnitude of punishment. Additionally, trial by jury is limited to particular offenses such as crimes against public officials, people, security, and arson.

In jury trial proceedings the jurors are not charged with rendering the general verdicts in the United States of "guilty" or "not guilty." Instead, Spain follows the continental European model, whereby the jury is presented with a list of questions to answer. The list is prepared by the judge and resembles a balance sheet of facts both for and against the defendant. The jury decides whether or not the evidence and testimony prove the questions on the list. The jury's role in determining guilt is reduced in the Spanish system because their fact-finding abilities are reduced to determining if the defendant committed a crime; not determining if a "crime" was committed in the juridical sense. Additionally, juries are required to give succinct rationale for their verdict.

Education and Training. In the National Police the initial training lasts for nine months followed by a year of practical training. Promotions are based on seniority, additional training, and performance. In the Franco era most police officers were seconded from the army. However, under the 1986 Organic Law this nexus was terminated and all candidate officers attend the Higher Police School at Ávila. The ranks of the plainclothes corps—commissioners, subcommissioners, and inspectors of first, second, and third class—are assimilated into the ranking system of the uniformed police: colonel, lieutenant colonel, major, captain, and lieutenant. To enter the Guardia Civil there are two methods. Half the positions are reserved for candidates with three years of specialized military service and the other half for students at the School of Young Guards. Prospective members undergo a rigorous selection process and much hardship in their boot camp phase.

Uniforms and Weapons. The uniform consists of light-brown trousers and dark-brown jackets. The principal weapons used by the uniform police are 9mm pistols, 9mm submachine guns, and 7.62mm rifles and various forms of riot equipment.

Police Statistics.

- Total Strength of the Police Force: 107,000
- Population per Police Officer: 377

CORRECTIONAL SYSTEM

There are eighty-six penitentiary institutions scattered throughout Spain. Except for Catalonia, a central Penitentiary Administration supervises all penitentiaries. In every penitentiary there is a school that provides at least an elementary education. Inmates are encouraged to pursue studies in prison and have the right to earn degrees in higher education during their sentence. Even members of the Euskadi Ta Askatasuna, a Spanish terrorist group, have been known to earn college degrees at the Basque Country University while in prison. The emphasis on education and individualized treatment highlights the importance placed on corrections in the Spanish prison system, as opposed to retribution.

Imprisoned persons are classified as being in first-, second-, or third-degree imprisonment. The degree of imprisonment determines whether or not an inmate will be placed in an open or closed penitentiary, as well as whether or not an inmate can go outside the institution for work. Prisoners with the most restrictions are placed in first-degree confinement. Those under first-degree confinement are most likely to work and take education classes. A majority of prisoners enter penitentiaries at the second-degree level and can progress through a combination of good behavior, acceptable psychiatric evaluations, and overall length of sentence.

Spain has institutions of last resort for people classified as juveniles. The minimum age at which an offender is dealt with as a juvenile is 12. The maximum age for an offender to be treated as a juvenile is 18. There are more than 43 institutions for people between the ages of 12 and 16. The internment of juveniles is considered a measure only to be taken after all other alternatives have been exhausted.

Prison Statistics.

- Total Prison Population: 60,963
- Prison Population Rate per 100,000: 141
- Pretrial Detainees: 22.8%
- Female Prisoners: 7.8%
- Juvenile Prisoners: 0.3%
- Number of Prisons: 77
- Official Capacity of the Prison System: 48,420
- Occupancy Level: 114.1%

Josep Canabate

Sri Lanka

Official country name: Democratic Socialist Republic of Sri Lanka
Capital: Colombo
Geographic description: Island in the Indian Ocean, 18 miles off the southeast coast of India
Population: 20,064,776 (est. 2005)

■ ■ ■

LAW ENFORCEMENT

History. An unpaid police force, the Vidanes was formed by the British in 1806. It comprised one or two headmen in each village, who received a percentage of property received from thieves as their reward. In 1833 a metropolitan police force was formed, and in 1843 a separate police was formed for the maritime provinces. All these forces were united in 1865 as the Ceylon Police Force under the Police Ordinance of that year. At the time of independence in 1948, the force had a strength of 5,000.

Structure and Organization. The Police Department is headed by an inspector general of police, who reports to the minister of home affairs. The force has over 300 stations under three range commands: the Northern Range, the Central Range, and the Southern Range. The Central Range includes the Colombo Metropolitan Division and the Police Training School. The Northern Range includes Jaffna and the districts where insurgent Tamils are in a majority. Below the range commands the operational territory is divided into provinces, divisions, districts, and stations. The more densely populated

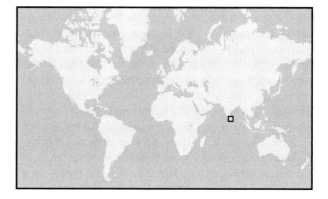

Western, Central, and Southern provinces each have more than one subdivision, while the thinly populated Eastern and North-Central provinces have only one division each. The three ranges are divided into fifteen divisions. As a rule, provinces and divisions are each headed by a superintendent, districts by assistant superintendents, and stations by inspectors.

The police establishment includes a special unit called the Criminal Investigation Department (CID) under a deputy inspector general. The CID has three operating divisions: the Special Branch, the Investigation Branch, and the Technical Unit.

Police stations in thirty-four major cities are linked through a system of radio communications operated from the radio control room in the police headquarters at Colombo. The radio control room also monitors the police emergency system, similar to 911 in the United States.

Dogs are used by police to investigate a crime scene where Senathurai Selvarajah and his wife, Relangi, were gunned down in Colombo, Sri Lanka, August 12, 2005. *The couple were supporters of the People's Liberation Organization of Tamil Eelam (PLOTE), a former separatist militant group that denounced violence around a decade ago and joined mainstream political groups in Sri Lanka. Authorities said Tamil Tiger rebels were suspected in the deaths of the Selvarajahs.* AP IMAGES.

Emergency duties are performed by a specially trained task force of about 450 men called the Depot Police. Located at Bambalapitiya, a suburb of Colombo, the Depot Police are capable of reacting rapidly to trouble anywhere on the island. In addition, they escort important public officials, provide honor guards at ceremonial state functions, and enforce law and order during the frequent communal disturbances.

The Police Department maintains in various subdivisions an auxiliary force called the Special Police Reserve, with an authorized strength of 3,000. Reservists are provided with uniforms, living allowances, and free rail transportation when called into service. Colombo Harbor security is under the Colombo Harbor Division, whose chief, an assistant superintendent, reports directly to the superintendent of the Colombo Division.

Police Statistics.

- Total Police Personnel: 21,941
- Population per Police Officer: 914

Education and Training. Applicants for a police service career must have completed at least high school and usually undergo a four-stage screening process, of which three are interviews and the fourth is a written examination. New recruits are sent to the Police Training School for six months of resident instruction. Transferred to Colombo from Kalutara in 1967, the school is headed by a director with the rank of a superintendent. Classes are held in three languages: Sinhala, Tamil, and English. The school maintains eight training stations, where students receive practical instruction. Outstanding officers are sent abroad for further training.

Uniforms and Weapons. All ranks wear khaki tunics and trousers with a blue cap or slouch hat. The force is generally unarmed, although a variety of weapons is available for use as required.

HUMAN RIGHTS

As a result of the ongoing civil war between the Sinhala majority and the Tamil minority, the human rights situation in Sri Lanka has been bleak for many years. Both the government and the rebels have tended to ignore human rights of civilians in the conflict. Violations of human rights include torture, disappearances, rape, and arbitrary arrest under emergency regulations. The Committee to Inquire into Undue Arrest and Harassment, which includes senior opposition party and Tamil representatives, examines hundreds of complaints against security forces. The National Human Rights Commission investigates human rights abuses. At the same time, the government has established a Prosecution of Torture Perpetrators Unit under the direct supervision of the attorney general.

CRIME

Crime Statistics. Offenses reported to the police per 100,000 population: 280. Of which:

- Murder: 8.2
- Assault:10.8
- Burglary: 54.7

CORRECTIONAL SYSTEM

The penal system is governed by the penal code of 1883, patterned after the Indian Penal Code of 1860. It was retained after independence with few modifications. Offenses are listed in general categories, each subdivided into specific violations. The scale of punishments ranges from death by hanging to whipping. Whipping is restricted to twenty-four lashes (6 for minors) inflicted in the presence of a medical officer. Female convicts are exempted from whipping.

All correctional institutions are administered by the Department of Prisons under the Ministry of Justice and regulated by the prisons ordinance of 1878. The operational head of the department holds the rank of commissioner.

Of the daily average prison population, nearly 70 percent are convicted prisoners. According to the Annual Administrative Report of the Commissioner of Prisons, nearly 30 percent of convicted prisoners are charged with excise offenses, including bootlegging; the next largest category is theft (14%), and the third causing grievous hurt (4%). First-time offenders make up 62 percent. By districts, Colombo accounts for nearly 34 percent, Kalutara in the Western province is a distant second with 9 percent. Nearly 75 percent are Sinhalese, Tamils 16 percent, and the balance is distributed among the other ethnic groups. These percentages correspond to the overall ethnic composition of the population. Based on length of confinement, 33 percent serve less than 1 month, 31 percent 1 to 3 months, 17 percent 3 to 6 months, and 8 percent 6 months to 1 year. Only 1 percent serve more than 1 year. By occupation, farmers are most represented with 26 percent, followed by unskilled workers at 24 percent, skilled workers at 10 percent, and the unemployed at 8 percent.

The department maintains an open-type correctional house for juvenile convicts at Wathapitiwela, called the Training School for Youthful Offenders (TSYO). It is patterned after regular residential schools and is divided into a number of houses, each house in the charge of a housemaster. There is another TSYO at Negombo, a closed-type school reserved for more troublesome juveniles requiring strict supervision.

The department also runs four prison camps, at Pallekalle, Anuradhapura, Kipay, and Taldena, where facilities are provided for agricultural training.

Prison Conditions. Prison conditions are poor and do not meet international standards because of overcrowding and lack of sanitary facilities. Conditions are worse in the 326 police detention facilities, where torture of political insurgents is reported, particularly during interrogation. Methods of torture included electric shock, beatings, suspension by the feet or wrists in contorted positions, burning, and near drowning. Detainees have reported broken bones and other serious injuries as a result of mistreatment.

Prison Statistics. There are 62 major prisons, 4 open prison camps, and 2 TSYOs. The Welikada Prison, the largest, holds nearly 2,500 inmates The total prison population is 20,975 and the prison population rate is 110 per 100,000 people. Pretrial detainees make up 47.6 percent and female prisoners 0.9 percent. The official capacity of the prison system is 7,641 and the occupancy level is 189.8 percent.

George Thomas Kurian

Sudan

Official country name: Republic of the Sudan
Capital: Khartoum
Geographic description: Largest country in Africa, located in North Africa below Egypt and bordering the Red Sea on the east
Population: 40,187,486 (est. 2005)

■■■

LAW ENFORCEMENT

History. The Sudan Police Force is exclusively composed of Northern Arabs. The Sudan Police Force had its beginnings in 1898, when a British captain was placed in the central administration for police duties with thirty British army officers under him to organize provincial police establishments. From 1901 to 1908 police administration was completely decentralized, but in the latter year the central government at Khartoum took over its direction. In 1924 Sir John Ewert of the Indian Police was invited to make a study and his recommendations resulted in the drafting of a new police ordinance. A police school was opened in Obdurman in 1925 for both officers and noncommissioned ranks. The force was transferred with new changes to the national government on independence in 1955. At that time the force consisted of 169 officers and 7,500 men.

Structure and Organization. With a strength of over 44,000 men and officers, the Sudan Police is headed by a commissioner, who reports to the Ministry of the Interior. The organization of the police headquarters in Khartoum has not changed much since colonial times.

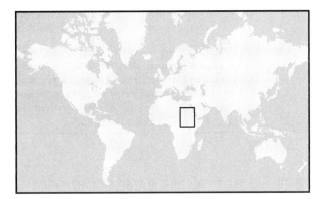

The headquarters division includes units for criminal investigation, administration, and training. Separate departments handle passports, immigration, and prisons. The department for security investigation reports directly to the minister of the interior.

The police establishment is distributed throughout the nine provinces and along the Sudan Railways, with special reinforcements in areas of potential trouble. Within each province the police are under the control of a commandant. The provincial police have both mounted and foot branches. The mounted police, mainly motorized, are still furnished with camels, mules, and horses for special assignments. Besides the regular force, there are a number of reserve companies completely motorized and organized along semimilitary lines. A separate unit, the Railway Police, guards trains and rail installations.

The Public Order Police, a new police unit established by the Islamic government, enforces the Sharia. Its mission includes enforcing proper social behavior as

Detainees wait to board trucks to transport them from a camp for displaced people to central Khartoum, May 24, 2005. *Thousands of police entered the camp to arrest suspects in connection with violent confrontations that occurred over the last week between police and residents resisting being moved out of the camp. Approximately 50 camp residents were arrested, according to State Minister of Interior Ahmed Mohamed Haroon, in the wake of clashes that left 14 policemen and three civilians dead.* AP IMAGES.

prescribed in the Koran, such as restrictions on the consumption of alcohol and immodest dress.

Other police units include the Border Guards, the Republican Guard, and the Customs Guard, the last under the Ministry of Finance and Economy. The Office of State Security, established in 1971 under the Ministry of the Interior, functions as a political police under the direct supervision of the president.

Below the commissioner the grades descend through deputy commissioner, assistant commissioner, commandant, superintendent, assistant superintendent, chief inspector, and inspector among the officer ranks. The lower ranks consist of *soul*, sergeant major, sergeant, corporal, and *nafar*. Pay for all grades is comparable to those in the armed forces.

Education and Training. All police officers are volunteers with recruits drawn mostly from among Sudanese Arabs. People from Nuba excel in police work.

The former Police School in Obdurman was transformed into a Police College in 1959. Senior officers are sometimes sent for training in Egypt.

Uniforms and Weapons. The police uniform consists of a light olive-green shirt and trousers worn with a dark-blue cap for the officers and olive green for the other ranks. Belts and badges of rank are also in dark blue. Traffic police officers wear white uniforms.

Police Statistics.

- Total Police Personnel: 50,121
- Population per Police Officer: 802

HUMAN RIGHTS

Members of the security forces are responsible for extra-judicial killings. They routinely beat, harass, arrest, detain incommunicado, and torture suspected opponents of the government. They and associated militias beat refugees and reportedly rape women abducted during raids in the southern provinces. Government planes have repeatedly bombed civilian targets in the south, Dinka villages have been raided, women and children have been abducted, and property has been looted and destroyed. Since the 1990s 15,000 Dinka women and children have been abducted. Some of those abducted have been sold into slavery or killed.

In accordance with the Sharia the Criminal Act mandates physical punishments including flogging, amputation, stoning, and crucifixion and the public display of bodies after execution.

CRIME

Crime Statistics. Offenses reported to the police per 100,000 population: 312. Of which:

- Murder: 10.2
- Assault: 46.3
- Burglary: 66.6
- Automobile Theft: 4.7

CORRECTIONAL SYSTEM

The ruling Islamic fundamentalists have imposed the Sharia as the law of the land on both Muslims and non-Muslims. The Sharia replaces the penal code promulgated by the British colonial rulers.

The general supervision of the Sudan Prison Service is the responsibility of the Ministry of the Interior acting through the commissioner of prisons. The four federal prisons in Khartoum North, Port Sudan, and Sawakin are directly administered by the commissioner, who is also responsible for five reformatories, the Kober Institution for the Insane, the Port Sudan Local Prison, and the Prison Service Training School in Khartoum North. The Sudan Prison Service maintains reformatory centers for juveniles, local government prisons, open and semiopen prisons, and provincial prisons. All provincial detention camps and jails are under the control of pro-

vincial authorities. Provincial prisons are classified at Local Class I and II, according to their size. Few Sudanese women commit serious crimes, so there are few female prisoners. Reform schools handle offenders under fifteen years of age, giving them regular schooling while in detention. Prison guards are trained at the Prison Service Training School.

Prison Conditions. The treatment of prisoners is reported to be generally inhumane. Most prisons are old and maintained poorly and most lack basic facilities, such as toilets. Health care and food are inadequate. Family visits are denied arbitrarily. Inmates are quartered in large barracks or dormitory rooms. Vocational and literacy training is compulsory. Within prisons there are small industries, and prisoners are paid a small sum for their labor, which is held in escrow until their release. After completing their sentences—often shortened by amnesty or probation—prisoners receive discharges rated according to their behavior in prison. The recidivism rate is less than 20 percent.

Prison Statistics.

- Total Prison Population: 12,000
- Prison Population Rate per 100,000: 36
- Pretrial Detainees: 10%
- Female Prisoners: 1.7%
- Juvenile Prisoners: 1.7%
- Number of Prisons: 125

George Thomas Kurian

Suriname

—■—

Official country name: Republic of Suriname
Capital: Paramaribo
Geographic description: Located in northern South America, bordering the North Atlantic Ocean between Guyana and French Guiana
Population: 438,144 (est. 2005)

■■■

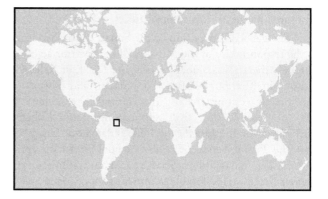

LAW ENFORCEMENT

Structure and Organization. The Armed Police Corps, which was founded during Dutch rule in 1865, has evolved over the years into a paramilitary force. It is headed by a commissioner of police who reports to the attorney general, but for operational purposes is under the Ministry of Justice and Police. Police training is provided by the Police Training School at Paramaribo. In remote communities in the interior the police conduct joint patrols with the military.

CRIME

Crime Statistics. Offenses reported to the police per 100,000 population: 17,819. Of which:

- Murder: 7.6

- Assault: 1,824.4

CORRECTIONAL SYSTEM

Prisons are administered by the director of prisons under the Ministry of Justice and Police. There are five prisons in the country, of which the largest is the Central Penitentiary Institution at Welgedacht.

Prison Conditions. Prison conditions are substandard. Violence among prisoners is common and authorities do nothing to stop that. Some facilities have been renovated to improve health and safety conditions. However, most facilities are old structures in dilapidated conditions. Detention cells in police stations where suspects are held temporarily are exempt from normal regulations and standards. Here, detainees are allowed no exercise and are not allowed to leave their cells. Guards mistreat the detainees, and the food, medical care, and other living conditions are deplorable. Conditions in women's and juvenile jails are slightly better.

Prison Statistics. The official capacity of the five prisons is 1,188, while the actual prison population is 1,933, yielding an occupancy level of 162.7 percent. The incarceration rate is 437 per 100,000 population. Of the total prison population, 41.4 percent are pretrial detainees, 5.9 percent are females, 9.7 percent are juveniles, and 19.3 percent are foreigners. In addition, there are a number of detention cells attached to police stations.

George Thomas Kurian

Swaziland

Official country name: Kingdom of Swaziland
Capital: Mbabane (Lobamba is the royal and legislative
  capital)
Geographic description: Landlocked country in south-
  ern Africa between South Africa and Mozambique
Population: 1,173,900 (est. 2005)

■■■

LAW ENFORCEMENT

History. The first police force in Swaziland was started
by King Sobuzha in 1880 and greatly expanded by his
son, King Mswati. It consisted of royal regiments
recruited from tribes loyal to the king. Each regiment
was commanded by an *induna*, and its men had the
power to make arrests for breaches of tribal law.

In 1895, when South Africa took over the administration of Swaziland, Chris Botha, the brother of
General Louis Botha, who became the first prime minister of the Union of South Africa, was given the task of
establishing a police force in the country. The force had a
short life as the Republican administration was withdrawn in 1899, soon after the start of the Boer War.

When the war ended in 1902, a victorious Britain
assumed control of Swaziland, and that same year a special
commissioner with a force of 150 South African constabulary personnel, both European and African, were sent to
the country to establish a provisional administration with
headquarters at Mbabane. The police constabulary was
under the commissioner's local control but subject to the
administration of the South African constabulary headquarters based at Carolina, in the Transvaal.

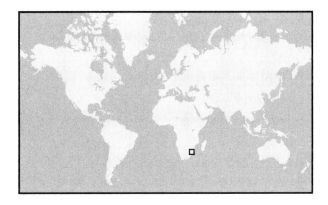

On February 22, 1907, the Swaziland Administration
Proclamation was proclaimed by Lord Selborne, the high
commissioner for South Africa. This legislation made provision for the formation of the Swaziland Police Force, and
on April 8, 1907, Captain C. H. Gilson was appointed
assistant commissioner of police for Swaziland, with headquarters at Mbabane. Twenty-one European officers were
transferred from the South African Constabulary to the
Swaziland Police, and 125 African personnel, mainly
Zulus from Natal, were recruited to bring the total to 146
officers and men.

A Police Training School was established about 1927.
In May 1965 the Police College at Matsapa was opened.
Up to 1933, the Swaziland Police also provided the staff
for the Prisons Department. From 1963 to 1966 the force
was reorganized and retrained and the establishment steadily increased until it numbered 644 in all ranks by 1967.

The Swaziland Police was a mounted force until
1953. It was renamed the Royal Swaziland Police in

1969, when the process of Africanization began, with over half of the expatriate senior officers being replaced by local officers. Since 1972 the posts of commissioner and deputy commissioner have been filled by Africans.

Structure and Organization. The Royal Swaziland Police is constituted under the Police and Public Order Act 29/57. It combines the functions of a civil police force with those of an armed constabulary. It is commanded by the commissioner of police, who is assisted at the headquarters in Mbabane by a deputy commissioner, an assistant commissioner, and staff officers.

The country is divided into four police districts. District headquarters are at Mbabane, Manzini, Lubombo, Siteki, Shiselweni, Hhohho, and Nhlangano. There are seventy-four police stations, police posts, and border posts distributed among the districts.

There are seven operational branches:

- Criminal Investigation Branch, including the Dog Squad, the Fraud and Vice Squad, the Drug Squad, and the Firearms Registry; forensic assistance is provided by the South African Police Criminal Bureau

- Fingerprint Bureau

- Photographic and Printing

- Traffic and Transport

- Intelligence

- Police Mobile Unit, which is commanded by a superintendent of police with four platoons; the unit serves as the permanent security guard for the king

- Communications

Education and Training. The Police College at Matsapa, near Manzini, offers basic training for recruits and advanced training for officers.

For recruitment as constables, candidates must meet certain minimum physical and educational standards. Men must be between twenty and thirty years of age and women between eighteen and twenty-five years of age, and hold at least a Junior Certificate of Education. Gazetted police officers and inspectors are appointed by the Civil Services Board, while subinspectors and constables are appointed by the commissioner of police. Vacancies above the constable level are filled by promotion.

Uniforms and Weapons. All ranks wear a winter uniform of blue serge and a blue cap. In the summer lower ranks wear a gray shirt, khaki shorts, and puttees, while inspectors and over wear khaki. On ceremonial occasions khaki units and trousers are worn with a khaki cap. In summer all ranks wear khaki tunic and shorts with a khaki cap.

The force personnel are armed with a baton or nightstick. During emergencies, however, they may be issued firearms.

Police Statistics.

- Total Police Personnel: 1,842

- Population per Police Officer: 637

HUMAN RIGHTS

The government's human rights record is poor. There are reports that the police torture and beat suspects and that the government fails to prosecute or otherwise discipline officers who commit abuses. During interrogation of suspects, police use a rubber tube to suffocate the suspects or the "Kentucky method," in which the arms and legs of the suspect are bent and tied with rope or chain.

CRIME

Crime Statistics. Offenses reported to the police per 100,000 population: 3,960. Of which:

- Murder: 18.1

- Assault: 471.7

- Burglary: 706.8

- Automobile Theft: 54.1

CORRECTIONAL SYSTEM

Swazi prisons are administered by the commissioner of prisons, who reports to the Minister of the Interior. The central prison is located in the capital while there are smaller prisons at the four police district headquarters and lockups and detention centers in the eighteen police stations distributed throughout the country.

Prison Conditions. Prison conditions generally meet international standards. However, detention centers are overcrowded and their conditions are unsatisfactory. Restrictions on the grant of bail result in overcrowding and other deplorable conditions. Women and children are held in separate facilities.

Prison Statistics.

- Total Prison Population: 3,245

- Prison Population Rate per 100,000: 324

- Pretrial Detainees: 49.6%

- Female Prisoners: 4.6%

- Juvenile Prisoners: 1.8%

- Number of Prisons: 12

- Official Capacity of the Prison System: 3,130

- Occupancy Level: 103.7%

George Thomas Kurian

Sweden

Official country name: Kingdom of Sweden
Capital: Stockholm
Geographic description: Southern and larger half of the Scandinavian Peninsula, bordering the Baltic Sea and Gulf of Bothnia
Population: 9,001,774 (est. 2005)

■■■

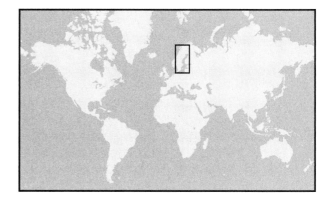

LAW ENFORCEMENT

History. Until 1965 Sweden had only local police forces who functioned in only 500 small police districts. Police work was hampered by restrictions on police movements from one district to another and the combination of the functions of district attorney and public distrainer in the police chief. In the 1930s a mobile auxiliary was created as a national police force with limited powers, primarily in the areas of traffic and serious crimes.

In 1984 the Riksdag approved a plan to reorganize the Swedish police system and create a new national force. On January 1, 1965, the Swedish Police (Rikspolis) was born. The law that created it reduced the number of police districts from 554 to 119 and the number of police posts from 989 to 510. The average strength of a police department was raised from 10 to between 20 and 50. The chief of police was also shorn of his functions as district attorney and public distrainer, thus enabling him to concentrate on police work proper. The public prosecutor's office was created, with 90 local districts, as was the distrainer's office, with 81 local districts.

Structure and Organization. The Rikspolis operates on three levels: national, regional, and local. The highest police authority in the kingdom is the National Police Board (NPB), which is answerable to the Ministry of Justice. The board is headed by the national police commissioner as chairman with the rank of director general, a deputy national police commissioner as vice chairman, and six members of the Riksdag representing different political parties. The NPB is responsible for the administration of the National Police Organization, the State Police College, the Police Council, the State Forensic Laboratory, and police training programs. The National Security Service and the National Criminal Investigation Department are units within the NPB.

The National Police headquarters in Stockholm is divided into four departments: A (Operations), B (Technical Services), C (Administration), and D (Security), the last of which reports directly to the commissioner's office.

Department A comprises Police Bureaus I and II. The former bureau deals with the work of uniformed police officers, including traffic control and surveillance. The Surveillance Section is assigned the task of allocating personnel to various police districts. Police Bureau II is concerned with investigation and detection. This bureau is divided into four sections: Planning, Local Records, Intrapolice Coordination, and Preliminary Investigations. It also deals with traffic accidents and police statistics.

The National Criminal Investigation Department is part of Police Bureau II. It has four squads: Squad A deals with murder and violent crimes, Squad B with narcotics, Squad C with larceny and theft, and Squad D with fraud.

Department B is divided into the Technical Bureau and the Training Bureau. The Technical Bureau has four sections: Equipment, Transport, Telecommunications, and Buildings. The Training Bureau is responsible for both training and recruitment.

Department C is divided into three bureaus dealing with administration, records, and staff, respectively. The Administration Bureau has sections dealing with budgeting and planning, purchasing, legal affairs, organization, service, and automatic data processing. Established in 1970, the Records Bureau keeps national criminal records, such as fingerprints, and records for passports, stolen vehicles, and wanted persons. The Staff Bureau is the personnel division of the Rikspolis and handles collective bargaining, contracts, appointments, dismissals, old age pensions, vacations, and salary classifications.

Department D has two bureaus dealing with national security. Bureau A deals with protection and control and Bureau B with detection and investigation.

The National Forensic Science Laboratory is attached to Police Bureau II of Department A, but is independent in technical matters. Bureau II of Department A is also the Swedish liaison for Interpol. Other police branches include the Intervention Police (Omradespolis) for crowd control and emergencies and the Aviation Police, which has a fleet of helicopters and airplanes.

Territorial organization starts with the counties, of which there are twenty-one. Each county, except for Gotland, has its own commissioner. The county government board can assume command of local police districts during emergencies. The county government is also in direct command of special county traffic surveillance groups, which are responsible for traffic surveillance across police district limits. Police functions are defined in the Police Act of 1984 as supplemented by police ordinances.

At the local end of the police administration are 118 police districts, most of them with 20 to 50 police officers. These are usually made up of both uniformed patrol officers and criminal investigation squads. The police authority in each district is the Police Board, headed by the police chief with the title of police commissioner. The local district has a constabulary or a Surveillance Department or a Criminal Investigations Department. The uniformed police of the constabulary carries out routine law enforcement and maintains communication links with the national headquarters. In the larger districts there are sections for the control of traffic, which in the smaller districts is the bailiwick of the surveillance units.

The local Criminal Investigation Department is divided into squads for investigation, larceny, fraud, and violence. A technical squad handles technical investigations. Units of at least three officers working in areas away from the central headquarters are empowered to make on-the-spot decisions.

A special local body of municipal representatives called the Police Committee acts as an advisory body in the local police commissioner's office.

The 1965 separation of the functions of police chief and public prosecutor led to a redefinition of police duties vis-à-vis the public prosecutor. Either the police or the public prosecutor may conduct preliminary examinations, and where it is carried out primarily by the police, the public prosecutor may also provide instructions.

Probably the best known Swedish innovation in policing is the social police. Introduced in the 1950s, the social police are plainclothes police officers who patrol the streets with social workers and focus on young people. They identify potential delinquents and offer them direct assistance or invoke the intervention of the Child Welfare Board.

Uniforms and Weapons. Normal working dress consists of a dark-blue jacket and trousers worn with a white-topped peaked cap. A similar uniform worn with a skirt and knee-length boots and an Africa Korps cap is worn by the women police. For car patrol, a hip-length over-blouse is worn instead of a jacket, and trousers are worn by women as well as men. Both wear a Scandinavian-type forage cap (*batmossa*). In summer the normal jacket may be replaced by a gray-blue short-sleeved tunic and in winter a heavy overcoat may be worn over the uniform, with an astrakhan cap. A Sam Browne belt is worn over all types of uniforms except for car patrol and from this is suspended a baton and a pistol holster. In all cases, a large patch is worn over the upper left arm showing the national crest surmounted by the word *Polis*. Badges of rank may appear on this patch or on the bottom of the jacket sleeve. Most officers in the higher echelons have badges showing rows of oak leaves between parallel bands.

A Swedish police officer readies his gun as tensions escalate between police and demonstrators rioting against the European Union (EU) summit in the streets of Göteborg, Sweden, June 15, 2001. The events took place in a city park outside the complex where the 15 EU leaders were holding their summit and two shooting victims were hospitalized afterward.
AP IMAGES.

Education and Training. Cadets are recruited by the Training and Recruitment Bureau of Department B. The district police chief accepts applications and conducts preliminary investigations, after which he or she forwards them to the National Police Board. If the board accepts, the recruit is sent to one of the several training schools, such as the National Institute of Technical Police or the police high schools at Stockholm or Lund. Basic training takes place over a 43-week period, including the Constable's Course for 32 weeks, practical work for 8 weeks, and the Constable's Course II for 3 weeks. Three to 5 weeks after the completion of the basic course, candidates enter the higher police course for 10 weeks.

Police training for the higher ranks is conducted at the Police College at Solna. After promotion to sergeant, the police officer takes a 12-week sergeant's course. An 8-week inspector's course is offered to those who need to learn about police organization. There is a 15-week superintendent's course and a 56-week commissioner's course at the Solna Police College. Specialized courses are offered at the Swedish Army Driving School for traffic controllers and at the Armed Forces Dog Training Center for dog handlers. In addition, the universities of Umeå and Växjö train police officers as part of their general curriculum. The Nordic Baltic Police Academy serves all Baltic states.

Police commissioners are recruited from law schools, but all other promotions are made from the rank and file. Police in Sweden are allowed to hold public office and belong to trade unions.

Police Statistics.

- Total Police Personnel: 27,145
- Population per Police Officer: 332

HUMAN RIGHTS

Sweden is a model for other nations in the scrupulous observance of human rights in law enforcement. Occasional violations of human rights trigger a number of corrective mechanisms, both internal to the department and through the national ombudsman's office.

CRIME

Crime Statistics. Offenses reported to the police per 100,000 population: 12,998. Of which:

- Murder: 4.5
- Assault: 42.5
- Burglary: 1,651.1
- Automobile Theft: 658.9

CORRECTIONAL SYSTEMS

The Swedish criminal justice system is governed by Riksdag legislation. The principal legislative enactments are the Code of Judicial Procedure and the penal code. However, not all crimes are listed in the penal code. A number of offenses are described in separate statutes, including traffic offenses and narcotics violations. Because Swedish law is not entirely codified, there is latitude for judicial interpretation. Thus, although Swedish criminal law belongs to the Romano-Germanic family, it shares with common-law systems a binding respect for judicial precedent.

The penal code, the most important source of criminal law, was promulgated in 1965 and has been revised many times since. The code is divided into three parts: Part 1 contains general provisions on the application of the law. Part 2 contains a list of the major crimes and specific elements that constitute each offense and the penalties that may be imposed in each case. The code divides offenses into four major categories: crimes against the person, crimes against property, crimes against the public, and crimes against the state. Since Sweden does not have a separate military criminal code, crimes committed by members of the armed forces are treated as crimes against the state. Part 3 of the code is concerned with principles for assessing sanctions. Articles in this part exempt juveniles under fifteen years of age and persons of unsound mind from criminal responsibility and provide for minor punishments for offenders below twenty-one years.

The Code of Judicial Procedure outlines the powers of the police authorities. Arrests are permitted without a detention order when a person is apprehended in the act of committing a crime. It also gives the police the right to search and seize and to restrain suspects from travel.

Sweden's correctional system has evolved over the years and embodies social democratic concepts in rehabilitation. Since the 1940s Sweden has led the way in reducing the number of actions classified as crimes and morally deviant behavior. The nature of the sanctions has also changed. Tax offenses, minor frauds, and minor property offenses are penalized by a fine, rather than imprisonment. Certain offenses, such as drunkenness, are consigned to medical and social workers. At the same time, in response to a dramatic increase in serious crime since the 1990s, the full force of the law has been brought to bear on certain other types of crime, such as narcotics trafficking, armed robbery, illegal possession of weapons, and certain types of environmentally destructive crimes, such as pollution. The use of imprisonment as a deterrent and punishment is being replaced by fines. Youth imprisonment was abolished in 1979 and internment was abolished in 1981. Finally, greater attention is being paid to crime prevention under the auspices of the National Council for Crime Prevention.

The corrections system is administered by the Swedish Prison and Probation Administration under the Ministry of Justice. It is composed of laypeople appointed by the minister of justice and is headed by a director general. Parole decisions are handled by the Correctional Service Board, which is chaired by a Supreme Court justice. This board also hears inmate appeals based on decisions made by the local supervisory boards. There are fifty such local supervisory boards, and they are responsible for parole and probation decisions in their respective districts. Each board is composed of five members and is chaired by a lawyer.

Since 1978 Sweden has been divided into thirteen correctional care regions. Each region is administered by a regional director, who is a professional probation officer. The regional director determines where a convicted offender will serve his or her sentence.

The total number of prisons is eighty-four. The principal correctional institutions are local and national facilities, some of which are open and some are closed.

The largest prison is at Kumla, which can house 224 inmates, while the smaller ones hold between 20 and 40 inmates. Swedish prisons are noted for their cleanliness and well-appointed living quarters and amenities. There is virtually no overcrowding, and each prisoner has his or her own cell.

There are three types of correctional facilities: remand prisons, local facilities, and national facilities. Each is designed for a specific purpose and for a specific type of offender. There are twenty-one remand prisons serving the entire country. Because of the limited number of remand prisons, some of the other prisons have a remand wing attached to them.

The forty-four local facilities are used primarily to house offenders sentenced to less than one year of imprisonment and inmates serving longer sentences, but who are approaching the end of their terms. Security measures are minimal at these centers. The primary purpose of local institutions is to keep the inmates as close to their families as possible.

Finally, there are nineteen national penitentiaries, which are administered directly by the National Prison and Probation Administration. These closed, maximum-security prisons house people sentenced to more than one year in prison.

The legal basis of the correctional system is found in the 1974 Act on Correctional Treatment in Institutions, which defines the purpose of corrections as "to promote the adjustment of the inmate in society and to counteract the detrimental effects of deprivation of liberty. Insofar as this can be achieved without detriment to the need to protect the public, treatment should be directed from the outset toward measures that prepare the inmate for conditions outside the institution." The act further declares that "inmates shall be treated with respect for their human dignity. They shall be treated with understanding for the special difficulties connected with a stay in an institution."

The 1974 act requires all inmates to be involved in some form of work, study, or training and provides for remuneration for such activities. Even the disabled are given remuneration for purchasing personal items. Solitary confinement is used rarely and under exceptional circumstances. Inmates who violate prison rules or who are simply recalcitrant may be warned or cited for a specific period that does not count toward the sentence. Inmates also have the right to form councils and to negotiate grievances with prison authorities. The act empowers prison authorities to grant furloughs to inmates for work, study, and leisure-time activities. The furlough scheme has been considerably expanded since the 1990s and is designed to facilitate the inmate's eventual reentry into society. Medical furloughs are granted if a person can receive better treatment in an outside hospital or clinic. Short-term and release furloughs are also regular features of the scheme. Short-term furloughs may be granted for a number of hours or days, primarily to enable the inmate to maintain ties with his or her family. Release furloughs are available for inmates eligible for parole. Inmates are allowed conjugal visits. Although correspondence may be scrutinized, it is not censored except in the case of high-security risks. Telephones are readily available, and inmates have access to a wide range of reading matter, including legal books and periodicals, and may borrow books from local public libraries. Finally, those within prison walls have the same right to social services as those without.

The largest high-security prison is at Kumla. Built in 1965, this prison holds 224 inmates and has a staff of 280. The high ratio of staff to inmates is typical of Sweden's correctional system. Kumla has a 21-foot wall around it, and its security is reinforced by an extensive television and radar monitoring system. Besides living blocks for regular prisoners, Kumla has two special blocks: one containing a hospital psychiatric ward, a temporary detention unit, and a disciplinary section, and the other for more dangerous inmates and security risks. Inmates are employed in one of the traditional prison workshops, or they can participate in one of the full-time educational programs. Generally, inmates are granted furloughs and conjugal visits as well as sojourns to local cultural and sporting events.

Tillberga is an open national prison where inmates are employed in the construction of prefabricated homes that are sold by a state-owned company. All workers are members of the construction union and are paid free-market wages negotiated by the union. However, they receive only 70 percent of the wages because they are not subject to the national income tax. Of this amount, the inmates actually receive only 25 percent; the rest is used to support the inmate's family and pay the cost of his or her food. The remaining sum is placed in a savings account, which he or she receives on release.

Under Sweden's privacy laws, newspapers cannot publish the names of people accused or convicted of crimes. Similarly, employers cannot ask a potential employee if she or he has served a prison term.

Parole is granted by the Correctional Services Board for inmates serving more than one year of imprisonment in a national prison and by local supervisory boards for others. It is never granted before at least three months of a sentence has been served. A probation officer is assigned to an inmate on eligibility for parole. A parolee is expected to maintain contact with his or her probation officer during the term of parole and is expected to maintain a residence and seek employment. The parolee

may also be subject to special directives, such as residing at a specific place, joining a job training program, or seeking medical or psychiatric care.

Sweden uses a number of noninstitutional programs to minimize the imposition of prison sentences and to prevent prison overcrowding. These include conditional sentences, probation orders, and fines. A conditional sentence is a form of probation for a period of up to two years, but the offender is not supervised by a probation officer. The sanction is a conditional warning to refrain from further criminal activity. A probation order is imposed on offenders who have committed an imprisonable offense and may be imposed for up to three years. It differs from the conditional sentence in that the offender is placed under supervision and may be sentenced to a short-term imprisonment (not exceeding three months) as well. Although the offender retains liberty while under supervision, he or she may be enjoined to pay fines or make compensation for damages, and the local supervisory board may issue other directives with which the probationer must comply. These directives usually include reporting periodically to the probation officer in any one of the sixty-three probation districts, and notifying the officer of place of residence and nature of employment or schooling. Fines are used extensively in Sweden as a penal sanction. Fines are of three types: standardized, fixed, and day fines. Day fines are determined by the per diem income of the offender and thus vary according to economic status. A person who fails to pay the day fine may have the fine converted to a sentence of imprisonment.

Despite the rising juvenile crime rate, Sweden's juvenile justice system is committed to social and medical treatment rather than traditional institutionalization. The age of criminal responsibility is fixed by the Code of Judicial Procedure at fifteen years. People below this age cannot be subject to criminal prosecution or penal sanction. The police, however, may interrogate a person under fifteen if the child's parents or guardians are present. Juveniles between fifteen and twenty years of age may be prosecuted and sentenced, but this is rarely done, especially if the suspect is under eighteen. If a prosecutor decides to bring charges against a person under the age of eighteen, the matter is turned over to the Child Welfare Board. Sweden does not have a separate juvenile court, and the Child Welfare Board performs some of the functions of a juvenile court. Each municipality has a board composed of five unpaid members elected by the municipal council for four-year terms. The board usually includes a minister, a lawyer, a school teacher, and a child specialist. The board has both a civil and criminal jurisdiction for juveniles under twenty-one years of age. The civil jurisdiction involves care proceedings where the child is neglected or abandoned or is delinquent. In criminal cases it is not concerned with establishing the offender's guilt, but with determining the appropriate treatment. The Social Services Act of 1982 requires that the board's decision to place a child in custody be reviewed by an administrative court of appeal. In cases where criminal charges are pressed, fines, probation, or suspended sentences are generally handed down. In exceptional cases a person under eighteen can be imprisoned, but can never be sentenced to life imprisonment. The penal code further provides a milder sanction for persons under twenty-one than it does for adults who commit the same offense.

Prison Statistics.

- Total Prison Population: 7,332
- Prison Population Rate per 100,000: 81
- Pretrial Detainees: 20.5%
- Female Prisoners: 6.2%
- Juvenile Prisoners: 0.3%
- Number of Prisons: 84
- Official Capacity of the Prison System: 7,099
- Occupancy Level: 103.3%

George Thomas Kurian

Switzerland

———■———

Official country name: Swiss Confederation
Capital: Bern
Geographic description: Landlocked country in central Europe, flanked by the Alps in the south
Population: 7,489,370 (est. 2005)

■■■

LAW ENFORCEMENT

History. In 1902 the Swiss Parliament enacted the Federal Department of Justice and Police Organization Act. The act was designed to unify civil and criminal law actions under one federal agency. Following its enactment the Justice Division consisted of a Divisional Head for Legislation and Administration of Justice, a Grade 1 deputy, a Grade 2 deputy, a secretary for the commercial register, a secretary for civil records, and a registrar.

After several years of consultations in various commissions and committees, the Parliament enacted the Swiss Civil Code, which established the law of person, family law, the inheritance law, and the law of property. In 1912 the cantons adopted the necessary legislation, and the new civil codes were put into full force. The legislation unified civil law practices throughout Switzerland. One of the hallmarks of the civil code is its democratic and down-to-earth style. It was the intention of its author, Eugen Huber, that the code should be geared toward the common person. He wanted it to be read and understood by ordinary citizens and to be expressed in clear and discernable language. The Swiss Civil Code has had considerable influence on the legal

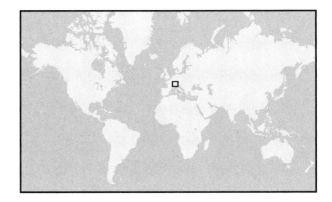

systems of other jurisdictions. A case in point is Turkey, which adopted a slightly modified version in 1926.

In 1923 the Federal Office for Land Registry (including the Surveyor's Office), which was a separate division in the Federal Department of Justice and Police, was brought into the Justice Division. This occurred following the enactment of federal land survey legislation that called for the systemization of land surveys and the introduction of land registries in the cantons. The Federal Surveyor's Office was subsequently moved twice more in the interests of synergy, first to the Federal Office for Spatial Development (1991) and finally to the Federal Office of Topography (1999). The family register provision is enacted into federal law. This law eventually made it possible for the civil registry to keep track via up-to-date records of the civil status of all Swiss nationals. The family register contains details of current family relationships and establishes who is a citizen of the municipality and canton and is thus entitled to Swiss citizenship. With this new process of registration, the government officials who maintain civil records have been able to provide a service that is unique in that it enables them to assist private individuals and official authorities whenever proof of civil status is required for the exercise of rights or the performance of obligations.

In 1942 a single Swiss Penal Code was established that eliminated the patchwork of cantonal codes. In 1967 appropriations legislation dealing with federal funding of penal and reform institutions was passed into law. Subsequently, as part of a reallocation of functions between the confederation and the cantons, the operating budgets were brought within the scope of the amended federal legislation that dealt with the funding of prisons and detention centers. The purpose of the legislation was to improve the quality of reform institutions and to coordinate the availability of places in reformatories.

In 1968, following years of assessment by a review commission (from 1958 to 1965), the Federal Council appointed a committee of legal experts to engage in a stage-by-stage reform of the family law sections of the federal civil code. The act had remained unchanged since 1912, and the changes that were made conformed to societal needs and attitudes that had evolved over the years.

In 1971 the federal penal code was amended to allow for alternative forms of criminal punishment. The law was also changed to allow for community service punishment for convicted juvenile offenders. New forms of crime made it necessary to create new offense classifications and changes to the penal code. In subsequent years additional crime categories were developed to deal with new and different types of criminal offenses such as insider trading (1988); money laundering (1990); membership of a criminal organization, power to seize criminal assets and reporting for financial intermediaries (1994); and cybercrime and check and credit card abuse (1995).

As part of the government's efforts to ease increasing tensions between the church and state, the special church-related provisions, which were originally established in the era of the Kulturkampf, were systematically abolished. In 1973 the removal of the Jesuits and monasteries article was approved by the people and cantons. In line with these changes the new federal constitution eliminated the rule barring members of the clergy from holding public office. Finally, in 2001 the electorate and the cantons voted to abrogate the diocese article, which provides that dioceses can be established only with the authorization of the confederation. This removed the last special church-related provision from the federal constitution.

The Justice Division was reorganized into three new main divisions. The first division is responsible for legislation in the field of public and administrative law and plays an advisory role in the drafting of all major legis-

lation by any section of the federal administration. The second division is primarily concerned with the operation of existing law. A special unit within this division prepares the appeal decisions of the Federal Council. This division is also responsible for legislation in the field of criminal law. The third division is responsible for legislation in the field of civil law and civil procedure law and execution. Attached to this division are the Commercial Registry Office, the Federal Office of Civil Status, and the Federal Office for Land Registry. Following Switzerland's ratification of the European Convention on Human Rights in 1974, a Council of Europe affairs unit was established within the Federal Office of Justice and its responsibility is to provide advice on any case brought against Switzerland plus representing the government before the European Court of Human Rights.

In 1979 the Administration Organization Act (AOA) did not include provisions that would create a new Federal Office for Legislation. The Federal Office for Legislation, if approved as a new agency, would have taken on the responsibility for developing and coordinating federal legislation at the constitutional level. Despite the failure of the AOA to include the establishment of the Federal Office for Legislation, the Federal Council adopted the position that the Justice Division should be involved in all legislative proposals that are to be considered at the federal level. The AOA changed the name of the Federal Justice Division to the Federal Office of Justice.

The reform of family laws with respect to amending the statutes governing marriage and divorce are addressed by the government. The new marriage act (1988) codifies the legal principle related to clarifying the equality of a husband and a wife in a marriage and makes both equally responsible for their joint well-being. The new Divorce Act introduces the possibility of divorce by mutual agreement. Additionally, either spouse can petition unilaterally for a divorce following separations that are minimally four years in length. No-fault divorce language is adopted that makes the issue of which spouse is to blame for a marriage breakup insignificant. The final step in the reform of family law legislation was a radical overhaul of the law of guardianship. In 1991, following many years of work, the first report on the reform of company law was submitted to the Federal Council. Accordingly, the Parliament enacted the revisions proposed to the Federal Council. The revisions are referred to as Title 26 of the Contract Law. The amended provisions contained the following objectives: increasing transparency, creating greater shareholder protection, improving the structure and function of corporate governance, and making methods of raising capital for companies that contain provisions safeguarding against possible abuses more accessible.

Because of years of amendments and changes in society, the federal constitution of 1874 had become significantly antiquated and contained many superfluous provisions. As a result, it was replaced by a completely new document. The new federal constitution approved by the people and the cantons in 1999 reflects the modern constitutional realities of Switzerland. The new constitution codified a number of previously unwritten laws. A number of constitutional amendments were also added by the Parliament.

In 2000 the reform of the justice system approved by the cantons paved the way for several fundamental changes related to rules of procedure and the courts system. The reform provided for the constitutional basis for the unification of both civil and criminal procedural law, and it conferred a constitutional right of access to an independent court for all citizens involved in legal disputes. It also provided the basis for a reform of the federal courts system. It proposed to restructure the federal judiciary completely to bring about an effective reduction in the workload of the Federal Supreme Court and the Federal Insurance Court.

As part of the reorganization of the Swiss police system at federal level, the Federal Office of Police was restructured as an agency solely responsible for police matters. The federal units not concerned with police matters were transferred to the Federal Office of Justice. These units were the Division for International Mutual Legal Assistance, the Swiss Criminal Records unit, the Gaming and Lotteries Unit, and Social Aids for Swiss Citizens Resident Abroad.

Structure and Organization. Switzerland is a confederation of twenty-six sovereign cantons. The cantons are not vested in the constitution of the federation. Each canton has its own constitution, legislature, government, and courts. As a general rule, jurisdiction and police powers are left to each individual canton.

On January 1, 2002, Switzerland enacted legislation empowering the federal government with investigatory jurisdiction to fight serious crimes nationwide. A new agency, the Criminal Federal Police, overseen by the Federal Office of Police was formed and charged with investigating organized crime, money laundering, corruption, and some white-collar crimes.

Principal Agencies and Divisions. The hierarchy of the Swiss police is broken down into three primary divisions: the Federal Police, the cantonal police, and the local or municipal police. The Federal Police are primarily responsible for investigating organized crime, money laundering, human smuggling, and drug trafficking. The cantonal police are responsible for criminal investigations, security (routine patrol, protection of life and property, and order maintenance), and traffic enforcement. If present, municipal or local police assist in standard law enforcement duties or may have insignificant assignments.

Differences can be seen in the structure of the cantonal authorities based on heritage. In general, German-speaking cantons separate division of labor into three categories: criminal, security, and traffic police. French-speaking cantons separate the division of labor into two categories: criminal (Sûreté) and Gendarmerie. The Gendarmerie corresponds to the German canton's security police and encompasses the traffic police.

Salaries. Officer salaries were observed in the canton of Basel-Stadt. Recruits at the Swiss Police School could expect to earn between 4,330 and 4,596 Swiss francs per month, depending on age. Additional social pay between 381 and 525 Swiss francs can be added based on the number of children in school. After graduation from the Swiss Police School officers can expect to earn between 4,396 and 5,545 Swiss francs per month.

Police at Work. Most of the cantons have officers working in various divisions throughout the police organization. The divisions vary from criminal patrol and investigation to traffic enforcement and investigation. There are also specialized units that are used, such as K-9, Mounted Patrol, and Sea Police. Of note, however, is the fact that Switzerland does not have a specialized unit for psychological criminal profiling. Speculatively, this may be because of the low number of serious assaults and murders.

Hierarchy and Ranks. The cantonal police are based on a paramilitary hierarchy and ranking structure. The *kommandant* (commander) is at the top of the ranking hierarchy. Each canton then has its own group of divisions, such as criminal division, traffic division, technical operations, and special operations, which are headed by lower-ranking supervisors and staffed with police officers and police service officers.

Police-Community Relations. The Swiss Crime Prevention Center directs a number of community-based programs informing the general public about topics of greater communal concern. The programs include "Hausliche Gewalt" (Stop), a program aimed at stopping domestic violence through education of controlling and intimidating behaviors, safety in old age, a program aimed at helping elderly Swiss citizens feel secure in their residence, and say no to drugs, an educating program designed to help drug users escape the downfalls of drug addiction.

The Swiss Crime Prevention Center also provides education regarding the areas of fraud (investment transactions, loan brokerage, and Nigerian con games), theft (bicycle, car theft, burglaries, pickpockets, and theft

A demonstrator cleans the protective shield of a riot police officer in Bern, Switzerland, January 22, 2005. *Small groups of protesters gathered to rally against the World Economic Forum taking place from January 26–30, 2005, in Davos, Switzerland.* AP IMAGES.

within the hospitality industry), violence (youth, family, school, and sexual), and drugs.

Local Police. Policing at the local level is canton specific. A number of cantons coordinate policing duties with municipal police agencies. The twenty-six cantons encompass over a hundred municipal police agencies. Some cantons use the municipal police agencies in traditional fashion, others delegate insignificant tasks to the municipal officers, while other cantons do not use municipal forces at all.

Special Police.

Sea Police. Several cantons have Sea Police, which are responsible for patrolling Switzerland's bodies of water.

Traffic Police. The Traffic division is an integral part of all the cantons. The traffic division may be broken down into subdivisions of patrol, accident, and technical. The Patrol Service Division oversees all the roadways by

ticketing for speeding and for other types of traffic violations. The Accident Service Division is responsible for complex traffic and accident investigations. The Technical Service Division is responsible for all the traffic controls and deployment of traffic police for large events.

Education and Training. Applicants may apply for admissions to police service between the ages of twenty and thirty-five years old, be in good physical and psychological condition, have excellent written and verbal skills (German), have knowledge of a foreign language, and possess an excellent driving record.

Law enforcement officers in Switzerland are not required to have a high school diploma or its equivalent. In fact, 70 percent have not completed high school. Training for law enforcement officers includes one year of academic and on the job training. Switzerland has one academy for specialized training and several other academies for basic law enforcement training.

Uniforms and Weapons. The basic uniform of a cantonal police officer is a dark-blue pant with a light- or dark-blue shirt. Patches are attached to the sleeve based on canton and assignment.

Transportation, Technology, and Communications. Vehicles vary from canton to canton; however, a mid-sized sedan such as the Volvo V70 is common to most localities. Other police vehicles include the Jeep Grand Cherokee, Honda CRV, Opel Monterey, Mercedes Vito, and Fiat Ducato. The vehicles are white with orange stripes or blue stripes horizontally traversing the vehicle's hood, fenders, and doors. The word *Polizei* is clearly marked on the hood and door panels.

The Swiss Police Technical Commission has working divisions on general technology and communications and electronics that keep the cantonal police organizations informed on new technology.

Surveillance and Intelligence Gathering. There is a need for a unity of doctrine when criminal activity and police actions involve several cantons. There has been an extensive effort to strengthen cooperation between the cantonal police organizations and between the cantonal police and the Federal Office for Police and the Attorney General's Office. The Conference of Cantonal Police Commanders of Switzerland and the Swiss Association of City Police Chiefs have made interagency communication and the adoption of a unity of doctrine a priority.

Police Officers Killed in the Line of Duty. Since 1919 a total of eleven Swiss law enforcement officers have been killed in the line of duty: Johann Altdorfer, Leonhard Heer, Rudolf Himmelberger, Stefan Jetzer, Gottfried

Kottmann, Hans Kull, Julius Muntwyler, Roland Niederberger, Friedrich Pluss, Friedrich Pfennigwert, and Peter Spitzer.

Police Statistics. There are twenty-six cantons and over a hundred municipal law enforcement agencies employing approximately 14,954 law enforcement personnel. The population per police officer is 501.

HUMAN RIGHTS

The Swiss government generally respects human rights, and the law and judiciary provide effective means of dealing with individual instances of abuse. There continue to be allegations by nongovernmental organizations of occasional police harassment directed against foreigners, particularly asylum seekers, including arbitrary detention. The government is continuing to take serious steps to address violence against women. Trafficking in women for forced prostitution has increased. Some laws still tend to discriminate against women. There continue to be reports of verbal abuse against foreigners by private citizens.

In one case, the Geneva prosecutor general dismissed a criminal complaint lodged against Geneva police by the Nigerian human rights activist Clement Nwankwo. He had accused the police of assaulting him on the street and subjecting him to degrading treatment in a police station following his arrest in 1997. While acknowledging that Nwankwo had been a victim of abuse of power, the prosecutor general concluded that disciplinary sanctions imposed on three officers following an administrative inquiry were sufficient punishment. In 1998 the Federal Supreme Court rejected Nwankwo's final appeal against his conviction for resisting the police at the time of the arrest, thus putting an end to all judicial proceedings. Nwankwo received no compensation, and the disciplinary actions against the three police officers were dropped without explanation. In October 1998 Nwankwo lodged a petition against Switzerland with the European Commission of Human Rights, claiming violation of two articles of the European Convention for the Protection of Fundamental Human Rights and Freedoms.

Swiss nongovernmental organizations believe that the Nwankwo case underscores overall problems with police treatment of foreigners, especially asylum seekers in Geneva and perhaps elsewhere. The cantonal government took measures in response to the incident, including launching an administrative inquiry into the conduct of the three police officers involved. The police successfully appealed the reprimand and warning that were imposed as a result of the inquiry. In 1998 the Association for the Prevention of Torture, a nongovern-

mental organization, organized a special seminar for police officers in Geneva. The federal government and the canton of Geneva financed the publication of a special brochure aimed at increasing respect for and awareness of the rights of all persons in custody. The brochure was distributed throughout the country.

In 1997, following its examination of Switzerland's third periodic report, the United Nations Committee against Torture expressed concern about "frequent allegations of ill treatment" inflicted in the course of arrests and police custody and a lack of independent mechanisms in the cantons to provide certain legal protections such as the possibility, "especially for foreigners," to contact their family or a lawyer in case of arrest and to be examined by an independent doctor on entering police custody, after each interrogation, and before being brought before an investigating magistrate or being released. The committee recommended the introduction of mechanisms to receive complaints of mistreatment by police officers against suspects and for the harmonization of the twenty-six different cantonal codes of penal procedure, "particularly with regard to the granting of fundamental guarantees in the course of police custody." In addition, the committee recommended that the authorities pay "the greatest possible attention" to the handling of cases of violence attributed to police officers to ensure the opening of investigations and, in proven cases, the imposition of possible sanctions. Responding to committee recommendations, in 1998 a team of experts appointed by the Federal Office of Justice presented a preliminary study identifying possible characteristics of a future federal-level code of penal procedures that would replace the cantonal codes. The study recommended granting fundamental protections to detainees in police custody, including the introduction of a legal right to inform relatives or third parties of their arrest. However, the committee did not recommend a provision for access to a lawyer from the time of arrest. The Federal Office of Justice issued a draft code in 2001.

The Brazilian national Luis Felipe Lourenco had been living illegally in the country and was arrested in 1998 by police in Geneva on charges of theft of a credit card. He allegedly was beaten by prison guards while in custody. The guards reportedly waited two hours before transporting Lourenco to the hospital, where he was diagnosed with a perforated lung and damage to his spinal cord. The Brazilian embassy reportedly asked the authorities to look into the incident. Inquiries are ongoing, but there has been no official report. Amnesty International criticized the police for brutality in its 1999 annual report. Lourenco claims to be partially paralyzed as a result of the injuries that he suffered at the hands of prison guards. The prison administration claimed that

Lourenco's injuries were incurred when he threw himself against a door.

Violence against women is a problem. According to a government-funded study on domestic violence, one-fifth of all women suffer in their lifetimes at least once from physical or sexual violence, and about 40 percent suffer from psychological or verbal abuse. The law prohibits wife beating and similar offenses. Spousal rape is a crime in the Swiss Penal Code. Victims of violence can obtain help, counseling, and legal assistance from specialized agencies or from nearly a dozen hot lines sponsored privately or by local, cantonal, and national authorities. Cantonal police have specially trained units to deal with violence against women, and victims are legally entitled to be heard exclusively by female police officers and judges. An estimated 680 women and 730 children took refuge in 14 women's shelters across the country during 1998. Those in charge of the shelters estimate that nearly as many were denied access because of lack of space and funding (Bureau of Democracy, Human Rights, and Labor 2000).

The difficulty in gathering information about the number of prosecuted, convicted, or punished spouse abusers stems in part from the fact that legal cases are handled by each canton and data are often not up to date. According to 1998 police criminal statistics, 320 men were investigated for rape offenses; in 1997, the last year for which data are available, 92 men were sentenced for rape (Bureau of Democracy, Human Rights, and Labor).

The Federation of Women's Organizations and many other women's nongovernmental organizations have heightened public awareness of the problem of violence against women. In 1998 two government-supported women's organizations that fight for equal gender rights jointly conducted the first national campaign against violence in relationships. This campaign received extensive media coverage.

Although the constitution prohibits all types of discrimination, and a 1981 amendment provides equal rights, equal treatment, and equivalent wages for men and women, a few laws still tend to discriminate against women. In 1996 a new federal law on equal opportunity for women and men came into force. The law includes a general prohibition on gender-based discrimination and incorporates the principle of "equal wages for equal work." The law also includes provisions aimed at eliminating sexual harassment and facilitating access to legal remedies for those who claim discrimination or harassment. The Federal Supreme Court has ruled that in a divorce settlement the primary wage earner must be left with sufficient income to remain above the poverty level. Since the man is the primary wage earner in most mar-

riages, when the income is too low to support both parties, it is usually the wife who must go on welfare.

On average women earn 20 to 30 percent less than men. Researchers find that discriminatory behavior by employers accounts for 40 percent of the overall wage gap between men and women. Women are also promoted less often than men. Individual cases of denial of equal pay for equal work are subject to the new law. In 1996, the most recent year for which data are available, 27.7 percent of the women between the ages of fifteen and sixty-one were not in the workforce; of those in the workforce, only 46 percent worked full time. Women held over 80 percent of all part-time jobs (Bureau of Democracy, Human Rights, and Labor).

According to nongovernmental organizational statistics, in 1999 there were 73 reported attacks against foreigners/minorities in the first seven months of the year, compared to 70 for the first half of 1998. These figures include instances of oral and written "attacks," which are much more common than physical assaults. Investigations of these attacks are conducted effectively and lead, in most cases, to the arrest of the people responsible. People convicted of racist crimes are commonly sentenced from three days' to three years' imprisonment with a fine of up to approximately $27,000 (Bureau of Democracy, Human Rights, and Labor).

Prostitution is legal, while working without a valid work permit is illegal. The penal code criminalizes sexual exploitation and trafficking in women; however, trafficking in women is a problem. The penal code criminalizes sexual exploitation and trafficking in persons. Police officials are concerned about a growing number of foreign women subject to abuse in sex trafficking rings. In the past victims came from Thailand, parts of Africa, or South America; by the turn of the twenty-first century an increasing number of women came from Hungary, Russia, Ukraine, and other states of the former Soviet Union. Many victims are forced to work in salons or clubs to pay for the cost of their travel and forged documents and find themselves in a state of dependency. Traffickers sometimes seize victims' passports. Generally, the victims do not read, write, or speak the country's languages and are afraid to seek help from the authorities.

Since 1905 the government has had an office to combat trafficking of girls for the purpose of commercial sexual exploitation. Over the years this office has evolved to include all forms of trafficking in persons. The Federal Office for Police has a human trafficking office as part of the criminal intelligence unit. In 1998 the government institutionalized the exchange of information on trafficking in persons with nongovernmental organizations. The

Department of Foreign Affairs launched programs intended to combat trafficking from eastern Europe. To confront modern forms of trafficking in women, especially via the Internet, the federal police have increased the number of their agents. In 1997 four persons were convicted of trafficking in women and thirteen were convicted of sexual exploitation; and in 1997–1998 police uncovered a large Thai trafficking organization. Its leader was arrested, tried, and convicted (Bureau of Democracy, Human Rights, and Labor).

CRIME

Organized Crime. Organized crime investigations are carried out primarily by the Federal Criminal Police. The primary interest of an organized crime investigation in Switzerland is on the international trade in illegal drugs, trafficking of people, and money laundering. Investigations into organized crime are carried out by investigators who are banking specialists, auditors, and information technology experts.

Crime Statistics. The most recent crime data available from Interpol is for 2002. Switzerland's crime statistics were summarized as follows:

Homicides	213
Sex Offenses	3,383
Rape	484
Serious Assaults	6,123
Thefts	271,867
Robberies and Violent Theft	2,445
Breaking and Entering	60,822
Automobile Theft	65,571
Other Thefts	1,523
Fraud	10,327
Counterfeit Currency	6,735
Drug Offenses	49,201
Total Number of All Infractions	350,294

SOURCE: *Interpol 2002.*

CORRECTIONAL SYSTEM

The Federal Department of Justice and Police is responsible for housing the Swiss prison population.

Prison Conditions. Reports on Switzerland indicate that prisoners are treated respectfully, with a minimum number of complaints. Overcrowding is kept to a minimum, possibly because of the minimal duration of most prison sentences. According to statistics regarding incarceration rates, most sentences are less than eighteen months long.

Prison Statistics.

- Total Prison Population: 6,021
- Prison Population Rate per 1,000: 81
- Pretrial Detainees: 41.5%
- Female Prisoners: 6.2%
- Juvenile Prisoners: 1.4%
- Number of Prisons: 157
- Official Capacity of the Prison System: 6,584
- Occupancy Level: 91.4%

MOST SIGNIFICANT ISSUE FACING THE COUNTRY

An issue facing Switzerland is how to address suicide tourism. Zürich's public prosecutor is drafting legislation that would restrict assisted suicide in Switzerland. In 2000 only three foreigners traveled to Zürich to commit suicide. This is a small figure, but it still remains an issue that the Swiss government feels it needs to address so that the problem does not increase in number. Because of the liberal laws in Switzerland, many foreigners are able to travel there and remain virtually unknown. Andreas Brunner, a Zürich prosecutor stated, "People are only here for one day before they die. We know nothing about them." This issue alone has created a problem for the Swiss government. Intelligence gathering is difficult and the Swiss government desires to be better educated in the profile of the type of person or persons who enter into another country to commit suicide. Along with investigations of suicide tourism, the Swiss government is also concerned with those who assist in these suicides. Each of these types of investigations in assisted suicide costs the canton between 2,428 and 5,000 Swiss francs (Capper 2004).

BIBLIOGRAPHY

Bureau of Democracy, Human Rights, and Labor. 2000. "Country Reports on Human Rights and Practices: Switzerland, 1999." U.S. Department of State. Available online at http://www.state.gov/www/global/human_rights/1999_hrp_report/switzerl.html (accessed January 2, 2006).

Capper, Scott. 2004. "Prosecutor Seeks to Outlaw 'Suicide Tourism.'" *Swissinfo* (February 27). Available online at http://www.swissinfo.org/sen/swissinfo.html?siteSect=105&sid=4748712 (accessed January 2, 2006).

Galli, Folco. 2002. "The Federal Department of Justice and Police Report." Federal Office of Justice, Berne, Switzerland, 2–32.

International Center for Prison Studies. 2005. "Prison Brief for Switzerland." King's College, University of London. Available online at http://www.kcl.ac.uk/depsta/rel/icps/worldbrief/europe_records.php?code=166 (accessed January 2, 2006).

Interpol. 2002. "International Crime Statistics: Switzerland." Interpol, Lyon, France.

Madigan, Kathleen. 2001. "Economic Trends." *Business Week Online* (October 1). Available online at http://www.businessweek.com/magazine/content/01_40/c3751027.htm (accessed January 2, 2006).

Officer Down Memorial Web Site. 2004. Available online at http://www.odmp.de/start/e_startframe.htm (accessed January 2, 2006).

Pagon, Milan, Bojana Virjent-Novak, Melita Djuric, Branko Lobnikar. 1996. "European Systems of Police Education and Training." National Criminal Justice Reference Service. Available online at http://www.ncjrs.org/policing/eur551.htm (accessed January 2, 2006).

Pauchard, Olivier. 2003. "The Rise and Fall of the Christian Democrats." *Swissinfo* (December 8). Available online at http://www.swissinfo.org/sen/swissinfo.html?siteSect=2201&sid=4513465 (accessed January 2, 2006).

Penal Reform International. 2002. "News from around the World." *PRI Newsletter*, pp. 48–49.

Swiss Crime Prevention Center. 2004. "Campaigns." Swiss Crime Prevention Center, Neuchâtel, Switzerland.

Debra Allee
Mark Clark
Michael Wills
Leslie Wills
Dwayne Wright
Nathan R. Moran
Robert D. Hanser

Syria

___

Official country name: Syrian Arab Republic
Capital: Damascus
Geographic description: Located in the Middle East, occupying the land between Mesopotamia and the Mediterranean
Population: 18,448,752 (est. 2005)

■ ■ ■

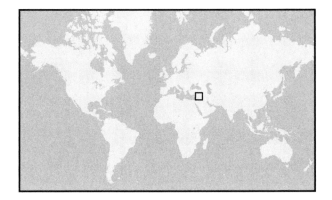

LAW ENFORCEMENT

History. Although the Syrian police was first established under the Ottoman and French periods, it underwent a radical transformation after independence and now owes little to either the French-inspired Gendarmerie or the Ottoman police.

Structure and Organization. Under the reorganization under Hafiz al-Assad, there are three security agencies: General Security, State Security, and Political Security, all under the Ministry of the Interior. Each works independently of the other. The police, like the military, is predominantly Alawite in composition.

The core police agency, the Public Security Police, operates under the Ministry of the Interior. It is headed by a director general and is organized territorially by administrative districts. Damascus has a metropolitan police under the direct jurisdiction of the director general. The headquarters is divided into four main branches: Administration, Criminal Investigation, Public Order, and Traffic.

The police are supplemented by two paramilitary forces: the Gendarmerie and the Desert Guard. The Gendarmerie had originally been formed under the French Mandate to police rural areas. The Desert Guard is responsible for guarding the border regions, especially those near Iraq. The People's Militia and the Detachments for the Defense of the Regime are quasi-military organizations, but they have been increasingly encroaching on police functions.

Education and Training. Education for all police ranks is provided at the central Police Training Schools in Damascus and Aleppo. There is also an Officers' College in Ḥimṣ where junior officers are enrolled for six-month courses in specialized subjects.

Police Statistics.

• Total Police Personnel: 8,708

• Population per Police Officer: 2,118

HUMAN RIGHTS

Syria, a major offender against human rights, has a long history of violations in this regard. These abuses include torture, arbitrary arrest and detention, prolonged detention without trials, and an inefficient and corrupt judiciary that never holds security personnel accountable for their actions. The government never investigates deaths in detention or disappearances. Amnesty International reports that authorities at Tadmur and other prisons regularly torture prisoners. The government often detains relatives of detainees or fugitives to force their confessions or surrender. Some of the inmates are held incommunicado for years before they are brought to trial.

CRIME

Crime Statistics. Offenses reported to the police per 100,000 population: 42. Of which:

- Murder: 1
- Burglary: 15.6
- Automobile Theft: 2.7

CORRECTIONAL SYSTEM

Prisons are administered by the director of the Prisons Service under the Ministry of the Interior. There are fifteen prisons in the country. In 2002 two major prisons at Tadmur and Mazzah were closed, and their prisoners were transferred to Saydnaya.

Prison Conditions. Prison conditions are substandard. However, there are rules for the segregation of women, children, and pretrial detainees from common housing with convicted criminals. Political and national security prisoners fare worse than common criminals.

Security officials demand bribes from family members who wish to visit their relatives in prison. Inmates are commonly denied food, medical care, and reading materials. The London-based Syrian Human Rights Commission reports the death of several detainees in prison as a result of torture. The government does not permit the independent monitoring of prisons.

Prison Statistics. Prison statistics are not published but the total prison population is estimated at 14,000 and the prison population rate is 93 per 100,000.

George Thomas Kurian

Taiwan

Official country name: Taiwan
Capital: Taipei
Geographic description: Island in the South China Sea, along with the Pescadores and the islands of Quemoy and Matsu, close to the Chinese mainland
Population: 22,894,384 (est. 2005)

■■■

LAW ENFORCEMENT

History. When the Kuomintang set up an independent state in Taiwan in 1949 immediately following the takeover of China by the Communists, it transferred to the new government the administrative structure of the Republic of China, including the administration of law enforcement. The police system was made up of three broad categories: General Police, Peace Preservation Corps, and Counterespionage Agency. Later, all these forces were unified in the National Police Administration under the Ministry of the Interior.

Structure and Organization. The National Police Administration's legal basis is the National Police Act. The act not only delineates the general responsibilities of the police—the maintenance and promotion of social order, the protection of property, and prevention of crime and delinquency—but also invests it with a role as a guardian of public safety and internal security.

Taiwan uses a traditional military rank structure; in ascending order, it is officer, sergeant, lieutenant, captain, and several grades of command officers in two categories: noncommissioned and commissioned. Commissioned

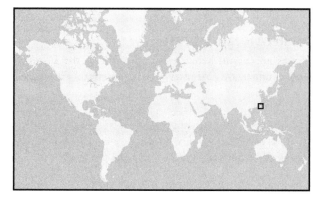

officers—lieutenant and above—perform staff and command assignments, while noncommissioned officers—sergeant and below—perform first-line supervision and line duties. Structurally, the force is divided into divisions: bureaus and corps or offices.

About 20,025 or 28 percent of police personnel work in specialized units and bureaus that provide enforcement, investigative, or support services at the national level. These units include:

- Entry and Exit Bureau, which enforces visa and entry laws and provides customs services

- Criminal Investigation Bureau, which provides investigative and forensic services

- Highway Police Bureau, which enforces traffic laws and regulates traffic

- Airport Police Bureau

- Railway Police Bureau

- National Park Police Corps

- Taiwan Security Police Corps, which provides security for government buildings and maintains order during civil disturbances

- Harbor Police, which serves the ports of Keelung, Taichung, Kaohsiung, and Hualien

- Foreign Affairs Division, which monitors foreigners resident in Taiwan

Municipal and Provincial Police. Most police officers work at the local, that is municipal and provincial, level. Approximately 10 percent—about 12,277—of all uniformed forces work in Taipei and Kaohsiung, the principal port. Municipal police forces are geographically grouped in precincts, substations, posts, and patrol beats.

There are twenty-three other provincial bureaus that account for the remaining police personnel. Provincial police bureaus have cities, towns, and villages within their jurisdictions. Each town or village has one or more precinct, substation, post, and patrol beat.

Because of overlapping jurisdictions of the national, provincial, and municipal police forces, the National Police Administration has established a coordinating body called the Police Administration and Planning Bureau. This bureau evaluates and develops systems, policies, and strategies, evaluates staffing levels, and makes workforce assignments. Other bureaus and offices of administration provide inspectional services, logistical support, budgetary services, command and communication centers, and forensic and scientific services.

Several documents define police powers in Taiwan besides the National Police Act. The most important of these documents is the Code of Criminal Procedure, which is supplemented by internal National Police Administration regulations. They define police behavior and set limits on police powers. Except for infractions of national or local laws, the police have no punitive powers other than fines and detention for up to fourteen days. Deadly force is restricted to extraordinary situations, such as protection of the life of a police officer. The police may stop and briefly detain a person for general questioning if they have reason to believe that he or she presents a clear danger to public safety. They may arrest a suspect on the basis of reasonable criminal evidence or if there is a likelihood of flight to avoid prosecution. The Code of Criminal Procedure guarantees a number of civil and human rights, such as a warrant before searching a home or car, the right to legal counsel, and the right to remain silent.

Generally speaking, the police appear to be well trained and disciplined, and they display high morale and professionalism. There is some evidence of graft and corruption, especially in cases involving gamblers and prostitutes, but it is not widespread. They are considerate and do not intrude unnecessarily into the lives of the citizens.

A special security force, the Peace Preservation Corps (PPC), operates under the Ministry of National Defense. It was established in 1949 to deal with the problem of communist infiltration and subversion. Among PPC functions are issuance of entry and exit permits, protection of public utilities against terrorism, prevention of smuggling, control of shipping, and counterespionage. Units of the PPC are organized in companies and are stationed in strategic locations, such as entrances to the mountain areas of aboriginal tribes.

Education and Training. Basic police education is provided in two institutions: the Taiwan Police College and the Central Police University.

Admission to either institution is based on physical, psychological, and academic qualifications. Both institutions combine academic training in criminal justice with field training in police work. They serve dual roles as police academies and institutions of higher learning. The curriculum covers a wide range of subjects: police administration, management, law, public safety, maritime law, visa and customs law, corrections, fire science, forensic science, information management, traffic management, and criminal investigation. The studies are divided into four categories: general academic courses, academic courses within a specific discipline, courses related to professional and ethical development, and physical and martial arts.

Each institution targets a specific geographical area. The Central Police University (CPU) is located in Gueishan District of Taoyuan County. Graduate degrees are offered through CPU's nine graduate schools:

- School of Administrative Management

- School of Crime Prevention

- School of Fire Science and Technology

- School of Forensic Science

- School of Information Management

- School of Traffic Management

- School of Law

- School of Criminal Investigation

- School of Maritime Police

The graduate program lasts for four years. Since 1994 the CPU has been offering a doctorate in crime prevention and corrections.

The Taiwan Police College (TPC) is a two-year institution located in Shan District of Taipei City. Graduates

A backer of Taiwan's opposition Nationalist Party encounters police officers as he demonstrates against the inauguration of President Chen Shui-bian at his party's headquarters in Taipei, Taiwan, May 20, 2004. The opposition was still challenging the results of a March 20 election in which Chen won a second presidential term by a slim margin. **AP IMAGES.**

earn an associate's degree and enter public service as entry-level noncommissioned officers.

Uniforms and Weapons. Police officers wear a black uniform in winter and a beige one the rest of the year. Shorts and shirts are worn in the hot months. A peaked cap is worn throughout the year. All members of the force carry a pistol and a truncheon.

Police Statistics.

- Total Police Personnel: 72,659
- Population per Police Officer: 315

HUMAN RIGHTS

Law enforcement personnel in Taiwan generally respect human rights, which are protected by the constitution and by the Judicial Yuan. There are occasional allegations of police abuse of detainees and judicial corruption. Detainees who are abused physically have the right to sue the police for torture, and confessions known to have been obtained through torture are inadmissible in court. Respect for human rights is part of the basic police training.

CRIME

Crime Statistics. Offenses reported to the police per 100,000 population: 799. Of which:

- Murder: 8.2
- Automobile Theft: 124.9

CORRECTIONAL SYSTEM

The criminal code, first enacted in 1928, was revised in 1935. It was adopted by the Nationalist government when it took over Taiwan in 1949. It is based on Continental rather than Anglo-Saxon jurisprudence.

Correctional institutions are administered by the Department of Corrections within the Ministry of Justice. They are divided into six categories: prisons, detention houses, vocational training institutions, juvenile reformatory schools, juvenile detention, and classification houses and detoxification centers. In 2002 there was 1 juvenile prison, 2 adult drug treatment facilities, 3 juvenile detention centers, 4 adult prisons, 19 adult correctional/vocational training institutions, and a number of juvenile classification houses and detoxification centers. Prisons hold inmates whose sentences run longer than 1 year. Detention houses house people awaiting trial or offenders sentenced to terms of less than 1 year. Reformatories hold juveniles between ages 14 and 18 who, under the law, may not be jailed with adults.

Each district court has an associated prison and a detention house, although they are not always located near the district capital. The Taipei Prison, for example, is located at Taoyuan, 10 miles west of the capital. The three major reformatories are at Taoyuan, Changhua, and Kaohsiung.

Administratively, each prison is headed by a warden and consists of five divisions: education and reform, work, health, guard, and general affairs. Facilities are quite extensive and include well-staffed medical sections and dispensaries, workshops, classrooms, and recreational areas. Each has one or more farms as well as full-scale factories. Under law, 25 percent of the profits from these enterprises is distributed to the convicts, 40 percent is set aside for working capital, 10 percent is put into the national treasury, and the balance is set aside to improve prison conditions.

There are no exclusive prison facilities for women, but each regular prison is segregated by sex. Convict mothers are permitted to bring their children under three years of age to live with them, and kindergarten facilities are provided for these children.

On entering the system, each prisoner is given a thorough physical and psychological examination and is categorized into one of four grades. Grade four is the lowest, reserved for dangerous criminals who are subject to strict, often solitary, confinement with no privileges. Grade-three prisoners have better quarters, with four people to a room, a double-decked iron cot, a stool, and a desk-table for each. They are required to attend classes, trained in prison shops to develop usable skills, and permitted a limited amount of free time to engage in sports or other recreational activities. Grade-two prisoners are housed in better quarters and have more privileges. They are allowed to mix with one another during the daytime and to participate in the full range of recreational activities. Grade-one convicts are comparable to what are commonly called trusties in the West. They

have single rooms for quarters; their free time is their own; there are no locks on the doors of their cells; and they may move within the confines of the prisons wearing ordinary clothes without restriction. Convicts of the first and second grades are permitted to receive visitors in special rooms. From time to time prison officials schedule family reunion parties, during which time prisoners get with their whole families. Prisoners may move up or down the grades on the basis of their conduct. Convicts are also given the opportunity to practice self-government, to elect a slate of officers and representatives to act as intermediaries before prison officials, and to form a council that administers a program of self-discipline among inmates.

Prison Conditions. Taiwan is one of the original signatories of the United Nations Standard Minimum Rules for the Treatment of Prisoners. The administration of penal institution conforms to the guidelines laid down by the United Nations Conference on the Prevention of Crime and the Treatment of Prisoners. The country's 4,000 custodial personnel are trained and their conduct is monitored by both human rights groups and internal watchdogs.

Taiwan has a progressive penal and rehabilitation philosophy. Inmates who have served one-third of their sentences are eligible for parole. Inmates serving life sentences are eligible for parole after ten years. In practice, parole is granted to 90 percent of the inmates. Inmates may participate in individual counseling and job training and are provided reentry assistance by private and government agencies. Community-based treatment programs also keep individuals on probation out of the prison system.

As a result of new construction, renovation, and expansion, overcrowding is no longer a serious problem. However, illegal aliens face long confinement in detention centers.

Prison Statistics.

- Total Prison Population: 57,275
- Prison Population Rate per 100,000: 252
- Number of Prisons: 86

George Thomas Kurian

Tajikistan

Official country name: Republic of Tajikistan
Capital: Dushanbe
Geographic description: Borders Afghanistan, China, Kyrgyzstan, and Uzbekistan
Population: 7,163,506 (est. 2005)

■■■

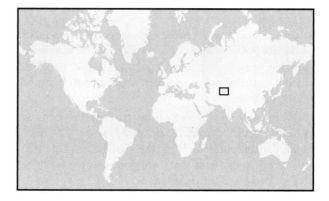

LAW ENFORCEMENT

History. The Tajiks come from ancient stock—the inhabitants of the Pamir Mountains claim to be the only pure descendants of the Aryan tribes who invaded India over 4,000 years ago, and the Saxon tribes of western Europe also originated there. Tajikistan's inaccessibility has protected it from most invaders, although Alexander the Great founded a city on the site of modern-day Khudzhand, calling it Alexandria Eskate (Alexandria the Furthest). However, the mountains effectively spared it from the Mongols, although it was under their aegis.

After the dissolution of the Mongol Empire, Tajikistan was successively ruled by the emirs of Samarkand, Bukhara, and finally Kokand. Russia took control of the Tajik lands in the 1880s and 1890s, but the Tajiks remained split among several administrative-political entities, and their territories were economically backward and were exploited for their raw materials.

In the aftermath of the 1917 Russian Revolution, the Tajiks rebelled against Russian rule; the Red Army did not establish control over them until 1921. Tajikistan was made an autonomous republic within Uzbekistan in 1924; in 1929 it became a constituent republic of the Soviet Union. The Tajiks continued to resist until the

early 1930s. During the fighting some 200,000 Tajiks fled to Afghanistan. Tajikistan's distance and remoteness again saved it during the Soviet era, when it escaped Moscow's heavy hand. In 1929 the Tajik state was upgraded to a full union republic, although Samarkand and Bukhara—where over 700,000 Tajiks still lived—remained in Uzbekistan.

In the 1930s canals and other irrigation projects vastly increased cultivated acreage and the population increased rapidly. Russian immigration was encouraged and many inhabitants of the Garm Valley and the Pamirs were forcibly moved to the southwest in the 1950s to help with the cotton growing, replacing those who had escaped into Afghanistan.

Independence came to Tajikistan with the dissolution of the Soviet Union in December 1991. The current system of governance emerged only after a period of turmoil in Tajikistan's recent political history. Immediately following independence, the country was drawn into civil war by the various factions vying for power. A major source of conflict was the disparity between the poorly developed regions in the south and those in the north, which had continued under the Soviet era.

The invasion of neighboring Afghanistan in 1979 by the Soviet Army created a complicated environment by the time Tajik independence arrived—the region was awash in weapons. Civil war continued in southern Tajikistan from 1992 until 1994, when the Tajik government and the United Tajik Opposition agreed to a cease-fire. Negotiations, which took place under the auspices of the United Nations, were difficult and prolonged, stretching over a three-year period. Russia and Iran, among others, participated as guarantor countries. The General Agreement on Restoration of Peace and National Consent in Tajikistan was finally signed in July 1997.

Fighting continued among some factions and, in a 1999 referendum, voters backed constitutional changes that would extend the president's term to seven years and allow the formation of Islamic political parties. By the end of 2000, a truce prevailed in most of Tajikistan. Some 30,000 to 50,000 were estimated to have died in the fighting, and war and neglect had devastated much of the country's infrastructure, making the nation one of the poorest in the world. Tajikistan remains dependent on help from Russia's military to preserve its tenuous stability and security. A drought in western and central Asia that began in the late 1990s has had particularly severe consequences in impoverished Tajikistan.

Post-Soviet developments in the former Central Asian republics had barely registered in the West. That changed after the terrorist attacks of September 11, 2001. Keen to prosecute its war against al Qaeda and the Taliban regime in Afghanistan, the United States started to canvas neighboring countries for facilities and military bases. Tajikistan, which shares a thousand-mile border with Afghanistan, was a prime candidate and much of the subsequent fighting in northern Afghanistan relied on U.S. supplies and personnel moved in from Tajikistan.

Structure and Organization. There is a great paucity of information regarding the police function in Central Asia generally and in Tajikistan specifically. Policing is guided by the Ministry of Internal Affairs, which is the most powerful armed institution in the country. The ministry is believed to have 28,000 personnel in a country of only 7 million people. The ministry shares policing authority with the National Security Service in areas such as narcotics, organized crime, and terrorism. The informal paramilitary units that sprang up around the country during the civil war are gone now. The procuracy is responsible for oversight of the ministry.

The branch of the Ministry of Internal Affairs in Khujand, a city with a population of 145,000, has around 500 staff members, including 47 officers in the criminal investigation police and about 100 ordinary police officers (militia).

Police at Work. Police officers spend much of their time illegally boosting their small official salaries. In 2003 the minimum wage in the country was 4 somoni (US$1.20) per month. For an ordinary police officer, the monthly wage amounted to about 17 somoni (US$5.50). High-ranking officers received 40 to 50 somoni (US$13 to $16) monthly. A regional judge in Tajikistan earned the equivalent of approximately US$20. Several prosecutors have admitted that they have had to find ways to pay their staff salaries themselves. And many police stations have developed small land holdings on which they farm animals and grow crops.

The combination of underfunding, low salaries, inadequate staffing, and little training contributes to an environment where corruption is already endemic. The traffic police have a particularly tarnished reputation in Tajikistan (as in most countries of the former Soviet Union). With many checkpoints along every major traffic route, police officers often stop passing cars and take money from drivers with no explanation. However, they are merely the most visible of a widespread and deeply penetrating corruption contagion.

One effect of the dismal economic situation is the great difficulty in recruiting candidates to staff city police departments. Only about 25 percent of ordinary police are from cities; most come from villages. That is, most personnel are not intimately familiar with the jurisdictions they are policing, are not as educated as the city dwellers, are less knowledgeable of the legal rights of the population, and are less capable of developing investigative techniques. The Ministry of Internal Affairs Academy is the main source of training, but most police officers believe that it is far from sufficient. Up to 70 percent of police officers have no specialized training.

The situation in Khujand paints a picture that is common around the country. The forty-seven officers of the criminal investigation police have only two cars and three radios at their disposal. The Chinese government is providing the ministry with technical assistance worth approximately $700,000, including fifty patrol vehicles.

The entire police force is dramatically underfunded and underequipped. There is little gasoline for the few cars available. The police are frequently forced to start their days by extorting gasoline from drivers for their patrol cars, thus forcing the police themselves to break the laws they are employed to enforce.

As for the rest of the department, officers are frequently forced to privately finance the purchase of uniforms and equipment, using personal mobile phones for communication for lack of police radios, and wearing

A Tajik police officer talks with others on patrol as they take a break from their tour of duty near the Ismail Somoni monument in Dushanbe, the capital of Tajikistan, April 7, 2004. Civil security issues in Tajikistan have been rapidly improving since 1997, when the secular government and predominately Islamic opposition agreed to stop a five-year civil war. **AP IMAGES.**

worn-out uniforms and nonregulation footwear because of shortages.

Corrupt practices are by no means limited to the lower ranks of the police force. The ministry suggests that it has initiated a campaign to clean up the ranks by dismissing corrupt officers and bringing charges against the worst offenders. In one of the worst cases, a lieutenant colonel was sentenced to twenty-five years' imprisonment in October 2002 for committing twenty crimes, including six murders, banditry, armed robbery, and drug trafficking. Realistic reform ends with these serious cases. Corruption is so embedded in the survival strategy of most police officers that rooting it out is all but impossible.

This systemic corruption, with police misuse of force, has created an abiding mistrust among the citizenry. By and large, the population views the police as ineffective, if not irrelevant, in protecting them from crime. It has also made the police an easy target for penetration by organized crime groups.

HUMAN RIGHTS

The government's human rights record is poor. Security forces torture, beat, and abuse detainees and other people, and they are frequently responsible for threats, extortion, and abuse of civilians. Prison conditions are harsh and life threatening, but the government agreed to permit the International Red Cross to make prison visits.

The government continues to use arbitrary arrest and detention, and arrests people for political reasons, including two top officials of a main opposition party.

Impunity and long pretrial detention are problems in Tajikistan as they are throughout the region. Law enforcement officers use torture to obtain confessions, which are used in trial without qualification. According to Amnesty International, people detained on capital charges say that they were tortured by police investigators. Allegations include torture by ferocious beating; rape with a truncheon, penis, or other objects; and electrocution of the ears, fingers, toes, and anus. The torture is said to have taken place when people were in police custody in so-called Temporary Detention Premises. Torture has also been reported by pretrial detainees held in investigative isolation prisons.

The torture of people in custody is prohibited by article 7 of the International Covenant on Civil and Political Rights. Testimony extracted under torture is inadmissible as evidence in court, according to article 15 of the Convention against Torture.

Tajikistan continues to use the criminal code of the former Tajik Soviet Socialist Republic (adopted in 1962), with amendments. Besides retaining capital punishment for a number of economic crimes (which is at odds with a trend evident since 1991 in other former Soviet republics to remove economic crimes from the scope of the death penalty), the list of peacetime capital offenses includes up to fifteen offenses to which capital punishment has been extended.

The death penalty in Tajikistan is regulated by the following published laws:

- The 1994 constitution of the Republic of Tajikistan proclaims the right to life. Article 18 states that no one may be deprived of his or her life except by a court-imposed sentence for an especially serious crime.

- The death penalty is not mandatory. The fifteen offenses that may be punished by death are listed in article 59 of the Tajik Criminal Code, adopted in 1998. Article 59 prohibits the imposition of a death sentence on anyone who was under eighteen years of age at the time of the offense and on pregnant women.

- The 2001 Tajik Criminal Execution Code explains how all prisoners are to serve their sentences.

The government routinely sentences criminal defendants to death in trials that violate norms of due process and human rights. During pretrial detention the police often beat and otherwise coerce suspects into making confessions, which are introduced into trial without qualification. Amnesty International reports that none of the thirty-three people sentenced to death in the first six months of 2003 received a fair trial.

Official secrecy surrounds the death penalty in Tajikistan. Prisoners are executed in secret after unfair trials, usually with little warning to their families. Relatives of death row prisoners are kept in a state of uncertainty about the fate of the person they love and are deprived of all rights once the prisoner has been executed, often discovering that clemency has been refused only after the prisoner has been removed without warning to the place of execution. They have no right to see the condemned person to say good-bye before the execution and are deprived of all rights once the prisoner has been executed—such as the possibility of collecting the prisoner's personal belongings or the body for reburial. They are frequently not told where the grave is located.

The death penalty is not a mandatory punishment. In each case it is applied at the discretion of the courts, which ordinarily are presided over by one professional judge and two lay "people's assessors." The courts have been given significant leeway in deciding matters of life and death, and in practice there is an element of arbitrariness in the justice administered by different courts, in different regions, under different presiding judges.

The criminal code states that the death penalty is an "exceptional measure," but practice shows it is not exceptional. Some Tajik legal scholars and government officials say that the courts resort to the death penalty for repeat offenders, others say it is for criminals who killed more than one victim, in line with unpublished instructions that date back to the Soviet era.

Prisoners in Tajikistan are executed by shooting. As soon as a prisoner has been shot, the law requires the director of the prison to inform the Ministry of Justice, which in turn informs the court that passed the sentence that its penalty has been carried out. It is then the responsibility of the court to notify the prisoner's local records office and, simultaneously, the prisoner's family. This procedure is set down in the 2001 Tajik Criminal Execution Code, although it is not always followed.

Relatives are allowed to ask the Ministry of Justice for monthly visits of two hours with the prisoner on death row, but they receive no warning of when the prisoner will be transferred from death row to be executed or when the execution has been scheduled to happen.

Once all appeals have failed and a sentence has come into legal force, all prisoners—including those under sentence of death—have the right within seven days to petition the president for clemency. Should a prisoner refuse to do so, the director of the death row prison and the state prosecutor are obliged to petition on the prisoner's behalf.

In death penalty cases a stay is put on execution until the president has decided on the petition. Before the introduction of the 2001 Tajik Criminal Execution Code, prisoners could be executed before the outcome of their petition was known, according to legislation inherited from the Soviet era. The president must decide on clemency within four months. If he decides to grant clemency, the death sentence is commuted to a prison term of up to twenty-five years.

Authorities infringe on citizens' right to privacy. The government restricts freedom of speech and has reinstituted restrictions on the press after it had initially relaxed such restrictions. Journalists practice self-censorship.

The government restricts freedom of assembly and association by exercising strict control over political organizations and by intimidating demonstrators. The government imposes some restrictions on freedom of religion and freedom of movement within the country. Violence against women and discrimination against women, people with disabilities, and religious minorities are problems. Child labor is a problem, and there are some instances of forced labor, including by children.

Government officials claim progress in investigating a number of political killings since the mid-1990s. The murderers of a British Broadcasting Company correspondent in 1995, a correspondent of the Russian TV

ORT in 1996, and the chairman of the State Television and Radio Committee in 2000 were convicted and sentenced in July 2003. The government formed a special investigative unit to look into crimes committed against journalists during the civil war and announced that a number of arrests had been made and charges filed. However, the government indicated that some of those under investigation were being detained without formal charges. Some of these individuals were held incommunicado.

Both the government and the opposition used landmines during the civil war. Landmine explosions in some unmarked minefields in the Karetegin Valley reportedly killed civilians in 2003. Landmines were laid along the northern segment of the border with Uzbekistan, which included some populated areas, and were not demarcated clearly in most places. The State Border Protection Committee reported that landmine explosions killed sixteen people along the Uzbek border during 2003. The media estimates that there have been 57 landmine deaths and that over 16,000 mines remain spread over 770 square miles.

CRIME

Crime statistics should always be handled with great care; in the case of Tajikistan and other former Soviet states they are relatively meaningless. Locked in an ideological battle with the West, Soviet reality urged the creation of fictitious figures across most sectors of the economy and society to portray a positive image to the outside world. The depiction of crime was one of the most important sectors for manipulation as the Soviet Union attempted to demonstrate the superiority of communism and its promise of the disappearance of crime. According to police officials, the practice of producing fraudulent statistics (*pripiska*) continues long after the demise of the Soviet Union. Latent crime has always been assumed to be rather high. Moreover, police officials come under considerable pressure to clear cases and produce favorable statistics. Filing citizen reports of crime can become a subjective procedure.

According to the Tajik minister of internal affairs, the percentage of crime solved during the first six months of 2000 was up 7.1 percent over the same period from 1999. The percentage of serious crime solved rose by 6.7 percent and economic crime by 15.6 percent. The minister did not discuss comparative data regarding the number of crimes actually committed throughout Tajikistan. In the capital, Dushanbe, however, 2,565 crimes were committed between January and June 2000, which is an increase of 295 over the first six months of 1999. However, at the same time serious crimes fell by 22.1 percent.

Police confiscated 260 tons of contraband aluminum destined for illegal export and intercepted 600 kilograms of drugs, including 300 kilograms of heroin.

Narcotics. With the official economy of Tajikistan a shambles, narcotics trafficking offers a viable alternative for criminal organizations, corrupt police officers, politicians, as well as the average citizen. Tajikistan itself produces few if any narcotic substances, but it remains a major transit country for heroin and opium from Afghanistan. Heroin and opium move through Tajikistan and Central Asia to Russia and western Europe. The volume of drugs following this route, through multiple land-based methods of transportation, is believed to be significant and growing.

The United Nations estimates that the amount of heroin from Afghanistan going through Tajikistan is roughly 40 to 50 metric tons a year. Hashish from Afghanistan also transits Tajikistan en route to Russian and European markets. During the first ten months of 2003, Tajikistan officials reported seizing 8,408 kilograms of illegal narcotics, including 5,137 kilograms of heroin, 1,966 kilograms of opium, and 1,179 kilograms of cannabis. In 2004 Tajikistan ranked third in the world for heroin seizures. Opium seizures also showed a slight increase compared to 2002's ten-month total of 1,025 kilograms. In December 2003 the Drug Information Center was established through the collaborative effort of the United States, the Ministry of Health, the Tajik State Medical University, and the World Health Organization. However, the number of young addicts continues to grow. Over 60 percent of Tajikistan's drug addicts fall into the eighteen to thirty age group.

Geography and economics continue to make Tajikistan an attractive transit route for illegal narcotics. The Pyanj River, which forms part of Tajikistan's border with Afghanistan, is thinly guarded and difficult to patrol. It is easily crossed, without inspection, at a number of points. Opium poppies and, to a much lesser extent, cannabis are cultivated in small amounts, mostly in the northern Aini and Panjakent districts. Law enforcement efforts have limited opium cultivation, but it has also been limited because it has been far cheaper and safer to cultivate opium poppies in neighboring Afghanistan. With the beginning of Poppy Operation in May 2003, more than two fields of opium poppies and 5,000 hemp plants have been found and destroyed. In June 2004 police in Dushanbe burned 600 kilograms of heroin that was confiscated in the course of 2003 and the first five months of 2004.

Abuse of heroin, opium, and cannabis in Tajikistan is a minor problem now, but it is growing in importance. Tajikistan's medical infrastructure is highly inadequate and cannot address the population's growing need for addiction treatment and rehabilitation.

Experts from Tajikistan's Drug Control Agency expected a bumper crop in 2004 on Afghan opium plantations, the major source of Tajikistan's drug worries. The new harvest was expected to produce more than 400 tons of heroin. Twenty heroin "minifactories" have sprung up near the Tajik border, each capable of producing 20 kilograms of heroin a day.

Organized Crime. Narcotics trafficking is not the only illicit activity in which organized criminal groups are heavily involved. Groups engage in trafficking human beings, firearms and explosives, smuggling precious materials such as gold and aluminum, and money laundering.

In Dushanbe and the surrounding areas organized crime continues to be a problem. Heavily armed rival clan-based factions are actively competing for control of markets and narcotics trafficking. Past incidents have included several spontaneous shootouts between factions in public marketplaces.

In 2001 the Supreme Court upheld guilty verdicts of murder, banditry, hostage taking, illegal possession of weapons, armed robbery, and other related crimes of eight members of an organized crime group active in Dushanbe and other regions of the country. The sentences varied from twelve years in prison to the death penalty.

The fight against organized crime is intricately entwined with the struggle for political power in Tajikistan. Organized crime leaders command considerable resources to effectively counter law enforcement efforts. Short-term reductions in crime statistics do not accurately reflect the true state of crime and the ability of crime groups to rebound.

The past plays a large role in the present struggle. Many of today's reputed crime bosses were prominent commanders during Tajikistan's bitterly contested civil war beginning in 1992. When the fighting ceased, the victorious Popular Front commanders divided Dushanbe into spheres of influence. Over time six pro-government commanders established themselves in Dushanbe as forces with which to be reckoned. These commanders are from such units as an elite brigade of Internal Troops of the Ministry of Internal Affairs, the Presidential Guard, a special rapid deployment force, and special border patrol groups.

The signing of the General Agreement on Peace in June 1997 formerly ended the war and established a framework for the reintegration of society. It also created new underworld rivalries. Under the peace agreement former leaders of the United Tajik Opposition were integrated into official structures. They moved swiftly to stake claims to their own spheres of influence in government committees controlling the oil and gas industries and other sectors of the economy. Turf wars have erupted among these commanders, politicians, and their respective clans. Traditional organized crime groups are deeply involved in these clan struggles. The power struggles have brought a spate of car bombings and assassination attempts of high government officials and rival group members.

Government officials also consider "outlaw extremist parties" to be organized crime groups. Chief among these has been Hizb ut-Tahrir. According to the head of the Ministry's Department for Combating Organized Crime, the group allegedly has committed such crimes as hostage taking and robbery. Essentially, the group is agitating for the establishment of an Islamic caliphate in Central Asia.

Trafficking in People. In August 2003 the Parliament approved amendments to the criminal code that make trafficking in people punishable by a term of imprisonment of five to fifteen years and the confiscation of one's property. The more general amendment defines trafficking in people broadly, while a second amendment specifically criminalizes trafficking in teenagers, defined as "the buying or selling of a minor with or without means and forms of coercion."

Traffickers may also be prosecuted under other laws prohibiting exploitation of prostitution, rape, kidnapping, buying and selling of minors, illegal limitations on arrival and departure in and out of the country, document fraud, and immigration violations. The penalties for these offenses are in most cases fines or imprisonment of five to fifteen years, although certain immigration violations carry a sentence of up to ten years, and rape is punishable by up to twenty years in prison or, in certain circumstances, a death sentence.

The Ministry of Internal Affairs formed a unit under the Criminal Investigation Department to deal with cases of trafficking, particularly to focus on fact-finding and investigation in cases of sexual exploitation. The unit reports that there are at least a dozen criminal organizations in the country involved in trafficking young girls to the Middle East.

Tajikistan is a source and transit point for trafficked people, primarily women. Trafficking within the country is also a problem. Media reports estimate that over 1,000 people were victims of trafficking in 2003. The actual figure is likely much higher. The Criminal Investigation Unit, as well as calls to hot lines, indicate that victims are most commonly trafficked to Russia, Central Asia, and the Persian Gulf states, including the United Arab Emirates, Yemen, Iran, and Saudi Arabia. Other trafficking destinations are other former Soviet countries,

Turkey, Syria, and Pakistan. There are also reports of the sale of infants. Most victims are female, ethnically Tajik, single, aged twenty to twenty-six, usually with at least one child (the children typically come under the care of extended family), and are new arrivals to Dushanbe or Khudzhand from a rural upbringing with little education. Ethnic minorities are overrepresented among victims, particularly those of Slavic origin.

Victims are commonly recruited through false promises of employment. "Advertising" is often done through social contacts, because traffickers employ their local status and prestige to help recruit victims. There are also cases of false weddings and, more rarely, kidnappings (usually in rural areas). Traffickers generally transport victims by air to the Middle East and by train to Russia and other former Soviet countries.

Traffickers tightly control arrangements for travel and lodging and employ contacts among tourism agencies. They sometimes employ document falsification services to evade entry restrictions in destination countries. Victims are commonly not separated from their travel documents until arrival in the destination country. Debt bondage is a common form of control. There are also reports of Tajik medical professionals—both men and women—trafficked to Yemen to work at medical clinics for substandard wages; traffickers reportedly seize their travel documents and force female medical personnel into prostitution.

Among the traffickers are individuals who rose to positions of power and wealth as field commanders—so-called warlords—during the civil war. Others, including women, are powerful local figures who use their wealth to cultivate patron-client relationships throughout their community; this creates a network that communicates supply and demand for trafficking victims.

Corruption is endemic in the country, and reports indicated that low-level government authorities working in customs, border control, immigration, police, and tourism receive bribes from traffickers. Furthermore, there is reason to believe that certain figures in the government act as patrons or protectors of individuals who are involved directly in trafficking. However, there is no indication of widespread institutional involvement in trafficking by the government.

CORRECTIONAL SYSTEMS

The Tajik prison system was transferred from the Ministry of Internal Affairs to the Ministry of Justice in 2002, following a trend throughout the former Soviet Union after 1991.

Over the past several years the number of inmates has grown by some 40 percent. The number of female inmates has increased as well. There is one women's facility; men and women are held separately. Pretrial detainees are held separately from those convicted. Separate juvenile reform facilities held juveniles.

Prison Conditions. Besides being overcrowded, prisons are generally unsanitary and disease-ridden. There is a shortage of food and medicine. Some prisoners die of hunger. Family members are allowed access to prisoners only after a guilty verdict, in accordance with the law. There is one prison specifically for members of the "power ministries" (police, state security, and military personnel).

The government permits some prison visits by international human rights observers. In December 2003 the government agreed to permit the International Red Cross to visit prisons.

Unfortunately, detailed information about the state of Tajik prisons across the country is not available. Because of the continued risk of being taken hostage, foreigners face difficulties in traveling extensively outside Dushanbe, and the local population mostly cannot take the time needed to assert their rights because of their struggle to earn a living.

Prison Statistics.

- Total Prison Population: 10,000
- Prison Population Rate per 100,000: 161
- Pretrial Detainees: 33%
- Number of Prisons: 18
- Official Capacity of the Prison System: 9,000
- Occupancy Level: 111%

BIBLIOGRAPHY

Amnesty International. Available online at http://amnesty.org (accessed January 3, 2006).

Bureau of Democracy, Human Rights, and Labor. 2004. "Country Reports on Human Rights Practices: Tajikistan, 2003." U.S. Department of State. Available online at http://www.state.gov/g/drl/rls/hrrpt/2003/27868.htm (accessed January 3, 2006).

"China Gives Tajikistan 2 Million Dollars in Food Aid." 2003. *Agence France-Presse* (March 13). Available online at http://www.reliefweb.int/rw/rwb.nsf/0/85746edb7f45155049256ce9000a3c28?OpenDocument (accessed January 3, 2006).

Eurasianet.org. 2000. "Tajik Minister Evaluates Crimes Figures." *Tajikistan Daily Digest.* Available online at http://www.eurasianet.org/resource/tajikistan/hypermail/200007/0018.html (accessed January 3, 2006).

Human Rights Watch. Available online at http://www.hrw.org (accessed January 3, 2006).

International Crisis Group. 2002. "Central Asia: The Politics of Police Reform." *Asia Report*, no. 42 (December 10). Available online at http://www.crisisgroup.org/home/index.cfm?id=1444&l=5 (accessed January 3, 2006).

Penal Reform International. 2002. "Transfer of Prison Service from the Ministry of Interior to the Ministry of Justice: International Experience." (October 14). Available online at http://www.penalreform.org/english/rights_dushanbe.htm (accessed January 3, 2006).

Redo, Slawomir. 2004. *Organized Crime and Its Control in Central Asia*. Huntsville, TX: Office of International Criminal Justice.

United Nations Office on Drugs and Crime. 2005. "Assessment of Organized Crime in Central Asia." Available online at http://www.unodc.org/unodc/en/organized_crime_assessments. html#africa (accessed January 3, 2006).

Joseph D. Serio

Tanzania

———•———

Official country name: United Republic of Tanzania
Capital: Dar es Salaam (Pending Capital: Dodoma)
Geographic description: Located in East Africa, border-
ing the Indian Ocean
Population: 36,766,356 (est. 2005)

■■■

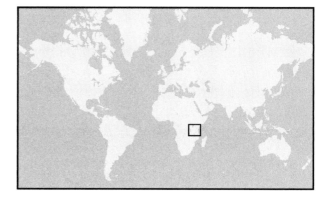

LAW ENFORCEMENT

History. Before the arrival of the Europeans, the native peoples policed themselves through village-based tribal institutions. During the German colonial period there was no regular police force, and police work was done by the army. The first police system was set up by the British in 1919 by extending the British East African Police to the new territory taken over from Germany. The police and the prisons were administered as a combined service until 1931. The top ranks were filled by the British, the middle ranks by the Asians, and the lower ranks by Africans.

The recruitment of native police was biased in favor of the "fierce and tough tribes" such as the Wanyamwazi and Wayao. The native policemen were subjected to harsh treatment as the best means of creating a loyal and disciplined force. Police operations were largely confined to townships. Policing of rural areas was largely left to the native chiefs, except in the case of white settler farms and plantations, which received periodic visits by provincial police chiefs.

At independence, the postcolonial state inherited the British structure intact. A British police officer continued to head the force until 1963, when the first Tanzanian

was appointed to head it. It was not until 1969 that the entire force was Africanized

In Zanzibar the sultan was protected by an armed guard from 1877, but a formal police force, including the Harbor Police, was created only in 1908. A mobile force as added in 1961.

Structure and Organization. Up to 1964 the police force was headed by a commissioner, who was always a Briton. However, following the union between Tanganyika and Zanzibar in April 1964 and the creation of a single police force for the federation, the commissioner was replaced by an African inspector general. Below him are three commissioners: one in charge of Zanzibar, one in charge of the mainland, and the third in charge of the Criminal Investigation Department. There are two major divisions at the headquarters: Administration and Operations and Training. Field units, such as Traffic, Air Wing, Marine, Signals, Railways, and Harbors, are under the latter.

Riot forces are positioned outside the U.S. Embassy in Dar es Salaam, Tanzania, in reaction to demonstrations held by Muslim youths, June 3, 2005. The protests occurred in the wake of news that U.S. soldiers allegedly destroyed copies of Islam's holy book, the Koran, in the Guantanamo Bay prison in Cuba. AP IMAGES.

Below the headquarters the force is organized on regional and district levels. The regional level is headed by the regional police commander, while the regional crime officer is in charge of criminal investigations. The officer in charge of the district and the officer in charge of criminal investigations perform similar functions in the district. The noncommissioned ranks (formerly known as the rank and file) include sergeants, corporals, and constables.

The administrative wing at the national headquarters is under a senior assistant commissioner, who reports directly to the deputy commissioner.

Since President Julius Nyerere's socialization policies, the police force is considerably politicized. Under the doctrine of party supremacy, all policemen must belong to the ruling party, and there are party cells at each level in the force, from district to headquarters.

To give a more specific ideological orientation to law enforcement, Nyerere created the People's Militia (Jeshi la Mgambo) as a parallel law enforcement organization.

Every member of the militia has powers of arrest similar to those of a constable. There is also the Field Force Unit, elements of which are strategically placed at regional and district capitals. There are also citizens' patrols (Sungusungu), which remain active in rural areas but have disappeared from urban areas.

Constitutionally, the central government controls the police force throughout the country. In practice, however, it appears that the Zanzibar Police Force, even though centrally funded, operates as a separate force under the direct control of Zanzibar authorities.

Education and Training. Recruits for the various branches of the police force are selected from the ranks of the National Service, and standards of selection are relatively high. Recruits are expected to be fluent in both Swahili and English and must be members of the ruling political party. All enlistments are voluntary.

Initial training is for fifteen months at the Police Training School at Moslin or the Police College at Dar es Salaam. Tanzania has the distinction of having one of the highest numbers of university-trained police officers in black Africa. A large number of police officers are also trained abroad. Tanzania also trains police officers of neighboring countries, such as Uganda.

Police Statistics.

- Total Police Personnel: 26,242

- Population per Police Officer: 1,401

HUMAN RIGHTS

Members of the police and security forces commit unlawful killings and mistreat suspected criminals. There are also reports that police officers routinely use torture, beatings, and floggings. In response to public complaints of widespread police corruption, the inspector general of police took a series of disciplinary actions against offending police officers. There is the Prevention of Corruption Bureau, which is tasked with combating police corruption, but it is widely perceived as ineffectual.

CRIME

Crime Statistics. Offenses reported to the police per 100,000 population: 1,714. Of which:

- Murder: 7.7%

- Assault: 1.7%

- Burglary: 96.6%

- Automobile Theft: 0.9%

CORRECTIONAL SYSTEM

The penal code that was introduced into British Africa was based on the Indian Penal Code with some modifications. These modifications were based on English common law rather than on local customary law. The code was not substantially revised after independence except for the innovation of minimum sentencing. The 1963 Minimum Sentencing Act made flogging a mandatory sentence for a variety of crimes and seriously curtailed the discretion of judges and magistrates in sentencing. Flogging had been a common punishment in colonial times, but many jurists found it incongruous that an independent nation would retain a form of punishment considered a brutal and degrading legacy of the past.

Until the coming of the Europeans, prisons were unknown in East Africa. Malefactors were punished according to the custom of the local group to which they belonged. Punishment of the offender was considered less important than compensation to the offended.

The first prisons in mainland Tanganyika were built by the Germans, who also used beheading, flogging, and hard labor as punishments. The British, who took over Tanganyika after World War I, built more prisons.

Prisons are administered by the commissioner of prisons under the Ministry of Home Affairs. Few new prisons have been built since independence. The total prison population is reported to be over 43,200, although the capacity of all prisons is only 22,000. The largest of the prisons is the Ukonga Prison at Dar es Salaam.

Prison Conditions. Conditions at all prisons and detention centers are deplorable by international standards. Visits are rarely allowed and all prisons suffer from overcrowding. Convicted prisoners are not allowed to receive food from outside sources even when the daily ration is inadequate. Inmates receive only limited medical care and have to depend on family members to provide medications. Serious diseases are common and result often in deaths. In 2002 seventeen prisoners suffocated to death in a jail cell in Mbeya. The cell was built to hold 30 inmates, but there were 112 in it at the time the deaths occurred. Women prisoners report that they are forced to sleep naked on the floor and are subjected to sexual abuse by wardens. Since there are only two juvenile detention centers in the country, most juveniles end up being kept with adults.

Prison Statistics.

- Total Prison Population: 43,244
- Prison Population Rate per 100,000: 116
- Pretrial Detainees: 49%
- Female Prisoners: 0.9%
- Juvenile Prisoners: 0.07%
- Number of Prisons: 120
- Official Capacity of the Prison System: 22,699
- Occupancy Level: 190.5%

George Thomas Kurian

Thailand

Official country name: Kingdom of Thailand
Capital: Bangkok
Geographic description: Located in Southeast Asia at the head of the Gulf of Thailand and extending south to Malaysia
Population: 65,444,371 (est. 2005)

■■■

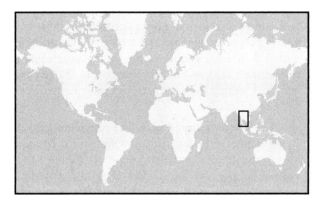

LAW ENFORCEMENT

History. Thailand has had organized police forces since the sixteenth century, but the first Western-style police was created with the help of British advisers in 1861. A Railway Police was created in 1894, followed by a Provincial Police Force in 1897. The latter became the Gendarmerie and the Patrol Department in 1915, and it was reorganized as the Royal Thai Police Department in 1932.

Structure and Organization. The Thai National Police Department (TNPD) is a division of the Ministry of the Interior and is charged with the enforcement of law throughout the kingdom. It is a unitary agency whose power and influence in politics have at time rivaled those of the army.

The formal functions of the TNPD cover more than law enforcement; they play an important role in counter-insurgency operations. In the event of a war of national emergency, the police personnel could be mobilized under the Ministry of Defense.

Based at first on British, Continental, and Japanese models, the TNPD was reorganized during the 1960s and 1970s under U.S. Agency for International Development programs and has adapted many U.S. practices and concepts. All components of the force are administered by the central headquarters in Bangkok, which also provides a centralized array of technical functions. The major operational units are the Provincial Police, the Border Patrol Police, the Metropolitan Police, the Central Investigation Bureau, and the Police Education Bureau. Of the total 119,679 police personnel, over half are in the Provincial Police, 14 percent are in the Border Patrol Police, and 15 percent are in the Metropolitan Police Force. Quasi military in character, the TNPD is headed by a director general who holds the rank of a general. He is assisted by three deputy directors general, all of whom have the rank of lieutenant general. Throughout the system, all ranks, except that of the lowest, the constable, correspond to those of the army. Ninety-five of the senior positions are occupied by officers who hold one of the three grades of general.

The Provincial Police. The Provincial Police is the largest segment of the TNPD in terms of both manpower and extent of territorial jurisdiction. It provides police services in every town and village throughout the kingdom except for Bangkok and territory contiguous to the national land borders. The Provincial Police is headed by a commander, who reports directly to the director general of the TNPD. For operational purposes, the Provincial Police is divided into seven regions:

- Region 1: Korat

- Region 2: Udon Thnai

- Region 3: Chiang Mai

- Region 4: Phitsanu Lok

- Region 5: Nakhom Pathom

- Region 6: Nakhon Sithammarat

- Region 7: Pattani

Since 1977 the regional commissioners who head the regional police have been granted considerable initiative and authority and have been given responsibility over railway, highway, marine, and forestry police operating within their jurisdictions. Under the regional commissioners there are provincial commanders in charge of the country's seventy-two provinces with headquarters in the provincial capitals.

The Border Patrol Police. The paramilitary Border Patrol Police (BPP) is an elite unit that enjoys considerable autonomy in its field operations, although it is technically part of the TNPD. Enjoying the direct patronage of the royal family, the BPP has links to the Royal Thai Army, and many of its commanders are former military officers.

Charged with border security along the land borders, the BPP deals with a variety of enemies, such as smugglers, bandits, illegal immigrants, infiltrators, and insurgents. As part of its mission, it maintains an extensive surveillance and intelligence network in the border districts. Despite its modest size in relation to other TNPD units, the BPP has become the country's primary and most effective counterinsurgency force. The basic operating unit is the line platoon of thirty-two men each, which functions as a security team. Each platoon is supported by one or more heavy weapons platoons stationed at each regional police headquarters as a mobile reserve support force. A special police aerial reinforcement unit airlifts BPP platoons to trouble areas during emergencies. Because of its superior skills and equipment, the BPP has been employed even to quell popular disturbances in the interior and in Bangkok.

The BPP has two subdivisions: the Border Patrol Air Support, which functions as a mobile tactical arm during emergencies and renders aid to people during natural disasters, and the Border Patrol Development Police, which works with villagers and hill tribes to improve their standard of life. It is involved in many civil action projects, such as schools, medical aid stations, air strips, and agricultural stations, designed to win the hearts and minds of rural peoples. By doing so, the BPP not only gains the goodwill of rural folks but also obtains valuable information and deprives insurgents of potential bases of support. A local law enforcement adjunct of the BPP, known as the Volunteer Defense Corps was founded in 1954 as a civilian militia to protect local inhabitants from guerrillas by denying them food and supplies and by gathering information on the modus operandi and movements of antigovernment groups.

There are seven divisional headquarters within the BPP: the General Staff Headquarters, which handles administration, the General Support Headquarters, which handles operational matters, the Special Training Headquarters, and four sector headquarters.

The Metropolitan Police. Because of its population and its status as the national capital, Bangkok is granted a special status as the headquarters of the Metropolitan Police. It operates under the command of a commissioner who holds the rank of a major general, assisted by six deputy commissions of the same rank. Operationally, the force is divided into three divisions: Northern Bangkok, Southern Bangkok, and Thon Puri. Together, there are forty police precincts in the three divisions, which are patrolled around the clock. Besides foot patrolmen, the Metropolitan Police maintains motorized units, a canine corps, building guards, traffic control specialists, and juvenile specialists. The Traffic Police Division also provides mounted escorts and guards of honor for the royal family and visiting dignitaries and serves as a riot control force to disperse unruly crowds.

The Central Investigation Bureau. The Central Investigation Bureau is the nation's principal intelligence-gathering organization and investigative agency. In the latter role it assists other branches of the TNPD in their criminal investigations by providing technical expertise and trained personnel. It has nine divisions.

1. Crime Suppression Division conducts criminal investigations, such as counterfeiting, fraud, illegal gambling, narcotics trafficking, secret societies, and organized crime, throughout the kingdom and controls the Emergency Squad, which remains under alert at all times.

2. Special Branch Division is concerned with national security and engages in clandestine and covert operations against subversive political groups.

Thai border officials patrol the banks of the Sungai Kolok River, which sits between Thailand and Malaysia, as a Thai-Muslim woman and her son drive by near the Manoh village of Narathiwat province in southern Thailand, September 6, 2005. *Tensions mounted between the two countries after Malaysia authorities stated that they would not help Muslim insurgents in Thailand, but vowed that they would not ignore ongoing violence that threatened border security. Muslim insurgents in Thailand, who complained about being treated as second-class citizens in a Buddhist-dominant country, started a campaign of violence 20 months ago and since then more than 950 have died.* **AP IMAGES.**

3. Criminal Record Division collects records and information and keeps dossiers on suspects and criminals, missing people, wanted people, and stolen property.

4. Scientific Crime Detection Division maintains forensic science laboratories and equipment. It examines DNA evidence, conducts polygraphs, takes photographs, identifies ballistic evidence, and tests handwriting evidence.

5. Registration Division consists of three subdivisions: the first handles firearms and vehicle licenses and registration; the second grants licenses to pawnshops and secondhand dealers, and controls hotels, prostitutes, and gambling; and the third handles motor vehicle driving tests and inspections.

6. Railway Police Division is responsible for preventing and detecting crime and ensuring the safety of passengers on the state-run railroads.

7. Marine Police Division is responsible for the suppression and detection of crime on the nation's territorial waters.

8. Highway Police Division controls and supervises vehicles and traffic on highways outside of Bangkok.

9. Forestry Police Division enforces forestry laws throughout the country, especially illegal timber cutting and smuggling.

The Police Education Bureau. The education and training of Thai police is the function of the Police Education Bureau. It runs several schools: the Police Officers' Cadet Academy, the Detective Training School, the Noncommissioned Officers Training School, the Border Patrol Police Training School, four Metropolitan Police training schools, and four Provincial Police Chaiya (victory) centers.

Director General's Office. Several divisions come directly under the control of the Director General's Office:

• The Secretariat is the central communications and information department and administrative center

• Office of the Inspector General formulates police rules and regulations and conducts disciplinary proceedings against police officers charged with human rights violations and corruption

- Legal Affairs Division handles cases against the police as well as intermural disputes with other agencies

- Police Prosecution Division prosecutes criminal cases in magistrates' courts

- Finance Division prepares the police budget and authorizes expenditures

- Quartermaster Division secures and maintains police equipment

- Foreign Affairs Division liaises with foreign police departments and with Interpol

- Immigration Department controls immigrants and aliens and apprehends and deports illegal aliens

- Research and Planning Division compiles records and statistics and conducts research into the nature of crime and means of crime prevention

- Communications Division operates radio and telephone networks and communication centers

- Technical Division is responsible for all police libraries and for publishing books and documents

- Police Fire Brigade Division is responsible for fire prevention and control within the metropolitan area and conducts research on fire-retardant chemicals

- Welfare Division provides welfare services for police personnel, including loans and educational grants

- Alien Registration and Taxation Division maintains a register of all resident aliens

- Police Aviation Division provides air support to police units

- Medical Division conducts medical and health programs for police personnel

Education and Training. The TNPD has an extensive training system. It runs some schools directly, such as the Police Officers' Academy at Sam Phran and the Detective Training School at Bang Khen. The Metropolitan Police runs a training school at Bang Khen and the Provincial Police runs training centers at Nakhon Pathom, Lampang, Nakhon Ratchasima, and Yala. The Border Police Patrol has schools specializing in counterinsurgency, such as the national school at Hua Hin and smaller schools at Udon Thani, Ubon Ratchathani, Chiang Mai, and Songkhla. Rank-and-file police officers are trained at the Police Education Bureau.

Police Statistics.

- Total Police Personnel: 119,679

- Population per Police Officer: 547

HUMAN RIGHTS

Corruption remains widespread among police officers. Low pay is one of the reasons cited for the widespread corruption. Many police officers are involved in prostitution and trafficking in women and children. The police are also charged by human rights organizations with rape, beatings, extortion, brutality, and threatening false charges. In some provinces police form their own killing teams and target canvassers belonging to opposition parties. In 2001 forty-eight people died while in police custody.

CRIME

Crime Statistics. Offenses reported to the police per 100,000 population: 351. Of which:

- Murder: 7.7

- Assault: 25.4

- Burglary: 9.9

- Automobile Theft: 3.3

CORRECTIONAL SYSTEM

The Thai Criminal Code of 1956 incorporates features borrowed from French, Italian, Japanese, English, and Indian models with some traces of native jurisprudence. Among other things it defines twelve kinds of offenses as felonies, including crimes against the Buddhist religion and the royal family. A death sentence is mandatory for certain kinds of offenses. The maximum prison term is twenty years.

Prisons are administered by the Department of Corrections within the Ministry of the Interior. The system includes 1 detention home, 3 reformatories, 5 regional prisons, 7 central prisons, 7 correctional institutions, and 23 prison camps. All metropolitan, provincial, and district police stations have jails used to confine offenders sentenced to terms less than one year.

The 7 central and 5 regional prisons house the bulk of long-term prisoners. The Khlong Prem Central Prison in Bangkok is the largest and oldest, with a capacity of 6,000 prisoners. The Nakhom Pathom Prison is a maximum-security institution for habitual criminals. One of the 23 prison camps is on Ko Tarutao, an island in the Strait of Malacca, and is administered separately.

Among the 7 correctional institutions, 1 at Ayutthaya and 1 at Bangkok house primarily youthful offenders 18 to 25 years of age serving terms of up to 5 years. The Women's Correctional Institution is also in Bangkok, while the Specialized Medical Correctional Institution for drug addicts and prisoners requiring medical care is in Pathum Thani province, northwest of the capital. Two minimum-security correctional centers are in Rayong and Phitsanulok.

Of the three reformatories, the Ban Yat Lao (sometimes called Lardyao) facility, just north of Bangkok, receives most of the more recalcitrant juvenile delinquents and has a capacity of about 2,000. Limited rehabilitation activities are undertaken there; those who fail to respond are sent to a second reformatory, near Rayong, which is operated as a prison farm. A third reformatory, at Prachuap Khiri Khan, southwest of Bangkok, accommodates the overflow from the other two institutions.

Additional special facilities for juvenile offenders, called observation and protection centers, are administered by the Central Juvenile Court and the Central Observation and Protection Center of the Ministry of Justice. Three of these centers are in Bangkok, Songkhla, and Nakhon Ratchasima. A center is attached to each juvenile court and assists it in supervising delinquent children charged with criminal offenses both before and after trial. Probation officers, social workers, and teachers are assigned to these centers.

Prisoners are classified into six classes, according to conduct. Those in the first three classes are considered eligible for parole and may be released when they have completed two-thirds, three-fourths, and four-fifths, respectively, of their terms.

As most prisoners are relatively uneducated, each facility runs special literacy classes. Some prisons also have vocational training programs and workshops. Products from prison labor are sold, and 35 percent of the net profit is returned to the individual prisoner. A small portion of this amount is credited outright to the prisoner for his or her pocket expenses, but the greater part is put into a savings fund to afford the prisoner the wherewithal for a new start on release.

Prison Conditions. There is severe overcrowding in Thai prisons mainly because of the large number of those convicted of drug offenses. Medical care is inadequate. The corrections department employs only 10 full-time doctors, 10 part-time doctors, 6 full-time dentists, and 47 nurses to serve 168,264 inmates. Prison authorities use solitary confinement and heavy leg irons to control and punish difficult prisoners. Prisoners captured after failed escape attempts are beaten severely. Conditions in immigration detention centers that are not administered by the Department of Corrections are particularly inhumane with credible reports of physical and sexual abuse by the guards.

Prison Statistics.

- Total Prison Population: 168,264
- Prison Population Rate per 100,000: 264
- Pretrial Detainees: 23.3%
- Female Prisoners: 18.4%
- Juvenile Prisoners: 0.5%
- Number of Prisons: 136
- Official Capacity of the Prison System: 110,900
- Occupancy Level: 151.7%

George Thomas Kurian

Togo

Official country name: Togolese Republic
Capital: Lomé
Geographic description: Western African, bordering the Bight of Benin between Benin and Ghana
Population: 5,681,519 (est. 2005)

■ ■ ■

LAW ENFORCEMENT

Structure and Organization. The Togolese Police comprise three branches: the Corps de Police Urbaine de Lomé, the Gendarmerie Nationale, and the National Police (formerly the Sûreté Nationale).

The Corps de Police Urbaine de Lomé is a municipal force under joint municipal and police control and organized in four commissariats, one for each arrondissement. A criminal investigation unit known as Brigade Criminelle is part of the corps.

The National Police, commanded by a director, has many sections, including Administration; Judiciary (the Judicial Police), Intelligence (Special Service), the Harbor Police, and the Railway Police. The National Police is also in charge of the Fire Service and the National Police School.

With a strength of 1,800 the Gendarmerie Nationale is deployed in one operational unit and five brigades: Air, Criminal Investigation, Harbor, Traffic, and Territorial. The Gendarmerie is also in charge of Central Criminal Archives and provides the presidential bodyguard.

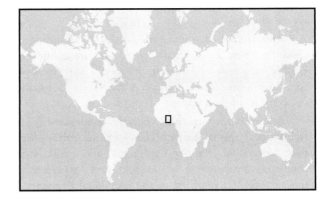

Police Statistics.

- Total Police Personnel: 2,756
- Population per Police Officer: 2,061

CRIME

Crime Statistics. Offenses reported to the police per 100,000 population: 11.

CORRECTIONAL SYSTEM

Prisons are administered by the director of the Penitentiary Administration of the Ministry of Justice.

Prison Conditions. Prison conditions are harsh and inhuman with serious overcrowding, poor sanitation, and unhealthful food. Lomé's Central Prison, for example, built for 350 inmates, houses 1,100. Medical facilities are inadequate and disease and drug abuse are widespread. Prison guards charge prisoners a small fee to shower, use the toilet, and have a mattress. Sick prisoners are charged for visiting the infirmary. Women are housed separately from men and juveniles from adults, but pretrial detainees are housed with convicted felons.

Prison Statistics. There are 12 prisons in the country, with a total prison population of 2,043. The incarceration rate is 46 per 100,000 population. Of the total number of inmates, 55.4 percent are pretrial detainees and 2.3 percent are female.

George Thomas Kurian

Tonga

Official country name: Kingdom of Tonga
Capital: Nuku'alofa
Geographic description: Archipelago in the South Pacific; part of Oceania
Population: 112,422 (est. 2005)

■■■

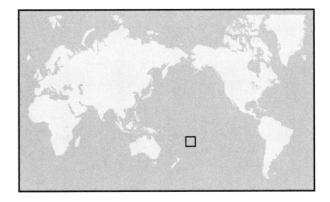

LAW ENFORCEMENT

History. When Tonga gained independence in 1970, it inherited an organized police force from the British administration. During the seventy years of British protection, Britain maintained a small colonial police force under a commissioner.

Structure and Organization. The Tonga Police Force is a national agency with jurisdiction over the entire kingdom. It is commanded by a commissioner of police from his central headquarters in Nuku'alofa. Below this command post the force is deployed in three territorial districts that coincide with the island groups of Tongatapu, Ha'apai, and Vava'u.

Most of the personnel are permanently stationed on the island of Tongatapu, where the bulk of the kingdom's population resides. Smaller islands do not receive adequate police protection not only because of the limited number of personnel but also because many of the islands are too small to justify a permanent post and communications with them are sporadic at best. The island of Niuatoputapu is so far to the north that a government vessel visits only once every

two months. Peace and order are maintained on such islands only through the authority of the local chiefs and the stabilizing influence of ancient traditions and customs.

The mission of the regular police includes a number of tasks besides the standard duties of law enforcement officers. Members of the force monitor sales in retail shops, issue licenses to whalers and fishermen, register bicycles, and serve as truant officers to the school system. They also regulate all matters relating to Tongan custom and tradition.

Education and Training. Police officers are recruited without any minimum standards of education or health. Successful applicants undergo no formal training, but are given lectures at police headquarters for a period ranging from five to eight weeks. There are neither police schools nor any refresher courses. Duty personnel usually devote about one hour a week to foot and arms drill and are required to attend lectures on practical police work. In the outer islands lectures are given by mobile teams sent from headquarters.

Uniforms and Weapons. Tongan police on regular duty wear uniforms consisting of khaki shirts and sarongs, a blue cummerbund fitted with a black belt, a navy-blue slouch hat, and black sandals. For ceremonial occasions, a white jacket is worn over the shirt, and the khaki sarong is replace by a white one. The force is unarmed, but batons are held in reserve and issued when required.

Police Statistics.

- Total Strength of Police Force: 306
- Population per Police Officer: 367

HUMAN RIGHTS

The government's human rights record is generally poor. Detainees are sometimes beaten by the police. In cooperation with government prosecutors, the police use repeated postponement of court dates and filing of frivolous charges as a means of intimidating government critics.

CORRECTIONAL SYSTEM

Tonga's penal system consists of a main prison at Hu'atolitoli, near Nuku'alofa, and three lesser jails located at Ha'apai, Vava'u, and Niuatoputapu. Prisoners sentenced to six months or more, regardless of their home island or where they committed their offenses, are incarcerated at the Hu'atolitoli institution. All sentences of more than one month may be remitted by as much as one-fourth for good behavior. This reduction is automatically granted at the time the prisoner enters the facility and may be revoked only if the inmate violates disciplinary standards.

Prison Conditions. Prison conditions are spartan but not harsh. Food and quarters are sanitary and adequate. Discipline is lightly applied, and security measures are not burdensome. Prisoners are required to perform labor on public works or on coral plantations owned by the government.

Prison Statistics.

- Total Prison Population: 116
- Prison Population Rate: 105
- Pretrial Detainees: 0.9%
- Female Prisoners: 3.4%
- Number of Prisons: 6
- Official Capacity of the Prison System: 139
- Occupancy Level: 81.3%

George Thomas Kurian

Trinidad and Tobago

Official country name: Republic of Trinidad and Tobago
Capital: Port-of-Spain
Geographic description: Caribbean islands between the Caribbean Sea and the North Atlantic Ocean
Population: 1,088,644 (est. 2005)

■■■

LAW ENFORCEMENT

History. Organized as the Trinidad Constabulary Force in the early decades of the twentieth century, the Trinidad and Tobago Police Service was known as the Trinidad and Tobago Police Force from 1938 to 1965. It assumed its present name under the Police Service Act of 1965, which is the legal basis for the mission, staffing, pay and allowances, and retirement system.

Structure and Organization. The Police Service Act established two schedules of police officers:

Commissioned Officers:

- Commissioner of Police
- Deputy Commissioner
- Assistant Commissioner
- Senior Superintendent
- Superintendent
- Assistant Superintendent

Noncommissioned Officers:

- Inspector

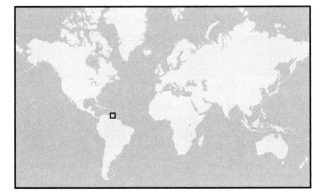

- Sergeant
- Corporal
- Constable

About 70 percent of the force is constables.

The Police Service is centralized at the national level, with headquarters at Port-of-Spain. It is headed by a commissioner of police assisted by three deputy commissioners, all of whom are appointed by the president on the advice of the prime minister. The deputy commissioner of administration supervises finance, personnel, training, the highway patrol in the northern part of the country, transport, telecommunications, and the mounted branch. The deputy commissioner for operations is responsible for police units throughout the country and the prevention and detection of crime. He is assisted by an assistant commissioner for crime, who supervises the Criminal Records Office and the Criminal Investigations Department. The third deputy commissioner

Female police officers march in the traditional Independence Day parade celebrated in Trinidad and Tobago, Queen's Park Savannah, Trinidad, August 31, 2003. *This year's festivities celebrated the islands' forty-first anniversary of independence from England.* AP IMAGES.

is in charge of the Special Branch, which is concerned with security and intelligence.

The country is divided for operational purposes into nine divisions under two branches: the Northern Branch, headquartered in Port-of-Spain, and the Southern Branch, headquartered in San Fernando. The headquarters of local stations are changed from time to time. Government quarters are provided for married commissioned and noncommissioned personnel in major stations. There is a Traffic Branch in Port-of-Spain and a training school in St. James Barracks, St. James, the former British military headquarters on the island. Special units include a larceny mobile patrol, charged with the control of thefts from landed estates, an estate police unit known as the Antisquatting Brigade, assigned to prevent illegal settlements on private lands, and the police band.

A volunteer reserve force, called the Special Reserve Police, was organized in 1939. Its members are attached to divisions of the regular police throughout the islands. The Special Reserve Police are under the jurisdiction of the commissioner of police and are commanded by a senior superintendent.

Besides the national Police Service, there is a small municipal force in Port-of-Spain. Its functions are limited to the protection of buildings, parks, and government installations in the city.

Although East Indians make up a plurality of the population, the Police Service is predominantly black, who make up over 90 percent of both the commissioned and noncommissioned cadres. The reasons for this racial imbalance are both historical and physical. East Indians, because of their smaller stature, generally do not measure up to the physical requirements for recruits, and qualifications and selection procedures also favor blacks. East Indians are also largely rural people who historically have been excluded from active participation in the Police Service.

The Trinidad and Tobago (Constitution) Order in Council of 1962 established a Police Service Commission, whose chairman is concurrently the chairman of the Public Service Commission. The other four members of the commission are appointed by the president on the advice of the prime minister.

The Police Service Act authorizes the formation of a police association empowered to function as a police union and represent police officers in discussions with the commissioner on matters relating to pay and grievances.

Education and Training. Police recruits are assigned to St. James Barracks for an initial training program. Training at the advanced level is also provided. Some officers are sent abroad for specialized training.

Uniforms and Weapons. The police uniform consists of a gray shirt and khaki shorts or a white tunic and blue slacks topped by a white helmet in daytime, and a blue tunic and blue peaked cap at night. Weapons are not carried during normal patrol, but rifles and bayonets are carried on ceremonial parades.

Police Statistics.

- Total Police Personnel: 4,657
- Population per Police Officer: 234

HUMAN RIGHTS

The police system generally respects the human rights of its citizens. However, police corruption is a major problem. The Police Complaints Authority, an independent body, receives complaints of police abuse or brutality, monitors investigations, and determines disciplinary measures, including dismissal. However, its power to impose discipline and dismiss offending officers is severely curbed by the Public Service Commission.

CRIME

Crime Statistics. Offenses reported to the police per 100,000 population: 1,170. Of which:

- Murder: 9.7
- Assault: 31
- Burglary: 452.7
- Automobile Theft: 80.6

CORRECTIONAL SYSTEM

The criminal code is based on doctrine of equity and general statutes that were in force in the United Kingdom on March 1, 1848. English common law and doctrines of equity originating between 1848 and 1962 are generally accepted by the courts, but are not necessarily binding.

The Prison Service Act of 1965 provides the legal basis for the correctional system. The service is headed by a commissioner of prisons and staffed, in order of precedence, by a deputy commissioner, senior superintendents, assistant superintendents, supervisors, welfare officers, and prison officers.

The country has eight prisons. The Royal Gaol in Port-of-Spain, the island prison on Carrera Island in the Chaguaramas, and the Golden Grove Prison near Arouca are among the largest. The first two are maximum-security prisons, while the third is an open prison designed for first-time offenders of minor crimes and others amenable to rehabilitation. A new maximum-security prison that opened in late 1998 has a capacity of 2,450. Offenders under sixteen are classified as juveniles and are not processed through the prison system but committed to an orphanage or industrial school.

Prison Conditions. Prison conditions in most prisons meet international standards. However, conditions are poor in the Frederick Street Prison in Port-of-Spain, which dates to the 1830s. Designed for 250 inmates, it houses 800. Diseases, such as HIV/AIDS, are rampant, and inmates have to buy their own medications. Overcrowding caused a riot in a Port-of-Spain facility in 2002.

Prison Statistics.

- Total Prison Population: 3,991
- Prison Population Rate per 100,000: 307
- Pretrial Detainees: 29.2%
- Female Prisoners: 3.1%
- Juvenile Prisoners: 1.2%
- Number of Prisons: 8
- Official Capacity of the Prison System: 4,348
- Occupancy Level: 111.9%

George Thomas Kurian

Tunisia

Official country name: Tunisian Republic
Capital: Tunis
Geographic description: Located in the North African littoral; juts into the Mediterranean Sea at the point where the narrows between Cape Bon and Sicily divide the Mediterranean Sea into eastern and western basins
Population: 10,074,951 (est. 2005)

■■■

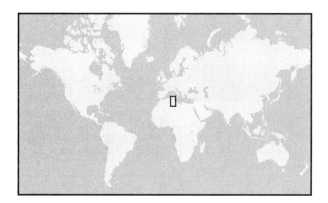

LAW ENFORCEMENT

History. During French colonial rule there were two law enforcement agencies in Tunisia: the Sûreté Nationale and the Gendarmerie. The Sûreté was an urban police and the Gendarmerie a rural police that became the Garde Nationale in 1956. Until 1967 both organizations operated independently, but the Garde had a closer relationship with the Tunisian National Army, especially in its types of equipment and training methods. Both forces were under the Ministry of the Interior. Following riots in the wake of the Arab-Israeli War of 1967, the Ministry of the Interior adopted a stronger role in police reorganization. The two forces were merged to form the Directorate of National Security Forces, under whom the directors of the Garde and the Sûreté were placed. Both forces have the same pay scales and conditions of service.

Structure and Organization.

The Sûreté Nationale. The Sûreté Nationale is the effective national police force that maintains public order, investigates crime, and controls traffic in cities and urban areas.

The Sûreté is organized generally along the lines of its French counterpart, with operational and investigative branches and support services. The section best known to the public consists of the uniformed urban police, segments of which are assigned to each of the governorates. All elements are under the supervision of the director general of the Directorate of National Security Forces in Tunis. A separate section of the Sûreté handles border control, immigration, political intelligence, security of the president, and general information. Other components are responsible for criminal files, Judicial Police, crime research laboratories, the Licensing Bureau, and the prison system.

The Traffic Police, a branch of the Sûreté, is limited to the large cities and includes women. Generally, the Traffic Police is the most visible of police units.

In the late 1960s, particularly after the ineffectual performance of the Sûreté against the anti-Jewish riots of 1967, the government established a special branch known as the Brigade of Public Order. With six battalions, recruited largely from the army's growing pool of reservists,

Tunisian security forces stand guard outside a government building, where the second United Nations' World Summit on the Information Society is scheduled to open the following day, November 15, 2005. The event, taking place in the city of Kram, received criticism from others who felt that Tunisia did not deserve the honor because of its history of censorship and human rights abuses. **AP IMAGES.**

the brigade specializes in control of riots, crowds, strikes, and other demonstrations.

A special section of the Sûreté known as the Directorate of Territorial Surveillance is responsible for intelligence and counterespionage activities and constitutes the equivalent of a secret service. It is responsible for much of the human rights violations for its reliance on torture and other means of repression.

Garde Nationale. The Garde Nationale was formed at independence to police rural areas, formerly the responsibility of the colonial Gendarmerie. The bulk of the Garde served in rural areas and the remaining served as highway patrol and as presidential bodyguards and ceremonial troops. Because of its size, training, equipment, and tactical deployment capability, the Garde is a versatile paramilitary force. It is also responsible for aiding the army in counterinsurgency operations when needed and in assisting in civic action projects and in emergency relief during disasters.

Education and Training. Sûreté personnel are public servants recruited in accordance with civil service regu-

lations. The force has six categories of personnel divided into several classes based on seniority and achievement. The highest is that of police superintendent, who is also authorized to exercise the powers of a magistrate in administrative, judicial, or municipal capacities. Most of them are recruited by means of a competitive examination; the rest are selected from among officers of the Garde Nationale, the army, and regional administrations. Frequent transfers tend to keep them under the influence of the central government and out of local politics.

The second highest rank, known as police officials, assist the superintendents in the performance of their duties and perform additional investigative and administrative tasks. Most are recruited by a special competitive examination and the rest from the Garde Nationale.

Police secretaries, the third rank, assist in investigation and administration. They are recruited on the basis of tests from applicants with at least six years of secondary education. Technical detectives, who make up the fourth rank, are charged with identification, documentation, and other technical police duties. Their recruitment is on the same basis as secretaries. Inspectors, the fifth-ranking group, work under the direction of superintendents and officials. Most inspectors are recruited by tests from civil service applicants with a high school diploma, and the rest by application or personnel with eighteen months' experience. The last category is the uniformed urban police corps, known as police constables. Of these, some are recruited form students at the Police Academy and others by competitive examinations.

Applicants accepted by the Sûreté are trained at its academy at Bir bu Ruqba. The duration of their courses varies with the service in which they are enrolled. Members of the force may be called on at any time to attend special training courses at the academy, and all except those in the grade of superintendent are required to participate in sports and physical education training.

Garde members are recruited in accordance with civil service regulations and consist mostly of former enlisted men and junior noncommissioned officers. Selected applicants train at the Garde training academy at Bir bu Fishah for at least six months.

Uniforms and Weapons. Khaki open-necked tunics and trousers are worn with a forage cap in summer and a blue uniform in winter. Pistols are carried by all ranks.

Police Statistics.

- Total Police Personnel: 28,717
- Population per Police Officer: 351

HUMAN RIGHTS

Members of the security forces routinely torture and physically abuse prisoners and detainees. They are intolerant of criticism by human rights activists. In 2000 and 2001 the National Council for Liberties in Tunisia reported five suspicious "accidental deaths" while in police custody. They were classified as accidents or suicides. The security forces use torture to coerce confessions. The forms of torture include electric shock, confinement to tiny, unlit cells, submersion of the head in water, beatings, suspension from the ceiling, cigarette burns, and food and sleep deprivation. There are also credible reports of sexual assaults. In 2002 the Tunisian Human Rights League prepared a report documenting human rights abuses by the security forces.

CRIME

Crime Statistics. Offenses reported to the police per 100,000 population: 1,419. Of which:

- Murder: 1.2
- Assault: 165.1

- Burglary: 60.1
- Automobile Theft: 10.2

CORRECTIONAL SYSTEM

Tunisian jurisprudence has undergone radical changes during the twentieth century as the government sought to modernize the legal system. The whole body of Tunisian law is now codified. The penal code was first enacted by beylical decree in 1913 and amended after independence in 1956. Similarly, the code of criminal procedure was introduced in 1921 but was amended extensively in 1968. Not surprisingly, both codes strongly reflect French legal traditions but are in many areas influenced by the Islamic Sharia.

The corrections system is the responsibility of the Ministry of Justice and is administered by a department of the Sûreté. It includes central prisons at Tunis, Bajah, Bizerte, Qabis, Qafsah, Al Qayrawan, Al Kaf, Safaqis, Susah, and Bardo and smaller facilities at less populated centers. Habitual criminals are usually sentenced to hard labor at the agricultural penitentiary at Jabal Faqirin. All these prisons were originally established by the French in the colonial era.

In most cases juvenile offenders are segregated from adults and women inmates from men. Selected prisoners serving less than five years are placed in open camps called reeducation centers for rehabilitation. Here, they perform useful work, for which they receive a token wage.

Prison Conditions. Prison conditions do not meet international standards. The most serious problem is overcrowding, Typically, 40 to 50 inmates share a 14-by-14-foot cell and 140 inmates share an 18-by-18-foot cell. Over 100 cellmates share a single water and toilet facility. Prisoners have to sleep on the floors. Human rights activists claim that political prisoners are placed in solitary confinement in special cellblocks. Political prisoners are regularly moved from prison to prison to make it harder for their relatives to remain in touch with them. Prisoners in several facilities undertake hunger strikes to protest subhuman conditions in the prisons. The government does not permit international organizations or the media to inspect or monitor prison conditions.

Prison Statistics.

- Total Prison Population: 23,165
- Prison Population Rate per 100,000: 253
- Pretrial Detainees: 22.7%

George Thomas Kurian

Turkey

—■—

Official country name: Republic of Turkey
Capital: Ankara
Geographic description: Anatolian Peninsula formerly known as Asia Minor, comprising southwestern Asia with the city of Istanbul and its Thracian hinterland in southeastern Europe, bordering the Black Sea and the Aegean Sea
Population: 69,660,559 (est. 2005)

■■■

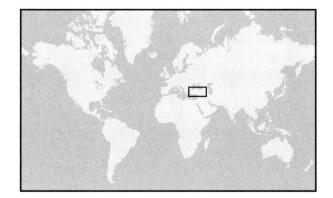

LAW ENFORCEMENT

History. According to article 2 under the General Principles of the Turkish constitution, the characteristics of the Republic of Turkey are defined as "a democratic, secular and social state governed by the rule of law." The criminal justice system can be examined under three main branches: National Police, judicial system, and corrections system. Each branch works separately under different administrative organizations. The National Police are affiliated to the Ministry of Interior, whereas the judicial and corrections systems function under the Justice Department.

"The history of Police started at the same time as the history of the Turks. During the governments of different Turkish nations, public order and public security have been provided by the State along with the national defense." It is better to classify the history of Turkish law enforcement into three periods: policing in old Turkish states, policing in the Ottoman period, and policing in modern Turkey.

Policing in Old Turkish States. During the tribal era, before the Turkish Islamic states, police had a militaristic structure and served under the military commander. The name Subasi was given to people who were in charge of the military. During wartime Subasi was leading and commanding his army; in peacetime he was providing the public safety of his region, which he was obligated to manage. However, public order and safety were directed according to certain rules and regulations in the old Turkish states. The Customs of Oguz Khan, the law of the Almighty Cenghiz Khan, and the Statutes of Timur were a few main examples of this period.

Policing in the Ottoman Period. Policing in the Ottoman era showed more organized structure compared to the early Turkish states. Indeed, the Ottoman dynasty ruled for 600 years between 1299 and 1922. Through this long history and the evolution thereof, Ottomans have combined the progress of Eastern and Western ideologies of organization and state structure. In the classical period of the state the main institution was the military, which consisted of both Turkish cavalry called *sipahis* and *kapikulu* soldiers, who were Christian youths from the Balkans who had been taken from their families at an early age and developed through education and training. In many circumstances the members of the *kapikulu* represented the elite in the society and formed the famous janissary (*yeniceri*, "new soldier") infantry, which was renowned for its military skills. During the late fourteenth century the janissary corps became the most important element of the Ottoman Army.

From the earliest period there were two authorities to administer a district: the bey, who came from the military class and represented the sultan's executive authority, and the Qadi, who came from the ulema (a name for a group of respected Islamic scholars) and represented the sultan's legal authority. The bey (military commander) could not inflict any punishment without first obtaining the Qadi's judgment, but the Qadi could not personally execute any of his own sentences. Especially in small towns and country areas, public order was maintained by three different groups: *kollukcular* (patrolmen), *yasakcilar* (prohibitors), and *bekciler* (night watchmen, sentries).

By the nineteenth century there were signs of weakness in every level of government as well as in the military. Finally, a janissary rebellion broke out in 1826. The new Ottoman Army was established in a few months after the extermination of the janissaries in Istanbul and was named Asakir-i Mansure-i Muhammediye (Triumphant Soldiers of Muhammad). This time a special unit, Asakir-i Redife, formed inside this new militarist structure and it was specifically assigned to maintain the public order in terms of policing. The commander of this new military police, the Serasker (captain), had the same authority as the commander of the janissary units in Istanbul. This new military police was directly affiliated to the new organized Ministry of Finance. However, in the provinces the security was being done by the cavalry units (*sipahis*) under the command of beys. This double structure continued until 1845. There was no unity for police organizations nationwide. "In March 20, 1845, the first police organization regulation (Polis Nizami) formed of 17 codes was made by the administration. The word 'police' was brought into official language for the first time in Ottoman history with this document and with a second official note, Mehmed Ali Pasha was assigned as the first chief of this new police force." In this progressive era the final change was made in 1879 by attaching the police to the new Ministry of Security (Zaptiye Nezareti); hence, the Gendarmerie and the police had been separated. The new Ministry of Security gathered the unity of command under its management. Centralization became a vital point in the new era of policing. At this point the first jurisprudence document regarding police management was published on December 6, 1896. The duties and responsibilities of the police organization were defined clearly in this official written article. According to the same regulation, police officers were classified as Ser-commissioner, second commissioner, third commissioner, assistant commissioner, and police officer.

During the Independence War (1919–1922) there were three organizations providing the internal security in the country: Gendarmerie, National Police, and Istanbul police forces.

Policing in Modern Turkey. Policing in modern Turkey started with the Republic of Turkey. In the modern era there are two organizations maintaining the internal security: National Police, as a law enforcement agency, and Gendarmerie, as a military branch. Ankara is the headquarters of both systems and all are affiliated with the Ministry of Interior. Both have their own jurisdictions, authority, and structural hierarchy. The Code of Amendments to the Law on Duties and Competencies of the Police defines the responsibilities of the police by stating: "The police protect the moral values, life of the people, and the property of society by securing the public."

Structure and Organization. Turkey can be divided into two types of administrative management: provincial and local. Therefore, all police departments function according to headquarters policy and commands. There are eighty-one provinces in Turkey; hence, each city has its own police department. "In each province, there is a provincial security directorate (police department) being responsible to both the governor of the province (who is also a representative of central government) and the General Directorate of Security in Ankara. In each town, a town security directorate (like a police station) work as accountable to the city security directorate and the governor." Depending on the size and population of the cities, the extent of the police departments varies. "The policing model in Turkey is put into the authoritarian model by a study. One of the characteristics of an authoritarian model of policing is that public participation is not allowed in policing either by the private or voluntary sector." The concept of the authoritarian model fits the definition of the police job in the National Police. In terms of policing applications the laws and regulations are strict, coercive, and demanding according to circumstances in Turkey.

The laws establishing the organization of police at the provincial and local levels distinguish three categories of functions: administrative, judicial, and political. In this context the administrative police perform the usual functions relating to the safety of persons and property:

enforcement of laws and regulations, prevention of smuggling and apprehension of smugglers, quelling of public disorder, fingerprinting and photographing, public licensing, controlling traffic and inspecting motor vehicles, apprehending thieves and military deserters, locating missing persons, and keeping track of foreigners residing or traveling in Turkey. The main distinction about the administrative police task is to prevent crime and to take serious precautions against any criminal activity in society. The government orders the public to abide the laws and regulations, which are enforced by the administrative police in the behalf of the administration. Put simply, the administrative police act as arms of central administration, which makes the laws and policies. The task of administrative police does not involve tracking criminals or doing crime scene investigations. Administrative police maintains social order.

Judicial police function directly with the administrators of justice. Small towns may not have this specific unit, so instead the administrative police serve as judicial police; the provinces have special divisions mostly attached to the offices of public prosecutors. The judicial police work with the courts and track down its investigations according to criminal procedure law. Assisting the prosecutor in investigating crimes, issuing arrest warrants, and finding evidentiary documents and materials for district attorneys are the main tasks of this force. The system Polnet serves as a domestic or international network system so a police officer from the southeast part of Turkey can easily access the same information as a police officer in Germany. This central computer information system provides immediate connection to other agencies, especially in terms of investigating property crimes. Technically, it is hard to make the distinction between administrative and judicial police in some levels. In certain situations administrative police have to work under the judicial police for gathering evidence or tracking criminals.

The authority of judicial police is not as broad as for police in the United States. The laws and regulations in Turkey place the police in a close relationship to public prosecutors in their region. Without the authorization of prosecutors, naturally an indirect connection with the judge, almost every police operation is accepted illegitimately. Besides, there is public criticism from all levels of society—media, legalists, and administrators—regarding the use of excessive force by police as well as criticism from the European Union. The Turkish National Police have been trying to adjust the whole system according to European Union conditions. Therefore, it is one of the best-computerized and well-equipped organizations of Europe.

Political police, at one point, were obliged to watch all activities and groups, including covert plans that might be identified as contrary to the security of the republic, but this function was terminated. Instead, counterterrorism units were established.

The policing model in Turkey is based on the authoritarian model. One of the characteristics of the authoritarian model of policing is that public participation is not allowed either by the private or voluntary sector. The concept of the authoritarian model fits the definition of the police functions spelled out for the National Police. The Turkish police model is similar to European countries, especially the German model. One of the possible supporting ideas to authoritarian model dissuasion might be the vision of the state among the public, because police act as the law enforcers of this enormous bureaucratic structural organization.

Education and Training. There are three types of schools that function for the National Police: Police University, Police College, and police training schools (police vocational schools of higher education). Faculty of Security Sciences is one of the main sections of the Police University and provides undergraduate higher education in four areas: legal studies, police professional studies, cultural studies, and applied studies. The Institute of Security Sciences of Police University is dedicated for graduate studies in four areas: criminal investigations, security administration and security strategies, international policing, and traffic investigations. The Institute of Security Sciences is a graduate school for individuals who possess a bachelor's degree from a military school, law school, or department of political science and finance. There are twenty police training schools in Turkey, and candidates are tested for their intelligence and knowledge in policing during the two-year course period. These police training schools are administered as two-year higher education units under the umbrella of the Police University in Ankara. Applicants to these schools have to have not only academic intelligence but also physical ability to be accepted (the Faculty of Security Sciences and the Institute of Security Sciences do not include any physical agility requirements). There is an equal opportunity for both genders to be a police officer in each school.

The Police College and Police University require highly standard test score results, which are applied by the national government. Police College students have direct access to continue their education in the Police University without any competitive selection phase.

In light of universal values and technological developments as well as their conformity to Turkish culture, the National Police try to form personnel by responding to all the needs of the twenty-first century's technological progress by making a great worldwide integration with

Metin Kaplan, an Islamic militant, is accompanied by Turkish police as he arrives at a courthouse in Istanbul, Turkey, April 4, 2005. Kaplan was extradited from Germany to stand trial in Turkey for charges of treason connected to a plot to fly an airplane into the tomb of Kemal Atatürk, the founder of modern Turkey. AP IMAGES.

other law enforcement agencies. The Turkish National Police educate brave, intelligent, and skeptical officers in terms of the quality of its organization.

There is the discussion of theory versus practice for the new graduates from the Police University. H. H. Cevik states, "The background that is provided and given by the police Academy to students who are candidates for future police chiefs has direct influences on the quality, direction and dimensions of policing work. After the students of the Police Academy (as candidates for administering the police organization at all levels) have graduated, they are directly appointed to operate their profession without being given a chance to observe policing exercises in police stations and other units, or having any experience before starting work. At the moment, although there is one year probational training, it has not actually been applied" (1999). The main point of this discussion is to give time for prospective police chiefs in the field of police work. New graduates from the Police University are limited in use of their power for one year. A field training officer, who has ten years of experience and a perfect record in the field, commands and trains these new fresh candidates during this one-year period. After this, they are appointed to police departments as sergeants, provided they have nothing negative in their record and medical report.

Gendarmerie. There is a clear jurisdiction distinction between the Gendarmerie and National Police. "Gendarmerie provides security outside the municipal boundaries of cities and provincial towns and guards Turkey's land borders against illegal entry and smuggling. It has jurisdiction over 90 percent of the territory of Turkey and 50 percent of the population; however their interaction with community is limited. In each province, the principal gendarmerie commander, a colonel or lieutenant colonel, advises the governor on matters of security and maintains direct charge of the district gendarmerie commands, usually headed by captains. The gendarmeries recruits are supplied through the military conscription system, and its officers and non-commissioned officers are transferred from the army."

JUDICIAL SYSTEM

The modern Turkish judicial system, which was adopted in 1926, is based on the Swiss Civil Code and the Italian Penal Code. The constitution was formed by the Turkish National Assembly in 1982 as the supreme law of the country.

According to article 9 of the constitution, "Judicial power shall be exercised by independent courts on behalf of the Turkish Nation." Besides the independence of courts, the security of judges and public prosecutors is guaranteed by the constitution and cited separately under the heading of "Judicial Power" of the constitution (articles 138–160), which certainly provides judicial and administrative protection for them by saying that "[n]o organ, office, authority or individual may attempt to intimidate, instruct or order, make suggestions or recommendations to or send notices to any judge concerning how they should exercise their powers in the courts." The most important factor that ensures the independence of the judiciary is the "Guarantee for Judges and Prosecutors" provided for in the constitution.

The Turkish legal system can be identified in three main structures: judicial (criminal), administrative, and military justice. All three judicial systems are regulated separately by the supreme power of the constitution.

The judicial courts form the largest part of the system; they handle most civil and criminal cases involving ordinary citizens. Each system includes courts of first instance and appellate courts. The superior courts are the Constitutional Court, the Court of Appeals, the Council of State, the Military Tribunal of Appeals, the Supreme Military Administrative Court, the Court of Jurisdictional Dispute, the Court of Accounts, and the Supreme Council of Judges and Public Prosecutors. The courts in Turkey are in fact divided into courts of justice, administrative courts, military courts, and Constitutional Court. Except for the Constitutional Court, they are further divided into lower and higher courts.

The Constitutional Court was established by the constitution of 1961. Its role is to examine all laws in respect to conformity with the constitution. The Constitutional Court reviews the constitutionality of laws and decrees at the request of the president or of one-fifth of the members of the National Assembly. Its decisions on the constitutionality of legislation and government decrees are final. The eleven members of the Constitutional Court are appointed by the president from among candidates nominated by lower courts and the High Council of Judges and Public Prosecutors.

The Court of Appeals (also known as the Court of Cassation) is the court of last instance for review of decisions and verdicts of lower-level judicial courts, both civil and criminal. Its members are elected by secret ballot by senior judges and public prosecutors. Below the Court of Appeals are the ordinary civil and criminal courts. At the lowest level of the judicial system are justices of the peace, who have jurisdiction over minor civil complaints and offenses. Every organized municipality (a community having a minimum population of 2,000) has at least one single-judge court, with the actual number of courts varying according to the total population. Three-judge courts of first instance have jurisdiction over major civil suits and

serious crimes. Either of the parties in civil cases and defendants convicted in criminal cases can request that the Court of Appeals review the lower-court decision. The Turkish courts have no jury system; judges render decisions after establishing the facts in each case based on evidence presented by lawyers and prosecutors.

Courts of Justice.

Civil Courts of the Peace. This is the lowest civil court in Turkey with a single judge. There is at least one in every town. Its jurisdiction covers all kinds of claims that include a certain amount of money, claims of support, requests by minors for permission to marry or to shorten the waiting period of marriage, eviction cases for rentals by lease, and all cases assigned to the court by the Code of Civil Procedure and other laws.

Civil Courts of First Instance. This is the essential and basic court in Turkey. Its jurisdiction covers all civil cases other than those assigned to the civil courts of the peace.

Commercial Courts. The commercial courts are the specialized branches of all civil courts of first instance, having jurisdiction over all kinds of commercial transactions and acts and affairs relating to any trading firm, factory, or commercially operated establishment. Where there are no commercial courts, the civil courts of first instance perform the functions of the commercial court.

Penal Courts of the Peace. This is the lowest penal court with a bench of one judge. They have jurisdiction over penal and municipal misdemeanors and all acts assigned by the Criminal Code, the Code of Criminal Procedure, the Code on the Application of the Criminal Code, and by other laws according to the assignment or to the degree of punishment stated by them.

Penal Courts of First Instance. Among the penal courts, this court with a single judge handles the essential local criminal work. Its jurisdiction covers all penal cases excluded from the jurisdiction of the penal courts of the peace and the central criminal courts.

Central Criminal Courts. This court consists of a presiding judge and two members with a public prosecutor. Offenses and crimes involving a penalty of over five years of imprisonment or capital punishment are under the jurisdiction of this court. There is one in every province.

State Security Courts. In accordance with article 143 of the constitution, the state security courts were established to deal with the offenses against the indivisible integrity of state with its territory and nation, the free democratic order, or against the republic whose characteristics are defined in the constitution, and offenses directly involving the internal and external security of the state.

Administrative Courts and the Council of State. The administrative court system consists of the Council of State, an appellate court, and various administrative courts of first instance. The Council of State reviews decisions of the lower administrative courts, considers original administrative disputes, and, if requested, gives its opinion on draft legislation submitted by the prime minister and the Council of Ministers. The president appoints 25 percent of the Council of State's judges. The other 75 percent are appointed by the High Council of Judges and Public Prosecutors. The Council of State is also the highest consultative body of the state and examines draft regulations and concessional contracts. It is responsible for resolving administrative disputes.

The Military Court System. The military court system exercises jurisdiction over all military personnel. In areas under martial law the military also has jurisdiction over all civilians accused of terrorism or "crimes against the state." The military court system consists of military and security courts of first instance, a Supreme Military Administrative Court, an appellate State Security Court, and the Military Court of Appeals, which reviews decisions and verdicts of the military courts. The decisions of the Military Court of Appeals are final. Military justice is carried out through the military courts and military disciplinary courts. These courts, unless the contrary is stated in the law, have jurisdiction to try military personnel for military offenses, for offenses committed by them against other military personnel or in military places, or for offenses connected with military service and duties.

CORRECTIONAL SYSTEM

From the administrative aspect it is possible to classify Turkish penitentiaries into two groups:

- The fully organized penitentiaries, which are stationed at the centers of aggravated felony courts, have the broader capacity. These penitentiaries have an administration, internal security, execution, health, psychosocial treatment, education, purifying, and workshop units in which directors, deputy general directors, administrative officers, accountants, doctors, dentists, psychologists, social workers, teachers, clerks, warehouse officers, and other necessary officials take place.

- The not-fully organized penitentiaries, which are stationed in towns, are the small-capacity ones.

The prisons are classified into three groups according to security aspects: maximum-security prisons (F-type prisons), medium-security prisons (E-type and special-type prisons), and minimum-security prisons (open prisons and juvenile reformations).

The prisons and remand houses, which are under authority of the Ministry of Justice, are stationed in the places determined by this ministry. In principle, the prisons and remand houses are established at the centers of courts.

The Gendarmerie, which is under the authority of the Ministry of Interior, maintains the external security of the prisons and the transferring of prisoners.

The penal institutions are under the authority of the General Directorate of Prisons and Detention Houses. A general director who is in charge of the directorate, 4 deputy general directors, 4 department chiefs, 11 examining judges, and 170 staff work at this directorate.

According to the Regulation on the Administration of Penal Institutions and Execution of Punishments, public prosecutors are responsible for the maintenance of order and security. The penal institutions are under the permanent supervision and control of public prosecutors in compliance with the laws, regulations, and circulars. Furthermore, the penal institutions are subject to periodical supervision of the controllers of the directorate and inspection of the ministry.

B-Penal Execution System. People who are subject to a detention order or a final decision containing a custodial sentence are placed in prison.

Prisoners are classified into groups according to the age, sex, type, crime, duration of punishment, and legal status. Various activities are carried out to rehabilitate the prisoners.

Prisoners may be given the following disciplinary punishments because of disruptive behaviors:

- Condemnation
- Deprivation of receiving visitors
- Deprivation of correspondence
- Solitary confinement

Disciplinary punishments containing collective, physical, cruel, degrading, and inhumane methods cannot be implemented.

The prisoner, the director, or at least two members of the disciplinary board have the right to appeal in twenty-four hours to the supervisory judge against the punishment decision.

There are various types of treatment activities in institutions:

- Literacy courses and elementary, high school, and university education

- Vocational training and creative activities (the prisoners are given a certificate at the end of the training process)

- Social, cultural, and sportive activities (cinema, theater, folk dances, music, library studies, debates, conferences, seminars, intelligence games, videos, television, computer courses, and so on)

- Religious education (this education aims to motivate the prisoners during the rehabilitation process)

Local institutions, nongovernmental organizations, professional institutions, and voluntary institutions contribute to these activities.

Prisoners who serve one-fifth of their imprisonment with good behavior may be selected for open prisons by the decision of the prison disciplinary board and prison administrative board and by the approval of the general directorate.

Prisoners who serve one-fifth of their imprisonment with good behavior may be granted excuse-permission from one to ten days, in case of their parents', spouses', or children's deaths. In urgent cases such as serious illnesses, fires, and earthquakes that have unfavorable damages on the close relatives of a prisoner, the prisoner may with the approval of the ministry be granted leave from one to ten days.

By contrast, prisoners who serve one-fourth of their imprisonment with good behavior and are selected for the open prison may be given seventy-two-hours of special leave (except travel duration).

Prison Statistics.

- Total Prison Population: 67,772

- Prison Population Rate per 100,000: 95

- Pretrial Detainees: 49%

- Female Prisoners: 3.5%

- Juvenile Prisoners: 3.6%

- Number of Prisons: 503

- Official Capacity of the Prison System: 70,994

- Occupancy Level: 95.5%

BIBLIOGRAPHY

Aydin, A. H. 1996. "Democracy and Policing." *Turkish Yearbook of Human Rights* 17–18, pp. 55–68.

Aydin, A. H. 1996. *Polis Meslek Hukuku.* Ankara, Turkey: Seckin Kitapevi.

Birinci, A. 1999. "The 'Firsts' in Turkish National Police." *Turkish Journal of Police Studies* 1 (3), pp. 9–16.

Cevik, H. H. 1999. "The Turkish Police and the Rule of Law." *Turkish Journal of Police Studies* 1 (3), pp. 73–84.

Emniyet Genel Müdürlüğü. 2005. Available online at http://www.egm.gov.tr (accessed January 16, 2006).

Metz, Helen Chapman, ed. 1996. *Turkey, a Country Study,* 5th ed. Washington, DC: Federal Research Division of the Library of Congress, p. 362.

Hakan Can

Turkmenistan

Official country name: Turkmenistan

Capital: Ashgabat

Geographic description: Located in the southwestern part of Central Asia, and bordered by Kazakhstan, Uzbekistan, Afghanistan, Iran, and the Caspian Sea

Population: 4,952,081 (est. 2005)

■■■

LAW ENFORCEMENT

History. Turkmenistan was annexed by Russia between 1865 and 1885 and became a Soviet republic in 1925. It finally achieved its independence on the dissolution of the Soviet Union in 1991. From a historical point of view the Turkmen are descendants of the Oguz Turks of the eighth to the tenth centuries. From an ethnological point of view the Turkmen are the most distinctive of the Turkish peoples of Central Asia. Mentioned in the Orkhon inscriptions of the eighth century, they belong to the Oguz tribal confederation that moved west in the tenth century and formed the Saljuq dynasties of Iran and Anatolia. In this sense the Turkmen are more akin to the Ottomans and the Azeri Turks than to the Turks of Central Asia. However, like the Kazakhs, their loyalties are extended to a wider circle, which encompasses clan and tribe, before it reaches the state. Turkmen are Sunni Muslims of the Hanafi sect. Conversion of the region to Islam began early and was complete by the tenth century. At the present, around 89 percent of the population is Muslim.

The establishment of Soviet power in Central Asia was determined largely by the events in the main theaters of the Russian civil war. From 1890 to 1917

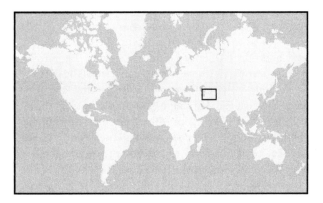

Turkmenistan was part of Russian Turkistan, a province that included Central Asia and its Muslim nationalities—the Kazakhs, the Uzbeks, the Kyrgyz, the Tajik, and the Turkmen. Within Turkistan, however, the Turkmen had a lesser status. Their lands were defined as the Transcaspian region and were ruled as a military colony. This neglect by Russia's government allowed the Turkmen to maintain their culture, language, and nomadic way of life with little interference. During the early part of World War I most of the area, except Tashkent, was in anticommunist hands, but British withdrawal in June 1919 and the defeat of General Aleksandr Kolchak in Siberia exposed it to penetration by the Communists. In 1922 the Communists founded the Union of Soviet Socialist Republics. Two years later they established the Turkmen Soviet Socialist Republic (SSR) as a full member of the Soviet Union. Two republics were so formed and admitted to the Soviet Union in May 1925: Uzbek SSR, in the eastern part, and Turkmen SSR, in the western part. After reclaiming Turkmen SSR in 1932, Joseph Stalin executed thousands of Turkmenistan's Communist leaders—including the president and the premier—whom he accused of helping the nationalists. Following this incident, the Communist regime in Ashgabat became completely obedient to the central Soviet government in Moscow.

After World War II the Soviets built new plants in central Asian cities, including Ashgabat and Chard Zhou (modern Türkmenabat). A workforce made up of ethnic Russians and ethnic Ukrainians emigrated to Turkmen SSR to take advantage of new jobs in the republic. Most Turkmen, however, remained rural and nomadic. Despite the immigration of factory workers, Turkmen SSR remained one of the Soviet Union's most isolated republics. In spite of the republic's isolation, economic development continued in the region. During the 1970s the Soviet government developed the region's energy resources, including oil and natural gas.

The Soviet leader Mikhail Gorbachev instituted several new policies after coming to power in 1985. Glasnost allowed more open criticism of the Communist Party and of the country's economic system. Perestroika eased government control over many small businesses, which could now set their own wages, prices, and production schedules. Turkmen Communist leaders, however, were slow to adopt these reforms. Annamurad Khodzhamuradov, who became Turkmen SSR's leader in 1986, remained loyal to the Soviet government but never accepted Gorbachev's reforms.

In 1990 Turkmen SSR declared that it would take greater control over local politics and economic policy. The government established the office of president and named Saparmurat Niyazov to the post. On October 27, 1991, Turkmenistan proclaimed its independence from the Soviet Union.

More than a decade after their independence, each of the Central Asian states is on its own particular path of political and economic development. While most have achieved at least partial integration within the international community, one stands out as an exception: the remote former Soviet republic of Turkmenistan, on the eastern shores of the Caspian Sea.

Structure and Organization. The national police force, estimated to include 25,000 personnel, is under the jurisdiction of the Ministry of Internal Affairs. The force is located in cities and settlements throughout the country, with garrisons in Ashgabat, Gyzylarbat, and Dashhowuz. Police departments do not have an investigative function in Turkmenistan; that role is filled by the procurator's offices in Ashgabat and other cities. The

police role is confined to routine maintenance of public order and to certain administrative tasks such as controlling the internal passport regime, issuing visas for foreign travel, and registering foreign guests. The Ministry of National Security (MNB), formerly the Committee on National Security, has the responsibilities formerly held by the Soviet Committee for State Security. The MNB is responsible for ensuring that the government remains in power and exercises wide discretion over issues such as exit visas, Internet access, and personal freedoms. The Ministry of Internal Affairs directs the criminal police, which works closely with the MNB on matters of national security. Civilian authorities maintain effective control of the security forces. The minister of the MNB does not formally supervise other ministries; however, the MNB exercises control over personnel changes and enforces presidential decrees.

Border Guards. About 5,000 personnel serve in the Turkmenistan Border Guard, which is commanded jointly by Turkmenistan and Russia. The Border Guard Command was established in 1992 to replace the Soviet-era Central Asian Border Troops District of the Committee for State Security of the Soviet Union. The Border Guards patrol the wild, mountainous Afghan and Iranian frontiers, which total over 1,000 miles and are rated the most sensitive borders of the country. The guards have small arms and some armored personnel carriers; experts evaluate them as an effective border force.

Education and Training. Police personnel are trained mostly on the job and many are recruited from military ranks. The Ministry of Internal Affairs runs a training school that is an institution of higher education. Law enforcement personnel are also recruited from law schools.

The Ministry of Justice receives training and equipment from the United States. Experts from the International Criminal Investigative Training Assistance Program (ICITAP), an organ of the U.S. Department of Justice, impart training in forensic procedures and investigative techniques to the specialists of the Ministry of Justice of Turkmenistan. The ICITAP develops country-specific packages to support the local law enforcement agencies. The ICITAP program in Turkmenistan is aimed at better training of the criminologists and improvement of their output by introduction of modern technologies.

At the national level, the primary security concerns are prevention of trafficking in drugs and other illegal commodities and combating organized and international crime. In December 1994 the MNB and the Russian Federation's Foreign Intelligence Service (a successor agency to the KGB) signed a five-year agreement for cooperation in state security and mutual protection of the political, economic, and technological interests of the two states.

CRIMINAL JUSTICE SYSTEM

The criminal justice system of Turkmenistan is deeply rooted in Soviet institutions and practices. As it did in the Soviet period, the Ministry of Internal Affairs continues to direct the operations of police departments and to work closely with the MNB on matters of national security.

The MNB continues as the main security force similar to the Soviet-era Turkmenistan Committee for State Security. The Ministry of Internal Affairs administers the regular police, working closely with the MNB in matters of national security. Criminal investigation is under procurator's offices, not regular police, who have only routine functions. As in the Soviet system, procurators investigate and prosecute crimes. The rule of law is hampered by the judiciary's subordinate position to the executive branch and a lack of independent judicial tradition.

JUDICIARY SYSTEM

As one of the three branches of government, the judiciary is charged with upholding the constitution and the Supreme Law, as the national codex of civil and criminal law is called. Power is concentrated in the president; the judiciary is wholly subservient to the regime, with all judges appointed for five-year terms by the president without legislative review.

The Ministry of Justice oversees the judicial system, while the Office of the Procurator General is responsible for ensuring that investigative agencies and court proceedings are in compliance with the constitution and the Supreme Law. The president appoints the republic's procurator general and the procurators in each province, and the procurator general appoints those for the smallest political jurisdictions: the districts and the cities. The court system is divided into three levels:

- Supreme Court
- Appellate courts
- Military courts

At the highest level, the Supreme Court consists of twenty-two members, including a president and associate judges, and is divided into civil, criminal, and military chambers. The Supreme court judges are appointed by the president. The Court hears only cases of national importance; it does not function as an appeals court. At the next level, appellate courts function as courts of

appeal in the six provinces and the city of Ashgabat. Sixty-one trial courts operate in the districts and in some cities, with jurisdiction over civil, criminal, and administrative matters. In courts at this level a panel of judges presides in civil and criminal suits, and typically one judge decides administrative cases. Outside this structure, military courts decide cases involving military discipline and crimes committed by and against military personnel. Also, the Supreme Economic Court performs the same function as the state arbitration court of the Soviet period, arbitrating disputes between enterprises and state agencies. The constitution stipulates that all judges at all levels are appointed by the president to terms of five years, and they may be reappointed indefinitely. Enjoying immunity from criminal and civil liability for their judicial actions, judges can be removed only for cause.

Observers of several trends in the administration of justice in this court system have concluded that rudimentary elements of legal culture are absent in the implementation of legal proceedings in Turkmenistan. First, the judiciary is subservient to the Ministry of Justice, and it is especially deferential to the wishes of the president. Second, because the Office of the Procurator General fills the roles of grand jury, criminal investigator, and public prosecutor, it dominates the judicial process, especially criminal proceedings. Third, disregard for due process occurs frequently when higher officials apply pressure to judges concerned about reappointment, a practice known as "telephone justice." Fourth, the legal system disregards the role of lawyers in civil and criminal proceedings, and the Ministry of Justice has not permitted an organized bar. Finally, the republic's citizenry remains largely ignorant of the procedures and issues involved in the nation's legal system. Turkmenistan's Parliament approved a new criminal code on June 12, 1998. The death penalty is provided for seventeen crimes, and the maximum custodial sentence is twenty years.

In February 2003 President Niyazov signed the "Betrayers of the Motherland" law, which characterizes any opposition to the government as an act of treason. Those convicted under the law face life imprisonment, are ineligible for amnesty or reduction of sentence, and may not receive visitors or food from outside sources. The law provides that a person accused of a crime may be held in pretrial detention for no more than two months that, in exceptional cases, may be extended to one year.

A warrant is not required for an arrest. The chairman of the Cabinet of Ministers, a position held by the president, has sole authority for approving arrest warrants. Authorities may detain individuals for seventy-two hours without a formal arrest warrant, but legally must issue a formal bill of indictment within ten days of detention. Detainees are entitled to immediate access to an attorney once a bill of indictment has been issued; however, in practice, they are not allowed prompt or regular access to legal counsel. Incommunicado detention is a problem.

The condition of the legal system and international doubts about human rights in Turkmenistan are indicators that this potentially prosperous former Soviet republic is far from a Western-style democracy, despite the stability its government has achieved and the eagerness with which Western investors have approached it. Future years will determine whether this is a transitional stage of independent democracy, whether liberation from the Soviet empire has produced a permanently authoritarian nation, or whether the independent stance of the mid-1990s will yield to closer ties and more economic and military reliance on the Russian Federation.

CRIME

War on Drugs. Like all other countries of the Central Asian region, Turkmenistan is facing an increasing domestic drug problem. Turkmenistan remains a key transit country for the smuggling of narcotics and precursor chemicals. The flow of Afghan opiates destined for markets in Turkey, Russia, and Europe frequently enters Turkmenistan from Afghanistan, Iran, Pakistan, Tajikistan, and Uzbekistan. The bulk of Turkmen law enforcement resources and manpower is directed toward stopping the flow of drugs from Afghanistan. Turkmen law enforcement at the Turkmen-Uzbek border is primarily focused on interdiction of smuggled commercial goods. Visits by U.S. government officials to crossing points on the Iranian border confirm that commercial truck traffic from Iran continues to be heavy. Caspian Sea ferryboat traffic from Turkmenistan to Azerbaijan and Russia continues to be a viable smuggling route; however, specific seizure statistics are unavailable.

Under a mutual cooperation agreement signed in September 2001, the United States and Turkmenistan have joined hands in antinarcotic efforts. In the ongoing support initiative, the ICITAP provides Turkmenistan with US$500,000 for the purchase of equipment and US$150,000 for supplementary measures to strengthen antinarcotic efforts and maintain law and order. Police and Customs units are given drug detection kits, vehicles, and communication devices. Furthermore, video equipment is purchased and provided for the Police Academy of Turkmenistan.

Some of this information seems to confirm what is reported by the Bureau for International Narcotics and Law Enforcement Affairs in its annual report on narcotics worldwide. In its 2003 report on Turkmenistan the bureau writes:

> Turkmenistan remains a key transit country for the smuggling of narcotics and precursor chemicals. The flow of Afghan opiates destined for markets in Turkey, Russia and Europe frequently enter Turkmenistan from Afghanistan, Iran, Pakistan, Tajikistan and Uzbekistan. The bulk of Turkmen law enforcement resources and manpower are directed toward stopping the flow of drugs from Afghanistan. Turkmen law enforcement at the Turkmen-Uzbek border is primarily focused on interdiction of smuggled commercial goods. Visits by USG officers to crossing points on the Iranian border confirm that commercial truck traffic from Iran continues to be heavy. Caspian Sea ferryboat traffic from Turkmenistan to Azerbaijan and Russia continues to be a viable smuggling route; however, specific seizure statistics have been unavailable. Turkmenistan Airlines operates international flights connecting Asghabat with Abu Dhabi, Bangkok, Birmingham, Frankfurt, Istanbul, London, Moscow, New Delhi, Almaty, Tashkent and Tehran.

During 2003 the government of Turkmenistan (GOTX) increased public pressure on law enforcement officials to slow narcotics traffic through Turkmenistan. Counternarcotics efforts are heavily focused along the mountainous Afghan border, but increased efforts have also been made along the Iranian border.

Narcotics. The GOTX continues to give priority to counternarcotics law enforcement. Despite poor equipment and insufficient transportation, Turkmen border forces are moderately effective in detecting and interdicting illegal crossings by armed smugglers. According to GOTX officials, there are female border guards along the Turkmen border checkpoints to search suspected female traffickers; nearly half of all traffickers being arrested at border crossings are female. Official statistics on narcotic seizures made in Turkmenistan are not published; however, efforts are netting larger seizures. Turkmen law enforcement continues to engage in operations to prevent the smuggling of acetic anhydride (AA), a heroin precursor chemical, through its borders. These efforts are primarily focused around the large rail and truck border crossing point at Serhetabad (formerly Kushka) on the Afghan border. Turkmen officials operating at this border point have made large seizures of AA headed for Afghanistan from as far away as India. In 2003 Turkmen authorities also arrested a number of internal body smugglers, mostly Turkmen or Tajik citizens, at legal crossing points on the Uzbek border. Seizures up to 400 kilograms of narcotics occurred along the Iranian and Afghan borders. Those convicted of possession of even small amounts of illegal drugs are routinely sentenced to eight to ten years in prison; however, these sentences are usually mitigated by the annual presidential amnesty, which is available to all but the most hardened criminals.

Turkmenistan's 1,100-mile Uzbek frontier remains thinly staffed by Border Guard forces when compared to its boundaries with Afghanistan and Iran. In addition, Turkmenistan's border with Uzbekistan has many legal crossing points that are ill equipped in comparison to those on its Afghan and Iranian frontiers. The Uzbek frontier has thus increasingly become an attractive alternative for smugglers seeking to circumvent more stringent controls on Turkmenistan's southern borders. In July 2004 Turkmenistan Border Patrol received two helicopters and one patrol boat under the ongoing border strengthening program that is designed to deter narcotics and contraband smuggling and ensure better border management.

Domestic drug abuse is steadily increasing, although concrete statistics are difficult to obtain. Turkmenistan remains vulnerable to financial fraud and money laundering schemes because of its dual exchange rate and the presence of foreign-operated hotels and casinos. There are troubling reports of involvement in narcotics trafficking by senior GOTX officials. Unofficial estimates suggest that as many as 20,000 people in Ashgabat alone are involved in the drug trade. Observers say that it is now possible to buy drugs in markets, discos, schools, and universities and that the peddlers are becoming less secretive about it. The problem of drug addiction is even more acute in rural areas, where living standards and education levels are lower than in the towns. The problem of drug dependency is exacerbated by local traditions, in which marijuana and opium are used as narcotic and folk remedies.

Turkmenistan's two major border control agencies, state customs, and the Border Guard are significantly handicapped in carrying out their drug enforcement duties by a systematic lack of adequate resources, facilities, and equipment. Most Turkmen border crossing points have only rudimentary inspection facilities for screening vehicle traffic and lack reliable communications systems, computers, unloading and x-ray equipment, and dogs trained in narcotics detection. Turkmenistan will continue to serve as a major transit route for illegal drugs and drug-making precursors until meaningful legal and political reforms are initiated and border control agencies are adequately funded.

Trafficking in Persons. The law does not prohibit trafficking in persons. The penal code prohibits prostitution, which is punishable by two years' imprisonment or hard labor. There have been unconfirmed and anecdotal reports of women from the country traveling to Turkey and the United Arab Emirates and working as prostitutes. There are no reports of trafficking within the country.

The government does not have programs in place to combat trafficking in persons, but it cooperates with the International Organization for Migration in educational efforts on this topic.

War against Terrorism. Turkmenistan supports the war on terrorism by allowing U.S. and international assistance to flow across its borders to Afghanistan. Access to this essential route has been a key to transporting food aid and other humanitarian assistance.

CORRECTIONAL SYSTEM

Prisoners are held under the "Betrayers of the Motherland" law. Most are held in the newly constructed maximum-security prison at Ovadan Depe (completed in June 2004), near Ashgabat, where access to prisoners is extremely limited. There are three types of prisons throughout the country:

- Educational-labor colonies
- Correctional-labor colonies
- Prisons

Prison Conditions. Prison conditions remain poor and unsafe, and authorities refuse all requests for access to prisons and prisoners by international observers. Prolonged pretrial detention and unfair trials are still being practiced. According to BBC and Interfax news agency reports, Turkmenistan has the sixth-highest prison population rate in the world following Kazakhstan. Facilities for prisoner rehabilitation and recreation are extremely limited.

In the correctional-labor colonies there are reports of excessive periods of isolation of prisoners in cells and "chambers." Hardened criminals and political prisoners are held at Ovadan Depe. In Gyzylgaya prison, located in the Kara-Kum Desert, prisoners work in the kaolin mine.

Men are held separately from women, and juveniles are held separately from adults. Prisoners who are connected to the November 2002 attack are reportedly held separately at Ovadan Depe. Former members of intelligence and security services are typically held in a dedicated facility at Akdash, near Türkmenbaşy. Pretrial detainees are usually held separately from convicted prisoners in detention centers; however, individuals connected to the November 2002 attack are held with convicted prisoners in detention centers before their eventual imprisonment.

In October 2000 President Niyazov announced an amnesty for 10,000 of the country's 19,000 prisoners, who were released on the Night of Nights during Ramadan. All those who committed crimes accidentally or for the first time and women and the elderly were granted amnesty on the eve of the Night of Nights.

Prison Statistics.

- Total Prison Population: 22,000
- Prison Population Rate per 100,000: 489
- Number of Prisons: 19

BIBLIOGRAPHY

Bashiri, Iraj. 1999. "Turkmenistan: An Overview." Institute of Linguistics, English as a Second Language, and Slavic Languages and Literatures, University of Minnesota. Available online at http://www.iles.umn.edu/faculty/bashiri/Courses/Turkmen.html (accessed January 16, 2006).

Bureau for International Narcotics and Law Enforcement Affairs. 2004. "International Narcotics Control Strategy Report: Turkmenistan, 2003." U.S. Department of State. Available online at http://www.state.gov/p/inl/rls/nrcrpt/2003/vol1/html/29838.htm (accessed January 16, 2006).

Burke, Justine. 2000. "Turkmen President Announces Mass Prisoner Amnesty." Eurasianet.org (October 27). Available online at http://www.eurasianet.org/resource/turkmenistan/hypermail/200010/0029.html (accessed January 16, 2006).

Joseph D. Serio

Tuvalu

———— ■ ————

Official country name: Tuvalu
Capital: Funafuti (administrative offices are located in Vaiaku on Fongafale Islet)
Geographic description: Group of nine coral atoll islands in Oceania, in the South Pacific Ocean
Population: 11,636 (est. 2005)

■ ■ ■

LAW ENFORCEMENT

Structure and Organization. The Tuvalu Constabulary is a centrally controlled and administered law enforcement agency under a chief police office assisted by superintendents, inspectors, noncommissioned officers, and constables. In addition, a unit known as the Island Police, a decentralized force of part-time policemen, complements the work of the constabulary.

Police Statistics.

- Total Police Personnel: 35
- Population per Police Officer: 332

CORRECTIONAL SYSTEM

Tuvalu has one minimum-security prison, located near the airport and segregated by sex. Only adults are held at this facility and children are remanded to their families. The men's section accommodates thirty-five inmates and the women's section twenty. In any given year, the number of inmates is far below capacity and in most years there are no female prisoners. There is also a single

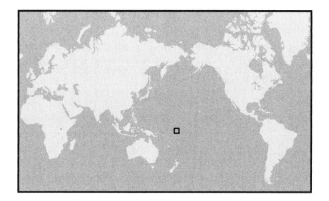

holding cell at the police station for detentions of less than twenty-four hours. Pretrial detainees are usually released on their own cognizance, except in cases where they are charged with violent crimes, such as homicide. Such exceptions have not happened yet.

Prison Conditions. Prison conditions meet international standards in terms of medical care, sanitation, and food.

Prison Statistics.

- Total Prison Population: 6
- Prison Population Rate per 100,000: 56
- Number of Prisons: 1
- Official Capacity of the Prison System: 55

George Thomas Kurian

Uganda

Official country name: Republic of Uganda
Capital: Kampala
Geographic description: Landlocked country in east central Africa, covering the headwaters of the Nile
Population: 27,269,482 (est. 2005)

■■■

LAW ENFORCEMENT

History. The forerunner of the Uganda Police Force was the armed constabulary, which was formed in 1900 with 1,450 Africans under the command of British district officers. In 1906 an inspector general was appointed as the commanding officer of all police detachments. Although established as a civil force, the police were from the outset frequently assigned military duties. During World War I the constabulary detachments patrolled the border between Uganda and German East Africa. In addition, police units were regularly assigned to peacekeeping patrols in Karamoja District to suppress cattle raiding and tribal skirmishes.

During the protectorate period and for the first few years after independence the semiautonomous federal states maintained their own police forces. The forces in Ankole, Bunyoro, and Toro were small, but the Uganda Police Force was a large, well-organized corps. The 1962 constitution provided that these forces were subject to the Uganda inspector general of police, but, in fact, he was able to exercise only nominal control over them. The 1967 constitution abolished the federal states, and the police forces in those states were either merged into

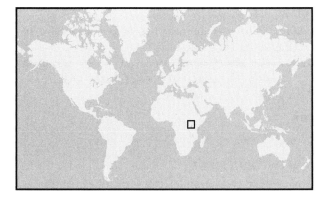

the Uganda Police Force or became local constabularies responsible to the district commissioners, but under the overall control of the inspector general.

Structure and Organization. The Uganda Police Force is a multitribal armed constabulary that, besides regular police work, performs intensive paramilitary duties, provides guard of honor detachments for visiting dignitaries, and assists public prosecutors in criminal courts.

The ratio of policemen to the population is 1 for every 1,948 inhabitants. A significant imbalance exists in the assignment of police among the districts, ranging from 1 to 100 in Kampala to 1 to 5,000 in Tezo District and 1 to 8,000 in Kigezi District. The heavy burden of law enforcement in the historically lawless outlying areas is placed on a relatively small force.

The Uganda Police Force is commanded by an inspector general who is appointed by the president on the advice of the Public Service Commission. The actions

A protestor is arrested and taken to Uganda's Central Police Station in Kampala after two days of riots in the area, November 15, 2005. *Several people protested the arrest of Colonel Kizza Besigye, an opposition leader of Forum for Democratic Change (FDC). That same day, a district magistrate decided that prosecutors had substantial evidence to support allegations of treason, concealment of treason, and rape against Besigye.* AP IMAGES.

of the inspector general of police are exempt from judicial inquiry or review, and he reports directly to the minister of internal affairs and the president.

The inspector general of police is directly assisted by four regional commanders, who manage police operations in their respective regions. A Police Council consisting of the inspector general of police, the permanent secretary of the Ministry of Internal Affairs, and four other members appointed by the minister oversees all aspects of recruitment and service. Senior police officials are appointed by the Public Service Commission after consultation with the inspector general of police.

The force is divided into several branches or units:

- Uniform Branch, assigned mainly to urban duties
- Special Branch
- Criminal Investigation Department
- Special Constabulary

- Special Force Unit
- Signals Branch
- Railway Police
- Police Air Wing
- Police Tracker Force
- Police Band
- Police Dog Section
- Public Safety Unit, formed in 1971 to combat armed robbery

The highlight of the corps is the Special Force Unit, formerly the Internal Security Unit. The Special Force Unit is a paramilitary organization trained in riot control and border patrol by Israeli instructors. Each unit consists of fifty men. The Police Tracker Force, the successor to the Karamoja Constabulary, is also organized along military lines. Its special assignment is the suppression of cattle raiding. The detective branch of the force is the Criminal Investigation Department, which maintains fingerprint, identification, and criminal records and operates the Photographic and Scientific Aids Section. Communications are handled by the Signals Branch. The Police Air Wing operates aircraft with VHF equipment for air-to-ground contact.

Education and Training. New recruits are assigned for initial training to the Police College in Kampala. Noncommissioned officers and constables are sent for promotion and refresher courses to the Police College at Naguru. Selected officers are also sent abroad, particularly to Australia, Israel, the United Kingdom, and the United States.

Police Statistics.

- Total Police Personnel: 14,000
- Population per Police Officer: 1,948

HUMAN RIGHTS

Uganda People's Defense Force, the key security force, is the source of most human rights violations in the country, including extrajudicial killings, disappearances, and torture. In 2002 the Police Human Rights Desk received 386 complaints of human rights violations. Some cases of abuse are investigated and some offenders are punished. There is a training program in place for police officials to respect internationally recognized human rights standards.

CRIME

Crime Statistics. Offenses reported to the police per 100,000 population: 316. Of which:

- Murder: 9.9

- Assault: 54.8
- Burglary: 19.3
- Automobile Theft: 8.3

CORRECTIONAL SYSTEM

The criminal justice system is governed by the 1930 criminal code, which was amended in 1968. The list of punishments includes death by hanging, imprisonment, whipping, and fines. Since 1968 the death sentence is mandatory for all persons convicted of armed robbery. Despite these deterrents, incidents of violent crime are increasing, especially in areas without significant police presence.

The prison service is part of the Public Service under the command of the commissioner of prisons. The commissioner, who reports to the minister of local government, is appointed by the president on the recommendations of the Public Service Commission.

The Prison Service operates 194 prisons, many of which are industrial and agricultural prisons with an emphasis on rehabilitation. There are special prisons for long-term prisoners and those placed in preventive detention as habitual criminals, that is, those convicted of a serious crime more than four times. Prisoners who are given the death sentence are confined in the Upper Prison at Murchison Bay in Kampala, where all executions are carried out. In addition, there are local prisons or jails administered by the district council administrations.

Prison Service recruits are trained at the Prisons Training School.

Prison Conditions. Uganda's prisons and police cells hold 21,900 prisoners. Prison conditions come closest to meeting international standards in Kampala, where inmates receive running water, medical care, and minimum sanitation. However, these prisons are also among the most overcrowded. The country's prisons hold three times their planned capacity. Although the law provides access to prisoners by their families, prison guards demand bribes to allow such visits and otherwise intimidate family members. Human rights groups receive complaints of torture, unhygienic conditions, and prisoners suffering from semistarvation. There are a number of reported deaths in custody, some as a result of torture. There is a high mortality rate in all prisons, many from malnutrition, but some from HIV/AIDS. Of the thirty-seven prisoners who died in 2002 in Kampala's Luzira Prison, thirty died of HIV/AIDS.

Prisoners at most prisons grow maize, millet, and vegetables. Skilled prisoners receive US$0.14 a day and unskilled prisoners US$0.06 a day. The Community Service Act reduces prison congestion by allowing minor offenders to do community service. Female prisoners are held in segregated wings, and rape is not generally a problem. Because of lack of space, juveniles are often kept in prison with adults. The prison system maintains one juvenile prison and four lower security remand homes. None of the juvenile facilities has school facilities or health clinics. Severe overcrowding is a problem in all juvenile facilities. The remand home in Kampala, designed for 45 inmates, holds 140 children. Prisoners as young as twelve perform manual labor from dawn until dusk.

Prison Statistics.

- Total Prison Population: 21,900
- Prison Population Rate per 100,000: 89
- Pretrial Detainees: 65.7%
- Female Prisoners: 4.3%
- Juvenile Prisoners: 4.2%
- Number of Prisons: 194; 45 central government and 149 local government
- Official Capacity of the Prison System: 8,530
- Occupancy Level: 186.4%

George Thomas Kurian

Ukraine

———■———

Official country name: Ukraine

Capital: Kiev

Geographic description: Located at a strategic position at the crossroads of Europe, sharing its border with Belarus, Hungary, Moldova, Poland, Romania, Russian, and Slovakia as well as the Black Sea

Population: 47,425,336 (est. 2005)

■ ■ ■

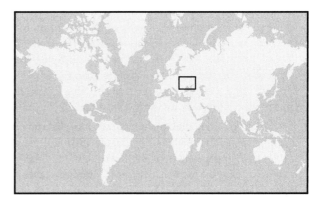

LAW ENFORCEMENT

History. When World War I erupted the first modern Ukrainian military formation, the Sich Riflemen, was formed in Western Ukraine. The riflemen swore allegiance to the Austrians to ensure the defeat of Russia. On January 22, 1918, an independent Ukrainian Republic was proclaimed in Kiev, which included the Right and Left Bank areas of the Dnieper River. On November 1, after the collapse of the Austro-Hungarian monarchy, the Western Ukrainian Republic was proclaimed in L'viv. It formally merged with the Ukrainian National Republic in Kiev on January 22, 1919.

Because of war with the Russian Bolsheviks and the Poles, Ukrainian independence was short lived. The Ukrainians themselves were not capable of uniting behind a single leader or policy of independence. Having been under both Polish and Russian rule, much of the Ukrainian intelligentsia was radicalized and predisposed to Vladimir Lenin's rhetoric. Nevertheless, Lenin recognized the potency of a Ukrainian national awareness and granted the Ukrainians a political identity in the form of the Ukrainian Soviet Socialist Republic (SSR), rather than absorbing them into the Russian Federated Soviet Socialist Republic. In 1922, except for Galicia and parts of Volhynia and smaller regions that were incorporated into Romania and Czechoslovakia, the Ukrainian SSR joined the Union of Soviet Socialist Republics (USSR).

Lenin's attempts to assuage Ukrainian nationalism through a measure of cultural autonomy were abandoned by Joseph Stalin; he imposed agricultural collectivization on Ukraine and requisitioned all grain for export. One result was the famine of 1932–1933 in which 7 million Ukrainians perished. In the late 1930s he persecuted the Ukrainian intelligentsia and destroyed the Ukrainian Orthodox Church. Nikita Khrushchev later said Stalin wanted all Ukrainians deported, but there were simply too many of them.

In 1941 all of Ukraine fell under the Germans' control when the Nazis invaded the Soviet Union. A group of Ukrainians in Western Ukraine took advantage of the Russo-German War and on June 30, 1941, proclaimed the restoration of the Ukrainian State in L'viv. The Nazis' reaction was one of mass arrests and extensive terror.

The republic suffered severe wartime devastation, especially as a battleground both in 1941–1942 (the German advance) and 1943–1944 (the Russian advance). Most of the Ukraine's 1.5 million Jews were killed by the Nazis during the war; many were shot outright in 1941.

By the end of World War II the Red Army reoccupied the Ukraine and in 1945 Stalin incorporated most of Western Ukraine into the Ukrainian SSR. Subsequently, mass arrests and deportations followed in the western territories. The Ukrainian Catholic Church was officially abolished by the Soviets in 1946. In April 1945 Stalin included Ukraine and Belarus among the forty-seven founding states of the United Nations, as a ploy to give the Soviet Union two extra votes.

During the 1950s and 1960s Ukrainians emerged as tacit junior partners of the Soviets in governing the Soviet Union. Khrushchev, although a Russian by birth, served as first secretary of the Ukrainian Communist Party during the 1930s and carried out the Stalinist purges in Ukraine. He went on to become head of the Communist Party of the Soviet Union in the 1950s and early 1960s. Leonid Brezhnev was born in the Ukraine and held important party posts there before being called to Moscow and serving as general secretary of the Communist Party into the early 1980s.

The Ukrainian parliament passed a declaration of sovereignty in July 1990, and in August 1991 it declared the Ukraine independent of the Soviet Union. Ukraine became a charter member of the Commonwealth of Independent States in December 1991. Leonid Kravchuk, a former-Communist-turned-nationalist, became Ukraine's first president. Parliamentary and presidential elections were held in 1994, and Kravchuk was defeated by Prime Minister Leonid Kuchma.

Since his election, Kuchma has implemented a few market reforms, but the economy remains dominated by huge, inefficient, state-run companies and has not improved significantly. Ukraine, briefly the world's third-largest nuclear power, also ratified the Strategic Arms Reduction Treaty and the Nuclear Nonproliferation Treaty (1994) and turned its nuclear arsenal over to Russia for destruction (completed 1996); in return the Ukraine received much-needed fuel for its nuclear power plants. The country's economic reforms and cooperation in disarmament helped it gain substantial Western aid and loans.

In the 1998 legislative elections communists won most of the seats. Kuchma was reelected in 1999 after defeating the Communist candidate, Petro Symonenko, in a runoff, and in December Viktor Yushchenko, the central bank chairman and an advocate of market reforms, was chosen as prime minister. In April 2000 voters in a referendum approved constitutional changes that increased the president's power over the legislature.

In September 2000 an opposition journalist was murdered. When tape recordings implicating Kuchma in his murder and other abuses of power subsequently were aired, Kuchma's support in Parliament eroded, and there were demonstrations in early 2001 calling for his resignation. The government refused to investigate the journalist's death and was accused of suppressing press coverage of the incident. The dismissal of Prime Minister Yushchenko in April 2001 by Parliament was a blow to reformers; he was succeeded by Anatoly Kinakh, an ally of President Kuchma. In the March 2002 legislative elections, Yushchenko supporters won roughly a quarter of the seats, as did supporters of the president. In November Kuchma dismissed Kinakh as prime minister and appointed Viktor Yanukovych to the post. In December 2003 the Ukrainian Supreme Court ruled that Kuchma could run for a third term because the election for his first term had occurred before the current constitution took effect.

The Ministry of Internal Affairs (MIA) of Ukraine originates from the period when Ukraine was a part of the Russian Empire. The Russian army of law and order existed until February 1917, at which time it undertook service on behalf of the provisional government. With the fall of the provisional government and rise of the Bolsheviks later that year, the police were retained to combat crime and guard prisoners. In the time of the Soviet Union, the MIA forces in Ukraine distinguished themselves not only in upholding traditional law and order but also by taking part in military operations from 1941 to 1945.

When Ukraine gained its independence in 1991, the objectives and priorities of law enforcement had been redefined. In accordance with the legislature's decree of September 30, 1991, No. 1465-XII, the internal forces of the Soviet Union, located on the territory of Ukraine, were transferred to the MIA of Ukraine with its full complement; at the same time, party control commissions and party committees were liquidated. Military political bodies have been reorganized into bodies of education and social legal work.

The MIA of Ukraine plays an important role in exercising control and supervision over guaranteeing of rights and freedoms of the citizens of Ukraine.

Structure and Organization. The MIA of Ukraine is the umbrella organization that oversees police activities in the country. The MIA is headed by the minister of internal affairs with several deputy ministers managing the various services and divisions. Each directorate or department of internal affairs is headed by a chief and is managed by his deputies—directors of the departments and services.

Most police units in Ukraine are referred to as "militia," deriving from the Soviet tradition that emphasized the fact that the police consists of ordinary citizens and exists to serve the people. According to article 7 of the Militia Act of 1990, the militia is a united system of agencies under the structural umbrella of the MIA and carries out administrative, preventive, investigative, criminal procedural, executive, and protective activities. It includes criminal investigation militia, public order militia, transport militia, state traffic inspection, security militia, and others.

Besides the militia, police functions are carried out by other divisions that also fall under the central authority of the MIA and are organized by geographic hierarchy:

- At the national level in the MIA

- Regional agencies (regional directorates of internal affairs; Kiev and Sevastopol City Directorates of Internal Affairs; the Main Directorate of Internal Affairs of the Crimean Republic; Directorate of Internal Affairs for Transport)

- District departments (district departments of regional directorates of internal affairs)

- City departments (city department [*gorodskoe upravlenye*] of the regional directorate of internal affairs)

- City precinct (precinct of the city department of the regional directorate of internal affairs)

The system of internal affairs agencies is headed up by the minister of internal affairs, who is directly responsible for overseeing the Minister's Apparatus, the Department of Management, and the Department of Internal Security. Deputy ministers run the following agencies and divisions:

- The Main Directorate for Fighting Organized Crime is responsible for setting policy, developing strategies, acquiring equipment, and maintaining appropriate staffing levels, among other things, to effectively address the problem of organized crime throughout the country

- The Department for Cooperation with the Supreme Council of Ukraine and the Public Relations Department are responsible for liaison activities between the national police and the legislature as well as coordinating mass media inquiries

- The Department of Information Technologies is charged with upgrading and improving the processing and dissemination of police information

- The Department for the Search for Fugitives, the State Service for Combating Economic Crime, the Department for Combating Illegal Drugs, the Criminal Investigation Militia for Juvenile Affairs, and the National Central Bureau of Interpol in Ukraine all fall under the auspices of a single deputy minister. As their names suggest, these departments make up the core of the police function with both domestic and international matters falling in their purview

- The Administrative Service of Militia, the State Automobile Inspectorate, the Main Directorate of Interior Troops, the Department of Citizenship, Immigration and Personal Registration Affairs, the Security Service, and the Department of Fire Safety are geared toward domestic safety and security; of particular interest is that the MIA in Ukraine, as in many other states of the former Soviet Union, has its own military to quell social unrest or political instability leading to attempted secession

- The Main Directorate of Investigations, Investigation Department, and the State Scientific-Research Forensic Expertise Center constitute the heart of the investigative function

- The Department of Personnel Management

- The Department of Logistics, Financial Resources, and Medical Care

All these services, agencies, and divisions performing special law enforcement administrative tasks have their own multilevel structure and are integrated in the previously mentioned departments and directorates of internal affairs. Directors of the services and divisions are subordinate to the chief of the Department or Directorate of Internal Affairs.

It should be noted that some of the agencies and divisions have subdivisions only on the regional level (e.g., Service for Combating Organized Crime) and some subdivisions are not directly subordinate to police departments or directorates (e.g., Interior Troop units).

Retirement Age. Terms of service depend on rank and gender. Men who are privates or low-level command personnel must retire by the age of forty-five. For women the mandatory retirement age is forty-five. With proper authorization, this age may be extended by five years.

Middle-, senior-, and high-command personnel may remain in service until the age of: 45 (except colonels); 50 (colonel); 55 (major general and lieutenant general); and 60 (colonel general). On reaching the mandatory age, the officer has to be discharged to reserve status and either register in a military service or retire. However, if necessary the term of service can be prolonged by five years or, in exceptional cases (taking into account the state of health), for a second time by five or ten years for those who have an advanced degree or high rank.

Middle-, senior-, and high-command personnel can be discharged for reasons of ill health, in the event of a downsizing of personnel, by their own volition, in connection with transfer to another ministry or agency, or if they do not meet the requirements of service or have committed a crime.

Police at Work. Positions in some of the departments and divisions include:

- Investigative departments—investigator, senior investigator, serious crimes investigator, assistant of the director, and director

- Departments of Criminal Search, Combating Economic Crime, Combating Organized Crime, and Combating Illegal Drug Trafficking—detective, senior detective, detective in the most important cases, senior detective in the most important cases, deputy of the director, and director

- Local Inspectors Service—local inspector, senior local inspector, and director

- Beat and patrol officers as well as the Local Inspectors Service are subordinate to the director of Administrative Service of Militia

To occupy a position in departments, directorates, or the MIA, each police officer should have the appropriate level of education, experience, and rank. The system of police ranks is based on the military structure:

High Command Personnel:

- Major General
- Lieutenant General
- Colonel General

Senior Command Personnel:

- Major
- Lieutenant Colonel
- Colonel

Midlevel Command Personnel:

- Second Lieutenant
- Lieutenant
- Senior Lieutenant
- Captain

Low-Level Command Personnel:

- Corporal
- Sergeant

- Senior Sergeant
- Master Sergeant
- Warrant Officer
- Senior Warrant Officer
- Private

The Ukrainian police is reported to be notoriously corrupt. In 2002, 58 criminal cases were brought against police officers and 334 against former police officers. An additional 828 employees were dismissed for malfeasance. Whole police units are reported to provide services to organized crime and to assist in the trafficking of women in exchange for money.

Local Police. The police of Ukraine are centralized and this remains one of the main features of the Ukrainian law enforcement system. However, steps have been taken to create local police units that are to be funded from local budgets and subordinate to local authorities as well as to the MIA. The presidential decree on the creation of a municipal militia was issued, and on April 3, 2004, the Supreme Council of Ukraine adopted amendments to the Militia Act and passed other laws concerning the creation of a municipal militia.

Traffic Police. The State Automobile Inspection (SAI) of the MIA is the primary agency tasked to oversee the operation of the traffic police. There is also the Directorate of Internal Affairs for Transport, which serves railroads. The SAI consists of several divisions:

- Department of Monitoring and Prevention

- Directorate of State Automobile-Technical Inspection, Control of Condition of Roads, and Informational Support, which includes the Department of State Automobile-Technical Inspection, Registration and Exams, and Control of Autotransport Sales; Department of Informational Support of Activity of SAI Divisions; and Department of Control of Transporting Dangerous Loads and Roads Condition

- Department of Road-Patrol Service

- Department of Economical Provision

- Office (Chancellery)

Also, there are departments of the SAI included in the directorates, city, districts, and departments of internal affairs.

The main tasks of the SAI are to ensure safety on the roads, control adherence to traffic laws, issue driver licenses, carry out searches for stolen vehicles, and combat traffic crimes. In 2001 SAI officers solved 4,500 criminal cases and 2,400 cases of drivers leaving the scene

Authorities take an unidentified detainee into custody following a violent exchange between supporters of Red Army veterans and supporters of Ukrainian partisans in downtown Kiev, Ukraine, October 15, 2005. *Red Army veteran supporters were protesting against assertions by Ukrainian partisans to deny them official recognition as World War II veterans. Partisans from the Ukrainian Insurgent Army battled both Nazis and Red Army soldiers during World War II as part of efforts to establish an independent Ukraine.* **AP IMAGES.**

of an accident, seized 2,200 weapons, and investigated 5,800 cases of illegal transportation of narcotics (totaling 4.4 tons).

Every year between 5,500 and 6,000 people die in traffic accidents and 38,000 are injured. A traffic accident occurs on average every fifteen minutes. According to the SAI, from 1997 to 2002 the number of traffic accidents dropped by 9 percent. With the collapse of the Soviet Union and the softening of the borders, Ukraine has found itself in the middle of a vast network of stolen car routes moving from west to east, typically destined for Russia.

Special Police. There are several units of special designation in the structure of the Ukrainian police. The Militia Troops Rapid Reaction Force, Berkut (Golden Eagle), is a highly mobile unit of special troops created for combating organized crime and ensuring public order during public events such as political demonstrations and rallies, sporting events, cultural programs, and religious observances. The rapid response forces were created in January 1992 and modeled after the militia troops of special designation. Berkut's activities are carried out by the Department of Patrol-Post Service, the transport

militia, and militia troops of special purpose subordinated to Department of Public Order Protection.

The Special Forces group, Sokol (Falcon), is attached to the Regional Directorate for Organized Crime Control of the MIA and designated to perform special operations regarding combating members of organized criminal groups.

The Titan group is a special task division of the State Security Service and the Gryfon (Griffin) group is a special task division of the militia responsible for overseeing the court system. There are also special task forces in the structure of the Interior Troops.

Education and Training. In 2002 there were 12 police institutions of higher education in Ukraine that hosted 110 doctors of science, almost 800 candidates of science, 23,400 cadets, and more than 24,000 students.

In general, the system of police education can be divided into several levels:

- Schools and special centers for training officers of lower rank and certain types of specialists

- Universities, academies, and institutes that graduate investigators, detectives, experts, and so on and midlevel staff; the institutions enjoying the best reputation for turning out high-quality graduates and producing good research are the National Academy of Internal Affairs in Kiev and the National University of Internal Affairs in Kharkiv

- Universities and academies providing special courses for professional development for all professionals particularly mid- and upper-level commanders

It should be noted that besides bachelor and specialist degrees, universities and academies offer masters and doctoral degrees in a variety of specialties. The educational process is set according to standards of higher education adjusted to address the specific nature of law enforcement activity. The quality of education is compatible with well-known civilian colleges and universities.

Recruitment and Conditions of Service. Conditions, terms, and rules of service are determined by the Statute on the Service of Private and Command Personnel of Internal Affairs Agencies of Ukraine adopted by a decree of the Cabinet of Ministers of the Soviet Union on July 29, 1991, with changes and amendments between 1992 and 2003.

Individuals having reached eighteen years of age and can perform the responsibilities expected of them can be accepted into the service of internal affairs agencies on a voluntary basis. Draftees are not taken into the internal affairs agencies except at those times when indicated by the legislature.

Ranks of private and those in low-command personnel are filled on a contractual basis by men who served in the army, others who are in armed forces reserves (except officers in reserve), and, in some cases, by women. The conditions of the contract are set by the minister of internal affairs.

Positions of middle-, senior-, and higher-command personnel are filled by those who have higher education and meet the requirements of the service. Middle-command personnel are filled by people from the low command who have middle or higher education, practical experience in the internal affairs agencies, and had good reputations during their time of service.

For excellent fulfillment of duties, high achievements in the service, courage and bravery demonstrated while fulfilling duties, and other special accomplishments, police officers can be recommended for state awards, medals, and recognition in accordance with the Disciplinary Statute of the internal affairs agencies.

Police officers are allowed to hold another job in internal affairs agencies and, in exceptional cases, in other ministries or agencies with the consent of the minister or the directors of the directorates of internal affairs. They are prohibited from involvement in any kind of entrepreneurial activity or from organizing strikes or participating in them. However, they can join public organizations or associations to protect their professional and socioeconomic interests.

Police officers are also allowed to study in educational institutions of the MIA and in higher schools of other ministries and agencies and take advantage of privileges afforded students.

Privates and command personnel work a forty-one-hour week and, if necessary, will work overtime during days off and holidays as well.

Promotion is decided on a competitive basis taking into consideration professional and personal qualities, accomplishments, and proven ability to carry out responsibilities. Rules for promotion are determined by statute. Certification of middle-, senior-, and higher-command personnel is held on every position every four years.

Uniforms and Weapons. The uniform of the Ukrainian police has changed several times in attempts to emulate the best police traditions of the leading European countries. Introduction of new uniforms followed several steps. In July 2000, the creation of new samples of the militia uniform was completed (full dress uniform and daily). In October 2000 the MIA adopted the conception of the new uniform for the MIA, and in November 2001 the Council of Ministers of Ukraine adopted the decree, "On Uniforms for the Officers of Internal Affairs, Servicemen of the Special Motorized Militia Units of Internal Troops of the MIA and for the Officers of the Tax Militia." In May 2002 the MIA issued the official rules for the proper wearing of the uniform. The complete set of the summer uniform was created in 2002.

The uniform of Ukrainian police officers was created in such way that unites an aesthetic look while contributing to the fulfillment of law enforcement tasks. To satisfy demands for mass production, the uniforms are made from Ukrainian materials, including new types of textiles. Responsibility for producing, buying, storing, and distributing the uniform belongs to the jurisdiction of the Logistics and Resource Supply Department of the MIA.

According to the Law on Militia, the militia has a right to use physical force, so-called special measures, and firearms. The use of force is forbidden against women with obvious signs of pregnancy, elderly people, people with obvious disabilities, and minors. An exception can be made in cases where a group of these people is committing an assault that threatens lives of citizens or militia officers or in cases of armed assault or resistance.

Firearms may be used in the following cases:

- To protect citizens from life-threatening assaults;
- To release hostages
- To resist an armed attack on a militia officer or members of his family or other attack if there is a threat to their lives or health
- To resist attacks on guarded locations, convoys, private residences, offices of state, and public organizations
- To detain a person who commits a serious crime and is trying to escape
- To detain a person who demonstrates an armed resistance or is trying to escape from custody
- To stop an armed person who threatens to use weapons and other objects that threaten the life of a militia officer
- To stop a vehicle in cases where the driver creates a life-threatening situation to a militia officer

The Ukrainian police service uses a variety of weapons. Depending on the task, police officers might use the TT (an old weapon rarely used), the Makarov (the most widely used weapon), the FORT series of pistols, the Kalashnikov submachine gun, carbines, and sniper rifles. The FORT series is quickly becoming the weapon of choice. For example, the FORT-12 is a 9mm pistol with a capacity of twelve rounds and can accommodate a laser-mounted guide.

The FORT series of weapons is produced by the State Research and Production Association. FORT was created in 1994 by the MIA for the express purpose of improving the firepower of Ukrainian law enforcement and other institutions.

Transportation, Technology, and Communications. There are three basic types of police vehicles: motor vehicles, helicopters, and boats. Since the 1990s the police service has introduced a variety of foreign-made vehicles to supplement and eventually replace the aging fleet of Russian-made Ladas and Moskviches. For example, the Ministry of Interior uses Mazda vans for special operations units, Volkswagen sedans in the traffic police as well as Volkswagens, BMWs, and Mercedes in a police capacity. The traffic police has also used the so-called dummy vehicle, a flat piece of metal placed on the side of the road to deter speeders.

The MIA manufactures a wide range of protection devices for its law enforcement personnel including polyfoam and polycarbonate helmets, a variety of protective vests, and bulletproof shields. Some of the armored garments produced by the MIA have been successfully tested by ballistic laboratories in Germany and the United States.

In addition, since 1992 the State Engineering Center, Spetsteknika, has produced means of communication and transport as well as forensic devices related to phonoscopy and ballistics, devices for the bomb squad, and special equipment for investigative units and rapid response teams, among other things.

Surveillance and Intelligence Gathering. Surveillance and Intelligence Gathering in law enforcement bodies is carried out in the form of operative-search activity (OSA). According to the Operative-Search Activity Act (1992), OSA is a system of public and nonpublic (covert) surveillance, intelligence, and counterintelligence measures carried out by operative and operative-technical means (article 2) for the purpose of discovering and documenting factual data concerning illegal acts by individuals and groups and intelligence collection and sabotage activities by special services of foreign countries to stop the violation of law and secure the interests of the public and the state.

Only special operative forces are entitled by law to carry out OSA. A number of state agencies have operational-search units including the MIA, the State Security Service, the Border Guard Troops, and the State Tax Service, among others.

When carrying out OSA, police operative units should adhere to principles of legality, respect for human rights and freedoms, and cooperation with executive authorities and the citizenry. Decisions to apply operative search measures can be made only when:

- There is the necessity to check legally obtained information regarding a crime committed or prepared by an unknown perpetrator; people are preparing to commit or have committed a crime; people are hiding from investigation, court, or avoiding execution; people are reported missing; intelligence and sabotage activity of foreign special services, organizations, or people is discovered; there is a real threat to life or health of court or law enforcement personnel because of their professional activity or threats to participants of the criminal justice system, members of their families, or close relatives

- There is a request of authorized state agencies and organizations regarding a background investigation of an individual in connection with access to state secrets and work with nuclear materials or on nuclear plants

- It is in the interest of public safety and national security

If there are grounds for OSA, decisions to initiate such investigations must be approved by the chief of the appropriate unit or his authorized deputy. Although OSA contains secret measures and can limit human rights and freedoms, it can happen only in circumstances set by law. Citizens of Ukraine and other people have the right to obtain a written explanation about the restriction of their rights and freedoms from operative-search bodies or appeal this action as established by law (article 9).

Secret penetration of residential premises or other property, collecting information through the use of technical devices, and controlling mail, telegraph, other correspondence, and telephone calls must be sanctioned by the court. Results of the previously mentioned operative-search measures are to be fully documented to be used as evidence at trial.

Police Officers Killed in the Line of Duty. In 2000, 54 officers were killed in the line of duty and 356 were injured. Two years later, the number killed had dropped to 40 and only 215 were injured.

Police Statistics.

- Total Strength of the Police Force: 125,000
- Population per Police Officer: 379

CRIME

In the 1990s there was significant growth in crime and then in the second half of the decade the situation began to stabilize. In 1995 the number of registered crimes was nearly 642,000, in 2000 that figure was down to 553,600, and in 2002, the number of general crimes was slightly more than 408,000. In 2002 the number of serious crimes fell by 1.6 percent, less serious crimes fell by more than 30 percent, and crimes against people fell by 17.8 percent.

During 2003, 385,800 crimes were discovered, 350,700 of which were so-called traditional crimes (172,600 serious). Approximately 260,000 offenders were identified and 351,900 people were recognized as victims. Data also show that the level of crime in Ukraine is comparatively low: per 10,000 people in Ukraine, 110.9 crimes; in Poland, 290; Russia, 205.1; Romania, 157.3; and Belarus, 117.3.

In 2003, generally speaking, 43,200 crimes were related to the economy (42,000 in 2002); 8,900 pertained to the budget; more than 3,000 in banking; 6,700 in agriculture; 3,900 in the fuel-energy complex; 3,600 pertaining to privatization; and 1,900 regarding foreign economic activity. Two hundred twenty-five incidents of operating fictitious firms were documented, 245 of money laundering, and more than 3,000 of bribery.

Statistics also show the high level of effectiveness of Ukrainian police response. The clearance rate in 2000 was 74 percent; of every ten homicides, nine were solved. In 2002 police solved 93.3 percent of murders.

Criminal Investigations and Forensics. Criminal investigation is performed according to the constitution of Ukraine, the Criminal Procedure Code, and other acts of the legislature. Investigations are carried out by a variety of agencies including departments within the MIA, the Prosecutor General's Office, the Security Service of Ukraine, and the Tax Militia of the State Tax Service. All investigators have the same status, rights, and obligations as set in the Criminal Procedure Code, though internal regulations and directives of agencies may add details and specifications. Most cases are handled by MIA investigators.

The post-Soviet period of Ukrainian independence is characterized by the strengthening and development of forensic service. The Explosive-Technical Service and the Criminalistics Research Center were attached to the Criminalistics Directorate of the MIA in 1995 and 1997, respectively. In 1998 the State Criminalistics Research Center of the MIA was created, uniting the Criminalistics Directorate, the Explosive-Technical Service, and the Criminalistics Research Center. In 2000 the Expert Service of Ukraine was established, uniting under a single organization the State Criminalistics Research Center of the MIA, the Criminalistics Research Centers attached to the Main Directorates, regional directorates, and the Directorate for Transport of the MIA, and the Criminalistics Departments attached to district and city departments.

The forensics units of the MIA perform investigations in a wide variety of areas including:

- Handwriting analysis and author profiles
- Documents, money (banknotes), and securities
- Photo-technical and portrait work
- Audio and video recordings
- Medical-biological
- Materials, substances, and products
- Hair, fibers, ballistics, and weapons
- Accounting
- Automobiles
- Arsons and explosions
- Food and plants

Narcotics. By 2003 detectives of the Department for Combating Illegal Drug Trafficking had discovered

57,400 crimes connected with illegal drug trafficking (among which 22,000 were serious), 3,800 groups of drug dealers had been eliminated, and more than 2,500 drug dens had been closed. Two hundred twenty-four illegal drug laboratories were eliminated, almost 22 tons of drug substances were seized, among which 110 kilograms of opium, almost 6 tons of marijuana, 3.4 kilograms of heroin, 76.5 grams of cocaine, and 3.5 kilograms of amphetamines (15,100 doses) were found.

The transit of narcotics through Ukraine is a serious problem. Combating narcotics trafficking is one of the most important tasks for the police, though a lack of economic resources seriously complicates efforts. Coordination between law enforcement agencies responsible for counternarcotics work is weak.

Ukraine is not a major drug-producing country; however, it is located along several important drug trafficking routes to Europe, making it an important transit country. Ukraine continues to experience an increase in drug trafficking from Afghanistan. Drugs pass through several countries before transiting Ukraine: Russia, Georgia, Armenia, Azerbaijan, Turkey, Romania, Moldova, and Poland are among these transit countries.

Criminal groups use Ukraine's seaports and rivers as part of the "Balkan Route" for smuggling narcotic drugs. Many available ports on the Black and Azov seas, river transportation routes, porous borders, and inadequately financed and underequipped border and customs control forces make Ukraine susceptible to drug trafficking. Shipments are usually destined for western Europe, and arrive by road, rail, or sea, which is perceived as less risky than by air or mail shipment.

Opium poppy is grown in western, southwestern, and northern Ukraine, while hemp cultivation is concentrated in the eastern and southern parts of the country. Small quantities of poppy and hemp are grown legally by licensed farms, which are closely controlled and guarded. The Cabinet of Ministers' approved such cultivation in late 1997. Despite the prohibition on the cultivation of drug plants (poppy straw and hemp), by 2003 over 5,000 cases of illegal cultivation by private households had been discovered.

Counternarcotics enforcement responsibility is given to the MIA, the State Security Service (SBU), the State Customs Service, and the Border Guards. The Drug Enforcement Department, an independent department within the MIA, reports directly to the minister of interior and is staffed by 1,725 personnel.

Corruption remains a major problem. Corruption in Ukraine is rarely linked with narcotics, although it decreases the effectiveness of efforts to combat organized crime, a major factor in the narcotics business. There were no prosecutions in 2003 on any charges of corruption of public officials relating to drugs. There were several cases of prison guards smuggling drugs into prisons. To combat corruption, the Ukrainian government has adopted an extensive set of laws and decrees. At the beginning of 2001 the government approved a national plan of action to combat corruption, but progress in implementation has been slow.

The number of officially registered drug addicts now exceeds 200,000, including over 4,000 teenagers, with over 18,000 new registrations in 2003. Sixty-eight percent of registered drug users are under thirty years of age, nearly 25 percent are women, and over 78 percent are unemployed.

Estimates of unregistered drug abusers vary widely, up to 1 million reported by local nongovernmental organizations. About 15,000 criminal offenses are committed annually by drug addicts. Drug addiction results in more than 1,000 deaths every year, according to officials. Marijuana and hashish continue to gain popularity with young people. Nevertheless, opium straw extract remains the main drug of choice for Ukraine addicts. Young people are using synthetic drugs more frequently, such as ephedrine, ecstasy, LSD, amphetamines, and methamphetamines. Hard drugs such as cocaine and heroin are still too expensive for most Ukrainian drug users, but there is a rise in heroin use because of the continued decrease in price. Efforts to combat narcotics continue to be hampered by a lack of resources (e.g., financing, personnel, and equipment).

Organized Crime. In 2003 special units combating organized crime revealed 634 organized groups and criminal organizations, which consist of 2,700 members who committed 6,200 crimes, including 60 murders and assassinations, 177 robberies, 455 armed robberies, and 1,400 thefts and burglaries. Fifty-three armed groups were eliminated. For comparison, in 2000, the activity of 960 criminal organized groups was stopped. These groups included 4,000 members that committed 7,700 crimes. In 2002 the Internal Affairs agencies eliminated 722 organized crime groups that committed 6,000 crimes.

In 2003 police determined the involvement of members of organized groups in the commission of 167 crimes connected with illegal weapons trafficking, 665 in drug trafficking, and 39 in money laundering. One thousand five hundred active participants and leaders of criminal groups were sentenced to prison.

The most dangerous element of the crime phenomenon is corruption and the strong cooperation among former Communist Party elite, members of the law enforcement and security apparatuses, and gangs of organized criminals. Much crime combines government officials' access to information or goods with the use or threat of force by organized criminals. The country's privatization program, for example, was undermined by former party officials and a criminal elite that appropriated state resources by stripping assets from banks and enterprises.

Drug traffickers, as well as other domestic and foreign crime groups, launder money through casinos, exchange bureaus, and the banks. And banks provide criminal groups with information about businesses' profitability and assets, which they use to extort money from them. Criminals and public officials often collude in this effort. Criminals, for example, extort money from businesses by threatening to sell the information they illegally obtain from banks to the tax police. Tax officials are sometimes willing to share their information about businesses with crime groups in return for a share of the money they extort from businesses.

Public officials in Ukraine are poorly paid and face many opportunities to benefit from their positions. Business activities are regulated by as many as 32 laws, about 30 presidential decrees, and more than 80 resolutions; 32 ministries and departments have the right to issue licenses for various activities. At the same time, taxes are high, creating incentives for businesses to pay off officials rather than pay taxes. A number of parliamentary deputies oppose tax cuts for fear that they will tempt many private firms out of the shadow economy, thus eliminating lucrative corruption-related opportunities for themselves.

The infiltration of the national and local legislatures by criminals has become a serious problem. In 2003 more than twenty members of Parliament could have been tried on criminal charges if they had been stripped of their parliamentary immunity. Forty-four legislators, elected to local political bodies, also had criminal backgrounds.

Trafficking in People. The law prohibits trafficking in people; however, trafficking in men, women, and girls is a significant problem. There are reports that some local officials are involved in trafficking.

The criminal code imposes firm penalties for trafficking in human beings, including for sexual exploitation and pornography. Article 149 mandates three to eight years in prison for trafficking. Under some circumstances—for example, trafficking of minors or groups of victims—traffickers may be sentenced to five to twelve years in prison, and traffickers of minors or members of organized trafficking groups may be sentenced to terms from eight to fifteen years.

According to the Ministry of Interior, 289 cases were filed against traffickers during 2003, up from 169 in 2002. Since 1998 a total of 604 criminal trafficking cases have been filed; these did not include cases opened under other applicable laws, such as brothel keeping, organized crime, and fraud. During the first six months of 2003, 33 cases were prosecuted, with 15 cases fully concluded. Of these cases, 13 resulted in convictions and 20 defendants were sentenced.

Trafficking is a national priority for law enforcement agencies, but these agencies often lack the financial and personnel resources to combat well-established criminal organizations that run trafficking operations. The MIA established special antitrafficking units at the national and oblast levels. These units became operational in 2000 and have had a growing impact, although they have suffered from lack of adequate resources and often are tasked to work on cases involving other crimes.

Police efforts have been hampered by a number of factors, including insufficient investigative resources, the reluctance of victims to give evidence against traffickers, and, in some cases, a lack of cooperation from officials in destination countries. The law permits the extradition of foreign nationals charged with trafficking when appropriate bilateral agreements with the country in question have been signed, when the crime was committed within the jurisdiction of another country, and when trafficking is a crime under the laws of the requesting country; however, there have been no cases of extradition of trafficking suspects. The constitution prohibits the extradition of citizens.

Ukraine is a major country of origin and transit for women and girls trafficked abroad for sexual exploitation. There are reports of men and boys being trafficked abroad primarily for labor purposes; however, the overwhelming majority of trafficking victims are women. No reliable figures are available on the extent of the problem, and estimates vary widely. There are reports that individual government employees (both law enforcement and other personnel such as orphanage employees) facilitate trafficking in people. It has been estimated that 420,000 women had been trafficked abroad between 1991 and 1998. Another estimate says that in 2003 between 8,000 and 10,000 individuals were trafficked abroad during the year.

Women and girls are trafficked to central and western Europe (including the Balkans, Austria, Italy, France, Germany, Switzerland, the Czech Republic, Hungary, Portugal, Spain, Poland, Greece, and Turkey), the United States, and the Middle East (including Israel, Lebanon, and the United Arab Emirates) for sexual exploitation. There are also reports that women and girls are trafficked to Australia, Japan, and South Africa.

Women who are trafficked out of the country are often recruited by firms operating abroad and subsequently are taken out of the country with legal documentation. They are solicited with promises of work as waitresses, dancers, or housemaids, or are invited by marriage agencies allegedly to make the acquaintance of a potential bridegroom. Once abroad, the women find the work to be different from what was represented to them initially. There are credible reports of widespread involvement of organized crime in trafficking.

Men are trafficked for agricultural labor and factory work. The main destination countries are Hungary, Poland, the Czech Republic, Slovenia, Russia, and western Europe. Men are promised reasonable wages, but are not paid and are frequently turned over to the police in the destination countries as illegal aliens if they complain. The Ministry of the Interior opens criminal cases against the employment agencies who organize the trafficking when it has a specific complaint from a victim.

There are unconfirmed reports that local officials abet or assist organized crime groups involved in trafficking. Nongovernmental organizations report that local militia and border guards receive bribes in return for ignoring trafficking. Some reports allege that local public officials abet or assist organized criminal groups in trafficking women abroad. In a 1999 report the United Nations Development Program identified graft of officials and political corruption as two of the factors causing the spread of trafficking and prostitution; however, data on the possible disciplining or prosecution of law enforcement and border control authorities for their involvement in trafficking was unavailable.

Although 278 victims testified against traffickers during 2003, victims were often reluctant to seek legal action against traffickers out of fear of reprisals or unwillingness to tell their stories publicly. Societal attitudes toward trafficking victims are often harsh, deterring women from pursuing legal action against traffickers. In addition, law enforcement officials do not provide sufficient protection to witnesses to encourage them to testify against traffickers, and traffickers are able to intimidate victims to withdraw or change their testimony. A witness protection law existed but was not fully effective because of shortages of funding. Under the law, names and addresses of victims of crimes may be kept confidential if they request protection because of fear for their lives.

CORRECTIONAL SYSTEM

Prisons fall under the direction of the Ministry of Justice.

Prison Conditions. Prison conditions in Ukraine remain harsh. Men and women are held in separate facilities, and juveniles are held separately from adults. Additionally, pretrial detainees are always held separately from convicted prisoners. In theory, regulations require more space

and some special accommodations, such as bathtubs, for women; however, in practice conditions are equally poor for men and women in both pretrial detention centers and regular prisons. The average space provided is just over 21 square feet per man and nearly 27 square feet per woman or juvenile. The law does not recognize political prisoners as a separate category of detainee.

Although information on the physical state of prison walls and fences as well as on pretrial detention blocks is officially considered to be a government secret, the press reports freely about harsh prison conditions. Due in part to severe economic conditions, prisons and detention centers are overcrowded and lack adequate sanitation and medical facilities. In 2003 almost 25,000 individuals were reportedly held in prison cells with neither windows nor toilets. In the Zhytomyr region funds earmarked to improve food standards for prisoners were misallocated. This is but a small example in a correctional system that is rife with corruption, misuse of positions by officials, and human rights abuses. As little as one hryvnia (approximately 20 U.S. cents) per day is spent to feed a single prisoner in some pretrial detention centers.

In one case it was reported that the European Court of Human Rights (ECHR) requested that the government pay from 5,300 to 15,900 hryvnia (US$1,000 to US$3,000) to six citizens who had been in inhumane conditions in prisons before their death sentences were commuted to life imprisonment. Additionally, the ECHR found that some inmates were denied the right to worship in some prisons.

Prisoners are permitted to file complaints with the ombudsman about the conditions of detention, but human rights groups report that they are punished for doing so. A member of the legislature told the human rights ombudsman that when he was an inmate, prison guards beat him with clubs and harassed him and other prisoners in the facility where he was detained in 2002. He stated that guards deprived complaining prisoners of correspondence and food packages. Conditions in pretrial detention facilities are also harsh. Inmates are sometimes held in investigative isolation for extended periods and are subjected to intimidation and mistreatment by jail guards and other inmates.

Overcrowding is common in these centers. The total capacity of these facilities is 36,000, but approximately 40,633 detainees were held in them as of November 2003. In April 2003 officials announced that the State Security Service had closed its pretrial detention centers. Prison officials confirmed that all pretrial detainees were subsequently transferred to its facilities.

Conditions in the Corrective Labor and Treatment Centers for Alcoholics (LTPs), operated by the State Penal Department, where violent alcoholics are confined forcibly by court decision, differ little from those in prisons. The government does not meet its earlier commitment to transfer all the LTPs to the Ministry of Health. Virtually no treatment for alcoholism is available in these centers. Despite a government decree directing the closure of LTPs by the end of 2000, as of 2003 two such centers continued to operate under the auspices of the State Department for Execution of Punishments.

According to official statistics from the Penal Department, there were 696 deaths in prisons during 2003, and 130 deaths in pretrial facilities. Poor sanitary conditions resulted in 300 deaths from diseases such as tuberculosis and 13 from dysentery. On June 19, 2003, the Rada passed a resolution that expressed concern about the serious problem of tuberculosis in prisons. In 2003 it was reported that as many as 14,000 inmates were infected with an active form of tuberculosis. In addition, 1,000 prisoners die from tuberculosis annually, and approximately 3,000 fatally ill patients are granted early release and sent home to die.

According to human rights groups, a reorganization of the Penal Department to ensure greater independence of the penal system has not affected the department's practices, and there is little civilian oversight of its activities. Although the government has implemented some programs for the retraining of prison and police officials, it has punished only a small minority of those who committed or condoned violence against detainees and prisoners. According to prison authorities, no criminal proceedings involving torture or mistreatment of prisoners were opened during 2003 and no employee of the penitentiary system was disciplined for improper treatment of detainees. However, 15 criminal cases were opened against employees and 6,318 employees were disciplined for other, unspecified, reasons. The human rights ombudsman continues to draw attention to the state of the penitentiary system by visiting prisons and raising prison-related issues in public. Following a visit to a detention facility in Crimea, officials built a courtyard to provide inmates, who previously were unable to exercise out of doors, with an area where they could engage in physical activity. A new Criminal Penal Code was signed into law and is intended to regulate prison life and provide safeguards against the mistreatment of prisoners. The government continues to allow prison visits from human rights observers; however, some of them report that at times it is difficult to obtain access to prisons to visit specific prisoners and that they are not allowed full access to prison facilities.

Prison Statistics.

- Total Prison Population: 198,900

- Prison Population Rate per 100,000: 417 (based on an estimated national population of 3.21 million in 2003)

- Pretrial Detainees: 21.4%

- Female Prisoners: 5.9%

- Juveniles Prisoners: 2%

- Foreign Prisoners: 1.6%

- Number of Establishments: 180

- Official Capacity of Prison System: 223,140

- Occupancy Level: 89.2%

Recent prison population trend (year, prison population total, prison population rate per 100,000 of national population):

1993	129,500	(248)
1996	202,590	(395)
1999	206,000	(413)
2001	198,885	(406)

BIBLIOGRAPHY

Amnesty International. Available at http://www.amnesty.org (accessed January 12, 2006).

"Demoscope Weekly." 2004. *Population and Society*, nos. 147–148 (February 23–March 7). Available online at http://www.demoscope.ru/weekly/2004/0147/analit05.php (accessed January 12, 2006).

Human Rights Watch. Available online at http://www.hrw.org (accessed January 12, 2006).

Ministry of Internal Affairs of Ukraine. 2005. Available online at http://mvsinfo.gov.ua (accessed January 12, 2006).

Public Relations Center of Ministry of Internal Affairs of Ukraine. 2004. Available online at http://mvsinfo.gov.ua/official/2004/01/012904_1.html (accessed January 12, 2006).

"The Report to People of Ukraine (About Operative and Official Activity of Internal Affairs Bodies of Ukraine in 2000)." 2001. *Militia of Ukraine* (January).

Statute of Service of Private and Command Personnel of Internal Affairs Agencies of Ukraine, adopted by Decree of Cabinet of Ministers of USSR, July 29, 1991, with changes and amendments, 1992–2003.

"Ukraine: Concerns about Ill-Treatment of Prisoners." 2002. Human Rights Education Associates (October 9). Available online at http://www.hrea.org/lists/hr-headlines/markup/msg00654.html (accessed January 12, 2006).

"The Year Is Behind: Counteraction to Criminals Is More Severe and Mobile. The Report of Ministry of Internal Affairs to People of Ukraine." 2003. *Militia of Ukraine* (February).

Volodymyr Smelik
Joseph D. Serio

United Arab Emirates

Official country name: United Arab Emirates

Capital: Abu Dhabi

Geographic description: Southeastern corner of the Arabian Peninsula, where it juts into the Strait of Hormuz, between the Gulf of Oman and the Persian Gulf

Population: 2,563,212, including 1,606,079 non-nationals (est. 2005)

■■■

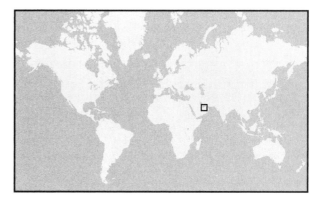

LAW ENFORCEMENT

History. Before 1971 the United Arab Emirates was a British protectorate known as the Trucial States. The police force was British in character, with a number of expatriate personnel. The Federal Police and security forces were authorized under the 1971 constitution and established by decree in 1974.

Structure and Organization. Each emirate has its own local police force. There is a Federal Police under the Ministry of the Interior, headed by a commissioner. The Federal Police is responsible for national security, administration, and nationwide and interemirate law enforcement, and addresses issues such as smuggling, terrorism, and counterfeiting. Local police forces are responsible for criminal investigation, traffic, and protection of public property. Law enforcement is essentially urban. In the hinterland, which is mostly desert, there is only limited police presence and then only periodically.

The Federal Police headquarters is in Abu Dhabi. It has a number of sections including administration,

criminal investigation, public security, and traffic. There is also an air wing with a number of helicopters.

Police Statistics.

- Total Police Personnel: 27,271

- Population per Police Officer: 94

HUMAN RIGHTS

Human rights are observed to a greater degree in the United Arab Emirates than in most Arab countries. However, there are serious problems because of the application of the repressive Sharia laws, the lack of democratic institutions and processes, and the absence of political parties and labor unions. In 2002 the Dubai Police established a Human Rights Department that conducts training courses for its members.

CRIME STATISTICS

Offenses reported to the police per 100,000 population: 2,604. Of which:

- Murder: 3
- Assault: 10.1
- Burglary: 5.1
- Automobile Theft: 23

CORRECTIONAL SYSTEM

Prisons are administered by a director of prisons under the Ministry of Interior. There are prisons in each emirate and a central prison in Abu Dhabi.

Prison Conditions. Prison conditions generally meet international standards, although conditions vary widely from emirate to emirate. Human rights observers are permitted to visit prisons. However, all of Abu Dhabi's prisons are overcrowded. Men and women, pretrial detainees and hardened criminals, and juveniles and adults are housed separately. Political and security prisoners face harsher conditions when they are transferred to the State Security Agency. At times, bureaucratic delays in processing and releasing prisoners result in detainees serving time beyond their original sentences.

Prison Statistics. The total prison population is 6,000, with an incarceration rate of 250 per 100,000 population. Of the inmates, 42 percent are pretrial detainees. The prison population is also heavily foreign, reflecting the preponderance of foreigners in the population.

George Thomas Kurian

United Kingdom

Official country name: United Kingdom of Great Britain and Northern Ireland
Capital: London
Geographic description: Located in western Europe, islands include the northern one-sixth of the island of Ireland between the North Atlantic Ocean and the North Sea, northwest of France
Population: 60,441,457 (est. 2005)

■■■

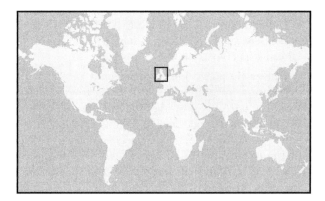

LAW ENFORCEMENT

History. It was between 600 to 1400 in England that Anglo-Saxon laws were written down. Laws were described as "the aggressive weapon of a new state" and remedy for wrongdoing was recognized as legitimately a matter of enforcement by the victim and his or her kin. Formal justice therefore took over from the previous system of private revenge or blood feud. Laws laid down the requirement that local communities must pursue criminals and offenders and deliver them to the royal courts; this was their public duty, in fact, harboring criminals was a serious offense punishable by death. This is the first true example of community policing. After the successful invasion of England in 1066, the king began to raise revenues from administering the criminal justice system by the imposition of fines and compensation. The mission statement of the Crown was to "promote the spiritual welfare of the people through the use of force against evil-doers," which was an early form of "to serve and protect."

In the twelfth century greater emphasis was placed on the role of the community and its accountability to the king through the system of "frankpledge," the local "watch," the "hue and cry," and the judgment of outlawry. Frankpledge, an oath of loyalty to the king, was the obligation of all citizens to pursue offenders and ensure the good behavior of other members of the community. Subsequently, sheriffs were appointed in counties as the first law officers to coordinate criminal cases and arrest suspects; they could also call out the *posse comitatus*, which consisted of all adult males, against "vagabonds and malefactors." The powers of sheriffs were then superseded by the appointment of other law officers such as coroners and sergeants of the peace. Laws of 1233 to 1285 obliged every town, borough, and city to set up a watch each night during the summer to arrest strangers and pursue those who sought to flee. "Constables of castle" were appointed by the Crown, but "constables" in towns were elected annually by the community they served. Constables had a range of military, policing, and revenue functions; these were the first police patrols. Other legal entities within towns and cities were the bailiffs and beadles, who had duties to exact fines, execute warrants, and deal with orphaned or foundling children.

Because of the social, health, and political problems of the thirteenth and fourteenth centuries, communal policing began to be replaced by a substantial body of appointed legal officers. In the mid-fourteenth century the justice of the peace role was created to deal with civil and criminal disputes and offenses; from this time until 1600 the roles of constable and justice of the peace evolved into the role they perform today. From 1600 many criminal law statutes were passed by the legislature, but it was not until the 1750s that the police first had real investigatory and crime prevention functions. At that time in London, Henry Fielding started the Bow Street runners that gained the reputation of expert thief takers.

In 1822 Robert Peel was appointed home secretary and the celebrated "general instructions" were written for the Metropolitan Police Service formed by the Metropolitan Police Act 1829. This period is recognized as the equivalent of the "industrial revolution" in the police service; it signaled the start of policing in the United Kingdom as we know it today.

Borough police forces commenced in 1835 and started rural policing in 1839. Policing from that time went on unchanged to the 1960s, when changes in society required a fundamental rethinking in operational policing. A Royal Commission was completed in 1960 that resulted in the Police Act of 1964. Transportation, organization, command, and control of the police service was changed forever and the fond image of the "bobby on the beat" was erased from reality.

Policing became more scientific and managed, leading to the temporarily popular "managing objectives" to the "managerialism" or increased focus on outputs and outcomes that are experienced today in policing and other public service organizations in the United Kingdom.

From the 1980s to the present day the police in the United Kingdom have become increasingly politicized. One can identify this through the approach taken to dealing with major incidents of public disorder (e.g., the miners' strikes through the 1980s) and attempts to articulate police professional standards and ethical principles, such as the Metropolitan Police Principles and the Association of Chief Police Officers' Statement of Common Purpose and Values of 1985 and 1992, respectively.

During the 1990s there were several high-profile examples of corruption and police incompetence. This led to a new focus and need for examination of policing principles and ethics. Several books were published to open up debate on the subject, which questioned why ethics are important and identified the ideal ethical police service.

In Europe several models of policing have emerged over the last two centuries. Most are described as democratic policing systems, but they move from the extreme of locally appointed, locally accountable systems such as those introduced in Belgium, to the locally appointed but centrally accountable in the United Kingdom, to the quasi military, centralized system in France and other European States.

There is a continuum between the cohesion of society and the model of policing that is appropriate for that society. To achieve greater accessibility of the police and interaction in the community, it is necessary to have readiness and understanding from the community that it will have to participate in its policing. The "best practice" model to establish a system of democratic policing in any country is thought to be the "tripartite" system, whereby accountability is separated by having the three pillars of governance: legislature, executive, and judiciary. This formula has been found to establish the necessary checks and balances in civil society to ensure that crime is punished and that the rights of individuals are respected.

Policing in the United Kingdom has been furthered by the introduction of rights-based law in the shape of the Human Rights Act of 1998 and other developments such as the new Oath of Office for police officers that incorporates a statement on human rights. The deployment and description of local and special police services in the United Kingdom are described in other sections of this entry, along with the impact of human rights law.

Structure and Organization. Administered centrally by the Home Department (or Home Office) of the UK government, the police service is organized on a local basis; thus, there are forty-four separate police forces in England, Wales, and Northern Ireland and eight in Scotland. There are also non–Home Office police forces with a national remit, focusing on specific areas of responsibility such as British Transport Police and Ministry of Defense Police. The total police strength is approximately 150,000 with additional support staff of 64,000. Each police force is divided into basic command units (BCUs), with about 200 to 300 police officers in each. There are approximately 400 BCUs in England and Wales.

There is a debate about changes brought about in the police service and the "police reform agenda," as it has been called, by the Labour government of Prime Minister Tony Blair. Following a general decline in confidence in the police, their overall effectiveness in dealing with incidents, and the emphasis of the Blair government on "new public management" and improving the quality of public services, changes have been brought in to make policing more effective and better "value for money."

Add to this a general dissatisfaction with police and the suspicion that internal discipline investigations are not being carried out to the satisfaction of complainants, the police reform agenda was carried through by the government by the provisions on the Police Reform Act 2002.

Various studies have been completed to pinpoint the key issues and sources of dissatisfaction with the UK police service. The Police Reform Act requires police forces to compile action plans to address the key issues and demonstrate their ability to continuously improve their performance. An additional agency, the Policing Standards Unit, was formed to inspect forces and work with them to identify and disseminate best practice and good performance.

Main Types of Policing in the United Kingdom. The police service in the United Kingdom undertakes all types of policing within the areas described earlier; therefore, there is no National Guard or Compagnie Républicaine de Sécurité type of organization as in the United States and France, respectively. Thus, a police officer might one day be completing community policing type of duties dressed in traditional police uniform and the next dealing with public disorder and wearing riot gear. Typically, police forces will be organized into specialist police functions with a number of officers delegated to traffic patrol and others to criminal investigation duties.

It is general knowledge that all police officers start at the bottom and work their way up the organization; there is no "direct entry." Therefore, the initial job description is the same for every entrant. Actually, the police service is probably the only job where the lowest level operative (constable) has more power and discretion than the person at the top of the organization (chief constable). As mentioned earlier, the office of constable is an ancient one in the United Kingdom.

UK National and International Policing Bodies. National policing organizations have been introduced to counter the global threat and reach of crime and to deal with organized and international crime. Such bodies as the National Crime Intelligence Service and the National Crime Squad dealing with cross-border, national, and international crime have been introduced. Also, other national functions such as the Police Information Technology Organization and the Police Standards and Skills Organization (PSSO) deal with information technology and continuous development. Centrex delivers police training on a national scale and the Police National Legal

Database assists forces to track legal issues. There are also international policing operations such as Interpol, Europol, and other international interfaces.

Local Police. Most police forces in the United Kingdom base their approach toward some form of community policing. The deployment of police officers throughout the country is on a localized basis, roughly on a county level per police force, although there are several metropolitan forces not compliant with county boundaries and several amalgamated forces covering several counties. Therefore, every town and even village may have its complement of police officers that look after local problems and issues and liaise directly with the local populace.

How the local police forces operationalize their brand of community policing is a matter for each chief constable and a good example of this is that of the West Mercia Constabulary, which has the four tracks of policing: local policing; responsive policing; policing partnerships, and targeted policing. Responsive policing is responding to emergencies and incidents. Policing partnerships are where the police link to other agencies and organizations to effect policing solutions. Targeted policing is the intelligence-led and targeted policing described earlier.

During the last century various changes were made to the governance and accountability of the police service. The changes culminated in the provisions of the Police and Magistrates' Courts Act 1994, which continued the principle of police authorities being a major part of the tripartite governance of the police service. This arrangement described the roles and responsibilities of the chief constable as the head of a local police force, the police authority, and its members, part appointed by government and part locally elected members, and the home secretary. The chief constable has sole operational command of the police force and no one can interfere with this operational independence. However, the police authority has political accountability and responsibility to the people of the area it serves and therefore holds the chief constable to account for performance and the quality of the police service. The home secretary sets national objectives and compiles a national policing plan that chief constables must take account of in their own Force Annual Policing plans. The chief constable has a statutory responsibility to report on the outcomes of the policing plan yearly. One aspect of the police reform agenda is that chief constables will be held to personal account on the performance of the police force under their command. In the worst case a chief constable could be replaced by the home secretary and interim managers placed in charge while the performance is improved to acceptable levels. The police authority also have controls over certain aspects of the funding of police forces.

Special Police.

Riot Police. As mentioned in a previous section in this entry, the UK police service does not have a separate organization of police officers that deal with public disorder or riots. When such incidents occur, police officers who normally fulfill everyday policing duties and have received special training are brought together to deal with such incidents. The police officers wear special protective clothing and equipment.

Emergency Services. In the United Kingdom there is a system of "integrated emergency management," which is fully covered by policies, practices, and procedures and is understood by all the emergency services: police; fire and rescue services; ambulance services and hospitals; and county/local council emergency planning units. The emergency services also have a responsibility to put into place plans for a response and contingencies in case of disasters of civil emergencies.

This system stems for the declaration of a major incident, which is a defined term. All the emergency services work together seamlessly and the overall efforts are coordinated by the police service.

In terms of the national picture there is the Civil Contingencies Secretariat that can coordinate efforts nationwide and link to government committees in crises.

The integrated emergency management system in the United Kingdom also governs the response to major and critical incidents through strategic, tactical, and operational levels. These are designated as gold, silver, and bronze levels, respectively, across all the emergency services. This methodology ensures common understanding, cohesion, coordination, and proper linkage and liaison between all emergency services and the three delivery levels. Therefore, there is a recognized and planned structure for the management of the incident and the incident command.

The integrated emergency management system has been used to good effect in many major and critical incidents that have occurred in the United Kingdom.

Mutual Aid Arrangements. The mutual aid arrangements between police forces in the United Kingdom exist for forces to support each other in times of emergency or need. The senior management in one police force, when planning for a major policing operation or during a major incident, will call on a neighboring police force to send reinforcements to assist. During times of national turmoil such as major industrial disputes the mutual aid requirement has covered the whole country. Also, in times of dire emergency the civil police may call on the military to assist, although this contingency is as a last resort and is hedged with caveats.

Education and Training.

Recruitment into the Police Service. There have been national political moves in the United Kingdom, through the "police reform agenda," to increase the number of police officers and police staff to address crime and disorder problems.

Despite national demographic data on the dwindling target population for police recruits, more people are applying to join the police service. However, the numbers of people applying from ethnic minority backgrounds is still not enough to truly reflect the makeup of society in general.

Diversity Issues. The police service has learned some hard lessons from the omission of recruitment and selection of ethnic minority police officers. Following the report by William Macpherson (1999) into the racist murder of Stephen Lawrence, the home secretary set up a task force to develop an action plan aimed at stamping out "institutional racism" in the UK police service. This included setting targets for individual police forces to achieve in the recruitment of ethnic minority recruits. In practice, the recruitment of police officers does not reflect the ethnic diversity that exists in the population of the country. There are also plans to retain, develop, progress, and promote ethnic minority officers. The Fourth Annual Report on Progress arising out of the Stephen Lawrence inquiry was published in March 2003; it said that community and race relations (CRR) training remains crucial in developing trust and confidence in ethnic minority communities. Proposals were put forward in the report for a future strategy for CRR training in the police sector.

Educational Standards of Police Officers. Society in general is changing and police officers must reflect their society; a society that is changing to an "information society"—one where citizens are literate in communication, reading, writing, and oral skills. Also, police officers must be able to understand information they receive and operate complex machinery such as computers and radios and drive automobiles in an exemplary fashion. This issue is demonstrated strongly in the detailed requirements stated in the PSSO Skills Foresight Report.

In setting exacting personal and professional standards for recruits into the police service, there is a question as to the educational standards required. The United Kingdom lags behind the United States in demanding high educational standards for law enforcement officers. The situation in the United Kingdom on education standards of police officers will be rectified by the introduction of common minimum standards, a competency framework, and standards protected by a national training strategy.

Police Service Practices on Assessment and Development Centers. In the 1990s promotion and selection centers were introduced in the police service to the Bramshill model. This model assumes that all people administering and assessing in the assessment center have been trained to a minimum standard set by the police service itself. This has the benefit of standardizing procedures and maintaining acceptable standards; it has the disadvantage of perpetuating a system that may not be delivering a quality product—that is, the right quality recruit or manager. The other disadvantage it has is that it is a pass-fail system and applicant candidates only know if they are successful after the assessment center.

Development Centers. Development centers are similar in nature to the assessment centers in wide usage throughout the police service for the purposes of selection and promotion. Exercises and competency-based interviews must still be properly validated and assessed against the National Competancy Framework (NCF) using trained assessors to ensure quality standards. Also, because sensitivity and openness are so important in the development process, only specially trained and selected individuals should give feedback to candidates.

Extended Police Family. In line with the police reform agenda it was recognized that policing was a community-based activity that should involve all sections of society. To be activated, an extended police family was recognized so that the community can truly be involved in its own policing through community-based projects and organizations. Also, a new type of patrol officer, the community support officer, was born. This type of officer has limited police powers and functions to patrol towns and cities on foot and to interact with communities and achieve public reassurance to lower the fear of crime.

Code of Conduct. The Code of Conduct introduced under the Police Act 1996 is aspirational in character as opposed to a punitive format. The headings of the code, which commenced operation on April 1, 1999, are as follows:

Promotion. Promotion in the UK police service is purely "through the ranks"; thus, all senior police officers have to start "at the bottom" of the organization and work their way up. There are promotion examinations to reach the ranks of sergeant and inspector and promotions are only ratified to these ranks after some form of interview. Increasingly, interviews are becoming competence-based interviews linking skills and abilities to the police

NCF. After the rank of inspector, some police forces require successful completion of an assessment center, again competence based, and others require an interview or both.

Issues in Police Training. Over the years there have been several examinations of police training in the United Kingdom, such as Her Majesty's Inspectorate of Constabulary (1999a), the Stubbs Report, and the home secretary's conclusions. Finally, there were the training needs identified by the police reform agenda that were linked to the work of the PSSO, the NCF, and the National Occupational Standards (NOS).

In the late twentieth century it was recognized that the existing police training system was not working effectively and that new models of delivery would be necessary. This led to many suggestions including a "virtual university" and a policing institute and forming a police national training organization (NTO), which would produce a competency framework and be the guardian of training standards. In fact, none of these suggestions was finally realized, although a fundamental review of police training was completed with the NTO, which achieved an agency status—Centrex—as a training provider and the formation of the PSSO as the organization to complete the work on the NOS and NCF.

The NTO did not materialize, but the police service joined with the criminal justice sector to form one NTO. The five strategic aims of an NTO are:

- Raising strategic capability

- Improving competitiveness

- Giving advice on training and education

- Qualifying the workforce

- Developing effective partnerships

The report *Managing Learning: A Study of Police Training* (Her Majesty's Inspectorate of Constabulary 1999a) also proposed that it was good practice to foster partnership arrangements for training delivery between police forces, local colleges, and institutes of higher education. It was also suggested that the tripartite partners (the Association of Chief Police Officers [ACPO], the Home Office, and the Association of Public Authorities) join with Centrex to develop training programs that could include participants from nonpolice organizations. In addition, the report suggested that not all police forces were effectively linking training and development to training needs analyses and force performance plans. This led to a system of accreditation of local police training schools by Centrex in terms of the quality of training delivered and the quality and expertise of their trainers.

The Stubbs Report recommended that there should be a police NTO, that NOS and an NCF be developed, and that training should be subject to cost-benefit analysis. It also recommended links to local training delivery providers such as colleges and that police forces should deliver specialist training more regionally or in "clusters." A training inspectorate was called for (now in place) and said that there should be changes to the funding arrangements, whereby the client police force could choose the training provider to deliver the training, either internally or externally.

Finally, the home secretary concluded the debate by summarizing all the recommendations into one strategy containing the following elements:

- A central police college
- Reorganized Police Training Council (strategic body)
- A police NTO
- A mandatory core curriculum for basic police courses
- A mandatory qualification framework (NCF)
- Greater regional collaboration
- Joint learning and community involvement
- Annual training plans and staff development plans
- Dedicated training units at local, regional, and national levels

Following on from this, and included in the police reform agenda of the early twenty-first century, the Police Reform Act added the following aspects to police training:

- Making high-quality lifelong learning opportunities to all staff at all stages of their career
- Raising professional standards
- Meeting the training needs of police officers and support staff efficiently and effectively and with increased flexibility of delivery
- Gaining the best value from the investment in police training

Clearly, police training had made some large steps forward in its development, but it was not finished. The PSSO was rapidly developing the NCF and the NOS and was seeking to "professionalize" the police through a system of continuous professional development. It stated, "It is clear from numerous reports on the subject of leadership and management in the Police Service that standards need to be raised.... We cannot leave the emergence of skilled and effective police leaders and managers to chance, expecting them to evolve their own style. The Police Service must make management and leadership a key development area."

Word from Her Majesty's Inspectorate of Constabulary. Her Majesty's Inspectorate of Constabulary reports *Managing Learning* (1999a) and *Training Matters* laid down the following key elements of police sector training and development:

- There must be a clear link between policing plans and training
- Learning requirements must be articulated
- Training and learning must be based on competence and outcomes
- There must be a link to external qualifications and opportunities for progression
- Investment must be on the basis of plans, exploiting all available sources
- There should be a comprehensive and coherent police system across the United Kingdom
- Training and development must be customer focused and employer led

Police National Competency Framework. The United Kingdom has introduced a nationally accepted police national competency framework. The PSSO, operating as an agency of the Home Office, has put the framework together for every rank and role in the police service, plus desired competencies for police support staff. This has proved to be a massive task but as of 2003 it was coming to fruition. A whole framework for general police work has been published and work is continuing on competencies for specialist roles. Police support staff have not been forgotten and a competency framework is also being produced for all levels of civilian staff. The NCF is delivered at three different levels (A, B, and C) according to the rank structure, with more complex and "strategic" behaviors being required at the higher C-graded management levels. The NCF comprises:

- A Behavioral Competency Framework
- A library of activities that includes knowledge and skills
- Thirty-three role profiles
- Six rank profiles
- A professional development review (PDR) process that uses the previously mentioned elements

The purpose of the NCF is to enable performance to be measured against clear standards and thereby allow "performance management" and personal development to take place. The eventual aim is to further professionalize the police service in the United Kingdom. The short-term aim of the NCF is to develop a generic framework to support an integrated human resource strategy for the purpose of improving operational performance by setting national standards for police officers and police staff. The PSSO is now working on the development of the NOS, which will build on the work of the NCF with occupational standards underpinning an activities library.

The Behavioral Competency Framework contains:

- Twelve behavioral competencies in three areas of leadership, working with others, and achieving results
- Each competency has a title, an overall definition, and two or three categories; research indicates the number of categories appropriate in each behavioral competency
- Each category represents a different complexity; for example, strategic perspective means something different to a constable and crime analyst than it does a chief constable, and the categories reflect this
- Each category has a definition and a number of positive behavioral indicators attached to it
- Each of the twelve behaviors has a set of negative indicators; these indicators remain the same at each category within the behavior

Research was conducted to ascertain the main tasks, responsibilities, functions, knowledge, and skills of police employees. This information was then used to build activity libraries—actual tasks carried out by the practitioners.

Each activity includes:

- An activity title with a qualitative statement that defines the professional standard required for effective performance
- A description of what effective performance looks like or what an individual actual does when performing effectively
- A description of the knowledge and skills required for effective performance of the activity, which could enhance the individual's effectiveness

Rank and role profiles can then be constructed for every member of the staff, such as for the dog handler constable.

Professionalism. Many times in the history of policing it has been said that police officers should become professionals. One definition suggests that a profession is a group that has the following characteristics:

- Possession of a body of systematic knowledge
- A commitment to the client

- An occupational association that grants rights to practice
- Exclusive entry based recognized credentials

As of 2003 the police service did not fit the criteria for a profession, but based on the stated intentions of the PSSO, it is working toward this status. In terms of a narrower view of professionalism, there is now a set of NOS and NCF in place; this is a start on the process. In addition, senior investigating officers have been appointed and accreditation of this role, along with the necessity to comply with continuous professional development, has been applied. There has also been the introduction of the National Crime Faculty and the Operations Faculty, located at Bramshill Police Staff College, building up the "body of knowledge" to advise police officers in the field on best practices of spontaneous policing operations.

Long-Term View from the PSSO. Clearly, in the long term it will be beneficial to the police service to have a well-trained and professional workforce. This should also lead to police officers having greater credibility and standing in the community.

Self-Development of Staff. Historically, police officers and support staff have not taken responsibility for their own self-development and have accepted training provided by the organization to assist their development. Critics believe this situation must change, whereby police staff take responsibility for their own self-development. The critics state that this is a necessity in any professional post, especially where the policies, practices, and procedures change at an ever-increasing speed. A number of publications have underlined other implications such as the increasing complexity and technological changes in policing.

Also a necessity in all professions, such as the medical and legal professions, is the requirement to complete continuous professional development (CPD) to maintain appropriate levels of knowledge and understanding within the context. Failure to complete CPD results in removal of the practitioner's name from the professional roll and results in the inability to practice. CPD programs should aid achievement of operational objectives and police force strategies and be in accordance with Investors in People requirements.

Professional Development Review. A wide range of views exist among police forces about appraisals and performance management systems, reflecting the difficulty in producing one agreed on approach. However, the following PDR system was agreed on in 1999 with the following parameters:

- The primary purpose is to improve performance
- It should use the NCF

- It is preferable to assess actual performance in a specific role, not just capability or behaviors

- The "point in time" writing process must be time efficient and unbureaucratic as possible

- It should be development focused but based on performance

The PDR process is therefore the national approach in the police service to fulfill the roles of annual appraisals, the performance management delivery process, the starting point for decisions relating to selection for post and promotion, and the method of assessing the performance of individuals who qualify for enhanced performance payments.

Delivery of Police Training. Police training is now delivered in a variety of ways, through:

- Centrex, the national police training organization

- Regional and national police training schools for specialist skills

- Each police force training school for local and general police skills

- External training providers

- Alternative learning strategies, such as open learning, online learning, e-learning

HUMAN RIGHTS

Human Rights Act 1998. One of the major commitments in the political manifesto of the Labour government, before they were voted into power in 1997, was that of the introduction of legislation to promote human rights and thus the Human Rights Act 1998 (HRA) was introduced. Previously, there had been no written "bill of rights" and, as a result, the rights and freedoms of individuals were not recognized or positively enforced. One of the objectives of the HRA was to introduce a written catalog of the minimum standards of human rights and freedoms in the nation. Once citizens knew and understood their fundamental rights and freedoms, they could be acknowledged and positively protected and enforced by regulatory agencies such as the police service. The HRA therefore merely adopted a number of articles and protocols from the European Convention on Human Rights (ECHR).

Does Human Rights Legislation Affect Operational Policing? Many people ask how human rights legislation affects operational policing and support functions. Every time a police officer or support staff member of the police service makes a decision, a person's rights may be affected. Every time a police officer uses bodily force, a power of arrest, search, seizure, surveillance, or interrogation methods another person's rights are affected; therefore, the police officer has to consider the use of that power and might have to justify its use in any subsequent legal proceedings. Every time a support staff member responds to inquiries or requests for assistance by telephone at the front counter or by other means of communication, he or she might infringe on another person's human rights; therefore, he or she needs to consider the provisions of the HRA.

Decision Making. When discretion is used in the operation of police powers, policies, or procedures or decisions are made to grant or not grant licenses and authorizations, where the rights of an individual or organization are affected, fairness in making decisions is paramount. There is now a greater emphasis on recording decisions, the rationale for making the decision, and the reasons other solutions and options were rejected. Police officers are asked by courts to justify their decision making and the use of discretion. In addition, there is an increased emphasis on audit and independent scrutiny of police actions; therefore, police officers need to scrupulously keep adequate and contemporaneous records of their decisions.

Contents of the Articles. The ECHR was written after World War II to establish peace and understanding in Europe. It covers all areas of civil liberties and freedom that could be expected to exist in democratic countries. A written bill of rights did not exist in the United Kingdom before the HRA. Legal practitioners did not see a need to formally document rights because they were implied in the English legal system.

European Convention on Human Rights. Human rights and freedoms are not foreign to jurisprudence in the United Kingdom; indeed, they are integral and a comfortable fit within the legal and law enforcement systems. It was British lawyers following World War II who, in fact, drew up the provisions of the ECHR and the text of the convention was adopted in 1950. The UK government formally ratified the convention in March 1951, but the articles were not assimilated into the English or Scottish legal system until the HRA. The first process on introduction was to test existing UK legislation for compliance against the European standard.

Police Ethics. This subject is examined in much greater depth in Peter Neyroud and Alan Beckley's *Policing, Ethics, and Human Rights* (2001). There is no servicewide accepted comprehensive document that contains a statement on ethics in policing in England and Wales. However, there are several documents that are akin to ethical codes, such as the Oath of Office of Constable, the Statement of Common Purpose and Values, and the "aspirational" Code of Conduct introduced on April 1, 1999, by the Police Act of 1996 contained in the Police Personnel Procedures. The Police Service of Northern Ireland have produced and published a Code of Police Ethics.

The oath of office has been updated in light of the recommendations of the Patten report (Patten 1999) on policing in Northern Ireland, which takes into account the renewed emphasis on human rights and the positive duty on police officers to uphold and protect the rights and freedoms of members of the public they serve.

ACPO Statement of Common Purpose and Values.

Code of Conduct (Police Personnel Procedures).
The Code of Conduct introduced under the Police Act of 1996 is in a completely different form from the Police Regulations it replaces. The code is aspirational in character as opposed to the punitive format of the repealed police regulations.

Police Service of Northern Ireland—Ethical Code.
The last word on the subject of police ethical codes is from Northern Ireland. Following the formation of the Police Service of Northern Ireland from the Royal Ulster Constabulary and as a result of the conclusions of the "Good Friday Agreement," the Patten report (Patten 1999) recommended that there should be a code of ethics for police officers in Northern Ireland. This document was published in 2003.

Complaints against Police. The arbiter of police ethics and accountability for English and Welsh police forces, the Police Complaints Authority was criticized for lack of independence, before being superseded by the Independent Police Complaints Commission (IPCC). As a result of this perceived flaw, the Patten report (Patten 1999) on policing in Northern Ireland suggested that the police service should "take steps to improve its transparency" through the appointment of a new Policing Board and complaints would be subject to scrutiny by a Complaints Tribunal and a Police Ombudsman. Police staff associations in England and Wales have long been calling for an independent system for investigating complaints against police. It was reported that the Police Complaints Authority, operating in England and in Wales as the watchdog of complaints against police, could adopt the Northern Ireland model. As a result of these developments a new body, the IPCC was introduced.

Police Inspectorates. Policing in the United Kingdom is subject to scrutiny in terms of the provision of a good-quality policing service by several organizations: Her Majesty's Inspectorate of Constabulary, the Police Standards Unit, and the Audit Commission, which is a general government watchdog inspecting "value for money" in the public sector.

CRIME

After several years of reductions in crime, the United Kingdom appears to be suffering an increase in crime since the turn of the twenty-first century; this is exacerbated by the fact that violent crime, particularly, is on the increase and detection rates are decreasing. There could be several explanations for this regression; one could be the aging society, another could be the lower levels of the numbers of police officers. This latter point is now being addressed by a high-profile police recruitment campaign headed by the Home Office. The police reform agenda has high expectations of the performance of the police service once the recruits are in place, as their objectives show.

The police service has also combated crime through new techniques such as intelligence-led policing. In addition, the police service has had to address "new" crimes using new techniques and equipment to ensure an effective response. For example, DNA identification techniques have led to crimes being detected many years after their commission and as of 2003 there were over 2 million samples being maintained in the national DNA database.

The number of carjackings is increasing, where drivers of expensive cars are targeted by criminals who threaten the driver with violence and then steal their car to sell it or disguise ("ringing") it. One of the biggest crime problems and one that has resulted in a large increase in street robberies is that of theft of mobile phones, particularly affecting young people. The government has tasked several police forces with the worst crime statistics in this area to target resources to respond to the problem. Identity theft is becoming a major crime problem, particularly through transactions with credit and debit cards. There are also examples of identity theft to obtain a new identity or passport. Major banks and credit card organizations are constantly trying to combat the losses caused by such crimes (much of which is hidden to maintain the credibility and confidence in banking) such as personal identification numbers and holograms to try to prevent cloning or counterfeiting credit cards. The government is also consulting the public on the possibility of issuing an identity card or "entitlement card" for all citizens. Such cards have not been a requirement in the United Kingdom since their abolition after World War II.

Forced marriages are common among ethnic minority citizens. The victims are usually women who go through a form of arranged marriage, sometimes without their knowledge and consent. This problem has been exacerbated by the availability of cheap transportation to other countries such as India and Pakistan, where this approach to marriage is part of the culture. A major problem is that of encouraging victims to actually report the crime and after that has been achieved, to protect the victim from the violence of thwarted family members.

Soccer "hooliganism" has been rife in the United Kingdom for several decades, but has declined since firm police action was taken and sports stadiums were redesigned. At its height, police discovered that this crime was being organized usually by young businesspeople to feed their excitement during the violent fights and clashes with police.

Organized Crime. Organized crime is rife in the United Kingdom, particularly in the cities, where it has been identified for many years. Low-level and local organized crime such as "protection rackets," prostitution, drugs, and property/tenant rackets exist and eventually lead to international crime. Gangs from southern and eastern Europe that specialize in prostitution and people trafficking have supplanted native criminal gangs in cities. Also, crime trends have been affected by the importation of violent and desperate criminals from various hotbeds of crime in foreign countries such as China, Africa, and the Caribbean.

During the 1990s there were examples of organized crime in single rights issues such as animal rights, football, and terrorism. Animal rights activists targeted laboratories and the homes of workers alleged to exploit animals, causing damage, harassment, and terror. There have also been violent crime incidents involving single issues such as homophobia and racism. The United Kingdom also suffered well-publicized terrorism incidents mainly resulting from the political situation in Northern Ireland.

Cross-Border and International Crime.
Drugs. Clearly one of the worst crimes of today is that of the drug trade. There are several echelons of this trade from the backstreet manufacturer of designer drugs to the international drug routes importing drugs from the poppy fields of Asia, across southern and eastern Europe to the United Kingdom. There are vast fortunes to be made from the drug trade, which deals in human misery and degradation. Criminals and, indeed, innocent "mules" are bringing in vast quantities of unlawful substances and controlled drugs daily through the various points of entry into the United Kingdom.

People Trafficking. The latest version of international crime is that of people trafficking, either with the

An officer observes two minutes of silence to pay honor to the victims of the July 7 London bombings, Aylesbury's northern road, England, July 14, 2005. The house in the background is being searched for evidence in connection with the bombings after policed raided it the previous night. **AP IMAGES.**

consent and connivance of the victim or without it. The people being transported are usually looking for a better life in a rich Western country where they become illegal immigrants. This sets them in a vulnerable situation as the traffickers can take advantage by charging high transportation rates and exploit the victims thereafter by using them as cheap labor or worse. Many women become victims of the international sex trade and are transported against their wishes into a life of prostitution and slavery.

Terrorism. The international crime of terrorism has been prevalent in recent decades, ranging from the local political troubles in Northern Ireland to the bombs on international flights such as the Lockerbie incident. Far and Middle Eastern terrorism is the latest manifestation, bringing with it the specter of suicide bombers and religious fanaticism.

International Crime—General. International crime has been called the victimless crime, as victims do not have any power to complain because of their weak situation. The other aspects of international crime are that victims are actually involved in the criminality to a certain degree; for example, drug users actually buy the drugs.

New Types of Crime.

Pedophile Crimes. A new type of crime has been established where pedophiles contact and "groom" their victims by contact through Internet chat rooms. Children are naturally trusting and might not tell an adult family member or friend what is happening. While communicating, the criminals can pretend they are a child, insist on secrecy, and set up a meeting with their victim. At this point the contact is made and the crime is committed, usually a serious sexual assault or homicide or a precursor to these outcomes. New means of investigating and combating these crimes are called for, necessitating the acquisition of new skills and equipment for the police service. New methods of investigation lag crimes by months and years and courts also need to be advised because new crimes mean new types of evidence, some of it "virtual." The police service in the United Kingdom has struggled to be abreast of trends in these types of crime and this has resulted in many young people becoming the victims of crimes. The crimes have been made possible by vast leaps in technological advances; the police service must strive to maintain progress at the same pace.

Cybercrime. In response to the new phenomena of cybercrime, the UK police service has introduced a high-tech crime unit. It is too early to judge the success of this initiative. However, judging from the long list and frequency of such crimes, further developments will be necessary to keep pace in this area of new crime.

CORRECTIONAL SYSTEM

The history of the Prison Service proper commences in the eighteenth century, when jailers made their living by charging for board and lodging. At that time no distinction was made between prisoners who were awaiting trial, debtors, or convicts awaiting transportation to the North American colonies. Conditions in prisons were described in 1777 by John Howard, a famous prison reformer, as "filthy, corrupt-ridden and unhealthy." In 1779 the practice of placing prisoners on "hulk" ships was introduced, which was superseded by transportation to a new location: Australia. The use of hulk ships continued until 1859 and at one time, Australia contained 70,000 prisoners.

Following much legislation, in the nineteenth century prisons were vastly improved, with the appointment of an inspectorate of prisons and the building of many new prisons. However, conditions in old prisons were still described as "appalling." This resulted in centralization of the management of prisons to the home secretary and in 1878 there was a Prison Commission that was tasked with organizing an efficient and uniform prison system.

The commission introduced a system of "separate confinement"—solitary confinement—and penal servitude. The prison uniform with its broad arrows (of current-day cartoon fame) was intentionally demeaning; also, facilities for personal hygiene were described as minimal. Prisoners worked together on a crank or treadmill and were given a meager diet; they were forbidden to talk. Communication with the outside world was strictly limited; there was, however, a system of early release for good behavior.

A watershed in prison reform was achieved by the Gladstone report in 1895 that recommended "the principle of prison treatment should have as its primary and concurrent objects, deterrence and reformation." The idea of rehabilitation was born and the isolation and forced unproductive labor of the previous era were abolished. Aftercare of prisoners following release and young offender institutes were introduced. The provisions of the Gladstone report were farsighted and were not repealed until 1948.

Further liberalization regimes ensued through the early twentieth century, when the broad arrow uniform was abolished along with the prison hair crop. Reasonable facilities were introduced for shaving and the silence rules were relaxed. Educational facilities were introduced besides rights relating to prison visits. The prison regime was also affected by the two world wars with an increase in conscientious objectors, aliens, and the call up of prison staff. As a result of overcrowding, new rules relating to remission were introduced.

In the postwar years the prison service suffered from chronic overcrowding that affected the expansion of training and facilities. Cells that were designed for one person were inhabited by two or even three inmates. Because of the shortage of staff, there was an increasing use of specialists such as psychologists and welfare officers. There followed a period of expansion of the prison estate by several new prisons, including open prisons and young offender institutes. In the late 1950s and 1960s there were several authoritative consultation documents and a commission on the role and responsibilities of prison staff. In 1963 the Prison Department of the Home Office was established with a regional management system. New security systems were also deployed in prisons such as closed-circuit television and other methods, including security classification of prisoners.

In 1971 boards of visitors to prisons were introduced to provide independent oversight of all establishments. Special attention was paid to the training, development, and rehabilitation of prisoners. The level of privileges and rights to visits were increased. However, this era was blighted by high tensions in prisons with several riots and demonstrations. Also, special problems were experienced with protests by convicted terrorist prisoners. A wide-ranging review of prisons reported in 1979 that changes were required on physical conditions for prisoners and staff, industrial relations, resources, staff pay, and conditions. The report praised the prison system for its positive and humanitarian traditions that it continues to this day.

Types of Correction Systems Today—Private and Public Sector. Her Majesty's Prison Service (HMP) in the United Kingdom comprises both public- and private-sector prisons. The Home Department (Ministry of the Interior) is the government department responsible for prisons. In England and Wales there are 157 establishments and in Scotland there are 3. Prison accommodation ranges from open prisons to high-security establishments to house convicted terrorists or dangerous criminals. When prisoners are sentenced, they are classified into different categories according to their security status; they are then allocated a place at an appropriate prison. Prisoners are also separated according to their gender and there are separate prisons for women or separate accommodation in mixed prisons. In 2003 the prison population in England and Wales was 72,853, an increase of 3 percent from the previous year; this is a worry as the trend of the number of incarcerations, in spite of efforts to reduce custodial sentences, has been heading upward.

An even more disturbing trend is that of the number of female prisoners convicted and given custodial sentences.

The long-term forecast of trends in the prison population shows that, in England and Wales, the prison population has increased from just over 60,000 in 2001 to 73,000 in 2003, and forecasts indicate the total will be over 90,000 by 2009.

These trends are a cause for concern in terms of the facilities and accommodations of the prison service estate. In 2003 the prison population was 11 percent higher (72,853) than the Certified Normal Accommodation of 65,571 and 2,999 lower than the Certified Operational Capacity. (For operational reasons, the maximum number of prisoners the estate can normally hold is up to 2,000 less that the certified operational capacity. This is because of constraints imposed by the need to provide separate accommodation for different classes of prisoners

[i.e., by sex, age, security category, and conviction status] and because of geographical distribution.)

Ethnicity of the Prison Population. Another cause for concern is that of the high proportion of ethnic minority prisoners that are a disproportionate percentage in comparison to the general population of the United Kingdom. This concern is linked to the high percentage of foreign nationals incarcerated compared to the overall UK population and the high percentage of black people within that group.

Deployment of Correction Systems across the United Kingdom. Prisons are located all around the country, and the policy is to attempt to sentence an offender to a prison near his or her home address to facilitate arrangements for family visits. The Prison Service is managed on a day-to-day basis by area managers located around the United Kingdom who have responsibility for a number of prison establishments in their geographical area. In England and Wales there are 11 area managers covering the 157 prisons; in Scotland there are 3 prisons, which are managed from Edinburgh. In Northern Ireland there are 3 establishments, which are managed from the head office in Belfast by an executive agency.

Description of Management Arrangements of the Correctional System. In the United Kingdom there have been increases in the prison population, which have led to an increase in the number of new prisons and refurbishment of old accommodations. Also, new measures have been introduced to use a wider range of sentencing options such as community sentences, prisoner "tagging," home detention curfew, and similar initiatives including early release of prisoners on license. Offenders serving short terms of imprisonment (4 years or less) are given automatic early release, those with longer terms must obtain Parole Board approval.

Prisoners in UK jails have certain privileges such as the right to write and receive mail, to be visited by friends and relatives, and to make telephone calls. These rights may be enhanced dependent on good behavior. Prisoners are also allowed to have radios, television, books, and other reading material. People who are "on remand," that is, in custody awaiting trial, have additional privileges to those available to convicted prisoners. There is a mandatory drug-testing regime in all prisons.

The HMP comes under the responsibility of the home secretary and is managed through the Home Office in London and the head office in that city. Day-to-day management of the HMP is devolved to areas around the United Kingdom. Each prison has a board of visitors that is appointed by the home secretary. The board is an independent body appointed from the local community that monitors complaints from prisoners and investigates the concerns of prison staff. Reports are forwarded to the home secretary.

In addition, prisons are subjected to an inspection regime by Her Majesty's Inspector of Prisons. This is an organization that inspects all prisons every three years and submits annual reports to Parliament on the state of conditions and facilities in prisons and the treatment of prisoners. Where the arrangements fail to satisfy a prisoner's requests or complaints, there is a remedy via the independent Prison's Ombudsman.

Sentencing Arrangements and Abolition of the Death Penalty. Twenty-five percent of convicted people of an indictable offense received a custodial sentence in 2001. In the United Kingdom the mandatory sentence for murder and certain other serious offenses is life imprisonment. In practice this does not mean the convicted person's whole life; the average term for life imprisonment is fourteen years' incarceration. In 2003 there were 5,413 life-sentence prisoners (9% of all sentenced prisoners; 5,244 men and 169 women). Of these, 165 were young people.

Most prisoners are released through a parole system back into the community; the most severe offenders were traditionally awarded a "tariff" term of imprisonment by the home secretary, a system that has been replaced by a recommendation from trial judges. The death penalty, following the commencement of the HRA and previous legislation, is no longer available for any offense in the United Kingdom unless war is declared. In fact, the last person to be executed in the United Kingdom was in 1965.

Prison Conditions. Statutory regulations govern all aspects of prison life. In particular, guidance is available for all prisoners on the internal disciplinary procedures to ensure fairness to those deprived of their liberty.

The introduction to the Prison Discipline Manual adequately explains the checks and balances it contains and the importance to be awarded to it by heads of prison establishments:

> Much misconduct in Prison Service establishments can be dealt with informally through good management or good staff-prisoner relations. However, the formal discipline system is central to the maintenance of good order and discipline. Discipline procedures are provided for by the Prison Rules 1999 and the Young Offender Institution Rules 2000, both as amended. The Rules set out all disciplinary offenses and punishments. They empower governors and controllers

of contracted out prisons to investigate all charges and they require prisoners to have a full opportunity to hear what is alleged against them and to present their case. Where alleged indiscipline amounts to a serious criminal offense the police will be asked to investigate and a prosecution may result.

This Manual contains both instructions and guidance on procedures related to the discipline system. Governors and controllers must comply with the instructions and must take account of the advice. The Manual should help all those involved—adjudicators, staff, prisoners and their representatives—in understanding the process. Its contents have been shaped by the decisions of the courts and by experience in the field. Adjudicators must manage hearings in accordance with the rules of natural justice and following the guidance in this Manual will offer the best prospect of that.

HMP Inspectorate. As discussed earlier, the role of Her Majesty's Inspectorate of Prisons (HMIP) was introduced in the late twentieth century. The HMIP's statement of purpose is "[t]o contribute to the reduction in crime, by inspecting the treatment and conditions of those in Prison Service custody, and Immigration Service detention, in a manner that informs Ministers, Parliament and others and influences advances in planning and operational delivery."

The most recent HMIP report stated that the most significant problem threatening the tests of a healthy prison—safety, respect, purposeful activity, and resettlement—was that of overcrowding. All prisons, both in the private and public sector, are subject to a rigorous inspection regime.

State of HMP Buildings and Implementation of Minimum Conditions Criteria. The trends discussed earlier are a cause for concern in terms of the facilities and accommodations of the prison service estate. In 2003 the HMP decided to keep prisoners in police cells. Keeping prisoners is such accommodations is far from ideal; although all prisoners' rights are respected, there are problems for relatives and visitors making visits to the prisoners who may be in situ for short periods only.

HMIP reports highlight several problems related to overcrowding:

- Vulnerable prisoners may not be identified

- Prisoners are not known to each other or to staff

- Prisoners are more likely to be locked in their cells for long periods

- Provides "fertile grounds for disturbance" as well as self-harm

- Basics of decency are curtailed

Recidivism Rates and Commentary on Crime in Prisons. The prison population is growing. Also, there is a tendency toward longer terms of imprisonment for comparable offenses. The implications of this are that more prisoners are spending more time in prison, thereby increasing the prison population.

Recidivism. There have been few research studies on recidivism in the United Kingdom, and those that have been completed have had uneven measures of success. In fact, one study of recidivism of sexual offenders recommended that official reconviction rates were not sufficiently accurate to establish the true picture. By using unofficial sources of data the study found that actual reconviction rates were 5.3 times the official statistics.

Outcomes from a £73 million project mounted by the Probation Service in England and Wales were reported to have failed to reform criminals. The project was intended to reform criminals by encouraging them to think about their victims; however, early results found that 70 percent were reconvicted after nine months. As there appeared to be no merit in the "think first" cognitive skills training, the program was cut from a target of 30,000 prisoners per year to 15,000.

Self-Harm and Suicide Statistics of Prisoners— Juvenile and Adult. In a recent HMIP report it was established that over 40 percent of respondents in male prisons said they felt unsafe at some time. In one prison 77 percent of women prisoners reported feeling unsafe. There were a total of seventy-two self-inflicted deaths in the first nine months of 2002, many of which were attributed to overcrowding.

Prison Conditions for Female Prisoners and Mother/Baby Provision. As a result of the alarming rise in women offenders, the UK government undertook a consultation exercise in 2001 to establish a strategy for women offenders. The report established that women offenders have many associated social problems relating to disadvantage and social exclusion. Therefore, a major cross-government initiative "Women's Offending Reduction Program 2002–2005" was launched. Factors such as health, economic stability, level of education, employment and training opportunities, family and community ties, and experience of abuse were widely accepted as criminogenic factors for women offenders.

The UK government introduced an action plan in 1999 relating to principles, policies, and procedures on mothers and babies/children in prison:

Table 1. Prison Statistics, United Kingdom

	England	Wales	Scotland/ Northern Ireland
Total Prison Population	76,070	6,721	1,307
Prison Population per 100,000	143	133	76
Pretrial Detainees	16.3%	16.8%	34.6%
Female Prisoners	5.9%	5.0%	3.0%
Juvenile Prisoners Under 18	3.0%	2.8%	5.7%
Number of Prisons	141	16	3
Official Capacity of Prison System	68,880	6,384	1,362
Occupancy Level	10.4%	104.6%	96.0%

The Main Principle: The purpose of a mother and baby unit in a prison is to enable the mother/baby relationship to develop while safeguarding and promoting the child's welfare.

Overarching Principles: The best interest of the child is the primary consideration at every level of policy making as well as when considering individual situations.

Prison Service policy will reflect the ECHR article 8, save where it is necessary to restrict the prisoner's rights for a legitimate reason, such as good order and discipline, or the safety of other prisoners or babies.

When making decisions about the best interest of the child, the long-term developmental needs of the child are given attention as well as the immediate situation.

Principles for Parents: Parents are enabled to exercise parental responsibility for their children whether the child is with them in prison or outside with other caregivers. Parental responsibility "means all the rights, duties, powers, responsibilities and authority which by law a parent of a child has in relation to the child and his property."

Parents and other significant caregivers are involved in decision making about their children.

Prison Statistics. Prison statistics are listed in Table 1.

BIBLIOGRAPHY

Association of Chief Police Officers. 1995. *Tackling Crime Effectively: Handbook*, vol. 1. London: Association of Chief Police Officers, HMIC, Home Office and Audit Commission.

Association of Chief Police Officers. 1996. *Report of the Working Group on Patrol*. London: Association of Chief Police Officers.

Association of Chief Police Officers. 1996. *Tackling Crime Effectively: Handbook*, vol. 2. London: Association of Chief Police Officers, HMIC, Home Office and Audit Commission.

Association of Chief Police Officers. 1999. *The Human Rights Audit Tool.* London: Association of Chief Police Officers.

Association of Chief Police Officers. 1999. *The Murder Manual.* London: Association of Chief Police Officers.

Association of Chief Police Officers. 1999. *National Standards for Covert Policing.* London: Association of Chief Police Officers.

Association of Chief Police Officers. 2000. *Keeping the Peace Manual.* London: Association of Chief Police Officers.

Association of Chief Police Officers. 2000. *National Intelligence Model.* London: National Criminal Intelligence Service.

Association of Police Authorities. 1998. *Objectives, Indicators, Targets: A Study of Policing Plans and Reports.* London: Association of Police Authorities.

Her Majesty's Inspectorate of Constabulary. 1997. *Thematic Inspection Report on Officer Safety.* London: Her Majesty's Inspectorate of Constabulary.

Her Majesty's Inspectorate of Constabulary. 1997. *Winning the Race.* London: Her Majesty's Inspectorate of Constabulary.

Her Majesty's Inspectorate of Constabulary. 1998. *What Price Policing? A Study of Efficiency and Value for Money in the Police Service.* London: Her Majesty's Inspectorate of Constabulary.

Her Majesty's Inspectorate of Constabulary. 1998. *Winning the Race: Revisited.* London: Her Majesty's Inspectorate of Constabulary.

Her Majesty's Inspectorate of Constabulary. 1999a. *Managing Learning: A Study of Police Training.* London: Home Office.

Her Majesty's Inspectorate of Constabulary. 1999b. *Police Integrity: Securing and Maintaining Public Confidence.* Report of Her Majesty's Inspectorate of Constabulary. London: Home Office.

Her Majesty's Inspectorate of Constabulary. 2000. "Policing London: Winning Consent." London: Home Office.

Her Majesty's Stationery Office. 1989. *Consolidated Guide to Police Probationer Training,* pts. 1–9. London: Crime Prevention Technical Unit.

Her Majesty's Stationery Office. 1989. "The New Look: A Guide to Probationer Training." London: Her Majesty's Stationery Office.

Her Majesty's Stationery Office. 1989. *Police Probationer Training Foundation Course—Trainers Guide.* London: Crime Prevention Technical Unit.

Her Majesty's Stationery Office. 1998. *Green Paper: The Learning Age.* London: Her Majesty's Stationery Office.

Home Office. 1981. *Racial Attacks: Report of a Home Office Study.* London: Home Office.

Home Office. 1983. *Manpower, Effectiveness, and Efficiency in the Police Service.* Circular 114/83. London: Home Office.

Home Office. 1991. *Safer Communities: The Local Delivery of Crime Prevention through the Partnership Approach.* London: Her Majesty's Stationery Office.

Home Office. 1993. *Inquiry into Police Responsibilities and Rewards (Sheehy Report),* vols. 1–2. Executive Summary CM2280.I and CM2280.II. London: Her Majesty's Stationery Office.

Home Office. 1993. *Performance Indicators for the Police.* Circular 17/93. London: Home Office.

Home Office. 1993. *Police Reform: A Police Service for the 21st Century.* London: Her Majesty's Stationery Office.

Home Office. 1994. *Role of HM Inspectorate of Constabulary.* Circular 67/94. London: Home Office.

Home Office. 1996. *Protecting the Public: The Government's Strategy on Crime in England and Wales.* London: Home Office, Cm. 3190.

Home Office. 1997. *Bringing Rights Home.* White Paper. London: Home Office, Cm. 3782.

Home Office. 1998. *Reducing Offending: An Assessment of the Research Evidence on Ways of Dealing with Offending Behaviour.* Home Office Research Study 187. London: Home Office.

Home Office. 1999. *Annual Report.* London: Home Office. Available online at http://www.Homeoffice.gov.uk/police.

Home Office. 1999. "The Government's Crime Reduction Strategy." Available online at http://www.Homeoffice.gov.uk/police.

Home Office. 1999. "Police Training: A Consultation Document." Available online at http://www.Homeoffice.gov.uk/police.

Home Office Research and Statistics Directorate. 1998. *Counting Rules for Recorded Crime: Instructions for Police Forces.* London: Home Office.

Macpherson, William. 1999. *The Stephen Lawrence Inquiry: Report of an Inquiry.* London: Her Majesty's Stationery Office.

Metropolitan Police. 1985. *The Principles of Policing and Guidance for Professional Behaviour.* London: Metropolitan Police.

Neyroud, Peter, and Alan Beckley. 2001. *Policing, Ethics, and Human Rights.* Portland, OR: Willan.

Patten, Christopher. 1999. *A New Beginning: Policing in Northern Ireland.* Report of the Independent Commission on Policing for Northern Ireland. London: Her Majesty's Stationery Office.

Royal Commission on Criminal Procedure. 1981. *Report of the Royal Commission on Criminal Procedure.* Cmnd. 8092. London: Her Majesty's Stationery Office.

Royal Commission on Criminal Procedure. 1992. *Report of the Royal Commission on Criminal Justice.* Cmnd. 2281. London: Her Majesty's Stationery Office.

Royal Commission on Criminal Procedure. 1998. *Criminal Statistics: England and Wales, 1997.* Cmnd. 4162. London: Home Office.

Alan Beckley

United States

Official country name: United States of America
Capital: Washington, D.C.
Geographic description: North America, north of Mexico and south of Canada, forms the coterminous United States; Alaska is to the west of Canada and Hawaii is in the North Pacific
Population: 295,734,134 (est. 2005)

■ ■ ■

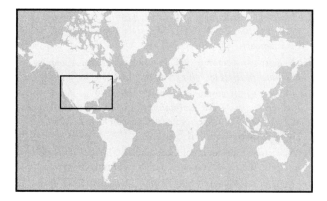

LAW ENFORCEMENT

History. The United States of America considers July 4, 1776, as the founding of the nation with the Declaration of Independence from Great Britain. The original thirteen states were considered colonies of Britain. They joined together to fight for independence during the Revolutionary War (1775–1782). The second Treaty of Paris in 1783 officially ended the war for independence. During the early years of the country, much effort was placed on establishing a federal government that would work in conjunction with the various states. It was 1791 when the U.S. Constitution and its Bill of Rights were adopted and put into action.

Prior to independence, social control and policing efforts throughout the colonies consisted of practices that were common in the colonists' homelands—local constables, sheriffs, and night watchmen. Night watchmen and constables, appointed or elected in villages and cities, were assigned a number of duties. For example, the constable in Plymouth, Massachusetts, in 1634, was the sealer of weights and measures, surveyor of land, jailer, and an announcer of marriages. County governments copied the English precedent of appointing sheriffs as their primary law enforcement officials. These sheriffs, like their British counterparts, were appointed through the political system (usually the colonial governor's office) and were not elected. Service as a night watchman or constable was an obligation of the adult males of the community. Although some communities experimented with paid constables, most colonists relied on volunteers to staff their law enforcement offices well into the 1700s. Some variations existed, however. For example, in New Amsterdam (later named New York when the British took over the city), a group of citizens equipped with rattles to warn of their watchful presence was referred to as the "rattlewatch." In 1658 New Amsterdam appointed eight paid watchmen to replace the volunteers, but it was not until 1693 that the first uniformed police officer was appointed by the mayor (Conser and Russell 2000). During the 1700s, policing in most colonial cities changed little, although historians note that the reliance on volunteer watchmen was becoming strained. The towns were becoming large enough to need reliable police but their best citizens habitually refused their turn and obligation to serve on the night watch. Some cities did pay their watchmen, but not enough to allow someone to earn his living by law enforcement. The idea of citizen participation in policing was breaking down, and something was needed to replace it. In 1749 the city of Philadelphia was permitted to levy a tax and appoint wardens with the authority to hire watchmen as needed. Only those interested in working on the watch for pay applied to the wardens (Johnson 1981).

The military presence of the British became an increasing factor as massive social and political discontent grew stronger toward the latter part of the 1700s. This military presence extended to the frontier in the Ohio Valley and Lake Erie during the French and Indian War (1756–1763). From 1765 through the end of the Revolutionary War (1783), the colonies faced several riots and disturbances, economic depression, and an ever-increasing imperial policy of Britain. The duties of public safety were given to military forces. Following the Revolutionary War, policing was turned back over to civilian authority (local government).

Some parts of the colonies had their own unique forms of policing. For example, southern governments enacted slave patrol legislation in the 1740s. These laws protected people from runaway slaves, inhibited insurrection, and authorized recapture of slaves. The slave patrols had the right to visit every plantation and to search houses for offensive weapons and ammunition. The infliction of corporal punishment was also permitted if any slave was found to have left his owner's property without permission. Some maintain that the slave patrols of the south were America's first modern-style police forces (Williams and Murphy 1990). By 1837 the Charleston (South Carolina) slave patrol, about 100 officers, was possibly the country's largest single police force at that time (Wintersmith 1974).

On the national level, the first U.S. Marshals were appointed following authorization by the Judiciary Act of 1789. They were to support the federal courts and to carry out all lawful orders issued by judges, Congress, or the president. Throughout their early years, they were assigned to enforce unpopular federal laws, which included collection of taxes on whiskey. A marshal served papers on distillers in western Pennsylvania in 1794, but before the incident ended, 13,000 state militiamen had to be summoned to put down what is known as the Whiskey Rebellion. U.S. Marshals' enforced the law banning the African slave trade following its passage in 1819 and later carried out the Fugitive Slave Law of 1850 (which required the return of runaway slaves to their owners). Marshals often met with local resistance, and sometimes their efforts were less than successful. Also, before the Civil War, Marshals tracked down counterfeiters (since the Secret Service did not exist until 1865). The U.S. Marshals may be best remembered for their efforts to bring some justice to the "wild west." Marshals pursued notorious train robbers, "gunfighters" and other outlaws (Conser and Russell 2000).

Major conflicts in the early 1800s and again in 1812 found the U.S. growing in strength and recognition as a major world government. In 1803, through the Louisiana Purchase, the country acquired the vast territory from Louisiana through the heartland and into the northwestern parts of the country. New territories were open for settlements and the country began to see great growth. War with Britain (1812–1814) reduced European attempts to maintain land in the country; and Florida was purchased from Spain in 1819 and became a state in 1845. In 1836 Texas won its independence from Mexico and became a state in 1845. In 1846, the United States declared war on Mexico because of territorial disputes over New Mexico. In 1848 the war with Mexico ended with the United States acquiring the area consisting of California, Nevada, New Mexico, Utah, Arizona, and parts of Colorado and Wyoming. During the expansion of the settlements to the western and southwestern parts of the country, there were periodic skirmishes and battles with the Native American tribes that inhabited the lands. Eventually, most Native Americans were assigned to specific territories referred to today as "reservations." These reservations have their own governing bodies or tribal councils and are coordinated through the Bureau of Indian Affairs.

During the 1830s to 1860s, most larger cities in the United States established paid police forces. Many of these departments were structured, in part, after the Metropolitan Police of London that had been formed in 1829. Major cities such as Philadelphia, Boston, and New York have interesting histories as to the emergence of a unified, 24-hour, police operation. Each had a social, economic, or political situation that caused reorganization and reform in the police department. During the 1850s, over 1.3 million people emigrated from Britain and Ireland to the United States As the country grew and developed, by the mid-1800s, the issue of slavery became internally divisive and eventually led to the Civil War (1861–1865). The Union military forces ultimately defeated the Confederate military, but not until a total of approximately 373,000 soldiers had been killed or died during the war and another 412,000 had been wounded. Following the Civil War, the country experienced growth in the metropolitan areas of the northern, eastern and western parts of the country. The area between the Mississippi River and the Rocky Mountains also experienced growth because of migration and settlements in the frontier. The United States declared war on Spain, over Cuba, in 1898 and later that year acquired Cuba, Puerto Rico, Guam, and the Philippines.

Local policing from the 1870s through the early 1900s was quite diverse throughout the United States and was dominated by local politics. The cities of the northern part of the country experienced growth from migrating minorities from the south (many were former slaves), foreign immigration and an expanding industrial base. In some communities, the primary problems were racial discord, segregation and discrimination. During this time period, whites victimized blacks with nearly total immunity. When whites were prosecuted, their sentences were less harsh than those for blacks committing the same offense. After the Civil War, the federal government reacted by passing the Civil Rights Act of 1866, which specified the rights of citizens regardless of race. It also allowed for lawsuits against persons who deprived a citizen of a civil right. This law led Congress to adopt the Fourteenth Amendment to the Constitution, which provided "equal protection" under the law. The Fifteenth Amendment, enacted shortly thereafter, addressed the voting rights of blacks. The Civil Rights Act of 1875 outlawed the exclusion of blacks from hotels, theaters, railroads, and other public accommodations (Williams and Murphy 1990). The police were often in the middle of many of the social problems of this time period and they were not yet known (nor trained) for professionalism and objectivity.

From 1905 to 1914, approximately 10.5 million immigrants from southern and eastern Europe entered the United States and settled mostly in the metropolitan areas. World events curtailed immigration to the United States when it entered World War I in 1917. The country's heavy industrial base grew and became more efficient during the war years and when the war ended in 1918, the country was again growing and prospering; by this time, it had a population of 103.5 million. During this time period, the policing field experienced its first major wave of modern reform efforts toward improved standardized training, better personnel qualifications and selection techniques, the application of science and technology to policing (such as telephone systems, two-way radios and fingerprint classification systems) and less political influence on police operations. Also, professional associations for managers and officers emerged. Women were also granted their first appointments with full police powers during the early 1900s. All of these events and trends influenced the development of more effective, better-managed police departments in many parts of the country. During the period from 1905 through the 1930s, over 40 states established state police or state highway patrols and 24 established bureaus of

investigation. In 1924 the Federal Bureau of Investigation (FBI) was reorganized to become a major investigative agency for the U.S. government.

The developing economic and industrial growth of the war years slowed after the war ended. The government cut back on spending during the early 1920s and great changes occurred throughout the country. Many companies began merging; labor unions lost membership and influence; a small portion of people amassed wealth; and about 80 percent of the wage earners were so poor, they were dropped from the tax rolls. By the end of the decade, the stock market collapsed and there were two runs on banks during the early 1930s. Unemployment reached nearly 25 percent by 1934. The time period from 1929 to 1939 was known as the Great Depression. The reform of the policing community continued during these years, in fact, the depression years attracted highly educated persons to the police field because it offered greater job security than the private sector. Policing efforts in larger cities were influenced by the era of Prohibition (1919–1933) in the United States when alcoholic beverages could not be manufactured, sold, transported or imported. Coupled with cultural movements like the granting to women of the right to vote, and the expansion of organized crime, prostitution, and drugs, the social order was becoming much more complex and crime was increasing. The Commission on Law Enforcement and Observance (also called the Wickersham Commission) was appointed in 1929 to investigate the entire field of criminal justice and lawlessness. Its report in 1931 called for additional reforms across the system.

The industrial and economic base of the country was emerging from the depression years in the late 1930s as much of Europe and other parts of the world were embroiled in war or preparing for hostilities. Many countries were ordering arms and war material from the United States. The United States entered World War II following the December 7, 1941, attack on Pearl Harbor, Hawaii, by Japan. War was declared on Japan and later on Germany and Italy. The war continued through 1945 until VE Day in May and the surrender of Japan in August. During World War II, the United States lost over 417,000 military personnel and 670,000 were wounded. Millions of service personnel subsequently returned to the United States and found employment in business and industry; over a million attended college on the GI Bill. During the war years, immigration to the United States was minimal. By 1950 the U.S. population was 150 million and growing because of the baby boom. From 1951 to 1953, the United States committed troops to the Korean Conflict and suffered 33,600 killed and over 103,000 wounded.

The 1960s brought great change to the United States on the social front. The population was about 180 million.

There was considerable racial conflict throughout the country. Major events occurred: the Cuban Crisis with the Soviet Union (USSR) raised fears of a nuclear war, the assassination of President John F. Kennedy occurred in 1963, and in 1968 Senator Robert Kennedy and Martin Luther King Jr. were assassinated. Social control mechanisms and governmental authority was questioned by a large segment of society. Economically, there was significant prosperity, and yet at the same time, significant poverty and increasing crime rates. Many social programs were instituted in the United States during the 1960s to improve social conditions of minorities and the poor. The Civil Rights Act in 1964 (CRA) prohibited discrimination in employment on grounds of race, color, religion, national origin, or sex. (Originally, the CRA of 1964 only applied to the private sector; it was expanded to the public sector and modified in 1972.) From the mid-1950s through the 1960s, racial unrest and the accompanying civil rights movement sparked racial riots and incidents across the United States, with the most violent in the South. The police who attempted to control these incidents were often untrained to handle crowds, especially racially diverse ones, and they often did not respond professionally. Nationally televised examples included the school desegregation incidents in the state of Alabama, civil rights marches in several cities, and the riots of the Democratic National Convention in 1968 in Chicago. Social unrest and crime conditions were so severe by 1965 that President Lyndon Johnson declared a "war-on-crime" and appointed the President's Commission on Law Enforcement and Administration of Justice. Officially charged to investigate the causes of crime, the commission was quite broad in its analysis. The summary report, *The Challenge of Crime in a Free Society*, was issued in 1967. Nine supplemental reports also were published: *The Police, The Courts, Corrections, Juvenile Delinquency and Youth Crime, Organized Crime, Assessment of Crime, Narcotics and Drug Abuse, Drunkenness*, and *Science and Technology*. These reports provided interesting reading, since each elaborated on the conditions found in the criminal justice system during the mid-1960s. All of the reports contained numerous recommendations for improvement of the policing system.

At the end of the 1960s, the country was embroiled in another military conflict—the Vietnam War. By the end of the conflict in early 1973, the United States had suffered 58,000 casualties and 153,000 wounded. The political scandal known as Watergate caused President Richard Nixon to resign in 1974. During the 1970s, the United States also experienced an energy crisis/gasoline shortages, wage and salary freezes, high inflation rates, high unemployment rates, high crime rates and tension in international relations with Russia, Iran, and the Middle East. On the policing front, a second wave of reform was sweeping the country. Billions of dollars were allocated to improve the criminal justice system through better training and education of personnel; improved equipment, technology and computer information systems; and expansion of agencies in terms of personnel and programs. Improving the professionalism of policing agencies was the focus of the efforts of the 1970s.

By 1980, the population of the United States had risen to 226 million. During the decade, the country experienced relative economic prosperity and technological prominence in the telecommunications and personal computing arenas. The cold war with the USSR, tensions in the Middle East and civil strife in Central America dominated the international scene. Crime rates and the ever-expanding drug culture were primary social concerns. By 1989 diplomatic relations with the USSR had improved, crime rates had leveled-off in the mid-1980s, but were starting to rise again and the government had declared "war" on illegal drugs.

During the 1980s, policing in the United States had continued to undergo reform and scrutiny. According to police historian Samuel Walker (1992), the police were "caught between old problems and new ideas." Old problems included the crime rates (down in the 1980s, then rising until the early 1990s when it started to decline) and varying types of crime (drug offenses, drive-by shootings, domestic violence, and juvenile crime) that upset the community. New ideas included problem-oriented policing, community policing, neighborhood crime prevention programming, and other enhanced community efforts. However, added to this puzzle are problems associated with police corruption and misconduct, rising fear of international and domestic terrorism, the application of military technology to civilian public safety and law enforcement, school violence, hate crime, and economic resources.

The 1990s opened with the country sending troops to the Gulf of Iraq following Iraq's invasion of Kuwait in 1991. As a whole, the country experienced considerable economic growth, low unemployment, stable and decreasing crime rates and a reduction in military spending during the decade. Immigration to the United States during the 1990s averaged about 6 million persons each year. However, the decade also brought renewed tensions from terrorist attacks as evidenced by the first bombing of the World Trade Center in New York City in 1993 and several major bombings overseas directed at American embassies or interests. In 1995 the bombing of the Murrah Federal building in Okalahoma City, Oklahoma, that killed 168 people indicated that disgruntled Americans could commit such acts. In 1999 the FBI placed the name of Osama bin Laden on its "Ten Most Wanted List" following an indictment related to the

1993 World Trade Center bombing. Also of concern was the rising number of undocumented (illegal) persons entering and residing in the United States.

On the policing front, the 1990s again brought national attention to police operations and tactics with the Rodney King incident in Los Angeles in 1991. In 1992 all the officers but one charged in the incident were found not guilty of all charges. Riots erupted and lasted for five days in the city resulting in more than 40 deaths, 2,382 injuries, over 5,000 buildings damaged or destroyed, an estimated 40,000 jobs lost and over $1 billion in property damage; 5,633 people were arrested. The riots spread to other cities across the country. Also in 1992, following a 51-day standoff near Waco, Texas, at the compound of the Branch Davidians, headed by David Koresh, federal agents assaulted the compound. A devastating fire, believed set by the occupants, resulted in the deaths of 80 people, including women and children in the compound. During 1998 to 1999, several fatal shooting incidents at schools throughout the United States also raised questions about the safety at those facilities and the law enforcement response to such incidents.

Since 2000 the defining events affecting the United States included the terrorist attacks of September 11, 2001, the military incursion into Afghanistan (October 2001) to strike al Qaeda terrorist training camps, and the invasion of Iraq (March 2003). The September 11 attacks on the World Trade Towers (New York City) and the Pentagon (Washington, D.C.) and the fourth airliner that crashed in western Pennsylvania killed a total of 2,995, injured 6,291 persons, and caused an estimated $33 billion in property damages. The government of the United States focused considerable effort and resources on the pursuit of terrorist groups responsible for the September 11 attacks or against governments believed to be sponsors of international terrorism. By the end of November 2002, a new Department of Homeland Security had been created in the executive branch of the government for the primary purpose of improving the country's ability to prevent, prepare for and respond to terrorist threats or attacks. In March 2003, a U.S.-led coalition of forces invaded Iraq to overthrow the regime of Saddam Hussein. Following September 11, 2001, law enforcement departments suffered personnel shortages (many officers who were in the National Guard and military reserves were called to active duty), reductions in budgets and increased demand for homeland security services. Reports in early 2004 indicated that terror alerts and homeland security efforts were costing major cities an additional $1 million to $7 million a week.

Structure and Organization. As of the end of 2003, the executive branch of the federal government of the United States consisted of 15 departments and 62 independent agencies. The executive branch is primarily responsible for public safety, internal and national security, and the delivery of all major services to the people of the country. It also contains the primary administrative and regulatory agencies of the country. The executive departments include the following:

- Department of Agriculture (USDA)
- Department of Commerce (DOC)
- Department of Defense (DOD)
- Department of Education (ED)
- Department of Energy (DOE)
- Department of Health and Human Services (HHS)
- Department of Homeland Security (DHS)
- Department of Housing and Urban Development (HUD)
- Department of the Interior (DOI)
- Department of Justice (DOJ)
- Department of Labor (DOL)
- Department of State (DOS)
- Department of Transportation (DOT)
- Department of the Treasury
- Department of Veterans Affairs (VA)

The independent agencies include:

- Amtrak (National Railroad Passenger Corporation)
- Broadcasting Board of Governors (Voice of America, Radio/TV Marti, and more)
- Central Intelligence Agency (CIA)
- Commission on Civil Rights
- Commodity Futures Trading Commission
- Consumer Product Safety Commission (CPSC)
- Corporation for National and Community Service
- Defense Nuclear Facilities Safety Board
- Environmental Protection Agency (EPA)
- Equal Employment Opportunity Commission (EEOC)
- Export-Import Bank of the United States
- Farm Credit Administration
- Federal Communications Commission (FCC)
- Federal Deposit Insurance Corporation (FDIC)
- Federal Election Commission (FEC)

- Federal Emergency Management Agency (FEMA)
- Federal Housing Finance Board
- Federal Labor Relations Authority
- Federal Maritime Commission
- Federal Mediation and Conciliation Service
- Federal Mine Safety and Health Review Commission
- Federal Reserve System
- Federal Retirement Thrift Investment Board
- Federal Trade Commission (FTC)
- General Services Administration (GSA)
- Institute of Museum and Library Services
- Inter-American Foundation
- International Broadcasting Bureau (IBB)
- Merit Systems Protection Board
- National Aeronautics and Space Administration (NASA)
- National Archives and Records Administration (NARA)
- National Capital Planning Commission
- National Council on Disability
- National Credit Union Administration (NCUA)
- National Endowment for the Arts
- National Endowment for the Humanities
- National Labor Relations Board (NLRB)
- National Mediation Board
- National Science Foundation (NSF)
- National Transportation Safety Board
- Nuclear Regulatory Commission (NRC)
- Occupational Safety and Health Review Commission
- Office of Compliance
- Office of Government Ethics
- Office of Personnel Management
- Office of Special Counsel
- Overseas Private Investment Corporation
- Panama Canal Commission
- Peace Corps
- Pension Benefit Guaranty Corporation
- Postal Rate Commission
- Railroad Retirement Board
- Securities and Exchange Commission (SEC)

- Selective Service System
- Small Business Administration (SBA)
- Social Security Administration (SSA)
- Tennessee Valley Authority
- Trade and Development Agency
- United States Agency for International Development
- United States International Trade Commission
- United States Postal Service (USPS)

The executive branch departments and agencies employ approximately 2,673,100 persons (excluding military personnel). The executive branch employs 97.6% of all federal civilian personnel. Additionally, there are approximately 1,475,125 persons (as of October 31, 2003) serving in the military branches (including the Coast Guard). Service in the military of the United States is voluntary.

Federal Law Enforcement Personnel and Agencies. The executive branch of the United States employs the vast majority of the federal law enforcement personnel. As of June 2002, there were 93,000 full-time federal personnel authorized to make arrests and carry firearms according to the Bureau of Justice Statistics. Compared with June 2000, employment of such personnel increased by about 6 percent. An additional 1,300 officers were employed in the U.S. territories. The data gathered by the Bureau of Justice Statistics represented 67 agencies and the numbers do not reflect the changes brought about by the creation of the Department of Homeland Security (Reaves and Bauer 2003).

The federal law enforcement community is very fragmented in terms of jurisdictional authority. Each agency has specific authority by statute. The primary duties for federal officers included criminal investigation (40%), police response and patrol (22%), corrections (18%), noncriminal investigation and inspection (14%), court operations (4%), and security and protection (1%). In terms of gender and racial composition, women accounted for 14.8% of federal officers in 2002. Minority representation was 32.4% in 2002, up from 30.5% in 1998. Hispanic or Latino officers comprised 16.8% of officers in 2002, and African American or black officers, 11.7%. Prior to the creation of the Department of Homeland Security in November of 2002, the Department of Justice employed 58% of all federal law enforcement personnel and the Treasury Department employed 23%. Currently, the Department of Homeland Security employs 38% and the Justice Department 37% (Reaves and Bauer 2003). Each of the federal agencies employing more than 500 full-time personnel is described briefly in the following pages. The agencies are arranged by size, from larger to smaller. The numbers reported here may not reflect the changes that took place in some of the agencies because of the creation of the Department of Homeland Security (special notations are included if the data were available). Agencies with 500 or more officers employed about 87,000, or 93%, of the federal officers covered by the Bureau of Justice Statistic's 2002 survey. Twelve federal agencies employed at least 100 personnel with arrest and firearm authority (Reaves and Bauer 2003). The number of officers, special agents, or investigators that is reported here is probably less than the current strength because most agencies have increased the number of personnel since September 11, 2001. Several hundred more law enforcement personnel were authorized in the 2003 and 2004 budget allocations of the federal government.

Immigration and Naturalization Service (INS): (Department of Homeland Security as of 2003, formerly part of the Department of Justice)—19,101 officers perform duties in three general areas: U.S. Border Patrol, consisting of about 9,830 officers detect and prevent smuggling and illegal entry of nondocumented persons into the United States at the ports of entry and along/nearby the 8,000 miles of U.S. boundaries; immigration inspectors, numbering about 4,529; and criminal investigators and immigration agents, numbering about 2,139 are responsible for investigating crimes under INS jurisdiction and 2,603 officers with detention and deportation duties. In March 2003, services formerly provided by the INS transitioned into the Department of Homeland Security (DHS) under U.S. Citizenship & Immigration Services (USCIS). The immediate priorities of the new USCIS are to promote national security, continue to eliminate immigration adjudications backlogs, and implement solutions for improving immigration customer services. The newly restructured Customs and Border Protection Agency within the Department of Homeland Security will include the Border Patrol, as well as INS, Customs and Agricultural Quarantine Inspectors. The U.S. Immigration and Customs Enforcement will include the enforcement and investigation components of INS, Customs, and the Federal Protective Services.

Federal Bureau of Prisons: (Department of Justice)—14,305 correctional officers maintaining the security of federal institutions. Their duties include supervising inmates, searching for contraband and responding to emergencies and disturbances. All of these officers are trained to use and carry firearms when necessary.

U.S. Customs Service: (Department of Homeland Security as of 2003, formerly part of the Department of the Treasury)—11,634 officers, 8,167 inspectors and 3,467 criminal investigators, interdict and seize contraband, process persons, vehicles, and items at more than 300 ports of entry, and administer certain navigational laws. The Customs Service has an extensive air, land, and marine interdiction force as well as an investigations component supported by its own intelligence branch. The Customs Service investigates violations of more than 400 laws related to customs, drugs, export control, and revenue fraud. It is the second oldest enforcement agency of the country, founded on July 31, 1789. For nearly 125 years, it funded virtually the entire U.S. government, and paid for the nation's early growth and infrastructure.

Federal Bureau of Investigation: (Department of Justice)—11,248 special agents are responsible for criminal investigation and enforcement related to more than 200 categories of federal crimes including bank fraud, embezzlement, kidnapping, and civil rights violations. It also has concurrent jurisdiction with the Drug Enforcement Administration (DEA) over drug offenses under the Controlled Substances Act. Since the September 11, 2001, terrorist attacks on the United States, the FBI has undergone major reorganization, internally, which modified the priorities of the agency to the following:

1. Protect the United States from terrorist attack.

2. Protect the United States against foreign intelligence operations and espionage.

3. Protect the United States against cyber-based attacks and high-technology crimes.

4. Combat public corruption at all levels.

5. Protect civil rights.

6. Combat transnational and national criminal organizations and enterprises.

7. Combat major white-collar crime.

8. Combat significant violent crime.

9. Support federal, state, county, municipal, and international partners.

10. Upgrade technology to successfully perform the FBI's mission.

The mission of the FBI is to protect and defend the United States against terrorist and foreign intelligence threats, to uphold and enforce the criminal laws of the United States, and to provide leadership and criminal justice services to federal, state, municipal, and international agencies and partners. To accomplish this mission, in fiscal year 2003, the FBI received a total of $4.298 billion, including $540.281 million in net program increases to enhance counterterrorism, counterintelligence, cybercrime, information technology, security, forensics, training, and criminal programs. Besides the more than 11,000 special agents, the FBI also employs over 15,900 support personnel in its 56 field offices and 400 satellite offices in the United States and its 45 legal attaché offices around the world.

U.S. Secret Service: (Department of Homeland Security as of 2003, formerly part of the Department of the Treasury)—4,256 special agents and officers have investigation and enforcement duties primarily related to counterfeiting, financial crimes, computer fraud and threats against dignitaries. It is well known for protecting the president and vice president and their immediate families. The Uniformed Division provides protection for the White House complex and other Presidential offices, the Main Treasury Building and Annex and foreign diplomatic missions. It was created originally in 1865 to combat counterfeiting, but it became the general investigative and law enforcement arm of the federal government until 1908 when Congress restricted its authority.

Administrative Office of the U.S. Courts: (Federal Corrections and Supervision Division)—4,090 probation officers (and another 410 were employed in districts where the court does not authorize officers to carry firearms while on duty) supervise federal offenders on probation and supervised release. They also conduct pre-sentence investigations to assess the offender's risk to the community, the harm done by the offender, the need for and ability to pay restitution and the offender's general background.

Drug Enforcement Agency: (Department of Justice)—4,020 special agents investigate major narcotics violators, enforce regulations governing the manufacture and dispensing of controlled substances and perform other functions to prevent and control drug trafficking. Other responsibilities include the management of a national drug intelligence program and the coordination and cooperation with federal, state, and local agencies and with foreign governments in programs designed to reduce the availability of illicit abuse-type drugs. The DEA's budget for fiscal year 2003 was about $1.9 billion.

U.S. Postal Inspection Service: 3,135 postal inspectors and police officers are responsible for criminal investigations covering more than 200 federal statutes related to the postal system. They also provide security for postal facilities, employees and assets, and escort high-value mail shipments.

Internal Revenue Service (IRS): (Department of the Treasury)—2,855 special agents within its Criminal Investigation Division are charged with enforcing the nation's tax laws. The IRS is the only federal agency that can investigate potential criminal violations of the Internal Revenue Code. IRS special agents lend their financial investigative expertise to money laundering and narcotics investigations conducted in conjunction with other law enforcement agencies at the local, state and federal levels. Operations and investigations are carried out through 6 regional offices, 35 field offices and 10 fraud detection centers.

U.S. Marshals Service: (Department of Justice)—2,646 marshals and deputy marshals' responsibilities include the receiving, custody, and transporting of all persons arrested by federal agencies; fugitive matters concerning escaped federal prisoners, probation and parole violators, persons under DEA warrants and defendants released on bond; managing the Federal Witness Security and Federal Asset Seizure and Forfeiture Programs; and security for federal judicial facilities and personnel. The Marshals Service is the oldest federal law enforcement agency; its authority established in 1789. For nearly 75 years, it was the primary enforcement agency of the federal government.

The director, deputy director and 94 U.S. marshals—appointed by the president or the attorney general—direct the activities of 95 district offices and personnel stationed at more than 350 locations throughout the 50 states, Guam, Northern Mariana Islands, Puerto Rico, and the Virgin Islands. The Marshals Service is involved in virtually every federal law enforcement initiative because of its responsibilities. The Service operates the Justice Prisoner and Alien Transportation System (JPATS) for transporting prisoners and criminal aliens. JPATS is one of the largest transporters of prisoners in the world, handling hundreds of requests every day to move prisoners between judicial districts, correctional institutions and foreign countries. On average, more than 270,000 prisoner and alien movements a year are completed by JPATS via coordinated air and ground systems. Since 1983 the Marshals Service has maintained the "15 Most Wanted" fugitives list that is a high-profile list of the most dangerous career criminals in the United States. Of the 167 individuals who have appeared on the list, 159 have been captured. Each year approximately 34,000 federal felons are apprehended because of investigations carried out by deputy marshals. The Marshals Service arrests more federal fugitives than all other law enforcement agencies combined. During fiscal year 2002, Marshals Service–sponsored task forces' arrested more than 27,000 state and local fugitives wanted on felony charges and the service successfully completed 334 extraditions from around the globe.

Bureau of Alcohol, Tobacco, Firearms & Explosives: (ATF)—2,335 officers enforces federal laws related to alcohol, tobacco, firearms, explosives, and arson. In 2003 ATF became a Justice Department agency and its name was changed to include the word *explosives.*

Although established in 1972 as a separate agency within the Treasury Department, many of its tax-related enforcement responsibilities have been carried out since 1789. ATF provides investigative support to the nation's state and local partners through the National Integrated Ballistic Information Network (NIBIN) that provides for the nationwide installation and networking of automated ballistic imaging equipment in partnership. The Comprehensive Crime Gun Tracing Initiative began in 2001 and provides nationwide firearms tracing capability. In fiscal year 2002, the ATF's National Tracing Center conducted over 240,000 trace requests of crime guns. ATF maintains four National Response Teams (NRT) comprised of highly trained and well-equipped special agents, forensic chemists and professional support staff that can be deployed within 24 hours to major explosion and fire scenes anywhere in the United States. The ATF International Response Team participates with the Diplomatic Security Service of the U.S. Department of State to provide technical and investigative assistance at international explosive and fire incidents. There are 36 ATF-trained explosives detection canine teams deployed with state, local, and other federal law enforcement agencies and 48 ATF-trained and certified accelerant detection canine teams deployed with state and local fire and police department. To date, ATF has trained over 310 international law enforcement organizations' explosives detection canine teams worldwide. ATF maintains three national laboratory facilities, in Maryland, Georgia, and California. ATF provides funding and instructor training for a key prevention program called Gang Resistance Education and Training (GREAT). GREAT is a life-skills competency program designed to provide middle-school children the ability to avoid gangs, resist conflict, make responsible decisions, and develop a positive relationship with the law enforcement community. In fiscal year 2002, ATF provided funding to 228 law enforcement agencies and 1,163 officers were certified to instruct in the GREAT program, providing GREAT instruction to 364,701 students.

National Park Service: (Interior Department)— 2,139 officers (1,549 park rangers and 590 park police officers) provide police services for the entire National Park System. Additional rangers serve seasonally, but are considered part-time employees. The history of the Park Police predates both the Department of the Interior and the National Park Service. Created in 1791 by President George Washington, the U.S. Park Police have been on duty in U.S. federal parks for more than 200 years. The U.S. Park Police have responsibilities for providing law enforcement services within the District of Columbia as well as other federal reservations, in the Washington metropolitan area, New York, and San Francisco. They are also frequently requested to provide protection for dignitaries, such as the president of the United States and visiting foreign heads of state, and assistance to other areas of the National Park Service and other law enforcement agencies during law enforcement emergencies.

Veterans Health Administration: (VHA)—1,605 officers provide law enforcement protection at 173 medical centers throughout the country. About 2,400 police officers have arrest authority in the VHA, but many do not have firearms authority. Begun in 1930 as a protective force, it was reorganized in 1972 into the Veterans Administration Police by an act of Congress. Today the Police and Security Service is the component of the Office of Security and Law Enforcement that is responsible for the protection of life and property and the maintenance of order on Veterans Administration facilities. The office conducts criminal investigations of offenses that occur on property owned or used by the department; it works regularly with several federal law enforcement agencies in areas such as information sharing, training, planning and policy development; its field inspectors visit each Veterans Administration Medical Center to conduct a careful review of the security and law enforcement posture of each facility; and it provides executive protection to the secretary of Veterans Affairs.

U.S. Capitol Police: 1,225 officers provide police services for the U.S. Capitol grounds and buildings. The Capitol Police have full law enforcement authority in an extended jurisdiction zone covering the area immediately surrounding the Capitol complex. Its mission is to protect and support the U.S. Congress in meeting its constitutional responsibilities. Congress created the U.S. Capitol Police in 1828 for the sole purpose of providing security for the U.S. Capitol Building. Over the years, its authority was extended to protecting life and property; preventing, detecting, and investigating criminal acts; and enforcing traffic regulations throughout a large complex of congressional buildings, parks, and thoroughfares. Additionally, the Capitol Police are responsible for protecting Members of Congress, Officers of the U.S. Senate, U.S. House of Representatives, and their families. Officers serve these individuals throughout the entire United States, its territories and possessions, and throughout the District of Columbia.

U.S. Fish and Wildlife Service: (Interior Department)—772 full-time personnel have duties related to patrol and enforcement of federal wildlife conservation and environmental laws in the National Wildlife Refuge system and of violations of federal wildlife protection laws and treaties. Federal wildlife law enforcement celebrated its centennial in 2000 with the 100th anniversary of the Lacey Act—the nation's first federal wildlife protection law. The Division of Law Enforcement focuses on combating international wildlife trafficking, unlawful commercial exploitation of native species, environmental contamination, and habitat destruction. Partnerships with states, tribes, and foreign countries make service special agents, wildlife inspectors, and forensic scientists part of a national and global network committed to protecting wildlife resources. The U.S. Fish and Wildlife Service manages the 95-million-acre National Wildlife Refuge System, which encompasses 542 national wildlife refuges, thousands of small wetlands and other special management areas. It also operates 69 national fish hatcheries, 64 fishery resources offices, and 81 ecological services field stations.

General Services Administration: (GSA)—744 officers of the Federal Protective Service (FPS) perform security, patrol and investigative duties related to federal buildings and property, and the employees and visitors using them. In 2003 the FPS was transferred to the Bureau of Immigration and Customs Enforcement, Border and Transportation Security Directorate of the Department of Homeland Security. The mission of FPS is to provide law enforcement and security services to over one million tenants and daily visitors to federally owned and leased facilities nationwide. The services' protection functions focus directly on the interior security of the nation, and require close coordination and intelligence sharing with the investigative functions within the Bureau. FPS is a full service agency with a comprehensive HAZMAT, WMD, Canine, and emergency response program as well as state-of-the-art communication and dispatch centers.

Forest Service: (Department of Agriculture)—658 officers provide police response, patrol and criminal investigation services for the National Forest System lands, facilities and users. Law enforcement personnel operate as full partners within the Forest Service organization in carrying out the agency's three primary objectives: protect the public, employees, natural resources, and other property under the jurisdiction of the Forest Service; investigate and enforce applicable laws and regulations that affect the National Forest System; and prevent criminal violations through informing and educating visitors and users of applicable laws and regulations.

State Department's Bureau of Diplomatic Security: 592 officers and special agents have the primary function of protecting visiting dignitaries. In the United States, the Bureau of Diplomatic Security investigates passport and visa fraud, conducts personnel security investigations, and protects the secretary of state and high-ranking foreign dignitaries and officials visiting the United States. Every diplomatic mission in the world operates under a security program designed and maintained by this bureau. It trains foreign civilian law enforcement officers in disciplines designed to reduce the threat and repercussions of terrorism throughout the world. Through close cooperation and interaction with other State Department offices, the bureau manages reciprocity and immunity issues for foreign diplomats in the United States. The bureau also provides protection to foreign missions through agreements with federal, state, and local law enforcement authorities. The Protective Liaison Division works closely with the Secret Service to provide foreign missions with protective security.

U.S. Mint: (Treasury Department)—375 officers provide police and patrol services for U.S. Mint facilities, including safeguarding the nation's coinage and gold bullion reserves. Established in 1792, the U.S. Mint Police are responsible for protecting over $100 billion in Treasury and other government assets stored in facilities located at Philadelphia; San Francisco; West Point, New York; Denver; Fort Knox, Kentucky; and the mint's headquarters in Washington, D.C. Officers have the primary responsibility for protecting life and property, preventing, detecting, and investigating criminal acts, collecting and preserving evidence, making arrests and enforcing federal and local laws.

Bureau of Indian Affairs: (Interior Department)—334 officers provide police services to Native American populations, through 37 agencies. Additionally, American Indian tribes operated 171 law enforcement agencies that employed at least 1 full-time sworn officer with general arrest powers. Tribally operated agencies employed about 2,303 full-time officers as of 2000. A major difference between tribally operated agencies and their state and local counterparts is jurisdiction over criminal offenses. Jurisdiction in Indian country may lie with federal, state, or tribal agencies depending upon the particular offense, the offender, the victim, and the offense location.

Amtrak: (National Railroad Passenger Corporation)—327 officers within its Police Division provide police response and patrol, and investigative services for the national railroad system.

Pentagon Force Protection Agency (PFPA): 327 officers of the Department of Defense was formerly known as the Defense Protective Service (DPS). The PFPA was established in May 2002 to expand the DPS mission of basic law enforcement and security to provide force protection against the full spectrum of potential threats through prevention, preparedness, detection, and response measures. The PFPA provides services to the 280-acre "Pentagon Reservation" and numerous other DOD activities and facilities in the national capital region.

Bureau of Land Management: (Interior Department)—235 officers provide police response, patrol, and criminal investigative services on 264 million acres of surface lands and 300 million acres of below-ground mineral estate managed by the department. Law enforcement personnel perform a wide variety of tasks, including: protecting cultural and historical sites from vandalism; locating and eradicating drug-manufacturing laboratories and marijuana fields; ensuring the humane treatment of wild horses and burros; guarding against the dumping of hazardous wastes and other pollutants; and preventing theft and damage of timber, rare cactus plants, minerals, and other valuable publicly owned resources.

Environmental Protection Agency: 220 special agents in its Criminal Investigation Division investigate violations of the nation's environmental laws.

Department of Energy: 212 officers (nuclear materials couriers) in its Transportation Safeguards Division protect nuclear weapon shipments from the manufacturer to designated locations.

Tennessee Valley Authority (TVA): 197 officers provide patrol and investigative services for TVA employees and properties, and the users of TVA recreational facilities.

Bureau of Engraving and Printing: 195 officers provide police services for the bureau's facilities including those where currency, stamps, securities, and other official U.S. documents are made.

Food and Drug Administration: 162 officers investigate violations of the federal Food, Drug, and Cosmetic Act and other public health laws.

National Marine Fisheries Service: (National Oceanic and Atmospheric Administration)—137 officers enforce federal laws and regulations that protect the nation's living marine resources.

Library of Congress: 127 officers provide law enforcement services in the library's buildings, protect staff and patrons, and assist in the protection of the library's property and collections.

Additionally, the Office of Inspector General exists in 57 federal offices, however, only 28 employed criminal investigators with arrest and firearm authority as of June 2002. Their primary responsibilities are to investigate violations and prevent and detect fraud, waste, and abuse within their respective agencies and programs. The largest inspector general office is found in the Department of Health and Human Services, with 436 investigative officers; the smallest is the Government Printing Office with eight (Reaves and Bauer 2003).

Police Statistics. At the state and local levels of government, it is very difficult to report exact statistics on how many law enforcement agencies operate in the United States. Because of the fragmented nature of the governmental system, no one agency or office is responsible for

maintaining accurate lists of information about the policing community in the United States. In some of the states, a central agency may collect and maintain statistics, however, the accuracy of such data varies. Because of local control over policing matters, agencies can be created or disbanded based on the will of the local governing officials. An agency can be formed in one community and abolished in another during the same week. Central registries of this activity are rare, although some reliable data is maintained by state offices responsible for the training and certification of officers. Thus, any count of the number of law enforcement agencies is an estimate and not an exact figure.

Since 1987 the Bureau of Justice Statistics in the Office of Justice Programs within the U.S. Department of Justice has been collecting data from law enforcement agencies under the Law Enforcement Management and Administrative Statistics (LEMAS) program. This program conducts surveys of the law enforcement community every three years. Because the survey consists of several thousand questionnaires and considerable data, there always is some time delay in reporting the results. The data reported in this chapter were the most recent available when the text was prepared, but the Bureau of Justice Statistics, Office of Justice Programs, in the U.S. Department of Justice continues to update these publications periodically.

State Agencies. There are 49 states that have at least one state-level policing agency with uniformed officers. Usually, this major agency is known as the "state police," "state patrol," or "department of public safety." Other state agencies may exist, however, that have responsibilities for specific areas of enforcement such as major criminal investigation, alcoholic beverage control, fish and wildlife protection, parks protection, health-care fraud, and environmental crimes. As with other governmental levels, the jurisdiction and authority of state agencies depend on legislative mandate. In general, those states with the title "state police" have broad policing authority throughout the state and have enforcement responsibilities over all types of offenses. Many states restrict the authority of their state-level policing agencies to specified areas of offenses, and if multiple agencies exist, they may be spread among several executive agencies within the state.

Of the state policing agencies, 37 (75%) have 500 or more full-time officers; 19 (38.7%) have 1,000 or more officers. The percentage of full-time employees that are sworn officers ranged from a low of 40.5 (Texas), to a high of 93.2 (Utah). The ratio of full-time officers to 10,000 population ranged from 1 (Florida) to 8.1 (Vermont), with 29 states falling in the 1.6 to 2.5 range.

The major functions performed by state policing agencies (from most prevalent to least) included the following:

- Accident investigation and traffic enforcement
- Patrol and first response
- Communications and dispatch
- Special Weapons and Tactics (SWAT)
- Search/rescue operations
- Narcotics/vice enforcement and training academy operations
- Fingerprint processing
- Major crime investigation (violent and property crime)
- Ballistics/laboratory testing

Special Jurisdiction/Purpose Police Agencies. A survey conducted in 2000 by the U.S. Department of Justice's Bureau of Justice Statistics, identified 1,376 special police agencies at both the state and local agency levels. Such agencies employed 69,650 full-time personnel, of which over 43,413 were sworn officers. These special police agencies constitute about 7.7% of all local and state agencies in the United States. This category of agency is very difficult to describe because it contains a variety of agencies. Such agencies usually have names that describe their uniqueness, such as mass transit, park district, gaming/racing, alcohol beverage control, metropolitan housing authority, campus/college, port authority, or airport police. Officers working in such special police agencies may possess general police authority only within the geographical limitations of their jurisdiction. Some of these agencies possess specific police authority over a large geographical area (for example, a state liquor control agent has authority throughout a state, but only over liquor-related offenses and regulations). Of all the special police agencies, about 50% are campus law enforcement agencies. Generally, with regard to campus law enforcement agencies, sworn and armed officers were more likely to be found at institutions under public rather than private control. Overall, about 93% of the agencies serving public institutions used sworn officers, and 81% used armed patrol officers, compared to 43% and 34% respectively among private institutions.

Local Agencies. Based on the 2000 survey conducted by the U.S. Department of Justice's Bureau of Justice Statistics, there are at least 17,700 local law enforcement agencies in the United States. Although there are many small agencies in the United States employing small numbers of officers, 72.5% percent of the sworn officers at the local level are employed in agencies of 50

or more sworn offices. These sworn officers are employed in only 2,209 agencies, or 12.4% percent of all local agencies. In the United States, there are about 9,214 agencies that employ fewer than 10 officers each; that is 51.8% of all local agencies in the country. Geographically, most of the country is policed by small local agencies.

There are some discrepancies between federal offices that collect information related to the strength of law enforcement agencies in the United States. In addition to the data collected and published by the Bureau of Justice Statistics, the FBI also publishes personnel data in their annual *Crime in the United States*. In 2002 the FBI estimated that there were 665,555 full-time sworn officers and 291,947 civilians providing law enforcement services in the United States. The average number of officers per 1,000 inhabitants would be 2.46. Of course, the ratio of officers to 1,000 inhabitants varies from jurisdiction to jurisdiction. In cities, the average was 2.3 officers per 1,000 population; in suburban counties, it was 2.7; and in rural counties it was 2.5. When cities were grouped by size, the range of officers per 1,000 was 1.8 for cities with 25,000–99,999 population to 3.2 for cities with fewer than 10,000 inhabitants (FBI 2002).

Local policing, the uniformed officer on the beat, is the most noticeable to the public on a daily basis. It is the local police who respond to general street crime and most traffic accidents. Local police authority is general in scope; they can enforce the general criminal code of the state plus appropriate county or city ordinances. They may be responsible for initiating federal charges in many jurisdictions; however, such situations are usually referred to federal authorities or investigated jointly. Nearly all local police departments have primary responsibility for initially investigating most types of crimes occurring in their jurisdiction. In some jurisdictions, the most violent or serious criminal offenses may be referred to other policing agencies, such as a county or state investigatory agency. The size of agencies does have some relationship to their primary function and responsibilities. The major functions carried out by local agencies are responding to calls for service, general patrol, criminal investigation, crime prevention, and homeland security. The larger agencies have specialized operations units to investigate sex crimes, drug, organized crime, terrorist activity, financial fraud and computer crime, and juvenile offenses. Specialized assignments to task forces, school resource functions, special weapons and tactics, squads, and criminal intelligence functions usually only occur in larger agencies also.

The concept of task forces has become very effective in recent years in the United States. A task force may utilize officers from many agencies in a region, including federal and state personnel. If smaller jurisdictions are involved, officers may be assigned to the task force for one or several day each week. By sharing human resources a task force can address crime issues over a larger geographical region. The types of task forces that function in the United States address issues such as violent crime, computer crime, narcotics, fraud, corruption and terrorism.

In the United States at the local level, not all police personnel are full-time employees. Throughout the country, various options exist within agencies for part-time officers who work limited hours weekly or only when needed to replace full-time officers. Part-time officers usually are paid an hourly wage. In many agencies, especially smaller ones, "reserve officers" or "auxiliary officers" may exist. They may be paid when on-duty, but they may be volunteering their time to the community. Terminology varies among the states, and what is deemed a reserve officer in one state may be called an auxiliary officer in another. Regardless of title, the key to their policing status is whether they are authorized to make arrests and carry a firearm. As indicated above, there were at least 43,000 part-time officers in the country in 2000 (and that figure may not include all the auxiliary and/or reserve officers).

Special Police. Another type of police officer that may appear in the protection of the public in the United States is referred to as special police. This is not to be confused with the public special purpose policing agencies discussed above. Some officers in uniform wear patches that may say Special Police, but they may not possess full arrest authority, and their authority to carry firearms may be limited to a very small geographical area, such as their place of employment. Many of the special police officers in the United States are actually private police who may be regulated by a public agency at the state level. Such private police may possess special police authority if a state legislature or city council has authorized it (such as the right to detain shoplifters, or the right to protect museums, libraries, art galleries, and so on). In many jurisdictions, these special police officers are considered private security personnel and possess no arrest authority at all, other than that possessed by the private citizen. It should be mentioned that in the United States, the right of a citizen to apprehend or arrest another person committing a criminal offense exists in most jurisdictions. The right is usually limited to serious offenses, such as felonies, and usually is regulated by statutory law of the state.

Education and Training. The education and training requirements for law enforcement personnel are not standardized across agencies because of the fragmented nature of policing in the United States. Federal agencies usually require a baccalaureate degree as the minimum education requirement; however, some agencies accept candidates who have some college education if they have several years of law enforcement experience. State and local agencies vary in the education requirement. The majority of state and local agencies require a minimum of a high school diploma or equivalent as the minimum for applying to their agency. Statistics are difficult to report on this issue since there is no central government agency that maintains such data nor are agencies required to report it. In at least two states, a state regulatory agency for certification and training has established two years of college as the minimum education requirement for peace officers. At the local level in the United States, an estimated 12% require two years of college as the minimum, while about 1% requires a baccalaureate degree. Since 1968 there have been several national commission reports that advocated increased education requirements for the nation's peace officers. Agencies have been hesitant to raise the educational entrance requirements because it may limit the pool of applicants for rural and small agencies and because it may reduce the number of minority applicants. In the United States, it is a violation of discrimination in employment law if requirements are not job-related or necessary. Research on the relationship between education and officer performance has been supportive for increased education; however, it also has been sporadic.

Training requirements also vary across the country and by level of government. Federal agencies often require 12–26 weeks of training for their new hires. A majority of federal officers receive some or all of their training through the Federal Law Enforcement Training Center (FLETC), headquartered in Glynco, Georgia. FLETC operates two satellite facilities (Artesia, New Mexico, and Charleston, South Carolina) and a third one is under development in Cheltenham, Maryland. The New Mexico facility trains federal officers in the western part of the country and focuses on Immigration and Border Patrol, Bureau of Prison officers and federal air marshals. In fiscal year 2002, more than 32,000 students graduated from FLETC facilities, including about 2,600 state and local officers. In 2003 the Training Center was transferred from the Treasury Department to the Department of Homeland Security. FLETC serves more than 70 federal agencies, as well as state, local, and international law enforcement communities. It has an annual budget of nearly $200 million. Classroom training for criminal investigators ranged from about 8 weeks to 22 weeks. For patrol officers, classroom training ranged from 4 weeks to 26 weeks. Field training requirements ranged from 2 weeks to 6 months for patrol officers, and as long as 2 years for investigators (Reaves and Bauer 2003).

Federal agents assigned to the FBI and DEA are trained at facilities located at Quantico, Virginia, on the

U.S. Marine Corps Base. The facility opened in 1972 and is situated on 385 wooded acres of land. The main training complex has three dormitory buildings, a dining hall, library, a classroom building, a Forensic Science Research and Training Center, a 1,000-seat auditorium, a chapel, administrative offices, a large gymnasium and outside track, along with a fully equipped garage. In addition to the main complex, there is a mock city known as Hogans Alley, which consists of facades replicating a typical small town. Just beyond Hogans Alley is a 1.1-mile pursuit/defensive driving training track. The extensive firearms training provided to all FBI/DEA and other law enforcement officers is conducted at the indoor firing range, the eight outdoor firing ranges, four skeet ranges, or the 200-yard rifle range.

The FBI New Agents' Training Unit (NATU) coordinates 16 weeks of instruction at the academy. New agent trainees are exposed to three components of curriculum: investigative/tactical, noninvestigative, and administrative. These three components total 643.5 hours of instruction, which are spread over four major concentrations: academics, firearms, operational skills and the integrated case scenario. New agents must pass 11 academic examinations, with a score of 85% or better, in the following disciplines: Legal (2 exams), Behavioral Science, Interviewing, Ethics, White Collar Crime, Organized Crime/Drugs/Violent Crime, Informants/Cooperating Witnesses, Interrogation, Forensic Science and National Foreign Intelligence Program. Additionally, FBI trainees must pass a physical training test involving (1) pull-ups, (2) sit-ups, (3) push-ups, (4) 120-yard shuttle run, and (5) two-mile run and a defensive tactics test. The defensive tactics test focuses on grappling and boxing, handcuffing, control holds, searching subjects, weapon retention, and disarming techniques. In terms of firearms training, each trainee must qualify twice with the bureau-issued handgun, and once with the shotgun; and must demonstrate familiarity with the submachine gun. During their 16 weeks of training trainees will fire between 3,000 and 5,000 rounds of ammunition.

The DEA and FBI use shared facilities at Quantico for physical fitness training, firearms, and tactical vehicle training, however, since 1999 the DEA has enjoyed its own training academy consisting of 185,000 square feet of space. The building includes a 250-bed dormitory; tiered classrooms; management, computer and break-out classrooms; an international translation-capable classroom; practical areas for fingerprinting, interviewing and wiretap training; and student support services, including a gift shop, nurse's station, mail room, laundry, dry cleaners, banking facilities, and a 250-seat cafeteria. Classrooms are equipped with rear screen, state-of-the-art audiovisual technologies. Each classroom has a camera mounted in the room so presentations in that classroom can be recorded or broadcast to every other classroom, and even to the dormitory if a student is ill and unable to attend class. The DEA Training Academy is used for Basic Agent training, Basic Diversion Investigator training, Basic Intelligence Research Specialist training, Basic Forensic Science training, professional and executive development training, certification training, and specialized training. The academy is also used to conduct drug law enforcement seminars for state and local law enforcement personnel, and through the use of specially equipped classrooms, international drug training seminars for foreign law enforcement officials. The academy's international classroom has the capacity to simultaneously translate an instructor's course of instruction into three different languages.

The typical DEA basic agent class sizes range from 40 to 50 trainees. The average age of trainees is 30 years. Approximately 60 percent of all trainees arrive with prior law enforcement experience, while 30 percent come from a military background. Every student must possess a bachelor's degree and nearly 20 percent have some postgraduate educational experience. The curriculum is a 16-week resident program that places strong emphasis upon leadership, ethics, and human dignity. Academic instruction provides the basics of report writing, law, automated information systems, and drug recognition, as well as leadership and ethics. Underpinning the instruction is a rigorous 84-hour physical fitness and defensive tactics regimen designed to prepare new special agents to prevail in compliant and noncompliant arrest scenarios. The firearms training program consists of 120 hours in basic marksmanship, weapons safety, tactical shooting, and deadly force decision training. In order to graduate, students must maintain an academic average of 80 percent on academic examinations, pass the firearms qualification test, successfully demonstrate leadership and sound decision making in practical scenarios, and pass rigorous physical task tests.

Most training facilities for state and local officers throughout the United States do not compare in size and complexity to the federal facilities. There is considerable variation in training facilities from state to state and within states; no general statement accurately describes the training facilities throughout the country. Across the United States, there is no standard curriculum or length of training for basic trainees. Again, differences are considerable because of the fragmented nature of the political jurisdictions, the variation in financial resources and philosophical differences. The main state agencies with uniformed officers average about 20 weeks of basic training. At the local level, the minimum hours of training for new officers is usually regulated by the state and the number of minimum hours varies from about 400 to 800 hours; the average is about 550. Regardless of the state mandated minimum hours, many large jurisdictions, especially large municipalities, average between 600 to 900 hours of initial or basic training. Almost all agencies require newly acquired officers to complete several weeks of orientation and field training following their basic training.

Salaries and Benefits. Annual salaries for law enforcement personnel vary considerably from the large cities to the rural sheriff's department; from the federal special agent to a local township constable. The typical salary is based on a 40-hour workweek. Entry-level salaries in large urban police departments serving populations over 250,000 average about $35,000. Rural sheriffs' departments offer an average starting salary in the low $20,000-range. Federal agents' starting salary is around $34,000-$41,000, depending on the agency and the locale of initial assignment. Small rural agencies may have starting salaries below $20,000. In addition to the stated salary, full-time employment normally includes paid (or mostly paid) health insurance, possibly dental and eye care, employer contributions to Medicare, Social Security or a pension plan, life insurance, and other insurances. Included in the typical benefit package for officers are the following: paid holiday, sick and vacation leave; paid overtime or compensatory leave (in lieu of overtime payment, hours may be accrued to be taken as paid leave); paid personal days; and paid military leave if in the National Guard or a military reserve unit. Other factors may increase an officer's pay; these include clothing/uniform allowances, hazardous duty pay, education incentives, court time, and shift differential.

Police Officers Killed in the Line of Duty. During the 1990s, an average of 166 officers died on duty each year. Preliminary figures for 2003 indicated that 148 law enforcement officers were killed in the line of duty in the United States, which was the same as for 2002. Of the 148 officers, 142 were male and 6 were female. Those officers worked in 38 of the 50 states, as well as Puerto Rico and one federal agency. According to the National Law Enforcement Officers Memorial Fund and the Concerns of Police Survivors, the states with the highest number of officer fatalities were: California (18); Georgia (10); Texas (10); Virginia (8); and Florida, Louisiana, and Tennessee (7). Of the 148 officers killed during 2003, preliminary data show that 53 died in automobile accidents; 52 were shot to death; 13 were struck by automobiles while on duty outside their vehicles; 11 died in motorcycle accidents; 6 succumbed to job-related illnesses; 4 drowned; 2 suffered fatal beatings; 2 fell to their deaths; 1 was stabbed to death; 1 died

in an aircraft accident; 1 was electrocuted; 1 was strangled; and 1 was hit by a train.

Dating back to the first known law enforcement fatality in 1792, there have been more than 16,000 federal, state, and local officers killed in the United States. All of those names are inscribed on the National Law Enforcement Officers Memorial, which is located in Washington, D.C.

Retirement Age. The retirement age for officers in the United States varies. Some departments have mandatory retirement at specific ages, such as 55, but most departments do not have mandatory retirement provisions. Most officers work 20 to 35 years before retiring and there have examples of officers working up to 50 years. Most departments have a retirement system; many are managed through statutory systems established at the state level. Normally, there is a minimum number of years of service required before an officer can retire. Usually, the amount of an officer's pension is determined by the combination of years of service and age and an average of the officer's highest three years of earnings. Each year of service is granted a certain percent, such as 2.2%; which is then multiplied by the number of years of service, such as 25; which is then multiplied by the average of the officer's highest three years of earnings, for example $45,000. The resulting annual pension would be: .022 (2.2%) x 25 years x $45,000 = $24,750. If this same officer had worked 30 years, the pension would be: $29,700. If the officer had worked 30 years with the highest average earnings of $50,000, the resulting annual pension would be $33,000. Pension systems often include medical insurance and death insurance benefits at various costs to the retired officer.

CRIME

There are two primary sources of data on the amount of crime in the United States. The most commonly known source is taken from offenses reported to police and is counted at the level of the local law enforcement agency. Collected and presented in the Uniform Crime Report or UCR, it is published annually by the FBI under the title *Crime in the United States*. The second method is known as the National Crime Victimization Survey (NCVS), initiated in 1973. It measures major crime through interviewing a sample of about 100,000 people in about 50,000 households. The NCVS is conducted for the Bureau of Justice Statistics (U.S. Department of Justice) by the federal Bureau of the Census. Each method has advantages and disadvantages.

The UCR data are compiled from participating law enforcement agencies that report monthly records of offenses reported to or discovered by police. Monthly reports have two parts. Part 1 Offenses are called Index Crimes and are those from which the FBI tracks the "Crime Index" that it reports to the nation through the media. The Crime Index includes the offenses of: arson, assault, burglary, forcible rape, larceny-theft, motor vehicle theft, robbery, and murder and non-negligent manslaughter. Most news reports published in the United States regarding the crime rates are based on this data. These offenses are used to gauge the crime "index," or its rate of decrease or increase. There are some problems with this method of counting, however. First, it covers only crime reported to law enforcement, and much of the crime committed in the United States is not reported. If victims do not trust police or the criminal justice system, or fear retaliation or humiliation, they may never report victimization. Hence, if victims change their behavior and report more crimes, the result may leave the impression that crime is increasing which may not be true. This is a significant problem. Second, if law enforcement agencies become more effective in discovering crimes, the rate will seem to increase because more crime was discovered. Third, the definitions of crimes are not the same from state to state and, in some cases, from year to year. For example, an offense such as entering an outbuilding (storage shed) might be a criminal trespass in Ohio, but a burglary in Georgia. One is a minor offense, while the other is serious. A fourth problem with the UCR is that it does not account for victimless crime, which is behavior defined as criminal, but engaged in by many who think it should not be. Generally, this includes prostitution, gambling, drug abuse, pornography, and others. For all of these reasons, the UCR alone is not sufficient for some researchers and criminologists to grasp the true rate of crime.

The second means to measure crime, the NCVS, essentially measures crimes that were committed against households, residents, and businesses. In conducting the survey, people are asked if they have been the victim of a crime in the past year and, if so, to describe it. Detailed information is acquired for victimizations. On the basis of this broad survey, estimates are generated for the nation as a whole. The NCVS provides interesting information. First, the rate of victimization is generally going down, not up. However, it is also clear that a significant amount of crime is not reported. The 2002 NCVS report, for example, indicated that the rate of reporting crime varied considerably across types of crime. Approximately 67% of thefts are not reported to the police, but only 37% of robberies are not reported. Victimization surveys also have their limitation because self-reported recollections are not reliable and each respondent is going to interpret events from his or her own perspective. She or he may see a situation as an assault when it was not. Another limitation of the NCVS, like that of the UCR, is its inability to capture information regarding white-collar crime and fraud, or information about crimes in which the respondent may have been involved. Respondents must be relied upon to report offender characteristics, and frequently the victim does not know this information. Information from the NCVS is important, but it is limited as well, and that must be kept in mind while interpreting the data.

Major Crime Rates. Nationally, the 2002 Crime Index for the United States included an estimated 11,877,218 offenses, which was a rise of less than one-tenth of a percent over 2001 figures. The Crime Index for 2002 was comprised of 12 percent violent crime and 88 percent property crime. Most violent crime rates remained about the same as 2001, however murder rose about one percent and forcible rape increased 4.7%. The percentage distribution of the major index offenses were: larceny-theft, 59.4%; burglary, 18.1%; motor vehicle theft, 10.5%; aggravated assault, 7.5%; robbery 3.5%; forcible rape, 0.8%; and murder, 0.1 percent.

The UCR (FBI) historically publishes a crime clock each year. The numbers at first glance appear quite serious, but it must be remembered that the United States is a very large nation. It should be interpreted as "somewhere in the United States, one crime index offense is committed every 2.7 seconds." Some local jurisdictions also calculate crime clocks to give their citizens a more realistic view of criminal activity in their jurisdictions; and the time element is significantly different when reduced to the local level.

Statistics can be very deceiving when one focuses on only one year. Both the UCR and the NVCS reports contain comparative data and statistics from previous years. UCR data, for example, when plotted over time, indicate that the crime rate in the United States has dropped since 1991 and some crimes are at a 30-year low. Even the 2002 NCVS report indicates that overall violent victimization and property crime rates were the lowest recorded since the inception of the NCVS in 1973.

The 2002 UCR also reported arrests and clearance rates for index crimes. An estimated 2,234,464 arrests for crime index offenses occurred which accounted for 16.3% of the total 13,741,438 arrests made in 2002. In other words, about 83.7% of all arrests in the United States are for nonindex offenses. The UCR also tabulates the "clearance rates" of offenses. An offense is cleared when an arrest is made and charges have been brought against the arrestee. An offense also is considered cleared by exceptional means if the offender has been identified and located and sufficient evidence for an arrest exists but circumstance beyond the control of law enforcement precludes making an arrest or charging the offender. In the United States in 2002, 20% of all crime index offenses were cleared by arrest or exceptional means. The rates vary according to offense. For 2002 the crime index offenses had the following clearance rates, nationally:

Murder	64%
Aggravated Assault	56.5%
Forcible Rape	44.5%
Robbery	25.7%
Larceny-Theft	18%
Motor Vehicle Theft	13.8%
Burglary	13%

There are also regional and jurisdictional differences in clearance rates because of the fragmented nature of the law enforcement system in the United States.

STATE PROFILES

The following sections provide an overview of the demographics, government, law enforcement community and corrections community in each state of the United States. Basic statistical data generally is from governmental sources such as the U.S. Bureau of the Census, the U.S. Department of Justice's offices, and other selected sources. Additional and more detailed information about each state can be accessed through various Web sites, many of which are listed in the reference section at the end of this article. The reader is reminded that statistical profiles of the law enforcement and corrections community will vary over time. Most of the data reported are for 2002 or 2003. These basic data do not vary greatly from year to year but the source of the data also has some limitations. For example, the data on crime statistics are based on officially reported crime; it is understood that not all crime is reported to the police. The data on the number of law enforcement agencies and full-time personnel in the various states are based on data reported to the FBI, except for a few states. However, again, not all agencies report their data, therefore, the data are not complete. For that reason it is understood that there are more agencies and more personnel than are reported for each state. Also, the data do not included part-time or reserve/auxiliary personnel.

The State of Alabama. Alabama is located in the southeastern part of the United States. It is bordered by Tennessee on the north, Georgia on the east, Florida and the Gulf of Mexico on the south, and Mississippi on the west. The state occupies a total area of 52,423 square miles including 1,673 square miles of water and it has a coastline of 53 miles and a shoreline of 607 miles. It is the 30th largest state in terms of area. Based on 2000 census figures, it ranks 23rd among the states in population. The capital of the state is the city of Montgomery with a population of 201,568. Other major cities and their populations include Birmingham, 242,820; Mobile, 198,915; Huntsville, 158,216; Tuscaloosa, 77,906; Hoover, 62,742; Dothan, 57,737; Decatur, 53,929; Auburn, 42,987; and Gadsden, 38,978. The state is divided into 67 counties.

The territory was organized in March 1817, and became the 22nd state on December 14, 1819. Alabama's constitution was adopted in 1901, which provided for an elected governor and a bicameral legislature. Today the legislature is made up of 35 members in a senate and 105 members in a house of representatives. As with all states in the United States, it elects two senators to the U.S. Congress, but the number of elected representatives to the House of Representatives is based on population; for Alabama it is seven.

The economy of the state primarily consists of agricultural and farming products of poultry and eggs, cattle, nursery stock, peanuts, cotton, vegetables, milk and soybeans. Its industrial base consists of paper, lumber and wood products, mining, rubber and plastic products, transportation equipment, and clothing apparel. The estimated 2002 population was 4,486,508. The percentage breakdown of the 2000 census was 71.1% White, 26.0 % Black or African American, 0.5% American Indian and 0.7% Asian. Persons reporting some other race were 0.7% and those reporting two or more races were 1.0%. Hispanics, who may be of any race, were 1.7% of the people. The 2000 census indicated that the population age 18 and over was 74.7%, 65 and over was 13.0% and the median age was 35.8.

The law enforcement community in Alabama consists of at least 380 agencies with a combined total of about 10,311 full-time officers and over 5,156 civilians. A breakdown of the agencies by governmental level and personnel strength based on 2002 data is listed in Table 1-1. There were 394 law enforcement officers assaulted in 2002. Officers in the state must complete at least 480 hours of basic training and 12 hours of continuing education annually. There were 370 officers assaulted in 2002. Two officers were killed feloniously in the line of duty and two died accidentally during 2002.

Crime Index offenses for 2002 for the state of Alabama totaled 200,331, which was a rate of 4,465.2 per 100,000 inhabitants. The numbers of major index offenses by category are listed in Table 1-2. At least 195,820 arrests were made in 2002 for all categories of crimes, with 25,619 being for index offenses. Of the index offense arrests, 3,912 arrests (15.3%) were persons under the age of 18.

Table 1-1. LAW ENFORCEMENT EMPLOYEE DATA, ALABAMA, 2002

Type of Agency	Number of Agencies	Total Personnel	Sworn	Civilian
All Agencies	380	15,467	10,311	5,156
State Agencies	6	1,406	759	647
County Sheriff's Offices	67	4,399	2,329	2,070
City Police	290	9,210	6,941	2,269
University Police Departments	17	452	282	170

SOURCE: http://acjic.state.al.us/SAC/cia02/02f-LawEnforcementEmployeeData.htm

Table 1-2. Crime Index Offenses, Alabama, 2002

Index Offense Category	Number of Offenses
Murder	303
Rape	1,664
Robbery	5,962
Assault	12,002
Burglary	42,578
Larceny	123,932
Auto Theft	13,890
Total Violent	19,931
Total Property	180,400
Total Crime Index	200,331

SOURCE: FBI, *Crime in the United States, 2002.*

The State of Alaska. Alaska is located in the northwestern part of the North American continent. It is bordered by Canada on the east and south. Also on the south is the Gulf of Alaska and the Pacific Ocean. The Bering Sea is to the west and the Arctic Ocean is to the north. The state is approximately 1,480 miles long and 810 miles wide and is not contiguous to any other states of the country. Alaska encompasses about 658,002 square miles, of which 86,051 square miles are water. It has about 6.640 of miles of coastline. It is the largest of the 50 states and more than twice the size of Texas, the second-largest state; but in terms of population, it ranks 48th. The capital of Alaska is Juneau with a population of about 31,262. Other major cities and their 2001 estimated populations include Anchorage, 261,446; Juneau, 31,262; Sitka, 8,788; Ketchikan, 8,295; Kenai, 7,039; Kodiak, 6,836; Wasilla, 5,568; Bethel, 5,449; and Barrow, 4,541. The state is divided into 16 boroughs. Alaska has 149 incorporated cities, including 12 home rule cities, 21 first-class cities and 116 second-class cities. There are 246 federally recognized tribal governments and one federal Indian reservation in the state.

On August 1, 1868, the United States purchased Alaska from Russia for $7.2 million, about two cents an acre; "Seward's Folly" many called it, after Secretary of State William H. Seward who negotiated the purchase. It was a territory until January 3, 1959, when it became the 49th state of the United States. Alaska's constitution was ratified in 1956 and became fully operational upon statehood. Today the legislature is made up of 20 members in a senate and 40 members in a house of representatives. As with all states in the United States, it elects two senators to the U.S. Congress, but the number of elected representatives to the House of Representatives is based on population; for Alaska it is one.

The oil and gas industry is the largest component of Alaska's economy. Oil revenues supply nearly 85 percent of the state budget. Gold and other mining, food processing, lumber and wood products, and tourism are other major industries. Alaska contains half the nation's coal reserves, and its largest silver and zinc mines. The tourism industry is Alaska's second-largest primary employer. In terms of agriculture, the major products include seafood, nursery stock, dairy products, vegetables and livestock. The estimated 2002 population was 642,955. Nearly half of the state's residents live in Anchorage, and most of the people live along the coasts and the river valleys. Some sections of the Interior and Arctic Slope regions remain uninhabited. In 2000 some 66 percent of all Alaskans lived in areas classified as urban. The percentage breakdown of the 2000 census was 69.3% White, 3.5% Black or African American, 15.6% American Indian and Alaska Native (Eskimo), 4.0% Asian and 0.5% Native Hawaiian and Other Pacific Islander. Persons reporting two or more races on the 2000 census were 5.4%. Hispanics, who may be of any race, were 4.1 percent of the people. Persons age 18 or older was 69.6% and persons 65 years old and over was 5.7%. The median age was 34.2.

The law enforcement community of Alaska is quite diverse and a statistical summary is presented in Table 2-1. The Alaska State Police functions as the primary agency across the state. Most municipalities have their own police department and there are another 90–100 villages that have officers. The jurisdiction of many of the agencies is quite large. For example, the North Slope Borough Police Department (NSBPD) is the fourth-largest municipal law enforcement agency in Alaska; it provides law enforcement services to the predominately Inupiat Eskimo communities of Barrow (the borough seat), Kaktovik, Nuiqsut, Anaktuvuk Pass, Atqasuk, Wainwright, Point Lay, Point Hope and the oil industrial complex at Prudhoe Bay. In total, the NSBPD serves a population of about 12,600 over an area of 88,281 square miles—a region larger than all but ten of the fifty states of the United States.

Table 2-1. LAW ENFORCEMENT EMPLOYEE DATA, ALASKA, 2002

Type of Agency	Number of Agencies	Total Personnel	Sworn	Civilian
All Agencies	41	1,857	1,161	696
State Agency	1	585	341	244
Borough	2	70	39	31
City Police	34	1,075	668	407
University Police Departments	2	35	24	11
Airport Safety Departments	2	92	89	3

SOURCE: FBI, *Crime in the United States, 2002.*

Table 3-1. LAW ENFORCEMENT EMPLOYEE DATA, ARIZONA, 2002

Type of Agency	Number of Agencies	Total Personnel	Sworn	Civilian
All Agencies	101	18,731	10,964	7,767
State Agencies	2	1,964	1,119	845
County	15	5,509	1,863	3,646
City Police	76	11,016	7,820	3,196
University Police Departments	8	242	162	80

SOURCE: FBI, *Crime in the United States, 2002.*

Police officers are required to complete 400 hours of basic training and 40 hours of supervised field training. Village police officers must complete a minimum of 48 hours. There were 115 officers assaulted in 2002. No officers were killed feloniously in the line of duty but two died accidentally during 2002.

Crime Index offenses for 2002 for the state of Alaska totaled 27,745 which was a rate of 4,309.7 per 100,000 inhabitants. The numbers of index offenses by category are listed in Table 2-2. At least 31,730 persons were arrested in Alaska for all categories of crimes, with 5,626 being for index offenses. Of the index offense arrests, 2,212 arrests (39%) were persons under the age of 18.

Table 2-2. Crime Index Offenses, Alaska, 2002

Index Offense Category	Number of Offenses
Murder	33
Rape	511
Robbery	489
Aggravated Assault	2,594
Burglary	3,908
Larceny-Theft	17,739
Auto Theft	2,471
Total Violent	3,627
Total Property	24,118
Total Crime Index	27,745

SOURCE: FBI, *Crime in the United States, 2002.*

The State of Arizona. Arizona is located in the southwestern part of the continental United States. It is bordered by Utah to the north, New Mexico to the east, Nevada and California to the west, and the country of Mexico to the south. Arizona encompasses about 114,006 square miles of area including 364 square miles of water. It has no coastline. It is the sixth-largest of the

50 states. The capital of Arizona is Phoenix with a 2000 population of 1,321,045. Based on 2000 census figures, it ranks 20th among the states in population, but its growth rate from 1990 was 40%; and the growth from 1980 to 1990 was 35%. In addition to Phoenix, the other major cities and their 2000 populations are Tucson, 486,699; Mesa, 396,375; Glendale, 218,812; Scottsdale, 202,705; Chandler, 176,581; Tempe, 158,625; Gilbert, 109,697; Peoria, 108,364; Yuma, 77,515; and Flagstaff, 52,894. The state is divided into 15 counties.

Arizona was admitted to statehood on February 14, 1912, as the 48th state. The state legislature is made up of 30 senators and 60 representatives. As with all states in the United States, it elects two senators to the U.S. Congress, but the number of elected representatives to the House of Representatives is based on population; for Arizona it is six. Additionally, in the state, there are 12 tribal governments.

The major industries of the state are copper and other mining, electric equipment, transportation equipment, machinery, printing and publishing, food processing, electronics and tourism. The primary agricultural products are cattle, cotton, dairy products, lettuce, nursery stock and hay. The estimated population for 2002 was 5,164,982. The percentage breakdown of the 2000 census was 75.5% White, 3.1% Black or African American, 5.0% American Indian, 1.8% Asian and 0.1% Native Hawaiian and Other Pacific Islander. Persons reporting some other race were 11.6% and those reporting two or more races on the 2000 census were 2.9%. Hispanics, who may be of any race, were 25.3% of the population in 2000. Persons age18 or older was 73.4% and persons 65 years old and over was 13.0%. The median age was 34.2.

All police officers must complete 585 hours of mandatory training. There were 2,201 officers assaulted in 2002, with personal injuries sustained in 17.1% of the assaults. Three officers were killed in the line of duty during 2002 (Department of Public Safety, 2003).

Crime Index offenses for 2002 for the state of Arizona totaled 348,467, which was a rate of 6,386.3 per 100,000 inhabitants. The numbers of index offenses by category are listed in Table 3-2. At least 298,631 arrests were made in Arizona in 2002 for all categories of crimes, with 48,900 being for index offenses. Of the index offense arrests, 13,508 arrests (27.6%) were persons under the age of 18.

Table 3-2. Crime Index Offenses, Arizona, 2002

Index Offense Category	Number of Offenses
Murder	387
Forcible Rape	1,608
Robbery	8,000
Aggravated Assault	20,176
Burglary	59,087
Larceny-Theft	201,541
Auto Theft	57,668
Total Violent	30,171
Total Property	318,296
Total Crime Index	348,467

SOURCE: FBI, *Crime in the United States, 2002.*

The State of Arkansas. Arkansas is located in the south-central part of the continental United States. It is bordered by Missouri to the north, Tennessee and Mississippi to the east, Louisiana to the south, and Oklahoma and Texas to the west. Arkansas encompasses about 53,182 square miles including 1,107 square miles of water. The Mississippi River flows the entire length of its eastern border. It is the 28th largest of the 50 states. The capital of Arkansas is Little Rock with a 2000 population of 183,133. Based on 2000 census figures, it ranks 33rd among the states in population. In addition to Little Rock, the other major cities and their 2000 populations are Fort Smith, 80,268; North Little Rock, 60,433; Fayetteville, 58,047; Jonesboro, 55,515; Pine Bluff, 55,085; Springdale, 45,798; Conway, 43,167; Rogers, 38,829; and Hot Springs, 35,750. The state is divided into 75 counties.

Arkansas was admitted to statehood on June 15, 1836, as the 25th state. It was organized as a territory in March 1819. The state legislature, the General Assembly, is made up of 35 senators and 100 representatives. Its present constitution was adopted in 1874. As with all states in the United States, it elects two senators to the U.S. Congress, but the number of elected representatives to the House of Representatives is based on population; for Arkansas it is four.

Table 4-1. LAW ENFORCEMENT EMPLOYEE DATA, ARKANSAS, 2002

Type of Agency	Number of Agencies	Total Personnel	Sworn	Civilian
All Agencies	207	8,373	5,569	2,804
State Agencies	1	735	505	230
County Sheriff's Offices	75	3,105	1,606	1,499
City Police	121	4,332	3,296	1,036
University Police Departments	10	201	162	39

SOURCE: FBI, *Crime in the United States, 2002*, and correspondence with Arkansas State Police.

Until the 1950s, Arkansas was primarily an agricultural state, but since then the economy has been dominated by manufacturing, services, and tourism. The major industries of the state are food processing, electric equipment, fabricated metal products, machinery, paper products, bromine, and vanadium. The primary agricultural products are poultry and eggs, soybeans, sorghum, cattle, cotton, rice, hogs, and milk. The estimated population for 2002 was 2,673,400. The percentage breakdown of the 2000 census was 80% White, 15.7% Black or African American, 0.7% American Indian, 0.8% Asian and 0.1% Native Hawaiian and Other Pacific Islander. Persons reporting some other race were 1.5% and those reporting two or more races on the 2000 census were 1.2%. Hispanics, who may be of any race, were 3.2% of the population in 2000. Persons age 18 or older was 74.6% and persons 65 years old and over was 14.0%. The median age was 34.2.

The law enforcement community in Arkansas consists of over 207 agencies employing about 5,569 officers according to data reported to the FBI (see Table 4-1). All police officers must complete 432 hours of mandatory training. There were 295 officers assaulted in 2002. One officer was killed feloniously in the line of duty during 2002 and one died accidentally.

Crime Index offenses for 2002 for the state of Arkansas totaled 112,672 which was a rate of 4,157.5 per 100,000 inhabitants. The numbers of index offenses by category are listed in Table 4-2. At least 107,467 arrests were made in Arkansas for all categories of crimes, with 11,877 being for index offenses. Of the index offense arrests, 2,517 arrests (21.2%) were persons under the age of 18.

Table 4-2. Crime Index Offenses, Arkansas, 2002

Index Offense Category	Number of Offenses
Murder	142
Forcible Rape	754

Robbery	2,524
Aggravated Assault	8,081
Burglary	23,229
Larceny-Theft	71,129
Auto Theft	6,813
Total Violent	11,501
Total Property	101,171
Total Crime Index	112,672

SOURCE: FBI, *Crime in the United States, 2002.*

Table 5-1. LAW ENFORCEMENT EMPLOYEE DATA, CALIFORNIA, 2002

Type of Agency	Number of Agencies	Total Personnel	Sworn	Civilian
All Agencies	462	113,827	74,174	39,653
State Agencies	10	11,468	7,868	3,600
County Sheriff's Offices	58	46,582	26,965	19,617
City Police	339	53,832	38,099	15,733
University Police Departments	47	1,332	806	526
Other Agencies	8	613	436	177

SOURCE: FBI, *Crime in the United States, 2002.*

The State of California. California is located in the western part of the continental United States. It is bordered by Oregon to the north, Nevada and Arizona to the east, the country of Mexico to the south, and the Pacific Ocean to the west. California encompasses about 163,707 square miles, including 7,734 square miles of water. Its coastline is about 840 miles and shoreline is about 3,427 miles. It is the third-largest of the 50 states. The capital of California is Sacramento with a 2000 population of 407,018. In addition to Sacramento, the other major cities and their 2000 populations are Los Angeles, 3,694,820; San Diego, 1,223,400; San Jose, 894,943; San Francisco, 776,733; Long Beach, 461,522; Fresno, 427,652; Oakland, 399,484; Santa Ana, 337,977; and Anaheim, 328,014. The state is divided into 58 counties.

California was admitted to statehood on September 9, 1850, as the 31st state. The state legislature is made up of 40 senators and 80 assembly members. Its present constitution was adopted in 1879. As with all states in the United States, it elects two senators to the U.S. Congress, but the number of elected representatives to the House of Representatives is based on population; for California it is 53.

The major industries of the state are electronic components and equipment, aerospace, film production, food processing, petroleum, computers and computer software and tourism. The primary agricultural products are vegetables, fruits and nuts, dairy products, cattle, nursery stock and grapes. The estimated population for 2002 was 35,116,033, making it the most populous state in the country. The percentage breakdown of the 2000 census was 59.5% White, 6.7% Black or African American, 1.0% American Indian, 10.9% Asian and 0.3% Native Hawaiian and Other Pacific Islander. Persons reporting some other race were 16.8% and those reporting two or more races on the 2000 census were 4.7%. Hispanics, who may be of any race, were 32.4% of the population in 2000. Persons age 18 or older was 72.7% and persons

65 years old and over was 10.6%. The median age was 33.3. Foreign-born persons were 26.2%.

The law enforcement community in California consists of at least 462 agencies employing about 74,174 officers according to data submitted to the FBI (see Table 5-1). Full-time peace officers must complete a minimum of 664 hours of mandatory basic training and an in-service requirement of 24 hours biannually. There were 6,893 officers assaulted in 2002 in California. Four officers were killed in the line of duty during 2002 and 6 were accidentally killed.

Crime Index offenses for 2002 for the state of California totaled 1,384,872, which was a rate of 3,943.7 per 100,000 inhabitants. The numbers of index offenses by category are listed in Table 5-2. At least 1,412,566 arrests were made in California for all categories of crimes, with 298,772 being for index offenses. Of the index offense arrests, 66,812 arrests (22.3%) were persons under the age of 18.

Table 5-2. Crime Index Offenses, California, 2002

Index Offense Category	Number of Offenses
Murder	2,395
Forcible Rape	10,198
Robbery	64,968
Aggravated Assault	130,827
Burglary	238,428
Larceny-Theft	715,692
Auto Theft	222,364
Total Violent	208,388
Total Property	1,176,484
Total Crime Index	1,384,872

SOURCE: FBI, *Crime in the United States, 2002.*

The State of Colorado. Colorado is located in the west-central part of the continental United States. It is bordered by Wyoming to the north, Nebraska to the northeast, Kansas to the east, Oklahoma to the southeast, New Mexico to the south, and Utah to the west. Colorado encompasses about 104,100 square miles, including 371 square miles of water. It is the eighth largest of the 50 states. Based on 2000 census figures, it ranks 24th among the states in population. The capital of Colorado is Denver with a 2000 population of 554,636. The other major cities and their 2000 populations are Colorado Springs, 360,890; Aurora, 276,393; Lakewood, 144,126; Fort Collins, 118,652; Arvada, 102,153; Pueblo, 102,121; Westminster, 100,940; Boulder, 94,673; and Thornton, 82,384. The state is divided into 63 counties.

Colorado was admitted to statehood on August 1, 1876, as the 38th state. It was organized as a territory in February 1861. Its present constitution was adopted in 1876. The state legislature is called the General Assembly and is made up of 35 senators and 65 representatives. As with all states in the United States, it elects two senators to the U.S. Congress, but the number of elected representatives to the House of Representatives is based on population; for Colorado it is seven.

The major industries of the state are scientific instruments, food processing, transportation equipment, machinery, chemical products, gold and other mining, and tourism. The primary agricultural products are cattle, wheat, dairy products, corn, and hay. The estimated population for 2002 was 4,506,542 with about 84 percent of the people living in areas defined as urban. The percentage breakdown of the 2000 census was 82.8% White, 3.8% Black or African American, 1.0% American Indian, 2.2% Asian and 0.1% Native Hawaiian and Other Pacific Islander. Persons reporting some other race were 7.2% and those reporting two or more races on the 2000 census were 2.8%. Hispanics, who may be of any race, were 17.1% of the population in 2000. Persons age 18 or older was 74.4% and persons 65 years old and over was 9.7%. The median age was 34.3.

The law enforcement community in Colorado consists of at least 233 agencies employing about 10,704 officers according to data reported to the FBI (see Table 6-1). All full-time peace officers must complete 445 hours of mandatory training; reserve officers must complete a minimum of 164 hours. There were 845 officers assaulted in 2002. No officers were killed feloniously in the line of duty during 2002; one died accidentally.

Crime Index offenses for 2002 for the state of Colorado totaled 195,936, which was a rate of 4,347.8 per 100,000 inhabitants. The numbers of index offenses

Table 6-1. LAW ENFORCEMENT EMPLOYEE DATA, COLORADO, 2002

Type of Agency	Number of Agencies	Total Personnel	Sworn	Civilian
All Agencies	233	15,489	10,704	4,785
State Agencies	3	1,016	761	255
County Sheriff's Offices	63	5,809	3,632	2,177
City Police	154	8,370	6,130	2,240
University Police Departments	13	294	181	113

SOURCE: FBI, *Crime in the United States, 2002.*

by category are listed in Table 6-2. At least 222,108 arrests were made in 2002 for all categories of crimes, with 33,788 being for index offenses. Of the index offense arrests, 10,300 arrests (30.5%) were persons under the age of 18.

Table 6-2. Crime Index Offenses, Colorado, 2002

Index Offense Category	Number of Offenses
Murder	179
Forcible Rape	2,066
Robbery	3,579
Aggravated Assault	10,058
Burglary	31,678
Larceny-Theft	125,193
Auto Theft	23,183
Total Violent	15,882
Total Property	180,054
Total Crime Index	195,936

SOURCE: FBI, *Crime in the United States, 2002.*

The State of Connecticut. Connecticut is located in the northeastern part of the continental United States, commonly referred to as New England. It was one of the original thirteen colonies. It is bordered by Massachusetts to the north, Rhode Island to the east, the Atlantic Ocean to the south, and New York to the west. Connecticut encompasses about 5,544 square miles, including 698 square miles of inland and coastal water area. Its shoreline extends 618 miles. It is the 48th largest of the 50 states. Based on 2000 census figures, it ranks 29th among the states in population. The capital of Connecticut is Hartford with a 2000 population of 121,578. The other major cities and their 2000 populations are Bridgeport, 139,529; New Haven, 123,626; Stamford, 117,083; Waterbury, 107,271; Norwalk, 82,951; Danbury, 74,848; New Britain, 71,538; West Hartford, 63,589; and Greenwich, 61,101. The state historically

Table 7-1. LAW ENFORCEMENT EMPLOYEE DATA, CONNECTICUT, 2002

Type of Agency	Number of Agencies	Total Personnel	Sworn	Civilian
All Agencies	97	9,741	7,788	1,953
State Agencies	2	1,825	1,272	553
City Police	88	7,634	6,301	1,333
University Police Departments	7	282	215	67

SOURCE: FBI, *Crime in the United States, 2002.*

was divided into 8 counties; however, county government was officially abolished in 1960.

Connecticut was the fifth of the original 13 states ratifying the Constitution of the United States on January 9, 1788. Settlement in Connecticut dates from the 1630s. The state legislature, the General Assembly, is made up of 36 senators and 151 representatives. The present constitution was adopted on December 30, 1965. As with all states in the United States, it elects two senators to the U.S. Congress, but the number of elected representatives to the House of Representatives is based on population; for Connecticut it is five.

The major industries of the state are related to transportation equipment, machinery, electric equipment, aircraft engines, spacecraft equipment, fabricated metal products, chemical products, and scientific instruments. The primary agricultural products are nursery stock, eggs, dairy products, and cattle. The insurance industry is the primary revenue producer for the state's economy. The estimated 2002 population for Connecticut was 3,460,503. The percentage breakdown of the 2000 census was 81.6% White, 9.1% Black or African American, 0.3% American Indian and 2.4% Asian. Persons reporting some other race were 4.3% and those reporting two or more races on the 2000 census were 2.2%. Hispanics, who may be of any race, were 9.4% of the population in 2000. Persons age 18 or older was 75.3% and persons 65 years old and over was 13.8%. The median age was 37.4.

The law enforcement community in Connecticut consists of at least 97 agencies employing about 7,788 officers according to data reported to the FBI (see Table 7-1). All police officers must complete a minimum of 646 hours of training plus physical assessments and 400 hours of department field training. There were 507 officers assaulted in 2002. No officers were killed feloniously in the line of duty nor died accidentally during 2002.

Crime Index offenses for 2002 for the state of Connecticut totaled 103,719, which was a rate of 2,997.2 per 100,000 inhabitants. The numbers of index offenses by category are listed in Table 7-2. At least 99,005 arrests were made in 2002 for all categories of crimes, with 17,013 being for index offenses. Of the index offense arrests, 3,795 arrests (22.3%) were persons under the age of 18.

Table 7-2. Crime Index Offenses, Connecticut, 2002

Index Offense Category	Number of Offenses
Murder	80
Forcible Rape	730
Robbery	4,060
Aggravated Assault	5,897
Burglary	17,088
Larceny-Theft	64,292
Auto Theft	11,572
Total Violent	10,767
Total Property	92,952
Total Crime Index	103,719

SOURCE: FBI, *Crime in the United States, 2002.*

The State of Delaware. Delaware is located in the northeastern part of the continental United States, commonly referred to as New England. It was one of the original thirteen colonies. It is bordered by Pennsylvania to the north, the Delaware Bay and Atlantic Ocean to the east, and Maryland to the south and the west. The state of New Jersey is across the Delaware Bay to the east. Delaware encompasses only 2,489 square miles of area of which 535 square miles are water. It has 28 miles of coastline and 381 miles of shoreline. It is the 49th largest of the 50 states. Based on 2000 census figures, it ranks 45th among the states in population. The capital of Delaware is Dover with a 2000 population of 32,135. The other major cities and their 2000 populations are Wilmington, 72,664; Newark, 28,547; Milford, 6,732; Seaford, 6,699; Middletown, 6,161; Elsmere, 5,800; Smyrna, 5,679; New Castle, 4,862; and Georgetown, 4,643. The state is divided into three counties.

Delaware was the first of the original 13 states ratifying the Constitution of the United States on December 7, 1787. The state legislature, the General Assembly, is made up of 21 senators and 41 representatives. The present constitution was adopted in 1897. As with all states in the United States, it elects two senators to the U.S. Congress, but the number of elected representatives to the House of Representatives is based on population; for Delaware it is one because of its small size and population.

Table 8-1. LAW ENFORCEMENT EMPLOYEE DATA, DELAWARE, 2002				
Type of Agency	Number of Agencies	Total Personnel	Sworn	Civilian
All Agencies	51	3,101	2,206	895
State Agencies	15	1,651	1,149	502
County Sheriff's Offices	1	532	335	197
City Police	34	842	676	166
University Police Departments	1	76	46	30

SOURCE: FBI, *Crime in the United States, 2002.*

Burglary	5,355
Larceny-Theft	18,555
Auto Theft	3,057
Total Violent	4,836
Total Property	26,967
Total Crime Index	31,803

SOURCE: FBI, *Crime in the United States, 2002.*

The major industries of the state include chemical products, food processing, paper products, rubber and plastic products, scientific instruments, printing, and publishing. The primary agricultural products are poultry, nursery stock, soybeans, dairy products, and corn. The estimated population for 2002 was 807,385. The percentage breakdown of the 2000 census was 74.6% White, 19.2% Black or African American, 0.3% American Indian and 2.1% Asian. Persons reporting some other race were 2.0% and those reporting two or more races on the 2000 census were 1.7%. Hispanics, who may be of any race, were 4.8% of the population in 2000. Persons age 18 or older was 75.2% and persons 65 years old and over was 13.0%. The median age was 36.0.

The law enforcement community in Delaware consists of at least 51 agencies employing about 2,206 officers according data reported to the FBI (see Table 8-1). All full-time peace officers must complete 22 weeks (about 880 hours) of basic training and they have a 16-hour in-service training requirement annually. There were 419 officers assaulted in 2002. No officers were killed feloniously in the line of duty nor died accidentally during 2002.

Crime Index offenses for 2002 for the state of Delaware totaled 31,803 which was a rate of 3,939.0 per 100,000 inhabitants. The numbers of index offenses by category are listed in Table 8-2. At least 25,217 arrests were made in 2002 for all categories of crimes, with 4,986 being for index offenses. Of the index offense arrests, 1,288 arrests (25.8%) were persons under the age of 18.

Table 8-2. Crime Index Offenses, Delaware, 2002

Index Offense Category	Number of Offenses
Murder	26
Forcible Rape	358
Robbery	1,154
Aggravated Assault	3,298

The State of Florida. Florida is located in the southeastern part of the continental United States. The Florida peninsula is a sizable landmass that juts out into the Atlantic Ocean. Most of the state is surrounded by water that includes the Gulf of Mexico to the west. The states of Georgia and Alabama border Florida to the north. The state encompasses 65,758 square miles of area, including 11,761 square miles of water. It has 1,350 miles of coastline and 8,426 miles of shoreline. It is the 22nd largest of the 50 states. Based on 2000 census figures, it ranks fourth among the states in population. The capital of Florida is Tallahassee with a 2000 population of 150,624. The other major cities and their 2000 populations are Jacksonville, 735,617; Miami, 362,470; Tampa, 303,447; St. Petersburg, 248,232; Hialeah, 226,419; Orlando, 185,951; Fort Lauderdale, 152,397; Hollywood, 139,357; and Pembroke Pines, 137,427. The state is divided into 67 counties.

Florida became the 27th state on March 3, 1845. It was organized as a territory in March 1821. The state legislature is made up of 41 senators and 120 representatives. The present constitution was adopted in 1969. As with all states in the United States, it elects two senators to the U.S. Congress, but the number of elected representatives to the House of Representatives is based on population; for Florida it is 25.

The major industries of the state include tourism, electric equipment, food processing, printing and publishing, transportation equipment, and machinery. The primary agricultural products are citrus, vegetables, nursery stock, cattle, sugarcane, and dairy products. The estimated population for 2002 was 16,713,149. The percentage breakdown of the 2000 census was 78.0% White, 14.6% Black or African American, 0.3% American Indian, 0.1% Native Hawaiian and Other Pacific Islander and 1.7% Asian. Persons reporting some other race were 3.0% and those reporting two or more races on the 2000 census were 2.4%. Hispanics, who may be of any race, were 16.8% of the population in 2000. Persons age 18 or older was 77.2% and persons 65 years old and over was 17.6%. The median age was 38.7.

Table 9-1. LAW ENFORCEMENT EMPLOYEE DATA, FLORIDA, 2002

Type of Agency	Number of Agencies	Total Personnel	Sworn	Civilian
All Agencies	407	69,762	41,511	28,251
State Agencies	28	3,617	2,777	840
County Sheriff's Offices	66	38,571	19,060	19,511
City Police	284	25,850	18,480	7,370
University Police Departments	16	690	460	230
Other Agencies	13	1,034	734	300

SOURCE: FBI, *Crime in the United States, 2002.*

The law enforcement community in Florida consists of at least 407 agencies employing about 41,511 officers according to data submitted to the FBI (see Table 9-1). All full-time peace officers must complete 672 hours of mandatory basic training and 40 hours of in-service every four years. There were 8,628 officers assaulted in 2002. One officer was killed feloniously in the line of duty and two died accidentally during 2002.

Crime Index offenses for 2002 for the state of Florida totaled 905,957, which was a rate of 5,420.6 per 100,000 inhabitants. The numbers of index offenses by category are listed in Table 9-2. At least 912,998 arrests were made in 2002 for all categories of crimes, with 182,530 being for index offenses. Of the index offense arrests, 47,936 arrests (26.3%) were persons under the age of 18.

Table 9-2. Crime Index Offenses, Florida, 2002

Index Offense Category	Number of Offenses
Murder	911
Forcible Rape	6,753
Robbery	32,581
Aggravated Assault	88,476
Burglary	177,242
Larceny-Theft	511,478
Auto Theft	88,516
Total Violent	128,721
Total Property	777,236
Total Crime Index	905,957

SOURCE: FBI, *Crime in the United States, 2002.*

The State of Georgia. Georgia is located in the southeastern part of the continental United States. The state of Florida borders Georgia to the south, Alabama to the west, Tennessee and North Carolina to the north, South Carolina to the northeast, and the Atlantic Ocean on the east. The state

encompasses 59,441 square miles of area, including 1,522 square miles of water. It has 100 miles of coastline and 2,344 miles of shoreline. It is the 24th largest of the 50 states. Based on 2000 census figures, it ranks tenth among the states in population. The capital of Georgia is Atlanta with a 2000 population of 416,474. The other major cities and their 2000 populations are Augusta-Richmond County, 199,775; Columbus, 186,291; Savannah, 131,510; Athens-Clarke County, 101,489; Macon, 97,255; Roswell, 79,334; Albany, 76,939; Marietta, 58,748; and Warner Robins, 48,804. The state is divided into 159 counties.

Georgia was founded in 1733, and was the last of the 13 original English colonies to be established in the United States. Georgia became the fourth state on January 2, 1788. The state legislature, the General Assembly is made up of 56 senators and 180 representatives. The present constitution was adopted in 1982. As with all states in the United States, it elects two senators to the U.S. Congress, but the number of elected representatives to the House of Representatives is based on population; for Georgia it is 13.

The major industries of the state include textiles and apparel, transportation equipment, food processing, paper products, chemical products, electric equipment, and tourism; it is the center of the world carpet industry. The primary agricultural products are poultry and eggs, peanuts, cattle, hogs, dairy products, and vegetables. The estimated population for 2002 was 4,188,014. The percentage breakdown of the 2000 census was 65.1% White, 28.7% Black or African American, 0.3% American Indian, 0.1% Native Hawaiian and Other Pacific Islander and 2.1% Asian. Persons reporting some other race were 2.4% and those reporting two or more races on the 2000 census were 1.4%. Hispanics, who may be of any race, were 5.3% of the population in 2000. Persons age 18 or older was 73.5% and persons 65 years old and over was 9.6%. The median age was 33.2.

The law enforcement community in Georgia consists of at least 431 agencies employing about 18,753 officers according data submitted to the FBI (see Table 10-1). All full-time peace officers must complete 404 hours of mandatory basic training and 20 hours of in-service training annually. There were 1,068 officers assaulted in 2002. One officer was killed feloniously in the line of duty and two died accidentally during 2002.

Crime Index offenses for 2002 for the state of Georgia totaled 385,830 which was a rate of 4,507.2 per 100,000 inhabitants. The numbers of index offenses by category are listed in Table 10-2. At least 232,233 arrests were made in 2002 for all categories of crimes, with 39,589 being for index offenses. Of the index

Table 10-1. LAW ENFORCEMENT EMPLOYEE DATA, GEORGIA, 2002

Type of Agency	Number of Agencies	Total Personnel	Sworn	Civilian
All Agencies	431	26,651	18,753	7,898
State Agencies	15	3,006	1,630	1,376
County Sheriff's Offices	118	13,215	8,888	4,327
City Police	253	9,322	7,201	2,121
University Police Departments	31	524	524	0
Other Agencies	14	584	510	74

SOURCE: FBI, *Crime in the United States, 2002.*

Table 11-1. LAW ENFORCEMENT EMPLOYEE DATA, HAWAII, 2002

Type of Agency	Number of Agencies	Total Personnel	Sworn	Civilian
All Agencies	4	3,553	2,799	754
County Offices	3	1,098	826	272
City & County of Honolulu	1	2,455	1,973	482

SOURCE: FBI, *Crime in the United States, 2002.*

offense arrests, 7,792 arrests (19.73%) were persons under the age of 18.

Table 10-2. Crime Index Offenses, Georgia, 2002

Index Offense Category	Number of Offenses
Murder	606
Forcible Rape	2,108
Robbery	13,432
Aggravated Assault	23,125
Burglary	73,932
Larceny-Theft	234,591
Auto Theft	38,036
Total Violent	39,271
Total Property	346,559
Total Crime Index	385,830

SOURCE: FBI, *Crime in the United States, 2002.*

The State of Hawaii. Hawaii is located in the Pacific Ocean approximately 2,400 miles west-southwest of San Francisco, California. The state consists of a 1,523-mile chain of islets and eight main islands—Hawaii, Kahoolawe, Maui, Lanai, Molokai, Oahu, Kauai, and Niihau. The state encompasses 10,932 square miles of area, including 4508 square miles of water. It has 750 miles of coastline and 1,052 miles of shoreline. It is the 43rd largest of the 50 states. Based on 2000 census figures, it ranks 42nd among the states in population. The capital of Hawaii is Honolulu with a 2000 population of 371,657. The other major cities and their 2000 populations are Hilo, 40,759; Kailua, 36,513; Kaneohe, 34,970; Waipahu, 33,108; Pearl City, 30,976; Waimalu, 29,371; Mililani Town, 28,608; Kahului, 20,146; and Kihei, 16,749. The state is divided into five counties.

Hawaii became the 50th state on August 21, 1959. It was organized as a territory of the United States in 1900, one year after it was annexed. The state legislature is made up of 25 senators and 51 representatives. The present constitution was adopted in 1950 but did not become effective until statehood in 1959. As with all states in the United States, it elects two senators to the U.S. Congress, but the number of elected representatives to the House of Representatives is based on population; for Hawaii it is two.

The major industries of the state include tourism, food processing, apparel, fabricated metal products, stone, clay, and glass products. The primary agricultural products are sugarcane, pineapples, nursery stock, livestock, and macadamia nuts. The estimated population for 2002 was 1,244,898. The percentage breakdown of the 2000 census was 24.3% White, 1.8% Black or African American, 0.3% American Indian, 9.4% Native Hawaiian and Other Pacific Islander and 41.6% Asian. Persons reporting some other race were 1.3% and those reporting two or more races on the 2000 census were 21.4%. Hispanics, who may be of any race, were 7.2% of the population in 2000. Persons age 18 or older was 75.6% and persons 65 years old and over was 13.3%. The median age was 36.2.

The law enforcement community in Hawaii consists of four agencies employing about 2,799 officers according date reported to the FBI (see Table 11-1). There were 223 officers assaulted in 2002. No officer was killed feloniously in the line of duty nor died accidentally during 2002.

Crime Index offenses for 2002 for the state of Hawaii totaled 75,238, which was a rate of 6,043.6 per 100,000 inhabitants. The numbers of index offenses by category are listed in Table 11-2. At least 45,929 arrests were made in 2002 for all categories of crimes, with 6,970 being for index offenses. Of the index offense arrests, 1,997 arrests (28.6%) were persons under the age of 18.

Table 11-2. Crime Index Offenses, Hawaii, 2002

Index Offense Category	Number of Offenses
Murder	24
Forcible Rape	372
Robbery	1,210
Aggravated Assault	1,656

Burglary   12,722

Larceny-Theft   49,344

Auto Theft   9,910

Total Violent   3,262

Total Property   71,976

Total Crime Index   75,238

SOURCE: FBI, *Crime in the United States, 2002.*

The State of Idaho. Idaho is located in the northwestern part of the continental United States. It is bordered on the northeast by Montana, the east by Wyoming, the south by Utah and Nevada, the west by Oregon and Washington, and the north by the country of Canada. The state encompasses 83,574 square miles of area, including 823 square miles of water. It is the 14th largest of the 50 states. Based on 2000 census figures, it ranks 39th among the states in population. The capital of Idaho is Boise with a 2000 population of 185,787. The other major cities and their 2000 populations are Nampa, 51,867; Pocatello, 51,466; Idaho Falls, 50,730; Meridian, 34,919; Coeur d'Alene, 34,514; Twin Falls, 34,469; Lewiston, 30,904; Caldwell, 25,967; and Moscow, 21,291. The state is divided into 44 counties.

Idaho was organized as a territory in March 1863 and became the 43rd state on July 3, 1890. The state legislature is made up of 35 senators and 70 representatives. The present constitution was adopted in 1890. As with all states in the United States, it elects two senators to the U.S. Congress, but the number of elected representatives to the House of Representatives is based on population; for Idaho, it is two.

The major industries of the state include food processing, lumber and wood products, machinery, chemical products, paper products, silver and other mining, and tourism. The primary agricultural products are cattle, potatoes, dairy products, wheat, sugar beets, and barley. The estimated population for 2002 was 1,341,131. The percentage breakdown of the 2000 census was 91.0% White, 0.4% Black or African American, 1.4% American Indian and 0.9% Asian. Persons reporting some other race were 4.2% and those reporting two or more races on the 2000 census were 2.0%. Hispanics, who may be of any race, were 7.9% of the population in 2000. Persons age 18 or older was 71.5% and persons 65 years old and over was 11.3%. The median age was 33.2.

The law enforcement community in Idaho consists of at least 114 agencies employing about 2,358 officers according to data reported to the FBI (see Table 12-1). All full-time peace officers must complete 427 hours of mandatory basic academy training and

Table 12-1. LAW ENFORCEMENT EMPLOYEE DATA, IDAHO, 2002

Type of Agency	Number of Agencies	Total Personnel	Sworn	Civilian
All Agencies	114	3,502	2,358	1,144
State Agencies	13	330	250	80
County Sheriff's Offices	41	1,567	855	712
City Police	60	1,605	1,253	352

SOURCE: FBI, *Crime in the United States, 2002.*

40 hours of agency field training. There were 191 officers assaulted in 2002. No officer was killed feloniously in the line of duty or died accidentally during 2002.

Crime Index offenses for 2002 for the state of Idaho totaled 42,547, which was a rate of 3,172.5 per 100,000 inhabitants. The numbers of index offenses by category are listed in Table 12-2. At least 72,595 arrests were made in 2002 for all categories of crimes, with 9,121 being for index offenses. Of the index offense arrests, 4,004 (43.9%) were persons under the age of 18.

Table 12-2. Crime Index Offenses, Idaho, 2002

Index Offense Category	Number of Offenses
Murder	36
Forcible Rape	497
Robbery	240
Aggravated Assault	2,646
Burglary	7,441
Larceny-Theft	29,060
Auto Theft	2,627
Total Violent	3,419
Total Property	39,128
Total Crime Index	42,547

SOURCE: FBI, *Crime in the United States, 2002.*

The State of Illinois. Illinois is located in the north central portion of the continental United States. It is bordered to the north by the state of Wisconsin, to the northeast by Lake Michigan, to the east by Indiana, to the southeast across the Ohio River is Kentucky and to the southwest and west across the Mississippi River are Missouri and Iowa. The state encompasses 57,918 square miles of area, including 4,508 square miles of inland water. It is the 25th largest of the 50 states. Based on 2000 census figures, it ranks fifth among the states in population. The capital of Illinois is Springfield with a 2000 population of

Table 13-1. LAW ENFORCEMENT EMPLOYEE DATA, ILLINOIS, 2002

Type of Agency	Number of Agencies	Total Personnel	Sworn	Civilian
All Agencies	751	50,441	36,389	14,052
State Agencies	5	4,238	2,444	1,794
County Sheriff's Offices	102	12,257	5,589	6,668
City Police	610	33,043	27,680	5,363
University Police Departments	29	721	508	213
Forest Preserve/Park Agencies	5	182	168	14

SOURCE: FBI, *Crime in the United States, 2002.*

111,454. The other major cities and their 2000 populations are Chicago, 2,896,016; Rockford, 150,115; Aurora, 142,990; Naperville, 128,358; Peoria, 112,936; Joliet, 106,221; Elgin, 94,487; Waukegan, 87,901; and Cicero, 85,616. The state is divided into 102 counties.

Illinois became the 21st state on December 3, 1818. It was organized as a territory in February 1809. The state legislature, the General Assembly, is made up of 59 senators and 118 representatives. The present constitution was adopted in 1970. As with all states in the United States, it elects two senators to the U.S. Congress, but the number of elected representatives to the House of Representatives is based on population; for Illinois it is 19.

The major industries of the state include machinery, food processing, electric equipment, chemical products, printing and publishing, fabricated metal products, transportation equipment, petroleum, and coal. The primary agricultural products are corn, soybeans, hogs, cattle, dairy products, and wheat. The estimated population for 2002 was 12,600,620. The percentage breakdown of the 2000 census was 73.5% White, 15.1% Black or African American, 0.2% American Indian, and 3.4% Asian. Persons reporting some other race were 5.8% and those reporting two or more races on the 2000 census were 1.9%. Hispanics, who may be of any race, were 12.3% of the population in 2000. Persons age 18 or older was 73.9% and persons 65 years old and over was 12.1%. The median age was 34.7.

The law enforcement community in Illinois consists of at least 751 agencies employing about 36,389 officers according data reported to the FBI (see Table 13-1). All full-time peace officers must complete a minimum of 400 hours of mandatory training, although there is an optional 480-hour course. Two officers were killed feloniously in the line of duty and two died accidentally during 2002.

Crime Index offenses for 2002 for the state of Illinois totaled 506,086, which was a rate of 4,016.4 per 100,000 inhabitants. The numbers of index offenses by category are listed in Table 13-2. At least 199,430 arrests were made in 2002 for all categories of crimes, with 41,490 being for index offenses. Of the index offense arrests, 10,983 arrests (26.5%) were persons under the age of 18.

Table 13-2. Crime Index Offenses, Illinois, 2002

Index Offense Category	Number of Offenses
Murder	949
Forcible Rape	4,298
Robbery	25,272
Aggravated Assault	47,695
Burglary	81,123
Larceny-Theft	301,892
Auto Theft	44,857
Total Violent	78,214
Total Property	427,872
Total Crime Index	506,086

SOURCE: FBI, *Crime in the United States, 2002.*

The State of Indiana. Indiana is located in the north-central portion of the continental United States. It is bordered to the northeast by Lake Michigan, to the north by the state of Michigan, to the east by Ohio, to the southeast and south across the Ohio River by Kentucky, and to the west by Illinois. The state encompasses 36,420 square miles of area, including 550 square miles of inland water. It is the 38th largest of the 50 states. Based on 2000 census figures, it ranks 14th among the states in population. The capital of Indiana is Indianapolis with a 2000 population of 791,926. The other major cities and their 2000 populations are Fort Wayne, 205,727; Evansville, 121,582; South Bend, 107,789; Gary, 102,746; Hammond, 83,048; Bloomington, 69,291; Muncie, 67,430; Anderson, 59,734; and Terre Haute, 59,614. The state is divided into 92 counties.

Indiana became the 19th state on December 11, 1816. It was organized as a territory in May 1800. The state legislature, the General Assembly, is made up of 50 senators and 100 representatives. The present constitution was adopted in 1851. As with all states in the United States, it elects two senators to the U.S. Congress, but the number of elected representatives to the House of Representatives is based on population; for Indiana it is nine.

The major industries of the state include steel, electric equipment, transportation equipment, chemical products, petroleum and coal products, and machinery. The primary agricultural products are corn, soybeans,

Table 14-1. LAW ENFORCEMENT EMPLOYEE DATA, INDIANA, 2002

Type of Agency	Number of Agencies	Total Personnel	Sworn	Civilian
All Agencies	253	17,292	10,742	6,550
State Agencies	2	1,923	1,237	686
County Sheriff's Offices	85	5,592	2,257	3,335
City Police	157	9,510	7,043	2,467
University Police Departments	8	251	189	62
Airport Authority Police	1	16	16	0

SOURCE: FBI, *Crime in the United States, 2002.*

Total Violent	22,001
Total Property	208,965
Total Crime Index	230,966

SOURCE: FBI, *Crime in the United States, 2002.*

hogs, cattle, dairy products, and eggs. The estimated population for 2002 was 6,159,068. The percentage breakdown of the 2000 census was 87.5% White, 8.4% Black or African American, 0.3% American Indian and 1.0% Asian. Persons reporting some other race were 1.6% and those reporting two or more races on the 2000 census were 1.2%. Hispanics, who may be of any race, were 3.5% of the population in 2000. Persons age 18 or older was 74.1% and persons 65 years old and over was 12.4%. The median age was 35.2.

The law enforcement community in Indiana consists of at least 253 agencies employing about 10,742 officers according date reported to the FBI (see Table 14-1). All full-time peace officers must complete a minimum of 600 hours of mandatory training. There were 1,214 officers assaulted in 2002. No officer was killed feloniously in the line of duty but one died accidentally during 2002.

Crime Index offenses for 2002 for the state of Indiana totaled 230,966 which was a rate of 3,750.0 per 100,000 inhabitants. The numbers of index offenses by category are listed in Table 14-2. At least 196,964 persons were arrested in 2002 for all categories of crimes, with 32,336 being for index offenses. Of the index offense arrests, 8,426 arrests (26.1%) were persons under the age of 18.

Table 14.2. Crime Index Offenses, Indiana, 2002

Index Offense Category	Number of Offenses
Murder	362
Forcible Rape	1,843
Robbery	6,612
Aggravated Assault	13,184
Burglary	42,605
Larceny-Theft	146,073
Auto Theft	20,287

The State of Iowa. Iowa is located in the north-central portion of the continental United States. It is bordered to the north by the state of Minnesota, to the east across the Mississippi River by Wisconsin and Illinois, to the south by Missouri, and to the west by Nebraska and South Dakota. The state encompasses 56,276 square miles of area, including 401 square miles of inland water. It is the 26th largest of the 50 states. Based on 2000 census figures, it ranks 30th among the states in population. The capital of Iowa is Des Moines with a 2000 population of 198,682. The other major cities and their 2000 populations include Cedar Rapids, 120,758; Davenport, 98,359; Sioux City, 85,013; Waterloo, 68,747; Iowa City, 62,220; Council Bluffs, 58,268; Dubuque, 57,686; Ames, 50,731 and West Des Moines, 46,403. The state is divided into 99 counties.

Iowa became the 29th state on December 28, 1846. It was organized as a territory in June of 1838. The state legislature is made up of 50 senators and 100 representatives. The present constitution was adopted in 1857. As with all states in the United States, it elects two senators to the U.S. Congress, but the number of elected representatives to the House of Representatives is based on population; for Iowa it is five.

The major industries of the state include food-processing, machinery, electric equipment, chemical products, printing and publishing, and primary metals. The primary agricultural products are hogs, corn, soybeans, oats, and cattle and dairy products. The estimated population for 2002 was 2,936,760. The percentage breakdown of the 2000 census was 93.9% White, 2.1% Black or African American, 0.3% American Indian, and 1.3% Asian. Persons reporting some other race were 1.3% and those reporting two or more races on the 2000 census were 1.1%. Hispanics, who may be of any race, were 2.8% of the population in 2000. Persons age 18 or older was 74.9% and persons 65 years old and over was 14.9%. The median age was 36.6.

The law enforcement community in Iowa consists of at least 231 agencies employing about 5,053 officers according data reported to the FBI (see Table 15-1). All full-time peace officers must complete a minimum of approximately 480 hours of mandatory training. There were 561 officers assaulted in 2002. No officers were

Table 15-1. LAW ENFORCEMENT EMPLOYEE DATA, IOWA, 2002

Type of Agency	Number of Agencies	Total Personnel	Sworn	Civilian
All Agencies	231	7,529	5,053	2,476
State Agencies	1	894	619	275
County Sheriff's Offices	98	2,981	1,477	1,504
City Police	129	3,546	2,882	664
University Police Departments	3	108	75	33

SOURCE: FBI, *Crime in the United States, 2002.*

Table 16-1. LAW ENFORCEMENT EMPLOYEE DATA, KANSAS, 2002

Type of Agency	Number of Agencies	Total Personnel	Sworn	Civilian
All Agencies	343	9,980	6,787	3,193
State Agencies	5	1,265	802	463
County Sheriff's Offices	105	3,611	1,980	1,631
City Police	219	4,818	3,816	1,002
University Police Departments	7	217	129	88
Other Agencies	7	69	60	9

SOURCE: FBI, *Crime in the United States, 2002.*

killed feloniously in the line of duty or accidentally during 2002.

Crime Index offenses for 2002 for the state of Iowa totaled 101,265, which was a rate of 3,448.2 per 100,000 inhabitants. The numbers of index offenses by category are listed in Table 15-2. At least 112,438 arrests were made in 2002 for all categories of crimes, with 18,840 being for index offenses. Of the index offense arrests, 6,587 arrests (35%) were persons under the age of 18.

Table 15-2. Crime Index Offenses, Iowa, 2002

Index Offense Category	Number of Offenses
Murder	44
Forcible Rape	797
Robbery	1,169
Aggravated Assault	6,378
Burglary	18,643
Larceny-Theft	68,411
Auto Theft	5,823
Total Violent	8,388
Total Property	92,877
Total Crime Index	101,265

SOURCE: FBI, *Crime in the United States, 2002.*

The State of Kansas. Kansas is located in the central portion of the continental United States. It is bordered to the north by the state of Nebraska, to the east across the Mississippi River by Iowa and Missouri, to the south by Oklahoma, and to the west by Colorado. The state encompasses 82,282 square miles of area, including 459 square miles of inland water. It is the 15th largest of the 50 states. Based on 2000 census figures, it ranks 32nd among the states in population. The capital of Kansas is Topeka with a 2000 population of 122,377. The other major cities and their 2000 populations include Wichita, 344,284; Overland Park, 149,080; Kansas City, 146,866; Olathe, 92,962; Lawrence, 80,098; Shawnee, 47,996; Salina, 45,679; Manhattan, 44,831; and Hutchinson, 40,787. The state is divided into 106 counties.

Kansas became the 34th state on January 29, 1861. It was organized as a territory in May 1854. The state legislature is made up of 40 senators and 125 representatives. The present constitution was adopted in 1859. As with all states in the United States, it elects two senators to the U.S. Congress, but the number of elected representatives to the House of Representatives is based on population; for Kansas it is four.

The major industries of the state include transportation equipment, food processing, printing and publishing, chemical products, machinery, apparel, petroleum, and mining. The primary agricultural products are cattle, wheat, sorghum, soybeans, hogs and corn. The estimated population for 2002 was 2,715,884. The percentage breakdown of the 2000 census was 86.1% White, 5.7% Black or African American, 0.9% American Indian, and 1.7% Asian. Persons reporting some other race were 3.4% and those reporting two or more races on the 2000 census were 2.1%. Hispanics, who may be of any race, were 7.0% of the population in 2000. Persons age 18 or older was 73.5% and persons 65 years old and over was 13.3%. The median age was 35.2.

The law enforcement community in Kansas consists of at least 343 agencies employing about 6,787 officers according to data reported to the FBI (see Table 16-1). All full-time peace officers must complete a minimum of 560 hours of mandatory basic training. There were 1,245 officers assa'ulted in 2002. No officers were killed feloniously in the line of duty or accidentally during 2002.

Crime Index offenses for 2002 for the state of Kansas totaled 110,997, which was a rate of 4,087.0 per 100,000 inhabitants. The numbers of index offenses by category are listed in Table 16-2. At least 54,136 arrests were made in 2002 for all categories of crimes, with 6,050 being for index offenses. Of the index offense arrests, 2,154 arrests (35.6%) were persons under the age of 18.

Table 16-2. Crime Index Offenses, Kansas, 2002

Index Offense Category	Number of Offenses
Murder	78
Forcible Rape	1,035
Robbery	2,165
Aggravated Assault	6,951
Burglary	19,679
Larceny-Theft	73,877
Auto Theft	7,212
Total Violent	10,229
Total Property	100,768
Total Crime Index	110,997

SOURCE: FBI, *Crime in the United States, 2002.*

The State of Kentucky. Kentucky is located in the east-central portion of the continental United States. It is bordered to the north by the Ohio River across which are the Illinois, Indiana and Ohio; to the east is West Virginia and Virginia, to the south is Tennessee, and to the west across the Mississippi River is Missouri and Illinois. The state encompasses 40,411 square miles of area, including 679 square miles of inland water. It is the 37th largest of the 50 states. Based on 2000 census figures, it ranks 25th among the states in population. The capital of Kentucky is Frankfort with a 2000 population of 27,741. The other major cities and their 2000 populations include Lexington-Fayette (county), 260,512; Louisville, 256,231; Owensboro, 54,067; Bowling Green, 49,296; Covington, 43,370; Hopkinsville, 30,089; Henderson, 27,373; Richmond, 27,152; and Jeffersontown, 26,633. The state is divided into 120 counties.

Kentucky became the 15th state on June 1, 1792. The state legislature, the General Assembly, is made up of 38 senators and 100 representatives. The present constitution was adopted in 1891. As with all states in the United States, it elects two senators to the U.S. Congress, but the number of elected representatives to the House of Representatives is based on population; for Kentucky it is six.

The major industries of the state include transportation equipment, chemical products, electric equipment, machinery, food processing, tobacco products, coal, and tourism. The primary agricultural products are horses, cattle, tobacco, dairy products, hogs, soybeans, and corn. The estimated population for 2002 was 4,092,891. The percentage breakdown of the 2000 census was 90.1% White, 7.3% Black or African American,

Table 17-1. LAW ENFORCEMENT EMPLOYEE DATA, KENTUCKY, 2002

Type of Agency	Number of Agencies	Total Personnel	Sworn	Civilian
All Agencies	383	10,035	7,719	2,316
State Agencies	14	2,217	1,362	855
County Sheriff's Offices	128	2,602	2,136	466
City Police	233	5,001	4,077	924
University Police Departments	8	215	144	71

SOURCE: FBI, *Crime in the United States, 2002.*

0.2% American Indian, and 0.7% Asian. Persons reporting some other race were 0.6% and those reporting two or more races on the 2000 census were 1.1%. Hispanics, who may be of any race, were 1.5% of the population in 2000. Persons age 18 or older was 75.4% and persons 65 years old and over was 12.5%. The median age was 35.9.

The law enforcement community in Kentucky consists of at least 383 agencies employing about 7,719 officers according to data reported to the FBI (see Table 17-1). Most full-time peace officers must complete a minimum of 660 hours of mandatory basic training and 40 hours of annual in-service training. There were 327 officers assaulted in 2002. One officer was killed feloniously in the line of duty and two died accidentally during 2002.

Crime Index offenses for 2002 for the state of Kentucky totaled 118,799, which was a rate of 2,902.6 per 100,000 inhabitants. The numbers of index offenses by category are listed in Table 17-2. At least 61,176 arrests were made in 2002 for all categories of crimes, with 10,226 being for index offenses. Of the index offense arrests, 1,925 arrests (18.8%) were persons under the age of 18.

Table 17-2. Crime Index Offenses, Kentucky, 2002

Index Offense Category	Number of Offenses
Murder	184
Forcible Rape	1,088
Robbery	3,063
Aggravated Assault	7,083
Burglary	27,855
Larceny-Theft	70,776
Auto Theft	8,750
Total Violent	11,418
Total Property	107,381
Total Crime Index	118,799

SOURCE: FBI, *Crime in the United States, 2002.*

The State of Louisiana. Louisiana is located in the south-central portion of the continental United States. It is bordered to the north by the state of Arkansas, to the east across the Mississippi River by Mississippi, to the south by the Gulf of Mexico and to the west by Texas. The state encompasses 51,843 square miles of area, including 8,277 square miles of inland water; it has a coastline of 397 miles and a shoreline of 7,721 miles. It is the 31st largest of the 50 states. Based on 2000 census figures, it ranks 22nd among the states in population. The capital of Louisiana is Baton Rouge with a 2000 population of 227,818. The other major cities and their 2000 populations include New Orleans, 484,674; Shreveport, 200,145; Lafayette, 110,257; Lake Charles, 71,757; Kenner, 70,517; Bossier City, 56,461; Monroe, 53,107; Alexandria, 46,342; and New Iberia, 32,623. The state is divided into 64 parishes.

Louisiana became the 18th state on April 30, 1812. It was organized as a territory in March 1804. The state legislature is made up of 39 senators and 105 representatives. The present constitution was adopted in 1974. As with all states in the United States, it elects two senators to the U.S. Congress, but the number of elected representatives to the House of Representatives is based on population; for Louisiana it is seven.

The major industries of the state include chemical products, petroleum and coal products, food processing, transportation equipment, paper products, and tourism. The primary agricultural products are seafood, cotton, soybeans, cattle, sugarcane, poultry, and eggs, dairy products and rice. The estimated population for 2002 was 4,482,646. The percentage breakdown of the 2000 census was 63.9% White, 32.5% Black or African American, 0.6% American Indian, and 1.2% Asian. Persons reporting some other race were 0.7% and those reporting two or more races on the 2000 census were 1.1%. Hispanics, who may be of any race, were 2.4% of the population in 2000. Persons age 18 or older was 72.7% and persons 65 years old and over was 11.6%. The median age was 34.0.

The law enforcement community in Louisiana consists of at least 207 agencies employing about 16,822 officers according to data reported to the FBI (see Table 18-1). All full-time peace officers must complete a minimum of 320 hours of mandatory basic training. There were 1,884 officers assaulted in 2002. Two officers were killed feloniously in the line of duty and one died accidentally during 2002.

Crime Index offenses for 2002 for the state of Louisiana totaled 228,528, which was a rate of 5,098.1 per 100,000 inhabitants. The numbers of index offenses by category are listed in Table 18-2. At least 216,444 arrests were made in 2002 for all categories of crimes, with 39,138 being for index offenses. Of the index

Table 18-1. LAW ENFORCEMENT EMPLOYEE DATA, LOUISIANA, 2002

Type of Agency	Number of Agencies	Total Personnel	Sworn	Civilian
All Agencies	207	22,366	16,822	5,544
State Agencies	2	1,610	1,011	599
Parish Sheriff's Offices	61	13,105	9,599	3,506
City Police	126	7,135	5,790	1,345
University Police Departments	18	516	422	94

SOURCE: FBI, *Crime in the United States, 2002.*

offense arrests, 9,132 arrests (23.3%) were persons under the age of 18.

Table 18-2. Crime Index Offenses, Louisiana, 2002

Index Offense Category	Number of Offenses
Murder	593
Forcible Rape	1,529
Robbery	7,123
Aggravated Assault	20,445
Burglary	45,350
Larceny-Theft	133,302
Auto Theft	20,186
Total Violent	29,690
Total Property	198,838
Total Crime Index	228,528

SOURCE: FBI, *Crime in the United States, 2002.*

The State of Maine. Maine is located in the far northeastern portion of the continental United States; it is part of the New England region. It is bordered to the northwest, north and northeast by the country of Canada, to the southeast and south by the Atlantic Ocean, and to the west by the state of New Hampshire. The state encompasses 35,387 square miles of area, including 4,523 square miles of inland water with 228 miles of coastline and 3,478 miles of shoreline. It is the 39th largest of the 50 states. Based on 2000 census figures, it ranks 40th among the states in population. The capital of Maine is Augusta with a 2000 population of 18,560. The other major cities and their 2000 populations include Portland, 64,249; Lewiston, 35,690; Bangor, 31,473; South Portland, 23,324; Auburn, 23,203; Brunswick, 21,172; Biddeford, 20,942; Sanford, 20,806; and Scarborough, 16,970. The state is divided into 16 counties.

Maine became the 23rd state on March 15, 1820. The state legislature is made up of 35 senators and 151 representatives. The present constitution was adopted in 1820. As with all states in the United States, it elects

Table 19-1. LAW ENFORCEMENT EMPLOYEE DATA, MAINE, 2002				
Type of Agency	Number of Agencies	Total Personnel	Sworn	Civilian
All Agencies	134	2,927	2,195	732
State Agencies	1	608	361	247
County Sheriff's Offices	16	395	287	108
City Police	113	1,846	1,497	349
University Police Departments	3	60	43	17
Other Agencies	1	18	7	11

SOURCE: FBI, *Crime in the United States, 2002.*

Burglary	6,965
Larceny-Theft	24,591
Auto Theft	1,429
Total Violent	1,396
Total Property	32,985
Total Crime Index	34,381

SOURCE: FBI, *Crime in the United States, 2002.*

two senators to the U.S. Congress, but the number of elected representatives to the House of Representatives is based on population; for Maine it is two.

The major industries of the state include paper, lumber, and wood products, electric equipment, food processing, leather products, textiles, and tourism. The primary agricultural products are seafood, poultry and eggs, potatoes, dairy products, cattle, blueberries, and apples. The estimated population for 2002 was 1,294,464. The percentage breakdown of the 2000 census was 96.9% White, 0.5% Black or African American, 0.6% American Indian, and 0.7% Asian. Persons reporting some other race were 0.2% and those reporting two or more races on the 2000 census were 1.0%. Hispanics, who may be of any race, were 0.7% of the population in 2000. Persons age 18 or older was 76.4% and persons 65 years old and over was 14.4%. The median age was 38.6.

The law enforcement community in Maine consists of at least 134 agencies employing about 2,195 officers according to data reported to the FBI (see Table 19-1). All full-time peace officers must complete a minimum of 720 hours of mandatory basic training. There were 259 officers assaulted in 2002. No officers were killed feloniously in the line of duty or accidentally during 2002.

Crime Index offenses for 2002 for the state of Maine totaled 34,381, which was a rate of 2,656.0 per 100,000 inhabitants. The numbers of index offenses by category are listed in Table 19-2. At least 54,880 arrests were made in 2002 for all categories of crimes, with 8,171 being for index offenses. Of the index offense arrests, 2,968 arrests (36.2%) were persons under the age of 18.

Table 19-2. Crime Index Offenses, Maine, 2002

Index Offense Category	Number of Offenses
Murder	14
Forcible Rape	377
Robbery	270
Aggravated Assault	735

The State of Maryland. Maryland is one of the Middle Atlantic States in the eastern portion of the continental United States. It is bordered to the north by the state of Pennsylvania; to the east by Delaware and the Atlantic Ocean; to the south by the District of Columbia, Virginia, and West Virginia; and to the west by West Virginia. The main part of Maryland is separated from Eastern Maryland by the Chesapeake Bay. The state encompasses 12,407 square miles of area, including 2,633 square miles of inland water and has a coastline of 31 miles and a shoreline of 3,190 miles. It is the 42nd largest of the 50 states. Based on 2000 census figures, it ranks 19th among the states in population. The capital of Maryland is Annapolis with a 2000 population of 35,838. The other major cities and their 2000 populations include Baltimore, 651,154; Frederick, 52,767; Gaithersburg, 52,613; Bowie, 50,269; Rockville, 47,388; Hagerstown, 36,687; College Park, 24,657; Salisbury, 23,743; and Cumberland, 21,518. The state is divided into 23 counties.

Maryland was one of the original 13 colonies and became the seventh to adopt the Constitution on April 28, 1788. The state legislature, the General Assembly, is made up of 47 senators and 141 delegates. The present constitution was adopted in 1867. As with all states in the United States, it elects two senators to the U.S. Congress, but the number of elected representatives to the House of Representatives is based on population; for Maryland it is eight.

The major industries of the state include electric equipment, food processing, chemical products, printing and publishing, transportation equipment, machinery, primary metals, coal, and tourism. The primary agricultural products are seafood, poultry and eggs, dairy products, nursery stock, cattle, soybeans, and corn. The estimated population for 2002 was 5,458,137. The percentage breakdown of the 2000 census was 64.0% White, 27.9% Black or African American, 0.3% American Indian, and 4.0% Asian. Persons reporting some other race were 1.8% and those reporting two or more races on the 2000 census were 2.0%. Hispanics, who may be of any race, were 4.3% of the population in 2000. Persons age 18 or older was 74.4% and persons 65 years old and over was 11.3%. The median age was 36.0.

The law enforcement community in Maryland consists of at least 123 agencies employing about 14,827

Table 20-1. LAW ENFORCEMENT EMPLOYEE DATA, MARYLAND, 2002				
Type of Agency	Number of Agencies	Total Personnel	Sworn	Civilian
All Agencies	123	19,516	14,827	4,689
State Agencies	13	4,191	2,798	1,393
County Sheriff's Offices	28	9,056	6,907	2,149
City Police	70	5,760	4,810	950
University Police Departments	12	509	312	197

SOURCE: FBI, *Crime in the United States, 2002.*

Table 21-1. LAW ENFORCEMENT EMPLOYEE DATA, MASSACHUSETTS, 2002				
Type of Agency	Number of Agencies	Total Personnel	Sworn	Civilian
All Agencies	329	19,749	16,425	3,324
State Agencies	1	2,742	2,354	388
City Police	299	16,090	13,406	2,684
University Police Departments	29	917	665	252

SOURCE: FBI, *Crime in the United States, 2002.*

officers according to data reported to the FBI (see Table 20-1). All full-time peace officers must complete a minimum of approximately 600 hours of mandatory basic training, plus firearms training and field training. Officers also have an annual in-service training requirement of 18 hours. There were 3,096 officers assaulted in 2002. Three officers were killed feloniously in the line of duty and three died accidentally during 2002.

Crime Index offenses for 2002 for the state of Maryland totaled 259,120, which was a rate of 4,747.4 per 100,000 inhabitants. The numbers of index offenses by category are listed in Table 20-2. At least 161,317 arrests were made in 2002 for all categories of crimes, with 24,028 being for index offenses. Of the index offense arrests, 7,229 arrests (30.1%) were persons under the age of 18.

Table 20-2. Crime Index Offenses, Maryland, 2002

Index Offense Category	Number of Offenses
Murder	513
Forcible Rape	1,370
Robbery	13,417
Aggravated Assault	26,715
Burglary	39,765
Larceny-Theft	143,320
Auto Theft	34,020
Total Violent	42,015
Total Property	217,105
Total Crime Index	259,120

SOURCE: FBI, *Crime in the United States, 2002.*

The State of Massachusetts. Massachusetts is located in the New England area (the northeastern portion) of the continental United States. It is bordered to the north by the states of Vermont and New Hampshire, to the east by the Atlantic Ocean, to the south by Rhode Island and Connecticut, and to the west by New York. The state encompasses 10,555 square miles of area, including 2,717 square miles of inland water and has a coastline of

192 miles and a shoreline of 1,519 miles. It is the 44th largest of the 50 states. Based on 2000 census figures, it ranks 13th among the states in population. The capital of Massachusetts is Boston with a 2000 population of 589,141. The other major cities and their 2000 populations include Worcester, 172,648; Springfield, 152,082; Lowell, 105,167; Cambridge, 101,355; Brockton, 94,304; New Bedford, 93,768; Fall River, 91,938; Lynn, 89,050; and Quincy, 88,025. The state is divided into 14 counties.

Massachusetts was one of the original 13 colonies and became the sixth state to ratify the U.S. Constitution on February 6, 1788. The state legislature, the General Court, is made up of 40 senators and 160 representatives. The present constitution was adopted in 1780. As with all states in the United States, it elects two senators to the U.S. Congress, but the number of elected representatives to the House of Representatives is based on population; for Massachusetts it is ten.

The major industries of the state include machinery, electric equipment, scientific instruments, printing and publishing, and tourism. The primary agricultural products are seafood, nursery stock, dairy products, cranberries, and vegetables. The estimated population for 2002 was 6,427,801. The percentage breakdown of the 2000 census was 84.5% White, 5.4% Black or African American, 0.2% American Indian, and 3.8% Asian. Persons reporting some other race were 3.7% and those reporting two or more races on the 2000 census were 2.3%. Hispanics, who may be of any race, were 6.8% of the population in 2000. Persons age 18 or older was 76.4% and persons 65 years old and over was 13.5%. The median age was 36.5.

The law enforcement community in Massachusetts consists of at least 329 agencies employing about 16,425 officers according to data reported to the FBI (see Table 21-1). All full-time peace officers must complete a minimum of approximately 800 hours of mandatory basic training. Officers have an annual in-service training requirement that varies from 20 hours to 5 days depending to their status and assignment. There were 337 officers assaulted in 2002. One officer was killed feloniously in the line of duty and no officers died accidentally during 2002.

Crime Index offenses for 2002 for the state of Massachusetts totaled 198,890, which was a rate of 3,094.2 per 100,000 inhabitants. The numbers of index offenses by category are listed in Table 21-2. At least 114,657 arrests were made in 2002 for all categories of crimes, with 26,930 being for index offenses. Of the index offense arrests, 5,576 arrests (20.7%) were persons under the age of 18.

Table 21-2. Crime Index Offenses, Massachusetts, 2002

Index Offense Category	Number of Offenses
Murder	173
Forcible Rape	1,777
Robbery	7,169
Aggravated Assault	22,018
Burglary	33,243
Larceny-Theft	107,922
Auto Theft	26,588
Total Violent	31,137
Total Property	167,753
Total Crime Index	198,890

SOURCE: FBI, *Crime in the United States, 2002.*

The State of Michigan. Michigan is located in the north-central portion of the continental United States. It is bordered to the north by the country of Canada, to the east is Lake Huron across which is Canada, to the south is Ohio and Indiana, and to the west is Lake Michigan across which is the state of Wisconsin. The state encompasses 96,810 square miles of area, including 40,001 square miles of water (including Lake Michigan). It is the 22nd largest of the 50 states in land area but 11th in total area. Based on 2000 census figures, it ranks eighth among the states in population. The capital of Michigan is Lansing with a 2000 population of 119,128. The other major cities and their 2000 populations include Detroit, 951,270; Grand Rapids, 197,800; Warren, 138,247; Flint, 124,943; Sterling Heights, 124,471; Ann Arbor, 114,024; Livonia, 100,545; Dearborn, 97,775; and Westland, 86,602. The state is divided into 83 counties.

Michigan became the 26th state on January 26, 1837. It was organized as a territory in January 1805. The state legislature is made up of 38 senators and 110 representatives. The present constitution was adopted in 1963. As with all states in the United States, it elects two senators to the U.S. Congress, but the number of elected representatives to the House of Representatives is based on population; for Michigan it is 16.

The major industries of the state include motor vehicles and parts, machinery, fabricated metal products, food processing, chemical products, mining, and tourism.

Table 22-1. LAW ENFORCEMENT EMPLOYEE DATA, MICHIGAN, 2002

Type of Agency	Number of Agencies	Total Personnel	Sworn	Civilian
All Agencies	546	28,080	21,006	7,074
State Agencies	2	2,976	2,055	921
County Sheriff's Offices	83	7,885	4,685	3,200
City Police	434	16,441	13,677	2,764
University Police Departments	19	530	351	179
Other Agencies	8	248	238	10

SOURCE: FBI, *Crime in the United States, 2002.*

The primary agricultural products are dairy products, apples, blueberries, cattle, vegetables, hogs, corn, nursery stock, and soybeans. The estimated population for 2002 was 10,050,446. The percentage breakdown of the 2000 census was 80.2% White, 14.2% Black or African American, 0.6% American Indian, and 1.8% Asian. Persons reporting some other race were 1.3% and those reporting two or more races on the 2000 census were 1.9%. Hispanics, who may be of any race, were 3.3% of the population in 2000. Persons age 18 or older was 73.9% and persons 65 years old and over was 12.3%. The median age was 35.5.

The law enforcement community in Michigan consists of at least 546 agencies employing about 21,006 officers according to data reported to the FBI (see Table 22-1). All full-time peace officers must complete a minimum of approximately 562 hours of mandatory basic training. There were 1,504 officers assaulted in 2002. Three officers were killed feloniously in the line of duty; none died accidentally during 2002.

Crime Index offenses for 2002 for the state of Michigan totaled 386,366, which was a rate of 3,874.1 per 100,000 inhabitants. The numbers of index offenses by category are listed in Table 22-2. At least 371,037 arrests were made in 2002 for all categories of crimes, with 51,794 being for index offenses. Of the index offense arrests, 13,115 arrests (25.3%) were persons under the age of 18.

Table 22-2. Crime Index Offenses, Michigan, 2002

Index Offense Category	Number of Offenses
Murder	678
Forcible Rape	5,364
Robbery	11,847
Aggravated Assault	36,417
Burglary	70,970
Larceny-Theft	214,367
Auto Theft	49,723
Total Violent	54,306

Total Property   335,060
Total Crime Index   386,366

SOURCE: FBI, *Crime in the United States, 2002.*

The State of Minnesota. Minnesota is located in the north-central portion of the continental United States. It is bordered to the north by Canada, to the east by Lake Superior and the state of Wisconsin, to the south by Iowa, and to the west by South Dakota and North Dakota. The state encompasses 86,943 square miles of area, including 7,326 square miles of inland water. It is the 12th largest of the 50 states in terms of area. Based on 2000 census figures, it ranks 21st among the states in population. The capital of Minnesota is St. Paul with a 2000 population of 287,151. The other major cities and their 2000 populations include Minneapolis, 382,618; Duluth, 86,918; Rochester, 85,806; Bloomington, 85,172; Brooklyn Park, 67,338; Plymouth, 65,894; Eagan, 63,557; Coon Rapids, 61,607; and Burnsville, 60,220. The state is divided into 87 counties.

Minnesota became the 32nd state on May 11, 1858. It was organized as a territory in March 1849. The state legislature is made up of 67 senators and 134 representatives. The present constitution was adopted in 1858. As with all states in the United States, it elects two senators to the U.S. Congress, but the number of elected representatives to the House of Representatives is based on population; for Minnesota it is eight.

The major industries of the state include machinery, food processing, printing and publishing, fabricated metal products, electric equipment, mining, and tourism. The primary agricultural products are dairy products, corn, cattle, soybeans, hogs, wheat, and turkeys. The estimated population for 2002 was 5,019,720. The percentage breakdown of the 2000 census was 89.4% White, 3.5% Black or African American, 1.1% American Indian, and 2.9% Asian. Persons reporting some other race were 1.3% and those reporting two or more races on the 2000 census were 1.7%. Hispanics, who may be of any race, were 2.9% of the population in 2000. Persons age 18 or older was 73.8% and persons 65 years old and over was 12.1%. The median age was 35.4.

The law enforcement community in Minnesota consists of at least 285 agencies employing about 8,104 officers according to data reported to the FBI (see Table 23-1). All full-time peace officers must complete a minimum of a two- or four-year degree from a certified program or possess a degree and complete the professional peace officer education program. The state requires 48 hours of in-service training every three years. There were 81 officers assaulted in 2002. One officer was killed feloniously in the line of duty and two died accidentally during 2002.

Table 23-1. LAW ENFORCEMENT EMPLOYEE DATA, MINNESOTA, 2002

Type of Agency	Number of Agencies	Total Personnel	Sworn	Civilian
All Agencies	285	12,583	8,104	4,479
State Agencies	1	796	525	271
County Sheriff's Offices	87	5,073	2,357	2,716
City Police	193	6,506	5,088	1,418
University Police Departments	2	66	45	21
Other Agencies	2	142	89	53

SOURCE: FBI, *Crime in the United States, 2002.*

Crime Index offenses for 2002 for the state of Minnesota totaled 177,454, which was a rate of 3,535.1 per 100,000 inhabitants. The numbers of index offenses by category are listed in Table 23-2. At least 164,144 arrests were made in 2002 for all categories of crimes, with 26,316 being for index offenses. Of the index offense arrests, 10,997 arrests (41.8%) were persons under the age of 18.

Table 23-2. Crime Index Offenses, Minnesota, 2002

Index Offense Category	Number of Offenses
Murder	112
Forcible Rape	2,273
Robbery	3,937
Aggravated Assault	7,106
Burglary	28,034
Larceny-Theft	122,150
Auto Theft	13,842
Total Violent	13,428
Total Property	164,026
Total Crime Index	177,454

SOURCE: FBI, *Crime in the United States, 2002.*

The State of Mississippi. Mississippi is located in the south-central portion of the continental United States. It is bordered to the north by Tennessee, to the east by Alabama, to the south by the Gulf of Mexico and Louisiana, and to the west by Louisiana and Arkansas. Most of its western border is formed by the Mississippi River. The state encompasses 48,434 square miles of area, including 1,520 square miles of inland water. It is the 32nd largest of the 50 states in terms of area. Based on 2000 census figures, it ranks 31st among the states in population. The capital of Mississippi is Jackson with a 2000 population of 184,256. The other major cities and their 2000 populations include Gulfport, 71,127; Biloxi, 50,644; Hattiesburg, 44,779; Greenville, 41,663; Meridian, 39,968; Tupelo, 34,211; Southhaven, 28,977;

Table 24-1. LAW ENFORCEMENT EMPLOYEE DATA, MISSISSIPPI, 2002

Type of Agency	Number of Agencies	Total Personnel	Sworn	Civilian
All Agencies	170	8,381	5,277	3,104
State Agencies	1	1,016	530	486
County Sheriff's Offices	62	2,824	1,395	1,429
City Police	102	4,307	3,186	1,121
University Police Departments	5	234	166	68

SOURCE: FBI, *Crime in the United States, 2002.*

Table 24-2. Crime Index Offenses, Mississippi, 2002

Index Offense Category	Number of Offenses
Murder	264
Forcible Rape	1,127
Robbery	3,356
Aggravated Assault	5,111
Burglary	29,593
Larceny-Theft	70,468
Auto Theft	9,523
Total Violent	9,858
Total Property	109,584
Total Crime Index	119,442

SOURCE: FBI, *Crime in the United States, 2002.*

Vicksburg, 26,407; and Pascagoula, 26,200. The state is divided into 82 counties.

Mississippi became the 20th state on December 10, 1817. It was organized as a territory in April 7, 1798. The state legislature is made up of 52 senators and 122 representatives. The present constitution was adopted in 1890. As with all states in the United States, it elects two senators to the U.S. Congress, but the number of elected representatives to the House of Representatives is based on population; for Mississippi it is five.

The major industries of the state include apparel, furniture, lumber and wood products, food processing, electrical machinery, and transportation equipment. The primary agricultural products are cotton, poultry, cattle, catfish, soybeans, dairy products, and rice. The estimated population for 2002 was 2,871,782. The percentage breakdown of the 2000 census was 61.4% White, 36.3% Black or African American, 0.4% American Indian, and 0.7% Asian. Persons reporting some other race were 0.5% and those reporting two or more races on the 2000 census were 0.7%. Hispanics, who may be of any race, were 1.4% of the population in 2000. Persons age 18 or older was 72.7% and persons 65 years old and over was 12.1%. The median age was 33.8.

The law enforcement community in Mississippi consists of 170 agencies employing about 5,277 officers according to data reported to the FBI (see Table 24-1). All full-time peace officers must complete a minimum of approximately 400 hours of mandatory basic training. There were 290 officers assaulted in 2002. One officer was killed in the line of duty and one died accidentally during 2002.

Crime Index offenses for 2002 for the state of Mississippi totaled 119,442, which was a rate of 4,159.2 per 100,000 inhabitants. The numbers of index offenses by category are listed in Table 24-2. At least 116,670 arrests were made in 2002 for all categories of crimes, with 15,033 being for index offenses. Of the index offense arrests, 3,458 arrests (23%) were persons under the age of 18.

The State of Missouri. Missouri is located in the midwest central portion of the continental United States. It is bordered to the north by Iowa; to the east by the Mississippi River across which are the states of Illinois, Kentucky and Tennessee; to the south by Arkansas; and to the west by Oklahoma, Kansas, and Nebraska. The state encompasses 69,709 square miles of area, including 811 square miles of inland water. It is the 21st largest of the 50 states in terms of area. Based on 2000 census figures, it ranks 17th among the states in population. The capital of Missouri is Jefferson City with a 2000 population of 39,636. The other major cities and their 2000 populations include Kansas City, 441,545; St. Louis, 348,189; Springfield, 151,580; Independence, 113,288; Columbia, 84,531; St. Joseph, 73,990; Lee's Summit, 70,700; St. Charles, 60,321; St. Peter's, 51,381; and Florissant, 50,497. The state is divided into 114 counties.

Missouri became the 24th state on August 10, 1821. It was organized as a territory in June 1812. The state legislature, the General Assembly, is made up of 34 senators and 163 representatives. The present constitution was adopted in 1945. As with all states in the United States, it elects two senators to the U.S. Congress, but the number of elected representatives to the House of Representatives is based on population; for Missouri it is nine.

The major industries of the state include transportation equipment, food processing, chemical products, electric equipment, and fabricated metal products. The primary agricultural products are cattle, soybeans, hogs, dairy products, corn, poultry, and eggs. The estimated population for 2002 was 5,672,579. The percentage breakdown of the 2000 census was 84.9% White, 11.2% Black or African American, 0.4% American Indian, and 1.1% Asian. Persons reporting some other race were 0.8% and those reporting two or more races on the 2000 census were 1.5%. Hispanics, who may be of any race, were 2.1% of the population in 2000. Persons age 18 or older was

Table 25-1. LAW ENFORCEMENT EMPLOYEE DATA, MISSOURI, 2002				
Type of Agency	**Number of Agencies**	**Total Personnel**	**Sworn**	**Civilian**
All Agencies	536	18,838	13,202	5,636
State Agencies	2	2,686	1,521	1,165
County Sheriff's Offices	112	4,745	3,172	1,573
City Police	406	11,008	8,219	2,789
University Police Departments	12	250	171	79
Other Agencies	4	149	119	30

SOURCE: FBI, *Crime in the United States, 2002.*

Table 26-1. LAW ENFORCEMENT EMPLOYEE DATA, MONTANA, 2002				
Type of Agency	**Number of Agencies**	**Total Personnel**	**Sworn**	**Civilian**
All Agencies	106	2,707	1,581	1,126
State Agencies	2	285	217	68
County Sheriff's Offices	56	1,533	680	853
City Police	46	841	655	186
University Police Departments	2	48	29	19

SOURCE: FBI, *Crime in the United States, 2002.*

74.5% and persons 65 years old and over was 13.5%. The median age was 36.1.

The law enforcement community in Missouri consists of at least 536 agencies employing about 13,202 officers according to data reported to the FBI (see Table 25-1). Full-time peace officers must complete a minimum of between 470 to 600 hours of mandatory basic training, depending on whether a class A or Class B license is obtained. There were 2,592 officers assaulted in 2002. One officer was killed feloniously in the line of duty and four died accidentally during 2002.

Crime Index offenses for 2002 for the state of Missouri totaled 261,077, which was a rate of 4,602.4 per 100,000 inhabitants. The numbers of index offenses by category are listed in Table 25-2. At least 304,921 arrests were made in 2002 for all categories of crimes, with 54,487 being for index offenses. Of the index offense arrests, 10,907 arrests (20.0%) were persons under the age of 18.

Table 25-2. Crime Index Offenses, Missouri, 2002

Index Offense Category	Number of Offenses
Murder	331
Forcible Rape	1,465
Robbery	7,024
Aggravated Assault	21,737
Burglary	42,721
Larceny-Theft	159,921
Auto Theft	27,878
Total Violent	30,557
Total Property	230,520
Total Crime Index	261,077

SOURCE: FBI, *Crime in the United States, 2002.*

The State of Montana. Montana is located in the northwestern portion of the continental United States. It is bordered to the north by Canada, to the east by North Dakota and South Dakota, to the south by Wyoming and Idaho, and to the west by Idaho. The state encompasses 147,046 square miles of area, including 1,490 square miles of inland water. It is the fourth largest of the 50 states in terms of area. Based on 2000 census figures, it ranks 44th among the states in population. The capital of Montana is Helena with a 2000 population of 25,780. The other major cities and their 2000 populations include Billings, 89,847; Missoula, 57,053; Great Falls, 56,690; Butte-Silver Bowl, 34,606; Bozeman, 27,509; Kalispell, 14,223; Havre, 9,621; Anaconda–Deer Lodge County, 9,417; and Miles City, 8,487. The state is divided into 56 counties.

Montana became the 41st state on November 8, 1889. It was organized as a territory in May 1864. The state legislative assembly is made up of 50 senators and 100 representatives. The present constitution was adopted in 1972. As with all states in the United States, it elects two senators to the U.S. Congress, but the number of elected representatives to the House of Representatives is based on population; for Montana it is one.

The major industries of the state include mining, lumber and wood products, food processing, and tourism. The primary agricultural products are cattle, wheat, barley, sugar beets, hay, and hogs. The estimated population for 2002 was 909,453. The percentage breakdown of the 2000 census was 90.6% White, 0.3% Black or African American, 6.2% American Indian, and 0.5% Asian. Persons reporting some other race were 0.6% and those reporting two or more races on the 2000 census were 1.7%. Hispanics, who may be of any race, were 2.0% of the population in 2000. Persons age 18 or older was 74.5% and persons 65 years old and over was 13.4%. The median age was 37.5.

The law enforcement community in Montana consists of at least 106 agencies employing about 1,581 officers according to data reported to the FBI (see Table 26-1). All full-time peace officers must complete a minimum of 480 hours of mandatory basic training. After basic training, officers can progress through five other levels based on additional training and schooling. No officer was killed feloniously in the line of duty and one died accidentally during 2002.

Crime Index offenses for 2002 for the state of Montana totaled 31,948, which was a rate of 3,512.9 per 100,000 inhabitants. The numbers of index offenses by category are listed in Table 26-2. At least 21,579 arrests were made in 2002 for all categories of crimes, with 4,440 being for index offenses. Of the index offense arrests, 1,656 arrests (37.3%) were persons under the age of 18.

Table 27-1. LAW ENFORCEMENT EMPLOYEE DATA, NEBRASKA, 2002

Type of Agency	Number of Agencies	Total Personnel	Sworn	Civilian
All Agencies	164	4,649	3,386	1,263
State Agencies	1	670	485	185
County Sheriff's Offices	91	1,467	902	565
City Police	70	2,472	1,967	505
University Police Departments	2	40	32	8

SOURCE: FBI, *Crime in the United States, 2002*.

Table 26-2. Crime Index Offenses, Montana, 2002

Index Offense Category	Number of Offenses
Murder	16
Forcible Rape	237
Robbery	283
Aggravated Assault	2,661
Burglary	3,289
Larceny-Theft	23,679
Auto Theft	1,783
Total Violent	3,197
Total Property	28,751
Total Crime Index	31,948

SOURCE: FBI, *Crime in the United States, 2002*.

The State of Nebraska. Nebraska is located in the center of the continental United States. It is bordered to the north by South Dakota, to the east by Iowa and Missouri, to the south by Kansas, and to the west by Colorado and Wyoming. The state encompasses 77,358 square miles of area, including 481 square miles of inland water. It is the 16th largest of the 50 states in terms of area. Based on 2000 census figures, it ranks 38th among the states in population. The capital of Nebraska is Lincoln with a 2000 population of 225,581. The other major cities and their 2000 populations include Omaha, 390,007; Bellevue, 44,382; Grand Island, 42,940; Kearney, 27,431; Fremont, 25,174; Hastings, 24,064; North Platte, 23,878; Norfolk, 23,516; and Columbus, 20,971. The state is divided into 93 counties.

Nebraska became the 37th state on March 1, 1867. It was organized as a territory in May 1854. Since 1934, the state legislature has been unicameral (one body) of 49 members elected on a nonpartisan basis for terms of four years (it is unique in the United States). The present constitution was adopted in 1875 although it was amended considerably in 1919–1920. As with all states in the United States, it elects two senators to the U.S. Congress, but the number of elected representatives to

the House of Representatives is based on population; for Nebraska it is three.

The major industries of the state include food processing, machinery, electric equipment, printing, and publishing. The primary agricultural products are cattle, corn, hogs, soybeans, wheat, and sorghum. The estimated population for 2002 was 1,729,180. The percentage breakdown of the 2000 census was 89.6% White, 4.0% Black or African American, 0.9% American Indian, and 1.3% Asian. Persons reporting some other race were 2.8% and those reporting two or more races on the 2000 census were 1.4%. Hispanics, who may be of any race, were 5.5% of the population in 2000. Persons age 18 or older was 73.7% and persons 65 years old and over was 13.6%. The median age was 35.3.

The law enforcement community in Nebraska consists of at least 164 agencies employing about 3,386 officers according to data reported to the FBI (see Table 27-1). Full-time peace officers must complete a minimum of 596 hours of mandatory basic training. There were 180 officers assaulted in 2002. No officers were killed feloniously in the line of duty nor died accidentally during 2002.

Crime Index offenses for 2002 for the state of Nebraska totaled 73,606, which was a rate of 4,256.7 per 100,000 inhabitants. The numbers of index offenses by category are listed in Table 27-2. At least 93,355 arrests were made in 2002 for all categories of crimes, with 11,970 being for index offenses. Of the index offense arrests, 4,404 arrests (36.8%) were persons under the age of 18.

Table 27-2. Crime Index Offenses, Nebraska, 2002

Index Offense Category	Number of Offenses
Murder	48
Forcible Rape	464
Robbery	1,359
Aggravated Assault	3,557

Burglary	10,329
Larceny-Theft	51,440
Auto Theft	6,409
Total Violent	5,428
Total Property	68,178
Total Crime Index	73,606

SOURCE: FBI, *Crime in the United States, 2002.*

Table 28-1. LAW ENFORCEMENT EMPLOYEE DATA, NEVADA, 2002

Type of Agency	Number of Agencies	Total Personnel	Sworn	Civilian
All Agencies	36	8,312	4,907	3,405
State Agencies	1	1,249	715	534
County Sheriff's Offices	16	1,465	999	466
City Police	14	5,364	2,994	2,370
University Police Departments	3	73	54	19
Other Agencies	2	161	145	16

SOURCE: FBI, *Crime in the United States, 2002.*

The State of Nevada. Nevada is located in the western portion of the continental United States. It is bordered to the north by Oregon and Idaho, to the east by Utah and northern Arizona, to the south, southwest, and west by California. The state encompasses 110,567 square miles of area, including 761 square miles of inland water. It is the seventh largest of the 50 states in terms of area. Based on 2000 census figures, it ranks 35th among the states in population. The capital of Nevada is Carson City with a 2000 population of 52,457. The other major cities and their 2000 populations include Las Vegas, 478,434; Reno, 180,480; Henderson, 175,381; North Las Vegas, 115,488; Sparks, 66,346; Elko, 16,708; Boulder City, 14,966; Mesquite, 9,389; and Fallon, 7,536. The state is divided into 16 counties.

Nevada became the 36th state on October 31, 1864. It was organized as a territory in March 1861. The state legislature is made up of 21 senators and 42 assembly members. The present constitution was adopted in 1864. As with all states in the United States, it elects two senators to the U.S. Congress, but the number of elected representatives to the House of Representatives is based on population; for Nevada it is two.

The major industries of the state include tourism, mining, machinery, printing and publishing, food processing, and electric equipment. The primary agricultural products are cattle, hay, dairy products, and potatoes. The estimated population for 2002 was 2,173,491. The percentage breakdown of the 2000 census was 75.2% White, 6.8% Black or African American, 1.3% American Indian, and 4.5% Asian. Persons reporting some other race were 8.0% and those reporting two or more races on the 2000 census were 3.8%. Hispanics, who may be of any race, were 19.7% of the population in 2000. Persons age 18 or older was 74.4% and persons 65 years old and over was 11.0%. The median age was 35.0.

The law enforcement community in Nevada consists of at least 36 agencies employing about 4,907 officers according to data reported to the FBI (see Table 28-1). Full-time, Category I, peace officers must complete a minimum of 480 hours of mandatory basic training. There were 452 officers assaulted in 2002. No officers were killed feloniously in the line of duty and one died accidentally during 2002.

Crime Index offenses for 2002 for the state of Nevada totaled 97,752, which was a rate of 4,497.5 per 100,000 inhabitants. The numbers of index offenses by category are listed in Table 28-2. At least 115,128 arrests were made in 2002 for all categories of crimes, with 18,783 being for index offenses. Of the index offense arrests, 4,072 arrests (21.7%) were persons under the age of 18.

Table 28-2. Crime Index Offenses, Nevada, 2002

Index Offense Category	*Number of Offenses*
Murder	181
Forcible Rape	928
Robbery	5,118
Aggravated Assault	7,629
Burglary	18,951
Larceny-Theft	47,459
Auto Theft	17,486
Total Violent	13,856
Total Property	83,896
Total Crime Index	97,752

SOURCE: FBI, *Crime in the United States, 2002.*

The State of New Hampshire. New Hampshire is located in the New England area of the continental United States. It is bordered to the north by Canada, to the east by Maine, to the south by Massachusetts, and to the west by Vermont. The state encompasses 9,351 square miles of area, including 382 square miles of inland water and it has 13 miles of Atlantic Ocean coastline and 131 miles of shoreline. It is the 46th largest of the 50 states in terms of area. Based on 2000 census figures, it ranks 31st among the states in population. The capital of New Hampshire is Concord with a 2000 population of 40,687. The other major cities and their 2000 populations include Manchester, 107,006; Nashua, 86,605; Derry,

Table 29-1. LAW ENFORCEMENT EMPLOYEE DATA, NEW HAMPSHIRE, 2002				
Type of Agency	Number of Agencies	Total Personnel	Sworn	Civilian
All Agencies	131	2,523	1,917	606
State Agencies	2	432	304	128
County Sheriff's Offices	2	49	26	23
City Police	127	2,042	1,587	455

SOURCE: FBI, *Crime in the United States, 2002.*

Table 29-2. Crime Index Offenses, New Hampshire, 2002

Index Offense Category	Number of Offenses
Murder	12
Forcible Rape	446
Robbery	413
Aggravated Assault	1,185
Burglary	4,838
Larceny-Theft	19,468
Auto Theft	1,944
Total Violent	2,056
Total Property	26,250
Total Crime Index	28,306

SOURCE: FBI, *Crime in the United States, 2002.*

34,021; Rochester, 28,461; Salem, 28,112; Dover, 26,884; Merrimack, 25,119; Londonderry, 23,236; and Hudson, 22,928. The state is divided into ten counties.

New Hampshire was one of the original 13 colonies and became the 9th state to ratify the U.S. Constitution on June 21, 1788. The state legislature, the General Court, is made up of 24 senators and 400 representatives. The present constitution was adopted in 1784. As with all states in the United States, it elects two senators to the U.S. Congress, but the number of elected representatives to the House of Representatives is based on population; for New Hampshire it is two.

The major industries of the state include machinery, electric equipment, rubber and plastic products, and tourism. The primary agricultural products are dairy products, nursery stock, cattle, apples, and eggs. The estimated population for 2002 was 1,275,056. The percentage breakdown of the 2000 census was 96.0% White, 0.7% Black or African American, 0.2% American Indian, and 1.3% Asian. Persons reporting some other race were 0.6% and those reporting two or more races on the 2000 census were 1.1%. Hispanics, who may be of any race, were 1.7% of the population in 2000. Persons age 18 or older was 75.0% and persons 65 years old and over was 12.0%. The median age was 37.1.

The law enforcement community in New Hampshire consists of at least 131 agencies employing about 1,917 officers according to data reported to the FBI (see Table 29-1). Full-time peace officers must complete a basic academy of no more than 12 weeks maximum and complete 8 hours of in-service annually. There were 219 officers assaulted in 2002. No officers were killed feloniously in the line of duty or accidentally during 2002.

Crime Index offenses for 2002 for the state of New Hampshire totaled 28,306, which was a rate of 2,220 per 100,000 inhabitants. The numbers of index offenses by category are listed in Table 29-2. At least 34,348 arrests were made in 2002 for all categories of crimes, with 2,896 being for index offenses. Of the index offense arrests, 1,146 arrests (39.60%) were persons under the age of 18.

The State of New Jersey. New Jersey is located in the eastern portion of the continental United States. It is bordered to the north by New York, to the east and south by the Atlantic Ocean, and to the west by Delaware and Pennsylvania. The state encompasses 8,722 square miles of area, including 1,303 square miles of inland water and it has 130 miles of coastline and 1,792 miles of shoreline. It is the 47th largest of the 50 states in terms of area. Based on 2000 census figures, it ranks ninth among the states in population. The capital of New Jersey is Trenton with a 2000 population of 85,403. The other major cities and their 2000 populations include Newark, 273,546; Jersey City, 240,055; Paterson, 149,222; Elizabeth, 120,568; Edison, 97,687; Woodbridge, 97,203; Dover, 89,706; Hamilton, 87,109; and Camden, 79,904. The state is divided into 21 counties.

New Jersey was one of the original 13 colonies and became the third state to ratify the U.S. Constitution on December 18, 1787. The state legislature is made up of 40 senators and 80 assembly representatives. The present constitution was adopted in 1947. As with all states in the United States, it elects two senators to the U.S. Congress, but the number of elected representatives to the House of Representatives is based on population; for New Jersey it is 13.

The major industries of the state include chemical products, food processing, electric equipment, printing and publishing, and tourism. The primary agricultural products are nursery stock, horses, vegetables, fruits and nuts, seafood, and dairy products. The estimated population for 2002 was 8,590,300. The percentage breakdown of the 2000 census was 72.6% White, 13.6% Black or African American, 0.2% American Indian, and 5.7% Asian. Persons reporting some other race were 5.4% and those reporting two or more races on the 2000 census were 2.5%. Hispanics, who may be of any race, were 13.3% of the population in 2000. Persons age 18 or

Table 30-1. LAW ENFORCEMENT EMPLOYEE DATA, NEW JERSEY, 2002

Type of Agency	Number of Agencies	Total Personnel	Sworn	Civilian
All Agencies	530	38,931	30,483	8,448
State Agencies	13	4,057	2,809	1,248
County Sheriff's Offices	23	5,228	4,034	1,194
City Police	479	25,094	21,202	3,892
University Police Departments	17	785	384	401
Other Agencies	24	3,767	2,054	1,713

SOURCE: FBI, *Crime in the United States, 2002.*

Table 31-1. LAW ENFORCEMENT EMPLOYEE DATA, NEW MEXICO, 2002

Type of Agency	Number of Agencies	Total Personnel	Sworn	Civilian
All Agencies	110	5,660	4,142	1,518
State Agencies	1	714	576	138
County Sheriff's Offices	32	1,321	1,033	288
City Police	66	3,374	2,390	984
University Police Departments	5	96	62	34
Tribal Police	6	155	81	74

SOURCE: FBI, *Crime in the United States, 2002.*

older was 75.2% and persons 65 years old and over was 13.2%. The median age was 36.7.

The law enforcement community in New Jersey consists of at least 530 agencies employing about 30,483 officers according to data reported to the FBI (see Table 30-1). Full-time peace officers must complete a minimum of 600 hours of mandatory basic training. There were 2,999 officers assaulted in 2002. No officers were killed feloniously in the line of duty and one died accidentally during 2002.

Crime Index offenses for 2002 for the state of New Jersey totaled 259,789, which was a rate of 3,024.2 per 100,000 inhabitants. The numbers of index offenses by category are listed in Table 30-2. At least 368,619 arrests were made in 2002 for all categories of crimes, with 51,333 being for index offenses. Of the index offense arrests, 13,027 arrests (25.4%) were persons under the age of 18.

Table 30-2. Crime Index Offenses, New Jersey, 2002

Index Offense Category	Number of Offenses
Murder	337
Forcible Rape	1,347
Robbery	13,905
Aggravated Assault	16,579
Burglary	43,898
Larceny-Theft	147,984
Auto Theft	35,739
Total Violent	32,168
Total Property	227,621
Total Crime Index	259,789

SOURCE: FBI, *Crime in the United States, 2002.*

The State of New Mexico. New Mexico is located in the southwestern portion of the continental United States. It is bordered to the north by Colorado, to the east by Oklahoma and Texas, to the south by Texas and Mexico,

and to the west by Arizona. The state encompasses 121,593 square miles of area, including 234 square miles of inland water. It is the fifth largest of the 50 states in terms of area. Based on 2000 census figures, it ranks 36th among the states in population. The capital of New Mexico is Santa Fe with a 2000 population of 62,203. The other major cities and their 2000 populations include Albuquerque, 448,607; Las Cruces, 74,267; Rio Rancho, 51,765; Roswell, 45,293; Farmington, 37,844; Alamogordo, 35,582; Clovis, 32,667; Hobbs, 28,657; and Carlsbad, 25,625. The state is divided into 33 counties.

New Mexico became the 47th state on January 6, 1912. It was organized as a territory in September 1850. The state legislature, the General Assembly, is made up of 42 senators and 70 representatives. The present constitution was adopted in 1911. As with all states in the United States, it elects two senators to the U.S. Congress, but the number of elected representatives to the House of Representatives is based on population; for New Mexico it is three.

The major industries of the state include electric equipment, petroleum and coal products, food processing, printing and publishing, stone, glass, and clay products, and tourism. The primary agricultural products are cattle, dairy products, hay, nursery stock, and chilies. The estimated population for 2002 was 1,855,059. The percentage breakdown of the 2000 census was 66.8% White, 1.9% Black or African American, 9.5% American Indian, and 1.1% Asian. Persons reporting some other race were 17.0% and those reporting two or more races on the 2000 census were 3.6%. Hispanics, who may be of any race, were 42.1% of the population in 2000. Persons age 18 or older was 72.0% and persons 65 years old and over was 11.7%. The median age was 34.6.

The law enforcement community in New Mexico consists of at least 110 agencies employing about 4,142 officers according to data reported to the FBI (see Table 31-1). Full-time peace officers normally complete about 800 hours of basic training and have a 40-hour biennial in-service requirement. There were 571 officers assaulted in 2002. No officers were killed feloniously in the line of duty and two died accidentally during 2002.

Crime Index offenses for 2002 for the state of New Mexico totaled 94,196, which was a rate of 5,077.8 per 100,000 inhabitants. The numbers of index offenses by category are listed in Table 31-2. At least 76,539 arrests were made in 2002 for all categories of crimes, with 8,677 being for index offenses. Of the index offense arrests, 2,181 arrests (25.1%) were persons under the age of 18.

Table 31-2. Crime Index Offenses, New Mexico, 2002

Index Offense Category	Number of Offenses
Murder	152
Forcible Rape	1,027
Robbery	2,206
Aggravated Assault	10,334
Burglary	19,634
Larceny-Theft	53,406
Auto Theft	7,437
Total Violent	13,719
Total Property	80,477
Total Crime Index	94,196

SOURCE: FBI, *Crime in the United States, 2002.*

The State of New York. New York is located in the northeastern portion of the continental United States. It is bordered to the north by Lake Ontario and Canada; to the east by Vermont, Massachusetts, and Connecticut; to the south by New Jersey and Pennsylvania; and to the west by Lake Erie and Canada. The state encompasses 54,475 square miles of area, including 7,251 square miles of inland water and it has 127 miles of coastline and 1,850 miles of shoreline. It is the 27th largest of the 50 states in terms of area. Based on 2000 census figures, it ranks third among the states in population. The capital of New York is Albany with a 2000 population of 95,658. The other major cities and their 2000 populations include New York, 8,008,278; Buffalo, 292,648; Rochester, 219,773; Yonkers, 196,086; Syracuse, 147,306; New Rochelle, 72,182; Mount Vernon, 68,381; Schenectady, 61,821; and Utica, 60,651. The state is divided into 62 counties.

New York became the 11th state on July 26, 1788. The state legislature, the General Assembly, is made up of 61 senators and 150 assembly members. The present constitution was adopted in 1777, but it had major revisions in 1938. As with all states in the United States, it elects two senators to the U.S. Congress, but

Table 32-1. LAW ENFORCEMENT EMPLOYEE DATA, NEW YORK, 2002

Type of Agency	Number of Agencies	Total Personnel	Sworn	Civilian
All Agencies	425	80,990	59,654	21,336
State Agencies	13	5,668	4,761	907
County Sheriff's Offices	53	7,278	5,630	1,648
City Police	327	67,010	48,578	18,432
University Police Departments	29	967	625	342
Other Agencies	3	67	60	7

SOURCE: FBI, *Crime in the United States, 2002.*

the number of elected representatives to the House of Representatives is based on population; for New York it is 31. The major industries of the state include printing and publishing, scientific instruments, electric equipment, machinery, chemical products, and tourism. The primary agricultural products are dairy products, cattle and other livestock, vegetables, nursery stock, and apples. The estimated population for 2002 was 19,157,532. The percentage breakdown of the 2000 census was 67.9% White, 15.9% Black or African American, 0.4% American Indian, and 5.5% Asian. Persons reporting some other race were 7.1% and those reporting two or more races on the 2000 census were 3.1%. Hispanics, who may be of any race, were 15.1% of the population in 2000. Persons age 18 or older was 75.3% and persons 65 years old and over was 12.9%. The median age was 35.9.

The law enforcement community in New York consists of 425 agencies employing about 59,654 officers according to data reported to the FBI (see Table 32-1). Full-time police officers must complete a minimum of 422 hours of mandatory basic training. There were 443 officers assaulted in 2002. Two officers were killed feloniously in the line of duty and three died accidentally during 2002.

Crime Index offenses for 2002 for the state of New York totaled 537,121, which was a rate of 2,803.7 per 100,000 inhabitants. The numbers of index offenses by category are listed in Table 32-2. At least 264,833 arrests were made in 2002 for all categories of crimes, with 47,530 being for index offenses. Of the index offense arrests, 12,590 arrests (26.5%) were persons under the age of 18.

Table 32-2. Crime Index Offenses, New York, 2002

Index Offense Category	Number of Offenses
Murder	909
Forcible Rape	3,885

Robbery	36,653
Aggravated Assault	53,583
Burglary	76,700
Larceny-Theft	318,025
Auto Theft	47,366
Total Violent	95,030
Total Property	442,091
Total Crime Index	537,121

SOURCE: FBI, *Crime in the United States, 2002.*

Table 33-1. LAW ENFORCEMENT EMPLOYEE DATA, NORTH CAROLINA, 2002

Type of Agency	Number of Agencies	Total Personnel	Sworn	Civilian
All Agencies	513	27,852	19,691	8,161
State Agencies	39	2,919	2,199	720
County Sheriff's Offices	101	11,271	6,457	4,814
City Police	340	12,747	10,433	2,314
University Police Departments	27	783	486	297
Other Agencies	6	132	116	16

SOURCE: FBI, *Crime in the United States, 2002.*

The State of North Carolina. North Carolina is located in the south-central Atlantic portion of the continental United States. It is bordered to the north by Virginia, to the east by the Atlantic Ocean, to the south by South Carolina and part of Georgia, and to the west by Tennessee. The state encompasses 53,821 square miles of area, including 5,103 square miles of inland water and has 301 miles of coastline and 3,375 of shoreline. It is the 28th largest of the 50 states in terms of area. Based on 2000 census figures, it ranks 11th among the states in population. The capital of North Carolina is Raleigh with a 2000 population of 276,093. The other major cities and their 2000 populations include Charlotte, 540,828; Greensboro, 223,891; Durham, 187,035; Winston-Salem, 185,776; Fayetteville, 121,015; Cary, 94,536; High Point, 85,839; Wilmington, 75,838; and Asheville, 68,889. The state is divided into 100 counties.

North Carolina became the 12th state on November 21, 1789. The state legislature, the General Assembly, is made up of 50 senators and 120 representatives. The present constitution was adopted in 1971. As with all states in the United States, it elects two senators to the U.S. Congress, but the number of elected representatives to the House of Representatives is based on population; for North Carolina it is 12.

The major industries of the state include tobacco products, textile goods, chemical products, electric equipment, machinery, and tourism. The primary agricultural products are poultry and eggs, tobacco, hogs, milk, nursery stock, cattle, and soybeans. The estimated population for 2002 was 8,320,146. The percentage breakdown of the 2000 census was 72.1% White, 21.6% Black or African American, 1.2% American Indian, and 1.4% Asian. Persons reporting some other race were 2.3% and those reporting two or more races on the 2000 census were 1.3%. Hispanics, who may be of any race, were 4.7% of the population in 2000. Persons age 18 or older was 75.6% and persons 65 years old and over was 12.0%. The median age was 35.3.

The law enforcement community in North Carolina consists of at least 513 agencies employing about 19,691 officers according to data reported to the FBI (see Table 33-1). Full-time peace officers must complete a minimum of 602 hours of mandatory basic training. There were 2,092 officers assaulted in 2002. No officers were killed feloniously in the line of duty but six died accidentally during 2002.

Crime Index offenses for 2002 for the state of North Carolina totaled 392,826, which was a rate of 4,721.4 per 100,000 inhabitants. The numbers of index offenses by category are listed in Table 33-2. At least 447,259 arrests were made in 2002 for all categories of crimes, with 76,017 being for index offenses. Of the index offense arrests, 14,336 arrests (18.9%) were persons under the age of 18.

Table 33-2. Crime Index Offenses, North Carolina, 2002

Index Offense Category	Number of Offenses
Murder	548
Forcible Rape	2,196
Robbery	12,205
Aggravated Assault	24,169
Burglary	99,535
Larceny-Theft	229,307
Auto Theft	24,866
Total Violent	39,118
Total Property	353,708
Total Crime Index	392,826

SOURCE: FBI, *Crime in the United States, 2002.*

The State of North Dakota. North Dakota is located in the north-central portion of the continental United States. It is bordered to the north by Canada, to the east by Minnesota, to the south by South Dakota, and to the west by Montana. The state encompasses

70,704 square miles of area, including 1,710 square miles of inland water. It is the 19th largest of the 50 states in terms of area. Based on 2000 census figures, it ranks 47th among the states in population. The capital of North Dakota is Bismarck with a 2000 population of 55,532. The other major cities and their 2000 populations include Fargo, 90,599; Grand Forks, 49,321; Minot, 36,567; Mandan, 16,718; Dickinson, 16,010; Jamestown, 15,527; West Fargo, 14,940; Williston, 12,512; and Wahpeton, 8,586. The state is divided into 53 counties.

North Dakota became the 39th state on November 2, 1889. It was organized as a territory in March 1861. The state legislature is made up of 49 senators and 98 representatives. The present constitution was adopted in 1889. As with all states in the United States, it elects two senators to the U.S. Congress, but the number of elected representatives to the House of Representatives is based on population; for North Dakota it is one.

The major industries of the state include food processing, machinery, mining, and tourism. The primary agricultural products are wheat, cattle, barley, sunflowers, milk, and sugar beets. The estimated population for 2002 was 634,110. The percentage breakdown of the 2000 census was 92.4% White, 0.6% Black or African American, 4.9% American Indian, and 0.6% Asian. Persons reporting some other race were 0.4% and those reporting two or more races on the 2000 census were 1.2%. Hispanics, who may be of any race, were 1.2% of the population in 2000. Persons age 18 or older was 75.0% and persons 65 years old and over was 14.7%. The median age was 36.2.

The law enforcement community in North Dakota consists of 89 agencies employing about 1,104 officers according to data reported to the FBI (see Table 34-1). Full-time peace officers must complete a performance based basic training program that can vary from 11 to 17 weeks and must complete 60 hours of in-service training each three-year period to remain licensed. There were 68 officers assaulted in 2002. No officers were killed feloniously in the line of duty or accidentally during 2002.

Crime Index offenses for 2002 for the state of North Dakota totaled 15,258, which was a rate of 2,406.2 per 100,000 inhabitants. The numbers of index offenses by category are listed in Table 34-2. At least 25,221 arrests were made in 2002 for all categories of crimes, with 2,810 being for index offenses. Of the index offense arrests, 1,420 arrests (50.5%) were persons under the age of 18.

Table 34-1. LAW ENFORCEMENT EMPLOYEE DATA, NORTH DAKOTA, 2002

Type of Agency	Number of Agencies	Total Personnel	Sworn	Civilian
All Agencies	89	1,542	1,104	438
State Agencies	1	187	126	61
County Sheriff's Offices	48	607	390	217
City Police	38	722	567	155
University Police Departments	2	26	21	5

SOURCE: FBI, *Crime in the United States, 2002.*

Table 34-2. Crime Index Offenses, North Dakota, 2002

Index Offense Category	Number of Offenses
Murder	5
Forcible Rape	163
Robbery	58
Aggravated Assault	270
Burglary	2,243
Larceny-Theft	11,501
Auto Theft	1,018
Total Violent	496
Total Property	14,762
Total Crime Index	15,258

SOURCE: FBI, *Crime in the United States, 2002.*

The State of Ohio. Ohio is located in the north-central eastern portion of the continental United States. It is bordered to the north by Michigan and Lake Erie, to the east by Pennsylvania, to the southeast by West Virginia, to the south by Kentucky, and to the west by Indiana. The state encompasses 44,828 square miles of area, including 3,875 square miles of inland water. It is the 34th largest of the 50 states in terms of area. Based on 2000 census figures, it ranks seventh among the states in population. The capital of Ohio is Columbus with a 2000 population of 711,470. The other major cities and their 2000 populations include Cleveland, 478,403; Cincinnati, 331,285; Toledo, 313,619; Akron, 217,074; Dayton, 166,179; Parma, 85,655; Youngstown, 82,026; Canton, 80,806; and Lorain, 68,652. The state is divided into 88 counties.

Ohio became the 17th state on March 1, 1803. It was organized as a territory in March 1861. The state legislature, the General Assembly, is made up of 33 senators and 99 representatives. The present constitution was adopted in 1851. As with all states in the United States, it elects two senators to the U.S. Congress, but the number of elected representatives to the House

Table 35-1. LAW ENFORCEMENT EMPLOYEE DATA, OHIO, 2002

Type of Agency	Number of Agencies	Total Personnel	Sworn	Civilian
All Agencies	555	33,621	23,664	9,957
State Agencies	2	3,118	1,955	1,163
County Sheriff's Offices	85	9,739	5,158	4,581
City Police	446	19,876	15,891	3,985
University Police Departments	17	596	416	180
Other Agencies	5	292	244	48

SOURCE: FBI, *Crime in the United States, 2002.*

Aggravated Assault	16,922
Burglary	99,164
Larceny-Theft	287,045
Auto Theft	42,767
Total Violent	40,128
Total Property	428,976
Total Crime Index	469,104

SOURCE: FBI, *Crime in the United States, 2002.*

of Representatives is based on population; for Ohio it is 19.

The major industries of the state include transportation equipment, fabricated metal products, machinery, food processing, and electric equipment. The primary agricultural products are soybeans, dairy products, corn, tomatoes, hogs, cattle, poultry, and eggs. The estimated population for 2002 was 11,353,140. The percentage breakdown of the 2000 census was 85.0% White, 11.5% Black or African American, 0.2% American Indian, and 1.2% Asian. Persons reporting some other race were 0.8% and those reporting two or more races on the 2000 census were 1.4%. Hispanics, who may be of any race, were 1.9% of the population in 2000. Persons age 18 or older was 74.6% and persons 65 years old and over was 13.3%. The median age was 36.2.

The law enforcement community in Ohio consists of at least 555 agencies employing about 23,664 officers according to data reported to the FBI (see Table 35-1). Full-time peace officers must complete a minimum of 552 hours of mandatory basic training. There were 874 officers assaulted in 2002. Three officers were killed feloniously in the line of duty and one died accidentally during 2002.

Crime Index offenses for 2002 for the state of Ohio totaled 469,104, which was a rate of 4,107.3 per 100,000 inhabitants. The numbers of index offenses by category are listed in Table 35-2. At least 247,686 arrests were made in 2002 for all categories of crimes, with 38,944 being for index offenses. Of the index offense arrests, 9,741 arrests (25.0%) were persons under the age of 18.

Table 35-2. Crime Index Offenses, Ohio, 2002

Index Offense Category	Number of Offenses
Murder	526
Forcible Rape	4,809
Robbery	17,871

The State of Oklahoma. Oklahoma is located in the south-central portion of the continental United States. It is bordered to the north by Kansas, to the east by Missouri and Arkansas, to the south by Texas, and to the west by parts of Texas and New Mexico. The state encompasses 69,903 square miles of area, including 1,224 square miles of inland water. It is the 20th largest of the 50 states in terms of area. Based on 2000 census figures, it ranks 27th among the states in population. The capital of Oklahoma is Oklahoma City with a 2000 population of 506,132. The other major cities and their 2000 populations include Tulsa, 393,049; Norman, 95,694; Lawton, 92,757; Broken Arrow, 74,859; Edmond, 68,315; Midwest City, 54,088; Enid, 47,045; Moore, 41,138; and Stillwater, 39,065. The state is divided into 77 counties.

Oklahoma became the 46th state on November 16, 1907. It was organized as a territory in May 1890. The state legislature is made up of 48 senators and 101 representatives. The present constitution was adopted in 1907. As with all states in the United States, it elects two senators to the U.S. Congress, but the number of elected representatives to the House of Representatives is based on population; for Oklahoma it is six.

The major industries of the state include transportation equipment, machinery, electric products, rubber and plastic products, and food processing. The primary agricultural products are cattle, wheat, milk, poultry, and cotton. The estimated population for 2002 was 3,493,714. The percentage breakdown of the 2000 census was 76.2% White, 7.6% Black or African American, 7.9% American Indian, and 1.4% Asian. Persons reporting some other race were 2.4% and those reporting two or more races on the 2000 census were 4.5%. Hispanics, who may be of any race, were 5.2% of the population in 2000. Persons age 18 or older was 74.1% and persons 65 years old and over was 13.2%. The median age was 35.5.

The law enforcement community in Oklahoma consists of at least 302 agencies employing about 7,108 officers according to data reported to the FBI (see Table 36-1). Full-time peace officers must complete a minimum of 326 hours of mandatory basic training plus

Table 36-1. LAW ENFORCEMENT EMPLOYEE DATA, OKLAHOMA, 2002				
Type of Agency	Number of Agencies	Total Personnel	Sworn	Civilian
All Agencies	302	10,585	7,108	3,477
State Agencies	2	1,451	852	599
County Sheriff's Offices	77	2,543	1,188	1,355
City Police	205	6,300	4,855	1,445
University Police Departments	16	260	188	72
Other Agencies	2	31	25	6

SOURCE: FBI, *Crime in the United States, 2002.*

Table 37-1. LAW ENFORCEMENT EMPLOYEE DATA, OREGON, 2002				
Type of Agency	Number of Agencies	Total Personnel	Sworn	Civilian
All Agencies	164	7,679	5,617	2,062
State Agencies	1	1,160	753	407
County Sheriff's Offices	36	1,815	1,327	488
City Police	126	4,646	3,492	1,154
Other Agencies	1	58	45	13

SOURCE: FBI, *Crime in the United States, 2002.*

all practicum work and exams, and complete 16 hours of annual continuing education. There were 843 officers assaulted in 2002. No officers were killed feloniously in the line of duty but one died accidentally during 2002.

Crime Index offenses for 2002 for the state of Oklahoma totaled 165,715, which was a rate of 4,743.2 per 100,000 inhabitants. The numbers of index offenses by category are listed in Table 36-2. At least 161,363 arrests were made in 2002 for all categories of crimes, with 22,663 being for index offenses. Of the index offense arrests, 6,770 arrests (29.9%) were persons under the age of 18.

Table 36-2. Crime Index Offenses, Oklahoma, 2002

Index Offense Category	Number of Offenses
Murder	163
Forcible Rape	1,573
Robbery	2,966
Aggravated Assault	12,885
Burglary	35,171
Larceny-Theft	100,185
Auto Theft	12,772
Total Violent	17,587
Total Property	148,128
Total Crime Index	165,715

SOURCE: FBI, *Crime in the United States, 2002.*

The State of Oregon. Oregon is located in the northwest portion of the continental United States. It is bordered to the north by Washington, to the east by Idaho, to the south by Nevada and California, and to the west by the Pacific Ocean. The state encompasses 98,386 square miles of area, including 2,383 square miles of inland water and it has 296 miles of coastline and 1,410 miles of shoreline. It is the ninth largest of the 50 states in terms of area. Based on 2000 census figures, it ranks 28th among the states in population.

The capital of Oregon is Salem with a 2000 population of 136,924. The other major cities and their 2000 populations include Portland, 529,121; Eugene, 137,893; Gresham, 90,205; Beaverton, 76,129; Hillsboro, 70,186; Medford, 63,154; Springfield, 52,864; Bend, 52,029; and Corvallis, 49,322. The state is divided into 36 counties.

Oregon became the 33rd state on February 14, 1859. It was organized as a territory in August 1848. The state legislature is made up of 30 senators and 60 assembly members. The present constitution was adopted in 1859. As with all states in the United States, it elects two senators to the U.S. Congress, but the number of elected representatives to the House of Representatives is based on population; for Oregon it is five.

The major industries of the state include lumber and wood products, tourism, food processing, paper products, machinery, and scientific instruments. The primary agricultural products are cattle, vegetables, nursery stock, fruits and nuts, dairy products, and wheat. The estimated population for 2002 was 3,521,515. The percentage breakdown of the 2000 census was 86.6% White, 1.6% Black or African American, 1.3% American Indian, and 3.0% Asian. Persons reporting some other race were 4.2% and those reporting two or more races on the 2000 census were 3.1%. Hispanics, who may be of any race, were 8.0% of the population in 2000. Persons age 18 or older was 75.3% and persons 65 years old and over was 12.8%. The median age was 36.3.

The law enforcement community in Oregon consists of at least 164 agencies employing about 5,617 officers according to data reported to the FBI (see Table 37-1). Full-time peace officers must complete a minimum of 10 weeks of mandatory basic training and 84 hours of in-service training every three years. There were 354 officers assaulted in 2002. One officer was killed feloniously in the line of duty and two died accidentally during 2002.

Crime Index offenses for 2002 for the state of Oregon totaled 171,443 which was a rate of 4,868.4 per 100,000 inhabitants. The numbers of index offenses by category are listed in Table 37-2. At least 111,337 arrests were made in 2002 for all categories of crimes, with 25,543 being for index offenses. Of the index offense arrests, 6,500 arrests (25.4%) were persons under the age of 18.

Table 37-2. Crime Index Offenses, Oregon, 2002

Index Offense Category	Number of Offenses
Murder	72
Forcible Rape	1,238
Robbery	2,742
Aggravated Assault	6,246
Burglary	25,696
Larceny-Theft	118,925
Auto Theft	16,524
Total Violent	10,298
Total Property	161,145
Total Crime Index	171,443

SOURCE: FBI, *Crime in the United States, 2002.*

The State of Pennsylvania. Pennsylvania is located in the middle Atlantic portion of the continental United States. It is bordered to the north by part of Lake Erie and the state of New York; to the east by New York and New Jersey; to the south by Delaware, Maryland and West Virginia; and to the west by Ohio. The state encompasses 46,058 square miles of area, including 1,239 square miles of inland water. It is the 33rd largest of the 50 states in terms of area. Based on 2000 census figures, it ranks sixth among the states in population. The capital of Pennsylvania is Harrisburg with a 2000 population of 48,950. The other major cities and their 2000 populations include Philadelphia, 1,517,550; Pittsburgh, 334,563; Allentown, 106,632; Erie, 103,717; Upper Darby, 81,821; Reading, 81,207; Scranton, 76,415; Bethlehem, 71,329; Lower Merion, 59,850; and Bensalem, 58,434. The state is divided into 67 counties.

Pennsylvania was one of the original 13 colonies and became the second state to adopt the U.S. Constitution on December 12, 1787. The state legislature, the General Assembly is made up of 50 senators and 203 representatives. The present constitution was adopted in 1968. As with all states in the United States, it elects two senators to the U.S. Congress, but the number of elected representatives to the House of Representatives is based on population; for Pennsylvania it is 21.

The major industries of the state include food processing, chemical products, machinery, electric equipment,

Table 38-1. LAW ENFORCEMENT EMPLOYEE DATA, PENNSYLVANIA, 2002

Type of Agency	Number of Agencies	Total Personnel	Sworn	Civilian
All Agencies	779	28,183	23,713	4,470
State Agencies	*	6,488	4,677	1,811
County Sheriff's Offices	15	741	610	131
City Police	696	20,092	17,781	2,311
University Police Departments	27	534	405	129
Other Agencies	13	328	240	88

SOURCE: FBI, *Crime in the United States, 2002.*
* Number of state agencies not reported.

and tourism. The primary agricultural products are dairy products, poultry, cattle, nursery stock, mushrooms, hogs, and hay. The estimated population for 2002 was 12,335,091. The percentage breakdown of the 2000 census was 85.4% White, 10.0% Black or African American, 0.1% American Indian, and 1.8% Asian. Persons reporting some other race were 1.5% and those reporting two or more races on the 2000 census were 1.2%. Hispanics, who may be of any race, were 3.2% of the population in 2000. Persons age 18 or older was 76.2% and persons 65 years old and over was 15.6%. The median age was 38.0.

The law enforcement community in Pennsylvania consists of at least 779 agencies employing about 23,713 officers according to data reported to the FBI (see Table 38-1). Full-time peace officers must complete a minimum of 750 hours of mandatory basic training and 12 hours of in-service training. There were 2,368 officers assaulted in 2002. Two officers were killed feloniously in the line of duty and one died accidentally during 2002.

Crime Index offenses for 2002 for the state of Pennsylvania totaled 350,446, which was a rate of 2,841.0 per 100,000 inhabitants. The numbers of index offenses by category are listed in Table 38-2. At least 421,600 arrests were made in 2002 for all categories of crimes, with 74,338 being for index offenses. Of the index offense arrests, 19,298 arrests (26.0%) were persons under the age of 18.

Table 38-2. Crime Index Offenses, Pennsylvania, 2002

Index Offense Category	Number of Offenses
Murder	624
Forcible Rape	3,731
Robbery	17,163
Aggravated Assault	28,060
Burglary	55,610
Larceny-Theft	212,441

Auto Theft	32,817
Total Violent	49,578
Total Property	300,868
Total Crime Index	350,446

SOURCE: FBI, *Crime in the United States, 2002.*

The State of Rhode Island. Rhode Island is located in the northeast portion of the continental United States. It is bordered to the north and northeast by Massachusetts, to the southeast and south by the Atlantic Ocean, and to the west by Connecticut. The state encompasses 1,545 square miles of area, including 500 square miles of inland water and it has 40 miles of coastline and 384 miles of shoreline. It is the smallest of the 50 states in terms of land area. Based on 2000 census figures, it ranks 43rd among the states in population. The capital of Rhode Island is Providence with a 2000 population of 173,618. The other major cities and their 2000 populations include Warwick, 85,808; Cranston, 79,269; Pawtucket, 72,958; East Providence, 48,688; Woonsocket, 43,224; Coventry, 33,668; North Providence, 32,411; Cumberland, 31,840; and West Warwick, 29,581. The state is divided into five counties.

Rhode Island was one of the original 13 colonies and it became the 13th state to ratify the U.S. Constitution on May 29, 1790. The state legislature is made up of 50 senators and 100 representatives. The present constitution was adopted in 1842. As with all states in the United States, it elects two senators to the U.S. Congress, but the number of elected representatives to the House of Representatives is based on population; for Rhode Island it is two.

The major industries of the state are fashion jewelry, fabricated metal products, electric equipment, machinery, shipbuilding and boat building, and tourism. The primary agricultural products are nursery stock, vegetables, dairy products, and eggs. The estimated population for 2002 was 1,069,725. The percentage breakdown of the 2000 census was 85.0% White, 4.5% Black or African American, 0.5% American Indian, and 2.3% Asian. Persons reporting some other race were 5.0% and those reporting two or more races on the 2000 census were 2.7%. Hispanics, who may be of any race, were 8.7% of the population in 2000. Persons age 18 or older was 76.4% and persons 65 years old and over was 14.5%. The median age was 36.7.

The law enforcement community in Rhode Island consists of at least 43 agencies employing about 2,485 officers according to data reported to the FBI (see Table 39-1). Full-time peace officers must complete a minimum of 620 hours of basic training. There were 432 officers assaulted in 2002. No officers were killed feloniously in the line of duty and none died accidentally during 2002.

Table 39-1. LAW ENFORCEMENT EMPLOYEE DATA, RHODE ISLAND, 2002

Type of Agency	Number of Agencies	Total Personnel	Sworn	Civilian
All Agencies	43	3,122	2,485	637
State Agencies	2	294	241	53
City Police	38	2,726	2,187	539
University Police Departments	2	91	47	44
Tribal Agency	1	11	10	1

SOURCE: FBI, *Crime in the United States, 2002.*

Crime Index offenses for 2002 for the state of Rhode Island totaled 38,393, which was a rate of 3,589.1 per 100,000 inhabitants. The numbers of index offenses by category are listed in Table 39-2. At least 42,140 arrests were made in 2002 for all categories of crimes, with 6,034 being for index offenses. Of the index offense arrests, 1,902 arrests (31.5%) were persons under the age of 18.

Table 39-2. Crime Index Offenses, Rhode Island, 2002

Index Offense Category	Number of Offenses
Murder	41
Forcible Rape	395
Robbery	916
Aggravated Assault	1,699
Burglary	6,415
Larceny-Theft	24,051
Auto Theft	4,876
Total Violent	3,051
Total Property	35,342
Total Crime Index	38,393

SOURCE: FBI, *Crime in the United States, 2002.*

The State of South Carolina. South Carolina is located in the south Atlantic portion of the continental United States. It is bordered to the north by North Carolina, to the east by the Atlantic Ocean, and to the south and west by Georgia. The state encompasses 32,007 square miles of area, including 1,896 square miles of inland water and it has 187 miles of coastline and 2,876 miles of shoreline. It is the 40th largest of the 50 states in terms of land area. Based on 2000 census figures, it ranks 26th among the states in population. The capital of South Carolina is Columbia with a 2000 population of 116,278. The other major cities and their 2000 populations include Charleston, 96,650; North Charleston, 79,641; Greenville, 56,002; Rock Hill, 49,765; Mount Pleasant, 47,609; Spartanburg, 39,673; Sumter, 39,643; Hilton

Table 40-1. LAW ENFORCEMENT EMPLOYEE DATA, SOUTH CAROLINA, 2002

Type of Agency	Number of Agencies	Total Personnel	Sworn	Civilian
All Agencies	260	12,128	8,787	3,341
State Agencies	*	1,446	1,116	330
County Sheriff's Offices	40	5,553	3,623	1,930
City Police	147	4,665	3,731	934
University Police Departments	17	411	274	137
Other Agencies	3	53	43	10

SOURCE: FBI, *Crime in the United States, 2002.*
* Number of state agencies not reported.

Table 40-2. Crime Index Offenses, South Carolina, 2002

Index Offense Category	Number of Offenses
Murder	298
Forcible Rape	1,959
Robbery	5,774
Aggravated Assault	25,730
Burglary	43,745
Larceny-Theft	123,196
Auto Theft	16,867
Total Violent	33,761
Total Property	183,808
Total Crime Index	217,569

SOURCE: FBI, *Crime in the United States, 2002.*

Head Island, 33,862; and Florence, 30,248. The state is divided into 46 counties.

South Carolina was one of the original 13 colonies and became the eighth state to ratify the U.S. Constitution on May 23, 1788. The state legislature is made up of 46 senators and 124 representatives. The present constitution was adopted in 1895. As with all states in the United States, it elects two senators to the U.S. Congress, but the number of elected representatives to the House of Representatives is based on population; for South Carolina it is six.

The major industries of the state include textile goods, chemical products, paper products, machinery, and tourism. The primary agricultural products are tobacco, poultry, cattle, dairy products, soybeans, and hogs. The estimated population for 2002 was 4,107,183. The percentage breakdown of the 2000 census was 67.2% White, 29.5% Black or African American, 0.3% American Indian, and 0.9% Asian. Persons reporting some other race were 1.0% and those reporting two or more races on the 2000 census were 1.0%. Hispanics, who may be of any race, were 2.4% of the population in 2000. Persons age 18 or older was 74.8% and persons 65 years old and over was 12.1%. The median age was 35.4.

The law enforcement community in South Carolina consists of at least 260 agencies employing about 8,787 officers according to data reported to the FBI (see Table 40-1). Full-time peace officers must complete a minimum of nine weeks of mandatory basic training. There were 490 officers assaulted in 2002. Five officers were killed feloniously in the line of duty and five died accidentally during 2002.

Crime Index offenses for 2002 for the state of South Carolina totaled 217,569, which was a rate of 5,297.3 per 100,000 inhabitants. The numbers of index offenses by category are listed in Table 40-2. At least 120,025 arrests were made in 2002 for all categories of crimes, with 20,597 being for index offenses. Of the index offense arrests, 4,804 arrests (23.3%) were persons under the age of 18.

The State of South Dakota. South Dakota is located in the north-central portion of the continental United States. It is bordered to the north by North Dakota, to the east by Minnesota and Iowa, to the south by Nebraska, and to the west by Wyoming and Montana. The state encompasses 77,121 square miles of area, including 1,224 square miles of inland water. It is the 17th largest of the 50 states in terms of area. Based on 2000 census figures, it ranks 46th among the states in population. The capital of South Dakota is Pierre with a 2000 population of 13,876. The other major cities and their 2000 populations include Sioux Falls, 123,975; Rapid City, 59,607; Aberdeen, 24,658; Watertown, 20,237; Brookings, 18,504; Mitchell, 14,558; Yankton, 13,528; Huron, 11,893; and Vermillion, 9,765. The state is divided into 67 counties.

South Dakota became the 40th state on November 2, 1889. It was organized as a territory in March 1861. The state legislature is made up of 35 senators and 70 representatives. The present constitution was adopted in 1889. As with all states in the United States, it elects two senators to the U.S. Congress, but the number of elected representatives to the House of Representatives is based on population; for South Dakota it is one.

The major industries of the state include food processing, machinery, lumber and wood products, and tourism. The primary agricultural products are cattle, hogs, wheat, soybeans, milk, and corn. The estimated population for 2002 was 761,063. The percentage breakdown of the 2000 census was 88.7% White, 0.6% Black or African American, 8.3% American Indian, and 0.6% Asian. Persons reporting some other race were 0.5% and those reporting two or more races on the 2000 census were 1.3%. Hispanics, who may be of any race, were 1.4% of the population in 2000. Persons age 18 or older was 73.2% and persons 65 years old and over was 14.3%. The median age was 35.6.

Table 41-1. LAW ENFORCEMENT EMPLOYEE DATA, SOUTH DAKOTA, 2002

Type of Agency	Number of Agencies	Total Personnel	Sworn	Civilian
All Agencies	130	2,016	1,267	749
State Agencies	2	350	180	170
County Sheriff's Offices	65	793	388	405
City Police	62	857	690	167
University Police Departments	1	16	9	7

SOURCE: FBI, *Crime in the United States, 2002.*

Table 42-1. LAW ENFORCEMENT EMPLOYEE DATA, TENNESSEE, 2002

Type of Agency	Number of Agencies	Total Personnel	Sworn	Civilian
All Agencies	437	23,962	15,174	8,788
State Agencies	*	2,982	1,551	1,431
County Sheriff's Offices	95	9,080	4,476	4,604
City Police	253	11,239	8,635	2,604
University Police Departments	14	426	329	97
Other Agencies	6	235	183	52

SOURCE: FBI, *Crime in the United States, 2002.*
* Number of state agencies not reported.

The law enforcement community in South Dakota consists of at least 130 agencies employing about 1,267 officers according to data reported to the FBI (see Table 41-1). Full-time peace officers must complete a 12-week basic certification course and an in-service domestic violence course once every four years after initial training. There were 36 officers assaulted in 2002. No officers were killed feloniously in the line of duty and none died accidentally during 2002.

Crime Index offenses for 2002 for the state of South Dakota totaled 17,342, which was a rate of 2,278.7 per 100,000 inhabitants. The numbers of index offenses by category are listed in Table 41-2. At least 28,112 arrests were made in 2002 for all categories of crimes, with 2,917 being for index offenses. Of the index offense arrests, 1,144 arrests (39.2%) were persons under the age of 18.

Table 41-2. Crime Index Offenses, South Dakota, 2002

Index Offense Category	Number of Offenses
Murder	11
Forcible Rape	361
Robbery	117
Aggravated Assault	861
Burglary	3,034
Larceny-Theft	12,139
Auto Theft	819
Total Violent	1,350
Total Property	15,992
Total Crime Index	17,342

SOURCE: FBI, *Crime in the United States, 2002.*

The State of Tennessee. Tennessee is located in the southeast central portion of the continental United States. It is bordered to the north by Kentucky and Virginia; to the east by North Carolina; to the south by Georgia, Alabama, and Mississippi; and to the west by Arkansas and Missouri. The state encompasses 42,146 square miles of area, including 926 square miles of inland water. It is the 36th largest of the 50 states in terms of area. Based on 2000 census figures, it ranks 16th among the states in population. The capital of Tennessee is Nashville with a 2000 population of 569,891 (includes and county of Davidson). The other major cities and their 2000 populations include Memphis, 650,100; Knoxville, 173,890; Chattanooga, 155,554; Clarksville, 103,455; Murfreesboro, 68,816; Jackson, 59,643; Johnson City, 55,469; Kingsport, 44,905; and Franklin, 41,842. The state is divided into 95 counties.

Tennessee became the 16th state on June 1, 1796. The state legislature is made up of 33 senators and 99 house members. The present constitution was adopted in 1870 but has been amended several times. As with all states in the United States, it elects two senators to the U.S. Congress, but the number of elected representatives to the House of Representatives is based on population; for Tennessee it is nine.

The major industries of the state include chemicals, transportation equipment, rubber, and plastics. The primary agricultural products are soybeans, cotton, tobacco, livestock and livestock products, dairy products, cattle, and hogs. The estimated population for 2002 was 5,797,289. The percentage breakdown of the 2000 census was 80.2% White, 16.4% Black or African American, 0.3% American Indian, and 1.0% Asian. Persons reporting some other race were 1.0% and those reporting two or more races on the 2000 census were 1.1%. Hispanics, who may be of any race, were 2.2% of the population in 2000. Persons age 18 or older was 75.4% and persons 65 years old and over was 12.4%. The median age was 35.9.

The law enforcement community in Tennessee consists of at least 437 agencies employing about 15,174 officers according to data reported to the FBI (see Table 42-1). Full-time peace officers must complete a minimum of 420 hours of mandatory basic training.

There were 2,136 officers assaulted in 2002. Two officers were killed feloniously in the line of duty and two died accidentally during 2002.

Crime Index offenses for 2002 for the state of Tennessee totaled 290,961, which was a rate of 5,018.9 per 100,000 inhabitants. The numbers of index offenses by category are listed in Table 42-2. At least 234,995 arrests were made in 2002 for all categories of crimes, with 36,020 being for index offenses. Of the index offense arrests, 5,963 arrests (16.6%) were persons under the age of 18.

Table 43-1. LAW ENFORCEMENT EMPLOYEE DATA, TEXAS, 2002

Type of Agency	Number of Agencies	Total Personnel	Sworn	Civilian
All Agencies	966	77,464	47,710	29,754
State Agencies	1	7,480	3,031	4,449
County Sheriff's Offices	251	25,423	11,459	13,964
City Police	615	40,713	30,920	9,793
University Police Departments	66	2,289	1,174	1,115
Other Agencies	33	1,559	1,126	433

SOURCE: FBI, *Crime in the United States, 2002.*

Table 42-2. Crime Index Offenses, Tennessee, 2002

Index Offense Category	Number of Offenses
Murder	420
Forcible Rape	2,290
Robbery	9,413
Aggravated Assault	29,439
Burglary	61,248
Larceny-Theft	161,610
Auto Theft	26,541
Total Violent	41,562
Total Property	249,399
Total Crime Index	290,961

SOURCE: FBI, *Crime in the United States, 2002.*

The State of Texas. Texas is located in the south Gulf portion of the continental United States. It is bordered to the north by New Mexico and Oklahoma; to the east by Oklahoma, Arkansas and Louisiana; to the south by the Gulf of Mexico and Mexico; and to the west by Mexico and New Mexico. The state encompasses 268,601 square miles of area, including 6,687 square miles of inland water. It is the second largest of the 50 states in terms of area. Based on 2000 census figures, it also ranks second among the states in population. The capital of Texas is Austin with a 2000 population of 656,562. The other major cities and their 2000 populations include Houston, 1,953,631; Dallas, 1,188,580; San Antonio, 1,144,646; El Paso, 563,662; Fort Worth, 534,694; Arlington, 332,969; Corpus Christi, 277,454; Plano, 222,030; and Garland, 215,768. The state is divided into 254 counties.

Texas became the 28th state on December 29, 1845. The state legislature is made up of 33 senators and 150 house members. The present constitution was adopted in 1876. As with all states in the United States, it elects two senators to the U.S. Congress, but the number of elected representatives to the House of Representatives is based on population; for Texas it is 30.

The major industries of the state include chemical products, petroleum and natural gas, food processing, electric equipment, machinery, mining, and tourism. The primary agricultural products are cattle, cotton, dairy products, nursery stock, poultry, sorghum, corn, and wheat. The estimated population for 2002 was 21,779,893. The percentage breakdown of the 2000 census was 71.0% White, 11.5% Black or African American, 0.6% American Indian, and 2.7% Asian. Persons reporting some other race were 11.7% and those reporting two or more races on the 2000 census were 2.5%. Hispanics, who may be of any race, were 32.0% of the population in 2000. Persons age 18 or older was 71.8% and persons 65 years old and over was 9.9%. The median age was 32.3.

The law enforcement community in Texas consists of at least 966 agencies employing about 47,710 officers according to data reported to the FBI (see Table 43-1). Full-time peace officers must complete a minimum of 600 hours of mandatory basic training. There were 5,062 officers assaulted in 2002. Five officers were killed feloniously in the line of duty and nine died accidentally during 2002.

Crime Index offenses for 2002 for the state of Texas totaled 1,130,292, which was a rate of 5,189.6 per 100,000 inhabitants. The numbers of index offenses by category are listed in Table 43-2. At least 1,036,323 arrests were made in 2002 for all categories of crimes, with 154,229 being for index offenses. Of the index offense arrests, 42,091 arrests (27.3%) were persons under the age of 18.

Table 43-2. Crime Index Offenses, Texas, 2002

Index Offense Category	Number of Offenses
Murder	1,302
Forcible Rape	8,508
Robbery	37,580
Aggravated Assault	78,628
Burglary	212,602

Larceny-Theft	688,992
Auto Theft	102,680
Total Violent	126,018
Total Property	1,004,274
Total Crime Index	1,130,292

SOURCE: FBI, *Crime in the United States, 2002.*

Table 44-1. LAW ENFORCEMENT EMPLOYEE DATA, UTAH, 2002

Type of Agency	Number of Agencies	Total Personnel	Sworn	Civilian
All Agencies	124	6,872	4,636	2,236
State Agencies	4	634	595	39
County Sheriff's Offices	29	3,155	1,671	1,484
City Police	82	2,869	2,246	623
University Police Departments	8	192	108	84
Other Agencies	1	22	16	6

SOURCE: FBI, *Crime in the United States, 2002.*

The State of Utah. Utah is located in the western portion of the continental United States. It is bordered to the north by Idaho and Wyoming, to the east by Wyoming and Colorado, to the south by Arizona, and to the west by Nevada. The state encompasses 84,904 square miles of area, including 2,736 square miles of inland water. It is the 13th largest of the 50 states in terms of area. Based on 2000 census figures, it ranks 34th among the states in population. The capital of Utah is Salt Lake City with a 2000 population of 181,743. The other major cities and their 2000 populations include, West Valley City, 108,896; Provo, 105,166; Sandy, 88,418; Orem, 84,324; Ogden, 77,226; West Jordan, 68,336; Layton, 58,474; Taylorsville, 57,439; and St. George, 49,663. The state is divided into 29 counties.

Utah became the 45th state on January 4, 1896. It was organized as a territory in September 1850. The state legislature is made up of 29 senators and 75 representatives. The present constitution was adopted in 1896. As with all states in the United States, it elects two senators to the U.S. Congress, but the number of elected representatives to the House of Representatives is based on population; for Utah it is three.

The major industries of the state include machinery, aerospace, mining, food processing, electric equipment and tourism. The primary agricultural products are cattle, dairy products, hay, and turkeys. The estimated population for 2002 was 2,316,256. The percentage breakdown of the 2000 census was 89.2% White, 0.8% Black or African American, 1.3% American Indian, and 1.7% Asian. Persons reporting some other race were 4.2% and those reporting two or more races on the 2000 census were 2.1%. Hispanics, who may be of any race, were 9.0% of the population in 2000. Persons age 18 or older was 67.8% and persons 65 years old and over was 8.5%. The median age was 27.1.

The law enforcement community in Utah consists of at least 124 agencies employing about 4,636 officers according to data reported to the FBI (see Table 44-1). Full-time peace officers must complete a minimum of 600 hours of mandatory basic training and 40 hours of in-service annually. There were 240 officers assaulted in 2002. One officer was killed feloniously in the line of duty and one died accidentally during 2002.

Crime Index offenses for 2002 for the state of Utah totaled 103,129, which was a rate of 4,452.4 per 100,000 inhabitants. The numbers of index offenses by category are listed in Table 44-2. At least 121,200 arrests were made in 2002 for all categories of crimes, with 20,091 being for index offenses. Of the index offense arrests, 7,658 arrests (38.1%) were persons under the age of 18.

Table 44-2. Crime Index Offenses, Utah, 2002

Index Offense Category	Number of Offenses
Murder	47
Forcible Rape	943
Robbery	1,140
Aggravated Assault	3,358
Burglary	15,124
Larceny-Theft	74,795
Auto Theft	7,722
Total Violent	5,488
Total Property	97,641
Total Crime Index	103,129

SOURCE: FBI, *Crime in the United States, 2002.*

The State of Vermont. Vermont is located in the New England portion of the continental United States. It is bordered to the north by Canada, to the east by New Hampshire, to the south by Massachusetts, and to the west by New York. The state encompasses 9,615 square miles of area, including 366 square miles of inland water. It is the 45th largest of the 50 states in terms of area. Based on 2000 census figures, it ranks 49th among the states in population. The capital of Vermont is Montpelier with a 2000 population of 8,035. The other major cities and their 2000 populations include Burlington, 38,889; Essex, 18,626; Rutland, 17,292; Colchester, 16,986; South Burlington, 15,814; Bennington, 15,737; Brattleboro, 12,005; Hartford,

Table 45-1. LAW ENFORCEMENT EMPLOYEE DATA, VERMONT, 2002

Type of Agency	Number of Agencies	Total Personnel	Sworn	Civilian
All Agencies	58	1,343	956	387
State Agencies	1	474	295	179
County Sheriff's Offices	8	117	81	39
City Police	49	752	580	172

SOURCE: FBI, *Crime in the United States, 2002.*

Table 45-2. Crime Index Offenses, Vermont, 2002

Index Offense Category	Number of Offenses
Murder	13
Forcible Rape	126
Robbery	77
Aggravated Assault	442
Burglary	3,489
Larceny-Theft	10,684
Auto Theft	769
Total Violent	658
Total Property	14,942
Total Crime Index	15,600

SOURCE: FBI, *Crime in the United States, 2002.*

10.367; Milton, 9,479; and Barre, 9,291. The state is divided into 14 counties.

Vermont became the 14th state on March 4, 1791. The state legislature, the General Assembly, is made up of 30 senators and 150 assembly members. The present constitution was adopted in 1783. As with all states in the United States, it elects two senators to the U.S. Congress, but the number of elected representatives to the House of Representatives is based on population; for Vermont it is one.

The major industries of the state include electronic equipment, fabricated metal products, printing and publishing, paper products, and tourism. The primary agricultural products are dairy products, cattle, hay, apples, and maple products. The estimated population for 2002 was 616,592. The percentage breakdown of the 2000 census was 96.8% White, 0.5% Black or African American, 0.4% American Indian, and 0.9% Asian. Persons reporting some other race were 0.2% and those reporting two or more races on the 2000 census were 1.2%. Hispanics, who may be of any race, were 0.9% of the population in 2000. Persons age 18 or older was 75.8% and persons 65 years old and over was 12.7%. The median age was 37.7.

The law enforcement community in Vermont consists of at least 58 agencies employing about 956 officers according to data reported to the FBI (see Table 45-1). Full-time peace officers must complete a minimum of 852 hours of mandatory basic training and 25 hours of in-service training annually. No officers were killed feloniously in the line of duty or accidentally during 2002.

Crime Index offenses for 2002 for the state of Vermont totaled 15,600, which was a rate of 2,530.0 per 100,000 inhabitants. The numbers of index offenses by category are listed in Table 45-2. At least 13,757 arrests were made in 2002 for all categories of crimes, with 1,826 being for index offenses. Of the index offense arrests, 489 arrests (26.8%) were persons under the age of 18.

The State of Virginia. Virginia is located in the mid-Atlantic region of the continental United States. It is bordered to the north by West Virginia, Maryland and the District of Columbia; to the east by Maryland, the Chesapeake Bay, and the Atlantic Ocean; to the south by North Carolina and Tennessee; and to the west by Kentucky and West Virginia. The state encompasses 42,769 square miles of area, including 3,171 square miles of inland water and it has 112 miles of coastline and 3,315 miles of shoreline. It is the 35th largest of the 50 states in terms of area. Based on 2000 census figures, it ranks 12th among the states in population. The capital of Virginia is Richmond with a 2000 population of 197,790. The other major cities and their 2000 populations include Virginia Beach, 425,257; Norfolk, 234,403; Chesapeake, 199,184; Newport News, 180,150; Hampton, 146,437; Alexandria, 128,283; Portsmouth, 100,565; Roanoke, 94,911; and Lynchburg, 65,269. The state is divided into 95 counties.

Virginia was the tenth of the original 13 colonies to ratify the U.S. Constitution on June 25, 1788. The state legislature, the General Assembly, is made up of 40 senators and 100 delegates. The present constitution was adopted in 1970. As with all states in the United States, it elects two senators to the U.S. Congress, but the number of elected representatives to the House of Representatives is based on population; for Virginia it is 11.

The major industries of the state include transportation equipment, textiles, food processing, printing, electric equipment, and chemicals. The primary agricultural products are cattle, poultry, dairy products, tobacco, hogs, and soybeans. The estimated population for 2002 was 7,293,542. The percentage breakdown of the 2000 census was 72.3% White, 19.6% Black or African American, 0.3% American Indian, and 3.7% Asian. Persons reporting some other race were 2.0% and those reporting two or more races on the 2000

Table 46-1. LAW ENFORCEMENT EMPLOYEE DATA, VIRGINIA, 2002

Type of Agency	Number of Agencies	Total Personnel	Sworn	Civilian
All Agencies	278	21,540	16,552	4,988
State Agencies	9	3,339	2,474	865
County Sheriff's Offices	95	9,005	6,965	2,040
City Police	151	8,388	6,605	1,783
University Police Departments	22	723	466	257
Other Agencies	1	85	42	43

SOURCE: FBI, *Crime in the United States, 2002.*

census were 2.0%. Hispanics, who may be of any race, were 4.7% of the population in 2000. Persons age 18 or older was 75.4% and persons 65 years old and over was 11.2%. The median age was 35.7.

The law enforcement community in Virginia consists of at least 278 agencies employing about 16,552 officers according to data reported to the FBI (see Table 46-1). Full-time peace officers must complete a minimum of 776 hours of mandatory basic training; deputy sheriffs must complete 936 hours, and complete 40 hours of in-service training biennially. There were 1,304 officers assaulted in 2002. One officer was killed feloniously in the line of duty and two died accidentally during 2002.

Crime Index offenses for 2002 for the state of Virginia totaled 229,039 which was a rate of 3,140.3 per 100,000 inhabitants. The numbers of index offenses by category are listed in Table 46-2. At least 251,047 arrests were made in 2002 for all categories of crimes, with 30,532 being for index offenses. Of the index offense arrests, 6,927 arrests (22.7%) were persons under the age of 18.

Table 46-2. Crime Index Offenses, Virginia, 2002

Index Offense Category	Number of Offenses
Murder	388
Forcible Rape	1,839
Robbery	6,961
Aggravated Assault	12,068
Burglary	31,757
Larceny-Theft	157,548
Auto Theft	18,478
Total Violent	21,256
Total Property	207,783
Total Crime Index	229,039

SOURCE: FBI, *Crime in the United States, 2002.*

The State of Washington. Washington is located in the northwest portion of the continental United States. It is bordered to the north by Canada, to the east by Idaho, to the south by Oregon, and to the west by the Pacific Ocean. The state encompasses 71,303 square miles of area, including 4,721 square miles of inland water and it has 157 miles of coastline and 3,026 miles of shoreline. It is the 18th largest of the 50 states in terms of area. Based on 2000 census figures, it ranks 15th among the states in population. The capital of Washington is Olympia with a 2000 population of 42,514. The other major cities and their 2000 populations include Seattle, 563,374; Spokane, 195,629; Tacoma, 193,556; Vancouver, 143,560; Bellevue, 109,569; Everett, 91,488; Federal Way, 83,259; Kent, 79,524; Yakima, 71,845; and Bellingham, 67,171. The state is divided into 39 counties.

Washington became the 42nd state on November 11, 1889. It was organized as a territory in March 1853. The state legislature is made up of 49 senators and 98 representatives. The present constitution was adopted in 1889. As with all states in the United States, it elects two senators to the U.S. Congress, but the number of elected representatives to the House of Representatives is based on population; for Washington it is nine.

The major industries of the state include aerospace, software development, food processing, paper products, lumber and wood products, chemical products, and tourism. The primary agricultural products are seafood, dairy products, apples, cattle, wheat, potatoes, and nursery stock. The estimated population for 2002 was 6,068,996. The percentage breakdown of the 2000 census was 81.8% White, 3.2% Black or African American, 1.6% American Indian, and 5.5% Asian. Persons reporting some other race were 3.9% and those reporting two or more races on the 2000 census were 3.6%. Hispanics, who may be of any race, were 7.5% of the population in 2000. Persons age 18 or older was 74.3% and persons 65 years old and over was 11.2%. The median age was 35.3.

The law enforcement community in Washington consists of at least 251 agencies employing about 9,868 officers according to data reported to the FBI (see Table 47-1). Full-time peace officers must complete a minimum of 720 hours of mandatory basic training. There were 1,129 officers assaulted in 2002. One officer was killed feloniously in the line of duty and one died accidentally during 2002.

Crime Index offenses for 2002 for the state of Washington totaled 309,931, which was a rate of 5,106.8 per 100,000 inhabitants. The numbers of index offenses by category are listed in Table 47-2. At least 237,512 arrests were made in 2002 for all categories of crimes, with 42,765 being for index offenses. Of the index offense arrests, 13,456 arrests (31.5%) were persons under the age of 18.

Table 47-1. LAW ENFORCEMENT EMPLOYEE DATA, WASHINGTON, 2002

Type of Agency	Number of Agencies	Total Personnel	Sworn	Civilian
All Agencies	251	13,747	9,868	3,879
State Agencies	1	2,034	1,105	929
County Sheriff's Offices	39	3,510	2,487	1,023
City Police	198	7,839	5.982	1,857
University Police Departments	7	143	118	25
Other Agencies	6	221	176	45

SOURCE: FBI, *Crime in the United States, 2002.*

Table 48-1. LAW ENFORCEMENT EMPLOYEE DATA, WEST VIRGINIA, 2002

Type of Agency	Number of Agencies	Total Personnel	Sworn	Civilian
All Agencies	352	3,959	3,028	931
State Agencies	*	1,089	721	368
County Sheriff's Offices	121	1,721	1,259	462
City Police	153	1,019	938	81
University Police Departments	10	128	108	20
Other Agencies	1	2	2	0

SOURCE: FBI, *Crime in the United States, 2002.*

* Number of state agencies not reported.

Table 47-2. Crime Index Offenses, Washington, 2002

Index Offense Category	Number of Offenses
Murder	184
Forcible Rape	2,734
Robbery	5,797
Aggravated Assault	12,249
Burglary	54,948
Larceny-Theft	193,526
Auto Theft	40,493
Total Violent	20,964
Total Property	288,967
Total Crime Index	309,931

SOURCE: FBI, *Crime in the United States, 2002.*

The State of West Virginia. West Virginia is located in the central eastern portion of the continental United States. It is bordered to the north by Ohio, Pennsylvania, and Maryland; to the east by Maryland and Virginia; to the south by Virginia; and to the west by Kentucky. The state encompasses 24,231 square miles of area, including 145 square miles of inland water. It is the 41st largest of the 50 states in terms of area. Based on 2000 census figures, it ranks 37th among the states in population. The capital of West Virginia is Charleston with a 2000 population of 53,421. The other major cities and their 2000 populations include Huntington, 51,475; Parkersburg, 33,099; Wheeling, 31,419; Morgantown, 26,809; Weirton, 20,411; Fairmont, 19,097; Beckley, 17,254; Clarksburg, 16,743; and Martinsburg, 14,972. The state is divided into 55 counties.

West Virginia became the 35th state on June 20, 1863. The state legislature is made up of 34 senators and 100 delegates. The present constitution was adopted in 1872. As with all states in the United States, it elects two senators to the U.S. Congress, but the number of elected representatives to the House of Representatives is based on population; for West Virginia it is three.

The major industries of the state include chemical products, mining, primary metals, stone, clay, and glass products, and tourism. The primary agricultural products are cattle, dairy products, poultry, and apples. The estimated population for 2002 was 1,801,873. The percentage breakdown of the 2000 census was 95.0% White, 3.2% Black or African American, 0.2% American Indian, and 0.5% Asian. Persons reporting some other race were 0.2% and those reporting two or more races on the 2000 census were 0.9%. Hispanics, who may be of any race, were 0.7% of the population in 2000. Persons age 18 or older was 77.7% and persons 65 years old and over was 15.3%. The median age was 38.9.

The law enforcement community in West Virginia consists of at least 352 agencies employing about 3,028 officers according to data reported to the FBI (see Table 48-1). Full-time peace officers must complete a minimum of 600 hours of mandatory basic training and 16 hours of in-service annually. No officers were killed feloniously in the line of duty or accidentally during 2002.

Crime Index offenses for 2002 for the state of West Virginia totaled 45,320, which was a rate of 2,515.2 per 100,000 inhabitants. The numbers of index offenses by category are listed in Table 48-2. At least 25,781 arrests were made in 2002 for all categories of crimes, with 3,508 being for index offenses. Of the index offense arrests, 566 arrests (16.1%) were persons under the age of 18.

Table 48-2. Crime Index Offenses, West Virginia, 2002

Index Offense Category	Number of Offenses
Murder	57
Forcible Rape	328
Robbery	657
Aggravated Assault	3,179
Burglary	9,677
Larceny-Theft	27,524

Auto Theft	3,898
Total Violent	4,221
Total Property	41,099
Total Crime Index	45,320

SOURCE: FBI, *Crime in the United States, 2002.*

The State of Wisconsin. Wisconsin is located in the north-central portion of the continental United States. It is bordered to the north by Lake Superior and the state of Michigan, to the east by Lake Michigan, to the south by Illinois, and to the west by Iowa and Minnesota. The state encompasses 65,503 square miles of area including 11,190 square miles of water because of the Great Lakes. It is the 23rd largest of the 50 states in terms of area. Based on 2000 census figures, it ranks 18th among the states in population. The capital of Wisconsin is Madison with a 2000 population of 208,054. The other major cities and their 2000 populations include Milwaukee, 596,974; Green Bay, 102,313; Kenosha, 90,352; Racine, 81,855; Appleton, 70,087; Waukesha, 64,825; Oshkosh, 62,916; Eau Claire, 61,704; and West Allis, 61,254. The state is divided into 72 counties.

Wisconsin became the 30th state on May 29, 1848. It was organized as a territory in July 1836. The state legislature is made up of 33 senators and 99 assembly members. The present constitution was adopted in 1848. As with all states in the United States, it elects two senators to the U.S. Congress, but the number of elected representatives to the House of Representatives is based on population; for Wisconsin it is nine.

The major industries of the state include machinery, food processing, paper products, electric equipment, fabricated metal products, and tourism. The primary agricultural products are cheese, dairy products, cattle, hogs, vegetables, corn, and cranberries. The estimated population for 2002 was 5,441,196. The percentage breakdown of the 2000 census was 88.9% White, 5.7% Black or African American, 0.9% American Indian, and 1.7% Asian. Persons reporting some other race were 1.6% and those reporting two or more races on the 2000 census were 1.2%. Hispanics, who may be of any race, were 3.6% of the population in 2000. Persons age 18 or older was 74.5% and persons 65 years old and over was 13.1%. The median age was 36.0.

The law enforcement community in Wisconsin consists of at least 316 agencies employing about 11,347 officers according to data reported to the FBI (see Table 49-1). Full-time peace officers must complete a minimum of 520 hours of mandatory basic training and 24 hours of in-service training annually. There were 575 officers assaulted in 2002. Two officers were killed feloniously in the line of duty and none died accidentally during 2002.

Table 49-1. LAW ENFORCEMENT EMPLOYEE DATA, WISCONSIN, 2002

Type of Agency	Number of Agencies	Total Personnel	Sworn	Civilian
All Agencies	316	15,848	11,347	4,501
State Agencies	5	1,011	787	224
County Sheriff's Offices	62	5,950	3,380	2,570
City Police	239	8,665	7,028	1,637
University Police Departments	10	222	152	70

SOURCE: FBI, *Crime in the United States, 2002.*

Crime Index offenses for 2002 for the state of Wisconsin totaled 176,987, which was a rate of 3,252.7 per 100,000 inhabitants. The numbers of index offenses by category are listed in Table 49-2. At least 409,682 arrests were made in 2002 for all categories of crimes, with 52,229 being for index offenses. Of the index offense arrests, 20,771 arrests (39.8%) were persons under the age of 18.

Table 49-2. Crime Index Offenses, Wisconsin, 2002

Index Offense Category	Number of Offenses
Murder	154
Forcible Rape	1,237
Robbery	4,713
Aggravated Assault	6,134
Burglary	27,926
Larceny-Theft	123,365
Auto Theft	13,458
Total Violent	12,238
Total Property	164,749
Total Crime Index	176,987

SOURCE: FBI, *Crime in the United States, 2002.*

The State of Wyoming. Wyoming is located in the northwest portion of the continental United States. It is bordered to the north by Montana, to the east by South Dakota and Nebraska, to the south by Colorado and Utah, and to the west by Utah and Idaho. The state encompasses 97,818 square miles of area, including 714 square miles of inland water. It is the tenth largest of the 50 states in terms of area. Based on 2000 census figures, it ranks 50th among the states in population. The capital of Wyoming is Cheyenne with a 2000 population of 53,011. The other major cities and their 2000 populations include Casper, 49,644; Laramie, 27,204; Gillette, 19,646; Rock Springs, 18,708; Sheridan, 15,804; Green River, 11,808; Evanston, 11,507; Riverton, 9,310; and Cody, 8,835. The state is divided into 23 counties.

Table 50-1. LAW ENFORCEMENT EMPLOYEE DATA, WYOMING, 2002

Type of Agency	Number of Agencies	Total Personnel	Sworn	Civilian
All Agencies	68	1,989	1,239	750
State Agencies	1	320	172	148
County Sheriff's Offices	23	719	404	315
City Police	40	861	598	263
University Police Departments	2	24	15	9
Tribal Agencies	2	65	501	15

SOURCE: FBI, *Crime in the United States, 2002.*

Table 50-2. Crime Index Offenses, Wyoming, 2002

Index Offense Category	Number of Offenses
Murder	15
Forcible Rape	148
Robbery	93
Aggravated Assault	1,108
Burglary	2,448
Larceny-Theft	13,303
Auto Theft	743
Total Violent	1,364
Total Property	16,494
Total Crime Index	17,858

SOURCE: FBI, *Crime in the United States, 2002.*

Wyoming became the 44th state on July 10, 1890. It was organized as a territory in May 1869. The state legislature is made up of 30 senators and 60 representatives. The present constitution was adopted in 1890. As with all states in the United States, it elects two senators to the U.S. Congress, but the number of elected representatives to the House of Representatives is based on population; for Wyoming it is one.

The major industries of the state include mining, chemical products, lumber and wood products, printing and publishing, machinery, and tourism. The primary agricultural products are cattle, sugar beets, sheep, hay, and wheat. The estimated population for 2002 was 498,703. The percentage breakdown of the 2000 census was 92.1% White, 0.8% Black or African American, 2.3% American Indian, and 0.6% Asian. Persons reporting some other race were 2.5% and those reporting two or more races on the 2000 census were 1.8%. Hispanics, who may be of any race, were 6.4% of the population in 2000. Persons age 18 or older was 73.9% and persons 65 years old and over was 11.7%. The median age was 36.2.

The law enforcement community in Wyoming consists of at least 68 agencies employing about 1,239 officers according to data reported to the FBI (see Table 50-1). Full-time peace officers must complete a minimum of 501 hours of mandatory basic training. Officers' in-service requirements vary until they reach the professional level, then it is 40 hours of training every two years. There were 74 officers assaulted in 2002. No officers were killed feloniously in the line of duty or accidentally during 2002.

Crime Index offenses for 2002 for the state of Wyoming totaled 17,858, which was a rate of 3,580.9 per 100,000 inhabitants. The numbers of index offenses by category are listed in Table 50-2. At least 34,060 arrests were made in 2002 for all categories of crimes, with 3,281 being for index offenses. Of the index offense arrests, 1,281 arrests (39.0%) were persons under the age of 18.

CITY PROFILES

The City of Albuquerque, New Mexico. Albuquerque is the largest city in the state of New Mexico and is the seat of Bernalillo County. It is geographically located in the west-central part of the state, 58 miles southwest of Santa Fe, where Interstates 25 and 40 intersect. Its elevation is about 4500 feet above sea level and it sits on the banks of the upper Rio Grande River. The 2000 population was 448,607, which made it the 35th largest city in the United States. The metropolitan area of Albuquerque has a population of over 712,000 residents making it the 61st largest metro area in the United States according to the 2000 census. The city encompasses about 181 square miles of area. The city is a center for health and medical services in the region; nuclear research, banking and tourism are important to the city's economy. Albuquerque is becoming a high-tech center and Intel Corporation's largest manufacturing facility is located there.

Albuquerque was originally settled in the 1600s but old town section of today's city dates to 1706. The city was named for the Duke of Alburquerque, the viceroy of New Spain. During the Civil War of the United States, the Confederate Army occupied it briefly, but it remained loyal to the Union.

According to the 2000 census, the population profile of the city was 71.6% White, 3.1% Black, 3.9% American Indian and Alaska Native, 2.2% Asian, 14.8% other race, 4.3% two or more races and 39.9% Hispanic/Latino. Approximately 75.5% of the population was age 18 and over and 12% were 65 and over; the median age was 34.9.

The Albuquerque Police Department has a budgeted strength of 1,325 positions, with about 955 sworn officers, to carry out its stated mission:

To strive to improve the quality of life in our city by protecting life and property, maintaining order, and reducing crime through education and prevention while upholding the Constitution and laws of the State of New Mexico, the United States, and the City of Albuquerque.

The department is organized based on four program strategies: (1) Neighborhood Policing, which includes community policing activities, responding to calls for service, crime prevention, traffic and tactical enforcement. Officers operate out of five command areas, each managed by a commander and staffed with anywhere from 82 to 119 officers. (2) Investigative Services, which includes the department's three specialized investigative units (special investigations, the criminal investigations division and the Metropolitan Crime Laboratory. (3) Central Support Services, which provides critical support to the Office of the Chief and its other divisions, such as human resources, financial management, fleet and facilities management, planning, communications, records management, court services, and internal affairs. (4) Off-Duty Police Overtime, which provides a mechanism to allow businesses and other external entities to employ sworn officers during their off-duty hours.

Officers begin their career with the Albuquerque Police Department as a police cadet attending a 25-week academy and earning $13.66 per hour (plus $50 monthly clothing allowance). After the academy, an officer's salary increases to $14.16 per hour for one year; then the salary increases to $16.66 per hour (plus $50 monthly clothing allowance). Salary incentives are available for a number of factors: college education, bilingual proficiency, shift differential, longevity and special assignment. Police officers who retire after 22 years and 10 months can receive 80% of their pay, based on the last three years of their employment.

Crime Index offenses for the city of Albuquerque totaled 35,762 for 2002.

The City of Atlanta. Atlanta is the capital city of and the largest city in the state of Georgia. It is geographically located in the northwestern part of the state at the base of the Blue Ridge Mountains near the Chattahoochee River. Major interstate highways leading into the city include I-20, I-75, and I-85. The 2000 population was 416,474, which made it the 39th largest city in the United States. The metropolitan area of Atlanta has a population of over 4 million residents and is the 11th largest metro area in the United States according to the 2000 census. The city encompasses about 132 square miles of area. Atlanta is the major commercial and transportation hub of the southeast United States; its international airport is one of the busiest in the world.

Atlanta was originally founded in 1837 under the name of Terminus; in 1843 it became incorporated under the name of Marthasville; in 1845 it was renamed Atlanta and incorporated as a city two years later. It became the capital of Georgia in 1868. During the Civil War of the United States, it was occupied by General William T. Sherman's troops in 1864 and it was burned and nearly totally destroyed. Atlanta was rebuilt after the war and grew rapidly due to the expansion of commerce and industry.

According to the 2000 census, the population profile of the city was 33.2% White, 61.4% Black, 0.2% American Indian and Alaska Native, 1.9% Asian, 2.0% other race, 1.2% two or more races and 4.5% Hispanic/Latino. Approximately 77.7% of the population was age 18 and over and 9.7% were 65 and over; the median age was 31.9.

The police department is led by a chief who is appointed by the mayor. The department has an authorized strength of over 1,732 sworn officers, but its actual strength as of January 2004 was 1,453. It employs about 847 civilians. It is a full-service police agency that has adopted a community-oriented philosophy and relies heavily upon community input and collaborative problem-solving strategies. Its major priorities today are youth-related crime, domestic violence, quality of life issues, homeland security and the perception of crime in Atlanta. The mission statement of the department is:

It is the mission of the Atlanta Police Department to improve the quality of life by providing a safe and secure environment and, within the framework of the Constitution, to enforce the laws, exercise regulatory authority and preserve the peace while protecting the rights of all and applying the highest standards of professionalism, integrity, and accountability, in partnership with the entire community.

The organizational structure of the department consists of three divisions (Field Operations, Criminal Investigations and Support Services Divisions) and one bureau (Bureau of Taxicabs and Vehicles for Hire). Citizen Advisory Councils and Neighborhood Planning Units representing 139 separate neighborhoods provide citizen input for departmental decisions while miniprecincts, foot patrols and bicycle patrols encourage personalized policing and frequent citizen-officer interaction.

One unique feature in the Atlanta Police Department is its Communications Network (COMNET), is a continuous link between private sector security providers and the department. It is a two-way, VHF radio network, established in 1990 to provide quick and efficient communications between the security providers and the department. The city recognizes that private security officers can often serve as the first line of notification for the police department, as they are visible, trained, and strategically posted by the company or property they are assigned to protect. COMNET links over 150 member sites that include campus police departments, federal agencies, the downtown improvement district, corporate and hotel security departments, retail loss prevention departments and property management companies.

Recruits attending the police academy must complete eighteen and a half weeks of training plus an additional six weeks of field training exposure with two weeks per watch in three of the six police zones. Officers also receive at least 20 hours of in-service training per year. Crime Index offenses for the city of Atlanta totaled 49,451 for 2002.

The City of Baltimore, Maryland. Baltimore is the largest city in the state of Maryland. It is geographically located in the north-central part of the state along the Chesapeake Bay at the mouth of the Patapsco River. It is 35 miles northeast of Washington, D.C. Major interstate highways leading into the city include I-70, I-95, and I-97. The 2000 population was 651,154, which made it the 17th largest city in the United States. The metropolitan area of Baltimore (which includes Washington, D.C.) has a population of over 7.6 million residents and is the 13th largest metro area in the United States according to the 2000 census. The city encompasses about 81 square miles of area. Baltimore's economy is based on a diverse blend of industry, shipping, financial, legal and nonprofit services. Tourism and scientific research are highly developed in the city. It was originally founded in 1729 and named for Lord Baltimore, the founder of Maryland. It was incorporated in 1797.

According to the 2000 census, the population profile of the city was 31.6% White, 64.3% Black, 0.3% American Indian and Alaska Native, 1.5% Asian, 0.7% other race, 1.5% two or more races and 1.7% Hispanic/Latino. Approximately 75.2% of the population was age 18 and over and 13.2% were 65 and over; the median age was 35.

The police department is led by a commissioner who is appointed by the mayor. The department has a strength of about 3,888 personnel, which includes 3,316 sworn officers and 572 civilians according to 2002 figures. The mission statement of the department is:

> The mission of the Police Department is to protect and preserve life and property; to understand and serve the needs of the City's neighborhoods; and to improve the quality of life by maintaining order, recognizing and resolving community problems, and apprehending criminals.

The organizational structure of the department consists of nine police districts where the majority of prevention and enforcement activities occur. Those districts report to the Patrol Division. That Division along with the Criminal Investigation Division and the Community Relations Section make up the Operations Bureau, which consists of the Patrol Division, the Criminal Investigation Division, and the Community Relations Section. The other major bureau of the department is the Administrative Bureau. Both Bureau Deputy Commissioners report to the Commissioner.

In recent years the department has undergone considerable reorganization, internal analysis, and refocusing of goals and objectives. Assisting in this effort has been the Grants and Government Relations Section, which in 2001 managed 35 grants totaling approximately $45 million. The section's oversight of the Court Liaison Program helped save the department over $1.3 million in overtime expenditures in 2001, according to the Annual Report.

Recruits attending the police academy complete 831 hours of training that address 508 objectives. The Education and Training Division consists of 46 instructors. Recruits earn 45 college credits from the City of Baltimore Community College for successfully completing the academy. The department offers 36 hours of mandatory in-service training but most of it is focused on recertification of weapons (firearms, batons, pepper-mace spray) and skills such as driving, basic investigation, and stop and frisk techniques. For first year officers, starting salary is about $35,784 and progresses to $45,800 within 5 years. Benefits include a health plan, life insurance, training, uniforms, a retirement plan, 14 paid holidays, paid vacations, sick leave, compassionate leave, blood assurance program, paid court time, and paid overtime.

Crime Index offenses for the city of Baltimore totaled 55,820 for 2002.

The City of Boston, Massachusetts. Boston is the capital city of and the largest city in the state of Massachusetts. It is the county seat of Suffolk County. Major interstate highways leading into the city include I-95, I-93, and I-90. The 2000 population was 589,141, which made it the 20th largest city in the United States. The metropolitan area of Boston has a population of over 6 million residents and is the seventh-largest metro area in the United States according to the 2000 census. The city encompasses about 48 square miles of area. Boston is a major commercial and transportation hub on the east coast of the country. Its commercial base includes banking and financial services, insurance companies, industrial and shipping concerns. It has 68 college and university institutions based there, and is the home of 25 inpatient hospitals.

Boston was incorporated as a city in 1822 but settlements date back to 1623. The city is rich with American history and the founding of the United States According to the 2000 census, the population profile of the city was 54.5% White, 25.3% Black, 0.4% American Indian and

Alaska Native, 7.5% Asian, 7.8% other race, 4.4% two or more races and 14.4% Hispanic/Latino. Approximately 80.2% of the population was age 18 and over and 10.4% were 65 and over; the median age was 31.1.

The police department is led by a commissioner who is appointed by the mayor. In 2004 the first woman commissioner (Kathleen M. O'Toole) was appointed. The department was organized in 1838 and considers itself the oldest police department in the United States. In 2002 the department was staffed with 2,143 officers and 628 civilians; a total of 2,771 personnel. The department was undergoing extensive reorganization in mid-2004. The mission of the Boston Police Department is summed in its official statement: "We dedicate ourselves to work in partnership with the community to fight crime, reduce fear and improve the quality of life in our neighborhoods. Our Mission is Neighborhood Policing."

One unique feature in the Boston Police Department is its new $70 million headquarters which is equipped with perhaps the most advanced identification imaging and ballistics identification technology in the country. It has a DNA laboratory (one of only 18 departments in the country with in-house DNA testing capacity), enhanced 9-1-1 and a computer-aided dispatch system linked to mobile data terminals.

Recruits attending the police academy must complete six months of training. The base salary of officers is $40,000 after three years. Benefits include 13 paid holidays per year, excellent promotional opportunities, a full retirement plan, and educational incentives. Crime Index offenses for the city of Boston totaled 35,706 for 2002.

The City of Chicago, Illinois. Chicago is the largest city in the state of Illinois, and the seat of Cook County. It is geographically located in the northeastern part of the state along the southwestern shore of Lake Michigan. Major interstate highways leading into the city include I-90, I-94, I-97, I-55, I-57, and I-88. The 2000 population was 2,896,016, which made it the third-largest city in the United States. The metropolitan area of Chicago has a population of over 9.1 million residents and is the third-largest metropolitan area in the United States according to the 2000 census. The city encompasses about 227 square miles of area. Chicago is a major industrial and shipping center of the Midwestern part of the United States. It is a commercial, financial, and retail trade center and home of the largest agricultural futures market in the world—the Chicago Board of Trade. O'Hare International Airport is a major air transportation hub. The first white settlers came to the area in the 1790s; the village was incorporated in 1833.

According to the 2000 census, the population profile of the city was 42.0% White, 36.8% Black, 0.4% American Indian and Alaska Native, 4.3% Asian, 13.6% other race, 2.9% two or more races and 26.0% Hispanic/Latino. Approximately 73.8% of the population was age 18 and over and 10.3% were 65 and over; the median age was 31.5.

The police department is led by a superintendent who is appointed by the mayor. The department has a strength of about 16,473 personnel, which includes 13,705 sworn officers, 1,680 civilians, and 1,088 crossing guards according to 2002 figures. The mission statement of the department is:

> The Chicago Police Department, as part of, and empowered by the community, is committed to protect the lives, property and rights of all people, to maintain order and to enforce the law impartially. We will provide quality police service in partnership with other members of the community. To fulfill our mission, we will strive to attain the highest degree of ethical behavior and professional conduct at all times.

The organizational structure of the department consists of 25 police districts where the majority of prevention and enforcement activities occur. The department has five bureaus: Operational Services, Investigative Services, Technical Services, Staff Services, and Administrative Services. The organization handled over 9,206,614 calls for all types of services, including 4,937,360 calls for 911 services.

In 2003 the Chicago Police Department celebrated its tenth anniversary of the Chicago Alternative Policing Strategy, a community policing/problem-solving approach to serving the citizens. This approach has a major focus on community meetings in order to build a partnership with the residents. Officers conducted and attended over 3,163 meetings in 2002 with an average attendance of 22 at each meeting.

Recruits must have at least 60 semester (90 quarter) hours of credit from an accredited college or university or have four years of military service. Once appointed, they must attend the police academy and complete 780 hours of training. Officers are considered probationary officers for an 18-month period. An officer's starting salary is $36,984, which increases to $47,808 after one year and to $50,538 after 18 months. The list of benefits includes: health insurance, tuition reimbursement up to 100% (including advanced degrees), prescription drug plan, vision and dental plan, paid sick leave, 20 paid vacation days, retirement plan, 13 paid holidays, home purchase assistance, annual uniform allowance of $1,500, and annual duty availability bonus of $2,520.

Compared to 2002, index crime in the city of Chicago for 2003 was down over 4 percent, with violent crime down over 10 percent. During 2003, index crimes dropped in every category.

The City of Columbus, Ohio. Columbus is the capital and largest city in the state of Ohio. It is the seat of Franklin County. It is geographically located in the central part of the state. The Scioto River runs through the city. Major interstate highways leading into the city include I-70 and I-71. The 2000 population was 711,470, which made it the 15th-largest city in the United States. The metropolitan area of Columbus has a population of over 1.5 million residents and is the 32nd largest metropolitan area in the United States according to the 2000 census. The city encompasses about 221 square miles of area. Columbus has a diversified economy; it is a port of entry and a major commercial and distribution center. It is a governmental and culture center of the state as well as a center for health research. Ohio State University is located in Columbus. The first white settlers came to the area in the 1797; it became the capital of the state in 1812 and was incorporated as a city in 1834.

According to the 2000 census, the population profile of the city was 67.9% White, 24.5% Black, 0.3% American Indian and Alaska Native, 3.4% Asian, 1.2% other race, 2.6% two or more races and 2.5% Hispanic/ Latino. Approximately 75.8% of the population was age 18 and over and 8.9% were 65 and over; the median age was 30.6.

The police department (technically the Division of Police within the Department of Public Safety) is led by a chief who is promoted from within through the civil service system. The chief reports to a public safety director who reports to the mayor. The department has a total strength of about 2,176 personnel, which includes 1,812 sworn officers, 364 civilians according to 2002 figures. The mission statement of the department is:

> We, the men and women of the Columbus Division of Police, are dedicated to improving the quality of life in our City by enhancing public safety through cooperative interaction with our community and with other public and private agencies. We are committed to reducing fear by maintaining order and peace. We are responsible for protecting life and property, enforcing laws, and taking all appropriate measures to combat crime. We are organized, staffed, and trained to maximize effective and efficient public service and to maintain a positive work environment. We work to fulfill the mission of the Columbus Division of Police in a manner that inspires the public's trust and confidence and protects the Constitutional rights of each citizen.

The department is organized into five subdivisions: Administrative, Investigative, Patrol East, Patrol West and Support Services; each commanded by a Deputy Chief. The individual subdivisions are further divided into bureaus or zones, each of which fulfills a more specific mission. A police commander supervises each zone or bureau. The zones or bureaus are subdivided into sections or watches and are commanded by a police lieutenant or civilian employee of equivalent position. The sections and watches are broken down into precincts, units, squads, crews, or teams; a police sergeant or a civilian supervises each. The organization handled over 2 million calls for all types of services in 2002, including 525,600 calls for 911 emergency services.

Recruits must complete a 28-week academy of basic training. An officer's starting salary is $34,611, which increases to $52,900 after four years. Fringe benefits include shift differential pay, health insurance, prescription drugs, dental plan, life insurance, 11 paid holidays, 15 paid sick leave, 2.4 weeks of paid vacation leave, 2.4 weeks each year vacation, increasing to 6.3 after 20 years of service, clothing and equipment allowance ($850 per year for uniformed officers; $1,200 for nonuniformed), personal liability insurance, retirement (25 years of service and age 48), college tuition reimbursement and annual service credit (beginning in the 6th year). Officers are eligible to take sergeant's exam after 3 years and there is a pay differential is 18% between ranks.

The index crime in the city of Columbus for 2002 totaled 66,261 offenses.

The City of Dallas, Texas. Dallas is the seat of Dallas County and second-largest city in Texas. It is geographically located in the northeast part of the state and is just 30 miles east of Ft. Worth. Major interstate highways leading into the city include I-20, I-30, I-35E, and I-45. The 2000 population was 1,188,580, which made it the eighth-largest city in the United States. The metropolitan area of Dallas-Ft. Worth has a population of over 5.2 million residents and is the ninth-largest metropolitan area in the United States according to the 2000 census. The city encompasses about 343 square miles of area. Dallas has a very diversified economy; it is a leading commercial, marketing, industrial, convention, and tourist center. The city was first settled in 1841 and was incorporated in 1856. The economy is highly diversified, and the city is the leading commercial, marketing, and industrial center of the southwest. The insurance business is important, and the service sector has experienced rapid growth. Dallas is also a popular tourist and convention city

According to the 2000 census, the population profile of the city was 50.8% White, 25.9% Black, 0.5% American

Indian and Alaska Native, 2.7% Asian, 17.2% other race, 2.7% two or more races and 35.6% Hispanic/Latino. Approximately 73.4% of the population was age 18 and over and 8.6% were 65 and over; the median age was 30.5.

The police department is led by a chief who is appointed by the mayor of the city. As of early 2004, the department was organized into five bureaus: Administrative Services Bureau, Support Services Bureau, Special Services Bureau, Investigations Bureau, and Patrol Bureau (consisting of six area divisions). The department has a total strength of about 3,533 personnel, which includes 2,977 sworn officers and 556 civilians. The mission statement of the department is the following:

> The Police Department, in serving the people of Dallas, strives to reduce crime and provide a safe city by: (1) providing assistance at every opportunity; (2) providing preventive, investigative and enforcement services; (3) increasing citizen satisfaction with public safety and obtaining community cooperation through the department's training, skills and effort; (4) realizing that the Police Department alone cannot control crime, but must act in concert with the community and the rest of the criminal justice system. In achieving this mission, the men and women of the Dallas Police Department will conduct themselves in an ethical manner. They will: (1) respect and protect the rights of the citizens as determined by the law; (2) treat citizens and their fellow employees courteously and with the same amount of dignity with which they expect to be treated themselves; (3) be examples of honesty and integrity in their professional and personal lives, thereby earning the public trust; (4) perform their duties with the knowledge that protection of the lives and property of all citizens is their primary duty; and (5) comply with the spirit and letter of the Code of Conduct.

Applicants to the department must possess forty-five semester hours of credit from an accredited college or university with a 2.0 grade point average. Recruits must complete a 32-week academy of basic training, followed by a 24-week field training program. An officer's base pay as a trainee is $36,806 ($38,006 if one has a degree). Upon graduation from the academy, the officer receives a one-time bonus of $1,000 and by year three the salary increases to $43,754 ($44,954 if degreed). Fringe benefits include educational incentive pay, detective pay ($100/month), language incentive pay ($75.00-100.00 per month), shift differential pay, patrol duty pay, health insurance, life insurance, retirement program and all equipment is provided.

The index crime in the city of Dallas for 2002 totaled 112,040 offenses.

The City of Denver, Colorado. Denver is the capital and largest city in the state of Colorado. It is the seat of Denver County. It is geographically located in the north-central part of the state at the foot of the Rocky Mountains where the South Platte River meets Cherry Creek. Major interstate highways leading into the city include I-70, I-76, and I-25. The 2000 population was 554,636, which made it the 25th-largest city in the United States. The metropolitan area of Denver has a population of over 2.5 million residents and is the 19th-largest metropolitan area in the United States according to the 2000 census. The city encompasses about 153 square miles of area. Denver has a diversified economy; it is a biotechnology, communications, transportation, manufacturing, and agriculture business center. The construction, real estate, and retail trade sectors are among the fastest-growing industries in the area. It is a governmental center for many federal agencies. The Denver International Airport is the largest airport in North America in terms of area (53 square miles); it was opened to passenger traffic in 1995. Gold was discovered in the area in 1858 and city incorporated in 1861; it became the territorial capital in 1867.

According to the 2000 census, the population profile of the city was 65.3% White, 11.1% Black, 1.3% American Indian and Alaska Native, 2.8% Asian, 15.6% other race, 3.7% two or more races and 31.7% Hispanic/Latino. Approximately 78.0% of the population was age 18 and over and 11.3% were 65 and over; the median age was 33.1.

The police department is led by a chief who is appointed by the mayor of the city. The department has a total strength of about 1,778 personnel, which includes 1,451 sworn officers, 327 civilians according to 2002 figures. The mission and vision statements of the department state the following:

> The mission of the Denver Police Department is to apply its knowledge, skills, and resources to foster an environment where all people live safely and without fear. Our Vision is of a police department that values its employees and the community it serves. We are committed to honesty and integrity, and dedicated to enforcing the law and maintaining peace, in partnership with the community.

The department is organized into operations and administration units with a deputy chief directing the functions of each. Operations is made up of the divisions of the Patrol, Criminal Investigation, and Special Operations. Administration is made up of the Division Chief of Technology and Support and the Bureaus of the Human Resource Management Bureau, the Financial Services Bureau, and the Administration Support Bureau.

Recruits must complete a 22–24-week academy of basic training. An officer's starting salary after graduation from the academy and during the nine-month probationary period is $39,144, which increases to $60,204 after three years of service. Fringe benefits include longevity pay, special assignment pay, bilingual officer designation pay ($100/month), health and dental insurance, life insurance, 11 paid holidays, 18 paid sick leave, 96 hours of paid vacation leave increasing over the years to 200 hours after 25 years of service, equipment allowance ($550/year), and protective-vest reimbursement up to $550.

The annual calls for service to the Denver Police Department total over 1.2 million. The index crime in the city of Denver for 2002 totaled 32,132 offenses.

The City of Detroit, Michigan. Detroit is the largest city in the state of Michigan and is the seat of Wayne County. It is geographically located in the southeast part of the state along the 27-mile Detroit River that connects Lake St. Clair with the Lake Erie. Across the river is Windsor, Ontario (Canada). Major interstate highways leading into the city include I-75, I-94, and I-96. The 2000 population was 951,270, which made it the 10th-largest city in the United States. The metropolitan area of Detroit has a population of over 5.4 million residents and is the 8th-largest metropolitan area in the United States according to the 2000 census. The city encompasses about 139 square miles of area. Detroit is one of the major manufacturing cities in the U.S. and is the center of the American automobile industry. In recent years the financial, insurance, and real estate fields have contributed greatly to the city's economy. Founded by the French in July 1701, it was not incorporated until 1815. Because of its early settlement and strategic location, it was prime territory during early wars with the French and British.

According to the 2000 census, the population profile of the city was 12.3% White, 81.6% Black, 0.3% American Indian and Alaska Native, 1.0% Asian, 2.5% other race, 2.3% two or more races and 5.0% Hispanic/Latino. Approximately 68.9% of the population was age 18 and over and 10.4% were 65 and over; the median age was 30.9.

The police department is led by a chief (Ella Bully-Cummings, the city's first black female chief) who is appointed by the mayor of the city. The five-member Board of Police of Commissioners, created in 1974 by City Charter, provides civilian supervisory oversight of the department. The department has a total strength of about 4,656 personnel, which includes 4,006 sworn officers, 650 civilians according to 2002 figures. The mission and vision statements of the department state the following:

Mission: Setting New Standards of Excellence in Policing through Integrity, Innovation, and

Training. Vision: Building a Safer Detroit through Community Partnerships

As of February 2004, the department's organizational structure included the Administrative Portfolio that includes the Management Services, Risk Management, Science and Technology and Training Bureaus; the Investigative Portfolio that includes the Central Services and the Professional Accountability Bureaus; the Operations Bureau that includes Customer Service Zones East and West, Metropolitan Division, Tactical Operation Section, Executive Protection, Police Athletic League and Auxiliary Services Unit; and several functions within the Chief's Portfolio.

The city in recent years has undergone an investigation by the U.S. Department of Justice that resulted in a court consent decree and court order for the appointment of an external federal monitor and support team. By the end of 2008, the department must make several major improvements that include prisoner holding cells renovation; improved medical care for prisoners; a computerized warning system to flag problem officers and training and auditing related to extensive new policies. It has been reported that settlements of police lawsuits exceeded $100 million between 1987 and 2001.

An officer's starting salary is approximately $30,000. Fringe benefits include medical, dental and optical plans, longevity pay, college tuition reimbursement, 20 days vacation per year, eight paid holidays a year, 12 sick days a year, a pension plan, department issued uniforms and equipment, court pay, shift differential pay, and uniform cleaning.

The index crime in the city of Detroit for 2002 totaled 85,035 offenses.

The City of Kansas City, Missouri. Kansas City is the largest city in Missouri. It is geographically located on the western boundary of the state on the banks of the Missouri River. Kansas City, Kansas, is across the river. The major interstate highways leading into the city are I-29, I-35, and I-70. The 2000 population was 441,545, making it the 36th-largest city in the United States. The metropolitan area of Kansas City has a population of over 1.7 million residents making it the 25th-largest metropolitan area in the United States according to the 2000 census. The city encompasses about 314 square miles of area. The economy of Kansas City is primarily based on telecommunications, banking and finance, service and agricultural industries. It is a major distribution and manufacturing center and ranks first in greeting-card publishing. Among the top employers are governmental agencies at the local, state, and federal levels.

A trading post originally established in 1821 grew to a settlement that was incorporated as the Town of Kansas in 1850. Its current name was adopted in 1889. The city played a major role in the westward movement of settlers and prospectors in the 1880s.

According to the 2000 census, the population profile of the city was 60.7% White, 31.2% Black, 0.5% American Indian and Alaska Native, 1.9% Asian, 3.2% other race, 2.4% two or more races and 6.9% Hispanic/Latino. Approximately 74.6% of the population was age 18 and over and 11.7% were 65 and over; the median age was 34.0.

A Board of Police Commissioners oversees the Kansas City Police Department, which is led by a chief of police. The department structure includes the chief's office and Legal Adviser and four bureaus: Administration, Patrol, Investigations and Executive Services. The agency has a total strength of 1,927 personnel, which includes 1,211 sworn officers and 716 civilian employees. The mission of the department is:

> The mission of the Kansas City, Missouri, Police Department is to protect life and property, preserve the public peace, prevent crime, and reduce fear and disorder in partnership with the community.

The starting salary for recruits attending the 24-week academy is about $32,688 a year, which increases to $35,256 during the six-month probationary period. Then the annual pay is $36,960. Fringe benefits include health and life insurance, 13–25 vacation days (depending on length of service), 18 sick days per year, 9 paid holidays, provided uniforms and equipment (except service weapon), uniform allowance ($50/month), educational tuition reimbursement program, college incentive pay, retirement system and shift differential pay.

The index crime in Kansas City for 2002 totaled 45,425 offenses.

The City of Las Vegas, Nevada. Las Vegas is the seat of Clark County, the largest city in Nevada, and one of the fastest-growing cities in the United States. It is geographically located in the southeastern part of the state. The major interstate highways leading into the city are I-15 and I-515. The 2000 population was 478,434, which made it the 32nd-largest city in the United States. The metropolitan area of Las Vegas has a population of over 1.6 million residents and is the 31st-largest metropolitan area in the United States according to the 2000 census. The city encompasses about 113 square miles of area. Las Vegas depends on tourism and conventions for its economy—hosting over 40 million visitors annually. It does have a favorable business climate because of low taxes; manufacturing, government, warehousing, and trucking are major sources of employment. Besides the gambling and tourist attractions in the city, other areas

nearby such as Hoover Dam, Death Valley National Park, and Lake Mead draw tourists. Spanish explorers are believed to have used the area in the early 1800s as a watering stop on the way to California. The Mormons settled the town in 1855 but later left. The U.S. Army established Ft. Baker there in 1864. The city really grew after the state legislature legalized gambling in 1931.

According to the 2000 census, the population profile of the city was 69.9% White, 10.4% Black, 0.7% American Indian and Alaska Native, 4.8% Asian, 9.7% other race, 4.1% two or more races and 23.6% Hispanic/Latino. Approximately 74.1% of the population was age 18 and over and 11.6% were 65 and over; the median age was 34.5.

Since July 1, 1973, the Las Vegas Metropolitan Police Department has been responsible for all police services within the city limits of Las Vegas and the unincorporated areas of Clark County. The police department is lead by an elected sheriff who serves a four-year term. The Las Vegas Metropolitan Police Department is the largest law enforcement agency in the state of Nevada and has a jurisdiction of 7,554 square miles. The department is organized into Law Enforcement Services which includes the Technical Services, Human Resources, Professional Standards and the Detention Services Divisions; and Law Enforcement Operations which includes two patrol divisions, the Investigative Services Division and the Special Operations Division. The agency has a total strength of about 3,900 personnel, which includes 2,000 sworn officers and 1,900 civilian employees (including detention officers). The department is responsible for the operation of the Clark County Detention Center.

Recruits must complete 781.5 hours of academy basic training, followed by an 18-week field training program. Fringe benefits include vacation leave (three weeks per year; four weeks after 15 yeas; five weeks after 20 years), sick leave (104 hours per year), 12 holidays per year, holiday pay, shift differential pay, special assignment pay, Spanish/bilingual pay, longevity pay (after 10 years), furnished uniforms and a uniform allowance of approximately $1,200 per year, retirement program, and health, dental and vision insurance.

The index crime in the city of Las Vegas for 2002 totaled 56,810 offenses.

The City of Los Angeles, California. Los Angeles is the seat of Los Angeles County and the largest city in California. It is geographically located in the southwest part of the state on the Pacific Ocean coast, about 145 miles from the Mexico border. The major interstate highways leading into the city are I-5 and I-10. The 2000 population was 3,694,820, which made it the second-largest city in the United States. The metropolitan area of Los Angeles has a population of over 16.3 million residents and is the second-largest metropolitan area in the United States according to the 2000 census. The city encompasses about 469 square miles of area. The economy of Los Angeles is very diversified. It is a major shipping, manufacturing, industry, and finance center; as well as home to a major portion of the entertainment industry. It attracts millions of tourists annually. Founded by Mexicans in the late 1700s, it was later ceded to the United States along with the state of California in 1848. The city of Los Angeles was incorporated in 1850.

According to the 2000 census, the population profile of the city was 46.9% White, 11.2% Black, 0.8% American Indian and Alaska Native, 10.0% Asian, 25.7% other race, 5.2% two or more races and 46.5% Hispanic/Latino. Approximately 73.4% of the population was age 18 and over and 9.7% were 65 and over; the median age was 31.6.

The Los Angeles Police Department serves the city and 17 other communities; it is responsible for providing police services to an area encompassing 467 square miles, representing 3.4 million residents. The Board of Police Commissioners oversees all operations of the department. The Board serves as the head of the Los Angeles Police Department, functioning like a corporate board of directors, setting policies for the department and overseeing its operations. The Board works in conjunction with the Chief of Police runs the department on a daily basis and reports to the Board.

The department is organized into four major offices: Chief of Staff/Professional Standards, Office of Operations, Office of Human Resources, and Office of Support Services and two bureaus: Consent Decree Bureau and Critical Incident Management Bureau. The agency has a total strength of about 13,110 personnel, which includes 9,600 sworn officers and 3,510 civilian employees. The budget is $839.2 million. The mission statement of the department is:

> It is the mission of the Los Angeles Police Department to safeguard the lives and property of the people we serve, to reduce the incidence and fear of crime, and to enhance public safety while working with the diverse communities to improve their quality of life. Our mandate is to do so with honor and integrity, while at all times conducting ourselves with the highest ethical standards to maintain public confidence.

Recruits must complete seven months of academy basic training, followed by one year of supervised field training. Starting salary for recruits is $47,710 ($49,631 if recruit has 60 college credits, $51,573 if recruit has a BS/BA degree); deputy chiefs earn up to $200,000. Fringe benefits include health and dental plans, pension plan, sick leave and disability (12 days of 100 percent paid sick leave, five days at 75 percent, and five days at 50 percent, upon hiring), vacation (15 days per year; 22 days after ten years), 13 holidays, longevity pay after 10 years, bilingual premiums (2.75%–5.5% additional premium) and uniform allowance ($850 per year).

Following an investigation by the U.S. Department of Justice, the city of Los Angeles voluntarily agreed to a consent decree approved in federal court, which provides for increased representation of blacks, Hispanics and women in the rank of police officer. In addition, the city is interested in increasing the number of Asian-Pacific police officers. Applicants who speak an Asian-Pacific and/or other foreign language(s) may be eligible for selective certification and bonus pay.

The index crime in the city of Los Angeles for 2002 totaled 190,992 offenses.

The City of Miami, Florida. Miami is the seat of Miami-Dade County and the second-largest city in Florida. It is geographically located in the southeast part of the state on the Atlantic Ocean coast. The major interstate highways leading into the city are I-75 and I-95. The 2000 population was 362,470, which made it the 47th-largest city in the United States. The metropolitan area of Miami has a population of over 3.8 million residents and is the 12th-largest metropolitan area in the United States according to the 2000 census. The city encompasses about 36 square miles of area. The economy of Miami relies heavily on international banking, finance, tourism, and cargo shipping. Many multinational and Fortune 500 companies have located in the area; the health-care sector and bio-medical technology, and plastics manufacturing are major employers.

According to the 2000 census, the population profile of the city was 66.6% White, 22.3% Black, 0.2% American Indian and Alaska Native, 0.7% Asian, 5.4% other race, 4.7% two or more races and 65.8% Hispanic/Latino. Approximately 78.3% of the population was age 18 and over and 17.0% were 65 and over; the median age was 37.7.

The Miami Police Department is led by a chief of police who reports to the city manager. The department is organized into three major divisions: Field Operations, Administration, and Investigations. Each has a number of subunits; and the Internal Affairs unit reports directly to the chief. The agency has an annual operating budget over $100 million and a total strength of about 1,408 personnel, which includes 1,075 sworn officers and 333 civilian employees. The mission and vision statements of the department are:

> Mission: Our mission, together with the communities of Miami, is to make our city a place

where all people can live, work and visit safely without fear. Vision: The Miami Police Department will maintain the highest standards of professional ethics and integrity. We are committed to the philosophy of community and neighborhood policing. We will build partnerships and coalitions with the business, corporate, and residential communities to identify and recommend solutions to problems with the goal of improving the quality of life in our neighborhoods. We will employ time-tested police methods and promising innovative approaches to better protect our communities. We value the cultural unity and differences of our communities, recognizing that there is strength in both. Our commitment is to provide professional service to our citizens, residents and visitors.

Recruits must complete 685 hours of academy basic training. Starting salary for recruits is $34,783 with periodic cost of living and performance-based pay increases and an automatic five percent pay increases yearly for the first 7 years. Fringe benefits include health and life insurance, pension plan, sick leave, vacation days, personal days, 11 holidays, tuition reimbursement plan, state funded educational incentives, uniform/clothing allowance and multiple longevity increases for 10, 15, 16, 20, 21, and 22 years of service.

The index crime in the city of Miami for 2002 totaled 33,952 offenses.

The City of New Orleans, Louisiana. New Orleans is the largest city in Louisiana. It is geographically located in the southeast part of the state on the banks of the Mississippi. Lake Ponchartrain lies north of the city. The major interstate highway leading into the city is I-10. The 2000 population was 484,674, which made it the 31st-largest city in the United States. The metropolitan area of New Orleans has a population of over 1.3 million residents and is the 34th-largest metropolitan area in the United States according to the 2000 census. The city encompasses New Orleans Parish, about 181 square miles of area. The economy of New Orleans relies heavily on its manufacturing base; it is home of one of the largest international ports in the county. The city is the corporate home of many oil companies with offshore operations in the Gulf of Mexico. Tourism is also a significant portion of the New Orleans economy and the city is famous for its French Quarter, with its mixture of French, Spanish, and native architectural styles. The city was founded by the French in 1718. After being ceded to Spain and then back to France again, it became part of the United States in the Louisiana Purchase of 1803.

According to the 2000 census, the population profile of the city was 28.1% White, 67.3% Black, 0.2%

American Indian and Alaska Native, 2.3% Asian, 0.9% other race, 1.3% two or more races and 3.1% Hispanic/Latino. Approximately 73.3% of the population was age 18 and over and 11.7% were 65 and over; the median age was 33.1.

The New Orleans Police Department is led by a superintendent who is appointed by the mayor. The department is organized into four bureaus, each of which is commanded by assistant superintendents: Operations; Technical Support; Policy, Planning and Training; and Public Integrity. Additionally, the Office of Fiscal and Personnel Management is managed by the chief financial officer. The city's geographical area is divided into eight districts. The agency has a total strength of about 2,000 personnel, which includes 1,613 sworn officers and 387 civilian employees.

Recruits must complete 476 hours of academy basic training, which is followed with 16 weeks of field training. Starting salary for recruits is $27,508 with and increase to $29,825 after the academy. Fringe benefits include the awarding of 21 college credits upon completion of police academy, health, dental and vision insurance, free/reduced college tuition programs, excellent retirement plan (25 years of service—83%, 30 years of service—100%), paid vacation and sick leave, uniform allowance, state supplemental pay, and longevity pay.

The index crime in the city for 2003 totaled 29,072 offenses.

The City of New York, New York. New York is the largest city in the state of New York and the largest city in the United States in terms of population. It is geographically located in the southeast part of the state where the Hudson River empties into the Atlantic Ocean coast. The major interstate highways leading into the city are I-78, I-80, I-87, and I-95. The 2000 population was 8,008,278. The metropolitan area of New York has a population of over 21.1 million residents and, of course is the largest metropolitan area in the United States according to the 2000 census. The city encompasses about 303 square miles of area. The economy of New York is quite diversified since it is the center of world finance, the arts, advertising, publishing, and communications. Its port is the largest on the east coast of the United States. New York is the home of the United Nations, and also a major international tourist center. Of course the terrorist attack on September 11, 2001, dealt a devastating blow to the city's sense of security and its economy.

New York was originally settled in 1614 with the name of New Amsterdam. The city passed from Dutch control to British and then to the United States after the Revolutionary War. The early Congress met in New York from 1785 to 1790. Greater New York City was charted in 1898.

According to the 2000 census, the population profile of the city was 44.7% White, 26.6% Black, 0.5% American Indian and Alaska Native, 9.8% Asian, 13.4% other race, 4.9% two or more races and 27.0% Hispanic/Latino. Approximately 75.8% of the population was age 18 and over and 11.7% were 65 and over; the median age was 34.2.

The New York City Police Department is led by a commissioner who reports to the mayor. The next ranking officer is then the chief of department who oversees the five field bureaus: Patrol Services, Detective, Transit, Housing, and Organized Crime. Additionally the following units report directly to the Chief: CompStat, Disorderly Control, Domestic Violence and the Operations Bureau. The department has 11 deputy commissioners: First Deputy, Strategic Initiatives, Counter Terrorism, Intelligence, Operations, Public Information, Community Affairs, Office of Equal Opportunity, Labor Relations, Trials and Legal Matters. The agency has a total strength of about 53,774 personnel, which includes 37,240 sworn officers and 16,534 civilian employees. The mission and vision statements of the department are:

> The Mission of the New York City Police Department is to enhance the quality of life in our City by working in partnership with the community and in accordance with constitutional rights to enforce the laws, preserve the peace, reduce fear, and provide for a safe environment.

Recruits must have successfully completed either: 60 college credits with a 2.0 grade point average from an accredited college or university, or two years of full-time, active military service in the U.S. Armed Forces with an honorable discharge and have a high school diploma or its equivalent. Recruits complete a six-month basic training academy for which 29 college credits can be earned. The average first year salary (with overtime and other special pay) is about $45,000 and it increases to about $70,000 after five years. Detectives average $88,000 annually, sergeants about $91,000 and lieutenants about $105,000. Fringe benefits include a medical plan, pension plan (50% of salary after 20 years of service; annual $12,000 variable supplement fund paid upon retirement), sick leave, 20 vacation days (27 after five years), personal days, holiday pay, college tuition reduction plan, up to 9 days graduate school educational leave, uniform/clothing allowance and longevity pay at every five-year increment.

The index crime in the city of New York for 2002 totaled 250,630 offenses.

The City of Phoenix, Arizona. Phoenix is the seat of Maricopa County and the largest city in Arizona. It is geographically located in the south-central part of the state on the Salt River. The major interstate highways leading into the city are I-10 and I-17. The 2000 population was 1,321,045, which made it the sixth-largest city in the United States. The metropolitan area of Phoenix has a population of over 3.2 million residents and is the 14th-largest metropolitan area in the United States according to the 2000 census. It is one of the fastest-growing cities in the country. The city encompasses about 475 square miles of area. The economy of Phoenix relies on commerce, agriculture, and manufacturing. Its major industries are aerospace technology, electronics, mining, and tourism. It is a governmental center for the region. Evidence of early Indian settlements date to 300 B.C.E; the current city traces its history to 1867 when it was settled and grew into an important trading center for the region. It was incorporated in 1881 and became the state capital in 1912 when Arizona was admitted to the union.

According to the 2000 census, the population profile of the city was 71.1% White, 5.1% Black, 2.0% American Indian and Alaska Native, 2.0% Asian, 16.4% other race, 3.3% two or more races and 34.1% Hispanic/Latino. Approximately 71.1% of the population was age 18 and over and 8.1% were 65 and over; the median age was 30.7.

The Phoenix Police Department is led by a chief of police who reports to the city manager. The department is organized into seven major divisions: Professional Standards, Patrol Operations South, Patrol Operations North, Patrol Support, Investigations, Technical Services, and Management Services. Each has a number of bureaus or precincts or subunits. The agency has a total strength of about 3,776 personnel, which includes 2,921 sworn officers (authorized) and about 855 civilian employees. The mission of the department is "To Ensure the Safety and Security for Each Person in our Community."

Recruits must complete a 16-week basic training academy. Starting salary for recruits is $37,020, which increases after the academy based on a number of factors. Fringe benefits include vacation leave (96 hours per year, 120 hours in years six through 10, 132 hours in years 11-15, 152 hours in years 16–20 and 180 hours per year after 21 years of service), personal leave (20 hours per year), 10 paid holidays per year, education/tuition reimbursement, training reimbursement (up to $500), health and life insurance and a retirement plan (50% at 25 years of service, with increased percentages for years beyond 25 years of service).

The index crime in the city of Phoenix for 2002 totaled 109,916 offenses.

The City of San Diego, California. San Diego is the second-largest city in the state of California. It is geographically located in the southwestern part of the state along the San Diego Bay and the Pacific Ocean; about 15 miles north of Mexico. The major interstate highways leading into the city are I-5, I-8, I-15, and I-805. The 2000 population was 1,223,400, making it the seventh-largest city in the United States. The metropolitan area of San Diego has a population of over 2.8 million residents making it the 17th-largest metropolitan area in the United States according to the 2000 census. The city encompasses about 324 square miles of area. The economy of San Diego is diversified; electronics, aerospace and missiles, medical and scientific research, oceanography, agriculture, and shipping are its major industries. Tourism is significant and it also a major hub for the U.S. Navy.

San Diego was originally settled in 1769 as a Franciscan mission. The city passed to Mexican control in 1822, then to the United States following the Mexican War. It was incorporated in 1850. According to the 2000 census, the population profile of the city was 60.2% White, 7.9% Black, 0.6% American Indian and Alaska Native, 13.6% Asian, 12.4% other race, 4.8% two or more races and 25.4% Hispanic/Latino. Approximately 76.0% of the population was age 18 and over and 10.5% were 65 and over; the median age was 32.5.

The San Diego Police Department is led by a police chief who reports to an assistant city manager. The department structure includes an executive assistant chief who supervises six assistant chiefs for the following functions: Neighborhood Policing Area 1, Neighborhood Policing Area 2, Neighborhood Policing Area 3, Operational Support, Special Services, and Policy and Planning; and a director of Administrative Services. The Chief's Office staff includes an Assistant to the Chief, Special Assistants to the Chief, Legal Advisor, Director of Neighborhood Code Compliance and a Confidential Secretary. The agency has a total strength of about 2,785 personnel, which includes 2,104 sworn officers and 681 civilian employees. The mission and vision of the department is:

> Our mission is to maintain peace and order by providing the highest quality police services in response to community needs by: apprehending criminals, developing partnerships, and respecting individuals. Our vision is: We are committed to working together, within the Department, in a problem solving partnership with communities, government agencies, private groups and individuals to fight crime and improve the quality of life for the people of San Diego.

The city has a national reputation for employing community- and problem-oriented policing in a highly committed and professional manner.

The starting salary for recruits attending the academy is about $36,804. The basic training academy is about six months in duration. Fringe benefits include flexible benefits plan (includes health, dental, vision), four-day work week, 12 paid holidays per year, 17 days paid annual leave per year (up to 27 days per year depending on length of service), retirement program, tuition reimbursement ($900 per year) and educational incentive pay, 30 days paid military leave per year, paid overtime, and special assignment pay.

The index crime in the city for 2002 totaled 50,124 offenses.

The City of San Francisco, California. San Francisco is the fourth-largest city in the state of California; its jurisdiction coincides with the County of San Francisco. It is geographically located in the central-western part of the state along the San Francisco Bay and the Pacific Ocean. The major interstate highways leading into the city are I-80 and I-280. The 2000 population was 776,733, making it the 13th-largest city in the United States. The metropolitan area of San Francisco has a population of over 7 million residents making it the fifth-largest metropolitan area in the United States (2000 census). The city encompasses about 47 square miles of area. The economy of San Francisco is dependent on tourism (up to 17 million visitors and conventioneers per year), shipping, biotechnology, commerce, and banking (over 60 foreign banks have offices in the city). The city is the home to the Golden Gate Bridge, Alcatraz Island (former prison), and the famous cable cars.

San Francisco was originally settled as a Spanish military post and Franciscan mission in 1776. The village was first named Yerba Buena and was renamed in 1848. Gold was discovered in the area in 1849 and the city was incorporated in 1850. The earthquake of 1906 devastated the city but it was rebuilt and continued to thrive. According to the 2000 census, the population profile of the city was 49.7% White, 7.8% Black, 0.4% American Indian and Alaska Native, 30.8% Asian, 6.5% other race, 4.3% two or more races and 14.1% Hispanic/Latino. Approximately 85.5% of the population was age 18 and over and 13.7% were 65 and over; the median age was 36.5.

The San Francisco Police Department is led by a police chief whom the mayor appoints. In April 2004, Heather Fong was appointed the first female chief of the department. The agency's structure is divided into four bureaus: Administration, Field Operations, Investigations, and Airport. The Field Operations is divided into two divisions: the Metro Division, which is comprised of five district stations encompassing downtown San Francisco; and the Golden Gate Division, which is comprised of district stations encompassing the outer areas and neighborhoods of the city, and the Traffic Company. The agency has a total strength of about 2,661 personnel, which includes 2,274 sworn officers and 387 civilian employees. The mission of the department is:

We, the members of the San Francisco Police Department, are committed to excellence in law enforcement and are dedicated to the people, traditions and diversity of our City. In order to protect life and property, prevent crime and reduce the fear of crime, we will provide service with understanding, response with compassion, performance with integrity and law enforcement with vision.

The starting salary for recruits attending the academy is about $56,559. The basic training academy is 1080 hours in duration. Fringe benefits include 10 vacation days (increasing to 15 after five years, 20 after ten years of service), 13 paid sick days a year, several healthcare plan options, bilingual pay, special assignment pay and retirement after 25 years of service.

The index crime in the city of San Francisco for 2002 totaled 42,671 offenses.

The City of Seattle, Washington. Seattle is the largest city in the state of Washington and the seat of King County. It is geographically located in the western part of the state between two bodies of water: Puget Sound on the west and Lake Washington on the east. The major interstate highways leading into the city are I-5 and I-90. The 2000 population was 563,374, making it the 24th-largest city in the United States. The metropolitan area of Seattle has a population of over 3.5 million residents making it the 13th-largest metropolitan area in the United States according to the 2000 census. The city encompasses about 84 square miles of area. The economy of Seattle is very diversified; its major industries include aircraft, shipbuilding, food processing, high technology and lumber/forest products. Its harbor is one of the major ports in the United States. Tourism is important to the city and it is the home of the landmark Space Needle.

Seattle was originally settled in 1851 and was incorporated as a city in 1869. The Great Northern Railway (in 1893) and discovery of gold in Alaska (1897) assured continued growth of the city. Today it is a regional center for commerce and industry and continues to attract population growth. According to the 2000 census, the population profile of the city was 70.1% White, 8.4% Black, 1.0% American Indian and Alaska Native, 13.1% Asian, 2.4% other race, 4.5% two or more races and 5.3% Hispanic/Latino. Approximately 84.4% of the population was age 18 and over and 12.0% were 65 and over; the median age was 35.4.

The Seattle Police Department is led by a police chief appointed by the mayor. The department structure includes the Deputy Chief of Administration (which oversees the Field Support Bureau, and the Training, Ethics & Inspections, Fiscal, Budget and Research &

Grants sections) and the Deputy Chief of Operations (which oversees the Patrol Operations 1 and 2 Bureaus, Criminal Investigations Bureau, and the Emergency Preparedness Bureau). The agency has a total strength of about 1,742 personnel, which includes 1,262 sworn officers and 480 civilian employees. The mission and vision of the department is:

Prevent Crime, Enforce the Law & Support Quality Public Safety by Delivering Respectful, Professional, and Dependable Police Services.

The starting salary for recruits attending the academy is about $41,244 and increases to about $51,376 after four years on the job. The basic training academy is 720 hours followed by 8 weeks of agency orientation and indoctrination; then the new officer serves four months with a field training officer. Fringe benefits include paid overtime, uniform allowance ($500 per year), retirement system, issued duty weapon (Glock .40 caliber), and medical/dental/vision insurance.

The index crime in the city for 2003 totaled 50,457 offenses.

The City of Washington, District of Columbia. Washington, D.C. is the capital of the United States. It is geographically located in the central Atlantic area of the eastern United States on the banks of the Potomac River. It was originally a 10-mile square area carved out of the states of Virginia and Maryland, but in 1846 the Virginia portion (now the city of Alexandria and the county of Arlington) was retuned to the state. The major interstate highways leading into the city are I-66 and I-395. The 2000 population was 572,059, making it the 21st-largest city in the United States. The metropolitan area of Washington, D.C. (which includes the city of Baltimore) has a population of over 7.6 million residents making it the fourth-largest metropolitan area in the United States according to the 2000 census. The city encompasses about 68 square miles of area. The economy of Washington, D.C. is primarily based on governmental functions and tourism. It is the home of the three branches of government and most of the related agencies. It is a cultural center and there are many national museums and monuments in the city. The capital of the United States was officially transferred to Washington, D.C. and originally settled in 1800. According to the 2000 census, the population profile of the city was 30.8% White, 60.0% Black, 0.3% American Indian and Alaska Native, 2.7% Asian, 3.8% other race, 2.4% two or more races and 7.9% Hispanic/Latino. Approximately 79.9% of the population was age 18 and over and 12.2% were 65 and over; the median age was 34.6.

The Washington, D.C. Police Department is led by a police chief appointed by the mayor. The agency has a total strength of 4,200 personnel, which includes 3,600 sworn officers and 600 civilian employees. The mission of the department is:

> The mission of the Metropolitan Police Department is to prevent crime and the fear of crime, as we work with others to build safe and healthy communities throughout the District of Columbia.

To qualify for appointment, applicants must have completed at least 60 semester hours of college credit. The starting salary for recruits attending the academy is about $39,644 a year, which increases to more than $43,375 a year after 18 months of service. The basic training academy is 24 weeks in duration. The probation period is 18 months (includes the academy). Fringe benefits include a health benefits package, group life insurance, vacation days (13 per year for the first three years, increasing to about 19 days for years 4–15 and 26 days after 15 years of service), 13 sick days per year, provided uniforms, educational tuition reimbursement program, retirement system (25 years of service), shift differential pay (3 or 4 percent), foreign language incentive pay (up to $1,300 per year) and a metropolitan housing assistance program.

The index crime in Washington, D.C. for 2002 totaled 44,349 offenses.

CORRECTIONAL SYSTEM

History. British colonists brought to the New World an ancient institution—the jail. Early in the nineteenth century, the new republic itself devised another type of institution that was to have a profound influence on corrections in this and many other countries: the penitentiary. The two types of institutions survive to this day.

Also in the nineteenth century, the United States developed noninstitutional methods of corrections: probation, parole, diversion, work and study release and other systems' designed either to keep offenders out of prison or to shorten their terms of incarceration or permit them to serve part of their time under supervision.

Colonial Jails. Colonial jails were primarily penal institutions where convicted persons faced death or corporal punishment, such as the whip, the branding iron or the stocks. The major function of the jail was to hold the prisoners until corporal punishment was meted out to them. However, the insane, the ill, the vagrant, deserted wives or children, the aged, and the poor were more numerous than the lawbreakers in the early jails. These people were incarcerated until some arrangement could be made to take care of them.

Inmates had to pay for their upkeep and when they could not, they were permitted to beg for food. Strong prisoners were used in heavy manual labor clad in conspicuous uniforms and wearing ball and chains. The first reform came in Philadelphia in the latter part of the eighteenth century owing, in large part, to a group of Quakers called The Philadelphia Society to Alleviate the Misery of Public Prisons, an institution that still exists today. The society urged that hardened criminals be separated from lesser offenders, that the sexes be segregated, and that the sale and consumption of liquor be prohibited.

In 1790 the Pennsylvania Legislature ordered the renovation of the Walnut Street Jail in Philadelphia on the basis of these principles. Hardened criminals were placed in single cells in a separate building apart from minor offenders. Women and debtors had their own building. Children were removed from the jail entirely. Food and clothing were supplied at public expense, and no liquor was allowed. Thus, with a rudimentary system of classifying prisoners and the provision of free essential services, the fundamentals of modern correctional management were introduced.

For a time, the new Walnut Street jail worked well. But soon, the number of inmates made it impossible to maintain the standards. Fifteen years later, the jail held four times the number of inmates the jail was designed for. Two visiting Frenchmen, Gustave de Beaumont and Alexis de Tocqueville, commented on the sad state of the prison in their reports.

As Walnut Street Jail became outmoded, Pennsylvania built a new one, the Eastern State Penitentiary at Cherry Hill in 1829. Its architecture was designed to advance the so-called silence system, under which no inmate was allowed to speak or otherwise communicate to another. The Cherry Hill prison was built with seven cellblocks radiating from a central rotunda like the spokes of a wheel. Each prisoner occupied a cell about 8 feet by 12 feet in dimension with running water and toilet facilities and an exercising yard about 8 feet by 20 feet surrounded by high brick walls. Walls between cells were thick and impenetrable to sound. The prisoners, therefore, neither saw nor heard anyone else except the keepers who inspected the inmates three times a day and an occasional chaplain. Meals were delivered through a hole in the door. In his cell, the prisoner worked at weaving carpentry, shoemaking, sewing, or other handcrafts. When he was not working, he was expected to read the Bible and meditate on his sins.

Another silent prison opened in Auburn, New York, but here, the prisoners were confined only at night. During the day, they worked together under surveillance, but could not speak to one another. The prisoners walked in lockstep, one hand on the shoulder of the man ahead, with all heads turned only in the direction of the guard. The Auburn system was a brutal one, with silence enforced by lashes and other punishments. But its prison-made goods sold well enough to cover prison expenses, making the New York legislature very happy.

However profitable, prisons are expensive to build. Cherry Hill cost about $500,000 for 250 prisoners, an enormous sum for that time. It was the most expensive public building in the New World and the first building in the country with flush toilets and hot air heating, conveniences that most homes did not have at that time. Despite the costs, Cherry Hill and Auburn became the models for many states in the latter part of the nineteenth century. Nationally, it was a time of prison building for all states in the Union.

Most of the nineteenth century prisons were built for maximum security. They were forbidding structures that Americans referred to as Bastilles. Even reformatories were maximum-security, such as the Elmira Prison in New York, which was originally designed for hardened criminals and later was converted into a reformatory. Not until the twentieth century did medium, and minimum-security institutions come into being as well as juvenile facilities.

The total number of prisons in the United States is 5,069, of which, 3,365 are local jails, 1,558 are state facilities, and 146 federal institutions. The total number of inmates is 2,033,331. A further 110,284 juveniles are held in custodial institutions and 1,912 in Indian country jails. The incarceration rate is 701 per 100,000 national population. The official capacity of the prison system is 1,817,628, of which, 677,787 are in local jails, 1,044,467 are in state facilities, and 95,374 in federal institutions. The occupancy rate, which determines if the system is overcrowded, is 106.4%, which is favorable relative to most countries. Of the total prison population, 19.7% are pretrial detainees, 8.1% females, and 0.5% juveniles. According to the National Prisoner Survey, 40% of the inmates are held in maximum-security facilities, 34% in medium-security facilities, and 26% in minimum-security facilities.

Nearly two-thirds of all state prisoners are held in closed prisons. Jails hold as many inmates on an average day as state correctional facilities. Jails are usually under city or county control, but five states—Alaska, Connecticut, Delaware, Rhode Island, and Vermont—now administer jails. Even though overcrowding is less serious in the United States than in most countries, it has been the subject of many judicial strictures. Judges have found that overcrowding violates a prisoner's constitutional rights, an acknowledgment that even prisoners have rights to decent and humane treatment. An additional problem, peculiar to the United States, is the fact that most guards are white while most prisoners are black, thus building up racial tensions and animosities. Most large prisons are also located in rural areas where prisoners are isolated from their families.

Corrections outside the institution originated in the 1840s. The concept was that not all persons who commit offenses need to be incarcerated and that many will return to law-abiding ways more quickly if they are not shut up out of contact with the free community. It was realized, further, that prisons are a burden on the taxpayer.

The oldest form of noninstitutional corrections is the probation. In 1841 John Augustus, a Boston boot maker, asked the court to release to him certain misdemeanants for training. Augustus and his fellow volunteers were so successful in reforming petty criminals that the Massachusetts legislature established the first state probation agency with a paid staff. Almost all states followed suit. In 1966 California began a program of state subsidies to local probation departments rewarding them for every case they took on without recourse to state penal facilities.

Parole allows an offender to be released under the continued custody of the state after his sentence has been partially served. Parole is the principal mode of release of prisoners today. Parole has been criticized on the basis that it returns hardened criminals prematurely to the streets. In some cases, this is a justified criticism. There is the celebrated case of Willie Horton in Massachusetts who was released on parole by Governor Michael Dukakis and who committed a brutal murder shortly thereafter. This incident is believed to have cost Dukakis his race for the White House in 1988. But, on the other hand, a majority of the parolees do not relapse and the fact that they are under state supervision during the parole period may deter most parolees from a continuing life of crime. Judges also have come to take an interest in parole as part of the rights of prisoners. Sentencing procedures complicate parole problems. The disparity of sentences imposed by different judges, depending on whether they are liberal or conservative, for identical offenses, is a source of bitterness among prisoners. The indeterminate sentence, under which an inmate does not know when he may be eligible for parole, is also controversial. In 1975 Maine became the first state to abolish parole and to require judges to impose flat sentences. Judges may select probation, fines, restitution, imprisonment or a combination of these penalties.

Prison Statistics. Total prison population: 2,131,180. Of this total, 713,990 were in local jails, 1,241,034 in state prisons, and 169,370 in federal prisons.

- Prison Population Rate per 100,000: 726

- Pretrial Detainees: 20.2%

- Female Prisoners: 8.7%

- Juvenile Prisoners under 18: 0.45%

- Number of Prisons: 5,069

- Official Capacity of the Prison System: 1,951,650

- Occupancy Level: 107.6%

Federal Correctional System. The federal corrections system is only a small part of the U.S. corrections system because, like law enforcement, correction's are a state subject under the Constitution. Nevertheless, just as there is a federal judiciary, there is a federal corrections system that runs parallel to the state system. This system is headed by the Bureau of Prisons within the Department of Justice. The bureau is headed by a director under whom are a number of agencies and divisions.

The Administrative Division develops plans, programs and policies concerning the acquisition, construction and staffing of new facilities as well as budget development and financial planning. The Correctional Programs Division is responsible for managing the correctional services operations and religious and psychological services. Federal Prisons Industries (under the trade name UNICOR) is a wholly owned government corporation whose mission is to provide employment and training opportunities for inmates. UNICOR manufactures a wide range of items from furniture to textiles. It also provides printing services for GPO and other agencies and data entry. The Health Services Division oversees all medical and psychiatric programs, environmental and occupational health services, food and nutrition services and farms.

The National Institute of Corrections provides technical assistance and training for local and state correctional agencies, grants for research, evaluation and program development. The Program Review Division oversees agency review functions, ensures internal controls, and prepares reports to the Attorney General. The Information, Policy and Public Affairs Division encompasses the Bureau's Information Systems, Policy Review, Research and Evaluation, Security Technology, Document Control, External Liaison, and Archives and Public Affairs. The Community Corrections and Detention Division is responsible for Community Corrections and Detention programs. The Bureau is subdivided into six geographic regions, each headed by a manager.

CORRECTIONS PROFILES FOR SELECTED STATES AND CITIES

Los Angeles County, California, Jail and Probation. The Mission Statement of the Los Angeles County Probation Department is to promote and enhance public safety, ensure victims' rights, and facilitate the positive behavior change of adult and juvenile probationers. The core purpose of the department is to enforce court-ordered sanctions for probationers, including the detention of juvenile offenders and the arrest of adult offenders; provide supervision and monitoring of probationers; prevent

and reduce criminal activity by developing and implementing strategies from early intervention through suppression. Shared ideas are freely discussed.

History of the Juvenile Department. In 1900 the Juvenile Court Commission was established by the Women's Clubs of Los Angeles and Judge Curtis D. Wilbur was appointed to supervise juvenile facilities and to select and pay the salary of the first Probation Officer. In 1903 the first California probation laws were enacted and Captain Augustus C. Dodds was appointed the first Los Angeles County Chief Probation Officer. In 1910 the first permanent juvenile detention facility opened on Eastlake Avenue in Los Angeles, the present site of Central Juvenile Hall. The El Retiro School for Girls was established in Sylmar in 1919, under the direction of the Probation Committee.

In August 1993, the department completed an initial study of its youthful offenders and found that 16% of the minors with "first time ever" petition requests accounted for 67% of the subsequent petition requests. This ongoing study is laying the groundwork for a new direction in delinquency prevention involving a multi-agency; multidisciplinary approach aimed at early identification and intervention of this chronic offenders group.

The Probation Commission, originally the Probation Committee, was created in 1903 and is one of the county's oldest official bodies. In April 1987 at the request of the County Board of Supervisors, the Legislature amended the Welfare and Institutions Code to change the title of the Probation Commission. In July this action was signed into law by the Governor as part of AB 1287. The Commissioners bring expertise from the private sector to the oversight and evaluation of policies and operations of the Los Angeles County Probation Department, and to those budgetary priorities and legislative proposals brought before the Board of Supervisors which impact the criminal justice system.

Detention and Corrections. Detention locations include the twin towers, central jail, and inmates reception center (IRC), all of which are clustered around the main arraignment court. Others include the North County Correctional Facility, Pichess Detention Center (The Ranch — north facility and east facility), Mira Loma Detention Center, and the Central Regional Detention Facility.

The Los Angeles County Sheriff's Department is the largest sheriff's office in the world. In addition to specialized services, such as the Sheriff's Youth Foundation, International Liaison and Employee Support Services, the Department is divided into ten divisions, each headed by a Division Chief.

The Correctional Services Division (COSD) was formed with the goal of enhancing the quality and number of educational, vocational, drug and alcohol, anger management, and religious programs available to the inmate population. COSD is comprised of the following: Inmate Reception Center, Medical Services Bureau, Food Services Unit, Jail Construction/Special Projects, Inmate Services Unit, and the Community Transition Unit. The Inmate Reception Center screens and evaluates all inmates for medical and mental health problems upon entry into the County jail system. Medical Services Bureau maintains Correctional Treatment Center licensure and provides in-patient medical, skilled nursing, and psychiatric services to inmates. The Food Services Unit provides quality meals for inmates and staff in accordance with government regulations for proper food preparation and required daily nutritional needs. CRDF programs provide goal-oriented inmates the opportunity to rehabilitate themselves through a strict regimen of behavior modification and educational programs. Inmate Services Unit works with the Inmate Welfare Commission to provide for the needs of inmates; Religious and Volunteer Services; Inmate Commissary; and Correctional Education. The Community Transition Unit partners with community based organizations to provide inmates a continuum of support services while transitioning back into the community. Headquarters for the Correctional Services Division is located at the Twin Towers Correctional Facility in downtown Los Angeles.

The Custody Operations Division along with the Correctional Services Division is responsible for the operation of the county's jail system and for the care, custody, security, and rehabilitation of all sentenced and pretrial inmates housed within the Los Angeles County Sheriff's Department jail facilities. The Custody Operations Division is commanded by Chief John L. Scott. The current facilities include: Mira Loma Detention Facility, North County Correctional Facility, Pitchess Detention Center North, Pitchess Detention Center East, Men's Central Jail, Twin Towers Correctional Facility, LAC/USC Medical Center and an administrative unit that provides support to both divisions.

King County, Washington, Department of Adult and Juvenile Detention. The King County Jail, Seattle Division is located at 500 5th Avenue, Seattle, Washington. The facility became operational in 1986. The bed capacity for the facility is 1,697 and the correctional staff number over 350. Over 300 community volunteers provide religious services, counseling, alcohol and drug treatment support, adult basic education, GED prep, and support upon release for inmates. Admissions during 2004 (through August) totaled 4,293. The average daily population in 2004 was 2,436.

The VINE program is an automated victim notification system that allows victims of domestic violence and other crimes to register to be notified of an inmate's release from jail, and to get information on charges and bail amount. VINE provides information on the custody status of inmates who have been booked into any King County Department of Adult Detention facility. Victims and the general public will be able to call the VINE system toll-free, to verify whether an inmate is in custody, and register to receive automatic telephone notification upon an inmate's custody status change. Callers will also be provided with information on additional victim assistance services. VINE is available in English, Spanish, Vietnamese, Russian, Tagalog, Chinese, and Amharic.

The Mission Statement is brief. "The Department of Adult and Juvenile Detention contributes to public safety by operating safe, secure, and humane detention facilities and community corrections programs, in an innovative and cost-effective manner." Similarly, the Vision Statement is brief. "The Department of Adult and Juvenile Detention is a nationally recognized, high-performance organization that supports criminal-justice and human-service agencies' efforts to maintain a safe, vibrant, and economically healthy community."

Located on Puget Sound in Washington State, and covering more than 2,200 square miles, King County is nearly twice as large as the average county in the United States. With more than 1.7 million people, it also ranks as the 12th most populous county in the nation. The Jail Register contains information on persons currently in custody, plus individuals booked or released within the past 24 hours, and includes information regarding their custody status, bail amount, and visiting schedule.

San Francisco, California, City and County. The population in 2000 was 776,733. The land area is 47 square miles with a population density of 16,526 persons per square mile.

The Sheriff's Office Custody Division handles Jail Facility Operations, station transfers of arrestees from police stations to the intake jail, and transportation of prisoners between facilities and courts. The San Francisco County Jail system houses an average daily population of 2,200 prisoners in five jails, County Jails 1, 2, 3, 7 and 8. The system includes an intake and release facility, County Jail 9, and a ward in San Francisco General Hospital, County Jail 5. Approximately 55,000 people are booked into the jails annually.

County Jail 8, the newest jail facility in San Francisco, was opened in December 1994, next to the Hall of Justice. This direct supervision facility has become a national model for program-oriented prisoner rehabilitation. Some 400 inmates participate in G.E.D., E.S.L. programs, alcohol and drug abuse counseling, and family unification.

County Jail 9 includes the new intake and booking facility. The building's dramatic architectural design was praised by Pulitzer Prize–winning architecture critic Allan Temko, who called it "a stunning victory for architectural freedom over bureaucratic stupidity."

County Jail 9 (425 7th Street, near Hall of Justice, San Francisco) is employed for classification, and County Jail 8 (Hall of Justice, 6th Floor, San Francisco) is for temporary housing. Inmates are permanently held in County Jail 1 (Hall of Justice, 6th Floor, San Francisco), County Jail 2 (Hall of Justice, 7th Floor, San Francisco), County Jail 3 (San Bruno), County Jail 7 (San Bruno), and County Jail 5 (San Francisco General Hospital).

The San Francisco Sheriff's Department is like no other sheriff's department in California, or possibly the nation. Michael Hennessey, in his 20-year tenure as Sheriff of San Francisco, has created and implemented programs focused on improving the life skills of prisoners so that when they return to their communities they are less likely to commit new crimes. A dedicated staff of Deputy Sheriffs and program personnel administers educational programs, drug and alcohol treatment, counseling, horticulture and community programs proven to cut recidivism and begin interaction and healing between offenders and communities. The department has the highest representation of women and minorities of any major law enforcement agency in the nation—more than 70% of total sworn staff.

The Mission Statement of the San Francisco Sheriff's Department is "to be an effective and integral part of the civil and criminal law enforcement efforts of the State of California, and the City and County of San Francisco. The Department will accomplish its mission through competent performance by its deputized personnel, and support staff, in accordance with the powers established by the laws of the State of California and the Charter and Ordinances of the City and County of San Francisco."

Jail Programs include education, skill development, and counseling and they are integral to the San Francisco county jail system. Prisoners are expected to participate in programs while in jail. Prisoners who progress satisfactorily in jail programs may be transferred during the latter part of their sentence to an alternative program. San Francisco is a national leader in using alternatives to incarceration. These programs include: home detention, Sheriff's Work Alternative Program, Post Release Educational Program, residential county parole, general education, substance abuse counseling, SISTERS (Sisters in Sober Treatment Empowered in Recovery), in custody therapeutic community, counseling and treatment, violence prevention, vocational training, arts, library services, and religious services.

Dekalb County, Georgia. On December 23, 1822, the Georgia legislature established the boundaries of DeKalb County, which included the location of land which would eventually be incorporated as the city of Marthasville. John S. Welch was commissioned as the first sheriff of DeKalb County. It was not until a year later, however, that Decatur was officially designated as the County Seat. George Harris was the first elected Sheriff of DeKalb County.

In 1848 a railroad official designated the railroad terminal as Atlanta, even though the surrounding town maintained its name of Marthasville. After a few years of freight being shipped with Atlanta listed as the destination, the city eventually changed its name to match that of the terminal. At one time, the county contained all of Atlanta and much of Fulton County. DeKalb County's population in 2001 was 665,133. Atlanta comprises a good portion of the county today.

Today, the fast-growing city remains a transportation hub, not just for the country, but also for the world: Hartsfield Atlanta International Airport is one of the nation's busiest in daily passenger flights. Direct flights to Europe, South America, and Asia have made metro Atlanta easily accessible to the more than 1,000 international businesses that operate there and the more than 50 countries that have representation in the city through consulates, trade offices, and chambers of commerce. The city has emerged as a banking center and is the world headquarters for 13 Fortune 500 companies.

Jail statistics in several categories include year to date totals of 36,419 Admissions; 34,873 Releases; 2,866 Average Daily Population; and average length of stay: 27.8.

Maricopa County, Arizona. The county was established on February 14, 1871, and currently has a population of approximately 3,200,000. The fiscal year 2002 budget was around $2.5 billion. It is 9,226 square miles in size, and is the 4th most populous county in the United States and 14th largest county in the United States.

The mission statement of the Maricopa County Sheriff's Office states that the office is "in partnership with our citizens and contract cities, will enforce state laws, deter criminal activity, protect life and property, maintain order, and operate a safe, constitutional jail system. Through innovative leadership and our dedication to providing quality services, the Sheriff's Office will maximize the use of its resources to provide the highest quality service which will aid in improving the quality of life for the citizens of Maricopa County. The office is also dedicated to providing a caring and supportive environment for our employees because they are the backbone of the system and have a need for continued growth and development through education and training. Each employee will have opportunities for career development, professional growth, and a challenging work environment."

No other detention facility in the country, state, or county can boast of 1,200 convicts in tents; no other county or state facility can boast of a gleaning program that results in costs of under 45 cents per meal per inmate; few others can say they have women in tents or on chain gangs and no other sheriff's office in the United States today has a volunteer posse of 3,200 men and women, people from the community who spend their time and money to train to be volunteers, helping to keep the county free from crime. From an enforcement perspective, the Maricopa County Sheriff's Office prides itself on serving and protecting the people who live in a huge county— 9,200 square miles—an area larger than some states.

There are three custody-related bureaus in the office: (1) The Custody Operations Bureau consists of seven divisions: Central Intake, Estrella Jail, Institutional Services, Laundry Services, Madison Street Jail, Tent City Jails, and Towers Jail; (2) the Custody Programs Bureau consists of five divisions: First Avenue Jail, Inmate Programs, New Jail Construction Unit, Special Projects, and Special Services; and (3) the Custody Support Bureau consists of seven divisions: Ancillary Services, Central Court, Classification, Detention Information Services, Durango Jail, Inmate Services, and Sexually Violent Persons Program.

The combined number of employees in the three custody bureaus is over 1,000. The combined number of inmates detained in the custody bureaus is 6,586. Together they comprise the 4th-largest jail system in the United States.

The custody division has initiated several programs: Community Gleaning, Girl Scouts Beyond Bars, Jail High School (Hard Knocks High), Job Placement Program, Stripes Program (inmates assisting Elections Department), Female Chain Gang (first and only), Vacancy Sign (sheriff pledges to always have room to book arrested individuals), Licensed Substance Abuse Program, Sack Lunches, Pink Underwear for inmates, Adult Education Program, and detainees in striped uniform.

Ramsey County, Minneapolis (St. Paul). The Ramsey County Sheriff's Department is a 400-member Department providing a wide array of law enforcement services to an urban community of 500,000 residents situated in a metropolitan area of over 2.5 million residents. These services include providing full police service to 7 contract communities, operating a pretrial detention center and performing a host of court services. There are three primary facilities for county inmates: Adult Detention Facility, Center Annex, and the Hospital Unit. Within the walls of the Ramsey County Jail Facilities are over 300 inmates. Many of the offenders arrested and placed

into custody are dangerous predators and purveyors of violence who have committed truly atrocious crimes against members of the community. Others are less dangerous, but also have been arrested for behavior outside the scope permitted by society. The Detention Division fulfills a vital role in the prevention and reduction of crime by lawfully incarcerating those arrested for or convicted of criminal behavior.

The CHORE Project involves the diversion of juvenile offenders to community service under the mentorship of the Ramsey County Sheriff's Department Community Affairs Officers. In a collaborative effort with Northwest Youth and Family Services, the juvenile offenders are assigned to a CHORE project with a Community Affairs Officer (CAO) mentor who will supervise the community service work. CHORE services are limited to public property projects. Under direct CAO mentor supervision, at risk youth are performing duties such as park cleanup, raking, pulling weeds, painting, and removing illegal signs.

Wayne County, Michigan. Wayne County is Michigan's largest county. It has a $1.9 billion annual budget and a workforce of over 5,000 people. It is the industrial engine that drives America, home to the world headquarters of General Motors, Ford, and many more. Wayne County's rich quality of life is impressively evident in each of 43 communities. With a population of over 2 million, Wayne is the eighth-largest county in the nation with a wonderful cross-section of cultural diversity. The county seat and largest city is Detroit. The county includes 120 miles of toll-free expressways, 209 miles of state super-highways, and five national freight railroad lines. Wayne County owns and operates two international airports: Detroit Metropolitan Airport and Willow Run Airport.

The Wayne County Sheriff's Office is the second-largest law enforcement agency in Michigan, with more than 1,300 officers among its ranks. Its mission is to protect and serve the citizens of Wayne County by serving as a regional law enforcement resource to the county's 43 local police departments. In addition to providing safe and secure jail bed space for more than 2,600 inmates, the department also provides critical services to all of its communities, including fugitive apprehension, Internet investigations, border enforcement, child rescue, drug and prostitution enforcement and many others.

Persons charged with offenses and committed for trial are detained in the Wayne County Jail pending trial, and persons sentenced to Jail upon conviction of an offense are confined in the Hamtramck Detention Facility (the Dickerson Jail). Medical facilities are available to provide care for minor and less aggravated cases of sickness and disease. Advanced care is provided to the inmate population with sheriff's personnel maintaining supervision at Aurora Hospital and Mercy Hospital, both in the city of Detroit.

The sheriff operates three jail divisions: Division 1, the Andrew C. Baird Detention Facility, was completed in 1984. This facility is 14 stories high, has 1,088 beds, 150 beds for the mental health wards, and 20 beds for the Infirmary Section. Division 1 houses the Central booking area and Classification section for the entire jail system; Division 2, Jail Division Two, the "Old County Jail," was originally constructed in 1929 and remains standing to this day. In 1963 construction was completed on the "Annex" side to this building, creating 251 new beds. In 1992 Division 2 was completely overhauled and now has the capacity to house 641. Division 3, the William Dickerson facility, opened in 1991 at a cost of $60,500,000. This jail has 804 beds and is a direct supervision (no bars) facility. The facility houses sentenced inmates, offers alternative programs, and provides such services as laundry to the entire jail system, including the Juvenile Detention Center and Food Service to the jails, Juvenile Center, and the House Senior Nutrition Program. The Dickerson Jail was built on 16.7 acres and is approximately 500,000 square feet in size.

The Wayne County Dose of Reality Tour was created to educate individuals who have gotten into trouble with drugs, alcohol or other criminal activity, to the potential consequences of their actions. It also serves as an excellent deterrent for youth that are beginning to head down that path. The tour features blunt, often shocking, presentations from jail inmates, as well as from victims of crime or drunk driving and their families. The ultimate goal of the program is to open the eyes of people to the reality that may await them if they do not change their ways.

In 2003 Sheriff Warren Evans established Operation Pride, a program that utilizes nonviolent inmates to provide community cleanup and beautification services to nonprofit agencies. Services include litter pickup, illegal dumping cleanup, community garden work and boarding up abandoned buildings. Inmates also provide snow clearing services for homebound senior citizens or the physically handicapped.

Cuyahoga County, Ohio (Cleveland). The county has 1.3 million residents, and is on the banks of Lake Erie. It includes the city of Cleveland, Ohio, and 59 other communities served by the county sheriff and jail.

The Cuyahoga County Corrections Center (CCCC) is a unique facility. The high-rise building, situated on one-half of a city block in downtown Cleveland at W. 3rd and Lakeside, consists of two independent structures united by a bridge on the fourth floor. Between the two buildings, there are approximately 1 million square feet of space dedicated to the housing of maximum security

prisoners, who are channeled into the CCCC from the City of Cleveland Municipal Court, as well as 13 other suburban courts and the Court of Common Pleas. The CCCC houses approximately ten different classifications of inmates from pretrial felons to sentenced misdemeanants; juveniles to adults, from county, state and federal jurisdictions. The average length of stay (ALS) for the pretrial inmate is approximately 32 days, while the ALS for the sentenced misdemeanor averages 130 days. Jail I, first occupied in July 1977, opened with a rated capacity of 956. Jail II, first occupied in November 1994, has a rated capacity of 480, making the original combined rated capacity of both Jail I and Jail II 1,436. The current average daily population is approximately 1,850. In April 1999, a renovation project costing $13.5 million was completed. During this renovation, full operations were maintained, making this the largest maximum security facility to maintain full operations while undergoing a complete renovation. This renovation resulted in an additional 303 beds, raising the rated capacity to 1,269 in Jail I for a combined total of 1,749 between Jail I and Jail II. The CCCC is managed by a dedicated Executive Staff comprised of the Director of Corrections, two Wardens, three Associate Wardens, Captain, Facility Services Manager, Mental Health Services Manager, and Health-Care Services Director. The daily operations are managed by 20 Sergeants who oversee 33 Corporals (lead workers) and a complement of 600 Corrections Officers (line staff). Together, this team, in conjunction with a full time medical staff which includes doctors, RNs, LPNs, MTAs, Psychiatric and Dental services, attends to a population dispersed over 85 housing units or "pods" (59 in Jail I and 26 in Jail II). The yearly departmental budget of approximately $54 million, 70% of which is dedicated to Corrections, includes the production of 6,000+ meals daily at an average cost of $0.70 per meal. Programs such as GED, Project Learn, AA, NA, CA, as well as in house religious services, library, recreation, and barbershop are made available to the entire inmate population. A schedule for these various programs is maintained so that all inmates have an equal opportunity to access them.

Suffolk County, Massachusetts. The Suffolk County Jail on Nashua Street opened in 1990 and is the replacement facility for the historical Charles Street Jail, which operated from 1851 until 1991. The Charles Street Jail was ordered to close in a 1973 federal court decision. The building was built for $54 million on 2.1 acres of land, and totals 249,540 sq. ft. The jail houses 700 pretrial detainees, of which 636 are male and 64 are female in 13 different housing units, with one unit designated for female offenders. The Suffolk County Jail has been accredited by the American Correctional Association since 1991 and has been reaccredited most recently at the end of 2000 for a three-year term. Transportation, booking and property also maintain effective operations of the facility with the constant movement of probation surrender inmates to a separate housing unit at the House of Correction. This move was necessary to combat the rising inmate population at the jail.

Annually, the kitchen staff serve more than 700,000 meals to detainees. The staff also takes time to prepare separate meals for days honoring different ethnic, religious, and cultural holidays. The jail continues to use the latest in correctional technology to maintain safe and secure housing units for pretrial detainees. Along with the House of Correction, the jail is fully compliant with all health and safety codes including the Americans with Disabilities Act. The command staff, along with all jail employees, continue to maintain a modern facility for the care and custody of detainees.

The Suffolk County Community Works Program sends properly classified inmates nearing the completion of their sentences into communities, under the constant watch of an armed Sheriff's deputy, to provide labor for many city, state and town projects. Cleaning vacant lots, beautifying roadway intersections, painting street lamps, boarding and securing abandoned homes and shoveling senior citizen housing walkways are just some of many innovative jobs the inmates complete.

The Suffolk County Sheriff's Department is committed to inmate rehabilitation and successful integration back to the community upon an individual's release. One of the components, which helps ensure a successful reentry, is employment. In recognizing this, Sheriff Andrea J. Cabral and the Sheriff's Department staff has effectively responded and created vocational and job training opportunities for offenders. Through several job fairs, as well as intensive vocational training in areas such as food sanitation, graphic arts, carpentry and a community works program. Offenders are provided extensive job training options to reduce their chance of recidivism. The Sheriff's Department also partners with several organizations to provide employment services to offenders, including college and university degrees, industrial education, and other services.

Social Services. Rehabilitation is an essential component to the mission at the Suffolk County Sheriff's Department. Either awaiting trial or incarcerated, offenders' receive comprehensive education and social service programs according to classification requirements. Services are provided at both the Suffolk County Jail at Nashua Street and the House of Correction through social service staff. Responsibilities for the division include classification, religious services, substance abuse programs, referrals and disciplinary hearings. There are several programs including, the Latino Health Institute, Alcoholics Anonymous,

Narcotics Anonymous, Women's Advocate, and HIV/AIDS programs.

The jail processed more than 13,000 pretrial detainees—men and women arrested—in 2003. Some detainees stay at the jail only for a few hours; others are housed for several months or, in some cases, years. The jail must provide a wide range of medical care to these detainees, including general medical attention, substance abuse counseling, psychiatric services, orthopedics and dentistry. The jail became the de facto detoxification, mental health and primary medical care facility for pretrial detainees in Suffolk County due to other county budget cuts. The jail's medical/psychiatric unit has room for 22 detainees and is always operating at full capacity. During the last six months of 2003, it saw a dramatic rise in the number of detainees who have mental health issues. The number of people seen by mental health practitioners rose from 2,757 in 2002 to 5,406 in 2003, an increase of 96 percent. In the first 10 months of 2002, there were 34 people committed to state mental health facilities. During one three-week period in 2003, there were seven inmates with mental health issues committed to state mental health facilities. In 2004, 15 percent of the men and 36 percent of the women housed at the jail were seen by medical staff and determined to have major mental health illnesses. In 2003 the jail treated 1,124 men and women who were in stages of detoxification, an increase of 109 percent from 2002. Not coincidentally, the vast majority (80%) of inmates with mental issues also have substance abuse problems.

The City and County of Denver, Colorado. Denver currently operates two separate jails. Both are overcrowded. Overcrowding impedes safe monitoring and control of inmates. Overcrowding in numerous cities and counties across the county has prompted lawsuits followed by federal court intervention capping jail populations. Under capping, inmates must be released early or sent to more expensive facilities elsewhere as new criminals are jailed.

All people arrested in Denver—about 55,000 a year—are taken to the City Jail, or a prearraignment detention facility. About two-third are released after paying fines, posting bond or completing a short sentenced. The balance are transferred—typically within 72 hours—to the County Jail to await trial. Designed for a capacity of 158 inmates, this jail houses more than 300 inmates on any given day, peaking at nearly 400 inmates on some nights. The County Jail holds people awaiting trial as well as convicted criminals serving sentences of less than two years.

Built in 1954 and expanded over time to house a maximum of 1,350 inmates, this jail has operated well beyond its capacity for several years. The County Jail houses in excess of 1,900 inmates everyday and tops

2,100 inmates in peak periods. The city has taken numerous steps to keep the jail population down. Recognizing that prevention is key to reducing crime, more dollars have funded after school programs, summer tutoring, recreation, and strengthening families. While important, these efforts alone cannot alleviate overcrowding. Diversion efforts such as electronic monitoring, early release programs, and substance-abuse treatment also minimize the number of people jailed. Although Denver has been a leader in these innovations, these efforts cannot keep pace with the rising jail population. In fact, the prospect of incarceration goes hand in hand with successful diversion activities.

Denver Community Corrections. With a current network of ten facilities in the Denver Metro area, Community Corrections is celebrating over forty years of successful coexistence with the Denver Sheriff Department. Catering to both adult male and female felony offenders within the state of Colorado, the Community Corrections facilities admit clientele ranging in age from 18 to 75. The facilities pride themselves not only on their safety methods and positive community standings, but also on their ability to successfully reintegrate ex-offenders into the community. They implement the use of counseling, cooperation and support from family members and intensive supervision while providing such necessities as shelter, food services, and emergency financial assistance. Positive behavior is rewarded through an incentive-based system of graduated privileges. Residents are permitted community access only with staff approval and for restricted periods of time. Monitoring is systematically applied to maximize safety, including the use of sophisticated electronic paging devices that track resident movements on a continual basis, and the application of Antabuse (an alcohol inhibitor), breath analysis and urinalysis testing. Personal searches, employer and regular facility checks are also utilized.

Residents are required to seek and maintain employment, and from these wages, required to pay any court restitution or child support orders. While these facilities and corresponding programs receive compensation from the Department of Safety, they also collect $13 per day subsistence, as required by law, from each client. For those participants unable to work, additional community services and extra chores are required.

Each facility is operated by experienced independent business organizations. They are responsible and accountable to the state for each client. The standards required by the Division of Criminal Justice must be met and maintained by each facility, which includes, but is not limited too, first and foremost, ensuring public safety. They must also meet stringent staff and facility requirements, provide for appropriate in-house client programming and management, and the design, implementation and facilitation of active participation in community services within their neighborhoods. All Community Corrections operations are monitored by regulatory agencies, including the Division of Criminal Justice, the Department of Corrections, the Denver County Community Corrections Board, and other departments within the state of Colorado and the City and County of Denver. The Denver Community Corrections programs are operated by the Denver Sheriff Department, (Phase 1 is known as the Mountain Parks Work Program) and there are three privately owned programs managed by the Correctional Management Inc., the Independence House and the Community Education Centers. In addition, Peer I and the Haven (drug treatment programs under the University of Colorado Health Sciences Center) also provide facilities for both men and women.

Under the auspices of the Department of Safety, Denver Community Corrections Programs have established unprecedented success rates working with criminal offenders. Admissions for the past five years total 11,000, breaking down to a yearly admission rate of approximately 2,200. Terminations over the past five years total 10,900, or 2,180 per year. The programs were successful in 71% of the cases, unsuccessful in 13% of the cases, 15% of the offenders' absconded, and 1% failed due to new charges.

Chicago, Illinois/Cook County. Cook County was established on January 15, 1831, by the Illinois state legislature. Chicago, then an unincorporated settlement with fewer than 60 residents, was designated the county seat. Due to a virtual absence of crime, a county courthouse and jail were not built until 1835. The first jail, located just North of the Chicago River, was a small wooden stockade that resembled a military fortress. Little is known about the structure's size and the inmates that were held there due to a fire that destroyed many of the county's early records (the Great Chicago Fire).

But, it is known that by 1850 the city's growing population and rising crime rate rendered the stockade obsolete. A larger court and jail facility was built just north of what is now 54 W. Hubbard Street. Only offenders awaiting trial for serious crimes were held at the county's Hubbard Street jail. Their trials proceeded quickly at the adjacent courthouse and those who were found guilty were sent to the state prison system to serve their sentence.

However, offenders who were arrested in Chicago for less serious crimes, like public drunkenness, fighting, and disturbing the peace, were not held at the county's jail. Instead, the city of Chicago was responsible for detaining them at the city "Bridewell" (an old English word for a jail used to house inmates on a short-term basis). Built in 1852 at Polk and Wells streets, the Bridewell was located near what was then the city's vice district. Inmates were rarely held there for more than several weeks.

In the subsequent years, the inmate count at the Bridewell grew just as quickly as Chicago's population. In 1871, just months before the Great Chicago Fire destroyed the Polk and Wells site, the Bridewell was moved to a new larger building at 26th and California, and officially renamed the Chicago House of Corrections. In its first year, the new facility's inmate population doubled. An average of 419 inmates were held there each day. Until prison and legal reforms were made in the early years of the twentieth century, juveniles as young as 7 years old were held at the House of Corrections with the general inmate population and female offenders were housed in isolation in the same building. By 1954, nearly 60% of the Jail's daily population had been sentenced to terms as long as five years. The county had the additional burden of conducting executions, which was traditionally a state function, and maintaining a death row for those inmates awaiting their date with the County Jail's electric chair.

As conditions at the County Jail continued to deteriorate, several community leaders and elected officials called for reforms in the county criminal justice system. In 1969 the Illinois state legislature finally acted. They voted into law a statute that created the Cook County Department of Corrections which combined the County Jail and the city's House of Corrections under one authority.

Today, the DOC administers eleven separate jail divisions, house nearly 9,000 inmates and employs more than 3,000 correctional offices and support staff. Though overcrowding is still a problem, the DOC, under the direction of County Sheriff Michael F. Sheahan, has developed a series of alternative programs. In 1993, Sheahan created the Department of Community Supervision and Intervention, which takes nonviolent jail inmates and places them in programs where they receive drug rehabilitation, high school equivalency courses and job training.

The Cook County Department of Corrections also relies on interns and volunteers to supplement staffing; 30 college students expanded their learning fields of criminal justice or social work as interns under the supervision of a seasoned Correctional Rehabilitation Worker. Tutoring, Bible study, self-enhancement and cultural enrichment programs, holiday treats (holiday dinner, candy, etc.), socks and soap are provided by more than 450 volunteers.

Detainees are encouraged to vote in local and national elections; voters' registration and absentee voting are provided and stringently monitored by the Cook County Board of Elections. Marriages are also performed by a judge in Criminal Courts on a monthly basis. Detainees, with the encouragement of officers, teachers, and civilian staff, participate in programs saluting ethnic holidays such as Kwanza and Cinco de Mayo. Professional entertainers and motivational speakers also make frequent presentations at the Department of Corrections.

The Cook County Department of Corrections is the largest (96 acres) single-site county predetention facility in the United States. Primarily holding pretrial offenders, the department admitted 86,110 detainees in 1996 and averaged a daily population of approximately 9,000. The Department of Corrections complex consists of 11 separate Divisions/units, each headed by a superintendent.

Houston, Texas, City Jail. The Houston Police Department Jail Division is responsible for booking, housing, feeding and processing all prisoners arrested by the Houston Police Department as well as other local law enforcement entities. Prisoner processing includes the fingerprinting, photographing and electronic identification of all offenders arrested for any charge except those charged with municipal code violations only. The Jail Division also facilitates the appearance of municipal code violators in the municipal court system for both arraignment and trial dockets. The Jail Division, in conjunction with the City Health Department, medically screens all prisoners upon their entrance to the jail facility and provides continuing medical services during the prisoner's incarceration in the jail facilities. One hundred nineteen thousand prisoners were booked into the city's jails during 1998. The Jail Division is primarily staffed with civilian jailers and classified police supervisors. Classified police officers assigned to the Jail Division transport prisoners to various destinations, primarily the county jail, outside the secure confines of the jail facilities.

Central Jail was built in 1951 and occupies space on four floors. Approximately 69,199 prisoners were booked at Central Jail during 1998. Southeast Jail opened in 1993 and is located in the Edward J. Stringfellow South Police Station. There were 49,686 prisoners booked at this location during 1998. Municipal Detention Center was relocated from 8400 Mykawa Road in January 1999. It was formerly referred to as the "Prison Farm" until 1986 when it was placed under the Houston Police Department by council action. The detention center houses only male prisoners who are serving jail time instead of monetary fines assessed by the municipal courts.

New York City.
Probation. The Department of Probation promotes public safety by providing supervision for the thousands of adults and juveniles placed on probation each year by judges in the Supreme, Criminal and Family Courts. In addition, Probation is responsible for preparing thousands of background reports each year that assist judges

in determining appropriate sentences for adult offenders and juvenile delinquents.

The mission statement of the New York City Probation Department is "to protect the community by intervening in the lives of offenders, holding them accountable and serving as a catalyst for positive change. We act in collaboration with the community and other justice partners. We provide information and services to the courts, give victims a voice in the justice system and help strengthen families."

The Statistical Tracking Analysis and Reporting System (S.T.A.R.S.) is designed to assess the department's ability to meet stated goals and objectives, strengths and weaknesses in completing the agency's mission-critical tasks, and standardize reporting of key agency indicators. The S.T.A.R.S. system, based on the system used by the Department of Correction to develop its T.E.A.M.S. process, will improve accountability at all levels of management within the department and reward individual managers for outstanding performances.

New York City Jails and Prisons. The New York City Department of Correction (DOC) averages a daily inmate population of between 14,000 to 19,000, more than the entire prison system in any of 35 states. Annually, between 120,000 and 130,000 are admitted to custody. The department employs just over 10,000 uniformed staff and 1,500 civilian staff. The department provides custody of males and females, 16 and older, who after arraignment on criminal charges, have been unable to post bail or were remanded without bail, pending adjudication of their criminal charges. These detainees constitute about two-thirds of the total inmate population.

The department also incarcerates those sentenced in the city to terms of up to one year, parole violators awaiting parole revocation hearings, and persons charged with civil crimes. Persons sentenced to prison terms of more than a year are held pending transfer to the State Department of Correctional Services. The majority of inmates are housed in one of the 10 facilities on Rikers Island, located in the East River adjacent to LaGuardia Airport.

Among the Rikers facilities are a jail for sentenced males, another for sentenced and detainee females, and a detention center for adolescent males (ages 16 to 18). Two floating detention centers are docked off the northern tip of Rikers Island. Each of these converted Staten Island ferries has an inmate capacity of 162 and serves as an annex to one of the seven other jails on Rikers all housing adult male detainees. Rikers facilities other than institutions housing inmates include a bakery, central laundry, tailor shop, print shop, maintenance and transportation divisions, marine unit, K-9 unit and a power plant. The department also operates six borough facili-

ties, 15 court detention facilities and four hospital prison wards.

The off-Rikers borough jails—one each in Manhattan and Queens, and two each in Brooklyn and the Bronx—have a combined capacity of approximately 4,000. One of the Bronx jails is an 800-bed barge moored off the South Bronx opposite Rikers Island. The island, technically, is part of the Bronx although it is zoned for postal purposes with Queens, to which is it is connected by a bridge.

The 15 court pens are located in the Criminal, Supreme and Family Court buildings in each borough. In Manhattan, an additional court pen is operated in the special Narcotics Court. These courthouse facilities hold inmates scheduled for the day's proceedings. Seriously ill inmates and those requiring intensive psychiatric observation are held in prison wards that the Department operates in Elmhurst General Hospital, Kings County Hospital and Bellevue Hospital. The North Infirmary Command on Rikers Island houses detainees with less serious medical problems and persons with AIDS not requiring hospitalization, as well as high security inmates. In addition, the department operates a semisecure chronic care unit at Goldwater Hospital on Roosevelt Island.

Total admissions for FY 2003 were 109,445 with an average daily population of 314,533. The average length of stay was 45.5 days for detainees and 40.7 days for those city sentenced. The average annual Cost Per Inmate was $58,288. The ethnic distribution of the population is African-American: 58.3%, Latino: 29.9%, White: 9%, and Other: 1.5%.

The Department of Correction's Emergency Services Unit (ESU) is the elite, tactical team the department relies on during emergencies that rise above the level which any individual facility has the capability to respond to. The primary tool of the ESU has been the Tactical Search Operation, which has made ESU so key in helping the department achieve its unprecedented record in reducing violence levels in recent years.

The NYPD has also established specific units which emphasize reducing gang related criminal activity. These units work hand-in-hand with the NYC Department of Correction's Gang Intelligence Unit (GIU). As police across the nation respond to gang activity, more and more gang members wind up in the correctional systems. Prisons and jails are quickly becoming concentrated gang environments and recruitment centers. Some estimates in certain areas put gang membership as high as six out of every 10 inmates. DOC has identified 12% of its daily inmate population as known gang members, a figure which has been steadily increasing.

Miami-Dade City, Florida, County Corrections and Rehabilitation

Mission Statement.

The Miami-Dade County Corrections and Rehabilitation Department serves our community by providing safe, secure and humane detention of individuals in our custody while preparing them for a successful return to the community.

Value Statements.

We will strive to be compassionate and courteous to all persons we come in contact with. We understand that our profession is one of service and we will be responsive to the changing needs of our community. We will be responsible for our conduct, both professionally and personally. We will be diligent, honest, fair and show strength of character. We hold ourselves to be accountable to the highest standards of ethical conduct and strive to be role models for all.

Code of Ethics.

As a law enforcement officer, my fundamental duty is to serve mankind; to safeguard lives and property, to protect the innocent against deception, the weak against oppression or intimidation, and the peaceful against violence or disorder; and to respect the constitutional rights of all men to liberty, equality, and justice.

Facilities. The Miami-Dade County Corrections & Rehabilitation Department is comprised of five correctional facilities: The Pre-Trial Detention Center, Women's Detention Center, Turner Guilford Knight Correctional Center, Training and Treatment Center, and the Metro West Detention Center. These facilities hold on average 7,000 inmates, who are awaiting trial or are serving sentences of 364 days or less. The department has a Boot Camp Program for youthful offenders, a Work Release Center and a medical unit at Jackson Memorial Hospital.

Miami-Dade Corrections & Rehabilitation Department was officially created on January 1, 1970. From its inception, the department has maintained a continuous pattern of growth and expansion. In order for the department to complete its daily mission, dedicated men and women perform a multitude of duties including security, maintenance, food preparation, training, clerical and many more.

Atlanta, Georgia.

History. Atlanta was founded in 1837 at the end of the Western & Atlantic railroad line (it was first named Marthasville in honor of the then-governor's daughter, nicknamed Terminus for its rail location, and then changed soon after to Atlanta, the feminine of Atlantic— as in the railroad). Today, the fast-growing city remains a transportation hub, not just for the country, but also for the world.

Atlanta has become the best example of the New South, a fast-paced modern city proud of its heritage. In the past two decades Atlanta has experienced unprecedented growth—the official city population remains steady, at about 420,000, but the metro population has grown in the past decade by nearly 40%, from 2.9 million to 4.1 million people. A good measure of this growth is the ever-changing downtown skyline, along with skyscrapers constructed in the Midtown, Buckhead, and outer perimeter (fringing I-285) business districts.

Department of Corrections. The Department of Corrections has four operating divisions that are responsible for the management of the Court Detention Center, Grady Detention Center, and City Detention Center. The main jail or Atlanta City Detention Center incorporates the progressive direct supervision model of design and management and was recognized by the American Concrete Institute as the best new high-rise building in Georgia in 1994. It is 17 stories tall and 471,000 square feet in size.

In 2002 the department provided custody for 54,065 offenders arrested by more than a dozen local, state, and federal law enforcement agencies. In 2002 the department managed 6,747 offenders sentenced by city courts to terms of confinement, boarded 939 federal prisoners to generate revenue which offset city costs, and averaged 1,214 offenders in custody per day.

Though a department with a critical and crucial function for the citizens of Atlanta, the Atlanta Department of Corrections finds its existence brief in comparison to other city agencies. The department was formerly known as the Prison Department which managed the City of Atlanta's 700 bed prison farm located within Northeast Atlanta on Key Road. Inmates at this facility, who served sentences for ordinance and traffic offenses, were routinely assigned to farming, livestock, cannery and dairy operation details. This enabled the detainees to benefit from vocational training and contribute to their sustenance.

In 1975 responsibility for the Atlanta jail and Grady Hospital Detention Center, was transferred to the Prison Department from the Atlanta Police Department to promote professionalism of the Correctional System. At the same time, the Prison Department was reorganized as the Bureau of Correctional Services within the Department of Human and Community Development, a reflection of the new emphasis placed on providing meaningful rehabilitative services to the highly recidivistic offender population. The bureau was later realigned to coexist under the Department of Public Safety with the police, fire and emergency management agencies.

In 1981 the city replaced its obsolete, traditional, 136-bed jail on Decatur Street. The new facility (Annex) incorporated a new design in detention facility construction. The design was a second generation podular design with 300-beds located on Peachtree Street in the southern portion of the central business district. In 1987 the Annex was expanded by double-bunking a portion of the cells to attain a maximum capacity of 516 beds. The additional bed space was primarily necessary to accommodate the growth of incarcerated offenders related to the advent of illicit drug usage.

In 1990 the Department of Public Safety was abolished and corrections operations were again configured under a single Department of Corrections. In 1995 the city opened its current high-rise jail. This new facility, the Atlanta City Detention Center (ACDC), is a third-generation jail that incorporates the progressive podular/direct supervision style of design and management. The Direct Supervision methodology allows more interaction between detainee and officer, lowering the number of inmate incidents. Originally providing 1,100 beds, its shell space was built-out two years later to house 1,300 inmates. The adjacent annex remained in operation and in tandem with the ACDC, allowed the consolidation of pretrial and sentenced offenders in one complex. The 50-year-old prison farm, though effective in the past, became too inefficient to manage the change in the detainee population and was consequently closed. During the construction of the ACDC, the city contracted to board 300 federal offenders per day over a 15-year period to generate external revenue which would help offset the debt service associated with the new jail.

In January 2003 the city transferred responsibility for the detention of arrestees charged with state offenses to the Fulton and DeKalb county jails, essentially reducing the scope of city correctional services by approximately one-third. The annex, no longer necessary for detention operations, was leased to a nonprofit organization to service a segment of the homeless population. The department continues to evaluate and revamp itself to address changing detainee demographics, technology advances and programs that assist with the reintegration of detainees to the community.

Special Units. Revered as the department's first responder for any life-threatening incident involving detainees/inmates, the Corrections Emergency Response Team consists of a special set of highly trained extremely motivated officers and supervisors, called to action at the hint of danger or emergency.

Fire Safety & Inspections Team Officers are given the responsibility of leaving their posts to respond to any hazardous or fire related incident of the department. Fire Safety Officers' receive specialized training in fire inspec-

tions and how to respond to emergency situations within the Atlanta City Detention Center.

City and County of Philadelphia, Pennsylvania. The mission of the Philadelphia Prison System (PPS) is to provide a secure correctional environment that adequately detains persons accused or convicted of illegal acts; to provide programs, services, and supervision in a safe, lawful, clean, humane environment; and to prepare incarcerated persons for reentry into society.

The PPS operates four major correctional facilities—the Curran-Fromhold Correctional Facility, the Detention Center, the House of Correction, and the Philadelphia Industrial Correctional Center—on State Road in northeast Philadelphia as well as several smaller Alternative and Special Detention facilities in various locations of the city. Philadelphia's correctional facilities confine adults who have been committed by the courts and juveniles who have been remanded to the adult penal system through either direct file or certification. In addition, prisoners from other correctional jurisdictions are detained within the PPS while attending court proceedings in Philadelphia.

As a county correctional system, the PPS houses inmates with sentences of two years or less. Some inmates with multiple consecutive sentences are incarcerated longer. About 61 percent of PPS inmates are awaiting trial, and the remaining 39 percent are convicted. To the degree possible, given their physical design, all PPS facilities operate on the concept of unit management, a prison management technique that reduces the need for inmate movement by delivering daily services, such as dining, medication, and sick call, on the housing unit, in an effort to promote safety, security, and inmate programming.

The Curran-Fromhold Correctional Facility and the under-construction Women's Detention Facility are designed, as well, to operate on the basis of direct supervision. Under this system, a correctional officer is assigned to each housing unit and works among inmates with no form of separation, allowing the officer to preempt developing problems. Inmates confined within the PPS have the opportunity to participate in a variety of educational programs conducted by the School District of Philadelphia as well as the PLATO computer-based education program conducted by the PPS. Additional literacy instruction is available through the Hooked-on-Phonics program and through volunteer tutors. Two faith-based programs are conducted by trained volunteers.

The Inmate Services Division provides a host of services to inmates, including counseling; job placement; addiction treatment; individual, family, and group therapy; sex offender services; psychological services; and recreational programs. Inmates have the opportunity to participate in multi-denominational religious services as well as African American history classes. A variety of self-help programs, including Alcoholics, Narcotics, and Cocaine Anonymous, are conducted by volunteer organizations, and a hospice program is conducted by the PPS.

The PhilaCor Division, of the PPS, administers 12 industrial training programs, and seven additional vocational training programs are provided by Jewish Employment and Vocational Service. Inmates may gain work experience in many other trades by participating in a variety of work and vocational training programs within the PPS. A complete range of medical, dental, and behavioral health services are provided through contract with Prison Health Services, Inc.

The PPS average daily inmate census grew by 7.2 percent from 7,121 in FY2001 to 7,637 in FY2002, before leveling off at 7,695 YTD through March 31 of FY2003. To help accommodate the female population, the city is constructing a 768-bed Women's Detention Facility (WDF) on the PPS campus. Scheduled to open July 1, 2003, WDF will house women of all custody levels. In addition to staff office space, this three-story facility, which will include a 143,000-square-foot housing building and a support building sized 75,000 square feet, will include an intake and discharge area and space for provision of all inmate services and programs. A separate initiative targeted for completion in early FY2004 is the construction of a $4.1 million 30,000-square-foot multipurpose building, which will house central administrative and support functions of the PPS. The average monthly census in 2002 varied between 7,300 and 7,800 inmates, with an average length of stay—76.1 days. There are approximately 1,750 employees in the entire system.

City of Las Vegas, Nevada. The Detention Services Division supervises the Mojave Detention Center. All individuals arrested on a misdemeanor offense within city limits are currently booked into the Detention Center. Individuals arrested by Immigrations and Naturalization Services or the U.S. Marshals Services are also booked into the Stewart and Mojave Detention Centers. Renovation of the Detention Center Intake Unit was completed on June 16, 2002. All functions were relocated to the Detention Center to include: All agency bookings, bail window and records management. The City Hall Jail is no longer operational as a receiving facility.

All inmates sentenced in the State of Nevada are sentenced to labor. Within the City Detention Center, inmates are assigned to a variety of jobs. The Family and Youth Services Community Trustee Crew assists employees at the Clark County Family and Youth Services kitchen with food preparation, service and sanitation.

Some join outside the facility work crews or work crews within the facility, which keep up sanitary conditions throughout the city, including parks, streets, the Downtown Transportation Center and downtown areas.

The culinary facility provides jobs daily for both male and female inmates. Through an agreement between the City of Las Vegas Detention Center and the Clark County Detention Center, 600 Clark County inmates are housed and supervised at the city facility until the county Jail expansion project is completed. While in custody, inmates receive a wide variety of support services including 24-hour medical care, personal and group counseling, weekly religious services, library access, commissary, visitation and recreational activities.

In a coordinated effort between the city of Las Vegas, the city of North Las Vegas and the Las Vegas Metropolitan Police Department, the Special Emergency Response Team (SERT) program was developed to provide a tactical response to emergency situations. The SERT team has proven to be valuable by assisting the three agencies involved in routine and emergency situations. The department's SERT team exists to assist in resolving high risk correctional facility incidents while minimizing the potential for injury or death to those involved. The team receives specialized training and equipment to enhance its ability to bring high risk incidents to a successful conclusion. The team, when called upon, has the responsibility of responding to a critical incident and aiding in its resolution. Officers assigned to the SERT program are assigned regular duties throughout the facility until called upon to serve this special function.

Georgia. The Georgia Department of Correction's provides an effective and efficient department through a highly dedicated and trained professional staff, who administer a balanced correctional system. The department's mission is to protect the public, serve victims of crime and reduce crimes committed by sentenced offenders by holding offenders accountable and providing safe and secure facilities, effective community supervision and effective methods of self-improvement for offenders. The department consists of 14,430 employees and is led by Commissioner James E. Donald. The major divisions are: Executive Office, Facilities Division, Probation Division, Human Resources Division, Administration Division, and the Georgia Correctional Industries.

The Corrections Division is responsible for the direct supervision of all offenders sentenced to the Georgia Department of Corrections. The Division operates: 37 state prisons, housing nearly 37,000 inmates, 9 transitional centers, 6 inmate boot camps, 1 probation boot camp, 19 probation detention centers, 13 diversion centers, 5 day reporting centers (including 4 which will open in the summer of 2004), and 120 probation offices. The Division oversees the custody of state inmates by contract in 3 private prisons and 24 county prisons. Overall, the Division is responsible for nearly 50,000 inmates and 134,000 probationers.

In the last year, 1,853 new Correctional Officers and 75 new Probation Officers graduated from the academy. 2,588 classes were conducted for 35,014 students. The Probation Unit conducted 354 classes for 6,965 students. The Employee Development Unit served 6,296 participants in 216 classes and conferences. The Management Development Unit graduated over 560 students from Agency and college-level courses. The Instructional Systems Unit conducted 391 classes for 5,137 students.

Risk Reduction Services is a unit within the Georgia Department of Corrections mandated to reduce recidivism by providing research-based programs. The goals of Risk Reduction Services is to provide constitutionally mandated or legally required programs, implement evidence based programs that target crime-producing behavior, focus on changing criminal thinking and reducing criminal behavior, and standardize "Best Correctional Practices" in Georgia. Offenders are identified and selected for risk reduction interventions via an assessment process which identifies offender risk and need. The primary targets of effective offender interventions are criminal thinking, substance abuse, education, and employment. A 1% reduction in recidivism results in a savings to the taxpayers of approximately $7 million.

Illinois. The Big Muddy River Correctional Center is a Level 3, high medium-security facility, located 1 mile south of Ina in Jefferson County. The facility opened in March 1993 and was designed to house 1,152 offenders. However, the average daily offender population is approximately 1,860. The facility consists of a total of 20 buildings, which comprise more than 39,000 square feet. The living units consist of four X-type housing units, one Receiving and Orientation Unit, one Segregation Unit and a 15-bed Health Care Unit. The facility sits on a 78-acre site, with 38 acres enclosed by fencing.

The Centralia Correctional Center has been operational since October 1980. It is a medium-security Level 4 facility housing male felons. The facility was originally designed with a rated capacity of 750 inmates. During FY 2003, the facility maintained an average daily population of 1,528 inmates. The architectural concept is unique in that the design is similar to a community college. Buildings and grounds were laid out to provide ample space for programming. Inmate services originate within a core of buildings with the housing units strategically placed around the central hub. This allows for easy monitoring of inmate movement during participation in programs and services.

In August 1983 the Safer Foundation accepted a contract from the Illinois Department of Corrections to operate a 60-bed male residential facility. The focus of Safer Foundation Crossroads Adult Transition Center is to assist convicted felons in the completion of their incarceration and successfully reenter into the community. There is a higher expectation that these residents will reestablish family contacts in the community and become more prepared educationally and financially upon release. Current capacity is 250 and average daily population is 321.

The Danville Correctional Center is a Level 3 high-medium male facility located in east central Illinois just off I-74 at the Indiana border. The facility received its first inmates in October 1985 and currently houses, on average, 1,814 inmates. The facility contains four X-type housing units, a Receiving and Orientation unit and an 87-bed Segregation Unit. The facility has an operating budget of approximately $28 million and employs 356 full-time staff in addition to contractual employees of School District 428, Lakeland College, Correctional Industries and Wexford Health Services. Danville Correctional Center was parent to the Ed Jenison Work Camp located approximately 50 minutes south of Danville in Paris. The 200-bed work camp opened in June 1993 and had provided thousands of manpower hours to local communities. The Ed Jenison Work Camp employed 82 full-time staff. Due to budget cuts, the Ed Jenison Work Camp closed its operation on September 30, 2002.

The Decatur Correctional Center is a Level 4 medium-security facility for female offenders that received its first inmates on January 24, 2000. Nearly two-thirds of the offenders have less than 12 months remaining on their sentences. Most of the remaining offenders have no more than 60 months left to serve. The mission of the center includes providing a continuum of programs and services to help female offenders reestablish and strengthen relationships with their children and enhance their ability to grow within the family structure. The facility offers female offenders a variety of programs aimed at achieving these goals that also address the diverse needs of the offenders, including medical, social, psychological and educational needs. All programs are intended to equip the female offender for a successful reintegration into the community.

The Dixon Correctional Center is Illinois's largest medium-security facility and is unique in its diversity. The administration of the facility is divided into specialized areas. The general population of medium-security males is divided into northeast, northwest and southeast housing units, a Health Care Unit housing older inmates with special needs, a unit for inmates with disabilities and an infirmary. The Special Treatment Center (STC) is designated medium-security and houses both mentally ill and developmentally disabled inmates. The STC's capacity is 520 inmates. The Dixon Psychiatric Unit (DPU) is a maximum-security unit, which serves as Illinois' primary psychiatric correctional facility. The capacity for this maximum-security unit is 212. Both the STC and DPU serve the needs of the mentally handicapped and developmentally disabled offenders by providing programs geared specifically toward a special needs population as well as a therapeutic environment. Dixon Correctional Center is situated on 462 acres of land just north of the city of Dixon, with 125 acres inside the perimeter fence. The facility operates its own power plant, sewage treatment plant, three deep wells and approximately 3.5 miles of underground tunnel systems. The facility sidewalks, signage, parking and other walkway areas are all in compliance with American with Disabilities Act requirements.

Dwight Correctional Center, originally the Oakdale Reformatory for Women, was opened Nov. 24, 1930. The Level 1 facility is situated on approximately 100 acres and houses adult female offenders. Dwight serves a multifaceted population consisting of reception and classification, segregation, protective custody, condemned and mental health units as well as a state-of-the-art medical facility designed to provide care to pregnant and critically or terminally ill inmates. Kankakee Minimum Security Unit (KMSU), a Level 7 facility, is a satellite facility of Dwight Correctional Center. It currently houses 100 offenders with an adult female capacity of 200 on 23 acres of land leased from the Illinois Department of Natural Resources. Offenders' housed at Kankakee provide public service work in community-based programs.

East Moline Correctional Center is a Level 6 minimum-security facility for adult males. The facility is located in northwest Illinois overlooking the Mississippi River. The facility was converted from a mental health facility in 1980 and houses an average daily population of 943 general population offenders and 159 offenders in the two work camps located on facility grounds. The facility is designed to provide multiple programs and services to the offender population thereby assuring offenders an opportunity for success in community reintegration. The center is a member of the Quad Cities Chamber of Commerce and works hard to be a community partner. The facility provides support to surrounding communities assisting with storm cleanup and general cleanup. East Moline Correctional Center continues to strive for individual accountability, increased staff performance and delivery of quality programs and services, thus ensuring a safe, secure and holistic correctional environment for staff and the offender population.

Fox Valley Adult Transition Center (ATC) opened in April 1972. In August 2000 the center was converted to a female facility under the Women and Family Services Division. The center consists of eight acres of timber and landscape, enhanced by flowers and other decorative arrangements that foster an environment conducive to self-improvement. Fox Valley ATC offers a variety of programs developed specifically for the female offender. The primary objective of the facility is to provide an integrated system of support and services for the female offender as she reenters the community and workforce.

John A. Graham is a Level 4 adult male correctional facility located 2 miles southeast of Hillsboro on Route 185. Graham is located on 117 acres and has 50 buildings within the facility. Graham was opened in 1980. At that time, Graham housed approximately 750 offenders. Graham currently houses an average daily population of 1,906 offenders. Graham houses several special populations including substance abuse treatment, sex offender treatment and inmates in a kidney dialysis program. Graham continues to offer numerous academic and vocational programs offered by School District 428 and Lake Land Community College. Classes include Adult Basic Education, GED, computer technology, construction occupation, custodial maintenance, auto body and automotive technology.

The Menard Correctional Center was established adjacent to the City of Chester on the banks of the Mississippi River in 1878. It is the second-oldest prison in Illinois and the state's largest maximum-security facility. Menard was originally designed to house 1,460 maximum-security males, but now has an average daily population of 3,315.

The Safer Foundation opened North Lawndale Adult Transition Center on June 1, 2000, under contract with the Illinois Department of Corrections. The center has a 200-bed capacity and is located at 2839 W. Fillmore on the west side of Chicago. The facility and the programs of the North Lawndale ATC are designed for offenders in work-release status transitioning from secure custody and preparing for parole. The security system within the facility enables staff to monitor residents' living areas, common areas, recreation areas and the streets in the area around the facility. From the beginning, North Lawndale adopted a philosophy that good programming is good security and good security is good programming. In practice, that means that residents who are active in programs create far less security problems than those who are not, and where there is structure and order, programs can be effectively implemented.

It has the largest Segregation Unit for a Level 2 facility in the state. Pinckneyville Correctional Center has an annual operating budget of $32,775,300 with

430 full-time state employees and an additional 60 contractual staff employed by School District 428, Rend Lake College and Health Professionals Limited.

Pontiac Correctional Center holds the distinction of being the eighth oldest correctional facility in the United States having opened in June 1871 as the Boys' Reformatory. It was renamed the Illinois State Penitentiary—Pontiac Branch in 1933 and in 1973 it received the name it bears today. Pontiac Correctional Center is comprised of two units with two security level classifications. The Maximum-Security Unit is classified Level 1 and principally houses problematic offenders in disciplinary segregation with limited privileges, Protective Custody, Orientation, Mental Health and Condemned Unit offenders with a sentence of death. Movement only occurs via direct staff escort. The Medium-Security Unit is classified Level 3 and houses medium and minimum-security status offenders. Average daily population is 1,660.

Tamms Correctional Center consists of a 200-bed Minimum-Security Unit (MSU) and a 500-bed Closed Maximum-Security Facility (CMAX). The facility is situated on 236 acres of land just north of Tamms on Route 127 in Alexander County. The MSU, which opened in 1995, provides work crews to numerous locations in southern Illinois and also serves as a work cadre for the CMAX facility. The CMAX facility, which opened in March 1998, has been designated to house the department's most disruptive, violent and problematic inmates. Inmates' approved for placement at CMAX have demonstrated an inability or unwillingness to conform to the requirements of a general population prison. Inmates' transferred to CMAX are required to stay for a minimum, predetermined length of time. Positive behavior, or a change in attitude to conform to stated rules and regulations, is considered in determining when an inmate returns to a general population environment. In addition, the state operates 20 additional prisons, correctional centers, work-camps, and other facilities.

Indiana. Inmates are 92.8% male, 7.2% female; 53.8% white, 39.2% black, 3.8% undetermined, 2.8% Hispanic, 0.2% American Indian/Alaskan Native, 0.1% Asian/Pacific Islander. The average age at intake is 31.1. There are 5,341 male and 546 female offenders on parole.

Minimum Security Facilities: (Level 1). These facilities have the least restrictive security measures. Housing is dormitory style. Offenders in these facilities typically are serving short sentences of nonviolent, non-weapons-based offenses. Also included as minimum security are work release program offenders, who leave the facility for outside employment, but return nightly.

Medium Security Facilities: (Level 2). These facilities have a moderate degree of security measures.

Housing is dormitory style. Offenders typically have shorter sentences than level 3 offenders. Medium security offenders are less aggressive than level 3s and 4s, have shorter sentences and a shorter criminal history.

High Medium Security Facilities: (Level 3). These facilities have a moderately high degree of security measures. Housing is celled space. Typically more aggressive offenders than level 1 and 2, could be serving longer sentences and have a long criminal history.

Maximum Security Facilities: (Level 4). These facilities have very restrictive security measures. Housing is celled space. Level 4 offenders typically have been convicted of violent or weapons based offenses. These offenders require close supervision and tight security to minimize risk to the public, staff and other offenders.

Iowa. The Iowa Department of Corrections operates 20 institutions with a combined population of 8,567 and with a design capacity of 6,989. These institutions include work farms, maximum security prisons, medium security prisons, a women's unit, and corrections centers of varying security levels.

Including those on work release, in out of state confinement, and other noninstitutional settings, the total system population is 9,443. The system includes 9 institutions divided into subunits such as treatment, work, farm, and confinement units.

Iowa Prison Industries (IPI) is a self-supporting division of the Iowa Department of Corrections, employs inmates throughout the State of Iowa. The high-quality products and services produced by these inmates are available for purchase by tax-supported institutions, government subdivisions, public and parochial schools, non-profit groups and their employees.

Victim and Restorative Justice Programs encourages victims' input in the criminal justice system by giving them opportunities to participate in decisions concerning an offender's liberty. The Office of Victim and Restorative Justice Programs also provides victims' support, information and restorative justice programs subject to set guidelines. Through the use of victim impact panels, offenders are made to undo the harm they committed, and take responsibility for their actions. The department also provides a number of services to inmates and their families similar to nation standards.

Kansas. During much of the past 18 years, KDOC managers and state policymakers have had to address the issue of providing adequate correctional capacity for steady and prolonged growth in the inmate population. In the late 1980s capacity did not keep pace with the population—which, along with related issues, resulted in a federal court order in 1989. The order was terminated in 1996 following numerous changes to the correctional system. During the last half of the 1990s, increases in the inmate population were matched by capacity increases, but capacity utilization rates remained consistently high. Since FY 1985, the inmate population has increased by 98% and capacity has increased by 170%. In 8 state institutions, the combined capacity is about 9,000 inmates. Of the 18 complete fiscal years up to FY 2004, the June 30 inmate population represented 97% or more of capacity on 14 occasions. Since 1995 the average June 30 capacity utilization percentage has been 98.5%. These institutions employ a staff of 1,135 individuals.

Offenders are employed not only in prison industries, but also in community service work. The system also provides offenders with the following services: Medical and mental health services, Sex offender treatment, Substance abuse treatment, Special education, Vocational education, Academic education, Values-based prerelease, Prerelease, and Work-release programs.

There were 4,216 offenders on parole in 2004, and an additional 4,142 (average daily population) in community correction's programs. There are currently 31 programs receiving state grants under the Community Corrections Act. Some programs serve a single county, while others are multi-county programs. Single-county programs include: Atchison County; Leavenworth County; Unified Government of Wyandotte County; Johnson County; Douglas County; Shawnee County; Reno County; Riley County; Sedgwick County; Sumner County; and Cowley County. Shawnee County and the 2nd District have a common administrator. There are also multicounty programs involving the same institutions.

Kentucky. As of January 1, 2003, the total population of the Kentucky Department of Corrections institutions (inmate population) was 15,934, of which, 1,282 (8%) were female. The population is 67% white, 32% black, and 6% Native American. The median age of the population is 33. Among other charges, 39% were incarcerated for violent crimes, 11% for sex offenses, 23% for drug crimes, 22% for drug crimes, and 1% for weapons related charges.

The Department of Corrections, in conjunction with the Kentucky Community & Technical College System, provides an extensive education program that includes a literacy program, adult basic education and GED preparatory classes and testing, in all 12 correctional institutions. In FY2003, a total of 378 GEDs and 293 vocational diplomas were issued during the school year. In addition, there were 546 inmates enrolled in the college program.

The department also offers a variety of vocational training opportunities in 39 different technical training programs. In FY2003, approximately 52% of the inmate population was involved in some type of educational or vocational training program. Comparable academic and vocational programs are also offered at the two facilities with which the department contracts to house inmates.

Kentucky currently contracts to house inmates at two privately owned and managed facilities. Marion Adjustment Center in St. Mary, Kentucky, is contracted to house up to 700 minimum-security inmates, and Lee Adjustment Center in Beattyville, Kentucky, is contracted to house up to 600 medium-security inmates.

Kentucky's Division of Correctional Industries is a self-supporting division of the Department of Corrections that employs approximately 800 inmates in the production of goods and services in 23 operations throughout the prison system.

The Average Daily Population (ADP) of inmates participating in the halfway house program is 565. This reintegration program allows inmates to become reacquainted with their families and community and gives them a head start in seeking employment. In addition, many inmates are enrolled in vocational school and college programs. The Class D Felon Program began in 1992, it allows Class D felons, excluding sex offenders, to be housed in local jails. Sixty-six county jails participate in this program and house over 3,000 Class D inmates. These inmates also provide valuable community service work to Kentucky's counties. Finally, there were 26,063 individuals on probation or parole in FY 2003.

Louisiana. In 2003 the Department of Corrections had a total inmate population of 36,612 with average sentence length of 21 years. The average age of the population is 35. Of the total, 27,114 are black, while 9,407 are white with 91 classified as "other." There are 88 inmates on death row, and 3,826 have life sentences, a factor which inflates the average sentence length. There are a total of 12 adult institutions (prisons) together with 11 correctional institutions of lesser security that service the population.

The Division of Probation and Parole-Adult, comprised of twenty-one district offices throughout the state and a headquarters office in Baton Rouge, functions as a community services division. Officers of the division supervise adult offenders who are released to the community on probation, parole, diminution of sentence, or medical furlough. They supervise inmates in ten community rehabilitation centers and the intensive parole cases from institutional IMPACT (Intensive Motivational Program of Alternative Correctional Treatment). Officers in the division provide investigative services to decision makers in the criminal justice system, including judges, the Parole and Pardon Boards, and the Governor's Office. They oversee collection of various criminal justice fees, supervision fees, and victim restitution.

Several of the state's prisons are host to chapters of the Jaycees, whose members are prisoners seeking to change their lives. The prisons also host a CORE program for inmate reentry into society. The primary components of this are education, training, substance abuse treatment, and value changes.

Examples of institutions include the Dixon Correctional Institute (DCI), located in East Feliciana Parish, opened in 1976 and was the first medium-security satellite prison in Louisiana. In 1993 DCI was accredited by the American Correctional Association and has maintained its accreditation since then. DCI is a multilevel security institution, with a maximum capacity of 1,340 inmates. The main compound is located approximately 30 miles north of Baton Rouge and encompasses 1,549 acres of pasture, 428 acres of timber, and approximately 450 acres reserved for crops in and around Jackson, Louisiana. DCI employs a work force of 556 with a general operating budget of 29.630 million dollars.

In 1976 the Louisiana State Penitentiary (LSP) lifted the traditional lid of censorship giving *The Angolite*, its official prisoner publication, freedom to publish whatever it desired, subject to the same standards governing professional journalism. It represented America's boldest experiment in journalism and freedom of expression in the world behind bars. The result was a provocative bi-monthly newsmagazine that went on to earn some of the nation's most coveted press awards. Various services are offered at the LSP. The Kids Activity Center was designed to encourage bonding between the fathers and the children that come to visit. It was felt that if the children and the fathers could share a book or another similar activity, it would strengthen the bond that had been weakened because of the father's absence from the home. The goal of the Parenting Skills program is to make a sustained lasting impact on crime prevention. This program focuses on educating current and future incarcerated parents, grandparents, and caregivers of methods in which to raise healthier and more nurtured children who will be less at-risk for criminal activity. A parenting skills curriculum is offered to all inmates at LSP who are within one year of release.

There is a large prison industry system manufacturing many products and producing farm goods as well. The Chaplains Department directly supervises all religious programming for the LSP. Many religious denominations are recognized without preferential treatment to any single group. Hundreds of citizen volunteers comprise the heart of religious programming available daily to the inmate population. The combination of inmate-led organizations and citizen volunteers unite to produce a variety of faith-based rehabilitative programs. Citizen volunteers facilitate bible studies, worship services, and prayer groups on a weekly basis. Inmate organizations with religious agendas create unique local churches led by inmate pastors. Finally, there is a substantial substance abuse program in place.

Maine. The Bolduc Correctional Facility has a staff of 65. The primary purpose of this minimum security institution is to promote a safe and healthy work environment for the community, staff and prisoners alike, while providing the necessary opportunities for change and personal growth that will positively affect an individual's reintegration to society.

The Central Maine Pre-Release Center opened in Hallowell in 1979, on the grounds of the former Stevens School complex, under the jurisdiction of what was then the Department of Mental Health and Corrections. The Department of Corrections continues to work very closely with the Hallowell Citizens Advisory Group who were included in the original planning process for this prerelease facility. To date, the department still upholds its pledge that sex offenders who have been convicted of a crime against a stranger will not be housed at the Central Maine Pre-Release Center. Currently, there are 58 minimum security adult males at the Central Maine Pre-Release Center. Prisoners at this unit participate in public restitution work crews and a work release program. During 2002, the aforementioned public restitution program provided approximately 22,000 man hours of free labor to citizens of the greater Kennebec County region. The facility is also the site for phase 2 of the department's residential substances abuse treatment program (Transitional Therapeutic Program). The facility, in conjunction with S.A.D. 16 and Adult Education, also offers approximately 50 hours of educational classes to the inmate population each week. Central Maine Pre-Release Center has developed a crime prevention program, which is designed for presentations in the public schools and other similar forums. The primary focal points of the Right Choices Program are substance abuse and anger related issues. The prisoners' message to the students is a simple one: learn to make better choices by being made aware of the consequences of our poor choices.

The Charleston Correctional Facility is located on the site of the former Charleston Air Force Station in Charleston, Maine. In 2001 the facility was downsized in a major restructuring of the Maine Department of Corrections. The purpose of the Charleston Correctional Facility is to confine and rehabilitate adult male prisoners classified as minimum and community security. The prisoners participate in educational and vocational programs as well as in paid industries programs and a unique work release program. The facility has a strong public restitution program that is designed to provide public restitution to local communities and the Maine Department of Transportation as part of a total progressive corrections program. The Charleston Correctional Facility public restitution program completes projects for local municipalities, state agencies, and nonprofit organizations annually. A total of 30,485 prisoner and staff hours were expended on projects during 2000. The Charleston Correctional Facility houses approximately 92 male prisoners.

The Downeast Correctional Facility, located at the former Bucks Harbor Air Force Station, was established by the legislature in September 1984. Funds were appropriated to purchase the facility for the confinement and rehabilitation of persons who have been duly sentenced and committed to the Department of Corrections and began receiving inmates in June 1985. The facility is a medium/minimum security institution with a prisoner count of 148.

It is the mission of the Maine Correctional Center (MCC) to improve public safety by decreasing the recidivism of both male and female prisoners by providing opportunities for correctional rehabilitation within a supervised and secure setting, while assuring the safety of the public, the staff and the prisoners. The correctional center is the Department of Corrections' primary Reception Center. Throughout their MCC commitment, prisoners are expected to accept increasing levels of personal responsibility for their conduct and for successful participation in rehabilitative programs. The MCC is a Medium/Minimum Security facility and houses both male and female prisoners. It was established by an act of the legislature on April 4, 1919. An appropriation of $45,000 was made to purchase land and buildings, located in Windham. Originally called the Reformatory for Men, it was later named the Men's Correctional Center. In 1976 the Stevens School was closed and the women were moved to the Maine Correctional Center (renamed). The population as of April 22, 2004, was composed of 501 males and 115 females. A multipurpose (male and female) housing unit opened in May 1989. A new women's unit (estimated capacity of 70) opened on July 25, 2002.

The mission of the Maine State Prison is to provide a safe, secure, and humane correctional environment for the incarcerated offender. Consistent with the mission of the Department of Corrections, the prison maintains appropriate control of offenders by providing various levels of security necessary to protect the public. This control is effected by utilizing the guiding principles of unit management and direct supervision concepts. The

Maine State Prison balances its security obligation with its obligation to promote rehabilitation by providing and implementing a comprehensive treatment plan for each offender which encourages that offender to reenter society as a law-abiding, productive citizen. The treatment plan includes, where appropriate, the opportunity and incentive for offenders to progress to less secure facilities where they may continue their personal growth and development. The Maine State Prison houses adult male prisoners classified as high risk, protective custody, close, medium, and minimum custody, with minimum custody prisoners held awaiting transition to minimum security facilities. As part of the move to the new facility, the Maine State Prison and the Department of Corrections went under the Unit Management Concept of managing prisoners. Unit Management divides the prisoner population up into smaller units managed by multidisciplinary Unit Teams.

Maryland. The Maryland Department of Public Safety and Correctional Services (DPSCS) has the primary responsibility for controlling, supervising, and providing services for defendants and offenders in custody. In addition, DPSCS creates statewide correctional and rehabilitative initiatives, and criminal justice training standards that are the foundation of Maryland's crime control efforts.

The Correctional Options Program (COP), a comprehensive program of graduated sanctions and services was established as a tool to divert carefully screened low-risk, drug-involved offenders from prison. It was designed to safeguard the public; assure that offenders are accountable for their actions; provide substance abuse, educational, vocational, and employment services; and strengthen participants' parenting, daily living, and social skills. COP is a front- and back-end alternative to incarceration which uses a broad spectrum of institution and community-based control mechanisms. As reported by NCCD, participants in COP were 22 percent less likely to return to prison during the 12 months following their release than offenders not participating in COP, and nonparticipants were twice as likely to recidivate as the result of a new offense.

In the 13 institutions, there are approximately 22,989 males (in 12 institutions) and 1,208 females (in one institution). In probation and parole, it was estimated that there would be 10,000 at the end of 2004, including those supervised in boot camps.

Massachusetts. A change in security level occurred in 1991, and the Bay State Correctional Center (BSCC) was designated a medium-security facility housing primarily "lifers and long termers." Thirty additional beds were added in 1995 raising the total capacity to 296, where it stands today.

Currently, BSCC is operating as a small general population medium-security facility. BSCC houses both long and short-term inmates, many of whom are elderly. BSCC is a fully handicapped accessible facility. In a collaborative effort with outside agencies, Bay State has always been committed to providing community service through a variety of programs. Many of the programs at Bay State serve to not only teach inmates skills but also to provide a service to the facility, the Department of Corrections and the community. In addition to those programs offered throughout the department, Bay State offers some of the following site specific programs. Prison Voices is an educational community outreach program that confronts school-age children, young adults and other interested members of the community with the reality and the consequences of becoming involved in criminal behavior. Greenhouse serves to enhance the appearance of not only the grounds, but also the office and program areas of the facility. Plants are donated to other institutions, the Norfolk Town Hall and the Norfolk Council on Aging. The program also provides flower arrangements to citizens having their 90th birthdays within the town of Norfolk as well as fresh garden vegetables to the local elderly.

In November 1972, Boston Pre-Release became the first prerelease (level 2) facility established in the Commonwealth of Massachusetts. The Boston Pre-Release Center is a 150-bed community based level three/two (3/2) correctional facility. It is a structured program, which allows gradual transition from prison life to the community by means of reintegration through releases to work, education, and counseling programs. Boston Pre-Release Center also operates several community work crews utilizing level (3) security inmates. These crews provide services to the local community, State Office buildings, and local state police barracks. Boston Pre-Release Center received its reaccreditation in May 2003 by the Commission on Accreditation for Corrections. Boston Pre-Release Center's Health Service Unit is also accredited by the National Commission on Correctional Health Care for its achievement in providing quality health care that meets the standards for health services.

Bridgewater State Hospital's mission is the establishment and maintenance of a safe, secure, and humane environment to all persons requiring specialized care and treatment. In all cases, the patients that are admitted to this facility may be charged with or convicted of crimes ranging from misdemeanors to major felonies. Massachusetts General Law requires that individuals who are determined to be in need of strict security because of the potential for endangering themselves or others be sent to Bridgewater State Hospital.

Each individual admitted to this facility shall be subject to a court-ordered evaluation under an applicable section of Mass General Law Chapter 123. The length of the observation period can range from twenty to forty days, based upon the purpose of the evaluation. Such evaluations are completed in the effort to determine the following: (1) competency to stand trial, (2) determination of criminal responsibility, (3) ability to await trial in a penal environment, (4) ability to serve a sentence in a penal environment, (5) need for further treatment and/or strict security following a finding of not guilty by reason of insanity, and (6) sentencing evaluation. Other programmatic opportunities available include academic and vocational education, structured recreation, leisure time activities, and general law libraries.

The Shattuck Hospital Correction Unit was established in 1974 as a federally funded pilot program to serve as the Massachusetts Department of Correction acute medical care facility. In 1995 the Lemuel Shattuck Hospital began an expansion plan of their own thereby affording the community and the Massachusetts Department of Correction a much wider variety of medical services which now are 33 in number. The increase in clinics triggered a need for more room in the Out-Patient Department Holding Area. In 1995 a major construction project in the Out-Patient Department Holding Area was completed. The capacity has increased from about 40 to 100 inmates. Between 40 and 80 inmates a day are serviced in the Out-Patient Department Holding area awaiting clinic appointments. The Shattuck Hospital Correction Unit has provided medical services to the Department for over a quarter of a century.

The Massachusetts Treatment Center, located within the Bridgewater Correctional Complex is a unique facility containing both civilly committed and sentenced sex offenders. The population consists of a capacity of 350 state inmates and 187 civil commitments. The facility was originally administered by the Department of Mental Health, with security being provided by the Department of Correction. Civil commitments resulted from a criminally convicted individual being legally determined to be a "sexually dangerous person" (SDP) as defined by M.G.L. Ch. 123A, resulting in a "day to life" commitment. In September 1990, the Massachusetts legislature repealed portions of Chapter 123A thereby discontinuing civil commitments to this facility. The administration of the facility became the responsibility of the Department of Correction in July 1995, also resulting from changes in legislation. In May 1997 this facility began admitting 300 state inmates in a new housing unit.

MCI-Cedar Junction is a maximum security prison for male offenders in the Commonwealth of Massachusetts. MCI-Cedar Junction also houses the Departmental Disciplinary Unit, or DDU. In the early 1950s, Department of Correction officials recognized the need to replace the antiquated Charlestown Prison, and the construction of MCI-Walpole began. Work on the maximum security penitentiary was completed in 1955, and the new prison officially opened less than a year later. The original perimeter consisted of a wall with eight observation towers. An additional tower was recently constructed for the new DDU. The wall is 20 feet high, with five strands of electrical wire along the top. In the mid-1980s, the townspeople of Walpole sought a change in the name of the prison, and legislative action resulted in renaming the facility MCI-Cedar Junction—an old railroad station in the town.

MCI-Cedar Junction treatment/program services offers its inmates the opportunity to take part in educational, treatment and reintegration programs. They include mental health, educational, and substance abuse programs, as well as instruction in personal medical care. The inmates also have the opportunity to become involved in employment programs while at MCI-Cedar Junction consisting of Industries, Food Service and janitorial positions. Industries is a correctional program designed to create inmate employment. The Industries Program at MCI-Cedar Junction is involved in the manufacture of motor vehicle license plates. Inmates' wages usually begin at $.50 per hour. This program enables inmates to develop employable work skills, which is the ultimate goal.

Since 1980 MCI-Concord has been designated as a medium security facility which serves as the Massachusetts Department of Corrections Reception and Diagnostic Center. Effective October 1995, MCI-Concord receives all new court commitments of male offenders.

After a specified period of time following an inmate's initial arrival into the prison system—usually twelve to sixteen weeks—an inmate will appear before the Classification Board, which will determine or recommend both a security rating and an institutional placement. The Classification Board will also make treatment recommendations designed to address the factors which may have led to commission of a crime. Participation in programs including substance abuse treatment, academic instruction, vocational programming, and counseling have done much to help offenders begin the reintegration process.

MCI-Framingham is a medium security correctional facility for female offenders, located 22 miles west of Boston. MCI-Framingham is the Massachusett's Department of Corrections only committing institution for female offenders. It is noted as the oldest female correctional institution in operation in the United States. The facility houses women at various classification levels, including state sentenced and county offenders, and awaiting trial inmates. The facility consists of four housing units within the compound, plus a two-story 120+ bed modular housing unit. In addition to meeting the security needs of a medium security facility, MCI-Framingham provides numerous program and treatment opportunities including mental health, medical, substance abuse, and family services, as well as educational, vocational, library, religious, recreation, and community service programs.

MCI-Norfolk is a medium security facility just south of Boston, with an average daily population of 1,250 inmates. Though it is rated medium security, MCI-Norfolk has a maximum security perimeter with a wall 5,000 feet long and 19 feet high, enclosing an area of 35 acres. Within the confinement of the wall, there is a minimum security environment of eighteen dormitory-style living units and two modular units divided by a large central grass quadrangle. Other buildings within the perimeter provide space for administrative and security personnel, health services, support staff and services, and other vocational and educational programs. Originally opened as the first "community-based" prison in the United States, the history and background of MCI-Norfolk is detailed and fascinating. The first of the MCI-Norfolk inmates were transferred from the state prison in Charlestown in 1927, and lived in houses in the Oval, which is currently at the southwest corner of the wall surrounding the compound. In its early years of operation, a major portion of the present institution, including the prison wall, was constructed by inmates who lived in the State Prison Colony. The more spacious and campuslike atmosphere and architecture permitted an approach to "community life" that was not available at other institutions, and represented a new step in Massachusetts Penology. In the mid-1950s, the name of the prison was officially changed to the Massachusetts Correctional Institute at Norfolk.

MCI-Norfolk is the largest facility of its type in the Commonwealth of Massachusetts. Eighty-percent of the inmate population at the facility is serving time for violent crimes. Of that 80 percent, approximately 275 inmates are serving life sentences for commission of murder in the first or second degree. The next largest crime category is armed robbery, followed by sex offenders.

MCI-Plymouth is located in the Myles Standard State Forest approximately 10 miles from Plymouth, 52 miles from Boston, and 29 miles from New Bedford. It is a 195-bed, level 3, minimum-security community correctional facility. The facility mission is to provide public safety through sound inmate accountability procedures while offering inmates opportunities for self-improvement to prepare for their reentry into the community.

All inmates work in a variety of job assignments at the facility and in the community on supervised work crews. Job assignments are intended to provide the offender with opportunities for positive behavioral change while developing work skills and dependable work ethics. Programs include the Correctional Recovery Program, Thinking for A Change, Public Safety Transition Program, AA meetings, NA meetings, and various religious services. The facility has partnered with the National Education for Assistance Dog Services (NEADS) which offers inmates an opportunity to train service dogs. NEADS is a nonprofit organization who provides service dogs for children and adults who are hearing and physically impaired.

MCI-Shirley is located approximately 42 miles northwest of Boston on the Shirley/Lancaster Line. The facility maintains 13 inmate housing units, a 28-bed full-service hospital unit, 59-bed segregation unit, gym, recreation areas, school, industries, laundry, vocational area, food services and programs. Although not all inmates in Level 4 are required to work, they do attempt to employ the maximum number in the specified areas. There are currently 485 inmate work assignments in Levels 3 and 4. Inmates are also encouraged to avail themselves to the many department and volunteer-driven programs.

The North Central Correctional Institution at Gardner, as it is now known, is located on 20 acres of hillside near the Gardner/Westminster town line. The dedication of this medium security facility was held on June 18, 1981, with the first ten inmates accepted into the prison two weeks later. Within the facility are eighteen buildings, with a perimeter consisting of two chain-linked fences topped with razor wire. The perimeter is manned by three towers and foot patrols of K9 teams. Reconstruction and renovation of the facility has continued for more than a decade, with many of the projects enabling the prison to increase the inmate population. As a result of these projects and renovations, over 1,000 inmates are now housed at NCCI-Gardner.

Twenty miles northwest of Boston, Massachusetts, is found the Northeastern Correctional Center, established in 1932, located on approximately 300 acres of farmland. The Northeastern Correctional Center is an all male prison that houses inmates for two levels of security (level three/minimum and level two/pre-release). The housing capacity for level three is 182 and 80 for level two inmates. The Northeastern Correctional Center is accredited by the American Correctional Association and managed by the Massachusetts Department of Correction and overseen by the Massachusett's Department of Public Safety.

Level-3 inmates, housed at the Northeastern Correctional Center, provide many hours of community services to the surrounding towns, cities, state, and government municipalities that is known as the Community Inmate Work Crew program. The prerelease program is designed to screen eligible level-2 inmates who are within eighteen months of their release and provide them with outside employment. The prerelease work program benefits the inmate by providing work with the goal to financially reestablish them once they are released from incarceration. The prerelease program also rewards the employer by offering the Work Opportunity Tax Credit. An employer can deduct 40 percent of the first $6,000 of gross wages for each inmate hired. A fluctuating staff of 87 correctional officers and administrative support personnel supervised and managed an inmate population that averaged 220 inmates per day in 2003.

Old Colony Correctional Center (OCCC) is a high-tech medium security facility located on 30 acres of land at the Bridgewater Correctional Complex, along with Bridgewater State Hospital, Southeastern Correctional Center, Massachusetts Boot Camp, and the Treatment Center. Since Old Colony is not a committing institution, inmates are transferred there from other Massachusetts Department of Correction facilities.

The actual construction of OCCC began in the summer of 1984, and the facility opened in October 1987. The prison originally consisted of nine cell blocks, six consisting of sixty cells while the remaining three contained thirty cells each. In May 1990, an additional sixty-cell modular unit was added. Each of the sixty-cell units have some double bunking because of a daily count consistently above suggested capacity. The facility has a secure perimeter, which consists of a 14-foot double chain link fence topped with razor wire. Between the double fences are high-tech motion detectors which are part of a microwave system which alerts tower and control room personnel when an intruder passes between the fences. These devices are sensitive enough to detect the motion of rain falling or wind blowing.

Historically, the name of Old Colony dates back to the founding of the United States, and fosters a sense of hope and "new beginning." In keeping with the Old Colony theme, the housing units within the institution are named after Revolutionary War heroes. Blocks are named for William Dawes, who joined Paul Revere in taking to horseback to warn that "The British are coming!" and for Crispus Attucks, a black Revolutionary and the first man to die in the famous Boston Massacre.

Pondville Correctional Center is located 36 miles southwest of Boston in the town of Norfolk, Massachusetts. It has a capacity of 204 inmates, of which 160 inmates are Level 3 (minimum) and 44 inmates are Level 2 (prerelease). The primary mission of Pondville Correctional Center is to protect the public's safety by incarcerating inmates and to provide inmates the opportunity for responsible reintegration and positive behavioral change. The focus of the facility's operations is twofold. First, inmates are required to work unless a medical condition exists which will require a waiver from work assignments. Second, inmates are provided vocational, educational, and self-help programming opportunities including Life Skills, Small Engine Repair, Violence Reduction, Public Safety Transition Program, Thinking for a Change, A.A., N.A., and various religious services. There are no walls or fences at this facility. Security is maintained through inmate counts and strict accountability procedures. Department policy mandates supervisory spot checks of community work crews, drug and alcohol testing, searches, and police notifications when inmates are in their community.

South Middlesex Correctional Center is a two-hundred bed facility for minimum status and prerelease female inmates within the Department of Correction. Originally, a facility for inmates with pre-release status, SMCC occupied the Hodder House, now a part of MCI-Framingham. On July 1, 2002, South Middlesex Correctional Center's population became all female. As a minimum-security and prerelease facility, SMCC is not within a secure perimeter and there are no lock-in cells. The work release inmate population at South Middlesex Correctional Center hold jobs within the surrounding community, and those workers are paid an average wage of $7 per hour. Many of the employment opportunities are offered by area fast-food restaurants. In turn, these inmates contribute 15% of their earnings to the Commonwealth of Massachusetts General Fund in order to help offset the cost of room and board.

The Souza-Baranowski Correctional Center (SBCC), located on 18 acres of land at the Shirley Correctional Complex in Shirley, Massachusetts, officially opened on September 30, 1998. This 500,000 square foot, high-tech, maximum security facility consists of 1,024 general population cells, 128 special management cells, and 24 health service beds. The security system is operated by 42 graphic interfaced computer terminals (GUI), which drive a keyless security system. The GUI controls 1,705 doors, lights, receptacles, water, intercom/public address, fire alarms and vehicle gates. Incorporating one of the largest camera matrix systems in the country, 366 cameras record live 24 hours a day. The perimeter surveillance system includes taut wire and microwave detection systems. SBCC offers a full range of educational, vocational, and substance abuse programming Correctional Industries provides employment opportunities within the confines of the facility. The SBCC was named in the memory of two correctional staff, Corrections Officer James Souza and Industrial Instructor Alfred Baranowski, who were killed at MCI Norfolk in 1972 during an aborted escape attempt by a convicted murderer.

Michigan. The Michigan Department of Corrections operates 42 prisons and 10 work camps. Additionally, it operates one boot camp. Total inmate population is 49,439 as of 2003. There is a total of 15,592 individuals on parole, and an additional 55,605 on probation. In Community Residential Programs (CRP), there are 1,132, with 459 in halfway houses, and 673 on electronic monitoring. Of the population as a whole, 35 is the average age for males, while 36 is the average age for women inmates. The population is 54.2% black, and 42.3% white, the rest are labeled as "other." The average cost per inmate per year is $24,680. In FY 2002 the budget was $1.6 billion.

The state secure-facilities network supervises a diverse offender population. The physical plants also span centuries, from the Michigan Reformatory in Ionia (built in the late 1870s) to the modern Bellamy Creek Correctional Facility, which was completed in 2001. The prisons are categorized into different security levels. A Secure Level I facility houses prisoners who are more easily managed within the network (even though they may have committed violent crimes). The state's only Level VI prison, Ionia Maximum Correctional Facility, houses prisoners who pose maximum management problems, are a maximum-security risk, or both.

The tools the department uses to protect the public are many and varied. Though it is probably not possible to "rehabilitate" anyone, self-help programs, including education and vocational training, are offered to offenders who want to change. Completion of high school is highly stressed. Services such as medical and mental health care are mandated by court rulings and are considered sound, humane corrections practice. Some programs, including public works, not only benefit offenders by giving them real-world job experiences, they also serve the communities. In addition, there is a large prison industries program which provides training and jobs for inmates.

Minnesota. The Department of Corrections operates 10 correctional institutions with a total population of 7,568 of which 449 (5.9%) are female. During FY 2003, 3,973 were released on parole, 156 on intensive supervision in the community, and 629 were discharged, for a total of 4,758 releases. In the same year, there were 5,568 commitments. The average sentence length is 31 months. Of the entire population, 22% were sentenced for drug offenses, 16.5% for sex crimes, 14% for homicide, 11% for assault, 8% for burglary, and 7.1% for robbery. The population is 57.2% white, 34% black, 6.5% Native American, and 2.3% Asian, with 3.3% Hispanic. Only 26.5% have a high school diploma or a GED, while 8.1% have a college degree. The rest of the population have less than a 11th grade education. The average age is 33.8.

The system operates a strong restorative justice component. The department works with interested communities assisting them in development of a restorative justice approach to community safety. Restorative justice is a framework for the criminal justice system that involves the community more broadly in the system. In addition to offender accountability through taking responsibility and making amends, restorative justice seeks to address victim needs, offender competencies, and community responsibility in repairing the harm done by crime. There is also a strong victims program, involving victims in every stage of the process, intervening where necessary, and providing links to other victim services.

Example institutions include the Minnesota Correctional Facility-Rush City, 7600 525th Street, Rush City, Minnesota, which opened in February 2000. The close-custody, level-four facility currently houses 1,011 offenders, most in double-bunked cells. Offender activities are conducted on a strict schedule. These activities include institution support jobs, prison industry jobs, education assignments, religious programming, and recreation and visiting times. The Minnesota Correctional Facility-Stillwater, 970 Pickett Street North, Bayport, built in 1914 as an industrial prison, is the states largest close-security, level four institution for adult male felons. Population is 1,300 as of March 2004. The Minnesota correctional system has a six-level classification structure ranging from level 1, which is minimum custody, to level 5, which is maximum custody. Level 2 is minimum, and level 3 is medium, and level 4 is close.

Mississippi. There are three state prisons in Mississippi: Central Mississippi Correctional Facility, Mississippi State Penitentiary, and the South Mississippi Correctional Institution.

The Central Mississippi Correctional Facility (CMCF) was established in 1986 and constructed in Rankin County. CMCF is located on 171 acres and includes thirteen housing units with a capacity of 3,233 beds. Offenders sentenced to the Mississippi Department of Corrections are brought to CMCF where they are processed through the Receiving and Classification unit. Each offender is thoroughly screened and tested for STD, HIV, and other medical conditions, provided a psychiatric evaluation and questioned regarding their educational level. The results of these tests, along with the offender's conviction and institutional behavior, help establish the classification of each inmate. Of the three state prisons, CMCF is the only facility to house female inmates. CMCF houses females classified to all custody levels, including A and B custody (minimum and medium security), C and D custody (maximum security) and death row. All female offenders sentenced to death are housed at CMCF. The prison also houses minimum and medium security male offenders (A and B custody), as well as some maximum security offenders (C custody). All male offenders sentenced to death are housed at the Mississippi State Penitentiary. CMCF III is a special needs facility for male offenders who have medical or physical conditions that require special treatment. CMCF III was the first state facility to achieve American Correctional Association accreditation. CMCF inmates provided more than 17,832 hours of free inmate labor during FY 2003 to adjacent municipalities and counties, as well as assisting other state agencies. There are approximately 646 employees at CMCF. Mississippi Prison Industries (MPIC) operates a tack shop, print shop, and sign shop at CMCF. MPIC employs approximately 82 inmates monthly. During FY 2003, MPIC utilized nearly 21,000 man-hours at these shops using both male and female inmates.

The Mississippi State Penitentiary (MSP) is Mississippi's oldest institution and is located on approximately 18,000 acres at Parchman, in Sunflower County. There are eighteen different housing units at MSP ranging in size from sixty beds at Unit 17 to 1,488 beds at Unit 29 (the major farming support unit). The total bed capacity at MSP is currently 5,768. MSP houses male offenders classified to all custody levels, including A and B custody (minimum and medium security), C and D custody (maximum security) and death row. All male offenders sentenced to death are housed at MSP. All female offenders sentenced to death are housed at the Central Mississippi Correctional Facility. MSP inmates provided more than 104,540 hours of free inmate labor during FY 2001 to adjacent municipalities and counties, as well as assisting other state agencies. There are approximately 1,720 employees at MSP. The majority of the farming activity involving Agricultural Enterprises takes place at MSP. During FY 2000, inmates worked a total of 708,864 hours in the agricultural program. Mississippi Prison Industries operates a work program at the MSP and utilizes more than 34,000 inmate man-hours in its textile, metal fabrication, and wood working shops. On a monthly average, 139 inmates work in these shops.

The South Mississippi Correctional Institution (SMCI) was established in 1989. It is the state's newest state prison. SMCI is located on 360 acres at Leakesville in Greene County. There are 19 housing units at SMCI with a capacity of 2,214 beds. SMCI houses male offenders who are classified to primarily A and B custody levels (minimum and medium security). SMCI also offers housing for approximately 140 offenders classified to C and D Custody level (maximum security). There are no female offenders housed at SMCI.

SMCI is the only state institution with a paramilitary "Boot Camp Program." The Regimented Inmate Discipline (RID) Program seeks to divert offenders from criminal behavior and instill a work ethic by incorporating a variety of rehabilitative and treatment elements as well as community service work projects. The foundation for the RID Program is based on the premise of instilling discipline, respect for authority, and self-esteem through a tough, structured "boot camp" environment. The RID Program consists of four phases lasting approximately five weeks each. There are eight treatment program components offered; five are mandatory and three optional. The mandatory components are: Discipline Therapy, Psychological Counseling, Alcohol and Drug Counseling, Pre Release Counseling, and Aftercare Strategies. Adult Basic Education, Discipleship Study, and Community Service Work Projects are optional treatment components offered. SMCI inmates provided more than 101,641 hours of free inmate labor during FY 2003 to adjacent municipalities and counties, as well as assisting other state agencies.

There are approximately 600 employees at SMCI. The SMCI Vocational Technical Department offers five vocational education programs that will enable offenders to become productive citizens upon their release from this facility. These programs are Auto Body, Auto Mechanics, Electrical, Plumbing and Pipefitting, and Welding. Program length for each program begins at approximately 1,300 hours to 2,650 hours. The SMCI Educational Department offers both Adult Basic Educational and General Education Development Classes providing students access to a full-time counselor. SMCI utilizes inmate labor to farm approximately 25 acres of fruits and vegetables that are used to subsidize food costs associated with feeding inmates.

There are 5 private prisons in Mississippi: East Mississippi Correctional Facility (1,000 beds); Delta Correctional Facility (Capacity is 1,000+); Marshall County Correctional Facility (1,000); Walnut Grove Youth Correctional Facility (750); and the Wilkinson County Correctional Center (995).

Missouri. As of May 29, 2004, there were more than 30,000 adult felons confined in Missouri's 21 correctional facilities and two-community release centers. The department also supervises 14,566 parolees and 50,702 probationers across the state. In all, the department is responsible for the care, custody, and supervision of approximately 95,000 adult offenders in Missouri. The Algoa Correctional Center (ACC) opened in 1932 and is located 6 miles east of Jefferson City. It is a medium-security (C-2) facility with a capacity of 1,635 male inmates. ACC was selected as one of three facilities to pilot the Long Distance Dads Parenting Program for male inmates.

The Boonville Correctional Center (BCC) is located at the former Missouri Training School for Boys and was constructed in 1889. The facility, located in Boonville, was transferred to the Department of Corrections on July 1, 1983. BCC is a medium-security (C-3) facility housing 1,256 inmates.

The Central Missouri Correctional Center is a (C-2) medium-security facility that houses 1,000 adult male offenders. The institution is located approximately 6 miles west of Jefferson City on Highway 179. It was formerly known as the Church Farm and is frequently referred to by that name also.

The Chillicothe Correctional Center (CCC) is a female facility named for its host city in the northwest part of the state. CCC houses inmates of all custody levels (C-1 to C-5) and has an operational capacity of 525. It was formerly a detention facility for juvenile female offenders.

The Crossroads Correctional Center (CRCC) is a maximum-security (C-5) male facility located adjacent to the Western Missouri Correctional Center in Cameron. It opened in March 1997 with an operational capacity of 1,500 inmates. CRCC was the first Missouri prison to install a lethal electric fence.

The Eastern Reception, Diagnostic and Correctional Center (ERDCC) is a 2,684-bed complex located northeast of Bonne Terre, Missouri. ERDCC serves as the point of admission for male offenders committed by the courts in eastern Missouri to the Missouri Department of Corrections. The ERDCC operates a cook/chill food facility, a unit that prepares and transports all regular and special diet meals to the Potosi, Farmington, and Missouri Eastern Correctional Centers and the St. Louis Community Release Center.

The Farmington Correctional Center (FCC) is a (C-2 & C-4) male facility with an operational capacity of 2,725 inmates and has been a correctional facility since 1986. FCC is situated on the grounds of the former Farmington State Metal Hospital. FCC is home to specialized programs for inmates with mental illness and sex offenses, and young men in the Regimented Discipline Program.

The Fulton Reception and Diagnostic Center (FRDC) is the intake and orientation center for male inmates assigned from central Missouri. The staff is responsible for the evaluation of inmates and their assignment to other correctional facilities custody levels C-1 to C-5. Assigning inmates to an appropriate facility increases public and institutional risk, and individual inmate needs such as aggressiveness, mental health, substance abuse, employment, and vocational. FRDC houses 1,302 inmates. Two hundred minimum-security prisoners are assigned as the facility workforce. The remaining 1,104 are reception inmates assigned transitionally during their evaluation and subsequently assigned to mainstream facilities appropriate to their risk and needs. FRDC also administers two other programs located on the grounds of the Fulton State Mental Hospital. The Biggs Correctional Unit is a 30-day evaluation center for inmates suffering from mental illness. This unit houses 20 male and 10 female inmates. This program is administered jointly with the Missouri Department of Mental Health.

The Missouri State Penitentiary is the oldest continuously operating correctional institution west of the Mississippi River. It was authorized by the General Assembly in 1832 and received its first offender in 1836. One housing unit completed in 1868 is still in use today and is now on the Historic Register of Buildings. The institution is distinguished by a high limestone wall with 15 officer towers surrounding a 47-acre compound. It is a maximum-security (C-5) institution housing nearly 2,000 male offenders. Due to its age and high maintenance costs JCCC is scheduled for replacement by a new facility near the Algoa Correctional Center in 2004.

The Maryville Treatment Center lies on 44 acres purchased by the Department of Corrections from the Sisters of St. Francis in June 1995. The facility began operation on December 3, 1996. The Institution is a minimum-security (Custody Level 2) correctional treatment facility with a designed capacity to house 525 offenders. Its mission is "to return recovering offenders to society as productive, responsible and law abiding citizens." That mission is accomplished by providing the offenders with long-term alcohol and substance abuse treatment in a therapeutic learning environment.

The Missouri Eastern Correctional Center (MECC) is a medium custody (C-3) facility located at Pacific, serving 1,100 male inmates. MECC offers the Missouri Sexual Offenders Program for male inmates with disabilities.

The Moberly Correctional Center (MCC), formerly known as the Missouri Training Center for Men, opened in 1963 and is a (C-3) medium custody institution serving 1,800 male inmates. MCC is home to the male dialysis center for those with special medical needs. The Northeast Correctional Center (NECC) opened in March 1998 housing 1,975 high custody (C-4) male inmates in Bowling Green. NECC also provides special housing and programming arrangements for male offenders under the age of 17.

The Ozark Correctional Center (OCC) is a minimum security (C-2) institution housing 695 male inmates located in Webster County near the community of Fordland. OCC features a long-term substance abuse therapeutic treatment environment program for all inmates. It was formerly a U.S. Air Force Base in the 1950s. An additional 45 inmates are housed at a satellite institution, Camp Hawthorn, located at the Lake of the Ozarks State Park. Inmates at Camp Hawthorn provide labor for various state park projects in the Lake of the Ozarks area. Camp Hawthorn is a satellite of the Ozark Correctional Center and is located at the Lake of the Ozarks State Park. This facility houses 45 inmates who provide labor for various state park projects in the Lake of the Ozarks area. The Potosi Correctional Center (PCC) is located on 140 acres approximately 2 miles east of Potosi. PCC is where capital punishment executions take place in Missouri. The first facility in the state to be built under the lease/purchase concept received its first inmates in February 1989. The facility was constructed and currently houses 800 capital punishment, maximum security and high-risk male inmates including those sentenced to death.

The South Central Correctional Center (SCCC) is situated on a 205-acre tract site northwest of Licking about 1 mile west of the city of Licking off U.S. Highway 63. SCCC employs 445 correctional professionals when fully staffed and has a capacity to confine 1,596 maximum-security male inmates. The Southeast Correctional Center is located 1 mile south of Charleston on Highway 105. SECC will confine 1,500 maximum-security and 96 minimum-security male inmates and employs approximately 445 correctional professionals at full capacity. SECC opened in September 2001.

The Tipton Correctional Center (TCC) is a medium-security (C-2) facility housing 1,088 male inmates. TCC is located about 1 mile north of Tipton and was formerly a female correctional facility. The Western Missouri Correctional Center (WMCC) is a medium security (C-3 and C-4) facility confining 1,975 male inmates. It is located on 385 acres off U.S. Highway 69 in Cameron. In June 2000, WMCC staff and inmates embarked on an aggressive recycling project to reduce trash hauling costs. In the first ten months of operation, WMCC recycled 438,887 pounds of solid waste such as metal, textile, paper and cardboard. In August 1994 the voters of the state of Missouri approved a general obligation bond that allowed for the conversion of the St. Joseph State Mental Hospital into a correctional facility. The facility opened in 1999, and confines 1,880 inmates. It serves as the intake center for male inmates coming from the western side of the state. Currently, the Park Building Treatment Center currently confines 480 inmates in either a 120-day Substance Abuse Treatment Program or the 180-day Offenders Under Treatment Program. Additionally, 100 inmates participate in community service work at several locations including the city of St. Joseph.

The Women's Eastern Reception, Diagnostic and Correctional Center (WERDCC) in Vandalia received its first inmates in January 1998. This facility confines 1,776 minimum to maximum (C-1 to C-5) female offenders and certified juveniles. WERDCC serves as the intake center for females entering the department from around the state and also includes a permanent inmate population. This Reception and Diagnostic unit processes female inmates for assignment to permanent population at WERDCC, Chillicothe Correctional Center or the community release center treatment programs for women in St. Louis or Kansas City. Processing includes orientation to prison life, risk assessment educational testing, psychiatric and medical evaluation, AIDS testing and a drug education program.

Montana. The Montana Department of Corrections operates 5 institutions and has an average daily population of 9,912, while 277 were on intensive supervision release, 613 at prerelease centers, 2,470 in secure custody, and 6,552 on probation or parole. This represents a 5.2% increase over FY2002. The top offense for 2003 among males was theft and for females, it was possession of drugs. 59% of males and 16% of females in secure custody were convicted of violent crimes while 49% (539) of prison admissions were for new convictions. The average age of adult inmates was 36 in FY 2002. The average age dropped to 35 for females and 35 1/2 for males in FY 2003. During 2002, 22% of the populations at Montana State Prison (287) and at Montana Women's Prison (16) were employed by Montana Correctional Enterprises. At Montana State Prison, 97 inmates passed the GED, 350 completed Chemical Dependency Treatment, and 125 completed Anger Management. Juveniles at Pine Hills Youth Correctional Facility, within 90 days of admission, raised their reading comprehension 1.2 grade levels, their language expression 2 grade levels, and their math computation 1.1 grade levels. At Pine Hills Youth Correctional Facility, 46 juveniles participated in Restitution Programs and 66 in Community Service Programs in FY 2002, paying $28,560 in restitution to victims. Residents of the Riverside Youth Correctional Facility completed 590 hours of Community Service. Probationers and Parolees made $1,827,638 in restitution payments.

Nebraska. In the fall of 1967, Legislative Bill 569 created the Work Release Program. It allowed a select group of inmates to be employed in the community and housed during nonworking hours in the institutions. A community residential program was established in 1971. The fall of 1991 saw construction begin on a new 200-bed institution. Opened in July 1993, the facility has four housing units (three male and one female) and is designed to house 44 women and 156 men. The CCC-L has been accredited by the American Correctional Association since 1981. Programs include: work detail, work release, educational release, furloughs, community activity passes (e.g. recreation, shopping, religious), ABE/GED and other programming (i.e., family counseling, mental health) may be arranged through community support programs and agencies. The average population is 284.

The Omaha Correctional Center (OCC) is a medium/minimum security facility located on a 37-acre site in East Omaha, just south of Epply Airfield. OCC was opened on April 24, 1984. At a total cost of approximately $17 million, the facility has an operational capacity of 731 inmates in single, double, and multiple occupancy rooms. The designed capacity is 396 inmates. Programs include: Mental Health Counseling, ABE/GED, College Courses, College Correspondence Courses, Residential and Non-Residential, Alcoholics Anonymous, self-betterment clubs, volunteer activities, prerelease programs, English as a Second Language (ESL), work programs to include traditional facility work programs, and Cornhusker State Industries. Its average population is 580 with a staff of 178.

The Nebraska Department of Correctional Services Diagnostic and Evaluation Center (DEC) was established by the Nebraska State Legislature in 1976 as part of Legislative Bill 984. Construction was completed in June 1979 and the new institution was opened in August 1979 as a 176-bed, maximum custody, reception, diagnostic, evaluation, assessment, classification and assignment facility. Due to the short length of stay at the institution, there are no industry programs and limited education programs. Each newly admitted inmate, following review of the admission order to ensure legal commitment, begins participation in an intensive medical, psychological, and social assessment process. This process culminates in the finalization of an individual classification study and specific programming recommendations to the Classification Officer relative to custody status and institutional placement. Varied program services are offered and encouraged through recreation and library programs. The maintenance of family and community ties is encouraged through the visitation, mail and telephone programs. Religious programming is also available to the inmate population. Several other opportunities including Alcoholics Anonymous, parenting classes, and a prerelease program are available for inmate participation. The average daily population is 366, with a staff of 142.

The Hastings Correctional Center is a detention center housing persons detained by ICE (Immigration and Customs Enforcement), which is a division of Homeland Security. The Hastings Correctional Center first opened on June 22, 1987. It originally housed community custody inmates, but soon became a minimum custody correctional facility. The Hastings Correctional Center stopped housing inmates and began housing immigration detainees in June 2002. The facility can house up to 185 detainees, with a staff of 80. Programs include: Academic Education (ABE/GED); Remedial Reading and Mathematics;

Pre-employment Training; English as a Second Language; College Level Courses; Industries—Wood Shop, Print Shop; Pre-Release; Non-Residential Substance Abuse; Inpatient Mental Health Program; and Inpatient Sex Offender Program. The average population is 452 and the staff is 232.

The Nebraska Correctional Center for Women (NCCW), located just west of York, Nebraska, is the only secure state correctional facility for adult women. Up to 80% of NCCW's population have self-reported substance abuse problems or history of involvement in domestic violence as an adult or as a child. Rather than merely addressing the symptoms, staff at NCCW attempt to focus on the roots of the problem(s). Education and training that encourages personal responsibility and fosters self-reliance is provided. NCCW houses all classifications levels of female inmates (except community A and B) including new commitments, court-ordered evaluators and safekeepers from county facilities. The average daily population is 274 with a staff of 89.

The Work Ethic Camp program is designed for first-time, nonviolent male and female offenders who would otherwise be prison bound. The program is based on a 120-day stay, but offenders may be kept up to 180 days. The offenders must be convicted as an adult of a felony offense. They will be sentenced to successfully complete the Work Ethic Camp as a condition of intensive supervision probation. Following their stay at the Work Ethic Camp, the offender will be returned to the community, and probation supervision will continue by local probation staff. The average daily population is 252, there is 70 on staff.

The Nebraska State Penitentiary (NSP) located in Lincoln is the oldest state correctional facility in Nebraska, opening in 1869. Until after World War I, it was the only adult correctional facility in the state. The NSP offers a variety of education/rehabilitation programs designed to enhance an inmate's chances for successful community adjustment upon release. These include Educational/Life Skills and Vocational Programs, Self-Improvement (Mental Health and Control Unit Program), Residential Treatment Community (RTC), Religious Programming and Self-Betterment Activities), and Support Services. The NSP is the site of major components of the Agency's Cornhusker State Industries program. The average daily population of the facility is 1,014 with a staff of 453. Also, the facility houses 130 male and 24 female inmates who are classified at Community A or B custody levels. Normally, inmates who are near the discharge of their sentence or pending parole hearings are selected for placement in CCC-O. The institution employs 24 full-time staff members that supervise or manage inmate programs. Programs include: Alcoholics Anonymous support groups, Narcotics Anonymous, Sub-

stance Abuse Counseling, Educational Class, Self-Change Group, Relapse Prevention Group, Aftercare Group, Academic Education Program (GED), Testing, Assessment, Tutoring, Referrals to Community based Counseling programs, and Christian Fellowship.

All inmates at the Tecumseh State Correctional Institution (TSCI) are males adjudicated as adults and classified as medium or maximum custody. (Approximately 30 minimum custody inmates are housed at TSCI for outside grounds, administration building and warehouse jobs.) The institution has a design capacity for 960 inmates, which includes 768 nonspecial management beds, 32 min. B, 32 SAU, 64 PC beds, and a 192-bed special management unit for Administrative Segregation, Disciplinary Segregation and Intensive Management inmates. Death Row inmates will be housed at TSCI, but the death penalty will continue to be administered at the Nebraska State Penitentiary in Lincoln, Nebraska.

TSCI uses a Unit Management concept designed to improve control and staff/inmate relationships by dividing the larger institution population into smaller, more manageable groups and to improve and personalize the delivery of rehabilitative services. Programs include: Mental Health Counseling, ABE/GED, College Correspondence Courses, Substance Abuse Counseling, Residential and Non-Residential, Alcoholics Anonymous, self betterment clubs, volunteer activities, prerelease programs, English as a Second Language (ESL), work programs to include traditional facility work programs, and Cornhusker State Industries. Inmates at the facility are afforded educational opportunities provided by Metropolitan Community College. Additionally, the facility attempts to meet the emotional and spiritual needs of the inmates through the programs and services of the religious activities. Treatment programming is always at capacity due to the sizable number of drug and sex offenders at the Tecumseh State Correctional Institution. The facility is always looking for committed citizens that have an interest in helping our inmates as volunteers. Volunteers are a vital part of the restorative programming. Through programming, the facility has been able to reduce inmate idleness. The average daily population is 858 and the institution has a staff of 391.

Nevada. There are currently 8 institutions, 10 conservation camps, and 1 restitution center administered by the Department of Corrections. In addition, there is one privately administered institution in Las Vegas. The state operates a large correctional industry. In 2003 it made a profit of nearly a half million dollars, which was returned to the state. They manufacture mattresses, draperies, printing services, metal products, furniture, and a host of other products.

There is also a large victim-services program. The Victim Services Unit within the Nevada Department of Corrections (NDOC) serves as a point of contact within corrections that is sensitive to the needs of crime victims. Through this office, crime victims, their family members, and interested or threatened parties can receive assistance with any of the following: registration of all crime victims for the notification of release of their offender from custody, victim notification of an inmate's release or escape, advocacy on behalf of victims concerning their particular needs in the correctional process, including but not limited to: situations involving harassment by inmates, compliance with court mandated conditions, general information regarding the status of offenders in the custody of or under the supervision of NDOC referrals for crime victims to other state, and federal and community based services. In addition, the unit provides notification of execution dates along with preparation and orientation for victims who choose to be present at an execution.

The Going Home Prepared program is designed to provide Serious and Violent Offenders in Nevada with prerelease and transitional services. The program was designed through a grant for $1.4 million from the U.S. Department of Justice and 7 other federal agencies.

Other programs offered at various institutions include educational opportunities, work opportunities, training, counseling, and substance abuse therapy.

The Ely State Prison has a designed capacity for 784, but carries, generally, an inmate population of 969. The Ely Conservation Camp has a maximum capacity of 150, which is its operating capacity currently. The High Desert State Prison is the largest major institution in the Department of Corrections. It is the first institution in what will become a large southern Nevada prison complex. High Desert was designed to incorporate much of the best technology available to corrections to provide for officer safety and the management and control of inmates. The complex totals approximately 1,576,000 square feet of space. The institution opened September 1, 2000, and became the reception unit for Southern Nevada.

The Lovelock Correctional Center contains four 168-cell housing units and two 84-cell units. Each 80 square foot cell has two bunks. There is also a dormitory outside the main compound to house minimum custody offenders who work in the Regional Warehouse and the institutional maintenance shops. The Nevada State Prison (NSP), located in Carson City, Nevada, is one of the oldest prisons still in operation in the United States. Established in 1862 when the Nevada legislature purchased the Warm Springs Hotel and 20 acres of land for $80,000, NSP has been in continuous operation since that time. Abraham Curry, who owned the hotel, was appointed as the first warden. Its design capacity is 591,

while its operating capacity is 791 inmates. There are a variety of inmate programs, including education, training, counseling, and therapy as well as religious programming. The Northern Nevada Correctional Center in Carson City has a design capacity of 922 and an inmate population of 1,174.

The Stewart Conservation Camp has a population of 240, its design limit. The Warm Springs Correctional Center (WSCC), Northern Nevada Restitution Center (NNRC) and the Silver Springs Conservation Camp, together make up a Tri-Facility Organization.

The NNRC is located at 2595 East Second Street in Reno, Nevada. NNRC is a community-based facility housing approximately ninety-five male inmates that meet stringent classification standards including a requirement that they have no history of violent or sex-related crimes and that they be within one year of probable parole release or expiration. This program offers an opportunity for inmates to establish employment in the community to better prepare themselves for release, address court ordered fees/fines, and meet restitution obligations.

The Southern Desert Correctional Center has a design capacity of 914, but actually houses 1,354 inmates, while the sister institution, Indian Springs Conservation Camp houses a maximum of 228 inmates. The Southern Nevada Correctional Center closed its doors in September 2000 when the High Desert State Prison opened. A maintenance staff of two remains to maintain the institution. The Rural Camp Warden and his administrative staff are also currently housed at the Southern Nevada Correctional Center. The Jean Conservation Camp is immediately adjacent to the institution and remained open as a women's facility when the institution closed. The camp was constructed from modular housing units originally used on the Alaskan pipeline construction project. These units have been replaced by a new 240 bed camp almost identical to the Stewart Conservation Camp.

The Southern Nevada Women's Correctional Facility was designed to hold 291, but currently holds 379 female inmates. Finally, the WSCC was authorized by and constructed through appropriations from the 1961 legislative session and was a women's prison until September 1997 when it was converted to a medium-security men's prison. The institution has been remodeled and expanded four times over the years. The completion of this project in July 1998 brought the budgeted capacity of WSCC from 260 to 510 inmates.

New Hampshire. At the end of 2003, there were 2,486 inmates in state prison facilities. The New Hampshire Department of Corrections (NHDOC) operates four facilities, including one specifically for women. The first prison was opened in 1812 and in that year housed one prisoner. Within 20 years, there were 101 prisoners. The total daily average for the system population in 2003 was 2,433 of which 105 were women. Of the total population, 136 were in community supervision. There are 1,161 employees in the system. Offenders can be charged with 77 various infractions of prison rules, including the possession of tobacco, which is prohibited in all NHDOC facilities.

The system received several grants to support inmate educational opportunities, including college courses taken inside the institution. Grants also support a substance abuse program. The Going Home Reentry Initiative, in the amount of approximately $1.8 million, was awarded to the DOC to support a pilot project in the city of Manchester designed to assist offenders with successfully transitioning from prison to the community. Services under this grant are available to offenders ages 18-35 that resided in Manchester prior to their incarceration at one of the state's prison facilities. Transition services for these offenders will include assistance in finding housing and employment, access to substance abuse treatment and mental health services, and access to further education and training for employment. The grant supports a total of 8 staff positions, including 4 Reentry Advocates to work directly with offenders transitioning into the Manchester community. The New Hampshire Department of Health and Human Services supports the Family Connections Project with another grant, assisting families of inmates.

Victim services include a number of support services, including notification of inmate custody changes, advocacy and support during inmate reduced custody processes, accompaniment and advocacy at parole hearings, protection from offender intimidation and harassment, outreach, information and referral, tours of correctional facilities, victim-offender dialogue (by victim request), and participation with IMPACT programming. This is an educational, self-improvement program available to inmates at Lakes Region Facility, NH State Prison for Men, and Northern NH Correctional Facility. Correctional staff and volunteers serve as IMPACT instructors. IMPACT classes include discussions, written exercises, and guest presentations to teach offenders about the physical, emotional and financial impacts of crime. The office supported 1,065 victims in 2003.

Community Corrections manages the Probation Academy program. The statewide program began in January 1996 as an alternative sentencing option for nonviolent, low-risk offenders. It is a one-year-long intensive and comprehensive program of both punishment and rehabilitation. The participant must satisfactorily complete a core curriculum of: living skills; parenting; stress management; money management; nutrition; counseling depending on need; educational/vocational courses depending on need; and substance abuse self-help programs.

New Jersey. The New Jersey Department of Corrections (NJDOC) is responsible for 14 major institutions—eight adult male correctional facilities, three youth facilities, one facility for sex offenders, one women's correctional institution, and a central reception/intake unit as well as a Stabilization and Reintegration Facility. These facilities collectively house approximately 26,386 inmates in minimum, medium and maximum security levels as of January 2004. This total includes 4,324 in the youth facility. The annual institutional cost per inmate is approximately $28,000. Approximately 14,000 inmates were committed to NJDOC institutions during the 2003 calendar year. It is anticipated that roughly 1,200 inmates per month will be incarcerated in 2004. Approximately the same number were released each year as are admitted. The median term for NJDOC inmates is six years. Forty-seven percent of all NJDOC inmates are serving terms of one-to-five years; 17 percent are serving terms of six-to-nine years; and 33 percent are serving maximum sentences of 10 years or more. Approximately 40% of all inmates were sentenced for violent crimes.

As of January 2003, 63 percent of all state correctional institutional offenders were African American, 19 percent were Caucasians, 17 percent were Hispanic and 1 percent represented other racial/ethnic backgrounds. (In these tabulations, a Hispanic is an individual of Mexican, Puerto Rican, Cuban, South American, or other Spanish culture or origin, regardless of skin color.)

In order to counter rising gang problems in the prisons, the Security Threat Group Management Unit (STGMU) was established to isolate problem gang members, control their behavior and prevent any activity. DEPTCOR is New Jersey's correctional industry program. An entity within the New Jersey Department of Corrections, DEPTCOR provides products and services manufactured by adults incarcerated in New Jersey's correctional system. DEPTCOR's factories and service industries throughout the state employ over 1,800 incarcerated males and females. These offenders are voluntarily assigned to meaningful work situations that help them develop useable skills and positive work habits. The Stabilization and Reintegration Program (SRP) is a comprehensive blend of military structure and discipline, education, work, substance abuse treatment, cognitive skills training, and intensive aftercare supervision. The role of the Office of Educational Services is to supervise, support and ensure delivery of educational services, recreational activities and law library services to the students it serves. The Department of Corrections provides mandatory educational services in all 14 of its primary facilities for grades K through 12 for every inmate under the age of 20. Education programs are on a voluntary basis for the remainder of the inmate population. The system also offers work crews to local governments, therapeutic services for inmates, and victim services including alerts and support.

New Mexico. Adult Prisons is the largest division in the New Mexico Corrections Department (NMCD) with an overall FY2003 budget of $165 million for inmate management and control. There are a total of 6,200 incarcerated adult offenders, 518 of whom are women. Nearly 3,500 of these inmates are of Hispanic origin, while 1,355 are white, 588 are Native American, and the rest are scattered over several ethnic groupings. The average daily population in 2004 was 6,607.

These offenders are housed in 10 different facilities: 5 public prisons and 5 private facilities. Security and nonsecurity staff are responsible for providing a humane, safe, secure and cost effective prison system. The Director of Adult Prisons is ultimately responsible for the secure operation of all adult institutions, including inmate initiatives, health service requirements and quality of life issues. Services available for inmates include addiction, education, health services, family services, faith based services, mental health services, and volunteer based services. The Office of Corrections Family Services was established as a central point of contact between the Corrections Department, family members, legislative entities, interdepartmental state agencies and the general public. Corrections Family Services promotes open lines of communication and provides clarification, direction, and resources for keeping families involved and informed. The office responds to inquiries regarding the Department's policies, procedures, and actions, in addition to facilitating problem resolution. The Corrections Industries Division (CID) enhances the rehabilitation, education and vocational skills of inmates through productive involvement in enterprises and public works of benefit to state agencies and local public bodies and to minimize inmate idleness. CID is administered without appropriated funds and is self-supporting. The Division is financed through a revolving fund, from which all operating expenses are paid. As the manufacturing and services arm of the Corrections Department, the Division employs 39 staff and supervisory personnel to manage an average of 375 inmates in 13 programs at eight different facilities around the state.

Community Corrections Programs primarily serve offenders in the community who are judged to be at higher risk to reoffend and thus have greater treatment needs. Community Corrections programs also serve as a diversionary program for probation/parole violators who would otherwise be incarcerated. Drug courts are designed to provide community-based treatment and supervision to selected offenders who are identified as having substance abuse issues. Drug courts work closely with the judges, prosecutors, defense attorneys, probation/parole authorities and other corrections personnel, law enforcement, pretrial service agencies, law enforcement, vocational rehabilitation, education and housing, and treatment providers.

New York. The Department of Correctional Services operates 70 institutions statewide, which hold approximately 70,000 inmates. The department's mission is to provide for public protection by administering a network of correctional facilities that: (1) retain inmates in safe custody until released by law; (2) offer inmates an opportunity to improve their employment potential and their ability to function in a noncriminal fashion; (3) offer staff a variety of opportunities for career enrichment and advancement; and, (4) offer stable and humane "community" environments in which all participants, staff and inmates, can perform their required tasks with a sense of satisfaction.

The number of inmates in New York State prisons stood at 71,472 by the close of calendar year 2000. This represents an increase of 2.1 percent or +1,471 inmates from the previous year and an increase of 489 percent from a low of 12,144 inmates on December 31, 1972. Prior to 1972, the prison population had declined following a series of executive, legislative, and judicial actions which diverted a number of offenders to other agencies. In 1973 admissions exceeded prison releases for the first time since 1963 and the prison population increased. This increase continued annually through 1996. Since 1972 the number of women in prison has risen at a higher rate than the increase for men. At the close of 1999, the female population stood at 3,508. This represents a rise of 784% over the 397 at the close of 1972. The male population has risen at a lower rate, but at a much greater volume, growing by 55,917 (+464%) from a 12,047 low in 1972 to 67,964 by the close of 1999.

There were 16,889 inmates released to parole supervision for the first time on their current sentence in 1999. The average time served by these offenders in combined Department and local jail custody was 36.6 months. Violent felony offenders had the highest average time served at 60.8 months. Juvenile offenders served an average time of 35.1 months, followed by other coercive felons at 33.4 months, drug felons at 29.6 months, property/other felons at 25 months and youthful offenders at 17.7 months. As expected, persons convicted of murder served the longest time, 254.7 months followed by first degree manslaughter at 124 months and first degree rape at 108.3 months. Of the total incarcerated, 51% are black, 16% are white,

31.3% are Hispanic, and the balance is classified as "other" (1.7%). While 8.7% of this population actually holds a college degree, only 47.4% can claim at least 11th to 12th grade education. Over 14.1% cannot claim an education above 8th grade with another 28.9% claiming a 9th or 10th grade education.

The division of Probation and Correctional Alternatives oversees probation and juvenile probation. There are approximately 250,000 individuals under supervision on any given day. Approximately 100,000 new cases are opened each year. The Division of Parole oversees all parolees. There are approximately 70,000 on parole. Parole Officers with institutional assignments conduct an assessment of the needs of each inmate and encourage the inmates' participation in programming in prison which meets these needs. They also provide discharge planning so that, upon release, parolees can be referred to community programs appropriate to identified needs. These Parole Officers conduct inmate group counseling sessions and Parole orientation classes for inmates. Additionally, they interview inmates in advance of their Board release interviews to gather information which is presented to the Board in summary reports together with recommendations for the granting or denial of parole release and possible conditions of release. After a parolee has been granted release, the Parole Officer continues to participate in Parole Board release planning through the Community Preparation Program. The Parole Officer provides the link between the institution and the community both through prerelease interviews conducted with inmates and through ongoing communication with the Field Area Office to which the parolee is to be released. These services are provided to inmates released by decision of the Parole Board and to those conditionally released. Community supervision is at the heart of the Division's mission. The Parole Officer with a field assignment is located in the community supervising offenders released from state correctional and youth facilities as well as those judicially sanctioned. Community protection requires that Parole Officers adhere to strict supervision standards. Additionally, it is essential to ensure that parolees comply with the terms and conditions of release. When the conditions of release are violated, the Parole Officer must take appropriate action.

North Carolina. The Department of Correction operates 23 prisons, with three more either planned or under construction. In addition, there are three small private prisons under contract with the state for special populations. On October 1, 2000, North Carolina's two-year experiment with privately run prisons came to an end as the Department of Correction assumed control of Amlico Correctional Institution in Bayboro and Mountain View Correctional Institution in Spruce Pine. Both facilities

were opened by Corrections Corporation of America (CCA) in 1998. CCA continues to own the facilities and leases them to the state. As of July 31, 2004, there was a total of 34,978 inmates in the system, of which 2,350 are women. Whites account for 11,863, while black inmates number 21,017. There are 649 Native Americans, 105 Asians, and 1,300 classified as either other or unknown. The probation population included 26,307 females, and 88,290 males while those on parole number 3,520.

The Cognitive Behavioral Interventions program attempts to change the thinking patterns of offenders. The program addresses concepts such as Cognitive Self-Change, Social Skills, Group Dynamics, Problem Solving, and Presentation skills. Through the Going Home Initiative, the state of North Carolina created a systemic prerelease, community transition and reentry infrastructure. Many services necessary to successful transition and reentry are available, however, they are not systemically coordinated as a seamless system among state and local government agencies, community-based organizations including faith-based initiatives, community-based treatment providers, the offender, the offender's family, victim advocates, or the community at large.

The goal of Job Start II is provide job skills for inmates prior to release, match them with jobs on the outside before release, and attach them to a mentor for follow-up and support. In this manner, reentry will be more successful and sustainable.

North Dakota. The Department of Correction and Rehabilitation Prisons Division includes three separate prisons located in three different areas. The North Dakota State Penitentiary was established in Bismarck in 1885, and houses 520 maximum- and medium-security male inmates. The goal of the prison is to keep the public safe, while also offering rehabilitative work, treatment, and educational programs that will effect change in the inmate's behavior. The James River Correctional Center was opened in 1998 on the grounds of the state hospital in Jamestown. This facility can house 160 male and 80 female medium security inmates. The Missouri River Correctional Center (MRCC) located 4 miles southwest of Bismarck, was first established in the 1940s as the State Farm. It has since grown to a 150-bed facility for minimum security males and females. Although some agricultural work is still performed there, the current purpose of the MRCC is to reintegrate offenders into society by offering work release and community treatment programming. The average daily population during 2002 was 1,160, with 823 new admissions and 798 releases during that year. The average sentence across the entire offender population was 43 months.

With the addition of the James River Correctional Center, as of April 1998, the Adult Services Division has been reorganized. It is now comprised of the ND Department of Corrections and Rehabilitation Prisons Division and the ND Department of Corrections and Rehabilitation Field Services Division (formerly Division of Parole and Probation). As of September 2000, the Field Services Division employs 72 professional staff in 14 district offices around the State of ND and 15 in the central office in Bismarck. The offender population under active supervision is 130 on parole, 2,719 on probation, 33 on community placement and 399 on Interstate Compact for a total of approximately 3,281.

The Corrections Rehabilitation and Recovery Program (CRRP) is a 25-bed male addiction treatment program. It is located at the NDSH in Jamestown. CRRP is a minimum of 100 days in residence for primary treatment with 4 levels of restrictions and earned privileges. The offender's release to the community includes up to 180 days of supervision and transition. This coordinated treatment and corrections strategy is a minimum of 100 days up to 280 days.

The Last Chance Program began during the fall of 1999, in Fargo, for the purpose of giving offenders "one last chance" to remain in the community, to participate and complete programming, and remain crime and violation-free. Though six to eight criminal offenders can reside at the Last Chance house, other offenders are able to participate while remaining in their homes. Placement in the Last Chance Program is restricted to those offenders who, "if not for their participation and successful completion of the program," would have their supervision revoked and face being sentenced to prison. Electronic monitoring systems are utilized by the Division to verify compliance with conditions of supervision such as curfew, house arrest, alcohol use, or home confinement. The division has access to active and passive monitoring systems. There are also a variety of educational, work, and counseling services for inmates.

Ohio. The Department of Rehabilitation and Correction currently has 32 institutions confining nearly 44,000 inmates. Three of those institutions house female inmates. The remaining institutions house male inmates of varying security levels. Ohio's first "supermax" prison, the Ohio State Penitentiary, opened in Youngstown in April 1998. Ohio also has two boot camps, one for each gender, aimed at young, first-time, nonviolent offenders. The State of Ohio also has two privately-operated prisons: the North Coast Correctional Treatment Facility in Grafton and the Lake Erie Correctional Institution in Conneaut. There are over 50,000 inmates on an average day, and commitments total over 20,000 per year. The population is almost equally divided between black and white inmates, with a small number classified as Hispanic or Native American.

The Division of Parole and Community Services, the community corrections division of the Ohio Department of Rehabilitation and Correction, consists of four primary areas: The Adult Parole Authority, the Bureau of Adult Detention, the Bureau of Community Sanctions, and the Office of Victim Services.

The community service program allows inmates an opportunity to give back to the community while at the same time supporting the Department's restorative justice initiative of making a contribution to society. The program alleviates boredom and tension in prison, resulting in a safer environment for both staff and inmates. Safer prisons help establish a sense of security within Ohio communities and give offenders a sense of pride and accomplishment as they provide needed services to various organizations throughout the state.

There is a strong victim services program, with support links to national groups, and information regarding inmate status. Beyond notification of inmate status, the office also provides crisis intervention for victims.

Oklahoma. The Department of Corrections operates 4 maximum-security prisons, 8 medium security installations, and 16 minimum-security prisons. In addition, it also has 15 work centers and 6 community correction facilities. There are 16,609 inmates in the prisons, 6,249 in private contract prisons, 28,912 on probation, and 4,808 on parole. The system totals 57,015 under some form of supervision. Of the inmate population, 58.4% are white, 28.1% black, and 8.5% are Native American. 90% of the inmate population is male. Of the population on probation, 75% are male and it is 65% white, and 19% black. On parole, 81% are male, 56% white and 31% black. Nearly 5,000 employees make up the system staff.

Services for offenders primarily are religious, educational, training, and alcohol and drug counseling. There is also an active victims program. Victims are notified when the inmate changes locations, is released/discharged, escapes, is recaptured or dies while incarcerated. Other services provided are the development of policy, training advising staff and inmates on victim sensitivity issues, maintaining a resource directory for crime victims, publishing a victim newsletter, supporting the victims at Pardon and Parole Board hearings, educating the public on department services and victim awareness, acting as a central source of information for victims, and assisting victim support groups statewide.

The Population Office is responsible for scheduling inmate movements throughout the Department of Corrections including contract facilities. During calendar year 2000, the Population Office received a total of 12,878 transfer requests, 1,411 requests for transfer to higher security, 6,105 requests for transfer to lower security,

4,329 lateral transfer requests (to same security level) and a total of 1,033 transfer requests were denied by the population office. LARC Case Management is responsible for the case management of all inmates received through the Assessment and Reception Center. During the calendar year 2000, a total of 7,681 inmates were received at ARC, 6,548 males and 1,133 females. A total of 7,767 initial classifications were completed before transfer to the Department of Corrections facilities and contract facilities. Reentry services include the coordination of a continuum of offender services that begin with program assessment at ARC, extends to program assignment at facilities, includes transition services to the community, with after-care services. Reentry coordination includes the facilitation of a transfer of information within the DOC regarding the programmatic completions and needs of the offender. Programmatic information will also be forwarded to other state and local agencies that need assistance with offender re-entry.

Oregon. The Oregon Department of Corrections (DOC) was created by the 64th Legislative Assembly in June 1987. The department has custody of offenders sentenced to prison for more than 12 months. Oregon houses offenders in 12 state prisons. The Oregon Department of Corrections is recognized nationally among correctional agencies for providing inmates with the cognitive, behavioral and job skills they need to become productive citizens. Oregon's recidivism rate is about 30 percent, well below the national average. The department currently has 3,704 employees and houses 12,264 inmates, of which 844 are female. There are a total of 11,475 on parole (1,498 women), and 17,389 on probation (4,903 women). The population in each category is overwhelmingly white, with a small number of Asian, African American, Hispanic, and Native American inmates. There are sex offender programs, educational opportunities, and counseling resources for inmates.

The Oregon Accountability Model (OAM) encompasses the simultaneous, coordinated and efficient implementation of many Department of Corrections initiatives and projects that provide a foundation for inmates to lead successful lives upon release. The Oregon Accountability Model has six components. Each of these components stands on its own as a project or a part of the corrections organization and culture. However, woven together, these six separate components strengthens the department's ability to hold inmates/offenders accountable for their actions and DOC staff accountable for achieving the mission and vision of the department.

The department is involved in a statewide project that focuses on transition as a seamless movement of offenders from the community to incarceration to com-munity supervision. The project limits duplication of services and increases effective and efficient use of partnerships. Seven of the department's prisons have been identified as reentry facilities. These prisons are strategically located to encourage reach-in by the community. Connections with the community before release are important factors in offenders' successes on the outside, and may include work, treatment, religion, and housing. Reentry prisons will be geared to preparing inmates for release during their last six months of incarceration.

Pennsylvania. The Department of Corrections operates 26 prisons and 14 community corrections centers in which it manages more than 40,000 inmates and employs 15,000 people. The rate of admission to the system grew by over 37% between 1992 and 2002, with 13,387 admissions in 2002. In that same period, parole violator admissions increased by over 53%. In August 2004, there were 40,524 inmates in the system, putting the system at 108% of capacity. There are also 46 privately operated community corrections centers. In those centers and the 14 state operated centers, there are a total of 2,762 individuals. All inmates are screened upon admission, and currently, more than 70% require some form of alcohol or drug treatment programs, a figure consistent with national averages. Recent outcome evaluations by Temple University suggest that the Therapeutic Community approach employed by the department reduced recidivism by more than 27%, again consistent with national evidence. Over 84% of the inmates participate in the religious services programs and there are 150 chaplains in the system staff. Over 2,700 citizens volunteer their time for various support services for inmates and victims. There are a wide variety of counseling, education, training and work programs available for inmates, and families can have "virtual visits" with the use of network based video conferencing. The Department has started a COR program for inmates just prior to release and following release. The Community Orientation and Reintegration program seeks to provide support services for inmates to make their transition successful.

Rhode Island. The mission of the Rhode Island Department of Corrections (RIDOC) is to contribute to public safety by maintaining a balanced correctional system of institutional and community programs which provide a range of control and rehabilitation options for criminal offenders.

The department operates 8 institutions, with two dedicated to female inmates. As of 2003, the capacity for the male system was 3,563 while the average population was 3,209. The female capacity was 340 with the average population at 217.

Correctional industries is a major component of inmate rehabilitation in Rhode Island. Using structured employment and training programs under the supervision of skilled civilian craftspeople, incarcerated men and women work in normal industrial or shop settings, learn various trades and develop good work habits. The tasks inmates perform are meaningful, challenging and demanding.

The Division of Rehabilitative Services is committed to the meaningful reintegration of offenders into the community. Program areas within this Division can be categorized into two sections: institutional or community corrections. Institutional corrections includes programming offered to the offender during incarceration, such as health services, education, substance abuse counseling and sex offender treatment. Community corrections refers to units such as Probation and Parole, Community Confinement, Furlough and Victim Services.

South Carolina. The state penal system began in 1866 when the state legislature transferred custody of those convicted of state law from county jails to the new department of corrections. The South Carolina Department of Corrections operates twenty-nine prisons statewide. Male institutions are categorized as either minimum security (level 1), medium security (level 2), or medium/maximum security (level 3); female institutions are categorized as level 4 and provide minimum through maximum security. An institution's security level is determined by the type of internal and external security features, housing within the institution, and level of security staffing. Inmates are assigned to institutions to meet their specific security, programming, medical, educational, and work requirements. There are currently 23,613 inmates in these institutions with an average daily population of 22,845 in 2003. The average age at admission is 30. Over 69% of the inmate population is African American, while only 30% is white. Over 78% are new inmates on admission. The average time served is less than 2 years overall.

The Division of Industries serves the Department of Corrections and the state of South Carolina by employing and training inmates. This training oriented work allows the inmates to return to society with skills that will enable them to become useful and productive citizens. In pursuit of this objective, the cost of incarceration is offset through inmate wages, and quality products and services are provided to qualified businesses and organizations at substantial savings. Products include a variety of furniture and other commodities.

A broad variety of services are also provided to victims of crime. The Division of Victim Services consists of five full-time employees. The program is housed in the Office of Executive Affairs, which reports directly to the Director. The organizational placement of the program is important. Having Victim Services on the Director's executive staff sends the message throughout the 31 institutions and among the 6,700 employees that they are to carry out their responsibilities with sensitivity and special attention to the rights of crime victims. Elevation of the program to division-level status gave victim services status equal to that of programs for inmates.

Pet therapy has been employed for inmates. The first group of retired racing greyhounds from Greyhound Pets of America (GPA) entered the Camille Griffin Graham Correctional Institution of the South Carolina Department of Corrections on October 21, 2002. This program is the first of its kind in the United States. All funding is handled by GPA. In the first year, 50 greyhounds have been housed and trained at the prison before going to their adoptive homes.

There is also a crime prevention program involving the department. "Operation Behind Bars" is a modified version of the old "Scared Straight" program which utilizes a more realistic approach with the participants rather than scare tactics. The program, targeted toward at risk youth and adults, allows each participant to tour a prison facility and then hear inmates give realistic accounts of actions that led to their criminal behavior, the effects of incarceration and day to day prison life. Currently, there are 11 prisons located throughout the state that participate in the Operation Behind Bars program. There were 71 people on death row in 2003 (34 African American and 37 white), with 2 executed.

South Dakota. The Adult Corrections System consists of the three main adult facilities, a prison annex, three trusty units, prison industries and parole. The state also runs local jails. In July 2004 there were a total of 3,052 inmates in the various facilities of the system. Of that, 2,174 were white, 756 were Native American, and 144 were African American. Predictably, the vast majority are male, 316 being female.

The Board of Pardons and Paroles is a nine-member appointed board charged with the authority to make decisions of parole, the revocation of parole, and parole policy and procedure. Three of the board members are appointed by the Governor of South Dakota, three are appointed by Attorney General, and the remaining three are appointed by the South Dakota Supreme Court. One of the appointees by each appointing authority must be an attorney. Each member of the board must be a resident of South Dakota and be appointed with the advice and consent of the Senate.

The prison industries unit produces garments, upholstery, furniture, license plates, data entry, and includes a printing shop and sign shop. Today, more than 600 inmates are employed in community service work projects statewide. Inmates not only work side by side with state employees on the day to day activities in state government, but also are working in communities, with nonprofit agencies, and with federal government agencies. The work experiences have provided them with the tools and skills to make them productive members of the community when they are released. Inmates are becoming proficient in all facets of the construction trades, office skills, auto body repair, metal fabrication, building maintenance, heating and air conditioning, horticulture, welding, conservation and upholstery.

In order to assist inmates' reentry into society, the department created the FORWARD program. The FORWARD program was created for inmates who are at risk to remain in prison beyond their parole date because they are not able to put together an acceptable parole plan. Inmates who are at high risk for parole violation or recidivism due to life skill deficits are also targeted in the programming. Inmates participate in the Life Skills Programming through FORWARD when they are within one year of release from prison through six months after release. The department also offers a victim's services program including support, offender status notification, and links to other support networks. The department also operates all juvenile programs in the state.

Tennessee. The Tennessee Department of Correction was one of the first departments in the country to become fully accredited by the American Correctional Association. Only a handful of departments nationwide are fully accredited. The Tennessee Department of Correction supervises more than 20,000 inmates and employs more than 5,000 people. There are 15 prisons in the state system, three of which are managed privately by the Corrections Corporation of America. Female inmates in the State of Tennessee are housed in two prisons, one which is located in Nashville and the other in Memphis. Male inmates are housed in the 13 other prisons located across the state. Those inmates in need of acute or continuing medical care are housed at the Lois M. DeBerry Special Needs Facility in Nashville.

There are currently 19,139 men and women incarcerated in state institutions, of these, 100 are on death row. There are also 35,636 felons on probation, 975 on ISP, 5,777 on community corrections programs, and 4,105 held in local (nonstate operated) jails.

Statistics show that 97 percent of all incarcerated felons are eventually released from prison. Hence, the department offers programs that will help educate and rehabilitate inmates. Services for inmates include educational opportunities. Currently, there are more than 16,000 inmates enrolled in educational programs. The department employs 52 academic instructors, 63 vocational instructors, 7 principals and 8 teaching assistants. Treatments include specific programs for sex offenders, anger management, cognitive therapy, and changing patterns of criminal thinking, among others.

In 2003 the department took a major step toward helping inmates reenter society by assigning a full-time prerelease coordinator to each state managed facility. While attending prerelease classes, inmates learn how to change criminal thinking patterns through a 22-session course called Thinking for a Change. They also attend a variety of life-skills classes on topics ranging from money management to parenting. The department, along with the Board of Probation and Parole, was recently awarded a $1 million grant to be used for an intensive reentry program called Tennessee Bridges.

In 1994 the General Assembly created TRICOR (Tennessee Rehabilitative Initiative in Correction) to put inmates to work in a real-life job setting. Overall, TRICOR offers more than 300 goods and services from office furniture to prison uniforms. Best of all, TRICOR fully funds itself and even generates revenue for the state. Each year, the program saved Tennessee taxpayers an estimated $3 million in operational costs. All TRICOR industries are located on prison property. More than 1,400 inmates work in support services roles inside all of the prisons.

Texas. The Texas Department of Criminal Justice created the Correctional Institutions Division (CID) in September 2003 through a merger of the Institutional Division, Operations Division, Private Facilities Division and the State Jail Division. The Correctional Institutions Division (CI Division) is responsible for the confinement of adult felony and state jail felony offenders who are sentenced to prison. The division oversees state prison facilities, pre-release facilities, psychiatric facilities, a Mentally Retarded Offender Program facility, medical facilities, transfer facilities, state jail facilities, and substance abuse facilities. There are expansion cellblock facilities, additional medical facilities, boot camps, and work camps colocated with several of the facilities mentioned above. The division is also responsible for Support Operations and ministering/monitoring privately operated facilities (private prisons, private state jails, a work program, preparole transfer facilities, intermediate sanction facilities, halfway houses, multiuse facilities, county jails, substance abuse facilities, and additional outpatient substance abuse facilities). There were approximately 18,000 offenders in privately operated facilities monitored by the CI Division during FY 2003.

At the end of 2002, there were a total of 668,226 offenders supervised by the Division. This includes

126,107 in prison, 438,202 in community supervision, 456 on death row, 84,328 on parole, 14,702 in state jails. The Division operates 115 institutions including 51 prisons, 7 private prisons and 17 state jails. Offenders can take advantage, if they qualify, of educational programs, counseling, job training, prison industries, and community service work.

Treatment programs include Inner Change, Freedom Initiative, Sex Offender Treatment Program, Substance Abuse Treatment Program, and Youthful Offender Program. There are also reentry programs, particularly for violent offenders. The division also offers significant assistance to crime victims including offender status notification, support for participation throughout the system (appeals, parole, etc.), and links and connections to other support services, including crime victim funds.

Utah. The Utah Department of Corrections consists of Three Main Entities: the Division of Institutional Operations, Utah Correctional Industries (UCI), and Adult Probation and Parole. The Department of Corrections Institutional Division has two prisons. The Central Utah Correctional Facility has a capacity of 1,125 and opened in 1990. The Utah State Prison, built in 1951, has a capacity of 4,500. Utah Correctional Industries Consists of 25 business partnerships, apprenticeships and training programs that help inmates develop skills to earn a sustainable wage upon release. The system offers basic education through high school, GED, literacy, life skills and other programs that educates offenders. Utah Correctional Industries offers a wide variety of training experiences, including computer assisted drafting, printing, woodworking, technical/vocational apprenticeships, and computers. The Utah prison system has increased by more than 500% between 1985 and 2002. At the same time, the state crime rate has dropped only recently, dipping about 5%. Currently, the cost per inmate year is $24,000 and the recidivism rate is about 60%, slightly better than the national average. Approximately 13,000 offenders are being supervised in communities, at a cost of approximately $2,000 per offender. The department also operates an independent Correctional Industries operation, which operates numerous manufacturing concerns, training offenders, and offering employment opportunities while incarcerated. They can furnish your office, conference room, library or other work area with industry standard products. Labor intensive services such as community work crews, general construction, roofing, asbestos abatement, and pavement crack sealing are offered as well. At UCI, citizens can purchase clothing, mattresses, interior and exterior signage, and a wide variety of printing services. In an effort to increase inmate employment numbers, the department is constantly looking for new products and services. In addition to the usual training and counseling program, there is an extensive sex offender treatment program.

Vermont. The Vermont Department of Corrections has 9 incarcerative facilities and 17 community-based facilities. The community-based facilities, also called field offices, are delineated by the services they focus on providing. There are Court and Reparative Service Units and Community Correctional Service Centers. These offices are sometimes colocated and sometimes at different addresses. In fiscal year 2003, the system had 14,488 inmates. Of that, 9,802 were on probation, and 815 were on parole. Another 1,573 were on intermediate sanctions. A major innovation by the department was creation of the Reparative Probation Program, which implemented Restorative Justice methods for handling some offenders. As of September 1998, after two years of operation, reparative boards had seen 2,421 offenders. 1,146 have successfully completed, and 233 negatively terminated and returned to court. The success rate is nearly 85 percent. Significant achievements include the establishment of reparative boards in every county of the State of Vermont, and the use of the reparative probation order by every court in the state. As of November 1, 1998, 259 Vermonters serve on 39 boards in 19 communities, and the numbers continue to grow.

The department supplies a host of programs and services to offenders, primarily risk management to address criminogenic factors in offenders, including sex offenders, domestic violence, substance abuse, and violence prevention. In addition, offenders are offered educational opportunities, and employment and training through the Vermont Correctional Industries—a separate entity that runs wholly from profits earned from the sale of products and services. In addition to reparative boards, the department employs volunteers for a variety of activities for offenders and victims.

Among others, victims services include: (1) crisis intervention, community referrals and assistance with concerns related to offender under the Department's jurisdiction, (2) information regarding the status of an offender under Department of Corrections supervision, (3) community education regarding policies and procedures of the Vermont Department of Corrections, and (4) referrals to appropriate federal, state, or local community resources, including victim service agencies.

Virginia. In 1796 a wave of reform swept the Virginia legislature, and Benjamin Latrobe was engaged to design a penitentiary house. Latrobe's facility was constructed on a site outside Richmond overlooking the James River. The facility, which received its first prisoners in 1800 and was completed in 1804, was known by generations of Virginians as the Virginia State Penitentiary or the "Pen." Today, the department of corrections is an agency of around 31,000 inmates, and nearly 13,000 employees.

2004 marked the 30th anniversary of the creation of the Virginia Department of Corrections. The department offers offenders a number of programs typical for modern prisons including education, training, work, treatment and counseling, and medical assistance.

The department operates 32 institutions, some are major institutions housing maximum to medium security prisoners, while correctional centers house medium- to minimum-security prisoners. There are also two locations with secure medical beds. It also contracts with private firms for transitional housing. The average daily population of the institutions is 25,087. There are also 47,465 on probation or parole including detention, diversion, day reporting, residential and transitional housing. They also house 500 inmates on contract from Connecticut. A unique program is the use of animal therapy in its Pound Puppies program, where inmates assist in the care of animals.

The system offers victim notification services that will keep victims aware of an offender's status. Volunteers play a significant role within the Department of Corrections. They assist in the areas of religion, substance abuse, support groups and counseling, life skills, family life programs, case management and transition programs. Volunteer opportunities exist within prison facilities and community-based correctional programs as well.

Washington. The Department of Corrections was created in 1981 by the Washington state legislature. As a partner with victims, communities and the criminal justice system, the department enhances public safety, administers criminal sanctions of the courts and correctional programs. The department consists of the Office of the Secretary and two operating offices, the Office of Correctional Operations and the Office of Administrative Services. The department employs over 7,000 men and women to administer and supervise over 17,000 offenders housed in 15 institutions and 18 work training and prerelease facilities. In addition, there are over 93,000 offender field cases, of which over 61,000 are supervised offenders in the community. There are 5 regions in the state. Each region is administered by a Regional Administrator, who provides oversight to that region's community corrections offices and facilities and reports to the Office of Correctional Operations.

The rated capacity for the 15 institutions in the system is 14,347, while the 2004 average daily population was 16,328, or 118% of capacity. Of that population, 91% are male, and 71% are white, while 20.8% are black, 3.9% are Native American, and 9.6% are of Hispanic origin. In addition, 2.7% are Asian. The average length of sentence is 21.2 months. There are 51,876 in the community corrections system. The system has a unique neighborhood probation program, where the probation officers live in the neighborhoods where their

caseload lives, keeping intense scrutiny on the population. The offending population is offered a wide array of educational opportunities, training, counseling, and medical assistance. Victim assistance includes support mechanisms and a victim notification program to alert victims of offender status.

West Virginia. The Division of Corrections, formerly a major division within the Department of Public Institutions, was established under Chapter 70, Acts of the Legislature in 1977. Under the executive reorganization of 1989, corrections became a division of the Department of Public Safety (now the Department of Military Affairs and Public Safety). The commissioner of the Division of Corrections directs the state's adult correctional system. In November 1997 oversight of the juvenile correctional institutions was transferred to the newly created Division of Juvenile Services. There are 13,700 total individuals in the system. This includes 8,300 on probation or parole, and 7,400 incarcerated. The annual cost per inmate is $20,834 or approximately $57 per day. Victim-related services include linking victims to support organizations and notifying victims of offender status and movement. Inmates may engage in the prison industries program, which provides income and skill training. The inmates manufacture a host of items including furniture, mattresses, linen, signs, inmate clothing, and welded items. They also provide services such as printing, upholstery, and digital printing. It is the mission of the West Virginia Division of Corrections to provide a safe, secure, and humane correctional system for the public, staff, and offenders. Compared to other state systems, it offers offenders fewer rehabilitation programs though education and work skill programs are offered at some locations. It operates 14 institutions along with several probation and parole locations, the latter of which are divided into northern and southern districts. The institutions include work release centers, as well as traditional medium- and maximum-security institutions.

Wisconsin. The Wisconsin Department of Corrections (DOC) operates 16 prisons with security ratings from minimum to supermaximum in locations throughout the State of Wisconsin. The Wisconsin Correctional Center System (WCCS), one of the 16 DOC institutions, is a decentralized network of 16 separate minimum-security facilities located across the state. The correctional centers are similar in that each is small in size (40 to 350 inmates) and are operationally self-contained. Only two of the facilities are fenced, and all are without traditional towers. Inmates are housed in single, double, or multiple occupant rooms. The inmates have general access to the facility's building and the grounds during designated hours of the day. Some of the correctional centers serve a specific program or population need; such as drug and alcohol treatment, education or boot camp type programming while others focus on work, community service, and similar roles.

Approximately 2,150 inmates are held in these centers. The Division of Adult Institutions operates 20 institutions statewide. In 2003 the population was 21,580 at its largest, in a system with a rated capacity of 17,769. The average age of male prisoners is 33 while the average female is 35. Of the total, 42.8% are white, 46% are black, 7.6% are Hispanic, and 2.7% are Native American. This population is over 10 times what it was in the 1970s. Due to financial constraints, the state has had to mothball new facilities for lack of funds to run them. The department offers services to inmates including educational, employment, and earning opportunities. The Community Corrections Division employs over 1,800 and has 56,652 on probation with another 11,059 on parole. The Juvenile Corrections division operates the state's entire juvenile probation and confinement system.

Wyoming. The Division of Prisons is responsible for the supervision control and custody of incarcerated felons located in four state-run correctional facilities, privately run adult community corrections facilities and out-of-state placements. Correctional facilities are located in Rawlins (Wyoming State Penitentiary), Riverton (Wyoming Honor Farm), Lusk (Wyoming Women's Center), and Newcastle (Wyoming Honor Conservation Camp/Wyoming Boot Camp). The division links and works directly with the courts, the Parole Board, Adult Community Corrections, probation and parole, and the public. The total inmate population is well over 1,800, triple the figure in 1984.

The Division of Field Services provides supervision for adults in the community who are on probation or parole, including an intensive supervision program. The division operates 20 field offices covering all 23 counties and also oversees four privately-run community correction facilities located in Casper, Cheyenne, Gillette and Rock Springs. The division provides presentencing investigation reports to assist the courts in the sentencing of offenders and provides staff and budget support to the governor-appointed seven member Board of Parole.

The Adult Community Corrections division contracts with community corrections boards which, in turn, contract for the housing of probationers, parolees and inmates with a private service provider for the operation of community corrections facilities located in Casper, Cheyenne, and Rock Springs and a private nonprofit service provider for the community correction facilities. The facilities provide the courts and parole board an alternative to incar-

ceration or traditional probation/parole supervision and they provide a transition option for the placement of offenders preparing to leave correctional facilities. In FY1998, there was an average daily population of 247 offenders and inmates in the four facilities.

The Intensive Supervision Probation program provides intensive supervision in the community for approximately 170 felony offenders (when the program is fully operational, it will supervise approximately 250 felony offenders). This program provides closer community supervision for those offenders who need it. It promotes public safety by increased surveillance and risk control strategies; promotes accountability to the victim; requires intensive treatment and educational programming focusing on offenders' problem areas; and it provides additional sanctioning options for the district court and the Board of Parole for certain prison-bound offenders. Among other programs, the state has recently reintroduced prison industries for training and cost reduction.

BIBLIOGRAPHY

Conser, James A., and Gregory D. Russell. 2000. *Law Enforcement in the United States*, Gaithersburg, MD: Aspen Publishers.

Federal Bureau of Investigation. 2002. *Crime in the United States, 2002.* Washington, DC: U.S. Department of Justice.

Hickman, Matthew J. 2002. *Census of State and Local Law Enforcement Agencies, 2000.* Washington, DC: Bureau of Justice Statistics, U.S. Department of Justice.

Johnson, David R. 1981. *American Law Enforcement: A History.* Saint Louis, MO: Forum Press.

Reaves, Brian A., and Lynn M. Bauer. 2003. *Federal Law Enforcement Officers, 2002.* Washington, DC: Bureau of Justice Statistics, U.S. Department of Justice.

Reaves, Brian A., and Andrew L. Goldberg. 1999. *Law Enforcement Management and Administrative Statistics, 1997: Data for Individual and Local Agencies with 100 or More Officers.* Washington, DC: U.S. Department of Justice.

U.S. Bureau of the Census. 2002. *Census of Governments.* Washington, DC: U.S. Bureau of the Census.

Walker, Samuel. 1992. *The Police in America: An Introduction,* 2nd ed. Boston: McGraw-Hill.

Williams, Hubert, and Patrick V. Murphy. 1990. "The Evolving Strategy of Police: A Minority View." In *Perspectives on Policing.* No. 13. Washington, DC: National Institute of Justice and Harvard University.

Wintersmith, Robert F. 1974. *Police and the Black Community.* Lexington, MA: Lexington Books.

REFERENCES

References (and for additional detail about the Albuquerque Police Department): http://www.cabq.gov/police/index.html and the City of Albuquerque 2004 Fiscal Budget; U.S. Bureau of the Census.

References (and for additional detail about the Atlanta Police Department): http://www.atlantapd.org/ and Linder & Associates Inc. (2004), Fragile Momentum: A Plan of Action for Rebuilding the Atlanta Police Department to Help Secure Atlanta's Position as Capital of the New South, New York: Linder & Associates Inc.; U.S. Bureau of the Census.

References (and for additional detail about the Baltimore Police Department): http://www.baltimorepd.org/ and the 2001 Annual Report available online; U.S. Bureau of the Census.

References (and for additional detail about the Boston Police Department): http://www.cityofboston.gov/police/; U.S. Bureau of the Census.

References (and for additional detail about the Chicago Police Department): http://www.cityofchicago.org/police and the 2002 Annual Report; U.S. Bureau of the Census.

References (and for additional detail about the Columbus Police Department): http://www.columbuspolice.org/ and the 2002 Annual Report; U.S. Bureau of the Census.

References (and for additional detail about the Dallas Police Department): http://www.dallaspolice.net/index.cfm; U.S. Bureau of the Census.

References (and for additional detail about the Denver Police Department): http://www.denvergov.org/Police/ and the 2002 Annual Report; U.S. Bureau of the Census.

References (and for additional detail about the Detroit Police Department): http://www.ci.detroit.mi.us/police/ and Egan, Paul (2003), "Detroit Cop Reform Tab May Top $100 Million," The Detroit News, http://www.detnews.com/2003/specialreport/0306/29/a01-205195.htm; U.S. Bureau of the Census.

References (and for additional detail about the Kansas City Police Department): http://www.kcpd.org/ and the 2002 Annual Report; U.S. Bureau of the Census.

References (and for additional detail about the Las Vegas Police Department): http://www.lvmpd.com/; U.S. Bureau of the Census.

References (and for additional detail about the Los Angeles Police Department): http://www.lapd.org/; U.S. Bureau of the Census.

References (and for additional detail about the Miami Police Department): http://www.miami-police.org/MiamiPD/Default.asp; U.S. Bureau of the Census.

References (and for additional detail about the New Orleans Police Department): http://www.new-orleans.la.us/home/nopd/ and Home Rule Charter; U.S. Bureau of the Census.

References (and for additional detail about the New York City Police Department): http://www.nyc.gov/html/nypd/home.html; U.S. Bureau of the Census.

References (and for additional detail about the Phoenix Police Department): http://phoenix.gov/POLICE/ and 2003 Budget Proposal; U.S. Bureau of the Census.

References (and for additional detail about the San Diego City Police Department): http://www.sannet.gov/police/; U.S. Bureau of the Census.

References (and for additional detail about the San Francisco City Police Department): http://www.sfgov.org/police; U.S. Bureau of the Census.

References (and for additional detail about the Seattle City Police Department): http://www.cityofseattle.net/police/ and the Seattle Police Department Policy Manual; U.S. Bureau of the Census.

References (and for additional detail about the Washington DC Metropolitan Police Department): http://mpdc.dc.gov/main.shtm; U.S. Bureau of the Census.

Joseph Conser
Gregory Russell
Ellen Lemley

Uruguay

———■———

Official country name: Oriental Republic of Uruguay
Capital: Montevideo
Geographic description: Located in southern South America on the northern bank of the Río de la Plata
Population: 3,415,920 (est. 2005)

■■■

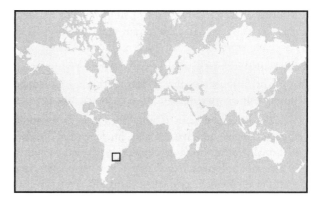

LAW ENFORCEMENT

History. The National Police of Uruguay was established in December 1829, a year after the country gained its independence, following the war between Brazil and Argentina. Article 168 of the 1967 constitution gives the president, acting through the minister of the interior, the responsibility for preserving public order. Article 173 authorizes him to appoint a chief of police for each of the nineteen departments, whom he may remove at will. These officers must have the same qualifications as senators.

Structure and Organization. The basic responsibility for law enforcement is divided between the National Police and the Maritime Police. The National Police is under the authority of the Ministry of Interior, which has the responsibility for public safety throughout the country except for the coastal areas and the shores of navigable rivers and lakes. The ministry is organized into four operating agencies (Montevideo Police, Interior Police, Highway Police, and National Corps of Firemen), three staff units (General Administration, Immigration Directorate, and Employees' Appeal Board), and a nationwide communications net. The annual police budget is about 5 percent of the national budget. Approximately 40 percent of the police force is assigned to urban areas, and the remainder to rural settlements. The chief of police of Montevideo controls three paramilitary organizations as well: the Republican Guard, the Metropolitan Guard, and the National Corps of Firemen.

The Republican Guard is a mounted unit with a strength of about 500 men and officers and commanded by an army officer. It is organized into a headquarters and service squadron of about 120 men, and two cavalry squadrons of about 190 men each. Its personnel are armed with sabers. The cavalry units are used for guard duty at police headquarters, for parades and ceremonial occasions, and for riot duty as a backup for the national police.

The Metropolitan Guard is a special elite force, with about 1,000 men in infantry-type units. Its equipment consists of machine guns, gas weapons, and fire hoses, all designed for riot situations and controlling crowds. Its members are distinguished by special training, and they are assigned as guards at public buildings such as the presidential palace and the General Assembly buildings and as escorts for important foreign dignitaries. The commander and deputy commander of the Metropolitan Guard are army officers.

The Technical Police is a branch of the Montevideo Police and has been in operation since 1945. Working in three shifts, it is on duty twenty-four hours a day. Technical operations include laboratory work, criminal identification, fingerprinting, and photography. The patronymic file contains details of all individuals charged with a crime in the past.

The Montevideo Police also includes the Feminine Police Corps. Formed in 1966 the unit provides assistance to tourists, interrogates and guards female delinquents, and transports them from police custody to the courts or prisons. Another branch is the Quick Action Unit, which undertakes operation against dissidents and guerrillas.

The Maritime Police, organized in 1925 under the Ministry of National Defense, is commanded by a director general, who is usually the second-ranking officer in the navy, and is staffed by active naval officers. The Maritime Police perform traditional Coastal Guard functions.

The National Highway Traffic Police are stationed throughout Uruguay in fourteen outposts called *destcamentos*.

The principal state security agency is the National Directorate of Information and Intelligence (Dirección Nationale de Informacion y Intelligencia), which consists of a number of specialized departments. It works in cooperation with the military intelligence agency, Antisubversive Operations Coordination Organ (Organismo Coordinador de Operaciones Antisubversivas).

Outside Montevideo there are nineteen police sections, each of which reports to the minister of interior and the chief of police. Each section has patrol zones called *radios*.

Education and Training. Police training is provided at the Police Training Academy in Montevideo, which was established in 1943. The training is conducted at two schools, one for cadets and officers and the other for enlisted men. The program for agents lasts for three months, for noncommissioned officers for one year, and for cadets for two years. The in-service qualification course for promotion for both commissioned and noncommissioned officers is for three months. In 1967 regional training courses were introduced.

Uniforms and Weapons. Lower ranks wear navy-blue blouses, gray shirts, and matching peaked caps with a high crown. Military-style uniforms are worn by officers.

Police Statistics.

- Total Police Personnel: 19,900
- Population per Police Officer: 172

HUMAN RIGHTS

Human rights are generally respected. An internal investigative police unit receives complaints of police abuse, but it is understaffed and can issue only recommendations for disciplinary actions. Police officers charged with less serious crimes may continue on active duty, but those charged with serious crimes are suspended until their cases are decided by the courts.

CRIME

Crime Statistics. Offenses reported to the police per 100,000 population: 3,002. Of which:

- Murder: 7.7
- Assault: 152.2
- Burglary: 52.3
- Automobile Theft: 130.1

CORRECTIONAL SYSTEM

The criminal justice system is governed by the penal code of 1889 as revised in 1934 by Law 9155. It consists of three books with a total of 366 articles. Thirty years without parole, rather than the death penalty, is the maximum punishment. A code for minors was enacted in 1934 and revised in 1938. It created the Juvenile Court in Montevideo.

The Ministry of Culture runs three federal prisons and a work colony. Each of the nineteen police departments has a jail for the temporary detention of prisoners, but after sentencing the prisoners are transported as soon as possible to one of the federal institutions, all of which are in the vicinity of Montevideo. Two of the prisons—known as Prison 1 and Prison 2—are for men, while Prison 3, known as the Establishment for the Correction and Detention of Women, is for female prisoners. The other federal facility is known as the Educational Colony for Work.

Article 70 of the penal code provides that inmates of rural minimum-security institutions may be employed in road building, quarrying, draining and clearing of land, and similar projects. Work is mandatory for all prisoners. Prisons are committed by basic regulations to provide training programs in crafts and trades. New prisoners are examined by members of the Criminological Institute, which was created in 1942 and which recommends suitable work or training for them. All inmates are paid wages in accordance with articles 72 and 73 of the penal code. Payments are not made until the prisoner is released, except for small payments that may be sent to dependents. The payments cannot be garnished for any reason, and they are payable to the heirs of the inmate if he or she dies during incarceration.

The Educational Colony for Work is in San Jose de Mayo, the capital of the San Jose Department, about 50 miles from Montevideo. It has maximum-, medium-, and minimum-security units in an area of 1,800 acres of arable land. There is a prerelease pavilion for prisoners about to complete their terms. Prisoners themselves are in charge of this facility, where inmates may bring their families to live with them. The colony buildings are surrounded by two moats 60 feet wide, with a 30-foot embankment between them and enclosed by a 10-foot wire fence carrying low-voltage electric current. Visits to the minimum-security inmates take place in the open; medium-security inmates are separated from visitors by a glass partition; and maximum-security inmates are separated from visitors by a reinforced glass partition, with telephones for communication. The prerelease pavilion is outside the moats.

Prison Conditions. Conditions in Uruguay's prisons have been deteriorating. Human rights groups have filed many complaints of abuse of prisoners, including beatings. There is also considerable overcrowding. A prison riot lasting several days left the Libertad Prison in ruins, but several hundred prisoners continue to be housed there. To relieve overcrowding, prison officials have been housing many prisoners in modified shipping containers or modular cells. Besides overcrowding, the penal system suffers from understaffing, corruption, and physical violence. The national prison director was convicted of taking bribes in exchange for transferring prisoners to better facilities. Narcotics, weapons, and cell phones are routinely smuggled into cells with the collusion of officials. Family visitors are strip-searched and subjected to invasive searches. Prison deaths rose sharply in 2003, generally from hanging, stabbing, and burning perpetrated by other inmates. Most of the prisoners infected with HIV/AIDS do not receive any treatment. Women are held in separate facilities except for Artigas, where they are held in a separate wing. Minors are held in institutions operated by the National Institute for Minors. Conditions in juvenile prisons are as bad as in those for adults.

Prison Statistics.

- Total Prison Statistics: 7,100
- Prison Population Rate per 100,000: 209
- Pretrial Detainees: 72.5%
- Female Prisoners: 6%
- Number of Prisons: 24
- Official Capacity of the Prison System: 3,386
- Occupancy Level: 150.8%

George Thomas Kurian

Uzbekistan

Official country name: Republic of Uzbekistan
Capital: Tashkent (Toshkent)
Geographic description: Located in Central Asia, it shares a border with Afghanistan, Kazakhstan, Kyrgyzstan, Tajikistan, and Turkmenistan
Population: 26,851,195 (est. 2005)

■■■

LAW ENFORCEMENT

History. A former Soviet national republic, Uzbekistan has been independent since 1991.

Structure and Organization.

Internal Security and the Organization of Police. The constitution provides for a presidential system with separation of powers among the executive, legislative, and judicial branches; however, in practice President Islam Karimov and the centralized executive branch that serves him dominate political life and exercise nearly complete control over the other branches. The Oliy Majlis (Parliament) consists almost entirely of officials appointed by the president and members of parties that support him. Despite constitutional provisions for an independent judiciary, the executive branch heavily influences the courts in both civil and criminal cases and does not ensure due process. From the center, responsibilities are delegated to regional departments and then to the next administrative levels—cities or districts, and to districts within cities.

The Ministry of Internal Affairs (MIA) controls the police. The police and other MIA forces are responsible

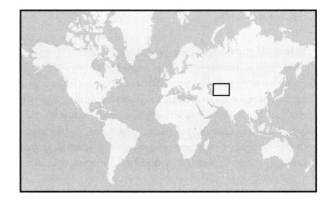

for most routine police functions. The National Security Service (NSS; the former Komitet Gosudarstvennoy Bezopasnosti [KGB; Committee for State Security]) deals with a broad range of national security questions, including corruption, organized crime, and narcotics.

The Uzbekistani police force (called Militia) is estimated to number about 25,000 individuals trained according to Soviet standards. The U.S. Department of Justice has begun a program to train the force in Western techniques. Interaction has also been expanded with the NSS, the chief intelligence agency, which is still mainly staffed by former KGB personnel. About 8,000 paramilitary troops are believed available to the NSS.

Most of the formal structures of law enforcement have survived from the Soviet period, with the MIA at the center. Since 1990 the MIA has grown to become the biggest armed organization in the country and the most powerful of all state institutions. Statistics on personnel and budget are state secrets, and estimates vary widely. However, human rights organizations suggest that there are probably about 200,000 MIA personnel in the whole country. By comparison, the military has around 70,000 and is due for a sharp reduction. Lawyers and human rights activists say there are 24,000 to 25,000 police just in Tashkent. However, it is believed that the ministry is bloated partly because it includes a variety of functions not related to normal policing, since the regulations state one police official should be deployed per 100 residents, which leads to a national figure of approximately 250,000 police.

Uzbekistan defines its most important security concerns not only in terms of the potential for military conflict but also in terms of domestic threats. Primary among those threats are the destabilizing effects of trafficking in narcotics and weapons into and across Uzbekistani territory. Although the government has recognized the dangers of such activities to society, enforcement is often stymied by corruption in law enforcement agencies.

In addition, the fire service comes under the MIA, as do all issues related to passports (such as issuance and renewal). The traffic police constitute a separate department within the ministry. The Uzbekistan Border Troop Command was established in March 1992, on the basis of the former Soviet Central Asian Border Troops District. In 1994 the Frontier Guard, as it is also called, came under the control of the MIA. The force, comprised of about 1,000 troops in 1996, is under the command of a deputy chairman of the NSS. The Frontier Guard works closely with the Russian Border Troops Command under the terms of a 1992 agreement that provides for Russian training of all Uzbekistani border troops and joint control of the Afghan border. These divisions are reproduced at each level of the MIA.

In general, the two key departments dealing with policing issues are the Service for Preservation of Public Order, which includes the patrol service, the police normally seen on the streets of major cities (usually referred to by their Russian name—*patrolnopostovaya sluzhba*), and the Criminal Police (*ugolovnyi rozysk*). There is also a special department tasked with combating corruption, racketeering, and terrorism.

In addition, the MIA has armed security forces, which are basically internal military units. It also has special forces that are designed to react quickly to serious security threats. These troops are based in every significant regional center and are for use mainly in cases of internal unrest.

They have also been used against militant groups who have penetrated Uzbekistan from Tajikistan, for example, in the Surkhandarya region in the south in 2000. They tend to be better trained and equipped than the regular army, but have little experience of dealing with peaceful demonstrators. In the event of any serious unrest, it seems likely that their response would be entirely based on use of force.

There is only limited oversight of the MIA and other security organs from civilian institutions. In theory, there is a parliamentary committee with such functions, but in practice it has no power and little access to information. The MIA has direct access to the presidential administration and does not answer to the government, except in the most formal sense. Oversight comes mainly from rival security and judicial organs.

National Security Service. The NSS is a much smaller organization than the MIA and is tasked with challenges to the existing constitutional system and terrorist activities. In practice, it fulfills much of the role of the KGB in the former Soviet Union. It spends a considerable amount of its time monitoring internal dissidents and peaceful opposition to the regime, intercepting communications, including e-mail, and monitoring international organizations and their employees. It reportedly makes wide use of informants, who compensate for its relatively small staff. The security services have political power unparalleled in Central Asia. The interior ministry exists almost as a state within a state, wielding huge influence not just in security policy, but over a range of other issues as well.

To deal with the threat against national security, three agencies—the NSS, the MIA, and the State Customs Committee—share jurisdiction. The international community has sought to provide technical and other assistance to Uzbekistan in this matter. In 1995 Uzbekistan established a National Commission on Drug Control to improve coordination and public awareness. A new criminal code includes tougher penalties for drug-related crimes, including a possible death penalty for drug dealers. The government's eradication program, which targeted only small areas of cultivation in the early 1990s, expanded significantly in 1995, and drug-related arrests more than doubled over 1994. In 1992 the U.S. government, recognizing Central Asia as a potential route for large-scale narcotics transport, began urging all five Central Asian nations to make drug control a priority of national policy. The United States has channeled most of its narcotics aid to Central Asia through the United Nations (UN) Drug Control Program, whose programs for drug-control intelligence centers and canine narcotics detection squads were being adopted in Uzbekistan in 1996. In 1995 Uzbekistan signed a bilateral counternarcotics cooperation agreement with Turkey and acceded to the 1988 UN Convention against Illicit Traffic in Narcotic Drugs and Psychotropic Substances.

The NSS is used regularly to check on MIA employees, and the bureaucracy has a formal oversight role. In

Police search the trunk of a car in the suburbs of the Uzbekistan capital Tashkent, May 14, 2005. *Heightened security measures were enforced in reaction to a recent outbreak of violence in Uzbekistan. The country's president, Islam Karimov, condemned these violent acts and claimed they were connected to Islamic extremists who hoped to establish a separate Muslim state across Central Asia.* AP IMAGES.

most cases, however, the latter is unwilling to challenge abuses within the police. In general, it works in tandem with them and is often bound to the MIA by corrupt ties and joint responsibility for abuses. There is little possibility for effective civil society oversight of the police.

Besides all different segments of the internal security organization, another one has been introduced based on the traditional establishment of the local community. In Uzbekistan most people in both urban and rural areas live in small communities known as *mahalla*; *mahalla* community bodies serve both administrative and social functions. The chairman of the *mahalla*, who is usually the community's elder, directs a small group of community activists. Increasingly, since the passage of the 1999 Law on the Mahalla, *mahalla* officials have been called on to carry out state security monitoring functions, drawing up lists of suspected religious and political dissidents. The high degree of mutual knowledge and interdependence among community members makes the *mahalla* a highly effective means of exercising pressure against suspects or their families. The *mahalla* can force a detainee, defendant, or convicted person or his or her family to submit to personal humiliation and at hate rallies promote their ostracism from the community.

Police Statistics.

- Total Strength of the Police Force: 35,000
- Population per Police Officer: 767

LEGAL SYSTEM

The constitution provides for an independent judiciary and states that the judicial authority of the Republic of Uzbekistan works independently of legislative and executive authorities, political parties, and other public associations; however, the judicial branch takes its direction from the executive branch and has little independence in practice. Under the constitution the president appoints all judges for five-year terms and has the power to remove judges. Removal of Supreme Court judges must be confirmed by the Parliament. Judges may be removed for crimes or failure to fulfill their obligations.

The following types of courts work in the Republic of Uzbekistan:

- Constitutional Court of the Republic of Uzbekistan
- Supreme Court of the Republic of Uzbekistan
- Higher Economic Court of the Republic of Uzbekistan

- Supreme and arbitration courts of the Republic of Karakalpakistan
- Regional (Viloyat) and Tashkent City Courts on civil and criminal cases
- Interdistrict district (city) courts on civil cases
- District (city) courts on criminal cases
- Economic Court of the Republic of Karakalpakistan
- Economic courts of regions (Viloyat) and Tashkent
- Martial courts

Courts can be specialized by categories based on the nature of cases. The establishment of extraordinary and emergency courts is not permitted. The legal proceedings in the Republic of Uzbekistan are performed in Uzbek and Karakalpak languages or in the language of most the population of the given district. People participating in proceedings with no knowledge of the language on which the legal proceedings is conducted are given the right of complete acquaintance with materials of proceedings and participation in trial actions through an interpreter and the right to act in court in their native language. The highest body of judicial authority in sphere of economic legal proceedings is the Supreme Economic Court of the Republic of Uzbekistan.

Courts of general jurisdiction are divided into three tiers: district courts, regional courts, and the Supreme Court. In addition, the Constitutional Court is charged with reviewing laws, decrees, and judicial decisions to ensure their compliance with the constitution. Military courts handle all civil and criminal matters that occur within the military. There is a system of economic courts at the regional level that handles economic cases between legal entities.

Decisions of district and regional courts of general jurisdiction may be appealed to the next level within ten days of ruling. Crimes punishable by death are murder, espionage, and treason. Officially, most court cases are open to the public, but may be closed in exceptional cases, such as those involving state secrets, rape, or young defendants. Unlike in past years, when trials of alleged Islamic extremists were often closed, local and international trial monitors and journalists are generally permitted to observe court proceedings during the year.

State prosecutors play a decisive role in the criminal justice system. They order arrests, direct investigations, prepare criminal cases, and recommend sentences. If a judge's sentence does not agree with the prosecutor's recommendation, the prosecutor has a right to appeal the sentence to a higher court. There is no protection against double jeopardy.

In the past judges whose decisions were overturned on more than one occasion could be removed from office. In 2001 the Parliament repealed this provision of the law, but other institutional controls remained in place, such as the executive's authority to decide which judges to reappoint. Consequently, judges in most cases continued to defer to the recommendations of prosecutors. As a result, defendants almost always were found guilty. Senior officials acknowledged the overwhelming power of the prosecutors and efforts to strengthen the independence of the judiciary continued after legislative reforms were enacted in 2000 and 2001.

Three-judge panels generally preside over trials. The panels consist of one professional judge and two lay assessors who serve five-year terms and are selected by either workers' collectives' committees or neighborhood (*mahalla*) committees. The lay judges rarely speak, and the professional judge often defers to the recommendations of the prosecutor on legal and other matters.

Defendants have the right to attend the proceedings, confront witnesses, and present evidence. The accused has the right to hire an attorney, and the government provides legal counsel without charge when necessary. Nonetheless, the right to an attorney in the pretrial stage is often violated, and judges in some cases deny defendants the right to their attorney of choice. Defense counsel is often incompetent, and effective cross-examination of even the most fatally flawed prosecution witnesses rarely occurs. Prosecutors normally attend only those sessions of the court in which they are scheduled to speak. Court reporters tend to take poor notes and often put down their pens when the defense is speaking. Some courts reportedly refuse to allow defense counsel access to trial transcripts on appeal.

The Uzbek legal system is based on civil law. A new two-part civil code was introduced in 1997. Other codes include the criminal code, the labor code, the civil procedure code, and the customs code. Presidential decrees also play an important part in the evolution of the system.

Investment-relevant laws include:

- The 1991 Law on Denationalization and Privatization, which governs privatization
- The edict On Additional Measures for Development of the Security Market, which created the state commission on securities and the stock exchange
- The 1996 Law on Joint-Stock Companies and the Protection of Shareholders' Rights, which governs the form and rules of the main corporate vehicles
- Two May 1998 laws, which extend and improve previous foreign investment legislation: the new Foreign Investment Law replacing a 1994 version, and the Law on Guarantees and Measures of Protection of Foreign Investors' Rights

On paper the system seems to have traveled some way from its Soviet past, but legal transition is still at an early stage. Bureaucracy and the judiciary's lack of independence mean that, even when the laws are satisfactory, the rules are not necessarily set in stone. Furthermore, the regulatory environment for foreign investment remains too complex and restrictive. And certain types of investment, such as portfolio investment, are unlikely because of the immaturity of the stock exchange.

In principle the 1998 Foreign Investment Law guarantees foreign investments against nationalization and expropriation, except in cases of natural calamities, accidents, and epidemics. In such cases investments may be subject to requisition in return for compensation. The Foreign Investment Law also protects foreign investors from legal change for a period of ten years from the date of their initial investment.

Commercial disputes involving foreign investors can be settled either by international arbitration (if the parties have agreed on this) or by an Uzbek commercial court. Uzbekistan is a party to the 1958 New York Convention on Recognition and Enforcement of Foreign Arbitral Awards. In the case of disputes with the state the country is also a party to the 1965 Washington Convention, so that arbitration can be sought from the International Center for Settlement of Investment Disputes. Outside the framework of these international agreements foreign judgments are generally not recognized in Uzbekistan.

The legal environment has improved tremendously since independence. Investment laws are drafted by professionals; there is a right of appeal from first-instance courts, as well as a right of judicial review of administrative action. However, the drawbacks of the country's political system make their mark on the legal system as well.

For example:

- The judiciary is not independent from the executive. This means that there is a potential for discrimination on grounds of nationalism or insufficient personal contacts. In these circumstances a level playing field cannot be ensured.

- Some basic legal requirements for an investor-friendly environment are not met. This applies especially, though not only, to currency convertibility regulations.

- Some rules are satisfactory in theory, but their implementation is insufficient, as in the cases of privatization or convertibility.

- Some requirements are simply too tight to make the environment viable for smaller investors, such as the minimum charter fund for businesses with foreign participation.

CORRECTIONAL SYSTEM

Prisons operate under the jurisdiction of the MIA. However, the Ministry of Justice also has limited jurisdiction on the prison system throughout the country. Despite the introduction of bail, accused persons are, with near uniformity, held in custody pending trial in pretrial detention facilities administered by the MIA. Under Uzbek law criminal investigations can be carried out by the police, the NSS, or the prosecution. The prosecution is also responsible for ensuring the legality of arrest and detention and of the investigative process; however, the prosecutorial functions of the prosecution clearly conflicts with its oversight function. No effective oversight mechanism exists to check the power of any of these agencies to abuse detainees' basic human rights with impunity.

Prisons are mainly separated based on gender and age. However, there is another separation implemented based on the type and severity of crime. Accordingly, several maximum-security prisons have been established, including Jaslyk Prison in Karakalpakistan.

Men and women are held in separate facilities. According to the Human Rights Watch, conditions are worse for male than for female prisoners, although a local human rights activist in frequent contact with the families of female prisoners reports that some inmates held in a women's prison in the Tashkent area are in ill health as a result of unsanitary conditions.

Juveniles are held separately from adults. The Human Rights Watch reports that conditions in juvenile facilities are generally much better than in adult prisons, although there are reports of inmates working in harsh circumstances. Pretrial detainees are held separately from those convicted of crimes; many of the worst incidences of abuse occur during pretrial detention. The government also operates labor camps, where conditions of incarceration are reported to be less severe than in prisons.

Prison Conditions. According to Amnesty International, prison overcrowding is a problem, with some facilities holding 10 to 15 inmates in cells designed for 4. Overcrowding may have been one of the reasons for annual large-scale amnesties since 2001, but the problem remains severe.

The Organization for Security and Cooperation in Europe's Office for Democratic Institutions and Human Rights initiated a prison reform program in cooperation with the MIA. After a series of delays since 2001, the International Committee of the Red Cross (ICRC) began an intensive regime of prison visits in September 2002. In June 2003 the ICRC reported that it was receiving satisfactory cooperation from authorities. The ICRC's visits were made on short notice and its teams of investigators were given adequate access to all prison facilities and could meet with prisoners without third parties. As of December 2003 the ICRC had conducted more than thirty visits to prisons and other places of detention, including Jaslyk Prison in Karakalpakistan, and had conducted a number of repeat visits. Foreign observers have also gained access to prisons to meet with individual detainees.

Prison Statistics.

- Total Prison Population: 48,100
- Prison Population Rate per 100,000: 184
- Pretrial Detainees: 11.5%
- Number of Prisons: 53
- Official Capacity of the Prison System: 56,300
- Occupancy Level: 113.5%

BIBLIOGRAPHY

Allworth, Edward A. 1990. *The Modern Uzbeks: From the Fourteenth Century to the Present—Cultural History.* Stanford, CA: Stanford University, Hoover Press Publications.

Amnesty International. 2002. "Annual Report, 2002: Uzbekistan." Available online at http://web.amnesty.org/web/ar2002.nsf/eur/uzbekistan!Open (accessed January 13, 2006).

Bureau of Democracy, Human Rights, and Labor. 2002. "Country Reports on Human Rights Practices: Uzbekistan, 2001." U.S. Department of State. Available online at http://www.state.gov/g/drl/rls/hrrpt/2001/eur/8366.htm (accessed January 13, 2006).

Bureau of International Information Programs. 2004. "State Department Terrorism Report: Europe-Eurasia." U.S. Department of State. Available online at http://usinfo.state.gov/topical/pol/terror/00041806.htm (accessed January 13, 2006).

Central Intelligence Agency. 2005. "World Factbook: Uzbekistan." Available online at http://cia.gov/cia/publications/factbook/geos/uz.html (accessed January 13, 2006).

Human Rights Watch. 2006. "Uzbekistan." Available online at http://hrw.org/doc?t=europe&c=uzbeki (accessed January 13, 2006).

International Crisis Group. 2002. "Central Asia: The Politics of Police Reform." *Asia Report*, no. 42. Available online at http://www.crisisgroup.org/home/index.cfm?id=1444&l=5 (accessed January 13, 2006).

Karimov, Islam. 1998. *Uzbekistan on the Threshold of the Twenty-first Century.* New York: St. Martin's.

Pliuskus, Vytautas. 2000. "Police Insignia: Uzbekistan." The Collection. Available online at http://police.collection.lt/search1.php?zodis=&salis=Uzbekistan&x=33&y=16#212 (accessed January 13, 2006).

Joseph D. Serio

Vanuatu

Official country name: Republic of Vanuatu
Capital: Port-Vila
Geographic description: Group of islands in Oceania, in the South Pacific Ocean
Population: 205,754 (est. 2005)

■ ■ ■

LAW ENFORCEMENT

History. Until independence, Vanuatu was an Anglo-French condominium known as New Hebrides. Responsibility for public security and maintenance of law and order was shared by the two colonial powers. Operational authority was not necessarily joint nor was it based on a demarcation of specific territories or functions. It was based, rather, on historic protocols. Matters involving French or British nationals were determined by the respective powers. In matters involving both nationalities or with natives, only jurisdiction was assigned to the national authority that took the original action or had a dominant interest in its outcome. Each national force operated independently with headquarters at Port-Vila on Efate Island.

Structure and Organization. Following independence, the British and French police authorities were merged to form the Vanuatu Police Force. The force is under a commandant who supervises four ranks of officers and men: superintendent of police, inspector, noncommissioned officers, and unrated constables, besides administrative personnel.

Below headquarters there are four operating territorial units whose headquarters are at Port-Vila,

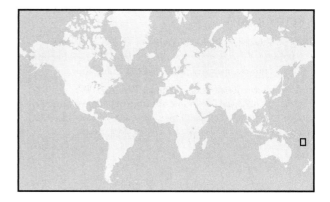

Santo (Luganville) on Espíritu Santo Island, Lakatoro on Malekula Island, and the major settlement on Tana Island. The Port-Vila district has responsibility for Efate Island and others in the south-central portion of the island group. It is assigned the largest force consisting of an inspector as commander and about forty-five constables. The Santo district covers all the northern islands of the group and has the second-largest force. The Lakatoro district covers all the islands in the north-central portion in the territory. The Tana district operates on Tana and Aneityum islands.

Besides the regular force, there is a paramilitary wing called the Vanuatu Mobile Force, which is under the control of the police commissioner.

Education and Training. There are no facilities for training, and trainees are sometimes sent to police schools on Fiji.

Police Statistics.

- Total Strength of the Police Force: 800
- Population per Police Officer: 257

HUMAN RIGHTS

The government generally respects human rights. There are some instances in which members of the Vanuatu Mobile Force use excessive force against rioters.

CORRECTIONAL SYSTEM

Few inmates are confined for long terms. Most serve sentences of a month or less, generally for drunkenness. All sentences are automatically remitted by one-third for good behavior. The prisons, though small, are well run and adequate. All convicted prisoners undergo some form of vocational training.

There is a rehabilitation center at Pialulub. It is a minimum-security facility where prisoners are permitted to have families and, after a training period, are paid wages and are permitted to participate in a savings program.

Prison Conditions. The central prison at Port-Vila is dilapidated and has little security. It holds about thirty prisoners, including one female prisoner.

Prison Statistics.

- Total Prison Population: 93
- Prison Population Rate per 100,000: 44
- Pretrial Detainees: 8.6%
- Female Prisoners: 5.4%
- Number of Prisons: 4

George Thomas Kurian

Vatican City

Official country name: The Holy See (State of the Vatican City)
Capital: Vatican City
Geographic description: Landlocked enclave of Rome in Italy
Population: 921 (est. 2005)

■■■

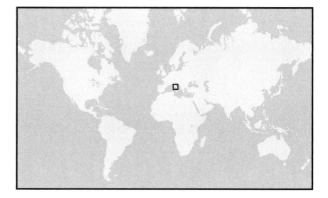

LAW ENFORCEMENT

History. The Vatican has two organizations that handle policing duties within the Holy See: the Guarda Svizzera Pontificia (Swiss Guard) and the Corpo della Gendarmeria dello Stato della Citta del Vaticano (Body of the Gendarmeria of the Vatican City State). While the former has existed since 1506, the latter has only been in existence, formally, since 1970 and was renamed in January 2002. Although the Swiss Guard is today presented as the "Pope's Army" and is given the title of a "military corps," the history of the Swiss Guard has changed substantially over the past 500 years. From its origins in 1506 until 1870 the Swiss Guard served as a military force. However, in 1870 the Swiss Guard's primary function changed from serving as a military force for the Vatican to serving as its guards. In 1929 its primary function was changed again and since that time the Swiss Guard has largely served as a police force, despite maintaining the tradition, history, and lineage of a military corps.

The official birthday of the Pontifical Swiss Guard is January 22, 1506, when 150 Swiss soldiers led by Captain Kaspar von Silenen entered the Vatican under the Porta del Popolo and were blessed by Pope Julius II, often referred to as the "Warrior Pope." As Pope Julius II's pontificate was marked by a reassertion of control over the Papal States, he often found himself at war with other countries. Having no soldiers of his own, Pope Julius hired Swiss mercenaries to serve as his army. Because of an impoverished economy in Switzerland, the Swiss greatest export became military soldiers who served for a fee. Pope Julius II had called on these Swiss mercenaries the previous year and because they had served with such dedication and devotion to the pope, he made them a permanent part of the Holy See and designated them as the Pontifical Swiss Guard.

Pope Julius II began using the Swiss Guard to take back Perugia and Bologna and wherever he went, they were always at his side serving as his personal body guards. As their service continued to be exemplary in the eyes of the pope, on July 5, 1512, he bestowed on them the special designation of "Defenders of the Freedom of the Church" and presented them with a standard, bearing the crossed keys with the inscription "Dominus mihi adiutor; non timebo quid faciat mihi homo" (The Lord is my help; I will not fear that which man can do to me). Toward the end of Pope Julius II's life, he increased the Swiss Guard from 189 soldiers to 300 and stated on his death bed that "they will remain faithful to us and to the Church of Rome as they always have been" (Serrano 1992, p. 45). Although Leo X, the next pope, could have reversed his predecessor's inclination toward a private Swiss military, he reaffirmed the Swiss Guard's presence with a celebration in its honor on April 11, 1513. However, while keeping the Swiss Guard, he dismissed all other Swiss soldiers who were serving as a military force for the Vatican.

During the papacy of Clement VII, Kaspar Roist, the second commandant of the Swiss Guard, served over a Swiss Guard that had been reduced back to the original number of 189 soldiers. In January 1527, because the Spaniards were closing in on Rome, Roist was ordered to abandon Rome and return to Switzerland. Commandant Roist refused and promised to defend the pope. On May 6, 1527, the Spaniards began their sack of Rome and ultimately closed in on the pope and his Swiss Guard. Captain Roist and his 189 Swiss Guardsmen fought valiantly, thereby allowing Pope Clement VII to flee to safety through the secret corridors connecting the Vatican to the Castle Saint Angelo. Only 42 of the 189 Swiss Guardsmen survived the attack. Eventually, Pope Clement VII was forced to surrender and only twelve of the Swiss Guard remained at his side.

The Swiss Guard was reconstituted by Pope Paul III in 1548 and eventually, with the appointment of Commandant Jost Segesser von Brunegg by Pope Pius V in 1566, the Swiss Guard was rebuilt into a well-established force within the Vatican. Throughout the 1600s and 1700s the Swiss Guard remained a force of approximately 120 guardsmen and served under many commandants from the Pfyffer family lineage. One such Pfyffer, Captain Franz Alois Pfyffer, defended Pope Pius VI during the French Revolution, when the pope was deposed and forced into exile in Siena, then Florence, Parma, Turin, and eventually Valence, where he died in 1799 of natural causes at the age of eighty-one. Pope Pius VII was then elected on March 14, 1800, and he returned to Rome with a new commandant, Karl Pfyffer von Altishofen, who reconstituted the Swiss Guard. However, in 1808 Napoléon Bonaparte returned, seized the Vatican, and placed Pius VII under arrest. The Swiss Guard was ordered to lay down its arms. When Napoléon was ultimately defeated on April 4, 1814, Pope Pius VII returned to Rome and Commandant Karl Pfyffer was once again called on to reconstitute the Swiss Guard.

The Vatican fell two more times during the nineteenth century. First in 1848, when a revolution declared Rome a republic and Pope Pius IX was forced to flee, and again in 1860, when the last of the Papal States were seized and the Vatican was reduced to its territory in Rome and some land on the outlying hills from Rome. Despite a pact with Napoléon III that these would remain papal lands, in 1870 the surrounding territory was taken and all that remained was the Vatican in Rome. At this point the Swiss Guard, although still designated a military force, was limited to guarding the Vatican City and the Pontifical Villa at the Castle Gandolfo (the pope's summer retreat) and providing personal security to the pope. The military era of the Swiss Guard was over.

During the Guard era (1870–1929) the Swiss Guard performed its duties under commandant's Alfred von Sonnenberg, Louis-Martin de Courten, Leopold Meyer von Schausensee, Jules Respond, and Alois Hirschbuhl. This time period was largely peaceful and on January 22, 1906, the 400th anniversary of the Swiss Guard was celebrated. World War I did cause some problems for the Swiss Guard as Europe began its "war to end all wars." Many male Swiss citizens were enlisting to fight in the war, which put a strain on the Swiss Guard. In 1914, for approximately one month, a group of theology students from a German-Hungarian college, who were not Swiss, were called on to fill the gaps while more Swiss males could be brought down from Switzerland.

The Guard era came to an end under the Lateran Pact, a series of three treaties, which were signed by the Holy See and the Kingdom of Italy on February 11, 1929. The pact gave full recognition to the Vatican that it was a city-state with absolute sovereignty. In light of this and its own internal changes, the Swiss Federal Council ruled, "Henceforth the Papal Guard cannot be considered to be a foreign armed-force as described in article 94 of the military penal code, because these troops are simply a police-force. Therefore, any man may join the service, as at present, without authorization from the Federal Council" (Serrano 1992, p. 113). Although the Vatican still recognized the Swiss Guard as a military force, the Swiss government ruled it a police force and this became the primary function of the Swiss Guard.

The police era (1929 to present) of the Swiss Guard has been marked by several events. Protecting the pope during World War II proved problematic with the Nazi occupation, but the Swiss Guard remained by the pope's side. Another event during this era marked a change in the Swiss Guard when Pope John XXIII set out on a pilgrimage to the Shrine of Mary in Loreto. The Swiss Guard accompanied the pope as a protective service and since then it has provided protective security for the pope whenever he leaves the Vatican. The event that most highlighted this duty came on May 13, 1981, when Mehmet Ali Agca, an alleged Turkish terrorist, shot and wounded Pope John Paul II as he was waving to the crowds in St. Peter's Square from his "Pope Mobile."

In 1970 two other guard forces, the Pontifical Noble Guard and the Palatine Guard of Honour, were disbanded and their duties were shifted to the Swiss Guard. These were mostly guard duties. That same year the Gendarmeria was formed as a police force largely responsible for traffic and pedestrian control in and around the Vatican City. Today, the Swiss Guard is responsible for security at the Vatican, protecting the pope, and serving in a police capacity within the Vatican City. While the Gendarmeria assist the Swiss Guard in these duties, as does the Rome Police, the Swiss Guard functions more as a police force for which the Swiss Federal Council had declared it in 1929.

Structure and Organization. As the Swiss Guard is not a large agency, there are few divisions. It is essentially divided into 33 members who serve in leadership/managerial roles, 2 who serve as official drummers, and 100 who serve as line officers or halberdiers. There are two specific duties for the Swiss Guard: protective detail, which guards the pope on his visits abroad and coordinates with law enforcement agencies wherever the pope is to visit, and the band, which performs at ceremonial functions. There are also several special duties given to certain members of the Swiss Guard and these include coordinating training, archives, Internet, finance, information media, the armory, the annual report, language training, sports and recreation, and the kitchen.

As of 2005 there were 133 members of the Swiss Guard, an increase of 43 members since Pope John Paul II's elevation to the papacy in 1978. The commandant is the commander of the guard and is given the rank of colonel. The captain commandant is given a special designation within the Vatican, as he is listed as a member of the papal household and a gentlemen of his Holiness. The commandant has a sergeant major, who serves at his side in the grade of lieutenant, as well as a chaplain, who serves in the grade of lieutenant colonel. Underneath the commandant is a lieutenant with the grade of lieutenant colonel, a second lieutenant in the grade of major, and another second lieutenant serving in the grade of captain. The next rank down is that of sergeant, and there are four who serve in the grade of second lieutenant. There are ten corporals serving in the grade of adjutant and twelve vice corporals serving in the grade of sergeant major. Finally, the other 100 members of the Swiss Guard are designated as halberdiers, with two designated as drummers, all of whom serve in the grade of sergeant.

Police at Work. On any given day in the Vatican two-thirds of the Swiss Guard are on duty in the mounting guard or posted at the entrances to the Apostolic Palace. They have daily inspections and briefings before going on duty and training is an integral part of their daily routine.

Salaries. A new recruit is paid approximately US$1,000 a month and room and board is provided for by the Vatican. Pay rises commensurate with duties and rank.

Retirement Age. There is no officially designated retirement age, but Swiss Guardsmen are granted a pension after eighteen years of service and may serve only twenty-five years in the pope's service.

Police-Community Relations. As a large portion of the Swiss Guardsmen's time is spent dealing with tourists, police-community relations is largely based on this type of interaction. The guardsmen are quite exceptional in assisting tourists in multiple languages.

Local Police. The Swiss Guard, despite being designated a military force, serves as the primary police in the Vatican. The Gendarmeria, composed of approximately 100 Italian men, also serves as a police force within and around the Vatican City, often assisting with traffic in the vicinity. In addition, both the Swiss Guard and the Gendarmeria work closely with the Rome Police because of the location of the Vatican, as well as with the State Police, which is administered by the Italian Division of Public Security, and the Carabinieri, the Italian National Police, which are administered by the Ministry of Defense.

Special Police.

Traffic Police. This function is primarily conducted by the Corpo della Gendarmeria dello Stato della Citta del Vaticano.

Education and Training. Members of the Swiss Guard must have attended the military school in Switzerland, hence they come to the Vatican already trained. On arrival, they are given additional training on policies and procedures and must become familiar with the Vatican City. The guardsmen are also provided continual training in the martial arts, the Italian language, firearms, protective services, and their religious faith, Catholicism. For those members of the Swiss Guard Band, they continue to receive lessons in their instruments.

Recruitment and Conditions of Service. Pope Pius IV in 1565 was the first to establish that only Swiss citizens could be members of the Swiss Guard. It was Pope Leo XII, through the advice of Commandant Karl Pfyffer von Altishofen, who established that only male Swiss citizens who were practicing Catholics between the ages of eighteen and twenty-five and no less than 5 feet 4 inches tall could serve as Swiss Guardsmen. The height requirement was changed to 5 feet 10 inches in the 1880s and in the early twentieth century the age was changed to nineteen to thirty years of age. Additional admission requirements state that individuals must hold a professional diploma or high school degree, they must have attended the military school in Switzerland, and they must demonstrate they have a good moral and ethical background by obtaining a certificate of good conduct from an ecclesiastical and a civil authority. In terms of marriage, Swiss Guardsmen may not enter the service married and to marry they must be at least twenty-five, have completed three years of service, and serve in the grade of corporal. Above all, they must also affirm that they are a faithful and practicing Roman Catholic.

On May 6 of each year, the day the Swiss Guard defended the pope in the sack of Rome, during the swearing-in ceremony, the chaplain reads an oath in the German language. Then, all new recruits are called forth one by one to place their left hand on the Swiss Guard Flag and raise their right hand splaying their thumb and first two fingers, which symbolizes the Holy Trinity of the Father, the Son, and the Holy Spirit. They are then asked to confirm their oath of office in their own native language by stating, "I, . . . , swear I will observe faithfully, loyally, and honorably all that has now been read out to me. May God and his saints assist me."

Uniforms and Weapons. The most noticeable aspect of the Swiss Guard is its dress uniform. The uniform that is most noted is a bright and attractive uniform with vertical stripes in the traditional Medici blue and yellow and complemented by red stripes on the sides of the uniform and red cuffs. In addition, a bright white collar is worn at the neck and a brown leather belt with a short saber and scabbard is worn at the side. The beret is the primary headgear worn with the uniform and its color signifies the soldier's grade.

Although the colorful uniform has long been attributed to Michelangelo, this appears to be a myth with no support in the historical record. In fact, it would be more likely that Raffaello had some involvement in the design as he was most instrumental in influencing Italian Renaissance fashion. The colorful uniform actually dates back to the fifteenth and sixteenth centuries and was a common uniform for foot soldiers, for which the purpose of the bright uniforms was to allow them to be recognized in the midst of battle. It is not known what the original uniform looked like and it has undergone many changes over the past 500 years.

The Swiss Guard also expands this uniform for special occasions, such as May 6, by adding ceremonial dress plates, white gloves, and a white pleated wrap around the neck. The beret is replaced with a metal helmet adorned with a colored plumage, white for the commandant and

sergeant major, purple for lieutenants, red for the halberdiers, and yellow/black for the drummers. In addition, the commandant's uniform is similarly designed, but is a darker crimson red uniform denoting his position.

Finally, it should be noted that while the colorful uniform of the Swiss Guard is the general image most people have, the guardsmen actually have an everyday uniform that is all blue and is complemented by a beret.

The boarding pike or what is often called a halberd, the traditional weapon of the Swiss Guard that dates back to its origins, is still the primary weapon today. The weapon is a 7-foot-long pole that comes to a point and approximately 1 foot down from the point is an axelike configuration. In addition, the Swiss Guardsmen carry about their waist a short saber during the performance of their duties while in dress uniform. Although not openly noticed, all members of the Swiss Guard are also trained in the use of handguns and various automatic and semi-automatic rifles that are kept available for emergencies and are carried during protective details.

Police Officers Killed in the Line of Duty. It is difficult to determine the number of Swiss Guardsmen killed in the line of duty, for in their early history they served more as a military and often faced death to protect the pope and defend the Papal States. There are, however, some noted deaths of Swiss Guardsmen killed in the line of duty. The first notable death was that of the first commandant of the Swiss Guard, Captain Kaspar von Silenen, who led the papal army against the Duke of Urbino, who had crossed the border into Rimini, Italy, with over 6,000 mercenaries. The odds were six to one, but Commandant von Silenen led the defense and died defending the Papal States. He was buried with honors in Rome on August 26, 1516.

The most tragic and honored day of the Swiss Guard was May 6, 1527. On this day the Spaniards began their infamous sack of Rome and 189 members of the Swiss Guard under the leadership of Captain Kaspar Roist defended the pope, which enabled him to escape to safety. One hundred and forty-seven Swiss Guardsmen were killed in the line of duty that day including Captain Roist, who was injured, taken by the Spaniards, and then executed in front of his wife, Elizabeth Klingler. This day remains the highest day of honor for the Swiss Guard and on the same day each year, the pope holds a ceremony to induct new members into the Swiss Guard.

The Swiss Pfyffer family during the seventeenth and eighteenth centuries provided a number of commandants for the Swiss Guard and then sustained an absence during the late nineteenth and early twentieth centuries. During World War II, after almost 100 years, a Pfyffer, Commandant Heinrich Pfyffer von Altishofen, was

An Italian police vehicle and two Swiss Guards patrol an entrance to the Vatican the day after a Swiss Guard commander was killed, May 5, 1998. *Colonel Alois Estermann, 43, Swiss Guard Commander, his wife, and a non-commissioned officer were all found shot to death in Estermann's apartment near the Vatican. Estermann had recently been nominated for commander of an elite division of the Swiss Guard by Pope John Paul II and was scheduled to have a special meeting with the pope that day.* AP IMAGES.

placed in charge of the Swiss Guard. His leadership came to an end when on March 12, 1957, while on duty in St. Peter's Basilica, he suffered a heart attack and died.

The most recent Swiss Guardsman killed in the line of duty was Captain Commandant Alois Estermann, who was murdered along with his wife, Gladys Meza Romero, in their apartment on May 4, 1998, several hours after having been promoted to the position of commandant. They were murdered by Swiss Guardsman Corporal Cedrich Tornay. Although controversy still surrounds this murder, the official report states that Tornay was upset because Estermann had passed him over for a decoration. In addition, he was reported to have had traces of cannabis in his blood system and a large cyst on his brain, which may have impaired his judgment. Estermann was the first Swiss Guardsman to reach the pope after he was shot in May 1981.

Transportation, Technology, and Communications. Although the size of the Vatican does not necessitate vehicles for nearly all duty is performed on foot, the Swiss Guard has access to vehicles and equipment when needed in terms of its protective detail for the pope.

The Swiss Guard has access to much of the latest technologies from satellite communications, cell phones, and protective detail communications to computers, Internet access, and its own Web page within the Vatican's Web site.

HUMAN RIGHTS

The protection of human rights is a requisite part of the Swiss Guardsmen and they are trained on the theology of human rights found in Catholic doctrine.

CRIME

Crime Statistics. The Vatican does not often experience a wide variety of crime. The primary offenses tend to be larcenies from pickpockets who prey on tourists. In 2002, for instance, there were 608 penal offenses mostly for simple larcenies. In addition, 397 civil proceedings were filed, most dealing with traffic offenses.

BIBLIOGRAPHY

Biasetti, Mario. 2003. *Soldiers of the Pope: The Story of the Swiss Guard*. Video. A Mario Biasetti Production distributed by Vision Video.

Papal Switzerland Guard. 2003. "Annual Report 2002." Vatican City: Vatican.

Papal Switzerland Guard. Available online at http://www.guardiasvizzera.org (accessed January 16, 2006).

Roman Curia. 2003. "The Swiss Guard." The Holy See. Available online at http://www.vatican.va/roman_curia/swiss_guard/ (accessed January 16, 2006).

Serrano, Antonio. 1992. *The Swiss Guard of the Popes*. Dachau, Germany: Bayerland.

Willard M. Oliver

Venezuela

— ■ —

Official country name: Bolivian Republic of Venezuela
Capital: Caracas
Geographic description: Located in northern South America, bordering the Atlantic Ocean and the Caribbean Sea
Population: 25,375,281 (est. 2005)

■■■

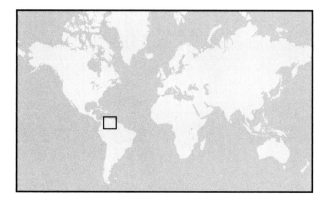

LAW ENFORCEMENT

History.

Guardia Nacional. The earliest antecedents of today's Venezuelan police date back to March 10, 1810, when the Supreme Junta of Caracas recommended the creation of an armed group to guard the Congress. On March 9, 1811, the Guardia Nacional (GN; National Guard) was created for this purpose. Later, the GN was also assigned to rural posts to combat incidents of theft and robbery. The original GN was disbanded in 1839 because of a lack of funds.

Under the aegis of General Antonio Páez, a new GN was formed on May 4, 1841. The new GN was charged with ensuring security and order, especially in the country's rural areas. The second GN shared the same fate as its predecessor: it was disbanded on March 12, 1847, because of a lack of funds.

On December 17, 1935, General Eleázar López Contreras became president of the republic. López urged state leaders to form police units in their jurisdictions to ensure security. A decision was reached to model the new police force after the Spanish Civil Guard (Guardia Civil Española). On August 4, 1937, the new police unit was created.

Cuerpo de Investigaciones Cientificas, Penales, y Criminalisitcas. After General Marco Pérez Jiménez was unseated from power at the beginning of 1958, the provisional government conceived the creation of a police unit that specialized in the investigation of crimes, the apprehension of criminals, and the examination of evidence. On February 20, 1958, the Technical Unit of the Judicial Police was created as an auxiliary unit of the judiciary. The unit began with only twelve people. However, guerrilla warfare in the 1970s and assessments of the unit by Chilean and English experts served as a catalyst for the unit's rapid expansion. This unit has operated under a variety of names, the most recent of which was given in 2001: Cuerpo de Investigaciones Cientificas, Penales, y Criminalisitcas (CICPC; Scientific, Penal, and Criminal Investigative Unit).

Dirección de los Servicios de Inteligencia y Prevención. The Dirección de los Servicios de Inteligencia y Prevención (DISIP; Directorate of Intelligence and Prevention Services) had similar beginnings as the CICPC when the provisional government was striving to achieve an acceptable level of national security. The predecessor of the DISIP was created on April 29, 1959. Known as the Dirección General de Policía (DIGEPOL; General Police Directorate), this unit was charged with exercising and coordinating police functions to preserve order in the national territories. During this era of Venezuelan history a volatile political climate contributed to the DIGEPOL's characterization as a police unit more than an intelligence unit. In 1969 the unit received its current name and was moved from the Ministry of Relations to the Ministry of Interior and Justice.

State Police. According to the Venezuelan constitution, the states are autonomous entities granted the right to organize their own police forces on the state and municipal levels. The police of the state of Aragua have the official title "Unit of Security and Public Order of Aragua State." In 1991 the Aragua state police began a tradition of in-house promotions in which police officers were able to ascend the ranks of the organization. Other state police agencies have since followed suit.

Structure and Organization. Venezuela has seven distinct branches of police:

1. Guardia Nacional, a completely volunteer force organized along military lines

2. Directorate of Intelligence and Prevention Services, a nonuniformed force termed by some analysts as the political police

3. Judicial police

4. Technical and judicial police, in charge of investigative work

5. Traffic police

6. Dirección de Identificación y Extranjería (DIEX; Directorate of Identification and Immigration)

7. State and municipal police forces of which there are 450

Guardia Nacional. The GN is unique in that it is purely a police agency but constitutes one of the country's four armed forces (similar in style to the Spanish Civil Guard from which it was modeled). Interestingly, this observation leaves a void in the constitutional requirement that the executive branch forms a uniformed national police agency. The GN has both police and military characteristics.

The GN has a variety of responsibilities including internal security. This activity involves guarding refugees and prisoners of war during states of emergency. Additionally, the GN serves as the country's border patrol. Other security functions can be broken down into six different areas:

- Security of installations including those that are considered of strategic importance

- Frontier security including the checking of foreign agricultural laborers

- Rural security that includes conducting operations to reduce incidents of drug trafficking

- Actions to ensure public order when other police agencies' resources are deemed insufficient for the task

- Penal security

- Transport security

Cuerpo de Investigaciones Científicas, Penales, y Criminalisitcas. In the government hierarchy the CICPC is directly subordinate to the Ministry of Interior and Justice. In legislation that sets forth the agency's mission, the CICPC is charged with collaborating with agencies of citizen security in the formation of control mechanisms and criminal records databases so that agencies can share information in the areas of drug trafficking, terrorism, and the disappearance of persons.

State Police. Twenty-two of Venezuela's states have a police force (Vargas state has no state police force). The state police are responsible for patrol work and public order, arrests, and community service. In many cases the GN plays a role in the selection of police commanders at the state level. Each state police force is regulated by a local police code.

The constitution establishes the state governor as the maximum authority over state police agencies. In the case of Aragua state the chain of command takes the following pattern after the state governor: governor secretary, commander general of security (ostensibly holds the rank of chief commissioner), and second commander of security (holds the rank of commissioner).

Caracas Metropolitan Police. Although Caracas has long counted on the presence of the police to ensure security and maintain public order, it was not until the city rapidly expanded in the 1960s that the Metropolitan Police took on its present form. The growth experienced in Caracas in the 1960s catalyzed the decision of the federal district governor of Miranda state (where Caracas is located) to create new city zones and to completely restructure the police. By 1970 the Caracas Metropolitan Police had 8,000 officers. By the end of the 1970s the

Police officers in Venezuela read an unofficial list of victims presumed dead after a chartered jet crashed approximately 400 miles west of Caracas, in the Western Zulia State, August 17, 2005. The plane was a tourist flight returning from the French Caribbean island of Martinique and all 160 people on board were killed. AP IMAGES.

police in Caracas established the country's first motorized unit, using jeeps to reach otherwise inaccessible neighborhoods. In 1979 a K-9 unit was also established.

Police-Community Relations. A number of different police agencies in Venezuela are involved in projects designed to strengthen ties to the community. The projects range from improving literacy in remote areas to the formation of neighborhood committees. In Aragua state the Brigada de Prevención y Rescate para Niños y Adolescentes (Brigade for the Prevention of and Rescue of Children) was formed on October 6, 2001.

The brigade's objective is to aid in the development of juveniles (ages five to fifteen) in such areas as human resources, sports, culture, and self-esteem. At least 290 juveniles are involved in this brigade.

Special Police. The Cuerpo de Vigilancia de Transito Terrestre (Land Transit Unit) is charged with organizing, directing, and controlling land transit in all of Venezuela's territory. This agency's chief responsibility is to maintain a healthy traffic flow and ensure that vehicles meet national standards. In addition, this unit supervises and controls the

activities of the Land Transit Volunteer Brigade and advises government officials on matters pertaining to land transit.

Education and Training. Basic training is provided for police entrants and officers at the Police Academy in El Junquito near Caracas. Training lasts for three years for judicial police and the GN, one year for traffic police, and six months for state and uniformed police. State, municipal, and traffic police have a two-tier entry and promotion system in which agents, corporals, and sergeants constitute the first tier and subinspectors to chief commissars make up the second tier. Judicial and political police only have the supervisory ranks while military police and the GN have military ranks.

Transportation, Technology, and Communications. The GN is responsible for some of Venezuela's most high-tech policing strategies. To combat drug traffickers who use planes for transport, the GN has developed an early warning system along the southern border and the Atlantic coast. The system consists of a network of air-based sensors placed at an altitude of 4,600 meters that send information to a substation on the ground. This warning system will be able to send information to six different stations once the project is completed and is likely to have a variety of other applications.

Police Statistics. The number of police officers at all levels is directly related to the jurisdictional size of Venezuela's police agencies. Thus, the GN has 35,000 officers. The police of Aragua state have 2,589 officers. Most officers in Aragua state are assigned to patrol duties (2,250), while the rest belong to other units such as the K-9 unit and the vehicle unit.

- Total Strength of the Police Force: 80,309
- Population per Police Officer: 316

CRIME

Criminal Identification and Forensics. In Venezuela forensics is the domain of the CICPC, which relies on three primary tools to conduct and maintain records on forensic investigation:

- Automated Identification System, which uses unique numerical identifiers
- Integrated Ballistics Identification System
- Automated System for the Identification of Fingerprints

The CICPC also works with the DIEX, which is part of the Ministry of Interior and Justice.

Crime Statistics. The Central Office of Statistics and Information publishes the annual report "Anuario Estadistico de Venezuela." The report is based entirely on information provided by the CICPC. In theory the CICPC receives crime reports from all Venezuelan police agencies. However, full cooperation is a goal that has yet to be reached.

CORRECTIONAL SYSTEM

The Venezuelan prison system consists of 29 prisons, of which 19 are pretrial facilities and 10 are for sentenced prisoners. It is headed by a director general who is in charge of custody and rehabilitation. There are three types of prisons: 17 judicial detention centers for those awaiting trial, 7 national jails and penitentiaries for convicted felons, and the National Institute for Female Reorientation located in Los Teques. Each prison, however, has separate wings for each kind of inmate. Minors are interned in separate institutions under the custody of INAN, an institute under the control of the Ministry of Health.

Prison Conditions. By law prisoners have the right to receive an opportunity to work, a basic education, and adequate medical attention. However, because of overcrowding they receive none of these. Most of the prisons have no place or program for work. As a result, most prisons breed corruption and crime. The large Caracas prison has a wing that houses homosexuals exclusively. Conditional liberty is granted to any prisoner who has completed three-fourths of his or her sentence or has reached seventy years of age and completed half of his or her sentence.

Prison conditions are harsh because of corruption and scarce resources. There is also considerable guard-to-prisoner and prisoner-to-prisoner violence. In the space of a year there were over 340 deaths and 1,419 injuries as a result of deliberate acts of violence. Gangs operate within prisons with the complicity of the guards. Inmates have to bribe guards for basic necessities such as food, space in a cell, and a bed. Gang-related violence and extortion are fueled by illegal trafficking in arms and drugs.

Prison Statistics.

- Prison Population Total: 21,432
- Prison Population Rate per 100,000: 83
- Pretrial Detainees: 26%
- Female Prisoners: 6.6%
- Number of Prisons: 29
- Official Capacity of the Prison System: 15,550
- Occupancy Level: 117%

Josep Canabate

Vietnam

---■---

Official country name: Socialist Republic of Vietnam
Capital: Hanoi
Geographic description: Easternmost country in continental Southeast Asia, bordering the South China Sea
Population: 83,535,576 (est. 2005)

■■■

LAW ENFORCEMENT

History. During French colonial rule public-order functions and institutions were patterned after those of metropolitan France. For police purposes, the region was divided into three areas: Tonkin (north), Annam (central), and Cochin China (south). Control was exercised by a French director general of police and public security stationed in Hanoi.

Overall responsibility for public order and safety in each region was in the hands of the Sûreté, which was directed by a regional chief of police responsible to the director general for technical and operational matters and to the regional governor for the disposition of the police forces. Ordinary police duties, such as patrol work, were performed by local policemen. All important command and administrative positions were held by French nationals. The French Sûreté Nationale supervised recruitment and training.

At the beginning of World War II large cities, such as Saigon, had municipal police departments administered by the mayor. After the Japanese occupied Vietnam in 1941 they permitted the old French police establishment to continue to function under the Vichy French administration. After the fall of Vichy France in 1945 a

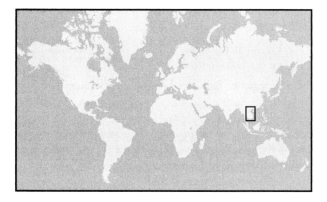

short-lived nationalist government was formed under the former playboy emperor Bao Dai, who retained the French connection. This regime was tolerated by the Japanese, but as Japan's position in the area deteriorated, Communist Viet Minh forces in the north, led by Ho Chi Minh, increasingly took control. In 1945 Bao Dai abdicated in favor a Viet Minh government. Meanwhile, the British, who at the Potsdam Conference in 1945 had been designated to accept the Japanese surrender of Vietnam, exercised police powers until the French Expeditionary Force arrived. During this interregnum, the country experienced much disorder. Communists infiltrated key positions in the military and the police. Most criminal files were lost and destroyed.

French efforts to reestablish police control over their colony were unsuccessful and were constantly thwarted by the Viet Minh. By June 1954, when the Indochina War ended with the partition of the country along the demarcation line, the police had ceased to be effective even in the cities. Bao Dai, who had been restored to power in the south, had turned over control of both the Security Police and the Municipal Police to the Binh Xuyen, a racketeering organization. It was given a monopoly of police functions, along with the right to run gambling, opium traffic, and prostitution in the metropolitan areas. The group also collected fees for visas and licenses and controlled the sale of rice, fish, and pork. Two large politico-religious sects, the Cao Dai and the Hoa Hao, controlled large areas of the countryside, maintaining their own police and security forces.

With the election of Ngo Dinh Diem as president, the state of near-anarchy began to mend. By April 1956 the armed forces of Binh Xuyen, Cao Dai, and Hoa Hao had been defeated and scattered. Americans began to be actively involved in rebuilding the police forces of the south. At first a police advisory group from Michigan State University replaced the French law enforcement personnel and later the U.S. Agency for International Development took over many of the operational functions.

In 1962 President Diem signed a decree integrating all the existing police forces into a single police agency, called the Directorate General of National Police, under the command of the director general of the National Police within the Department of the Interior. The Directorate General was composed of the headquarters proper, six regional directorates, and a municipal directorate, which included the Saigon Metropolitan Police and the surrounding province of Gia Dinh. The regional directorate headquarters were at Hue, Nha Trang, Ban Me Thuot, Bien Hoa, My Tho, and Can Tho. They were charged with the supervision of the police units located within the provinces making up the region, as well as the municipal police forces in the larger towns, such as Hue, Da Nang, Nha Trang, Cam Ranh, Da Lat, and Vung Tau. Each province was under a police chief.

The headquarters of the director general was in Saigon, where he was assisted by a staff consisting of a deputy director and four assistant directors, one each for administration, intelligence, telecommunications, and operations. Also at the assistant director general level were the chiefs of the two major counterinsurgency operations: the National Police Field Forces and the Resources Control Service. Directly under the director general were the Internal Activities Division and the Internal Affairs Branch, the latter concerned with irregularities within the police departments.

The assistant director for operations was responsible for supervision of the activities of the Judicial Police, Administrative Police, Rehabilitation Service, Immigration Service, Uniform and Traffic Police Service, and Order Police, formerly the Combat Police.

Each of the six regional directorates was a scaled-down version of the Directorate General and was headed by a director whose immediate assistants were a deputy director, a chief of administration, a chief of uniformed police, and a chief of special police. The Saigon Municipal Directorate enjoyed a special position within the system as the largest—with about 10,000 men—and as dealing with the most severe law enforcement problems. It was organized into a headquarters, eight precincts, the Harbor Police, the Airport Police, the Traffic Police, and the Gia Dinh Provincial Police.

In the north the People's Police Force took over the law enforcement functions from the French. The centrally controlled force, known as the Bo Cong An, was organized under the minister of public security. The force was organized hierarchically, with the chain of command running down to the smaller territorial units—provinces, cities, districts, and villages. Larger cities, such as Hanoi and Haiphong, were divided into wards, stations, and posts. After the conquest of the south in 1975, the northern police system was extended to the vanquished south.

Structure and Organization. As in other Communist states, the police structure and operations are never released to the public and have to be pieced together from scattered accounts in the press. At the provincial level, there is a police force branch organized into several sections to deal with matters pertaining to political conformity, internal security, passports and identity cards, counterintelligence, and administration. Smaller groups having similar responsibilities are maintained at the district level. A group of special agents, subdivided into cells, is concerned with counterrevolutionary activities. Each village administrative committee has a security section composed of trusted party members charged with the surveillance of suspects. The security sections receive considerable information through complaints and denunciations made by local people—a practice encouraged by the Communist Party and the constitution as one of the duties of a good citizen. Villages also maintain their own local watchmen for patrol and guard duties.

The rank structure for officers and noncommissioned officers is prescribed in the decree of law of July 16, 1962. It indicates a strong military influence on the service. The decree prescribes three ranks for officers. The highest is the general's rank with two additional grades for lieutenant general and major general; field rank has four grades (senior colonel, colonel, lieutenant colonel, and major), and the company rank has four grades (senior captain, captain, senior lieutenant, and lieutenant). Noncommissioned officers are divided into three ranks: senior sergeant, sergeant, and corporal. A temporary rank called aspirant comprises those preparing for promotion to officer rank. The equivalent of a military private is referred to an a policeman.

Included in the commissioned ranks are the following:

- Army officers who are graduates of the Officers School who are transferred to the police force

- Party cadres and specialists and cadres in public service who are transferred to the police force

- Graduates from police cadre training schools of the Ministry of Public Security

- Reserve police officers who are recalled to active duty

- Noncommissioned policemen who have distinguished themselves in service or have shown outstanding loyalty to the party or have accomplished some notable feat in the discharge of their duties

The 1962 decree stipulates that the appointment of officers and men is based as much on their political record and on the "services rendered to the revolution" as their professional skills. Nominations to aspirant and commissioned ranks are made by the minister of public security and to the noncommissioned officers' ranks by the Council of Ministers. Nominees for lieutenant must be graduates of a police cadre training school or non-commissioned officers or soldiers with a distinguished record of valor, skill, and proficiency in combat.

Promotions are based on the needs of the police force, political records, achievement records, and the length of service in grade. The service normally required in each grade is 2 years from corporal up to lieutenant, 3 years from lieutenant to captain, 4 years from captain to lieutenant colonel, and 5 years from lieutenant colonel to higher grades. The same authorities who are authorized to appoint are also authorized to promote or demote. In emergency cases, a police unit commander with the rank of a senior captain or higher may dismiss a subordinate two ranks below him and nominate another officer as replacement. Age limits for different ranks are 38 to 48 for lieutenant, 43 to 53 for captain and senior captain, 48 to 58 for major, 53 to 63 for lieutenant colonel and colonel, 55 to 63 for senior colonel, and 58 to 65 for major general.

The 1962 decree accorded broad powers to the police force for enforcing state political, military, and economic policies. Their political duties include the defense of the socialist regime and the destruction of counterrevolutionaries. Their specialized duties include the apprehension of hooligans, bandits, thieves, embez-zlers, speculators, and other criminals; control and reform of counterrevolutionaries; safeguarding of public property; ensuring security of land, river, air, and sea transport; census enumeration; issuing of passports and travel permits; control of production, sale, and use of radio and television sets; control of hotel, printing, engraving, and other trades; and control of weapons, poisons, and explosives. Periodically, policemen and officers receive awards for exceptional performance of any of these duties.

Nonprofessional law enforcement units are reported in the press. They include People Protection Squads, Enterprise Protection Force (active in factories, government buildings, and communes), Municipal Security Protection Force, Neighborhood Protection Civil Guard Agency, Capital Security Youth Assault Units, Township Public Security Force, and Civil Defense Force.

Armed Public Security Force. Founded on March 3, 1959, the Armed Public Security Force is a second police agency functioning under army control. Although its responsibilities overlap those of the regular police in some areas, its functions are more specific and special-ized, such as protecting ports and coastal areas, borders, factories, construction sites, communication and trans-portation centers, public utility installations, mines, and cooperatives. It is the training agency for the district police and the militia. It also engages in public works and civic projects. It helps farmers during planting and harvesting seasons, combats floods and droughts, con-structs communication routes and irrigation works, con-ducts rescue missions, clears jungles, builds canals, camps, and access roads, and even helps to deliver babies in rural areas. These ostensibly public-spirited missions in fact help to reinforce its primary task of maintaining constant surveillance over the population.

The Armed Public Security Force is organized along military lines into sections, platoons, companies, battalions, and larger formations, depending on the availability of personnel and the security requirements of the region.

Education and Training. All men of military age are eligible to join the police force if they can pass basic literacy, intelligence, and health tests and if their loyalty is vouched for by a party official. Former soldiers who become reservists at the expiration of their service terms and soldiers discharged on reaching age forty-five form the core of the force. Officers are obtained mainly from the army either by direct transfer or by granting com-missions to graduates from army officer training schools. A majority of the enlisted men have some previous military training.

Training is carried out under the supervision of army officers. The courses are limited to military subjects, such as those commonly given to infantry units and include marksmanship, grenade throwing, reconnaissance, and

A traffic officer directs vehicles in front of the Hanoi Stock Market building during its official opening in Hanoi, Vietnam, March 8, 2005. It was the opening of the country's second stock market, following the debut of the first one in Ho Chi Minh City five years before. **AP IMAGES.**

tactics. Pervading all types of training is political indoctrination and ideological awareness-raising.

Uniforms and Weapons. Uniforms are similar to those used in the military. Collar tab insignia for officers and noncommissioned officers have a green base instead of the red base found in army uniforms. Shoulder boards also have a green base instead of the brown base used for army officers and the gray base is used for army noncommissioned officers.

Armament and weapons are similar to those in the army infantry units. The principal weapons are submachine guns, automatic rifles, rifles, pistols, and hand grenades.

HUMAN RIGHTS

As in other Communist states, Vietnam has a deplorable human rights record. Security forces commit serious abuses including arbitrary detention and beatings of religious and political dissidents. The government restricts or abridges a number of civil rights, including the right to free speech, free exercise of religion, the right to gather and

to travel, and the right to privacy. Many of the restrictions are based on grounds of national security or societal stability. Citizens are arrested and detained arbitrarily if the authorities believe that they are a threat to national security or have publicly dissented from official policy.

CRIME

Crime Statistics. Offenses reported to the police per 100,000 population: 74. Of which:

- Murder: 1.5
- Burglary: 8.5

CORRECTIONAL SYSTEM

The penal code consists of a body of decrees, legislation, and rulings, some of which date from the colonial period. Judicial concepts and practices combine Vietnamese, Chinese, French, and Soviet-era elements. In the absence of a uniform code of criminal law, sentences vary greatly for the same offense, and political considerations often intrude on judicial decisions. Crimes against the state are dealt with more seriously than other types of crimes.

Information on the prison system is scanty. Prison installations and facilities, with only a few exceptions, consist almost entirely of those inherited from the French. The major prisons are in Ho Chi Minh City, Hanoi, Haiphong, Nam Dinh, and the prison island of Con San, 140 miles south of Hanoi. The Chi Hoa in Ho Chi Minh City is considered the largest. Each provincial and district capital has a detention center and a jail to confine prisoners during interrogation. There are some Soviet-style labor camps in outlying areas.

Prison Conditions. Vietnamese penal philosophy emphasizes isolation of offenders—rather than punishment—as a prelude to rehabilitation and reformation. As in other socialist countries, prisoners are exposed to relentless indoctrination to determine whether they are salvageable. Punishments tend to be harsh. Those in solitary confinement are stripped and locked in a small, windowless cell for days or weeks at a time and are given one small bowl of rice for lunch and dinner and one bucket of water. Police sometimes beat suspects while arresting or interrogating them. Conditions of pretrial prisoners are reportedly even more harsh. Some political and other prisoners are denied visitation rights. Prisoners are required to work, but are denied wages. Political and religious prisoners are held in remote prisons, such as Z30a at Xuan Loc in an isolated part of Dong Nai province.

Prison Statistics.

- Total Prison Population: 55,000
- Prison Population Rate per 100,000: 71
- Female Prisoners: 5.5%

George Thomas Kurian

Yemen

Official country name: Republic of Yemen
Capital: Sanaa
Geographic description: Consisting of the southeastern littoral of the Arabian Peninsula, bordering the Arabian Sea, the Gulf of Aden, and the Red Sea, between Oman and Saudi Arabia
Population: 20,727,063 (est. 2005)

■ ■ ■

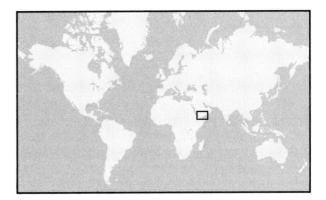

LAW ENFORCEMENT

History. Yemen represents the fusion of two different entities: North Yemen and South Yemen. North Yemen was liberated from the Ottomans in 1918 and went through several political stages to become a republic in the 1960s. South Yemen was a British protectorate until 1968. The first police force in South Yemen was the Aden Police Force set up in 1939 by the British. After the Marxist takeover of the country, all traces of British influence were purged from this force and a new Public Security Force was set up in its place. Policing in North Yemen was more a tribal than a government matter until the fall of the imams and the establishment of a republic.

Structure and Organization. There are three main divisions of the Public Security Force: Criminal Investigation Department, Riot and Security Police, and Rural Police. The national police are divided into four zones: Central at Sanaa, Eastern at Ta'izz, Southern at Aden, and Western at Hodeida. They are under the Ministry of the Interior, but there is provision for dual control and administration at the governorate level. The Public Security Force and the Armed Police are quasi-military mobile forces armed with light, crew-served weapons and small arms and equipped with radio. The Rural Police are scattered over more than 100 police posts. Many of the policemen lack professionalism and training and are designed only to undertake token law and order functions. In towns like Sanaa, Aden, and Hodeida the urban police also respond to public requests for medical and other emergency assistance and carry out other routine police duties. Beyond the Public Security Force there is an internal security unit under the Ministry of State Security.

In the northern and central Zaydi areas internal order and security are the responsibility of the tribal sheikhs.

Education and Training. The Police Academy for officers is located in Sanaa, and there are three training units for enlisted personnel in Hodeida, Ta'izz, and Sanaa. Officers and senior enlisted personnel are sent to police schools in Saudi Arabia, Kuwait, and Egypt.

Police Statistics.

- Total Police Personnel: 9,318

- Population per Police Officer: 2,224

CRIME

Crime Statistics. Total offenses reported to the police per 100,000 population: 63. Of which:

- Murder: 5.3

- Assault: 3.2

- Burglary: 1.2

- Automobile Theft: 3.6

CORRECTIONAL SYSTEM

Before independence crime was not a major problem and was handled in accordance with tribal justice. The principal jail in the south is the Al Manusrah Prison in Aden. In the north the major prisons are at Sanaa, Hodeida, Ibb, and Dhamār.

Prison Conditions. Prison conditions are poor and do not meet internationally recognized standards. Prisons are overcrowded, sanitary conditions are primitive, and food and health care inadequate. The cells lack bedding or mattresses. Inmates rely on relatives for food and medicine. Prison authorities exact bribes from prisoners or refuse to release prisoners who have completed their sentence until family members pay a bribe. Tribal leaders use the prison system to lock up their enemies. Conditions are equally deplorable in women's prisons, where children are incarcerated with their mothers. Female prisoners may be released from prison only if so authorized by their male relatives. Female prisoners are also subjected to sexual harassment and violent interrogation.

Prison Statistics.

- Total Prison Population: 14,000

- Prison Population Rate per 100,000: 83

George Thomas Kurian

Zambia

Official country name: Republic of Zambia
Capital: Lusaka
Geographic description: Landlocked country in southern Africa, east of Angola
Population: 11,261,795 (est. 2005)

■■■

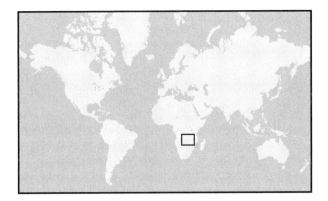

LAW ENFORCEMENT

History. Before independence in 1964 Zambia was known as Northern Rhodesia, and the Northern Rhodesia Police Force set up by the colonial authorities were responsible for law enforcement in the towns. The Native Authorities were charged with law and order in rural areas, but in most cases the only police presence outside of the main towns consisted of an unarmed messenger serving court summons. In serious situations the Northern Rhodesia Police could be called on by the Native Authorities. At the time of independence the national police force had a strength of 6,000.

In 1964 the Northern Rhodesia Police Force was transferred to Zambia and became the Zambia Police Force. Most European and Asian officers remained with the force for many years thereafter, allowing an orderly transfer of functions to native Zambians.

Structure and Organization. The first Zambian constitution established the Zambia Police Force as one of the public (civil) services administered by the Public Service Commission. The 1973 constitution removed the police and prison services from the jurisdiction of the Public Service Commission and established the Police and

Prison Service Commission consisting of a chairman and between three and six members. In 1979 the Police and Prison Commission was combined with three other commissions under the title of Civil Service and placed under the supervision of a minister of state in the Office of the Prime Minister. The actual line of command flows through an inspector general of police, whose staff includes a commissioner, a deputy commissioner, and a senior assistant commissioner. Criminal investigations are under the command of a senior assistant commissioner, while all other departments are under the command of another assistant commissioner. Administrative control of the force is vested in the Ministry of Home Affairs.

As the sole national law enforcement agency, the strength of the Zambia Police Force has grown from 6,000 at independence to over 18,000, and is augmented by over 2,000 members of the Zambia Police Reserve. Its main headquarters is in Lusaka. It has five functional departments: Administration, Staff, Criminal Investigation, Communications, and Training. Operationally, the force is broken down into nine territorial divisions that are coterminous with the provinces. Provincial units are commanded by an assistant commissioner or senior superintendent. There are also four special divisions: the Mobile Unit, headquartered at Kamfinsa (near Ndola); the paramilitary battalion, headquartered at Lilayi (near Lusaka); the Police Training School, also at Lilayi; and the Tazara Police, headquartered at Lusaka. The last is a special security force that protects the Tanzania-Zambia Railway.

Subordinate units include divisional police, district police, and police posts established in towns and villages. Grade structures conform to the colonial pattern and are grouped into three basic categories: superior officers, subordinate officers, and other ranks. In the larger towns the subordinate officers supervise the activities of sergeants and constables and manage the so-called charge offices, where public complaints are received and police records are maintained. Subordinate officers, sergeants, and constables participate in beat duty and operate motorized patrols.

In dealing with major unrest the police are assisted by the Mobile Unit or the Paramilitary Battalion. The latter is divided into four operational companies, each of which consists of four platoons with a total strength of 1,000. The Mobile Unit has a similar structure.

The Mounted Section is often visible on ceremonial occasions, when it escorts the president. Besides ceremonial assignments, it also combats cattle rustlers. The Marine Service operates a variety of small boats and craft in antismuggling patrols along the lakes Tanganyika and Mweru in the northeastern part of the country and anti-infiltration patrols on Lake Kariba in the south.

A rather unusual feature of the Zambia Police Force is the Prosecutions Branch. Almost all criminal prosecutions in magistrate courts are conducted by police prosecutors under the general supervision of the director of public prosecutions. Police officers above the rank of subinspector are appointed as public prosecutors after a nine-month course, at the end of which they must pass an examination in criminal law and procedures and rules of evidence. The Prosecutions Branch is headed by a senior superintendent attached to the Lusaka headquarters.

Education and Training. The Police Training School at Lilayi provides initial training for new police recruits and offers promotion courses, refresher training, motor vehicle and motor cycle courses, traffic courses, and instructor training for all ranks. The school is commanded by a senior superintendent. Basic training for recruits lasts 26 weeks. To be accepted as a recruit, a candidate must be between 18 and 25, at least 5 feet 6 inches tall for men and 5 feet 2 inches tall for women, and have a form-three school certificate. The training school includes a dog training school with a large kennel that has trained German shepherds.

Uniforms and Weapons. The uniforms of the lower ranks consists of a gray shirt and khaki shorts worn with a black fez. The officers wear khaki shorts and trousers with a blue peaked cap. Sergeants and corporals wear chevrons on the upper arms. Officers wear badges of rank on the epaulettes. The Zambia Police Force is authorized to carry weapons in the performance of its duties, but the law places explicit restrictions on the use of firearms.

Police Statistics.

- Total Police Personnel: 18,442
- Population per Police Officer: 611

HUMAN RIGHTS

Police personnel commit unlawful killings and frequently beat and otherwise abuse those in their custody. The lack of professionalism, investigative skills, and discipline in the police force are serious problems. There are reports that the police release prisoners in exchange for bribes, detain debtors in private monetary disputes in exchange for a portion of the payment owed, and extort money from drivers and truckers at unauthorized roadblocks. A Police Complaints Authority has been established under the amended Police Act. A Police Professional Standard Unit has also been established to investigate cases of police corruption, arbitrary arrest and detention, and other unprofessional conduct by police personnel. The Police Training School provides human rights training for new recruits as well as serving officers.

CRIME

Crime Statistics. Offenses reported to the police per 100,000 population: 666. Of which:

- Murder: 9.8
- Assault: 9.5
- Burglary: 153.5
- Automobile Theft: 9.6

CORRECTIONAL SYSTEM

The basic source of Zambian criminal law is the penal code, which is divided into two parts: general provisions and crimes. The code states that the "principles of English law" apply in Zambia's courts. For example, the burden of proof in a criminal trial rests on the government, proof beyond any reasonable doubt is required, and an accused person may not be placed in double jeopardy. Children under eight cannot be charged with a crime and those between eight and eighteen receive less severe punishment if convicted. The range of punishments is carefully defined, although the courts generally have some latitude in sentencing. Conviction for murder carries a mandatory death sentence. Corporal punishments are prescribed in certain cases and consist of whipping with a rod or cane.

The responsibility for prisons is vested in the Prison Service of the Ministry of Home Affairs. The minister is advised by the constitutionally appointed Police and Prison Service Commission. There are fifty-three institutions under the control of the Prison Service. Twelve prisons are distributed among the provincial capitals and are designed to house male inmates only. Kabwe, a maximum-security prison, is designated for hardened criminals; Kasama Prison in Northern province is for female convicts whose sentence exceeds three months; and Katambora Reformatory, near Livingstone, is for juvenile offenders. Prison staff are trained at the Training School in Kabwe.

Prison Conditions. By law adult inmates are separated from juveniles, males from females, and first-time offenders from recidivists. Prison conditions are harsh. Severe overcrowding, combined with poor sanitation, inadequate medical facilities, meager food supplies, and lack of potable water result in serious outbreaks of diseases. In 2003 more than ninety-one inmates died from tuberculosis or dysentery. In some prisons starvation occurs because the prison service has inadequate funding for food.

Prison Statistics.

- Total Prison Population: 13,200
- Prison Population Rate per 100,000: 122
- Pretrial Detainees: 38.6%
- Female Prisoners: 1.5%
- Juvenile Prisoners under 19: 0.7%
- Number of Prisons: 53
- Official Capacity of the Prison System: 5,500
- Occupancy Level: 240%

George Thomas Kurian

Zimbabwe

Official country name: Republic of Zimbabwe
Capital: Harare
Geographic description: Landlocked country in southern Africa, between South Africa and Zambia
Population: 12,746,990 (est. 2005)

■■■

LAW ENFORCEMENT

History. When the British South Africa Company settled in and eventually annexed Mashonaland, it organized a private police force, the British South Africa Company Police. In 1896 it became independent of the company as the British South Africa Police (BSAP), which was both an unarmed constabulary and a standing army. When an army was finally created in 1939, the BSAP gave up its military duties, but retained its paramilitary functions until the creation of Rhodesia and Nyasaland in 1953. When the federation was dissolved in 1963, the BSAP had an approximate strength of 8,000. It included a reserve of 35,000 partially trained policemen, three-fourths of whom were white. Most of the African recruits were from the minority Ndebele, who had strong military traditions. They wore military-style uniforms and made considerable use of their authority to bear down on the citizens. They increased their meager income by extracting bribes, by playing confidence games on the gullible, and by outright theft. A large stick or *sjambok* (whip) was the policeman's symbol of authority, and it was freely used. On independence in 1980 the BSAP became the Zimbabwe Republic Police Force (ZRPF).

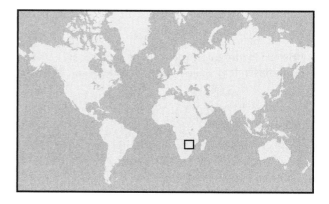

Structure and Organization. The central headquarters of the ZRPF is in Harare, where the headquarters of the Criminal Investigation Department (CID), the Forensics Laboratory, and the Traffic Branch are also located. There are three provincial headquarters—Harare North, Harare South, and Mashonaland South—and three district headquarters—Harare Central, Harare South, and Harare Rural. Other district headquarters are at Gweru, Kwekwe, and Mutare. The Police Reserve headquarters is at Morris Depot, Harare.

Bulawayo, the headquarters of Matabeleland, houses the Matabeleland provincial headquarters, three district headquarters (Bulawayo Central, Bulawayo Western, and Bulawayo Rural), a CID branch, and a provincial training and reserve headquarters. Police camps exist at Gweru and Mutare.

The force is commanded by a commissioner, who is assisted by two deputy commissioners, one for administration and the other for crime and security. Operationally, there are eight branches: a uniformed branch dealing with patrol, crime prevention, accident investigation and highway patrol, a woman's branch, an administration branch, a criminal investigation department, a dog section, and a signals branch.

Territorially, the force is divided into six provinces, each with between one and five districts that, in turn, are divided into stations. The number of stations in a district may range from seven to fourteen. Provinces are commanded by senior assistant commissioners or assistant commissioners, the districts by chief superintendents or superintendents, and the stations by chief inspectors or section officers. In the field there are several grades: patrol officer (senior grade), patrol officer, sergeant major, sergeant (senior grade), sergeant, and constable.

Education and Training. The main training facilities are the Willowvale Police Training Center, the Morris Police Training Depot, and the Tomlinson Police Training Depot, all in Harare.

Uniforms and Weapons. The basic uniform in winter is a khaki tunic and trousers, worn with a leather belt. In summer shorts and a bush jacket are worn with leather leggings and boots. On occasion a short-sleeved gray shirt is worn in place of the bush jacket. Normal headgear is a khaki peaked cap. Women wear a royal-blue dress or tunic and skirt with a dark-blue Robin Hood hat. The force is normally unarmed but may be supplied with rifles, pistols, and shotguns during emergencies.

Police Statistics.

- Total Police Personnel: 15,160
- Population per Police Officer: 841

HUMAN RIGHTS

Zimbabwe has one of the worst human rights record in Africa. There is a systematic government-sanctioned campaign of violence and intimidation against persons opposed to the rule of President Robert Gabriel Mugabe. Security forces routinely kill and torture political opponents and white farmers whose farms are unconstitutionally expropriated. Supporters of the Zimbabwe African National Union (ZANU), the ruling party, occupy white-owned commercial farms and abduct, torture, rape, and kill their owners as well as any one who protests these illegal actions. There are reports of politically motivated disappearances. Youth militias consisting of ruffians and thugs are organized by the government to threaten its enemies. The government has packed the

courts and undermined the independence of the judiciary. According to the Zimbabwe Human Rights Forum (ZHRF), in 2002 fifty-eight political activists opposed to Mugabe were killed and thirty-five were abducted and never heard from again. Human rights groups report that there are torture chambers in government offices, police stations, and schools to brutalize opposition supporters. The ZHRF reported 1,061 cases of torture during 2003 as part of a government-inspired campaign of violence. In a number of rural areas ZANU supporters conduct *pungwes* (forced nightly political gatherings) in which hundreds of villages are rounded up, driven to remote areas, and forced to renounce opposition to the president.

CRIME

Crime Statistics. Offenses reported to the police per 100,000 population: 5,619. Of which:

- Murder: 9
- Assault: 198.4
- Burglary: 435.9
- Automobile Theft: 1.4

CORRECTIONAL SYSTEM

The corrections system is administered by the Zimbabwe Prison Service under the Ministry of Justice, Legal, and Parliamentary Affairs.

Prison Conditions. As a result of overcrowding and unsanitary conditions, the prisons breed all kinds of diseases, such as cholera, diarrhea, and HIV/AIDS. HIV/AIDS contributes to many deaths in prison—1,051 since 1998. The number of female prisoners has been growing for crimes of prostitution, embezzlement, fraud, and petty theft. There are an estimated 2,000 women in prison. Many of these women are obliged to raise their children in prison. Juveniles are held separately from adults and pretrial detainees from hardened criminals.

Prison Statistics. The prison service runs 41 prisons and penitentiaries with a total population of 21,000, of whom 29.6 percent are pretrial detainees, 1 percent are juveniles, and 4.8 percent are foreigners. The prisons are designed to hold only 16,000, and the occupancy level is 131.3 percent of capacity.

George Thomas Kurian

Appendixes

Police Codes of Ethics

MEMBER CODE OF ETHICS

SOURCE IACP Constitution.

INTRODUCTION *With some 14,000 members in the United States and 67 other countries, the International Association of Chiefs of Police is the most universally representative police association. Responding to a proposal by a Vice President, Lee Brown, that the IACP develop a code tailored to the professional enhancement of police executives, the IACP Staff and Parliamentarian Francis Looney drafted a code that was extensively discussed before being adopted by the Board of Officers and then ratified by the Executive Committee. It is incorporated in the Association's Rules as Rule XXXIV.*

CODE OF ETHICS

The members of the International Association of Chiefs of Police collectively adhere to the principle that a standard of professional conduct for its membership is desirable and that through vigilant enforcement of these standards, the professionalism and performance of police executives internationally will be enhanced.

Basic Tenets

Section 1:

The membership of the International Association of Chiefs of Police (hereafter IACP) is dedicated to the principles of effective and democratic government through the appointment of police executives by appropriately constituted elected or appointed officials. Members will maintain a constructive and practical approach to their duties within the parameters of the policies set by the governing body and appropriate statutes and ordinances.

Section 2:

IACP members shall be dedicated to the highest ideals of honor and integrity to maintain the respect and confidence of their governmental officials, subordinates, the public, and their fellow police executives.

a. Members should conduct themselves so as to maintain public confidence in their profession, their department, and in their performance of the public trust.

b. Members should conduct their official and personal affairs in such a manner so as to give the clear impression they cannot be improperly influenced in the performance of their official duties.

Section 3:

IACP members shall adhere to the highest standards in application and maintenance of employment.

a. At all times, members shall completely and accurately represent their credentials, including prior employment, education, certifications, and personal history.

b. Members seeking a police executive position should demonstrate professional respect for incumbents and those seeking the same position. Professional respect does not preclude honest differences of opinion. It does preclude attacking a person's motives or integrity in order to be appointed to a position. Members should not seek employment in a jurisdiction having an incumbent chief law enforcement administrator who has not resigned, retired, or been officially notified of termination.

c. Members who officially accept an appointment as chief law enforcement administrator should not fail to report to that position. This does not preclude the possibility of a member considering several offers or seeking several positions at the same time; but once a bona fide offer has been accepted, that commitment should be honored.

d. Members should commit to at least two years of service in any position, barring any unforeseen actions by the governing body or severe personal problems. This minimum period permits implementation of programs and opportunity for their effectiveness to be realized.

Section 4:

Members of the IACP represent that the primary function of the police executive is to serve the best interests of a respective jurisdiction and the law enforcement profession.

a. Members of the IACP are committed to fair and impartial enforcement of laws and ordinances and respect for fundamental human rights.

b. Members of the IACP are dedicated to innovative and participative management, at all times seeking to improve their departments, increase productivity, and remain responsive to the needs of their jurisdiction.

c. Members of the IACP shall continually strive to improve their personal knowledge and abilities and that of their fellow chiefs through independent study, courses, meetings, and seminars. This responsibility extends to the members of their department.

d. Members of the IACP believe that all supervision and management should be fair and equitable for all levels of employees and that all statutes and personnel regulations should be honored. All actions relating to selection, retention, promotion, and transfers should be based on ability and equal opportunity.

e. All policies, procedures, and rules regulating conduct of officers should be in writing and available to all personnel. This includes disciplinary and grievance policies and operating procedures of the department.

f. Members of the IACP shall encourage friendly and courteous service and strive to improve communications with all members of the public, at all times seeking improvement in the quality and image of public service.

g. Members of the IACP shall be committed to advancing the principles of respect for individual dignity and respect for constitutional rights of all persons with whom their departments come in contact.

h. Members of the IACP recognize that they should refrain from participation in the election of the employing governing body and from all partisan political activities which would impair their ability to serve all segments of their community. This standard is not to be construed to prevent any member from voting or expressing a personal opinion where appropriate.

i. Members of the IACP recognize that their position requires them to provide leader ship by example, including adherence to all governmental and departmental written directives as applicable.

j. Members of the IACP represent that their function is to administer their agencies within the framework of the policies articulated by their governing body and state and national law. Any actions directed toward change in those policies, including lobbying, shall be conducted in an open and constructive manner with the knowledge of their employers.

Section 5:

Members of the IACP believe that professional standards include the regulation of personal and financial conduct.

a. Members shall not seek favor or personal gain through misuse of confidential information or their public time or facilities.

b. Members shall not directly or indirectly solicit any gift, or accept or receive any gift, whether in the form of money, services, loans, travel, entertainment, hospitality, promises, or in any other form, under circumstances in which it could reasonably be inferred the gift was intended to influence them, or could reasonably be expected to influence them, in the performance of their duties or was intended as a reward for any official action on their part.

c. Members shall not invest or hold any investment, directly or indirectly, in any business, commercial, or other private transaction which creates a conflict with their official duties.

d. Members shall not disclose to others, or use to further the personal interest of themselves or others, confidential information acquired by them in the course of their official duties.

e. Members shall not engage in, solicit, negotiate for, or promise to accept private employment or render services for private interests or conduct a private business when such employment, service, or business creates a conflict with, or impairs the proper discharge of, their official duties.

f. Members shall not, acting in their official capacity, endorse commercial products by agreeing to the use of their picture, endorsement, or quotation in paid advertisements, whether for compensation or not. Members further should not permit any endorsement of commercial products by department employees acting in their official capacity, whether for compensation or not.

Enforcement

The following procedures will be adhered to in all actions arising under this code of ethics:

Section 6:

The President will appoint an Ethics Committee of at least three members of the Executive Committee and/or Past Presidents to hear alleged code violations. The President shall name one of the three members to be Chair of the committee.

Section 7:

a. The Chair of the Ethics Committee will be designated to receive all complaints. Complaints regarding IACP members' conduct can be brought by any member of the IACP or by any responsible individual or organization outside of the membership. The Chair will review all complaints and conduct whatever investigation and inquiry deemed necessary to determine whether sufficient cause exists to conduct a hearing into the allegation. If there is an apparent or possible violation of the code of conduct, the Chair will make a written recommendation to the Executive Committee that a hearing be conducted. The Executive Committee will approve or disapprove the Chair's recommendation.

b. Complaints of a frivolous or an unfounded nature may be dismissed by the Ethics Committee, with the written concurrence of the President. All dismissals of frivolous or unfounded nature shall be in writing and supported by the results and conclusions of the Chair's investigation. Consistent or repeated frivolous complaints by an IACP member against other members may subject that member to disciplinary action by the IACP upon motion by the committee, with the written concurrence of the Executive Committee.

Section 8:

IACP members will be held to the standards of behavior set forth in Rule 4, Basic Tenets of this Code, and specifically, but not exclusively, to the standards set forth in Rule 4, Sections 2, 3, 4 and 5. This includes adherence to the laws they are sworn to uphold.

Members will also be subject to disciplinary action for behavior other than that specified in the aforementioned provisions that brings disrepute upon their department or their profession.

Section 9:

Upon receiving the Executive Committee's approval to initiate disciplinary action, the Chair will schedule a hearing before the Ethics Committee.

Section 10:

The alleged violator will be notified by registered letter by the Chair at least two weeks before the meeting. The alleged violator may request a continuance for a specified duration upon written motion to the Chair of the Ethics Committee. No IACP member shall be granted more than two such continuances. If the alleged violator does not request a continuance, the hearing may be conducted in the alleged violator's absence.

Section 11:

The date, time, and site of the hearing shall be determined by written order of the President.

Section 12:

The hearings shall be conducted as follows:

a. The Chair shall conduct the hearing.

b. The hearing will be conducted in a formal manner approximating a governmental administrative legal proceeding. The degree of formality will be determined by the Executive Committee depending on the nature of the allegations.

c. Attendance at the hearing will be restricted to the alleged violator, members of the Executive Committee, and members of the Ethics Committee. Witnesses will not be permitted to the hearing room except when offering testimony.

d. The alleged violator may present witnesses on their behalf. The party alleging the violations may testify or present witnesses on their behalf, or may offer testimony by means of affidavits submitted to the Chair of the Ethics Committee prior to the date of the hearing.

e. Either party may examine and cross-examine witnesses. In addition, members of the hearing panel and the Executive Committee members may ask questions directly of the witnesses.

f. All hearings shall be recorded or transcribed verbatim.

Section 13:

a. The Ethics Committee, after hearing all information, shall recommend one of four potential courses of action. Any action taken requires an affirmative two-thirds vote. Decisions will be based on a standard of the preponderance of the evidence.

b. The four possible courses of action are:

1. Unfounded. The alleged violation did not occur. An unfounded determination will be considered a dismissal of all charges with prejudice.

2. Exonerated. The incident occurred but was not a violation of the standards set forth in this code.

3. Sustained. The preponderance of the evidence presented to the hearing board supports the allegation, and the violation is a breach of the standards set forth in the code.

4. Deferral. The hearing has been deferred due to the unforeseen unavailability of information or witnesses.

Section 14:

In the event of a sustained classification, the Executive Committee shall levy one of three sanctions, based on the nature and severity of the violation and the recommendations and findings of the hearing panel contained in the Chair's written report to the Executive Committee. The Executive Committee may levy one of the following three penalties under Article 2, Section 12, of the IACP constitution.

a. Censure. A letter to the violator citing the section of Rule 4 violated and the Association's disapproval.

b. Suspension. A letter to the violator, citing the section violated, and advising the violator that they are suspended from IACP membership and privileges for a period of time determined by the Executive Committee, after which the individual may apply to the Executive Committee for readmission to IACP. No public notification will be made by IACP except with the express approval of the Board of Officers or the Executive Committee.

c. Expulsion. A letter to the violator, citing the section violated, and advertising that the violator is expelled permanently from IACP membership and privileges.

THE POLICING PRINCIPLES OF THE METROPOLITAN POLICE

SOURCE *From* The Principles of Policing and Guidance for Professional Behaviour. *New Scotland Yard, London: Public Information Department, Metropolitan Police, 1985.*

INTRODUCTION *The Principles represent the first major attempt of the London Metropolitan Police to restate the "Primary Objects of Police" that were enunciated on its formation in 1829. Sponsored by the incumbent Commissioner, Sir Kenneth Newman, they represent the most significant articulation of police standards that has thus far been attempted, combining maxims and commentary in a sustained and coherent statement. Handsomely produced, but poorly marketed, The Blue Book, as it was popularly called, failed to win internal acceptance, and by 1990, it had been superseded by what came to be the nationally sponsored Association of Chief Police Officers (ACPO) "Statement of Values and Common Purpose."*

THE POLICING PRINCIPLES OF THE METROPOLITAN POLICE

The Police Objectives

The primary aims and duties of the Metropolitan Police are to uphold the Rule of Law, to protect and assist the citizen and to work for the prevention and detection of crime and the maintenance of a peaceful society, free of the fear of crime and disorder. They will carry out these aims and duties in consultation and cooperation with others in the community.

The Rationale

This rationale explains and expands the main phrases in the statement of police objectives, that is to say: "upholding the rule of law" "protecting and assisting the citizen" "cooperation with others" "maintenance of a peaceful community" and "fear of crime and disorder."

Upholding the Rule of Law

The aim of "upholding the Rule of Law" encompasses two distinct but inter-related duties: the duty of upholding the law of the land (as enacted by Parliament or as established by common law) and maintaining The Queen's Peace; the related duty of keeping strictly within prescribed powers, abstaining from arbitrary action and respecting the individual rights and freedoms of all citizens.

The Law and The Queen's Peace

In discharging the duty of maintaining a state of public tranquility. Where a conflict arises between the duty of the police to maintain order and their duty to enforce the law, the solution will be found in the priority which is to be given in the last resort to the maintenance of public order, and in the constant and commonsense exercise of police discretion. Priority will also be given to dealing with those crimes which most harm or cause anxiety to the public.

In upholding the law, the main emphasis of policing will be upon prevention. This principle has obtained since the establishment of the Force in 1829 when the primary objects were formalized as follows:

> It should be understood at the outset that the principal object to be attained is the prevention of crime. To this great end every effort of the police is to be directed. The security of person and property, the preservation of the public tranquility and all other objects of a police establishment will thus be better effected than by detention and punishment of the offender after he has succeeded in committing the crime.

This statement remains a valid description of the police function and one which will continue to guide the Metropolitan Police. But in the light of rapid social and cultural changes in recent years, there is a need to expand the statement and to develop the interpretation of the "prevention of crime" and the "preservation of public tranquility." The revised scope of these concepts should take account of developments within the community in broad-based consultation and participation in the control of crime.

"Prevention" is the chief concern of the Metropolitan Police and one which will govern decisions on how manpower and equipment is allocated. Skill in the "detection" of offenses is also important in deterring offenders and in protecting life and property. It will be the aim of the Metropolitan Police to enhance their effectiveness in detection by improving the collation of intelligence and analysis of crime, as well as the preparation and presentation of cases.

Respect for Individual Rights

In carrying out their duties, police will be governed by the following principles, which are central to the Rule of Law:

a. That a respect for citizens's individual rights and freedoms and the avoidance of arbitrary or unlawful action are fundamental to the constitutional meaning of the Rule of Law and thus to the whole meaning and purpose of police duty;

b. That The Queen's Peace will be endangered if citizens perceive police action to be inconsistent with the fundamental values of British society. These values emphasize a just balance between order and freedom and mark an abhorrence of unfair or arbitrary action by the State or its officials;

c. That the fundamental values of British society are underpinned by procedure and legal rules and assumptions. Of particular importance in the context of police duty are: the presumption of innocence; the right to free speech; the right to free association; restrictions on powers of arrest and detention; the right to silence; the right of access to legal advice; the prohibition of discriminatory behavior towards individuals, classes of person and minority groups; the observance of suspects's rights; the requirement of reasonableness when acting upon suspicion; integrity in the collection and presentation of evidence; respect for human dignity; the need to use only such force as is necessary to accomplish a legitimate purpose; and the thought that in safeguarding these principles, the constitutional facet of the Rule of Law is an unifying theme in the regulation of police conduct; if upholding the Rule of Law is a primary aim of police, then observance of the principles must follow;

d. That the British ideal is that policing should be shaped by the consent of the population. Such consent is conditional upon the observance by police of the individual's rights and liberties. Only in this way will the respect of the public be retained and the duties and functions of police be capable of being effectively discharged;

e. The effectiveness of the police will be undermined if their actions are perceived to be inconsistent with the Rule of Law;

f. That respect for the law is intimately connected with the public's perception of police standards and behavior. It is, therefore, essential that in both word and deed, police officers reflect the fundamental values of British democracy, demonstrating total impartiality to all, regardless of race, color, creed or social position.

Protecting and Assisting the Citizen

The police have a duty to: protect persons and property; befriend anyone who needs their help; assist with major or minor emergencies;control road traffic and advise local authorities on related matters; assure the safety of the Royal Family and maintain security at a wide variety of public events; and undertake a variety of regulatory and supervisory duties, on behalf of Government departments and others.

Cooperation with Others

There is now abundant evidence that police action alone is insufficient to reduce crime. The aim of gaining the cooperation of others, therefore, goes beyond earning respect and approval for policing and extends to involving the active assistance of the public in preventing crime and helping to preserve the peace.

It is a principle of British law that the police are only members of the public who are paid to give full attention to duties, many of which are incumbent on every citizen in the interests of community welfare and orderly existence. It is, therefore, the duty of every citizen to cooperate with the police in the prevention of crime. In modern circumstances, however, there is a need for an organized framework for promoting positive cooperation between the police and the public for reducing crime, and the continuing aim of the Metropolitan Police must be to work with others to develop collaborative strategies against crime and disorder. This aim includes invoking the assistance of statutory and voluntary agencies and local authorities. Many of the apparently isolated incidents to which police are called are symptoms of more general substantive problems with roots in a wide range of social and environmental conditions. The aim of the Metropolitan Police will, therefore, be to work with other agencies to develop what is known as a "situational" or "problem-solving" approach to crime prevention, where, rather than merely dealing with individual acts of law-breaking, careful analysis is made of the total circumstances surrounding the commission of types of crime, taking account of wide-ranging social and environmental factors, in order better to understand, and counter, the causes of those acts.

In pursuance of this aim, the police will endeavor to work closely with consultative committees with a view to: sharing information and jointly analyzing crime and public order problems; anticipating trends of crime and disorder; identifying and discussing alternative means of reducing crime and disorder; identifying community interests and helping to co-ordinate the activities of formal and informal groups within a neighborhood; and implementing and monitoring specific courses of action.

In summary, the Metropolitan Police aims to be forward-looking as well as outward-looking, considerate of the present and future needs of the community and helpful towards schemes of social development and renewal, while at the same time requesting a constructive contribution by others to the solution of those aspects of the problems encountered by the police.

Cooperation and consultation with others is, however, circumscribed by the fact that the police have a duty impartially to uphold the law. They are not subject to political control in operational matters nor in individual prosecutions. The Metropolitan Police does, however, fully recognize the importance of consultation and cooperation with the community in discharging its duties.

Maintenance of a Peaceful Community

In pursuing the aim and duty of maintaining a peaceful community, members of the Metropolitan Police will view their role as one involving cooperation with others in the creation and maintenance of a way of life in communities which strikes the optimum balance between the collective interests of all citizens and the personal rights of all individuals. The creation of this kind of community requires a collaborative effort by all social agencies organized within the framework of a clear social policy which seeks out alternative or complementary options to conventional law enforcement.

In cases of potential riot or disorder, police will think first in terms of mediation, short term intervention and the prevention of physical conflict. If, despite these efforts, disorder erupts, police will act firmly and decisively, meeting force with such force as is necessary and reasonable in the circumstances to prevent crime and to protect life and property. It will be the policy of the Force to develop professional skills with a view to containing disorder with the least possible injury to all the people involved. The safety of citizens is paramount, but the police response will be governed also by the policy that police casualties will be avoided, as far as possible, by the use of reasonable force against people who threaten to injure police officers.

Fear of Crime and Disorder

The Metropolitan Police will pay special attention to the phenomenon of the fear of crime and disorder. Research suggests that the fear of crime has emerged as a distinct causative factor in the process of neighborhood decline, and its accompanying destabilization within the community.

There is now evidence that citizens's fear of crime is connected not only with actual crime rates and with persons perceived as potential criminals, but also the appearance of a neighborhood. Perceptions are based on the features of the physical environment such as vandalism, litter, graffiti and derelict or abandoned property. Perceptions are also formed by the sight and experience of disorderly people such as those suffering from drink or drugs, as well as from any generalized flouting of laws designed to maintain the well-being of the community.

In areas where this menacing, disorderly or lawless atmosphere grows apparent, retail profits become depressed and shops and businesses are inclined to move elsewhere; property declines in value and the municipal rate base is eroded. Such "disinvestments" feeds on itself, and, joining with other factors including the fear of crime, accelerates the spiral of decay. The impression given is that nobody cares for the area; apathy is fostered which, because it undermines public will to become involved and cooperate, lowers the effectiveness of the police.

Local authorities can reinforce public confidence and tranquility by tackling dereliction and can reduce opportunities for crime in many ways. The police should help and advise them in such crime prevention activity.

Addressing the fear of crime has important crime-preventive significance. Therefore the Metropolitan Police will endeavor to work with others:

i. to place crime in accurate perspective (fear being based often on exaggerated assessments of danger);

ii. to promote public self-help and confidence through the medium of consultative committees, crime prevention panels, neighborhood watch schemes and victim support schemes;

iii. to make police action supportive of, and complementary to, borough improvement schemes;

iv. to cooperate with local planners in schemes for "designing-out" crime and promoting informal social controls;

v. to deploy police foot patrols where they will help to reinforce other measures designed to stimulate confidence and self-help;

vi. to improve analysis and assessment of environmental factors which give rise to crime, fear of crime and neighborhood decline.

Organizational Implications

This revised and updated statement of the purpose and philosophy of the Metropolitan Police implies the need for complementary changes in organization and direction within the Force. Whilst many of the principles set out in the police objectives are of an enduring character, the organizational implications will change in response to a constant appraisal of the police environment. The Metropolitan Police is, therefore, pursuing a program of carefully managed change to achieve a strategy harmonious with community needs. The focal points for this strategy are at divisional level where objectives and priorities will be identified in partnership with consultative committees and social agencies.

Organization and Direction

The organization and direction of the Force should:

i. Provide for strategic policy-making to guide the Force consciously and systematically towards future goals and should involve the entire organization in that process;

ii. allow for sufficient devolution of responsibility to divisions to permit operational commanders at these levels to respond flexibly and effectively to local needs and priorities;

iii. allow for such decentralization of decision-making and allocation of resources as will facilitate problem-oriented rather than incident-oriented strategies against crime and disorder at divisional level;

iv. ensure that subordinate officers in divisions are fully involved in the strategy so as to encourage their commitment to it in terms of actions and attitudes;

v. give priority to those functions involving direct contact between police and public;

vi. limit specialist units to functions requiring continuity of experience and superior expertise and encourage the deployment of "generalist" personnel;

vii. achieve at all levels by good management a continuous improvement in the cost-efficient and effective use of resources, wherever possible measuring performance against planned objectives;

viii. ensure by maintaining good internal and external communication that policies are clearly understood, that police problems and Force performance are properly appreciated and that the Force is sensitive and responsive to the needs and feelings of the public;

ix. at all times encourage and reward professional competence and integrity and foster these qualities, and adherence to professional excellence, by careful recruitment, development and motivation of staff;

x. encourage in its officers the lawful and compassionate exercise of individual discretion;

xi. acknowledge mistakes willingly and openly, learning from then and taking remedial action.

Overall, the organization and direction of the Force should be aimed a creating an outward-looking service with an appreciation of the connection between policing functions and those of other public agencies and readiness to adapt to changing social and cultural conditions.

GUIDANCE FOR PROFESSIONAL BEHAVIOR

PART ONE

Our Duty as Constables

A constable is a citizen, locally appointed, but with authority under the Crown to protect life and property, to prevent and detect crime, to preserve the Queen's Peace, and to prosecute offenders under the law.

Training School Definition

The Office of Constable

The office of constable is an ancient and honorable one, with a rich an colorful history. Since the passing of the Metropolitan Police Act there ha been further legislation to clarify the powers and duties of the office much case law has appeared, much Parliamentary debate has taken place and, especially in recent years, much thought has been given and mud writing has been published, which emphasizes that those who occupy the distinguished office are operationally independent in that they are held to law to have full discretion over whether or not to exercise their power providing that they act reasonably.

This curious operational independence, which brings with it a high degree of personal independence, and therefore a high degree of personal responsibility, is very important to you and me for it places upon us obligations to our fellow citizens which have flourished in modern times and which show no sign of diminishing.

The fact that the office you hold is unique and that it has a clear legal base, is borne out by the terms of the Constable's Oath or Declaration. When you and I joined the service we swore or declared: *I solemnly and sincerely declare and affirm that I will well and truly serve our Sovereign Lady the Queen in the Office of Constable without favor or affection, malice or ill-will, and that I will, to the best of my power, cause the peace to be kept and preserved, and prevent all offenses against the persons and properties of Her Majesty's subject, and that while I continue to hold the said office I will, to the best of my skill and knowledge, discharge all the duties thereof faithfully according to law.* You will see that this declaration, which binds you throughout your service, has three main parts.

Firstly, it defines your principal duties as being to keep the peace and to prevent crime. Secondly, it obliges you always to be impartial by acting without favor or affection, malice or ill-will—the very root of your operational independence. Thirdly, it indicates clearly that as a servant of the Sovereign you own your duty to the community as a whole and to every individual member of it.

Thus it is clear that, though not a Government servant, you are a public servant, and you are charged with performing all the duties of your office whatever they might by law become from time to time, and that you are pledged to strict impartiality.

This may seem as an onerous responsibility. We must see what principles we can define for ourselves, which will help us to form our judgments and to guide our conduct and attitudes. One basic principle can be defined very easily, and straight away. It arises out of our place as citizens in a free society.

The Important Role of the Constable in our Free Society

As a result of the history and traditions of our country, we all enjoy many freedoms which we would be wise to cherish, even if only as a matter of self interest as citizens. And as police officers we are obliged as a duty by a benign exercise of our powers, to sustain constantly and if possible to enhance, the democratic rights and freedoms which we all share.

One of the basic characteristics of a democracy is, of course, that government is carried out with the consent of the majority of those governed—consent in the sense that people have the power to change it if they disapprove, that they support the laws made on their behalf by the government and, equally importantly, that they consent to the way in which those laws are enforced.

Therefore, in the context of our consideration of the contribution which the citizen-constable makes to the public good, it is important that we should not look upon the enforcement of the law as an end in itself. Enforcement serves many ends, one of the most important of which is to assist in creating that state of civilized tranquility which enables individuals to enjoy their rights and attain their lawful aspirations. To do this we need the help of the public.

Throughout our history this has been accepted as a wise attitude for us, as constables, to adopt. Experience, some of it bitter, has taught us that our fellow citizens do not take at all kindly to officiousness on the part of anyone. They avoid the zealot and the bully, and they are far too robust, and love their freedoms far too much, to put up for long with any fervent or unrelieved control—as many an enemy in the past has discovered to his cost.

This means that any unreasonable, abrupt and over-zealous action by us will not achieve an orderly society, except perhaps in the very short term, but will rapidly lose for the Force its public support. And, since a police service without public support will not be able to police by consent, and in the long term will not be able to police at all, one of the very cornerstones of democratic government will have been put at risk.

On the other hand, by acknowledging always that you are a friend, a guide and a servant of your fellow citizens, and never their master, by adopting an appropriately firm but conciliatory and helpful manner to everyone you meet, and by acting always in ways which are manifestly fair and lawful, so naturally attracting public acceptance of police activity, you and your service colleagues can help to sustain our democratic way of life and build up a store of public goodwill to be drawn on in the future.

It is vital therefore that you are aware constantly of the potential that each of your actions has for good or harm and of the importance for the success of policing and of democracy, not only of those actions themselves but of the style you adopt when going about your business. You are part of the complex machinery by which this country remains democratic and free—and an understanding of that should color your every action.

So, although we will go on to deal with some other aspects of our society and develop maxims from those, we can discern even at this early stage of our discussion a general principle which we should keep in the forefront of our minds—that is, that policing is a public service and not just a law enforcement task; the way in which we perform that service makes an important contribution to our democratic and free way of life. A clear duty can be defined from this: "It is your duty to act always for the general public good, as a helpful and reasonable public servant, and not merely as an enforcer of the law."

The Importance of Discretion

A constable, though he must obey lawful and reasonable orders from any senior rank, does not hold his office and exercise his powers at the behest of a more senior officer, who in any case, whatever his title, is constitutionally a constable also. Nor is he answerable to any government official, or to the Home Office or to Parliament. He is answerable to the law and holds his office independently of anyone else; on taking his declaration of office, he has assumed obligations which accrue to him personally.

You will see from this that in making your declaration you have taken on a personal duty which you cannot then betray and an individual discretion which you must exercise with wisdom and skill.

We must therefore discuss whether there are any principles which can be followed to help us exercise discretion sensibly. To do this in a way which can be followed by all members of the Force, we had better start with some basic issues. Initial police training ensures that newly appointed constables have a level of competence adequate to enable them to deal with everyday police problems. They will know, for example, when dealing with an assault of a trivial nature, that any possible injury should be noted, that names and addresses should be exchanged, and that the parties should be advised of their legal remedies. Basic knowledge of this sort brings technical competence, and much of the instruction given to the Force is aimed at increasing the general level of technical competence—by defining as clearly as possible the correct legal procedures to be applied in a particular set of circumstances.

But police officers cannot do their full duty to their fellow citizens by applying standards of technical competence alone. Dearly, if all offenses brought to the attention of police or discovered by police were to result in legal action, courts and police officers would spend most of their time dealing with minor matters at the expense of more serious ones, and the public, and those in other parts of the criminal justice system, would be quick to voice their dismay. Informal action, outside the courts, is often a more effective way of keeping the peace and maintaining order, and is therefore much more in the public interest. And as there are several categories of offences which are often not best dealt with by formal criminal proceedings, it is a cool head, good judgment and a tolerant attitude which are of greatest importance to you.

So, even the youngest and most inexperienced must use sensible discretion when patrolling the streets, in deciding which offences to report, which to warn an offender for, and, on occasions, which to allow to pass without action.

These decisions, which have to be taken often without the advantage of guidance by a supervisor or more experienced colleague, are for you only. They are the first stages in the prosecution process, and are therefore very important matters, demanding fine judgment on your part.

The importance of recognizing that an officer must in certain circumstances be free to decide an issue for himself was acknowledged when the first instructions were issued to the Metropolitan Police in 1829. These were the opening words of the contemporary Instruction Book:

The following general instructions for the different ranks of the Police Force are not to be understood as containing certain rules of conduct applicable to every variety of circumstances that may occur in the performance of their duty; something must necessarily be left to the intelligence and discretion of individuals.

The basic responsibility of your position has not changed in any substantial way, then, in the hundred and fifty or so years since professional policing began; in that time many millions of decisions about whether or not to institute proceedings have been made by individual constables, and the lives of many millions of individual members of the public have therefore been affected to one degree or another.

On the whole the standard of decision making has been remarkably high, although there have been occasional examples of gross ineptitude or malpractice by police when exercising their powers, which have caught the public eye—sometimes spectacularly. Nevertheless, the great majority of decisions are seen by most as being closely in step with public attitudes to different classes of crime and offenses, and with public opinion about how different kinds of offenders should be dealt with. And the standard has been very consistent over the years, too, notwithstanding that changes in the extent and complexity of the law, and in the aspirations and attitudes of society, and in the very pace of life in our great city, have made the exercise of your discretion so much more demanding a task than that which faced your predecessors.

Because the exercise of police power has such an important effect on everyday affairs, it has been from time to time a central issue in cases heard at the Court of Appeal. The result of these cases is that a constable is deemed to have full discretion over whether or not top start the legal process by reporting or arresting an offender, and the decision he takes in any particular case will be supported by the law, provided it can be shown to have been lawfully taken on reasonable grounds. What may amount to reasonable grounds is discussed later.

Thus, yours is not just an individual discretion, it is also a wide discretion—and that brings with it a very wide responsibility.

It may in addition bring much difficulty for you, because the discretion, though wide, is certainly not unfettered and the limits are not all that easy to discern, particularly for younger officers.

On the one hand, for instance, if you were to decide to take an offender before the court for a minor offence in respect of which there were many mitigating circumstances, either known to you or to be discovered by simple enquiry, you may be sure that you would attract disfavor. The least you might expect for your unreasonableness is a hearty rebuke from the court and you might suffer some other kind of discomforts also—from your senior officers, or even, if it could be thought that you had acted maliciously, in the form of some legal action taken against you by the victim of your over-zealousness.

On the other hand, a decision by you not to take any action in circumstances where reasonableness demands clearly that you should do so, can amount to a neglect of duty under the discipline code. In exceptional circumstances your inaction could amount to a crime, that of neglect by a public officer, if you fail quite unreasonably to prevent a crime.

Deliberate and culpable neglect by a public officer (in this context the term includes a constable) of any duty imposed on him by statute or common law, can amount to a criminal offense of misconduct. It is, as we will see, the duty of every police officer to prevent crime; he must not, willfully and without reasonable justification, neglect to carry out that duty, since it is one which is imposed by common law upon all those who hold the office of constable. A recent example of gross neglect of that sort is given in the case of The Crown against Dytham in 1979. A constable saw a man being kicked and beaten in the gutter outside a club from which the man had just been ejected. The man was kicked to death but the constable did not attempt to intervene and stop the attack or to summon assistance. Instead he was heard to say something about it being time for him to finish duty, and he left the scene. This was a disgraceful neglect which rightly led to his conviction and punishment. Of course, such extreme neglect is exceptional, and amounts to rather more than a failure to exercise reasonable discretion. Indeed no discretion arises in a case of that kind, for the duty to act should in the eyes of any reasonable person be so clear, and the surrounding circumstances so unequivocal, as not to give rise to choice.

On the face of things then, it would appear that the exercise of reasonable judgment is all that is required in normal circumstances to keep you comfortably within the bounds of your discretion. But, although that is generally so, there are more problems with this than at first meet the eye, as your experience will show you.

What may be thought entirely reasonable by one person, may not be seen in the same light by another. The issue of whether or not a particular offense should be pursued, and if so with what vigor, is potentially of such importance and public interest, that it is sensible for us to consider it further.

Reasons for Exercising Discretion

Discretion is the art of suiting action to particular circumstances. It is the policeman's daily task.—Lord Scarman

Police discretion is certainly an art rather than a science; it would be impossible to describe, with anything like scientific accuracy, all of the factors you should have in mind when exercising judgment. Nevertheless, you may find it helpful if we discuss some examples, in order that we can identify the principles which underlie the art. They are very simple examples, perhaps, but they will enable us to identify the kinds of principles you must weigh in your balance before deciding what to do.

Let us suppose that you are an officer in uniform, leaving the police station. You pass a number of cars parked in contravention of a waiting restriction. Should you trace and report the drivers, or should you not? There are a number of factors which will influence your decision, depending on circumstances. Here are some of them:

1. Are the cars on your beat? (If they are not, and you can reasonably foresee that the officer who patrols that beat will deal with them, or that they will be dealt with in another way, for instance by Traffic Wardens, and there are no aggravating circumstances, then this becomes a reason for taking no action, and for getting on with your own duty).

2. If they are on your beat, do you have another more important or more urgent duty to perform? (If you have, then that is a reasonable factor for you to weigh. Police business amounts all too often to striking a balance between pressing and conflicting priorities).

3. Are the cars causing such obstruction or danger that they require removal? (If they are, you might need to discount some other consideration, like having other business to get on with, and do something about the cars).

4. How long is it before the parking restriction expires? (If the time is nearly over, you are not likely to achieve any great public purpose by engrossing yourself with such minor offences. Nor are the motorists likely to thank you for your trouble.)

5. What is the feeling of local people about the illegal parking of cars? (If you know the feeling is high, it may be sensible, despite your having other work to do, or despite anything else, to do something about the cars).

We could go on, for there are many other questions and factors which may arise, even in such a simple example as this. None of them is likely to clinch the issue on its own, and each will have some weight depending, as always, on the circumstances. Your problem in a case of this particular kind will be solved largely by your skill in balancing conflicting policing priorities together with your knowledge of what the public regards as important.

Let us take another very simple example. A boy is playing with his football in the street. He is fooling about generally and deliberately throws the ball through a nearby house window, out of which one of his friends is grimacing and hurling gleeful insults. You are passing and are satisfied that what you have seen amounts to criminal damage. Should you take action against the boy? In this case your judgment will depend more on your understanding of the boy and the people involved. While our first problem was one of priorities, this is much more a human problem.

You will first want to establish, as far as possible, what the owner wishes to do about his window, where the offending boy lives, whether he or his parents are willing to pay for the broken window, and whether this will placate the owner. The boy's history will also be very relevant. Is this something he has done before—perhaps even been convicted for it? What is the best way to stop him offending again if there are indications that he is the type of boy who may do so?

Having ascertained and considered all these things, you may very well decide that you should not proceed against the boy; perhaps much more is likely to be achieved by resolving the matter in a neighborly way between the parties at the scene, if that can be done, than by any other course.

Certainly, if you were to have reported the drivers of the cars, or taken proceedings against the boy, without thinking about any of the factors which we have mentioned, you would have been failing properly to exercise your discretion, and thus to perform your duty; in exactly the same way, you would have been neglectful if you had merely walked away from the cars, or ignored the boy. And therein lies perhaps the only principle that can be laid down for you, with certainty, about every incident you deal with: whatever confusion and lack of definition there may be in the factors surrounding an incident, and however unsure you may be about the weight which should be given to a particular factor, your clear duty, whenever time and the pressure of events allow, is to consider them as honestly and reasonably as you can. If necessary and if it is possible you may seek such advice as you can get from others, and then decide the issue by using your judgment to the best of your ability.

There is a further source of help for you. The Attorney General has issued guidelines to all those involved in the process, to indicate the range of factors which should be borne in mind when deciding whether a prosecution should be initiated or continued. Arising from this, a procedure has been developed by which adults who have been arrested for an offence may in appropriate circumstances be cautioned, released and no further action taken.

Some of the advice contained in the Attorney General's guidelines is not directly relevant to the decisions which you may have to take on the street, it is germane more to later decisions, taken about sometimes very complex matters, after reports and investigations are complete. But other parts are very relevant to all cases, such as the requirements to consider: the relative triviality or seriousness of the offense, the attitude of the complainant towards prosecution, the character, age and mental or physical condition of the accused person, the staleness of the offense, the attitude of the public towards the offense alleged, the prevalence of the offense in that area.

You should study the guidelines. They are an important aid to the proper use of your discretion.

And whatever else you may find it right to take into account, you should always include that general question which arises from your prime duty to prevent crime—which course of action will most effectively prevent a repetition of this offense? And also the general question which arises out of your office of constable—which course will be seen by my fellow citizens as humane, reasonable and in the general public interest?

From this first part of our discussion about discretion we can glean another Duty: It is your duty when exercising police powers, to avoid peremptoriness; to weigh carefully all surrounding factors, and to judge these in the light of the Attorney General's Guidance.

But that cannot be the end of it, for there are some occasions when the incidents you are faced with on the streets do not call for any contemplation, but for action. When you see a serious offense, a robbery, or an act of violence, or a breach of the peace, you do not need to hesitate in order to contemplate earnestly upon the likely reaction of victims, or to debate for long with yourself the best way to serve the public interest in these particular circumstances—you get on with it, and arrest those responsible.

In some ways, and certainly in the context of the exercise of careful and tolerant judgment, incidents such as these are relatively easy to deal with. But you must take care to ensure that the requirement for you to show resolution and decisiveness in cases of this kind, which can, if you are successful, lead very rightly to public acclaim, does not lead you to arrogant over-confidence, or to take an unduly dismissive attitude towards the possible plight of the offender, or of others involved. As we shall see in due course, the offender as well as anyone else is entitled to careful and sensitive handling by you.

Of course, crimes such as unprovoked serious assaults, robberies and other violent thefts, are so appalling and seemingly so indefensible, that only the interests of the victim and of public justice need trouble you at the time you take your initial action. But first impressions are not always accurate, and after the detailed circumstances and individual motives of a case have been explored, a different picture can sometimes emerge. It is not unknown for an act of violence or a breach of the peace, or even what was on the face of it a quite disgraceful crime, in the end to be revealed as an indication as much of the offender's misfortune as it is of the victim's.

There is a distinct requirement here for you to be humane and to strike a careful balance of attitudes not just towards those directly involved in any incident you come across, victim of offender, but towards the interests of the general public also. Moreover it is your clear duty to strive to increase your professional skill and your understanding of others, so as to do it all the better.

That is a tall order, the younger and less experienced may think. But there is no need to be over-anxious. Time helps all of us and we can take comfort from the fact that there are sometimes so many conflicting influences surrounding even a relatively simple incident that the most experienced and wise of us has difficulty in deciding the issue. Moreover, none of us can ever be confident that our decisions will always be right, although good judgment comes more easily as learning and professional skill grow, and as experience widens.

The events which influence an individual police officer's character, and mould his judgment, will have been experienced at different times and with different intensities; it is likely therefore that views in the service, about what is correct in a particular case and what is not will conflict, even between contemporaries. You will find that these differences of view are sometimes quite sharp, and occasionally confusing. But they are not necessarily out of place in a service as broad based and as complex as ours.

For instance, one officer, though performing his duty quite conscientiously, may think that having a drink before driving is not in itself always a reprehensible matter; he may consider it unnecessary for him to explore that aspect of a case unless the circumstances in which a driver is discovered indicate that the driving may have been impaired. Another officer, perhaps with extensive personal experience of the pain and tragedy of road accidents, may think that drinking and driving is a cause of so many of them, that whenever there is the slightest evidence that drink has been taken he must exercise his powers.

Differences of that kind, which have as their basis differing attitudes to individual culpability or different opinions about the degree of gravity in a class of offenses, are matters which can, for the most part, be settled by Force organization and by the checks and balances inherent in our prosecution system. Training, too, can play an important part in encouraging common attitudes where this is necessary, though it is not the purpose of training to seek to abolish all differences of attitude amongst police officers. Some differences, providing of course that they do not distort police activity in an unfair way, are

not only tolerable, but healthy, and can contribute to productive debate within the service and to the progressive development of policy.

In this context you may wonder whether your own stance must always be consistent, and whether, when off duty, you are entitled to adopt an attitude to offenses and offenders different from that which governs your thinking when on duty. The answer is yes, for good reasons which a couple of simple examples will again show us.

If you are off duty and driving your car at 30mph in a road restricted to that speed, and you are overtaken by a car traveling at 40 mph, should you attempt to stop the car and report the motorist for speeding? Providing there are no aggravating circumstances, such as danger to other road users, quite clearly you should not. Apart from the inadequacy of any evidence of speed you may be able to give to a court and the possible danger involved in one private car stopping another, your action might be seen by the motorist, and any interested bystanders, as officious, or worse. Unreasonable of them you may say, and you may be right; nevertheless confrontation is a distinct probability and your intervention might well lead to an unseemly row. Neither you, nor the motorist, nor the service, would be the better for that.

When off duty, proper use of your discretion requires you to overlook such traffic offenses and other minor infringements of the law. Inaction in such cases would not be neglectful—it would be good sense. Of course intervention would be appropriate, indeed would be a matter of duty, if human life was at risk, a serious offense was imminent, or peace was seriously endangered and your action could preserve it, but careful restraint and prudence should be your rule at all times.

For a second example we can take a subject on which there is a variety of views among many responsible members of society, which is reflected in the views of police officers: the smoking of cannabis. What should you do if you see that people, at a party, are smoking a substance which you think may be cannabis? This is a very difficult decision for anyone to make. It is much easier to advise what you should not do; you should not attempt to arrest as many cannabis users as you can see. Indeed, prudence may tell you that you should not take any action at all at the party, because you will not be able to take effective action. Your decision, in this, as in all things, on or off duty, should be made with a sharp eye to what is feasible, and likely to achieve your purpose, as well as to what is strictly legal or morally correct.

Depending on how flagrant the smoking has been, whether there was encouragement given to others to smoke, or whether there was any attempt to sell cannabis, you may decide to stay, and attempt to identify any person who might have been supplying cannabis so that action can be taken against him later, if that is appropriate. On the other hand, if it was clear that the smoking was not widespread and took place merely for the personal satisfaction of a few, and you were, in any case, not sure that the substance was a controlled drug, you may decide to do nothing except perhaps, leave a note for a collator or a drugs squad officer, outlining what you have seen or suspect.

You would also not want to neglect your obligation to your host in all this. Your decision about how, if at all, to approach him, would of course be influenced by the extent to which you knew him, how sure you could be of his good reputation and intentions, and what evidence there was of foreknowledge on his part. Certainly, if you were to have taken some action thoughtlessly about his party without telling him of it, he would be bound, on discovering that, and if he was free of guilt himself, to question your purpose. He would regard you as uncivilized to say the least, and this would be so, particularly if the party had taken place at his home and had comprised principally his close friends or family. It is only if there was some clear ground for suspecting complicity by your host that you could, in such circumstances, justify taking action behind his back. Much the best course, if the situation allows it, would be to tell him what you have seen and explain carefully what action you propose to take. His reaction to that can be an important factor for you when deciding how to handle things.

As is nearly always the case with the exercise of police powers, none of the above courses of action could be judged to be wholly wrong or wholly right in the circumstances described. It is quite possible that another person, who was present or who learned afterwards of your action or inaction, could take a view different from yours.

But if challenged about what you did or did not do, you would be able to say with some justice that you had assessed the issue as sensibly as you could, that you had considered as a priority what was practicable and would serve the public interest, and had given no more weight than was reasonable to your personal view of the culpability of the offenders and the seriousness of the offense. No one could contradict you; you could be content that you had reasonably discharged the functions of your office, even though, you might yourself think afterwards, with the marvelous wisdom which hindsight brings to us all, that it would have been better to have done things in a slightly different way.

From this discussion we can see that many of the differences in approach to situations in which there is scope for discretion are dependent on whether an officer, by reason of experience and understanding of human nature, tends on any occasion more towards zeal or towards indulgence. Minor differences of opinion in this area are understandable, but major ones are not and a generally correct balance must be maintained. Both over-zealousness and undue tolerance are wrong, the former leading to conflict through the unnecessary use of authority, the latter to public dissatisfaction about a lack of police action. These extremes must be avoided when making difficult personal decisions, and we shall see later, when we come to discuss our duty as a Force, how important this principle can be for the maintenance of public tranquility.

We are able here to discern another three principles to be followed when we are contemplating the exercise of our powers: to be humane, having regard to public interests in addition to those of victim and offender; to be prudent and restrained, paying full regard to what is practicable, particularly when off duty; and to avoid equally undue zeal and undue tolerance.

It is necessary to show confidence and sure-footedness in another matter. You must be free of improper influence when exercising your powers and, just as importantly, you must take pains to be seen to be free.

As a police officer you are very much in the public eye and your fellow citizens will be quick to notice, and to comment upon, any activity of yours, on of off duty, which they perceive as being likely, however remotely, to affect your honesty and your impartiality.

There are some provisions of the Police Regulations and the Discipline Regulations which are very relevant here. For instance, you will know that you must not engage in political activity. You may not do other things, such as acquire a business interest, without the consent of the Force. Disciplinary rules prescribe that you discharge promptly any lawful debt and avoid any pecuniary liability. Force instructions require you to decline, and report, any gratuity or reward which is offered to you.

These instructions, and others like them, are intended to help you maintain your impartiality and to give the public a clear indication that this is what the service is determined its members should do. There can be no doubt about this. The Police Regulations tell us:

A member of a police force shall at all times abstain from any activity which is likely to interfere with impartial discharge of his duties or which is likely to give rise to the impression amongst members of the public that it may so interfere.

The rules may be simple and clear enough for everyone to understand, but the reality of life is often much more subtle, so that reasonable compliance with the rules, in such a way as to avoid a clumsy or pompous attitude to those offering genuine friendship and warmth, is not at all easy. Sometimes you will find that careful thought, and not a little shrewdness, are required if you are to differentiate between kindly and disinterested acts, and those which are more sinister, being designed to test for weakness on your part. And, as always with these things, the older and more experienced you are, the easier it will be to recognize the difference between the two. A few more examples might help in teasing out the principles.

One clearly defined perquisite for police, which is acknowledged by all involved, is the facility which enables you to travel free, if you wish, on most London Transport services by using your warrant card as a "season ticket." This has been considered to be in the public interest because you carry a particular responsibility to help keep order and to enforce the transport regulations when you travel in this way. The public knows that this facility exists, knows the reasons for it, and is therefore content that your integrity and honesty of purpose are not thereby put at risk.

Other forms of benefit are offered by reputable organizations to the police, without thought of advantage. Travel firms or insurance companies, will sometimes offer substantial discounts to police officers because they want to attract reputable customers who will (indeed must) promptly pay their debts and who are a better commercial risk in other ways—for example, as safe drivers or prudent property owners.

Then there are other firms which offer a form of "discount" to almost any customer who asks for it, without any expectation of favor in return. These should give you no trouble, and taking advantage of these concessions is no more than your right in the market place.

There are, however, some firms or businesses which are not so scrupulous and which try to inflate their commercial reputation by implying a police connection in their titles, in their advertising, or in the course of pressing their services on their customers. You need trade only once with such people to do the favor required, allowing them afterwards to boast of your custom as evidence of their reliability or soundness. This is not a small point; a transaction of that kind may not compromise you, indeed you may not know what is done or said afterwards by the business, but your reputation, and that of the service, can be seriously damaged if other customers receive short measure or shoddy service.

So, if a discount or other advantage is offered to you, and not to others, without any discernible and reasonable justification for singling you out, take great care, lest unwittingly you are "led by the nose" for someone else's advantages of this kind.

You must be sensible about other advantages also. Of course the casual offer of a cup of tea, and the like, by a local resident or trader is innocent enough, and cordiality here can help to cement a healthy relationship with local people, thus enhancing your understanding of local affairs and problems. But things can get gradually more significant almost without your noticing it, and you must take care not to stumble in this difficult area.

Such things as an offer of free food at an eating place, free services from a local trader, or free drinks from a licensee, are quite a different proposition and they are potentially more difficult to handle if, as is sometimes the case, the "offer" takes the form of reluctance, or refusal, to accept payment when you proffer it. An "offer" of this sort must not be accepted, even if you believe that it does not have any ulterior motive, and stems only from kindliness, or genuine admiration, for you and the service.

There may be many who see what you do, or do not do; any onlooking member of the public is bound to regard the incident as an improper inducement to influence you in the donor's favor. Not to put too fine a point on it, it will be seen as a bribe. And so would you see it that way, if you were in the same position. There will be many, too, who learn afterwards of what happened, the "innocent" donor has no need to be quiet, the "guilty" has every reason to boast, and will condemn your taking advantage of your office.

You must put the maintenance of your good reputation before all else, and refuse. Of course you must do this as gracefully as you can, and careful steps are sometimes needed so as not to accuse unfairly or dismay those involved. Quiet firmness is required in the form you employ for your refusal. No fuss is necessary. Tact and good humour, the thoughtful police officer's constant companions, will help you to avoid giving offense to a person who might be merely well motivated and kindly.

What matters most of course is not so much the manner of your refusal, though this is important, but the substance of your decision. This must always be clearly expressed so that there can be no confusion about your attitude. If you keep in mind your constable's declaration of impartiality, you will not find it difficult to make decisions of this sort. After all, you and I would not have the slightest doubt about what should be done in more serious cases which clearly enter the world of criminality. If, for example, we were to be offered a sum of money to refrain from arresting someone, we would know without hesitation what to do; indicate that we were not to be bought, then take action quickly. Failure to do that would be, as we know, a criminal offense on our part, and, if discovered, we would rightly be held in great contempt both by the public and by our police colleagues alike.

It is clear then that we must take care that we are not bought, bit by bit, for there is no difference in the end. Downfall will be equally disgraceful whether it comes as a result of conscious corruption on our part, or by a gradually increasing carelessness about personal standards leading, even inadvertently, to our abusing our powers and positions. Selfishness in police officers, and a pursuit of personal advantage, is not only reprehensible in themselves but carry the distinct danger that they will undermine the honesty of purpose which our fellow citizens demand of us.

But again that is not the end of it. There are other, less substantial, and less easily discerned, factors which we must take into account. The public forms an opinion, good or not, about the standard of police integrity not only by considering how police officers are seen to behave in regard to material things such as we have mentioned, but also on a number of other factors.

First there is the public view of how insular or how public-spirited are the internal relationships and loyalties which police officers build up with each other within the Force, and whether these affect police judgment. These relationships are germane more to the way we perform our duties as a Force and therefore can be dealt with later when we discuss those duties.

A second consideration is very relevant here; the way the public regards links which individual police officers might build with individuals or groups outside the service.

Of course a police officer, like every other citizen, is a free agent-When off duty, friendships, acquaintances, and social activities are not normally a matter for the Force to bother about, or for any colleague to concern himself with. Indeed, we serve in a Force which is seeking to introduce greater freedom and participation, both in its management and in the way it embraces public aspirations and opinions. And in recent years the society we serve has come more and more to value openness and frankness and the ability to associate freely without undue interference. We are just as entitled, of course, to those freedoms.

But the declared promise we gave as constables to exercise our powers impartially makes it sensible for us to be circumspect and careful, and to have regard, in this context as in all others, to the impression the public may gain from what we do.

Relationships with individuals are not so difficult a matter. Clearly, none of us would have any time for an officer who fell into close association with a person of dissolute habits, or with an active criminal, indeed acquaintances of that kind could leave the officer open to a disciplinary charge. But this is not to say that you must steer clear of the friendship of someone just because they have been involved in an offence at some time. Not a bit of it, for such an attitude would surely brand you, and the Force, as hopelessly puritan and stern, without much understanding of the ways of others. You would be much the poorer, too, for you would be cutting yourself off from a large slice of the lively world we live in. Many former offenders have benefited from the friendship of a sensible and caring police officer, and many police officers have been enriched and sustained, sometimes for life, by such friendship.

So it is once again a matter of balance for you to strike as a free citizen, taking others as you find them, treating them for what they are and not for what they might once have been. All you need ensure is that you do not put yourself in a position where you may be compromised or where the public is likely to doubt reasonably whether your impartiality can be relied upon.

Much the same principle must apply to any relationship with, or membership of, a group. The Force positively encourages its officers to take a full part in the social life around them, for their own sake as a means of enhancing their awareness of the community they serve, and for the sake of the Force which is anxious to be seen as a caring contributor to the public good. The community gains from this; a number of very worthwhile undertakings, particularly those related to the well-being of young people and the socially disadvantaged, would not survive half so well without the energy and drive volunteered by police officers. Good citizenship, ingrained in so many officers, finds yet another outlet in this way.

Accordingly, you will feel as free as any other citizen to take part in any society or organization—social, sporting, cultural or charitable—which captures your attention and enriches your social pleasure. These are pursuits which cause no adverse or critical concern to the Force or to the public, the members of which are much reassured about the humanity of their police force when they observe its members taking part in such things.

Nevertheless there are a couple of areas which can give rise to public apprehension about police participation. There will be, for instance, natural disquiet about police membership of any organization with a party political connotation, however slight or indirect that might be, or one which, while thought by many members of the public, and many police officers to be very worthy—such as a movement for animals's rights or a peace group—pursues its objectives with such earnestness that it is likely eventually to fall foul of the law. The public rightly expects police officers to avoid a connection with an organization of that kind, as of course, does the service itself.

Similarly members of the public are sometimes uneasy when they learn that a police officer is a member of, or a contributor to, any private club or institution whose purpose, or conditions of participation are not generally known or published, or whose activities are kept away from public view. Unnecessary conjecture and, sometimes, suspicion, can arise. Although the aims of the group may be estimable, and the conjecture without foundation, it is important that any police officer who participates should consider how he might dispel any apprehension felt by his fellow citizens, and his fellow constables, about his probity.

The police Regulation which we mentioned earlier (requiring us to avoid, on or off duty, any activity likely to interfere with our impartiality or to give the impression that it might do so) is a particularly burdensome one in this context, for it is all too easy for an onlooker to believe that an officer who is a member of such a group will show favor to other members. And it is not uncommon for fellow police officers to take the same view, harboring the additional suspicion, that they, not being members, will receive less favorable treatment at the hands of supervisors who are members than they deserve in such matters as promotions or postings. Thus an officer must pay the most careful regard to the impression which others are likely to gain of his membership, as well as to what he actually does, however inhibiting he may find this to be when arranging his private life.

One group which has been the subject of conjecture of this kind, and one which has unique features that add to the difficulties for police officers, is the institution of freemasonry. It will help us to appreciate the special obligations which fall on us if, in concluding our discussion of the principles which govern the exercise of police powers, we look at the impressions that police participation in freemasonry can give, both within and outside the service.

What matters should an officer consider if he is thinking of becoming a freemason?

To begin with, he will want to weigh the advantages. If accepted as a member, he may take satisfaction from participation in a long-established institution which embraces people of many kinds from all walks of life, and which includes in its upper echelons some of the most distinguished people in the land. He may expect too, that membership will bring social pleasure and companionship with his fellow masons, some of whom may well be his fellow police officers. With them, he may take proper pride in the charitable efforts of his lodge, and in the pursuit of the ideal of freemasonry which is "the improvement of man both as an individual and as a member of the community."

And it is important, when considering freemasonry in the context of the police service, to remember that many officers, of different ranks, have been able to reconcile their private commitment to freemasonry with their public duty without difficulty. We should remember too, that much of the conjecture about the influence of freemasonry upon our service has not been supported by evidence. The accusers, including some police officers who criticize freemasonry, have often been wrong.

There is, of course, a long established principle that no-one should accuse, unless he can prove, and there is an obligation, as we shall see later when we come to discuss our duty as a Force, that police should adhere wholeheartedly to the Rule of Law which requires "reasonableness when acting on suspicion." When, as happens occasionally, a police officer becomes so obsessed with freemasonry that he seeks on the flimsiest of evidence of lay blame at its door for all sorts of ills which cannot reasonably be connected with it, he is acting not just unfairly, but unprofessionally.

Nevertheless, it is necessary with freemasonry, as with any institution including, of course, the police service itself, to strike a distinction between the ideal and the reality. Some of the assertions have been supportable. The activities of some freemasons have been thought, on reasonable grounds, to be motivated by self-interest and not committed to the aims of freemasonry, so adding to the suspicion that all may not be well in this very private institution. Therefore, although an officer who is a freemason may take great care to ensure that membership does not influence him in the exercise of his police powers, he may find it impossible to convince a member of the public, or a colleague who is not a freemason, that this is always so.

There are a number of other factors also which weigh against him. Firstly, there is the marked exclusivity of the institution and the mystery which surrounds the method by which a person is judged by freemasons to be suitable for membership of a lodge. Then there is the oddness of the initiation ceremony itself, with its strange rites which smack to some of immaturity, being reminiscent of the secret societies of boyhood. There is some oddness too, in these modern days, about the requirement for freemasons to respect social distinctions and the status quo to such an extent as to sustain the notion that "while some must rule, others must obey and cheerfully accept their inferior positions." And finally, and most importantly in the context of police participation, there is the freemason's solemnly sworn obligation never to reveal the secrets of the craft, including that which tells him how he can indicate his affinity to another freemason in a way that will not be discerned by onlookers.

All of these carry considerable weight. They militate against the acceptance, by colleagues and citizens alike, of an officer, who is a freemason as a man on whose fairness it is possible to rely always, and unquestioningly.

Nothing in our discussion should be taken as a criticism of freemasonry in itself. Of course, some of the factors we have looked at apply to other private and selective bodies in the group which we have in mind, but the unique combination of them in this institution does cause extreme difficulty for a police officer. It is difficulty of a kind not faced by another professional person who is a freemason. The police officer's special dilemma is the conflict between his service declaration of impartiality, and the sworn obligation to keep the secrets of freemasonry. His declaration has its statutory obligation to avoid any activity likely to interfere with impartiality or to give the impression that it may do so; a freemason's oath holds inevitably the implication that loyalty to fellow freemasons may supersede any other loyalty.

Thus, an officer who is approached about membership should consider these factors most carefully before deciding what to do. It is a matter for his judgment of course, and no supervisor should presume to instruct him, for to do so would be thought an unwarranted interference with private life. But advice and guidance is a very different matter and the discerning officer will probably consider it wise to forego the prospect of pleasure and social advantage in freemasonry so as to enjoy the unreserved regard of all those around him. It follows from this that one who is already a freemason would also be wise to ponder, from time to time, whether he should continue as a freemason; that would probably be prudent in the light of the way that our Force is striving, in these critical days, to present to the public a more open and wholehearted image of itself, to show a greater readiness to be invigilated and to be free of any unnecessary concealment or secrecy.

Here again, just as with the other things we have dealt with in this part of our discussion, there are no hard and fast rules, and no unarguably correct answers. Your judgment about what stance you should take in these very difficult issues—which, in the past, have tested, and even beaten, some of the wisest and most experienced officers—will be much helped if you remember that your declaration of office as a constable must be paramount. The responsibility it brings to be impartial does not cease when you leave a police station at the finish of your daily duty, it must pervade all that you do, privately or publicly, and it must supersede any other loyalty you may have.

From this, and from the ringing terms of the declaration, we can get the final, and perhaps the most important, principle which we must follow when exercising our powers: To be, and be seen to be, unfettered by obligation, deciding each issue without fear or favor, malice or ill-will.

In summary then, there are a number of duties which flow directly from the constitutional position of the constable, and from the public's expectation of how we should use our discretionary powers:

1. It is your duty to act always for the general public good, as a helpful and reasonable public servant, and not merely as an enforcer of the law.

2. It is your duty when exercising police powers:to avoid peremptoriness;

3. to weigh carefully all surrounding factors, and to judge these in the light of the Attorney General's guidance;

4. to be humane, having regard to public interests in addition to those victim and offender;

5. to be prudent and restrained, paying full regard to what is practicable, particularly when off duty;

6. to avoid equally undue zeal and undue tolerance;

7. to be, and be seen to be, unfettered by obligation, deciding each issue without fear or favor, malice, or ill-will.

PART TWO

OUR DUTY AS A FORCE

The Objectives of the Force

Since 1829, writers on police affairs contention have drawn attention to the necessity for police forces to define the objectives and priorities which they see for themselves, to indicate the methods which they plan to use in order to achieve those objectives, and to measure whether they have done so.

Clear definition and rational planning of this sort is seen as eminently sensible in the Metropolitan Police, for two reasons. Firstly, it enables the Force as a whole to husband carefully, and effectively, its limited resources of manpower and equipment. Secondly, the methods we have introduced to attain that purpose allow much greater participation, at a local level, in the process of agreeing, setting, and achieving the highest standards of service and efficiency.

For us, as individuals, this second aspect of our new system may be the most fulfilling and challenging, not least because it moves us away from an authoritarian method of management to one which is more participative. There are many general advantages also. Firstly, by setting agreed objectives, we can make more purposeful the actions of individual police officers and local groups of officers. Secondly, by a willing disclosure of our intentions and our working practices, we can greatly increase public understanding of the problems which face us, the limitations which scarcity of resources places upon us, and the ways in which the public can help.

And this "new" thinking about policing objectives, coupled with the original objects drawn up by our first Commissioners, Rowan and Mayne, whose declarations still underpin all that we do, has been drawn into a statement of corporate purpose, our "principles of policing", which are printed elsewhere in this book. You should study it closely. It lies at the heart of everything that we do as a Force. All of our detailed objectives and priorities are framed in support of it.

The statement should become the cornerstone of your personal policing philosophy. It is worth repeating:

> *The primary aims and duties of the Metropolitan Police are to uphold the Rule of Law, to protect and assist the citizen and, in consultation and cooperation with others in the community, to work for the prevention and detection of crime and the achievement of a peaceful society free of the fear of crime and disorder*

The aims and duties stated are not of course "new" in the sense that they have not governed us before. Nor could they be, for they are based inevitably on the traditional duty which accrues to the constable. Our Force has its own statutory base and individuality, of course, and its own unique accountability; arising largely because of its importance as the Force which polices the seat of Government and the center of commerce, there are special duties imposed upon it and upon individual members. And some of its members, our civil staff, though fully committed to the aims of the Force and dealing very closely with the public, do not exercise police powers. Nevertheless, the Force is essentially a collection of constables; whatever else, a collection of constables must, collectively, have no lesser standards than individual constables.

We are on familiar ground then, in view of our earlier discussion about the declaration of office and the duties of individual constables. We can look upon the core statement as articulating tried and tested objectives which have been re-defined to give a fresh degree of emphasis and a new relationship between them, to reflect the complexities of modern life and to take account of our social evolution since professional policing began in 1829.

Further discussion of some of the aspects of the statement will show what a rapidly growing complex of duties nowadays falls upon us, and will enable us to recognize the professional good sense of working always to attract public support. We will also be able to develop our thoughts about police conduct.

Our Primary Duties, the Rule of Law and the Fear of Crime

The phrase "Rule of Law" is a general term, of wide meaning, incorporating a number of the ideals and principles which are crucial to the process of government and justice in a free society. It includes also some of the provisions on human rights propounded by bodies such

as the Council of Europe and the United Nations. We will discuss these important matters later on.

The duty of upholding the Rule of Law means, therefore, a number of things for us in the police service. We must, as the phrase clearly implies, apply the law of the land, as enacted in statutes, or as established by Common Law, and maintain the Queen's Peace. But as we shall see, to uphold the Rule of Law in its full sense when enforcing the law, we must keep strictly within prescribed powers, abstain from arbitrary action, and respect the individual rights and freedoms of all citizens.

We know that one of our main emphasis in maintaining the peace, and applying the law, must be upon prevention, as was the case in 1829 when the principal object was formulated as follows: *It should be understood at the outset that the principal object to be attained is the prevention of crime. To this great end every effort of the police is to be directed. The security of person and property, the preservation of the public tranquility and all other objects of a police establishment will thus be better effected than by detection and punishment of the offender after he has succeeded in committing the crime.*

Though that object remains today just as valid as it was on the day it was written, in recent years it has been sensible to acknowledge that skill in the detection of crime, as well as in its prevention, is important in our quest to deter offenders, and to protect and assist the citizen. Moreover, as our statement indicates to us, our society cannot be considered at ease, and truly protected by us, if our fellow citizens are bedeviled by a fear of crime and disorder.

Recent research shows that fear of crime has emerged as a matter which contributes to the process of neighborhood decline, thus affecting the stability of the community. Fear of crime in the mind of the average citizen is produced not only by the actual rate of crime and the number of people perceived as potential criminals, but also by the physical appearance of the locality. We have all worked in areas of decay where litter, graffiti, and derelict buildings abound, and where vandalism seems uncontrolled. All this increases the citizen's feeling of insecurity, as does the inordinate presence in the streets of disorderly and unpredictable people such as those suffering from the effects of habitual drink or drugs—a presence which is itself another symptom of social decay.

In areas where this menacing, disorderly or lawless atmosphere grows apparent, the more affluent move out, shops lose profitability as a result, and they move; businesses move away as schools in the locality diminish, property declines in value and the municipal base is eroded. All this feeds on itself, as many police officers have seen at first hand to their dismay, and there is a despairing spirit. This sometimes leaves people unhappy, fearful and unwilling to cooperate with any institution, including the police. And if we do not enjoy public cooperation and support in these areas, we cannot expect to police very effectively.

It is clear that we must work very closely with local authorities and other agencies to put this right, by ensuring that such measures as we are able to take to control disorder and prevent and detect crime go hand in hand with any local efforts to improve the appearance and economic viability of run-down areas. Only by first restoring a feeling of security and confidence, can economic investment and regeneration occur in the worst of our inner-city areas.

You will see that working publicly and cooperatively in this way and addressing diligently the fear of crime, is not only good citizenship in that it serves to improve the lot of our fellows, but it is also very good professional sense.

So, enlisting public support for our efforts is important if we are to control disorder and to prevent crime. But, as we know, nothing in police life is simple to achieve, and there is another dimension to the prevention of crime which we must consider. There is a balance, a very delicate one, that we are obliged sometimes to strike between the prevention of crime on the one hand, and the preservation of public tranquility on the other.

On occasion, it is not possible to achieve fully the one without risk of endangering the other, and our understanding of public wishes about the prevention of crime, what level of crime they consider tolerable, and what they do not, has not always been faultless. It has been necessary in recent times for us to work hard as a Force to develop mechanisms to consult more effectively with the varied communities in London, so that we can judge more accurately just what a community's aspirations are in that direction.

The spur for much of this arose out of the riots in London during 1981, when there were serious public disturbances in Brixton. Police officers who were there will not forget them easily. Neither will anyone who was serving then forget the public outcry afterwards about who was to blame. The police, for their alleged misbehavior before the riots, came in for a considerable share of the outrage and the acrimony, particularly from some minority ethnic groups, many of whose representatives saw the police as enemies. It is accepted now, by police as well as by others, that this view had some justification. But there was other, less easily discernible, causes, as is now well accepted also, and the enquiry which was conducted under the Police Act by Lord Scarman points to ways in which co-operative effort can help to avoid any repeat of the tragic disorder. Lord Scarman's report, a document of great substance and penetration, has led to important changes in police strategies and attitudes.

The innovations which flowed from Lord Scarman's enquiry need to be developed wholeheartedly, for they should enable us to be more forward-thinking and perceptive in discerning what it is that a community requires of its police. We should now be better equipped to decide, in consultation with the community, and in the light of the law of the land, how to strike our sometimes difficult balances in a particular area.

In other words, with public help through our consultative machinery, our Force should be able to perform better that primary duty mentioned earlier which falls to us as constables and as citizens: the maintenance of a state of civilized tranquility which facilitates the enjoyment of individual rights, and which allows the unfettered attainment of lawful aspirations. Thus, by considering both the general discussion we have had about the duty of the constable, and the development of the aims of the Force which we have described, it is possible for us to define our collective and individual duty: It is a duty to prevent and detect crime, to keep the peace, to assuage fear of crime and disorder, and, wherever possible, to enlist the help of our fellow citizens in achieving those ends.

Society's Fundamental Rights and Values

We can be sure that we will be much helped in developing our understanding of public attitudes, and in improving our growing rapport with those we serve, by addressing ourselves enthusiastically to those other important duties which fall upon us under the Rule of Law: to work always within prescribed powers, to avoid arbitrary action, and to respect individual rights.

Working "within prescribed powers" and avoiding "arbitrary action" mean that we must act within the law, and within any agreed codes of practice which govern police conduct, and that we must keep clearly within the bounds imposed by the fundamental rights and values maintained by British society as a whole—the rights and valued which you and I cherish for ourselves as fellow citizens.

The twelve most important rights and values, for the purposes of our present discussion, are:

1. respect for human dignity;

2. the right to free speech;

3. the right to free association;

4. prohibition of discriminatory behavior towards individuals, classes of persons and minority groups;

5. the requirement of reasonableness when acting upon suspicion;

6. the requirement to use only such force as is necessary to accomplish a legitimate purpose;

7. restrictions on powers of arrest and detention;

8. the observance of suspects's rights;

9. the right of access to legal advice;

10. integrity in the collection and presentation of evidence;

11. the right to silence;

12. the presumption of innocence.

Adherence to these great principles is a duty which, of course, arises on moral grounds, but there is, in addition, a distinct professional advantage, and therefore a public advantage, to be gained from careful attention to our attitudes in this context.

Police officers who comply with society's demands about how police should behave, who wholeheartedly support and defend society's own values, and who adhere scrupulously to society's rules about fairness, are able reasonably to demand in return that their fellow citizens should actively support policing aims. They can expect too, that people will comply voluntarily with the law, and with police authority, when it is properly exercised.

The idea that there is an unspoken contract of this sort between police and public is not new. It has always been part of the philosophy of the citizen/policeman. But in recent years it has become increasingly important to sustain the idea as society has become more dispersed and as communities in some areas have decayed and lost cohesion.

Police officers number only a hundred thousand or so in this country. We are charged with policing, helping and guiding many millions of people of widely different backgrounds, skills, religions, aspirations, cultures and habits; a marvelous mix of interesting folk—exciting, exasperating, and probably quite unlike anything that has gone before. This means that the pursuit by police of public acceptance and cooperation, which has always been a matter of good professional and practical sense, has now become a matter of urgent duty.

There tumbles from the twelve principles of the Rule of Law we have mentioned a bundle of maxims, many of which are of traditional importance for the police, and most of which apply as much to the Force as to the individual officer. A couple of the maxims are so important to us that we must deal with them later as separate entities.

But first there are nine principles of the Rule of Law which are well supported by criminal law and legal practice, and which ought, on that account alone, to have the wholeearted support of police officers.

The right to free speech, freedom of association, and to legal advice, the right to silence and to be presumed innocent until guilt is proved, the requirements of reasonableness when acting on suspicion, the observance of the rules relating to the rights of suspects and to powers of arrest and detention, and the requirement for integrity in the collection and presentation of evidence, are rightly made the subject of legal rules and codes of practice which oblige police to comply or risk rejection of their case, and even penalty.

Regrettably, the fact that some of the codes and rules are couched in very restrictive terms has occurred not so much because fairness cannot otherwise be achieved, but because of the necessity to define things with great accuracy in order to prevent misinterpretation or malpractice.

There have been cases in which suspects have been unfairly treated, or the rules of practice have been broken. In the worst cases police evidence has been deliberately false and contrived, leading to miscarriages of justice.

Disgraceful conduct of that kind is wrong, manifestly unprofessional and often criminal. It works very much against the interests of the public, and of you and me as police officers.

Let there be no doubt that the careless, thoughtless, irresponsible or downright wicked actions of a few, in the selfish hope of some short-term advantage, can hurt cruelly the many, for such behavior leads to a gradual reduction in the general reliance which courts and juries feel able to put on police evidence.

When this happens, the personal reputations of fine officers can be wrongly sullied, perfectly proper evidence which ought to sustain a conviction can be suspected and rejected by courts, allowing the guilty to escape their just deserts, and the good name of our Force, and the police service, to be seriously damaged. Dire penalties for us, and the public, to pay for the work of fools, you will agree. Therefore we have a clear duty in this context which we can express as follows:

It is a duty to uphold the rule of law by sustaining wholeheartedly:

the right to free speech;

the right to free association;

the right of access to legal advice;

the right to silence;

the presumption of innocence;

and by scrupulous compliance with:

the requirement of reasonableness when acting upon suspicion;

the rules pertaining to the rights of suspects;

the restrictions on powers of arrest and detention; and the requirement for integrity in the collection and presentation of evidence.

These are all matters of sensible police professionalism and each of them is covered to one degree or another in our police orders and instructions, as well as in the law. But, of course, shrewdness, penetration, and the ability to stick to our purpose are necessary if we are to investigate crimes effectively and to enforce the law against the unscrupulous and the wicked. These attributes too are included in police training and are rightly taught alongside the requirements specified in the above duty.

The public has something of a double-edged expectation of us here. They expect that we should not, on the one hand, be easily fooled (indeed, that we should not be fooled at all) or put off by the wily and the sly, and that we should, on the other hand, be fair and be seen to be fair, by impeccable application of the rules to everyone we deal with including, of course, the wily and the sly.

And just as we are expected to be ready to pit our strength against the violent and the disorderly, and keep ourselves fit in order to do so, so we are expected to pit our wits against the cheat and the villain, and to keep our wits sharpened for that purpose.

At a glance these things seem to run against each other, but there is no real dilemma here if we remember the compelling necessity for honesty in all that we do.

In order to prevent any decline in the regard which society has for our truthfulness and integrity, we must follow the rules and codes, in fact and in spirit, with enthusiasm and careful competence.

If we fail to do that then all the shrewdness, stamina and sharpwittedness we can muster will count for naught; the wrongdoer will escape, and our professionalism will be left very much in doubt. It is therefore not only a requirement of duty, of morality, and of the law—it is professional to keep to the rules.

Respect for Human Dignity and Prohibition of Discriminatory Behavior

Running as a thread through our discussion so far, and through the duties which we have defined, is the requirement that we should be impartial, fair, and sympathetic to the dilemmas of others. That requirement looms large in our training systems, is emphasized in our Force orders, and it is enshrined in the Rule of Law principles demanding respect for human dignity and the prohibition of discriminatory behavior.

The requirement is reflected in general police practice, too. You might well be able to think of examples of good and humane work by officers who have decided complex issues and who have taken action in pressing and trying circumstances, with quiet seemingly unhurried judgment

and a fine regard for the needs of others. A calm and careful approach to duty accords with the real spirit of your office of constable; you should do to your fellow citizen only that which you would happily see done to yourself, and you should advance a patient and careful respect for individual dignity, showing courtesy to all.

Although sometimes this seems to be easier said than done in these comparatively hectic days, it has been a duty since professional policing began. The Instruction Book of 1829, speaking on the attitude of a police officer, said: *While prompt to prevent crime and arrest criminals, he must look on himself as the servant and guardian of the general public and treat all law abiding citizens, irrespective of their race, color, creed or social position, with unfailing patience and courtesy. By the use of tact and good humour the public can usually be induced to comply with directions and thus the necessity for using force, with its possible public disapproval, is avoided.*

This puts the requirement into an essentially practical context. It is certainly true, as your experience will have shown you, that much difficulty can be avoided by a kindly word, or a sympathetic ear. But if only there were always enough time, you might say.

In London, where pressures abound, one of the greatest an officer has to suffer is pressure of time. The amount of work that has to be done can sometimes give little opportunity for leisurely courtesy and understanding. An officer who, for example, is at the scene of his fourth or fifth burglary in a day, and knows that after dealing with that, he has to go on to others, may be tempted to become off hand and brusque, because he thinks that that is "businesslike" and will give the appearance of efficiency.

But to victims of the burglary the occasion will be far from routine; it may be for them the first time a police officer has dealt with them, and the incident will long remain in their memories, as an impression of how the police, in general, behave. Patience is not just the right and civilized thing here, it makes professional sense; support and approval from the community will not be forthcoming without it.

Of course it is important that we should be courteous and patient with everyone with whom we deal, whatever their appearance, their style of life, or whatever demand they seek to make of us.

And it is particularly important that we should take care of the ill or the infirm, as well as the aged, and the otherwise vulnerable. Some elderly people, the housebound, those living alone, and not only those who are in disadvantaged inner city areas but those living in London's "better" areas as well, become dismayed and confused with the pace of life, with the bustle and noise, and the boisterous rumpus of the younger people around them. They are sometimes too frightened to go out, particularly at night, and they deserve the attention of hardy folk like police officers. The reassurance and the support which we can give them by doing our duty, sometimes just by being seen about the place, will do much to restore their confidence and their ability to tolerate what is to them a new style and speed of life.

We know, as well, how important it is to offer compassion and ready help to anyone undergoing trauma or experiencing grief. Many a man or woman, and a child too, has been able to tolerate grief and pain that much more readily because of the immediate support of a staunch, sympathetic and dependable police officer. The strong arm of the law, used gently, can be a great comfort. Never forget its power, and be ready always to offer it to anyone who may require it.

We have a particular duty, too, to others who may need special and patient attention because they do not readily understand our customs or our language, particularly those from among our recent immigrant groups. Then there are our minority ethnic groups, many born in the United Kingdom. Many feel themselves very much at risk of being subjected to racial attacks and discrimination—even from us, as well as from the public at large—and they can become very apprehensive that the police, and society, may not be able to protect them properly.

Members of ethnic minorities may have fears and difficulties not generally experienced by most and, partially because of this, the attitude to police of black youngsters, particularly those of West Indian origin, has given much cause for concern of late. Incidents, some of which are capable of rational explanation, as well as those giving some grounds for apprehension about police over-zealousness or misbehavior, have been elevated to scandals. Events such as festivals and parades, which ought to have been peaceful and joyous occasions, have given undue trouble when black youngsters have turned to crime and disorder, often using police as targets.

The fact that there are many possible reasons for this including, of course, the increasing feeling of rejection and frustration amongst black youngsters, and the irresponsibility of the youngsters' behavior, is important but beyond the immediate scope of this text.

We should acknowledge that there is an uncritical readiness in some of us to think poorly of the black community, not only the young. There is an over-generalized assumption, on occasions, of their involvement in violent crime, deceit and collaboration in avoiding detection and rescuing lawfully detained prisoners; lack of intelligence and the ability to articulate, and absence of the motivation to work. Similarly, some black community comment on the police features allegations of racial prejudice, harassment and abuse, use of excessive force,

falsification of evidence, and indifference to the problems of black people.

Allegations of this nature, coming from both "sides," feed off each other. Examples of positive conduct both by police and by black community alike struggle for recognition against such a background and it is hard to persuade some that a rational assessment, rather than labels of convenience and generality, is both fair and just.

The police will need to work hard and patiently to increase their understanding of minority ethnic groups, especially the young blacks, and, at the same time, to do what they can to encourage the young and old from such groups to understand ourselves.

Initially we need to aim for greater involvement of all sections of the community in policing, whether this means asking for their help with training or encouraging participation in neighborhood watch schemes, and we should ensure that we, as constables, respond with thoughtfulness and enthusiasm. In the long term the increasing level of recruitment into the Force of men and women from our minority ethnic groups and our improved appreciation of "policing skills" should help, particularly if these can be supported by the actions and statesmanship of civil leaders and others in public life.

But all the efforts made will be of little value if public pronouncements of good intent are not carried through into practice in our day to day contact with the community we serve.

Patience, civility and a careful regard for every person's self-esteem will right the position in the end. Clearly: It is a duty to show compassionate respect for the dignity of the individual and to treat every person of whatever social position, race or creed, with courtesy and understanding.

The Use of Force

We are the only public service which, as a matter of duty, when making arrests or preventing criminal offenses, is required, and empowered, to lay hands on citizens.

Daily, throughout the country, there will be thousands of incidents in which this needs to be done. Hundreds of arrests are made each day, many of them involving drunken, drugged, or seriously disturbed people. Every week in this country thousands of police officers are taken from their normal work and mustered for duty at demonstrations, marches, football matches and other sporting events, in such a way that they can more readily be used to control and, if necessary, lay hands upon to arrest or eject thousands of their fellows.

In no other part of the country does this happen quite to the extent that it occurs in London; our city is so often the focus for discontent and protest, as well as rowdy celebration. Yet most of this takes place without serious trouble or hurt, because of the willingness of the individual police officer good humouredly to mediate and calm. Though there may be an initial struggle, the vast majority of arrests are accomplished unremarkably and peacefully, as are nearly all confrontations between policeman and citizen. That is a credit to society, and to the police, whose restraint and skill, strategies and tactics, have often received acclaim.

But occasionally things go wrong and violence flares. Then the readiness of the Force, its training to deal with public disorder, its equipment, and most importantly of all its tactics, are put to the test, sometimes severely so, in its attempt to restore order with the minimum of force.

In this area great strides have been taken during recent years. Since the 1981 riots, and Lord Scarman's recommendation that we must be better equipped and trained to deal with disorder, the co-ordination and control of resources in the Force and the husbanding of officers into small but flexible units, we have been able to respond much more quickly and effectively to potential threats to the peace.

Violence Occurs Nevertheless

In its various ugly forms violence is all too prevalent a part of the hurly-burly of the police officer's daily life in some areas. Many assaults take place. Every day police officers are injured in London. All these incidents are hurtful and unpleasant, and occasionally some are very serious indeed, leading to grave incapacity and, tragically, even to death. Rightly, there is always public concern about these assaults; much is said, and many new initiatives are proposed, in the quest to reduce the level of violence in our society though, alas, progress seems painfully slow to those of us who have to face it daily.

And when things go badly awry, on an individual or on a Force basis, and police are accused of assault or brutality, the spotlight rightly falls on us. Out of even relatively simple cases, great debates arise. Accusation and counter accusation abound. The actions of individual officers are probed, again and again. Explanations, though they be true or false, are hoisted up to the light and penetrated and shaken, sometimes with scant regard to the fact that at the time, the officer had not the facility of this fine hindsight and was obliged to judge things in an instant to react immediately.

But that is the way of police life, of course, and it is proper and right that there should be careful public invigilation of our use of force. And the more so since on a number of occasions we have been found wanting; incidents ranging from careless overreaction and burly

excess, to deliberate and wicked assault have been leveled, and proved, against individual officers.

All the more important then that we should develop our ability to remain calm and restrained, and to apply force economically and humanely. You should regard it as a matter of personal pride to be able to arrest a violent offender, quell a breath of the peace, or deal expeditiously with a disturbed or drunken man quietly, skillfully, and with the minimum of fuss. Your training has just that in view, and it is important that police officers should develop the expertise, and maintain their physical fitness, to do these things well.

Your experience will show you that, as your skills improve, so your confidence grows, and the chances of your receiving an injury diminish. You will learn, too, that you should beware the loose-lipped and boastful police officer who makes too much of every incident.

An officer who reacts spectacularly to every sign of resistance to what he wants to do, particularly when in the company of other officers, and who afterwards is full of noise and coarse boasting is, you can be sure, an officer who lacks skill, and courage, is unsure of himself, and perhaps on the edge of losing his nerve and becoming a bully. He will let us down if we do not act. He needs help, counsel, and further training to meet the high standards of restraint and professional efficiency in the use of force which the public is entitled to demand of us.

You should strive to exhibit those attitudes whatever the pressures and the provocation. The more often you succeed in doing this the greater will be your resolution when next faced with violence, and the more impressive your example to other officers.

And the Force is putting much effort into fulfilling if s obligation in this context that is to develop the training methods, tactics and policies, which will help you fulfill your difficult, individual obligations.

In recent years there have been great strides in the training given in self- defense, and the economic application of physical restraints. The necessity for each officer to be fit, both physically and psychologically, is now well recognized, and the Force is developing new methods of discerning, and then helping, the debilitating symptoms of stress.

Hand in hand with this, there has been considerable progress in the way the Force selects, equips, trains, and assesses those officers who are authorized to use firearms. The tactics and strategies which might be employed by senior officers directing incidents where firearms may need to be used, are the subject of constant review and refinement.

But all of this, excellent and carefully developed though it may be, alters not one jot the obligation which falls, individually, upon each of us. The decision to use force at the appropriate level, is one which falls, no matter how complex and spectacular, or how simple and unobtrusive the incident may be, upon the individual constable.

You will see that the obligation to decide for yourself, and if necessary to account afterwards to society through the law, arises in this context as it does in all others from your office of constable.

Our last principle springing from the Rule of Law, then, is one which allows us to draw together a number of different threads: It is a duty to show both resolution and restraint if faced with violent resistance, and to use, with consummate skill, only such force as is necessary to accomplish a legitimate purpose.

Summary

During this second part we have examined the aims and objects of the Force and have been able in the light of this, and of our discussion about the position of the constable, to define four duties, as follows:

i. It is a duty to prevent and detect crime, to keep the peace, to assuage fear of crime and disorder, and, wherever possible, to enlist the help of our fellow citizens in achieving those ends.

ii. It is a duty to uphold the Rule of Law by sustaining wholeheartedly:

the right to free speech;

the right to free association;

the right of access to legal advice;

the right to silence;

the presumption of innocence;

and by scrupulous compliance with:

the requirement of reasonableness when acting upon suspicion;

the rules pertaining to the rights of suspects;

the restrictions on powers of arrest and detention; and the requirement for integrity in the collection and presentation of evidence.

iii. It is a duty to show compassionate respect for the dignity of the individual and to treat every person of whatever social position, race or creed, with courtesy and understanding.

iv. It is a duty to show both resolution and restraint if faced with violent resistance, and to use, with consummate skill, only such force as is necessary to accomplish a legitimate purpose.

PART THREE

OUR DUTY TO EACH OTHER

Personal Standards and Group Loyalty

Because we deal primarily with people who find themselves in heightened or dramatic circumstances, it is not surprising that most of the skills, attitudes and qualities demanded of us are those which will succeed in times of crisis. Those to whom we are responsible, our fellow citizens, want us to show, consistently, as a matter of ordinary daily duty, the qualities to which they themselves doubtless aspire but which they do not always show.

If they did, what need of constables?

It is, thank goodness, part of the human condition to endeavor to improve. Police officers are, by obligation and perhaps by inclination also, in the vanguard of that quest for improvement. But we are all of us fallible, and, as our fellow citizens sometimes fall short of ordinary standards, so do we sometimes fall short of the even higher standards expected of us.

Let us look at the standards we are expected to keep and the qualities we are expected to show. It is a formidable list.

From the duties we have constructed out of our position as constables we find that as public servants we should be tolerant, careful, thoughtful, well-balanced, humane, prudent, practical, wise and incorruptible.

From the duties which arise for us, as members of a force, we see that we must be public spirited, scrupulously fair, valiant defenders of public ideals, tough, alert, courteous, compassionate, and both resolute and restrained.

And we need not rest our view of this only on the assessment of ourselves which we have made in this book. Police duties and the qualities required to accomplish them have been the subject of many enquiries, committees, and commissions. We have lots of evidence of what the public expects. Perhaps the best summation of what is required comes from the most recent Royal Commission on Police:

> *Discretionary duties demand powers of observation and memory and a well-developed sense of personal responsibility. The constable is expected to act with authority, commonsense, courage and leadership... Physical toughness, mental alertness, a long-established reputation for honesty and fair-dealing, tact, kindness, courtesy and a sense of humor: such qualities are taken for granted.*

Therein lies the nub, perhaps. They are taken for granted by the vast majority of people, or at least our daily exhibition of this formidable list of qualities is considered unremarkable by the man on the street.

Unremarkable, that is, until one of us is discovered to be well short of the mark, perhaps to the extent of committing a disciplinary or criminal offense. Then there is excitement enough, and we are reminded, time and again, that public interest in the standard of our behavior, although not much in evidence when all is well, does in fact run deep, and any shortcoming on our part is a matter of great concern for all.

This is a good sign, and far from making us despair should give us pleasure.It is an accolade, indeed, that the community demands the very highest standards of us, and that the great majority, silent from day to day, trust us to achieve those standards, being quick to take interest only when we do not do so, and then showing hurt and outrage if our failure is serious.

We can take a proper pride in our high ideals in the same way as our public takes a proper pride in us. No group of people in any other walk of life has quite the same, all pervasive obligations to their fellows—on duty and off duty.

But what duties do we owe each other, and how can we ensure that our standards are kept?

A main requirement is for us to show mutual support, particularly when the going is rough, and to be ever ready to aid a colleague, mentally as well as physically. Group loyalty in our service is strong. It can have a wonderfully supporting effect for the less able and less experienced of us, and it is so important for the well-being of the Force that it is the task of those who hold supervisory posts to arrange our organization and our policies so that their combined effect is to create and sustain such a spirit.

You will find, that the group spirit and high morale in the Force is, perhaps, the most enjoyable side of police life. It is your duty to foster it, and to help younger colleagues to get enrichment from it And you should consider it a matter of personal pride to help them reach our high standards, by yourself giving careful leadership to new entrants, and by setting them a wise and good example.

To this end we each have an obligation to work to increase our professional skills, and to widen our experience, so that we can better advise and support our colleagues as well as perform our duties more effectively.

And we have a duty, too, to keep ourselves in top physical condition, not only to sustain a good collective spirit and a cheerful resilience, and fitness always does that, but also to be able to support each other firmly at times of pressing need. A flabby, easily exhausted police officer, who has neglected himself and is out of condition, is a disaster when police are called to action. He is no good to any of us, or to the public.

In the context of our duty to each other, we have another main requirement. We must, for the sake of the service and as a matter of duty, be careful invigilators of those around us in the service.

This is a clear and particular obligation, perhaps even the most important obligation, for those of us who hold rank. But it is also a general duty which falls on all of us equally, whatever our rank and whatever our position in the Force. The group loyalty we have mentioned, though vital for an effective force and worth cherishing on that account alone, can work to our disadvantage. Unless such loyalty is carefully managed, it can become a harmfully insulating mechanism for police officers if they find themselves under siege from a world which is too critical, boisterous or hectic. A defensive mechanism like this can sometimes so warp judgments that officers in a small group will turn against the rest of us, rejecting our ideals and values and emphasizing their own.

Then, as has happened a number of times in the history of the police service, that group comes to work against public and service interests. The intellectual freedom, which so enriches the constable, becomes arrogant. It is assumed that the general rules of behavior do not apply to the group. They make their own rules. They become conspiratorial, secretive, looking upon other members of the Force as their antagonists. Such a group, if not removed, will hurt us all.

We have a duty to guard against this sort of development, and to assist each other by careful leadership and forthright statesmanship to create throughout our Force an atmosphere of openness and cooperation, which will not allow cancerous growth of that kind to flourish.

When faced with malpractice by any officer your duty is clear. Although in such a case you must, of course, apply all those restraints and considerations which we have mentioned earlier as being necessary principles governing all police action, there is no room for equivocation of any kind when you see wrongdoing by a police officer, or when you obtain any other credible evidence of it.

With your growing experience of colleagues, and your knowledge of police practice, you should not have too much difficulty in differentiating between what is over-zealousness, or laziness, or error of judgment, or genuine mistake, and what is wickedly neglectful or even criminal.

And you may not shield yourself from your duty by closing your eyes, or falling silently behind your group loyalty. You must speak out, and act. Failure to do so would not just be neglectful on your part, it would be so serious an evasion of your duty as an individual constable as to attract the most severe punishment.

And rightly so, for herein lies the real greatness of your office. Your duty to act fearlessly, and impartially, is unqualified. It is as much a duty, one might say even more a duty, for you to act against a fellow officer who is a criminal, as it is for you to take action against anyone else. If it should be your misfortune to find yourself in this position, do your duty resolutely. Take no account of the empty protests, breast-beating or excuses of any foolish officers who may side with the one you accuse, and demand that you should shield him. They are wrong. You are right. The Force and the great majority of its members who are jealous of its fine ideals and principles, will support you enthusiastically. And so, too, will the public stand by you.

From this important discussion we can define a complex but fundamental duty: It is a duty to guard the good reputation of the Force, to work constantly to maintain its high ideals, to encourage others to do so by good example and leadership, and to contribute to its excellence by showing resolution and honesty if faced with police malpractice.

To Protect and Assist the Citizen

The only part of our Statement of Policing Principles which we have yet to examine is the individual, and joint, duty to "protect and assist the citizen."

It is appropriate for us to deal with this in the last part of our examination—in the context of our duty to each other. As we will see, it is a very important aspect of our duty and affords the best opportunity to give a clear indication to each other of our public spiritedness and of commitment to our collective ends.

Protecting and assisting the citizen is a broad-based duty, embracing many activities; it also serves always to cement good relationships with individual citizens and with community groups.

As your training will have shown you, the police have a general duty to administer a variety of regulatory and supervisory legal measures which directly, or indirectly, assist the public. For example, we must work to administer and enforce traffic law so as to keep our roads safe and to maintain free passage on highways and other public places. Public safety in the general sense is very much our business also. These general regulatory duties take up quite the majority of police time. They do not often hit the headlines, but they demand of us the same sorts of skills, the same sure-footed and unflappable attention to the needs of others, and the same understanding and tolerance of what is sometimes inadvertent breaking of the law. But sometimes, breaches are deliberate and then the same firm commitment to the public purpose is necessary as in our more spectacular duties. There would be much disruption of life, and occasionally

great danger to the public, if we were not assiduously to apply ourselves to these matters. In London we have also unique duties concerning the security of the Royal Family, the protection of foreign diplomats and visitors, and those responsibilities which we exercise because our city houses the seat of Government.

But perhaps most important of all in this context, we have, by tradition and convention and in step with forces outside London, a duty to befriend the public whenever they need help. In everyday terms, this can range from our well-known willingness to provide information about the correct time, or where to catch a bus, or guidance on a particular law, to the opposite extreme of offering immediate and compassionate assistance at times of illness, tragedy or grief.

People who are in distress are entitled to sympathetic guidance and comfort from us, and we must never be slow to give it. We are an emergency service, nearly always first on the scene, and we must be ready both as a Force and as individuals to assist unhesitatingly and skillfully, in cases of accident and disaster. Our training, our contingency planning, our equipment, and our communication systems, are all geared sensibly to facilitate this.

Imaginative action and considerable innovation are called for if we are to be fully competent in this respect. Many are the times when, at scenes of accidents and other disasters, police officers have displayed tireless endeavor and quiet leadership of an exemplary kind, being able thereby to turn chaos to order, and panic to calm.

We must, therefore, take care as individuals, and as a Force, to develop our professional skills, our knowledge of our ground, and our resourcefulness, in order to meet unexpected problems quickly. We are strong and fit, and used to working as a team, so that our fellow citizens have come, by tradition, to see us as staunch and reassuring friends to whom they can turn whenever they are faced with danger and uncertainty.

From this widespread endeavor a clear principle arises: It is a duty to befriend and assist the citizen by giving sympathetic guidance and comfort to all in distress, and to advance staunch leadership when the public is faced with disaster or uncertainty.

OUR FINAL DUTY

We have examined at length in this book the requirement that we must improve our professional skills, and our human qualities, in order to serve our fellow men better and to encourage each other, by example, to do so.

In doing this we have mentioned some of the failings and wrongdoings of police officers who do not reach our high standards in instances which help us discern precisely where our duties lie.

Now that we have discerned where they do lie, we can see also that, as we have said, the duties are unique. No one else shares them. As the Royal Commission on the police said in 1960:

The constable must be vigilant both to use his authority adequately and instantly as occasion demands, and at the same time never to exceed it. We are satisfied that this individual responsibility is more onerous than any delegated to, or assigned by, a member of any comparable profession or occupation. Responsibility of this kind, to be properly and reasonably exercised, demands high moral standards and a nice exercise of judgment.

Unique then. And more...

The police function to which you and I are dedicated is perhaps the most worthwhile and most noble function in any free society. For you and I have this in common, that we represent government by consent.—Sir Robert Mark

So unique and noble. And you will know that that surely is right, for just as you might have had the misfortune in your time to observe police officers who are not so good, you will have had the pleasure of working with many, many more who are very good indeed, and some whose actions are so consistently above reproach as to defy adequate description. Moreover you will have heard about, indeed, may have been fortunate enough to serve with, officers who on occasion have responded to the demands of duty with such incomparable skill, and such disregard for themselves, as to take your breath away with admiration.

The general public, as well as the service, rightly admires the many police officers who, in pursuit of criminals, at scenes of disasters, when protecting or saving life, and elsewhere, have risked their own lives and limbs in order to pursue their duty to the very limits of their ability.

And we in the service are particularly proud, for pride here is surely no sin, of those fine men and women who have made the supreme sacrifice by giving their lives for others.

We are privileged, you and I, to be members of this great service and to have such marvelous companions as these. We must never forget them. We must always honor them. We must each of us strive to our utmost to emulate their greatness and to display, as they did, implacable resolution and courage. We must, therefore, have as our highest and most noble duty: To be brave and selfless in the face of danger and to serve the community, if need be, to the limits of our capacity.

CONCLUSION

In analyzing the office of constable and the Statement of Policing Principles we have been able to define nine duties. Some are straightforward and stand alone. Others are very complex. One or two are closely linked with each other. To list them in the order we developed them in the text would not quite fill our purpose of constructing a Code of Professional Duties, because the duties do not necessarily follow the one from the other. They read more easily when broken into the two main categories of those duties which indicate what we must do, and those which indicate how we must do it.

A CODE OF PROFESSIONAL DUTIES

Duties of function

It is your duty:

1. To prevent and detect crime, to keep the peace, to assuage fear of crime and disorder, and, wherever possible, to enlist the help of our fellow citizens in achieving those ends.

2. To uphold the rule of law by sustaining wholeheartedly:

   the right to free speech;

   the right to free association;

   the right of access to legal advice;

   the right to silence;

   the presumption of innocence;

   and by scrupulous compliance with:

   the requirement of reasonableness when acting upon suspicion;

   the rules pertaining to the rights of suspects;

   the restrictions on powers of arrest and detention; and the requirement for integrity in the collection and presentation of evidence.

3. To show compassionate respect for the dignity of the individual and to treat every person of whatever social position, race or creed, with courtesy and understanding.

4. To show both resolution and restraint if faced with violent resistance, and to use, with consummate skill, only such force as is necessary to accomplish a legitimate purpose.

5. To befriend and assist the citizen by giving sympathetic guidance and comfort to all in distress, and to advance staunch leadership when the public is faced with disaster or uncertainty.

Duties of Method

It is your duty to strive:

6. To be brave and selfless in the face of danger and to serve the community, if need be, to the limits of your capacity.

7. To act always for the general public good, as a helpful and reasonable public servant, and not merely as an enforcer of the law.

8. When exercising police powers:

   to avoid peremptoriness;

   to weigh carefully all surrounding factors, and to judge these in the light of the Attorney General's guidance;

   to be humane, having regard to public interests in addition to those of victim and offender;

   to be prudent and restrained, paying full regard to what is practicable, particularly when off duty;

   to avoid equally undue zeal and undue tolerance;

   to be, and be seen to be, unfettered by obligation, deciding each issue without fear or favor, malice or ill-will.

9. To guard the good reputation of the Force, to work constantly to maintain its high ideals, to encourage others to do so by good example and leadership, and to contribute to its excellence by showing resolution and honesty if faced with police malpractice.

GLOBAL STANDARDS TO COMBAT CORRUPTION IN POLICE FORCES/ SERVICES

SOURCE http://www.interpol.org/Public/corruption/ standard/Default.asp.

INTRODUCTION *In 1998 Interpol's General Secretariat held the First International Conference on Corruption-Related Crimes. One of the recommendations made during the Conference was the formation of a group that would shape and carry out the agency's anti-corruption strategy. The Interpol Group of Experts on Corruption (IGEC) is made up of representatives from the regions that Interpol serves, and one of their accomplishments was the draft of "Interpol's Global Standards to Combat Corruption." The standards were adopted by Interpol in 2002.*

GLOBAL STANDARDS TO COMBAT CORRUPTION IN POLICE FORCES/ SERVICES

Article 1

Objectives

a. To ensure that the police forces/services of each Member State of Interpol have high standards of honesty, integrity and ethical behaviour in and in connection with the performance of their policing functions.

b. To promote and strengthen the development by each Member State of Interpol of measures needed to prevent, detect, punish and eradicate corruption in the police forces/services within its national boundaries and to bring to justice police officers and other employees of police forces/services who are corrupt.

Definitions

Corruption includes:

a. The solicitation or acceptance, whether directly or indirectly, by a police officer or other employee of a police force/service of any money, article of value, gift, favour, promise, reward or advantage, whether for himself/herself or for any person, group or entity, in return for any act or omission already done or omitted or to be done or omitted in the future in or in connection with the performance of any function of or connected with policing.

b. The offering or granting, whether directly or indirectly, to a police officer or other employee of a police force/service of any money, article of value, gift, favour, promise, reward or advantage for the police officer or other employee or for any person, group or entity in return for any act or omission already done or omitted or to be done or omitted in the future in or in connection with the performance of any function of or connected with policing.

c. Any act or omission in the discharge of duties by a police officer or other employee of a police force/service which may improperly expose any person to a charge or conviction for a criminal offence or may improperly assist in a person not being charged with or being acquitted of a criminal offence.

d. The unauthorized dissemination of confidential or restricted police information whether for reward or otherwise.

e. Any act or omission in the discharge of duties by a police officer or other employee of a police force/service for the purpose of obtaining any money, article of value, gift, favour, promise, reward or advantage for himself/herself or any other person, group or entity.

f. Any act or omission which constitutes corruption under a law of the Member State.

g. Participation as a principal, co-principal, initiator, instigator, accomplice, accessory before the fact, accessory after the fact or in any other manner in the commission or attempted commission or in any conspiracy to do or omit to do any act referred to in the preceding provisions of this Article.

Police force/service means each police force/service or other official body with a responsibility to perform policing functions within the national boundaries of the Member State.

Article 3

Principles

a. To make corruption within police forces/services a high-risk crime.

b. To promote and maintain a high standard of honesty, integrity and ethical behaviour within the police forces/services of each Member.

c. To foster the recruitment and training as police officers of persons of high levels of integrity, honesty, ethical standards and expertise.

Article 4

Measures

Each Member of the Organization commits to:

a. making corruption by a police officer or other employee of a police force/service a serious criminal offence;

b. having legislation enacted to allow the proceeds of corruption and related crimes to be forfeited;

c. establishing and maintaining high standards of conduct for the honest, ethical and effective performance of policing functions;

d. Such standards should be mandatory and be directed towards an understanding and application of honest, ethical and appropriate behaviour, the avoidance of conflicts of interest, the proper use of public resources in and in connection with the fair and impartial application of the law, the performance of policing functions, the reporting of acts of corruption in and in connection with the performance of policing functions, and the establishment and strengthening of public confidence in police officers and police forces/services as part of the system of justice;

e. Such standards should accept that it is an obligation of the police force/service to seek out and effectively deal with corruption within the police force/service;

f. Such standards should impose an obligation on police officers and other employees of a police force/service to report to the appropriate person or authority acts or omissions which constitute or may constitute corruption within the police force/service;

g. setting up and maintaining effective mechanisms to oversee and enforce the high standards of conduct required in and in connection with the performance of policing functions;

h. bringing into being or causing to be brought into being such legislative, administrative and other measures as may be necessary to prevent, detect, punish and eradicate corruption in the police forces/services;

i. conferring or causing to be conferred on a designated authority, whether internal or external, such powers to carry out investigations and bring to justice without fear, favour, affection or ill-will those who engage in corruption and dishonesty in the course of or in association with the carrying out of policing functions, and adequately resourcing and funding such authority;

j. providing for a system for the recruitment of officers for such designated authority who are of high integrity and which ensures that such officers are not disadvantaged by recruitment to any such designated authority;

k. providing adequate safeguards to prevent abuse of powers by those engaged in the anti-corruption system and to minimize unnecessary infringements of individual rights; having a system for instructing police officers and others engaged in and in connection with the performance of policing functions of the standards and ethical rules applicable to the performance of such functions;

l. establishing and enforcing procedures for the declaration and registration of the income, assets and liabilities of those who perform policing functions and of appropriate members of their families;

m. establishing a mechanism such as an oversight body or bodies to monitor the systems and measures established for preventing, detecting, punishing and eradicating corruption within the police forces/services and the adequacy, application and effectiveness of such systems and measures;

n. requiring public reporting at least once each year of the work and findings in relation to the monitoring of the systems and measures referred to in Article 4(k) and their adequacy, application and effectiveness;

o. putting in place deterrents to the bribery of those performing policing functions;

p. establishing mechanisms to encourage participation by civil society in activities and efforts to prevent corruption in the police forces/services;

q. having and maintaining effective systems for the recruitment of police officers of high levels of integrity, honesty, ethical standards and expertise;

r. ensuring that the systems for recruitment, posting, promotion and termination of police officers and other employees of the police forces/services are not arbitrary but are based on fairness, openness, ability and performance;

s. having and maintaining a system for the training, including on-going training, of police officers and other employees in the police forces/services which reinforces the high standards of conduct referred to in Article(c);

t. taking all practicable steps to ensure that the rates of remuneration for police officers and other employees of the police forces/services are such as to enable them and their families to maintain a reasonable standard of living without having to resort to other employment or to corruption;

u. having and maintaining systems for the procurement of goods and services that are based on openness, efficiency, equity and certainty of the rules to be applied and that seek the best value for money;

v. having and maintaining systems of revenue collection, money and property handling and for the control and preservation of evidence that ensure that those collecting or handling public money, dealing with evidence or handling property are accountable and that the systems are such as to deter corruption;

w. having an effective system that obliges police officers and other employees of the police forces/services to report corruption, that enables them and members of civil society to report corruption, and that protects those who report corruption in good faith;

x. continuing research in relation to current best practice for the prevention, detection, punishment and eradication of corruption in and in connection with the performance of policing functions;

y. reviewing at appropriate and regular intervals the measures and systems for the prevention, detection, punishment and eradication of corruption in and in connection with the performance of policing functions;

z. using their best endeavours to ensure that the mechanisms and systems for the prevention, detection, punishment and eradication of corruption in and in connection with the performance of policing functions in its police forces/services are kept abreast of current practice as recognized by the General Assembly of Interpol;

aa. reporting at least once each two years, or at such shorter intervals as the General Assembly may resolve, on the measures taken and the mechanisms and systems in place to implement the standards set out in this protocol and the effectiveness of such mechanisms, systems and measures;

ab. permitting the monitoring by and co-operating with such person or persons as may be appointed by the Secretary General for the purpose of monitoring the mechanisms, systems and measures in place in relation to its police forces/services to achieve the objectives and meet the standards referred to in this protocol and the effectiveness of such mechanisms, systems and measures.

Article 5

Review

The operation of this protocol shall be reviewed by the General Secretariat of Interpol on an ongoing basis and is to be the subject of a report to each session of the General Assembly that is held after the expiration of two years from the adoption of this protocol.

ETHICS HANDBOOK

SOURCE *U.S. Department of Justice, 2002.*

INTRODUCTION *The following handbook, intended* inter alia *for the guidance of FBI employees, brings together the substance of various directives, regulations, and laws that might be considered of occupational ethical significance. In May 2002 the U.S. Department of Justice Departmental Ethics Office issued the sixth edition.*

CONFLICTS OF INTEREST

General Rule

You should avoid situations where your official actions affect or appear to affect your private interests, financial or non-financial.

Statutory Prohibition

You may not participate personally and substantially in a matter in which you, your spouse, minor child or general partner has a financial interest. This prohibition also applies if an organization in which you serve as an officer, director, trustee, or employee has a financial interest; or if a person or organization with which you are negotiating for future employment has a financial interest.

18 U.S.C. § 208

Impartiality Standard

Generally, you should seek advice before participating in any matter in which your impartiality could be questioned. You may not participate without authorization in a particular matter having specific parties that could affect the financial interests of members of your household or where one of the following is a party or represents a party: someone with whom you have or are seeking employment, or a business, contractual or other financial relationship; a member of your household or a relative with whom you have a close relationship; a present or prospective employer of a spouse, parent or child; or an organization which you now serve actively or have served, as an employee or in another capacity, within the past year.

5 CFR 2635.502

Purchase of Forfeited Property

Without written approval, you may not purchase or use property that has been forfeited to the Government and offered for sale by the Justice Department.

5 CFR 3801.104

Extraordinary Payments

If you received a payment in excess of $10,000 from a former employer that was not pursuant to an employee benefit plan, you must disqualify yourself from matters affecting that former employer for two years unless you receive a waiver.

5 CFR 2635.503

Remedies for Conflicts

If you have a financial conflict of interest or believe your impartiality might be questioned, you must either disqualify yourself from taking action that could affect your interest, or see your Deputy DAEO about the following alternatives:

In the case of a financial interest, you may seek a waiver of the prohibition under 18 U.S.C. § 208(b), or divest yourself of the interest. Your component head may grant you a waiver if your financial interest is found to be not so substantial as to affect the integrity of your services to the Government. (If you are directed to divest an interest, you may be eligible to defer the tax consequences of divestiture).

18 U.S.C. § 208(b)(1)
5 CFR 2634.1001–.1004

In a case where your impartiality might be questioned, you may obtain a formal determination from your component head that the Department's interest in your participation outweighs the concern that the integrity of the Department's operations would be questioned.

5 CFR 2635.502(d)

When participating in a matter affecting your financial interests, you have an unlimited exemption for holdings in a diversified mutual fund and for certain employee benefit plans where the holdings may be affected by the matter. In addition, you have an exemption of $50,000 for aggregated interests in sector mutual funds that may be affected by a matter in which you participate. You also have an exemption for interests in publicly-traded securities not to exceed $15,000 in parties to a matter and $25,000 in non-parties affected by the matter. And, you have an exemption of $25,000 per asset when participating in a matter of general applicability, such as regulations and most legislation, with a combined limit of $50,000 in all entities affected by the general matter.

5 CFR 2640.201–.202

Nepotism

You may not appoint, employ, or promote a relative to a position in the Department, or advocate a relative for appointment, employment, promotion or advancement.

5 U.S.C. § 3110

Financial Disclosure

You may be required to file a financial disclosure report which will be used to identify potential or actual conflicts of interest. Check with your Deputy DAEO if you are uncertain of your filing status.

5 CFR 2634

OUTSIDE ACTIVITIES
General Rule

You should not engage in any outside employment or other outside activity that conflicts with your official duties. Employees are prohibited from engaging in outside employment that involves criminal matters, the paid practice of law or matters in which the Department is or represents a party. Only the Deputy Attorney General may waive these prohibitions.

5 CFR 2635.802
5 CFR 3801.106

Approval for Certain Outside Activities

You are required to obtain written approval for certain outside employment including the practice of law that is not otherwise prohibited or any outside employment involving a subject matter related to the responsibilities of your component.

5 CFR 3801.106

Representing Others

You may not receive compensation for the representation of anyone before an agency or court of the Federal

Government on a matter in which the U.S. is a party or has a substantial interest. This prohibition applies whether or not you render the representation yourself.

18 U.S.C. § 203

You also may not represent someone before an agency or court of the Federal Government, with or without compensation, on a matter in which the U.S. is a party or has a substantial interest.

18 U.S.C. § 205

There are exceptions to the above statutes for representing your immediate family, testifying under oath, representing another employee in personnel administration proceedings, and representing employee organizations in certain matters.

Fundraising

You may engage in fundraising in your personal capacity as long as you do not solicit your subordinates or persons having business with the Department. There is an exception for mass mailings that do not target the above persons. You may not engage in fundraising in your official capacity unless authorized by statute, executive order or regulation. There is an exception for giving an official speech at a fundraiser.

5 CFR 2635.808

Service as an Expert Witness

You may not serve as an expert witness in your private capacity in any proceeding before the United States in which the U.S. is a party or has an interest unless specifically authorized.

5 CFR 2635.805

Official Speaking and Writing

You may not be paid by anyone but the Government for speaking or writing undertaken as part of your official duties.

18 U.S.C. § 209

Outside Teaching, Speaking and Writing

When you are teaching, speaking or writing in your private capacity, you may not use nonpublic information, nor should there be any use of your official title except as a biographical detail or where there is a disclaimer. Generally, you may not be compensated for teaching, speaking, or writing that relates to your official duties. However, there is an exception for teaching in certain educational settings. If you are a career employee, or a non-career employee classified at GS-15 and below, what relates to your duties is a present assignment or one assigned during the past year, or a policy, program or operation of your component. If you are a noncareer

employee above GS-15, what relates to your duties is broader. You may not use your official time or that of a subordinate to prepare materials. Some components require advance review and clearance for certain written work and speeches.

5 CFR 2635.703, .705 & .807

If you are in a non-career position above GS-15 you must have advance authorization from the DAEO before engaging in teaching for compensation.

5 CFR 2636.307

Outside Earned Income

If you are a full-time Presidential appointee, you may not receive earned income for any outside activity performed during that appointment. If you are a noncareer official in a position classified above GS-15, your outside earned income is limited to 15% of the salary for Executive Level II. Also, if you are a political appointee classified above GS-15, you are subject to other restrictions related to providing fiduciary services for compensation.

5 CFR 2636.302–.306

ACCEPTING THINGS OF VALUE

Gifts, Entertainment and Favors from Outside Sources You may not solicit or accept a gift given because of your official position or from a prohibited source to include anyone who:

> Has or seeks official action or business with the Department;
>
> Is regulated by the Department;
>
> Has interests that may be substantially affected by the performance of your official duties; or
>
> Is an organization composed mainly of persons described above.

A gift does not include items such as publicly available discounts and prizes, commercial loans, food not part of a meal such as coffee and donuts, and items of little value such as plaques and greeting cards.

Unless the frequency of the acceptance of gifts would appear to be improper, you may accept:

> Gifts based on a personal relationship when it is clear that the motivation is not your official position.
>
> Gifts of $20 or less per occasion not to exceed $50 in a year from one person.
>
> Discounts and similar benefits offered to a broad class, including a broad class of government employees.
>
> Most genuine awards and honorary degrees although in some cases you will need prior approval.

Free attendance, food, refreshments and materials provided at a conference or widely attended gathering or certain other social events which you attend in your official capacity, with prior approval. If you are invited to an event by someone other than the sponsor, the cost must not exceed $260 and at least 100 people must be expected to attend.

Gifts based on an outside business relationship such as travel expenses related to a job interview.

5 CFR 2635.202–.204

You should return gifts not meeting the exceptions or contact your Deputy DAEO on how to dispose of them. Perishable items may be given to charity or shared by your office, with approval.

5 CFR 2635.205

Supplementation of Salary

You may not receive any supplementation of your government salary from any source except the Government for performing your official duties.

18 U.S.C. § 209

Foreign Gifts

You are allowed to accept certain gifts from foreign governments if they do not exceed a minimal value presently set at $260. See your Deputy DAEO for information on how to report the acceptance of a foreign gift.

5 U.S.C. § 7342

Gifts to Superiors

You may not give, or solicit a contribution for, a gift to an official superior, and you may not accept a gift from an employee receiving less pay than you if the employee is a subordinate. There is an exception for voluntary gifts of nominal value made on a special occasion such as marriage, illness or retirement. You also may give an individual gift to a superior costing $10 or less, and contribute to shared food and refreshments on other less significant occasions.

5 CFR 2635.302 & .304

Travel

Generally, you may not accept reimbursement for travel and related expenses from any source other than the Government when you are traveling on official duty. However, with prior written approval, you may accept travel expenses incidental to attendance at meetings or similar functions related to your duties from non-Federal sources pursuant to the GSA regulations cited here. You may not accept travel expenses for a spouse accompanying you on official travel. Consult your Deputy DAEO on obtaining approval for yourself.

41 CFR 304

You may retain for personal use benefits from commercial sources, including bonus flights, that result from your official travel. You may keep a bonus offered when you volunteer to take a later flight as long as the delay does not interfere with the conduct of your duties and you do not charge the Government for additional costs but you may not keep such a bonus if you are bumped from a flight. In most cases, you may not fly first class when on official business.

41 CFR 301

POLITICAL ACTIVITIES

Most Employees May:

Register and vote as they choose.

Assist in voter registration drives.

Express opinions on candidates and issues.

Be a candidate for public office in nonpartisan elections.

Contribute money to political organizations, in general.

Attend and be active at political rallies and meetings.

Attend political fundraisers.

Join and be an active member of a political party or club.

Circulate and sign nominating petitions.

Campaign for or against referendum questions, constitutional amendments and municipal ordinances.

Distribute campaign literature in partisan elections.

Make campaign speeches for candidates in partisan elections.

Campaign for or against candidates in partisan elections.

Hold office in political clubs and parties.

No Employees May:

Be a candidate in a partisan election.

Engage in political activity while on duty, in a government office, while wearing an official uniform or using a government vehicle.

Solicit political contributions from the general public or collect contributions except from a fellow member of a Federal labor or employee organization who is not a subordinate.

Solicit or discourage the political activity of anyone who has business with the Department.

Use official authority or influence to interfere with an election.

Wear political buttons while on duty.

5 U.S.C. §§ 7321–26
5 CFR 734

Under the statute, members of the Career Senior Executive Service, employees of the Criminal Division and the FBI and administrative law judges are subject to stricter rules under the pre-1994 law whereby they are prohibited from participating actively in political management or political campaigns. These stricter rules apply to all DOJ political appointees under Department policy.

In certain communities, including the suburbs of Washington, D.C., an employee may run as an independent candidate in a local partisan election and solicit and receive contributions. An election is partisan if any candidate for an elected public office is running as a representative of a political party whose candidates for presidential elector received votes in the last presidential election.

5 CFR 733

MISUSE OF OFFICIAL POSITION

General Rule

You may not use your public office for your own private gain or for that of persons or organizations with which you are associated personally. Your position or title should not be used to coerce; to endorse any product or service; or to give the appearance of governmental sanction. For example, you may use your official title and stationery only in response to a request for a reference or recommendation for someone you have dealt with in Federal employment or someone you are recommending for Federal employment.

5 CFR 2635.702

Use of Government Property and Time

Generally, you should be mindful of your responsibility to make an honest effort to use government property and official time, including the time of a subordinate, for official business only. However, as a Justice Department employee, you are generally authorized to make minimal personal use of most office equipment and library facilities where the cost to the Government is negligible.

5 CFR 2635.704
28 CFR 45.4

Government Vehicles

Generally, an official purpose does not include your transportation to and from the workplace; however, there are some statutorily authorized exceptions to this rule.

31 U.S.C. §§ 1344 & 1349(b)

Use of Nonpublic Information

You may not engage in a financial transaction using nonpublic information or allow the use of such information to further your private interests or those of another.

Nonpublic information is information you gain on the job and which has not been made available to the general public and is not authorized to be made available on request. (There are also statutory prohibitions on the misuse of information involving national security, trade secrets, private individuals and government procurement.)

5 CFR 2635.703

POST-EMPLOYMENT RESTRICTIONS

Negotiating for Future Employment

You may not take official action on a matter affecting the financial interests of an organization with which you are negotiating or have an arrangement for a job. Generally, you would disqualify yourself from a matter in order to negotiate for a job, and employees participating in a procurement have to report to certain officials in writing before negotiating with a contractor competing for that procurement. You may also have to disqualify yourself when you are merely seeking employment, which includes sending a resume. You should get advice from your Deputy DAEO about seeking and negotiating for employment before you begin a job search.

18 U.S.C. § 208
41 U.S.C. § 423
5 CFR 2635.602

Restrictions for After You Leave Government

There are statutory prohibitions on former government employees that generally prevent you from "switching sides" after leaving the Government. The following are the main restrictions, but see your Deputy DAEO for others:

Lifetime Ban

You are prohibited from communicating to or appearing before an employee of an agency or court of the Federal Government on behalf of another person, with the intent to influence, on a particular matter involving specific parties in which you participated personally and substantially while with the Government and in which the United States is a party or has an interest.

18 U.S.C. § 207(a)(1)

Two-year Ban

You are prohibited for two years from communicating to or appearing before an employee of a Federal court or agency on behalf of another person, with the intent to influence, on a particular matter involving specific parties which you know was pending under your responsibility during your last year of government service and in which the United States is a party or has an interest.

18 U.S.C. § 207(a)(2)

One-year Ban

If you are an Executive Level official or an ES 5 or 6 in the SES (or a comparable level of another pay system) you are subject to an additional restriction that generally prohibits you from communicating to or appearing before an employee of the Justice Department or your component on a matter on which you seek official action on behalf of another person.

18 U.S.C. § 207(c)

One-year Ban for Certain Procurement and Contracting Officials

If you served in a certain critical position or made certain critical decisions on a procurement on a contract in excess of $10 million, you may not receive compensation from that contractor for one year.

41 U.S.C. § 423

SPECIAL APPLICATIONS

Entering Employees

In certain circumstances, you may not be able to maintain a financial relationship with a former employer or accept a severance payment or moving expenses from a private source. Consult your Deputy DAEO for advice. If you are an attorney, you will have to disqualify yourself in cases you handled before entering the Government, and from other matters involving your former law firm or clients for a certain period, usually several years. Generally, you will not be allowed to remain on leave of absence from a law firm or another business entity while with the Department. See your Deputy DAEO about any repayment of your capital contributions over time or about retaining an interest in a contingent fee.

18 U.S.C. §§ 203,208 & 209
5 CFR 2635.502

PROFESSIONAL CODES

Post Employment Compensation

There are restrictions on your receiving compensation, even after you leave, based on another's representations before the Federal government that took place while you were still a government employee.

18 U.S.C. 203

Special Government Employees

If you are a special government employee, that is, you expect to serve for no more than 130 days in a 365-day period, you are subject to most of the rules in this booklet. However, in some cases, they are applied stringently. Consult your Deputy DAEO.

Attorneys

If you are an attorney with the Department, you are expected to comply not only with the rules in this booklet, but also with relevant professional codes of conduct. Consult your Deputy DAEO or the Professional Responsibility Advisory Office for advice on which codes apply and what they require.

ETHICAL STANDARDS IN LAW ENFORCEMENT

SOURCE *LEAPS, 1973.*

INTRODUCTION *The Law Enforcement Association on Professional Standards, Education, and Ethical Practice (LEAPS) was founded in 1970, in St Louis, Missouri. Its membership of more than 200 was comprised of police practitioners and academics with college degrees who were "united to promote professional standards and ethical practice in police services." The Standards, released on June 26, 1973, received some support and in one case at least (Jamestown, NY) were incorporated into a police manual. In 1974 LEAPS merged with the New York based Academy of Police Science (founded in 1958) to form the American Academy for Professional Law Enforcement (AAPLE). The Standards carried over to the new organization, which eventually redrafted them as its own.*

PREAMBLE

The worth of the law enforcement profession is measured by its contribution to the welfare of man, by its concern for excellence, and by the guidance it provides its members toward a high level of ethical practice. The purpose of the present principles of ethics are: to better serve the public; to elevate the standards of the profession and to strengthen public confidence in law enforcement; to encourage law enforcement officers to fully appreciate the total responsibilities of their office; to earn the support and cooperation of the public; and to ensure the effectiveness of service to society.

Principle 1: Responsibility

The officer, committed to the welfare of the public, through the rule of law and professional service, places high value on objectivity and integrity an maintains the highest standards in the services the officer provides.

a. The officer believes in the dignity and worth of the individual and in the constitutional right of all persons to liberty, equality, and justice under the law.

b. The officer is entrusted with a special authority and responsibility to enforce the laws of society and to carry out this mandate with courtesy, fairness, consideration, and compassion.

c. Officers in a command or supervisory position will carry out their duties in a manner that is consistent with the highest degree of professional effectiveness, efficiency, and responsibility.

Principle 2: Competence

Professional competence is an obligation shared by all law enforcement officers, in the interest of the public and of the profession as a whole, from the selection throughout their professional career.

a. The officer should strive to attain a high degree of academic education, preferably the bachelor's degree, and to continue education and training throughout one's career. While education and training does not guarantee competence, such personal development equips an officer to meet the demands of his profession.

b. Where compatible with individual career paths, command and supervisory officers should develop ongoing and timely programs of training and should encourage and assist officers to pursue higher education.

Principle 3: Professional and Legal Standards

The law enforcement officer in the practice of his profession shows sensible regard for the social codes and moral expectations of the community in which he works. An officer should be aware that unethical behaviors have a far-reaching, detrimental effect on all law enforcement officers and agencies and on the communities they serve.

a. Conduct at all times should be such that an officer brings credit to his profession.

b. Unethical behaviors such as fabricating, altering, or withholding evidence to effect an arrest or gain a conviction as well as theft, graft, and acceptance of bribes or gratuities cannot be tolerated.

c. If an officer observes unethical, improper, or unlawful behavior by a colleague, he is required to determine the facts in the case, to rectify the situation and, if appropriate, to report the case to his immediate supervisor or to a review committee for investigation and action. Officers who fail to take legally prescribed action when confronted with misconduct share the burden of guilt.

Principle 4: Public Statements

Truth, objectivity, and due regard for the rights and privacy of the individual must characterize all statements of law enforcement officers who supply information to the public, either directly or indirectly.

a. In regard to court testimony, the officer shall present evidence honestly and without bias or prejudice. The sole objective shall be to give evidence as the officer has knowledge of it. The officer shall not identify with the prosecution or defense, but provide evidence on the basis of actual fact.

Principle 5: Confidentiality

Safeguarding information about an individual or group that has been obtained by the law enforcement officer in the course of duty or investigation is a primary obligation of the officer. Such information is not communicated to others, unless certain important conditions are met.

a. No information shall be maintained or transmitted to another about the private life of an individual which does not relate specifically to the problem of law violation.

b. Security and privacy shall be assured all individuals whose records are maintained in order that such records shall be used only in criminal justice proceedings.

c. Information on individuals shall not be processed or integrated with other record systems except to inform criminal justice agencies on matters pertaining to law violation.

d. Only those with a legal right of access shall have access to any criminal justice agency records or record systems.

Principle 6: Professional Relationships

The officer should maintain high standards of conduct in professional relations with those he serves, with fellow officers, with professional colleagues in other organizations in the criminal justice system, and with those in other public service agencies.

a. The officer should maintain professional confidence as a trust.

b. When engaged in official actions, the officer is obligated to inform individuals of the nature of their relationship except in those instances where to do so would defeat the ends of justice.

c. It is unethical for any officer or agency to establish a protective allegiance with individuals so as to obscure their complicity in a criminal act.

d. Physical and psychological abuses of authority shall not be tolerated.

e. Pressure by a department on an individual officer to make a quota of arrests or to insure a quota of citations should be condoned.

f. It is the professional responsibility of law enforcement agencies to develop effective referral systems for non-criminal actions coming to their attention.

g. The officer shall act responsibly when called on to make professional recommendations, the importance of which may affect the welfare of an individual or society.

h. An officer should hold that high standards of conduct in interprofessional relationships are essential to professional competence.

i. In the interest of harmony and efficient public service, the officer has an obligation and responsibility to cooperate with other professionals in the criminal justice system.

Principle 7: Education and Training Practices

Law enforcement instructors and educators should encourage students in their quest for knowledge and in their development of professional skills, giving them every assistance in the free exploration of ideas.

a. The instructor should properly advise students to ensure that they understand opportunities and requirements in the field.

b. The instructor in discussing law enforcement techniques should impress upon the student the importance to all applicable principles governing practices, and of the retention of such principles in accord with his organization's regulations.

c. An instructor of law enforcement should stress to his students the importance of the system context in which criminal justice agencies operate, emphasizing that agencies should contribute to the goals of the entire criminal justice system.

d. The present ethical standards in law enforcement shall be reviewed with students. A student who serves in any law enforcement capacity, as a cadet or a recruit, is expected to follow the ethical standards of the profession.

Principle 8: Research and Writing

Practitioners and educators in law enforcement have the responsibility of developing a body of knowledge and conducting research to improve service, to provide the best information for professional practice, and to publish their results and conclusions so that the profession and the public is well informed.

Principle 9: Recruitment and Employment Practices

A law enforcement agency will not discriminate against any officer, employee, or applicant for employment because of race, sex, creed, color, or national origin. The agency will take affirmative action to ensure that all such applicants are fairly considered for employment, and that employees are treated during employment with equal opportunity.

a. Such employment practices and policy shall be related to, but not be limited to, the following: employment, upgrading and promotion, demotion or transfer, recruitment or recruitment advertising, layoffs or termination, rates of pay or other forms of compensation, and selection for training or education, including apprenticeship.

b. Agencies shall post in conspicuous places, available to employees and applicants for employment, notices setting forth the provisions of this nondiscrimination clause.

c. Agencies will permit access to its records and accounts by a body of local or state government or the U.S. Department of Justice officials for the purposes of investigation to ascertain compliance with this non-discrimination clause.

d. All criteria used by agencies in their recruitment and selection processes shall be clearly related to the duties, requirements, and responsibilities of the law enforcement task.

ETHICAL STANDARDS IN LAW ENFORCEMENT

SOURCE *American Academy for Professional Law Enforcement, 1976.*

INTRODUCTION *The American Academy for Professional Law Enforcement (AAPLE) was formed in 1974—the result of a merger of the New York based Academy of Police Science and the St. Louis-based Law Enforcement Association on Professional Standards, Education and Ethical Practice. AAPLE's mission was to foster "professional standards" in the provision of "law enforcement services to the public." It sought to do this "through education and training aimed at providing the maximum effective service and promotion of highest professional ethics in serving clients and dealing in inter-professional activities with colleagues." A note to the standards indicates that it is "based on provisions of 'Ethical Standards in Law Enforcement' developed as a consequence of LEAPS, Second National Symposium on Police Ethical Practice with subsequent amendments, June 26, 1973." It is further stated that "the new materials in Sections 5.0, 6.0, 9.0, and 10.0 were suggested by Professor William*

P. Brown. Section 6.0 c.f. and 10.0 are based on the provisions of the Draft Code of Conduct for Law Enforcement Officials adopted by the United Nations Committee on Crime Prevention and Control and as reported by Amnesty International."

PREAMBLE

The worth of the law enforcement profession is measured by its contribution to the welfare of man. Police officers are entrusted with a legal authority and responsibility to enforce the laws of society and to carry out this mandate with courtesy, fairness, consideration, and compassion.

The purposes of these principles of ethics are: to elevate the standards of the profession and to strengthen public confidence in law enforcement; to encourage law enforcement officers to fully appreciate the total responsibilities of their office; to earn the support and cooperation of the public; and to ensure the effectiveness of service to society.

ETHICAL STANDARDS OF LAW ENFORCEMENT

1.0 Responsibility

The officer is entrusted with special authority and responsibility to enforce the laws of society and to give assistance in a specified manner to individuals in need. He is required to carry out this mandate with courtesy, fairness, consideration, and compassion.

a. The officer should manifest a belief in the dignity and worth of every individual and in the constitutional right of each person to liberty, equality, and justice under law.

b. The officer should manifest commitment to the welfare of the public. That interest is best served when high value is placed on objectivity and integrity and on achieving the highest standards of professional service.

c. Officers in a command or supervisory position should carry out their duties in a manner that is consistent with a full recognition of their responsibilities and an effort to achieve them with the highest degree of professional effectiveness and ethical awareness.

2.0 Competence

The need for continual striving for increased professional competence is an obligation shared by all law enforcement officers. That responsibility begins when they enter the police service and continues throughout their professional career.

a. While education and training does not guarantee competence, the emphasis on the personal develop-

ment that it manifests does tend to equip an officer to better meet the changing demands of his profession. Therefore, there is an ethical obligation to strive to obtain the benefits that academic education and training can bring, and there should be the recognition that this emphasis should continue throughout one's professional career.

b. Command and supervisory officers have the responsibility to aid the officers under their supervision in developing ongoing and timely programs of professional development. Agencies and command personnel should assist officers in obtaining professional development.

3.0 Professional and Legal Standards

The law enforcement officer in the practice of his profession should show sensitivity towards the social codes and moral expectations of the community in which he works. However, it should be recognized that in some instances a local standard will be at variance with overriding legal principles or recognized standards of professional ethical conduct towards, for example, unpopular defendants. An officer should be aware that unethical behaviors have a far-reaching, detrimental effect on all law enforcement officers and agencies and on the communities they serve.

a. Conduct at all times should be such that an officer brings credit to his or her profession.

b. Unethical behaviors such as fabricating, altering, or withholding evidence to affect an arrest or gain a conviction as well as theft, graft, and acceptance of bribes or gratuities cannot be tolerated.

c. No officer should by his acquiescence or approval support unethical, improper or unlawful behavior by a colleague.

d. If an officer observes seriously improper or unlawful behavior by a colleague, he is required to report the case to his immediate supervisor or to other designated organizational channels for investigation and action. If the officer's supervisor is involved in this seriously improper or unlawful behavior either by direct participation or by condoning its performance by another, the officer should follow the legally prescribed course of action for reporting the activity. When a department does not support officers who do take such action, an ethical officer should seriously consider his career potential in such an organization. (However, it should be recognized that ethical people have lived through eras of widespread organizational impropriety. In such instances the need may be to concentrate strictly on high quality performance and personal non-involvement in impropriety.)

4.0 Public Statements

Truth, objectivity, and due regard for the rights and privacy of the individual must characterize all statements of law enforcement officers who supply information to the public, or other officers, either directly or indirectly. In regard to court testimony, the officer shall present evidence honestly and without bias or prejudice. The sole objective shall be to give evidence as the officer has knowledge of it. The officer shall not identify with the prosecution or defense, but provide evidence on the basis of actual fact.

5.0 Confidentiality

Police frequently gain access to confidential information that can be seriously detrimental to an individual or group. Safeguarding that information is a primary obligation of the agency and of any police officer who is aware of it. Confidential information should not be communicated to others unless certain important conditions are met:

a. It is lawful to do so.

b. No information about the private life of an individual that does not relate specifically to the problem of law violation shall be transmitted to another.

c. Security and privacy shall be assured all individuals whose recordsare maintained in order that such records shall be used only in criminal justice proceedings. Information that is a matter of public record may be released when the law so requires.

d. Information detrimental to individuals, particularly that which is based on unsubstantiated evidence, should not be processed or integrated with other records systems except to inform criminal justice agencies on matters pertaining to law violation.

6.0 Professional Relationships

High standards of conduct in interprofessional relationships are essential to professional competence. The profession and the agency should seek, and the officer should maintain, high standards of conduct in professional relations with those he or she serves, with fellow officers, with professional colleagues in other organizations in the criminal justice system, and with those in other public service agencies.

a. Except when involved in an undercover investigation, an officer who works in a professional relationship with other persons should seek a dear and public-interest-serving purpose in those relationships. Professional relationships may be complex, but unwarranted ambiguity promotes ineffectiveness and the avoidance of responsibility.

b. It is unethical for any officer or agency to establish a protective allegiance with an individual or group so as to obscure complicity in a criminal act.

c. In the performance of their duty, law enforcement officials should respect and protect human dignity and maintain the human rights of all persons.

d. Law enforcement officials may never use more force than necessary in the performance of their duty.

e. No law enforcement official may inflict, instigate, or tolerate any cruel, inhuman, or degrading treatment or punishment, nor may any law enforcement official invoke exceptional circumstances such as internal political instability, the need to show official action in response to great public concern or any other public emergency as a justification of cruel, inhuman, or degrading treatment or punishment.

f. Law enforcement officials having custody of persons needing medical attention should secure such attention and take immediate action to meet the needs of the person in custody.

g. It is entirely proper for an agency to require enforcement concentration or de-emphasis for objective and stated reasons. Agency executives have the responsibility to assure that such pressure is realistic and is accompanied by such quality standards that arrest or citation is fully justified. The emphasis should always be on the legitimate relationship of police response to public action rather than on mere quantitative measure of police response (quotas).

h. It is the professional responsibility of law enforcement agencies to develop effective referral systems for non-criminal actions coming to their attention.

i. The officer shall act responsibly when called on to make professional recommendations that may affect the welfare of an individual or society.

j. In the interest of harmony and efficient public service, the officer has an obligation and responsibility to cooperate with other professionals in the criminal justice system.

7.0 Education and Training Practices

Law enforcement instructors should emphasize the ethical responsibility in policing for both the agency and the individual officer. They should encourage students in their quest for knowledge and in their development of professional skills, giving them assistance in the free exploration of ideas. The quest for truth is essential to the achievement of justice.

a. The instructor should properly advise students to ensure that they understand opportunities and requirements in the field, as well as limitations.

b. The instructor in discussing law enforcement techniques should impress upon the student the importance and problems of putting theory into practice, of adherence to all applicable principles governing practices, and of the retention of such principles in accord with organization regulations.

c. An instructor of law enforcement should stress to the students the importance of the systems contexts in which criminal justice agencies operate. It should be emphasized that agencies contribute to the goals of the criminal justice systems, as well as to the service and management systems in the jurisdictions in which they perform their duties.

d. The present ethical standards in law enforcement shall be reviewed with students. A student who serves in any law enforcement capacity (for example, as a cadet or a recruit or as intern, student participant or researcher) is expected to follow the ethical standards of the profession.

8.0 Research and Writing

Practitioners and educators in law enforcement have the responsibility of developing a body of knowledge and conducting research on the police contribution to the public welfare, to provide the best information for professional practice, and to publish their results and conclusions so that the professional and the public is well informed.

9.0 Recruitment and Employment Practices

A law enforcement agency will not discriminate against any officer or employee or applicant for employment because of race, sex, creed, color, or national origin. The agency will take affirmative action to ensure that all applicants are fairly considered for employment, and that employees are treated during employment with equal opportunity.

a. Such employment practices and policy shall be related to, but not limited to, the following: employment, upgrading and promotion, demotion or transfer, recruitment or recruitment advertising, layoffs or termination, rates of pay or other forms of compensation, and selection for training or education, including apprenticeship.

b. Agencies shall post in conspicuous places, available to employees and applicants for employment, notices setting forth the provisions of this non-discrimination clause.

c. Agencies should maintain appropriate records and accounts as to their compliance with non-discrimination policies and should facilitate legitimate access to them.

d. All criteria used by agencies in the recruitment and selection processes shall be clearly related to the duties, requirements and responsibilities of the law enforcement task.

10.0 The Context of Professional Support

Law enforcement as a profession should be willing to offer its ethical and effective practitioners support when they are attacked for their compliance with the professional standards.

a. A law enforcement official who, in fulfilling the obligations of this code, erroneously exceeds the limits of law despite honest and conscientious assessment, is entitled to the full protection of his agency and of the jurisdiction which employs him or her.

b. A law enforcement official who complies with the provisions of this code deserves the respect, the full support and the collaboration of the community and of the law enforcement agency in which such official serves, as well as the support of the law enforcement profession.

POLICE CODE OF CONDUCT

SOURCE *Police Chief, October, 2002.*

INTRODUCTION *After thirty years of service, efforts were made to "replace" the 1957 IACP Law Enforcement Code of Ethics. The new code—longer, less idealistic, and more pragmatic—was adopted by the IACP Executive Committee on October 17, 1989, during IACP's 96th Annual Conference in Louisville, Kentucky. The committee that authored the new code acknowledged "the assistance of Sir John Hermon, former chief constable of the Royal Ulster Constabulary, who gave full license to the association to freely use the language and concepts presented in the RUC's 'Professional Policing Ethics,' Appendix I of the Chief Constable's Annual Report, 1988, presented to the Police Authority of Northern Ireland, for the preparation of this code." But the new code had a mixed reception. Its length disturbed some, and its diminished idealism troubled others, and the 1957 code remained a "sentimental" favorite. And so, at the 98th Annual IACP Conference in Minneapolis, Minnesota, October 5-10, 1991, the 1989 Code was renamed the Police Code of Conduct, and a slightly revised version of the 1957 Code was "reinstated" as The Law Enforcement Code of Ethics.*

POLICE CODE OF CONDUCT

Primary Responsibilities of a Police Officer

A police officer acts as an official representative of government who is required and trusted to work within the law. The officer's powers and duties are conferred by statute. The fundamental duties of a police officer include serving the community, safeguarding lives and property, protecting the innocent, keeping the peace and ensuring the rights of all to liberty, equality and justice.

Performance of the Duties of a Police Officer

A police officer shall perform all duties impartially, without favor or affection or ill will and without regard to status, sex, race, religion, political belief or aspiration. All citizens will be treated equally with courtesy, consideration and dignity.

Officers will never allow personal feelings, animosities or friendships to influence official conduct. Laws will be enforced appropriately and courteously and, in carrying out their responsibilities, officers will strive to obtain maximum cooperation from the public. They will conduct themselves in appearance and deportment in such a manner as to inspire confidence and respect for the position of public trust they hold.

Discretion

A police officer will use responsibly the discretion vested in his position and exercise it within the law. The principle of reasonableness will guide the officer's determinations, and the officer will consider all surrounding circumstances in determining whether any legal action shall be taken.

Consistent and wise use of discretion, based on professional policing competence, will do much to preserve good relationships and retain the confidence of the public. There can be difficulty in choosing between conflicting courses of action. It is important to remember that a timely word of advice rather than arrest—which may be correct in appropriate circumstances—can be a more effective means of achieving a desired end.

Use of Force

A police officer will never employ unnecessary force or violence and will use only such force in the discharge of duty as is reasonable in all circumstances.

The use of force should be used only with the greatest restraint and only after discussion, negotiation and persuasion have been found to be inappropriate or ineffective. While the use of force is occasionally unavoidable, every police officer will refrain from unnecessary infliction of pain or suffering and will never engage in cruel, degrading or inhuman treatment of any person.

Confidentiality

Whatever a police officer sees, hears or learns of that is of a confidential nature will be kept secret unless the performance of duty or legal provision requires otherwise.

Members of the public have a right to security and privacy, and information obtained about them must not be improperly divulged.

Integrity

A police officer will not engage in acts of corruption or bribery, nor will an officer condone such acts by other police officers.

The public demands that the integrity of police officers be above reproach. Police officers must, therefore, avoid any conduct that might compromise integrity and thus undercut the public confidence in a law enforcement agency. Officers will refuse to accept any gifts, presents, subscriptions, favors, gratuities or promises that could be interpreted as seeking to cause the officer to refrain from performing official responsibilities honestly and within the law.

Police officers must not receive private or special advantage from their official status. Respect from the public cannot be bought; it can only be earned and cultivated.

Cooperation with Other Police Officers and Agencies

Police officers will cooperate with all legally authorized agencies and their representatives in the pursuit of justice.

An officer or agency may be one among many organizations that may provide law enforcement services to a jurisdiction. It is imperative that a police officer assist colleagues fully and completely with respect and consideration at all times.

Personal-Professional Capabilities

Police officers will be responsible for their own standard of professional performance and will take every reasonable opportunity to enhance and improve their level of knowledge and competence.

Through study and experience, a police officer can acquire the high level of knowledge and competence that is essential for the efficient and effective performance of duty. The acquisition of knowledge is a never-ending process of personal and professional development that should be pursued constantly.

Private Life

Police officers will behave in a manner that does not bring discredit to their agencies or themselves.

A police officer's character and conduct while off duty must always be exemplary, thus maintaining a position of respect in the community in which he or she lives and serves. The officer's personal behavior must be beyond reproach.

THE EVOLUTION OF THE INTERNATIONAL ASSOCIATION OF CHIEFS OF POLICE'S LAW ENFORCEMENT CODE OF ETHICS

SOURCE *"Law Enforcement Code of Ethics of the International Association of Chiefs of Police, 1957,"* Codes of Ethics Online, *1957. Copyright held by the International Association of Chiefs of Police, 515 North Washington Street, Alexandria, VA 22314 USA."IACP Law Enforcement Code of Ethics, 1991,"* Police Chief, *October, 2002."Canons of Police Ethics,"* Police Chief, *October, 2002.*

INTRODUCTION *Perhaps the most widely used of all police codes, the 1957 Law Enforcement Code of Ethics has its roots in the 1928 "Square Deal" Code that O.W. Wilson prepared for the Wichita Police Department. Wilson returned to Berkeley in 1947 and in the early 1950s was a member of the Peace Officers' Research Association of California (PORAC). As part of a program to enhance the professional status of policing, a PORAC subcommittee, which included Wilson, was formed to draft a code of ethics. A draft was presented at the May 1955 Conference of the Californian Peace Officers Association (CPOA), and it was adopted, subject to some further refinements. The changes were approved in October 1955 by the CPOA Executive, at which time PORAC also adopted it. Then in December 1956 at a meeting of the Executive Committee of the National Conference of Police Associations, it was adopted by that body. Finally, after several months of study by a subcommittee of the International Association of Chiefs of Police (IACP), the Law Enforcement Code of Ethics for Californian Peace Officers was adopted and ratified without significant change at the 64th IACP Conference in Honolulu, Hawaii, September 29 through October 3, 1957. The IACP subcommittee (comprised of Andrew J. Kavanaugh, Franklin M. Kreml, and Quinn Tamm) charged with examining the Californian Code also prepared the Canons of Police Ethics for release in conjunction with the code. In 1989, the IACP adopted a new Law Enforcement Code of Ethics, ostensibly to "replace" the original code. The controversy that*

followed resulted in two changes, ratified at the 98th Annual IACP Conference in Minneapolis, Minnesota, October 5 through 10, 1991: (1) the 1957 code was edited, to ensure consistency with the newer version; and (2) the newer version was retitled as the Police Code of Conduct. No longer, therefore, does it "replace" the 1957 Law Enforcement Code of Ethics. Adopted by many agencies in the United States and overseas, the Law Enforcement Code of Ethics remains the "standard" code, and is often made the centerpiece of training programs in police ethics.

LAW ENFORCEMENT CODE OF ETHICS OF THE INTERNATIONAL ASSOCIATION OF CHIEFS OF POLICE ADOPTED 1957

As a law enforcement officer, my fundamental duty is to serve mankind; to safeguard lives and property; to protect the innocent against deception, the weak against oppression or intimidation, and the peaceful against violence or disorder; and to respect the Constitutional rights of all men to liberty, equality and justice.

I will keep my private life unsullied as an example to all; maintain courageous calm in the face of danger, scorn or ridicule; develop self restraint; and be constantly mindful of the welfare of others. Honest in thought and deed in both my personal and official life, I will be exemplary in obeying the laws of the land and the regulations of my department. Whatever I see or hear of a confidential nature or that is confided to me in my official capacity will be kept ever secret unless revelation is necessary in the performance of my duty.

I will never act officiously or permit personal feelings, prejudices, animosities or friendships to influence my decisions. With no compromise for crime and with relentless prosecution of criminals, I will enforce the law courteously and appropriately without fear or favor, malice or ill will, never employing unnecessary force or violence and never accepting gratuities.

I recognize the badge of my office as a symbol of public faith, and I accept it as a public trust to be held so long as I am true to the ethics of the police service. I will constantly strive to achieve these objectives and ideals, dedicating myself before God to my chosen profession . . . law enforcement.

IACP LAW ENFORCEMENT CODE OF ETHICS, 1991

As a law enforcement officer, my fundamental duty is to serve the community; to safeguard lives and property; to protect the innocent against deception, the weak against oppression or intimidation and the peaceful against violence or disorder; and to respect the constitutional rights of all to liberty, equality and justice.

I will keep my private life unsullied as an example to all and will behave in a manner that does not bring discredit to me or to my agency. I will maintain courageous calm in the face of danger, scorn or ridicule; develop self-restraint; and be constantly mindful of the welfare of others. Honest in thought and deed both in my personal and official life, I will be exemplary in obeying the law and the regulations of my department. Whatever I see or hear of a confidential nature or that is confided to me in my official capacity will be kept ever secret unless revelation is necessary in the performance of my duty.

I will never act officiously or permit personal feelings, prejudices, political beliefs, aspirations, animosities or friendships to influence my decisions. With no compromise for crime and with relentless prosecution of criminals, I will enforce the law courteously and appropriately without fear or favor, malice or ill will, never employing unnecessary force or violence and never accepting gratuities.

I recognize the badge of my office as a symbol of public faith, and I accept it as a public trust to be held so long as I am true to the ethics of police service. I will never engage in acts of corruption or bribery, nor will I condone such acts by other police officers. I will cooperate with all legally authorized agencies and their representatives in the pursuit of justice.

I know that I alone am responsible for my own standard of professional performance and will take every reasonable opportunity to enhance and improve my level of knowledge and competence.

I will constantly strive to achieve these objectives and ideals, dedicating myself before God to my chosen profession . . . law enforcement.

CANONS OF POLICE ETHICS

Article 1. Primary Responsibility of Job

The primary responsibility of the police service, and of the individual officer, is the protection of the people of the United States through the upholding of their laws; chief among these is the Constitution of the United States and its amendments. The law enforcement officer always represents the whole of the community and its legally expressed will and is never the arm of any political party or clique.

Article 2. Limitations of Authority

The first duty of a law enforcement officer, as upholder of the law, is to know its bounds upon him in enforcing it. Because he represents the legal will of the community, be it local, state or federal, he must be aware of the limitations and proscriptions which the people, through law, have placed upon him. He must recognize the genius of the American system of government that gives to no man, groups of men, or institution, absolute power, and he must ensure that he, as a prime defender of that system, does not pervert its character.

Article 3. Duty to Be Familiar with the Law and with Responsibilities of Self and other Public Officials

The law enforcement officer shall assiduously apply himself to the study of the principles of the laws which he is sworn to uphold. He will make certain of his responsibilities in the particulars of their enforcement, seeking aid from his superiors in matters of technicality or principle when these are not clear to him; he will make special effort to fully understand his relationship to other public officials, including other law enforcement agencies, particularly on matters of jurisdiction, both geographically and substantively.

Article 4. Utilization of Proper Means to Gain Proper Ends

The law enforcement officer shall be mindful of his responsibility to pay strict heed to the selection of means in discharging the duties of his office. Violations of law or disregard for public safety and property on the part of an officer are intrinsically wrong; they are self-defeating in that they instill in the public mind a like disposition. The employment of illegal means, no matter how worthy the end, is certain to encourage disrespect for the law and its officers. If the law is to be honored, it must first be honored by those who enforce it.

Article 5. Cooperation with Public Officials in the Discharge of Their Authorized Duties

The law enforcement officer shall cooperate fully with other public officials in the discharge of authorized duties, regardless of party affiliation or personal prejudice. He shall be meticulous, however, in assuring himself of the propriety, under the law, of such actions and shall guard against the use of his office or person, whether knowingly or unknowingly, in any improper or illegal action. In any situation open to question, he shall seek authority from his superior officer, giving him a full report of the proposed service or action.

Article 6. Private Conduct

The law enforcement officer shall be mindful of his special identification by the public as an upholder of the law. Laxity of conduct or manner in private life, expressing either disrespect for the law or seeking to gain special privilege, cannot but reflect upon the police officer and the police service. The community and the service require that the law enforcement officer lead the life of a decent and honorable man. Following the career of a policeman gives no man special perquisites. It does give the satisfaction and pride of following and furthering an unbroken tradition of safeguarding the American republic. The officer who reflects upon this tradition will not degrade it. Rather, he will so conduct his private life that the public will regard him as an example of stability, fidelity, and morality.

Article 7. Conduct toward the Public

The law enforcement officer, mindful of his responsibility to the whole community, shall deal with individuals of the community in a manner calculated to instill respect for its laws and its police service. The law enforcement officer shall conduct his official life in a manner such as will inspire confidence and trust. Thus, he will be neither overbearing nor subservient, as no individual citizen has an obligation to stand in awe of him nor a right to command him. The officer will give service where he can, and require compliance with the law. He will do neither from personal preference or prejudice but rather as a duly appointed officer of the law discharging his sworn obligation.

Article 8. Conduct in Arresting and Dealing with Law Violators

The law enforcement officer shall use his powers of arrest strictly in accordance with the law and with due regard to the rights of the citizen concerned. His office gives him no right to prosecute the violator nor to mete out punishment for the offense. He shall, at all times, have a clear appreciation of his responsibilities and limitations regarding detention of the violator; he shall conduct himself in such a manner as will minimize the possibility of having to use force. To this end he shall cultivate a dedication to the service of the people and the equitable upholding of their laws whether in the handling of law violators or in dealing with the law-abiding.

Article 9. Gifts and Favors

The law enforcement officer, representing government, bears the heavy responsibility of maintaining, in his own conduct, the honor and integrity of all government institutions. He shall, therefore, guard against placing himself in a position in which any person can expect special consideration or in which the public can reasonably assume that special consideration is being given. Thus, he should be firm in refusing gifts, favors, or gratuities, large or small, which can, in the public mind, be interpreted as capable of influencing his judgment in the discharge of his duties.

Article 10. Presentation of Evidence

The law enforcement officer shall be concerned equally in the prosecution of the wrong-doer and the defense of the innocent. He shall ascertain what constitutes evidence and shall present such evidence impartially and without malice. In so doing, he will ignore social, political, and all other distinctions among the persons involved, strengthening the tradition of the reliability and integrity of an officer's word.

The law enforcement officer shall take special pains to increase his perception and skill of observation, mindful that in many situations his is the sole impartial testimony to the facts of a case.

Article 11. Attitude toward Profession

The law enforcement officer shall regard the discharge of his duties as a public trust and recognize his responsibility as a public servant. By diligent study and sincere attention to self-improvement he shall strive to make the best possible application of science to the solution of crime and, in the field of human relationships, strive for effective leadership and public influence in matters affecting public safety. He shall appreciate the importance and responsibility of his office, and hold police work to be an honorable profession rendering valuable service to his community and his country.

CODE OF PRACTICE FOR POLICE COMPUTER SYSTEMS

SOURCE *"The Data Protection Act: The Data Protection Principles,"* http://www.opsi.gov.uk/ACTS/acts1998/80029—l.htm#sch1ptI, *1998. "The Data Protection Act: Interpretation of the Principles in Part I,"* http://www.opsi.gov.uk/ACTS/acts1998/80029—m.htm#sch1ptII, *1998.*

INTRODUCTION *Produced as a 33 page document, the Association of Chief Police Officers (ACPO) Code of Practice for Police Computer Systems reflects the growing use of computerized data in policing and the complex ethical and practical problems involved in collecting, holding, and using and disclosing that data. Drawn up to help police meet the requirements of the UK Data Protection Act (1984), the code is structured around eight principles, each enunciated in the act, each followed by its interpretation in the act. What then follows (but is not included here) is a detailed statement of the "Method of Compliance," relating each principle to police activity. Also included in the code (but not below) are sections on monitoring and inspection, registration, exemptions, sanctions, complaints, and procedures for reviewing the code.*

THE DATA PROTECTION PRINCIPLES

PART I

The Principles

1. Personal data shall be processed fairly and lawfully and, in particular, shall not be processed unless—

   (a) at least one of the conditions in Schedule 2 is met, and

   (b) in the case of sensitive personal data, at least one of the conditions in Schedule 3 is also met.

2. Personal data shall be obtained only for one or more specified and lawful purposes, and shall not be further processed in any manner incompatible with that purpose or those purposes.

3. Personal data shall be adequate, relevant and not excessive in relation to the purpose or purposes for which they are processed.

4. Personal data shall be accurate and, where necessary, kept up to date.

5. Personal data processed for any purpose or purposes shall not be kept for longer than is necessary for that purpose or those purposes.

6. Personal data shall be processed in accordance with the rights of data subjects under this Act.

7. Appropriate technical and organisational measures shall be taken against unauthorised or unlawful processing of personal data and against accidental loss or destruction of, or damage to, personal data.

8. Personal data shall not be transferred to a country or territory outside the European Economic Area unless that country or territory ensures an adequate level of protection for the rights and freedoms of data subjects in relation to the processing of personal data.

DATA PROTECTION ACT: INTERPRETATIONS OF THE PRINCIPLES IN PART I

The first principle

1. —(1) In determining for the purposes of the first principle whether personal data are processed fairly, regard is to be had to the method by which they are obtained, including in particular whether any person from whom they are obtained is deceived or misled as to the purpose or purposes for which they are to be processed.

(2) Subject to paragraph 2, for the purposes of the first principle data are to be treated as obtained fairly if they consist of information obtained from a person who—

a. is authorised by or under any enactment to supply it, or

b. is required to supply it by or under any enactment or by any convention or other instrument imposing an international obligation on the United Kingdom.

2. —(1) Subject to paragraph 3, for the purposes of the first principle personal data are not to be treated as processed fairly unless—

a. in the case of data obtained from the data subject, the data controller ensures so far as practicable that the data subject has, is provided with, or has made readily available to him, the information specified in sub-paragraph (3), and

b. in any other case, the data controller ensures so far as practicable that, before the relevant time or as soon as practicable after that time, the data subject has, is provided with, or has made readily available to him, the information specified in sub-paragraph (3).

(2) In sub-paragraph (1)(b) "the relevant time" means—

a. the time when the data controller first processes the data, or

b. in a case where at that time disclosure to a third party within a reasonable period is envisaged

   i. if the data are in fact disclosed to such a person within that period, the time when the data are first disclosed,

   ii. if within that period the data controller becomes, or ought to become, aware that the data are unlikely to be disclosed to such a person within that period, the time when the data controller does become, or ought to become, so aware, or

   iii. in any other case, the end of that period.

(3) The information referred to in sub-paragraph (1) is as follows, namely—

a. the identity of the data controller,

b. if he has nominated a representative for the purposes of this Act, the identity of that representative,

c. the purpose or purposes for which the data are intended to be processed, and

d. any further information which is necessary, having regard to the specific circumstances in which the data are or are to be processed, to enable processing in respect of the data subject to be fair.

3. —(1) Paragraph 2(1)(b) does not apply where either of the primary conditions in sub-paragraph (2), together with such further conditions as may be prescribed by the Secretary of State by order, are met.

(2) The primary conditions referred to in sub-paragraph (1) are—

a. that the provision of that information would involve a disproportionate effort, or

b. that the recording of the information to be contained in the data by, or the disclosure of the data by, the data controller is necessary for compliance with any legal obligation to which the data controller is subject, other than an obligation imposed by contract.

4. —(1) Personal data which contain a general identifier falling within a description prescribed by the Secretary of State by order are not to be treated as processed fairly and lawfully unless they are processed in compliance with any conditions so prescribed in relation to general identifiers of that description.

(2) In sub-paragraph (1) "a general identifier" means any identifier (such as, for example, a number or code used for identification purposes) which—

a. relates to an individual, and

b. forms part of a set of similar identifiers which is of general application.

The second principle

5. The purpose or purposes for which personal data are obtained may in particular be specified—

a. in a notice given for the purposes of paragraph 2 by the data controller to the data subject, or

b. in a notification given to the Commissioner under Part III of this Act.

6. In determining whether any disclosure of personal data is compatible with the purpose or purposes for which the data were obtained, regard is to be had to the purpose or purposes for which the personal data are intended to be processed by any person to whom they are disclosed.

The fourth principle

7. The fourth principle is not to be regarded as being contravened by reason of any inaccuracy in personal data which accurately record information obtained by the data controller from the data subject or a third party in a case where—

a. having regard to the purpose or purposes for which the data were obtained and further processed, the data controller has taken reasonable steps to ensure the accuracy of the data, and

b. if the data subject has notified the data controller of the data subject's view that the data are inaccurate, the data indicate that fact.

The sixth principle

8. A person is to be regarded as contravening the sixth principle if, but only if—

a. he contravenes section 7 by failing to supply information in accordance with that section,

b. he contravenes section 10 by failing to comply with a notice given under subsection (1) of that section to the extent that the notice is justified or by failing to give a notice under subsection (3) of that section,

c. he contravenes section 11 by failing to comply with a notice given under subsection (1) of that section, or

d. he contravenes section 12 by failing to comply with a notice given under subsection (1) or (2)(b) of that section or by failing to give a notification under subsection (2)(a) of that section or a notice under subsection (3) of that section.

The seventh principle

9. Having regard to the state of technological development and the cost of implementing any measures, the measures must ensure a level of security appropriate to—

a. the harm that might result from such unauthorised or unlawful processing or accidental loss, destruction or damage as are mentioned in the seventh principle, and

b. the nature of the data to be protected.

10. The data controller must take reasonable steps to ensure the reliability of any employees of his who have access to the personal data.

11. Where processing of personal data is carried out by a data processor on behalf of a data controller, the data controller must in order to comply with the seventh principle—

a. choose a data processor providing sufficient guarantees in respect of the technical and organisational security measures governing the processing to be carried out, and

b. take reasonable steps to ensure compliance with those measures.

12. Where processing of personal data is carried out by a data processor on behalf of a data controller, the data controller is not to be regarded as complying with the seventh principle unless—

a. the processing is carried out under a contract—

    i. which is made or evidenced in writing, and

    ii. under which the data processor is to act only on instructions from the data controller, and

b. the contract requires the data processor to comply with obligations equivalent to those imposed on a data controller by the seventh principle.

The eighth principle

13. An adequate level of protection is one which is adequate in all the circumstances of the case, having regard in particular to—

a. the nature of the personal data,

b. the country or territory of origin of the information contained in the data,

c. the country or territory of final destination of that information,

d. the purposes for which and period during which the data are intended to be processed,

e. the law in force in the country or territory in question,

f. the international obligations of that country or territory,

g. any relevant codes of conduct or other rules which are enforceable in that country or territory (whether generally or by arrangement in particular cases), and

h. any security measures taken in respect of the data in that country or territory.

14. The eighth principle does not apply to a transfer falling within any paragraph of Schedule 4, except in such circumstances and to such extent as the Secretary of State may by order provide.

15. —(1) Where—

a. in any proceedings under this Act any question arises as to whether the requirement of the eighth principle as to an adequate level of protection is met in relation to the transfer of any personal data to a country or territory outside the European Economic Area, and

b. a Community finding has been made in relation to transfers of the kind in question, that question is to be determined in accordance with that finding.

(2) In sub-paragraph (1) "Community finding" means a finding of the European Commission, under the procedure provided for in Article 31(2) of the Data Protection Directive, that a country or territory outside the European Economic Area does, or does not, ensure an adequate level of protection within the meaning of Article 25(2) of the Directive.

RECOMMENDATION OF THE COMMITTEE OF MINISTERS TO MEMBER STATES ON THE EUROPEAN CODE OF POLICE ETHICS

SOURCE https://wcd.coe.int/com.instranet.InstraServlet?Command=com.instranet.CmdBlobGet&DocId=212764&SecMode=1&Admin=0&Usage=4&InstranetImage=62073, *September 19, 2001.*

INTRODUCTION *In 2001, the Council of Europe's Directorate General for Legal Affairs made a recommendation to adopt the European Code of Police Ethics to support law enforcement reform in member states. The code was adopted by the Committee of Ministers on September 19, 2001. The appendix to the recommendation contains the actual text of the ethics code. The implementation of the code is reviewed and supported by the Council for Police Matters (PC-PM), whose seven members met for the first time in November 2004. The PC-PM serves as the advisory body for the COE's European Committee on Crime Problems.*

COUNCIL OF EUROPE

COMMITTEE OF MINISTERS

Recommendation Rec(2001)10 of the Committee of Ministers to member states on the European Code of Police Ethics

Adopted by the Committee of Ministers on 19 September 2001 at the 765th meeting of the Ministers' Deputies

The Committee of Ministers, under the terms of Article15.*b* of the Statute of the Council of Europe,

Recalling that the aim of the Council of Europe is to achieve greater unity between its members;

Bearing in mind that it is also the purpose of the Council of Europe to promote the rule of law, which constitutes the basis of all genuine democracies;

Considering that the criminal justice system plays a key role in safeguarding the rule of law and that the police have an essential role within that system;

Aware of the need of all member states to provide effective crime fighting both at the national and the international level;

Considering that police activities to a large extent are performed in close contact with the public and that police efficiency is dependent on public support;

Recognising that most European police organisations—in addition to upholding the law—are performing social as well as service functions in society;

Convinced that public confidence in the police is closely related to their attitude and behaviour towards the public, in particular their respect for the human dignity and fundamental rights and freedoms of the individual as enshrined, in particular, in the European Convention on Human Rights;

Considering the principles expressed in the United Nations Code of Conduct for Law Enforcement Officials and the resolution of the Parliamentary Assembly of the Council of Europe on the Declaration on the Police;

Bearing in mind principles and rules laid down in texts related to police matters—criminal, civil and public law as well as human rights aspects as adopted by the Committee of Ministers, decisions and judgments of the European Court of Human Rights and principles adopted by the Committee for the Prevention of Torture and Inhuman or Degrading Treatment or Punishment;

Recognising the diversity of police structures and means of organising the police in Europe;

Considering the need to establish common European principles and guidelines for the overall objectives, performance and accountability of the police to safeguard security and individual's rights in democratic societies governed by the rule of law,

Recommends that the governments of member states be guided in their internal legislation, practice and codes of conduct of the police by the principles set out in the text of the European Code of Police Ethics, appended to the present recommendation, with a view to their progressive implementation, and to give the widest possible circulation to this text.

Appendix to Recommendation Rec(2001)10 on the European Code of Police Ethics
Definition of the scope of the code

This code applies to traditional public police forces or police services, or to other publicly authorised and/or controlled bodies with the primary objectives of maintaining law and order in civil society, and who are empowered by the state to use force and/or special powers for these purposes.

I. Objectives of the police

1. The main purposes of the police in a democratic society governed by the rule of law are:

- to maintain public tranquillity and law and order in society;

- to protect and respect the individual's fundamental rights and freedoms as enshrined, in particular, in the European Convention on Human Rights;

- to prevent and combat crime;

- to detect crime

- to provide assistance and service functions to the public.

II. Legal basis of the police under the rule of law

2. The police are a public body which shall be established by law.

3. Police operations must always be conducted in accordance with the national law and international standards accepted by the country.

4. Legislation guiding the police shall be accessible to the public and sufficiently clear and precise, and, if need be, supported by clear regulations equally accessible to the public and clear.

5. Police personnel shall be subject to the same legislation as ordinary citizens, and exceptions may only be justified for reasons of the proper performance of police work in a democratic society.

III. The police and the criminal justice system

6. There shall be a clear distinction between the role of the police and the prosecution, the judiciary and the correctional system; the police shall not have any controlling functions over these bodies.

7. The police must strictly respect the independence and the impartiality of judges; in particular, the police shall neither raise objections to legitimate judgments or judicial decisions, nor hinder their execution.

8. The police shall, as a general rule, have no judicial functions. Any delegation of judicial powers to the police shall be limited and in accordance with the law. It must always be possible to challenge any act, decision or omission affecting individual rights by the police before the judicial authorities.

9. There shall be functional and appropriate co-operation between the police and the public prosecution. In countries where the police are placed under the authority of the public prosecution or the investigating judge, the police shall receive clear instructions as to the priorities governing crime investigation policy and the progress of criminal investigation in individual cases. The police should keep the superior crime investigation authorities informed of the implementation of their instructions, in particular, the development of criminal cases should be reported regularly.

10. The police shall respect the role of defence lawyers in the criminal justice process and, whenever appropriate, assist in ensuring the right of access to legal assistance effective, in particular with regard to persons deprived of their liberty.

11. The police shall not take the role of prison staff, except in cases of emergency.

IV. Organisational structures of the police

A. General

12. The police shall be organised with a view to earning public respect as professional upholders of the law and providers of services to the public.

13. The police, when performing police duties in civil society, shall be under the responsibility of civilian authorities.

14. The police and its personnel in uniform shall normally be easily recognisable.

15. The police shall enjoy sufficient operational independence from other state bodies in carrying out its given police tasks, for which it should be fully accountable.

16. Police personnel, at all levels, shall be personally responsible and accountable for their own actions or omissions or for orders to subordinates.

17. The police organisation shall provide for a clear chain of command within the police. It should always be possible to determine which superior is ultimately responsible for the acts or omissions of police personnel.

18. The police shall be organised in a way that promotes good police/public relations and, where appropriate, effective co-operation with other agencies, local communities, non-governmental organisations and other representatives of the public, including ethnic minority groups.

19. Police organisations shall be ready to give objective information on their activities to the public, without disclosing confidential information. Professional guidelines for media contacts shall be established.

20. The police organisation shall contain efficient measures to ensure the integrity and proper performance of police staff, in particular to guarantee respect for individuals' fundamental rights and freedoms as enshrined, notably, in the European Convention on Human Rights.

21. Effective measures to prevent and combat police corruption shall be established in the police organisation at all levels.

B. Qualifications, recruitment and retention of police personnel

22. Police personnel, at any level of entry, shall be recruited on the basis of their personal qualifications and experience, which shall be appropriate for the objectives of the police.

23. Police personnel shall be able to demonstrate sound judgment, an open attitude, maturity, fairness, communication skills and, where appropriate, leadership and management skills. Moreover, they shall possess a good understanding of social, cultural and community issues.

24. Persons who have been convicted for serious crimes shall be disqualified from police work.

25. Recruitment procedures shall be based on objective and non-discriminatory grounds, following the necessary screening of candidates. In addition, the policy shall aim at recruiting men and women from various sections of society, including ethnic minority groups, with the overall objective of making police personnel reflect the society they serve.

C. Training of Police Personnel

26. Police training, which shall be based on the fundamental values of democracy, the rule of law and the protection of human rights, shall be developed in accordance with the objectives of the police.

27. General police training shall be as open as possible towards society.

28. General initial training should preferably be followed by in-service training at regular intervals, and specialist, management and leadership training, when it is required.

29. Practical training on the use of force and limits with regard to established human rights principles, notably the European Convention on Human Rights and its case law, shall be included in police training at all levels.

30. Police training shall take full account of the need to challenge and combat racism and xenophobia.

D. Rights of police personnel

31. Police staff shall as a rule enjoy the same civil and political rights as other citizens. Restrictions to these rights may only be made when they are necessary for the exercise of the functions of the police in a democratic society, in accordance with the law, and in conformity with the European Convention on Human Rights.

32. Police staff shall enjoy social and economic rights, as public servants, to the fullest extent possible. In particular, staff shall have the right to organise or to participate in representative organisations, to receive an appropriate remuneration and social security, and to be provided with special health and security measures, taking into account the particular character of police work.

33. Disciplinary measures brought against police staff shall be subject to review by an independent body or a court.

34. Public authorities shall support police personnel who are subject to ill-founded accusations concerning their duties.

V. Guidelines for police action/intervention

A. Guidelines for police action/intervention: general principles

35. The police, and all police operations, must respect everyone's right to life.

36. The police shall not inflict, instigate or tolerate any act of torture or inhuman or degrading treatment or punishment under any circumstances.

37. The police may use force only when strictly necessary and only to the extent required to obtain a legitimate objective.

38. Police must always verify the lawfulness of their intended actions.

39. Police personnel shall carry out orders properly issued by their superiors, but they shall have a duty to refrain from carrying out orders which are clearly illegal and to report such orders, without fear of sanction.

40. The police shall carry out their tasks in a fair manner, guided, in particular, by the principles of impartiality and non-discrimination.

41. The police shall only interfere with individual's right to privacy when strictly necessary and only to obtain a legitimate objective.

42. The collection, storage, and use of personal data by the police shall be carried out in accordance with international data protection principles and, in particular, be limited to the extent necessary for the performance of lawful, legitimate and specific purposes.

43. The police, in carrying out their activities, shall always bear in mind everyone's fundamental rights, such as freedom of thought, conscience, religion, expression, peaceful assembly, movement and the peaceful enjoyment of possessions.

44. Police personnel shall act with integrity and respect towards the public and with particular consideration for the situation of individuals belonging to especially vulnerable groups.

45. Police personnel shall, during intervention, normally be in a position to give evidence of their police status and professional identity.

46. Police personnel shall oppose all forms of corruption within the police. They shall inform superiors and other appropriate bodies of corruption within the police.

B. Guidelines for police action/intervention: specific situations

1. Police investigation

47. Police investigations shall, as a minimum, be based upon reasonable suspicion of an actual or possible offence or crime.

48. The police must follow the principles that everyone charged with a criminal offence shall be considered innocent until found guilty by a court, and that everyone charged with a criminal offence has certain rights, in particular the right to be informed promptly of the accusation against him/her, and to prepare his/her defence either in person, or through legal assistance of his/her own choosing.

49. Police investigations shall be objective and fair. They shall be sensitive and adaptable to the special needs of persons, such as children, juveniles, women, minorities including ethnic minorities and vulnerable persons.

50. Guidelines for the proper conduct and integrity of police interviews shall be established, bearing in mind Article 48. They shall, in particular, provide for a fair interview during which those interviewed are made aware of the reasons for the interview as well as other relevant information. Systematic records of police interviews shall be kept.

51. The police shall be aware of the special needs of witnesses and shall be guided by rules for their protection and support during investigation, in particular where there is a risk of intimidation of witnesses.

52. Police shall provide the necessary support, assistance and information to victims of crime, without discrimination.

53. The police shall provide interpretation/translation where necessary throughout the police investigation.

2. Arrest/deprivation of liberty by the police

54. Deprivation of liberty of persons shall be as limited as possible and conducted with regard to the dignity, vulnerability and personal needs of each detainee. A custody record shall be kept systematically for each detainee.

55. The police shall, to the extent possible according to domestic law, inform promptly persons deprived of their liberty of the reasons for the deprivation of their liberty and of any charge against them, and shall also without delay inform persons deprived of their liberty of the procedure applicable to their case.

56. The police shall provide for the safety, health, hygiene and appropriate nourishment of persons in the course of their custody. Police cells shall be of a reasonable size, have adequate lighting and ventilation and be equipped with suitable means of rest.

57. Persons deprived of their liberty by the police shall have the right to have the deprivation of their liberty notified to a third party of their choice, to have access to legal assistance and to have a medical examination by a doctor, whenever possible, of their choice.

58. The police shall, to the extent possible, separate persons deprived of their liberty under suspicion of having committed a criminal offence from those deprived of their liberty for other reasons. There shall normally be a separation between men and women as well as between adults and juveniles.

VI. Accountability and control of the police

59. The police shall be accountable to the state, the citizens and their representatives. They shall be subject to efficient external control.

60. State control of the police shall be divided between the legislative, the executive and the judicial powers.

61. Public authorities shall ensure effective and impartial procedures for complaints against the police.

62. Accountability mechanisms, based on communication and mutual understanding between the public and the police, shall be promoted.

63. Codes of ethics of the police, based on the principles set out in the present recommendation, shall be developed in member states and overseen by appropriate bodies.

VII. Research and international co-operation

64. Member states shall promote and encourage research on the police, both by the police themselves and external institutions.

65. International co-operation on police ethics and human rights aspects of the police shall be supported.

66. The means of promoting the principles of the present recommendation and their implementation must be carefully scrutinised by the Council of Europe.

DECLARATION ON THE POLICE, RESOLUTION 690

SOURCE http://www.coe.int/T/E/Human_Rights/Police/
5._Reference_Documents/
b._Resolution_690_(1979)_on_Decl_police.asp,
1979.

INTRODUCTION *The declaration of the police was prepared by the legal affairs committee of the Council of Europe, and it was adopted in May 1979 by the Parliamentary Assembly of the Council of Europe (resolution 690). Subsequently, with only the qualified support of the Council's committee of ministers, the resolution/declaration was transmitted to the governments of member states. Accompanying the resolution were the committee of ministers critical "observations," based in part on comments received from various specialist bodies to whom the committee had submitted the declaration. Partly because of the problematic nature of some clauses in the declaration, and the division of policing authority in many of the member states, the declaration has not yet achieved the official acceptance that was originally sought for it.*

RESOLUTION 690 (1979) [1]

on the Declaration on the Police

The Assembly,

1. Considering that the full exercise of human rights and fundamental freedoms, guaranteed by the European Convention on Human Rights and other national and international instruments, has as a necessary basis the existence of a peaceful society which enjoys the advantages of order and public safety;

2. Considering that, in this respect, police play a vital role in all the member states, that they are frequently called upon to intervene in conditions which are dangerous for their members, and that their duties are made yet more difficult if the rules of conduct of their members are not sufficiently precisely defined;

3. Being of the opinion that it is inappropriate for those who have committed violations of human rights whilst members of police forces, or those who have belonged to any police force that has been disbanded on account of inhumane practices, to be employed as policemen;

4. Being of the opinion that the European system for the protection of human rights would be improved if there were generally accepted rules concerning the professional ethics of the police which take account of the principles of human rights and fundamental freedoms;

5. Considering that it is desirable that police officers have the active moral and physical support of the community they are serving;

6. Considering that police officers should enjoy status and rights comparable to those of members of the civil service;

7. Believing that it may be desirable to lay down guidelines for the behaviour of police officers in case of war and other emergency situations, and in the event of occupation by a foreign power,

8. Adopts the following Declaration on the Police, which forms an integral part of this resolution;

9. Instructs its Committee on Parliamentary and Public Relations and its Legal Affairs Committee as well as the Secretary General of the Council of Europe to give maximum publicity to the declaration.

APPENDIX

Declaration on the Police

A. Ethics [2]

1. A police officer shall fulfil the duties the law imposes upon him by protecting his fellow citizens and the community against violent, predatory and other harmful acts, as defined by law.

2. A police officer shall act with integrity, impartiality and dignity. In particular he shall refrain from and vigorously oppose all acts of corruption.

3. Summary executions, torture and other forms of inhuman or degrading treatment or punishment remain prohibited in all circumstances. A police officer is under an obligation to disobey or disregard any order or instruction involving such measures.

4. A police officer shall carry out orders properly issued by his hierarchical superior, but he shall refrain from carrying out any order he knows, or ought to know, is unlawful.

5. A police officer must oppose violations of the law. If immediate or irreparable and serious harm should result from permitting the violation to take place he shall take immediate action, to the best of his ability.

6. If no immediate or irreparable and serious harm is threatened, he must endeavour to avert the consequences of this violation, or its repetition, by reporting the matter to his superiors. If no results are obtained in that way he may report to higher authority.

7. No criminal or disciplinary action shall be taken against a police officer who has refused to carry out an unlawful order.

8. A police officer shall not co-operate in the tracing, arresting, guarding or conveying of persons who, while not being suspected of having committed an illegal act, are searched for, detained or prosecuted because of their race, religion or political belief.

9. A police officer shall be personally liable for his own acts and for acts of commission or omission he has ordered and which are unlawful.

10. There shall be a clear chain of command. It should always be possible to determine which superior may be ultimately responsible for acts or omissions of a police officer.

11. Legislation must provide for a system of legal guarantees and remedies against any damage resulting from police activities.

12. In performing his duties, a police officer shall use all necessary determination to achieve an aim which is legally required or allowed, but he may never use more force than is reasonable.

13. Police officers shall receive clear and precise instructions as to the manner and circumstances in which they should make use of arms.

14. A police officer having the custody of a person needing medical attention shall secure such attention by medical personnel and, if necessary, take measures for the preservation of the life and health of this person. He shall follow the instructions of doctors and other competent medical workers when they place a detainee under medical care.

15. A police officer shall keep secret all matters of a confidential nature coming to his attention, unless the performance of duty or legal provisions require otherwise.

16. A police officer who complies with the provisions of this declaration is entitled to the active moral and physical support of the community he is serving.

B. Status

1. Police forces are public services created by law, which shall have the responsibility of maintaining and enforcing the law.

2. Any citizen may join the police forces if he satisfies the relevant conditions.

3. A police officer shall receive thorough general training, professional training and in-service training, as well as appropriate instruction in social problems, democratic freedoms, human rights and in particular the European Convention on Human Rights.

4. The professional, psychological and material conditions under which a police officer must perform his duties shall be such as to protect his integrity, impartiality and dignity.

5. A police officer is entitled to a fair remuneration, and special factors are to be taken into account, such as greater risks and responsibilities and more irregular working schedules.

6. Police officers shall have the choice of whether to set up professional organisations, join them and play an active part therein. They may also play an active part in other organisations.

7. A police professional organisation, provided it is representative shall have the right:

   • to take part in negotiations concerning the professional status of police officers;

   • to be consulted on the administration of police units;

   • to initiate legal proceedings for the benefit of a group of police officers or on behalf of a particular police officer.

8. Membership of a police professional organisation and playing an active part therein shall not be detrimental to any police officer.

9. In case of disciplinary or penal proceedings taken against him, a police officer has the right to be heard and to be defended by a lawyer. The decision shall be taken within a reasonable time. He shall also be able to avail himself of the assistance of a professional organisation to which he belongs.

10. A police officer against whom a disciplinary measure has been taken or penal sanction imposed shall have the right of appeal to an independent and impartial body or court.

11. The rights of a police officer before courts or tribunals shall be the same as those of any other citizen.

C. War and other emergency situations—occupation by a foreign power [3]

1. A police officer shall continue to perform his tasks of protecting persons and property during war and enemy occupation in the interests of the civilian population. For that reason he shall not have the status of "combatant", and the provisions of the Third Geneva Convention of 12 August 1949, relative to the treatment of prisoners of war, shall not apply.

2. The provisions of the Fourth Geneva Convention of 12 August 1949, relative to the protection of civilian persons in time of war, apply to the civilian police.

3. The occupying power shall not order police officers to perform tasks other than those mentioned in Article 1 of this chapter.

4. During occupation a police officer shall not:
   - take part in measures against members of resistance movements;
   - take part in applying measures designed to employ the population for military purposes and for guarding military installations.

5. If a police officer resigns during enemy occupation because he is forced to execute illegitimate orders of the occupying power which are contrary to the interests of the civilian population, such as those listed above, and because he sees no other way out, he shall be reintegrated into the police force as soon as the occupation is over without losing any of the rights or benefits he would have enjoyed if he had stayed in the police force.

6. Neither during nor after the occupation may any penal or disciplinary sanction be imposed on a police officer for having executed in good faith an order of an authority regarded as competent, where the execution of such an order was normally the duty of the police force.

7. The occupying power shall not take any disciplinary or judicial action against police officers by reason of the execution, prior to the occupation, of orders given by the competent authorities.

[1]. *Assembly debate* on 1 February 1979 (24th Sitting of the 30th Session) (see Doc. 4212, report of the Legal Affairs Committee). *Text adopted by the Assembly* on 8 May 1979 (2nd Sitting of the 31st Session).

[2]. Parts A and B of the declaration cover all individuals and organisations, including such bodies as secret services, military police forces, armed forces or militias performing police duties, that are responsible for enforcing the law, investigating offences, and maintaining public order and state security.

[3]. This chapter does not apply to the military police.

CODE OF ETHICS OF THE OFFICE OF THE SHERIFF

SOURCE http://www.lakecountysheriff.com/admin/admin.htm.

INTRODUCTION *The National Sheriffs' Association (NSA) was founded in 1940 and currently has approximately 50,000 members. It provides professional services to the law enforcement community, as well as a Victim Witness Program, National Neighborhood Watch, and Jail Officer Management studies. On June 4, 1986, the NSA Standards, Ethics, Education, and Training (SEET) Committee adopted a new Code of Ethics at its 46th Annual Conference. It was published in the bimonthly* Sheriffs' Roll Call, *and comments were solicited. After a further report by the SEET Committee to the NSA Board of Directors, the Code was adopted, along with an enforcement policy, at a meeting of the membership on June 24, 1987, at Grand Rapids, Michigan.*

CODE OF ETHICS OF THE SHERIFF

As a constitutionally/statutorily elected Sheriff, I recognize and accept that I am given a special trust and confidence by the citizens and employees whom I have been elected to serve, represent and manage. This trust and confidence is my bond to ensure that I shall behave and act according to the highest personal and professional standards. In furtherance of this pledge, I will abide by the following Code of Ethics.

I shall ensure that I and my employees, in the performance of our duties, will enforce and administer the law according to the standards of the U.S. Constitution and applicable State Constitutions and statutes so that equal protection of the law is guaranteed to everyone. To that end I shall not permit personal opinions, party affiliations, or consideration of the status of others to alter or lessen this standard of treatment of others.

I shall establish, promulgate and enforce a set of standards of behavior of my employees which will govern the overall management and operation of the law enforcement functions, court related activities, and corrections operations of my agency.

I shall not tolerate nor condone brutal or inhumane treatment of others by my employees nor shall I permit or condone inhumane or brutal treatment of inmates in my care and custody.

I strictly adhere to standards of fairness and integrity in the conduct of campaigns for election and I shall conform to all applicable statutory standards of election financing and reporting so that the Office of the Sheriff is not harmed by the actions of myself or others.

I shall routinely conduct or have conducted an internal and external audit of the public funds entrusted to my care and publish this information so that citizens can be informed about my stewardship of these funds.

I shall follow the accepted principles of efficient and effective administration and management as the principle criteria for my judgments and decisions in the allocation of resources and services in law enforcement, court related and corrections functions of my Office.

I shall hire and promote only those employees or others who are the very best candidates for a position according to accepted standards of objectivity and merit. I shall not permit other factors to influence hiring or promotion practices.

I shall ensure that all employees are granted and receive relevant training supervision in the performance of their duties so that competent and excellent service is provided by the Office of the Sheriff.

I shall ensure that during my tenure as Sheriff, I shall not use the Office of Sheriff for private gain.

I accept and will adhere to this code of ethics. In so doing, I also accept responsibility for encouraging others in my profession to abide by this Code.

Text Acknowledgements

COPYRIGHTED EXCERPTS IN *WORLD ENCYCLOPEDIA OF POLICE FORCES AND CORRECTIONAL SYSTEMS, SECOND EDITION* WERE REPRODUCED FROM THE FOLLOWING SOURCES:

"Member Code of Ethics, International Association of Chiefs of Police," IACP Constitution. Reproduced by permission.—"The Policing Principles of the Metropolitan Police," From *The Principles of Policing and Guidance for Professional Behaviour*. New Scotland Yard, London: Public Information Department, Metropolitan Police, 1985. Reproduced by permission.—"Interpol's Global Standards to Combat Corruption," http://www.interpol.org/Pubic/corruption/standard/Default.asp, Reproduced by permission.—Ethical Standards in Law Enforcement, LEAPS, 1973. Reproduced by permission.—Ethical Standards in Law Enforcement, American Academy for Professional Law Enforcement, 1976. Reproduced by permission.—"Law Enforcement Code of Ethics of the International Association of Chiefs of Police," "IACP Law Enforcement Code of Ethics," and "Canons of Police Ethics," *Police Chief, October, 2002. © 2002. Reproduced with permission.—"The Data Protection Act: Interpretation of the Principles in Part I," http://www.opsi.gov.uk/ACTS/acts1998/80029–m.htm#sch1ptII, 1998. © Crown copyright 1998. Reproduced under the terms of Crown Copyright Policy Guidance issued by HMSO.—"The Data Protection Act: The Data Protection Principles," http://www.opsi.gov.uk/ACTS/acts1998/80029–l.htm#sch1ptI, 1998. © Crown copyright 1998. Reproduced under the terms of Crown Copyright Policy Guidance issued by HMSO.—"Recommendation of the Committee of Ministers to Member States on the European Code of Police Ethics, Council of Europe Committee of Ministers," http://cm.coe.int/ta/rec/2001/2001r10.htm, September 19, 2001. Reproduced by permission of the Council of Europe.—"Declaration on the Police, Resolution 690," http://www.coe.int/T/E/Human_Rights/Police/5._Reference_Documents/b._Resolution_690_(1979)_on_Decl_police.asp, 1979. Reproduced by permission of the Council of Europe.—"Law Enforcement Code of Ethics of the International Association of Chiefs of Police, 1957," Codes of Ethics Online, 1957. Copyright held by the International Association of Chiefs of Police, 515 North Washington Street, Alexandria, VA 22314 USA. Reproduced by permission.—"Code of Ethics of the Office of the Sheriff,"* http://www.lakecountysheriff.com/admin/admin.htm. Reproduced by permission of the National Sheriff's Association.

Police Origins Worldwide

Afghanistan
1880s

Algeria
1962

Andorra
Andorran Police, 1931

Angola
People's Police Corps of Angola, 1978

Anguilla
Anguillan Police, 1972

Antigua and Barbuda
Antigua and Barbuda Police, 1886

Argentina
Federal Police, 1880

Australia
1788

Austria
City Guard, 1569

Bahamas
Royal Bahamas Police Force, 1840

Bahrain
Bahrain Police, 1926

Bangladesh
Provincial Police, 1861

Barbados
Barbados Police Force, 1835

Bermuda
1879

Bolivia
1886

Botswana
Bechuanaland Mounted Police, 1884

Brunei
Straits Settlement Police, 1905

Burundi
Judicial Police, 1967

Cambodia
1970

Cameroon
Cameroon National gendarmerie, 1960

Canada
Quebec, 1651

Chad
Surete, 1961

Chile
Queen's Dragoons, 1758

China
Public Security, 1949

Colombia
1858

Congo
National Gendarmerie, 1961

Cyprus
1960

Denmark
Copenhagen, 1590

Dominican Police
National Police, 1936

Ecuador
Municipal Police, 1830

El Salvador
National Guard, 1912

Ethiopia
1935

Finland
Servants of the Town, 1700s

France
Commissaire-Enqueteurs, 615; Marechausee, 1544

Gambia
River Police, 1855

Germany
1732

Ghana
Gold Coast Militia and Police, 1844

Gibraltar
Gibraltar Police, 1830

Greece
Gendarmerie (Khorofylaki), 1833

Grenada
Grenada Militia, 1783

Guyana
Guyana Police Force, 1891

Honduras
Special Security Corps, 1963

Hong Kong
Royal Hong Kong Police Force, 1841

India
Sind Constabulary, 1843

Indonesia
Dutch Algemeene Politie, pre-1947

Iran
Gendarmerie, 1911

Iraq
Iraq Police Force, 1919

Ireland
Provincial Police, 1822

Israel
Palestine Police Force, 1922

Italy
Carabinieri, 1814

Ivory Coast
Gendarmerie, 1854

Jamaica
Jamaica Constabulary, 1867

Japan
1871

Jordan
1956

Kenya
1886

Korea, South
Paramilitary Constabulary, 1945

Laos
1945

Lesotho
Lesotho Mounted Police, 1872

Liberia
National Police, 1924

Liechtenstein
Liechtenstein Corps, 1933

Luxembourg
Marechausee, seventeenth century

Malawi
Malawi Police Force, 1921

Malaysia
Colonial Police, 1806

Malta
Malta Police, 1814

Mauritius
Mauritius Police, 1859

Monaco
1867

Mozambique
Public Security Force, 1975

Nepal
Raksha Dal, c. 1952

Netherlands
1795

New Zealand
Armed Constabulary, 1846

Nigeria
Lagos Police Force, c. 1890s

Norway
Local Police, twelfth century; first chief constable, 1686

Oman
Askars Tribal Police; Muscat Police, 1931

Panama
National Police Corps, 1904

Paraguay
Paraguayan Police, 1951

Peru
Civil Guard, early twentieth century

Philippines
Philippines Constabulary, 1901

Poland
National Police, 1918

Portugal
Sixteenth century

Puerto Rico
Civil Guard, 1868

Qatar
Qatar Police, 1948

Russian Federation
The Cheka, 1917

St. Helena
Constabulary, 1865

St. Lucia
St. Lucia Police, 1834

Senegal
National Gendarmerie, 1843

Seychelles
1775

Sierra Leone
Sierra Leone Police, 1829

Singapore
Singapore Police, 1827

Somalia
Armed Constabulary, 1884

South Africa
Cape Constabulary, nineteenth century

Spain
Carabineros, 1829

Sri Lanka
Vidanes, 1806

Sudan
Sudan Police, 1898

Suriname
Armed Police Corps, 1865

Tanzania
British East Africa Police, 1919

Thailand
Tamruat, sixteenth century

Trinidad and Tobago
Trinidad Constabulary, early 1900s

Turkey
Jandarma, 1845

Tuvalu
Gilbert and Ellis Islands Armed
Constabulary, 1892

Uganda
Armed Constabulary, 1900

United Arab Emirates
1974

United Kingdom
Tithings, 800; London Metropolitan
Police, 1829

United States
Schout Fiscal, 1640s

Uruguay
National Police of Uruguay, 1829

Vatican City
Swiss Guard, 1506

Western Samoa
Western Samoa Police, 1900

Yemen
Aden Police Force, 1937

Rankings

OFFENSES REPORTED TO THE POLICE PER 100,000 POPULATION

1. Burkina Faso	9
2. Nepal	9
3. Mali	10
4. Guinea	18.4
5. Congo, Republic of	32
6. Syria	42
7. Myanmar	64.5
8 Yemen	65
9. Cote d'Ivoire	67
10. Vietnam	74
11. Iran	77
12. Cameroon	78
13. Gambia	89
14. Bangladesh	90
15. Mauritania	95.4
16. Niger	99
17. Mexico	108
18. Madagascar	112
19. Gabon	114
20. Indonesia	120.9
21. Senegal	123
22. China	128
23. Guinea-Bissau	129
24. Central African Republic	135
25. Angola	143.5
26. Somalia	144
27. Saudi Arabia	149
28. Burundi	156
29. Eritrea	161.9
30. Mozambique	166
31. Albania	168.8
32. Azerbaijan	176
33. Algeria	178
34. Iraq	197
35. Peru	218
36. Djibouti	252
37. Ethiopia	258.3
38. Kiribati	261
39. Armenia	264.4
40. Georgia	286
41. Benin	297
42. Togo	311
43. Nigeria	312
44. Uganda	316
45. Tajikistan	317
46. Pakistan	318
47. Uzbekistan	328
48. Oman	331
49. Thailand	351
50. Morocco	366
51. Sri Lanka	380
52. Honduras	392
53. Bosnia and Herzegovina	402
54. Paraguay	418
55. Panama	419
56. Kenya	484
57. Guatemala	510
58. Turkey	547
59. Sao Tome and Principe	558
60. Ecuador	587
61. India	594
62. Malaysia	604
63. Argentina	631
64. Bolivia	660

65. Portugal	661	120. Poland	2901
66. Zambia	666	121. Uruguay	3002
67. Cyprus	689	122. Lebanon	3063
68. Haiti	701	123. Slovenia	3138
69. Papua New Guinea	766	124. Monaco	3430
70. Brazil	779.1	125. Korea, South	3494
71. Singapore	783	126. Estonia	3565
72. Colombia	790	127. Greece	3641
73. Taiwan	799	128. Egypt	3693
74. Malawi	850	129. St. Kitts and Nevis	3808
75. Costa Rica	868	130. Barbados	3813
76. El Salvador	879	131. Swaziland	3962
77. Kazakhstan	932	132. St. Vincent	3977
78. Brunei	932.9	133. Czech Republic	4142
79. Moldova	957	134. St. Lucia	4386
80. Kyrgyzstan	987	135. Italy	4214
81. Mongolia	1010	136. Spain	4446
82. Libya	1065	137. Bahamas	4870
83. Nicaragua	1069	138. Antigua and Barbuda	4977
84. Qatar	1079	139. Hungary	5011
85. Macedonia	1102	140. Seychelles	5361
86. Venezuela	1106	141. United States	5374
87. Ukraine	1115	142. Aruba	5461
88. Hong Kong	1122	143. Netherlands Antilles	5574
89. Trinidad and Tobago	1170	144. Zimbabwe	5619
90. Bulgaria	1170.7	145. Guadeloupe	5793
91. Croatia	1216	146. Austria	6095
92. Jordan	1256	147. France	6097
93. Serbia and Montenegro	1268	148. Israel	6254
94. Guyana	1277	149. Luxembourg	6280
95. Belarus	1282.4	150. Martinique	6305
96. Kuwait	1346	151. Australia	7003
97. Chile	1366	152. Switzerland	7030
98. Bahrain	1390	153. South Africa	7140.8
99. Tunisia	1419	154. Germany	7682
100. Ireland	1696	155. Netherlands	7808
101. Tanzania	1714	156. Canada	8121
102. Slovakia	1740	157. Botswana	8281
103. French Polynesia	1799	158. French Guiana	8396
104. Malta	1841	159. Belgium	8478
105. Jamaica	1871	160. Grenada	8543
106. Namibia	2006	161. Bermuda	8871
107. Lithuania	2029	162. Denmark	9300
108. Latvia	2097	163. Greenland	9360
109. Reunion	2097	164. Dominica	9567
110. Romania	2206	165. Norway	9769
111. Marshall Islands	2273	166. United Kingdom	9823
112. Puerto Rico	2339	167. Sweden	12982
113. Maldives	2353	168. New Zealand	13854
114. Lesotho	2357	169. Finland	14350
115. Fiji	2370	170. Suriname	17819
116. Ukraine	2604.7	171. Russia	20514
117. Andorra	2616	172. Iceland	31332
118. Mauritius	2712		
119. Tonga	2727		

SOURCE: *The Illustrated Book of World Rankings,* George Thomas Kurian, ed.

POPULATION PER POLICE OFFICER

1. Kuwait	80	
2. Nicaragua	90	
3. Brunei	100	
4. Cape Verde	110	
5. Nauru	110	
6. Antigua and Barbuda	120	
7. Mongolia	120	
8. Seychelles	120	
9. Bahamas	125	
10. Iraq	140	
11. Serbia and Montenegro	140	
12. United Arab Emirates	140	
13. Mali	160	
14. Uruguay	170	
15. Bahrain	180	
16. Cyprus	180	
17. Panama	180	
18. Equatorial Guinea	190	
19. Guyana	190	
20. Israel	210	
21. Andorra	220	
22. Reunion	220	
23. Hong Kong	221	
24. Grenada	230	
25. Malta	230	
26. Singapore	230	
27. Hungary	237	
28. Mauritius	240	
29. St. Vincent and the Grenadines	250	
30. Ecuador	260	
31. Barbados	280	
32. Saudi Arabia	280	
33. Trinidad and Tobago	280	
34. Laos	280	
35. Belize	290	
36. Tuvalu	290	
37. Dominica	300	
38. St. Kitts and Nevis	300	
39. Ireland	310	
40. Paraguay	310	
41. United States	318	
42. Venezuela	320	
43. Angola	325	
44. Kiribati	330	
45. Netherlands Antilles	330	
46. Sweden	330	
47. Tonga	330	
48. Tunisia	340	
49. United Kingdom	350	
50. Bermuda	370	
51. Poland	370	
52. Greece	380	
53. Puerto Rico	380	

54. Haiti	400
55. Marshall Islands	400
56. Sao Tome and Principe	400
57. Fiji	407
58. Colombia	420
59. Jamaica	430
60. Oman	430
61. St. Lucia	430
62. Australia	438
63. Vanuatu	450
64. American Samoa	460
65. Korea, North	460
66. Austria	470
67. Chile	470
68. Costa Rica	480
69. Japan	480
70. Korea, South	506
71. Netherlands	510
72. Lebanon	530
73. Thailand	530
74. Afghanistan	540
75. Somalia	540
76. Zambia	540
77. Albania	550
78. Dominican Republic	580
79. Egypt	580
80. Spain	580
81. Denmark	600
82. Sierra Leone	600
83. Swaziland	610
84. Ghana	620
85. Solomon Islands	620
86. France	630
87. Jordan	630
88. New Zealand	630
89. Belgium	640
90. Czech Republic	640
91. Finland	640
92. Switzerland	640
93. Cuba	650
94. Myanmar	650
95. Liechtenstein	660
96. Norway	660
97. Portugal	660
98. Guatemala	670
99. Italy	680
100. Mauritania	710
101. Pakistan	720
102. Papua New Guinea	720
103. Taiwan	720
104. Peru	730
105. Senegal	730
106. Sudan	740
107. Botswana	750

108. Zimbabwe	750	132. Gabon	1290
109. Malaysia	760	133. Tanzania	1330
110. India	820	134. China	1360
111. Luxembourg	829	135. Kenya	1500
112. Algeria	840	136. Liberia	1570
113. Morocco	840	137. Turkey	1570
114. Sri Lanka	860	138. Malawi	1670
115. Congo	870	139. Yemen	1940
116. South Africa	870	140. Syria	1970
117. Congo, Democratic Republic of	910	141. Togo	1970
118. Iceland	940	142. Cambodia	1980
119. Comoros	960	143. Uganda	1990
120. Chad	990	144. Niger	2350
121. El Salvador	1000	145. Bangladesh	2560
122. Nepal	1000	146. Central African Republic	2740
123. Honduras	1040	147. Madagascar	2900
124. Ethiopia	1100	148. Benin	3250
125. Indonesia	1119	149. Gambia, The	3310
126. Lesotho	1130	150. Cote d'Ivoire	4640
127. Guinea	1140	151. Rwanda	4650
128. Nigeria	1140	152. Canada	8640
129. Philippines	1160	153. Maldives	35710
130. Cameroon	1170		
131. Argentina	1270		

SOURCE: *The Illustrated Book of World Rankings,* George Thomas Kurian, ed.

General Bibliography

POLICE HISTORY

Clayton, Anthony, and David Killingray. 1989. "Khaki and Blue: Military and Police in British Colonial Africa." *Center for International Studies Africa Series 51.* Ohio University Press.

Critchley, T. A. 1978. *History of Police in England and Wales.* Rev. ed. London: Constable.

Dhillon, K. S. 1998. *Defenders of the Establishment: Ruler-supportive Police Forces of South Asia.* Indian Institute of Advanced Study.

Emsley, Clive. 1996. *English Police: A Political and Social History,* 2nd ed. Harlow, Essex: Longman.

Enders, Mike, and Benoit Dupont. 2001. *Policing the Lucky Country.* Annandale, New South Wales: Hawkins Press.

Harring, Sidney L. 1983. *Policing a Class Society: The Experience of American Cities, 1865-1915.* New Brunswick, NJ: Rutgers University Press.

Jeffries, Charles. 1952. *Colonial Police.* London: Max Parrish.

Lee, W. L. Melville. 1901. *History of Police in England.* London: Methuen.

Rawlings, Philip. 2002. *Policing: a Short History.* Cullompton: Willan Publishing.

Reith, Charles. 1956. *New Study of Police History.* London: Oliver and Boyd.

Roth, Mitchel P. n.d. *Historical Dictionary of Law Enforcement.* Westport, CN: Greenwood Press.

Senior, Hereward. 1997. *Constabulary: The Rise of Police Institutions in Britain, the Commonwealth and the United States.* Toronto: Dundurn Press.

Vila, Bryan J., and Cynthia Morris. 1999. *Role of Police in American Society: A Documentary History.* Westport, CN: Greenwood Press.

POLICING IN SPECIFIC COUNTRIES

Brogden, Mike, and Clifford D. Shearing. 1993. *Policing for a New South Africa.* London: Routledge.

Chappell, Duncan, and Paul R. Wilson. 1996. *Australian Policing: Contemporary Issues,* 2nd ed. Sydney: Butterworths.

Ellison, Graham, and Jim Smyth. 2000. *Crowned Harp: Policing Northern Ireland.* London: Pluto Press.

Hills, Alice. 1999. *Policing Africa: Internal Security and the Limits of Liberalization.* Boulder, Colorado: Lynne Reinner Publishers.

Horton, Christine. 1995. "Policing Policy in France." *PSI Research Report 782.* London: Policy Studies Institute.

Jemibewon, David M. 2001. *Nigeria Police in Transition: Issues, Problems, and Prospects.* Ibadan, Nigeria: Spectrum Books.

Kadar, Andras. 2001. *Police in Transition: Essays on the Police Forces in Transition Countries.* Budapest: Central European University Press.

Langworthy, Robert H., and Lawrence F. Travis. 1998. *Policing in America: A Balance of Forces.* 2nd. ed. Upper Saddle River, NJ: Prentice Hall.

Marin, Rene J. 1997. *Policing in Canada: Issues for the 21st Century.* Aurora, Ontario: Canada Law Books Inc.

1165

Opolot, Ejakait S. E. n.d. *Police Administration in Africa: Toward Theory and Practice in the English-speaking Countries.* Lanham, MD: University Press of America.

Parker L. Craig. 2001. *Japanese Police System Today: A Comparative Study,* 2nd ed. Armonk, NY: M.E. Sharpe.

Raghavan, R.K. 1999. *Policing a Democracy: A Comparative Study of India and the US.* New Delhi: Manohar Publishers.

Reiner, Robert. 2000. *Politics of the Police,* 3rd ed. Oxford: Oxford University Press.

Ryder, Chris. 2004. *Fateful Split: Catholics and the Royal Ulster Constabulary.* London: Methuen.

Seagrave, Jayne. 1997. *Introduction to Policing in Canada.* Scarborough, Ontario: Prentice Hall.

Shaw, Mark. 2002. *Crime and Policing in Post-apartheid South Africa: Transforming Under Fire.* London: Hurst and Company.

Singh, Joginder. 2002. *Inside Indian Police.* New Delhi: Gyan Publishing House.

POLICE THEORIES AND INTRODUCTIONS TO POLICING

Bayley, David H. 1998. *What Works in Policing.* New York: Oxford University Press.

Bittner, Egon. 1990. *Aspects of Police Work.* Boston: Northeastern University Press.

Brandl, Steven G., and David E. Barlow. 2004. *Police in America: Classic and Contemporary Readings.* Belmont, CA: Wadsworth/Thomson Learning.

Burke, Roger Hopkins. 2004. *Hard Cop, Soft Cop: Dilemmas and Debates in Contemporary Policing.* Cullompton, Devon: Willan Publishing.

Dempsey, John S. 1998. *Introduction to Policing.* 2nd ed. Belmont, California: West Wadsworth Publishing.

Dunham, Roger G., and Geoffrey P. Alpert. 1989. *Critical Issues in Policing: Contemporary Readings.* Prospect Heights, IL: Waveland Press.

Edwards, Charles. 1999. *Changing Policing Theories for 21st Century Societies.* Annandale, NSW: Federation Press.

Gaines, Larry K. and Gary W. Cordner. 1998. *Policing Perspectives: An Anthology.* Los Angeles: Roxbury Publishing.

Leishman, Frank, Barry Loveday, and Stephen P. Savage. 2000. *Core Issues in Policing,* 2nd ed. Harlow Longman.

Lyman, Michael D. 2002. *Police: An Introduction.* 2nd ed. Upper Saddle River, New Jersey: Prentice-Hall.

Mawby, R. I. 1990. *Comparative Policing Issues: The British and American System in International Perspective.* London: Unwin Hyman.

Mawby, R. I. 1999. *Policing Across the World: Issues for the Twenty-first Century.* London: UCL Press.

Newburn, Tim. 2003. *Handbook of Policing.* Cullompton, Devon: Willan Publishing.

Reichel, Philip L. 2002. *Comparative Criminal Justice Systems: A Topical Approach,* 3rd ed. Upper Saddle River, NJ: Prentice-Hall.

Reiner, Robert. 1996. *Policing. Volume 1: Cops, Crime and Control: Analysing the Police Function.* Aldershot: Dartmouth Publishing.

Robinson, Cyril D., Richard Scaglion, and Michael J. Olivero. 1994. "Police in Contradiction: The Evolution of the Police Function in Society." *Contributions in Criminology and Penology 44.* Westport, CN: Greenwood Press.

Thurman, Quint C., and Jihong Zhao. 2004. *Contemporary Policing: Controversies, Challenges, and Solutions: An Anthology.* Los Angeles: Roxbury Publishing.

Wright, Alan. 2002. *Policing: An Introduction to Concepts and Practice.* Cullompton: Devon Willan Publishing.

COMMUNITY POLICING

Adams, Thomas F. 2001. *Police Field Operations,* 5th ed. Upper Saddle River, NJ: Prentice-Hall.

Alpert, Geoffrey P., and Alex R. Piquero. 2000. *Community Policing: Contemporary Readings.* Prospect Heights, IL: Waveland Press.

Bullock, Karen, and Nick Tilley. 2003. *Crime Reduction and Problem-oriented Policing.* Cullompton, Devon: Willan Publishing.

Kidd, Virginia, and Rick Braziel. 1999. *COP Talk: Essential Communication Skills for Community Policing.* San Francisco: Acada Books.

Kratcoski, Peter C., and Duane Dukes. 1995. *Issues in Community Policing.* Cincinnati: Anderson Publishing.

Lab, Steven P. and Dilip K. Das. 2003. *International Perspectives on Community Policing and Crime Prevention.* Upper Saddle River, NJ: Prentice-Hall.

Miller, Linda S., and Karen M. Hess. 2002. *Police in the Community: Strategies for the 21st Century,* 3rd ed. Belmont, CA: Wadsworth/Thomson Learning.

Oliver, Willard M. 2000. *Community Policing: Classical Readings.* Upper Saddle River, NJ: Prentice-Hall.

Peak, Kenneth J., and Ronald W. Glensor. 2001. *Community Policing and Problem Solving: Strategies and Practices,* 3rd ed. Upper Saddle River, NJ: Prentice Hall.

Roberg, Roy R., John Crank, and Jack Kuykendall. 2000. *Police and Society,* 2nd ed. Los Angeles: Roxbury Publishing.

Robinson, Deborah Mitchell. 2002. *Policing and Crime Prevention.* Upper Saddle River, NJ: Prentice-Hall.

Skogan, Wesley G., and Susan M. Hartnett. 1997. *Community Policing: Chicago Style.* New York: Oxford University Press.

Skolnick, Jerome H., and David H. Bayley. 1988. *Community Policing: Issues and Practices Around the World.* Washington, D.C.: U.S. Department of Justice.

Stevens, Dennis J. 2001. *Case Studies in Community Policing.* Upper Saddle River, NJ: Prentice-Hall.

Stevens, Dennis J. 2002. *Policing and Community Partnerships.* Upper Saddle River, NJ: Prentice-Hall.

Stevens, Dennis J. 2003. *Applied Community Policing in the 21st Century.* Boston, MA: Allyn and Bacon.

Thurman, Quint, and Edmund F. Mcgarrell. 1997. *Community Policing in a Rural Setting.* Cincinnati: Anderson.

Trojanowicz, Robert, Victor E. Kappeler, and Larry K. Gaines. 2001. *Community Policing: A Contemporary Perspective,* 3rd ed. Cincinnati: Anderson Publishing.

Trojanowicz, Robert C., and Bonnie Bucqueroux. 1998. *Community Policing: How to Get Started.* 2nd ed. Cincinnati: Anderson Publishing.

Watson, Elizabeth M., Alfred R. Stone, and Stuart M. Deluca. 1998. *Strategies for Community Policing.* Upper Saddle River, NJ: Prentice-Hall.

ZERO TOLERANCE AND PROBLEM-ORIENTED POLICING

Braga, Anthony A. 2002. *Problem-oriented Policing and Crime Prevention.* Monsey, NY: Criminal Justice Press.

Bratton, William J., et al. 1998. "Zero Tolerance: Policing a Free Society." *Choice in Welfare Series 35.* London: Institute of Economic Affairs, Health and Welfare Unit.

Brito, Corina Sole, and Tracy Allan. 1999. *Problem-oriented Policing: Crime-specific Problems, Critical Issues and Making POP Work,* Volume 2. Washington, D.C.: Police Executive Research Forum.

Brito, Corina Sole, and Eugenia E. Gratto. 2000. *Problem-oriented Policing: Crime-specific Problems, Critical Issues and Making POP Work,* Volume 3. Washington, D.C.: Police Executive Research Forum.

Burke, Roger Hopkins. 1998. *Zero Tolerance Policing.* Leicester: Perpetuity Press.

Clarke, Ronald V., and John E. Eck. 2003. *Become a Problem Solving Crime Analyst: In 55 Small Steps.* London: Jill Dando Institute of Crime Science.

Goldstein, Herman. 1979. "Improving Policing: A Problem-oriented Approach." *Crime and Delinquency,* Vol. 25.

Goldstein, Herman. 1990. *Problem-oriented Policing.* New York, London: McGraw-Hill.

Karmen, Andrew. n.d. *New York Murder Mystery: The True Story Behind the Crime Crash of the 1990s.* New York: New York University Press.

Kelling, George L., and Catherine M. Coles. 1996. *Fixing Broken Windows: Restoring Order and Reducing Crime in our Communities.* New York: Free Press.

Kelling, George L., and William H. Sousa. 2001. "Do Police Matter? An Analysis of the Impact of New York City's Police Reforms." *Civic Report 22.* New York: Manhattan Institute for Policy Research, Center for Civic Innovation.

Knutsson, Johannes. 2003. "Problem-oriented Policing: From Innovation to Mainstream." *Crime Prevention Studies 15.* Monsey, NY: Criminal Justice Press.

Mcardle, Andrea, and Tanya Erzen. 2001. *Zero Tolerance: Quality of Life and the New Police Brutality in New York City.* New York: New York University Press.

Silverman, Eli. 1999. *NYPD Battles Crime: Innovative Strategies in Policing.* Boston, MA.: Northeastern University Press.

Shelley, Tara O'Connor, and Anne C. Grant. 1998. *Problem-oriented Policing: Crime-specific Problems, Critical Issues and Making POP Work.* Washington, D.C.: Police Executive Research Forum.

Taylor, Ralph B. 2001. *Breaking Away from Broken Windows: Baltimore Neighborhoods and the Nationwide Fight Against Crime, Grime, Fear, and Decline.* Boulder, CO: Westview Press.

Toch, Hans, and Douglas J. Grant. 1991. *Police as Problem Solvers.* New York: Plenum.

Walklate, Sandra, and Karen Evans. 1999. *Aldershot* Ashgate.

Wilson, James Q., and George L. Kelling. March 1982. "Broken Windows: The Police and Neighborhood Safety." *Atlantic Monthly.*

POLICE PATROL

Braithwaite, Helen, Neil Brewer, and Peter Strelan. 1998. *Conflict Management in Police-citizen Interactions.* Sydney: McGraw-Hill.

Brown, Michael K. 1988. *Working the Street: Police Discretion and the Dilemmas of Reform.* New York: Russell Sage Foundation.

Cooper, Christopher. 1999. *Mediation and Arbitration by Patrol Police Officers.* Lanham, MD: University Press of America.

Iannone, Nathan F. 1975. *Principles of Police Patrol.* McGraw-Hill.

Kelling, George L., Tony Pate, Duane Dieckman, and Charles E. Brown. 1974. *Kansas City Preventive Patrol Experiment: A Technical Report.* Washington, D.C.: Police Foundation.

Kemp, Charles, Clive Norris, and Nigel G. Fielding. 1992. *Negotiating Nothing: Police Decision-making in Disputes.* Aldershot: Avebury.

Mcbride, Mike. 1998. *Crime Patrol: To Recognise and Arrest Criminals: The Operational Guide to Proactive Patrolling.* Woking: New Police Bookshop.

Remsberg, Charles. 1986. *Tactical Edge: Surviving High-risk Patrol.* Northbrook, IL: Calibre Press.

Shapland, Joanna, and Jon Vagg. 1988. "Policing by the Public." *Social Science Paperbacks 401.* London: Routledge.

POLICE RELATIONS WITH THE PUBLIC—COMMUNITY REASSURANCE, FEAR OF CRIME, PARTNERSHIPS, AND CRIME PREVENTION

Bean, Philip, and Jo Campling. 2001. *Mental Disorder and Community Safety.* Basingstoke: Palgrave.

Crawford, Adam, and Mario Matassa. Criminal Justice Review Group. 2000. "Community Safety Structures: An International Literature Review." *Criminal Justice Review Group Research Report 8.* London: Stationery Office.

Davies, Pamela, Peter Francis, and Victor Jupp. 2004. *Victimisation: Theory, Research and Policy.* Basingstoke: Palgrave Macmillan.

Goold, Benjamin J. 2004. *CCTV and Policing: Public Area Surveillance and Police Practices in Britain.* Oxford: Oxford University Press.

Homel, Ross. 1997. "Policing for Prevention: Reducing Crime, Public Intoxication and Injury." *Crime Prevention Studies 7.* New York: Criminal Justice Press.

Hughes, Gordon, Eugene Mclaughlin, and John Muncie. 2002. *Crime Prevention and Community Safety: New Directions.* London: SAGE Publications.

Johnston, Les. 2001. "Crime, Fear and Civil Policing." *Urban Studies,* vol. 38 .

Jones, Trevor, and Tim Newburn. 2001. "Widening Access: Improving Police Relations with Hard to Reach Groups." *Police Research Series Paper 138.* London: Home Office, Policing and Reducing Crime Unit.

Sung, Hung-En. 2002. *Fragmentation of Policing in American Cities: Toward an Ecological Theory of Police-citizen Relations.* Westport, CN: Praeger.

Tonry, Michael, and David P. Farrington. 1995. "Building a Safer Society: Strategic Approaches to Crime Prevention." *Crime and Justice 19.* Chicago: University of Chicago Press.

POLICE AND THE MEDIA

Doyle, Aaron. 2003. *Arresting Images: Crime and Policing in Front of the Television Camera.* Toronto: University of Toronto Press.

Lawrence, Regina G. 2000. *Politics of Force: Media and the Construction of Police Brutality.* Berkeley, CA: University of California Press.

Leishman, Frank, and Paul Mason. 2003. *Policing and the Media: Facts, Fictions and Factions.* Cullompton: Willan Publishing.

Mawby, Rob C. 2002. *Policing Images: Policing, Communication and Legitimacy.* Cullompton, Devon: Willan Publishing.

Perlmutter, David D. 2000. *Policing the Media: Street Cops and Public Perceptions of Law Enforcement.* Thousand Oaks, CA: SAGE Publications.

Rafter, Nicole. 2000. *Shots in the Mirror: Crime Films and Society.* New York: Oxford University Press.

Ross, Jeffrey Ian. 2000. *Making News of Police Violence: A Comparative Study of Toronto and New York City.* Westport, CN: Praeger.

Wilson, Christopher P. 2000. *Cop Knowledge: Police Power and Cultural Narrative in Twentieth-century America.* Chicago: University of Chicago Press.

POLICE ETHICS, CORRUPTION, AND MISCONDUCT

Alderson, John C. 1998. *Principled Policing: Protecting the Public with Integrity.* Winchester: Waterside Press.

Bal, Ihsan, and Bedri M. Eryilmaz. 2002. *Police Professional Ethics.* Ankara: Police Academy Publications.

Banks, Cyndi. 2004. *Criminal Justice Ethics: Theory and Practice.* Thousand Oaks, CA: SAGE Publications.

Burns, Ronald G., and Charles E. Crawford. 2002. *Policing and Violence.* Upper Saddle River, NJ: Prentice-Hall.

Council of Europe. 2002. *European Code of Police Ethics: Recommendation 10 Adopted by the Committee of Ministers of the Council of Europe and Explanatory Memorandum.* Strasbourg: Council of Europe Publishing.

Crank, John P., and Michael A. Caldero. 2000. *Police Ethics: The Corruption of Noble Cause.* Cincinnati: Anderson Publishing.

Crawshaw, Ralph, and Leif Holmstrom. 2001. *Essential Texts on Human Rights for the Police: A Compilation of International Instruments.* The Hague: Kluwer Law International.

Crawshaw, Ralph, Barry Devlin, and T. Williamson. 1998. *Human Rights and Policing: Standards for Good Behaviour and a Strategy for Change.* The Hague: Kluwer Law International.

Delattre, Edwin J. 2002. *Character and Cops: Ethics in Policing,* 4th ed. Washington, D.C.: AEI Press.

Dixon, David. 1999. *Culture of Corruption: Changing an Australian Police Service.* Annandale, New South Wales: Hawkins Press.

Finnane, Mark. 1994. *Police and Government: Histories of Policing in Australia.* Melbourne: Oxford University Press.

Kleinig, John. 1996. *Ethics of Policing.* Cambridge: Cambridge University Press.

Kleinig, John. 1996. *Handled with Discretion: Ethical Issues in Police Decision Making.* Lanham, MD: Rowman and Littlefield.

Kleinig, John, and Margaret Leland Smith. 1997. *Teaching Criminal Justice Ethics: Strategic Issues.* Cincinnati: Anderson Publishing.

Kleinig, John, and Yurong Zhang. 1993. *Professional Law Enforcement Codes: A Documentary Collection.* Westport, CN: Greenwood.

Klockars, Carl B., Sanja Ivkovic Kutnjak, and Maria R. Haberfeld. 2004. *Contours of Police Integrity.* Thousand Oaks, CA: SAGE Publications.

Lersch, Kim Michelle. 2003. *Polcing and Misconduct.* Upper Saddle River, NJ: Prentice-Hall.

Nelson, Jill. 2001. *Police Brutality: An Anthology.* New York: W. W. Norton.

Newburn, Tim. 1999. "Understanding and Preventing Police Corruption: Lessons from the Literature." *Police Research Series Paper 110.* London: Home Office, Policing and Reducing Crime Unit.

Neyroud, Peter, Alan Beckley, Paul M. Collier, and Julia Clayton. 2001. *Policing, Ethics and Human Rights.* Cullompton, Devon: Willan Publishing.

Palmiotto, Michael J. 2001. *Police Misconduct: A Reader for the 21st Century.* Upper Saddle River, NJ: Prentice-Hall.

Paoline, Eugene A. 2001. *Rethinking Police Culture: Officers' Occupational Attitudes.* New York: LFB Scholarly Publishing LLC.

Sherman, Lawrence W. 1974. *Police Corruption: A Sociological Perspective.* Anchor Press.

Villiers, Peter. 1997. *Better Police Ethics: A Practical Guide.* London: Kogan Page.

POLICE CULTURE

Chan, Janet B.L. 1997. *Changing Police Culture: Policing a Multicultural Society.* Cambridge: Cambridge University Press.

Chan, Janet B. L., Chris Devery, and Sally Doran. 2003. *Fair Cop: Learning the Art of Policing.* Toronto: University of Toronto Press.

Coady, Tony, Steve James, Seumas Miller, and Michael O'keefe. 2000. *Violence and Police Culture.* Melbourne: Melbourne University Press.

Crank, John P. 1998. *Understanding Police Culture.* Cincinnati: Anderson Publishing.

Muir, William K. 1977. *Police: Streetcorner Politicians.* University of Chicago Press.

Prenzler, Tim, and Janet Ransley. 2002. *Police Reform: Building Integrity.* Annandale, New South Wales: Hawkins Press.

Reuss-Ianni, Elizabeth. 1983. *Two Cultures of Policing: Street Cops and Management Cops.* New Brunswick/ London: Transaction Books.

POLICE AND ETHNIC MINORITY RELATIONS

Bell, Jeanine. 2002. *Policing Hatred: Law Enforcement, Civil Rights, and Hate Crime.* New York: New York University Press.

Bland, Nick, Gary Mundy, Jacqueline Russell, and Rachel Tuffin. n.d. "Career Progression of Ethnic Minority Police Officers." *Police Research Series Paper 107.* London: Home Office, Policing and Reducing Crime Unit.

Bolton, Kenneth, and Joe R. Feagin. 2004. *Black in Blue: African-American Police Officers and Racism.* New York: Routledge.

Carlson, Daniel P. n.d. *When Cultures Clash: The Divisive Nature of Police-community Relations and Suggestions for Improvement.* Upper Saddle River, NJ: Prentice-Hall.

Fredrickson, Darin D., and Raymond P. Siljander. 2002. *Racial Profiling: Eliminating the Confusion Between Racial and Criminal Profiling and Clarifying What Constitutes Unfair Discrimination and Persecution.* Springfield, IL: Charles C. Thomas.

Fridell, Lorie, et al. 2001. *Racially Biased Policing: A Principled Response.* Washington, D.C.: Police Executive Research Forum.

Heumann, Milton, and Lance Cassak. 2003. *Good Cop, Bad Cop: Racial Profiling and Competing Views of Justice.* New York: Peter Lang.

Jones-Brown, Delores D., and Karen J. Terry. 2004. *Policing and Minority Communities: Bridging the Gap.* Upper Saddle River, NJ: Pearson Prentice Hall.

Macdonald, Heather. 2003. *Are Cops Racist?* Chicago: Ivan R. Dee.

Marlow, Alan, and Barry Loveday. 2000. *After Macpherson: Policing after the Stephen Lawrence Inquiry.* Lyme Regis: Russell House Publishing.

Perry, Barbara. n.d. *Hate and Bias Crime: A Reader.* London: Routledge.

Rowe, Michael. n.d. *Policing, Race and Racism.* Cullompton, Devon: Willan Publishing.

Russell, Katheryn K. 1998. *Color of Crime: Racial Hoaxes, White Fear, Black Protectionism, Police Harassment and other Macro Aggressions.* New York: New York University Press.

Shusta, Robert M., Deena R. Levine, Philip R. Harris, and Herbert Z. Wong. 2002. *Multicultural Law Enforcement: Strategies for Peacekeeping in a Diverse Society,* 2nd ed. Upper Saddle River, NJ: Prentice Hall.

Stone, Vanessa, and Rachel Tuffin. 2000. "Attitudes of People from Minority Ethnic Communities Towards a Career in the Police Service." *Police Research Series Paper 136.* London: Home Office, Policing and Reducing Crime Unit.

Walker, Samuel, Cassia Spohn, and Miriam Delone. 2003. *Color of Justice: Race, Ethnicity, and Crime in America,* 3rd. ed. Belmont, CA: Wadswoth/Thomson Learning.

WOMEN IN THE POLICE

Brown, Jennifer, and Frances Heidensohn. 2000. *Gender and Policing: Comparative Perspectives.* Basingstoke: Macmillan.

Heidensohn, Frances. 1995. *Women in Control? The Role of Women in Law Enforcement.* Oxford: Oxford University Press.

Gerber, Gwendolyn L. 2001. *Women and Men Police Officers: Status, Gender, and Personality.* Westport, CN.: Praeger.

Hagen, Susan, and Mary Carouba. 2002. *Women at Ground Zero: Stories of Courage and Compassion.* Indianapolis: Alpha Books.

Scarborough, Kathryn E., and Pamela A. Collins. 2002. *Women in Public and Private Law Enforcement.* Boston, MA: Butterworth-Heinemann.

Schulz, Dorothy Moses. 1995. *From Social Worker to Crime Fighter: Women in United States Municipal Policing.* Westport, CN: Praeger.

Segrave, Kerry. 1995. *Policewomen: A History.* London: McFarland.

Silvestri, Marisa. 2003. *Women in Charge: Policing, Gender and Leadership.* Cullompton, Devon: Willan Publishing.

Westmarland, Louise. 2001. *Gender and Policing: Sex, Power, and Police Culture.* Cullompton, Devon: Willan Publishing.

POLICE LEADERSHIP AND MANAGEMENT

Adlam, Robert, and Peter Villiers. 2003. *Police Leadership in the Twenty-first Century: Philosophy, Doctrine and Developments.* Winchester: Waterside Press.

Berry, Geoff, Jim Izat, R. I. Mawby, Lynne Walley, and Alan Wright. 1998. *Practical Police Management,* 2nd ed. London: Police Review Publishing.

Brodeur, Jean-Paul. 1998. *How to Recognise Good Policing: Problems and Issues.* Thousand Oaks, CA: SAGE Publications.

Dantzker, M. L. 1997. *Contemporary Policing: Personnel, Issues and Trends.* Boston, MA: Butterworth-Heinemann.

Drennan, James W. 2003. *Police Leadership and Labour Relations: A Reform Perspective.* Toronto: Emond Montgomery Publications.

Fox, William, Belinda Van Wyk, and Marius Fourie. 1998. *Police Management in South Africa.* Kenwyn, South Africa: Juta.

Henry, Vincent E. 2002. *Compstat Paradigm: Management Accountability in Policing, Business and the Public Sector.* Flushing, New York: Looseleaf Law Publications.

Hoover, Larry T. 1995. *Quantifying Quality in Policing.* Washington, D.C.: Police Executive Research Forum.

Hoover, Larry T. 1998. *Police Program Evaluation.* Washington, D.C.: Police Executive Research Forum.

Roberg, Roy R., Jack Kuykendall, and Kenneth Novak. 2002. *Police Management,* 3rd ed. Los Angeles: Roxbury Publishing.

Swanson, Charles R., Leonard Territo, and Robert W. Taylor. 2001. *Police Administration: Structures, Processes, and Behavior,* 5th ed. Upper Saddle River, NJ: Prentice-Hall.

Thibault, Edward A., Lawrence M. Lynch, and Bruce R. Mcbride. 2001. *Proactive Police Management,* 5th ed. Upper Saddle River, NJ: Prentice-Hall.

Whisenand, Paul M. 2001. *Supervising Police Personnel: The Fifteen Responsibilities,* 4th ed. Upper Saddle River, NJ: Prentice-Hall.

Whisenand, Paul M., and Fred R. Ferguson. 2001. *Managing of Police Organizations,* 5th ed. Upper Saddle River, NJ: Prentice-Hall.

POLICE TRAINING

Charles, Michael T. 2000. "Police Training: Breaking All the Rules." *Implementing the Adult Education Model into Police Training.* Springfield, IL: Charles C. Thomas.

Haberfeld, Maria R. 2002. *Critical Issues in Police Training.* Upper Saddle River, NJ: Prentice-Hall.

O'keefe, James. 2004. *Protecting the Republic: The Education and Training of American Police Officers.* Upper Saddle River, NJ: Pearson Prentice-Hall.

Palmiotto, Michael J. 2003. *Policing and Training Issues.* Upper Saddle River, NJ: Prentice-Hall.

Palombo, Bernadette Jones. 1995. "Academic Professionalism in Law Enforcement." *Current Issues in Criminal Justice 11,* Garland Reference Library of Social Science 998. New York: Garland.

PRIVATE POLICE

Button, Mark. 2002. *Private Policing.* Cullompton, Devon: Willan Publishing.

Jones, Trevor, and Tim Newburn. 1998. *Private Security and Public Policing.* Oxford: Clarendon Press.

Pastor, James F. 2003. *Privatization of Police in America: An Analysis and Case Study.* Jefferson, NC: McFarland.

Rigakos, George S. 2002. *New Parapolice: Risk Markets and Commodified Social Control.* Toronto: University of Toronto Press.

POLICING OF DRUGS

Abadinsky, Howard. 2001. *Drugs: An Introduction,* 4th ed. Belmont, CA: Wadsworth.

Bean, Philip. 2001. *Drugs and Crime.* Cullompton, Devon: Willan Publishing.

Conklin, John E. 2003. *Why Crime Rates Fell.* Boston, MA: Allyn and Bacon.

Davis, Robert C., and Arthur J. Lurigio. 1996. *Fighting Back: Neighborhood Antidrug Strategies.* Thousand Oaks, CA: SAGE Publications.

Elvins, Martin. 2003. *Anti-drugs Policies of the European Union: Transnational Decision-making and the Politics of Expertise.* Basingstoke: Palgrave Macmillan.

Kopp, Pierre. 2004. "Political Economy of Illegal Drugs." *Studies in Crime and Economics 1.* London: Routledge.

Lee, Gregory D. 2004. *Global Drug Enforcement: Practical Investigative Techniques.* Boca Raton, FL: CRC Press.

Lyman, Michael D. 2001. *Practical Drug Enforcement,* 2nd ed. Boca Raton, FL: CRC Press.

Massari, Monica, and Gruppo Abele. 2003. *Synthetic Drugs Trafficking in Three European Cities: Major Trends and the Involvement of Organised Crime.* Turin: Gruppo Abele.

Murji, Karim. 1998. *Policing Drugs.* Aldershot: Ashgate.

Natarajan, Mangai, and Mike Hough. 2000. "Illegal Drug Markets: From Research to Prevention Policy." *Crime Prevention Studies 11.* Monsey, NY: Criminal Justice Press.

TERRORISM

Alexander, Yonah. 2002. *Combating Terrorism: Strategies of Ten Countries.* Ann Arbor: University of Michigan Press.

Bevelacqua, Armandop, and Richard Stilp. 2002. *Terrorism Handbook for Operational Responders.* New York: Delmar Publishing.

Clutterbuck, Richard. 1994. *Terrorism in an Unstable World.* London: Routledge.

Combs, Cindy C. 2003. *Terrorism in the Twenty-first Century,* 3rd ed. Upper Saddle River, NJ: Prentice-Hall.

Combs, Cindy C., and Martin Slann. 2002. *Encyclopedia of Terrorism.* New York: Facts on File.

Currie, Stephen. 2002. *Terrorists and Terrorist Groups.* San Diego, CA: Lucent Books.

Cutter, Susan L., Douglas B. Richardson, and Thomas J. Wilbanks. 2003. *Geographical Dimensions of Terrorism.* New York: Routledge.

Freedman, Lawrence. 2002. *Superterrorism: Policy Responses.* Oxford: Blackwell Publishing.

Griset, Pamala L., and Sue Mahan. 2003. *Terrorism in Perspective.* Thousand Oaks, CA: SAGE Publications.

Granot, Hayim, and Jay Levinson. 2002. "Terror Bombing: The New Urban Threat." *Practical Approaches for Response Agencies and Security.* Tel Aviv, Israel: Dekel Publishing.

Kushner, Harvey W. 2003. *Encyclopedia of Terrorism.* Thousand Oaks, CA: SAGE Publications.

Laqueur, Walter. 2003. *No End to War: Terrorism in the Twenty-first Century.* New York: Continuum.

Martin, Gus. 2003. *Understanding Terrorism: Challenges, Perspectives, and Issues.* Thousand Oaks, CA: SAGE Publications.

Moghaddam, Fathali M., and Anthony J. Marsella. 2004. *Understanding Terrorism: Psychosocial Roots,*

Consequences, and Interventions. Washington, D.C.: American Psychological Association.

Silke, Andrew. 2003. *Terrorists, Victims and Society: Psychological Perspectives on Terrorism and its Consequences.* Chichester: John Wiley and Sons.

Thackrah, J.R. 2004. *Dictionary of Terrorism,* 2nd ed. London: Routledge.

Wilkinson, Paul. 2000. *Terrorism Versus Democracy: The Liberal State Response.* London: Frank Cass.

EMERGENCY PROCEDURES

Alexander, David A. 2002. *Principles of Emergency Planning and Management.* Harpenden: Terra Publishing.

Bolz, Frank, Kenneth J. Dudonis, and David P. Schulz. 2002. *Counterterrorism Handbook: Tactics, Procedures, and Techniques,* 2nd ed. Boca Raton, FL: CRC Press.

Fernandez, Louie, and Martin Merzer. 2003. *Jane's Crisis Communications Handbook.* Alexandria, VA: Jane's Information Group.

Haddow, George D., and Jane A. Bullock. 2003. *Introduction to Emergency Management.* Boston, MA: Butterworth-Heinemann.

Jensen, Robert A. 2000. *Mass Fatality and Casualty Incidents: A Field Guide.* Boca Raton, FL: CRC Press.

Lanceley, Frederick J. 2003. *On-scene Guide for Crisis Negotiators,* 2nd ed. Boca Raton, FL: CRC Press.

Maniscalco, Paul M., and Hank T. Christen. 2003. *Terrorism Response: Field Guide for Fire and EMS Organizations.* Boston, MA: Prentice Hall.

McMains, Michael J., and Wayman C. Mullins. 2001. *Crisis Negotiations: Managing Critical Incidents and Hostage Situations in Law Enforcement and Corrections,* 2nd ed. Cincinnati: Anderson Publishing.

Tarlow, Peter E. 2002. *Event Risk Management and Safety.* New York: John Wiley and Sons.

ORGANIZED CRIME

Abadinsky, Howard. 2003. *Organized Crime,* 7th ed. Belmont, CA: Wadsworth/Thompson.

Albanese, Jay S., Dilip K. Das, and Arvind Verma. 2003. *Organized Crime: World Perspectives.* Upper Saddle River, NJ: Prentice-Hall.

Allum, Felia, and Renate Siebert. 2003. "Organized Crime and the Challenge to Democracy." *ECPR Studies in European Political Science 28.* London: Routledge.

Blunden, Bob. 2001. *Money Launderers: How They Do It, and How to Catch Them at It.* Chalford: Management Books.

Boer, Monica den. 2002. *Organised Crime: A Catalyst in the Europeanisation of National Police and Prosecution Agencies?* Maastricht: European Institute of Public Administration.

Edwards, Adam, and Peter Gill. 2003. *Transnational Organised Crime: Perspectives on Global Security.* London: Routledge.

Fijnaut, Cyrille, and James B. Jacobs. 1991. *Organized Crime and Its Containment: A Transatlantic Initiative.* Deventer, Netherlands: Kluwer.

Fiorentini, Gianluca, and Sam Peltzman. 1995. *Economics of Organised Crime.* Cambridge: Cambridge University Press.

Gilmore, William C. n.d. *Dirty Money: The Evolution of Money Laundering Counter-measures.* Strasbourg: Council of Europe Press.

Hill, Peter B.E. 2003. *Japanese Mafia: Yakuza, Law, and the State.* Oxford: Oxford University Press.

Jamieson, Alison. 2000. *Antimafia: Italy's Fight Against Organized Crime.* Basingstoke: Macmillan.

Kaplan, David E., and Alec Dubro. 2003. *Yakuza: Japan's Criminal Underworld,* 2nd ed. London: Robert Hale.

Kyle, David, and Rey Koslowski. n.d. *Global Human Smuggling: Comparative Perspectives.* Baltimore: Johns Hopkins University Press.

Levi, Michael, and Alaster Smith. 2002. "Comparative Analysis of Organised Crime Conspiracy Legislation and Practice and Their Relevance to England and Wales." *Home Office Online Report 17/02.* London: Home Office, Research Development and Statistics Directorate.

Lintner, Bertil. 2002. *Blood Brothers: The Criminal Underworld of Asia.* New York: Palgrave Macmillan.

Lyman, Michael D., and Gary W. Potter. 2004. *Organized Crime,* 3rd ed. Upper Saddle River, NJ: Pearson Prentice Hall.

Passas, Nikos. n.d. *Organized Crime.* Aldershot: Dartmouth Publishing.

Ruyver, Brice de, Gert Vermeulen, and Tom Vander Beken. 2002. *Strategies of the EU and the US in Combating Transnational Organized Crime.* Antwerp: Maklu.

Viano, Emilio. 1999. *Global Organized Crime and International Security.* Aldershot: Ashgate.

Vukson, William B.Z. 2001. *Organized Crime and Money Laundering.* Toronto: G7 Books.

POLICE USE OF CRIMINAL INTELLIGENCE

Bennett, Wayne W., and Karen M. Hess. 2004. *Criminal Investigation,* 7th ed. Belmont, CA: Wadsworth/Thomson.

Billingsley, Roger, Teresa Nemitz, and Philip Bean. n.d. *Informers: Policing, Policy, Practice.* Cullompton, Devon: Willan Publishing.

Bloom, Robert M. 2002. *Ratting: The Use and Abuse of Informants in the American Justice System.* Westport, CN: Praeger Publishers.

Boer, Monica den. 1997. *Undercover Policing and Accountability From an International Perspective.* Maastricht: European Institute of Public Administration.

Field, Stewart, and Caroline Pelser. 1998. *Invading the Private: State Accountability and New Investigative Methods in Europe.* Aldershot: Ashgate.

Gill, Peter. 2000. "Rounding Up the Usual Suspects?" *Developments in Contemporary Law Enforcement Intelligence.* Aldershot: Ashgate.

Gilmour, Raymond. 1999. *Dead Ground: Infiltrating the IRA.* London: Warner Books.

Madinger, John. n.d. *Confidential Informant: Law Enforcement's Most Valuable Tool.* Boca Raton, FL: CRC Press.

Mallory, Stephen L. 2000. *Informants: Development and Management.* Incline Village, NV: Copperhouse Publishing.

Motto, Carmine J., and Dale L. June. 2000. *Undercover,* 2nd ed. Boca Raton, FL: CRC Press.

Ratcliffe, Jerry. 2004. *Strategic Thinking in Criminal Intelligence.* Annandale, New South Wales: Federation Press.

Ritch, Van. 2003. *Rural Surveillance: A cop's Guide to Gathering Evidence in Remote Areas.* Boulder, CO: Paladin Press.

DOMESTIC VIOLENCE

Buzawa, Eve S., and Carl G. Buzawa. 2003. *Domestic Violence: The Criminal Justice Response,* 3rd ed. Thousand Oaks, CA: SAGE Publications.

Erez, Edna, and Kathy Laster. 2000. "Domestic Violence: Global Responses." *International Review of Victimology,* vol. 7 no. 1-3. Bicester: AB Academic Publishers.

Feder, Lynette. 1999. "Women and Domestic Violence: An Interdisciplinary Approach." *Women and Criminal Justice,* vol. 10 no. 2. New York: Haworth Press.

Hanmer, Jalna, and Catherine Itzin. 2000. *Home Truths about Domestic Violence: Feminist Influences on Policy and Practice: A Reader.* London: Routledge.

Her Majesty's Crown Prosecution Service Inspectorate and Her Majesty's Inspectorate of Constabulary. 2004. *Violence at Home: A Joint Thematic Inspection of the Investigation and Prosecution of Cases Involving Domestic Violence.* London: H.M.C.P.S.I..

Hoyle, Carolyn. 1998. *Negotiating Domestic Violence: Police, Criminal Justice and Victims.* Oxford: Clarendon Press.

Jenkins, Pamela J., and Barbara Parmer Davidson. 2001. *Stopping Domestic Violence: How a Community Can Prevent Spousal Abuse.* New York: Kluwer Academic/Plenum Publishers.

Lockton, Deborah, and Richard Ward. 1997. *Domestic Violence.* London: Cavendish.

Loue, Sana. 2001. *Intimate Partner Violence: Societal, Medical, Legal, and Individual Responses.* New York: Kluwer Academic/Plenum Publishing.

Paradine, Kate, Jo Wilkinson, and the National Centre for Policing Excellence–Her Majesty's Crown Prosecution Service Inspectorate and Her Majesty's Inspectorate of Constabulary. n.d. *Protection and Accountability: The Reporting, Investigation and Prosecution of Domestic Violence Cases: A Research and Literature Review.* London: H.M.C.P.S.I..

Plotnikoff, Joyce, and Richard Woolfson. n.d. "Policing Domestic Violence: Effective Organisational Structures." *Police Research Series Paper 100.* London: Home Office, Policing and Reducing Crime Unit.

Roberts, Albert R. 1996. *Helping Battered Women: New Perspectives and Remedies.* New York: Oxford University Press.

Summers, Randal W., and Alan M. Hoffman. 2002. *Domestic Violence: A Global View.* Westport, CN: Greenwood Press.

Stanko, Elizabeth A. 2002. *Violence.* Aldershot: Ashgate.

POLICING OF PUBLIC ORDER, PROTESTS, AND RIOTS

Baxter, Norman. 2001. *Policing the Line: The Development of a Theoretical Model for the Policing of Conflict.* Aldershot: Ashgate.

Bessel, Richard, and Clive Emsley. 2000. *Patterns of Provocation: Police and Public Disorder.* New York: Berghahn Books.

Cannon, Lou. 1999. *Official Negligence: How Rodney King and the Riots Changed Los Angeles and the LAPD.* Boulder, CO: Westview Press.

Della porta, Donatella, and Herbert Reiter. 1997. "Policing of Mass Demonstration in Contemporary Democracies: The Policing of Protest in Contemporary Democracies." *EUI Working Papers RSC 97/1.* San Domenico, Italy: European University Institute.

Fillieule, Olivier, and Fabien Jobard. 1997. "Policing of Mass Demonstration in Contemporary Democracies: The Policing of Protest in France: Towards a Model of Protest Policing." *EUI Working Paper RSC no. 97/4.* San Domenico Italy: European University Institute Badia Fiesolana.

Gale, Dennis E. 1996. *Understanding Urban Unrest: From Reverend King to Rodney King.* Thousand Oaks, CA: SAGE Publications.

Hunt, Darnell M. 1997. *Screening the Los Angeles Riots: Race, Seeing, and Resistance.* Cambridge: Cambridge University Press.

Ingleton, Roy D. 1996. *Arming the British Police: The Great Debate.* London: Frank Cass.

Jefferson, Tony. 1990. *Case Against Paramilitary Policing.* Milton Keynes: Open University Press.

Kraska, Peter B. 2001. *Militarizing the American Criminal Justice System: The Changing Roles of the Armed Forces and the Police.* Boston, MA.: Northeastern University Press.

Mcphail, Clark, John Mccarthy, and David Schweingruber. 1997. "Policing of Mass Demonstration in Contemporary Democracies: Policing Protest in the United States From the 1960s to the 1990s." *EUI Working Paper RSC 97/3.* San Domenico, Italy: European University Institute.

Neale, Jonathan. n.d. *You are G8, We are 6 Billion: The Truth Behind the Genoa Protests.* London: Vision Paperbacks.

Waddington, David. 1992. *Contemporary Issues in Public Disorder: A Comparative and Historical Approach.* London: Routledge.

Waddington, David, Karen Jones, and Chas Critcher. 1989. *Flashpoints: Studies in Public Disorder.* London: Routledge.

Waddington, P. A. J. 1991. *Strong Arm of the Law: Armed and Public Order Policing.* Oxford: Oxford University Press.

Waddington, P. A .J. 1997. "Policing of Mass Demonstration in Contemporary Democracies: Controlling Protest in Contemporary Historical and Comparative Perspective." *EUI Working Paper RSC 97/6.* San Domenico, Italy: European University Institute.

Waddington, P. A. J. 2001. "Policing of Public Order." *Police Practice and Research,* vol. 2 no. 1-2. Harwood Academic Publishers.

INTERNATIONAL POLICING PEACEKEEPING, POLICE COOPERATION, INTERPOL, AND EUROPOL

Anderson, Malcolm, and Joanna Apap. 2002. "Police and Justice Co-operation and the New European Borders." *European Monographs 40.* The Hague: Kluwer Law International.

Deflem, Mathieu. 2002. *Policing World Society: Historical Foundations of International Police Cooperation.* Oxford: Oxford University Press.

Hall, Ben, and Ashish Bhatt. 1999. *Policing Europe: EU Justice and Home Affairs Co-operation.* London: Centre for European Reform.

Hansen, Annika S. 2002. "From Congo to Kosovo: Civilian Police in Peace Operations." *Adelphi Papers 343.* Oxford: Oxford University Press.

Holm, Tor Tanke, and Espen Barth Eide. 2000. "Peacebuilding and Police Reform." *International Peacekeeping,* vol. 6 no. 4. London: Frank Cass.

Koenig, Daniel J., and Dilip K. Das. 2001. *International Police Cooperation: A World Perspective.* Lanham, MD: Lexington Books.

Mitsilegas, Valsamis, Jorg Monar, and Wyn Rees. 2003. *European Union and Internal Security: Guardian of the People?* Basingstoke: Palgrave Macmillan.

Occhipinti, John D. 2003. *Politics of EU Police Cooperation: Toward a European FBI?* Boulder, CO: Lynne Rienner Publishers.

Pakes, Francis J. 2004. *Comparative Criminal Justice.* Cullompton, Devon: Willan Publishing.

Santiago, Michael. 2000. "Europol and Police Cooperation in Europe." *Criminology Studies 11.* Lewiston, NY: Edwin Mellen Press.

Sheptycki, J.W.E. 2002. *In Search of Transnational Policing: Towards a Sociology of Global Policing.* Aldershot: Ashgate.

Williams, Phil, and Dimitri Vlassis. 2001. "Combating Transnational Crime: Concepts, Activities and Responses." *Transnational Organized Crime,* vol. 4 no. 3–4. London: Frank Cass.

CYBERCRIME

Arnaldo, Carlos A. 2001. *Child Abuse on the Internet: Ending the Silence.* New York/Paris: Berghahn Books/ UNESCO Publishing.

Boon, Julian, and Lorraine Sheridan. 2002. *Stalking and Psychosexual Obsession: Psychological Perspectives for Prevention, Policing and Treatment.* Chichester: John Wiley and Sons.

Calder, Martin C. 2004. *Child Sexual Abuse and the Internet: Tackling the New Frontier.* Lyme Regis: Russell House Publishing.

Casey, Eoghan. 2004. *Digital Evidence and Computer Crime: Forensic Science, Computers and the Internet,* 2nd ed. San Diego: Elsevier Academic Press.

Furnell, Steven. 2002. *Cybercrime: Vandalizing the Information Society.* Harlow: Addison-Wesley.

Newman, Graeme R., and Ronald V. Clarke. 2003. *Superhighway Robbery: Preventing E-commerce Crime.* Cullompton, Devon: Willan Publishing.

Newton, Michael. 2004. *Encyclopedia of High-tech Crime and Crime-fighting.* New York: Checkmark Books.

Taylor, Max, and Ethel Quayle. 2003. *Child Pornography: An Internet Crime.* Hove: Brunner-Routledge.

Vacca, John R. 2003. *Identity Theft.* Upper Saddle River, NJ: Prentice Hall PTR.

Wall, David S. 2003. *Cyberspace Crime.* Aldershot: Ashgate.

WHITE COLLAR CRIME

Croall, Hazel. 2001. *Understanding White Collar Crime.* Buckingham: Open University Press.

Davies, Pamela, Peter Francis, and Victor Jupp. 1999. *Invisible Crimes: Their Victims and Their Regulation.* Basingstoke: Macmillan.

Green, Gary S. 1997. *Occupational Crime,* 2nd ed. Chicago: Nelson Hall Publishers.

Shover, Neal, and John Paul Wright. 2001. *Crimes of Privilege: Readings in White-collar Crime.* New York: Oxford University Press.

Sjogren, Hans, and Goran Skogh. 2004. *New Perspectives in Economic Crime.* Cheltenham: Edward Elgar.

Smith, Russell G. 2002. *Crime in the Professions.* Aldershot: Ashgate.

Weisburd, David, and Elin Waring. 2001. *White-collar Crime and Criminal Careers.* Cambridge: Cambridge University Press.

POLICE AND PSYCHOLOGY—INTERVIEWING, DECEPTION, AND EYEWITNESSES

Ainsworth, Peter B. 2001. *Offender Profiling and Crime Analysis.* Cullompton, Devon: Willan Publishing.

Ainsworth, Peter B. 2002. *Psychology and Policing.* Cullompton, Devon: Willan Publishing.

Canter, David, and Laurence J. Alison. 1998. "Interviewing and Deception." *Offender Profiling Series 1.* Aldershot: Ashgate.

Canter, David, and Laurence J. Alison. 2000. "Profiling Property Crimes." *Offender Profiling Series 4.* Aldershot: Ashgate.

Carson, David, and Ray Bull. 2003. *Handbook of Psychology in Legal Contexts,* 2nd ed. Chichester: John Wiley.

Godwin, Grover Maurice. 2000. *Hunting Serial Predators: A Multivariate Classification Approach to Profiling Violent Behavior.* Boca Raton, FL: CRC Press.

Goldstein, Alan M., and Irving B. Weiner. 2003. *Handbook of Psychology. Volume 11: Forensic Psychology.* Hoboken, NJ: John Wiley and Sons.

Gordon, Nathan J., and William L. Fleisher. 2002. *Effective Interviewing and Interrogation Techniques.* San Diego: Academic Press.

Gudjonsson, Gisli H. 2003. *Psychology of Interrogations and Confessions: A Handbook.* Chichester: John Wiley and Sons.

Holmes, Ronald M., and Stephen T. Holmes. 2002. *Current Perspectives on Sex Crimes.* Thousand Oaks, CA: SAGE Publications.

Holmes, Ronald M., and Stephen T. Holmes. 2002. *Profiling Violent Crimes: An Investigative Tool.* 3rd ed. Thousand Oaks, CA: SAGE Publications.

Kapardis, Andreas. 2003. *Psychology and Law: A Critical Introduction,* 2nd ed. Cambridge: Cambridge University Press.

Keppel, Robert D., and William J. Birnes. 2003. *Psychology of Serial Killer Investigations: The Grisly Business Unit.* San Diego: Academic Press.

Kleiner, Murray. 2002. *Handbook of Polygraph Testing.* San Diego: Academic Press.

Kurke, Martin I., and Ellen M. Scrivner. 1995. *Police Psychology into the 21st Century.* Hillsdale, NJ: Lawrence Erlbaum.

Leo, Richard A., and George C. Thomas. 1998. *Miranda Debate: Law, Justice and Policing.* Boston: Northeastern University Press.

Memon, Amina, Aldert Vrij, and Ray Bull. 2003. *Psychology and Law: Truthfulness, Accuracy and Credibility,* 2nd ed. Chichester: John Wiley and Sons.

Milne, Rebecca, and Ray Bull. 1999. *Investigative Interviewing: Psychology and Practice.* Chichester: John Wiley and Sons.

National Research Council, Committee to Review the Scientific Evidence on the Polygraph, and Stephen E. Fienberg. 2003. *Polygraph and Lie Detection.* Washington, D.C.: National Academies Press.

Poole, Debra A., and Michael E. Lamb. 1998. *Investigative Interviews of Children: A Guide for the Helping Professionals.* Washington D.C.: American Psychological Association.

Rossmo, D. Kim. 2000. *Geographic Profiling.* Boca Raton, FL: CRC Press.

Russell, Harold E., and Allan Beigel. 1999. *Understanding Human Behavior For Effective Police Work,* 3rd ed. New York: Basic Books.

Yeschke, Charles L. 2003. *Art of Investigative Interviewing: A Human Approach to Testimonial Evidence,* 2nd ed. Boston, MA: Butterworth-Heinemann.

Zulawski, David E., and Douglas E. Wicklander. n.d. *Practical Aspects of Interview and Interrogation,* 2nd ed. Boca Raton, FL: CRC Press.

POLICING OF VIOLENCE

Capozzoli, Thomas K., and Steve R. Mcvey. 2000. *Kids Killing Kids: Managing Violence and Gangs in Schools.* Boca Raton, FL: St Lucie Press.

Daye, Douglas D. 1996. *Law Enforcement Sourcebook of Asian Crime and Cultures: Tactics and Mindsets.* Boca Raton, FL: CRC Press.

Fein, Robert A., et al. 2002. *Threat Assessment in Schools: A Guide to Managing Threatening Situations and to Creating Safe School Climates.* Washington, D.C.: United States Secret Service.

Geberth, Vernon J. 1996. *Practical Homicide Investigation: Tactics, Procedures, and Forensic Techniques,* 3rd ed. Boca Raton, FL: CRC Press.

Gilligan, James. 2001. *Preventing Violence.* London: Thames and Hudson.

Hazelwood, Robert R., and Ann Wolbert Burgess. 2001. *Practical Aspects of Rape Investigation: A Multidisciplinary Approach,* 3rd ed. Boca Raton, FL: CRC Press.

Huff, C. Ronald. 1996. *Gangs in America,* 2nd ed. Thousand Oaks, CA: SAGE Publications.

Innes, Martin. 2003. *Investigating Murder: Detective Work and the Police Response to Criminal Homicide.* Oxford: Oxford University Press.

Kemshall, Hazel, and Jacki Pritchard. 1999. "Good Practice in Working with Violence." *Good Practice 6.* London: Jessica Kingsley.

Moffatt, Gregory K. 2000. *Blind-sided: Homicide Where it is Least Expected.* Westport, CN: Praeger.

Morewitz, Stephen J. 2003. *Stalking and Violence: New Patterns of Trauma and Obsession.* New York: Kluwer Academic/Plenum Publishers.

O'brien, Bill. 2001. *Killing for Pleasure: The Global Phenomenon of Mass Murder.* London: John Blake Publishing.

Schell, Bernadette H., and Nellie M. Lanteigne. 2000. *Stalking, Harassment, and Murder in the Workplace: Guidelines for Protection and Prevention.* Westport, CN: Quorum Books.

Smith, M. Dwayne, and Margaret A. Zahn. 1999. *Studying and Preventing Homicide: Issues and Challenges.* Thousand Oaks, CA: SAGE Publications.

Smith, Peter K. 2003. *Violence in Schools: The Response in Europe.* London: Routledge Falmer.

Turk, William L. 2004. *School Crime and Policing.* Upper Saddle River, NJ: Pearson Prentice-Hall.

Vossekuil, Bryan, et al. 2002. *Final Report and Findings of the Safe School Initiative: Implications for the Prevention of School Attacks in the United States.* Washington, D.C.: United States Secret Service.

Weisel, Deborah Lamm, et al. 1997. *Police Response to Gangs: Case Studies of Five Cities.* Washington, D.C.: Police Executive Research Forum.

Wong, Marleen, James Kelly, and Ronald D. Stephens. 2001. *Jane's School Safety Handbook.* Alexandria, VA: Jane's Information Group.

POLICE STRESS

Blau, Theodore H. 1994. *Psychological Services for Law Enforcement.* New York: Wiley.

Brown, Jennifer, and Elizabeth Campbell. 1994. *Stress and Policing: Sources and Strategies.* Chichester: John Wiley and Sons.

Finn, Peter, and Julie Esselman Tomz. 1996. *Developing a Law Enforcement Stress Program for Officers and Their Families.* Washington, D.C.: U.S. Department of Justice, Office of Justice Programs.

Henry, Vincent E. 2004. *Death Work: Police, Trauma, and the Psychology of Survival.* New York: Oxford University Press.

Kates, Allen R. 1999. *CopShock: Surviving Posttraumatic Stress Disorder (PTSD).* Tucson: Holbrook Street Press.

Raphael, Beverley, and John P. Wilson. 2000. *Psychological Debriefing: Theory, Practice and Evidence.* Cambridge: Cambridge University Press.

Territo, Leonard, and James D. Sewell. 1999. *Stress Management in Law Enforcement.* Durham, NC: Carolina Academy Press.

Toch, Hans. 2002. *Stress in Policing.* Washington, D.C.: American Psychological Association.

Violanti, John M. 1996. *Police Suicide: Epidemic in Blue.* Springfield, Illinois: Charles C. Thomas.

Violanti, John M. and Douglas Paton. 1999. *Police Trauma: Psychological Aftermath of Civilian Combat.* Springfield, IL: Charles C. Thomas.

Index

Academies *continued*
    in France, 403
    in Germany, 426
    in Ghana, 433–434
    in Greece, 442–443
    in Guatemala, 453
    in Guinea, 456
    in Haiti, 462
    in Honduras, 465
    in Hungary, 469
    in Iceland, 475
    in India, 479–480, 481
    in Indonesia, 486
    in Iran, 491
    in Iraq, 493
    in Ireland, 498–499
    in Israel, 505–506
    in Italy, 512, 514, 515
    in Jamaica, 523
    in Japan, 5, 531
    in Jordan, 538
    in Kazakhstan, 542
    in Kenya, 550
    in Kuwait, 567
    in Latvia, 582
    in Lesotho, 590
    in Liberia, 592, 593, 594
    in Libya, 597
    in Lithuania, 600, 604
    in Macedonia, 615, 616, 617
    in Madagascar, 621
    in Malaysia, 627
    in Mexico, 644–645
    in Moldova, 652
    in Morocco, 663
    in Nepal, 672
    in Netherlands, 679, 680
    in New Zealand, 686
    in Nigeria, 700, 702
    in Oman, 711
    in Pakistan, 715
    in Panama, 720
    in Papua New Guinea, 723
    in Paraguay, 725
    in Philippines, 734, 741
    in Puerto Rico, 769
    in Qatar, 771
    in Romania, 775, *775*
    in Rwanda, 790
    in Saint Vincent and the
        Grenadines, 796
    in Saudi Arabia, 803
    in Senegal, 806
    in Serbia and Montenegro, 810
    in Seychelles, 815
    in Singapore, 819, 820, 821
    in Slovakia, 825
    in Slovenia, 832
    in Somalia, 840
    in South Korea, 558, 559

    in Swaziland, 857
    in Sweden, 862
    in Syria, 874
    in Taiwan, 877–878
    in Tajikistan, 881
    in Tanzania, 889
    in Thailand, 893, 894
    in Tunisia, 905
    in Turkey, 908–909
    in Uganda, 921
    in Ukraine, 928
    in United Kingdom, 59
    in United States, 964–965
    in Uruguay, 1064
    in Venezuela, 1082
    in Yemen, 1089
    in Zambia, 1092
Academy of Police Science (U.S.),
    1135, 1137
ACC. *See* Algoa Correctional Center
Accident insurance, for prisoners in
    Greece, 445
Accidents
    car (*See* Car(s), in accidents)
    nuclear, in Chernobyl, 199
Accountability
    in balanced-and-restorative justice,
        50
    in law enforcement, in United
        Kingdom, 938, 939–940
*Account of the Origin and Effects of a
    Police Set on Foot by the Duke of
    Newcastle on a Plan Suggested by the
    Late Henry Fielding,* 4
Accra (Ghana), 433, 434
ACDC. *See* Atlanta City Detention
    Center
Acetic anhydride (AA), 916
ACLU. *See* American Civil Liberties
    Union
ACP. *See* Azeri Communist Party
ACPO. *See* Association of Chief Police
    Officers of England, Wales, and
    Northern Ireland
Acquired immunodeficiency syn-
    drome. *See* HIV/AIDS
ACT. *See* Australian Capital Territory
    (ACT) Police Force
Act Number 1 (1894, South Africa), 27
Act Number 169/1999 Coll. (Czech
    Republic), 339
Act Number 265/2001 Coll. (Czech
    Republic), 338
Act Number 283/1991 Coll. (Czech
    Republic), 335

Act on Commercial Activity Number
    455/1991 Coll. (Czech Republic),
    336
Act on the Local Police Number 553/
    191 Coll. (Czech Republic), 336
Addis Ababa (Ethiopia)
    correctional system in, 382
    law enforcement in, 380, 381
Aden Police Force, 1089
Adlam, Robert, 62
Administration Organization Act
    (AOA) (1979) (Switzerland), 867
Administration and Planning Bureau,
    Police (Taiwan), 877
Administrative courts, in Turkey, 911
Administrative Makhzani (Morocco),
    662, 663
Administrative Offenses Code
    (Belarus), 201, 202
Administrative Office of the U.S.
    Courts, 959
Administrative police
    in Egypt, 362
    in Jordan, 536–537
    in Kenya, 549, 550
    in South Korea, 557
Adoption, international, 125
ADS. *See* Anti-Drug and Smuggling
    Unit
AFEAU. *See* Agrupación de Fuerzas
    Especiales Antiterroristas Urbanas
Afewerki, Isaias, 371
Afghan International Administration
    (AIA), 134
Afghanistan, **133–135**
    correctional system in, 133, 134–135
    drugs from
        in Azerbaijan, 184
        in Belarus, 203
        in Georgia, 419
        in Kazakhstan, 544
        in Kyrgyzstan, 574
        in Latvia, 584
        in Norway, 707
        in Russia, 783, 784
        in Tajikistan, 884, 885
        in Turkmenistan, 916, 917
        in Ukraine, 931
        United Nations targeting,
            135, 544, 884
    human rights in, 134
    illegal immigrants from, 179
    law enforcement in, 133–134
    refugees from, in Hungary, 471
    Soviet invasion of, 881
    Taliban in, 134, 714, 881
    U.S. involvement in police training
        in, 133, 134

VOLUME 1: 1–614; VOLUME 2: 615–1176

AFI. *See* Agencia Federal de Investigaciones

AFIS. *See* Automated Fingerprint Identification System

Africa. *See also* specific countries
  colonialism in
      extent of, 11
      police during, 12–13
  correctional system in
      health care in, 89–90
      history of, 79
      penal colonies in, 76
  law enforcement in, history of, 8, 12–13

African Americans
  in civil rights movement, 84, 955
  and law enforcement, history of, 954

Afrique Occidentale Francaise (Federation of French West Africa), 318

Agca, Mehmet Ali, 1075–1076

Agencia Federal de Investigaciones (AFI) (Mexico), 643

Age requirements, for police
  in Australia, 171
  in Austria, 177
  in Canada, 268
  in Czech Republic, 336, 337
  in Denmark, 344
  in Germany, 426
  in Netherlands, 679
  in Philippines, 740
  in Portugal, 761
  in Slovakia, 825
  in Slovenia, 832
  in Somalia, 840
  in Swaziland, 858
  in Ukraine, 928

Age statistics
  for police, in Estonia, 376
  for prisoners
      in Estonia, 378
      in South Korea, 564

Agricultural colonies, in Italy, 518–519

Agriculture. *See* Farms

Agriculture and Fishing, Ministry of (Netherlands), 678

Agriculture and Forestry Police (Italy), 510

Agrupación de Fuerzas Especiales Antiterroristas Urbanas (AFEAU) (Colombia), 299

AIA. *See* Afghan International Administration

AIDS. *See* HIV/AIDS

Aid 65 (Portugal), 761

Airplanes
  bombings of, 97, 98, 102
  crashes of
      in Luxembourg, *611*
      in Venezuela, *1082*
  hijacking of
      nonterrorist, 97, 98, 99
      terrorist, 96, 97–98, 99
  police
      in Canada, 269, 272
      in Colombia, 301
      in Netherlands, 678
      in Peru, 728
      in Somalia, 839
  terrorist attacks on, **96–99**

Airport police. *See also* Aviation police
  in Croatia, 324
  in Fiji, 384
  in Netherlands, 678
  in Philippines, 737
  in Senegal, 806
  in Seychelles, 814
  in Singapore, 820
  in South Korea, 558

Air Service (Czech Republic), 335, 337, 338

Air Services (Italy), 514

Air Wing, Police (Kenya), 549

Ajzenstadt, Mimi, 120

Akaki Prison (Ethiopia), 382

Akayev, Askar, 570, *571*

AK-47 rifles, in aviation terrorism, 98

Alabama, 968
  crime in, 968, *969*
  law enforcement in, 968, *969*

Åland Islands, law enforcement in, 388–389

Alash Orda (Kazakhstan), 540

Alaska, 969–970
  crime in, 970, *970*
  law enforcement in, 969–970, *970*

Alawite (ethnic group), 874

Albania, **136–139**
  correctional system in, 139
  crime in, 139
  human rights in, 138–139
  law enforcement in, 136–138
  Serbia and Montenegro in conflict with, 137, 138, *138*, 807
  U.S. involvement in police training in, 137–138

Albanian Mafia, 136, 137, 138, 139

Albanian National Police (ANP), 136, 137–138

Albanians
  in Danish crime, 346

in organized crime, 38, 136, 137, 138, 139
  as refugees in Italy, 513
  in Slovak crime, 826

Albert I (prince of Monaco), 53

Albuquerque (New Mexico), 1009–1010

Albuquerque Police Department, 1009–1010

Alcalde (city judge), in Paraguay, 725

Alcatraz, U.S. Penitentiary at (California), 83

Alcohol
  ban on
      in Botswana, 232, 237
      in United States, 954
  crime related to, in Estonia, 376
  driving under influence of
      in Austria, 176
      in Hungary, 469
      in New Zealand, 686
      in Norway, 705
      in Slovenia, 831

Alcohol, Tobacco, Firearms and Explosives, Bureau of (ATF) (U.S.), 959–960

Alcohol detoxification
  in Kazakhstan, 542
  in Lithuania, 606
  in United States, 1029

Alderson, John, 62

Alem Baqaqn Prison (Ethiopia), 382

Alexander I (czar of Russia), 2, 386, 778

ALF. *See* Animal Liberation Front

Alfred (king of England), 2

Algeria, **140–141**
  correctional system in, 141
  crime in, 141
  human rights in, 141
  law enforcement in, 140–141

Algoa Correctional Center (ACC) (Missouri), 1047

Alien and Border Police (Czech Republic), 335, 336

Aliens. *See* Foreigners; Immigrants

Aliens Directorate (Greece), 440

Aliens Division (Denmark), 343

Alien smuggling. *See* Human trafficking, of illegal immigrants

Aliyev, Heydar, 182, 183

Aliyev, Ilham, 182, 183, 186

All India Services, 477

All-Russian Extraordinary Commission for Combating Counterrevolution and Sabotage (Soviet Union). *See* Cheka

VOLUME 1: 1–614; VOLUME 2: 615–1176

1180   WORLD ENCYCLOPEDIA OF POLICE FORCES AND CORRECTIONAL SYSTEMS, 2ND ED.

VOLUME 1: 1–614; VOLUME 2: 615–1176

1182   WORLD ENCYCLOPEDIA OF POLICE FORCES AND CORRECTIONAL SYSTEMS, 2ND ED.

VOLUME 1: 1–614; VOLUME 2: 615–1176

1184   WORLD ENCYCLOPEDIA OF POLICE FORCES AND CORRECTIONAL SYSTEMS, 2ND ED.

VOLUME 1: 1–614; VOLUME 2: 615–1176

1186   WORLD ENCYCLOPEDIA OF POLICE FORCES AND CORRECTIONAL SYSTEMS, 2ND ED.

VOLUME 1: 1–614; VOLUME 2: 615–1176

1188   WORLD ENCYCLOPEDIA OF POLICE FORCES AND CORRECTIONAL SYSTEMS, 2ND ED.

VOLUME 1: 1–614; VOLUME 2: 615–1176

VOLUME 1: 1–614; VOLUME 2: 615–1176

1192   WORLD ENCYCLOPEDIA OF POLICE FORCES AND CORRECTIONAL SYSTEMS, 2ND ED.

VOLUME 1: 1–614; VOLUME 2: 615–1176

1194   WORLD ENCYCLOPEDIA OF POLICE FORCES AND CORRECTIONAL SYSTEMS, 2ND ED.

VOLUME 1: 1–614; VOLUME 2: 615–1176

1196   WORLD ENCYCLOPEDIA OF POLICE FORCES AND CORRECTIONAL SYSTEMS, 2ND ED.

VOLUME 1: 1–614; VOLUME 2: 615–1176

1198   WORLD ENCYCLOPEDIA OF POLICE FORCES AND CORRECTIONAL SYSTEMS, 2ND ED.

VOLUME 1: 1–614; VOLUME 2: 615–1176

WORLD ENCYCLOPEDIA OF POLICE FORCES AND CORRECTIONAL SYSTEMS, 2ND ED.

1199

VOLUME 1: 1–614; VOLUME 2: 615–1176

1200   WORLD ENCYCLOPEDIA OF POLICE FORCES AND CORRECTIONAL SYSTEMS, 2ND ED.

VOLUME 1: 1–614; VOLUME 2: 615–1176

1202   WORLD ENCYCLOPEDIA OF POLICE FORCES AND CORRECTIONAL SYSTEMS, 2ND ED.

VOLUME 1: 1–614; VOLUME 2: 615–1176

1204   WORLD ENCYCLOPEDIA OF POLICE FORCES AND CORRECTIONAL SYSTEMS, 2ND ED.

VOLUME 1: 1–614; VOLUME 2: 615–1176

1206   WORLD ENCYCLOPEDIA OF POLICE FORCES AND CORRECTIONAL SYSTEMS, 2ND ED.

VOLUME 1: 1–614; VOLUME 2: 615–1176

1208   WORLD ENCYCLOPEDIA OF POLICE FORCES AND CORRECTIONAL SYSTEMS, 2ND ED.

F

FAA. *See* Federal Aviation Administration

Face recognition technology
in Belgium, 210–211
future of, 42

Faeroe Islands
correctional system in, 347
law enforcement in, 342–343, 345

Falcón, Ramón, 150, 151

Falcone, Giovanni, 72, 511, 516

FALN. *See* Fuerzas Armadas de Liberación Nacional

Falun Gong (Chinese spiritual movement), 295–296

Families of Victims of Involuntary Disappearances (Philippines), 745

Family, extended police, 20

Family Allowance Act (1953) (Chile), 285

Family Islands, 189

Family law, in Switzerland, 867

Family register, in Switzerland, 866–867

Family services, in correctional systems, in United States, 1053

FAR. *See* Forces Armées Royales

FARC. *See* Fuerzas Armadas Revolucionarias de Colombia

Farmington Correctional Center (FCC) (Missouri), 1047

Farms
collective
in Kazakhstan, 540, 541
in Kyrgyzstan, 569–570
prison
in Bolivia, 224
in Jamaica, 524
in Kenya, 552
in South Africa, 844

Farnham, Eliza W. B., 80

Fatigue, occupational, in Finland, 392

Faulds, Henry, 28–29

FBI. *See* Federal Bureau of Investigation

FCC. *See* Farmington Correctional Center

FDC. *See* Forum for Democratic Change

Fear, of crime, 1106–1107, 1118–1119

Federal Agency of Investigation (Mexico), 643

Federal Aviation Administration (FAA) (U.S.), 96–97

Federal Bureau of Investigation (FBI) (U.S.), 958–959
on antiabortion terrorism, 103

budget for, 958–959
on crime statistics, 966–967
criminal investigation by, 28, 954, 958
in cybercrime, 32–33, 34, 35
on cyberterrorism, 33
Dominican police training by, 354
education and training in, 964–965
establishment of, 27–28
ethics handbook for, 1130–1135
vs. Europol, 38
history of, 28
Identification Division of, 28
Internet Fraud Complaint Center of, 32
on juvenile crime, 116
mission of, 958
Patriot Act (2001) on, 106
on police statistics, 963
in Puerto Rico, *768*

Federal Bureau of Prisons (U.S.), 83, 84, 85, 86, 958

Federal College of Public Administration (Germany), 426

Federal Correctional Institution (U.S.), 85–86

Federal correctional system, in United States, 1024

Federal Crime Agency (Germany). *See* Bundeskriminalamt

Federal governments
of Estonia, structure of, 372–373
of Finland, structure of, 387–388
of United States
in correctional system, 1024
in criminal investigation, 27–28
in law enforcement, 7

Federal Investigation Agency (FIA) (Pakistan), 713, 714

Federal Judicial Police (Mexico), 643

Federal Law Enforcement Training Center (FLETC) (U.S.), 964

Federal Penitentiary Service (Argentina), 154

Federal police
in Argentina, 150, 151
in Australia, 166
in Austria, 174, 176, 177
in Belgium, 210, 213
in Brazil, 239, 240–241
in Canada, 265 (*See also* Royal Canadian Mounted Police)
in Germany, 424
in Indonesia, 483
in Malaysia, 625–626
in Mexico, 643–644
in Nigeria, 697

in Pakistan, 713, 714
in Switzerland, 868
in United Arab Emirates, 935
in United States
education and training of, 964–965
history of, 6
salaries for, 966
structure and organization of, 956–962

Federal Police Commission (Ethiopia), 381

Federal Preventive Police (Mexico), 643–644

Federal Prison Industries, Inc., 84

Federal Protective Service (FPS) (U.S.), 961

Federal Reserve Units (FRUs) (Malaysia), 625–626

Federal Road Police (Brazil), 239, 241

Federal Security Force (Pakistan), 713, 714

Federal Security Service (FSB) (Russia), 784

Federated Malay States Police (Malaysia), 624, 625

Federated States of Micronesia (FSM). *See* Micronesia, Federated States of

Federation Court Police (Bosnia and Herzegovina), 226

Federation of French West Africa, 318

Federation Intelligence and Security Service (Bosnia and Herzegovina), 228

Federation of Malaya Police, 625

Federation of Women's Organizations (Switzerland), 871

Ferri, Enrico, 518

Fetha Negast (Law of Kings) (Ethiopia), 381–382

Feudalism, in Japan, 533

FIA. *See* Federal Investigation Agency

Field Constabulary (Papua New Guinea), 723

Field Force (Gambia), 412

Field Force Unit (Tanzania), 889

Fielding, Henry, 3–4, 938

Fielding, John, 4, 7

Fielding, Nigel, 19

Field and Traffic Support Bureau (Canada), 271

Fiji, **384–385**
correctional system in, 385
human rights in, 385
law enforcement in, 384–385

VOLUME 1: 1–614; VOLUME 2: 615–1176

1210 WORLD ENCYCLOPEDIA OF POLICE FORCES AND CORRECTIONAL SYSTEMS, 2ND ED.

VOLUME 1: 1–614; VOLUME 2: 615–1176

VOLUME 1: 1–614; VOLUME 2: 615–1176

1214   WORLD ENCYCLOPEDIA OF POLICE FORCES AND CORRECTIONAL SYSTEMS, 2ND ED.

VOLUME 1: 1–614; VOLUME 2: 615–1176

1216   WORLD ENCYCLOPEDIA OF POLICE FORCES AND CORRECTIONAL SYSTEMS, 2ND ED.

VOLUME 1: 1–614; VOLUME 2: 615–1176

1218   WORLD ENCYCLOPEDIA OF POLICE FORCES AND CORRECTIONAL SYSTEMS, 2ND ED.

VOLUME 1: 1–614; VOLUME 2: 615–1176

1220   WORLD ENCYCLOPEDIA OF POLICE FORCES AND CORRECTIONAL SYSTEMS, 2ND ED.

VOLUME 1: 1–614; VOLUME 2: 615–1176

1222   WORLD ENCYCLOPEDIA OF POLICE FORCES AND CORRECTIONAL SYSTEMS, 2ND ED.

VOLUME 1: 1–614; VOLUME 2: 615–1176

1224   WORLD ENCYCLOPEDIA OF POLICE FORCES AND CORRECTIONAL SYSTEMS, 2ND ED.

VOLUME 1: 1–614; VOLUME 2: 615–1176

1226   WORLD ENCYCLOPEDIA OF POLICE FORCES AND CORRECTIONAL SYSTEMS, 2ND ED.

VOLUME 1: 1–614; VOLUME 2: 615–1176

1228   WORLD ENCYCLOPEDIA OF POLICE FORCES AND CORRECTIONAL SYSTEMS, 2ND ED.

VOLUME 1: 1–614; VOLUME 2: 615–1176

1230   WORLD ENCYCLOPEDIA OF POLICE FORCES AND CORRECTIONAL SYSTEMS, 2ND ED.

VOLUME 1: 1–614; VOLUME 2: 615–1176

1232   WORLD ENCYCLOPEDIA OF POLICE FORCES AND CORRECTIONAL SYSTEMS, 2ND ED.

VOLUME 1: 1–614; VOLUME 2: 615–1176

1234   WORLD ENCYCLOPEDIA OF POLICE FORCES AND CORRECTIONAL SYSTEMS, 2ND ED.

VOLUME 1: 1–614; VOLUME 2: 615–1176

1236   WORLD ENCYCLOPEDIA OF POLICE FORCES AND CORRECTIONAL SYSTEMS, 2ND ED.

VOLUME 1: 1–614; VOLUME 2: 615–1176

1238   WORLD ENCYCLOPEDIA OF POLICE FORCES AND CORRECTIONAL SYSTEMS, 2ND ED.

VOLUME 1: 1–614; VOLUME 2: 615–1176

1240　　WORLD ENCYCLOPEDIA OF POLICE FORCES AND CORRECTIONAL SYSTEMS, 2ND ED.

VOLUME 1: 1–614; VOLUME 2: 615–1176

1242   WORLD ENCYCLOPEDIA OF POLICE FORCES AND CORRECTIONAL SYSTEMS, 2ND ED.

VOLUME 1: 1–614; VOLUME 2: 615–1176

1244   WORLD ENCYCLOPEDIA OF POLICE FORCES AND CORRECTIONAL SYSTEMS, 2ND ED.

VOLUME 1: 1–614; VOLUME 2: 615–1176

1246   WORLD ENCYCLOPEDIA OF POLICE FORCES AND CORRECTIONAL SYSTEMS, 2ND ED.

VOLUME 1: 1–614; VOLUME 2: 615–1176

1248   WORLD ENCYCLOPEDIA OF POLICE FORCES AND CORRECTIONAL SYSTEMS, 2ND ED.

VOLUME 1: 1–614; VOLUME 2: 615–1176

WORLD ENCYCLOPEDIA OF POLICE FORCES AND CORRECTIONAL SYSTEMS, 2ND ED.

1249

VOLUME 1: 1–614; VOLUME 2: 615–1176

1250   WORLD ENCYCLOPEDIA OF POLICE FORCES AND CORRECTIONAL SYSTEMS, 2ND ED.

VOLUME 1: 1–614; VOLUME 2: 615–1176

1252   WORLD ENCYCLOPEDIA OF POLICE FORCES AND CORRECTIONAL SYSTEMS, 2ND ED.

VOLUME 1: 1–614; VOLUME 2: 615–1176

1254   WORLD ENCYCLOPEDIA OF POLICE FORCES AND CORRECTIONAL SYSTEMS, 2ND ED.

VOLUME 1: 1–614; VOLUME 2: 615–1176

1256   WORLD ENCYCLOPEDIA OF POLICE FORCES AND CORRECTIONAL SYSTEMS, 2ND ED.

VOLUME 1: 1–614; VOLUME 2: 615–1176

1258   WORLD ENCYCLOPEDIA OF POLICE FORCES AND CORRECTIONAL SYSTEMS, 2ND ED.

VOLUME 1: 1–614; VOLUME 2: 615–1176

1260   WORLD ENCYCLOPEDIA OF POLICE FORCES AND CORRECTIONAL SYSTEMS, 2ND ED.

VOLUME 1: 1–614; VOLUME 2: 615–1176

1262   WORLD ENCYCLOPEDIA OF POLICE FORCES AND CORRECTIONAL SYSTEMS, 2ND ED.

VOLUME 1: 1–614; VOLUME 2: 615–1176

1264   WORLD ENCYCLOPEDIA OF POLICE FORCES AND CORRECTIONAL SYSTEMS, 2ND ED.

technology used in, 100, 101,
109–110, 111
in United Kingdom, 946
aviation, 97, 98, 102
eco-terrorism, 103
London bombings (2005),
102, *470*
Pan Am flight 103 bombing
(1988), 97, 98, 102
in United States, 955–956
antiabortion, 101, 103–104,
105, 109
aviation, 97 (*See also*
September 11, 2001)
eco-terrorism, 100, 103, 108,
109, 110
fight against, 102, 112–114
law enforcement response to,
112–114
political-cause, 97, 100,
102–103
Puerto Rican independence
movement, 104, 113
right-wing, 100, 104–108,
109, 110
war on, ix, 102
weapons in, 98, 100–101, 110–111
in Yemen, 102
TETRA. *See* Terrestrial Trunked Radio
Tetra (radio system) (Serbia and
Montenegro), 811
Texas, 1003
correctional system in, 1031,
1058–1059
crime in, 1003, *1003–1004*
law enforcement in, 1003, *1003,*
1014
mounted police in, 8, 9
Texas Department of Criminal Justice,
1058–1059
Texas Rangers, 8, 9
Texas State Department of Corrections,
85
TFDP. *See* Task Force Detainees of the
Philippines
Thailand, **891–895**
border conflict with Malaysia, *893*
correctional system in, 894–895
crime in, 894
human rights in, 894
human trafficking for sexual
exploitation in, 871, 894
international penitentiary congress
in, 94
law enforcement in, 891–894
Thai National Police Department
(TNPD), 891–892, 894
Thai people, in Danish crime, 346

Thames River Police (England), 4
Thana (station house)
in Bangladesh, 194, 195
in Pakistan, 714
Theft. *See also specific types*
in Germany, 424
in Norway, 708
in Philippines, 744
in Portugal, 764
Sharia (Islamic law) on, 804
in Singapore, 822
Themistocles, 436
Theodosian Code, 75
Theodosius II (Roman emperor), 75
Theoharis, Athan, 28
Third Position (philosophy), 107
Third world nations. *See* Developing
countries
Thomas Larrea Prison (Ecuador), 360
Threat assessment, by Europol, 39
Tiananmen Square incident (1989)
(China), 289, 295
Tibet, 288
Tihar Jail (India), 482
Timor-Leste Police Service (TLPS),
356
Tipton Correctional Center (TCC)
(Missouri), 1048
Tirailleurs (Morocco), 660
Titan group (Ukraine), 927
Tithing system, 2
TLPS. *See* Timor-Leste Police Service
TNPD. *See* Thai National Police
Department
Tocqueville, Alexis de, 1022
Togo, **896–897**
correctional system in, 896–897
crime in, 896
law enforcement in, 896
Tokyo (Japan)
Aum Shinrikyo terrorist attack in,
101, 111
law enforcement in, 528–529
history of, 5, 525
organizational structure of,
527
Tokyo Metropolitan Police
Department, 525, 528–529
Toledo Manrique, Alejandro Celestino,
729, 731
Tonga, **898–899**
human rights in, 899
law enforcement in, 898–899
Tonga Police Force, 898
Tonton Macoutes (Haiti), 462
Tornay, Cedrich, 1078

Toronto (Canada), 265, 266
Torture
in Afghanistan, 135
in Algeria, 141
in Angola, 145
in Argentina, 154
in Armenia, 159
in Bahrain, 192
in Bangladesh, 194
in Belarus, 206, 207
in Bolivia, 223
in Bulgaria, 250
in Burundi, 258
in Cambodia, 260
in Cameroon, 262
in China, 295–296
in Congo, Democratic Republic of,
309
definition of, 213
in Dominican Republic, 355
in Egypt, 364
in Equatorial Guinea, 369
in Georgia, 417, 420
in Guinea, 456
in India, 482
in Iran, 492
in Iraq, 494, 495
in Israel, 506–507
in Jordan, 538
in Kazakhstan, 543
in Kenya, 551, 552
in Laos, 578
in Lebanon, 588
in Lesotho, 590
in Liberia, 594
in Libya, 597
in Madagascar, 621
in Malaysia, 627, 628
in Mauritania, 637
in Mexico, 645
in Moldova, 654
in Morocco, 663
in Nepal, 670, 672
in Nigeria, 702
in North Korea, 556
in Pakistan, 716, 717
in Paraguay, 726
in Portugal, 760, 761
in Saudi Arabia, 803
in Senegal, 806
in Solomon Islands, 837
in Somalia, 840
in South Africa, 843
in Sri Lanka, 852
in Sudan, 854
in Swaziland, 858
in Syria, 875
in Tajikistan, 882
in Tanzania, 889

VOLUME 1: 1–614; VOLUME 2: 615–1176

1266   WORLD ENCYCLOPEDIA OF POLICE FORCES AND CORRECTIONAL SYSTEMS, 2ND ED.

VOLUME 1: 1–614; VOLUME 2: 615–1176

1268   WORLD ENCYCLOPEDIA OF POLICE FORCES AND CORRECTIONAL SYSTEMS, 2ND ED.

VOLUME 1: 1–614; VOLUME 2: 615–1176

1270   WORLD ENCYCLOPEDIA OF POLICE FORCES AND CORRECTIONAL SYSTEMS, 2ND ED.

VOLUME 1: 1–614; VOLUME 2: 615–1176

1272   WORLD ENCYCLOPEDIA OF POLICE FORCES AND CORRECTIONAL SYSTEMS, 2ND ED.

VOLUME 1: 1–614; VOLUME 2: 615–1176

1274   WORLD ENCYCLOPEDIA OF POLICE FORCES AND CORRECTIONAL SYSTEMS, 2ND ED.